Effective VisualAge® for Java™, Version 3

Includes Coverage of Versions 3.02 and 3.5

Scott Stanchfield
Isabelle Mauny

WILEY COMPUTER PUBLISHING

John Wiley & Sons, Inc.
New York • Chichester • Weinheim • Brisbane • Singapore • Toronto

Publisher: Robert Ipsen
Editor: Theresa Hudson
Developmental Editor: Kathryn A. Malm
Managing Editor: Angela Murphy
New Media Editor: Brian Snapp
Text Design & Composition: Benchmark Productions, Inc.

This book is printed on acid-free paper. ♾

Published by John Wiley & Sons, Inc.
Published simultaneously in Canada.

Library of Congress Cataloging-in-Publication Data:

ISBN 0-471-31730-6

Printed in the United States of America.
10 9 8 7 6 5 4 3 2 1

For Nancy, Nicole, Alex, Trevor, and Claire Marie

–Scott

"Sorry, can't come this weekend, need to work on the book." How many times have you heard this, and always kept the faith, when I was losing it. I will never thank you enough for your support, kindness, and above all for being my second family. *Je vous aime.* Thank you for being there.

–Isabelle

CONTENTS

ACKNOWLEDGMENTS

The authors wish to thank the following folks for their assistance in developing this book. Without their cooperation, we would never have been able to provide the quality of content we wanted. Thanks to all of you for your time and support! If we inadvertently missed someone, please rest assured that it is only because you've been dealing with two authors whose brains tend to vapor lock at inopportune times.

Nancy and the Kids

First and foremost, I've (Scott) got to thank my wife Nancy and my four cuddly kids, Nicole, Alexander, Trevor, and Claire for their support and understanding over the past year and a half. Thanks for your patience, and know that daddy won't have to say, "Gotta work on the book now" anymore.

Isabelle's Friends

"Sorry, can't come this weekend, need to work on the book." How many times have you heard this, and always kept the faith, when I was losing it. I will never thank you enough for your support, kindness, and above all for being my second family. *Je vous aime.* Thank you for being there.

Technical Reviewers

We'd like to acknowledge our technical reviewers, *Tim deBoer* and *Judah Diament.* Without their help, we would have had several silly or unclear sections. If you can understand what we're trying to say in this book, you can blame them. Tim is an outstanding technical support guru for VisualAge for Java, and Judah is an avid VisualAge for Java user and active participant in the VisualAge for Java newsgroups.

IBM Folks

Next, we must thank all of the wonderful IBM people who have answered our questions, provided inspiration, and helped with all of the book production activities (many of which we didn't know existed.) The list of involved IBMers is huge, and we thank them all, but we feel we must mention the following folks who went the extra mile for us:

> *Sheila Richardson*, for suckering us into the wormhole that is book authorship, and helping us obtain the rights for providing the software on the CD.
>
> *John Botsford*, for providing all the software we could swallow, version after version of it.
>
> *Tim deBoer* and *Christophe Elek*, for their excellent technical support, humor, and insights into upcoming product features.

Angus McIntyre, VisualAge for Java marketing chief, for providing insight into IBM's marketing plans, being very open with us on product direction, and helping to rid the world of the "beach ads".

Susan Carpenter, for some truly excellent copyediting, helping us feel confident that the book will look and sound good without accidental changes of semantics.

Greg Adams, (who works at OTI, but works on VisualAge for Java), for his help in seeing what's happening behind the scenes of VisualAge for Java, and his help on the team programming chapter.

Becky Nin, Mary Lehner, Hetty Dougherty and Brian Farn for their invaluable help on the Database Programming chapter. You have made an amazing job there.

Sheldon Wosnick, Elson Yuen for our interesting discussions on servlets and JSP programming!

Terry McElroy, "contract-master" extraordinaire, for handing all of the wonderful legal paperwork in such an incredibly timely fashion, and helping it make sense to us so we could concentrate on the writing.

Alex Koutsoumbos, VisualAge marketing genius from down under (as in Australia), for introducing Scott to some truly great Australian beer (not Foster's) and providing a great contact for what's going on with VisualAge in another country.

Stephanie Parkin, *Ralph Earle*, and the rest of the cool gang and IBM's VisualAge Developer Domain (http://www.software.ibm.com/vadd), for nudging me to write articles on Model-View-Controller. And, with their gracious permission, we've included these articles as Chapters 15 and 16 of this book.

Wiley Folks

Kathryn Malm and *Theresa Hudson*, our ever-vigilant editors at John Wiley & Sons, for putting up with constant delays and understanding the demands of our full-time jobs. While we may have aged them twenty-two years (each) during the time we've written this book, we hope the end result was worth their drained life force.

INTRODUCTION

Developing programs in the Java language just got easier! VisualAge for Java provides the tools you need for productive and effective programming. *Effective VisualAge for Java, Version 3.5* is our vision of how you can get the most out of VisualAge for Java, from simple tricks to help you when editing code by hand, to advanced techniques to simplify visual programming. Our goal is to expand your view of what this fantastic tool can do for you, allowing you to spend less time writing code.

How This Book Is Organized

When we designed this book, we decided to concentrate on the VisualAge for Java *tool*, rather than the Java Language. There are already several excellent books on the Java Language (we mention some in Appendix E, "Additional Resources"), and we assume that you're comfortable with the language. Rather than spend half the book on the language and the other half on the tool (and covering each weakly), we wanted to cover only the language concepts that are critical to understanding of the tool.

As the title of this book suggests, we're doing more than just showing you *what* VisualAge for Java can do for you. This book explains *how*, *why*, and *when* you should choose certain tools, and several useful design patterns that can make you a truly effective Java language developer.

We recommend that you read the book in the order in which the chapters are presented. Several of the layer concepts in the book build on knowledge learned earlier. Keep in mind that even if you already know many of the concepts covered in a chapter, you'll still learn some new techniques by reading that chapter. VisualAge for Java is a very complex tool, and there's often much more functionality present than it seems.

Getting to Know VisualAge for Java

We start with the basics of using the VisualAge for Java environment, explaining several tools you can use to create, edit, and execute your Java language programs. As you write your programs, you'll want to take advantage of the version control (software configuration management) and file system export/import facilities available in the environment.

Chapter 1, VisualAge for Java Concepts

What is VisualAge for Java, and why is it the perfect choice for Java language development? Start by exploring Integrated Development Environments, and how VisualAge for Java helps you concentrate on the Java language, rather than the details of how the Java platform is implemented on your operating system.

Chapter 2, Creating Code

To write applications and applets, you need to create projects, packages, classes, interfaces and methods. In this chapter, we show you how to create, edit, and execute these program elements.

Chapter 3, Navigating Your Code

VisualAge for Java provides several ways to view and edit your code. In this chapter, we explore the browsers that VisualAge provides, as well as searching and customizing your Workspace.

Chapter 4, Using Version Control

Unlike most other IDEs, VisualAge for Java provides its own built-in version control (also known as software configuration management.) In this chapter we explore the basics of version control, as well as applying team version control in VisualAge for Java, Enterprise Edition.

Chapter 5, Testing and Debugging

Once you write your program, you'll probably need to work out a few bugs. VisualAge for Java provides two debuggers: one that's integrated into the IDE, and one for use outside the IDE. This chapter explores using both debuggers, and examines the Scrapbook to help test your applications.

Chapter 6, Integrating with the File System

VisualAge for Java is a fantastic development environment, but eventually you'll need to send your code out to the file system for others to use, or bring code into the IDE to work on. This chapter covers the export and import functions, allowing you to move code out of and into the IDE. This chapter also explains how you can use your own resource files, such as images and property files, inside the IDE.

JavaBeans Components

Sun's JavaBeans Component Model (or more simply, Beans) provides a great architecture for developing reusable software components. The following chapters focus on Beans and how you can develop them inside VisualAge for Java.

Chapter 7, Introduction to JavaBeans Components

Because understanding the JavaBeans Component Model is so critical to effective use of VisualAge for Java, we explain the model in detail in this chapter. We explore the concepts and code involved preparing you to create and use Beans in the IDE.

Chapter 8, The BeanInfo Editor

VisualAge for Java's BeanInfo Editor provides a simple yet powerful interface for creating and maintaining JavaBeans Components. We explore how to add and delete properties, event sets, and methods, without writing and code.

Chapter 9, Extension and Composition

There are two ways you can use beans in VisualAge for Java: extension and composition. Extending beans enhances their attributes and behavior, while composing beans combines the strength of several independent beans to build a more complex bean. This chapter explains the concepts of bean extension and composition, and when you might want to choose one over the other.

Visual Programming

VisualAge for Java provides the most advanced visual builder tool available: the Visual Composition Editor, or VCE. This section of the book concentrates on visual programming in the VCE, from basic GUI construction to use of advanced patterns like Model-View-Controller. While the VCE is an excellent GUI builder, keep in mind that it's not just for GUIs; you can build non-visual beans in the VCE as well!

Chapter 10, Bean Composition in the VCE

This chapter covers the basic concepts of the VCE, including the beans palette, beans list and property sheets. We explain how to break down a bean into smaller pieces, and create new GUI applications and Applets follows, using the VisualAge for Java SmartGuides.

Chapter 11, Layout Management

The first real step in creating a GUI is designing the layout of that GUI. In this chapter, we examine how to use the Java platform's layout managers, combining them to create more interesting GUIs. Much of this chapter covers the concepts and design strategies involved when using layout managers in VisualAge for Java; you should read this chapter even if you feel you already understand layout management.

Chapter 12, Connections

The VCE represents event handling via connections between beans. In this chapter, we explore the various types of connections and when you want to use each type.

Chapter 13, Variables and Instances

One of the things that sets the VCE apart from other visual builder tools is that you can work with variables, representing various instances of beans. This gives you a great deal of power when using the VCE, including the ability to "tear off" properties from inside other beans, and provide "plugs" to easily connect multiple beans together.

Chapter 14, Design Patterns for the VCE

This chapter discusses several patterns to help you make more effective use of the VCE. You need to strike a balance between using too few connections and potential connection spaghetti. The chapters presented in this chapter help you factor common processing and use a small amount of code to reduce the number of connections you need to define.

Chapter 15, Model-View-Controller in the VCE

One of the most powerful patterns you can use in your application is Model-View-Controller (MVC). This chapter explains MVC, and walks you through a detailed example of implementing MVC in the VCE.

Chapter 16, Advanced Model-View-Controller Techniques

You can take the Model-View-Controller paradigm much further than the simple application developed in the previous chapter. By using proxy models and views, you can easily adapt any kind of data for use in your application.

Chapter 17, Factory Beans

This chapter unravels the mysterious factory bean, explaining its purpose in the VCE and demonstrating a few scenarios where it can be quite useful.

Chapter 18, Using AWT and Swing in the VCE

The VCE provides excellent support for the AWT and Swing GUI libraries. This chapter shows how to work with some of the more complex components, as well as special techniques like creating a Panel subclass for easier radio button use.

Chapter 19, Handwritten Code versus Generated Code

This chapter explains the code that VisualAge for Java generates. The structure of GUI code and generated beans is explored, showing how the code maps to your BeanInfo Edition or VCE session.

Chapter 20, Bean Customization

You can make your beans more useful to other programmers by providing property editors and customizers for them. This chapter explains how to write, install, and use property editors and customizers, providing a friendlier interface for programmers that use your beans.

Advanced Programming

This part of the book covers advanced topics, including server-side and database programming. We strongly recommend that you read Chapters 1 through 6 before this part, as knowledge of many of the basic VisualAge for Java concepts is assumed in these chapters.

Chapter 21, Database Programming

This chapter focuses on using Data Access Beans (DAB) and SQLJ in VisualAge for Java. Several examples walk you through the details of creating a database application, using DAB in visual composition and SQLJ in your code.

Chapter 22, Developing Distributed Applications

In this chapter, we move into the realm of distributed programming, discussing some basic architectural issues and employing RMI and CORBA within VisualAge for Java.

Chapter 23, Developing Enterprise JavaBeans

Sun's Enterprise JavaBeans (EJB) architecture provides a powerful distributed object framework. Using the EJB development environment provided in the Enterprise Edition of VisualAge for Java, we explore EJBs from development through deployment and testing.

Chapter 24, Developing Servlets and JavaServer Pages

Many websites use Servlets and JavaServer Pages (JSP) to prepare data for user requests. In this chapter, we examine the tools for developing Servlets and debugging JavaServer Pages.

Chapter 25, Tool Integration

You can extend VisualAge for Java using its Tool API to write Java code. This chapter provides the most complete coverage available on the tool api, describing all classes, interfaces, and methods, and showing examples of how to perform common tasks using the API.

Appendices

We conclude the book with a few appendices, providing some useful tidbits to aid you in your quest for effective use of VisualAge for Java.

Appendix A, Internationalization

Other countries are no longer great distances. Widespread use of the Internet brings foreign countries as close as a dial-up connection. Providing an application that presents itself to a user in their language and using their local customs gives you a strong competitive edge in the global marketplace. This appendix describes the basic concepts behind creating an international application, and shows you how to use VisualAge for Java to take a giant leap toward a more flexible application.

Appendix B, Maintenance and Troubleshooting

Sometimes even good products experience problems or perform sluggishly. This appendix describes several things you can do to tune your VisualAge for Java installation, and recover from problems.

Appendix C, Overview of Changes in VisualAge for Java

This appendix lists the major changes between VisualAge for Java, version 3.02 and version 3.5.

Appendix D, The CD-ROM

We provide an appendix that describes the software provided on the CD-ROM, with brief installation instructions for each tool or product.

Appendix E, Additional Resources

While we cover a great many topics in this book, we cannot answer every possible question you may have. This appendix lists some useful resources for more information on VisualAge for Java.

Who Should Read This Book

This book is for everyone who wants to be a productive Java language developer. If you're currently using VisualAge for Java, you'll find many extras in the environment, as well as see effective ways to apply theses tools. If you're not a VisualAge for Java user, this book will walk you through the environment, helping you to see what the tool can do so you can be effective from the first time you use the tool.

This book assumes you have a firm understanding of the Java Language. A few topics, such as the JavaBeans Component Model, are covered in detail, but keep in mind that this is not a book on the Java Language; this is a book on using VisualAge for Java. If you find your Java knowledge isn't sufficient, we recommend you look at some of the books mentioned in Appendix E, "Additional Resources."

Special Conventions Used in This Book

To help you see when we're referring to controls and menu options in VisualAge for Java, we highlight text that contains their names in bold face. You should look for controls on the screen that match those names. For example, if you see text like

File->Quick Start->Features->Add Feature

you should

1. Open the **File** menu.
2. Choose **Quick Start.**
3. Select **Features** in the left pane of the Quick Start dialog.
4. Select **Add Feature** in the right pane of the Quick Start dialog.

We use bold text to help separate the narrative from the names of controls.

VisualAge for Java Version 3.5 Content

As we were preparing to publish this book, IBM released version 3.5 of VisualAge for Java. There are several usability changes and a few new features added. For a list of changes between version 3.02 and version 3.5, please see Appendix C, "Overview of Changes in VisualAge for Java."

Most of the screen captures presented in this book were captured using VisualAge for Java version 3.02. When the accompanying discussion requires screens specific to version 3.5, the screens were captured using version 3.5. Because of this, you may notice a few items on the screen that appear different than the version of VisualAge for Java you're using. These items may include a few extra tabs at the top of the screen, as well as an extra toolbar icon in version 3.5.

This book includes the major changes in version 3.5, such as the new Servlet SmartGuide and enhanced inner class support. Some new features, such as XMI support (which allows communication between VisualAge for Java and a tool like Rational Rose) do not appear as we considered them out of this book's scope.

Note that there are some features, such as Servlet Builder, that have been removed from version 3.5. This book contains coverage of these features for those who choose to keep using VisualAge for Java 3.02.

In some sections of this book, we'll refer to the installation directory of VisualAge for Java. You can specify whatever directory you want when installing, or accept the default directory. The default installation directory varies, depending on which version of VisualAge for Java:

```
c:\IBMVJava                                -- version 3.02
c:\Program Files\IBM\VisualAge for Java   -- version 3.5
```

What's on the CD-ROM

This book includes a CD-ROM that contains the following software:

VisualAge for Java, Professional Edition, version 3.5. This is the *full professional version* of VisualAge for Java, with no limits on the number of classes or development time.

Instantiations VA Assist, Trial Edition. A superb plug-in tool for VisualAge for Java, providing several usability enhancements to make you a more productive programmer.

Sample code from this book. All code samples presented in this book are provided on the CD-ROM.

Other VisualAge for Java plug-in tools. Other freely available plug-in tools are provided, as examples of the tool API and to help boost productivity.

The contents of the CD-ROM are described in detail in Appendix D, "The CD-ROM".

Web Sites Related to This Book

There are two Web sites that relate directly to this book:

Effective VisualAge for Java. The official site for this book is **www.wiley.com/compbooks/stanchfield.** This site will contain information about the book and any corrections or additions to the book's content.

VisualAge for Java Tips and Tricks. Scott Stanchfield runs this site, containing interesting tips and tricks that can help you become a more effective VisualAge for Java user. Much of the content at this site in included in this book, but additional content, such as details on VisualAge's generated code, appear here. See **javadude.com/vaj.**

Summary

While reading this book, remember that VisualAge for Java is a very complex set of tools, often providing several ways to perform a given task. In this book, we'll explain your options, and often recommend a preferred method. *We recommend you try each option and find the one that works best for you.* We wrote this book to expand your options and knowledge of the. The choices are there for you to make, providing a flexible and comfortable environment.

About the Authors

Scott Stanchfield Born and bred in Ann Arbor, Michigan, Scott Stanchfield found his niche in computer science. Developing software for companies such as IBM, McCabe & Associates and MetaWare Incorporated, he honed his computer skills. Turned to the dark side by a friend at MageLang Institute (now jGuru.com), Scott's career in teaching Java began. Early on, Scott was forced to use VisualAge for Java, and quickly learned to love it. Through his tips and tricks site and participation in the VisualAge newsgroups, Scott has earned a reputation as a VisualAge expert.

Isabelle Mauny is an architect and consultant for IBM's European technical sales support team. With 8 years experience in the application development arena, Isabelle teaches, demonstrates, and develops e-business applications using the VisualAge for Java and WebSphere Application Server products.

VisualAge for Java Concepts

1

Welcome to VisualAge for Java! You've chosen the most productive environment available for Java programming, and you won't be sorry about that choice! VisualAge for Java does things differently than you may be used to, but as you'll see while reading this book, those differences provide development power. This book helps you unleash that power, showing you not just the basics of using the environment, but ways to use the environment better.

We'll start by discussing the concepts of an IDE and how VisualAge for Java differs from the current trend in IDEs. We'll tell you how those differences are benefits, but it *can* take a little time for you to adjust. Then, we'll walk you through a simple example to immerse you in the environment.

What Is an IDE?

IDE stands for *Integrated Development Environment*. An IDE is a collection of tools with similar interfaces and helpful dialogs that can help you be more productive when developing source code. To appreciate an IDE, you need to step back and think about life before IDEs existed.

At the heart of all Java language programs are classes and interfaces, collectively known as *types*. Programmers create types by editing a file that contains the code for those types in an editor. The programmer can then compile those types using a compiler and run the resulting program.

While this process is straightforward, it can be cumbersome. There are several problems with the process:

Each tool has a different interface. The developer must learn the editor, compiler, debugger, and interpreter. Because each tool has a different interface, they cannot leverage existing knowledge.

Some tools have too many options. Think about how many options the average compiler has. Think about the run-time environment. The trouble is, you have to learn all of those options or constantly look them up in the documentation. Was that option -d or -D or -debug or -Debug?

You can forget to compile. This is one of the most insidious problems you can face as a programmer. You compile all files but one. Because the Java Language provides a dynamic run-time environment, the newly compiled code can still load in out-of-date compiled code.

You must keep track of all pieces of your application. When it's just you and the file system, you need to provide all of the organization.

Finding related information can be difficult. If you want to find where method funky() is called, you need to use yet more tools (with different interfaces and options) to analyze your code.

You constantly rewrite tedious plumbing. *Plumbing* refers to code that you must write repeatedly in nearly every program to get the job done. Usually plumbing is low-level code that you could write in your sleep. If you're only using an editor, you get to write new plumbing in every program, and this process becomes terribly tedious.

You need to know everything. Most editors only know how to listen to your typing. They don't care whether you type in a valid statement or not. It's up to you to type in the correct code. What's the name of the method I need? What parameters does this method want? It's up to you to look up the answers.

You must manually find the location of syntax errors. "Missing semicolon on line 42 near someVariable." Compilers tell you what's wrong, but you must hunt through your code to find the spot and fix the problem.

Enter the IDE

Through the years, programmers learned ways to improve the development process. Early achievements came in editing and organization. Editors became more powerful and provided programmable macros, helping to relieve tedious code. The *make* utility provided organization by ensuring that changed source was recompiled.

All of these changes started building toward the notion of an integrated development environment. The interfaces between the various tools started blurring. It was hard to tell where the editor stopped and the debugger started. Modern IDEs provide the following functionality:

The editor and debugger feel the same. In the editor, you can set breakpoints. While debugging, you can edit code.

Integrated compilation and execution, as menu options or key presses. Most of the tools you need to build and run your program are easily available. You do not need to open a command prompt to compile or execute the code.

You can access language-specific assistance. IDEs may support a single language or a small group of languages. They often provide custom support, such as context-sensitive help, syntax highlighting, and code completion. Keywords and comments appear in different colors or fonts. Pressing F1 can display help on the word under the cursor. Valid methods to call can appear in a pop-up menu after pressing "." in the editor.

You have a single source for customization. Rather than setting options for each tool independently, you access a single dialog that asks which options you want. All the tools feel like part of the same package.

You can perform simple project management. All modern IDEs support the notion of a *project*. In its simplest form, a project is a group of files, usually in the same directory. The IDE provides commands to compile all files contained in a project, and many IDEs provide a make-like "compile only those files that have changed" function.

You can easily browse and cross-reference your code. Most IDEs now provide some sort of browsing and cross-reference capability. You can ask where method *funky()* is used or where class *Thimble* is defined. This makes development much easier, especially when you need to make a change that can affect several other files.

You can easily control many versions of your code. Most IDEs provide integration with version control tools, also known as Software Configuration Management (SCM) tools. This makes it easy to take snapshots of your code, when releasing to your customer, or whenever you hear yourself saying "so far, so good". If anything goes wrong, you can always back out the change. Most IDEs implement this support as calls to an existing SCM tool. Others, like VisualAge for Java, provide a built-in SCM tool.

You can generate complex and tedious code. As IDEs evolved, many provided dialogs that generate code. Each dialog supports a specific type of task. Some dialogs create properties for JavaBeans components. Other dialogs might create a new type of event. Some create an application skeleton. These dialogs help relieve the tedium of plumbing in your application. In many environments, these dialogs are called *wizards*. In VisualAge for Java, we refer to these dialogs as *SmartGuides*.

You can visually design applications. Advanced IDEs provide visual builder tools. These come in two flavors: GUI builders and visual builders. Most IDEs simply provide a GUI builder. A GUI builder is a tool that enables you to drag and drop components, drawing your Graphical User Interface. Some of these also enable you to draw lines between components to represent event handlers. Visual builders are a more generic form of GUI builders. You can use them to draw GUIs *and* non-GUIs. Visual builders, like the one provided with VisualAge for Java, provide a great deal of power for application construction.

NOTE

There is a difference between "smart editors" and IDEs. Some editors, like emacs and Codewright, are very powerful. Nevertheless, they are *not* IDEs. They may provide some help for developing languages, and simple menu items that call a compiler, but they do not form a true IDE. The editor is *adapting* other tools for easy access, as opposed to *integrating* those tools as part of the same environment. You can often perform the same actions as in many IDEs, but you need to learn how to interact with each tool independently.

IDE Benefits

IDEs provide several benefits for new users and "power users" alike. The most obvious benefit is reduction of learning curve, the amount of time it takes to adjust to using the tool. When all of the tools you need to use feel the same, it's much easier to find the right keys to press or menus to choose for each tool. In a non-IDE environment, you may need to consult the manual to determine how to save your work. In an IDE, the same command works in all situations.

Learning curves can be quite daunting. Take, for instance, a user who is dropped at a UNIX or DOS command prompt. The cursor blinks. The user blinks. Where do you start? What do you type? Often the only choice is to read a manual or a book to determine how to write a program and edit code.

An IDE reduces the learning curve by presenting most of the options as menu choices. The user just needs to look at each menu. If the user wants to start a new program, and sees menu option **File->New**, they can probably figure out what they need to do.

Users who have already learned the environment can also benefit. They can use code generators to reduce the amount of code they need to write (as well as help ensure that code is correct). They can use visual builders to create and maintain GUIs (a picture is quite literally worth hundreds of words). They can use the browsing capabilities to find where they need to make changes. Finally, they can find new features in the IDE without consulting the manuals.

Files, Be Gone!

Computer programs start with files, right?

Why? Must they?

File-based development is perhaps the oldest paradigm in computer programming. A paradigm is, quite simply, "the way things are done." People become trapped in paradigms, just because they assume it's the proper or only way to do a job. After following the paradigm it becomes natural, something that requires little thought about the process.

It's time for a paradigm shift. Before you can proceed with VisualAge, you need to change the way you think about "the way things are done."

Since the dawn of computer storage devices, programmers have edited files, typing in source code for their programs. We compile or assemble these files to create executable programs. That's just "the way things are done." However, does this make sense? Obviously, we need *somewhere* to put the source code, and files have filled that need. However, *files are artificial.*

What Java language construct does a file map to?

Is it a class or interface? No. You can have several classes or interfaces in a single file (although only one can be declared public).

Is it a package? No. You can define several different files in the same package.

Is it an applet or application? No. Several files could contain parts of the same applet or application.

Files impose an artificial structure to our programs. Wouldn't it be great to work with Java language constructs rather than files? Edit a class! Edit a method! Edit a package! That's the approach taken by VisualAge for Java.

Through the Eyes of VisualAge for Java

VisualAge for Java has a very different view of the world than most other IDEs. Rather than helping you edit code that you store in files, VisualAge stores its code in a database.

Why a database, you ask? Think about what databases are good at: storing related data for fast access. Individual pieces can be accessed quickly in many different ways. Relationships between data can help a user create complex queries, examining that data from many different angles.

Think about a few of the relationships that exist in the Java language:

- Packages contain classes and interfaces.
- Classes and interfaces import packages.
- Classes and interfaces contain methods and variables.
- Classes, interfaces, and methods can reference other classes and interfaces.
- Methods can call other methods.

There are many more relationships between program elements, but just thinking about these few relationships can expose some of the power that a database can bring to a development environment. You can cross-reference just about anything in your program. Where is variable *addButton* defined? What methods call method getGardenHose()? What classes do I need to run this application? The possibilities are amazing. VisualAge for Java takes advantage of this power in ways you may not have imagined.

VisualAge for Java stores your source code in a database. This database is called the *repository*. The repository tracks the code and relationships between elements of that code. Yet, the repository goes the further step of tracking *versions* of that code. It is a complete software configuration management system for your Java language programs.

NOTE

VisualAge for Java isn't the first environment to take this approach to programming. VisualAge for Java is derived from IBM's VisualAge for Smalltalk product (and much of VisualAge for Java is written in Smalltalk!). Smalltalk environments have always tended toward a much more object-oriented approach to development, and this approach also works quite well for the Java language.

Repository, Workspace, and Workbench

Figure 1.1 shows the relationship of the *repository*, the *workspace*, and the *Workbench*. These three components store your source and compiled code, and provide a visual representation to work with. In this section, we describe these three components and the responsibilities of each.

The Repository

The repository contains *all* versions of *all* Java language constructs that you develop. It tracks methods, classes, interfaces, and packages, as well as their relationships to each other. If you have source code for your Java language constructs, that source is stored in the repository. If the source exists, the compiled bytecode is not stored in the repository. The only time compiled bytecode appears in the repository is if you do *not* have its source (which is the case for many third-party libraries that you might add to the repository).

The repository also stores version information, such as versions of individual methods, which method versions belong with each version of a class, and which class versions belong with each version of a package. (Version control becomes much more complex, and is covered in detail in Chapter 4, "Using Version Control.") Finally, the repository stores information about user interface designs.

Figure 1.1 The relationship between repository, workspace, and Workbench.

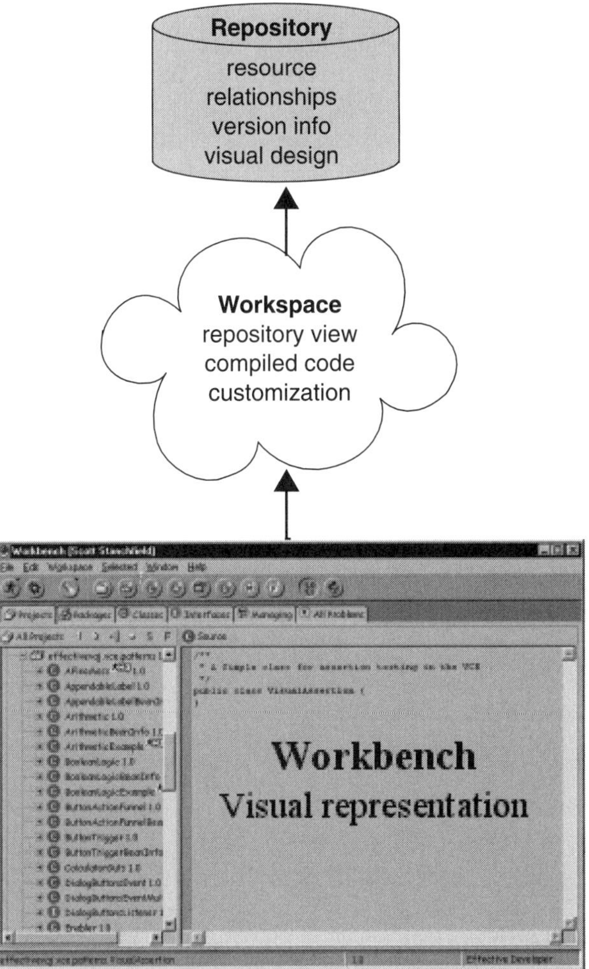

The Workspace

The workspace is a user's "current slice" of the repository. The workspace is *non-visual*; it is a mapping into the repository of what the user wants to look at. While the repository stores *all* versions of your code, the workspace focuses on a single version of any class, interface, package, or method. You can change *which* version you are currently using at any time, but the workspace will only reference a single version at any given time. Note that we use the word *reference* here. The workspace does *not* make a copy of the source code. The source code is *always* stored in the repository. The workspace just keeps track of which version of the source code you are using.

If you have source code for a Java language class or interface, that source is stored in the repository. When source is available, *only* the source is stored in the repository. Whenever you point the workspace to a version of some Java language source in the repository, VisualAge for Java *compiles* that source and stores the resulting bytecode in the workspace. This has several benefits:

- Most users only use the latest version of the code. Old bytecode doesn't need to be kept.
- Each user sees exactly the bytecode they need.
- If the user needs to view a different version of bytecode, it can always be recompiled from the source. There is no need to save that bytecode.
- Bytecode can change based on other classes that the user has in his workspace. For example, constants in other classes could change values between different versions of the other class, as can the compiled method signature stored when determining which method is being called in another class. (Different overloaded methods could be provided in different versions of other classes.) This makes it impossible to store bytecode in the repository for a given version of Java language source, because the bytecode can be dependent on specific versions of *other* Java language source. Note that this is an effect of the Java language definition, *not* something specific to VisualAge for Java.

If you do not have Java language source available, the bytecode is stored in the repository.

The workspace also keeps track of various customizations you have made to the IDE, affecting how you view, edit, and execute the data in the repository and how VisualAge for Java generates code.

The Workbench

The third component, the Workbench, provides a visual representation of the workspace. The Workbench is your primary graphical user interface for communicating with VisualAge for Java. It provides several ways to view and edit your Java language source, always giving you a view of *everything* in your workspace. As we'll see throughout the following chapters, there are many other ways to work with your source code in VisualAge for Java, looking at everything in a package, a single class, or a single method.

Remember: The work*space* is the invisible mapping of which items in the repository you want to work with. The Work*bench* is the graphical user interface that allows you to manipulate the items in your work*space*.

Figure 1.2 Sharing a repository.

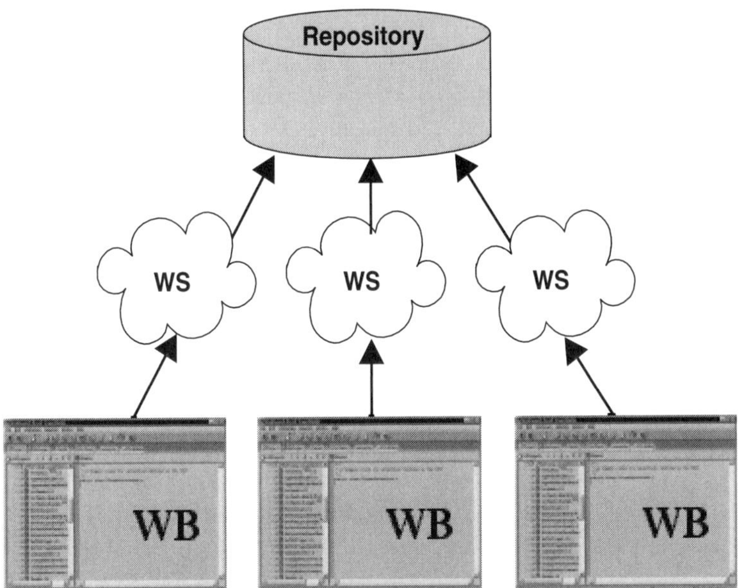

Teamwork in VisualAge for Java

One of the advantages to the repository/workspace/Workbench architecture is how easily it becomes a team-programming environment. All programmers can work with the same repository, each having their own workspace and Workbench. Look at Figure 1.2. By using the same repository, programmers can look at and execute each other's code very easily. By having separate workspaces (WS in Figure 1.2) and Workbenches (WB in Figure 1.2), the programmers can choose which versions they want to use. This flexibility allows all programmers to work on the same code at the same time *or* work on different versions.

In Chapter 4, we'll examine how you can share code. We'll also cover how you can version the code to provide "checkpoints" that you can return to for bug fixes, if you decide to abandon changes that you've been trying out, or if you want to find out what's changed between two versions of your code.

Method-Level Interaction

Most file systems and IDEs work with a *file* as their unit of compilation and version control. We've already discussed that VisualAge for Java uses a repository database instead of files, but the storage and compilation is much more interesting than that.

VisualAge for Java works with code at the *method* level. You edit methods. You version methods. You compile methods. This is a significant improvement over file-level or even class-level systems, especially when you consider version control.

Think of a class as a collection of specific versions of methods, and the benefit becomes obvious. You can change which versions of methods you use in a class. You can delete methods. You can re-add methods. Compare this to how you would need to work with file-level version control. You would have to extract the different versions of the files, find the code you want, and paste a copy of it into the current version of the class. With VisualAge for Java, you simply tell it to use a certain version of a method.

When you edit code in VisualAge for Java, you edit individual methods and class definitions. You see only a single method in the source code pane, or you see the class definition (including its variables and import statements). This may seem very strange, but after a few weeks, most users find they don't want to see more than a single method at a time. This is much more productive than needing to constantly scroll up and down to move between methods. You simply choose the method you want to work with, edit, and save it. Of course you *can* have multiple windows open at once, enabling you to work with more than one method at a time.

New in version 3.5!

3.5 Version 3.5 of VisualAge for Java introduces full-source editing capability. If you really miss editing an entire class as a single file, you can open the class in a full source view. The order of the class' methods is preserved, whether you had imported the class or created it inside VisualAge for Java. We'll discuss full source editing in Chapter 3, "Navigating Your Code."

However, we recommend that you try to shake the "full source" paradigm when editing your code. While you're probably very used to working with the entire source for a class at once, most people who have used VisualAge for Java and have gotten used to the method-level paradigm find they prefer it.

Incremental Compilation

VisualAge for Java also compiles a bit differently than other environments. Most IDEs provide easy access to compile your Java language source files, and possibly compiling an entire set of files that you're developing. However, *easy* compilation does not mean *effective* compilation.

Think about your development cycle. When you're creating a new application, you may write code for several hours or even days before you first try to compile it. What happens when you compile it? You usually get errors, and plenty of them.

What's the chance that the errors you see relate to code that you've recently written? Chances are good that you worked on the code several hours ago, and this can make it difficult to remember what you were thinking when you wrote that code, such as why you were making a change and what other parts of the program that change affects.

VisualAge for Java employs *incremental compilation* to make your time more productive. Each time you save a change to a method, class, interface, or package, VisualAge for Java compiles *that piece* as well as any pieces that depend on it.

Think about the benefits of this approach:

You no longer need to run a separate compile. This means that you cannot forget to compile any piece of your application, and there is one less key to press or menu item to select.

All dependent pieces are compiled. Whenever you save a change to a method, all pieces that depend on that method are compiled. For example, any methods that call the changed method are recompiled if the method's parameters change. Because of this, you can instantly see impacts, such as where you need to add additional parameters. Whenever you change variables in a class, the methods in the class that use those variables are recompiled as well. Whenever you change a class definition, classes and methods that reference the changed class are recompiled. Your entire workspace stays up to date with all changes that you have made.

Only dependent pieces are compiled. Because VisualAge for Java works at the method level, it can choose *exactly* which parts of your code need to be recompiled. Sometimes, it will only compile the method you have changed. Other times, it will compile that method and a few others that call it. This limited compilation scope can greatly improve the speed at which compilation takes place. Most often, you won't notice the compilation time when saving a method.

You see problems instantly. Because VisualAge for Java compiles methods after you save them, you receive immediate feedback on the change you have just made. This ensures that the reason for the change is still fresh in your mind, and you'll immediately see the errors made during that change. You also see which other methods and classes in your workspace are affected by that change, so you can change them while still in the mindset of the change.

You can change code while debugging. Often referred to as incremental debugging, you can edit and save methods *while your program is running*. The next time that the running program hits the changed code, the changes are executed. This can allow you faster turnaround if you need to make several changes while debugging. You don't need to constantly stop and restart the program for many changes.

There is no way to disable incremental compilation. Some users request this because they "want to be in control." Some feel that this must slow down productivity. The benefits and speed of VisualAge for Java's incremental compilation really counter these claims, as you will rarely notice the compilation. The benefits of instantly seeing problems and impacts are enormous, and the vast majority of users couldn't imagine working without them.

Hello World!

To whet your appetite, let's walk through a traditional "Hello, World!" example in VisualAge for Java. This simple application prints "Hello, World!" to the console and exits. If you follow this example, you'll see your basic interaction with VisualAge for Java when creating classes that you edit by hand. In later chapters, we'll explore other ways to work with your source code, using different browsers to view your code at various levels, as well as using VisualAge for Java's code generation capabilities to generate graphical user interfaces and JavaBeans components.

Every Java application or applet starts as a class. VisualAge for Java provides a code generator that creates classes for you, as well as equipping that class with helpful stub methods, import statements and interface implementation clauses. To create a class in VisualAge for Java, invoke the Create Class SmartGuide by clicking the C-button on the tool bar, shown in Figure 1.3.

> **NOTE**
>
> IBM uses the term *SmartGuide* to refer to code generation dialogs. You may have heard the term *wizard* used to refer to similar dialogs in other applications.

The Create Class SmartGuide is a two-page dialog that asks you to enter the details of the class definition. The first page, shown in Figure 1.4, asks for the location of the class, its superclass, and how you want to work with the class after it has been created.

Enter the following information on the first page of the dialog:

Project: My First Project

Package: my.first.pkg

Class Name: HelloWorld

Figure 1.3 Invoking the Create Class SmartGuide.

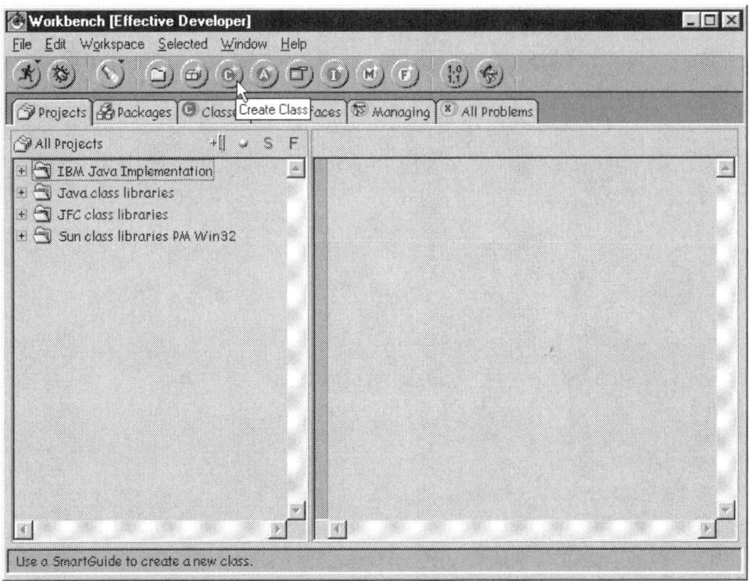

Leave the superclass as java.lang.Object. This is the root class of all Java language classes, and if you specify it as the superclass, VisualAge for Java will *not* add an "extends" clause to your class definition.

Make sure the two check boxes, **Browse the class when finished** and **Compose the class visually**, are not selected.

When you click the **Next** button, you move to the second page of the dialog, shown in Figure 1.5.

The second page of the Create Class SmartGuide enables you to specify classes and packages to import, interfaces that you want the class to implement, and which stub methods you would like VisualAge to generate in your application.

In this example, select the **main()** method so that VisualAge for Java provides a stub for it. After selecting the **main()** check box, click **Finish** to complete the class information. VisualAge for Java creates the class and closes the Create Class SmartGuide.

Expand the tree on the left side of the Workbench window so you can see the main() method inside the HelloWorld class. Select the main() method by clicking once on it in the tree. VisualAge for Java displays the source code for *only* the main() method in the right side of the Workbench. Add the following code into the main() method, as seen in Figure 1.6.

```
System.out.println("Hello, World!");
```

Figure 1.4 Specifying the project, package, and class name.

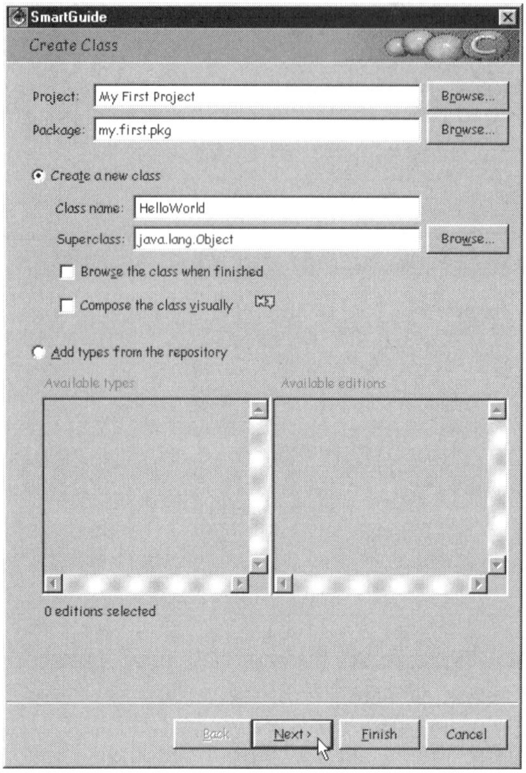

> **NOTE**
>
> If your Workbench window does not look as shown in Figure 1.6, you can choose the **Window->Flip Orientation** command to change how the window is split.

After changing the method, bring up the pop-up menu in the source code pane. You can do this on Windows by right-clicking anywhere in the source code. (Other platforms have different ways of bringing up pop-up menus.) Choose **Save** from the pop-up menu to save the changes to the main method. (See Figure 1.7.)

When you choose **Save**, VisualAge for Java saves the code and compiles it at the same time. If you have any errors, a dialog will present them to you, and the method will be marked with a small red X to indicate it contains an error. If you have any errors, check the code carefully. It should look exactly as follows:

```
/**
 * Starts the application.
 * @param args an array of command-line arguments
 */
public static void main(java.lang.String[] args) {
    // Insert code to start the application here.
    System.out.println("Hello, World!");
}
```

The code in bold text is the line that you added. If there are any mistakes, correct them and save the method again.

When you have an error-free application, you can run it. The easiest way to run an application in VisualAge for Java is to select the application class (or any of its methods) and click the "Running Man" icon on the tool bar. Figure 1.8 demonstrates how to run this application.

Figure 1.5 Asking VisualAge to create a main() method.

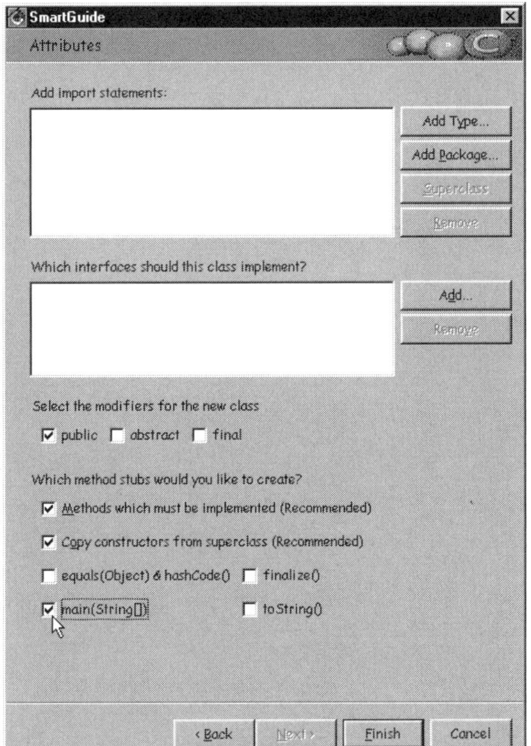

Figure 1.6 Editing the main() method.

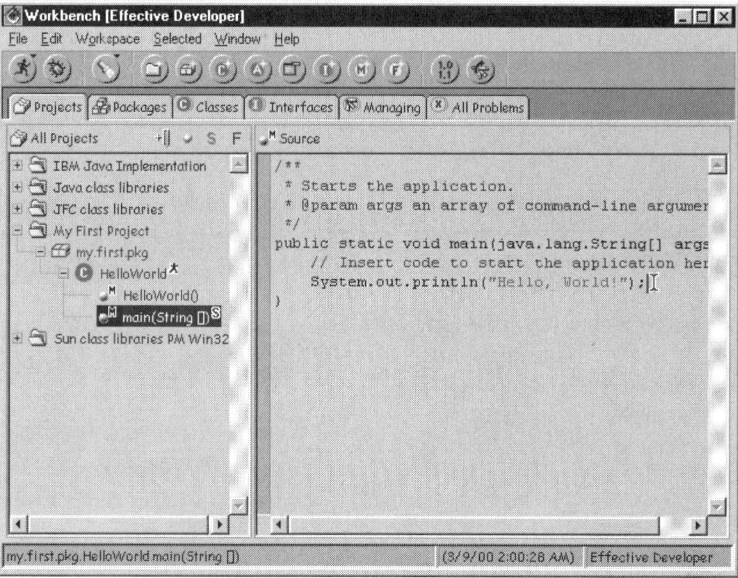

Figure 1.7 Saving the changes to the main() method.

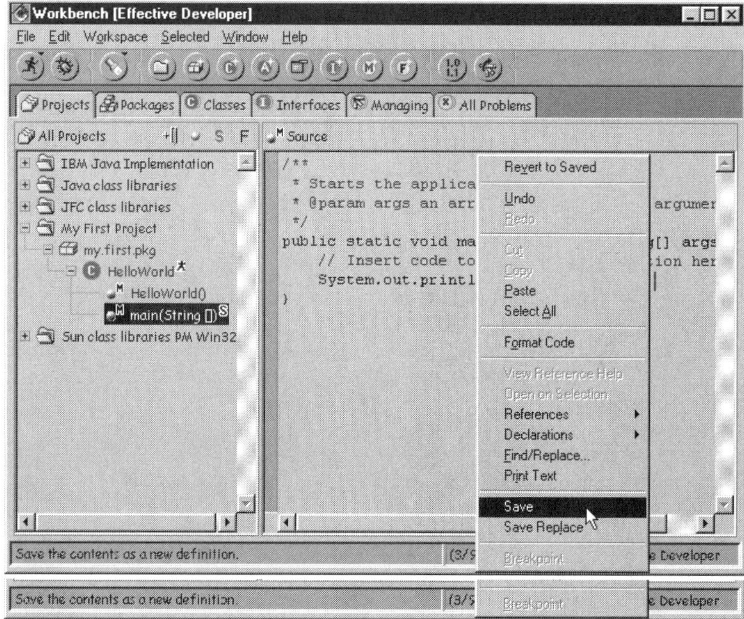

Figure 1.8 Running the HelloWorld application.

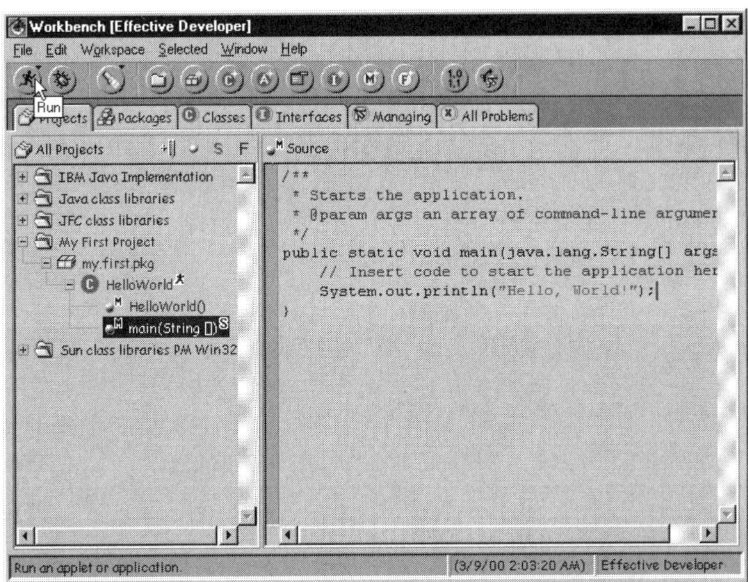

When the application runs, you'll see a window appear and then quickly hide behind the Workbench window. This is the Java console output. The window pops up because your program is writing console output (using System.out), and hides because VisualAge for Java wants to keep focus in the window you last selected, the Workbench.

Look at the console output. You may need to select the window using the task bar or by clicking in a visible portion of it to bring it to the foreground. The console output should look as seen in Figure 1.9.

The console window displays your output: "Hello, World!" Throughout this book, we'll see other ways to use the console, viewing the output of multiple programs, stopping running programs, or typing input that a program requests.

Summary

In this chapter, we've seen the key concepts of the VisualAge for Java IDE. VisualAge for Java differs from other IDEs in many ways, all of which help it to be the most productive IDE you'll ever use.

If VisualAge for Java is new to you, you'll no doubt feel very uncomfortable with it right now. *This is perfectly normal.* Most users become accustomed to it within a few weeks, but the benefits are enormous.

Figure 1.9 Your "Hello, World!" output.

We wrote this book to show you the tools that VisualAge for Java provides and effective ways of using those tools. Simply knowing that you have a hammer, saw, and screwdriver isn't enough; you need to see when these tools are useful, and the most effective ways to use them. Throughout this book, we'll present the tools, interspersed with tips, techniques, and design patterns to help make you a truly effective VisualAge for Java developer.

Creating Code

2

In this chapter, we'll look at how you create code inside VisualAge for Java. For starters, we'll look at manual creation of code. Later chapters will cover creating code using various code-generation dialogs and the Visual Composition Editor.

Looking at Your Code in the Workbench

VisualAge for Java provides several ways to look at your code. You can look at all of your code at once or only code that exists in a particular package or class. The environment is totally flexible. You can use the view of your code that makes you most comfortable for development or testing at any given time. You can easily switch back and forth between different views of your code. In this chapter, we discuss the basics of working with code inside VisualAge for Java. In Chapter 3, "Navigating Your Code," will look at several different ways of viewing your code.

Projects, Packages, Types, and Methods

VisualAge for Java organizes your code into projects, packages, types, and methods.

> **Types** are classes and interfaces that you develop or reference in your programs.
>
> **Methods** are methods defined inside types that you work with.
>
> **Packages** are Java language packages, groups of associated types.
>
> **Projects** are groups of packages. Note that projects are *not* Java language constructs. Projects are present in VisualAge for Java for organizational purposes only.

VisualAge for Java separates each of these types of constructs. At any given time, you edit a method, type, package, or project. All you see in the editor is that single construct. When editing a method, you see only that method. When editing a type, you see only the declaration of that type, including import statements and variables defined within that type. When editing a package or project, you see only comment text for that package or project.

Projects contain packages. Packages contain types. Types contain methods.

This organization and separation helps you concentrate on only the construct you actually need to edit. In Chapter 4, "Using Version Control," you will see that this organization and separation can greatly assist management of multiple versions of your code.

Choosing Appropriate Names

Before we discuss creating code, let's talk about a simple naming convention that can help people understand your code more easily.

Naming conventions are ways of helping people understand your code based solely on the names you choose. Some naming conventions are more restrictive than others. For example, Hungarian notation requires prefixes on all variable names that help identify the type of the variable. Other naming conventions are more relaxed, but still provide important hints about names. The naming convention that we recommend you use is very simple. It's merely a matter of which letters you capitalize in your names.

Sun Microsystems uses this simple naming convention in their Java language source code, and recommends that other Java language programmers do the same. You can find more details on this naming convention and other coating standards that Sun recommends at http://java.sun.com/docs/codeconv/index.html.

Basic Conventions

Names should contain only upper and lowercase letters and digits. If a name is composed of multiple words, each successive word should start with an uppercase letter. You should not use underscores to separate words in names.

In general, you should make names long enough to describe the function of construct, but no longer. The Java language allows you to make names any length. Use as many letters as you feel necessary to uniquely define the function of the construct, without using words such as *the*, *a*, or *an*. (Note that there are some valid places to use *the* or *a*. We will see some of these in Chapter 15, "Model-View-Controller in the VCE.")

Types

All types should start with an uppercase letter, and each successive word should start with an uppercase letter. For example:

```
Button
AddressBookModel
ImpossibleMissionAssignment
```

> **NOTE**
>
> It is extremely important that you not include "$" characters in your type names. The Java language uses the "$" character for qualification of inner-class names.

Variables and Methods

All variables and methods should start with a lowercase letter, and each successive word should start with an uppercase letter. For example:

```
currentAccount
personToAddToAccount
withdrawFromAccount()
getName()
setName()
```

> **NOTE**
>
> You can easily tell the difference between a variable and method name, because methods are always followed by parentheses.

Variable names such as *i*, *j*, *x*, and *y* are generally accepted for use as loop counters and coordinates. For other types of variables, you should choose names that are as descriptive as you can possibly make them.

Packages

Package name conventions are extremely important for two reasons:

- The Java2 platform is very picky about potentially ambiguous package names.
- Carefully chosen package names can avoid collisions between code developed in different companies using the same type names.

Suppose you have a package named my.pet.Squirrel. This package could contain any classes you wish. Suppose you also have a package named my.pet that contains class Squirrel. In this case, the fully qualified name my.pet.Squirrel is ambiguous. Just by looking at the name, you cannot determine if you mean the package my.pet.Squirrel or the class Squirrel in package my.pet. Because of this potential conflict, package names should be completely lowercase. In addition, due to differences in how platforms store file and directory names, keeping the name entirely lowercase limits potential problems when moving code between platforms.

Suppose you create a class named gui.Button. When you use your class, your application works fine. You deliver your application, including gui.Button to a user. At first, the application performs as expected. However, the user downloads another application from another developer. The other developer also has a class named gui.Button. Suddenly your application stops working! The problem is that because the fully qualified names of both classes are the same, the first one found in the CLASSPATH is used for both applications. To correct this problem, you should prefix your package name with your domain name, reversed. We reversed the domain name to keep the more generic parts of the name first. This also helps reduce the number of directories you need on your system to store the code.

Package names should be entirely lowercase, prefixed with your reversed domain name. For example,

```
com.javadude.tabsplitter
com.jguru.sample
edu.umich.stanchfield.scott.cs420.project.part1
```

> **NOTE**
>
> *Never* use the default package for any deliverable code! The default package is only really useful when first learning the Java language. You can use the default package to allow you to write code before you learn about packages. Whenever you want to send code to anyone else, you should place that code in a properly named package to avoid conflicts with other code that your user has installed.

Projects

Because projects are not Java constructs, there's no execution restriction on their names. We recommend that you use mixed case names with spaces between words. Note that projects can only include characters that are valid in Windows file names.

Workbench Layout

Let's start exploring the Workbench. The Workbench window is your main interface into VisualAge for Java. If it's not visible, you can always find it by choosing menu option **Window->Workbench**. You can see what the Workbench looks like in Figure 2.1.

Figure 2.1 The components of the Workbench.

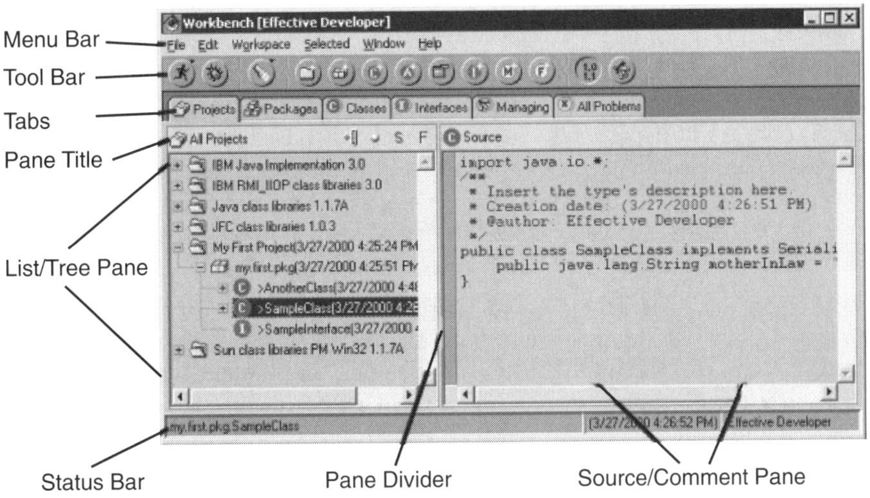

Menu Bar
Tool Bar
Tabs
Pane Title
List/Tree Pane
Status Bar
Pane Divider
Source/Comment Pane

> **NOTE**
>
> Figure 2.1 shows the Workbench in VisualAge for Java, Enterprise Edition, version 3.5. Version 3.5 contains a few new controls, such as the Resources tab, and the Enterprise Edition may contain the EJB (Enterprise JavaBeans) tab. If you are using and earlier version of VisualAge for Java, or the Entry or Professional Edition, some of these controls may not appear on your screen.
>
> Most of the screen captures that appear in this book were captured using Enterprise Edition, version 3.02. Screen captures from version 3.5 are used whenever the additional controls are important to the accompanying discussion.

What are all of these items?

Menu bar. You can choose several commands from the menus on the menu bar. We'll discuss many of them throughout the book, but you should browse through the options for yourself to see what's available.

Tool bar. Several common commands are available as buttons on the tool bar. You can turn the tool-bar display on or off using the customization options. We'll show you how to do this in Chapter 3.

Tabs. The tabs at the top of the screen enable you to switch between the various pages in the Workbench. In this chapter, we'll be staying on the first page, the Projects view. Note that you can move the tabs to the bottom of the screen if you prefer. We'll show you how to do this in Chapter 3.

Pane title. These title bars help you identify which pane is which. They also provide some controls to help you filter the view in that pane. We'll discuss these controls in Chapter 3. If you double-click in a pane title, that pane maximizes to fill the entire page view. Double-click in the pane title again and the other panes reappear. (You can also maximize a pane by pressing Ctrl-M if the pane has focus. You can change the Ctrl-M key mapping if you would like. See *Key Bindings* later in this chapter for details.)

List/Tree pane. This pane presents a list, tree, or graph of program elements. To work with an element, you select it by left-clicking on it, or bring up a pop-up menu for it by right-clicking on it. When a single element is selected, its source or comment will appear in the Source/Comment pane.

Status bar. The status bar presents data about the selected program element, or, if in the Visual Composition Editor, information about the currently selected bean. (The Visual Composition Editor is covered in Chapter 10, "Bean Composition in the VCE.")

Pane divider. You can resize the panes by dragging the pane divider. If you want a pane to completely fill the page, you can double-click its pane title.

Source/Comment pane. This is your text editor. If the selected program element is a class, interface, method, or field, the source for that element appears here. We discuss how to use the editor under "Editing Your Code" later in this chapter.

Creating Projects

Everything you work on in VisualAge for Java is contained within a Project. A project is simply a group of packages that you're working on for a given application or library. Projects are represented by the folder icon in the Workbench.

You can create a project by clicking the Add Project button on the tool bar. Clicking this button invokes the Add Project SmartGuide, as seen in Figure 2.2. You can also invoke the Add Project SmartGuide by bringing up a pop-up menu in the All Projects pane and choosing **Add->Project**.

> **NOTE**
>
> IBM uses the word "SmartGuide" to refer to its code-generation dialogs. You may have heard these types of dialogs called "wizards" in other IDEs.

Figure 2.2 Entering the project name.

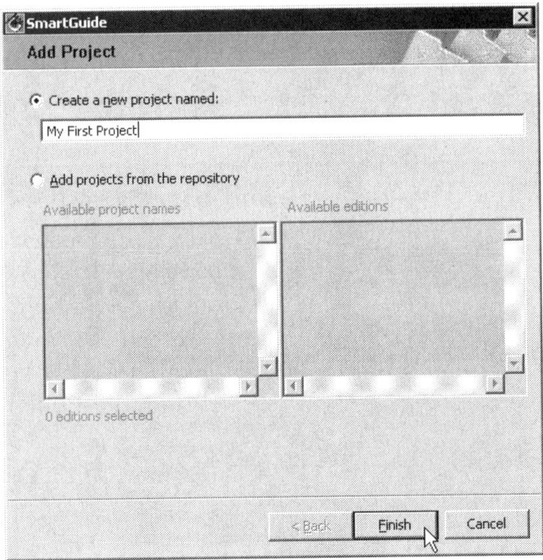

The Add Project SmartGuide gives you two options. You can either create a new project or add an existing project from the repository. Figure 2.2 shows use of the first option. You can type any name you want for the project (using valid file-name characters) and click Finish to create the project.

> **NOTE**
>
> Spaces *are* allowed in the project name!

Adding Elements from the Repository

Later we'll see how you can delete program elements (such as projects) from the workspace. VisualAge for Java will remove the element from your workspace but not from the repository. The deleted elements remain in the repository so that you or other programmers can access them later. This enables you to keep only the objects you need in your workspace, adding and deleting elements as needed.

You can add existing elements to the workspace by choosing the **Add ... from the repository** option of the SmartGuide. Projects, packages, classes, interfaces, and methods can be added using this option. For example, you can choose the **Add projects from the repository** option of the Add Project SmartGuide to choose projects to add. There is a similar option for each other type of program element.

Figure 2.3 Choosing an existing project.

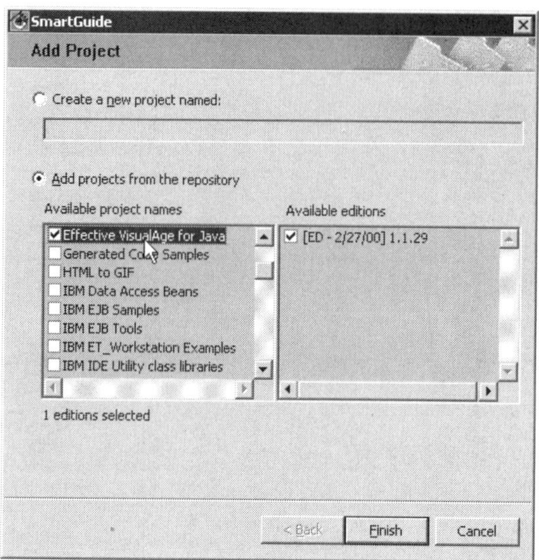

Figure 2.3 shows selection of the Effective VisualAge for Java project. When you select a project from the list on the left, multiple edition numbers will appear in the list on the right. You can select only one edition to add to your workspace. You select a project and edition number and then click **Finish** to add that project to your workspace.

Creating Packages

Packages are collections of classes and interfaces. VisualAge for Java represents a package as a box with string.

You can create a package by pressing the Add Package button on the tool bar. (You can also access this SmartGuide by choosing **Add->Package** from the All Projects pane pop-up menu.) This invokes the Add Package SmartGuide. To create a package, you enter a project name (by typing it or choosing it from a list by using the Browse button) and type the name of the package you want.

Note in Figure 2.4 that a small error message appears in the bottom left corner. You will see this message appear as you type the package name, any time you press a "." character. VisualAge validates the name on each keystroke, so at the time the name appears with a "." at the end, the package name is not valid. Keep typing; the error should disappear. For this example, however, we typed a truly invalid package name, because the word *package* is a reserved word in Java. For this example, change the package name to my.first.pkg, and click **Finish** to create the package.

> **TIP**
>
> If the project already exists, you can select it in the Workbench *before* pressing the Add Package button. When the SmartGuide appears, the project name field is pre-filled with the selected project.
>
> Note also that the project you type does not need to exist prior to invoking this SmartGuide. If you type a project that does not exist, VisualAge for Java will create it for you. Thus, if you need to create a new project and package, you can simply use the Add Package SmartGuide to add both at once.

To add an existing package, select the **Add package from repository** option and choose the package to add. This will add the selected package edition to the selected project in the workspace.

Finally, you can choose the **Create a default package** option. This will create a package named "Default Package for *project-name*" inside the project. You should *never* use this option for any real work. All real classes and interfaces should reside in a named package to avoid collisions with other code.

Figure 2.4 Specifying an invalid package name.

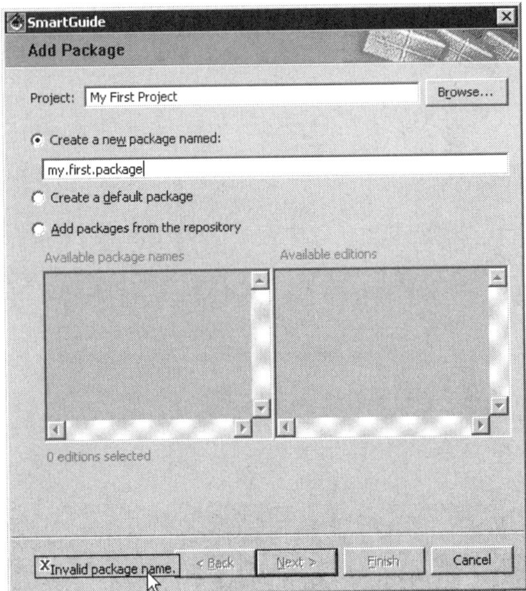

Creating Classes

VisualAge for Java represents classes using the symbol shown in the margin. You can create a class by clicking the Add Class button on the tool bar. See Figure 2.5.

Project. The name of the project in which the class will be generated. You can supply an existing project name, or enter a new one. The project will be created for you before the class is created. If you click the **Browse** button to the right of this field, you can select an existing project in the workspace from a dialog.

Package. The name of the package in which you want to create the class. If you specify an existing package and it is already loaded in a project, the project name is loaded automatically in the **Project** field. Otherwise, the package is created and loaded in the specified project. If you click the **Browse** button to the right of this field, you can select an existing package in the workspace from a dialog.

Class Name. The name of the class you want to create. VisualAge for Java will warn you if you don't start the class name with an uppercase

Figure 2.5 Entering the class name and superclass.

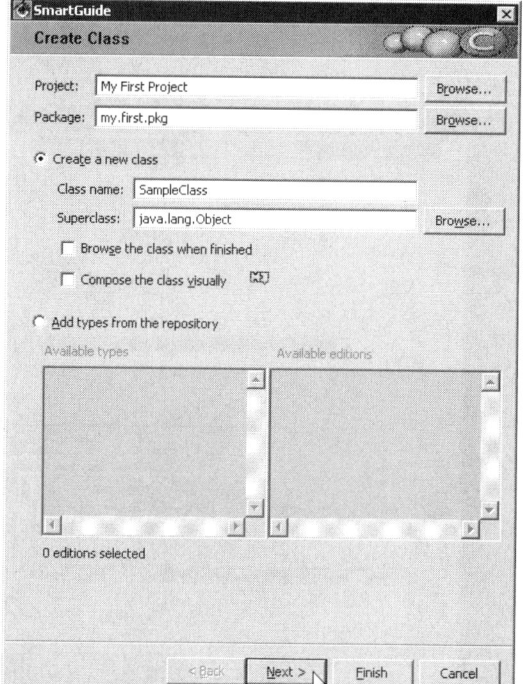

letter. You can turn this warning off, but we recommend you adhere to this simple naming convention and keep the warning turned on.

Superclass. The name of the class from which you want to inherit. The default class is java.lang.Object. If you leave this field as java.lang.Object or blank, VisualAge will not add an extends clause to the class definition. If you enter any other class name, VisualAge adds an extends clause for the specified class.

> **NOTE**
>
> You can use the class selection dialog to choose the superclass. This dialog, shown in Figure 2.6, also appears for many other dialogs in VisualAge for Java. You choose a class by typing the first few letters of the class name (or by typing a pattern); the list of possible class names appears. Do not type the package name, *just* the class name itself. You then select the class name you want and the package that contains it. If a given class name exists in multiple packages, there will be more than one package in the list. Make sure you always check to be sure the correct package is selected.

Figure 2.6 Selecting a class.

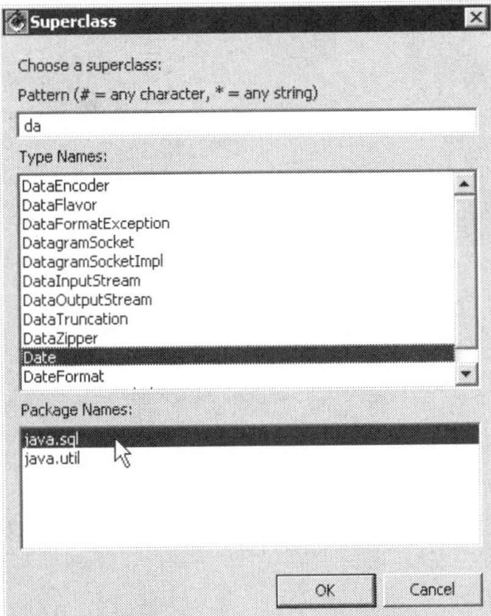

Browse the class when finished. If you choose this option, a class browser opens after the class is created. We discuss class browsers in Chapter 3.

Compose the Class Visually. If you select this option, the class browser opens to the Visual Composition Editor (VCE) page. We discuss visual composition in Chapter 10 "Bean Composition in the VCE."

You can also add existing classes using the **Add types from the repository** option. Note that you will only be allowed to add types that exist in the selected package in the repository.

When you click **Next**, you move to the Attributes page of the Add Class SmartGuide. You *can* click **Finish** at this point, but we strongly recommend you go to the Attributes page to specify imported packages and implemented interfaces. The Attributes page appears in Figure 2.7.

Add Import statements. You can supply a list of packages or types that the class you are creating imports. You must use the **Add Type** and **Add Package** buttons to fetch this information from the list of types and packages loaded in the workspace. You can use the **Superclass** button to copy the

Figure 2.7 Entering class attributes, imports, and interfaces.

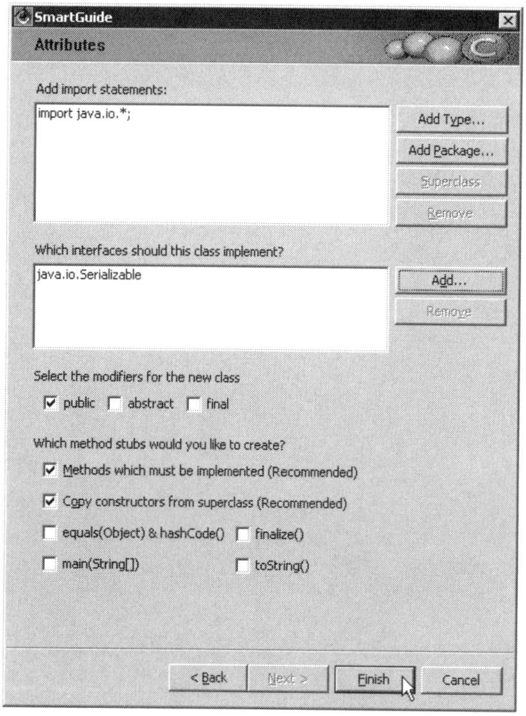

import statements from the class superclass. If you add an import statement that you do not want, select it and click the **Remove** button.

Which interfaces should this class implement. You can specify a list of interfaces that the class must implement. If an interface was selected at the time you started the Add Class SmartGuide, the interface name will already appear in this list. (You can select multiple interfaces, and they will all appear here.) Use the **Add** button to start a dialog that lets you choose interfaces from those loaded in the workspace.

Select the modifiers for the new class. You can specify whether the class should be **public**, **final**, **abstract**, or a combination of these modifiers.

Method stubs to create. These options automatically create stub methods. Stub methods are defined methods that have an empty body. After the class is created, you only have to fill in the details of these methods. Methods required when implementing an interface and methods belonging to abstract superclasses are generated automatically if the **Methods which must be implemented** option is selected. Constructors defined in the superclass can be copied in the new class. Finally, the following methods can be created on demand:

- **equals(Object) and hashCode().** Override both methods if you wish to use your class as a key in a hash table. The equals() method could also be used to test object equivalence based on the object contents and not on the object handle.
- **main().** Select this option if you are creating a class that is a Java application.
- **finalize().** Override this method if you want to run any code before your object is garbage-collected.
- **toString().** This method is useful when debugging an application. Override this method to display pertinent information about the inner state of the object at run time. See Chapter 5, "Testing and Debugging," for further information.

Once you have provided all the necessary information, click **Finish** to create the class.

If you specified a project or package that does not exist, they will be created for you.

Creating Applications and Applets

You can also create Application and Applet classes using the application and create applet icons. We discuss these SmartGuides in detail in Chapter 10.

Creating Interfaces

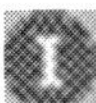

VisualAge for Java represents interfaces using the interface icon. The SmartGuide for creating interfaces is similar to the one used to create classes.

Creating Fields

VisualAge for Java represents fields using the field icon. There are three ways to create fields (instance or class variables) in a class:

- The Create Field SmartGuide.
- Typing the field directly into the class definition.
- Adding JavaBeans properties in the BeanInfo Editor.

The Create Field SmartGuide

You can create a field by pressing the Add Field button on the tool bar. This invokes the Create Field SmartGuide, seen in Figure 2.8.

Field name. The name of the field. A field usually starts with a lowercase letter.

Field type. The type of the field. If you click on the **Browse** button, you get the list of all types that are currently loaded in the workspace.

> **NOTE**
>
> If you're trying to choose a primitive type do *not* click the **Browse** button. Only class and interface names appear in the class selection dialog. Instead, choose the type using the drop-down list in this field or type the primitive type name.

Array and Dimension. Indicates if the field should be an array, and how many dimensions deep it is.

Initial value. The initial value of the field, declared in the class definition. Primitive Java types (int, short, boolean, and so forth) are initialized automatically to a default value if they are data members of a class. The default values are defined in the Java language. You should indicate a value if you use non-primitive types or when you want to specify value other than the default one.

Access modifiers. Indicates whether this field should be **private, public, protected,** or **none** (no modifier added).

Other modifiers. Indicates whether this field should be **final, static, volatile, transient,** or any combination of these.

Access with getter and setter methods. Select this option if you decide that a field should be accessed only through get and set accessor methods. This is usually a good practice. Depending on who should have the

Figure 2.8 The Create Field SmartGuide.

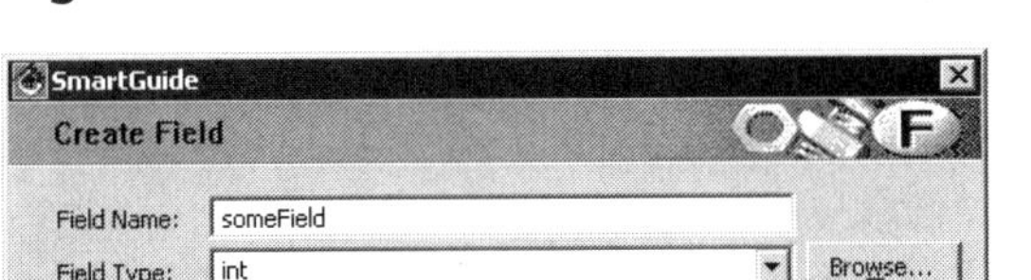

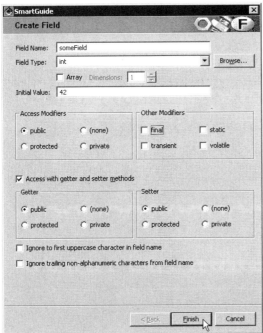

right to access this field, you can declare the getter and setter as **public, protected, private,** or **none** (no modifier added). By default, VisualAge for Java capitalizes the field name and prefixes it with *get-* or *set-* to generate the method names (whatever the field type is). If the field does not start with a letter (for example, an underscore), the *set-* and *get-* prefixes are added directly to the field name. If you want to use a different name, you need to modify the generated code. For example, for a field named numberOfTracks, the code for the getter and setter methods looks like this:

```
public short getNumberOfTracks() {
    return numberOfTracks;
}
public void setNumberOfTracks(short newValue) {
    this.numberOfTracks = newValue;
}
```

Ignore to first uppercase character in field name. If you define a field named fieldArtist, the getter and setter methods' names would be getArtist() and setArtist(), respectively.

Ignore non-alphanumeric trailing characters from field name. If you define a field named artist_, the getter and setter methods' names would be getArtist() and setArtist(), respectively.

Direct Field Entry

The simplest way to create fields in your class or interface is to simply type them into the class or interface definition. To do this, select the class or interface in the All Projects pane, and type the code for the field in the Source pane. For example, if you wanted to add an integer field named x, with an initial value of 5, you would add the code to the class definition as shown in bold in the following example:

```
import java.io.*;

/** This is a sample class */
public class SampleClass implements Serializable {
    private int x = 5;
}
```

When you save the class definition, VisualAge accepts the field. You can save the class definition by bringing up a pop-up menu in the Source pane and choosing **Save**.

WARNING

If you omit the semicolon when adding a variable definition, VisualAge may not be able to save the definition. If VisualAge complains about problems parsing the code, watch for missing semicolons or a missing type or variable name. For example:

```
import java.io.*;

/** This is a sample class */
public class SampleClass implements Serializable {
    private int = 5;
}
```

This is a common typo; missing the type or variable name is easy to do, and VisualAge will complain bitterly. To correct it, add the missing type or variable name and save it.

Fields for JavaBeans Component Properties

If you want to create a JavaBeans property, you should use the BeanInfo editor to create the property, rather than the Create Field SmartGuide. See Chapter 7, "Introduction to JavaBeans Components," for general information on JavaBeans properties, and Chapter 8, "The BeanInfo Editor," for details on creating properties in VisualAge for Java.

Creating Methods

VisualAge for Java represents methods using the method icon. There are several ways to create methods in VisualAge for Java. You can use SmartGuides to create them, type code by hand, or copy methods from other classes. In this section, we explore each of these method-creation techniques.

The Create Method SmartGuide

You can create a method by pressing the Add Method button on the tool bar. This invokes the Create Method SmartGuide, shown in Figure 2.9.

You have four choices in this SmartGuide:

Figure 2.9 The Create Method SmartGuide.

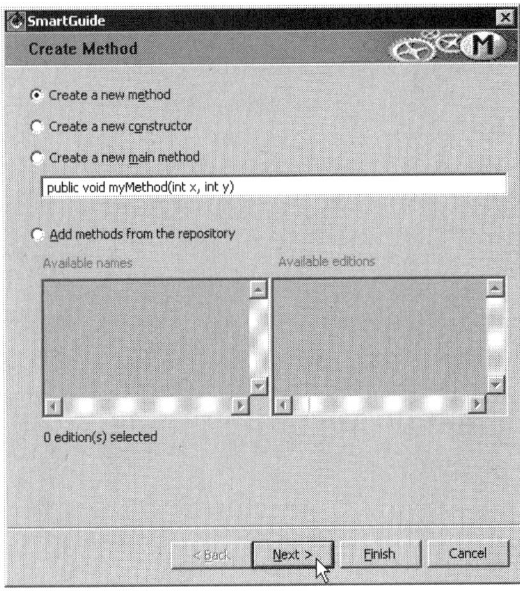

Create a new method. Adds any method you would like to the selected class. You must specify the name of the method to create.

Create a new constructor. Adds a new constructor to the selected class. You do not need to enter the name of the method.

Create a new main method. The easy way to add a main() method to a class. You do not need to enter the name of the method.

Add methods from the repository. Adds an existing method to the class. The lists below this option display any methods that used to exist in the selected class but have been deleted. This makes it safe to delete methods from a class, because you can easily add it back later if you change your mind.

Clicking **Next** moves you onto the Attributes page, seen in Figure 2.10.

On the Attributes page, you have the following options:

Method name. Allows you to specify the name of the method. This will be filled in with the name of the method that you typed on the first page of the SmartGuide.

Return type. Allows you to specify the return type of the method.

Array. Select this box if the return type of the method is an array.

Figure 2.10 Method attributes.

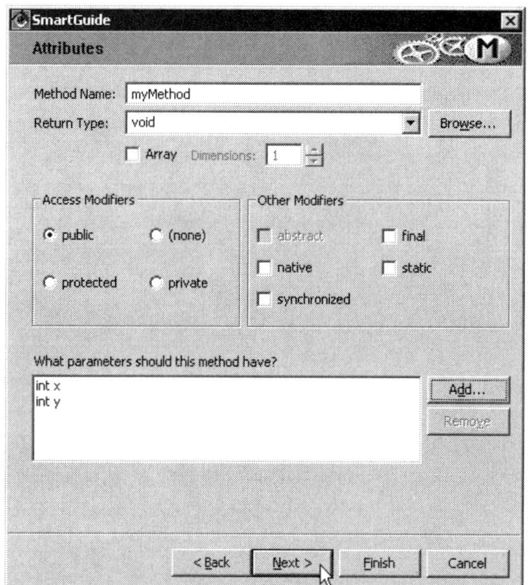

Dimensions. Available only when the **Array** option is selected, this option specifies how many dimensions the return-type array has. The number of dimensions is the same as the number of [ ] pairs that you would type after the type name.

Access Modifiers. Specify the access level of the method: **public**, **(none)**, **protected**, or **private**.

Other Modifiers. Allows you to specify additional modifiers that are added to the front of the method declaration.

What parameters should this method have? If you specified parameters on the first page of the method SmartGuide, they will appear here. You can **add** or **remove** parameters from this list. The order in which the parameters are listed is the order in which they will appear in the method declaration.

Click **Next** to proceed. The last page of the method SmartGuide allows you to specify which exceptions this method will throw. After entering any exceptions, click **Finish** to create the method.

> **TIP**
>
> The method SmartGuide is really useful for two tasks: adding a main() method, or adding an existing method from the repository. We recommend that you not use it to create other methods or constructors, because it usually ends up taking longer to move through the dialog than it does to type the method manually.

Manual Method Entry

An alternate technique for entering methods is to just type the method directly in the class or interface definition. For example, suppose you wanted to add a method named doTheHustle() to a class named SomeClass. You would select SomeClass and type the new method in the Source pane.

```
import java.io.*;

/** This is a sample class */
public class SomeClass implements Serializable {
    public void doTheHustle() {
        ...
    }
}
```

When you save the method (by choosing **Save** from the Source pane's pop-up menu), VisualAge rips it out of the class definition and stores it as a separate method. The method is listed in the All Projects pane under the class.

Creating a Method Using Save

In VisualAge for Java there are two ways to save source: *Save new* and *Save replace*. The difference between the two is the effect they have when you change the signature of a method.

VisualAge for Java keeps track of methods in a given type by the method signature. The signature is the combination of the method name and the types of its parameters. The Java language uses the signature to distinguish one method from another. VisualAge for Java, following the *Java Language Specification*, considers methods with different signatures to be different methods.

Whenever you edit a method, you may or may not change the signature. You might add or remove parameters, change a type of one of the parameters, or change the name of the method. VisualAge can interpret the change in two ways:

Save new. If you choose **Save** from the pop-up menu in the Source pane, VisualAge performs a Save-new action. This action tells VisualAge that you want to create an entirely new method when you change the signature. If you change a method's signature and perform a Save-new, the changes to the old method are saved in a new method, and the old method does not change.

Save replace. If you choose **Save replace** from the pop-up menu of the Source pane, VisualAge saves the changes to the method. If the signature changes, VisualAge *deletes* the old method from the workspace and saves the changes as a new method in the type. (You can recover the deleted method by choosing the **Add existing methods from the repository** option in the add method SmartGuide.)

Using Save-new, you can create methods by making a few changes to an existing method, including changing the signature. In general, you will usually want to perform a Save-replace, because you will usually be adding or removing a parameter instead of overloading a method.

Method Templates

This feature adds a new method, *void newMethod()*, to the class. When you use this function, the user-defined method comment defined in the Workbench options (described in Chapter 3) is put in the head of the method. This is the only advantage over writing the code manually.

To create a method template, select the type to which you want to add a method, and choose **Method Template** from its pop-up menu, as shown in Figure 2.11. (You can also press Ctrl-T after selecting a type.) After the new method appears, you can edit and save it as you would like.

Figure 2.11 Creating a method using the method template command.

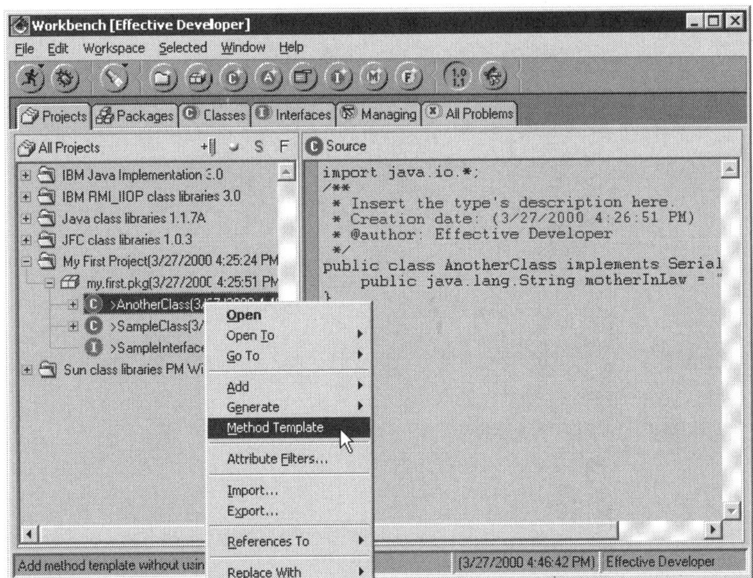

> **TIP**
>
> Make sure you choose **Save replace** when saving the new method, or you will end up with two methods: newMethod() and the method you wanted to create.

Generating Required Methods

Often, you will not realize that you need to make a class implement an interface until after you have created it. You can easily add an implements clause to the class definition by typing it in, but you still need to write the methods for the interface.

The problem is that it is very easy to mistype the method signatures. Fortunately, VisualAge for Java provides a function to automatically add skeleton code for each method that the interface requires. To use this option:

1. Add an implements clause to the class you want to modify. This tells the compiler that you intend to provide the methods defined in the specified interface.
2. Choose **Generate->Required Methods** from the pop-up menu for the class, as seen in Figure 2.12.

Figure 2.12 Generating methods required by interfaces or abstract superclasses.

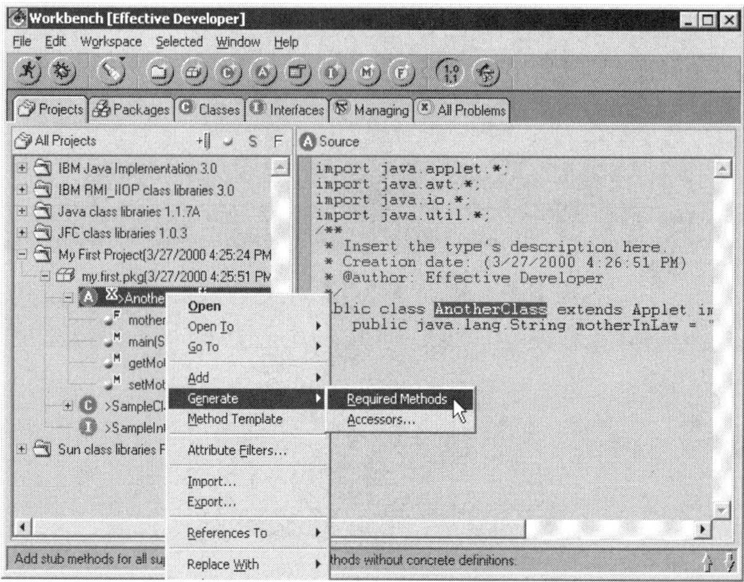

VisualAge adds a skeleton method for each method defined in the interface. You can then edit these methods to provide the functionality you need.

Creating Accessor Methods for Fields

It is possible to define or redefine accessors for existing fields. You can generate accessors for fields defined in a class or for one single field. If getter and setter methods are already defined, you can preserve or redefine them. Bring a pop-up menu for a class or field, and select **Generate->Accessors**, as shown in Figure 2.13.

This invokes the Generating Accessors dialog, shown in Figure 2.14.

The list of fields is displayed at the top of the window. If accessors are found for a field, an [existing get/set] message is displayed near the field name.

You can press the **Select fields without accessors** button to select all fields that do not currently have accessors in the fields list. If you started the Generate Accessors tool from a field, the corresponding entry in the list is pre-selected. The instance, static, and final check boxes let you filter which fields should appear in the list.

If you select the **Replace existing accessors** option, a new edition of the get and set methods is created, replacing any existing get or set method for the field in question. If you have modified the original accessor code, you can retrieve your changes from the repository.

Figure 2.13 Starting the Generate Accessors SmartGuide.

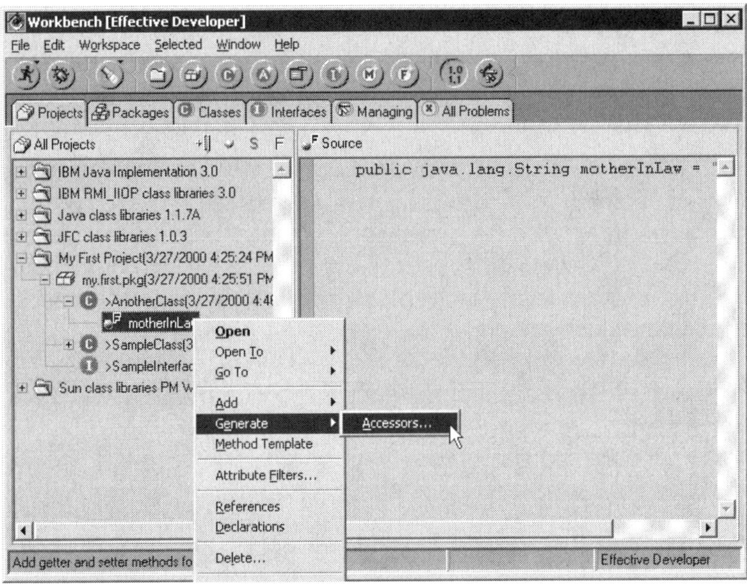

Figure 2.14 Choosing accessors to create.

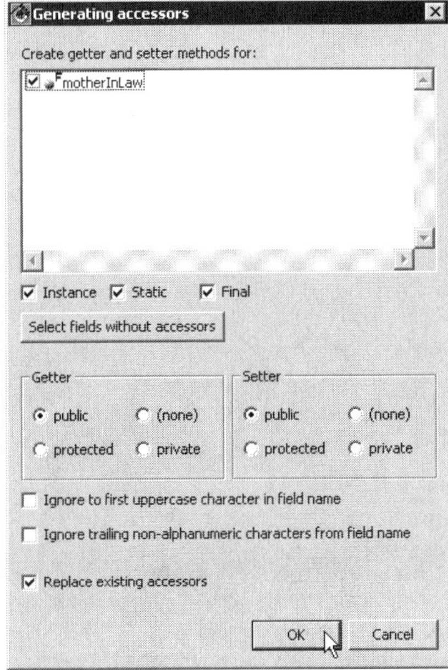

Overriding Methods

In Chapter 3, we discuss an easy way to override methods. We won't discuss it further here.

Editing Your Code

VisualAge for Java provides a very basic editor, with a few very advanced features. While it may not compare to an editor like emacs or SlickEdit, you really don't need all of the extra power these other editors provide. Most of the extra functionality you would use in these other editors is replaced by functions of the VisualAge for Java IDE. In this section, we explore the functionality of the editor so you can get the most productivity out of it.

Basic Editing

Let's start by looking at the basics of the editor. If you're already familiar with other editors in Windows, you probably already know how to perform these actions. You can change the key mapping (see *Key Bindings* later in this chapter) if you would rather use different key combinations than we discuss here. Two default key mappings are provided: the standard VisualAge for Java keys, and an emacs-like key mapping.

Cursor Movement

Code movement begins with the arrow keys.

Arrow keys move the cursor up, down, left or right in your code.

Ctrl-Arrow keys moves the cursor in that direction by an entire word. Ctrl-Up or Ctrl-Down move the cursor up or down a single line.

Home moves the cursor to the start of the current line.

End moves the cursor to the end of the current line.

Ctrl-Home moves the cursor to the top of the current source or comment.

Ctrl-End moves the cursor to the bottom of the current source or comment.

Alt-Home moves the cursor to the top of the current page of code.

Alt-End moves the cursor to the bottom of the current page of code.

PgUp scrolls the source or comment up one page.

PgDn scrolls the source or comment down one page.

Mouse wheel up/down pages up or down in the source or comment.

You can also move the cursor by clicking anywhere in the code or by moving the horizontal and vertical scrollbars with the mouse.

> **NOTE**
>
> If you are using a wheeled mouse, rolling the wheel acts like page-up and page-down commands in the currently-selected pane. If this does not work for you, make sure you have the latest mouse drivers, especially for the Microsoft Intellimouse.

> **New in version 3.5!**
>
> 3.5 If you rest the mouse cursor over a variable or class name when working with VisualAge for Java, version 3.5, a tool tip appears that describes the variable or class name. This can be very helpful when examining code that you're not familiar with. Note that this feature only appears to work if you don't have focus in the source/comment pane. The easiest way to do this is to click on the name of the current method in the tree pane, then float the cursor over the variable or class name in the source/comment pane.

Selecting Code

There are several commands in the editor that act upon selected code. You can select code using any of the following actions.

Shift-Arrow Keys extend or reduce the current selection in the direction you move the cursor. For example, if you want to select a line, move the cursor to the beginning of the line (by pressing Home) and press Shift-Down.

Ctrl-Shift-Arrow Keys extend or reduce the current selection by a word (left or right arrow) or by a line (up or down arrow).

Ctrl-A selects all text in the Source/Comment pane.

Shift-Home selects all text from the current cursor position to the start of the line.

Shift-End selects all text from the current cursor position to the end of the line.

Ctrl-Shift-Home selects all text from the current cursor position to the beginning of the text.

Ctrl-Shift-End selects all text from the current cursor position to the end of the text.

Alt-Shift-Home selects all text from the current cursor position to the top of the currently viewed page of text.

Alt-Shift-End selects all text from the current cursor position to the bottom of the currently viewed page of text.

Shift-PgDn extends the selection to the next page of text.

Shift-PgUp extends the selection to the previous page of text.

In addition, you can use the mouse to select code as follows:

Dragging the mouse selects the text underneath the cursor.

Double-clicking on a word selects the word underneath the cursor.

Double-clicking to the right of an opening delimiter selects all text to the matching closing delimiter. The delimiters on which this works are the left parenthesis, left curly brace, left square bracket, and double quotation marks.

Double-clicking to the left of a closing delimiter selects all text to the matching opening delimiter. The delimiters on which this works are the right parenthesis, right curly brace, right square bracket, and double quotation marks.

Single-clicking in the selection area to the left of the text selects the line of text. The selection area can be seen in Figure 2.15.

Figure 2.15 The selection area.

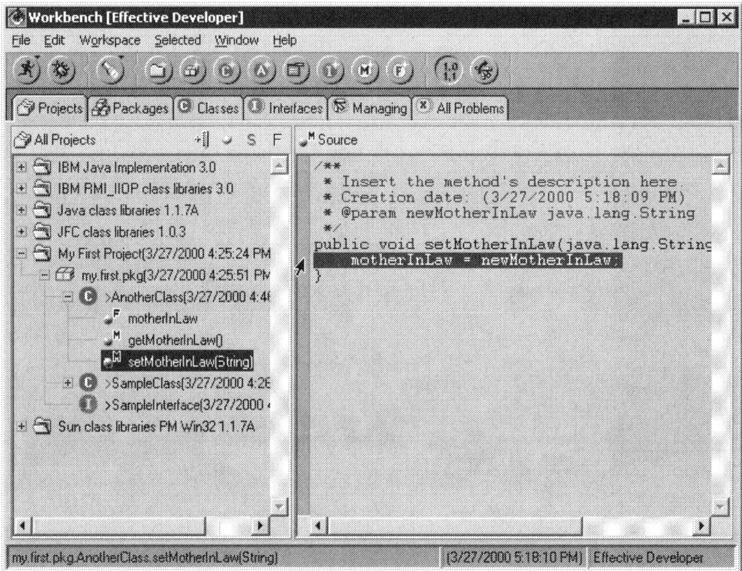

Copy/Cut/Paste

You can perform the following actions to move code in your text.

Ctrl-C or Ctrl-Insert copies the selected text to the system clipboard.

Ctrl-X or Shift-Delete cuts the selected text, removing it from the Source/Comment pane and placing it in the system clipboard.

Ctrl-V or Shift-Insert places the current clipboard text at the cursor location in the Source/Comment pane. If you have text selected in the Source/Comment pane, the selected text is *replaced* by the clipboard text.

You can also access the cut/copy/paste commands from the Edit menu or from the pop-up menu in the Source/Comment pane.

Undo and Redo

VisualAge for Java keeps track of the last twenty changes you have made to your text. You can undo any of these changes by pressing Ctrl-Z or selecting **Edit->Undo**. If you want to redo a change that you have undone, you can press Ctrl-Y or select **Edit->Redo**.

Saving Your Changes

You can save your changes using the Save new or Save replace commands. By default, Save new is mapped to Ctrl-S, and Save replace is mapped to Ctrl-Shift-S. See *Creating a Method Using Save* earlier in this chapter for details on the difference between Save new and Save replace.

> **NOTE**
>
> We strongly recommend that you *reverse* the mapping of these keys. It is much more common to add a parameter to a method than overloading that method. By swapping the key mappings, you can use Ctrl-S for all editing activities except overloading, and Ctrl-Shift-S for overloading methods. See *Key Bindings* later in this chapter for details on changing your mapped keys.

If you try to switch methods (by clicking on another method in the Tree/List pane) *before* saving your changes, VisualAge will ask if you want to save the changes in a small dialog. You can choose:

Yes to save the changes you've made and switch to the new method.

No to discard the changes you've made, and switch to the new method.

Cancel to forget about changing to the new method and return to editing the current method.

> **TIP**
>
> Get used to pressing Ctrl-S after you're done editing. If you press Ctrl-S *before* selecting another method to edit, you won't need to react to the additional "Do you want to save changes" dialog.

Searching in the Source/Comment Pane

VisualAge for Java has several searching facilities. You can search for text in the Source/Comment pane, search for program elements in the workspace, search for text in the workspace, or perform management queries to find out what your developers have been working on. In this section, we'll talk about searching in Source/Comment pane. In Chapter 3 we'll discuss the other searching functions in VisualAge for Java.

There are two types of searches provided when editing code:

Find/Replace provides search for a specific string with the option to replace that string.

Incremental Find helps you locate text using a minimal number of keystrokes.

Let's see how these functions work.

Find/Replace

When you press Ctrl-F in the editor, or select **Edit->Find/Replace**, VisualAge for Java will display the Find/Replace dialog, seen in Figure 2.16.

This dialog allows you to enter some text to find, and, optionally, text to replace the found text. The options in this dialog are:

Find what. Enter the text you want to locate in this field.

Replace with. If you want to replace the found text, enter the replacement in this field.

Direction. Choose Down or Up to search for the text below or above the current cursor position, respectively.

Match case. Select this box if you only want to find the text when it exactly matches the **Find what** string. If this box is not selected, letters in the found string can be either upper- or lowercase.

Whole words. Select this box if you don't want to find the string as part of a larger word. For example, suppose you enter "radio" as the **Find**

Figure 2.16 The Find/Replace dialog.

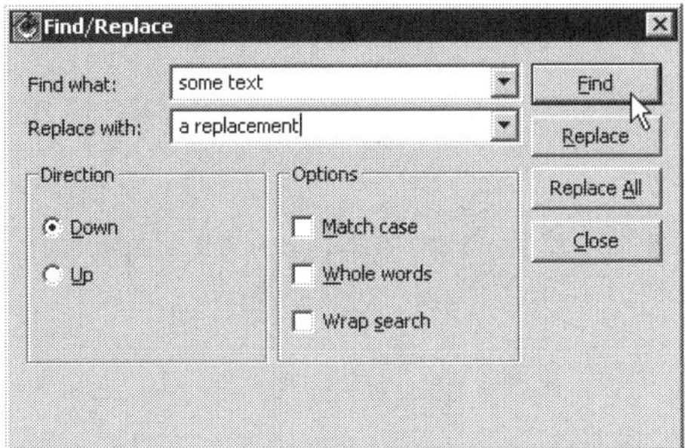

what string: If this box is selected, the find will not stop on "radioButton" in the text.

Wrap search. Select this box if you want to keep searching past the end or beginning of the text. The search will wrap to the opposite end of the text and continue in the same direction. This is usually a good option to check.

Find. When you click this button, the search proceeds to the next piece of text matching the search criteria.

Replace. When you click this button, the currently selected occurrence of the search text is replaced, and the next occurrence is found. If you haven't found the text yet, this button acts the same as the Find button.

Replace all. When you press this button, all occurrences of the **Find what** string are automatically replaced with the **Replace -with** string. Be careful with this option, because it may replace partial strings in the text as well. (You may want to select the **Whole words** option when using **Replace all.**)

Close. If you press this button, the Find/Replace dialog is closed.

Incremental Find

Incremental find works a little differently than a traditional find. If you are looking for a rather long string, a traditional find can be cumbersome, because you must type a lot of text in the **Find what** field. Incremental find helps by locating the first text after the cursor position that matches the characters you have typed. Each time you type a new character, the find may progress to another piece of text.

You invoke incremental find by pressing Ctrl-I in the Source/Comment pane. After pressing Ctrl-I, "I-Search" is displayed in the status bar. You then start typing letters, each of which will appear in the status bar. If the current selection matches the letters typed, it remains the current selection. Otherwise, the search proceeds further in the text for the first piece of text that matches the letters typed so far. Often, you can find the text you're seeking with only a few keystrokes. If you end up typing the entire name, you can keep pressing Ctrl-I to find the next occurrence that matches the letters typed.

Code Completion

One of the advanced features of the VisualAge for Java editor is code completion. This feature is what really sets an environment like VisualAge for Java apart from traditional text editors.

You start code completion by pressing Ctrl-space or Ctrl-L while editing. VisualAge for Java presents a pop-up window that contains possible completions based on the text you've typed so far.

For example, suppose you type *Sy* followed by Ctrl-space. VisualAge presents the pop-up window shown in Figure 2.17.

You can choose the proper completion by double-clicking it in the list or pressing the arrow keys and then Enter. If the list is rather large, you can continue typing letters to narrow it. In the above example, if you type the letter S, the completion list narrows to only those items that start with *Sys-*.

The list of completions is based on the semantics of the text preceding the cursor. For example, if you had typed *System.out* followed by Ctrl-space, the list would contain only methods and variables in the PrintStream class (because System.out is a class variable of type PrintStream). This makes code completion

Figure 2.17 The code completion pop-up window.

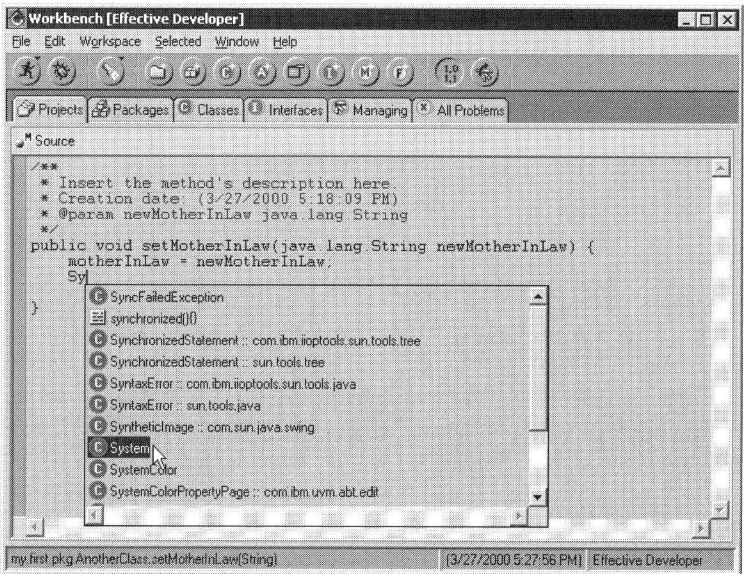

an excellent way to see what methods are available. Rather than constantly looking at the javadoc for a class to find the proper method to call, you can use code completion to see what methods are available.

> **TIP**
>
> Code completion is your friend. Force yourself to use it a lot when you're starting to learn VisualAge for Java. It can save you a great deal of typing and, more importantly, reduce the number of typos you make when writing your code.

Keyword Completion

Keyword completion is a form of code completion that lets you choose templates for your code. You define templates by choosing **Window->Options->Coding->Keyword completions** from the menu bar. You can see this dialog in Figure 2.18. Enter any text you want for the completion, adding <|> (less than, vertical bar, greater than) inside the code to represent where you want the cursor to appear after the completion.

Using the definition shown in Figure 2.18, you can type *for* in the editor, followed by Ctrl-space, and see the possible keyword completions. You select which for-template you want and press Enter. If you choose the for(;;){} template, the following code is inserted in the editor:

```
for(;;) {

}
```

The cursor will be placed before the first semicolon.We discuss more of the Options dialog in Chapter 3.

Macros

A more general completion is the macro facility. You can define any text that you want to act as a macro, and its replacement. A good example is a replacement for the often-used statement:

```
System.out.println();
```

If you hate to type that as much as we do, you'll be happy to know that you can define a macro as shown in Figure 2.19. You can get to the macro definitions by selecting **Window->Options->Coding->Macros**.

Once you're in the macros page, click **Add** to create a new macro definition. VisualAge will prompt you for the name of the macro (we recommend "sop" for

Figure 2.18 Defining keyword completions.

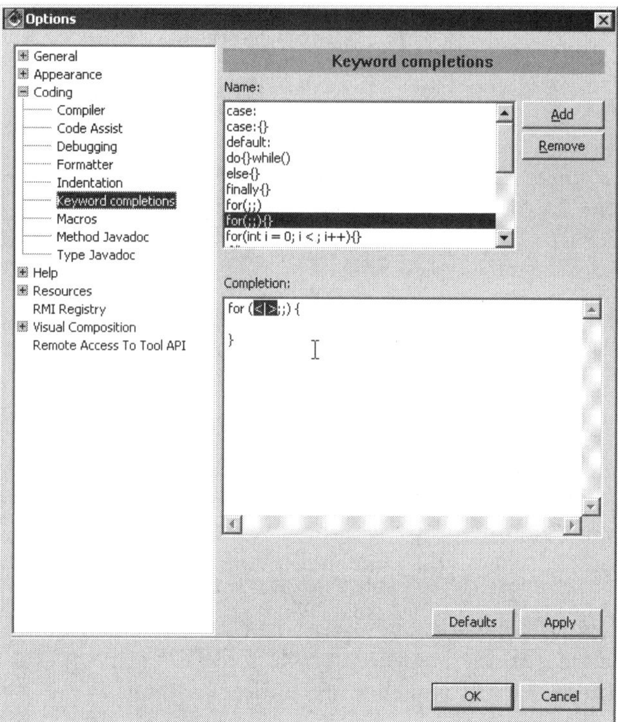

this example). Then you enter the expansion. In this example, we entered the following as the expansion:

```
System.out.println(<|>);
```

This means that choosing "sop" in the code completion pop-up window will enter System.out.println(); in the text, with the cursor placed between the parentheses.

We discuss more of the Options dialog in Chapter 3.

> **TIP**
>
> When creating a macro, try to choose a name that will be unique with as few leading letters as possible. In this example, "sop" is a great choice, because it's unique in the VisualAge environment. "sysop" is less desirable, because you need to type more letters to get a unique completion.

Figure 2.19 Defining custom macros.

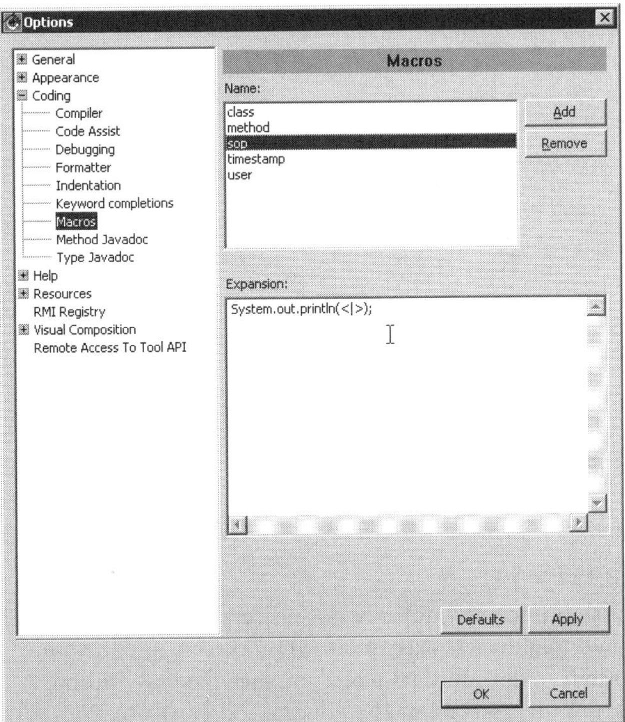

Compilation Errors

Whenever you save a method or type in VisualAge for Java, it is automatically compiled. If your code contains errors, VisualAge reports this in several ways. By default, VisualAge provides a warning dialog, seen in Figure 2.20, that alerts you of any code errors. If you see this dialog, you have three choices:

Save the code with the errors. You can always fix them later.

Correct the errors using one of the suggested corrections in the dialog.

Cancel the save action. This drops you back into the editor where you can fix the changes and try saving again.

In some cases, VisualAge will tell you that the changes cannot be saved. This usually occurs when editing a type definition if you have mismatched curly braces. In a case like this, you must fix the problem and try to resave.

Figure 2.20 Correcting an error in the error dialog.

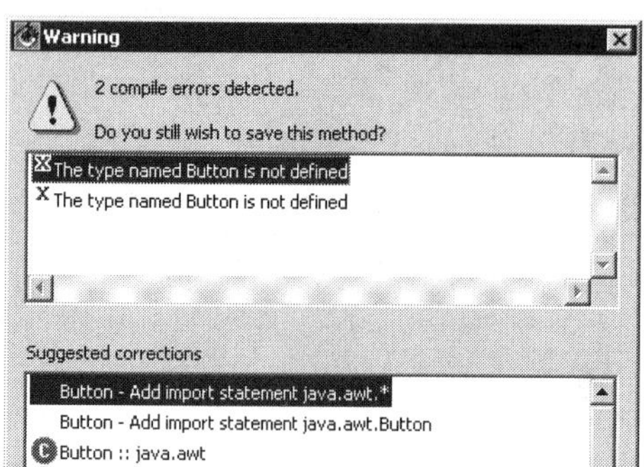

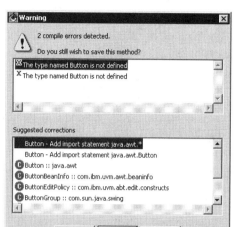

Other Ways to Tell if You Have Errors

To many people, the error dialog is a major annoyance during development. Often, you'll write code to call a method that doesn't exist and then proceed to add that new method. Unfortunately, the warning dialog appears when you save the first method, telling you what you already know: The second method doesn't exist.

VisualAge for Java provides several cues that there are errors in a method or type definition besides the warning dialog. Take a look at Figure 2.21. This is what the Workbench might look like after you edit and save a method. Note the indicators that you have an error:

A gray X appears next to the class name. This means that there is an error in one of the methods in the class. If this had been a red "X" on the class name, it would mean the class definition itself contains an error.

A red X appears next to the method name. This means that the method contains an error.

The offending text is selected in the source pane. The text is selected, which gives you a great visual cue that there is a problem.

The error message appears in the status bar. The text describing the first error in the method appears here so you can see what the compiler is complaining about.

With so many indications that there is an error, do we really need the error dialog? The only real advantage to the error dialog is the automatic-correction feature. However, this is usually less useful than it might seem. For the most part,

Figure 2.21 Some not-so-subtle hints that you have a problem.

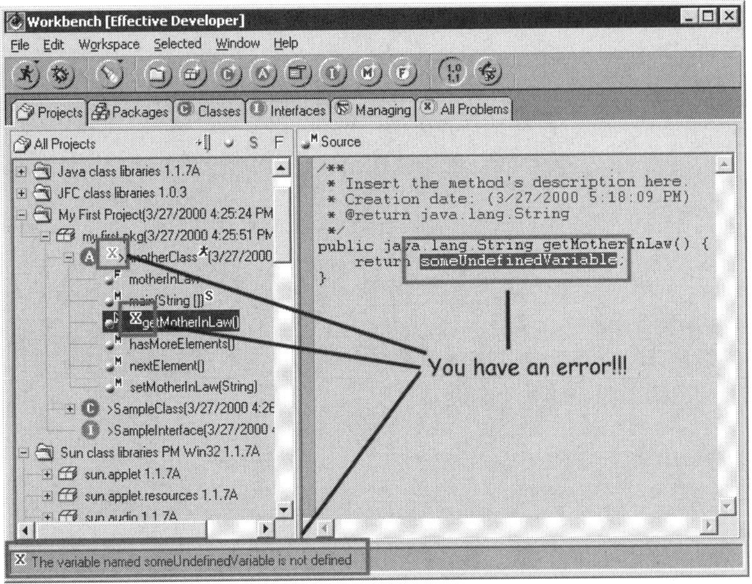

the only time it helps is to add missing import statements to the class definition, and that type of error usually only occurs a few times for each class.

So how can we get rid of the annoying error dialog?

Getting Rid of the Error Dialog

To prevent the error dialog from appearing, choose **Window->Options->Coding** (as seen in Figure 2.22) and clear the **Report problems before saving** check box. You'll still see the other indicators shown in Figure 2.21, but the warning dialog will not appear.

We discuss more of the Options dialog in Chapter 3.

Formatting Your Code

VisualAge for Java provides a Format code option, available by pressing Ctrl-W or by choosing **Edit->Format code.** This reformats code based on several options in the Options dialog that we'll discuss in Chapter 3.

However, you should not use this option very often for the following reasons:

- The formatter places all parameters to method calls on a single line. This often makes the code contain very long lines.
- The formatter removes any blank lines that do not precede a comment line.

Figure 2.22 Shutting off the error dialog.

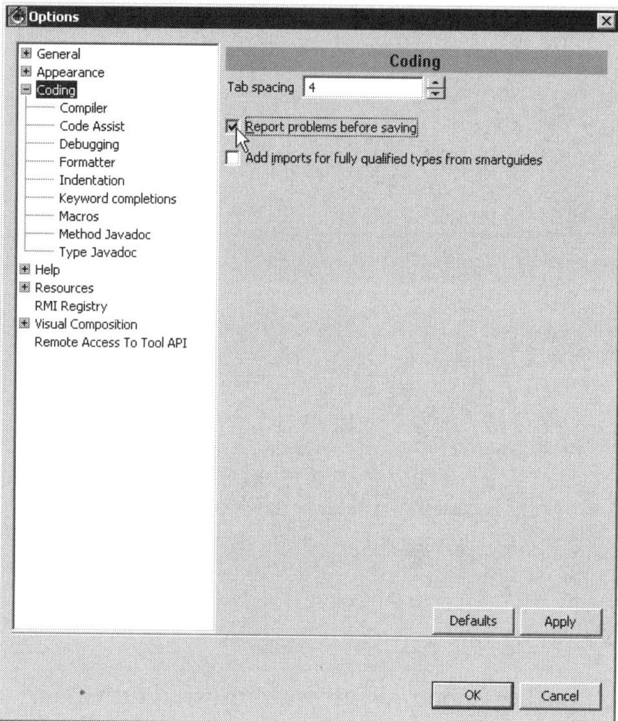

> **TIP**
>
> We recommend that you use the Format code command only if the code is in really bad shape or you're having trouble finding mismatched curly braces. After an initial format, we recommend that you handle the formatting yourself.

Key Bindings

You can change the way the keyboard interacts with VisualAge for Java in the Key Bindings dialog, seen in Figure 2.23. You can get to this dialog by choosing **Window->Options->General->Key Bindings**. To change key bindings, click on the key sequence to change and press the new key sequence.

You can create your own profiles for key settings by clicking the **Add** button at the top of the dialog. VisualAge for Java comes with two profiles, one for the

Figure 2.23 Changing key bindings.

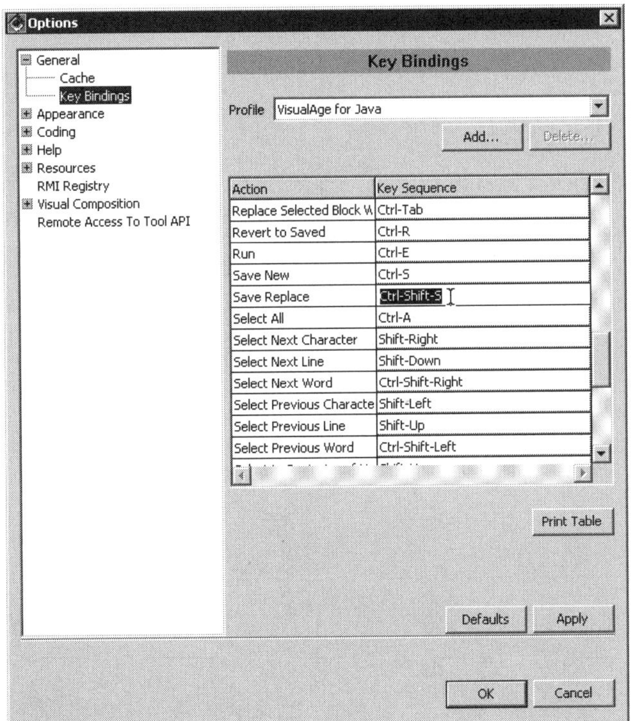

default bindings that we describe in this chapter, and one that mimics the emacs text editor.

We discuss more of the Options dialog in Chapter 3.

The Whatis Command

While working in VisualAge for Java, you can press F6 to invoke the Whatis command. Whatis allows you to find out what a given key is mapped to. For example, if you wanted to know what Ctrl-C currently does, you would press F6 followed by Ctrl-C. VisualAge displays "Control-c runs the command Copy" in the status bar.

Miscellaneous Commands

The following commands are available during editing and don't really fall under any other category.

Goto Line Number

If you want to go to the seventeenth line in the code you're editing, press Ctrl-G. This displays a dialog asking which line you want to go to.

> **TIP**
>
> This command is actually more useful if you want to find out how many lines a method contains. When you press Ctrl-G, the Goto Line dialog displays the value range of line numbers. The higher number is the number of lines in the method.

Open Selection

If you select a type name in your code and press F3, VisualAge for Java will open a class or interface browser for the selected type. We discuss class and interface browsers in Chapter 3.

> **NOTE**
>
> You must actually *select* the type name, not simply have your cursor on top of it.

Revert to Saved

If you have made some changes to a method or type and want to completely discard them, you can choose the Revert-to-Saved command by pressing Ctrl-R or choosing **Edit->Revert to Saved.**

> **WARNING**
>
> Be careful of this command. There is no verification that you meant to revert the changes. Always keep in mind that Ctrl-R is Revert to Saved, *not* Replace as it is in some editors.

Commenting Code

You can comment out a selected block of code by pressing Ctrl-/ (Ctrl and slash). This places single-line comment delimiters in front of each selected line. You can uncomment lines that begin with single-line comment delimiters by selecting those lines and pressing Ctrl-\ (Ctrl and backslash).

Indenting Code

You can indent code by selecting the lines to indent and pressing the Tab key. You can remove indentation of selected lines by pressing Shift-Tab.

Sorting Selected Lines (version 3.5 and later)

3.5 Version 3.5 of VisualAge for Java provides a line-sorting option. This option is not available via a menu, nor is it bound to a key by default. You add a key binding for "Sort Selected Lines" through the options dialog's "Key Bindings" page as discussed above.

To use this feature, select the lines you want to sort and press the key you bound for "Sort Selected Lines."

Program Element Properties

Each program element has a properties dialog. You can access these dialogs by choosing **Properties** from the pop-up menu of a method, class, interface, package, or project. Most of the properties dialogs just give you information about the version of the program element. Class property dialogs provide some options that you may need to set when running a class as an application or applet.

Applet Parameters

If the selected class is an applet, the properties dialog will contain an Applet page as seen in Figure 2.24.

The Applet page lets you define how VisualAge for Java runs this applet, and the details it uses when generating an HTML file. (See Chapter 6, "Integrating with the File System," for details on creating HTML as part of exporting code to the file system.) VisualAge for Java doesn't use an HTML file to run applets internally. It uses the information you specify here to determine how large to display the applet and what parameters to pass to the applet.

The applet parameters page specifies the default parameters to be used whenever you run the applet. In VisualAge for Java, version 3.5, you can override these values for a single run by choosing **Run->In Applet Viewer with** option to execute the applet. We'll discuss running applets in detail under the section *Running Your Code* later in this chapter.

Note the **Save in repository (as default)** option. If you check this box, the specified information is stored in the repository. Anyone else who accesses the class will see these parameters. Be very careful about using this option in a team environment!

Program Parameters

If your class has a main() method, you will see the Program options tab. Selecting this tab displays the page shown in Figure 2.25.

Figure 2.24 The applet parameters page.

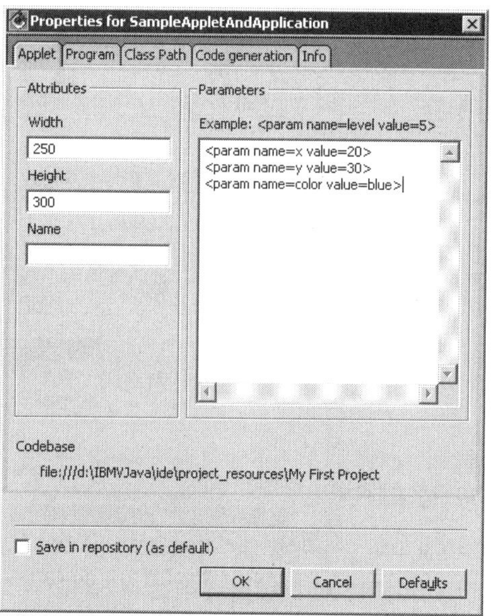

Figure 2.25 The program parameters page.

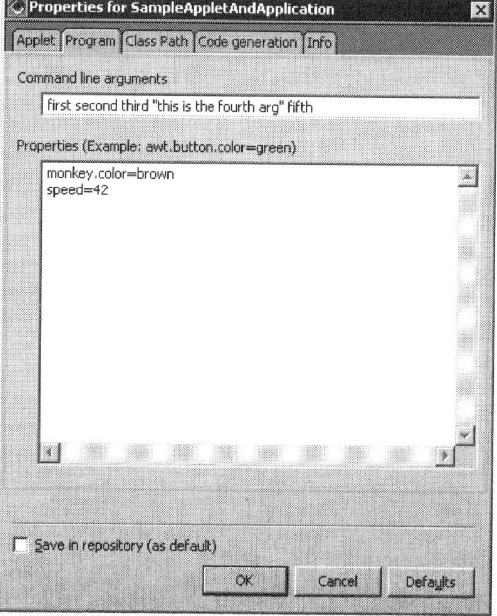

On this page, you can specify the command-line arguments to your application, as well as any system properties that you want to set. (System properties are normally passed by adding -D options to the command line before the application class name, and can be accessed inside your application by calling the System.getProperty() method.)

The program parameters page specifies the default parameters to be used whenever you run the application. In VisualAge for Java, version 3.5, you can override these values for a single run by choosing **Run->Run main with** option to execute the applet. We'll discuss running applications in detail under the section *Running Your Code* later in this chapter.

NOTE

Each word in the command line arguments field is considered an argument, and becomes a separate String in the String[] that is passed to your main() method. If you want to have one of the arguments be a multi-word string, you must enclose that argument in double-quotes. In the example in Figure 2.25, we are passing five arguments using the command:

```
Stringfirst second third "this is the fourth argument" fifth
```

These arguments are passed into your main() as follows:

```
args[0] = "first"
args[1] = "second"
args[2] = "third"
args[3] = "this is the fourth argument"
args[4] = "fifth"
```

Class Path Parameters

When you compile and run Java programs, you need to tell the compiler and interpreter where to look for the classes you use. In most environments, you need to set a CLASSPATH variable for this purpose. The CLASSPATH setting acts as a list of starting points for locating your classes.

VisualAge for Java does things a bit differently. First, it separates the CLASSPATH concept into two parts:

- When compiling code, the compiler looks at *all* code in the Workspace to find the required classes and interfaces.
- When executing code, the interpreter looks in *specific locations* to find the required classes and interfaces. You specify these locations in the Class Path tab of your class.

The first thing these rules mean to you is that any code required for compilation *must* reside in the workspace. In other words, any classes that you reference other than those named in a Class.forName() call, must be imported into your workspace, or the compiler will complain that the classes were not found.

The second thing this means is that for each executable class (classes that have a main() or are applets) you must set its class path if it requires other classes.

> **TIP**
>
> If you try to run an application and get a ClassNotFoundException or a NoClassDefFoundException, you probably need to change the class path. Note that you must change the class path of the application you *start*, not the classes that you use.

The class-path parameters page is shown in Figure 2.26.

In this dialog, you specify where VisualAge for Java should look to find referenced classes, interfaces, and resources. The project that contains the application and the Java Class Libraries projects are always searched automatically for referenced types. This means that if your application uses only types in the standard Java libraries, or types in the same project, you don't need to change anything.

Figure 2.26 The class-path definition page.

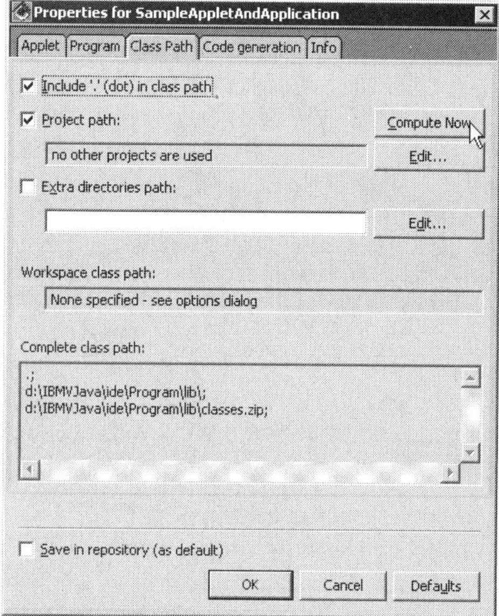

If you need to reference types in other projects, you need to set the project path. You can set the project path in two ways:

Pressing the **Compute Now** button will determine which projects are needed based on referenced types. This cannot determine types that are referenced in Class.forName() calls; if you use Class.forName(), you may need to edit the project path manually.

Pressing the **Edit** button provides a dialog that lists all projects in your workspace. You select which projects you want and press Ok.

Generally, all you need to do is to press the **Compute Now** button, and the class path will be correctly set.

If you need to reference external resources, such as images or property files, you may need to set an extra directories path. The extra directories path enables you to specify directories and JAR files outside VisualAge for Java that should be searched. Note that the external directories path is only used at run time; it has no effect on compilation of your code. A common use for the extra directories path is to specify the JDBC driver that you want to use in a database application.

Please see Chapter 6 for more details on handling resource files in your application.

The workspace class-path is described in Chapter 3.

Code Generation Parameters

VisualAge for Java provides a visual application builder tool called the Visual Composition Editor. One of its functions is to generate event-handling code for JavaBeans components. (JavaBeans components are discussed in Chapter 7 and the Visual Composition Editor is discussed in Chapter 10.)

When generating events, VisualAge offers three possible code-generation options, as seen in Figure 2.27:

Do not use any inner classes. If you select this option, the class you are composing (known as the composite bean) listens to its contained components. This composite bean determines which component fired the event and reacts appropriately. The problem with this approach is that you are making the inner event-handing details of the class available to the general public.

Use one inner class for all events. If you select this option, the VCE generates a single inner class inside the composite bean. This inner class determines which component fired the event and performs the required action. Because this class is an inner class is defined inside the composite bean, the event-handling details are hidden from the outside world.

Use an inner class for each event. If you select this option, a separate anonymous inner class is generated for each event that must be handled. All processing is hidden, but at this point in time the generated code is incorrect.

Figure 2.27 The code generation page.

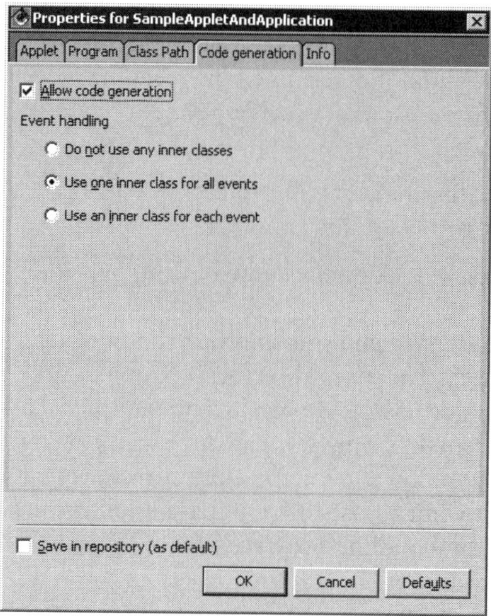

> **WARNING**
>
> The **Use an inner class for each event** option currently does not generate proper code. Do not use this option! The problem is that the generated code assumes that the order in which event handlers are added to a bean is the same as the order in which they will be notified. The JavaBeans specification does not guarantee this. While this handling may work for many beans, it can cause problems with other beans. We recommend that you choose the **Use one inner class for all events** option.

> **NOTE**
>
> The **Allow code generation** option should usually be selected. If you clear it, you will not be able to save your visual designs in the Visual Composition Editor.

Figure 2.28 The general information page.

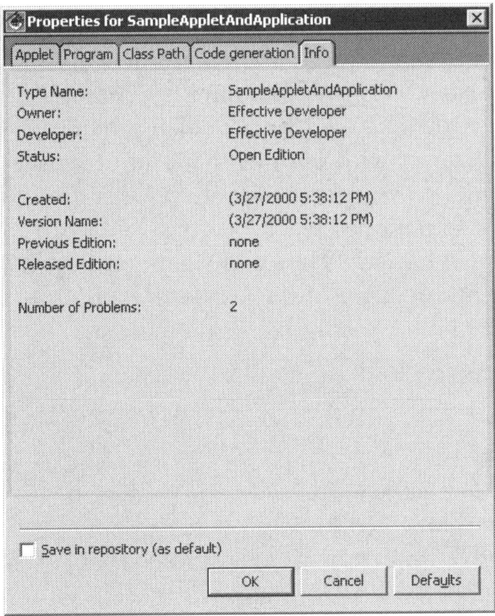

Class Information

The final page of the Properties dialog is the information page. This page, shown in Figure 2.28, describes the class' status and version. A similar information page exists for all program elements.

Running Your Code

Running your application or applet is easy in VisualAge for Java. You simply select the class to run and click the Running Man button on the tool bar.

> **NOTE**
>
> If a package or project contains only one application or applet, you can also select that package or project and click the Running Man button.

If the class is an applet, it will appear in an applet-viewer window. If the class is an application (has a main() method), it will do whatever the application code tells it to do. Note that a class can be both an application and an applet. If you click the running man and the class is both an application and an applet, it will be run as though it were an applet. You can also select **Run->Run main** or **Run->In Applet Viewer** from a class' pop-up menu to explicitly state how you want to run the class.

If you need to pass parameters to your application or applet, see the *Applet Parameters* and *Program Parameters* sections earlier in this chapter for details on how to set up the parameters. VisualAge for Java, version 3.5, also provides **Run->Run main with** and **Run->In Applet Viewer with** options that automatically bring up the appropriate parameters page. When you enter parameters and press **Ok**, the application or applet runs using those parameters.

If you want to run a class again, you also have the choice of right-clicking on the Running Man button. This presents a pop-up menu of the last several applications that you have run. You can choose the application to run from this list.

> **NOTE**
>
> If you receive a ClassNotFoundException or a NoClassDefFoundException when running your application, you probably need to set the class path for the application. Please see *Class Path Parameters* earlier in this chapter for details on setting up a class path.

The Console

If your application or applet writes to the system console, or requires user input from the console, the VisualAge for Java console appears, seen in Figure 2.29.

> **NOTE**
>
> The console tends to hide itself behind other VisualAge for Java windows. You will probably see it pop up briefly then hide itself. You will need to find it on the Windows task bar or whatever other window location system is provided on your machine.

The output of all programs that you run appears in the same console window. You can switch between different programs by clicking on the appropriate entry. The entries are listed based on the time you run them.

Entries that have a T icon in front of them (see Figure 2.29) are applications or applets that have terminated. If the entry does not have a T, it's still running. You can stop an application by choosing **Terminate** from the entry's pop-up

Figure 2.29 The VisualAge for Java console.

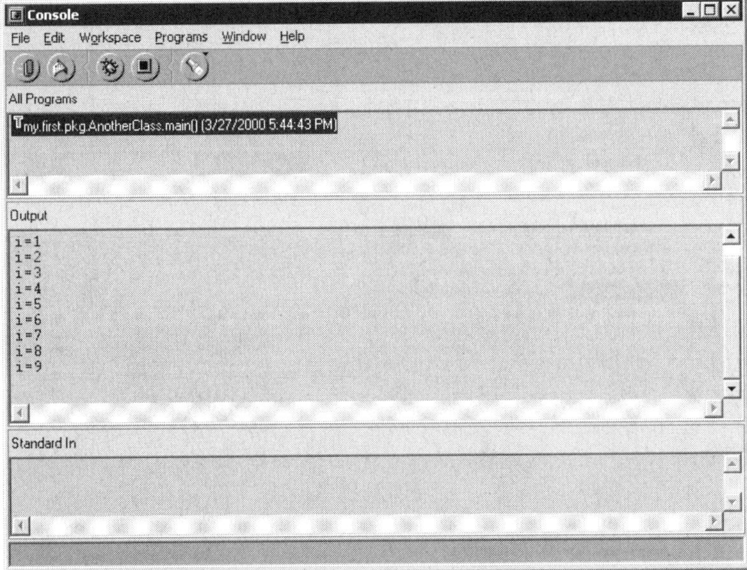

menu. You can clear an entry by choosing **Remove** from its pop-up menu. You can also select **Remove all terminated** from the pop-up menu and all applications that are finished will be removed.

If you close the console window, all output is discarded.

> **WARNING**
>
> If you run a program several times and some of those runs have not terminated, you will see the first active output in the console window. What this means to you is that if you make some changes and rerun the application, you may see old output. If you ever see old output in the console, double-check to see which output you're actually viewing.

Reorganizing Program Elements

Each program element can be copied, moved, or renamed. You use the **Reorganize** submenu from a program element's pop-up menu to perform those actions. The **Reorganize** menu has the following menu items:

Copy. Allows you to copy an element to another location. For example, you can copy a method to another class, or copy a class to another package.

Rename. Allows you to rename a program element.

Move. Allows you to move a program element to another location. For example, you can move a method to another class, or move a class to another package.

Fix/Migrate. Renames package references in a type, package, or project.

> **WARNING**
>
> You should *never* write to the console from an applet if you want the user to see the text. Most browsers either hide the console or disable it by default. This means that the user will never see your output! If you're writing an applet, *all* output should be displayed in the applet GUI. For the same reasons, you should not use console input in an applet. All input should be requested through the applet GUI.

When you copy, rename, or move program elements, the original program element is kept in the repository, and you can retrieve it at any time.

If you are using the Enterprise Edition, you must be a privileged user of the source or the target program elements to be able to perform any reorganizing operation. Any of those operations result in the creation or deletion of a program element: For example, if you copy a type to a package A, you must be a group member of package A. If you move a type from package A to package B, you must own package A and be a group member of package B. In fact, you need the right to delete a type from package A, and the right to create a type in package B. We discuss these ownership details in Chapter 4.

Copying Elements

The following program elements can be copied in the workspace:

- A package can be copied to another project.
- A type can be copied to another package.
- A method can be copied to a another type.

You have the choice whether or not to rename the copy. Let's take a look at a quick example. Suppose you want to duplicate the AudioCD class in the effective-vaj.env.ide.beans package. Follow these steps to perform this action:

1. Bring up the pop-up menu for the **AudioCD** class.
2. Select **Reorganize->Copy**, as seen in Figure 2.30.

Figure 2.30 Copying a program element.

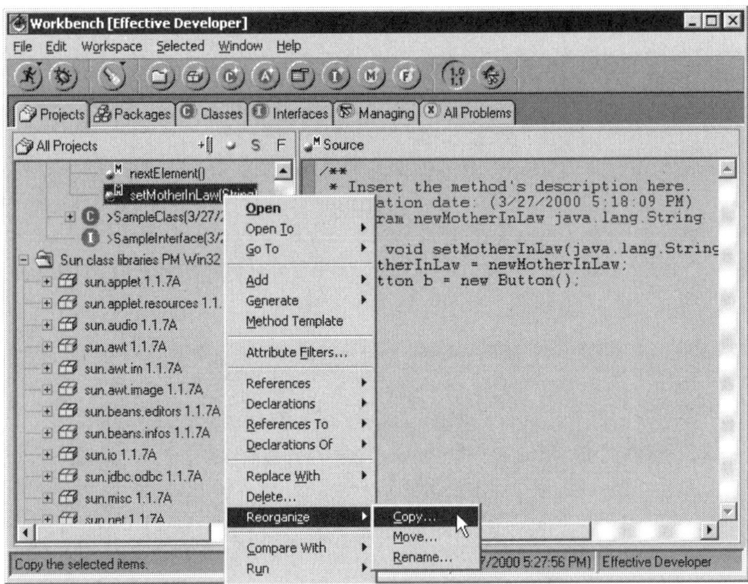

3. Leave the target package name as is.
4. Select the **Rename the copy** check box. If you leave this option unchecked, the tool simply exits when you click **Ok**.
5. Click **Ok**, and enter **CompactDisc** in the copy dialog that opens.
6. Click **Ok** to perform the copy.

The result of the copy operation is that a new class named CompactDisc is created in the same package with the same content as the AudioCD class. (The only difference is that the class and constructor names have changed to CompactDisc.)

You could have specified a name that corresponds to an existing program element in the repository. In this case, a warning is displayed. If you click **Ok**, a new edition of the program element is created in the repository. If you select the **Don't show this message again** check box, similar situations that occur in the future will not be flagged. You can reactivate this warning by modifying the IDE help options, as described in Chapter 3.

Moving Elements

You can move packages, types, and methods. To do this, select **Reorganize->Move** from a program element's pop-up menu. This is similar to doing a copy, except that the original program element is deleted from the workspace. When you start a move, a list of possible targets is displayed. For example, the list of packages loaded in the workspace is displayed when you move a type. You cannot specify a non-existing program element as the target for a move.

Renaming Elements

You can rename any program element, such as methods. To do this, select **Reorganize->Rename** from a program element's pop-up menu.

For types and methods, you also can edit the code manually to change its current name: However, using the renaming functionality lets you search for all references to the current element across the workspace. Results are displayed in the Search Results window. The Replace Matches window is started. Use it to replace all occurrences of the program element.

> **WARNING**
>
> Be careful when you rename projects. Remember that the VisualAge for Java class path is closely related to projects. You will need to update the class path of any executable class referencing classes in this project. In addition, resources attached to the project folder will not be copied automatically to the new project folder. You will have to do this manually. When such a situation occurs, VisualAge for Java displays a warning message.

Fixing or Migrating References

If you change the name of a package containing a class, anyone that uses that class must update their code. This can be a complex task, because you need to replace the class name in many places. It can be even more difficult if the referenced class was used in a visual design, because you need to open the referring class to the VCE and change the references there.

Fortunately, Version 3.0 of VisualAge for Java provides a batch method of performing package name changes. This function is accessible from the **Reorganize->Fix/Migrate** option for types, packages, and projects. When you choose **Reorganize->Fix/Migrate**, the dialog shown in Figure 2.31 is displayed.

In this dialog, you specify which package patterns to replace. After you specify the **From** and **To** fields, click **Add** to add the replacement to the list. Make sure you add all pairs you need to; a common mistake is to type entries in the **From** and **To** fields and click **Next** before clicking **Add**. If you do this, all replacements except the last one are executed.

3.5 VisualAge for Java, version 3.5, provides option Include JDK1.2 renamed packages. If you select this option, several packages are automatically added to the migration dialog. These packages include the renamed Swing packages, and are particularly useful for migrating from an earlier version of VisualAge for Java.

Press the **Next** button to move to the exclusions page of the dialog, seen in Figure 2.32.

Figure 2.31 Choosing package references to rename.

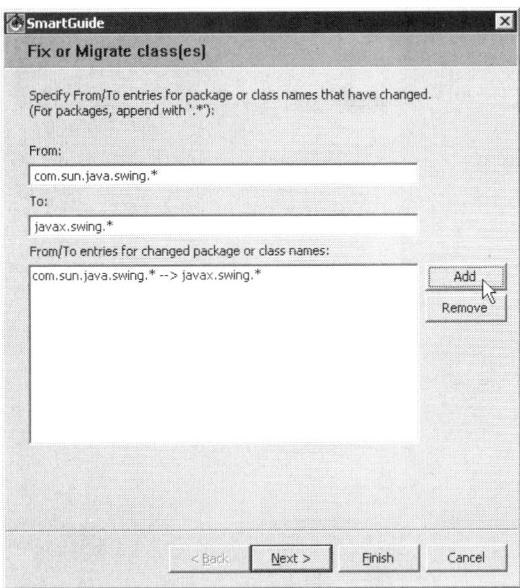

Figure 2.32 Omitting some packages from the renaming.

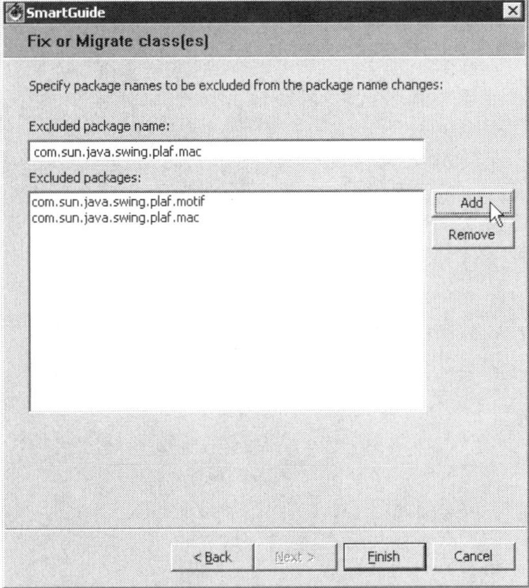

NOTE

All references to the listed packages and their "subpackages" are renamed. For example, if you want to migrate an application from using Swing 1.0.3 to Swing 1.1.1, you would specify com.sun.java.swing.*->javax.swing.*, as seen in Figure 2.31. All references to com.sun.java.swing are renamed, as are references to com.sun.java.swing.event, com.sun.java.swing.table, com.sun.java.swing.text, and so on. Some renames might not be appropriate, so be sure to specify exceptions on the next page of the dialog!

On this page of the dialog, you specify subpackages that you want to exclude from the renaming. In our Swing migration example, you want to exclude the com.sun.java.swing.plaf.motif and com.sun.java.swing.plaf.mac packages from the renaming.

WARNING

The order in which you perform migration can make a difference in migration success. Simply migrating a project or package may not work properly. If a class that you need to migrate depends on another class that needs to be migrated, you can end up with indefined class references.

For example, suppose that you had created a class named MyJPanel that extends com.sun.java.swing.JPanel (through the Visual Composition Editor) in an earlier version of VisualAge for Java. In a different package, you create AnotherJPanel, a class that extends MyJPanel (again, through the Visual Composition Editor). If you import these classes into VisualAge for Java version 3.5, both classes will contain errors, as the Swing package names have changed.

If you migrate AnotherJPanel before MyJPanel, the migrations will leave AnotherJPanel with an error. If you migrate MyJPanel first, the migration will succeed.

Our basic advice is to first try migrating at the project level. If classes contain errors after the migration, replace the project with its previous version and try migrating the packages that didn't contain migration errors first. (You can find details on version control in Chapter 4.)

When you click **Finish**, VisualAge runs through all types and methods in the selected project, package, or type and renames the package references. In addition, any types that were visually composed in the VCE are modified so that their visual design reflects the package name change. This rename process can take quite a while; this might be a good time for a coffee break.

Summary

In this chapter, we've uncovered the basics of code creation in VisualAge for Java. We've explored how you can create projects, packages, types, and methods from the point of view of the Workbench. Keep in mind that there are always several ways to approach a task in VisualAge for Java. We have presented the most common techniques for approaching software development in this environment.

In the next chapter, we'll look at alternative ways to browse your code, how you can search for program elements, and how you can customize VisualAge for Java to better suit your development needs.

NAVIGATING YOUR CODE

3

VisualAge for Java provides many ways to examine code. Part of the philosophy of the environment is that there is no single best way to perform a given task. You must always consider the context of the task. Sometimes, you may be working on a single project while other times on many different projects. Sometimes, you may want to see several methods in separate windows, while other times you may want to see only a single method at a time. The VisualAge for Java product developers felt it was important to give you flexibility in how you perform your tasks.

Throughout this book, we'll give some advice and best practices on using VisualAge for Java. Keep in mind that although we feel these practices are quite useful, you may find ways of using the tool that better suits your needs. Play with the tool. By playing around and trying different ways to do development tasks, you'll find what techniques work best for you. Try our suggestions, but if you find a different technique that you prefer, use it!

In this chapter, we'll present the different ways you can view and manipulate your code in VisualAge for Java. For now, we'll concentrate on non-GUI Java applications. That is, we won't talk about the Visual Composition Editor yet. (The Visual Composition Editor is covered in detail starting in Chapter 10, "Bean Composition in the VCE.")

Browsers, Pages, and Panes

VisualAge for Java separates your work area into browsers, pages, and panes. Most of the windows you'll work with in VisualAge for Java are *browsers*. A browser is a window that lets you examine and possibly modify code. Browsers give you a view of the code in your workspace, possibly showing all code in the workspace, or just code in a given project, package, class, or method. We'll examine each of these types of browsers shortly.

A *page* is a screen of data presented within a browser. Each page can be accessed by clicking on the tabs at the top or bottom of the browser. Generally, each page gives you a look at certain types of program elements, such as classes, packages, or methods. Each page will have different menu items available to match the type of data displayed in that page.

A *pane* is a section of a page, letting you see a source editor or a list, tree, or graph of program elements. You can view a single pane at once (by double-clicking in its title bar or pressing Ctrl-M to maximize it) or multiple panes. You can resize panes by dragging the bars that separate them. You can change the pane orientation by selecting **Window->Flip Orientation.**

In this section, we'll explore each type of pane and the actions you can take on items displayed within that pane. Note that the source editor was described in Chapter 2, "Creating Code," so we will not cover it in detail in this chapter.

Tree Panes

Most panes contain a tree that shows you the structure of your program elements. Figure 3.1 shows an example of a tree pane, in this case, the All Projects pane from the Projects tab of the Workbench.

This tree shows a project named *A Sample Project*, which contains a package named sample.pkg. In VisualAge for Java, all packages must be contained within a project in the workspace. Projects are not a Java concept; they are a VisualAge for Java concept, used to group packages for easy association while working on them. As seen in Figure 3.1, packages contain classes, and classes contain fields and methods.

Each type of program element is represented by a different type of icon, and additional icons help show attributes or modifiers that are present in the class, method or field. Figure 3.1 shows the following icons:

Yellow folder. Represents a project.

Yellow box. Represents a package.

Green circle containing a "C". Represents a class.

Green "C" outside of a circle. Represents an inner class. Note that the inner class name will be qualified with its containing class name. For example, class EventHandler defined inside class MyClass will appear as MyClass$EventHandler. Note that only top-level inner classes will appear in the tree; local inner classes (those defined in a method) will not appear in the tree as their location makes a difference for their use.

Empty circle surrounding a variable or method icon. The variable or method is defined inside an inner class.

Green circle containing a white "A". Represents an applet class.

Green "A" following a class or method name. The class or method is declared abstract.

Brown "T" following a field. The field has been declared transient.

Red "V" following a field. The field has been declared volatile.

Dark red "S" following a field or method. The field or method has been declared static.

Figure 3.1 A tree pane.

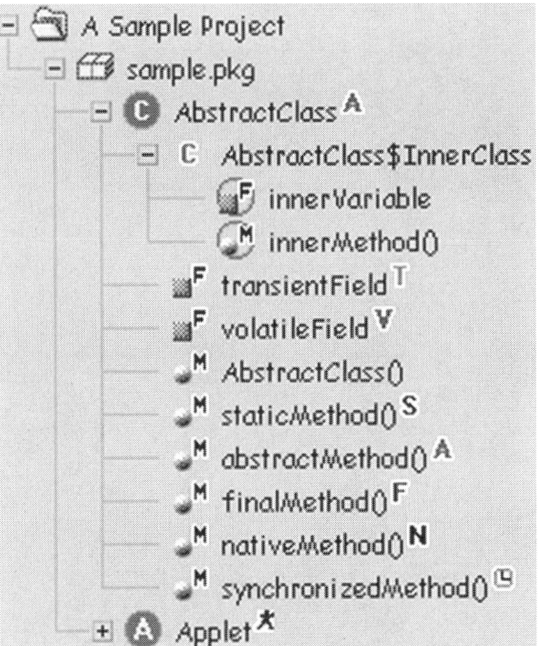

Dark red "F" following a class, field, or method. The class, field, or method has been declared final.

Blue "N" following a method. The method has been declared native.

Brown clock symbol after a method. The method has been declared synchronized.

Small black "running man" after a class. The class is executable; it contains a main() method or is an applet.

This tree is continued in Figure 3.2, showing more of the icons that you'll see when using VisualAge for Java.

Figure 3.2 shows the following icons:

Piece of paper after a class or interface. The class or interface was imported without source code.

Blue triangle before a method or field. The method or field has no access modifier.

Red square before a method or field. The method or field has been declared private.

Yellow diamond before a method or field. The method or field has been declared protected.

Figure 3.2 The access modifier icons.

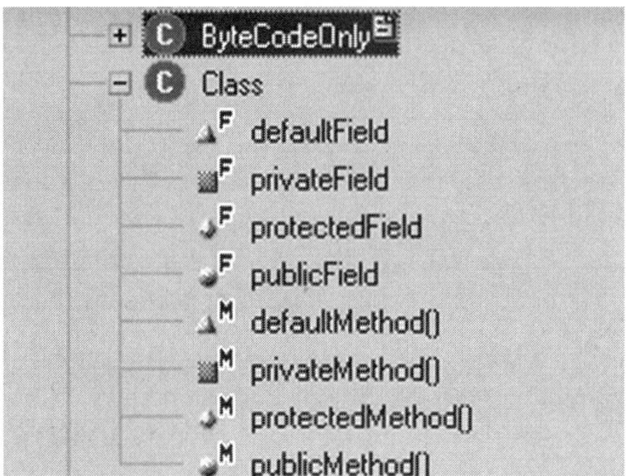

Green circle before a method or field. The method or field has been declared public.

Small blue "F" after the access modifier symbol. The name represents a field or variable in the class or interface.

Small blue "M" after the access modifier symbol. The name represents a method in the class or interface.

This tree is continued in Figure 3.3, showing more of the icons you'll see when using VisualAge for Java.

Figure 3.3 shows the following icons:

Red "X" before a class name. The class definition contains a compiler error.

Gray "X" before a class name. A method within the class contains a compiler error.

Red "X" before a method name. The method contains a compiler error.

Gray triangle containing a black "!". A method within the class contains a compiler warning.

Yellow triangle containing a black "!". The class or method contains a compiler warning.

Purple circle containing a white "I". Represents an interface.

Yellow puzzle piece after a class name. The class was composed in the Visual Composition Editor (VCE—see Chapter 10 for details).

Figure 3.3 Errors and other icons.

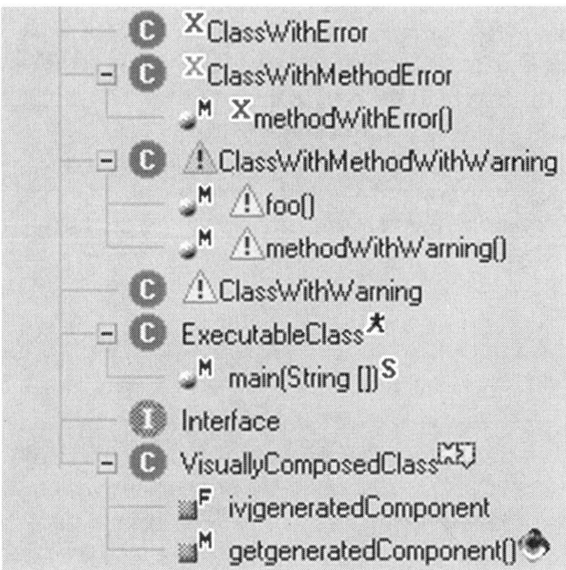

Multi-color diamond with eye and arrow after a method. The method was generated by the VCE and will be regenerated when you save the visual composition again.

Expanding and Collapsing Nodes

Each node in the tree may be a branch or a leaf. Branch nodes contain more nodes within them. For example, a project can contain packages, or a package can contain types. If a node contains child nodes, it will have a "+" or "-" box next to it (see Figure 3.1). Pressing the "+" box will expand the node, showing its children. Pressing a "-" box will collapse the node, hiding its children. Leaves are nodes without children; they have no "+" or "-" box before them.

You can also expand and collapse nodes using the arrow keys on the keyboard. If you click on a node that has children and press the right-arrow key, the node will be expanded. If you press the left arrow key when an expanded node is highlighted, the node will be collapsed. If you press the left arrow key on a collapsed node, the selection moves to the *parent* node in the tree.

Finally, pressing the up and down arrow keys move the selection up and down the tree without changing the expansion state of any nodes. If you press a letter on the keyboard, you are moved to the next name that starts with that letter in the tree.

Opening Elements in a New Browser

You can open any element except fields in its own browser window. By default, you can do this by double-clicking on a non-field program-element (project, package, class, interface, or method) or by choosing **Open** from the pop-up menu for that object. The new browser window opens with that element as the root of the browser. You will see only program elements within that root element in the new browser window.

You can also choose from the **Open to** submenu of the pop-up menu of a program element. **Open to** lists the pages available with the browser for that type of program element, and lets you open the browser starting on the selected page.

Filtering the View

There are several options that let you control what program elements appear in the tree.

First, the elements are limited by the type of browser. If you're looking at the Workbench window, *all* program elements will be available. If you're looking at a package browser, only program elements within that package will be available.

Next, the available elements depend on which page you are viewing. For example, some browsers have a Classes page, allowing you to look at only the classes defined in the root element for the browser. Many browsers also have an Interfaces page, which limits the view to only interfaces defined within the root program element.

Each browser also lets you filter the listed program elements by their attributes. Choosing the **Attribute Filters** option from the pop-up menu of any item in the tree displays the dialog shown in Figure 3.4.

To start with, all filters are selected, meaning that all elements within the program element root will be displayed. Deselecting any of the options causes elements with those attribute modifiers not to appear. (If an element has more than one modifier, it will appear if *any* of those modifiers are selected.)

Figure 3.4 The Attribute Filters dialog.

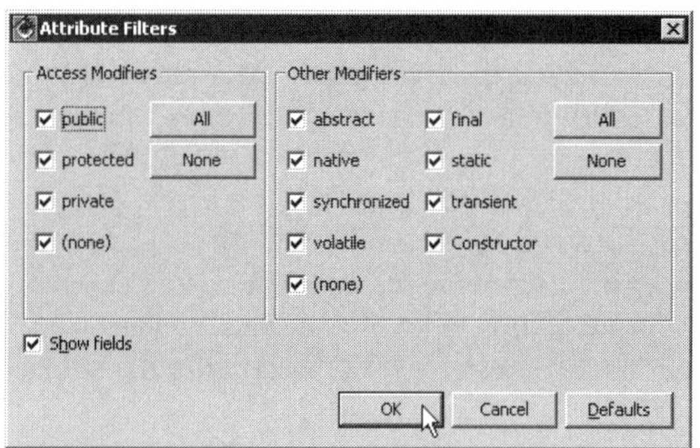

The Access Modifiers section of the dialog specifies methods to appear based on their access level. If you deselect **protected**, for example, all protected methods are hidden. Clicking **All** in this section selects all modifiers; clicking **None** in this selection deselects all modifiers.

- **public** fields and methods
- **protected** fields and methods
- **private** fields and methods
- (**none**) fields and methods without an access modifier

The Other Modifiers section helps filter out methods based on the following attributes:

- **abstract** methods
- **native** methods
- **synchronized** methods
- **volatile** fields
- **final** fields and methods
- **static** fields and methods
- **transient** fields
- class **Constructors**
- (**none**) methods or fields with no extra modifiers

Finally, the **Show fields** check box enables you to show or hide fields in the tree. Some developers like to see the fields in the tree, while others feel it clutters the tree. The choice is up to you.

Figure 3.5 shows a close-up of the upper-right corner of a tree pane (in this case, it's the All Projects pane in the Projects tab of the Workbench). The controls in this part of the pane provide quick access to some useful filters.

Figure 3.5 The quick filter buttons.

There are four buttons in this section of the window:

Add BookMark (plus-sign and bookmark symbol). Marks the current location. This is available only in the Projects page of the Workbench and is discussed under *Setting Bookmarks* later in this chapter.

Public Members Only (green circle). If pressed, only public fields and methods will appear in the tree.

Static Members Only (red "S"). If pressed, only static fields and methods will appear in the tree.

Show Fields (blue "F"). If pressed, fields will appear in the tree.

List Panes

Some panes display only a list of program elements rather than display them in a tree. Take a look at Figure 3.6.

The top three panes, titled All Packages, Types, and Members, are lists of program elements. Whenever you see lists side-by-side as you see in Figure 3.6, the lists are related from left-to-right.

Starting with the leftmost (or topmost if you flipped orientation), you select a program element. In this example, we're selecting packages. When you select the element, the next pane to the right (or below for a flipped orientation) will be filled with program elements inside the selected program element. In this example, we selected a package in the left/top pane, and the list of types contained within

Figure 3.6 List panes.

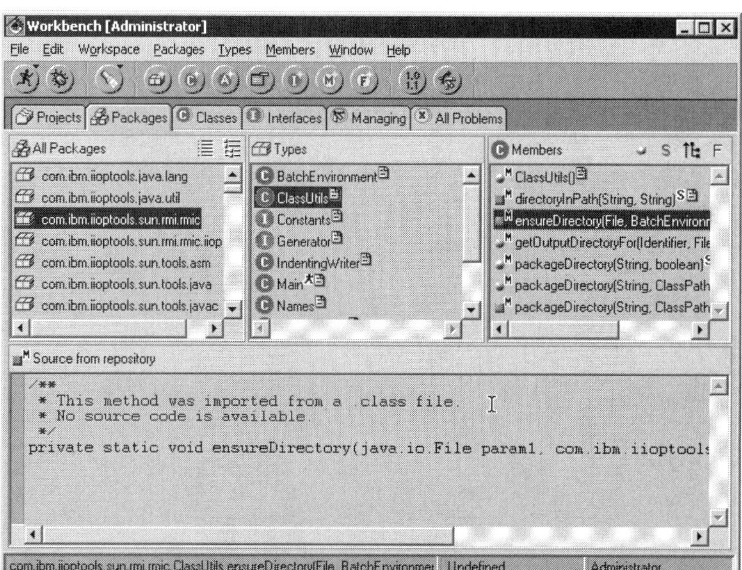

> **NOTE**
>
> If you have selected **Window->Flip Orientation,** the related panes will appear top-to-bottom along the left edge of the screen as shown in Figure 3.7.

that package appears in the Types pane to the right/below. Similarly, when you select a program element in the middle pane, the pane to its right/below is filled with program elements within the selected element. In this example, we select a type in the middle pane and the list of members in that type appears in the Members pane.

Graph Panes

Some panes provide a third view, as seen in Figure 3.8.

While this view may look impressive, in reality it's pretty useless for navigating your code. Note the scrollbar on the left side of the pane. If you slide it down, it scales the pane's contents, as seen in Figure 3.9.

Moving the left scrollbar up and down usually elicits "oohs" and "ahhs" from onlookers, until you ask, "Can you read anything?" While this view is great for marketing ("Look what VisualAge can do"), it's totally useless for development.

Figure 3.7 Flipped orientation of the list panes.

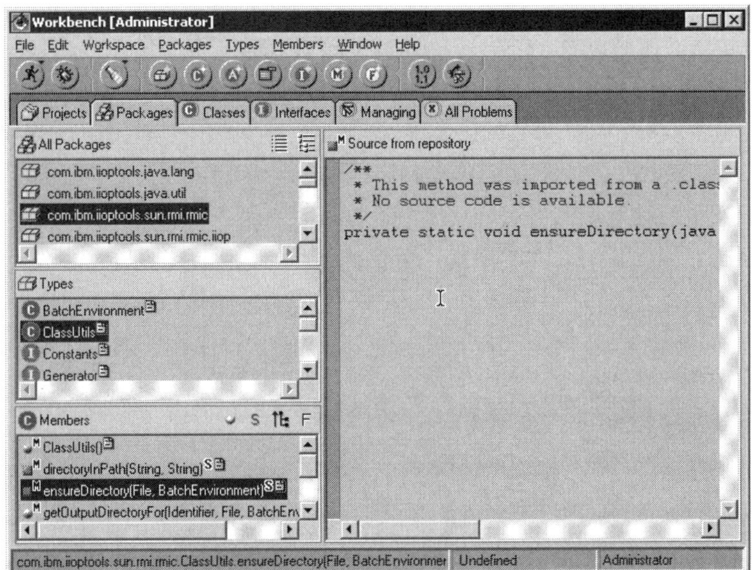

Figure 3.8 A graph view of the class hierarchy.

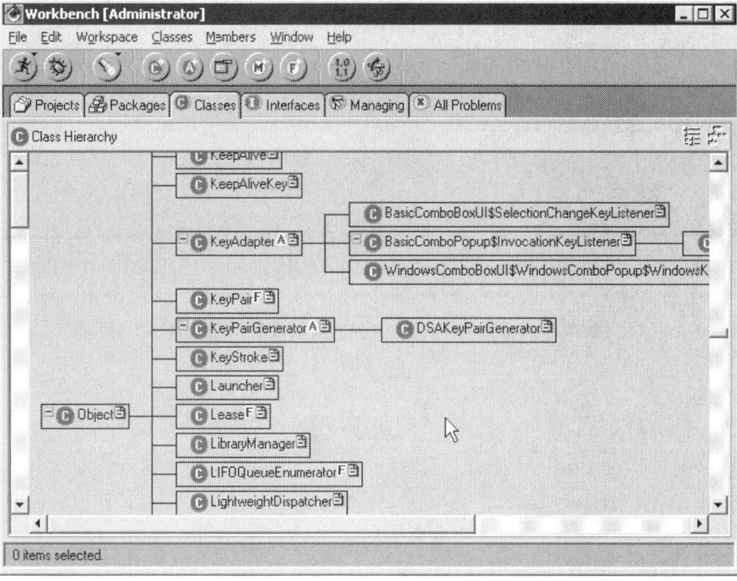

Figure 3.9 Wow... the class hierarchy!

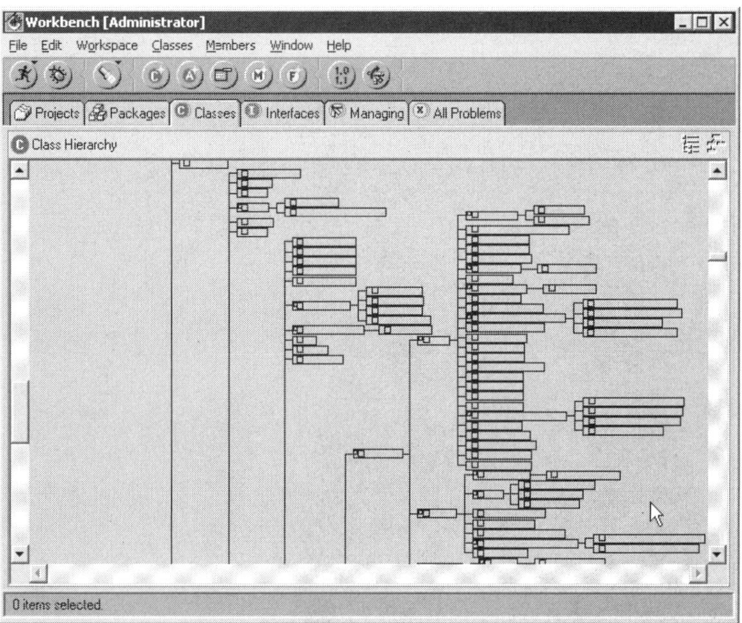

Figure 3.10 Version branch view.

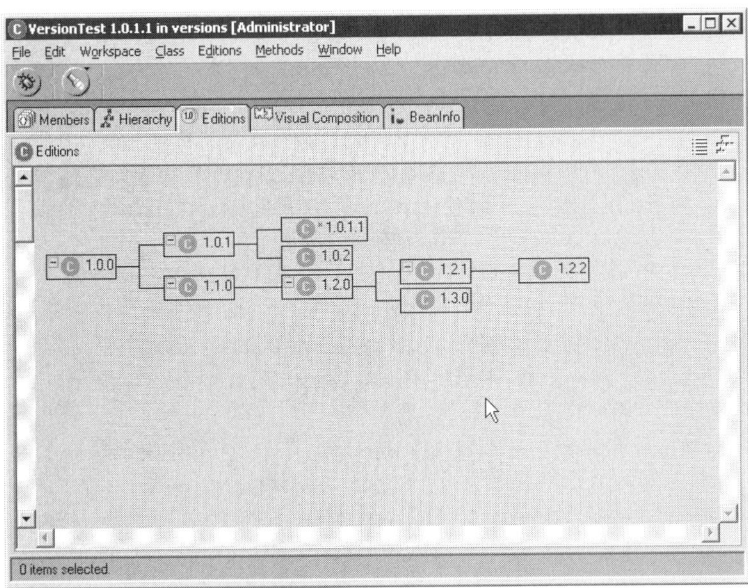

However, the graph view *is* useful in one sense. If you want to see how different *versions* of your code are related, you can use the graph view of the Editions page of a browser. For example, Figure 3.10 shows a graph of branched versions of a class.

This is an incredibly useful view, because you can see exactly how your code has branched and which versions are related to other existing versions. We'll discuss versioning in Chapter 4, "Using Version Control."

Actions on Program Elements

Any program element, whether it's displayed in a tree, list, or graph, can be manipulated by choosing items from its pop-up menu. On many systems, like Windows, you can access the pop-up menu by right-clicking on the entry in the tree, list, or graph. Other operating systems may have other ways to access the pop-up menu, sometimes also known as the context menu.

In the following sections, we describe the actions that are available on each type of program element and where we'll talk about them in this book.

Projects

When you open the pop-up menu for a project, you'll see the following options:

Open. Opens a project browser window (discussed in *The Project Browser* later in this chapter) for the selected project.

Open to. Opens a project browser window to a specified page. The **Open to** submenu contains items mapping to each page in the project browser.

Go to. Selects a project, package, or type by name. This option is discussed in *The Go To Command* later in this chapter.

Add. Allows you to add a program element in the selected project. This option acts the same as the tool-bar buttons for adding projects, packages, classes, interfaces, and methods, discussed in Chapter 2. If you choose this option from a project's pop-up menu, the selected create SmartGuide will automatically fill in the selected project name in the project field. You can change the project if you like, but this provides a convenient way to add items in a selected project.

Attribute filters. Allows you to limit which program elements are displayed in the tree, list, or graph. We discussed this option in *Filtering the View* earlier in this chapter.

Import. Allows you to load external code into your workspace or repository. This option is covered in detail in Chapter 6, "Integrating with the File System."

Export. Allows you to send code from your workspace or repository to the file system or another repository. This option is covered in detail in Chapter 6.

Replace with. Allows you to change which version of the selected project is loaded into your workspace. We discuss versioning in Chapter 4.

Delete. Deletes the project from the workspace. The project will no longer appear in any browsers, but still exists in the repository.

Reorganize. Allows you to rename a project or fix program elements contained in a project. These options are covered in Chapter 2 under *Reorganizing Program Elements.*

Manage. Controls versioning and ownership of the project. We discuss these topics in Chapter 4.

Compare with. Allows you to examine the differences between two versions of a project or between two projects in the workspace. We discuss this in *Comparing Program Elements* later in this chapter.

Run. Allows you to execute your application or applet. This option is discussed in Chapter 2.

Document. Allows to you print and generate JavaDoc HTML pages from your code. These options are discussed under *Printing and Creating Javadoc* later in this chapter.

Tools. Displays any available tools that can be run against a project. If there are no tools installed that act on projects, the Tools submenu will not appear. Tools are discussed in Chapter 25, "Tool Integration."

Copy to Clipboard (version 3.5 and later). Copies the name of the project to the clipboard. You can then paste the name of the project in an editor or anywhere else that accepts text.

Properties. Displays the Properties dialog for your project. This option is discussed in Chapter 2.

These options are also available from the **Selected** menu in the Projects page of the Workbench.

Packages

When you select the pop-up menu for a package, you'll see the same options as those available for Projects, with the following additions for version 3.5 of VisualAge for Java. The difference is that they apply to the selected package instead of to a project.

3.5 **Open Source View (version 3.5 and later).** This option opens a new window that contains a tab at the top for each class or interface in the selected package. Each tab contains the full source of the class named in that tab.

The options in this pop-up menu are also available from the **Packages** menu in any window that contains a Packages pane.

Classes and Interfaces

When you select a pop-up menu for classes or interfaces, you'll see the same options that are available for projects and packages, with the following additions:

Generate. Allows you to automatically create method stubs for inherited abstract methods and get/set methods for fields. These options are discussed in Chapter 2. VisualAge for Java, version 3.5, adds a new option in this submenu for generating a stream-unique version id for serializable classes. (This is the same functionality provided by the program serialver that comes with Sun's JDK distribution.)

Method Template. Quickly creates a new method. This option is discussed in Chapter 2.

References to. Performs a search for program elements that reference the selected class or interface. This is discussed under *Searching Your Workspace* later in this chapter.

Externalize Strings. Extracts String literals from your code, replacing them with references to resource bundles for internationalization. This option is discussed in Appendix A, "Internationalization."

In addition, the pop-up menu for interfaces adds an **Implementors** (sic) option that performs a search for classes that implement the selected interface.

The options in this pop-up menu are also available from the **Types** menu in any window that contains a Types pane.

Fields

The pop-up menu for fields provides most of the options for a class, using the names **References** and **Declarations** to perform searches for references to the field and to declarations of fields with the selected field's name.

The options in this pop-up menu are also available from the Members menu in any window that contains a Members pane.

Methods

Methods provide the same pop-up menu as classes with some changes to the search items. See *Searching Your Workspace* later in this chapter for details.

The options in this pop-up menu are also available from the Members menu in any window that contains a Members pane.

Cloning and Locking Windows

Sometimes you may want to have a second copy of a browser open. You can get another copy of a window by selected **Window->Clone**. The second copy is marked by a ":2" in the title bar of its window, the third copy by ":3", and so on.

> **WARNING**
>
> Do *not* edit the same program element in multiple windows at the same time. VisualAge for Java does not handle this gracefully. If you try to edit a method in two windows and save it in one of the windows, VisualAge will warn you that the results may be inconsistent. If you ignore the warning, the last save wins. If you make changes in one window, then make changes in a second window, save the first window, and then save the second window, the results will be *only* the changes made in the second window. There will be another edition of the method containing the first changes, but there is no auto merge and the windows' contents are not kept in sync.

If you're working with a window a lot and don't want to accidentally close the window, choose the **Window->Lock** option. This option stops you from clicking the X button in the upper-right corner of the window to close it. If the window is the last remaining VisualAge for Java window, it will ask if you want to quit VisualAge for Java. Otherwise, it will bring up a dialog stating that the window must be unlocked before you can close it.

Multiple Windows versus Single Window

By default, each browser in VisualAge for Java opens in a separate window. You can change this default by setting **Window->Options->General->Option an item in->Current Browser**. If you change this setting, anytime you use **Open** or **Open to** on a program element, the current window is replaced by the new browser.

In addition, two new buttons are added to the tool bar: Back (arrow pointing left) and Forward (arrow pointing right). These buttons act like the Forward and Back buttons in a Web browser; they let you move to the previously displayed browser and back.

The Workbench

As we saw in Chapter 2, the Workbench is your main window into your workspace.

> **NOTE**
> If you're getting "workspace" and "Workbench" confused, please see Chapter 1, "VisualAge for Java Concepts."

The Workbench gives you a view of all code in your workspace. You can work with your code on seven different pages:

Projects. Lists all projects in the workspace in a tree.

Packages. Lists all packages in the workspace in a list or tree.

Classes. Lists all classes in the workspace in a tree or graph.

Interfaces. Lists all interfaces in the workspace in a list.

EJBs (Enterprise Edition only). Lists all Enterprise JavaBeans components in the workspace in a tree.

Managing. Lists all program elements in the workspace in lists for easy version management.

All Problems. Lists all problems in code in the workspace in a tree.

In the following sections, we explore each of these pages of the Workbench.

The Projects Page

The Projects page provides a view of all projects in your workspace. It consists of two panes:

All Projects. A tree containing all projects in the workspace. Underneath each project are all packages contained within the project. Underneath each package are classes and interfaces defined in that project. Underneath each class or interface are methods and fields defined inside them.

> **NOTE**
>
> The EJBs page will appear only if *all* of the following conditions are met:
>
> - You have installed the Enterprise Edition of VisualAge for Java.
> - You are running on Windows NT or Windows 2000.
> - You specified that you want Enterprise JavaBeans support when you installed VisualAge for Java.
> - You added the EJB Development Environment feature inside VisualAge for Java.
>
> Details on the Enterprise JavaBeans Development Environment (including its installation) are covered in Chapter 23, "Developing Enterprise JavaBeans." We will not talk about it in this chapter.

Comment or **Source.** An editor pane that allows you to edit a comment (for packages and projects) or the code for the selected class, interface, method or field.

Figure 3.11 shows the Projects page of the Workbench.

> **NOTE**
>
> If you accidentally close your Workbench window, you can open it again by choosing **Window->Workbench**.

Setting Bookmarks

The Projects page provides a feature that you cannot use in any other part of VisualAge for Java. You can set *bookmarks* to keep track of any location in your workspace. This allows you to easily switch between up to nine different program elements by selecting a number in the title bar of the All Projects pane.

To set a bookmark, select a project, package, class, interface, method, or field and click the Add Bookmark button. A small number, 1-9, will appear in the title bar for the All Projects pane representing the selected program element. You can return to that location anytime by clicking on the number.

To remove a bookmark, right-click on the number and choose **Remove Bookmark->*name*** (where *name* is the number of the bookmark to remove).

Figure 3.11 The Projects page of the Workbench.

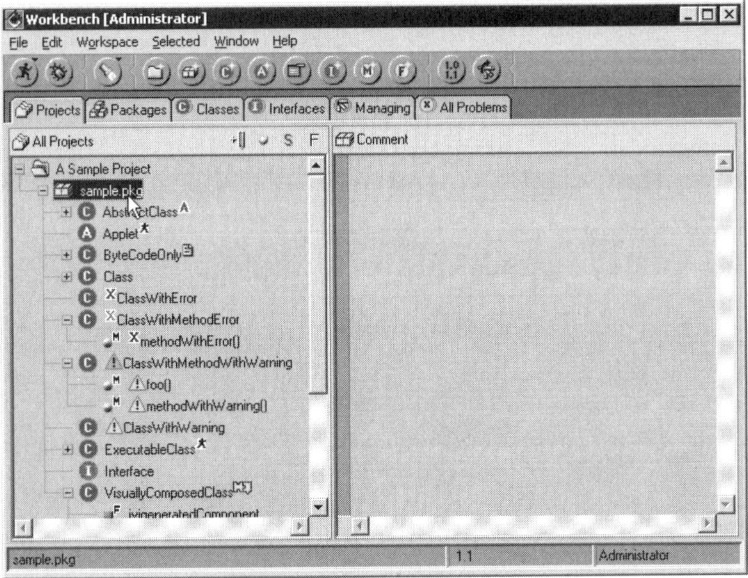

The Packages Page

The Packages page, shown in Figure 3.12, organizes code in the workspace by package. You can select any package from the All Packages pane, and its classes and interfaces will be displayed in the Types pane. Select a type, and its methods and fields will be displayed in the Members pane. In addition, the class definition will appear in the Source pane for you to edit. Select a method or field, and that method or field will appear in the Source pane for you to edit.

List versus Tree Views

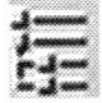

The default view of the packages is a straight list of all packages in the workspace, sorted alphabetically. This list can be awkward to deal with, so VisualAge for Java provides an alternate view. If you click the Tree Layout button in the title bar of the All Packages pane, the view changes to the view shown in Figure 3.13.

This view of the packages in the workspace can be very useful. You can expand branches to see "subpackages" or collapse branches to hide "subpackages." Suppose you only want to deal with packages that start with com.mycompany. Expand the "com" node and the "mycompany" node, and you'll see their "subpackages."

As you look at the tree in Figure 3.13, you may notice a difference in the color of some nodes. The darker nodes in the Figure appear gray on the screen, while the lighter nodes appear yellow. Yellow nodes represent "real" packages.

Figure 3.12 The Packages page of the Workbench.

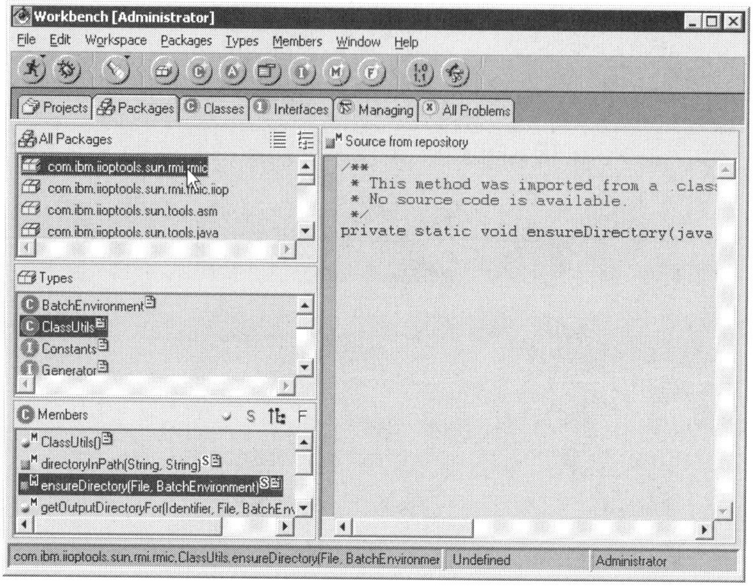

NOTE

We place "subpackages" in quotation marks because there is no such thing as a subpackage in the Java language. In the Java language, there is absolutely *no* relationship between a package like *java.awt* and a package like *java.awt.event*. As far as the language is concerned, the "." character might as well be the letter x. The "." is just like any other character.

It just happens that in the standard implementations of the Java Runtime Environment (JRE), the code for classes in those packages share a common root directory structure.

In VisualAge for Java, they represent "subpackages" as child nodes in the package tree. This is meant as a notational convenience; no relationship between child and parent nodes in the tree should be inferred.

Gray nodes represent placeholders in the tree hierarchy. If you click on a gray node, you won't see any classes or interfaces in the Types pane. If you click on a yellow node, you *will* see classes and interfaces in the Types pane.

Figure 3.13 The tree view of the Packages page.

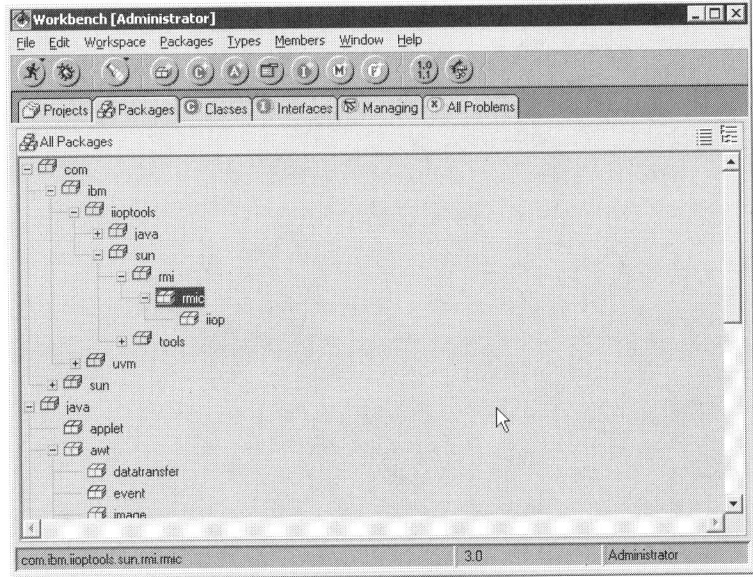

Inheritance Filters

In the Members pane, you will see all of the fields and methods defined in the selected class. Several pages in the VisualAge for Java browsers provide a Members pane, and they all have a very useful *inheritance filter*.

Often, when you're working with a class, all you want to see are methods and fields defined in that class. Other times, it would be nice to see inherited methods. Whenever VisualAge for Java provides a Members pane, you can specify which methods you would like to see.

The easiest way to do this is to click the Root Minus One button on the title bar of the Members pane, as shown in Figure 3.14.

By choosing this option, you'll see all methods in your class and all methods inherited except those in java.lang.Object. The java.lang.Object class is the root of all class inheritance in the Java language, so "Root Minus One" means "everything between this class and Object, not including Object."

The Root Minus One inheritance is the most commonly used inheritance filter, but you can further customize which methods should appear by choosing the **Inheritance Filters** option from the pop-up menu in the Members pane. This displays the dialog shown in Figure 3.15.

In this dialog, you have the following options:

All Inherited Methods. All methods defined in your class and in all superclasses will appear, including those in java.lang.Object.

Figure 3.14 The Root Minus One filter.

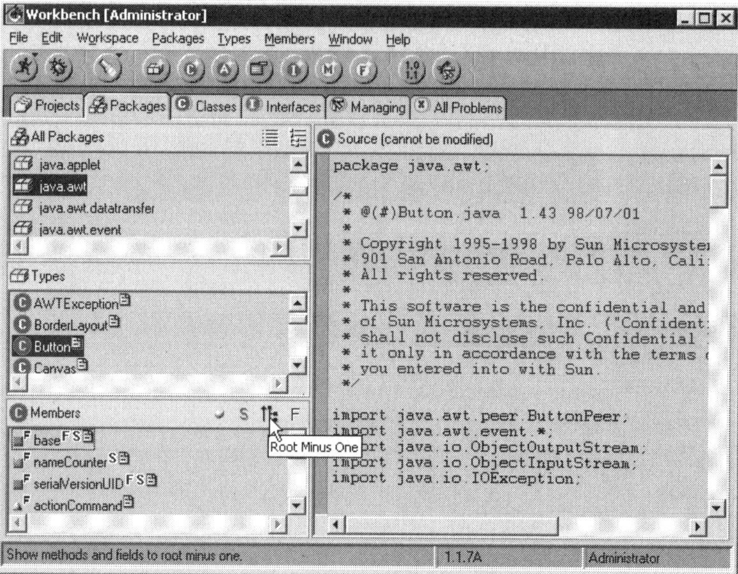

To Root Minus One. All methods defined in your class and in all superclasses will appear, *except* those in java.lang.Object.

To Named Class. All methods defined in your class and up through the chosen class will appear.

To Named Interfaces. All methods defined in your interface and up through the chosen interfaces will appear. This option applies only to interfaces.

No Inheritance. Only methods defined in your class will appear.

Figure 3.15 The Inheritance View Filters dialog.

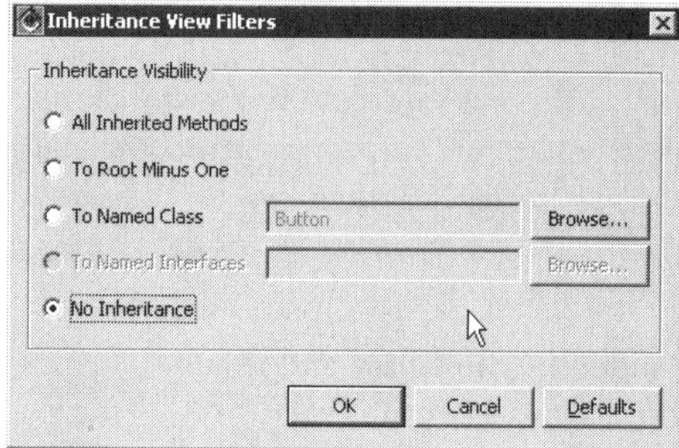

Overriding the Easy Way

The inheritance filters option gives you an easy way to override methods. The most difficult thing about overriding methods is getting the signature right. You can use the inheritance filters to make sure you *can't* get the signature wrong. Here's how you do it:

1. Select the class in which you want to create the overridden method.
2. Set the inheritance filter to include the method to override. Usually Root Minus One is a good choice, and is easily selected via its button, as seen in Figure 3.14.
3. Edit the method, changing its implementation to be whatever you want.
4. Save the method.
5. When asked, select the target class in which to save the method.

When you start editing the method, VisualAge thinks you're editing the method in the superclass. When you save it, VisualAge asks what your intention was. Did you want to actually edit the superclass method? Or were you trying to override the method, saving it in the subclass? By choosing the subclass, you override the method by just changing its implementation.

The Classes and Interfaces Pages

The Classes and Interfaces pages of the Workbench provide lists of all classes and interfaces in the workspace. Figure 3.16 shows the Classes page. The Interfaces page is similar, except that the interfaces appear in a list instead of a tree.

The classes appear in the tree based on their hierarchy. This can be rather cumbersome to use in the Workbench, but this type of view can be very useful in a more limited browser, such as a project or package browser. We'll discuss these browsers later in this chapter.

The Managing Page

The Managing page of the Workbench, seen in Figure 3.17, gives you an easy place to examine the version control status of all of your classes. We'll discuss this page more in Chapter 4.

The All Problems Page

Because VisualAge for Java stores all of its code in a database, it can generate some useful reports for us. One of the reports it provides is the All Problems page of the Workbench. In this view, all code that contains compilation errors or warnings appears in a tree. Each problem class, interface, or method lists its problems, as seen in Figure 3.18.

You can select any code that contains errors, edit that code in the Source pane, and save it to correct the problem. The All Problems page acts like a to-do list, letting you see what code needs work. You can move between errors by

Figure 3.16 The Classes page of the Workbench.

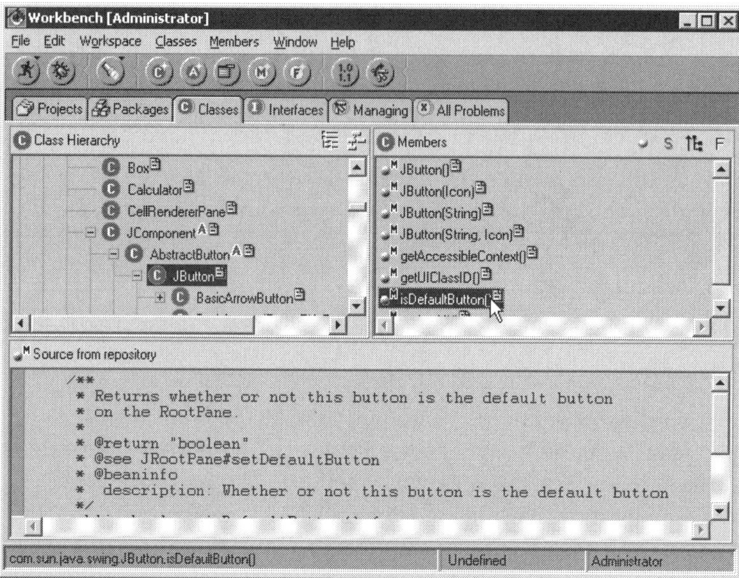

Figure 3.17 The Managing page of the Workbench.

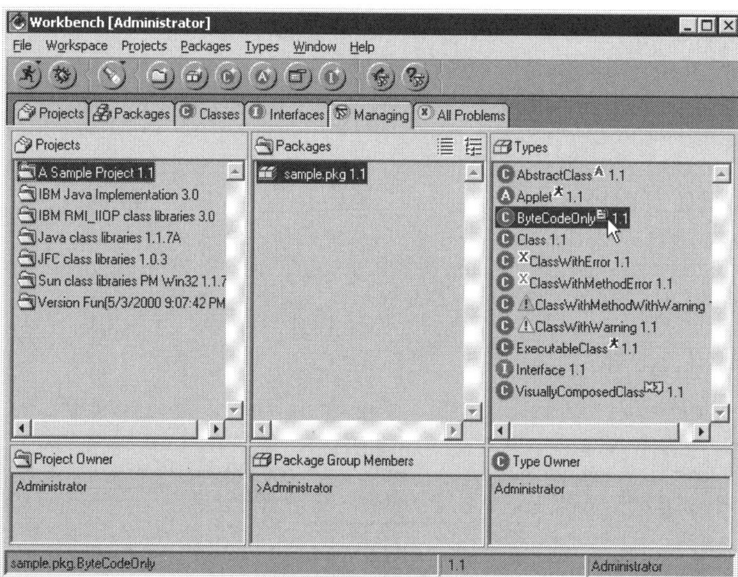

Figure 3.18 The All Problems page of the Workbench.

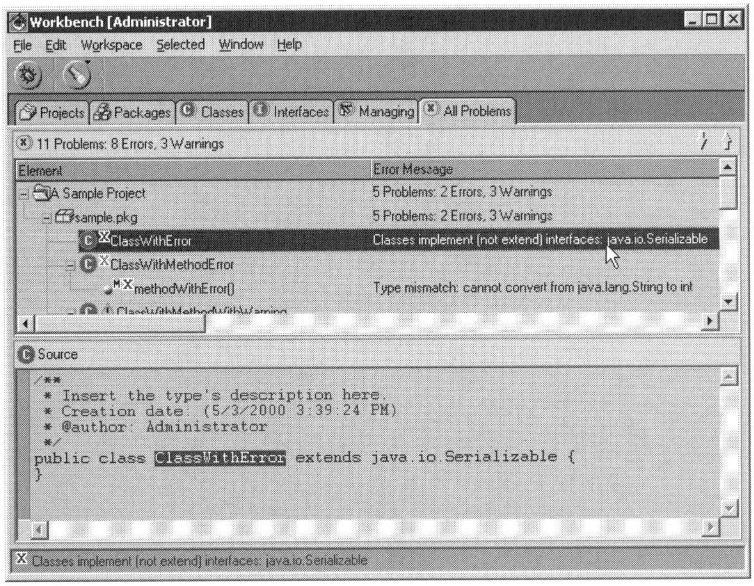

clicking on the up and down arrow icons that appear in the upper-right corner of the error-listing pane.

The Project Browser

A project browser lets you view the code in your workspace that is part of a particular project. This filters out all other code, enabling you to concentrate on only the code you want to work with. You can open a project browser by double-clicking a project from the Workbench, by choosing **Open** or **Open to** from a project's pop-up menu, or by choosing **Workspace->Open Project Browser**.

A project browser like the one shown in Figure 3.19 appears.

The project browser has the same options and pages as the Workbench, with a few exceptions:

- You cannot set bookmarks.
- You see only the code contained within the specified project.
- An Editions page lets you see all versions of the code that are present in the repository (see *The Editions Page* later in this chapter).
- A Resources page lets you work with resource files associated with the project. See Chapter 6 for details on using resource files in VisualAge for Java.

Figure 3.19 A project browser.

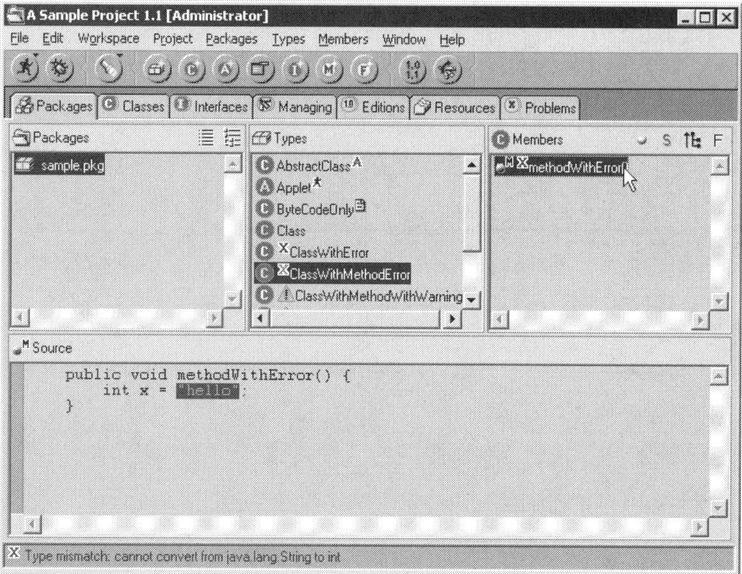

The Editions Page

The Editions page lists the versions of a project that are available in the repository. You can use this page to see which versions are available, or pick **Add to Workspace** from the pop-up menu of an edition to swap it into the workspace. The Editions page appears in Figure 3.20.

> **NOTE**
>
> The icons for packages, classes, methods, and fields are gray. Gray icons mean that if you interact with these program elements, you are interacting with a *shadow* of the element in the repository. You *cannot* save changes to a shadow, but you can look at the shadows as much as you would like.
>
> If you want to make changes to a version of a project that is not in the workspace, you must swap it into the workspace to make those changes. Make sure you version the code that is currently in the workspace before swapping in the other code. Version control issues like this are covered in Chapter 4.

Figure 3.20 The Editions page.

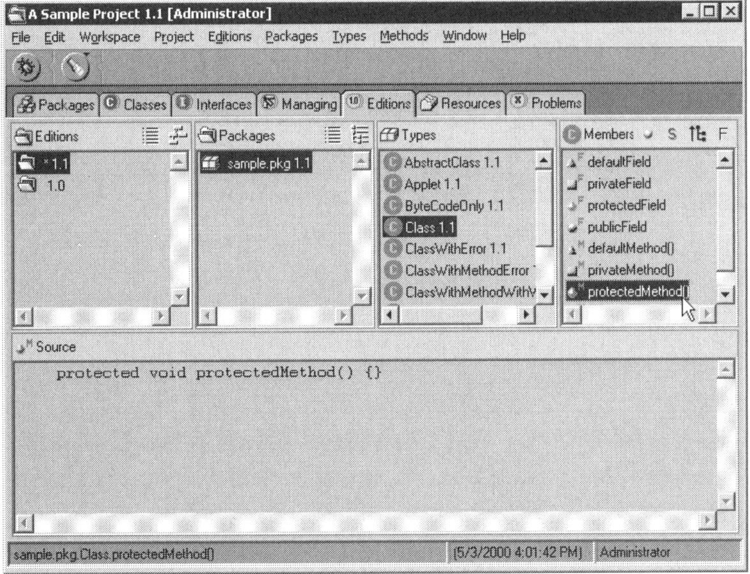

The Package Browser

The package browser is similar to the project browser but limits the scope of code to a single package in the workspace. You open a package browser by double-clicking on a package in any other browser, by choosing **Open** or **Open to** from a package's pop-up menu, or by choosing **Workspace->Open Package Browser**. A sample package browser appears in Figure 3.21.

The package browser does *not* have a resources page, because resource files are always associated with projects in VisualAge for Java.

> **NOTE**
>
> Some of the class icons in the Class Hierarchy pane are filled in, while others are not. The filled C icons are classes that are within the scope of the browser. For example, for a package browser, only classes in the current package will have filled icons. For a project browser, only classes in the project will have filled icons. The classes with non-filled icons are there to show you superclasses that are not in the scope of the browser. You can view or edit them, but they're only there to complete the hierarchy view.

Figure 3.21 A package browser.

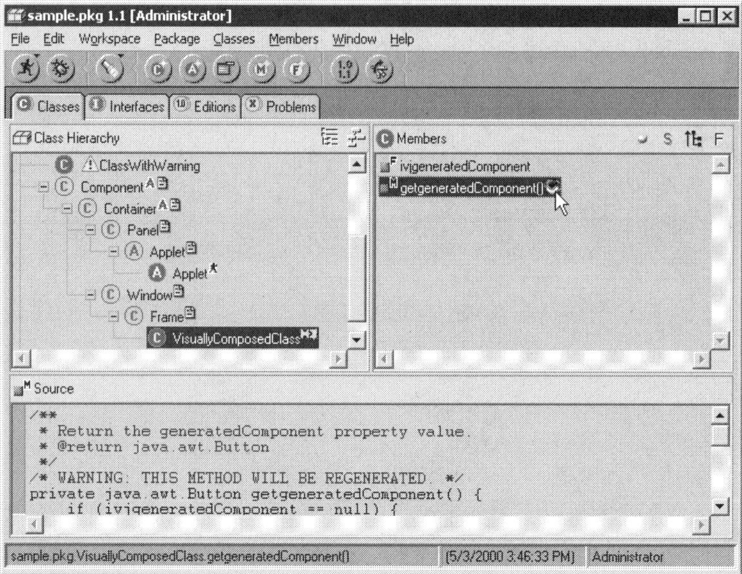

The Class Browser

A class browser limits the scope of the browser to a single class. You can open a class browser by double-clicking on a class in any other browser, by choosing **Open** or **Open to** from the pop-up menu for a class, or by choosing **Workspace->Open Type Browser** and selecting a class. A sample class browser appears in Figure 3.22.

The class browser follows the same format as the project and package browsers, with two new pages:

Visual Composition. Helps you design a class by dragging, dropping, and connecting JavaBeans components. We discuss the Visual Composition Editor (VCE) starting in Chapter 10.

BeanInfo. Helps you add and remove JavaBeans features. We discuss the BeanInfo editor in Chapter 8, "The BeanInfo Editor."

The Interface Browser

An interface browser is similar to a class browser but provides only the Members and Editions pages (VisualAge for Java, version 3.5, also provides a hierarchy page). It is intended for viewing a single interface and can be opened by double-clicking on an interface, choosing **Open** or **Open to** from the pop-up menu for an interface, or by choosing **Workspace->Open Type Browser** and selecting an interface.

Figure 3.22 A class browser.

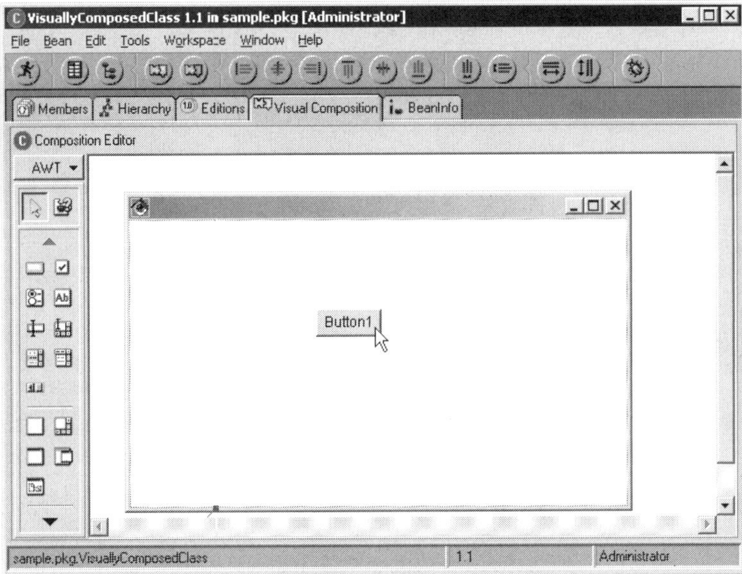

The Method Browser

A method browser limits the scope to a single method in the workspace. They can be quite useful for looking at other methods while editing a method in another browser. You can open a method browser by double-clicking on a method in any other browser, or by choosing **Open** from the pop-up menu for a method. A sample method browser appears in Figure 3.23.

Searching Your Workspace

VisualAge for Java provides several ways to search for data in your workspace, from simple textual searches to cross-reference searches to help find usage or declaration of any program element. We'll explore several search methods in this section.

Using the Class Selection Dialog

The first type of search we'll cover is finding a class or interface needed in a SmartGuide. For example, suppose you're creating a new class and you need to specify the superclass. When you click the **Browse** button on the Create Class SmartGuide (as seen in Chapter 2), you'll see the dialog presented in Figure 3.24.

This dialog enables you to find a class based on its name. You type in a pattern at the top of the dialog, choose a name that matches the pattern, and then choose the proper package. You'll be seeing this dialog a lot when you're using

Figure 3.23 A method browser.

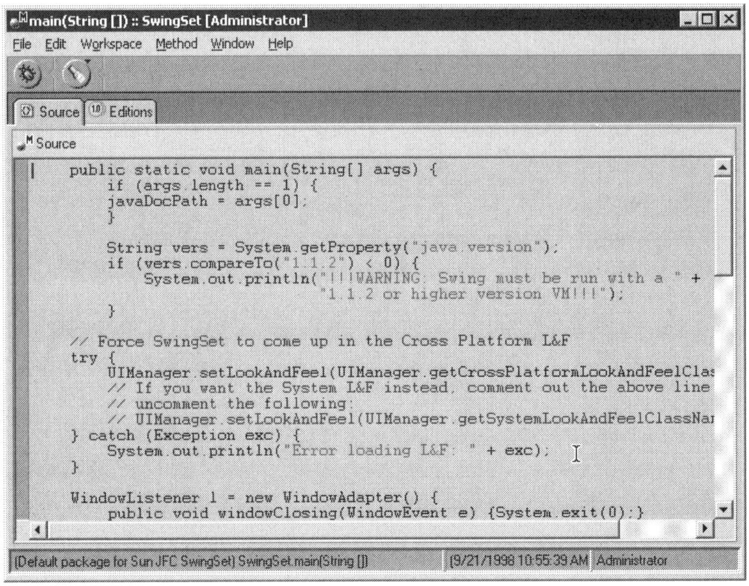

> **WARNING**
>
> Do *not* edit the *same* method in multiple windows at the same time. VisualAge for Java does not handle this gracefully. If you try to edit a method in two windows, and save it in one of the windows, VisualAge will warn you that the results may be inconsistent. If you ignore the warning, the last save wins. If you make changes in one window, then make changes in a second window, save the first window, and then save the second window, the results will be *only* the changes made in the second window. There will be another edition of the method containing the first changes, but there is no auto merge and the windows' contents are not kept in sync.

VisualAge for Java, so get used to it. As you enter more characters in the pattern field, the list is shortened to reflect only the names that match the pattern.

The Go To Command

For every tree, list, or graph pane, there is a **Go to** command in its pop-up menu. You can choose **Go to** for a project, package, or type. After you choose **Go to,** you'll see a selection dialog like the one shown in Figure 3.24 to select a project,

Figure 3.24 The class selection dialog.

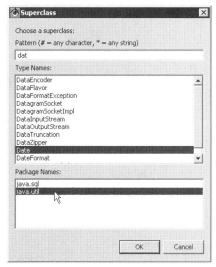

Superclass

Choose a superclass:

Pattern (# = any character, * = any string)

dat

Type Names:

DataEncoder
DataFlavor
DataFormatException
DatagramSocket
DatagramSocketImpl
DataInputStream
DataOutputStream
DataTruncation
DataZipper
Date
DateFormat

Package Names:

java.sql
java.util

OK Cancel

> **NOTE**
>
> When entering a pattern, do *not* enter the package name. You only want to enter the class name or part of it.
>
> After you select a class name, make sure the correct package is selected at the bottom of the dialog. Classes with the same name could exist in several packages. You need to make sure you have the correct one.

package, or type. After you select a program element, VisualAge will select that element in the list.

Searching for Program Elements

The search tool enables you to find a string across the workspace. You can access the search tool by clicking the flashlight icon on the tool bar. You can reduce the scope of the search to the class hierarchy or create a working set in which to search. Some predefined search patterns are available; you can use them to perform impact analysis for the various elements of your code. The Search/Replace window is useful to find and replace a string within a source pane. The Search/Replace window can be used to perform global search/replace across the workspace. Search results are displayed in the Search Results window.

Doing a Simple Search

You can open the Search window by clicking the flashlight icon on the tool bar, choosing the **Edit->Search** menu item, or pressing F4. This displays the Search dialog, as seen in Figure 3.25.

Search is performed based on the following information:

Search string. You can use an asterisk (*) as a wildcard to represent one or many characters in the string. If you had selected a program element before starting the search, the program element is loaded in the list by default. You can use the drop-down list to select a string that was previously used in a search.

Element. The program element can be a type (that is classes and types), a method, a constructor, or a field.

Usage. You can search references to and/or declarations of a program element.

Scope. It can be the workspace, the hierarchy, or a working set. If the scope is set to **class hierarchy**, you need to select a class by using the **Choose** button. The scope is composed of the chosen class, its subclasses and superclasses, as well as the interfaces it implements. A good usage of hierarchy search is to find which classes in a project extend a class you have defined, or which classes that extend your class override a certain method.

Begin the search by clicking the **Start** button. If you click the **Stop** button, the search is stopped and results found so far are added to the Search Results

Figure 3.25 The Search dialog.

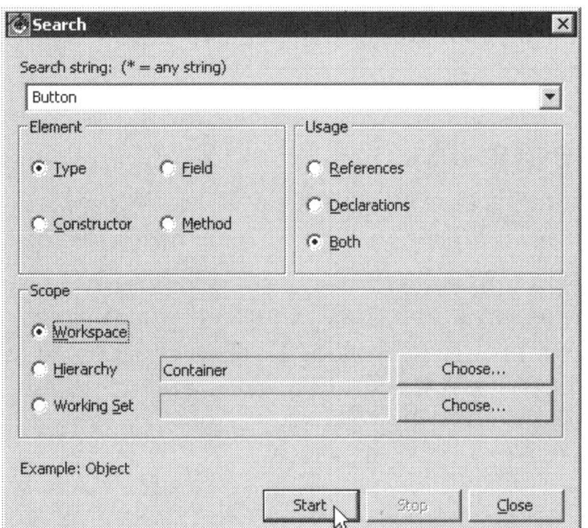

window. If you click the **Close** button, the search is stopped and no results are displayed.

> **WARNING**
>
> Choose the scope of the search carefully; in particular, workspace searches can be very slow if you are looking for something very common, such as toString() for example.

Defining Working Sets

Working sets are used to reduce the scope of a global search. A working set is a collection of program elements the scope in which VisualAge will perform the requested search. Working sets are saved in the workspace; therefore, you retrieve them between working sessions. To define a new working set, you need to supply the following information, as shown in Figure 3.26:

The working set name. Enter a string that uniquely identifies this working set.

A list of program elements. Select a combination of projects, packages, and types that should be used in the search.

Working sets are used when you search information, or when you use the global search/replace function.

Figure 3.26 Defining a working set.

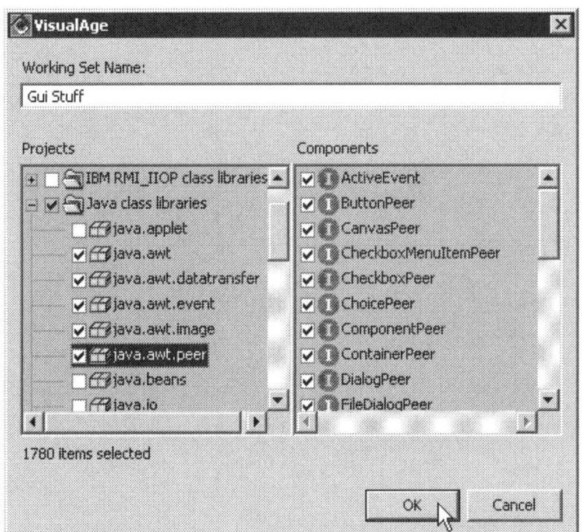

Search Results Window

The Search Results window (shown in Figure 3.27) is the central location in which all search results are displayed. As long as you don't close the window, search descriptions and results are accumulated in the Search Results window. If you want to make sure to keep search results during a working session, we recommend that you lock the Search Results window to avoid accidentally closing it. You can do this by selecting **Window->Lock Window**.

The top of the Search Results window is divided into two panes. The left pane contains a list of search descriptions and the right pane is used to display search results. A source pane is used to display the source code of program elements that match a specific search pattern.

A search description respects the following pattern: *SearchString – [Scope Type-Scope Details]*. The scope type can be **workspace, hierarchy**, or **working set**; the scope details can be the class or working set name. You can perform a search again by selecting a search description and using the **Search Again** pop-up menu item. You can remove a description list for the list by using the **Remove from list** pop-up menu item. Both options are available also from the **Descriptions** menu.

The list of search matches is displayed by selecting a search description. If several matches were found, you can use the arrows at the top right of the window to navigate between matches. You can also use the Ctrl-N and Ctrl-P shortcuts. If there is only one match, the next and previous match shortcuts are inactive. Search results can be sorted by method or class name using the tool-bar icons.

Figure 3.27 The Search Results window.

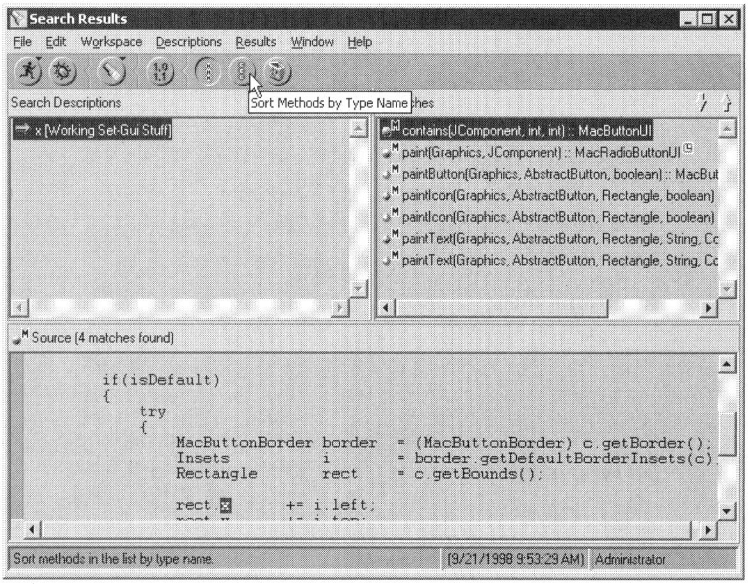

You can use the results of a search to replace occurrences of a string: Choosing **Replace Matches** from the pop-up menu of any entry in the Matches pane opens the find/replace window. The result set is used as the scope to the find/replace window. Changes made by the find/replace tool can be saved automatically. This feature is helpful if you want to rename an interface and change the implement statement in every class that implements that interface. First, you search for all implementers of the interface; then you use **Replace Matches** to change the interface name in every class.

Results can be copied to the clipboard. This is particularly useful, because you cannot print a report directly from the Search Results window. To print search results:

1. Perform a search.
2. Choose **Copy Results** to Clipboard from the pop-up menu of any match.
3. Open the Scrapbook (**Window->Scrapbook**).
4. Paste the report into an empty page.
5. Save or print the file.

A results summary might look like this:

```
Search Results (5/16/99 5:13:06 PM)
doPost [Hierarchy-References/Declarations]
  HttpServlet::doPost(HttpServletRequest, HttpServletResponse)
```

Impact Analysis

A common task when making changes to a program is to see what you need to change in your code. Finding out what needs to change is called *impact analysis*. Because all of the code you are working on is contained in one single place (the workspace), it is very easy to obtain impact-analysis information for your code. For example, you can find exactly where the classes you have developed are used, where a method is declared and used, or where a field is initialized or modified. Impact analysis can be done at the type, method, or field level.

Several common tasks follow:

Searching for Interface Implementers. After selecting an interface in any code browser, you can use the **Implementors** (sic) command to search for classes that implement this interface across the workspace. You can also invoke this command in an interface browser from the Interfaces menu.

Searching for Types References. After selecting a class, you can use the **References To->This Type** menu item to search for references to this class across the workspace. You cannot set the scope of the search when using this menu item. If you want to refine the search, use the Search window.

Searching for Field References. If you select a class or interface, you can use **References To->Fields** to search for references to fields defined in the class or inherited from a superclass. You can filter fields for which you want to search, and select the scope of the search. Both references and declarations of the field are searched.

You can also perform field-search directly by selecting a field name, and by using the **References** and **Declarations** menu item in the field pop-up menu. In this case, the scope of the search is the workspace.

Searching for Methods References. By selecting a method in any code browser and choosing **References**, you can search for references to a specific method. A submenu allows specifying the scope of the search.

Searching for Methods Declarations. By selecting a method in any code browser and choosing **Declaration**, you can search for declarations of a specific method. A submenu allows you to specify the scope of the search.

You can also perform more a precise search by analyzing the body of a method. For example, you can search for fields that a method accesses, methods sent by a method, or types referenced by a method. All of those options are available as contextual menu options on a method. You can search for references to and declarations of the program elements referenced in a method. This can be a good debugging feature. For example, suppose that you are modifying a class variable, but it does not have the value it should have when your code is invoked. By using this option, you can quickly know who else is modifying this field. You can specify the scope of the search for each of those commands.

Using Find/Replace

The find/replace window can be used to find or replace strings within a Source pane. Several options enable you to choose the search direction (up, down), how case should be handled, and if the search should wrap when the end of the Source-pane text is reached. If you select a string in the Source pane prior to calling find/replace, the find field is initialized with that string.

Using Text Search/Replace

The Text Search/Replace function is very similar to find/replace functionality with the exception that it enables you to expand the scope of the find/replace to the workspace. It actually combines a search and a find/replace. You can invoke the Search/Replace window by choosing **Workspace->Text Search/Replace** from the menu bar. You need to supply the following information, as shown in Figure 3.28.

Find what. The string for which you want to search. A history of the strings you have already provided is available in a drop-down list.

Figure 3.28 Text search and replace.

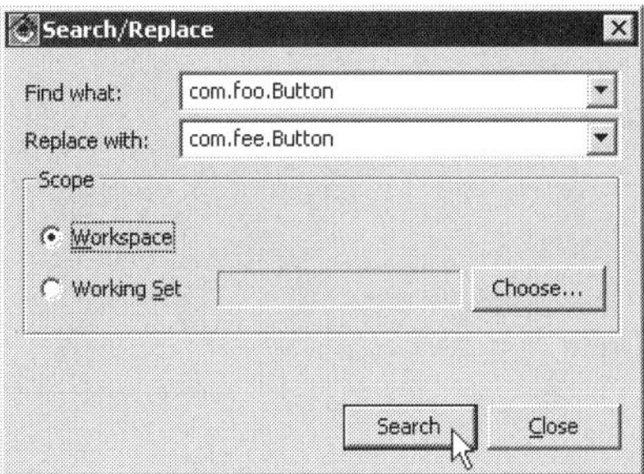

Replace with. The string with which you want to replace the found string. A history of the strings you have already provided is available in a drop-down list.

Scope. The scope can be set to the workspace or to a working set.

The Log

VisualAge for Java provides a log window that may present error messages or status of some tools. The log window appears as shown in Figure 3.29. You can access the log window by choosing **Window->Log.**

You can add your own messages to the VisualAge for Java log from tools that you write. See Chapter 25 for details on writing your own tools.

Figure 3.29 The Log window.

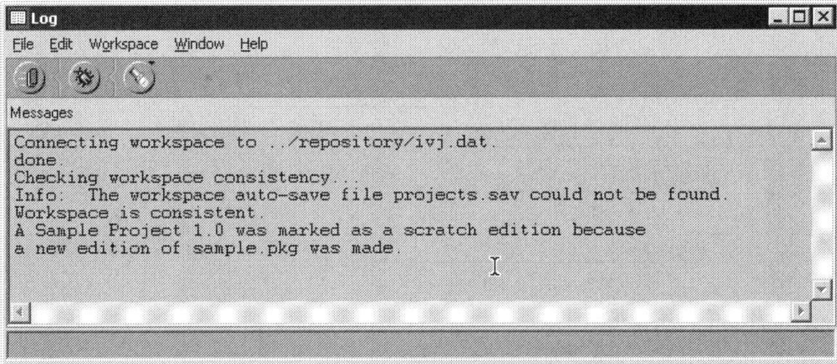

Customizing VisualAge for Java

You can change several things about the way VisualAge for Java behaves. The main interface to your customization is by choosing **Window->Options**. This displays the Options dialog, seen in Figure 3.30.

The Options dialog is divided into two parts. On the left side, there is an index of all options pages. On the right side, the currently selected page is displayed. In Figure 3.30, the General page is displayed. We'll describe the options on each page of the dialog in the following sections.

Each page in the Options dialog contains a **Defaults** button and an **Apply** button. The **Defaults** button will restore the *page* settings to their factory default values. The **Apply** button commits the current *page's* changes. The **Ok** button commits all changes and closes the dialog, while **Cancel** discards changes and closes the dialog.

Figure 3.30 The Options dialog.

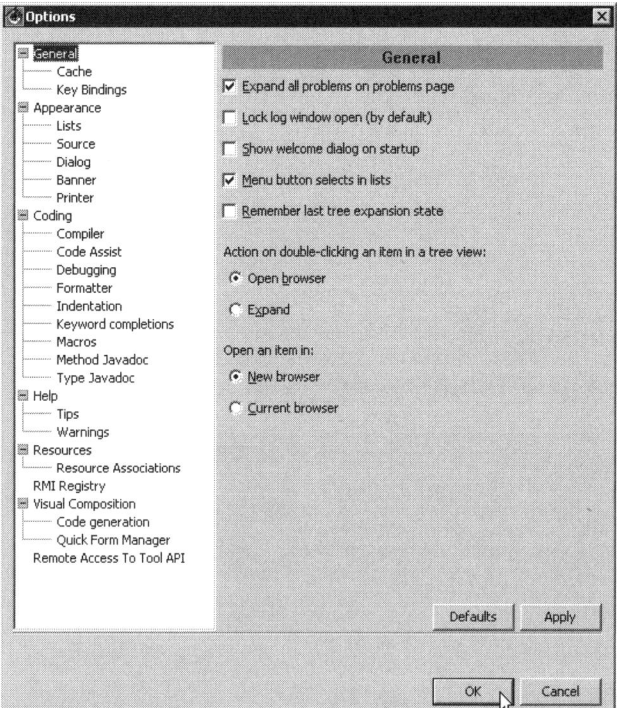

General

The General page of the Options dialog contains the following options:

Expand all problems on problems page. If selected, the tree that contains the list of problems in each browser's Problems page will start fully expanded. Otherwise, you will see only the projects in the tree and need to expand them to see the problems.

Lock log window open (by default). If selected, the Log window starts locked. This means that you won't be able to close it unless you unlock it first (or choose **Unlock** in the warning dialog that appears when you try to close the log window). We recommend that you keep this box cleared.

Show welcome dialog on startup. If selected, an annoying little dialog appears every time you start VisualAge for Java, asking, "What do you want to do?" We recommend that you clear this box before the dialog drives you mad.

Menu button selects in lists. If selected, whenever you right-click in a tree, list, or graph to bring up a pop-up menu, the item under the mouse is selected. If cleared, the selection does not change, and the pop-up menu relates to the selection, which is not necessarily the item under the mouse cursor. We recommend you keep this box selected.

Remember last tree expansion state. If checked, VisualAge remembers the entire expansion state of all trees. Thus, if you collapse a project and re-expand it, you'll see the packages expanded as they were previously. If cleared, whenever you collapse a project, VisualAge forgets which program elements under it were expanded. If selected, VisualAge uses a little more memory, but not too much.

Action on double-clicking an item in tree view. If you choose **Open browser** (the default), the appropriate browser window is opened for a program element when you double-click on the element). If you choose **Expand**, the tree node expands or collapses. We recommend that you keep this set to **Open browser**, because you can expand or collapse by pressing the "+" or "-" keys, as well as by using the keyboard arrow keys.

Open an item in. If left on the default setting, a new window appears whenever you open a new browser. If set to **Current browser**, the current window is replaced with the new browser, and back/forward buttons are added to the tool bar (similar to an Internet web browser).

General->Cache

The General->Cache page of the Options dialog contains the following options:

Disk Cache. The number of classes that VisualAge will keep in a temporary cache on the disk. This helps VisualAge load them more quickly.

The default is 800, but if you use a large class library, you may want to set this number higher to avoid reloading the code from the repository every time you run your programs.

Memory Cache. The number of classes that VisualAge will keep in memory (when they're not being used). This further reduces the load time for applications at the expense of memory. If you've got extra memory, you may want to increase this amount. However, if you're also using tools like WebSphere and DB2 (or some other database and application server), you'll need to be careful about this setting, because WebSphere and DB2 use a lot of memory themselves.

Clear Disk Cache. Click this button to clear the classes that occupy the disk cache.

Clear Memory Cache. Click this button to clear the classes that occupy the memory cache. This operation does *not* take actually place until you restart VisualAge for Java.

General->Key Bindings

The General->Key Bindings page of the Options dialog enables you to define how you want to use the keyboard to work with VisualAge for Java. Select or create a profile to use and then change the key mappings by clicking on Key Sequence and pressing the new key sequence you want. Two profiles exist: one for the default VisualAge for Java settings and another that simulates many key presses in emacs.

We discuss key bindings in more detail in Chapter 2.

Appearance

The Appearance page of the Options dialog contains the following options:

Tab location in browsers. You can specify whether you want the tabs for pages within a browser to appear at the top or bottom of the window.

Show toolbars. Clearing this box will hide the tool bars. This is useful if you're running with a smaller resolution screen and want some more screen space. You can still access all of the tool-bar commands from menus.

Show pane titles. Clearing this box will hide the pane title-bars, giving you more screen space for code.

Include return type in method label. Selecting this box will show the return type in front of methods in the tree or list. Although some people like this option, for many, it makes the alphabetization of the method names difficult to see.

Include type name in field label. Selecting this box will show the type of each field in front of the field in the tree- or list-panes.

Initially show static fields in inspectors. When using an inspector in the debugger, selecting this option will show class variables (static fields). If cleared, only instance variables (non-static fields) will appear. See Chapter 5, "Testing and Debugging," for details on using the VisualAge for Java debugger.

Reset window sizes. Click this button to reset the sizes of all windows to the initial sizes provided with VisualAge for Java.

Reset window pane proportions. Click this button to reset the location of the divider bars in all windows to their factory defaults.

Appearance->Lists

The Appearance->Lists page (and the other pages under Appearance) of the Options dialog allow you to change the font settings in VisualAge for Java. We recommend that if you change the Appearance->Code settings, you choose a non-proportional (monospaced) font like Courier or Lucida Console.

Coding

The Coding page of the Options dialog contains the following options:

Tab spacing. The number of spaces that a tab should represent in the Source pane.

Report problems before saving. If selected, an annoying dialog appears whenever you have errors in your code and save. We recommend that you turn this option off. Although the dialog provides some nice correction capabilities (such as adding missing import statements automatically), the corrections aren't needed often enough to warrant the annoyance of constantly seeing this dialog and having to press Enter.

Add imports for fully-qualified names from smartguides. Whenever you specify a type in a SmartGuide that is in a different package, the type must either be fully qualified (the default) or you must add an import statement for the type. If the option is selected, VisualAge will automatically add an import-on-demand statement like

```
import java.util.*;
```

to the class definition whenever you specify a type in other packages. The type reference (in an extends clause, for example) will appear *without* package-qualification.

Coding->Compiler

The Coding->Compiler page of the Options dialog contains the following options:

Unreachable code errors. If selected, the compiler will warn you about code that cannot be reached. We recommend you always select this box, because this is the default behavior of all other Java compilers.

Report method names conflicting with constructors. If selected, VisualAge will warn you if you write code like the following:

```
public class SomeClass {
    private int x;
    public int getX() {return x;}
    public void SomeClass() {
        x = 42;
    }
}
```

Although this may *appear* to be a constructor definition, it is not. The Java language says that if you provide a return type (void, in this case), the code is a method *regardless* if it has the same name as the class it's defined in. In other words, when you write code like:

```
SomeClass anInstance = new SomeClass();
System.out.println(anInstance.getX());
```

you'll see 0 as the result, *not* 42 as you might expect. This is *not* a compilation error, and most Java compilers don't warn you about it. If you select **Report method names conflicting with constructors**, the VisualAge for Java compiler will provide a compilation error if you make such a mistake. To fix the error, simply remove the return type on the constructor. We *strongly* recommend that you select this box.

Coding->Code Assist

The Coding->Code Assist page of the Options dialog contains the following options:

Automatically insert is there is only one completion. If you press Ctrl-Space (or whatever you have code completion bound to) and there is only one possible completion for the text you've typed, it will automatically be inserted without showing the code-completion list.

Key used to select item in completion list. Specifies which keys can be used to select the completion that you want from the list that appears when you invoke code completion. You can choose Return, Tab, Space, or any combination.

Coding->Debugging

The Coding->Debugging page of the Options dialog contains the following options:

Show system programs in debugger and console. If cleared, programs that run as part of the IDE will not appear in the debugger or console. Normally, you want to keep this box cleared. However, if you're testing JavaBeans property editors or customizers, you'll want to select this box to debug them and see their output in the console.

Show creation time of running programs. If selected, the debugger will show what time each program was started. We recommend that you keep this box selected, because it helps to distinguish between two running instances of the same program.

Source path for dynamically loaded classes. If you're debugging external code, you can set the location of its source code here.

Reset recent breakpoint conditions. Click this button if you want to clear the list of breakpoint conditions that you can set by modifying a breakpoint. We describe breakpoint settings in Chapter 5.

Trace class initialization for running programs. Enables you to see how classes are being initialized while running a program. We describe this option in Chapter 5.

Coding->Formatter

The Coding->Formatter page of the Options dialog contains the following options. Note that these options only affect how the code formatter (Ctrl-W) works. They will not affect how newly created classes appear.

Compound statements begin new line. If cleared, compound statements are "cuddled." For example, an if-else statement might look as follows:

```
if (condition) {
    statement;
} else {
    statement;
}
If the option is selected, the "else" starts a new line:
if (condition) {
    statement;
}
else {
    statement;
}
```

Opening braces begin new line. If cleared, opening curly braces will appear on the same line as the statement they belong to. In the following examples, **Compound statements begin new line** is also selected. For example:

```
if (condition) {
    statement;
}
else {
     statement;
}
If the option is selected, the opening curly braces start on a
new line. For example:
if (condition)
{
    statement;
}
else
{
    statement;
}
```

3.5 **Compact assignment statements (version 3.5 and later).** If selected, spaces before the equal sign in an assignment statement are removed. For example:

```
x = 42; // "non-compact" assignment
x= 42;  // "compact" assignment
```

3.5 **Keep 'else if' on same line (version 3.5 and later).** If selected, the formatter will place "else if" on the same line. If unselected, the formatter will move the "if" to its own line. For example:

```
// "keep 'else if' on same line unselected:
if (condition1)
  someAction();
else
  if (condition2)
    anotherAction();

// "keep 'else if' on same line selected:
if (condition1)
  someAction();
else if (condition2)
  anotherAction();
```

3.5 **Keep existing layout (version 3.5 and later).** The style of the existing class is preserved.

Coding->Formatter->Spacing (version 3.5 and later)

The Coding->Formatter->Spacing page of the Options dialog contains the following dialog. Note that these options only affect how the code formatter (Ctrl-W) works. They will not affect how newly created classes appear. (Note that this tab only appears in version 3.5 of VisualAge for Java.)

Keep blank lines. If set to "Keep one", multiple blank lines in a row will be reduced to a single blank line when you format the source. If set to "Remove all", all blank lines will be removed from the source when it is formatted.

Represent indentation with. If set to "Tab", tab characters are added to the file to for indentation of statements. If set to "Spaces", multiple spaces will be added for indentation purposes.

Number of spaces per tab. The number of spaces that are used to represent each level of indentation.

> **NOTE**
>
> This "Number of spaces per tab" setting is independent of the "Tab spacing" setting in the Coding page of the options dialog. This setting controls the amount of space for each indentation level. You can set a different amount of space in the Coding page, which represents how much space is inserted when you press the Tab character.

Coding->Indentation

The Coding->Indentation page of the Options dialog contains the following options. These options apply whenever you type code or use the code formatter.

No indentation. No automatic indentation is performed

Simple auto indent. Indentation is increased for each opening brace you type

Smart auto indent. Indentation is increased for each opening brace, and decreased for each closing brace that you type

Coding->Keyword Completions and Coding->Macros

The Coding->Keyword Completions page of the Options dialog enables you to define keyword completions and macros. See Chapter 2 for details on keyword completion and macros.

Coding->Managing (version 3.5 and later)

3.5 The Coding->Managing page of the Options dialog lets you specify an initial version name that will appear in the "One Name" field when a user first versions a program element. This can be any string you want. See Chapter 4 for details on creating versions of your code.

Coding->Method Javadoc and Type Javadoc

The Coding->Method Javadoc and Coding->Type Javadoc pages enable you to define the comments that automatically appear at the top of created classes, interfaces, and methods. These comments will only appear for methods if you use the method SmartGuide or method template option to create methods. Method and class creation are covered in Chapter 2.

Help

The Help page of the Options dialog contains the following options:

Use file association. If selected, the normal file association for HTML pages on your operating system is used to determine which Web browser to use to display VisualAge for Java help.

Specify browser path. If selected, you can specify any Web browser you want to use for VisualAge for Java help.

Normally, you will want to *Use file association*. You would only want to set *Specify browser path* if you need to use a different browser for VisualAge for Java help than you would for normal Web viewing (which is probably quite rare).

Help->Tips and Help->Warnings

The Help->Tips page of the Options dialog enables you to enable or disable several tips and warning in the VisualAge for Java IDE. We strongly recommend you do not disable tips and warnings through this dialog. You should wait until the messages come up and see if you find them useful or not.

Resources

The Resources page of the Options dialog contains the following options:

Workspace class path. Enables you to specify external directories and JAR files that contain code and resources that you need when running programs in the IDE. See Chapter 2 for details on setting class paths. Note that this path *only* affects run time. If you need a class to be available to compile your program, the class *must* exist in the workspace (you must import it). The workspace class-path is most often useful for inclusion of common resources like images, and for including a JDBC driver that you want to use in your applications.

Shared project_resources directory. Here you can specify a network path that contains resource files that are *shared* by all users of a team repository. Note that this does *not* change existing projects. Existing projects will still use the local project_resources directory *unless* you change their Properties to use the shared project resources directory (select Properties from the pop-up menu for a project). See Chapter 6 for details on resources.

New projects should use shared resources. If selected, any new projects that you create will be set to use the specified shared project_resources directory.

Resources->Resource Associations

The Resources->Resource Associations page of the Options dialog enables you to specify external programs or Java classes that will be used to process resource files. Resource files appear in the Resources page of Project browsers. See Chapter 6 for details on resources. You can also specify tools to use against resources. See Chapter 25 for details.

RMI Registry

RMI is Java Remote Method Invocation. The RMI registry is a simple naming server that allows a client application to locate a remote object. You can read about RMI at http://java.sun.com/products/jdk/rmi.

The RMI Registry page of the Options dialog contains the following options:

Start RMI registry on VisualAge startup. If selected, the RMI registry will automatically start when you start VisualAge for Java. We recommend that you select this box only if you use RMI regularly, otherwise, you should start and stop the registry manually.

Use default RMI port. If selected, the RMI registry in VisualAge will listen at the default port for RMI (1099).

Use a custom RMI port. If selected, you can specify whatever port you would like the RMI registry to listen to.

Restart RMI Registry. Click this button to start the RMI registry.

Stop RMI Registry. Click this button to stop the RMI registry.

Visual Composition

The Visual Composition page of the Options dialog contains the following options:

Inherit BeanInfo of bean superclass. If selected, any new BeanInfo classes that you create by using the BeanInfo editor (see Chapter 8) will "inherit" the feature definitions of the bean's superclass. It does this by defining the getAdditionalBeanInfo() method of the generated BeanInfo class to point to the superclass' BeanInfo. We strongly recommend that you keep this option selected. The only time you would want to clear this option is if you want to hide the features of a bean's superclass. If you do clear this box, make sure you select it again after you're done defining the non-inheriting BeanInfo class.

BeanInfo search path extensions. You can specify packages in your workspace that contain BeanInfo classes here. See Chapter 7, "Introduction to JavaBeans Components," for details on how BeanInfo classes are found.

Design time class path extensions. You can specify external directories or JAR files to use in the Visual Composition Editor here. This is useful if you're using property editors or customizers that require resource files (like images) or JDBC access.

Visual Composition->Code Generation

The Visual Composition->Code Generation page of the Options dialog contains the following options. See Chapter 10 for details on the Visual Composition Editor.

Event handling. Specifies what type of code the Visual Composition Editor (VCE) should generate to create event handlers.

- **Do not use any inner classes.** If selected, the VCE will generate code to make the composite bean (the class you're visually composing) handle the events directly. The composite bean will implement the required event listener interfaces and provide code to dispatch to event handlers.
- **Use one inner class for all events.** If selected, the VCE will generate a single inner class inside the composite bean that listens for and dispatches events to the generated event handlers.
- **Use an inner class for each event.** If selected, the VCE will generate an inner class for each event connection you create in the VCE.

> **WARNING**
>
> The **Use an inner class for each event** option currently generates incorrect code. We strongly recommend that you do not use this option for event-code generation.

Generate meta data method. If selected, the VCE will generate a method called getBuilderData(). This method contains no code, but it has a large comment in it that encodes the visual design information used in the VCE. If you select this option, any class you save in the VCE after you set this option will contain a getBuilderData() method and can be exported as source code without losing the visual design. See Chapter 10 for more information about visual designs.

Visual Composition->Quick Form Manager

The Visual Composition->Quick Form Manager page of the Options dialog enables you to register and remove quick forms for use in the Visual Composition Editor. Please see Chapter 11, "Layout Management," for details on quick forms.

Remote Access to Tool API

The Remote Access to Tool API page of the Options dialog enables you to start a remote tool API server in VisualAge for Java. This book does not cover remote Tool API access; please see Remote Tool Integration under the VisualAge for Java online help. Choose **Help->Concepts->Remote Tool Integration** from the IDE.

Tools and Features

You can further customize VisualAge for Java by creating your own plug-in tools and bundled features. See Chapter 25 for details on defining and using features and tools.

Summary

In this chapter, we've explored the basics of browsing code in the IDE, searching and cross-referencing program elements, and customizing the IDE to help you use it more productively. The IDE is very flexible. There are many ways to perform any given task; find the techniques that make you comfortable and most productive!

In the next chapter, we move on to a critical concept in VisualAge for Java: version control. VisualAge for Java provides built-in version control, using a unique paradigm that is incredibly useful and scaleable. When developing code in VisualAge for Java, use the version-control tools often. The more often you version your code, the easier it is to recover past work and undo changes.

4 Using Version Control

In this chapter, we explore how to use VisualAge for Java's source code management features during the development process. In particular, we cover how to manage versions, maintain program elements integrity, and handle parallel development. The first part of the chapter concentrates on the Professional Edition; the second part describes the tasks involved in using the Enterprise Edition, where multiple users share a repository. We don't pretend to teach team programming in one chapter, but rather, we give you the right base upon which to build.

For an in-depth look at team version control in VisualAge for Java, we recommend you read the IBM Redbook, *VisualAge for Java Enterprise Version 2 Team Support*. You can download this Redbook from www.redbooks.ibm.com. Search for SG24-5245-00 once you are at the Redbooks home page. Note that this Redbook was written for version 2 of VisualAge for Java, but the version control has not changed for version 3.5.

Where Does VisualAge Keep Code?

VisualAge for Java uses a central repository to store all the code that you create. Each developer works with a view into this code called the workspace.

The Repository

The repository is the central location in which all of the code that you either have created or imported from existing libraries is stored. This repository can be local/personal (accessible locally on your workstation) or remote/team (managed by a team server). Normally, only source code is stored in the repository; however, if you import .class files, the bytecodes are also stored in the repository. When you modify code in the IDE and save it, the source code is automatically saved in the repository, and the compiled bytecodes are imported in the workspace. Repository contents can be browsed (not edited) from the Repository Explorer, which you start from **Window->Repository Explorer**.

VisualAge for Java can't start without a valid repository. At start-up, an attempt is made to connect the local workspace to the repository defined in the VisualAge for

Java configuration file. Local repositories are located in \IBMVJava\ide\repository. You set the name of the repository you to which you want to connect by changing the [JavaDevelopment] entry in the \IBMVJava\ide\program\ide.ini file. You can specify either a relative or absolute path to the local repository: Paths must be relative to the \IBMVJava\ide\program directory. The following definition addresses a local repository called ivj.dat (which is the default name):

```
[JavaDevelopment]
;Local Configuration
ServerAddress=
DefaultName=../repository/ivj.dat
OpenReadOnly=false
```

> **NOTE**
>
> You can also change the location of the repository by choosing **Window->Repository Explorer** and then **Admin->Change Repository**.

If you specify a server address, an attempt is made to connect to the team server process running on that machine. The team server is in charge of handling concurrent connections to a repository from multiple clients, as depicted in Figure 4.1. A team server can manage one or more repositories. You connect to a remote repository by specifying a machine name and a repository file name. The machine name can be either a host name (such as *eagle*) or an IP address (such as *10.0.0.1*). When you connect to a remote repository, DefaultName must point to a path that is local to the server. For example, if the repository is located on the C:\ drive on the server machine, you must specify C:\ivj.dat for DefaultName. If you have mapped this remote drive to a local Z:\ drive on your machine (using the *net use* command or NFS), do not use the local Z:\ drive name, but the server C:\ drive name, like this:

```
[JavaDevelopment]
; Server Configuration
Server Address=eagle
DefaultName=C:\ivj.dat
OpenReadOnly=false
```

> **NOTE**
>
> It is recommended that you address a repository location using an absolute path rather than a relative path to the repository file (in the ide.ini file).

The size of the repository file is limited to four gigabytes. The team server executable is available on a wide number of platforms including Windows NT, IBM AIX, SUN Solaris, or Novell. The format of the repository is independent of the operating system you use. Therefore, a repository can be moved from one system to another without any problems.

The Workspace

The workspace contains all of the program elements that a single developer needs. You add program elements to the workspace by loading them from the repository. The first time you start the IDE, only the Java class libraries and VisualAge for Java supporting classes are loaded into the workspace. The Workbench is a view of the workspace contents.

The contents of the workspace are stored in a file called ide.icx, located in the \IBMVJava\ide\program directory. The workspace file is saved when you explicitly ask for it, or when you exit VisualAge for Java. This file *must* be saved for the repository and the workspace to be consistent. There is no way to exit VisualAge for Java without saving the workspace, even if you haven't changed any code! If for any reason, VisualAge is stopped before you are able to save the workspace, an attempt is made to rebuild the workspace from the repository data at next start-up. See the *Understanding the IDE Startup Process* section later in this chapter for details on how this works.

Figure 4.1 Local and team configurations.

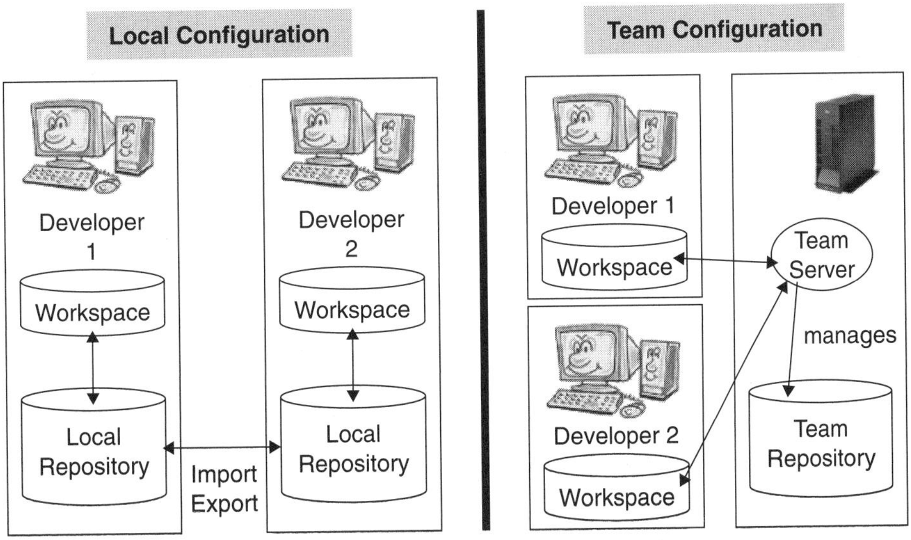

> **TIP**
>
> The size of the workspace directly influences VisualAge for Java's performance, because the contents of this file are loaded in memory at start-up. Keep in this file only the code you need for your current development.

To load the code from the repository to the workspace, you must call the Add action. To remove code from the workspace, you must call the Delete action. Those terms can be confusing as you may think that the workspace contents are really deleted. Actually, they are just unloaded from your workspace, but still available in the central repository.

If worse comes to worse, you can recreate your workspace from the original installation. Original workspace and repository files are available on the installation CD-ROM in the ivj3x/Backup folder. You can then rebuild the workspace contents by loading projects and packages from the repository. This also means that the repository is an important file that you must back up often! We'll talk more on back-up policies in Appendix B, "Maintenance and Troubleshooting."

Enterprise versus Professional Edition

In the Professional Edition of VisualAge for Java, version control is used by a single developer. Several developers cannot share the repository. The repository is then qualified to be *local*. In the Enterprise Edition, the repository can be installed on a server and shared by the development team. In this case, the repository is then qualified as being *remote*. A Professional Edition's workspace can be connected only to a local repository, while an Enterprise Edition's workspace can be connected to a local or remote repository.

The Professional Edition can be connected only to a repository called ivj.dat located in the \IBMVJava\ide\repository directory. This implies that if you have a team of 10 developers and you want them to share code using a central repository, you must buy 10 licenses of the Enterprise Edition, and not one license of the Enterprise Edition and nine licenses of the Professional Edition.

Overview of Versioning

Forget about everything you know on version control: VisualAge for Java is different! First, you version program elements and not files; all program elements have editions, including methods. Projects, packages, and types can be versioned. Whenever your code has reached a state to which you want to revert, you create a *versioned edition* of that code. A versioned edition is a frozen edition that cannot be changed. If you want to modify a versioned program element, you first need to create an *open edition*.

How VisualAge Associates Program Elements

The first thing you need to understand is that VisualAge for Java groups program elements when you version them. Whenever you save a method, an open edition of that method is created. Whenever you version a class, *that class version is associated with the method editions it currently references in the workspace*. Whenever you version a package, it associates the package version with the class or interface versions contained within it.

This is a very elegant solution, and it gives you a lot of power during development. If you want to change a class so it uses an older version of one of its methods, you simply replace the edition of the method. Using file-based version control, you would need to grab the old and new versions of the file, and paste a copy of the old method from the old version into the new version of the file.

Think of classes and interfaces as collections of methods (as well as the declaration of the class), packages as collections of classes and interfaces, and projects as collections of packages. Whenever you version an element, it forever associates that version of that element to the versions of the elements contained within it.

Performing Version Control Tasks

To illustrate those principles, let's walk through an example scenario. Angus is a brilliant consultant who created a one-man company, Fictive Consultants. A large bank, MoneyMaker, wants him to create a prototype of an Internet banking solution. The requirements of the bank are simple: A customer who connects to the bank Web site must be able to log on and view the balance of all of its accounts at the bank. Angus has been working with VisualAge for Java since version 1.0, and he decides to use the Professional Edition to create the prototype.

Creating Projects and Packages

First, Angus creates a project called *MoneyMaker Internet Banking*. This project is used to group packages relative to the Internet banking prototype. Next, he creates three packages to hold the prototype classes. All package names start with com.fictive.ib. One package is used to group servlets, another to group the beans used by JavaServer Page elements. Finally, a *utils* package is created to hold all supporting classes. Next, Angus creates classes in the different packages: a logonServlet and a listAccountServlet, an InvalidLogonDataException class, as well as Account and Customer classes. Angus ends up with the structure shown in Figure 4.2. The initial project baseline is now ready.

Versioning Life Cycle

When you create a program element, it is always an open edition. Therefore, Angus can modify his contents. Whenever he reaches a state in development to which he wants to be able to revert to, he creates a *versioned edition* by using **Manage->Version**

Figure 4.2 Original class structure.

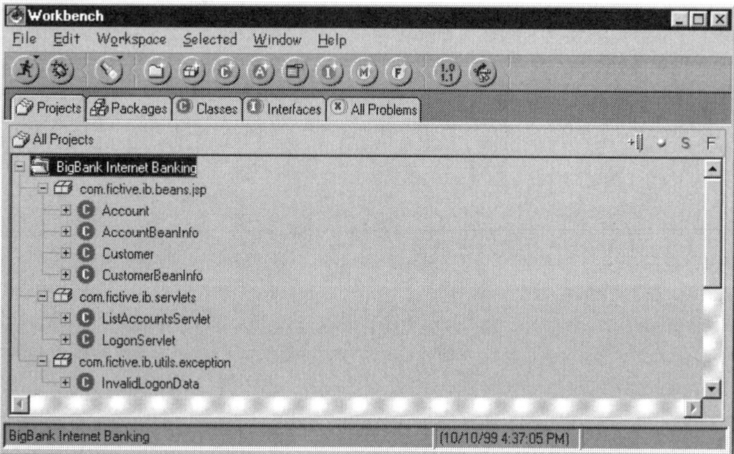

on the type's pop-up menu. You can consider a versioned edition as a snapshot of your code at a certain point in time. Code does not need to be error-free or even compilable to be versioned. You should not create a versioned edition each time you successfully enter a line of code, but rather each time you reach a stable state. As a basic rule of thumb, version your code whenever you hear yourself utter, "Yes! It (almost) works!" This ensures that no matter how badly you distort the code, you can always go back to the last working version. You also can decide to version your work when you leave the office at night, for example. In the rest of this chapter, the terms *version* and *versioned edition* are used to designate the same state.

Each versioned edition must have a name. You can specify a name, or let VisualAge for Java generate this name for you, as shown in Figure 4.3. You can select multiple program elements to version them all at one time. The version name is applied to all the selected items, unless you have selected the Name Each option. If a selected item already has a version with the same name, a dialog lets you choose a different name.

VisualAge for Java is rather smart when it comes to generating version names. Suppose you have chosen a version tag to be *AM-0310-V0.1* the first time you versioned a program element. Next time you version this program element, VisualAge for Java automatically proposes *AM-0310-V0.2* as a version name. In general, VisualAge for Java increases by one the last digit or character of the version name: for example, *AM-0.1a* becomes *AM-0.1b*. However, be careful what you specify as the last part of a version number. For example, if you name a version 1.0a1, VisualAge for Java can automatically name the following versions 1.0a2, 1.0a3, and so forth up to 1.0a9. *However*, VisualAge treats each character as a digit, so the next version would be 1.0b0! To work around this behavior, you separate letters from numbers in your version number, preferably using a space or dot. For example, you could use 1.0a.1 and VisualAge for Java will only increment the last part of the version name. After 1.0a.9, you would see 1.0a.10.

> **TIP**
>
> Use meaningful version names. For example, begin the version's name with your initials. If you export this code to a repository format, other developers who import the code have a visual cue of who wrote it. This is even more important in the Enterprise Edition, where several developers can work on different editions of the same class. Other useful information includes the version creation's date.

Once you have created a version, the program element can't be modified. An open edition must be created first. VisualAge for Java creates an open edition automatically each time you make a change to the program element, for example, if you modify a method in a type.

Methods are handled a bit differently. You can't create versions of a method, but an open edition of the method is created each time you save it, as shown in Figure 4.4. Those intermediate editions only disappear when you compact the repository (see the section *A Bit of Administration* later in this chapter).

Figure 4.3 Versioning a type.

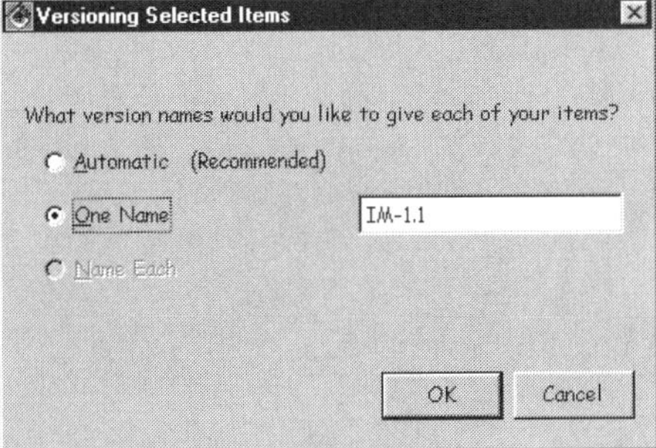

Figure 4.4 Editions page in the method browser.

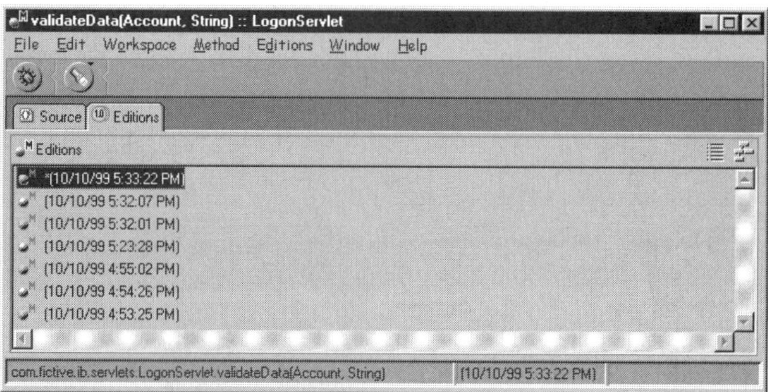

All editions are kept in the repository, but only *one* of those editions can be loaded in the workspace. At any time, you can exchange the current edition with another. For example, Angus has created a validateLogonData() method in the logonServlet class. He versions the class, slightly modifies it, and realizes the previously versioned edition was much better. To revert to the previous edition, he selects the logonServlet class, then selects **Replace With->Previous Edition** from the pop-up menu. The current edition is replaced with the previous one. You can revert to any edition by using **Replace With->Another Edition**.

Working with Editions

You can view *all* editions by selecting a program element and invoking **Open To->Editions** (including for methods). Information listed on the Editions page is taken from the repository and cannot be modified. These are *shadow* program elements, represented by grayed icons. If you open any of these editions, a *shadow browser* appears. In a shadow browser, all icons are gray to help you see that this is a shadow; moreover, the title of the browser begins with "Shadow of". If you edit program elements in a shadow browser, you will not be able to save them.

> **TIP**
>
> If you accidentally edit a program element in a shadow browser, VisualAge for Java will not let you save it. We recommend that you copy the code you changed and paste it into a Scrapbook page or another text editor on your system. You can then edit the "live" version of it in your workspace and paste in your changes.

The Editions page lets you perform two essential tasks: load a specific edition in the workspace and compare editions. If you select an edition, you can use the **Add to Workspace** pop-up item to replace the current edition by the selected one. This is equivalent to using the **Replace With->Another Edition** option.

If you want to know the differences between two editions, select them (press and hold the Ctrl key as you click all that apply) and choose **Editions->Compare** from the pop-up menu. The Compare window lets you view a list of differences, for example, added or removed methods, or code changes in the body of a method. You can also compare project and package editions.

Packaging the Application

Angus is now ready to package a JAR file to deploy at the bank. First, he creates an "Angus 1.0" version of the project. This creates versions for all contained packages and their types. This version is the new project baseline. If Angus makes some changes to version "Angus 1.0," and then the customer asks for a change on the prototype delivered at the bank, he will be able to revert to the "Angus 1.0" version and fix the code. However, Angus will then have to merge the changes made in both branches: the one with new features and the one with fixes.

Reconciling Changes

What Angus faces is very frequent in development. You version a project, package it, and deliver it. This version is the baseline to add features for the next version. In the mean time, customers start complaining and open defects against your code. You now have two streams of development. Fixes to version 1.0 go in a fix pack, and added features can only be part of the next major release. However, fixes also have to be in the next release! Somewhere in the development process, you must merge the changes from both development streams. Reconciling changes is done in the comparing window.

Angus has created the Account class. After delivering version "Angus 1.0," he decides to implement a toString() method for that class. Next day, MoneyMaker IT director calls him to suggest that declaring the getPinNumber() accessor as public is a potential security flaw. Angus has now two editions coming from the same baseline: one that contains fixes (Angus Fix 1.1), and another one that contains new features (Angus Features 1.1). To reconcile changes, he must choose any of the versioned editions as the reference edition, create an open edition from that version, and import changes from other editions in that new open edition. Then, he versions the open edition, which becomes Angus 1.1; it contains changes from both "Angus Fix 1.1" and "Angus Features 1.1". This version is the new baseline.

If Angus loads the "Angus Features 1.1" edition in his workspace and compares it to the "Angus Fix 1.1" edition, he sees the differences shown in Figure 4.5. In the left pane, you can see the code for the Angus Features 1.1 edition of the Account class; in the right pane, the code for the "Angus Fix 1.1" edition. The code in the right pane is compared to the code on the left pane. If a difference states "Removed method," it means that the type in the left pane has a method that the type in the right pane does not have. The toString() method exists in the "Angus Features 1.1" edition, not in the "Angus Fix 1.1" edition, therefore it is considered as a removed method in the "Angus Fix 1.1" edition. Angus can safely ignore that difference by selecting the difference, and choosing **Ignore**. Then, he selects the other difference and chooses **Load Right**. The result is an open edition of the Account class that contains the toString() method and a private getPinNumber() method. The next step is to version this class to create the "Angus 1.1" versioned edition, which is the new development baseline.

Reconciling changes is not an easy task. It involves quite a lot of planning and manual tasks. Although it is difficult to totally avoid situations where reconciliation is necessary, you can limit those problems by having a limited number of developers working on the same class. You should also avoid having multiple developers working on the same method of a class. If changes in a method conflict, you must manually edit the method's contents, which is an error-prone process.

Working with a Team

The MoneyMaker Corporation is happy with the prototype, and wants to build a larger application. To face demand, Angus needs to hire two Java developers, Scott and Isabelle. Since the Professional Edition does not let developers share a repository, Angus decides to migrate to the Enterprise Edition.

Using the Enterprise Edition requires that you define users. You can think of the Professional Edition as the Enterprise Edition with one developer, where all of the code is owned by a single user. In the Professional Edition, the notion of users is transparent to you; in the Enterprise Edition, you have to define users before starting any development.

Figure 4.5 Comparing editions.

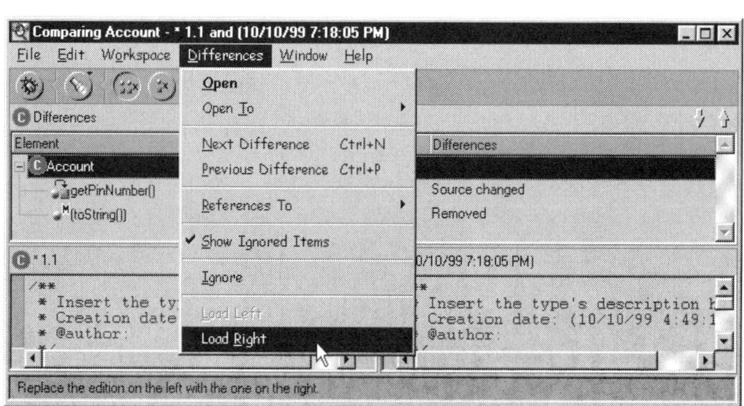

> **NOTE**
>
> A simpler (and cheaper) solution is to manually export the code from a developer's repository into another developer's repository. This can work for a small team, but is rather painful as soon as you are developing an application with a larger team of developers.

A base enterprise repository has one predefined user, Administrator. Administrator is in charge of installing the team server, creating users, and administering the repository. The administrator role *must be reserved* for administration, not to author code!

Setting Up the Team Environment

Before his developers arrive, Angus sets up the environment. When VisualAge for Java is first installed, only the Administrator user is available. As Administrator, Angus must create a VisualAge for Java user for each team member. This task is available from the Quick Start window (invoked with F2 or **File->Quick Start**) in the Team Development category. The following information needs to be supplied to create a user, as shown in Figure 4.6:

Unique name. A string to uniquely identify this user. This value is the differentiation between users.

User name. The name that will appear in the Workbench.

Network name. You can configure the team server to use passwords to connect to the repository. The network login name is used as the logon user ID. Administrator can define a list of user IDs and passwords in a file, or use native operating system user definitions. In this configuration, the network login name must exactly match the native user ID. Please refer to the online documentation for team server configuration's instructions.

Other team members can now start using VisualAge. The first time they connect to the repository, they can pick their name from the users list. The workspace belongs to the user you first selected, until you explicitly change the workspace owner from **Workspace->Change Workspace Owner** in the menu bar. Changing the workspace owner really means you are becoming that user and therefore need to assume all the roles that the user has.

Migrating from Professional to Enterprise Editions

Once users have been created, Angus must import the MoneyMaker Internet Banking project from the Professional Edition repository into the Enterprise

Figure 4.6 Creating users in a team environment.

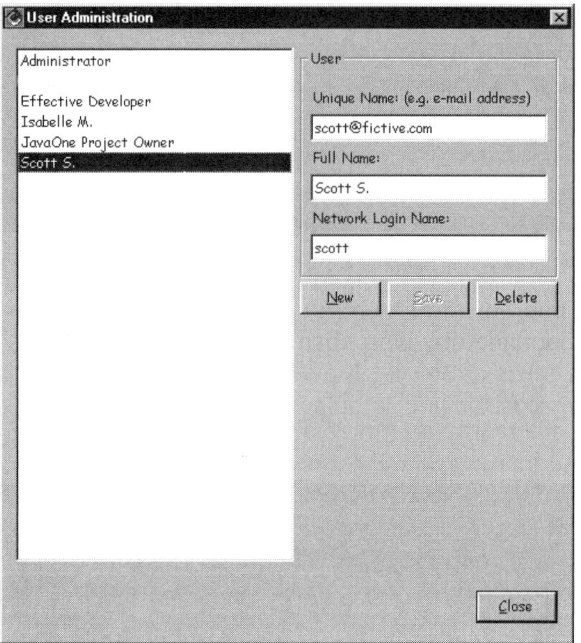

Edition repository. This is just a matter of exporting the code on one side and importing it on the other side. You can do this is several ways:

Import the whole project in the team repository. In this solution, you can connect to the Professional Edition repository from the Workbench and import into the team repository all editions of the code you have developed so far in the Professional Edition. By using a repository file format, you preserve all edition information as well as any project metadata, such as the metadata linked to the Visual Composition Editor. The main drawback is that all code is now owned by the team repository administrator, who now needs to change ownership for projects, packages, and types.

Export the whole project in a JAR file. You can also export the latest working solution of the code to a JAR file, and re-import that code from your Workbench. The code would then be marked as owned by the user who imported the code, for example, Angus. If you own the code, it is much easier to change ownership of components. However, you lose previous version information, and you would have to be sure that you had saved all visual designs with the Generate meta data method option selected.

Import the whole project in a local repository. In this solution, you would first import the whole project from the Professional Edition into a *local* repository. This way, you would not have to cope with the problem of convincing the team repository administrator to help you; you are the administrator of your local repository and have complete control over the code. Then, you would export the project from the local repository to the enterprise repository.

In the following sections, we concentrate on the third solution. For details on importing and exporting repository interchange files or JAR files, please refer to Chapter 6, "Integrating with the File System."

You Need Discipline and Communication

VisualAge for Java requires developers to be disciplined in the development process and, above all, to communicate. You will have problems using this environment if you do not respect those simple rules.

The first thing you must know is that there is no locking mechanism. Any developer can load a class into their workspace, start creating open editions, and version them. You can't prevent a developer from working on a specific edition of your code. However, we assume that in an organized development team, developers have been assigned specific tasks to work on, and that they have no reason to grab each other's code, and start modifying it! However, if you are used to a check-in or check-out mechanism that prevents a developer from working on a file which some other developer has checked out, this may come as a surprise.

Integrity of a program element is ensured by *ownership*. A user is designated as the program element owner. For a type, the owner must ensure that the class/interface conforms to specifications, is functional, and well tested. If two developers have worked in parallel on a same type, the owner is responsible for reviewing and merging changes made to that type (using the change's reconciliation process we saw a bit earlier). Developers need to talk to the owner, explaining the changes they have made, for the owner to review and accept them. You will not be notified if another developer is modifying a type you own. This does not mean that a developer can overwrite changes made by another developer, but that it is important for developers to talk about the changes they are making to a same type.

Forming the Team

There are several *roles* to distribute in the team: who is the *project leader*, who are the *owners* for the project, packages, and types, and who are the *developers*. As the company's senior consultant, Angus decides to act as the project leader. He owns the overall MoneyMaker project, and therefore is responsible for the overall integrity of the application. Since this is a small team, he also owns all packages in that project. For each package, he must choose a development team—the package group members. Only package group members can create, delete, and own types in a package.

> **NOTE**
> Don't confuse users with roles. A user can have multiple roles. For example, one user can be the project leader, a package owner, and a class developer.

Developers and Owners

When you create a type in a package, you become the type *owner*, as well as the type *developer*. If Isabelle creates a class LogonCheck in the com.fictive.ib.utils package, she becomes the owner and the developer of that class. Next, she versions the class, and Scott creates an open edition from the versioned edition. Scott is now the developer of this open edition of the class. Although Isabelle still owns the LogonCheck class, she can't modify the code created by Scott, because she is not the *developer* of that edition. Only the developers of an open edition can version this edition. You can check the developer and owner names of any program element by opening their properties and looking at the Info page. You can also look at the bottom-right corner of the Workbench window.

Setting Component Ownership

The MoneyMaker Internet Banking project was first developed using the Professional Edition, and all the program elements were marked as owned by Administrator during import. Angus connects to the repository as Administrator by selecting **Workspace->Change Workspace Owner**, and switches to the Managing page.

> **NOTE**
> In general, ownership can be transferred but not taken. This explains why you have to be the Administrator user to change ownership for this project and its packages. The only exception is for classes. Any package group member can take ownership of a class in that package.

By selecting the project and choosing **Manage->Change Owner**, Administrator specifies the *Angus M.* user as the new project owner. Only a package group member can own a package: Therefore, Administrator needs to add the *Angus M.* user as a package group member. Next, he sets the *Angus M.* user as the package owner by choosing Select as owner in the pop-up menu.

Angus is now ready to build his development team by assigning developer and owner roles. First, Angus must switch users and become the *Angus M.* user by using **Workspace->Change Workspace Owner** again.

> **NOTE**
> The steps above are specific to a migration from the Professional to the Enterprise Edition. If Angus were starting development with the Enterprise Edition, he would just create the project and the packages and would automatically become the owner for those. The following steps would then be the same.

In the team, Scott takes care of developing servlets while Isabelle concentrates on all utility classes and reusable types. Therefore, Scott owns all types in the com.fictive.ib.servlets package, while Isabelle owns all other types. Angus selects the com.fictive.ib.servlets package, and chooses Add in the Package Group Members pane. A dialog opens with the list of users defined in the repository: He selects *Scott S.* Angus then repeats the process for the two other packages, and adds *Isabelle M.* as a package group member for those packages.

Once you are a package group member, you have the right to author, delete, and own classes in this package. However, you do not need to be a package group member to create an open edition of an existing class and work with it. For example, Isabelle can create an open edition of a servlet and work with it. However, she can't create a new servlet in the com.fictive.ib.servlets package.

Finally, Angus declares the *Scott S.* user as the owner of all types in the com.fictive.ib.servlets package by selecting all types and choosing **Manage->Change Owner** in the pop-up menu. Similarly, he sets the *Isabelle M.* user as the owner for all the types in the two other packages. The resulting organization is depicted in Figure 4.7.

Development Cycle

A program element's life cycle is a bit different in a team environment. You still version your code to save a certain state, create an open edition from that code, make changes, and version again. If we go back to our scenario, Angus—as the project owner—must create an open edition of the MoneyMaker Internet Banking project. Then, he must create an open edition of the three packages so that Isabelle and Scott can start working on their types. The two developers will then create open editions of the existing types, create new types, and version their code whenever they feel it is necessary.

There is an extra step, though: *releasing*. In a team environment, versions are private. Team members who are reusing types should not load in their workspace types that have not been released, that is, fully approved by their owner. In other words, to import in your workspace code that you just reuse—that is, code you did not develop yourself—you should always use the released edition by choosing **Replace with->Released Edition.**

Figure 4.7 MoneyMakers project organization.

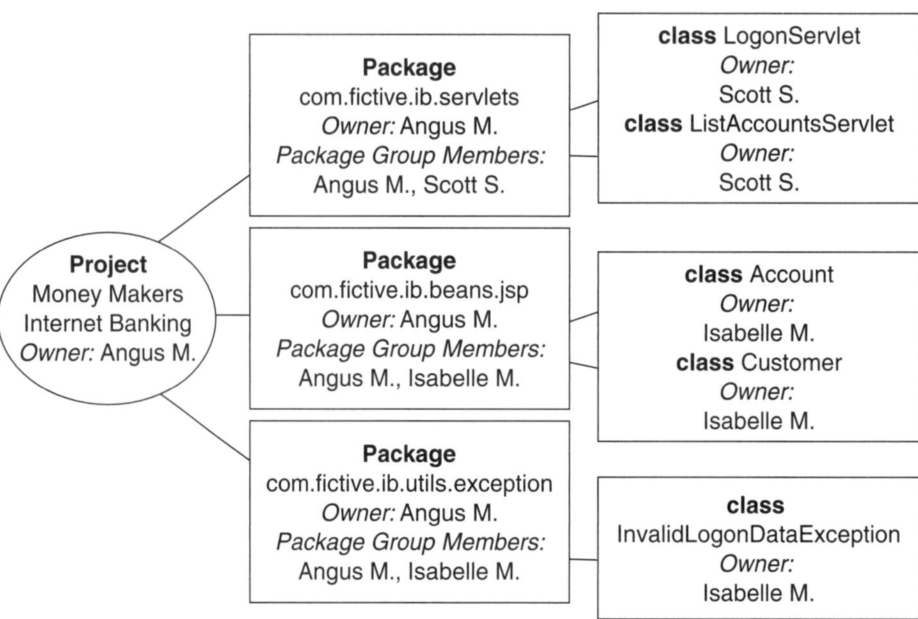

Only owners can release code. They need to look at the types they own, approve changes, reconcile multiple editions, and create a new version that will be released to other team members. For example, it is Scott's responsibility to ensure that all servlets are properly tested and to release the code. A released edition is created from a versioned edition. You must first version some code, and then release it. If you are the code owner, those two actions can be done at once, by selecting the Release Selected Items option when you version a type.

A package can be versioned only when all of the types it contains have been released. Similarly, a project can be versioned only when all of the packages it contains have been released. Angus must wait until Scott and Isabelle both have released the types they own before he can version and release all packages and version the project. It is the project leader's responsibility to communicate to other team members that a new release is available and must be loaded in their workspace.

Creating Rolling Baselines

Normally, you must version a program element before releasing it. However, versioning packages is something you should do only at the end of the development process when you are ready to deliver the application. Once a package is versioned, you can't add a class to that package. You must create an open edition of the package to be able to modify it. This clutters the repository with unnecessary editions.

To circumvent that problem, VisualAge for Java lets you release packages *without versioning them*. To release a package, all of the types it contains must be versioned and released. Then, you can select a package and release it. Once all packages in a project are released, you can load the project released contents by choosing **Replace With->Released Contents** in the pop-up menu.

Such a development baseline (where the project and packages are not versioned) is called a *rolling baseline*. A rolling baseline is useful when you want to share your code with another team that depends on your code. If another team used the MoneyMaker Internet Banking project, Angus would first ask his teammates to version and release their code. Then, he would release the packages into the current project. Other users would then select the MoneyMaker Internet Banking project and choose **Replace->With Released Contents**. They would then work with the latest tested version of the code, and Angus's team would continue to modify the types contained in all packages without the need to create open editions of their containing packages.

Creating Scratch Editions

Scratch editions are indicated by < > enclosing the edition name. You are likely to create scratch editions inadvertently, mostly by modifying a type contained in a versioned package. A scratch edition exists *only* in the workspace. You can consider a scratch edition as a test version of a package or project. Suppose Scott has loaded in his workspace utility classes developed by Isabelle and wants to make a small change to the Account class for testing purposes. This class is part of a versioned package: Scott can't create an open edition of the package, because Angus owns it.

Nevertheless, he can modify the class. This creates a scratch edition of the package in his workspace. The scratch edition is not visible to anyone but Scott, and acts as a holding version for the contents. Once he is finished with the test, Scott can version the Account class if necessary and then revert to the previous edition of the package by using **Replace->With Previous Edition**. Eventually, Scott can talk to Isabelle and persuade her to integrate his changes in the next development baseline.

Delivering the Application

When you are ready to deliver an application, you create a *static baseline*. Isabelle and Scott must version and release all of the types they own. Then, Angus must version and release all packages and, finally, version the project. This time, it is important that you version the packages, because you want to make sure no changes can be made to that reference baseline. You want to make sure you can come back to version 1.0 of the MoneyMaker Internet Banking project even if version 3.0 is under development.

Then, you start the top-bottom development process again: The project owner creates an open edition of the project, packages owners create new versions of the packages, and base developers can start working.

Grouping Multiple Projects (version 3.5 only)

VisualAge for Java, version 3.5, introduces a new concept: solution maps. You can use solution maps to group multiple project editions. For example, you could split the MoneyMakers Internet Banking application in three projects, and associate those projects in a solution map. Whenever you load a solution map, VisualAge for Java automatically loads its associated projects and their contents (i.e., packages and types).

Creating Solution Maps

Suppose that Angus has split the application into two projects, MMIB Framework, and MMIB HomeBanking. The MMIB HomeBanking project requires the MMIB Framework project. Angus will now create a solution map to associates those two projects. Solution maps are not visible from the workspace: they can only be manipulated from the Repository Explorer. To create a solution map, Angus needs to:

1. Start the Repository Explorer from **Workspace->Repository Explorer.**
2. Switch to the Solutions page, and invoke **Names->New Solution** from the menu bar. You can also right-click in the Solutions pane, and invoke **New Solution.**
3. Provide a name for the solution map, such as **HomeBanking.**
4. A HomeBanking entry should now appear in the Solutions pane.

Once you have created a solution map, you must add projects to it, also known as contents. To add a project to a solution map, right-click in the contents pane, and invoke Add Project... or invoke **Contents->Add Project** from the menu bar. You can add any edition of a project to a solution map. However, you will not be able to version a solution map until all its contents (i.e., projects) are versioned. Therefore, we recommend adding only versioned editions of projects to a solution map. To add the MMIB Home Banking and MMIB Framework projects to the HomeBanking solution map, Angus must:

1. Right-click inside the Contents pane, and invoke **Add Project.**
2. Select the MMIB Home Banking project, and one of its versioned editions. The edition currently loaded in the repository is marked with a * (star).
3. The MMIB Home Banking project is now listed in the Contents pane.

4. Repeat the steps above to add the MMIB Framework project to the HomeBanking solution map. The Repository explorer should now be similar to the one shown in Figure 4.8.

Once you have added projects to a solution map, you can easily choose which edition will be associated to a solution by using the Release options shown in the Figure 4.8. If you want to associate the edition that is currently loaded in the workspace to a solution map, you can use the **Release Workspace Edition** option. If you want to use any other edition, use the **Release Other...** option.

You can definitely group all projects in a solution map by versioning it. If you version the HomeBanking solution map shown in Figure 4.8, you will associate the MMIB Framework IM-13/10.5 and MMIB Home Banking IM-13/10.2 versioned editions to that solution map. Whenever you will load that edition, the corresponding projects' editions will be loaded. To version a solution map, select the solution map edition, and invoke **Version** from its contextual menu.

Solution Maps and Ownership

The user who creates a solution map owns it. Only solution maps owners have the right to version a solution map. If you own a solution map, you can transfer ownership by selecting an edition, and invoking **Change Owner...** from its contextual menu.

Exporting and Importing Solution Maps

You can import/export solution maps as repository files (.dat files). Similarly to projects or packages, only versioned solution maps can be exported in a repository file. If you export a solution map, all the projects it contains will be exported. Similarly, all projects associated to a solution map will be imported when you import a solution map. When a solution map is successfully imported in the

Figure 4.8 The HomeBanking solution map.

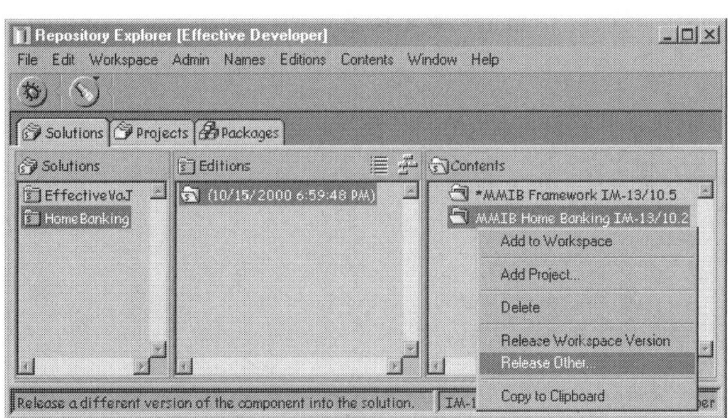

repository, it appears automatically on the Solutions page. You can load the solution map contents in your workspace by selecting a solution map edition, and invoking **Add to Workspace** from its contextual menu. For more information about import and export, please refer to Chapter 6.

Managing Resources (version 3.5 only)

3.5 Starting with VisualAge for Java, version 3.5, you can more easily manage resources files. If you select a project and invoke **Open To->Resources**, you will be able to manage resource files for this project, particularly adding/deleting resource files. Whenever you version a project, resource files will be "released" in this version, and copied in a safe place on the file system. Whenever you load a specific project edition, the associated resource files are loaded as well. Resource files are not managed in the repository: they are kept in on the file system.

You can also manage resources in an external SCM tool from a project's resource page. Refer to the *Integration with External SCM Tools* section later in this chapter for details.

Extracting Repository Information

As a project leader, Angus needs to keep track of what his developers are doing: how many classes are versioned and released, and by whom. Type owners need to find out whether other team members have created editions of the types they own. The Management Query tool shown in Figure 4.9 allows you to search through the repository and extract this information. This tool is available from the Quick Start window in the Team Development category. You can also start it from **Workspace->Management Query** in the menu bar.

Figure 4.9 The Management Query window.

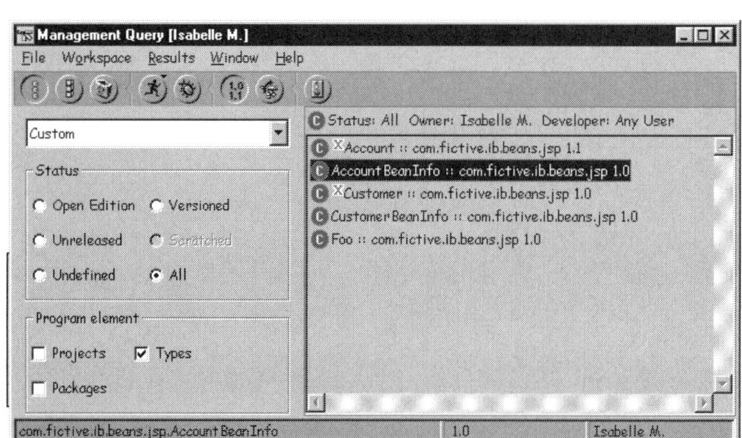

The Management Query tool comes with predefined queries. A query is qualified by the program element it applies to, the scope of the search, the status of the program element (versioned, released, and so on), and a user name. For example, you can find all unreleased types that you own. This information is useful to know which types you must look at when creating a rolling baseline. Versions, releases, and open editions can be created directly from the search results pane.

Search results can be copied to the clipboard from the **Results->Copy to Clipboard** menu. For example, you can paste the results in a Scrapbook page, save them to a file, or keep them in the Scrapbook as notes for yourself. Search results are similar to this:

```
Management Query (10/11/99 2:09:35 AM)
Status: All  Owner: Scott S.  Developer: Any User
     ListAccountsServlet :: com.fictive.ib.servlets 1.0
     LogonServlet :: com.fictive.ib.servlets 1.0
```

A Bit of Administration

Administrator is in charge of the well-being of the repository. After some time, the repository becomes cluttered by unused editions and program elements. Some administration tasks have to be performed regularly to avoid excessive growth of the repository and possible repository corruption. These are backing up the repository, purging program elements, and compacting the repository.

Purging Program Elements

Project and package owners should periodically *purge* unneeded program element editions. Purging program elements marks them for deletion. You can't see them from the Repository Explorer anymore, but they are still physically in the repository. If you have made a big mistake and purged a project that half the team needs, you can *restore* it from the repository. You must be Administrator or the program element owner to be able to purge a program element.

> **WARNING**
>
> By purging a program element, you delete all of its editions from the repository. Purging is a delicate operation: Make sure you know what you are doing! Make sure *nobody else* in the team uses that program element, or ask him or her to delete this element from their workspace.

Once you have taken all necessary precautions, you can open the Repository Explorer window, select the program element to be purged, and choose **Purge** from the pop-up menu. If you select **Names->Restore**, a dialog displays a list of purged elements you can restore.

Compacting the Repository

After you have purged program elements, Administrator can physically remove them from the repository by compacting the repository. In addition to deleting purged program elements, compacting also removes all open editions from the repository. Compacting creates a copy of the current repository, but skips *all open editions* and purged elements.

During a compact, any class or interface editions (versioned or not) that are not associated with a non-purged package are deleted. As long as at least one package version uses a class or interface version, that class or interface version is kept. As long as at least one class or interface version uses a method edition, that method edition is kept.

Compacting the repository is a task that should be well planned with the development team. It is a good idea to do a compact soon after a release, to start a development cycle with a clean repository. All users must be disconnected from the repository before the operation starts. In addition, no one must connect to the repository while a compacting operation takes place! You can corrupt the repository and lose your data. To ensure this, Administrator can use the *emadmin list* command to check that nobody is connected before starting compacting, stop the team server process, and restart it with the maximum user option set to 1. Refer to the team programming online information for a description of the team server's start-up options (from **Help->Reference->Team Server Administration**).

> **TIP**
>
> Keep the old repository in a safe place. A panicked developer who has lost data will be coming at you!

Managing Multiple Repositories

It is recommended that you split your development over multiple repositories. For example, as Angus's team grows, he would create a team repository for each of the individual teams working in a large project. A team would take care of creating visual components, another team would create a framework that all other teams would build upon. Each team would import the projects or packages they need directly from the remote repository. For example, Scott would import the framework classes that he needs in his servlets from the framework.dat file located on the team server.

Having multiple repositories is also convenient if you wish to work from home. You might want to have a local repository to connect to when working at home, and a remote repository where all of the team code resides. You can import the subset of code you need to your local repository, continue to work at home, and re-export it to the team repository back at work. You should make sure that all of the code you want to take code home has been versioned *before* importing it to your local repository. This will avoid potential conflicts of two developers working on the same open edition in parallel (they are actually working on local copies of the code) and versioning it under different names.

TIP

If you are using local repositories for each user, we strongly recommend that you include your initials or user name in version names. This way, if multiple developers create version 1.1 of some class at home, each has a distinct version name. Note that event if all three had used "1.1" as the version name, all versions would be kept when imported into the shared team repository. It's just harder to determine which version 1.1 is which.

Understanding the IDE Start-Up Process

At VisualAge for Java startup, the workspace is connected to the repository. Pointers are created between the bytecodes stored in the workspace and the source code stored in the repository. But what exactly happens under the covers?

If you look inside the \IBMVJava\ide\program directory, you can see a few files with a .sav extension: projects.sav, features.sav, and eventually busy.sav. The projects.sav file is a text representation of the workspace contents: the list of projects, packages, and types loaded in the workspace. Each program element is associated with an ID, which identifies the object in the repository. This file is updated whenever you load a project, add a package, or version a type.

When you start VisualAge for Java, an empty busy.sav file is created. It is deleted if you shut down the IDE properly. If you stop VisualAge for Java a bit abruptly, the busy.sav remains on the file system. On the next system start-up, VisualAge for Java looks for this file. If busy.sav is present, VisualAge for Java uses the information stored in projects.sav to rebuild a workspace consistent with the repository.

NOTE

The projects.sav file should never be manually edited or deleted. However, deleting the busy.sav file proved to be useful in some situations where the IDE would not restart. Use this tip as a last resort when everything else failed.

Figure 4.10 VisualAge for Java and SCM workflow.

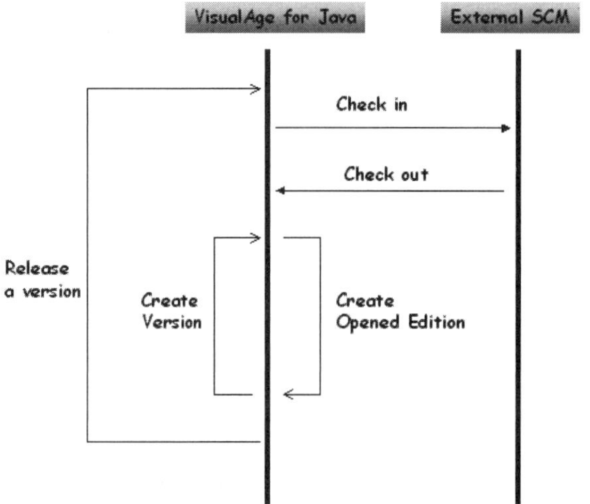

Integration with External Software Configuration Management (SCM) Tools

The use of an external tool can be justified in two ways. First, you can store only Java source code in the repository. How can you version documentation or non-Java code? Second, VisualAge for Java integrated version control is very convenient for day-to-day work. However, you can't easily manage changes. How can you know which defects and features have been fixed between versions 1.0 and 1.1? Many external tools provide defect-tracking mechanisms that might prove very useful.

Coupling VisualAge for Java with a traditional source control management (SCM) tool is a good solution. You use VisualAge for Java for daily work. Developers create versions of their types, using fine grain comparison and merging tools. Only when types are released will they be stored in the external SCM tool. Only the released edition is the official edition used by all team members. Other editions will never be included in an official release. Therefore, only those editions should go in an external SCM, as depicted in Figure 4.10.

VisualAge for Java lets you add, check in, and check out types to SCM tools accessible through the Source Code Control (SCC) interface. This interface is available only on the Windows platform. Rational ClearCase Version 3.2 (Version 3.02) or 4.0(Version 3.5), Merant PVCS Version Manager V6.0 or 6.6, Microsoft Visual Source

Safe 6.0, and IBM TeamConnection Version 3.0 are the four officially supported products. To bridge to a source control system, you must first define a connection:

1. Select the program element you want to add to version control and choose **Tools->External SCM->Change Connection.**
2. Provide a project name and a working directory. The list of resources that corresponds to a project as defined in your SCM tool is displayed when you click on the **Change** button. The working directory is used as a root for exporting the code and loading it in the SCM tool, shown in Figure 4.11.

After a connection is defined, you can select a program element (project, package, type) and put it under source control. You need to add it the first time, then check it in, check it out, or get the latest edition. For this example, we used an evaluation copy of Intersolv PVCS 6.0. We first defined a project called MoneyMaker in PVCS, set up the connection, and added types contained in the com.fictive.ib.servlets package to that project. Once types are added to the project, you can see them from the PVCS tool, as shown in Figure 4.12.

What Has Changed in version 3.5?

3.5 With VisualAge for Java, version 3.5, the bridge to SCM tools has been totally rewritten. The new support lets you add/check in/check out types (classes/interfaces) *and resources* to an external SCM tool.

In the original design of the new bridge, it has been assumed that a user would either use the "native" team programming *or* an SCM tool, but not both! This will work very well in the Professional Edition, especially since it does not have the notion of users. However, if you use the Enterprise Edition, it will make things a bit more difficult to manage.

When you put a project under external version control, this external version control tool must become your *primary* version control manager. In other words, although you may use some of the basic native team environment features, such as versioning, it is assumed that you will not use other features of the Enterprise Edition team programming, especially ownership.

Figure 4.11 Create an SCM connection.

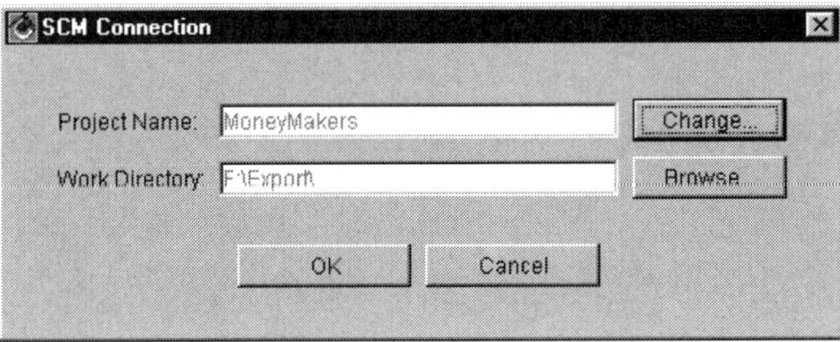

Figure 4.12 VisualAge for Java files in PVCS.

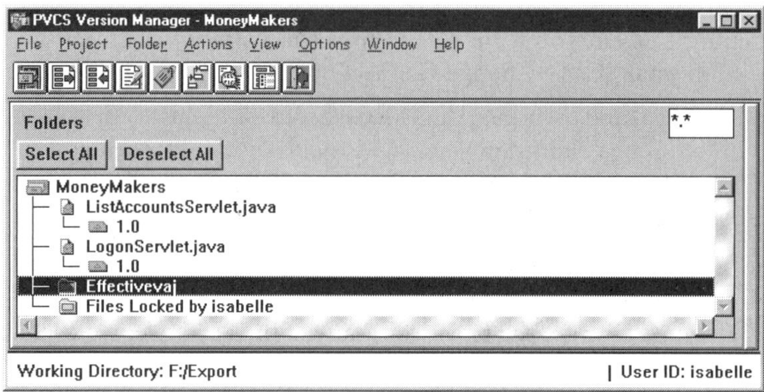

Actually, it is *critical* for a project under external version control and for all its contents (packages and types) to be owned and developed by a unique user. In fact, *each time* you check in or check out a type, the *project* that contains this type will be *versioned*, which implies that all types and packages in this project will be versioned and released. Therefore, *the same user* must be used to work in this project, should it be for creating or owning types and packages! You may want to define a user, for example SCMUser, which will own all projects you wish to put under external version control, as well as their contents.

NOTE

Since a project is versioned each time you check out or check in a type, your repository will be cluttered with numerous useless editions after some time. Make sure to purge those editions and compact your repository regularly. Also, avoid checking out/checking in too often: Use the team environment versioning to keep intermediate editions, and perform a check in when you would usually release the type.

Here is a common development scenario when using an external version control tool:

1. You put a project under version control by selecting it and invoking **Tools->External Version Control->Add to Version Control**. You are then asked to choose which interface you want to choose (Microsoft SCCI or VisualAge Team Connection). If you choose the SCCI interface, you are offered a choice of available SCM tools known on your system, such as Merant PVCS or Rational Clearcase.

2. Once you have chosen which tool you want to use, you are able to synchronize the contents of your VisualAge for Java project with a PVCS project for example. This synchronization works both ways. If the VisualAge for Java project is empty, and some files are present in the PVCS project, they are imported in the VisualAge for Java project. If types are defined in the VisualAge for Java project and the existing SCM project is empty, they are exported to the SCM tool. If you have types defined in both, the current VisualAge for Java project will be versioned and unloaded from the workspace, then replaced with the PVCS project contents (you will be warned first!).
3. Once the VisualAge for Java project contents and the external SCM contents are synchronized, you can start working in VisualAge for Java by checking out the files you want to edit. It is important that you *first* check out from VisualAge and *then* edit in VisualAge. If you modify a type without first checking it out, you will receive a warning and the type will be marked as de-synchronized with the SCM tool. However, you can always re-synchronize both tools by selecting a project and invoking **Tools->External Version Control->Refresh Project**. Again, this synchronization works both ways.

WARNING

Keep in mind that the external version control tool is your primary version manager. You want to check out types to prevent anybody else from working on this code while you are working on it. If you don't follow this simple rule, you may have to manually reconcile your changes with changes made by your teammates.

4. When you have done all edits, you can check-in the type back into the SCM tool. The project will be versioned, the default version name being SCCI_Controlled_xx.
5. To edit a type, first check the type out, and then modify the code.

NOTE

The new SCM bridge uses the Remote Access Tools API. This API server must been running before you can connect to any SCM tool. You can start the Remote Tools Access API Server from the workspace options dialog that can be started using **Workspace->Options**.

Summary

This chapter introduced you to the various tasks related to version control involved when developing code in VisualAge for Java. We also introduced some strategies to bridge to external SCM tools. In the next chapter, we describe the features of the integrated debugger and present the Scrapbook, a tool to test snippets of Java code.

TESTING AND DEBUGGING

5

VisualAge for Java comes with two debuggers: the integrated debugger and the distributed debugger. The integrated debugger is part of the IDE. It lets you debug interpreted Java only. The distributed debugger is a separate program and can be installed from the VisualAge for Java CD-ROM. The distributed debugger lets you debug both compiled and interpreted Java, as well as other compiled languages such as C, C++, or COBOL. Applications that you debug with the distributed debugger can run on a variety of platforms, including OS/390, AS/400, Solaris, or AIX. While the integrated debugger can only debug locally, the distributed debugger can attach to any remote Java virtual machine.

In this chapter, we describe extensively the integrated debugger features and cover the basics of the distributed debugger. We also describe the scrapbook, a utility to test and debug snippets of Java code.

The Integrated Debugger

The integrated debugger starts automatically when it encounters a breakpoint in the code you are executing, or when an uncaught exception occurs. You can start the debugger manually (even if no Java program is running) by selecting **Window->Debug->Debugger** from the menu bar, or the debugger icon in the tool bar. There are three pages in the debugger window: Debug, Breakpoints, and Exceptions. The debugger opens by default to the Debug page. If you choose **the** Breakpoints or Exceptions option, VisualAge for Java opens to the corresponding page.

The debugger also includes utility classes that let you use some of the debugger features programmatically from your code. Inserting com.ibm.uvm.tools.DebugSupport.halt() in your code will stop the execution of the current thread and start the debugger window, identical to hitting a breakpoint. This is mainly useful to debug a snippet of code running in the Scrapbook. If you are debugging your application, you probably want to use breakpoints instead. Setting breakpoints does not require any code change, and breakpoints can easily be added to or removed from your application.

NOTE

If you use DebugSupport.halt() statements in your code or any facility offered by the DebugSupport class, make sure to clear them before deploying your code. The DebugSupport class can be used only when the code is executed within VisualAge for Java.

The Debugger Window

The debugger window consists of three pages:

Debug page. Lists active programs and their associated threads.

Breakpoints page. Lists all breakpoints set in the workspace or on external .class files.

Exceptions page. Enables you to specify exceptions for which you want to stop execution when they are first thrown.

The Debug Page

The Debug page is the main working page. From here, you can view a list of the running programs and their threads. Figure 5.1 shows the debugging of a multi-threaded program. The StartDaemon class starts up three threads that have been set up to be daemons. This is an almost useless piece of code, but it helps demonstrate the key features of the debugger. The class, DaemonCreator, has just a run() method, as follows:

```
public void run() {
 int yieldCount = 0;
 while (true) {
  yield();
  yieldCount++;
  System.out.println("Daemon "+getName()+" ran: "+yieldCount+"
times.");
  System.out.flush();
 }
}
```

As you can see in Figure 5.1, the debug page is divided in two panes: the All Programs/Threads pane and the Source pane. The All Programs/Threads pane displays the program and their associated threads in a tree view. When a thread is paused, you can expand the tree to see the methods' call stack. For each thread, a string such as `Thread[Daemon 1,2,Daemons Group] (Daemon Alive) Breakpoint #3` is displayed where:

Daemon 1 is the thread name. Note that this name was given in the Thread constructor. If you have not specified any name, `Thread-i` is displayed.

2 is the thread priority.

Daemons Group is the name of the group the thread belongs to.

Daemon Alive is the thread status. If the thread is not a daemon, only `Alive` is displayed.

Breakpoint #3 is the name of the breakpoint that stopped the thread execution. If you manually select a thread and pause it, `User Selected` is displayed instead.

> **TIP**
>
> To see in the debugger and console the time at which a program was created, you can set the corresponding option in the **Coding->Debugging** page of the IDE customization window. This can help you determine if you are actually running the version of the code that you thought you were running.

Whenever a thread is paused, the call stack is displayed under the thread name. If you select a method, the corresponding source code is shown in the Source pane. To view the call stack trace as text, select a method, right-click, and choose the Copy Stack option. The stack is copied in the clipboard. You can then paste it (for example, in the Scrapbook) to look at it. The stack for this example looks like this:

```
Debugger Stack Trace Report:
Thread[Daemon 1,2,Daemons Group] (Daemon Alive) User Selected
  PrintStream.flush()
    this=(java.io.PrintStream) java.io.PrintStream@2c1b
  DaemonCreator.run()
    this=(effectivevaj.env.debug.DaemonCreator) Thread Group:
java.lang.ThreadGroup[name=Daemons Group,maxpri=10]
Thread Name: Daemon 1
Priority: 2
yieldCount=(int) 187
```

The last three lines are the results of the execution of the toString() method on the DaemonCreator object. In general, it is a good idea to override the toString() method to easily get information on an object's inner state in the debugger. See the *Inspecting Variables* section later in this chapter for more details.

The Breakpoints Page

The Breakpoints page enables you to view all types of breakpoints: those that have been set in code loaded in the workspace or in external .class files, as shown in Figure 5.2. From the Breakpoints page, you can:

Set breakpoints on external .class files. This option is available from the **Methods->External .class file breakpoints** menu action or from the tool bar. See the *Setting External Breakpoints* section later in this chapter for more details.

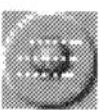

Clear one or multiple breakpoints. You can select one or multiple breakpoints, and choose **Methods->Clear** (by holding the Ctrl key and clicking the left mouse button) or use the Clear icon in the tool bar.

Clear all breakpoints. You can clear all breakpoints by choosing **Methods->Clear All**, or use the ClearAll icon in the tool bar.

The Exceptions Page

The Exceptions page enables you to choose a list of exceptions for which you want to stop execution at the place they are thrown, as opposed to stopping execution when the exception is caught (for example, in a catch block). Please refer to the *Handling Exceptions* section later in this chapter for details on this feature.

Figure 5.1 The Debug page.

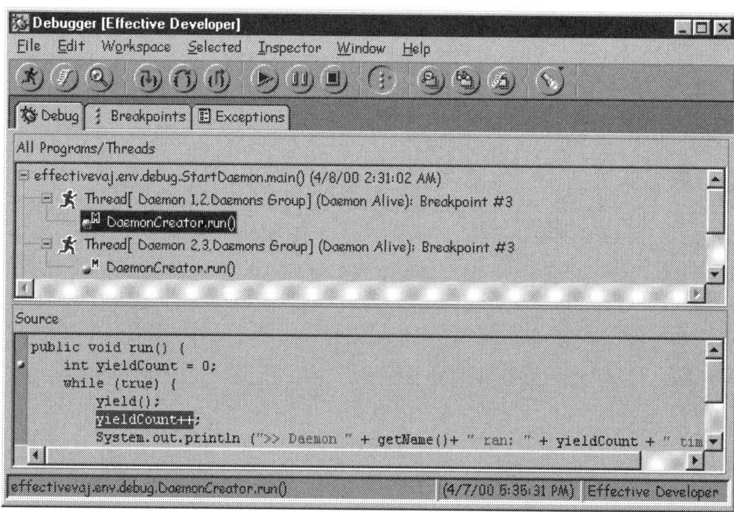

Figure 5.2 The Breakpoints page.

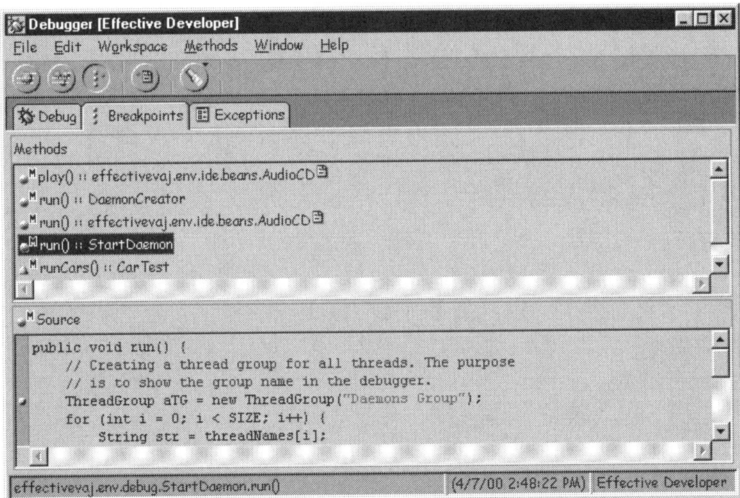

All classes that inherit from the Throwable class are listed. You can sort them alphabetically by class name, package name, or hierarchy. The list of available exceptions can be very long, and browsing through the list is a difficult way to select an exception. Fortunately, you have alternatives to find the exception you want to catch:

Type in the first few letters of the exception name. The corresponding entry in the list will be selected as you type more letters to qualify the exception name. As shown in Figure 5.3, typing *i* selects the first exception in the list that starts with I, typing *v* selects IVJException, and so on. When you are positioned on the right exception name, you can press the space bar to select it. This also resets the search buffer.

Change the view to be sorted by package name. You can search for a package by typing the first few letters of the package name. This is a better solution if you are looking for a user-defined exception.

Sort the exceptions by hierarchy. Use this view to select an exception and all of its subclasses. You can use the Selected-Select Including subclasses menu entry to select an entire inheritance tree, or the equivalent icon in the tool bar.

Managing Breakpoints

The integrated debugger supports line breakpoints. You can set a breakpoint on a line by double-clicking on a line of code in any Source pane or by typing Ctrl-B

Figure 5.3 The Exceptions page.

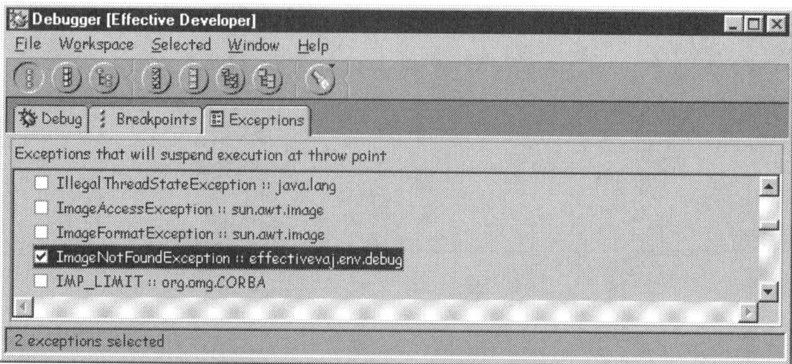

when the cursor is on a statement. This adds a bullet in the left margin of the Source pane. You can also add and modify breakpoints during a debugging session without restarting the program or thread execution.

If you double-click on an invalid location, a breakpoint is created in the nearest valid location. You will find a different behavior in constructors, shown in Figure 5.4. In this example, we have double-clicked on the setDaemon() line of code, but the breakpoint is shown on the last line of the constructor. At execution, though, you are able to step over the statements contained in the constructor. The workaround for this problem is calling DebugSupport.halt() wherever you want the breakpoint.

Breakpoints are linked to a statement and not to a line number. If you modify code that had defined breakpoints, the breakpoints symbol will disappear when you edit the code, but reappear when you save. Breakpoints are kept across

Figure 5.4 Putting breakpoints in constructors.

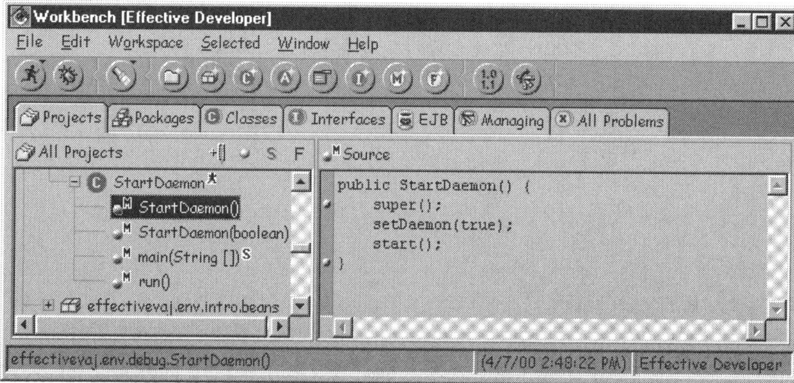

> **WARNING**
> You can set breakpoints in saved code only. If you try to put a breakpoint on unsaved code, nothing will happen, and you will not get an error message.

debugging sessions and working sessions. In other words, breakpoints are saved when you stop VisualAge for Java.

Once a breakpoint is set, you can clear it by double-clicking on the same line of code again (or by right-clicking over the breakpoint symbol and choosing Clear). You can also modify its definition to refine the conditions under which the corresponding thread is suspended. You may modify a breakpoint so that the execution is suspended for a particular thread, when an expression evaluates to true, or on an iteration number. You can combine any of those three possibilities, such as stopping on a certain thread when an expression evaluates to *true* or stopping when the expression is true and the breakpoint has been hit three times.

Configuring Thread Breakpoints

A *thread breakpoint* suspends the execution of a particular thread. For example, the StartDaemon class starts three DaemonCreator threads. Each DaemonCreator thread executes a run() method that prints out some information. We would like to step only in the run() method of Daemon 2.

The first step is to set a breakpoint on the first line of the run() method of the DaemonCreator class; that is the first statement *after* the threads have been started. It is mandatory that the threads already run: The breakpoint modification dialog allows you to select only running threads. Once the program starts, the three threads are stopped on the first line of the run() method. Then, follow these steps to add a thread breakpoint:

1. Double-click on the desired line of code in the run() method to create a new breakpoint.
2. Right-click on the breakpoint and choose Modify. The dialog shown in Figure 5.5 appears.
3. At the top of the window, select **In Selected Thread.**
4. In the list of programs, select the appropriate program.
5. In the list of threads, select the appropriate thread. You can only select one thread.
6. Click **Ok.**
7. 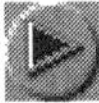
Now, select the three threads in the Threads pane and click Resume to restart. Only Daemon 2 will stop when encountering the breakpoint, and you can now step in the run() method for Daemon 2 while the two other daemons are running.

Figure 5.5 Configuring thread breakpoints.

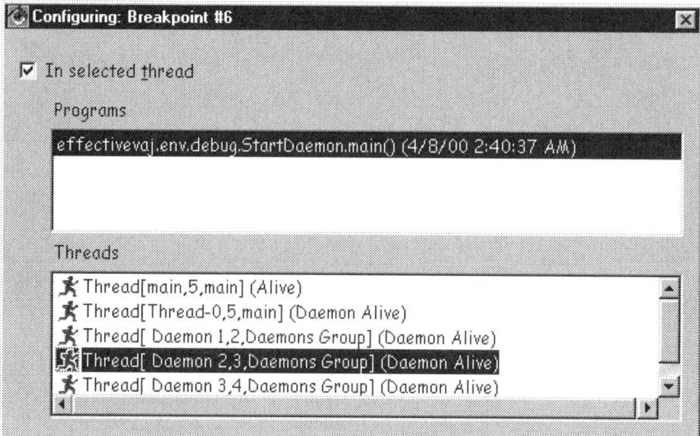

Attaching Expressions to Breakpoints

You can configure a breakpoint to run a code segment (also called an expression). Each time the breakpoint is hit, the attached code is executed. If the result of the execution evaluates to false, the debugger is not started. If the result evaluates to *true*, the current thread is paused. You can use *any* valid boolean expression, such as

```
i == n+2, or this.getValue()!= var1.getValue().
```

If you type an invalid expression, an error is displayed when you try to save the breakpoint. Use this feature to stop on a specific loop iteration or variable value. You can also use expression breakpoints to insert traces in your code without modifying it. Specifying

```
System.out.println (" trace")
false
```

would execute the first statement but continue execution, since the final expression evaluates to *false*. To remove the trace, you remove the breakpoint. To configure an expression breakpoint:

1. Right-click over an existing breakpoint, and choose **Modify.**
2. Select the **On Expression** check box.
3. Type an expression in the text area below. Note that this text area is a real source code editor: You can use code completion as shown in Figure 5.6, keyword completion, or macros. The code you type can contain several statements. If the last expression that you use does not return true or false, then you must add false or true at the end of the expression.

   Up to 10 recently used expressions are kept in the Recent Expressions drop-down list. You can reset this list to its default value from the IDE

Figure 5.6 Using expression breakpoints.

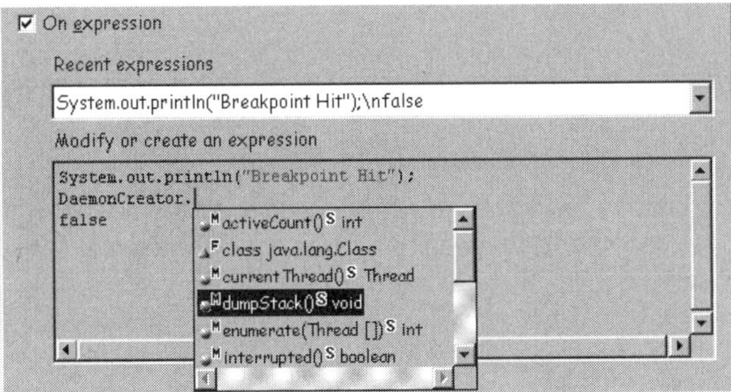

customization window, in the **Coding->Debugging** page, by clicking **Reset recent breakpoint conditions.**

Configuring Iteration Breakpoints

A breakpoint can also configured to stop execution on a specific iteration, that is, after the breakpoint has been reached *n* times. If you specify 10, the code execution stops only the tenth time you pass on that breakpoint. To configure an iteration breakpoint:

1. Right-click over an existing breakpoint and select **Modify.**
2. Select the **On Iteration** check box.
3. Type an integer greater than 0 in the text area.

> **NOTE**
> You can only use integers as iteration numbers, not variable names.

Iterations are counted across runs of your code. If you passed a breakpoint twice in one run and restart the application, the *next* iteration of that breakpoint is considered iteration *number three*. To restart the iteration count, right-click on the breakpoint symbol for the breakpoint, and select **Reset iterations count.**

Globally Enabling or Disabling Breakpoints

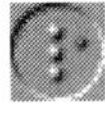

If you have an application with breakpoints but want to run the application without stopping, you can disable or enable the breakpoints globally, rather than remove all breakpoints, using the Global EnableBreakpoints option. This option is available from the Workbench menu bar in **Window->Debug->Global Enable Breakpoints.** If the debugger is opened, you can also use the equivalent tool bar icon.

> **TIP**
>
> When the Global Enable Breakpoints option is set, all breakpoint symbols change from pale blue to pale gray. However, the color change is subtle. If you don't understand why your program does not stop on breakpoints, make sure the option is not enabled in the menu bar.

The Debugger Commands

The integrated debugger lets you step into and step over a statement. By calling step over (F6), you execute the next executable statement and stop execution. When you step over a method, all of the statements contained in that method are executed, and the execution stops at the beginning of the next statement. By calling Step Into (F5), you go into the next executable statement and stop execution on the first line of that statement. Consider the following lines of code:

```
public String toString() {
    return zThread Group: " + getThreadGroup() +
           "\n Thread Name:  " + getName() +
           "\n Priority: " + getPriority();
}
```

This code is composed of multiple statements. The next executable statement is highlighted in the editor pane. If the getThreadGroup() statement is highlighted and you call Step Over, the getThreadGroup() statement is executed, and the next executable statement —"\n Thread Name:"— is highlighted. If you call Step Into instead, you step into the getThreadGroup() method. As more methods are stepped into, the thread's call stack expands.

In addition to those basic functions, you can also:

Step to return. Run the code up to the return statement and stop before returning to the calling method. This function is convenient when you want to skip execution until the end of a large method. The shortcut for this command is F7.

Run to cursor. Stop execution at the location of the cursor. You have to select a statement for this to work: Simply positioning the cursor somewhere in the code won't work. For example, to jump to an *if* statement, just highlight the *if*. The shortcut for this command is F9.

Rewinding Execution

The integrated debugger lets you rewind execution, that is, go back in the execution of you code. This is a very powerful feature of the debugger. Consider the following segment of code:

```
public void myMethod() {
  methodA();
}
public void methodA() {
  // Some more code goes here.
  methodB();
}
```

Suppose you put a breakpoint in myMethod, step into methodA, and then step in methodB. Then you realize you actually wanted to step over the code in methodA right before methodB is called. Because methodA is in the call stack of the thread, you can select it and choose **Drop to Selected Frame**. The program execution is resumed at the beginning of methodA. By using the **Drop to Selected Frame** option, you avoid stopping the program and re-executing it until methodA is invoked.

> **NOTE**
>
> Changes to variables made before rewinding execution *are not undone.* For example, if you change variable foo to 42 in methodB, dropping to methodA does not reset foo to its previous value.

Handling Threads

A thread is suspended automatically when a breakpoint is hit or when an uncaught exception is thrown. You can also manually suspend a thread to view its call stack (to see what it is currently doing) and inspect variables.

To suspend thread execution, select the thread in the All Programs/Threads pane and click on the Suspend icon. After a thread is suspended, the methods call stack appears underneath in a tree view. The list of visible variables and their values is also available in the variable pane on the right. You can select multiple threads to suspend them simultaneously if you use the Ctrl key and the left mouse button.

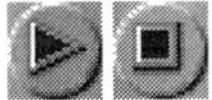

In the same way, you can restart and stop execution by using the **Selected->Resume** (F8) and **Selected->Terminate** functions, or by using the Resume and Terminate icons. Note that stopping a thread will often stop the complete program.

Monitoring and Inspecting Variables

After a thread is suspended, you can inspect its visible variables. Variables appear in the Variables pane on the Debug page. If you need more space to view variables and their values, you can open a separate window by using the **Window->Visible Variables** option shown in Figure 5.7. The variables and value panes will be added back automatically to the Debug page when you close the window.

If you select a variable, its current value is displayed in the Value pane. If the variable is an instance of a class (and not a primitive type), the toString() method will be called by default on that instance. If you don't override the toString() method in your class, the toString() method defined in java.lang.Object is called.

Variable values also can be displayed as hover help by suspending the mouse pointer over a variable for a few seconds. The string displayed is the result of the execution of the toString() method. You should override the toString() method in your classes to return a string that displays information relevant to the inner state of the instance.

> **WARNING**
>
> If applicable, make sure to handle exceptions in the toString() method; it could be executed before the instance variables are initialized. For example, if you write something like
>
> ```
> public String toString() {
>   //Should test if make is null!
>   return ("Car Make: " + make.getName());
> }
> ```
>
> you will encounter problems when *make* is null. A NullPointerException will be caught by the IDE. As a rule of thumb, toString() should just print information, not execute code.

Figure 5.7 The Visible Variables window.

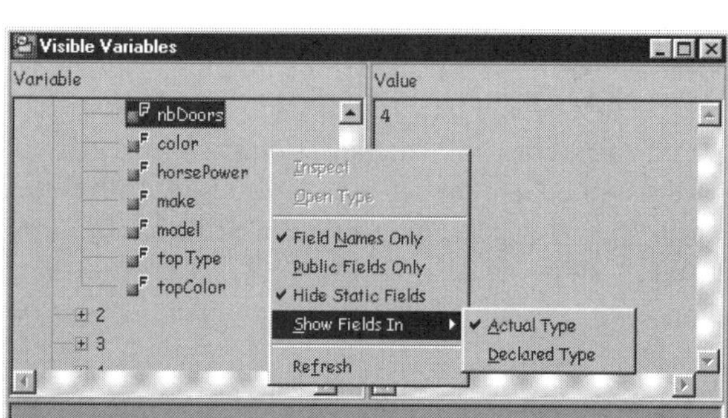

You can filter the information shown in the Variables pane from the Variables pane's pop-up menu, as shown in Figure 5.7. From there, you can choose to:

- Show variable names only, or also show their type: The default is to hide variable types.
- Show only public fields: The default is to show all non-static fields, whatever their modifier value (public, protected, or private).
- Hide static fields: The default is to hide static fields. Make sure this option is not selected if you can't see static fields in the Variables pane.
- Show fields as their actual types or their declared types.

This last bullet deserves a bit more explanation. For example, create a class Car with five attributes (nbDoors, color, make, model, horsePower), and a Convertible class that inherits from Car, with two supplemental attributes (topType, topColor). Now create a program that manipulates an array of Cars and fills it with Convertibles. If the **Show Actual Type** option is selected, then attributes from both classes are shown, as in Figure 5.7. If the **Show Declared Type** is selected, then only attributes from the Car class are shown.

Watching Variables and Expressions

The Watches window (from **Window->Watches**) enables you to watch a variable or expression value. To use this feature, type in a variable name or expression in the Expression column. When the program execution is suspended, the expression is evaluated and the resulting value shown in the Value column. The value string is the result of the toString() method execution.

> **NOTE**
>
> Sometimes, expression values are not automatically refreshed. You can then use the **Refresh** action in the window pop-up menu, shown in Figure 5.8, to manually refresh the value.

The **Inspect** and **Open Type** actions enable you to open an Inspector window and a class browser, respectively, on the current expression value. For example, invoking **Open Type** on the carsGroup[1].getColor() expression value opens a class browser for the java.awt.Color class.

The Inspector Window

The Inspector window starts whenever you invoke the Inspect action from the Scrapbook, the Watches window, or the Variables pane. You can open an Inspector

Figure 5.8 The Watches window.

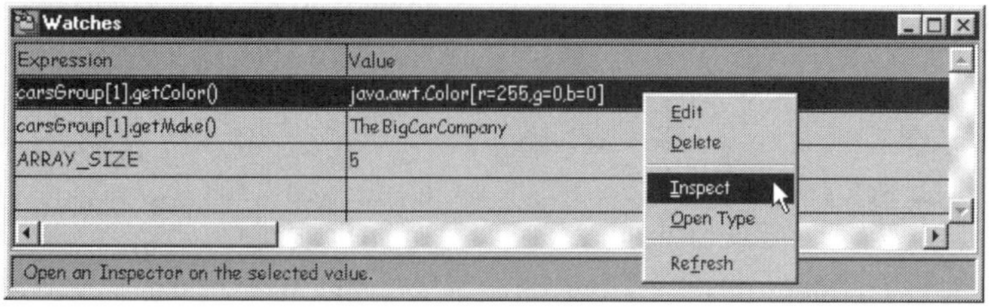

window on any variable by selecting it in the integrated debugger's Source pane and invoking Inspect. The main advantage in viewing variables values in an Inspector window rather than in the Variables pane is that multiple Inspector windows can be opened at once. The inspector will close itself when the thread terminates or when the variable is not available in the current execution context.

You can also call an Inspector window programmatically using the inspect(Object o) method from the com.ibm.uvm.tools.DebugSupport class. This is a very good candidate for an expression breakpoint. To view the contents of a variable without stopping the program execution, you can create a breakpoint and attach the following segment of code to it:

```
com.ibm.uvm.tools.DebugSupport.inspect (instanceName);
false
```

TIP

To view the value of multiple fields at once, select all the fields as shown in Figure 5.9.

The Evaluation Window

You can use the Evaluation window to evaluate snippets of code. Code runs in the Evaluation window as if it was part of the currently resumed method. You can insert any valid expression in the Evaluation window and then select it and choose to run, display, or inspect it. Run will just execute the statement; Display will run and show the execution results if any are available, as shown in Figure 5.10; and Inspect will open an inspector on the available results.

You could also type in or select an expression in the debugger's Source pane directly and run, display, or inspect it. However, the execution results would be inserted in the Source pane, therefore polluting the source code. If you copy and paste the code in the evaluation window, results are inserted in that window instead.

Figure 5.9 The Inspector window.

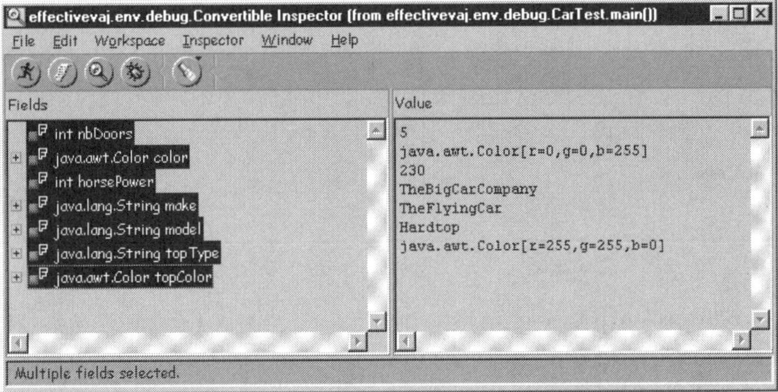

> **WARNING**
>
> If you type an assignment statement in the evaluation window, or run a method that changes the values of some variables, those changes actually take place in the running program. Be careful when executing code this way, as it could change the behavior of the running program.

Modifying Code While Debugging

The integrated debugger lets you change the code while debugging it. Not only can you change the value of variables, but you also can change the actual contents of a method. Most debuggers do not allow this; They force you to stop the debugging session, make changes in the code, recompile it, and re-execute the program to check that the changes fixed a problem. Being able to modify the code without restarting the whole debugging session can save you a lot of time in the testing phase.

Figure 5.10 The Evaluation window.

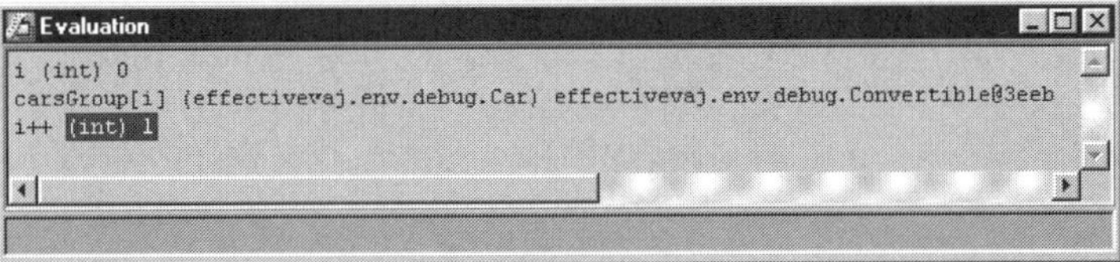

Modifying Method Contents

You can modify the contents of a method directly in the debugger's editor pane. Alternatively, you can revert to a previous edition of a method saved in the repository by selecting the method and choosing **Replace With** in the pop-up menu. After you save changes, execution resumes at the beginning of the method. If this method is run by several threads (for example run()), then execution resumes for all threads.

> **WARNING**
>
> The execution will be resumed from the beginning of the method, but changes to variables made until you changed the method contents are *not* undone. In other words, if you execute a loop that increments an instance variable, the value of that variable will still be the same when execution resumes.

Modifying Variable Values

Similarly, you can modify a variable's value from the Inspector or Variables pane. You can type in any expression that returns any value from which the variable can be initialized. This is the only way to modify non-primitive types. To modify a variable, you need to:

1. Select the variable in the Visible Variables window, or open an Inspector on the variable.
2. Go to the Value pane and type an expression that can be used to initialize the variable. For example, use Color.yellow for a variable of type java.awt.Color, new java.lang.String ("newValue") for a String, as in Figure 5.11, or new Short(12).shortValue() for a short. Note that the Value pane is a full editing window. You can use code completion, keyword completion, and macros as usual!
3. Right-click and select **Save**. The variable is now initialized with the new value.

> **NOTE**
>
> You can also modify a variable value from the Evaluation window: For example, typing carsGroup[1].setMake(new String("The Big Car Company")), selecting it, and invoking Run modifies the make field value.

Handling Exceptions

The integrated debugger is invoked automatically when an uncaught exception is thrown. However, it always stops on the outermost uncaught exception. Consider this segment of code:

```
public void openImageFile(String imageFilename)
            throws ImageNotFoundException {
 try {
   FileInputStream fis = new FileInputStream(imageFilename);
   FileDescriptor fd = fis.getFD();
 }
 catch (java.io.IOException ioe) {
  throw new ImageNotFoundException(ioe.getMessage());
 }
}
```

If you invoke the openImageFile() method by passing a nonexisting image file name as a parameter, the ImageNotFoundException is thrown and the execution stops in the openImageFile method. However, this is not where the actual exception occurred. The actual exception is IOException: If you want to stop the execution of the program when the IOException is thrown, you must:

Figure 5.11 Modifying a string variable.

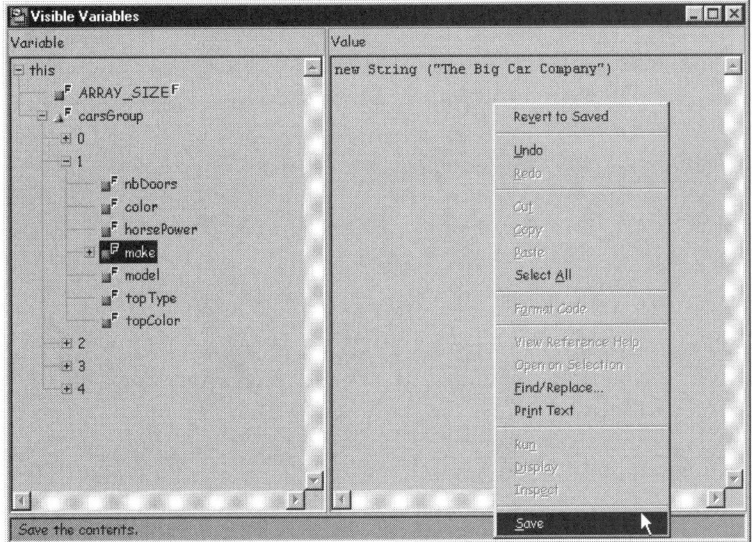

1. Switch to the Exceptions page.
2. Select the IOException. See *The Exceptions Page* section earlier in this chapter for navigation tips in this page).

If you re-invoke the openImageFile() method, the debugger stops execution at the source of the exception that is in the open method of the FileInputStream class.

> **WARNING**
>
> Be careful when catching exceptions. Unchecked exceptions (or run-time exceptions) are not meant to be caught, and many programs or libraries use exceptions as a standard way of programming. For example, catching a FileNotFoundException may prevent Swing-based programs from working, and the WebSphere Test Environment won't start if you are catching the NullPointerException. Make sure to deselect all exceptions from the Exceptions page when you are done debugging your program.

Debugging External Classes

The integrated debugger lets you easily create breakpoints in classes that are loaded in your workspace. You can also create breakpoints in classes that are dynamically loaded by your code (for example, using Class.forName()) or stored outside of the workspace. Code loaded externally must be referenced on the workspace class path or on the system class path. If you want to be able to step in the source code, you must also set the source code class path on the **Coding ->Debugging** page of the IDE customization window. To create a breakpoint on an external .class file, you need to:

1. Switch to the Breakpoints page in the debugger.

2. Choose **Methods->External .class file breakpoint** or the corresponding tool bar icon.
3. Select the directory or archive file when the .class file is located.
4. Select the methods you want to stop into, as shown in Figure 5.12. Breakpoints can only be set at method entry; that is, execution stops as soon as you step into the method. If the source code can be found on the source code class path, you will be able to debug the code as if the code were in the workspace. However, you will not be able to modify code while debugging. You can only see source code at execution time, though; if you select the breakpoint in the Breakpoints window, a message similar to the following is displayed:

```
/**
 * This method is located in an external .class file.
 * No source code is available.
 */
public java.lang.String toString()
```

After you have selected the methods you want to step into, you can start the program execution.

Debugging System Programs

VisualAge for Java starts a number of programs when you invoke a tool or debug code. Those programs are called system programs. Usually, those programs are hidden from the user: You do not see them in the debugger or console window. However, there are occasions when you want to display system program output and exception trace.

An example of system program is the Visual Composition Editor (VCE). A system program is created each time you use the VCE to edit a class. When you open a class browser to the Visual Composition page, the class's default constructor in invoked: If this default constructor fails, the VCE will fail to open. In this case, viewing the system program output is your only way to check what's going on. Similarly, when you drop a bean on the VCE free-form surface, this bean is instantiated in the context of this system program. If the default constructor of the bean fails to execute, the eventual trace and exceptions stack appear under the VCE system program. Bean property editors and customizers are also run with this system program's execution context.

Figure 5.12 Setting an external breakpoint.

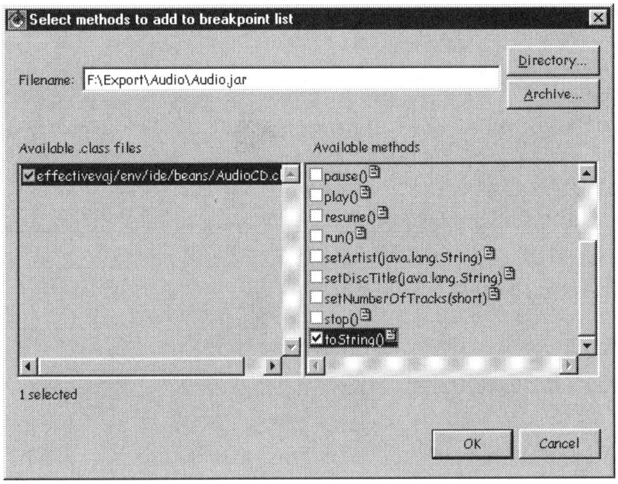

If you select **Show system programs in debugger and console** from the **Coding->Debugging** page of the IDE Customization window, system programs are displayed in the debugger and the console window. System programs are identified in the debugger by the System keyword. Setting this option is useful when debugging a problem occurring in the VCE, but it should be unset whenever you do not need it.

Debugging Program Initialization

The **Trace class initialization for running programs** option in the **Coding->Debugging** page of the IDE customization window allows you to create a trace of all classes that are loaded and initialized during a program execution. This is somewhat similar to the *–verbose* option of the JDK's java command. After this option is set, you can see the trace by selecting a running program. In general, you should not set this option, because it considerably slows down the program's execution.

The trace disappears as soon as the execution is over. You could put a breakpoint near the end of the program in order to copy and paste the trace in a window where you can analyze it. When the trace is on, the Class Trace On message appears in the Debugger title. An example of output trace follows:

```
effectivevaj.env.debug.CarTest.main() (10/3/99 11:50:59 PM)
Class Load and Initialization Trace
<Initialized: java.lang.Thread>
<Initialized: java.lang.ThreadGroup>
<Initialized: effectivevaj.env.debug.CarTest>
<Initialized: effectivevaj.env.debug.Car>
<Initialized: effectivevaj.env.debug.Convertible>
<Initialized: java.lang.Runtime>
```

The Scrapbook

The *Scrapbook* is a tool that enables you to write snippets of code and run them without writing the code as part of a class definition. For example, if you wish to test the Car and Convertible class behavior, you do not need to create a CarTest class with a main() method. You can instead create an instance of the Car class, and invoke its methods to test them. The Scrapbook is extremely useful when unit-testing your classes.

You start the Scrapbook by choosing **Window->Scrapbook** from any window in VisualAge for Java.

Handling Scrapbook Pages

The Scrapbook window is composed of one or several pages. You add pages to the Scrapbook using **Page->New** (Alt-N), or each time you open a text-based file.

The Scrapbook opens by default with one page called Page1. If you open a file from the file system, the file name is used as the page name, for example, *CustomerProfile.java*, as seen in Figure 5.13.

Each Scrapbook page is a full editing window. The capabilities available in the Workbench's source editor pane are accessible to you here, such as code completion or token highlighting.

Text written in a page can be saved to the file system. This is actually the only way to retrieve the code you have written in a Scrapbook page, because the contents of a page are not saved into the repository. You can explicitly save a page by selecting **File->Save** on the menu bar. VisualAge for Java also prompts you to save the contents of a page when you exit the Scrapbook window. Because you can save the contents of the page in a text file, you can also use the Scrapbook to keep notes during development.

> **NOTE**
>
> If you exit VisualAge for Java *without* closing the Scrapbook, page contents are restored when you restart the tool.

Interacting with the Code

There are three options for interacting with your code:

Run the code. The code is compiled in the compilation context, and executed. The shortcut for the Run command is Ctrl-E.

Display the results of running the code. The selected code is compiled and executed. If the execution returns any results, they are printed in the page. The shortcut for the Display command is Ctrl-D.

Figure 5.13 Creating Scrapbook pages.

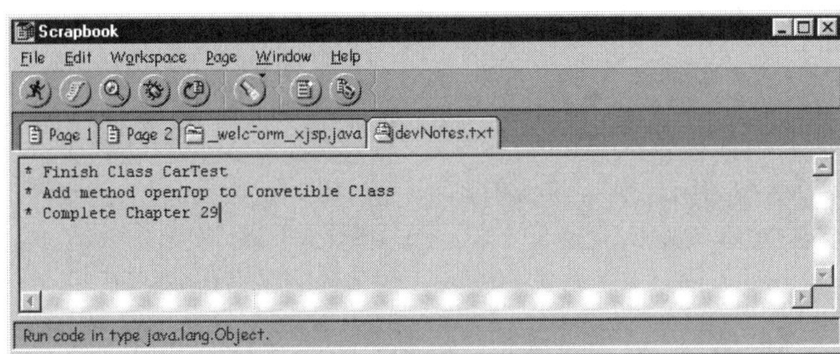

Inspect the results of running the code. The selected piece of code is compiled and executed and an Inspector window is opened for the result. The shortcut for the Inspect command is Ctrl-Q.

Before you can interact with a piece of code, you need to select it. You can select all the contents of the scrapbook window by using Ctrl-A.

Understanding Java Contexts

Code executes in the Scrapbook within a certain context. You set the context of each Scrapbook page by using **Page->Run In**. This option lets you choose a class name: Code executed in this Scrapbook page runs as if it were part of that class. Behind the scenes, VisualAge for Java creates a doIt() method and runs the code you type in the Scrapbook page as if it belonged to that method. If you set the context to be the Convertible class, you have access to all private data members and methods of that class, and to non-public classes that belong to the same package. You also implicitly inherit from any imports made in this class. If you have imported the java.io package in the Convertible class, you will not have to specify java.io when using types like FileInputStream or Serializable. The default context is java.lang.Object.

Run-Time Behavior

Each Scrapbook page runs a different context: You either create a different page to change the context, or change the current context by using **Page->Run In**. A new virtual machine is started each time you execute code in a page: You could, for example, test a distributed application by running the server and client programs on different pages.

If a program is busy running a piece of code, a corresponding message is displayed in the Scrapbook status area. Moreover, a small clock icon is displayed on the page tab. If the code does not terminate by itself, you must terminate the running page program from the debugger, or use **Page->Restart Page** on the menu bar. Scrapbook running programs appear in the debugger under the name of the page (for example, Page1).

Importing External Code

You can import Java source code into the workspace by using **File->Import** on the menu bar. You can use the Scrapbook to test before import: Open a source file, check if it suits to your needs, eventually fix it, and then import it. By using the straight import function into the workspace, you will not have a chance to modify and test the code before importing it.

Only valid class definitions will be imported in the workspace. If you do not specify a package name for the class by using the Java package statement, the code is imported in the project's default package.

NOTE

There is a major difference between terminating a Scrapbook program from the debugger and restarting a page from the Scrapbook. In addition to stopping all threads, restarting a page reinitializes all static variables. If you just stop the program from the debugger, static variables are not reinitialized. Their values are kept across sessions. This feature can be very useful if you want to reuse a static variable across sessions (for example, a database connection). However, for other static variables such as a reference counter, you want to make sure to restart the page to reset their values.

NOTE

If you try to import Java source code that has structural errors in the repository, you will get a chance to import it in a Scrapbook page to fix it. This feature is described in details in Chapter 6, "Integrating with the File System."

The Distributed Debugger

The distributed debugger is a complement to the integrated debugger. It lets you debug code after it has been deployed into a production or test environment. While the integrated debugger can only debug code running in VisualAge for Java's virtual machine, the distributed debugger can attach to any remote virtual machine. If you are a user of the IBM WebSphere application servers, you can use the distributed debugger to debug servlets, JavaServer Page files, and enterprise beans running in those application servers.

Using the integrated debugger, you can only debug interpreted Java. With the distributed debugger, you can debug both interpreted and compiled Java, as well as other compiled languages such as C, C++, Fortran, or COBOL. In this section, we focus on debugging interpreted Java code.

The integrated debugger comes with an extension called Object Level Trace (OLT). The OLT tools can be used to trace calls between the components of distributed applications that are running in the WebSphere application servers. Multiple OLT servers running on a network send information to a single client: This lets you trace the execution of an application across a network. For example, you can view interactions between servlets running on serverA and enterprise beans running on serverB from a single client GUI. For more information about

OLT, please refer to the distributed debugger online documentation as well as the WebSphere Application Server documentation.

The purpose of this section is to give you a brief overview of the distributed debugger: This is quite a complex product, which would deserve its own chapter. The list of features presented in this section is not exhaustive: Our goal is to get you going with this debugger, which is often ignored in the product (because it installs separately). In the following sections, we briefly describe the debugger architecture and walk you through a simple debugging session. You can go through another sample in Chapter 21, "Database Programming."

The distributed debugger is packaged with VisualAge for Java, Enterprise Edition, but you need to install it separately. In the following sections, we assume you have installed the distributed debugger under C:\IBMDebug.

Debugger Architecture

The distributed debugger is implemented in a client/server architecture. It is composed of two main components: the debugger server and the debugger client. The debugger client is the GUI part of the debugger:It connects to a running debugger server through TCP/IP. If the client and the server components run on the same machine, the debugging session is qualified as local. Otherwise, it is qualified as remote.

The debugger server (also known as the debug engine) runs on the same system as the program that you want to debug. It is available on a variety of platforms, such as IBM AIX, SUN Solaris, Windows NT, or IBM OS/390. To start a debugging session, you must first run the debugger server and then attach the debugger client. In local debugging mode, both components are started simultaneously when you invoke the debugger using the *idebug* command. In remote debugging mode, you need to start the debug engine on the remote machine and attach the GUI to it after it starts running. You can also put the GUI in daemon mode, where the GUI will wait for the server to start, and automatically attach to it. The debugger client is available only on Windows NT and IBM AIX.

Debugging Interpreted Java Code

To debug interpreted Java code, you must start the Java virtual machine using the *java_g –debug* command. You can start the virtual machine first and then attach to it from the debugger, or let the debugger start the virtual machine with all the right parameters for you. When you start a virtual machine with the *java_g –debug* command, an agent password is displayed: Make note of this password, because you will need it to attach the debugger engine to the running JVM.

The distributed debugger does not let you modify code and variable values dynamically in the interpreted Java mode (you can modify code only when debugging compiled programs).

Exporting Code for Debugging

Suppose you want to debug the StartDaemon program we used at the beginning of this chapter. You need to export it as a JAR file or in a directory, and make sure you select Include debug attributes in .class files. This will annotate the bytecodes for debugging. Moreover, you must export Java source files if you want to step into the source code. For details on code export, please refer to Chapter 6.

The directory or JAR file to which you export the code must be added to the class path. For example, if you export the DaemonCreator classes to a C:\VAJTest\daemon.jar file, you must either add this JAR file to the system class path or modify the class path before invoking the debugger, like this:

```
SET CLASSPATH=C:\VAJTest\daemon.jar;%CLASSPATH%
```

Similarly, if you export the code to a directory, you must add this directory to the class path. Make sure to add the directory to which you exported the code to the class path, not the directory in which the .class files are located. For example, if you export the effectivevaj.env.debug.Daemons class to C:\VAJTest, you must add C:\VAJTest to the classpath, not C:\VAJTest\effectivevaj\env\debug. You should also make sure that all libraries used by your program are listed on the system class path. In the following steps, we assume you have exported all the code to a C:\VAJTest directory.

Starting the Debugger

In this example, we simply tell the distributed debugger to debug the StartDaemon class. The debugger server will start a virtual machine in debug mode, attach to it, and start the debugger client. To achieve this:

1. Start the debugger by invoking idebug, which is located in C:\IBMDebug\bin.
2. In the load program dialog, switch to the Interpreted (Intel/AIX) tab, and click Browse.
3. Select the C:\VAJTest directory in the class component window.
4. Expand the effectivevaj folder in the bottom pane until you reach the StartDaemon class (the one that contains the main entry point).
5. Click **Ok** to validate.
6. Click **Load** to start the debugging session. The debugger client opens.

The Debugger Client

Using the debugger client, you can debug multiple programs at the same time. Each program is represented by a tabbed page, as shown in Figure 5.14. Each page is divided into panes. When you debug interpreted Java, the following panes are available:

Stacks pane. Displays the call stack for each running thread.

Breakpoints pane. Lists all breakpoints set in this debugging session. A profile is created for each program that you debug: if you select the Use Program Profile option when loading a program, the breakpoints are restored from the information kept in the profile.

Packages pane. Displays the list of packages that are used by your running program.

Source pane. Displays the source code for your program. By default, the debugger looks for code in the same place it got the byte-codes from (in our case, from C:\VAJTest). To load the source code from another location, you can define a DER_DBG_PATH variable to point to the source code.

Setting Breakpoints

The distributed debugger lets you set line and method breakpoints in interpreted Java. When you use a method breakpoint, execution stops when the method is called. You set a line breakpoint by double-clicking on a line of code or by pressing F9. You set method breakpoints by selecting the Breakpoints pane and choosing **Breakpoint->Set Method** from the menu bar. Alternatively, you can browse the effectivevaj.env.debug package from the Packages pane, select the method you want to stop on, and choose Set Method Breakpoint from the pop-up menu.

Breakpoints can be disabled from the breakpoint pop-up menu by choosing **Breakpoint->Disable**, or by pressing Ctrl-F9. If you do not need a breakpoint for a moment, it is better to disable it than to delete it: It will be easier to enable the breakpoint again than to recreate it.

Figure 5.14 Debugger client GUI.

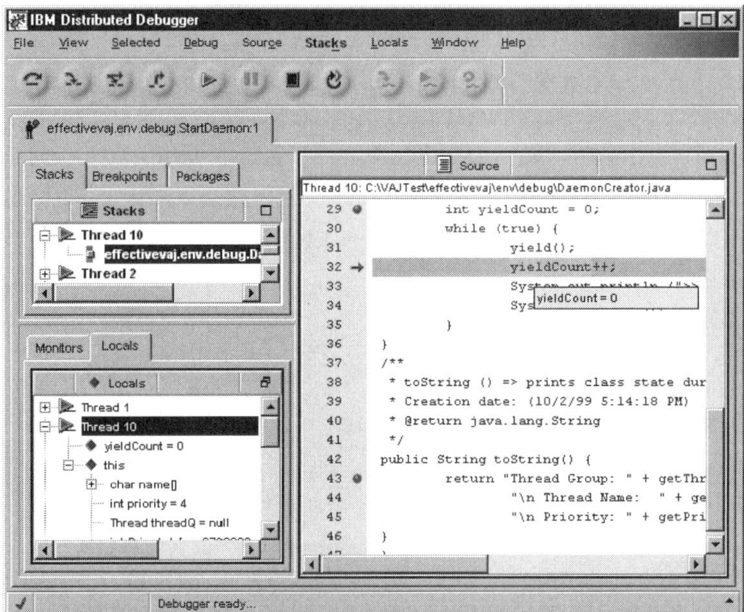

NOTE

Other breakpoint types, such as storage breakpoints or deferred breakpoints, are available when debugging compiled programs. Please refer to the C:/\IBMDebug/\help/\en_US/\debugger/\concepts/\cbwbrkpt.htm file for details.

Stepping In the Code

The distributed debugger has a slightly different behavior than the integrated debugger when it comes to stepping into code. In the integrated debugger, the "stepping unit" is the statement: For example, "Name" + getName() has three statements: "Name" (which is using the String class behind the scenes), the call to the getName() method, and the "+" that appends the results of getName to the "Name" string. You will have to call Step Over three times to execute the complete line of code. In you want to get into the getName() method, you will have to step over once to execute the "Name" statement; then step into the getName() method.

In the distributed debugger, the stepping unit is the line. If you step over the "Name" + getName() line of code, you execute the whole line of code and jump to the next line. If you call Step Into, the debugger steps into the first method call (that is, into getName()). If no debug information is available for that method, the debugger tries to load the source code instead, and displays a "Source not available" message if the source code can't be found on the class path. This behavior is specific to interpreted Java: When debugging C or C++, a disassembly view would be used.

To avoid stepping into methods for which you do not have debug information, use *Step Debug*. Consider the following line of code:

```
out.println (" Daemon Info: " + getName() + toString());
```

In this sample, getName() is a method from the Thread class that you are not really interested in stepping into; Moreover, it has not been compiled with debug information. The method you want to step into is toString(). If you call Step Into, the debugger tries to find debug information for getName() and displays a message that the source can't be found. If you call Step Debug instead, the debugger finds out that the first method that contains debug information is toString() and stops execution at the beginning of this method.

Lastly, you can use *Step Return* to complete the execution of a method and stop execution right after the line that called this method. For example, if you are in the toString() method and call Step Return, the toString method is run to completion and the execution stops right after the out.print("") line that called toString().

Monitoring Variables and Expressions

The Monitors pane lets you monitor variables and expressions values during program execution. When debugging interpreted Java, you are not allowed to alter variable values. The integrated debugger is much more flexible and powerful when you want to change code or data on the fly. To change the representation of variables values, you can select the variable and choose Representation. You add variables and expressions to the program monitor by:

- Selecting a variable or expression in the Source pane (for example, yieldCount), and select **Add to Program Monitor** from the pop-up menu.
- Choosing **Monitors->Monitor Expression** from the menu bar: The expression you type is evaluated, and, if valid, added to the monitor.

> **TIP**
>
> To easily view the value of a variable, highlight a variable name and leave the mouse pointer over it for a couple of seconds. The current variable value appears in a pop-up window, as shown in Figure 5.14.

Summary

In this chapter, you have learned how to use the integrated debugger features: set breakpoints, handle exceptions, modify code while debugging, and inspect variable values. We also reviewed how to test snippets of code in the Scrapbook and debug interpreted Java in VisualAge for Java's distributed debugger. In the next chapter, we explain how to export and import code in the VisualAge for Java IDE, as well as present some strategies for deploying applets and applications.

Integrating with the File System

6

Code developed with VisualAge for Java is stored in the repository. You must use the export functions in order to share your code with other developers or to deploy an application. Similarly, you must import code of third-party libraries to use them while developing your code in VisualAge for Java.

In this chapter, we explain how to export and import Java bytecode, source code, and repository interchange files, as well as how to deal with resource files. We also explain how to produce HTML documentation for your code.

3.5 Throughout this chapter, we have identified VisualAge for Java, version 3.5 changes by using this icon.

General Concepts

You can import and export code from the file system in three formats:

- Java source code (.java files)
- Java byte-codes (.class files)
- VisualAge for Java repositories (.dat files)

Importing and exporting can be done from the **File->Import** and **File->Export** menu items. The import and export functions are also available from any program element's pop-up menu. When exporting or importing code, there are three options to choose from:

Directory. Choose this option to export or import code to or from a directory.

Jar File. Choose this option to package an application in a Java archive (JAR) file or read types and resources from a JAR file.

Repository. Choose this option to exchange data between VisualAge for Java repositories.

Exporting Code

Projects, packages, and types can be exported to the file system. You can export working code or code with errors if you export as Java source code. If you export .class files, the code must compile without errors; VisualAge compiles the source as it exports and stores the resulting bytecode in the target directory or JAR file. Please refer to the section *Using Repository Interchange Files* later in this chapter for further information about creating repository interchange files.

You can export code from the Export SmartGuide, which can be started from the **File->Export** menu item, or by choosing **Export** from a program element's popup menu. We recommend that you select what you want to export before starting the SmartGuide. You can choose additional items to export once inside the SmartGuide, but it is easier to select one or multiple program elements in the Workbench. When you choose to export a project, all types contained in the packages loaded in that project are selected for export. If you export a package, all types contained in that package are selected for export. You also can export an individual type.

When you export code to .java or .class files, the code is exported from the workspace, *not* from the repository. Code that you export to repository interchange files is taken from the repository, not from the workspace. This means that you export the edition (versioned or opened) that is currently loaded in the workspace. Scratch editions, which exist only in the workspace and not in the repository, can be exported only to .java or .class files, not to repository interchange files.

For example, suppose that you want to export the effectivevaj.ide.intro.beans package to the file system for testing purposes. First, you need to choose a directory into which to export the code. We recommend that you add this directory to the system CLASSPATH variable so you can compile and run those classes from the command line.

> **NOTE**
>
> In general, you should add to your system CLASSPATH environment variable any directory or JAR file that contains types your code depends on. You can also supply additional class path information by using the –classpath option of the java command.

For this example, we use the c:\VAJTest directory. To export the code, follow these steps:

1. Select the effectivevaj.ide.intro.beans package and choose **Export** from its pop-up menu. This starts the Export SmartGuide.

2. Choose **Directory** as the export destination and click **Next**. The dialog shown in Figure 6.1 appears.
3. Enter c:\VAJTest in the directory text field, or use the **Browse** button to select an existing directory. If the directory c:\VAJTest does not exist, it is created at export time. Next, you need to select what you want to export: .java (source code), .class (compiled code), or resources. After you have selected an option, the **Details** button next to that option lets you choose which items to export. Because you had selected the effectivevaj.ide.intro.beans package before calling the SmartGuide, only three of the types contained in the Effective VisualAge for Java project are selected.
4. Select the **.class** check box to export compiled code as well. Because you do not want to export any existing resources, you can leave the corresponding option cleared. Refer to the section *Managing Resource Files* later in this chapter for details on how to handle resource files.

Figure 6.1 The Export SmartGuide.

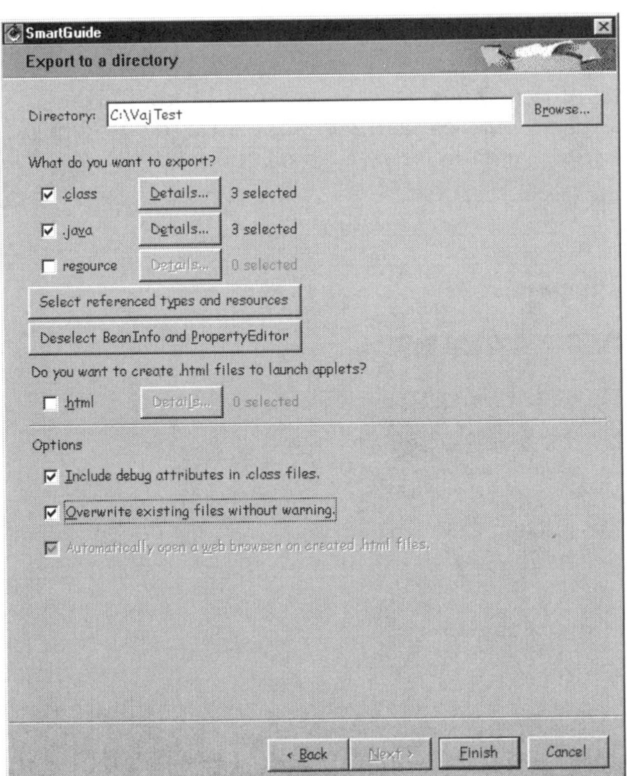

5. If you want to export additional classes, you can click on the **Details** button next to the **.class** check box to bring up a selection dialog, shown in Figure 6.2. This dialog lets you pick types to export from all projects loaded in the workspace. If you select a project, all types in that project are selected. Don't select a project unless you really want to export *all* types contained in that project. Select individual types instead.
6. If your code uses classes contained in another project, you can use the **Select Referenced Types and Resources** button to find by transitivity all types and resources used by the types you already selected. Types loaded dynamically (using Class.forName() for example) will *not* be found. You must manage these dependencies manually.

NOTE

In general, you should not export code that is not yours. In other words, if your code uses a third-party class library, you should not export the code from that library. You should export your code, and add the JAR or .zip file that is delivered with the third-party library to the system CLASSPATH variable to make sure those classes are found at run time. If you use libraries provided with VisualAge for Java, do not export them, either. All run-time files can be found under x:\IBMVJava\eab\runtime30. This directory is added to the system CLASSPATH variable during VisualAge for Java installation.

Figure 6.2 Export Details page.

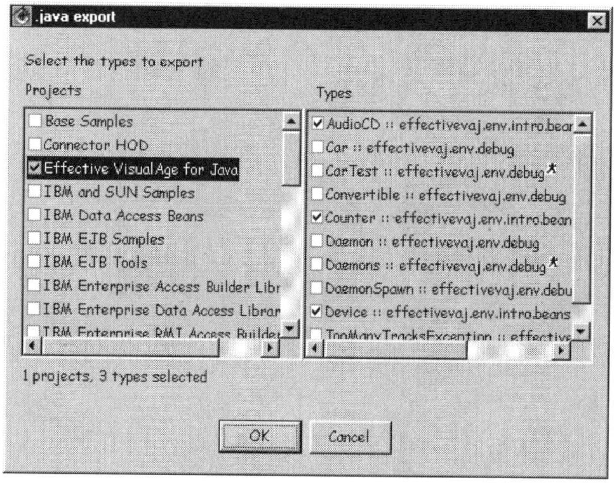

7. Finally, you can decide to **overwrite existing files** without getting a warning if the files already exist on the file system. If you leave this option unchecked, you will be prompted with a confirmation dialog.
8. You are now ready to export your code (we will review other available options in the next sections). Click on **Finish.** If the export directory does not exist, you are asked to confirm its creation.

Notice that in the export directory, the package names have been translated into directories, as shown in Figure 6.3.

Exporting HTML for Applets

Applets can only be executed within an HTML file. VisualAge for Java creates a sample HTML file when you select the **.html** check box on the Export SmartGuide, as shown in Figure 6.1. Then use the **Details** button next to the .html check box to select which applets should be executed in the generated HTML file. The .html option is available only if you have also selected the .class option.

Let's consider a project called *IBM and SUN Samples*, which contains two packages. The sunw.demo.juggler package contains the Juggler applet, and the COM.ibm.ivj.examples.hanoi package contains the HanoiApplet applet. If you export this project to a directory and select the **.html** option, the following applet index file is generated:

```
<HTML>
<HEAD><TITLE>Applet Index</TITLE></HEAD>
<BODY>
<H1>Applet Index</H1>
<hr>
<dd><a href=HanoiApplet.html>HanoiApplet</a>
<dd><a href=Juggler.html>Juggler</a>
</BODY></HTML>
```

Figure 6.3 Exported files.

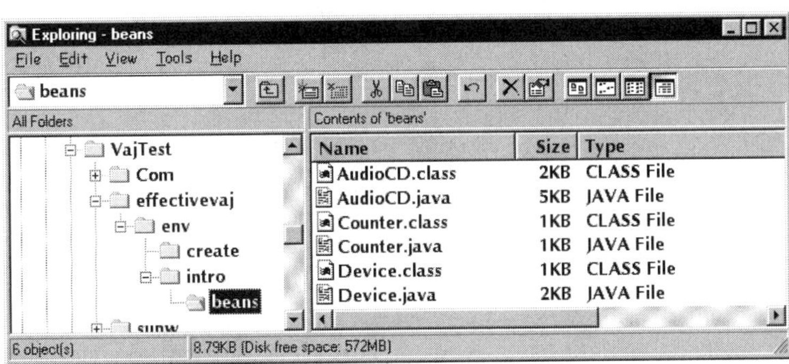

If you select the **Automatically start a browser on created HTML file** option, the default HTML browser is started for this index file as soon as the code export ends.

Each referenced HTML file enables you to start the corresponding applet and eventually look at the applet source file if you had chosen to export **.java** files together with the **.class** files, as shown in Figure 6.4. The tool uses the applet properties such as applet parameters and sizing properties (HEIGHT, WIDTH) for HTML generation.

> **NOTE**
>
> You must make sure that the HEIGHT and WIDTH parameters are large enough to handle the entire applet dialog. Otherwise, you will see only a gray box in the browser.

Those properties are available on the Applet tab of the applet properties window. To access this menu, select the applet class, bring up its pop-up menu, and choose **Properties**. The APPLET tag generated for HanoiApplet looks like this:

```
<APPLET CODE=COM.ibm.ivj.examples.hanoi.HanoiApplet.class WIDTH=400
HEIGHT=200>
<param name=numberOfDisks value=5>
```

> **NOTE**
>
> If you export a JApplet (based on the Swing classes), you must install the Swing classes in a location where your browser can find them. For Netscape Navigator, a solution is to manually copy swingall.jar, which contains all Swing classes, to the program\java\classes directory. For Internet Explorer, you must copy swingall.jar under c:\windows\java\classes, or c:\winnt\java\classes for Windows NT. You may also automatically download the Swing runtime by using the Java plug-in, available from JavaSoft at http://javasoft.com/applets.

Consideration for JavaBeans Components

VisualAge for Java can be used to create JavaBeans components and their companion classes, such as BeanInfo classes or property editors. By default, those companion classes are selected for export. However, you need them only if you want to use those beans to develop other applications in another Java IDE. If you

Figure 6.4 Generated HTML file for HanoiApplet.

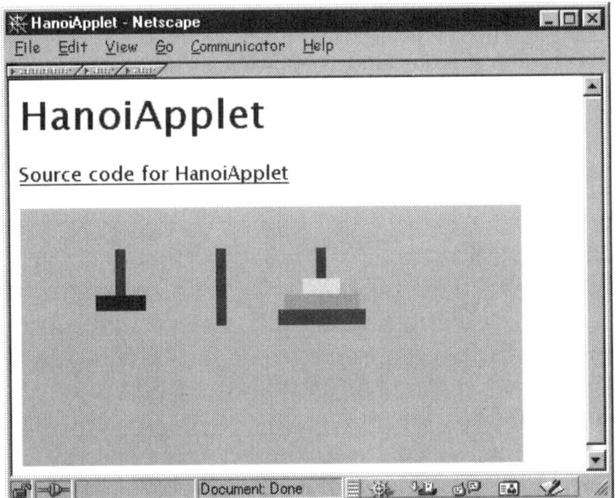

are exporting code for deployment to end users, you do not need those classes. You can then use the **Deselect BeanInfo and PropertyEditor** button to remove those classes from the types list.

Strategies for Debugging

If you export code that you intend to debug with an external debugger, you must select the **Debug Attributes in .class files** option. This will add the necessary debug information in the .class files. You won't be able to debug your program if you do not select this option. If you want to step through source code while debugging, you also need to export the .java files and make sure they are located in a directory or JAR file which is on the project's class path.

Preserving Visual Composition Data

If you use the Visual Composition Editor (VCE), you need to be careful when exporting code. This tool uses special metadata to describe the connections and GUI components properties. If you want to be able to rebuild this information from files exported in the source code format (.java file), you must set an option in the IDE customization window. This option is available on the **Window->Options->Visual Composition Editor->Code generation page.** If you check the **Generate meta data method** option, an extra getBuilderData() method is added to the class.

The alternative to generating the getBuilderData() method is to export as a repository interchange file. We'll discuss this under *Using Repository Interchange Files* later in this chapter. This would require that the packages or projects that contain the code be versioned, which is not always practical in a team environment.

> **NOTE**
>
> You must regenerate the code of any existing class to force the creation of that method. This can be done by choosing **Bean->Re-Generate Code** from the Visual Composition window.

Deploying JAR Files

If you are ready to deploy an applet or application, JAR files are probably a better choice than directories as export targets. JAR files can be used to group all kind of files, although they are frequently used to package .class files and resource files at deployment time. JAR files can also be compressed for faster download over a network, because they use the same algorithm as ZIP tools. To generate a JAR file containing the types in the effectivevaj.ide.intro.beans package, follow these steps:

1. Select the effectivevaj.ide.intro.beans package, and choose **File->Export** or select **Export** from the package's pop-up menu.
2. Select **Jar file** as the export destination.
3. Enter c:\VAJTest\effectiv.jar as the JAR file name.
4. Since we are exporting the code for deployment, you only need to select the .class option. If you plan to use the code in another Java IDE and modify it, you must also select the **.java** option.
5. JAR files are used to package Java beans. A special file, the manifest file, describes the contents of the JAR file. You can use the **beans** option to mark a class with the Java-Bean: True option in this manifest file. Select the **beans** option, and click on the **Details** button.
6. Select the AudioCD and Counter classes, and click **Ok.** VisualAge for Java creates the manifest file with entries similar to this one:

   ```
   Name: effectivevaj/env/intro/beans/AudioCD.class
   Java-Bean: True
   ```

7. If the size of the JAR file is an important factor, you can select the **Compress the .JAR file contents** option. This is particularly important for JAR files containing applets that will travel over a network. The generated JAR file can be viewed using any tool supporting the .zip format, as shown in Figure 6.5.
8. If you are using VisualAge for Java, version 3.5, you also have the option to seal a JAR. Sealed JAR files are new in Java2. By sealing a JAR, you ensure that if classA uses classB, and classB is in the same

sealed JAR/package as classA, classA will always use this specific classB, and not another classB that would be referenced on the CLASSPATH. This is important for security issues (you are guaranteed to use your classB, not another malicious classB) and for version management purposes. With multiple vendors offering the same classes, sealing a JAR ensures that classB is at the same version level than classA, regardless of a more recent/older classB available on the CLASSPATH.

You can either seal an entire JAR file or individual packages. If you choose the **Seal the JAR** option, you are given the opportunity to choose some packages that will not be sealed. If you prefer to seal only a few packages, then select the **Do not Seal the Jar** option, and press the **Seal Packages...** button to individually select the packages that will be sealed.

Importing Code

Now that we have seen how to export code, we can concentrate on importing code to the repository. Only types that you load dynamically (using Class.forName(), for example) can be left on the file system, and referenced through the workspace class path. In any other case, you must import the code in the repository. For example, if ClassA creates an instance of ClassB by using the *new* operator, the ClassB definition must be imported to the repository; otherwise, the code will not compile properly, and ClassA will be marked with problems. You can import both compiled and source code into the repository; code that you imported from .class files can't be modified afterwards.

Each time you import code, it is stored in the repository; types are compiled and loaded in the workspace. If you import classes or packages that already exist,

Figure 6.5 Viewing the generated JAR file.

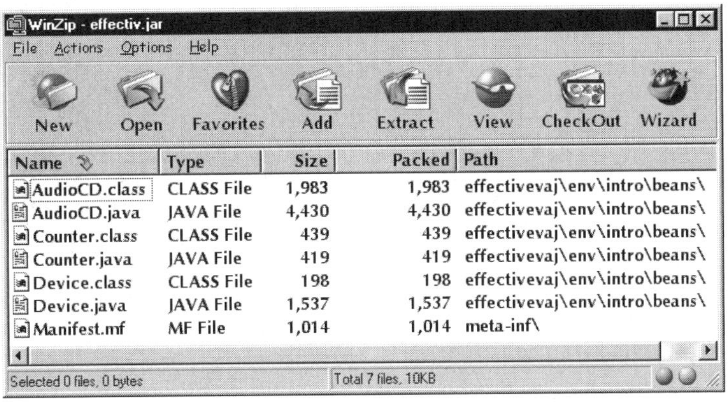

WinZip - effectiv.jar

File Actions Options Help

New Open Favorites Add Extract View CheckOut Wizard

Name	Type	Size	Packed	Path
AudioCD.class	CLASS File	1,983	1,983	effectivevaj\env\intro\beans\
AudioCD.java	JAVA File	4,430	4,430	effectivevaj\env\intro\beans\
Counter.class	CLASS File	439	439	effectivevaj\env\intro\beans\
Counter.java	JAVA File	419	419	effectivevaj\env\intro\beans\
Device.class	CLASS File	198	198	effectivevaj\env\intro\beans\
Device.java	JAVA File	1,537	1,537	effectivevaj\env\intro\beans\
Manifest.mf	MF File	1,014	1,014	meta-inf\

Selected 0 files, 0 bytes   Total 7 files, 10KB

an open edition is created automatically. You can still revert to the previous edition if the newer edition is not satisfactory.

The Import SmartGuide is very similar to the Export SmartGuide. To check what happens when code is imported, you can practice with the different JAR files located under x:\IBMVJava\ide\project_resources\jars, which are part of the standard install. These packaged samples come with the base JDK. One of them is called molecule.jar. In the following steps, you will import it into a new project called Base Samples:

1. Open the Import SmartGuide by selecting **File->Import**.
2. Select **Jar file** as the import source.
3. Use the **Browse** button to locate the molecule.jar file in the x:\IBMVJava\ide\project_resources\jars directory.
4. The molecule.jar does not contain any source code; therefore only the **.class** and **resources** options are selected.
5. Next, select which types and resources you want to import. If you import a JAR file, any file that does not have a .class or .java extension is considered as a resource and is copied to the resources directory. If you click the **Details** button for resources, you can see that the JAR contains .xyz files.
6. The following options are available for import:

   Project Name. The name of the project in which the package and its types should be loaded. You can either use the **Browse** button to select an existing project or type a project name. Enter *Base Samples* in this field. Note that if you have a project selected before you start the Import SmartGuide, it will appear in this field automatically.

> **NOTE**
>
> If you try to import classes that specify a package that exists in your workspace but in a different project, VisualAge for Java will ask how you want to handle them. You cannot import them into the specified project (a given package can only exist in a single project in the workspace at a time). You can either cancel the import *or* request that VisualAge import the code *into the package in the other project.*

   Create New Editions. For versioned projects or packages. Versioned editions are frozen and can't be modified. Therefore, an open edition must be created. If you do not set this option, you will be asked to confirm whether an open edition should be created. Otherwise, open editions are automatically created whenever necessary.

> **NOTE**
>
> In the Enterprise Edition, only the project owner can add packages to existing projects. Similarly, only package group members can add types to existing packages. Make sure you have all necessary rights *before* importing the code, or the import will fail.

Overwrite Existing Resources. Select this option if you do not want to be warned when importing resource files over existing ones.

Version the Code. Check this option to version the code as soon as the import is terminated. You can allow the tool to generate a version tag or specify your own.

7. If the JAR file contains classes marked as beans in the manifest file, the dialog shown in Figure 6.6 starts automatically. From this dialog, you can add those beans to the Visual Composition Editor palette. You can add the molecule bean to an existing category or a new one. To create a Molecule Beans category, click the **New Category** button and enter the category name in the newly created field. Then, make sure the molecule bean is selected and click on **Add to Category** button.

Figure 6.6 Adding beans to the VCE palette.

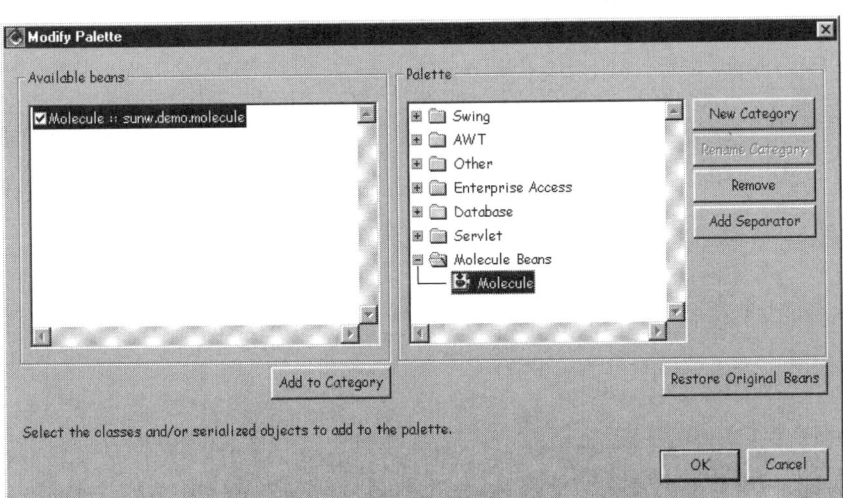

Importing from a Directory

To import from a directory, you must first select a directory to import from, and then select which files you want to import from that directory. When you click on the **Browse** button to the right of the Directory field, you can select a root directory from which you select files to import. For example, choose the C:\VAJTest directory as a root import directory. Then, select which type of files you want to import (the **.class** and **.java** options are mutually exclusive during import; choose **.java** when source is available). Finally, click on **Details** to navigate under C:\VAJTest and select which files you want to import. The dialog in Figure 6.7 is displayed.

Only files of the type you have chosen (**.class** and **.java**) are available for selection. By default, all files that match the type you have chosen are selected for import. If you want to select a subset of those files, you must navigate in the tree of directories using the dialog's left pane. The selection model is such that selecting the top of the tree selects the whole tree. If you want to import all classes in the hanoi directory, you need to expand the tree down to the hanoi directory and select it. This action selects all parent directories up to the root. If you click on a leaf name (for example, hanoi), then classes inside that directory are shown in the right pane. You can then individually select the files to import.

For example, if you wanted to import only the Device.java and CDAudio.java files, you would first deselect the C:\VAJTest directory (to unselect

Figure 6.7 Importing code from a directory.

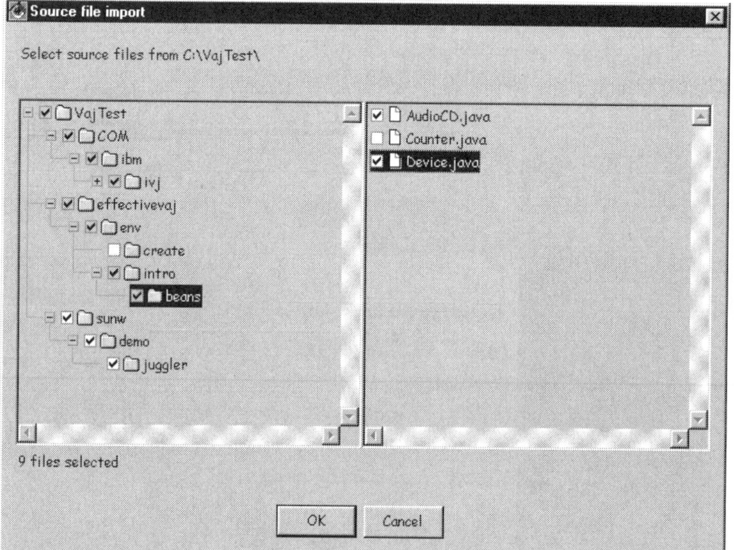

all files), navigate in the left pane to the effectivevaj.env.intro.beans directory, and click on the beans folder to display the list of files in the right pane. Select the Device.java and CDAudio.java files to import them.

> **TIP**
> Selection is made by clicking in the little square on the left of directories and files names, not by clicking on the name itself.

Importing Files with Errors

Some source files that contain compilation errors can't be imported into the repository. When VisualAge imports code, it must be able to determine where it can separate methods from the class definition. Some errors, such as missing curly braces or, in some cases, a missing semicolon after a variable defined in a class, can make this separation impossible. If VisualAge for Java detects compilation errors such as these, it proposes to import the code in the Scrapbook, shown in Figure 6.8. This gives you a chance to fix the problem and import the code into the workspace from the Scrapbook. To successfully import a source file that has these types of problems, you must:

1. Select the files in the list to import into a Scrapbook page. If multiple files have errors, they will be loaded in separate Scrapbook pages.
2. Try to fix the compilation errors, save them, and select **File->Import to Workspace** to import the code into a given project. The code is compiled prior to being imported. If the code still has problems, the corresponding compilation error description will be shown in the Scrapbook page.

Using Repository Interchange Files

The last export/import format we haven't covered is *repository interchange files* (.dat). These files have the same format as the VisualAge for Java repository. You would typically export to a repository file each time you want to back up a project or exchange your code with another developer. All metadata information stored in the repository, such as VCE information and program element properties, is saved when you export to an interchange file. The same repository interchange file can be used to store multiple editions of your code; exporting version 1.1 does not erase version 1.0, but adds version 1.1 to the existing repository file. Each time you release a project, you can export the full project to a repository file and therefore save all released editions in a single repository file. This is a simple back-up strategy.

Figure 6.8 Importing files with problems into the Scrapbook.

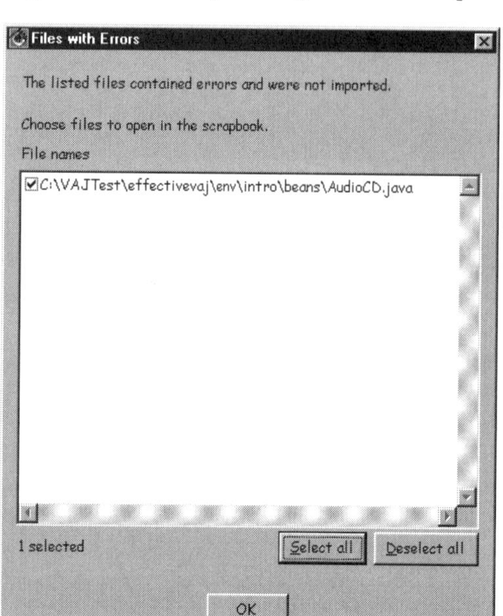

User information is saved in the interchange file as well. If you import code developed by a user that does not exist in your repository, that user is automatically created.

You can export only *versioned* editions of projects and packages to an interchange file. This does not mean that your code must be complete and error-free. Types with errors can be versioned as well.

NOTE

If you import a version of a program elements that has the same name as a version already in the repository, VisualAge checks to see if they're actually the same code. If they are the same code, VisualAge ignores the import. If they are not the same code, VisualAge imports the new code. This can result in two different program element versions with the same version name. Whenever you use an option like **Replace With->Another Edition**, both editions will be listed. To help ease confusion, we recommend that you add developer initials to the version numbers, so if two developers import the same version of a program element, you can easily tell which is which.

Exporting Interchange Files

Interchange files are useful for transferring code from one repository to another, for example to continue working on a project from home. Suppose that you want to work on the Effective VisualAge for Java project on your home computer:

1. Version the Effective VisualAge for Java project.
2. Select the Effective VisualAge for Java project and choose **File->Export**.
3. Choose **Repository** as the export destination.
4. If you are using the Enterprise Edition, you can either export interchange files locally or to a team server. In this example, we will export the file locally.
5. Supply c:\VAJTest\effectiv.dat as the repository name. You *must* put the .dat extension if you want it; the tool does not add it automatically. At import time, VisualAge for Java looks for files with that extension. However, the import will work even if the extension is not .dat.
6. You have the option to export projects or packages. Make sure the **Projects** option is selected, and click its **Details** button. The dialog in Figure 6.9 opens. If you are using VisualAge for Java, version 3.5, you can also export solution maps. A solution map groups several projects that are related to each other. If you export a solution map, you export all projects contained in that solution map.
7. Select all versions you want to export, and click **Ok.**
8. Click **Finish** to start the export.

Figure 6.9 Choosing versions to export.

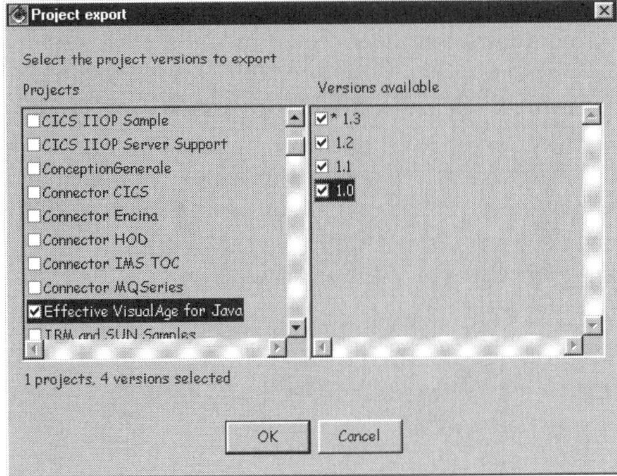

Importing Interchange Files

Importing interchange files is similar to exporting them. Pick a .dat file, select which solution maps, projects or packages you want to import, and select which versions you need.

> **NOTE**
>
> If you haven't selected the **Import most recent version to workspace** option, the code is added to your repository *but not to your workspace.* You may think the import did not work: actually, it did. All you need to do is select **Add->Project** or **Add->Package** and choose the **Add types from repository** option to load the program elements you just imported.

Migrating from Professional to Enterprise

If you are migrating a repository interchange file that was created in the Professional Edition to an Enterprise Edition repository, all imported code is marked as owned by Administrator. You will need to manually transfer ownership to other users from the Managing page. For each program element, you must select the element and change the owner to a user that exists in your repository. This task has to be done by Administrator.

Remember that Administrator should not author code in the workspace, only administer it.

Managing Resource Files

Any image file, properties file, or configuration file required by an application that is not Java source or bytecode is considered a resource file. Resource files are stored outside VisualAge for Java and can be edited, deleted, and renamed from the project's browser Resources page, shown in Figure 6.10.

When you create a project, a folder with the same name is created under the \IBMVJava\ide\project_resources directory. This folder is considered the project's codebase. VisualAge for Java looks for resources relative to that directory. Suppose that you have a properties file that you open from a class loaded in the Base Samples project, like this:

```
// Loading Properties file using the default locale.
PropertyResourceBundle NLSData = (PropertyResourceBundle)

PropertyResourceBundle.getBundle("NLS_Strings");
```

Figure 6.10 The base samples project resources.

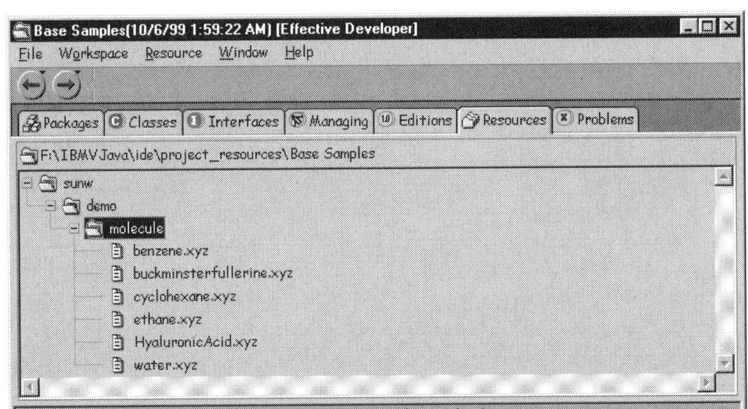

In this case, VisualAge for Java searches for an NLS_Strings.properties file in the \IBMVJava\ide\project_resources\Base Samples directory. If an application located in a specific project uses resource files, you must copy those files to the project's resources directory. Otherwise, they will not be found at execution time.

TIP

Use the import SmartGuide to ensure that the resources are copied to the correct directory. Select the Resources option only, the project name, and the resources you want to import. The files will be copied to the correct file directory for the project.

Loading Resources in Your Program

Whenever you need to load a resource in your Java program, you should use the getResource() method of the Class class to locate the file. For example, suppose that you wanted to load an image called dog.gif for use on a Swing JButton bean. You could write the following code:

```
URL url = getClass().getResource("/images/dog.gif");
JButton button = new JButton(new ImageIcon(url));
```

This asks the current class loader (the Java class that locates your classes, usually on the class path) to find images/dog.gif. Using the previous code and assuming your application is in the project Base Samples, you should put dog.gif in \IBMVJava\ide\project_resources\Base Samples\images\dog.gif. There is a problem with this strategy, though. When you use this code outside VisualAge for Java, if there happened to be an images/dog.gif existing for another application that was found first in the class path, the wrong dog.gif would be loaded.

To solve this problem, we *remove the leading slash* in the getResource() call as follows:

```
URL url = getClass().getResource("images/dog.gif");
JButton button = new JButton(new ImageIcon(url));
```

If the string passed to getResource() does not start with a slash, getResource() adds the package name in front of the resource name. In this example, if we assume the class calling the getResource() method is in package my.dog, you would place the dog.gif in \IBMVJava\ide\project_resources\Base Samples**my\dog**\images\dog.gif. Note the inclusion of the package name, highlighted in bold text. This prevents conflicts between applications as long as the applications exist in separate packages. We strongly recommend you use this approach to load resource files like images needed by your application.

Sharing Resources

By default, resource files are stored locally, that is, on each developer's machine. However, a team of developers who is working on a same project often needs to share resources. Developers can achieve this by using a shared resource directory. To share resources in a team, the administrator must:

1. Create a shared directory on a server (for example, C:\ProjectResources). This directory needs to be shared (or exported on UNIX) so that every developer can access it remotely.
2. Create a subdirectory under C:\ProjectResources for each project containing programs that will load resource files from that directory. For example, create a C:\ProjectResources\Base Samples directory for storing all resources associated with the project Base Samples.

Then, each developer must mount the C:\ProjectResources on his/her machine (for example, as r:) via the *net use* command or using a distributed file system such as NFS, and configure VisualAge for Java, as follows:

1. Declare the shared directory in VisualAge for Java by selecting **Window ->Options**; navigate to the Resources category and enter r: in the shared project resources directory field. If you select the **New projects should use shared resources** option, all new projects are configured to use the shared project resources directory rather than the local one.
2. Configure existing projects to use the shared rather than the local project resources directory by opening the project properties window: Select the

project, right-click, and choose **Properties**. On the Resources tab, select the **Shared project_resources directory** option. Once this option is selected, VisualAge for Java searches for all resources in r:\<Project Name>, for example, r:\Base Samples. Note that VisualAge for Java searches resources on the shared *or* the local project resources directories but not in both. For example, if the resource can't be found on the shared directory, VisualAge for Java does not look in the local directory.

3. Move all local resources to the shared directory.

Resources and Export/Import

At export time, VisualAge for Java copies selected resources from the project's codebase to the export destination, preserving the directory structure, even if you export to a JAR file. For example, if you export the Base Samples project and its resources to the c:\VAJTest directory, the water.xyz file is exported to the c:\VAJTest\sunw\demo\molecule directory.

> **NOTE**
>
> At run time outside VisualAge for Java, resources are found using the CLASSPATH variable. If you want to load the sunw/demo/molecule/water.xyz file, C:\VAJTest must be added to the class path.

At import time, resources are automatically added to the project's resources folder.

Resources and Repository Interchange Files

When you export code to a repository interchange file, resource files are not taken into account. A repository file can contain only Java source code and bytecode. Dealing with resource files when importing or exporting interchange files is a manual process. You must separately import or export resource files and ensure that they are backed up together with the repository. For example, if you want to export resources related to the Base Samples project, you must:

1. Select the Base Samples project and choose **File->Export.**
2. Select **Directory** as the export target.
3. Give a target directory name, such as C:\VAJTest.
4. Check only the **resources** option.
5. Press the **Details** button to select the resources you want to export.
6. Click on **Finish** to start the export.

Creating HTML Documentation

The Javadoc tool is one of the most useful tools in Java. Javadoc parses special comments in your Java code and will generate HTML documentation based on those comments. The Javadoc tool looks for comments that are delimited by /** and */ (note the two asterisks). You must place those comments *immediately before* the type or method declaration, typically *after* any import statement. A Javadoc comment may contain any valid HTML tag (such as <p>, <h2>) as well as specific Javadoc tags that start with the @ symbol. For example, all sample types contained in this book have a Javadoc comment similar to this one:

```
/**
 * <h3>Effective VisualAge for Java</h3>
 * <h4>by Scott Stanchfield and Isabelle Mauny.</h4>
 *
 * <p><b>Chapter: 1</b> Introduction to the VisualAge for Java IDE.
 * <p><b>Package:</b> effectivevaj.env.ide.beans
 * <p><b>Class:</b> A simple class to illustrate the IDE Concepts.
 * <p> Creation date: <timestamp> </P>
 *
 *
 * <h4>DISCLAIMER:</h4>
 * <p>...</p>
 */
```

The timestamp and user macros will be expanded automatically when the comment is added to a new type definition. Once you have created Javadoc comments in your code, you can invoke the Javadoc tool and generate the HTML documentation right from the VisualAge for Java IDE. To generate HTML documentation using Javadoc:

1. Select the packages or types for which you want to create documentation. You can also select a project to generate documentation for all packages contained in that project.
2. Choose **Document->Generate Javadoc**. The dialog in Figure 6.11 appears.
3. Specify the output directory. This directory *must* exist, or the export will fail. You must manually create the Javadoc output directory before generating the documentation. The default Javadoc directory is \IBMVJava\ide\javadoc.
4. The output options let you select whether you want to include the @author, @version, and @deprecated tags. Although those tags are helpful during development, you may not want to include them in the final version of the documentation. By default, Javadoc generates an HTML file that contains a list of all packages, their associated types, and links to those types. If you do not want to generate this file, you must clear the **Generate Package**

Figure 6.11 Choosing Javadoc generation options.

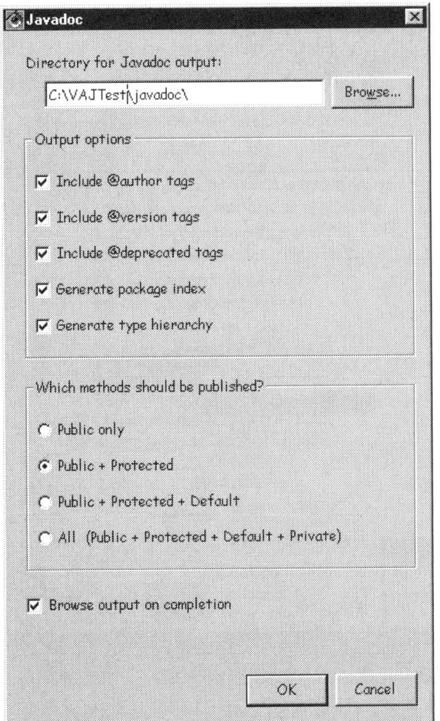

Index option. Similarly, clear the **Generate Type Hierarchy** option if you do not want to create the HTML file that describes the type relationship within a package (inherited classes and implemented interfaces).

5. If the **Browse Output on Completion** option is selected, your default browser will start automatically. Figure 6.12 shows an example of the generated documentation.

Changing Method and Type Javadoc Comments

Type Javadoc comments appear in front of all classes and interfaces generated with the corresponding SmartGuides. Method Javadoc comments appear in front of all methods that are added using the method template command or Create Method SmartGuide. To change the default Javadoc comments, proceed as follows:

1. Open the IDE customization window by selecting **Window->Options**.
2. Switch to the Coding category and customize the Type Javadoc and Method Javadoc comments. *Do not use /** and */ delimiters; they are added automatically when a type or method is created.*

Figure 6.12 Javadoc sample output.

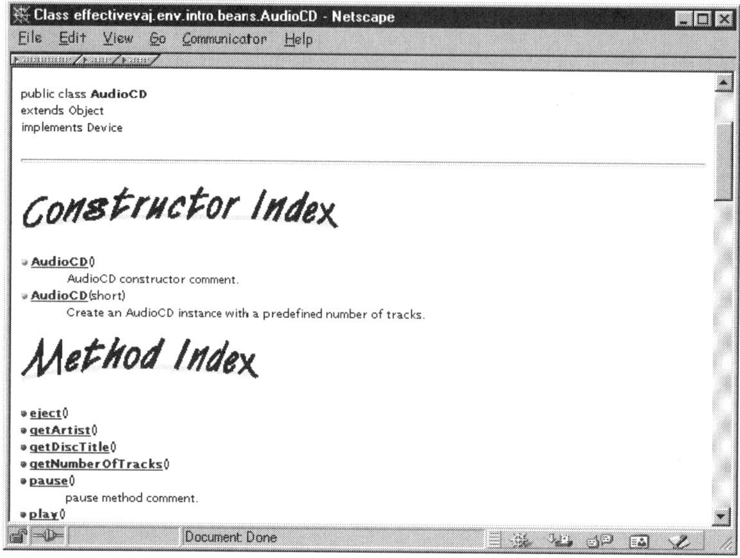

> **TIP**
>
> You can also insert type and method Javadoc comments by using the <class> and <type> macros in any editor window. The contents of these macros are different from the type and method Javadoc comments: You must edit them from the IDE customization window (Coding->Macros category).

Summary

In this chapter, you learned how to export and import Java code and resources files to and from the file system. You need to perform those tasks to deploy your code, or import existing libraries in the repository to use them. We also reviewed how to produce HTML documentation by creating special code comments and using the Javadoc tool. This chapter completes the first part of the book, which focuses on the VisualAge for Java IDE. In the next part, we introduce you to JavaBeans components and how to handle them in the IDE. This next chapter serves as a basis for the second half of this book, which focuses on component-based programming.

INTRODUCTION TO JAVABEANS COMPONENTS

7

Because the JavaBeans component model is so integral to VisualAge for Java, JavaBeans concepts are covered in depth in this chapter. If you are already familiar with the JavaBeans component model, you should still read this section to make sure you understand all relevant concepts.

This chapter presents several code samples and naming patterns. Keep in mind that VisualAge for Java will generate nearly all of the code discussed in this chapter. It is important that you understand the concepts involved, but do not worry too much about the code.

Beans Are Vain Classes

JavaBeans components, or simply *beans*, are classes that are proud of what they are, and they let the world know it. Using certain naming conventions and possibly a helper class, a bean identifies its attributes and behavior to any interested party. *Bean-builder* tools or other applications use that knowledge to customize beans and glue them together through event registration.

You have most likely seen this type of behavior in the form of bean-builder tools. You drag and drop GUI components in a design area, change their attributes, and specify interactions between them. However, you might wonder how those tools can know so much about the components. In fact, those tools are much simpler than they appear, thanks to the JavaBeans component model.

The power of beans is not limited to designing user interfaces. A bean can be a nonvisual component, such as a data structure or a proxy for a remote database. Bean-builder tools manipulate beans, helping to build applications without requiring you to write code. Moreover, beans are not only useful in application design tools; they can prove useful in run-time environments as well.

What Makes a Class a Bean?

All beans must meet two requirements:

- They must be public classes (so any class can inquire about it).

- They must support persistence of their state.

The bean specification enables this persistence through the java.io.Serializable or java.io.Externalizable interfaces. This requirement enables an application such as a bean-builder tool to restore a "pickled" instance of a bean, an instance created before running the application.

If you plan to always restore the bean from its serialized state, no other requirements must be met. However, it is generally desirable to create new instances of a bean by using a new expression. To enable this, the bean must provide a public no-argument (otherwise known as default) constructor.

> **TIP**
>
> Many bean-builder tools, including VisualAge for Java, interpret the bean specification as *requiring* public no-argument constructors. Others require persistence. Because of this, *always* make your beans persistent and define a public no-argument constructor. If you do not make your bean serializable, it *may not* be usable in other bean-builder tools.

Of course, simply making a class persistent and possibly providing a public no-argument constructor does not make the bean terribly interesting. For a bean to be useful, it should provide information about its attributes and behavior.

Bean Features

The bean specification defines three types of bean *features*. Features are aspects of a bean that could prove interesting to another application or class, describing the state and behavior of the bean. The three types of bean features are:

Properties. Exposed pieces of the bean's state.

Event Sets. A stimulus from the bean, signaling that something, such as a change of state, has occurred. The bean broadcasts this information to its listeners.

Methods. Public methods, callable from other beans or applications.

All bean features *must* be public. This allows any other bean to inspect or modify properties, register itself as an event listener, or call provided methods. This does not mean that the actual data inside the class needs to be public, nor do *all* methods in the class need to be public. Only the parts of a bean that describe its features must be public.

Through use of simple naming conventions, a bean enables applications to determine which features it supports. Tools discover bean features solely through the *names* of the public methods defined in a bean class. A beans-enabled tool can use the Java language reflection API to determine which public methods a class defines; the tool can also determine available bean features based on the names of their methods. Some beans also provide an explicit class called a *BeanInfo* class that describes features in more detail, but this is not necessary. This additional information can enhance design-time use of the bean but has no affect on the run-time behavior of the bean.

Properties

Properties describe part of the state of its bean, usually information that can distinguish different instances of a bean. There are two types of properties: simple and indexed.

> **NOTE**
> A property can be either simple *or* indexed; it cannot be both.

Simple Properties

Simple properties act like individual bits of data, describing the state of a bean. You define simple properties using sets of methods that match the following patterns:

```
public TypeName getPropertyName()
public boolean isPropertyName()
public void setPropertyName(TypeName value)
```

> **NOTE**
> You can define the isPropertyName() method for boolean properties only.

TypeName is the name of a class or primitive type, and *PropertyName* is the name of the property. The presence of a *get* or *is* method defines a readable property. A *set* method defines a writeable property. The property name is actually a lowercased version of whatever follows the get or set in the method declaration. For example, suppose a bean defines the following method:

```
public Color getEyeColor()
```

This defines a readable property named *eyeColor* of type java.awt.Color.

Note that there can be *both* a *get* and *is* method for a boolean property; the *is* method is allowed for readability. Normally, you define the *get* and *set* methods, but sometimes the *get* method doesn't read naturally. For example, writing

```
if (list.isEmpty()) {...}
```

is more readable than

```
if (list.getEmpty()) {...}
```

The beauty of this model is its simplicity. Many programmers already use *get* and *set* methods to access their data, so defining properties is no different from their current style.

A tool that recognizes *get* and *set* methods can present a list of properties to a user, enabling the user to specify property values. The tool generates code to pass the specified values to the set methods.

Because the tool is only querying the names of the methods, *there does not need to be any actual data corresponding to the property.* A property could simply be a computation or an alternate means to validate and set other data inside the class. An isEmpty() method might simply count items in a referenced list, or a getMaximumValue() method might return an integer such as five.

Indexed Properties

Indexed properties are an extension of simple properties that allow multiple values for that property. The property *acts* like an array, even if there is no actual data for that property or if the data is stored in a non-array structure.

You define indexed properties using four methods:

```
public TypeName[] getPropertyName()
public TypeName getPropertyName(int index)
public void setPropertyName(TypeName[] value)
public void setPropertyName(int index, TypeName value)
```

Recognizing these methods, a bean-builder tool can present a (possibly editable) list of values for setting the property.

Bound and Constrained Properties

While these names may conjure images of Harry Houdini, *bound* and *constrained* properties have nothing to do with ropes, shackles, or chains.

Bound and constrained properties fire events that report any modification to their state. Bound properties notify registered listeners *after* their state has changed, while constrained properties notify listeners *before* they change, allowing those listeners to veto the change. You can bind and constrain simple or indexed properties.

Bound or constrained properties greatly enhance the flexibility of a bean. Bound properties enable you easily to keep property values in different beans synchronized. VisualAge for Java provides techniques to take advantage of bound properties. Constrained properties allow you to plug in validation ,in the form of listener objects, rather than hardcoding that validation into the property code itself.

Bound Properties: Reporting Property-State Changes

A bound property fires a PropertyChangeEvent (defined in package java.beans) when its state changes. PropertyChangeListeners register themselves with the bean to receive notification of those changes. The java.beans package provides support for this processing through its PropertyChangeSupport class. For example, consider a simple property *phoneNumber*, defined as follows:

```
private String phoneNumber;

public void setPhoneNumber(String phoneNumber) {
  this.phoneNumber = phoneNumber;

}

public String getPhoneNumber() {
  return phoneNumber;
}
```

> **NOTE**
>
> Sometimes the statement
>
> ```
> this.phoneNumber = phoneNumber;
> ```
>
> can be quite confusing to read, especially when first learning the Java language. We use it here because it is an accepted common practice. The *this* qualification on the first phoneNumber means, "I'm talking about the *instance* variable *phoneNumber*." This is necessary to distinguish it from the current active use of phoneNumber, the *parameter* phoneNumber.

This simple property definition directly sets and gets its data. To bind this property, you need to provide the following:

- Methods to register(add) and remove PropertyChangeListeners
- Code to fire a PropertyChangeEvent to the registered listeners

Because the code to perform those functions is identical for every bound property, you can delegate those functions to an instance of PropertyChangeSupport.

A resulting Person bean containing the phoneNumber property could look as follows:

```
package effectivevaj.bean.intro.boundproperty;

import java.beans.PropertyChangeEvent;
import java.beans.PropertyChangeListener;
import java.beans.PropertyChangeSupport;
import java.io.Serializable;

/**
 * A sample Person bean that defines a bound property
 */
public class Person implements Serializable {
  // Create a PropertyChangeSupport instance
  //   to which we'll delegate our bound-property
  //   functionality
  private transient PropertyChangeSupport

  /** Let classes listen for property changes */
  public void addPropertyChangeListener(
                PropertyChangeListener l) {
    if (pcs == null)
      pcs = new PropertyChangeSupport();
    pcs.addPropertyChangeListener(l);
  }

  /** Let classes stop listening to property changes */
  public void removePropertyChangeListener(
                PropertyChangeListener l) {
    if (pcs == null)
      pcs = new PropertyChangeSupport();
    pcs.removePropertyChangeListener(l);
  }

  // Define a read/write/bound property named
  //   phoneNumber
  private String phoneNumber;

  /** Define property phoneNumber as readable String */
  public String getPhoneNumber() {
    return phoneNumber;
  }
```

```
  /** Define property phoneNumber as writeable String
   *  phoneNumber is bound, firing PropertyChangeEvents
   *  whenever its value changes
   */
  public void setPhoneNumber(String phoneNumber) {
    // save the old value
    String oldNumber = this.phoneNumber;
    // set the new value
    this.phoneNumber = phoneNumber;
    // report the change
    if (pcs != null)
     pcs.firePropertyChange("phoneNumber",
                                 oldNumber, phoneNumber);
  }
}
```

The bold text in the previous example highlights the code that binds the phoneNumber property. As discussed in Chapter 8, "The BeanInfo Editor," VisualAge for Java can generate all of this code for you.

After binding phoneNumber, you can keep the telephone numbers of two people synchronized by creating listeners. For example, suppose that you have a married couple, Scott and Nancy, who share a telephone number. When one spouse changes the telephone number, the telephone number should change for the other person as well.

The following code acts as glue between two Person beans, *scott* and *nancy*. Create event listeners (using anonymous inner classes) to listen for changes to the phoneNumber property of each bean. Whenever the phoneNumber of scott changes, set the phoneNumber of nancy. You provide the same type of handling for changes to the phoneNumber in nancy as well.

```
package effectivevaj.bean.intro.boundproperty;

import java.beans.PropertyChangeEvent;
import java.beans.PropertyChangeListener;

/**
 * Test the Person bean's bound phone number property
 */
public class PhoneSync {
  /**
   *  Test the bound phoneNumber of the Person bean
   *  Create two people that share a phone number and
   *    create property-change listeners that will keep
   *    their phone numbers synchronized
```

```
 */
public static void main(String[] args) {
  // create two people who share a phone number
  final Person scott = new Person();
  final Person nancy = new Person();

  // when scott's phone changes, change nancy's
  scott.addPropertyChangeListener(
    new PropertyChangeListener() {
      public void propertyChange(PropertyChangeEvent e) {
        if (e.getPropertyName().equals("phoneNumber"))
          nancy.setPhoneNumber(scott.getPhoneNumber());
      }
    }
  );

  // when nancy's phone changes, change scott's
  nancy.addPropertyChangeListener(
    new PropertyChangeListener() {
      public void propertyChange(PropertyChangeEvent e) {
        if (e.getPropertyName().equals("phoneNumber"))
          scott.setPhoneNumber(nancy.getPhoneNumber());
      }
    }
  );

  // Run a little test...
  System.out.println("Initial phone numbers");
  System.out.println("Scott: "  + scott.getPhoneNumber());
  System.out.println("Nancy: "  + scott.getPhoneNumber());
  System.out.println();

  System.out.println("Set Scott's number to 555-1212");
  scott.setPhoneNumber("555-1212");

  System.out.println("Scott: "  + scott.getPhoneNumber());
  System.out.println("Nancy: "  + scott.getPhoneNumber());
  System.out.println();

  System.out.println("Set Nancy's number to 555-7777");
  nancy.setPhoneNumber("555-7777");

  System.out.println("Scott: "  + scott.getPhoneNumber());
```

```
    System.out.println("Nancy: "  + scott.getPhoneNumber());
  }
}
```

Creating PropertyChangeListeners for each Person bean automatically updates both Person beans when either telephone number changes. This technique will be used during visual composition to achieve several interesting effects, including keeping a model synchronized with a GUI. The results of running PhoneSync follow:

```
Initial phone numbers
Scott: null
Nancy: null

Set Scott's number to 555-1212
Scott: 555-1212
Nancy: 555-1212

Set Nancy's number to 555-7777
Scott: 555-7777
Nancy: 555-7777
```

VisualAge for Java can generate code to perform exactly this task. This is discussed in Chapter 12, "Connections."

Constrained Properties: Property Validation by Delegation

Constrained properties allow registered listeners to veto a proposed change. The bean fires a PropertyChangeEvent *before* the property state is changed, and the listeners can object to the change by throwing a PropertyVetoException. The exception prevents the state from changing and informs the code that called the set method of the veto.

Constrained properties perform property validation through *external* objects. Rather than hardcoding validation inside the set method, delegate the validation to registered listeners. Consider the benefits of this approach. If you design a text-field GUI component that has a constrained text property, you can plug in any validation you want.

In one use, you could plug in the following validation criteria:

- All characters must be numbers.
- There must be exactly seven characters.

In a different instance, you could plug in different validations:

- The first character must be alphabetic.
- The text must be a single word.
- The text must contain at least one number.
- The text must be greater than six characters.

Each validation process is contained in a separate VetoableChangeListener and registered with the text field. If *any* of the separate validations is not successful, the setText() method will fail. This is preferable to making a new subclass of the text field simply to add different validation in its setText() method. Think of all the subclasses that you would need to provide validation. Suppose that you wanted to check that the value entered in a text field or a combo box were a date. You would need to subclass each of those classes to perform the validation. If you made their text or value properties constrained, you would need only to define the data-check logic in one validator class.

The java.beans package provides another concrete-implementation class, VetoableChangeSupport, to assist with constrained-property event processing. Constraining a property is very similar to making it bound.

The following code defines a constrained property called *phoneNumber*. Similar to the earlier bound property example, delegate the listener tracking and event firing to another object, one of class VetoableChangeSupport.

```
package effectivevaj.bean.intro.constrainedproperty;

import java.io.Serializable;
import java.beans.PropertyChangeEvent;
import java.beans.VetoableChangeListener;
import java.beans.VetoableChangeSupport;
import java.beans.PropertyVetoException;

/**
 * A sample Person bean that defines a constrained property
 */
public class Person implements Serializable {
  // Create a VetoableChangeSupport instance
  //   to which we'll delegate our constrained-property
  //   functionality
  private transient VetoableChangeSupport vcs;


  /** Let classes listen for property changes */
  public void addVetoableChangeListener(
                VetoableChangeListener l) {
    if (vcs == null)
      vcs = new VetoableChangeSupport(this);
    vcs.addVetoableChangeListener(l);
  }

  /** Let classes stop listening to property changes */
```

```
    public void removeVetoableChangeListener(
                    VetoableChangeListener l) {
      if (vcs == null)
        vcs = new VetoableChangeSupport(this);
      vcs.removeVetoableChangeListener(l);
    }

    // Define a read/write/constrained property named
    //  phoneNumber
    private String phoneNumber;

    /** Define property phoneNumber as readable String */
    public String getPhoneNumber() {
      return phoneNumber;
    }

    /** Define property phoneNumber as writeable String
     *  phoneNumber is constrained, firing
     *  PropertyChangeEvents whenever its value is
     *  about to change
     */
    public void setPhoneNumber(String phoneNumber)
                 throws PropertyVetoException {
      if (vcs != null)
        // report the impending change
        vcs.fireVetoableChange("phoneNumber",
                                 this.phoneNumber, phoneNumber);
      // change to the new value
      this.phoneNumber = phoneNumber;
    }
  }
```

The bold text highlights the changes necessary to support a constrained property. Again, VisualAge for Java can generate all of this code for you. You will see how in the next chapter.

Registered VetoableChangeListeners can throw a PropertyVetoException, which halts the setPhoneNumber processing, throwing the exception to the caller of setPhoneNumber().

As a simple example, restrict a Person's telephone number to exactly seven numeric characters. The strategy to implement this is as follows:

- Constrain the phoneNumber property (defined previously).

- Create the class StringLengthCheck to ensure that a String is within a minimum-maximum range, as follows:

```
package effectivevaj.bean.intro.constrainedproperty;

import java.beans.PropertyVetoException;
import java.beans.PropertyChangeEvent;
import java.beans.VetoableChangeListener;

/**
 * A VetoableChangeListener that validates that a String's
 *   length falls within a given range
 */
public class StringLengthCheck
       implements VetoableChangeListener {

  private int minimum, maximum;

  /** constructor – gather the min-max range for
   *                 the legal string length
   */
  public StringLengthCheck(int min, int max) {
    minimum = min;
    maximum = max;
  }

  /** VetoableChangeListener notification - check to see
   *     if the length of the new string value is within
   *     the minimum/maximum range
   */
  public void vetoableChange(PropertyChangeEvent e)
         throws PropertyVetoException {
    if (e.getPropertyName().equals("phoneNumber")) {
      String number = (String) e.getNewValue();
      if (number == null)
        throw new PropertyVetoException("No new value!", e);
      int len = number.length();
      if (len < minimum || len > maximum)
        throw new PropertyVetoException(
                  "Improper length: must be in range " +
                  minimum + "-" + maximum, e);
    }
  }
}
```

- Create class NumberStringCheck to ensure that all characters are numeric, as follows:

```
package effectivevaj.bean.intro.constrainedproperty;

import java.beans.VetoableChangeListener;
import java.beans.PropertyChangeEvent;
import java.beans.PropertyVetoException;

/** A VetoableChangeListener that validates that a
  *   String's value is completely numeric
  */
public class NumberStringCheck
       implements VetoableChangeListener {

  public void vetoableChange(PropertyChangeEvent e)
         throws PropertyVetoException {
    if (e.getPropertyName().equals("phoneNumber")) {
      String number = (String) e.getNewValue();
      if (number != null) {
        int len = number.length();

        for (int i = 0; i < len; i++)
          if (!Character.isDigit(number.charAt(i)))

              throw new PropertyVetoException(number +
                     " contains non-numeric characters", e);
      }
    }
  }
}
```

- Add instances of StringLengthCheck and NumberStringCheck to the Person bean as VetoableChangeListeners, as follows:

```
package effectivevaj.bean.intro.constrainedproperty;

import java.beans.PropertyVetoException;

/**
 * Test our constrained phoneNumber property
 */
public class PhoneValidate {
```

```
/** A convenience method to handle the exceptions for us */
protected static void setPersonsPhoneNumber(Person person,
                                            String number){
  try {
    person.setPhoneNumber(number);
    System.out.println("Set number to " + number);
  }
  catch (PropertyVetoException e) {
    System.out.println(e);
  }
}

/**
 * Runs a simple test of our constrained phone property
 */
public static void main(String[] args) {
  Person scott = new Person();
  scott.addVetoableChangeListener(
          new StringLengthCheck(7, 7));
  scott.addVetoableChangeListener(new NumberStringCheck());

  // test a non-numeric phone number
  setPersonsPhoneNumber(scott,"111aaaa");

  // test a long phone number
  setPersonsPhoneNumber(scott,"5551111111111");

  // test a normal phone number
  setPersonsPhoneNumber(scott,"5551212");

  // create a new person that only checks that the
  //   phoneNumber is numeric
  Person nancy = new Person();
  nancy.addVetoableChangeListener(new NumberStringCheck());

  // test a non-numeric phone number
  setPersonsPhoneNumber(nancy,"111aaaa");

  // test a long phone number
  setPersonsPhoneNumber(nancy,"5551111111111");
 }
}
```

As you can see from the previous test, not only can you plug in several validations, but you can also use *different* sets of validations for each *instance* of a class. The previous example will print the following to System.out:

```
java.beans.PropertyVetoException: 111aaaa contains
  non-numeric characters
java.beans.PropertyVetoException: Improper length: must be
  in range 7-7
Set number to 5551212
java.beans.PropertyVetoException: 111aaaa contains
  non-numeric characters
Set number to 5551111111111
```

How Can a Tool Tell if a Property Is Bound or Constrained?

Tools such as VisualAge for Java have two ways to determine if properties are bound or constrained. They can make educated assumptions, or they can find out for certain through a BeanInfo class.

If a tool sees that a bean defines method

```
public void addPropertyChangeListener(PropertyChangeListener l)
```

it assumes that *all* contained properties are bound. While that is a bit over-assuming, it really does not hurt use of the bean. If the bean has any properties that are not bound, it is the bean-developer's responsibility to provide a BeanInfo class that explicitly states which properties are not bound.

Constrained properties are similar, but assumptions are safer. Whenever the tool sees that a property's set method throws a PropertyVetoException, the tool can assume the property is constrained.

Remember that properties can be *both* bound *and* constrained. In practice, most properties are only bound, and very few are only constrained.

Event Sets

Beans may or may not fire events. If they support bound or constrained properties, they will fire events; they can also fire other types of events.

Event firing requires the following elements:

- An event class to transmit information about the event
- An interface that describes how the bean will notify interested parties, known as listeners
- A data structure to track listeners
- Registration methods to add and remove listeners
- Code to fire the events

For example, suppose that you were creating a WeatherStation bean that notifies any interested parties when the sun rises or sets. This example is used throughout the following sections.

An Event Class

The first requirement for event firing is a class to represent information about the event. The SunEvent object contains the time of the event and a boolean property that tells us if the event represents the sun rising or setting.

Event classes should be immutable. Immutable objects are ones that cannot be changed. Event firing passes a reference to a single event instance to each listener in an *unspecified* order. It is important that those listeners cannot modify the event, or it could change the way processing continues for other listeners. Note that the following class is not a bean, because its superclass does not implement java.io.Serializable. If you like, you can define the event object as a bean, but in practice this is rarely done.

Note that the event object must extend class java.util.EventObject. EventObject provides the getSource() method so you can determine the event origin. By extending EventObject, those objects can be handled generically in other methods, and some tools, like VisualAge for Java, take advantage of this when creating generic methods to forward events.

```
package effectivevaj.bean.intro.eventsets;

import java.util.Date;
import java.util.EventObject;

/**
 * An event that represents the Sun rising or setting
 */
public class SunEvent extends EventObject {
  private boolean risen;
  private Date date;

  public SunEvent(Object source, boolean risen, Date date) {
    super(source);
    this.risen = risen;
    this.date = date;
  }

  /** return a String representation of the date */
  public String getDate() {
    // return only a String representation
    //   so the user cannot modify the real date
    return date.toString();
```

```
  }

  /** return whether the sun rose or set */
  public boolean isRisen() {
    return risen;
  }
}
```

EventObject requires a source (a reference to the object that fired the event), which is set to the WeatherStation bean when firing the event. Whenever events are fired, an instance of the EventObject class is created and passed to each registered listener.

VisualAge for Java can generate a basic event class for you, but you will need to fill in the details, such as the date and its risen status (whether the sun rose or set) in this class. This is explored in Chapter 8.

An Event-Listener Interface

Event listeners are classes that have registered interest in an event that a bean can fire. The bean notifies listener classes by calling certain methods in those listener classes. But how does the bean know which methods to call?

When defining the event, you also define a contract between the event source and its listeners. This contract specifies which methods the event source will call. Any listeners *must* implement those methods. Sounds like a perfect use for a Java language interface.

Therefore, define an interface that specifies the contract. Because each listener must implement that interface, the event-source bean can determine which methods it can call. Continuing the example, define a simple interface for the sun events.

Note that the following interface extends the java.util.EventListener interface. EventListener requires *no* methods. It is just a tag that indicates an interface is acting as an event listener. This assists determination of the events a bean can fire.

```
package effectivevaj.bean.intro.eventsets;

import java.util.EventListener;

/** A contract between a SunEvent source and
  *   listener classes
  */
public interface SunListener extends EventListener {
  /** Called whenever the sun changes position
    *   in a SunEvent source object
    */
  public void sunMoved(SunEvent e);
}
```

Any SunEvent listeners are required to implement a single method, sunMoved(). Normally, event-listener methods should take a single parameter: the event object. However, if you have a strong need, the bean specification allows (but strongly discourages) different parameters.

As you may have anticipated, VisualAge for Java can also generate the listener interface for you. More on this appears in Chapter 8.

An Event-Source Bean

Now you define the source of the sun events, the WeatherStation. This class needs to track its listeners and fire the events. This is implemented as follows, and a simple GUI to trigger the SunEvents is provided:

```
package effectivevaj.bean.intro.eventsets;

import java.util.Vector;
import java.util.Date;
import java.util.Enumeration;
import java.awt.Button;
import java.awt.Frame;
import java.awt.GridLayout;
import java.awt.event.ActionListener;
import java.awt.event.ActionEvent;
import java.awt.event.WindowAdapter;
import java.awt.event.WindowEvent;
import java.io.Serializable;

/** A sample event source - this class fires SunEvents
  *   to anyone watching. A simple GUI is provided
  *   with "rise" and "set" buttons that cause the
  *   SunEvents to be fired.
  */
public class WeatherStation extends Frame
                                implements Serializable {
  private transient Vector listeners;

  /** Provide a simple GUI that triggers our SunEvents
    */
  public WeatherStation() {
    super("Sun Watcher");
    setLayout(new GridLayout(1,0));
    Button riseButton = new Button("Rise");
    Button setButton = new Button("Set");
    add(riseButton);
    add(setButton);
```

```
    // make the "Rise" button fire "rise" SunEvents
    riseButton.addActionListener(new ActionListener() {
      public void actionPerformed(ActionEvent e) {
        fireSunMoved(true);
      }
    });

    // make the "Rise" button fire "set" SunEvents
    setButton.addActionListener(new ActionListener() {
      public void actionPerformed(ActionEvent e) {
        fireSunMoved(false);
      }
    });

    // Provide a means to close the application
    addWindowListener(new WindowAdapter() {
      public void windowClosing(WindowEvent e) {
        System.exit(0);
      }
    });

    pack();
  }

  /** Register a listener for SunEvents */
  synchronized public void addSunListener(SunListener l) {
    if (listeners == null)
      listeners = new Vector();
    listeners.addElement(l);
  }

  /** Remove a listener for SunEvents */
  synchronized public void removeSunListener(SunListener l) {
    if (listeners == null)
      listeners = new Vector();
    listeners.removeElement(l);
  }

  /** Fire a SunEvent to all registered listeners */
  protected void fireSunMoved(boolean rose) {
    // if we have no listeners, do nothing...
    if (listeners != null && !listeners.isEmpty()) {
      // create the event object to send
      SunEvent event =
```

```
          new SunEvent(this, rose, new Date());

        // make a copy of the listener list in case
        //    anyone adds/removes listeners
        Vector targets;
        synchronized (this) {
          targets = (Vector) listeners.clone();
        }

        // walk through the listener list and
        //    call the sunMoved method in each
        Enumeration e = targets.elements();
        while (e.hasMoreElements()) {
          SunListener l = (SunListener) e.nextElement();
          l.sunMoved(event);
        }
      }
    }
}
```

The bold text provides the support for tracking listeners and calling their event-handler methods. Of course, VisualAge for Java can generate this code as well. Details are in the next chapter.

The event source can now notify interested listeners. The synchronized keywords and cloning are necessary to avoid possible problems if the list of listeners changes while you are notifying listeners. Pressing the Rise and Set buttons fires an appropriate SunEvent to any registered listeners.

Typically, developers will create a fire method similar to the previous fireSunMoved() method, but the method is not required. The event-firing code can appear in any method you prefer. VisualAge for Java will create a method similar to this fire method, taking a SunEvent as its argument.

A Sample Event Listener

In the example, the weather channel informs any interested parties about the sun rising or setting. Continuing this example, Mrs. Jones assigns her class the task of graphing the behavior of the sun. They must watch a weather channel to find out at exactly what time the sun rose and set each day, logging this information in their notebook. This example can be modeled using a Student class as follows:

```
/** A sample SunListener, logging when the sun rises and sets
  */
public class Student implements SunListener {
  private String name;
```

```
  /** constructor - get the student's name */
  public Student(String name) {
    this.name = name;
  }

  /** sunMoved method comment. */
  public void sunMoved(SunEvent e) {
    log(name + "\tlogs : " +
        (e.isRisen() ? "rose" : "set") +
        " at " + e.getDate());
  }

  /** A simple log method - just print the text */
  protected void log(String text) {
    System.out.println(text);
  }
}
```

Note that Student implements SunListener, defining the details of a sunMoved() method. Any number of Students may watch the weather channel to hear the time of sunrise and sunset.

```
package effectivevaj.bean.intro.eventsets;

/**
 * A simple test of the SunEvent source and listeners
 */
public class WeatherTest {
  /** Run a test on the weather station, using Scott's
   *    kids as sample students
   */
  public static void main(String[] args) {
    // create a new sun event source
    WeatherStation w = new WeatherStation();

    // add some students to listen for sun rise/set
    w.addSunListener(new Student("Nicole"));
    w.addSunListener(new Student("Alex"));
    w.addSunListener(new Student("Trevor"));
    w.addSunListener(new Student("Claire"));

    // display the GUI for the weather channel
    w.setVisible(true);
  }
}
```

Running WeatherTest and pressing the Rise and Set buttons results in something like the following:

```
Nicole logs : rose at Thu Apr 29 14:55:21 PDT 1999
Alex   logs : rose at Thu Apr 29 14:55:21 PDT 1999
Trevor logs : rose at Thu Apr 29 14:55:21 PDT 1999
Claire logs : rose at Thu Apr 29 14:55:21 PDT 1999
Nicole logs : set at Thu Apr 29 14:55:22 PDT 1999
Alex   logs : set at Thu Apr 29 14:55:22 PDT 1999
Trevor logs : set at Thu Apr 29 14:55:22 PDT 1999
Claire logs : set at Thu Apr 29 14:55:22 PDT 1999
```

WARNING

The above listener methods run in a specific order each time an event is fired. This is because we stored the listeners in an ordered data structure. There is no guarantee of event-notification order in the bean specification! Unless a bean documents its event-firing behavior as ordered, you should not assume any particular order of notification. Beans could store their listeners in any data, and they may report them in a different order every time they fire an event.

Also note that event firing is *synchronous*. That is to say, the event source calls only one event handler at a time. Most beans fire their events in this manner (although there is nothing to stop you from writing a bean that fires events asynchronously). Because of this, you should perform only *short* operations in your event handlers. Think of it this way: The next listener has to wait for you, so you should be courteous and return as quickly as possible. If you need more complex operations, spawn another thread from your event handler.

VisualAge for Java can generate event-handling code as well, and we will discuss this in Chapter 12.

Determining Which Events Are Fired

Events are useful when writing code by hand, but they require a lot of code. Fortunately, bean-builder tools can provide assistance in generating this code. But how can a bean-builder tool determine which events can be fired so it can assist?

Recall that methods define properties using certain naming conventions; Events are defined in a similar manner. Bean-builder tools look for methods with the following naming pattern:

```
public void addSomeName(SomeName l)
public void removeSomeName(SomeName l)
```

When a tool sees a method that matches this naming pattern, it checks to see if SomeName is an interface that implements EventListener. (Remember that tag that was added to the SunListener interface?) A method matching this pattern defines an *event set*.

Once identified, the bean-builder tool examines the event listener interface to see which methods it requires. Those methods are possible events that the bean can fire. Using this information, the bean-builder tool can tell the user which events a bean can fire, enabling the user to associate an event from one bean with an action on another. How the bean-builder tool can use this information to help a user generate an application is described later.

Methods

The last type of bean features is *methods*. You may have guessed by now that bean methods are leftovers; that is, they are any public methods that remain after you determine properties and event sets. Bean-builder tools can present a list of methods to the programmer, stating available actions for any given bean. Bean tools do not treat method features as anything special. Normally you just connect to them as the result of some event being fired.

Bean-Builder Tools and Beans

Now that you know how tools can recognize bean features, let's explore how those bean-builder tools use beans.

Bean-builder tools typically have a tool bar or palette that holds pictures of commonly used beans. The user selects one of those beans and drops it in a design area that represents the class being built. The user can drop multiple beans in the design area; some tools allow only graphical user-interface beans, while other tools allow any beans.

The user can ask for a *property sheet* for any bean in the design area. Property sheets are dialogs that contain a list of property names and values. The bean-builder tool determines which properties are available and then calls the appropriate get method to display the current values of those properties. The user can then modify writeable properties (properties with set methods) in a property sheet to represent the initial state of that particular bean instance. Of course, the program can modify the property values during execution by invoking their set methods. When a bean-builder tool generates source code for a bean, it creates *new* statements for each bean as well as calls to each *set* method to set the property values specified in the property sheet. The code that VisualAge for Java generates is examined in Chapter 19, "Handwritten Code versus Generated Code."

Most bean-builder tools enable the user to specify interactions between beans. Those interactions start with one bean firing an event, and end by calling a method or setting a property in another (or the same) bean. Some tools provide wizards to specify this interaction, while others enable the user to draw lines between components, choosing the source event and target feature via pop-up menus. The bean-builder tool can generate an event listener to respond to those events and call the appropriate target method. VisualAge for Java provides the most advanced bean-builder tool available, the Visual Composition Editor. We will discuss it in detail starting in Chapter 10, "Bean Composition in the VCE."

Introspection and the Role of BeanInfo Classes

Introspection is the process of determining which features a bean supports. In its most basic form, introspection is simply a process of using the Java core reflection classes to determine which public methods the bean defines and match those methods against the bean naming patterns.

The introspection process examines the bean class and proceeds to each superclass. The process inspects public methods in each class, adding them to the list of features. If any duplicate features exist, subclass definitions take precedence. Often this provides the desired functionality; sometimes it can fall short.

How can features be hidden from the user of a bean-builder tool? How can you allow only expert users to see some features, while non-expert users see only very basic features? How can you change the way the user interacts with the properties in a property sheet, or enable several properties to be set as a group? Explicit metadata is required to address those and other issues, describing exactly what you want. The bean specification calls this metadata *BeanInfo*. BeanInfo are classes that are delivered along with beans. Any bean may have a BeanInfo class, which describes in detail the features provided by that bean.

BeanInfo classes are associated with a bean by a simple naming convention. The name of the BeanInfo class is the name of the bean with "BeanInfo" as its suffix. For example, a bean named Person could have a PersonBeanInfo class that describes it. BeanInfo classes all implement the java.beans.BeanInfo interface, which requires methods that return arrays of PropertyDescriptors, MethodDescriptors, and EventSetDescriptors as well as general information about the bean itself.

If the introspection process discovers a BeanInfo class, it queries that BeanInfo class to determine features instead of examining public method names. The FeatureDescriptors (PropertyDescriptors, MethodDescriptors, and EventSetDescriptors) provide the names and descriptions of the features. Each FeatureDescriptor can contain additional information, stating if a feature should be hidden or considered expert. The bean-builder tool uses the FeatureDescriptor information to filter the features that are available. PropertyDescriptors can also specify a *property editor*, one means of customizing the way a user edits a property's value in the bean-builder tool.

Finally, the BeanInfo class provides a BeanDescriptor, which describes the bean overall, possibly including a Customizer (which provides customized editing for the entire bean) and icons to represent the bean in the bean-builder tool's palette.

Keep in mind that once you define a BeanInfo class, *it* is in charge of describing bean features. If you add new methods to your bean, bean builder tools will not know about them unless you add the features to the BeanInfo class as well. This is discussed in more detail in Chapter 8.

BeanInfo classes are tedious to write, but fortunately, VisualAge for Java generates them for you. The next chapter examines how easy VisualAge for Java makes bean development by generating features and BeanInfo classes.

Summary

JavaBeans components, while very simple, provide a great deal of information. They can implicitly or explicitly tell tools, like a bean-builder tool, their functionality. Those other tools can help a user assemble a set of beans, or provide automatic integration of beans to customize the program. The flexibility and simplicity of design makes them quite desirable and useful in real world programming.

The next chapter moves on to the tools that VisualAge for Java provides to work with beans, starting with the innocent-looking BeanInfo editor.

THE BEANINFO EDITOR 8

While simple in concept, beans require quite a bit of code. Fortunately, VisualAge for Java provides excellent tool support for bean creation and maintenance.

There are three options for working with beans in VisualAge:

Write code by hand. Not terribly desirable. The code for this option was presented in the previous chapter.

Define bean features using the BeanInfo editor. Generates code for all features. This is covered in this chapter.

Compose beans using visual composition. Combine features of other beans. This is covered in Chapter 10, "Bean Composition in the VCE."

Because VisualAge for Java is an incredibly flexible tool, you can combine these approaches when developing your beans. However, we strongly recommend that you isolate visually composed code and handwritten code; we discuss this in detail in Chapter 15, "Model-View-Controller in the VCE."

Birth of a Bean

A bean can be instantiated by reconstituting a serialized image or calling the *new* operator. Reconstituting beans is useful if the default initialization code is complex and time-intensive. You initialize the bean in another program and then "pickle" it by writing out the state of the instance using object serialization. Later, the program that uses the bean "unpickles" it, recreating its original state. The program can still set properties via the bean's set methods, of course.

If this serialization approach will *always* be used, support for serialization is the only requirement for the bean. However, it is much more common to enable a user to use the *new* operator to create a bean instance. To enable this, the bean must have a public no-argument constructor. Unless there is a very strong reason not to, you should always provide a public no-argument constructor for your beans. Remember that you can always add other constructors that *do* take parameters.

These other constructors can be used by classes that do not follow the BeanInfo specification.

The bean specification requires that all beans be persistent. Starting with that requirement, let's implement an example Person bean *without writing any code.*

The Person bean in this example will have the following features:

name. A readable, writeable, and bound String property

phone. A readable, writeable, bound, and constrained String property

Start developing the Person bean as you would any class in VisualAge for Java; use the Add Class SmartGuide to create a new class, as shown in Figure 8.1.

Create class effectivevaj.bean.beaninfo.simple.Person, extending java.lang.Object. Figure 8.2 shows use of the Add Class SmartGuide when creating a bean.

After you set up the initial information, you need to move to the second page of the Add Class SmartGuide by pressing the **Next** button. On the second page of the SmartGuide, choose to implement the java.io.Serializable interface, as seen in Figure 8.3.

This creates a class with both bean basics: It is and has a public no-argument constructor. A user can create an instance of it using the new operator or by reconstituting a serialized image. However, without any features, it is not a terribly useful bean.

The remedy is to use VisualAge for Java's BeanInfo editor.

The BeanInfo Editor

VisualAge for Java provides a BeanInfo editor in its class browser. The BeanInfo editor creates BeanInfo classes and automates creation of bean features. You can add new bean features and modify existing bean features. This editor is the most often overlooked feature in VisualAge for Java, and it provides one of the most important functions in the tool.

If, while reading the last chapter, you started thinking "Beans sound like a lot of work," the BeanInfo editor will quickly become your best friend. Clicking a few buttons and typing a few names creates properties, event sets, and methods.

So far, in this example you have created a Person bean. It does not have any features or a BeanInfo class. The BeanInfo editor will create both.

Figure 8.1 Invoking the Add Class SmartGuide.

Figure 8.2 Creating our Person bean.

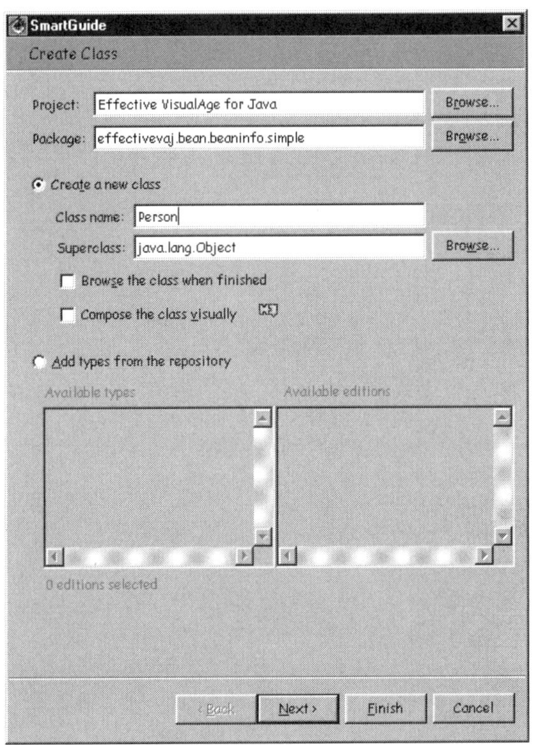

Basic Use of the BeanInfo Editor

To start the BeanInfo editor, choose **Open To->BeanInfo** from a class' pop-up menu (or from the Selected menu when a class is selected), as shown in Figure 8.4.

The result for the Person bean in shown in Figure 8.5. The bottom pane shows the BeanDescriptor information for the Person bean. The BeanDescriptor information gives the following general information about a bean.

Customizer Class. The name of a class that acts as a SmartGuide to edit all properties of the bean.

Description. A simple description of the bean, possibly used by bean builders when a user asks for a more descriptive name of a bean.

Display Name. A textual name of the bean. Bean-builder tools may use this as a tool tip or as a label in a palette.

Expert. If true, requests that a bean-builder tool display the bean only if the user is an expert.

Figure 8.3 Make sure you implement Serializable!

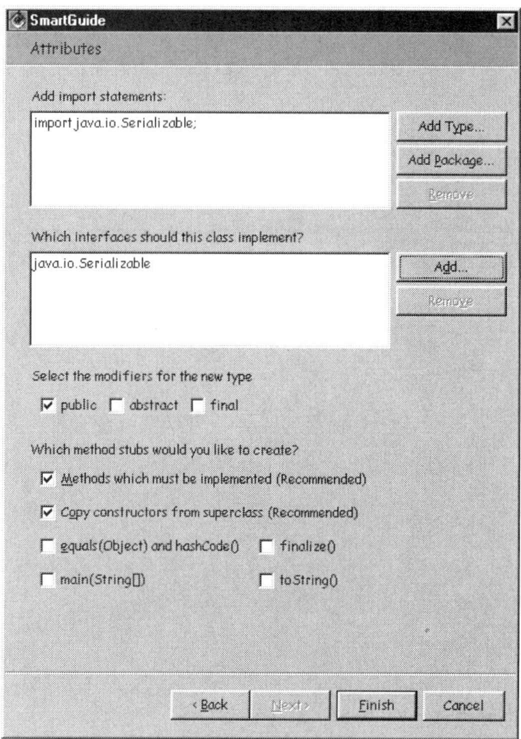

Hidden. If true, requests that a bean-builder tool not display the bean.

Hidden State. If true, the bean-builder tool must use serialization to store and recreate the bean instance. Hidden State means that the bean has some state information the program cannot set via set methods.

Icons. Color and monochrome icons used by a bean-builder tool to represent the bean in a palette or other location.

You can change any of these values and select **Save** from the pop-up menu in the bottom pane. Note that you must click on an unselected section of the bottom pane to display the pop-up menu. The BeanInfo editor creates a new BeanInfo class to store the information.

The newly created BeanInfo class explicitly lists all feature information. The only features that will be visible during introspection will be those explicitly listed in the BeanInfo class. This means that if you write code to create a new property, it will not appear as a bean feature unless you explicitly add it to the BeanInfo class.

Figure 8.4 Invoking the BeanInfo editor.

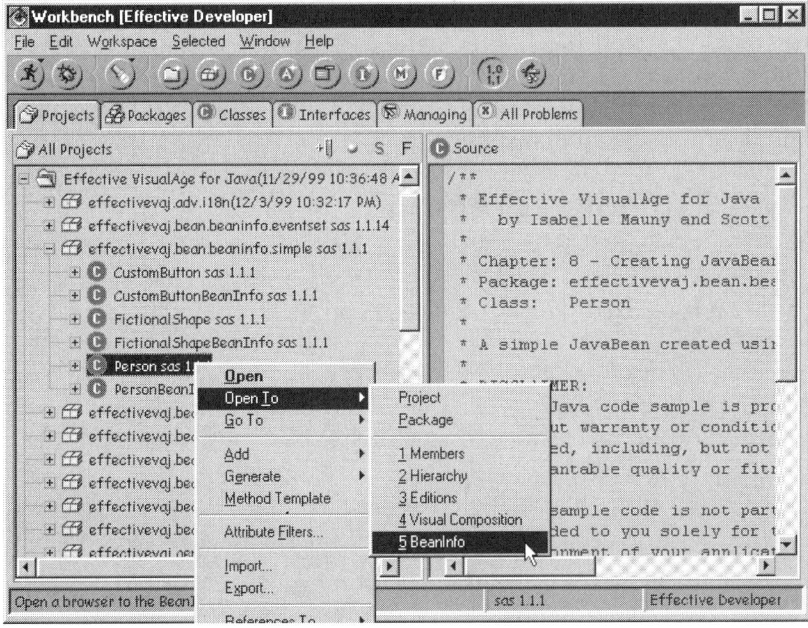

Figure 8.5 The Person bean in the BeanInfo editor.

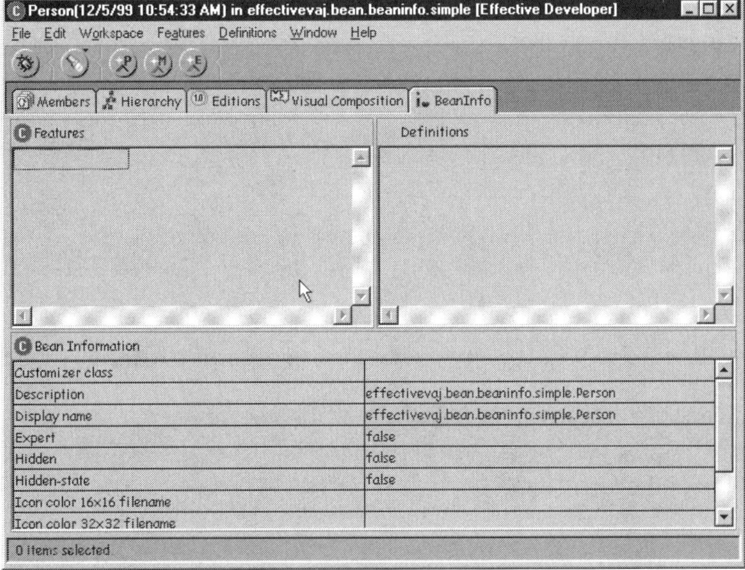

Working with Properties

When developing beans using VisualAge for Java, there are two ways to create new properties. You can write get and set methods for the new properties, or ask VisualAge for Java to generate them for you. First, we will discuss how to manage properties from within the BeanInfo editor. Later, we will see how to add existing properties to the BeanInfo class.

Adding and Extending Properties

Because bean property methods follow predictable method names, VisualAge for Java can easily create these methods for you. You specify the name and type of the property, whether it is indexed, simple, bound, or constrained: VisualAge for Java creates the code for you.

To add a property, press the Create Property Feature button on the tool bar, as shown in Figure 8.6, or choose New Property Feature from the Features menu. The New Property Feature SmartGuide, shown in Figure 8.7, will appear, ready to create the property methods.

This SmartGuide gathers information from you about the property you want to create:

Property Name. The simple name of the property you want to create. Note that the bean specification states that property names should begin with a lowercase letter.

Property Type. A primitive type or class name, defining the type of the property.

Readable. If checked, specifies that the property is readable. VisualAge will generate a get method for it.

Writeable. If checked, specifies that the property is writeable. VisualAge will generate a set method for it.

Indexed. If checked, specifies that the property should act like an array of values.

Bound. If checked, the set method will fire PropertyChangeEvents to PropertyChangeListeners *after* the property value changes. This will add

Figure 8.6 Invoking the Create Property Feature SmartGuide.

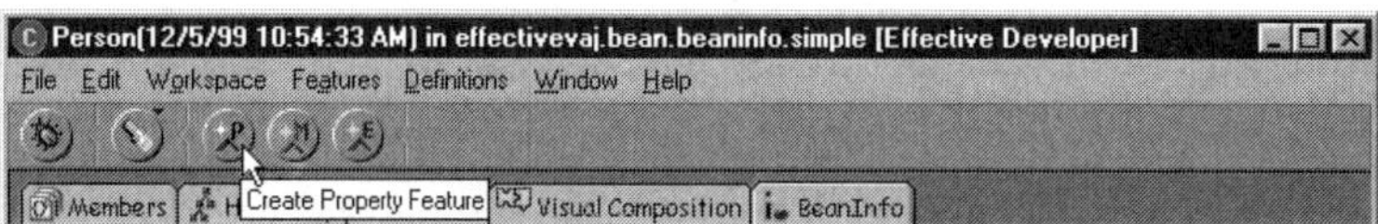

Figure 8.7 Defining a new property.

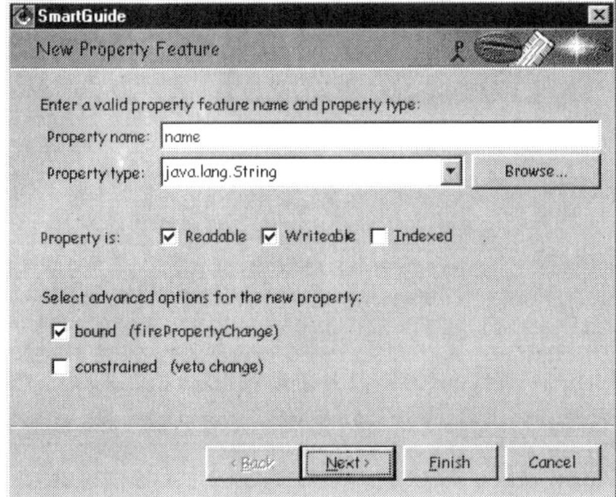

the appropriate support as well—an instance of PropertyChangeSupport and methods to add and remove PropertyChangeListeners.

Constrained. If checked, the set method will fire PropertyChangeEvents to VetoableChangeListeners *before* the property value changes, and define the set method to throw PropertyVetoException. This will add the appropriate support as well—an instance of VetoableChangeSupport and methods to add and remove VetoableChangeListeners.

This example creates a name property, using java.lang.String for its type, and makes it readable, writeable, and bound.

Pressing the **Next** button displays a second page, shown in Figure 8.8, that asks for descriptive information about the property. If you do not need the extra descriptive information, press the **Finish** button instead.

The information contained on this page is extra information that only a BeanInfo class can provide. A bean-builder tool uses this information to describe a property to its user, possibly hide the property, and define how the user interacts with that property. This information contains:

Display name. An alternate name used in the property sheet. This should be a short, readable name for the property. For example, if you have a property named *userName*, you might want to set the display name to "user name" (note the space), making it more readable.

Short description. A short description of the property, usually displayed in a tool tip or status line. A userName property might have a description like "a string that uniquely identifies this person when logged into the system."

Figure 8.8 Extra property information.

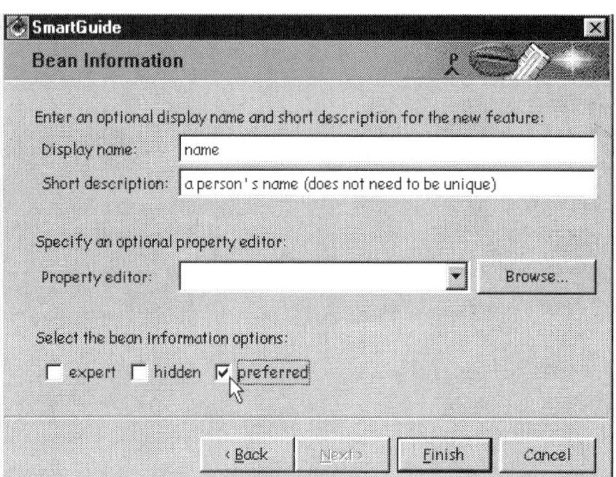

Property editor. The name of another class that defines user interaction when modifying the property's state. This is discussed in more detail in Chapter 20, "Bean Customization."

Expert. If checked, a property that requires detailed knowledge or interest. This enables a bean-builder tool to provide two levels of user interaction. Initially, novice users might feel more comfortable accessing only nonexpert features. Once users become familiar with the bean, they can elect to work with all available features. For example, a database-access bean could provide a property called numberOfRowsToCache. Only expert users who understand database caching should modify the value, so you would mark it expert.

Hidden. If checked, a feature not presented to the user. The feature is still available to the user through method calls (after all, features *are* defined as public methods) but not from the visual design area. This is useful if the property should only be used "under the covers" by other beans; you still create public methods for the properties, but the end-user might be unaware that they exist.

Preferred. If this is true, the property will be more readily accessible to the user. It will usually appear in pop-up menus rather than requiring the user to select it via a window. *This is an extension specific to VisualAge for Java.* The bean specification allows extra attributes for use in a particular bean-builder tool. These attributes are specified by a String name, and a bean-builder tool must explicitly ask for that name. Other bean-builder tools will ignore these extensions, because they do not know what name to ask for.

> **NOTE**
> We recommend that you consider whether this property will need to be accessed frequently. If so, check the **Preferred** box. You can always change its preferred status later, but if you know a property will often be involved in connections, it is much faster to check this box now.

After you press the **Finish** button, VisualAge for Java creates the methods required for the property. In this example, VisualAge for Java generates the setName() and getName() methods.

Because most properties have instance variables that store their values, VisualAge for Java creates an instance variable for every property. The name of this variable is field*PropertyName*, and the get and set methods simply return or modify its value. When defining a *name* property that is neither bound nor constrained, VisualAge for Java generates the following code. The code for bound and constrained properties is discussed later in this chapter.

```
private String fieldName = new String();

/**
 * Gets the name property (java.lang.String) value.
 * @return The name property value.
 * @see #setName
 */
public String getName() {
  return fieldName;
}

/**
 * Sets the name property (java.lang.String) value.
 * @param name The new value for the property.
 * @see #getName
 */
public void setName(String name) {
     fieldName = name;
}
```

Although the class has access to the field*PropertyName* variable, you should access the property *only* through its get and set methods. This makes it easy to change the implementation of the property later and ensures that bound and constrained properties fire their respective events whenever modified.

NOTE

VisualAge for Java uses fully qualified class names when generating most of your code. The reason for this is simple: If the names were not fully qualified, VisualAge for Java would need to add import statements to your code. Such added import statements could conflict with existing imports, or already exist in your code.

In general, tools that generate code must generate fully qualified names if the user can edit that code. The tool has no way of knowing the intent of the user code. Does the user really mean the same Button class in his import, or might he want to change his imported Button class without affecting the visually composed Button?

Bound Properties

Bound properties are particularly useful in VisualAge for Java. When visually composing a bean, you can connect two bound properties, generating PropertyChangeListener code to keep those properties' values synchronized. You should generally make your properties bound; there is little overhead if there are no listeners, but there can be significant advantages if a user wants to react when the property value changes.

When you bind a property, VisualAge for Java generates additional code, and the set method becomes slightly more complex. VisualAge for Java also generates an instance of PropertyChangeSupport as well as methods to add and remove PropertyChangeListeners. For the name property example, VisualAge generates the following code. Note that the instance variable and get method remain unchanged.

```
private String fieldName = new String();
protected transient java.beans.PropertyChangeSupport
          propertyChange;

/**
 * Accessor for the propertyChange field.
 */
protected java.beans.PropertyChangeSupport
             getPropertyChange() {
  if (propertyChange == null) {
    propertyChange = new
      java.beans.PropertyChangeSupport(this);
  };
  return propertyChange;
}
```

```
/**
 * The addPropertyChangeListener method was generated to
 *    support the propertyChange field.
 */
public synchronized void addPropertyChangeListener(
          java.beans.PropertyChangeListener listener) {
  getPropertyChange().addPropertyChangeListener(listener);
}

/**
 * The removePropertyChangeListener method was generated to
 *    support the propertyChange field.
 */
public synchronized void removePropertyChangeListener(
          java.beans.PropertyChangeListener listener) {
  getPropertyChange().removePropertyChangeListener(listener);
}

/**
 * The firePropertyChange method was generated to support
 *    the propertyChange field.
 */
public void firePropertyChange(String propertyName,
                               Object oldValue,
                               Object newValue) {
  getPropertyChange().firePropertyChange(propertyName,
                                         oldValue,
                                         newValue);
}

/**
 * Gets the name property (java.lang.String) value.
 * @return The name property value.
 * @see #setName
 */
public String getName() {
  return fieldName;
}

/**
 * Sets the name property (java.lang.String) value.
 * @param name The new value for the property.
 * @see #getName
 */
```

```
public void setName(String name) {
  String oldValue = fieldName;
  fieldName = name;
  firePropertyChange("name", oldValue, name);
}
```

Notice that the getPropertyChange() method does not define a property; it is protected, not public. VisualAge for Java generates methods like this one for several objects. The code inside the method performs *lazy instantiation*; we create the actual property change instance the first time we call the get method. Lazy instantiation has two important advantages:

- If your program never calls the get method, the program does not create the object.
- Order of initialization is not an issue. You can call the get method without worrying whether the object already exists.

The other methods and the change to the setName() method are exactly what you expect for a bound property. The firePropertyChange() method is a convenience method provided so you can easily fire a property-change event if something other than the set method can change the property. We will take advantage of this in the next chapter.

Because the generated code strictly adheres to the bean specification, *the bound property will function in any JavaBeans-compliant bean-builder tool.* You are not generating VisualAge-specific beans.

In Chapter 12, "Connections," you will see exactly how useful bound properties can be. They are an extremely valuable asset and can greatly simplify your program.

Constrained Properties

The code generated for constrained properties is similar to that for bound properties. If a property is *both* bound and constrained, the above code still applies, but VisualAge for Java generates additional code to control the possibility of property-value vetoes.

For the example person bean, the phone property is bound *and* constrained. When creating the property in the New Property SmartGuide, check the *constrained* box as shown in Figure 8.9.

The following code shows the changes for the constrained phone property. Note that some of the bound-property code is omitted for sake of brevity.

```
protected transient java.beans.VetoableChangeSupport
                    vetoPropertyChange;
private String fieldPhone = new String();

/**
```

Figure 8.9 Constraining a property.

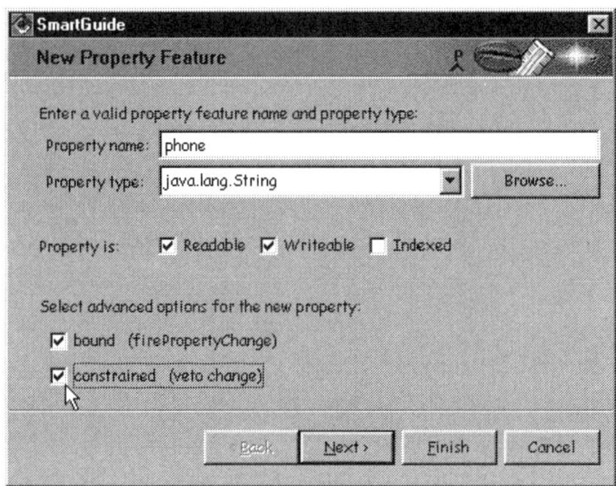


```
 * The addVetoableChangeListener method was generated to
 *    support the vetoPropertyChange field.
 */
public synchronized void addVetoableChangeListener(
         java.beans.VetoableChangeListener listener) {
  getVetoPropertyChange().addVetoableChangeListener(
                              listener);
}

/**
 * The fireVetoableChange method was generated to support
 *    the vetoPropertyChange field.
 */
public void fireVetoableChange(String propertyName,
                               Object oldValue,
                               Object newValue)
            throws java.beans.PropertyVetoException {
  getVetoPropertyChange().fireVetoableChange(propertyName,
                                             oldValue,
                                             newValue);
}

/**
 * Gets the phone property (java.lang.String) value.
 * @return The phone property value.
 * @see #setPhone
 */
```

```
public String getPhone() {
  return fieldPhone;
}

/**
 * Accessor for the vetoPropertyChange field.
 */
protected java.beans.VetoableChangeSupport
            getVetoPropertyChange() {
  if (vetoPropertyChange == null) {
    vetoPropertyChange =
      new java.beans.VetoableChangeSupport(this);
  };
  return vetoPropertyChange;
}

/**
 * The removeVetoableChangeListener method was generated
 *   to support the vetoPropertyChange field.
 */
public synchronized void removeVetoableChangeListener(
          java.beans.VetoableChangeListener listener) {
  getVetoPropertyChange().removeVetoableChangeListener(
                                  listener);
}

/**
 * Sets the phone property (java.lang.String) value.
 * @param phone The new value for the property.
 * @exception java.beans.PropertyVetoException
 *            The exception description.
 * @see #getPhone
 */
public void setPhone(String phone)
            throws java.beans.PropertyVetoException {
  String oldValue = fieldPhone;
  fireVetoableChange("phone", oldValue, phone);
  fieldPhone = phone;
  firePropertyChange("phone", oldValue, phone);
}
```

Again, the generated code adheres to the bean specification and will function in any compliant bean-builder tool. Note the additional code in the set method: The vetoableChange event is fired to ask for dissent. If one of the VetoableChangeListeners does not like the change, it throws a PropertyVetoException. Because this exception can be thrown (and is not a RuntimeException), the set method must declare that it can throw it.

VisualAge for Java can generate the appropriate code, but you need to work a little harder to take advantage of them. Watch the VisualAge for Java Tips and Tricks site, www.javadude.com/vaj. We plan to post some validation frameworks in the future.

Modifying Properties

After you have created a property, you can easily modify its attributes. If you select a property in the Features pane of the BeanInfo editor, the lower pane displays the attributes of that feature, as seen in Figure 8.10.

These settings affect descriptions in the BeanInfo class only; they do not modify the generated bean code. The property attributes are:

Bound. Indicates whether this property is bound. Changing this value will not change the set method; it is simply a cue to a bean-builder tool. If you have non-bound properties listed as bound, the bean-builder tool will think they fire PropertyChangeEvents and allow the user to work with them as such. If you have *any* non-bound properties, make sure you mark them as such in the BeanInfo.

Figure 8.10 Modifying property attributes.

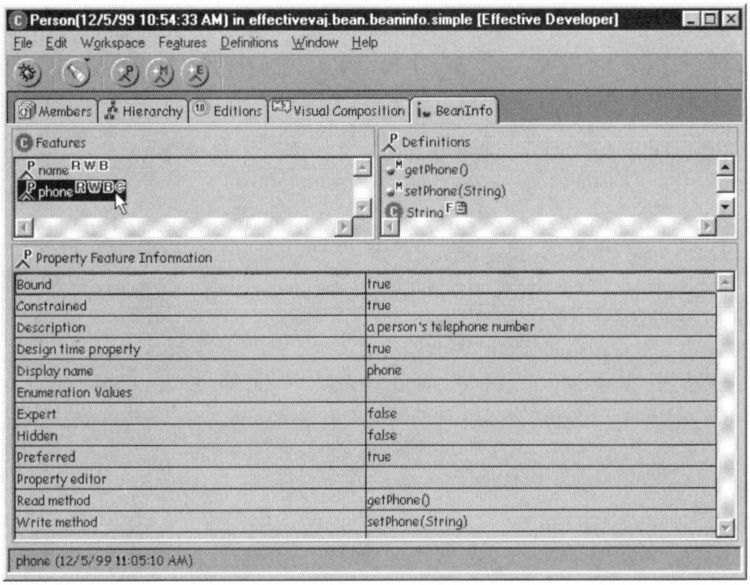

Person(12/5/99 10:54:33 AM) in effectivevaj.bean.beaninfo.simple [Effective Developer]

File Edit Workspace Features Definitions Window Help

Members | Hierarchy | Editions | Visual Composition | BeanInfo

Features
name RWB
phone RWBC

Definitions
getPhone()
setPhone(String)
String F

Property Feature Information

Bound	true
Constrained	true
Description	a person's telephone number
Design time property	true
Display name	phone
Enumeration Values	
Expert	false
Hidden	false
Preferred	true
Property editor	
Read method	getPhone()
Write method	setPhone(String)

phone (12/5/99 11:05:10 AM)

Constrained. Indicates whether this property is constrained. Again, changing this value will not change code in the set method for the property.

Description. A textual description of the property, used in tool tips or status lines when the user selects the property.

Design time property. Determines if the property should appear on a property sheet. A design-time property is one whose value can be set when the user is dropping the bean in the design area. If this is false, the property will not appear in the property sheet but may still be available when connecting beans together.

Display name. The name by which the property will be displayed in the property sheet or other lists of available properties.

Enumeration values. Provides a simple dialog where you can assign names and values for a property. This is a convenient option for use within VisualAge for Java, replacing the need for a property editor that defines getTags(). (See Chapter 20 for details on property editors.)These enumeration values will *not* be available outside of VisualAge for Java! If you want to provide this customization for your bean outside VisualAge for Java, you *must* provide a property editor. We strongly recommend you not use this option.

Expert. Indicates whether the property should be considered an expert property. If true, the user must specify that they are an expert to see the property.

Hidden. Indicates whether the property should be presented to the user in the bean-builder tool. If this is false, the user of a bean-builder tool will not see the property.

Preferred. If this is true, the property will be more readily accessible to the user in the VCE.

Property editor. The name of a class to use to edit the property in a property sheet. We will discuss property editors in Chapter 20.

Read method. The name of the method to invoke to access the current value of the property. By convention, this method is get*PropertyName*(), but if there is a strong need to change it, you can. One possible reason is that you might not want properties edited without a corresponding BeanInfo class. By defining nonstandard names for the read and write methods, the property will not appear in a bean-builder tool unless a BeanInfo class is present to tell it that the property exists (and which methods can access it). Generally, we strongly recommend against changing the read and write methods.

Write method. Defines the name of the method used to change a property's value. By convention, this is set*PropertyName*().

While you can change these values, keep in mind that the changes affect only the BeanInfo class, *not* the bean itself.

Deleting Properties

You can remove a property from your bean in several ways:

Change the property to be hidden. This does not really delete the property; it just prevents a user from changing the property's value in a bean-builder tool.

Remove the property definition from the BeanInfo class. Again, the property still exists, but the user cannot access it in a bean-builder tool as long as the BeanInfo class exists.

Delete the get and set methods from the bean class. This truly removes the property from the bean.

We have already seen how you can change the hidden status of a property: Just set the hidden attribute of the property in the BeanInfo editor. We will now discuss how to remove the property. To initiate the second or third forms of deletion, select the property in the Features pane of the BeanInfo editor and choose **Delete** from the property's pop-up menu (or the Features menu). You will then see the Delete Features window, shown in Figure 8.11.

> **NOTE**
>
> If you choose to delete the get and set methods for a property outside of the BeanInfo editor, you will still need to delete the property information in the BeanInfo page. If you do not delete the information from the BeanInfo page as well, the BeanInfo class will be out of sync with your bean and you will receive IntrospectionErrors when using it in a bean-builder tool. This could cause other problems as well.

In addition, this does not delete the generated support for bound and constrained properties. If you no longer have *any* bound properties, you can delete the following:

- The declaration of the propertyChange instance variable
- The generated getPropertyChange() method
- The generated add- and removePropertyChangeListener() methods
- The generated firePropertyChange() method

Figure 8.11 Deleting properties.

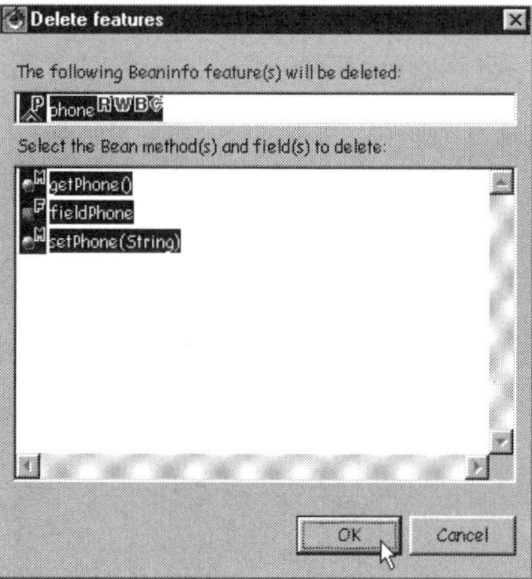

Similarly, if no remaining properties are constrained, you can delete the following:

- The declaration of the vetoPropertyChange instance variable
- The generated getVetoPropertyChange() method
- The generated add/removeVetoableChangeListener() methods
- The generated fireVetoableChange() method

We recommend that you version the bean before deleting any of these methods. You can then undo the change if the methods are still required.

Changing the Type of a Property

By far, the most common mistake made in the BeanInfo editor is forgetting to change the type of a property from java.lang.String when creating it. If this happens, you must change the type of the property to the type you really want. There are two ways to do this:

- Change the referenced type name to the desired type name in the field*PropertyName* variable and the get and set methods
- Delete and recreate the property

If you have not added any code to the get or set methods, deleting and recreating the property is the easiest way to change its type.

Changing a Property's Bound or Constrained Status

You can change the bound and constrained attributes for a property in the BeanInfo editor, but this does *not* change the set method for that property. If you want to unbind or unconstrain a property, you have two choices:

Remove the code that makes the property bound or constrained. If you have made significant code changes to the get or set method of a property, this is the probably the safest means to remove the bound or constrained behavior. If there are no more bound or constrained properties, you can also delete the add- and remove PropertyChangeListener methods from the bean as described previously.

Delete the property and recreate it. If you have not added code to the get or set method of a property, or the added code can easily be recreated, you can simply delete and recreate the property.

In addition, if you decide to *add* the bound and constrained behavior, you can either add the code by hand or delete and recreate the properties. In the case of adding this behavior, it is far easier to delete and recreate the property.

For deletion and recreation to succeed, you must fully delete the property, not just make it hidden or remove it from the BeanInfo class.

Working with Event Sets

The BeanInfo editor provides two ways to support event sets:

- Adding support to fire existing events
- Creating new events as well as support to fire them

In both cases, VisualAge for Java can generate all of the code necessary to make a bean behave as an event source.

Adding Support for Existing Events

Suppose that you were creating a custom Button bean, and you wanted to support ActionEvents in the same manner as java.awt.Button does. If you were to write the code yourself, this would require a means of tracking the listeners, and code to fire the event. In VisualAge for Java, you can have the BeanInfo editor create this functionality.

As an example, suppose that you opened a CustomButton class in the BeanInfo editor. You can add a new event set by pressing the Create Event Set Feature button on the tool bar or by choosing **New Event Set Feature** from the **Features** menu, as shown in Figure 8.12. This displays the dialog shown in Figure 8.13.

Figure 8.12 Invoking the Create Event Set Feature SmartGuide.

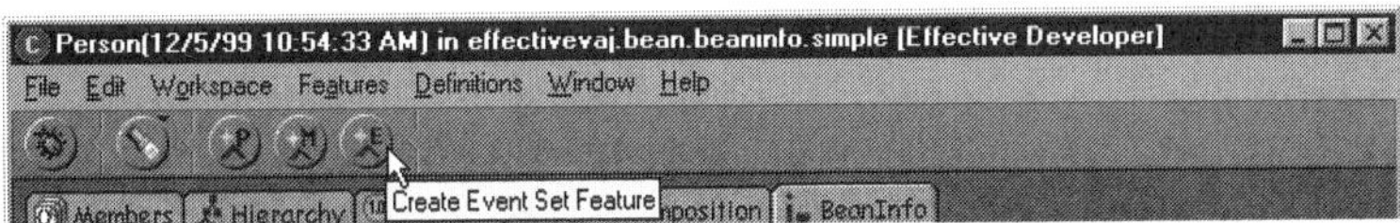

Figure 8.13 Creating a new event set.

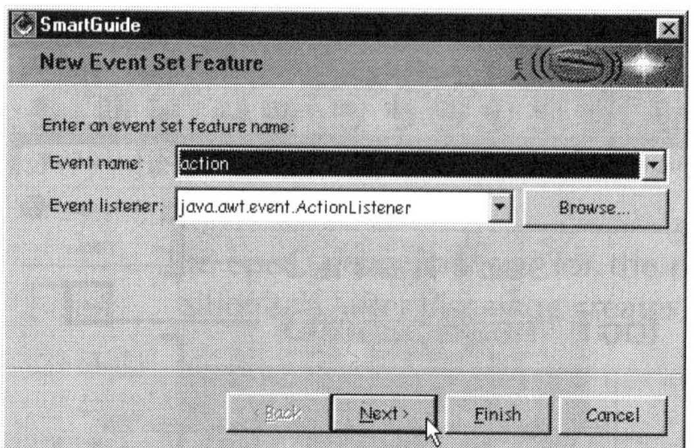

Choose the name of the event, in this case *action*, and VisualAge for Java will select the corresponding listener interface. Pressing **Next** enables you to specify a name and description for the event.

After you press Finish, VisualAge for Java generates the code necessary to treat the CustomButton class as an event source for the ActionEvent. The generated code follows:

```
protected transient java.awt.event.ActionListener
                        aActionListener = null;

public void addActionListener(
              java.awt.event.ActionListener newListener) {
  aActionListener = java.awt.AWTEventMulticaster.add(
                              aActionListener, newListener);
  return;
}

public void removeActionListener(
              java.awt.event.ActionListener newListener) {
  aActionListener = java.awt.AWTEventMulticaster.remove(
                              aActionListener, newListener);
  return;
}

/**
 * Method to support listener events.
 */
protected void fireActionPerformed(
                java.awt.event.ActionEvent e) {
```

```
    if (aActionListener == null) {
      return;
    };
    aActionListener.actionPerformed(e);
  }
```

The generated code can vary slightly depending on the type of event. For example, an AWTEventMulticaster tracks the listeners if it supports the listener type; otherwise, a Vector tracks the listeners.

> **NOTE**
>
> Event multicasters are *thread-safe* tree-like structures. They track two listeners (which could be other multicasters) and, through their design, prevent problems if listeners are added or removed during event firing. The code behind the Multicasters is discussed in Chapter 19, "Handwritten Code versus Generated Code."

VisualAge for Java generates a fire method for each method in the listener interface. To fire events, call the appropriate fire method. For example, you could add a simple MouseListener to the button to click (press) the button:

```
// instance variable in CustomButton
// consider the button pressed if the user
//   presses and releases inside the button
private boolean wasPressed = false;

// somewhere in the CustomButton constructor
addMouseListener(new MouseAdapter() {
  public void mousePressed(MouseEvent e) {
    wasPressed = true;
  }
  public void mouseReleased(MouseEvent e) {
    if (wasPressed && contains(e.getX(), e.getY())) {
      fireActionPerformed(
        new ActionEvent(CustomButton.this,
                        ActionEvent.ACTION_PERFORMED,
                        getLabel()));
    }
    wasPressed = false;
  }
});
```

By calling fireActionPerformed(), you inform any registered ActionListeners that the button was clicked.

Creating New Events

Creating a new event is as simple as adding an existing event. The SunEvent example from Chapter 7, "Introduction to JavaBeans Components," is used here to illustrate this.

Generating Event Support Classes

To create a new event, first create an event source. In this case, create a WeatherStation bean (extending java.awt.Frame and implementing java.io.Serializable again) and open it in the BeanInfo editor. Once there, choose **New Listener Interface** from the **Features** menu as shown in Figure 8.14. (Note that there is no tool-bar button for this function.)

After you select **New Listener Interface**, the dialog shown in Figure 8.15 appears. You only need to enter the Event name; VisualAge for Java fills in the other field values automatically. Unless you have a very specialized need, you should not modify the other fields.

As you type sun in the Event Name field, VisualAge for Java fills in all other fields automatically. This SmartGuide will create the event listener interface, the event class, and a multicaster class to track listeners. Pressing **Next** displays a window that prompts for the names of the implementation methods that the event listener interface requires, as shown in Figure 8.16.

Figure 8.14 Invoking the New Listener Interface SmartGuide.

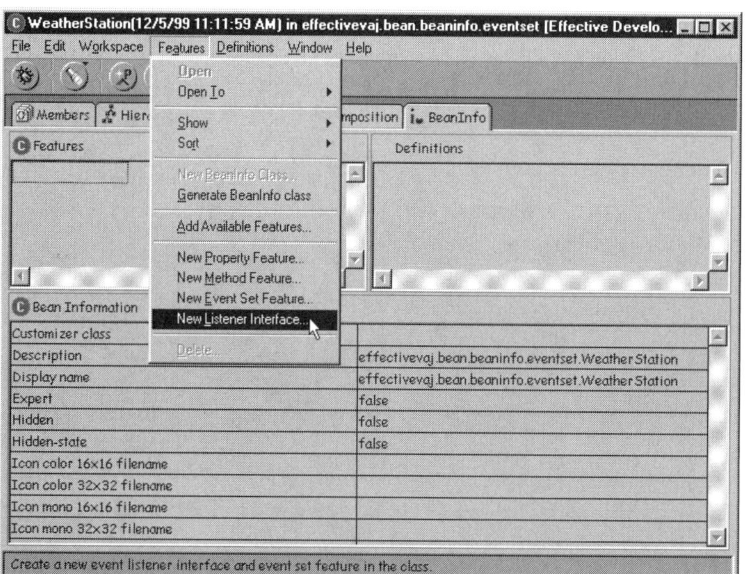

Figure 8.15 Creating a new event listener.

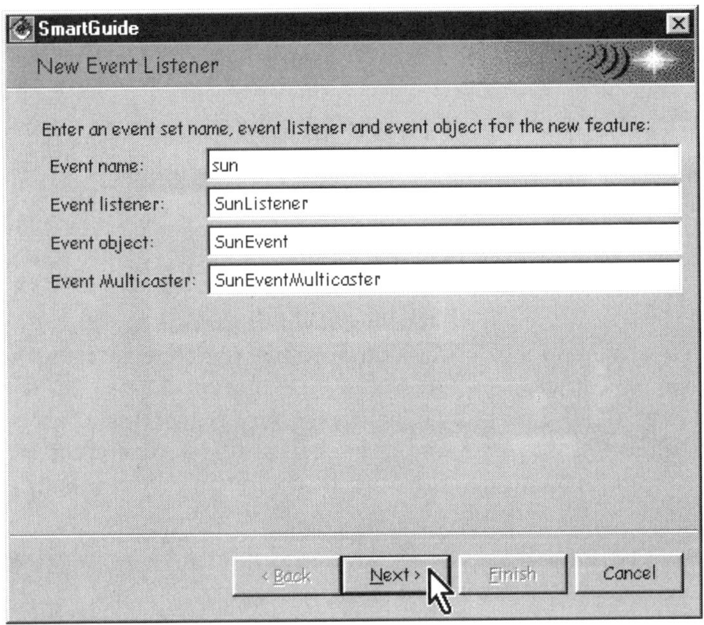

Figure 8.16 Defining listener methods.

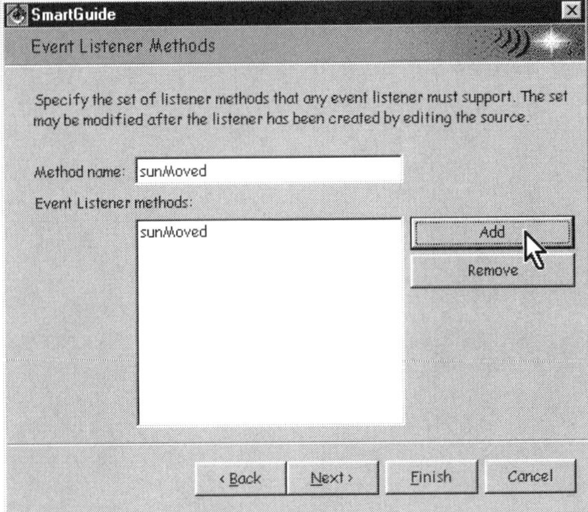

Specify the names of the methods you want in the interface and press the **Add** button. When finished, press the **Next** button to continue to the dialog shown in Figure 8.17.

You can specify details about the event set and press **Finish** to generate the code.

VisualAge for Java generates the event class, an event listener interface, and an event multicaster class. It also adds the necessary code to make the bean an event source. The code to fire the sun event is similar to that for firing action events above.

Adding Details to the Generated Event Class

Now you have a SunEvent, SunListener, and SunEventMulticaster. However, the generated event object is nothing but a subclass of java.util.EventObject; you need to add information to it, namely the date and status of being risen or not.

Open the SunEvent in the BeanInfo page. Note that SunEvent is not a bean, but you can still use the BeanInfo editor to create the get methods, treating the *date* and *risen* values like read-only properties. Start by creating a new read-only property named *date*, of type java.util.Date. Create the property as shown in Figure 8.18.

Two things to watch when creating this property:

- Make sure you change the property type. A very common error is to forget to change the property type, generating a String property rather than the type you wanted.

Figure 8.17 Extra event set information.

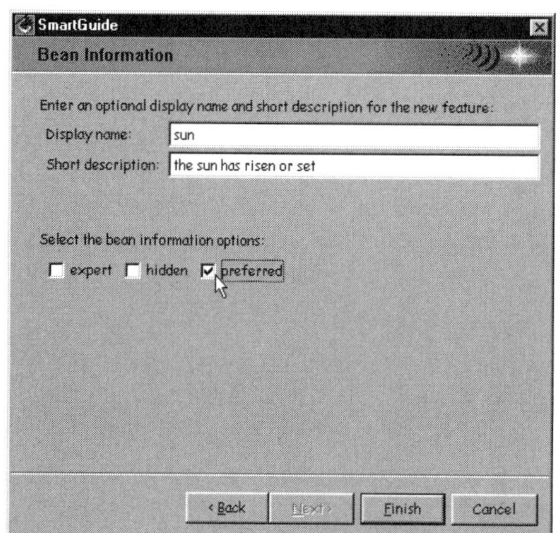

Figure 8.18 Creating the date property.

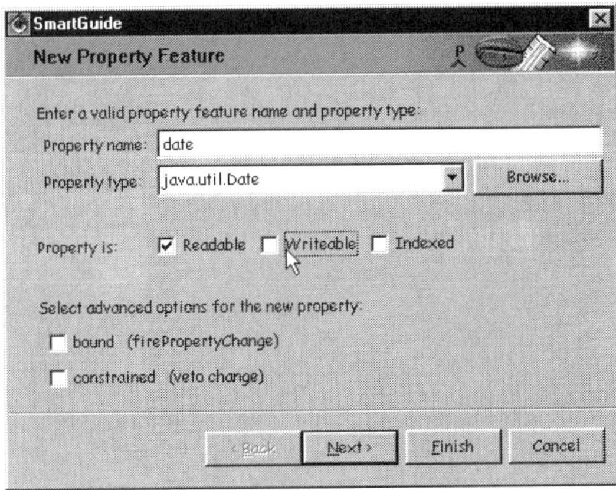

- If you use the **Browse** button to select the Date class, make sure you choose the *correct* Date class. Note that the window initially selects java.sql as the package. See Figure 8.19.

Create a boolean property *(risen)* in a similar manner. Be careful when creating boolean properties: Do *not* use the **Browse** button, as you would be selecting

Figure 8.19 Make sure you choose the correct package.

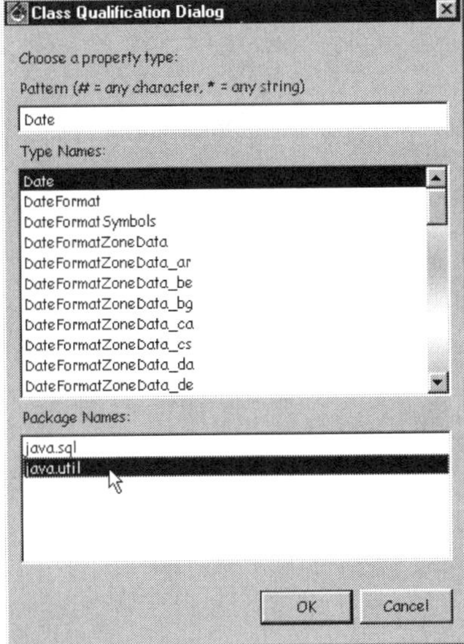

class java.lang.Boolean instead of primitive type boolean. (If you need to create a Boolean property for this or another bean, this is fine, but make sure you are choosing the correct type for the property at hand: boolean or Boolean.)

Next, provide a constructor that sets these properties. To do this, edit the SunEvent's constructor; change its code to look as follows. Note that this requires either importing java.util.Date in the class definition or explicitly qualifying it in this constructor.

```
public SunEvent(Object source, Date date, boolean risen) {
  super(source);
  fieldDate = date;
  fieldRisen = risen;
}
```

Because this is not being used as a bean, you can delete the generated SunEventBeanInfo class after creating these read-only properties. Remember that the event class is not being used as a bean: You will not be dropping it into a bean-builder tool, just using it to pass information between an event source and target.

Note that VisualAge for Java generated a getRisen() method, rather than an isRisen() method. The preferred style for boolean properties calls for an is method, so rename the getRisen() method to isRisen().

Firing the Generated Events

Finally, add a bit of code to WeatherStation's constructor to fire the sun events as before:

```
public WeatherStation() {
  super("Sun Watcher");
  setLayout(new GridLayout(0, 1
  Button riseButton = new Button("Rise");
  Button setButton = new Button("Set");
  add(riseButton);
  add(setButton);

  // make the "Rise" button fire "rise" SunEvents
  riseButton.addActionListener(new ActionListener() {
    public void actionPerformed(ActionEvent e) {
      fireSunMoved(new SunEvent(this, new Date(), true));
    }
  });

  // make the "Rise" button fire "set" SunEvents
  setButton.addActionListener(new ActionListener() {
```

```
    public void actionPerformed(ActionEvent e) {
      fireSunMoved(new SunEvent(this, new Date(), false));
    }
  });

  // Provide a means to close the application
  addWindowListener(new WindowAdapter() {
    public void windowClosing(WindowEvent e) {
      System.exit(0);
    }
  });

  pack();
}
```

This is the same as the WeatherStation constructor in Chapter 7 with the exception of the bold lines. The fireSunMoved() method that VisualAge for Java generates takes a different parameter from the handwritten fireSunMoved(). VisualAge for Java wants to pass a SunEvent, so you need to create it yourself.

To test the new implementation, copy the Student and WeatherTest classes from the previous chapter (in package effectivevaj.intro.eventsets). The results are the same as when writing the event code by hand. Compare the amount of work to implement by hand versus by using the BeanInfo editor. As you write more event sources, you will quickly see how productive the BeanInfo editor can be.

Deleting Event Sets

You can delete event sets in a similar manner as properties. Make sure you select the *event set*, not the individual events. By selecting the event set, the BeanInfo editor can present you a list of all fire methods, as well as the add- and delete-listener methods and the listener tracking variable.

Working with Methods

You can create methods in the BeanInfo editor, but it is generally easier to create them by typing them directly in the class definition or using the **Add->Method Template** command. The advantage to adding a method through the BeanInfo editor is that it enables you to add descriptive information about the parameters to the method, automatically adding knowledge of that method to the BeanInfo class. However, it generally takes more work to do so. You are better off creating the method outside the BeanInfo editor and resynchronizing the bean to list the new method. See *Synchronization of a Bean and its BeanInfo* later in this chapter for details.

Figure 8.20 Invoking the Create Method Feature SmartGuide.

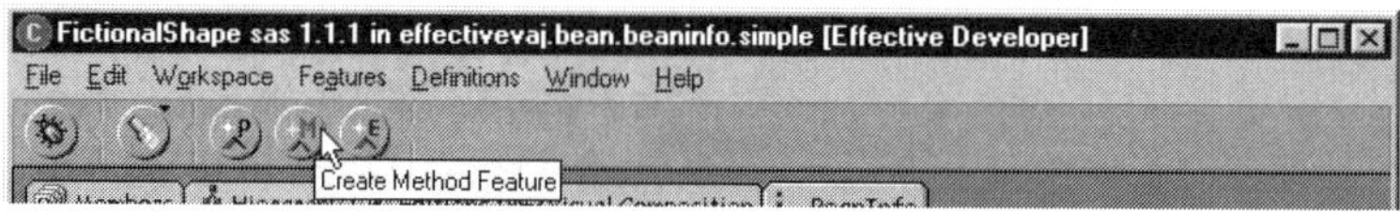

Creating Methods through the BeanInfo Editor

Pressing the Create Method Feature button, shown in Figure 8.20, on the tool bar of the BeanInfo editor or selecting **New method feature** from the **Features** menu displays the New Method Feature SmartGuide. This SmartGuide, seen in Figure 8.21, is significantly different from the Create Method SmartGuide discussed earlier. The main difference is in how you specify parameters.

You specify the name, return type, and number of parameters. Pressing the **Next** button displays a page for each parameter. On each parameter page, shown in Figure 8.22, you specify the name, type, and description of each parameter.

You can press **Next** to enter a description of the method, or press **Finish** to create the method and the associated BeanInfo descriptor. Note that this only creates an empty method; the code within the method is your responsibility.

Deleting Methods

You can delete methods in the same manner as you can properties and event sets. Note that in some cases, VisualAge for Java might not completely update the BeanInfo class after deleting a method. In these cases, you will need to choose **Generate BeanInfo class** from the **Features** menu to ensure consistency. (You can determine that you need to regenerate the BeanInfo class if the BeanInfo class has an error in it, flagged with a red X, after removing the method.)

Figure 8.21 Creating a new method.

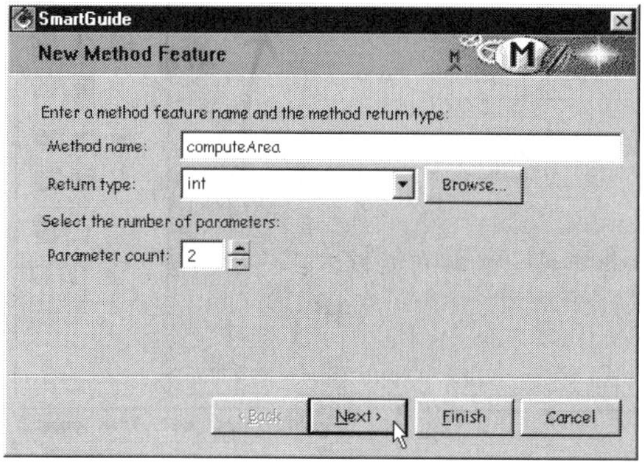

Figure 8.22 Defining a method parameter.

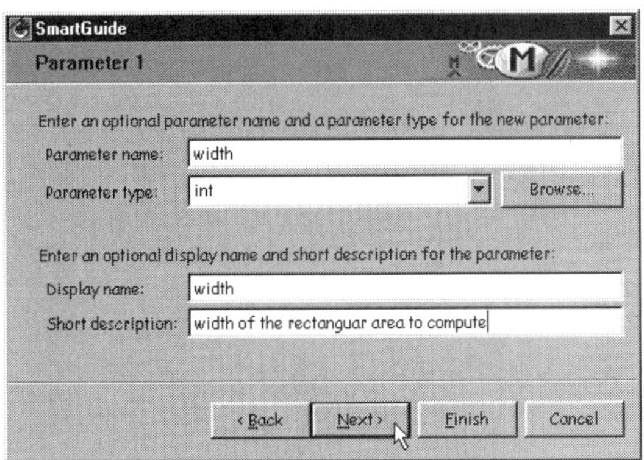

Synchronization of a Bean and Its BeanInfo

Sometimes the BeanInfo class and its corresponding bean lose their synchronization. The most likely cause of this is adding or removing methods outside of the BeanInfo editor. If your bean is not displaying all of the bean features it should, or the BeanInfo class is flagged with errors (red or gray Xs), you should ask VisualAge to resynchronize. In addition, if you see IntrospectionErrors while using a bean in the VCE, it most likely means the bean is out of sync with its BeanInfo.

To request resynchronization, choose **Generate BeanInfo class** from the **Features** menu. This will update the BeanInfo class to match what you see in the BeanInfo editor.

Adding Features to a BeanInfo Class

If you add features outside of the BeanInfo editor (by creating methods), or have added features to the superclass that are not currently visible, you can explicitly add those features to the BeanInfo class.

Choosing **Add Available Features**, shown in Figure 8.23, from the Features pane's pop-up menu (or from the **Feature** menu on the menu bar) presents a list of all introspected bean features, shown in Figure 8.24, that are not currently represented in the BeanInfo class. Select the features you want to add (use Ctrl-click to select multiple features) and press the **Ok** button to add them to the BeanInfo class. Once added, you can edit the feature information for them (attributes such as hidden, expert, and property editor) as you would any feature.

Adding features in the BeanInfo editor does *not* modify code in your bean. It only adds FeatureDescriptors to its BeanInfo class. This is especially useful if you subclass an existing bean and want to modify the BeanInfo class for a superclass feature (marking it preferred, for example).

Figure 8.23 Invoking the Add Available Features SmartGuide.

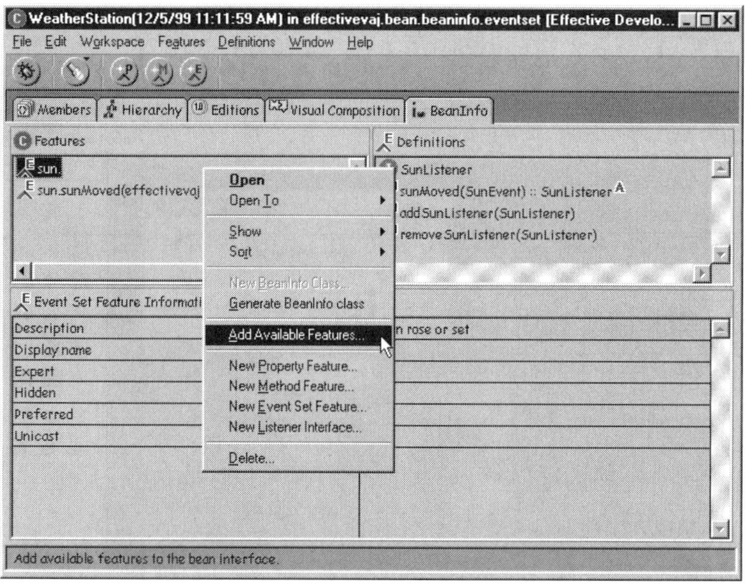

Figure 8.24 Adding a feature to the BeanInfo class.

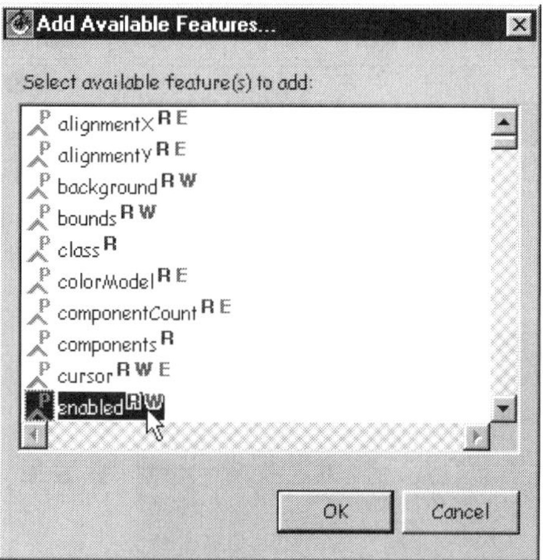

Summary

VisualAge for Java provides some of the best bean code generation capability available today. By making it easy for you to create and modify beans, it *encourages* their use. Take advantage of this: Think beans!

We now start to move from code to visual building. The first thing we need to discuss is the concept of extension versus that or composition. Once you understand the difference and the value in each, you are ready to begin using the really powerful tools in VisualAge for Java.

Extension and Composition 9

One of the keys to productive program development is reuse. Many classes, like Java's Vector and GUI components, are reusable by themselves. Other classes seem to have some or most of the behavior that you need. We would like some way to reuse that common behavior: Why rewrite the same code or visual design more than once?

Extension and composition can give you that behavioral reuse. *Extension* involves subclassing an existing bean and then adding to or modifying its features. *Composition* involves including instances of other beans whose features you want to leverage. You compose a larger bean by building it out of smaller beans. Both methods are powerful if you know when to use them.

This chapter discusses extension and composition, and provides a few common scenarios. With extension or composition, you can reuse any bean, though the extent of the reusability depends on the code in the original bean. We discuss some strategies to help ensure your beans are as reusable as possible.

VisualAge for Java is very bean-centric. If you strive to make many of your classes into beans, VisualAge for Java can provide a great deal of support for working with, extending, and composing those beans.

> **NOTE**
>
> Extension and composition are *not* mutually exclusive. It is common to extend a bean *and* enhance its functionality by delegating to other beans. This is the root of the effectiveness of visual composition. You can extend existing beans and drop delegate beans into a visual design area. The delegates perform some of the processing for you, such as computing partial values or displaying part of a user interface.

Creating Beans through Extension

Extension of beans is the key to successful bean reuse. Rather than trying to anticipate every possible use of a bean and provide features for all those uses, you start with the basic features you need for your current application. In later applications, you can subclass the beans and either add new features or override the old features to provide the enhanced functionality.

The most common reason to extend a bean is to change its behavior. The behavior change could be minimal, such as validating a new property value, for example. It could be more significant, such as adding new data to the bean or causing it to fire new events.

General Strategies for Easily Extendible Beans

Creating a reusable bean does not happen magically; you must plan for effective bean reuse. In this section we present some strategies to help you write easily extended beans without causing extra work or bloating your code.

Some textbooks claim that when you create a class, you should make it *complete*. A complete class is one that provides every possible or desirable way to interact with it. Reusable classes can be used anywhere; because you have anticipated all possible uses, they do not need to be modified.

If you are laughing right now, you are not alone. There are several problems with this concept:

Anticipating all possible uses is an impossible task. Someone will always find a way to abuse your class. The concept that you can be all-knowing is just plain silly.

Even if you *could* anticipate all possible uses, imagine what this does to code size. Your program, a simple phone book, should be only a few kilobytes in length. Anticipating that your PhoneNumber class could be used in to hold rate information, automatically determine if you need a dialing prefix, or other uses bloats the code *with no benefit to the current program*. Not to mention, chances are good that no one *will* use these extra features, and if anyone *does* need them, you probably missed a critical feature for their application, and they may create a new class from scratch.

All of that extra code clouds the design of your current program. When a reviewer or maintainer picks up your code, they must read through all of that extra code to find the methods you actually need to perform your task. This makes their jobs that much more difficult, not to mention the other, unused code, distracts them from reviewing or changing the used code.

To ensure that beans are maximally reusable *without* causing extra work or bloating the code, follow these simple rules:

All data *must* be private. When you create a bean, that bean class should be the *only* class that can directly modify its instance variables. Any other classes must use public set methods to make such a change. This preserves consistency of the state and allows useful extensions such as bound properties.

Most data should appear as properties. Unless there is a strong reason otherwise, (such as caching information in data or providing support for another property), make the data available as a property. You can restrict access to the property by making it read-only or by hiding it from visual composition through its BeanInfo class. Remember that get and set methods define *properties*, not the actual data. Exposing the data as properties allow subclasses to override the property methods if needed.

Most methods should be public or protected. Private methods should be a rarity in your classes. The reason for this is any subclass can override public and protected methods. When all data is private, overridden methods are safe; the subclass cannot modify the data without calling the superclass method. This allows maximum flexibility while maintaining integrity. To change behavior, a subclass overrides a method, replacing or modifying its behavior.

Modified behavior changes the parameters before calling the superclass method or changes the return values after calling the superclass method.

Replaced behavior does not call the superclass method, but it could call any support methods that are public or protected. Unless there is a *very* strong reason (one you could argue in front of the Supreme Court), you should completely avoid private and package-access methods.

NOTE

The exception to the above statement is generated code. Whenever a tool, like VisualAge for Java's Visual Composition Editor (VCE) generates code, it must be exceedingly careful about interaction with subclasses. If a subclass happens to provide a method that the VCE needs to generate, the result is either a compiler error or the subclass overrides the method, possibly destroying the GUI. Because of this, generated code often must use private methods.

Following these rules enables you to create simple, yet very reusable beans. No code bloat exists, because you perform only the tasks you need for the current project. Later projects can extend the bean, adding data or modifying behavior, with no impact to the base bean.

A Simple Extension

To help explain extension, let's look at an example. Suppose that you define a Person bean with a *name* property. This initial Person bean stores the name as an instance variable and returns it when asked. You can decide later that you want to have a new type of Person whose name always starts with an uppercase letter. No matter what name was passed to its setName() method, make sure it starts in uppercase, fixing the value if necessary.

Start with the existing Person bean, which looks as follows:

```
package effectivevaj.bean.extension.simple;

import java.io.Serializable;

public class Person implements Serializable {
  private String fieldName;

  public String getName() {
    return fieldName;
  }

  public void setName(String name) {
    fieldName = name;
  }
}
```

Suppose that you wanted to make sure the person's name always began with a capital letter. You could provide a subclass that changes the way the setName() method works. Recall that this can be done in VisualAge for Java via the Members tab of the class browser. This general technique is discussed in Chapter 2 "Creating Code," using inheritance filters to choose the methods to edit.

1. Create a CapitalizingPerson bean, extending the Person bean. Do this by using the Add Class SmartGuide (the green C icon on the toolbar) and set its superclass to effectivevaj.bean.extension.Person.
2. Open the CaptializingPerson bean to its Members tab.
3. Set method visibility **To Root Minus One**, by pressing the Root Minus One button above the methods list, as shown in Figure 9.1.

   Setting the visibility **To Root Minus One** shows all methods defined in any class above Person, other than Object. In this example, it is used to help override a method in Person. This is the *safest* way to override methods, as you *cannot* get the method signature wrong. You just click on the method, edit, and save. Poof! Overridden method!
4. Next, edit the setName() method as follows:

Figure 9.1 Setting visibility *to* root minus one.

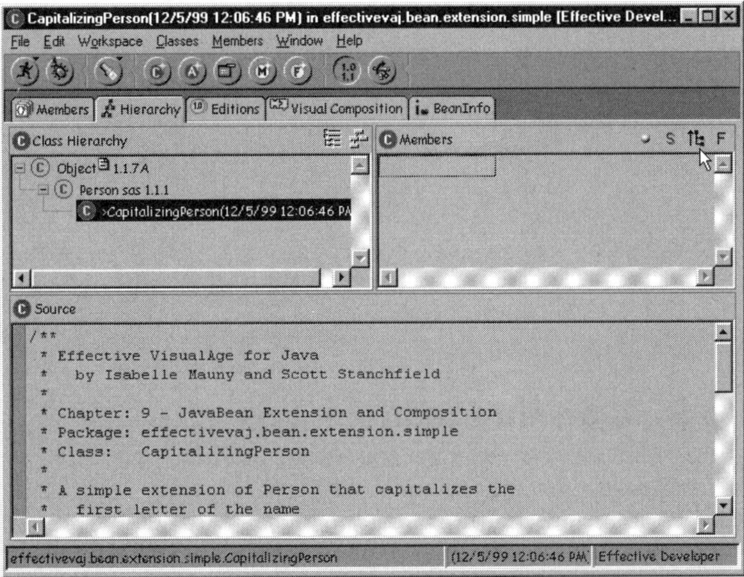


```
/**
 * Sets the name property (java.lang.String) value.
 * Before setting, ensure the first character is upper case
 * @param name The new value for the property.
 * @see #getName
 */
public void setName(String name) {
  if (name != null && name.length() > 0)
    super.setName(Character.toUpperCase(name.charAt(0)) +
                       name.substring(1));}

  if (name != null && name.length > 0)
    super.setName(Character.toUpperCase(name.charAt(0)) +
                       name.substring(1));
```

5. Press Ctrl-S to save the changes. When VisualAge asks in which class you want changes saved, as shown in Figure 9.2, select **CapitalizingPerson.**

The CapitalizingPerson class performs extra work but still uses its superclass' setName() method to set the property. This is a critical point. When extending beans, add functionality but let the superclass do its normal work when possible, especially if you are not sure what the superclass does in the method.

Figure 9.2 Selecting target for method override.

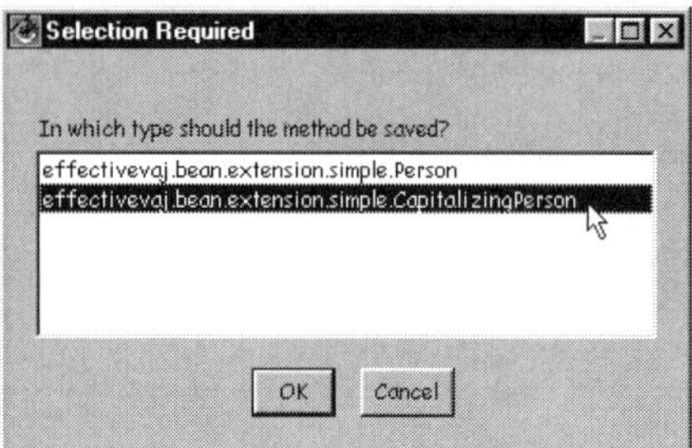

Extending to Bind an Unbound Property

This is a specific case of bean extension but is useful enough to warrant detailed discussion. Many beans have properties that would be more useful if bound. As we will see in Chapter 12, "Connections," VisualAge for Java provides powerful support for bound-property use during visual composition.

For example, java.awt.TextField's *text* property is not bound. Instead, it fires a separate event, TextEvent, whenever its text changes. It would be much more useful if the text property were bound, so we could take advantage of bound-property support during visual composition.

To bind the text property, intercept the TextField's TextEvent and fire a PropertyChangeEvent for the text property. Let's create a subclass of TextField that listens to its own TextEvent. You also need to tell its BeanInfo class that the text property is now bound. To create a BoundTextField:

1. Create a new subclass of TextField called BoundTextField, shown in Figure 9.3. Set it to implement TextListener on the second page of the wizard shown in Figure 9.4.
2. Open BoundTextField to the BeanInfo editor.
3. Create a new property called *dummy* of any type and make it bound, as in Figure 9.5. This causes VisualAge to create the extra support for bound properties. This is a useful trick to obtain the PropertyChangeSupport instance and add/removePropertyChangeListener() methods.
4. Delete the dummy property, as shown in Figure 9.6. This leaves the new class with only the bound property support.
5. Choose **Add Available Features** from the Features menu.
6. Select the text property, as shown in Figure 9.7, and press **Ok** to add it to the BeanInfo class.

Figure 9.3 Creating BoundTextField.

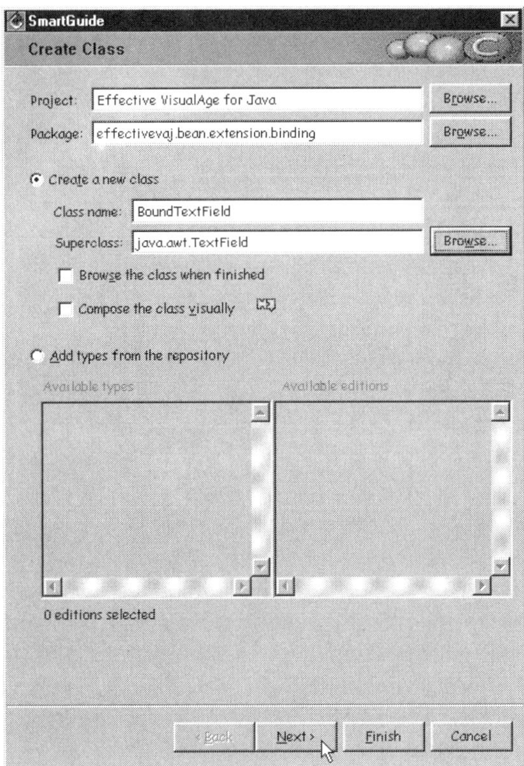

7. Select the text property and change its bound attribute to true, as shown in Figure 9.8. This tells the bean builder tools that it can use the property as a bound property.
8. Add code to the textValueChanged() method to fire the PropertyChangeEvent:

```
public void textValueChanged(TextEvent e) {
  firePropertyChange("text",null,getText());
}
```

9. Change the constructors to have the TextField listen to itself for change notification:

```
/**
 * BoundTextField constructor comment.
```

Figure 9.4 Make BoundTextField implement TextListener.

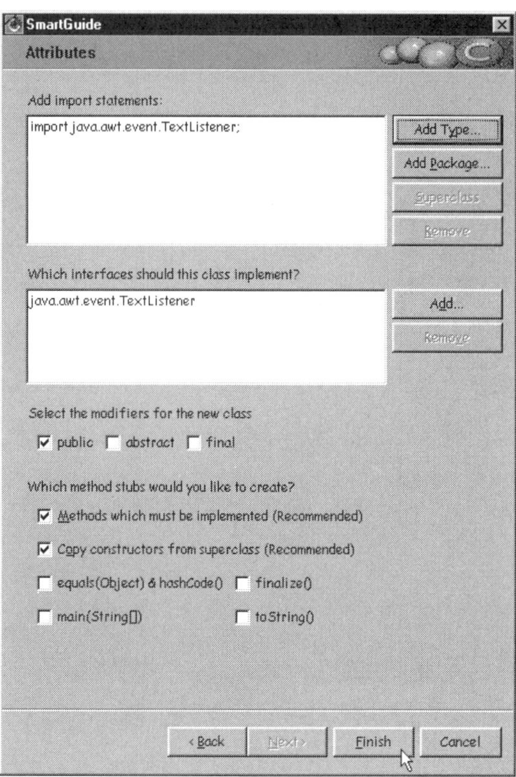

Figure 9.5 Creating a dummy property for bound-property support.

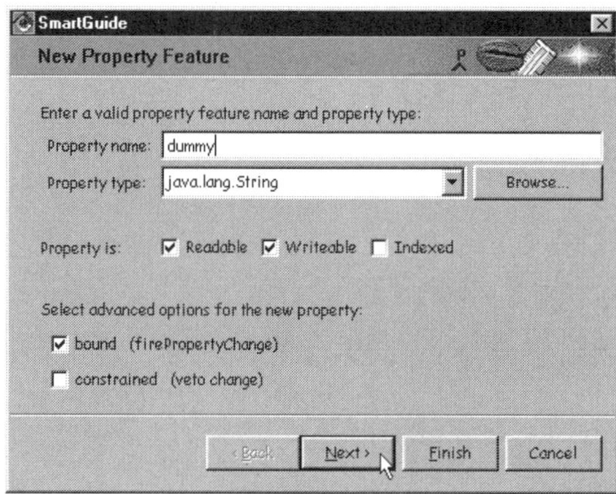

Figure 9.6 Deleting the dummy property.

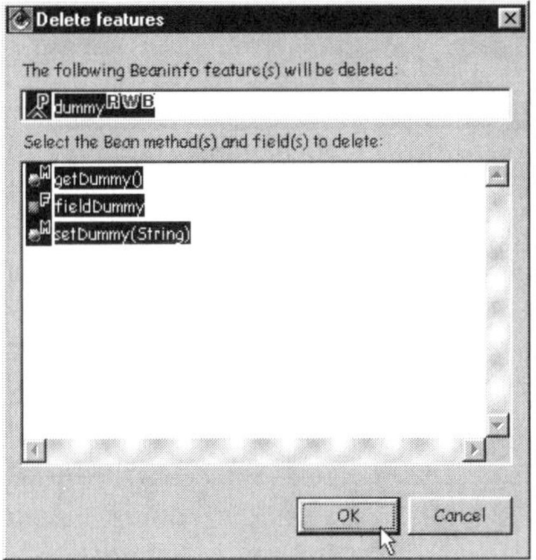


```
 */
public BoundTextField() {
  super();
  addTextListener(this);
}

/**
 * BoundTextField constructor comment.
 * @param columns int
 */
```

Figure 9.7 Adding the text property.

Figure 9.8 Flagging *text* as a bound property.

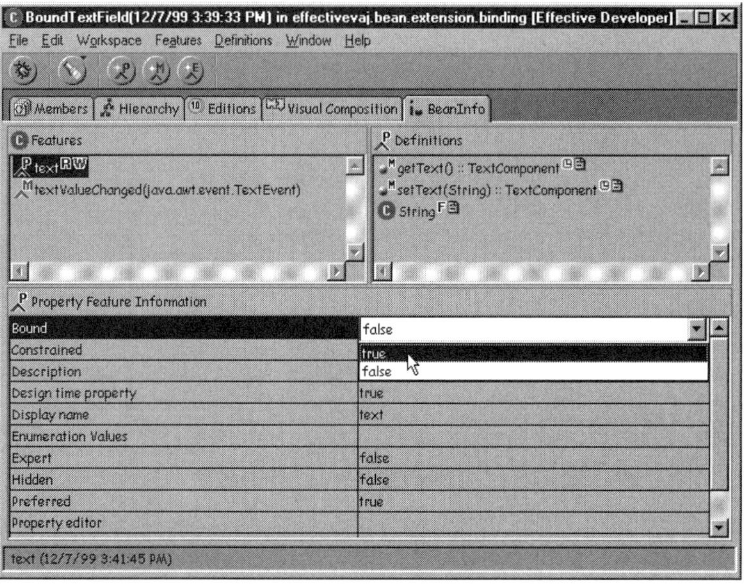


```
public BoundTextField(int columns) {
  super(columns);
  addTextListener(this);
}

/**
 * BoundTextField constructor comment.
 * @param text java.lang.String
 */
public BoundTextField(String text) {
  super(text);
  addTextListener(this);
}

/**
 * BoundTextField constructor comment.
 * @param text java.lang.String
 * @param columns int
 */
public BoundTextField(String text, int columns) {
  super(text, columns);
  addTextListener(this);
}
```

The text property is now bound! We will demonstrate how useful this is inside VisualAge for Java in Chapter 12.

Binding Swing Components

Swing components require some extra attention. Swing is an extended GUI library developed by Sun. Swing is a code component in Java version 1.2 and above, and an add-on component for earlier versions of Java. VisualAge for Java version 3.0 includes Swing version 1.0.3. VisualAge for Java version 3.5 includes Java version 1.2.2.

Most Swing GUI components extend class JComponent, which already has a firePropertyChange() method. Because of this, you need to modify the process described previously when binding Swing components. Fortunately, it is even easier to bind properties of Swing components

For example, let's bind the text property of JTextField. This process applies to com.sun.java.swing.JTextField (Swing 1.0.x, in VisualAge for Java version 3.0) or javax.swing.JTextfield (Java 1.2 and above, in VisualAge for Java version 3.5). (We will discuss the different Swing packages in Chapter 18, "Using AWT and Swing in the VCE.")

Bind JTextField's text property as follows:

1. Create a subclass of JTextField called BoundJTextField. Make it implement Swing's DocumentListener class (in package com.sun.java.swing .event or javax.swing.event). Make sure that **Methods which must be implemented** is selected on the second page of the wizard. This will generate stubs for the required DocumentListener methods.
2. Add code to fire the PropertyChangeEvent to the insertUpdate(), changedUpdate(), removeUpdate() methods:

```
public void changedUpdate(DocumentEvent arg1) {
  firePropertyChange("text", null, getText());
}

public void insertUpdate(DocumentEvent arg1) {
  firePropertyChange("text", null, getText());
}

public void removeUpdate(DocumentEvent arg1) {
  firePropertyChange("text", null, getText());
}
```

3. Add code to each constructor to make BoundJTextField listen to its own model. Note that whenever you deal with changes in Swing components, you should always look at the model (in this case, the *document* property) for change notification.

```
/**
 * BoundJTextField constructor comment.
 */
public BoundJTextField() {
  super();
  getDocument().addDocumentListener(this);
}

/**
 * BoundJTextField constructor comment.
 * @param arg1 int
 */
public BoundJTextField(int arg1) {
  super(arg1);
  getDocument().addDocumentListener(this);
}

/**
 * BoundJTextField constructor comment.
 * @param arg1 java.lang.String
 */
public BoundJTextField(String arg1) {
  super(arg1);
  getDocument().addDocumentListener(this);
}

/**
 * BoundJTextField constructor comment.
 * @param arg1 java.lang.String
 * @param arg2 int
 */
public BoundJTextField(String arg1, int arg2) {
  super(arg1, arg2);
  getDocument().addDocumentListener(this);
}

/**
 * BoundJTextField constructor comment.
 * @param arg1 javax.swing.text.Document
 * @param arg2 java.lang.String
 * @param arg3 int
 */
public BoundJTextField(Document arg1, String arg2,
```

```
                             int arg3) {
    super(arg1, arg2, arg3);
    getDocument().addDocumentListener(this);
}
```

4. Open BoundJTextField to the BeanInfo editor, and choose **Generate BeanInfo Class** from the Features menu to create a BeanInfo class.
5. Add the available feature *text* as we did for BoundTextField, and flag the text property as bound.

Now the JTextField's text property is bound. We will use these bound text fields in Chapter 12 to help us synchronize the text property with properties in other beans. They will also be critical for easy application of the model/view/controller paradigm, discussed in Chapter 15, "Model-View-Controller in the VCE."

Creating Beans through Composition

Composition is the act of creating a new bean as a collection of other beans. The new bean does not *inherit* functionality, but it can *delegate* tasks to its constituents.

Think of a typical large company. The corporate structure of such a company is usually hierarchical. Managers hire employees to perform tasks. Some of these employees could be managers as well, hiring more employees below them. When a top-level manager has a task to complete, such as "produce the next version of product X," he delegates the task to his subordinate employees. Perhaps he asks one to estimate the cost of producing that version. The employee tasked with the cost could be a manager himself, who delegates parts of the task to employees who determine cost of design, development, marketing, and release preparation.

Your bean can delegate *any* of its features to other classes. From the outside, it appears as though your bean is performing the requested task. However, it actually asks some other beans to perform parts of its task and collates the results. To examine this concept, let's create beans for the previous scenario.

A Simple Delegation Scenario

For this example, create a class named Task that represents the requested work. This will be an empty class:

```
package effectivevaj.bean.extension.delegation;

public class Task {
}
```

In a real application, Task would contain data that the experts could examine when making their cost estimates.

Next, define the beans that perform the real tasks. Start with a CostEstimator interface, which defines a how other classes can ask for a cost estimate for a specified task. Each CostEstimator-implementing bean returns the cost that *his* area requires for the project. Define four such implementers:

DesignGuru. Determines estimated cost to design the application

DevelopmentGuru. Determines estimated cost to code the application

MarketingGuru. Determines the estimated advertising budget for the application

ReleaseGuru. Determines the estimated cost to produce the CDs, packaging and distribute the application

The big boss at our fictional company assigns to an EstimationManager the overall responsibility for determining the cost of the application. The EstimationManager delegates this job to each of his gurus and sums the results.

You can now create all four gurus, each defining an estimateCost() method. This method would normally examine the Task passed to it and determine an appropriate cost estimate. For this simple example, each guru returns a fixed price when asked, as implemented in the following code:

```
package effectivevaj.bean.extension.delegation;
import java.io.Serializable;

public class DesignGuru implements Serializable {
  public double estimateCost(Task t) {
    return 40000.00;
  }
}

public class DevelopmentGuru implements Serializable {
  public double estimateCost(Task t) {
    return 30000.00;
  }
}

public class MarketingGuru implements Serializable {
  public double estimateCost(Task t) {
    return 10000.00;
  }
}

public class ReleaseGuru implements Serializable {
  public double estimateCost(Task t) {
    return 20000.00;
  }
}
```

Note that you make each of these classes implement Serializable, defining them as beans.

Create an EstimationManager class (just extending Object) and open it to the BeanInfo editor. The above gurus all report to the EstimationManager. Do this by adding a property to the EstimationManager for each guru. Using the BeanInfo editor's Create Property Feature SmartGuide, add the following properties:

designer. A readable, writeable, and bound DesignGuru

developer. A readable, writeable, and bound DeveloperGuru

marketer. A readable, writeable, and bound MarketingGuru

releaser. A readable, writeable, and bound ReleaseGuru.

Binding these properties makes it very easy to enable reassignment of roles. This reassignment would fire a PropertyChangeEvent, and EstimationManager could listen for the change and recalculate the cost based on the new individuals in those roles. Bound properties cost you little in terms of code and performance, but make your application much more flexible when you or someone else wants new functionality.

Finally, edit the EstimationManager's estimateCost() method:

```
public double estimateCost(Task t) {
  return getDesigner().estimateCost(t)  +
         getDeveloper().estimateCost(t) +
         getMarketer().estimateCost(t)  +
         getReleaser().estimateCost(t);
}
```

This is the essence of delegation. Track the delegates (the objects that perform the tasks) and call them to assist your task. A simple driver to test the delegation follows:

```
package effectivevaj.bean.extension.delegation;

/** A simple test of our estimation delegation */
public class EstimationTest {
  /** Create an EstimationManager and assign employees
   *    to him. Then ask how much a Task will cost.
   */
  public static void main(String[] args) {
    EstimationManager manager = new EstimationManager();

    manager.setDesigner(new DesignGuru());
    manager.setDeveloper(new DevelopmentGuru());
    manager.setMarketer(new MarketingGuru());
    manager.setReleaser(new ReleaseGuru());
```

```
    double cost = manager.estimateCost(new Task());
    System.out.println("Estimate is " + cost);
  }
}
```

When run, this test produces the anticipated result:

```
Estimate is 100000.0
```

Summary

Extension and composition are powerful concepts, helping you build new functionality from existing code. Before beginning new development, examine your existing code to see if you can reuse it. Often you can extend an existing class and change its behavior slightly to perform the required task. Other times you can combine the functionality of several classes into one, possibly modifying the results.

Extension and composition provide the root of the effectiveness of visual composition. You can extend existing beans and drop delegate beans into a visual design area. The delegates perform some of the processing for you, such as computing partial values or displaying part of a user interface.

With this in mind, let's turn our attention toward a powerful tool in VisualAge for Java—the Visual Composition Editor.

Bean Composition in the VCE

10

VisualAge for Java is primarily a bean development environment. Most of the tools provided work best when your class is a bean, even though facilities are provided for non-bean classes such as Enterprise JavaBeans and servlets. As we have already seen, you can develop beans via the BeanInfo editor, but that is just a start. The real power of VisualAge lies in its Visual Composition Editor (VCE).

The VCE is a visual programming environment. You can drag and drop beans in a design window and draw lines between those to set up event handling. The result is a new, bigger bean you can drop in a design window to help create other, still bigger beans. The VCE, shown in Figure 10.1, provides bean *composition*, truly using beans as building blocks to form more complex beans, applications, and applets.

This chapter introduces the basic structure of the VCE and walks through the creation of a sample application and applet. The remaining chapters in this section of the book cover the details of working with beans and visual design patterns that can improve your productivity and the maintainability of your beans.

I Didn't Mean to Do That!

Before we show you how to use the VCE, let's think about safety and error correction. It is very easy to make mistakes during visual composition. Most of these mistakes involve moving components that you did not want to move, changing properties for the wrong component, or accidentally deleting components.

Before you start changing a visual composition, *version the class*. It is much easier to drop back to a previous version than recreate the entire design from scratch. Generally, it is a good idea to version anytime you hear yourself say "Cool! That works!" (Versioning is covered in Chapter 4, "Using Version Control.")

However, if you forgot to version, or have not done so recently, there is still hope for recovery. The VCE provides an undo feature with a rather deep memory. As soon as you notice a mistake, choose **Edit->Undo**, or press Ctrl-Z. You can repeatedly undo to back out multiple changes. If you undo too many times, you can

Figure 10.1 The Visual Composition Editor.

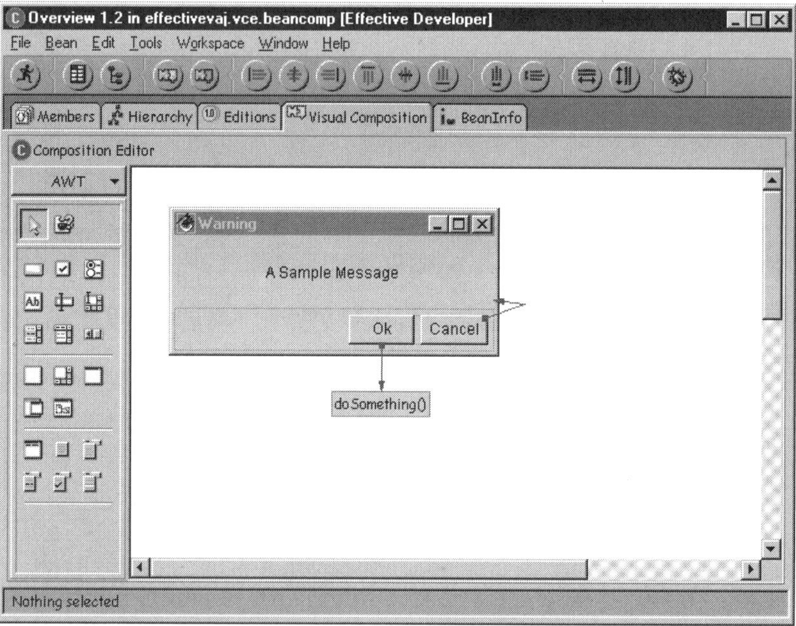

also redo the changes you want to keep by choosing **Edit->Redo**. Undo and redo enable you to restore a GUI that seemed to magically disappear in the smallest of mouse movements, or an accidental brush of the Delete key.

> **TIP**
>
> *Save early, and save often.* Some platforms that support VisualAge have a tendency to randomly crash. While not a pleasant thought, it is an important thing to keep in mind.

When developing your bean, *save it often*. We cannot stress this point strongly enough. Save a bean by selecting **Bean->Save Bean**, or, more simply, by pressing Ctrl-S. When you save your bean, the VCE generates code based on the current visual design.

Occasionally, you will change the interface of a bean used in a visual design. If this happens, the previously generated code might no longer be valid. To correct this, you can open a visual design and choose **Bean->Regenerate Code**.

Basic VCE Operation

Before we get to the details, we should look at the general VCE operation so you can see how each piece fits in. You use the VCE to build a *composite bean*, the class you are visually editing. We call this a composite bean because we build it by combining other beans. The bean being edited *is composed* of other beans.

The VCE provides a general working area, called the *design area* (also called the *free-form surface*) into which you drop beans. Think of the design area as your blueprint for the composite bean. Any beans that you drop in the design area become part of the composite bean. You compose GUIs by dropping visual beans inside container beans, applying layout managers for proper positioning. Use of layout managers is discussed in Chapter 11, "Layout Management."

> **NOTE**
>
> Visual beans are beans that extend java.awt.Component (directly or indirectly) and have a visible user interface when run. Container beans extend java.awt.Container (a subclass of java.awt.Component), enabling you to place other visual beans inside them. Nonvisual beans do not extend java.awt.Component. You can drop any bean in the design area.

You select beans to drop from the *beans palette*. The beans palette lists many commonly used beans and also enables direct specification of a bean class name for choosing a bean. After dropping a bean, you can customize it using a *property sheet*, a table that lists property names and values for that bean.

Once you have built a GUI, you can connect beans together based on the events that they fire. For example, you can create a connection that calls the put() method of a hash table whenever the user presses a certain button. We discuss connections in detail in Chapter 12, "Connections."

The Beans Palette

The left pane of the VCE is the *beans palette*, shown in Figure 10.2. The beans palette contains images of several beans, similar to how an artist's palette contains several paint colors. You can select a bean from the palette and drop it in a visual design, making the palette suitable for frequently used beans.

The palette contains several pages that enable you to organize the types of beans you most frequently use. When you first install VisualAge for Java, the palette contains pages for AWT beans, Swing beans, and some miscellaneous beans like the Factory Bean (discussed in Chapter 17, " Factory Beans"). You can switch

Figure 10.2 The beans palette.

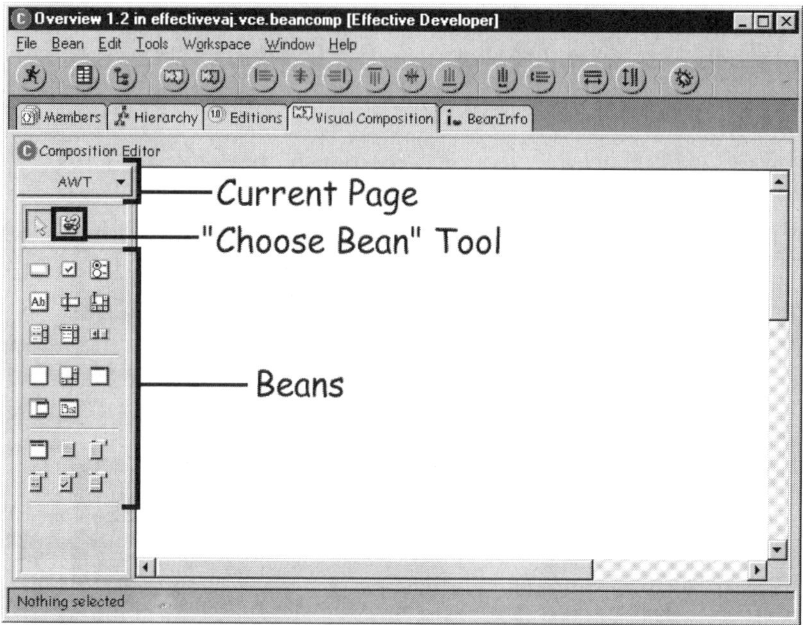

pages via the drop-down choice box at the top of the palette. You also can customize the palette, adding your own beans and pages.

All beans in the palette reside in the workspace. If you remove a bean from the workspace, VisualAge automatically deletes it from the palette. As we will see in Chapter 25, "Tool Integration," you can define *features*, bundled projects with installation information that can automatically add entries to the palette.

You can select beans in one of two modes: *single-use* or *sticky*. Single-use mode is the normal way you add a bean. It enables you to choose a bean and drop a single instance of it into the design area. Sticky mode enables you to choose a bean, and drop multiple instances of it in the design area. To use single-use mode, click on a bean in the palette, then click the target location in your visual design. To use sticky mode, hold the Ctrl key while you click on a bean in the palette. This enables you to place several instances of that bean in the visual design without reselecting it from the palette. Exit sticky mode by selecting a different bean, or clicking the arrow icon. We will discuss how you add beans to the design under *Dropping Beans* later in this chapter.

The beans palette is very convenient for developing with frequently used beans. However, you would not want to place *every* bean you create in it. Putting all of your beans in the palette would make the size of the palette unwieldy. In addition, you might need to use some beans only a few times.

To prevent palette bloat, the VCE provides a way to select beans that are not in the palette. The Choose Bean command enables you to select *any* bean that resides in your workspace *by name* for placement in your visual design. It is represented by the Choose Bean icon and, when pressed, invokes the Choose Bean dialog shown in Figure 10.3.

> **NOTE**
>
> You can access the Choose Bean command only through this icon; there is no menu option available for it.

The Choose Bean dialog requests the name of the class and the name to give the instance that you are creating. It also asks for the *type* of design element you are creating. The bean type can be any of three values:

Class. Creates an *instance* of the bean in the design. You must specify a valid bean for the **Class Name** entry; it must have a public default (no-argument) constructor so that the VCE can create an instance of it.

Variable. Creates a *variable* of the bean class type in the design. You can specify *any* class or interface name for the type; it does not need to be a bean, because the VCE does not create an instance of it. The differences between using variables and instances are discussed in Chapter 13, "Variables and Instances."

Serialized. Creates an *instance* of the bean in the design. Rather than specifying a class name, you specify the name of a file that contains a

Figure 10.3 The Choose Bean dialog.

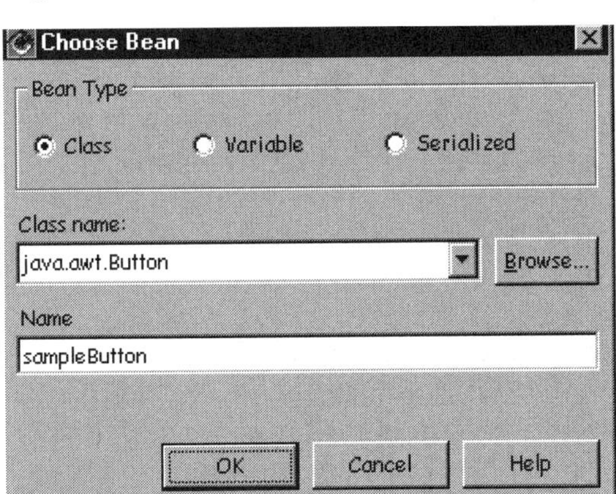

serialized image of the bean you want. The VCE will deserialize this file to create the bean instance.

Once you have selected a bean using this dialog, you can add it to your design in the same manner as though you had selected the bean from the beans palette. (We discuss dropping beans under *Dropping Beans* later in this chapter.) If you want to drop chosen beans in sticky mode, press and hold the Ctrl key and click the Choose Bean icon.

Customizing the Beans Palette

You can add beans to the Beans Palette in three ways:

- Add individual beans to the palette
- Add several beans from a single project to the palette
- Import a JAR file that contains beans

After adding a bean to the palette, it is ready to select and drop in the design area.

Adding Individual Beans to the Palette

You can add any bean to any page of the palette. To do this, select **Modify Palette** from the **Bean** menu or from the palette's pop-up menu, as seen in Figure 10.4.

This invokes the Modify Palette dialog, seen in Figure 10.5. From this dialog, you can add a class to any category, add or remove categories, and reorder or delete beans from categories.

To add a class, type its name in the **Class name** field, or select it by clicking the **Browse** button. To add a pre-pickled class (one saved through serialization), choose the **Serialized** radio button and type the file name in the **File name** field (the **Class name** field changes its name to **File name** when the **Serialized** radio button is selected). After selecting the class or serialized file, select a category from the list on the right and click **Add to Category**.

To reorder beans in a category, drag the bean to the position you desire. To delete beans from a category, select it and click **Remove**. Want a new page in the palette? Select **New Category**. You can also rename categories or remove them. Finally, if you would like to visually separate groups of beans in a category, click **Add Separator** and drag it to the desired location. Separators appear as horizontal lines in the palette.

Adding Several Beans from a Project to the Palette

If you have several beans in a project that you would like to add to the palette, adding them one at a time can be quite a burden. Fortunately, VisualAge for Java provides a simple way to select beans from a project. Instead of choosing **Modify Palette**, choose **Add Beans from Project** from the palette pop-up menu, as shown

Figure 10.4 Modifying the beans palette.

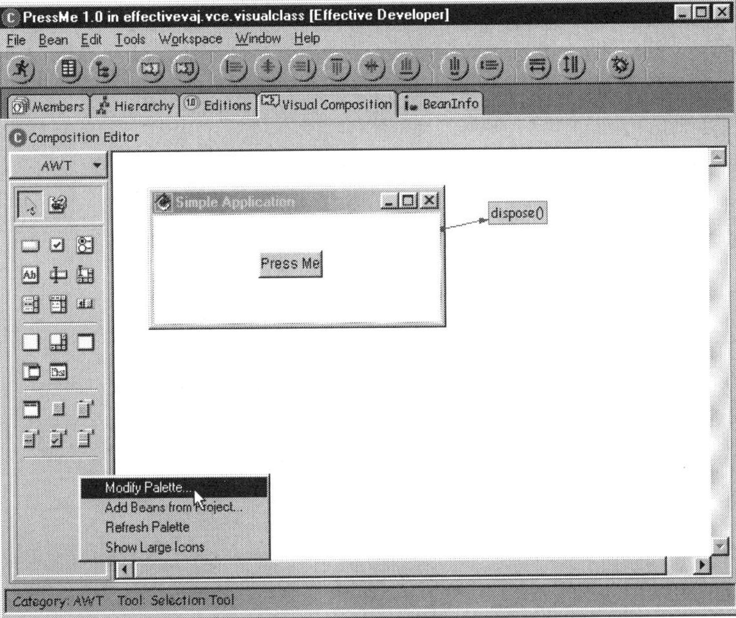

in Figure 10.4. Note that this option is not available from the **Bean** menu. This invokes a modified version of the Modify Palette dialog, seen in Figure 10.6.

Figure 10.5 The Modify Palette dialog.

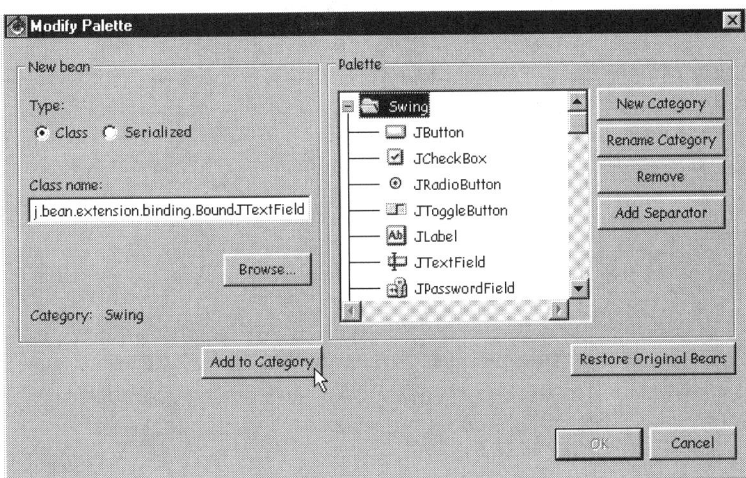

Figure 10.6 The alternative Modify Palette dialog.

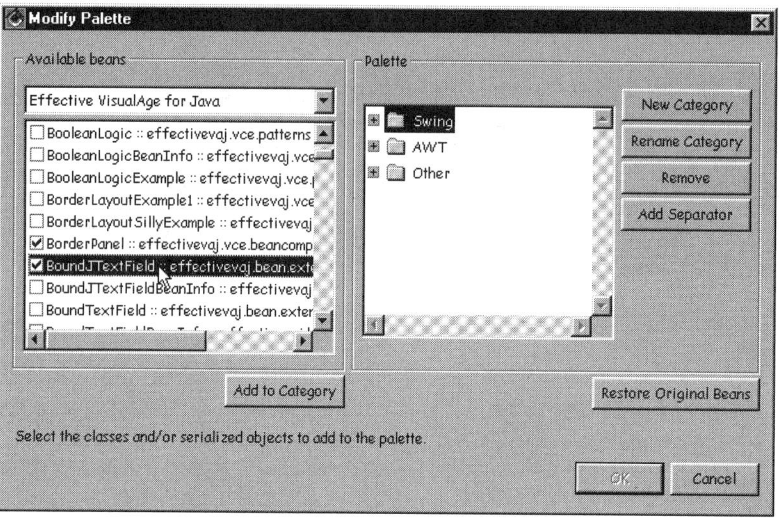

This version of the dialog enables you to select a project from the drop-down list, and then check which beans you want to add to the palette. You can add several beans to a category at once. If you want to add beans to different categories, select all that you want in one category, select the category, and click **Add to Category**. Then select the beans to go to the other category, select the other category, and click **Add to Category**.

Adding to the Beans Palette During JAR Import

All JAR files contain a manifest file. Depending on the contents of the JAR, the manifest might specify some of the classes in that JAR as beans. If so, VisualAge for Java will give you the opportunity to add these beans automatically to the beans palette. After importing the contents of a JAR, the Modify Palette dialog appears again. This version of the Modify Palette dialog is similar to adding beans from a project. All classes marked as beans in the manifest appear in the list, enabling you to add them to the palette.

The Design Area

The design area is shown in Figure 10.7. The design area is where you build your application by arranging beans inside the area. You can drop visual and nonvisual beans in the design area. You can use the design area to compose visual beans (user interface components) into a larger user interface for your application. However, the VCE is much more flexible than other user-interface builder tools.

You can also drop *non*visual beans in the design area, visualizing your program logic, or providing communication between visual beans in a user interface and the nonvisual business logic of your code.

To edit a class in the VCE, choose **Open to->Visual Composition** from its pop-up menu, shown in Figure 10.8. If you or someone else has previously edited the class in the VCE, double-clicking on a class will also open it to the VCE. If you already have a class browser open for the bean, you can click on its Visual Composition tab to start the VCE.

> **NOTE**
>
> By default, double-clicking opens a class to its class browser. You can change this option in the General page of the Options dialog to expand/collapse the class' subtree in the class list.

If the class is a subclass of java.awt.Component (it could be several subclasses deep), the *superclass* component is displayed in the design area. If the class is *not* a subclass of Component, the design area is initially empty.

Figure 10.7 The design area.

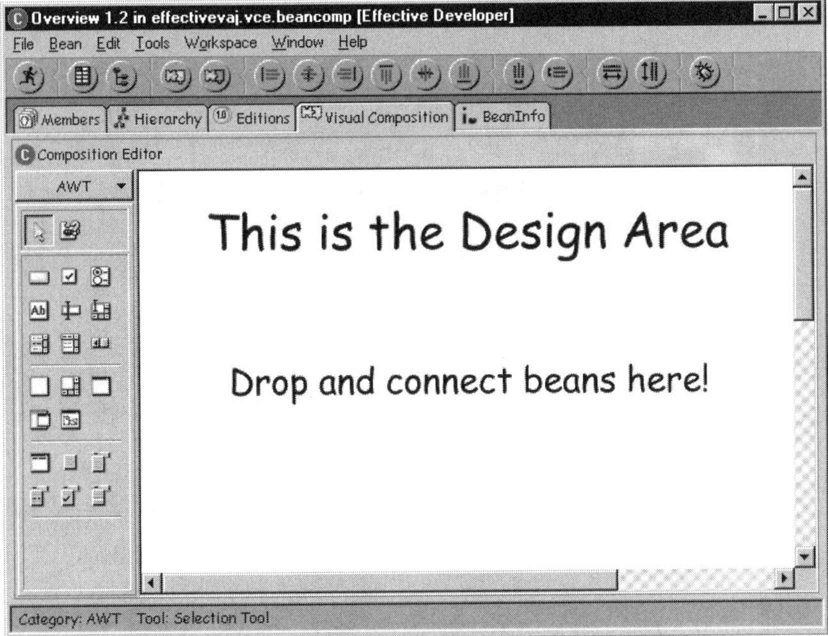

We start exploring the design area by discussing basic bean manipulation. You can manipulate and customize beans directly, interacting with the visual representations of the beans in the design area, or indirectly through the beans list (discussed under *The Beans List*, later in this chapter).

Dropping Beans

When you select a bean from the beans palette or through the Choose Bean dialog, the cursor changes to a crosshair. To add the bean to your visual design, drop it in the design area by clicking on the location in which you want to place it. If you press and *hold* the mouse, rather than click and release it, you can drag the component to its target location and then release the mouse to position it. When the bean is dropped, the cursor returns to its normal appearance. If you selected the sticky mode, the cursor will remain a crosshair, ready to drop more instances of that bean, until you select a different bean or press the arrow icon.

> **TIP**
>
> We strongly recommend that you always *press and hold* the mouse button when dropping components, especially when you drop a component into a container that has a layout manager. The press-and-drag combination enables you to see where the component will be placed, and displays "hint lines" for the various layouts. This function is described in more detail in Chapter 11.

Where you can place beans in the design area depends on the following criteria:

- Is the selected bean *visual* or *nonvisual*? Visual beans are those that extend class java.awt.Component (directly or indirectly). The VCE (complying with the bean specification) considers any other bean nonvisual.
- What is under the cursor when you drop a bean in the design area? Is the cursor over a bean? Is it over a component that extends java.awt.Container? Is it over a non-visual bean?

Based on these criteria, Table 10.1 shows the result of dropping a new bean in the design area.

If you drop a visual bean into a container bean, the new bean becomes as a *child* of that container. This has the same effect as writing code to add the component to a container. For example, if we dropped a button labeled "I'm nifty" into a panel, the generated code is similar to the following

```
Panel someParent    = new Panel();
```

Figure 10.8 Open to visual composition.

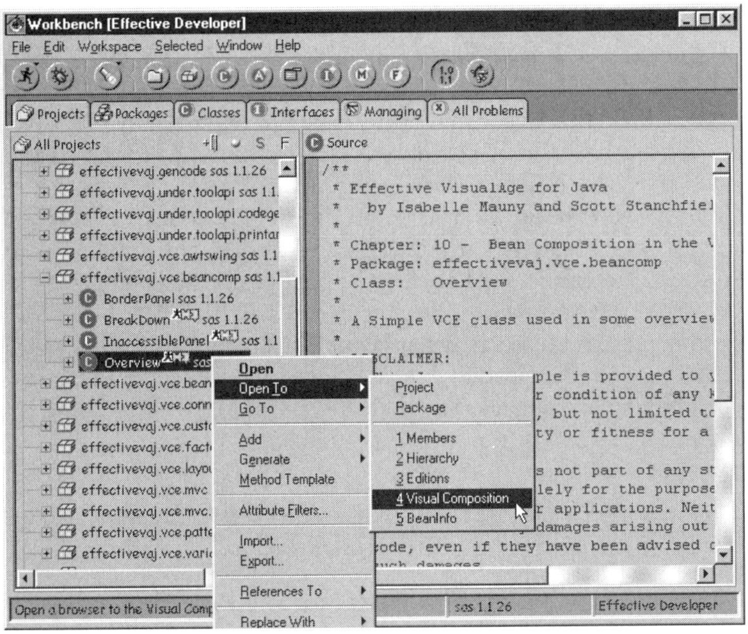

```
Button niftyButton = new Button("I'm nifty");
someParent.add(niftyButton);
```

If the parent container has an associated layout manager, different versions of the add() method are used to set the appropriate layout constraints. For example, if the layout manager were BorderLayout, the generated code would use an add() call like the following:

```
someParent.add(niftyButton, BorderLayout.NORTH);
```

Table 10.1 Result of Dropping a Bean in the Design Area

Type of bean being dropped	If dropped in a Container...	If dropped on an empty part of the design area	If dropped on non-Container component
Visual (subclass of java.awt .Component)	Dropped bean becomes a child of that Container	Becomes an independent bean in the design area	Illegal (cannot drop)
Nonvisual	Illegal (cannot drop)	Becomes an independent bean in the design area	Illegal (cannot drop)

In this example, BorderLayout.NORTH is a layout constraint that tells the border layout that we want the component to reside in the top section of the panel it manages. The use of layout managers in the VCE is discussed in Chapter 11.

If you attempt to drop a nonvisual bean in a container, or there is already a visual bean at that location in the container, the VCE indicates that this drop is illegal by changing the cursor to a slashed circle, as shown in Figure 10.9.

If you drop a visual or nonvisual bean in an empty section of the design area, it appears as an independent bean. It is not contained within any other bean, enabling you to drop nonvisual beans anywhere *and* drop *visual* beans to compose parts of your user interface separately. This provides a great deal of flexibility when composing your user interface. Rather than drop all beans into the main component (perhaps a frame, window or dialog), you can build smaller chunks of the user interface and then drag those smaller parts into the main component. As we discuss later in this chapter, composing your user interface in smaller pieces can make the task significantly more manageable.

Selecting Beans

You can modify, move, or delete selected beans that reside in the design area. To select a bean, click on it in the design area. The VCE draws a selection outline

Figure 10.9 An illegal drop.

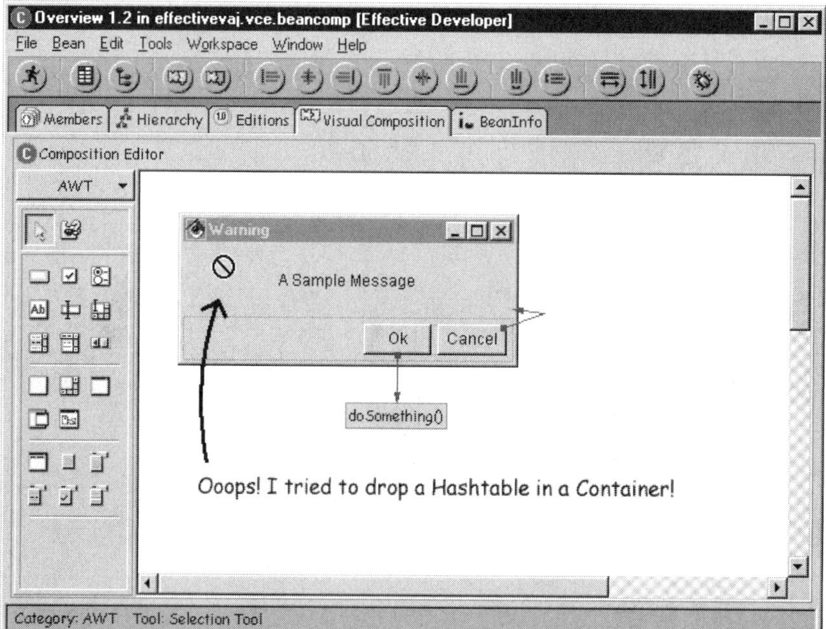

around the bean. If the bean is a visual component, the VCE also draws selection anchors around the component, as shown in Figure 10.10.

The selection anchors enable you to resize visual beans. When you move the mouse cursor over a selection anchor, the cursor changes. Note that the resize cursor has *two* arrows, shown in Figure 10.11. If you see *four* arrows, you would be moving the bean rather than resizing it.

To select multiple beans, hold the Shift or Ctrl key while you click on the beans. *We recommend you use only the Shift key for multiple selection* (see the warning below). As you select successive beans, the previously selected beans' selection anchors change color, as shown in Figure 10.12. White anchors indicate a selected component. Black anchors indicate the *anchor* component in the selection. Performing an operation such as right aligning components uses the anchor as the reference point. This is discussed in more detail in Chapter 11.

NOTE

You cannot resize beans that are contained in a container *that has an associated layout manager.* It is the responsibility of a layout manager to size and position its container's child beans.

Note that you can select multiple beans if they are all in the *same* parent container. If you select multiple beans, one of which is outside the current parent container, all of the previously selected beans will be unselected.

WARNING

Use the Shift key, rather than the Ctrl key, to select multiple beans. The Ctrl key is also used to copy components. If you select several components and drag the mouse even slightly while selecting them, the VCE copies them. You can easily end up with three or four times as many components as you want. If you accidentally copy beans while selecting them, press Ctrl-Z (by default) or choose **Edit->Undo**.

Pop-up Menus for Beans in the Design Area

Each dropped bean has a pop-up or context menu associated with it, as shown in Figure 10.13. Some of the options on the pop-up menu are covered in detail in this chapter; the other options are covered in other chapters.

Figure 10.10 A selected bean.

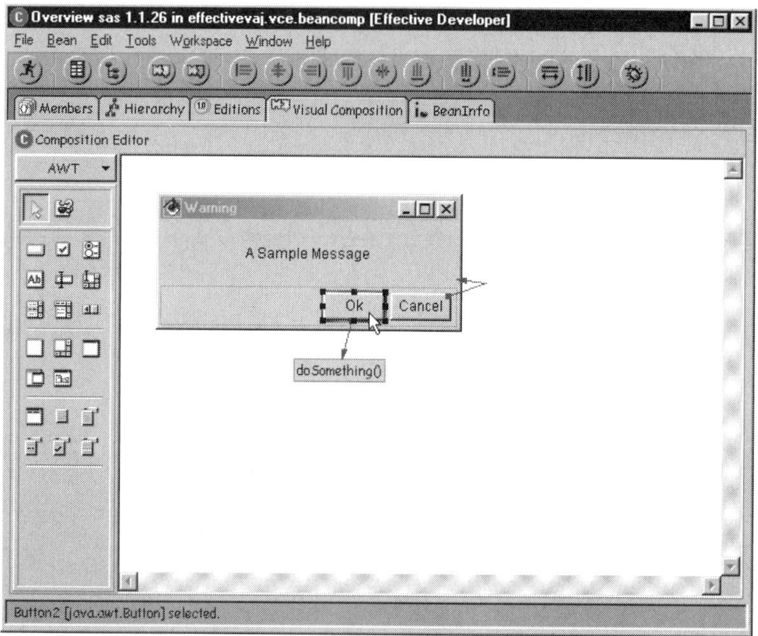

Figure 10.11 Resizing a bean.

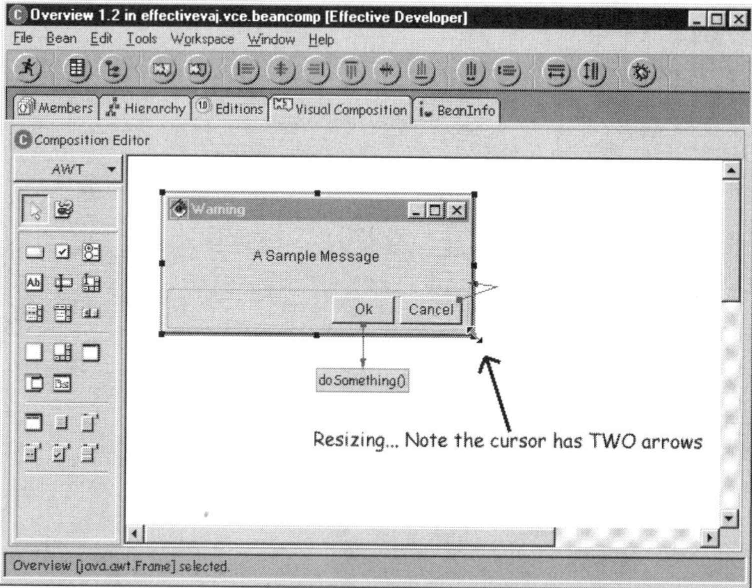

Figure 10.12 Selecting multiple beans.

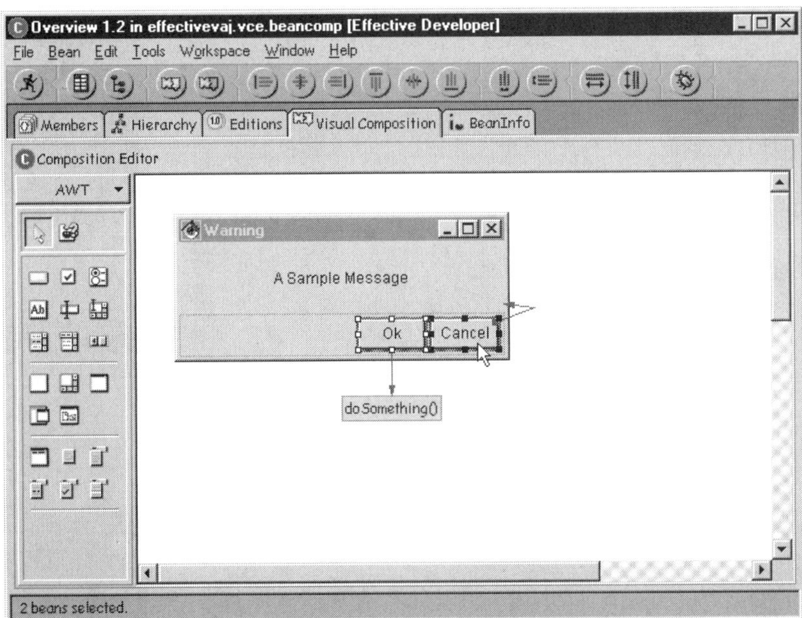

The pop-up menu contains several options:

Properties. Displays a property sheet for the selected bean(s) (see *Property Sheets*, later in this chapter).

Event-to-Code. Generates event-handling code for a bean's event to call a method in the composite bean (see Chapter 12).

Quick Form. Generates a GUI and connections from a bean to that GUI (see Chapter 11).

Open. Opens a class browser for the selected beans' type (see *Changing the Definition of a Used Bean*, later in this chapter).

Promote Bean Feature. Generates new features in the composite bean that delegate to contained beans (see *Promoting Features*, later in this chapter).

Morph Into. Changes the type of a bean, or changes the bean from an instance to a variable (see Chapter 13).

Change Bean Name. Changes the instance variable name used for the bean (see *Naming Beans*, the next section in this chapter).

Delete. Deletes the selected beans (see *Deleting Beans*, later in this chapter).

Connect. Generates event handling code for an interaction between beans (see Chapter 12).

Figure 10.13 Bean's pop-up menu.

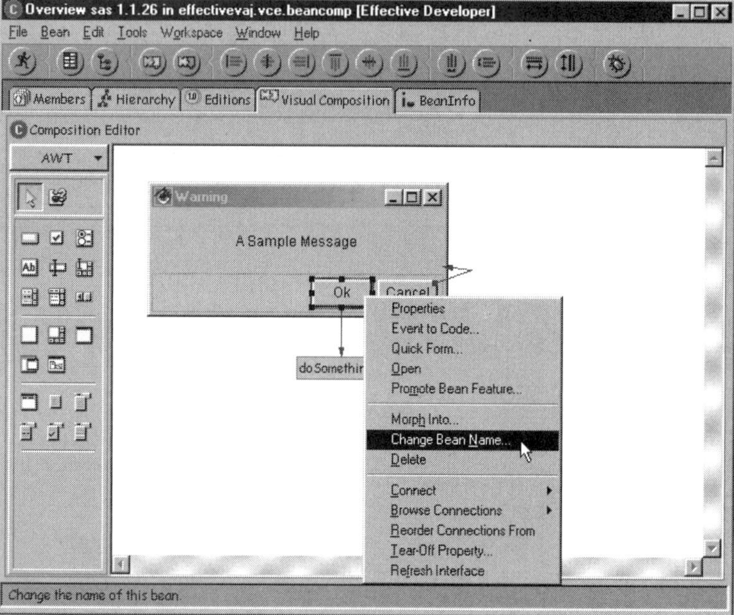

Browse Connections. Enables you to specify which connections are visible (see Chapter 12).

Reorder Connections From. Enables you to specify the order in which connections should execute (see Chapter 12).

Tear-Off Property. Generates a new variable to provide direct access to a feature within the selected bean (see Chapter 13).

Refresh Interface. Asks the VCE to re-read the introspection information for a changed bean definition (see *Changing the Definition of a Used Bean*, later in this chapter).

Open the pop-up menu by using the standard mouse or key sequence for your platform. For example, the default mouse setup under Windows defines the right mouse button to open the pop-up menu.

Naming Beans

An instance variable in the composite bean represents each bean that you drop in the design area. These instance variables, with some generated methods, make up the bean composition code. We discuss this generated code in detail in Chapter 19,

"Handwritten Code versus Generated Code." At this point, you need to know one thing about the generated code: The VCE bases the name of the generated instance variable on your selected Bean Name for the bean instance.

When you initially drop a bean, its bean name is its class name with a unique number appended to it. For example, if you drop three Button beans in the VCE, the VCE generates beans named *Button1*, *Button2*, and *Button3*. The VCE also generates instance variables *ivjButton1*, *ivjButton2*, and *ivjButton3* to hold a reference to those Buttons.

> **NOTE**
> The ivj- prefix stands for "IBM VisualAge for Java."

The source code is much more readable if you change these default names to more useful names. For example, you might want an *okButton* and a *cancelButton* rather than *Button1* and *Button2*.

To change the bean name, choose **Change Bean Name** from the beans' pop-up menu (shown in Figure 10.13) and enter the new name. The next time you save the bean, the VCE generates code using the newly entered name. You can also change the bean name from the bean's property sheets (discussed under *Property Sheets*, later in this chapter).

Moving Beans

To move a bean, select it and drag it to its new location. As you drag the component, the cursor changes its appearance to the movement cursor, which has four arrows as shown in Figure 10.14.

Be careful where you place the cursor! If it is on a selection anchor, the cursor changes to a resize cursor, which only has two arrows. If you are anywhere else in the selected component and begin to drag it, you get the four-arrow movement cursor.

If part of the component is visible, you can drag from *any* visible part of the component. However, if contained components completely fill it, or other components are in front of it, you will only be able to drag it by carefully grabbing its selection outline between anchor points. The cursor will change its appearance when you move it over the outline, as shown in Figure 10.15. *Do not* press the mouse button to drag the component until you see this cursor. If the component is completely behind other components, the beans list provides an alternative method of selecting and dragging a component. We discuss this under *The Beans List*, later in this chapter.

Figure 10.14 Moving a bean.

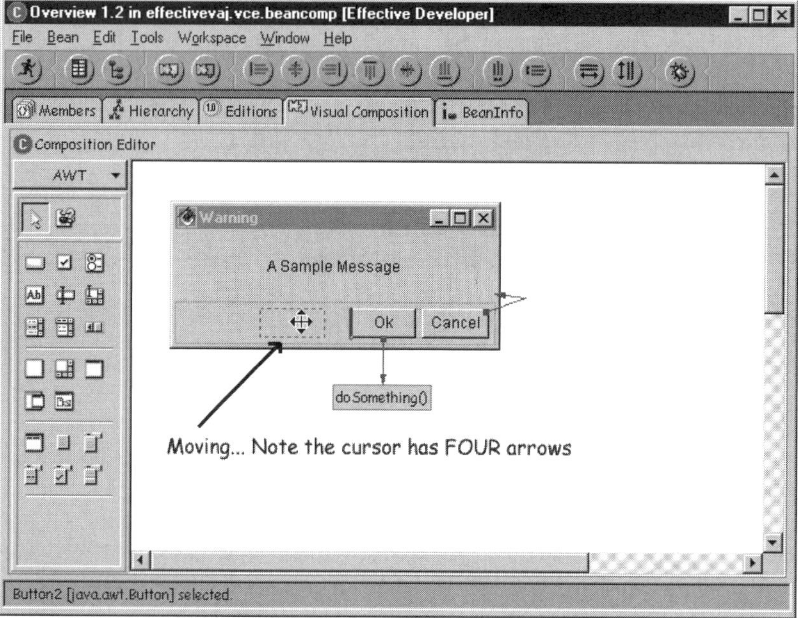

Copying Beans

Sometimes you drop and customize a bean (see *Property Sheets* later in this chapter) and decide you need another that is identical to it. For example, you may need two panels that use the same layout, or two buttons with the same foreground and background colors. Rather than dropping a new component in the design area and customizing it, you can *copy* an existing component to create a new component with the same property values.

There are two ways to copy a bean:

- Select a bean and choose **Edit->Copy** (or use the appropriate shortcut key on your platform, such as Ctrl-C on Windows). Then choose **Edit->Paste**, which turns the cursor into a crosshair so you can drop the new instance. Similar to Copy, there is a shortcut key for Paste for each platform, such as Ctrl-V on Windows.
- Hold the Ctrl key and drag the component.

Both methods have the same effect: The VCE adds a new instance of the bean with the same property values as the copied bean. If the copied bean is a container that has child components, the VCE copies the container and all of its contained components. This could be an entire *sub-GUI*, nested containers and components that form a section of your user interface.

Figure 10.15 Grabbing a filled container bean by its border.

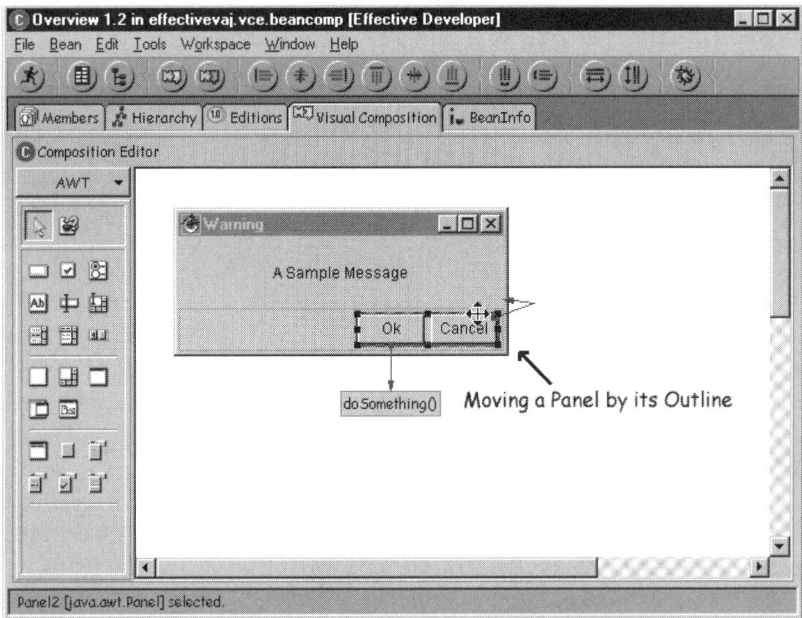

You can also copy beans from one VCE session to another. For example, suppose that you have a Name/Address form as part of a VCE design that you would like to copy and make a few changes to in another VCE design. You could copy it from the first VCE session using **Edit->Copy**, switch to the other VCE session, and use **Edit->Paste** to add it to the other GUI.

> **NOTE**
>
> Be careful when you copy part of a GUI from one VCE design to another. If the sub-GUI that you are copying can be useful in other places, you could benefit from making that sub-GUI its own class. This allows you to make changes to a single visual design and all users see the update.

Deleting Beans

Beans can be removed from a VCE design by selecting them and choosing **Delete** from their pop-up menu (shown in Figure 10.13). You can also delete selected components by pressing the Delete key.

If you want to delete the component but add it in another VCE session, you can choose **Edit->Cut** (Ctrl-X on Windows) to delete it but keep a copy of it on the system clipboard. You can then **Edit->Paste** it into another VCE session.

> **NOTE**
>
> If you accidentally delete beans, you can always get them back using **Edit->Undo** or the undo key (by default, Ctrl-Z in Windows).

Morphing Beans

Sometimes you create an instance of the wrong bean class. This most often happens between AWT and Swing components, where you drop a Button bean when you meant to drop a JButton bean. Fortunately, this mistake can be corrected.

The VCE provides a **Morph Bean** function (seen on a bean's pop-up menu in Figure 10.13) that changes a bean's type. "Morph" is a common shortened form of "To undergo metamorphosis," and usually refers to a computer graphics technique where one picture is changed to another by warping the image and changing its colors.

In its simplest form, morphing a bean only changes the type of the bean. However, you may not realize you want to change the bean until after you have carefully placed it, set several properties, and created connections between it and other beans. If property settings or connections (discussed in Chapter 12) are involved, the Morph Bean function examines the current and target type of the morph. If the set properties and connections are compatible (that is, the properties and connections exist in both the original and target types), the new bean retains them. If there are any incompatible connections, the VCE asks if you want to delete them.

It may seem strange to ask if you want to keep invalid connections, but the VCE does this in case you selected the wrong target type. You can always morph the bean a second time to correct the problem.

Changing the Definition of a Used Bean

Occasionally, you may want to edit a dropped bean's definition in another window. For example, suppose that you use a MyButton bean and decided to add a *hiliteColor* property to it.

To edit a used bean, open the dropped bean by selecting **Open** from its pop-up menu (shown in Figure 10.13). The Open option opens a class browser for the selected beans. You can then edit the code, modify features in the BeanInfo editor, or change the visual design.

Depending on the operation performed, the VCE may not detect that the bean definition has changed. You would know that this has happened if a new feature does not appear in the VCE, such as a new property not appearing in a property sheet, or a method or event not appearing in a connection dialog. If, for example, you add a property to a bean and the VCE does not appear to detect it, use the **Refresh Interface** option on that beans' pop-up menu. This asks the VCE to redetermine the introspection information for the bean, which will pick up the added property. Note that this is not always necessary, because the VCE automatically updates the bean definition when possible. If you want to be sure that the VCE sees any BeanInfo changes you make, you can always use **Refresh Interface** after editing a bean that is used in an open VCE session.

The Beans List

The beans list, shown in Figure 10.16, describes the containment structure of beans located in the design area. You open the beans list by pressing the Beans List icon on the toolbar or by selecting **Tools->Beans List** in the VCE.

Each bean dropped in the design area appears in the beans list. If you add the bean to a container, that bean will appear in a *subtree* of the parent container.

The beans list gives you an alternative interface for composing your bean. You can drop new beans on top of containers to add them, rearrange components by dragging them around in the tree, or delete them by selecting a bean and pressing the Delete key. The beans list provides all pop-up menu options for each bean, enabling you to perform the same tasks in the beans list as you could in the design area.

The beans list is also a valuable selection tool. Suppose you had designed a user interface where a Panel bean, managed by GridLayout, contained several Button beans. Figure 10.17 shows this panel as the CENTER component of a BorderLayout.

Note how the Button beans completely fill their parent panel. There is no way to select the parent panel in the design area. However, you can select the parent panel in the beans list by clicking on it, as shown in Figure 10.18.

Figure 10.16 The beans list.

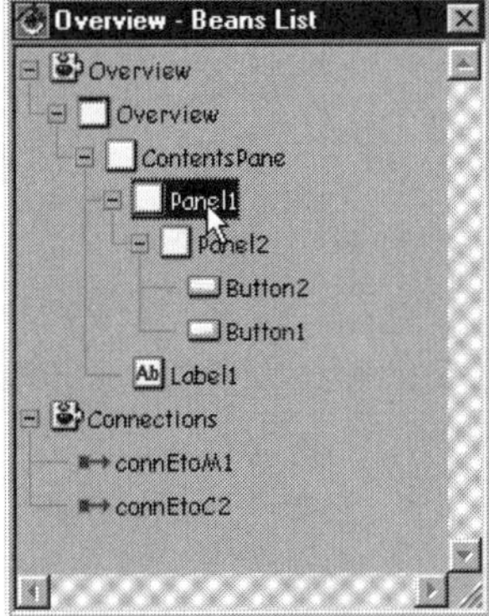

Figure 10.17 An inaccessible panel.

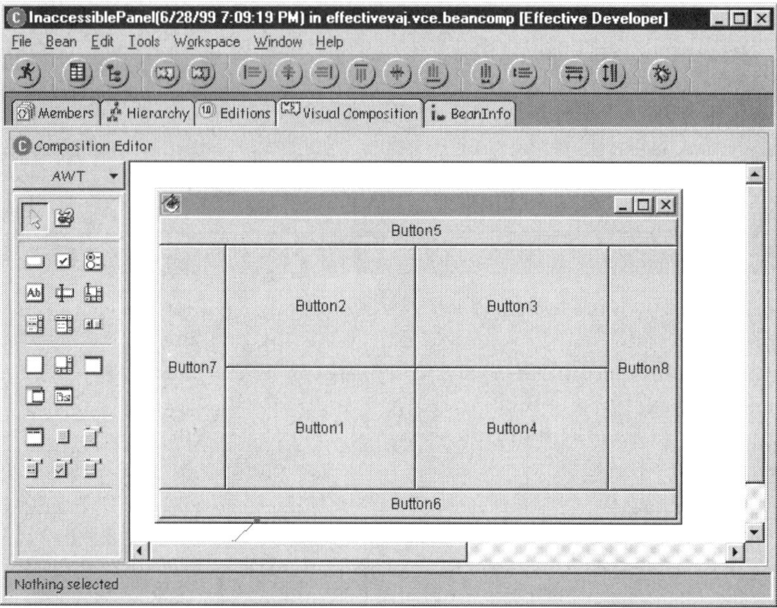

Figure 10.18 Selecting an inaccessible panel.

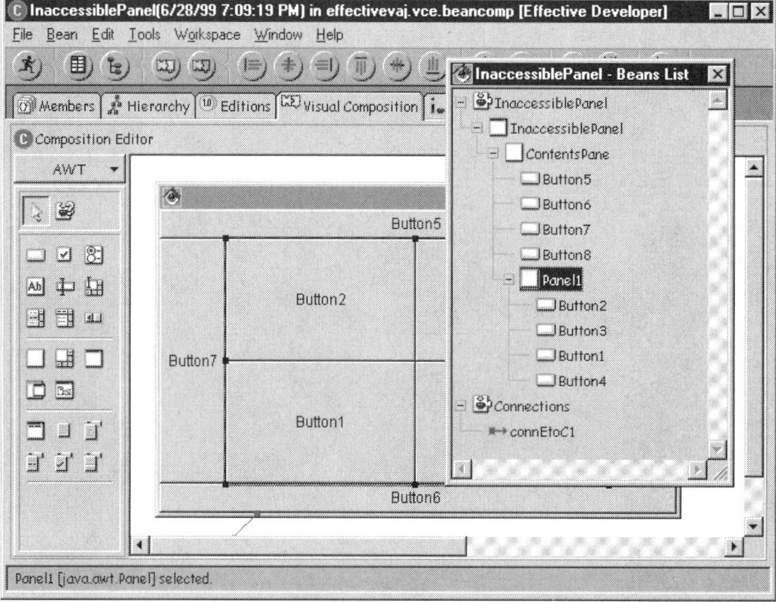

When you select a component in the beans list, the VCE also selects it in the design area. Note how the VCE selects the CENTER panel. You can now move or resize the parent panel by grabbing its outline in the design area with the mouse. This is a very important technique, as it enables you to access components that you cannot directly select in the design area.

There are a few drawbacks to using the beans list. First, you cannot select multiple beans. If you want to select multiple beans you must do so directly in the design area. (This, of course, means that you can select multiple beans only if they are visible.) Second, you cannot perform operations between the beans list and the design area. For example, you cannot drag a component from the beans list to a different parent container in the design area.

At the bottom of the beans list is a list of connections (event-handling code represented by lines) used in your visual design. This provides easy access to connections, as well as helping you locate which connections are which in the visual design. We discuss connections in Chapter 12. Note that you cannot create connections between a bean in the beans list and a bean in the design area.

Property Sheets

You can customize beans that you place in the design area to make them more useful. After you drop a bean, all of its properties have default values for that bean type. Several buttons labeled *Button1*, *Button2*, and so forth do not make a good user interface. You need to change a bean's properties (such as a Button's label) to help distinguish that bean from other instances of the same bean type.

A *property sheet,* shown in Figure 10.19, is used to customize a bean in the VCE. A property sheet lists all of the visible properties for a bean in a table. You can see the current values for the properties and change their values. The VCE lists any properties defined in a bean that are *not* marked hidden by the bean's BeanInfo class. Note that some properties might be marked expert properties, and will only appear if you select the Show expert features checkbox.

To access the property sheet, you can do any of the following:

- Double-click on a bean in the design area or beans list.
- Choose **Properties** from the pop-up menu for a bean.
-  Select bean(s) and click the **Properties** button on the tool bar.
- Select bean(s) and choose **Tools->Properties.**

At the top of the property sheet is a drop-down list of all beans in your design area. You can switch between beans by selecting a different bean from this list, shown in Figure 10.20, or by selecting a different bean in the design area or beans list.

Figure 10.19 A property sheet.

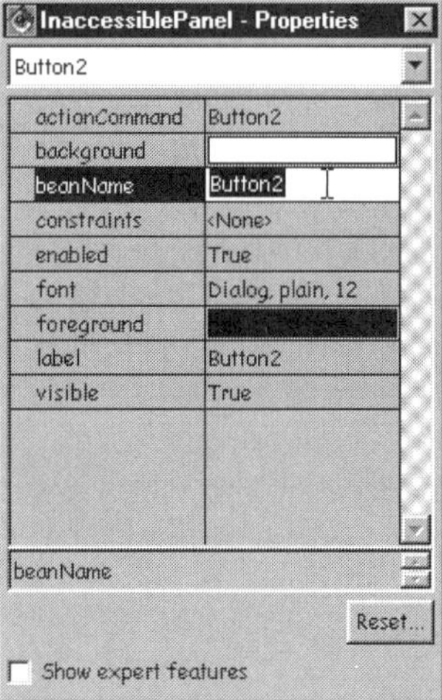

The property sheet contains a list of all bean properties defined in the selected bean. These properties are determined using introspection (discussed in Chapter 7, "Introduction to JavaBeans Components"); examining the methods in the class that start with "get" and "set"; or asking a BeanInfo class for a list of properties. The listed property names derive directly from the method names (*label* comes from the getLabel() method, for example) or from the display name attribute in the BeanInfo.

Figure 10.20 Selecting the bean to customize.

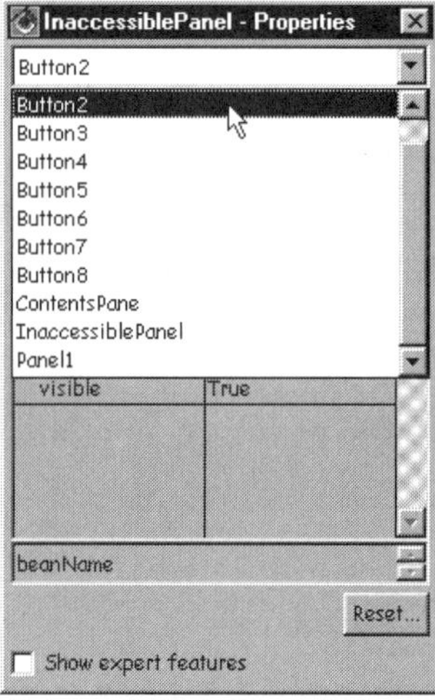

To the right of each property name is a field that displays that property's current value. Click on the value to modify the property. Many properties have simple textual inputs, as shown in Figure 10.21.

Other properties provide a *property editor* to enable better user interaction when setting a value. For example, a property that should accept a limited set of values could provide a drop-down list of those values, like the one shown in Figure 10.22. You can create your own property editors to provide easier or more controlled ways to change property values. Creation of your own property editors is covered in Chapter 20, "Bean Customization."

Immediately below the list of properties is the property description area. If you provide a short description in the BeanInfo for a property, the description area displays it when you click on a property in the property sheet, as shown by the highlighted box in Figure 10.22. If you do not provide a short description, or a BeanInfo class does not exist for the bean, the property name appears in the description area.

Expert and Hidden Properties

The list of properties displayed for the Button example is short. The property sheet provides property filtering based on the *expert* attribute in the Button class' BeanInfo. By default, the property sheet displays only non-expert properties, because most developers do not need to access the expert properties. If you do not see a property you need to modify, select the **Show expert features** checkbox at the bottom of the property sheet, as shown at the bottom of Figure 10.22.

Figure 10.21 Simple property value change.

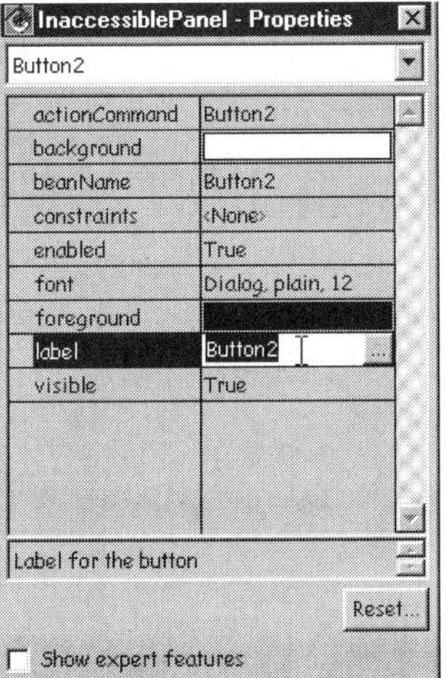

Figure 10.22 Property editor, property description, and expert checkbox.

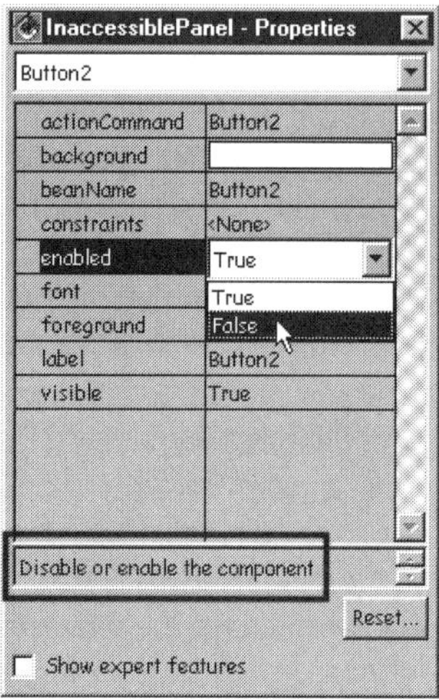

Even when you enable **Show expert features**, some properties do not appear in the property sheet. Any properties listed as *hidden* by BeanInfo will *never* appear in the property sheet. These properties are accessible via their get and set methods (which you can call in your handwritten code), but the property sheet excludes them because there is usually no reason for a developer to change their values visually. We recommend that you try to expose all of your data as properties, which makes it very easy for subclasses to override the property methods to extend or replace behavior. However, just because you have made the data available via property methods does not mean that users of the bean should be able to access them in a visual builder tool. Marking properties as hidden is the proper way to protect such properties from change in a visual builder tool.

Multiple Selection and the Property Sheet

Remember that you can select multiple beans in the design area. The property sheet displays "<Multiple selection>" in its drop-down list to enable simultaneous edits. Notice that some of the properties have been ghosted (that is, grayed out), while others have not. The ghosted properties are ones that currently have *different values* for at least one selected bean. Non-ghosted properties contain the same value in all selected beans. Figure 10.23 shows two multiple-selection scenarios. The first property sheet is for two selected Button beans. The second property sheet is for selected Button and Label beans. Note that some properties are ghosted, while others are not.

You can modify any of the listed properties, and all selected beans adopt the entered values. However, if the selected beans are of different types, the property sheet is limited to only the properties that all selected beans define. For example, if you select a Button and a Label, the property sheet shrinks to only those properties defined in both Button and Label.

Resetting Property Values

Sometimes, setting a property value can be a mistake, one that needs correction.

Many beans have a default value for properties if you have not explicitly entered a value. For example, all Swing components have a writeable preferredSize property. If you have not set the preferredSize property of a Swing component, the bean computes its value, possibly taking into account the size of fonts and images to display. If you explicitly set the preferredSize property, your value is used; the bean no longer computes preferredSize.

> **NOTE**
>
> *Never* explicitly set preferredSize for any bean. Doing so locks in the current size of the bean, and later changes in font size or displayed text will not display properly if the font is too big or the text will not fit in the old preferredSize!

Figure 10.23 Multiple-bean property sheets.

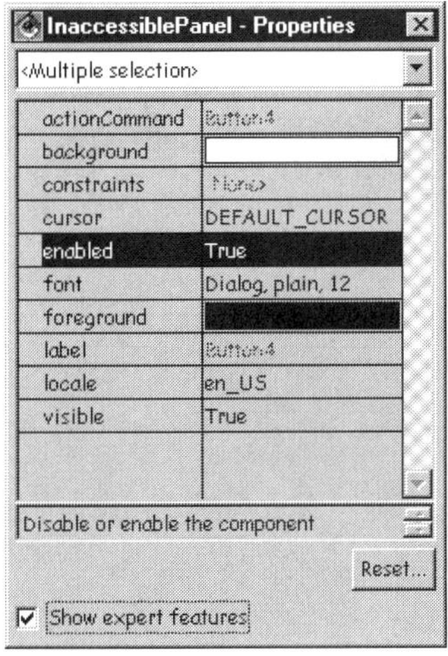

Multiple Buttons

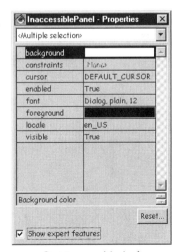

Button and Label

In VisualAge for Java, version 2, once you set a property value there was no way to unset it. In version 3, a **Reset** button, shown in Figure 10.24, restores properties' default values.

When you click the **Reset** button, the VCE displays a dialog that contains a list of all properties you have set. Check the properties you want to reset, and click **Ok** to reset those property values.

> **NOTE**
>
> The reset function will work only for multiply selected beans if the set of changed properties is *exactly* the same for all selected beans.

Using Beans to Compose Beans

Bean composition is the key to effective design in VisualAge for Java. If you strive to make most (if not all) of your classes beans, VisualAge will help you use those beans as building blocks for larger and larger beans.

Break It Down!

The first rule of visual composition is to not try to do everything in a single design session. Dropping all of your beans to create your application in a single session

Figure 10.24 Resetting property values.

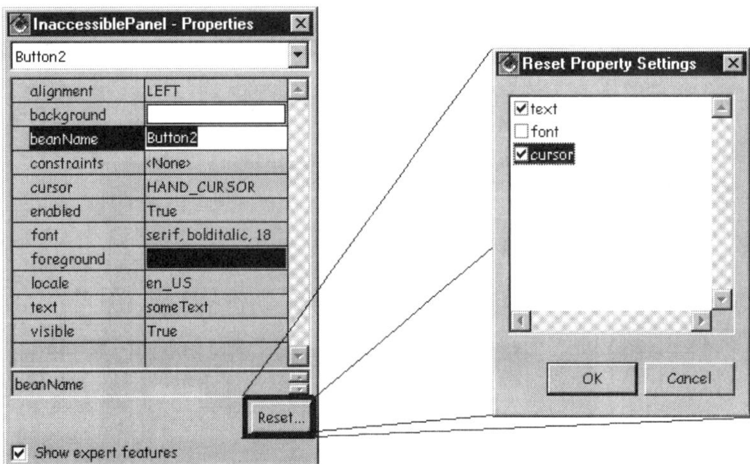

usually creates a cluttered visual design, and when you add connections to perform event handling, the design becomes very difficult to read.

Decompose your design into smaller, more workable beans. You can combine *those* beans to create larger beans. The larger bean design becomes much simpler, as it contains only a few smaller beans. This is especially useful if you have parts of several user interfaces that are similar, because you can *reuse* these similar parts in other user interfaces. For example, we could divide the simple GUI in Figure 10.25 into several smaller pieces. Note how this Ok/Cancel panel might be reusable in several dialogs.

Promoting Features

When you break down the design into smaller beans, you will need to be able to access the internal details of those smaller beans from the larger bean. Each bean is essentially a closed black box; you can access or modify the bean only through its public features. You can ask for its property values, listen for its events, and call its methods. You cannot access its private variables or methods.

When you design part of your application as a separate bean, the walls of that black box hide all of its contained components. For example, suppose you designed a partial user interface bean to represent the Ok and Cancel buttons that most dialogs need. Figure 10.26 shows the sub GUI that extends Panel called DialogButtons.

Figure 10.25 A simple GUI and a possible breakdown.

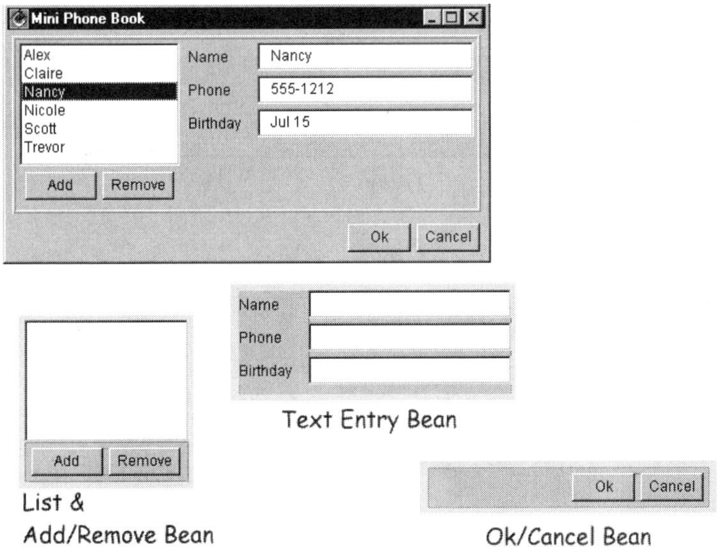

Promoting a Property

Because DialogButtons extends Panel, all of Panel's properties are visible to any users of it. However, users of DialogButtons cannot change the text on the Ok and Cancel buttons or listen to events fired by those buttons. The buttons are *implementation details* of the DialogButtons bean, represented as private variables and methods within the DialogButtons class. Suppose that a user wanted to change the text of the Ok button to Done. The label property of the Button needs to be exposed so it can be set. If we wanted to do this through the code, we could define an *okButtonLabel* property for our DialogButtons bean as follows:

```
public void setOkButtonLabel(String text) {
  getokButton().setText(text);
}
public String getOkButtonLabel() {
  return getokButton().getText();
}
```

> **NOTE**
>
> The getokButton() method provides access to the *okButton* bean that you dropped in the VCE. It is discussed in more detail in Chapter 19.

These two methods delegate the property logic to *okButton*. We define an *okButtonLabel* property for the DialogButtons bean, making the label property of okButton accessible. We would physically type the above two methods to implement this. However, being brilliantly lazy programmers, we cannot stand for that, so we use the VCE's Promote Bean Feature option, shown in Figure 10.27.

Promoting an existing feature generates a *new* feature in the bean you are creating in the VCE. The new feature delegates its function to the *promoted* feature. When you choose **Promote Bean Feature**, the dialog in Figure 10.28 appears.

To provide access to the okButton label property, select the label property and click the >> button to shift it to the list of Promoted Features.

When you click the **Ok** button, the VCE generates code to promote the feature, just like the code presented previously. After it generates the promotion code, *make sure you save the bean in the VCE as well.*

It is important to note that promotion is a *one-time* code generation. You cannot demote a feature; you need to delete the generated methods that delegate to the real components, as well as the BeanInfo entries that describe them. You can do this by deleting the promoted feature in the BeanInfo editor for the class.

Promoting an Event

Properties are not the only promotable features. You can also promote events, though the generated methods are a bit different.

Figure 10.26 Simple Ok/Cancel dialog panel.

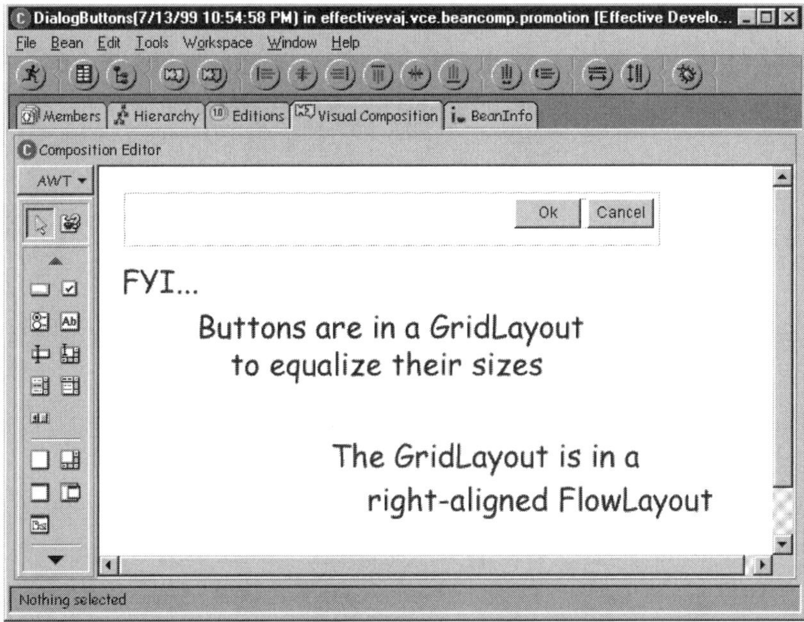

Figure 10.27 Promoting bean features.

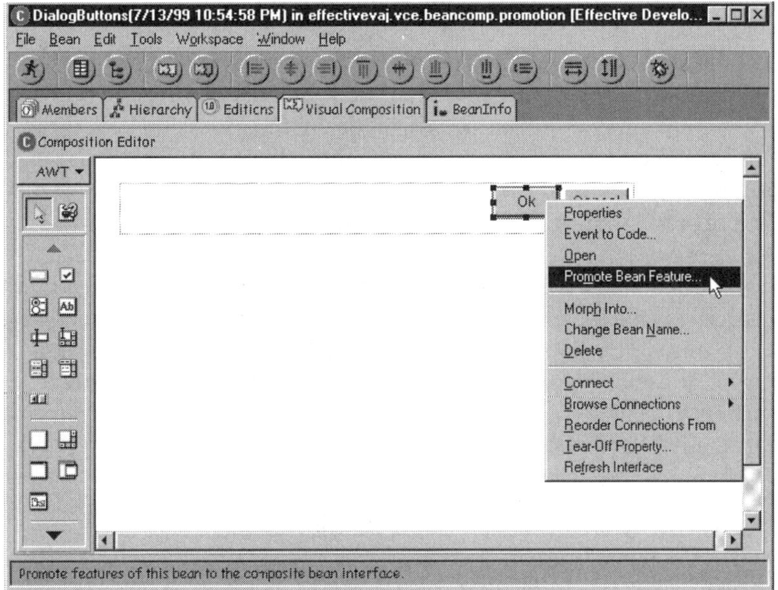

Figure 10.28 Select features to promote.

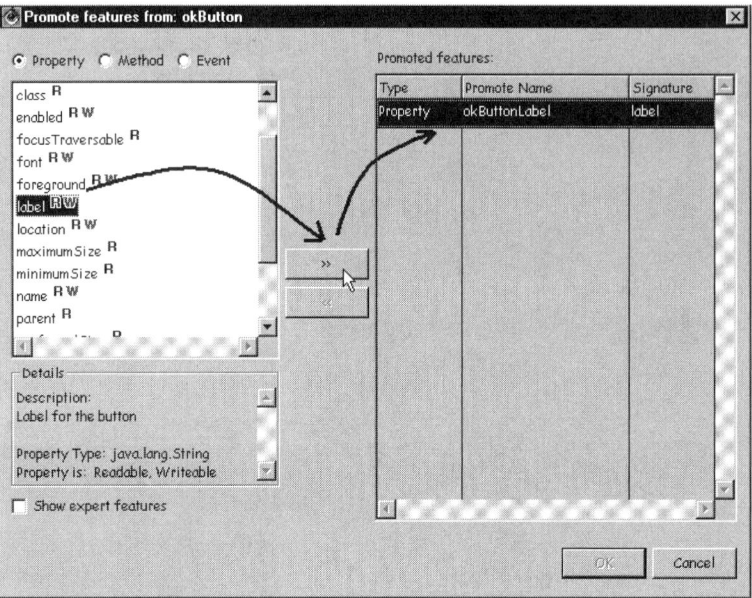

Expanding upon the example, suppose that you would like to enable an outside bean to find out when the user clicks the Ok and Cancel buttons. Once again, select **Promote Bean Feature** from the pop-up menu for okButton. When the Promoted Features Dialog appears, note that the list does not include the previously promoted label property. Again, promotion is a one-time code generation. Any features you promote this time are *added* to the promoted features; features previously promoted remain promoted, unless you delete the generated code.

Now, select **Event** as the type of feature, and choose the *actionPerformed* event, similar to how we promoted the label property. The only difference is that we choose the **Events** radio button at the top of the dialog and select *actionPerformed* to promote.

Click the **>>** button to shift the actionPerformed event to the Promoted Features list. Note the long, ugly name it creates for it in Figure 10.29. The name is generated based on the bean name and promoted feature. The name not only looks long and unwieldy, it does not describe well the function that the promoted feature provides.

Change the name to simply *okPressed* by double-clicking on the given name and modifying it; then click the **Ok** button.

The VCE generates several things to promote the event handling:

- A new event listener interface named DialogButtonsListener. This interface contains a single method, okPressed().

- Methods to register DialogButtonListeners with the DialogButtons bean.
- A Method to fire the okPressed event. This method notifies any registered listeners.
- A connection in the VCE to call fireOkPressed() when okButton fires actionPerformed. (Connections are discussed in detail in Chapter 12.)

> **WARNING**
>
> Be careful *not* to press the Enter key when changing feature names. If you were promoting multiple features at once, pressing Enter after changing the first feature name would automatically press the **Ok** button. When done typing a name, just click the mouse on another feature to edit it.

After saving the bean, running the bean will cause it to watch okButton and fire okPressed events when the Ok button is clicked.

To complete the example, we do the same thing for *cancelButton*, naming the promoted event *cancelPressed*. This adds support to fire cancelPressed, including updating the listener interface and adding a fireCancelPressed() method. The

Figure 10.29 Generated names *can* be ugly.

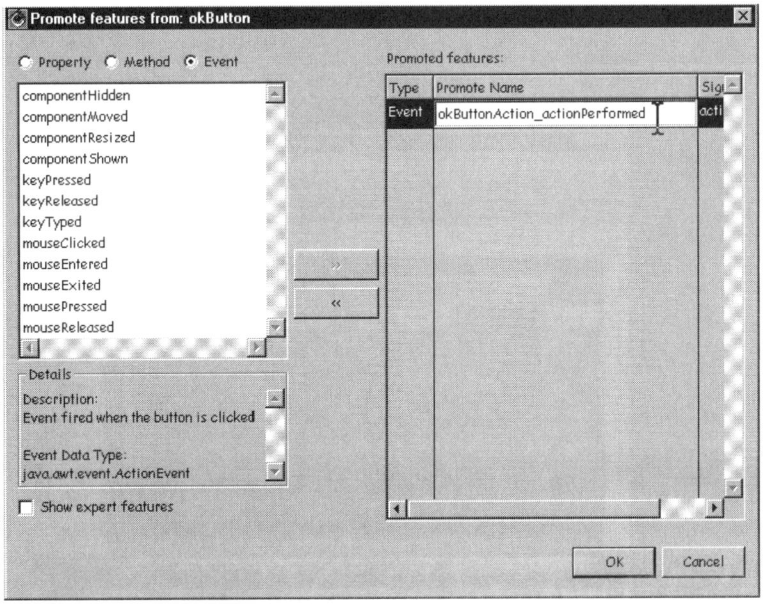

final VCE design appears in Figure 10.30. Note that it is very simple, and the outside world only cares that they can drop it into another GUI (probably at the bottom of a Dialog) and that they can register for okPressed and cancelPressed events.

> **NOTE**
>
> The fireOkPressed and fireCancelPressed connections in Figure 10.30 are passed instances of java.util.EventObject. Depending on your intended use of the bean, you can change these parameters to an instance of a specific event type. The details of setting connection parameters are covered in Chapter 12.

The DialogButtons bean can be dropped into any other GUI, preferably as the South component of a BorderLayout. Its okButtonLabel property can be changed in the composer by double-clicking on the dropped DialogButtons instance. The resulting GUI reflects the change. You can create connections from the DialogButtons instance stating when Ok is clicked, do some action, and when Cancel is clicked, do another action.

Figure 10.30 The final DialogButtons bean.

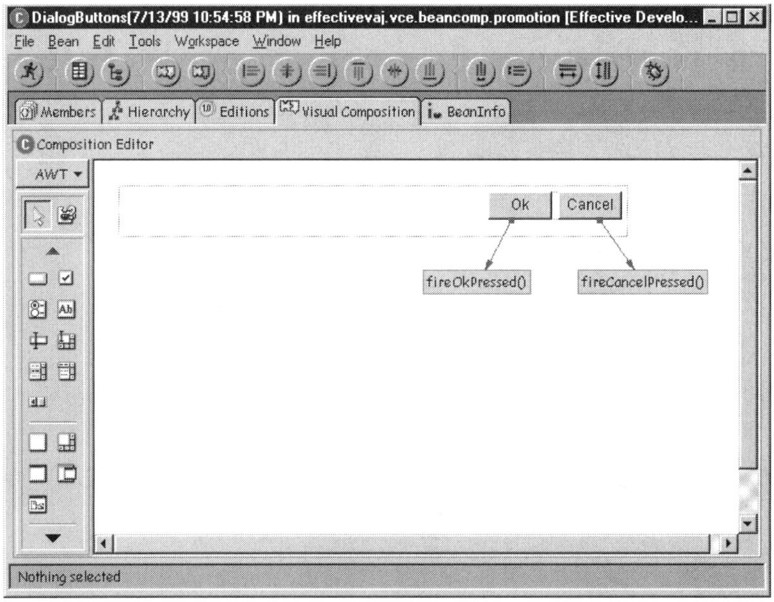

One final thought on this design. Because events are fired to indicate when the user decided to click Ok or Cancel, the user interface of DialogButtons can be changed to anything you want. As long as those events still fire, the bean that contains it is not affected. More powerful design techniques such as this one are covered over the next several chapters on Visual Composition techniques.

Creating an Application or Applet

One of the most common tasks you will need to perform is to create a base application or applet. There are several ways to perform these tasks:

Create an applet or application "from scratch" (typing in the code by hand). Not terribly desirable, but possible to do in VisualAge for Java. You are completely responsible for filling in the details of what the application does, though you can open the class to the Visual Composition Editor to compose the application.

Create an applet using the Create Applet SmartGuide. The SmartGuide gives you a head start at the basic applet structure, and can help set up parameters and a thread for animation.

Create an application using the Create Application SmartGuide. This SmartGuide creates an AWT- or Swing-based application framework. You can specify menus, a tool bar, status bar, and other basic application needs.

If you are already familiar with Java, you already know how to write the code for an application or applet by hand. Because this book assumes this knowledge, our discussion only covers the automated means of generating GUI-based applications and applets.

Creating a Visual Application from Scratch

If you decide that the Create Application SmartGuide does not give you what you are looking for, you can always create your own application from scratch, with the help of the VCE.

There are a few tricks to creating an effective application. We will walk through creation of a simple visual application that displays a Button that prints "Hello World" when the button is clicked.

Create a Visual Class

Begin by creating a class using the Create Class Smart Guide. To create this class:

1. Click the Create Class button on the tool bar to start the Add Class SmartGuide.
2. Enter PressMe as the class name, and java.awt.Frame as the superclass, as shown in Figure 10.31. If we were creating a Swing-based application, we would use com.sun.java.swing.JFrame (VisualAge for Java, ver-

sion 3.0) or javax.swing.JFrame (VisualAge for Java, version 3.5) as the superclass. Once you have typed the basic information into the first page of the Create Class SmartGuide, click **Next** to continue to the next page.

> **NOTE**
>
> We have selected "Compose this class visually." This requests that VisualAge open a class browser for the new class, starting on the Visual Composition tab, after VisualAge creates the class.

3. Add import statements for packages java.awt.*, java.awt.event.*, java.beans.*, and java.io.*. Import java.io.Serializable. These entries are shown in Figure 10.32. Note that we import Serializable because we want this to be a bean. Anytime the VCE generates code for a class in

Figure 10.31 Create Class SmartGuide (page 1).

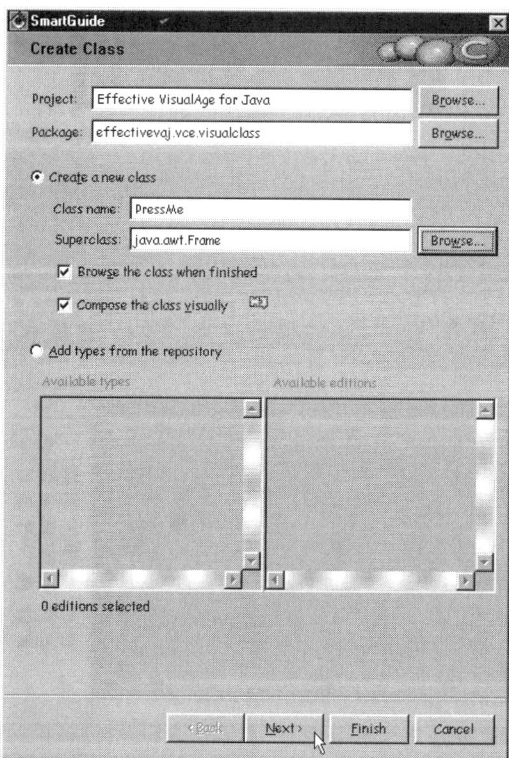

these packages, it will only use the name of the class rather than fully-qualify the class name in the generated code. At this point, do *not* select the main() checkbox. If left unchecked, VisualAge generates a simple main() when you save your work in the VCE.

4. Press **Finish** to create the class.

> **NOTE**
>
> A bug in version 3.0 (and 3.5) causes it to still use fully qualified names on *new* expressions. All other class usage should use only the class name.

Visually Compose the Class

After creating the class, VisualAge opens it to the Visual Composition page. Once inside the VCE, you see the superclass of PressMe, an AWT frame, shown in Figure 10.33.

To create our application, we need to perform several visual composition tasks. Our application needs a title on its frame and a button labeled "Press Me" to click. We also need to set up some event handling, so that when the user clicks the Press Me button, the application prints "Hello World" to the console.

To perform these tasks:

1. Double-click the frame's title bar to bring up its property sheet. Note that you *must* double-click within the *title bar* of the Frame, as it already contains another component.
2. In the property sheet, type "Simple Application" for the frame title, as shown in Figure 10.34.
3. Click on the Button bean. In the default palette setup, it is the first bean under the selection arrow and Choose Bean icon (Figure 10.35).
4. Drop an instance of Button in the middle of the empty space of the frame shown in Figure 10.36. Note that we are not using a layout manager for this example. This is *not* a good idea for a real application, but because we do so here because we do not discuss layout managers until Chapter 11.
5. Double-click the button and set its label property to "Press Me" and its bean name to *pressMeButton* as shown in Figure 10.37.
6. Save the bean by pressing Ctrl-S.

Figure 10.32 Create Class SmartGuide (page 2).

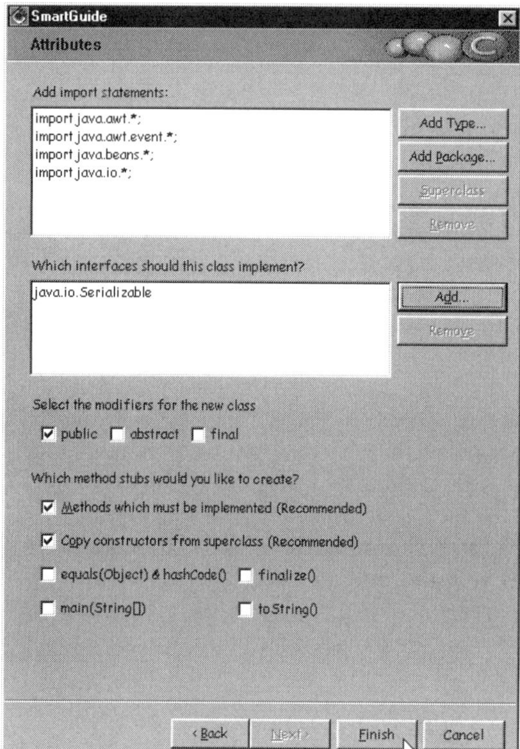

7. Once you have saved the bean, switch to the Hierarchy tab in order to edit some methods. For this example, we write code to perform the event handling. Event handling can also be done (usually more easily) by using a connection, discussed in Chapter 12.
8. Edit the constructor for the class, PressMe(). Edit PressMe() to contain the following code:

```
/**
 * PressMe constructor comment.
 */
public PressMe() {
  super();
  initialize();
  getpressMeButton().addActionListener(new ActionListener() {
    public void actionPerformed(ActionEvent e) {
      System.out.println("Hello World");
```

Figure 10.33 The initial PressMe application.

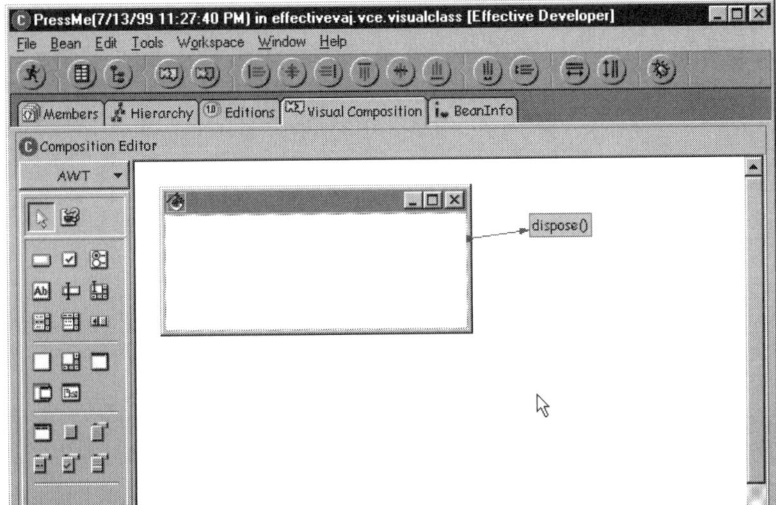


```
        }
    });
}
```

The initialize() method creates the GUI for your application. The getPressMeButton() method accesses the Button that you dropped in the visual design. We discuss these methods in detail in Chapter 19. Run the application and click the Press Me button. "Hello World" is printed to the console window.

The Create Applet SmartGuide

The Create Applet SmartGuide creates applets based on the AWT Applet class, the Swing JApplet class, or another existing applet subclass. You invoke the Create Applet SmartGuide from any browser by selecting **Add->Applet** from a pop-up menu, from the Quick Start window (**File->Quick Start->Basic->Create Applet**), or from the Create Applet tool bar button.

The Applet SmartGuide contains six pages:

Create Applet. Enables you to specify the basic attributes of the applet, including the name and type of the applet.

Applet Properties. Enables you to specify general attributes about how your applet will execute. (Can it be run as an application? Does it start its own thread?)

Figure 10.34 Setting the frame title.

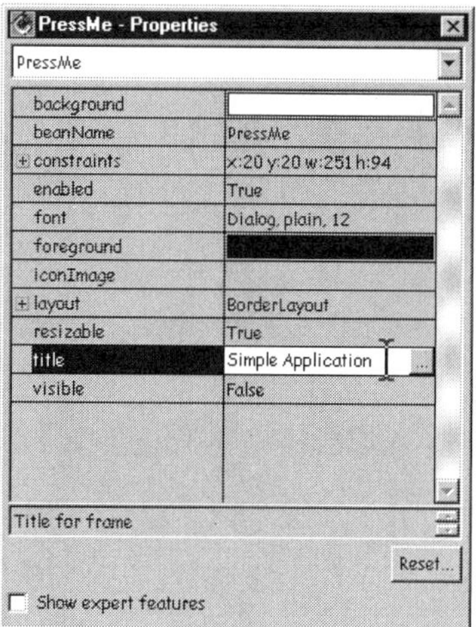

Events. Enables you to set up stub methods for common events.

Code Writer. Enables you to create sample applet code, providing methods you can modify for your applet.

Figure 10.35 Grab a Button bean.

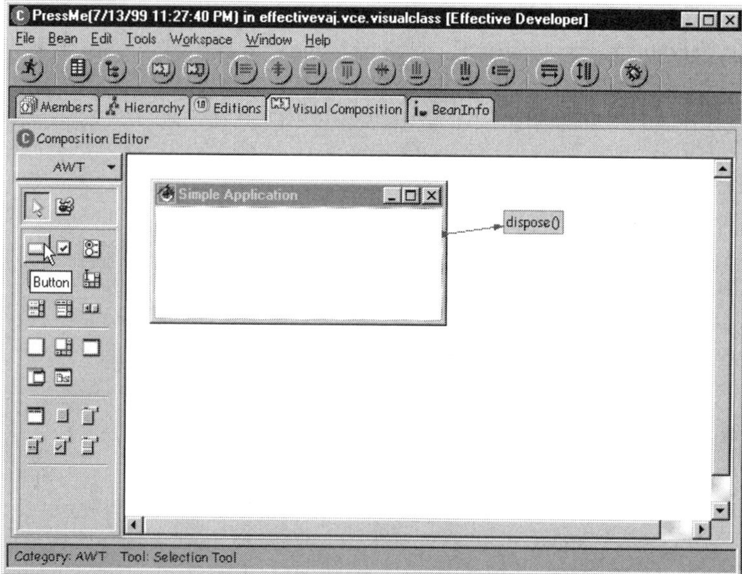

Figure 10.36 Drop a button.

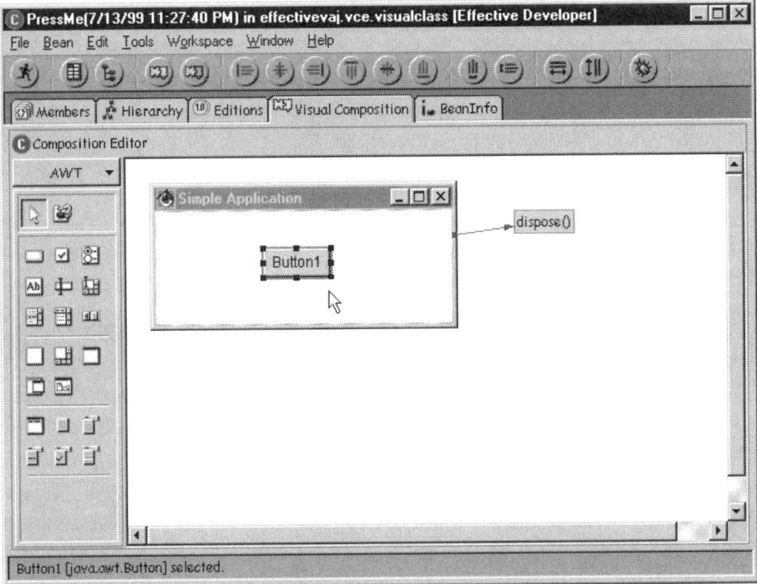

Figure 10.37 Change the button's label.

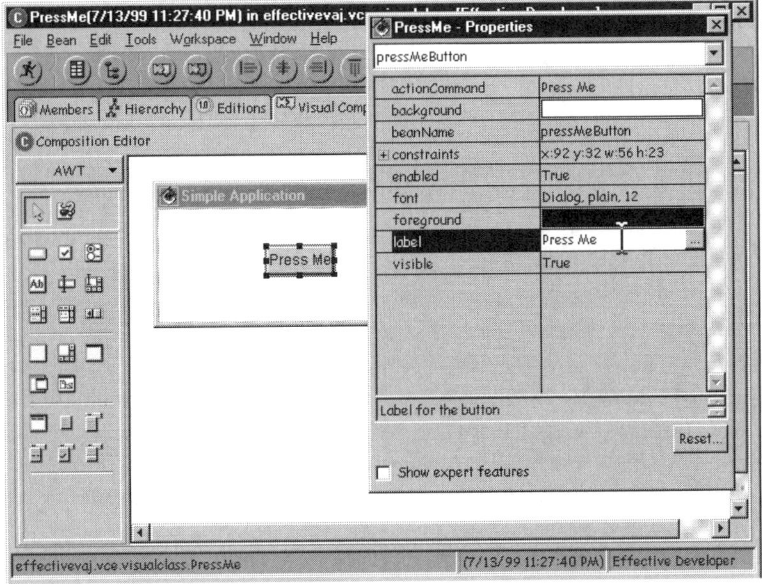

> **NOTE**
>
> Does the "Press Me" text seem crowded to you? That's because we are not using a layout manager here. Chapter 11 discusses this in more detail.

Parameters. Enables you to specify the parameters that the applet can accept.

Applet Info. Enables you to describe the applet.

The Create Applet SmartGuide is one of the most complete SmartGuides available in VisualAge for Java. You can click Finish in any of these pages to start code generation, but we recommend you always proceed through *all* pages to ensure you know what will be generated.

The Create Applet Page

The Create Applet page, shown in Figure 10.38, is the first page that appears when you start the Create Applet SmartGuide. You need to specify the following information to create an applet:

Project name. The project in which you want to create the applet. Use the **Browse** button to select the project from the list of projects loaded in the workspace.

Package. The package in which you want to create the class. If you specify an existing package that is already loaded in a project, the **Project name** field automatically reflects that project name. Otherwise, the SmartGuide creates the package in the specified project when you create the applet. If you do not specify a package name, the SmartGuide creates a default package in the project. Remember that using a default package is generally not a good idea, as classes within it can easily conflict with other developers' code.

Applet Name. The name of the applet class you want to create. You cannot use the name of a class or interface that already exists in the version of the package that is loaded into the workspace. For this example, we use VisualApplet.

Superclass name. The name of the class that the applet should extend. You have three options: Inherit from the AWT Applet class, inherit from the Swing JApplet class, or specify an existing applet class. If you choose the last option, use the **Browse** button to choose from the list of applet classes loaded in the workspace. For this example, we create an AWT Applet.

Figure 10.38 Create Applet page.

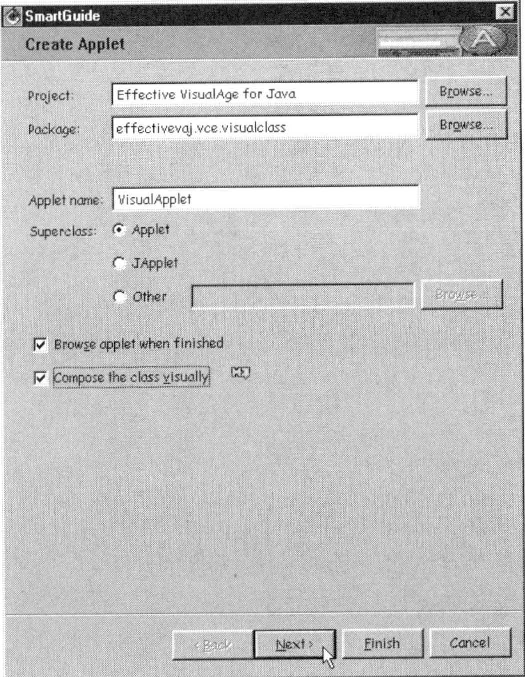

Browse the class when finished. Selecting this option opens a class browser after class creation. Using this option depends on whether you like to develop directly in the Workbench or in a class browser.

Compose Visually. If you select this option, the applet automatically opens in the Visual Composition Editor after VisualAge creates it.

Clicking **Finish** from any page of this SmartGuide creates an applet definition similar to the following:

```
public class BasicApplet extends com.sun.java.swing.JApplet {
  Font font = new Font("Dialog", Font.BOLD, 24);
  String str = "Welcome to VisualAge";
  int xPos = 5;
}
```

The Create Applet SmartGuide creates a minimal set of methods: getAppletInfo(), init(), and paint(). The getAppletInfo() method returns a string that describes the applet, the init() method calls the super class init() method, and the paint() method displays the *str* string in the applet window.

The Applet Properties Page

The Applet Properties page, shown in Figure 10.39, enables you customize how the applet runs. You specify two options in this page: whether the applet can run by itself (as an application), and whether the applet should start a thread for concurrent processing.

> **Running the applet by itself.** This option enables running the applet as an application. The generated main method creates a frame to contain the applet, calling the applet's init() and start() methods. Other generated code listens for the application to exit and calls the applet's stop() and destroy() methods.
>
> **Create a threaded applet.** If you decide that your applet must run in a thread, the generated applet class implements the Runnable interface, and adds a field of type Thread to the class definition. The run method contains the thread execution loop. This is where you would place your concurrent processing. The start() and stop() methods control the life of the created thread.

Figure 10.39 Applet Properties page.

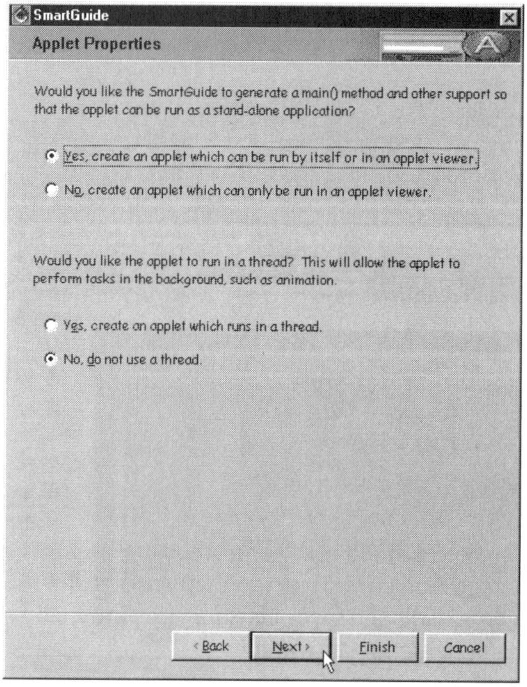

The Events Page

If the applet needs to respond to user input, such as keyboard or mouse events, it can register itself as a listener of those events. From the Events page, you can select which events the applet should listen to. The applet will provide the appropriate listener methods that you can modify to process the user input. See Figure 10.40.

You can choose the following options on this page of the Create Applet SmartGuide:

Keyboard events. If selected, the applet implements the KeyListener interface, and the corresponding methods are added to the applet interface.

Mouse events. If selected, the applet implements the MouseListener interface, and the corresponding methods are added to the applet interface.

Mouse movement events. If selected, the applet implements the MouseMotionListener interface, and the corresponding methods are added to the applet interface.

The Code Writer Page

The Code Writer page (Figure 10.41) enables you to specify whether to add a sample piece of code to the applet. The default option is to add this sample code, so in

Figure 10.40 Applet Events page.

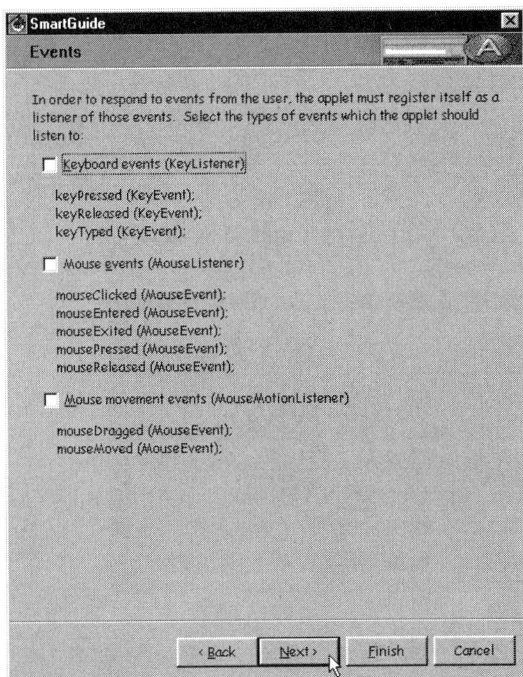

Figure 10.41 Code Writer page.

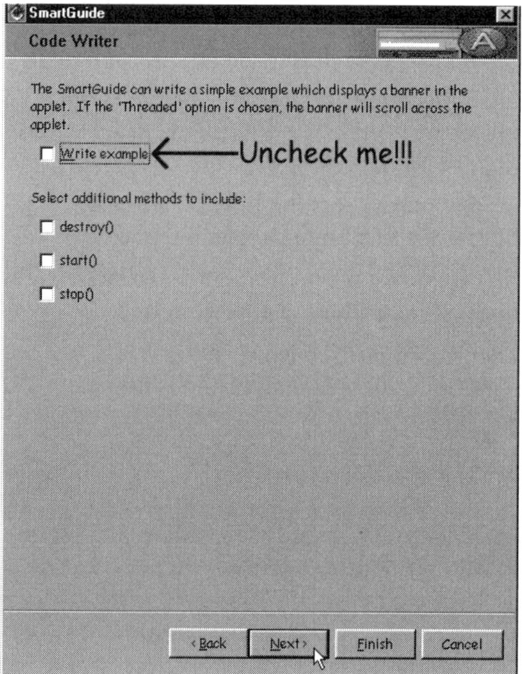

most cases you should deselect it. You specify the additional methods to generate: destroy(), start(), and stop(). Note that the start() and stop() methods are selected and ghosted if you have previously chosen to run the applet in a thread, as they must be generated to properly control the thread.

The start(), stop() and destroy() method options generate only stub methods (methods that have no code in their bodies) that call the superclass versions of them. If you want these methods to do *anything*, you must edit the generated code.

The Parameters Page

Specify application initialization parameters on the parameters page, shown in Figure 10.42. You can retrieve these parameters using Applet's getParameterInfo() method. By default, the parameter list has one entry. Click **Add** or **Remove** to manage items in the list. For example, you can create a basic JApplet subclass with two parameters, FIRSTNAME and LASTNAME. A parameter requires a name, default value, type, and description. Specifying information as shown in Figure 10.42, the getParameterInfo() method looks like this:

```
public String[][] getParameterInfo() {
```

Figure 10.42 Setting applet parameters on the Parameters page.

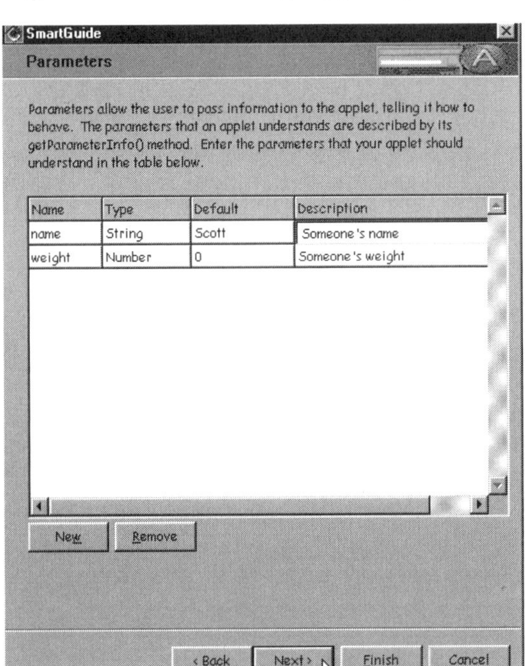


```
    String[][] info = {
      {"FIRSTNAME", "String", "The user's first name"},
      {"LASTNAME", "String", "The user's last name"}
    };
    return info;
}
```

> **NOTE**
>
> If you plan to visually compose the application and use connections to define the processing, do *not* select any of these options. These options create some stub methods that can conflict with the methods the VCE needs to generate for connection processing.

Adding getParameter() calls in your code accesses the values that set in the HTML <param> tags for the applet. The default values appear in Applet

Properties sheet (select Properties from the VisualApplet class' pop-up menu in the Workbench), as seen in Figure 10.43.

The Applet Info Page

The applet info page, shown in Figure 10.44, enables you to modify the string returned by the getAppletInfo() method. By default, this string is the concatenation of the class name and the type comment defined in the IDE options (found under **Window->Options->Coding->Method Javadoc**).

The Create Application SmartGuide

The Create Application SmartGuide quickly generates a basic GUI application with predefined controls, such as a tool bar, a status bar, or a splash screen. The Application SmartGuide creates applications based on AWT or Swing components. The generated application extends java.awt.Frame, javax.swing.JFrame, or com.sun.java.swing.JFrame. You can choose to add a tool bar, menu bar, status bar, splash screen, and an About dialog to the application. The logic of the application uses Visual Composition Editor connections, providing a quick start to your visual application.

Figure 10.43 Applet properties hold parameter defaults.

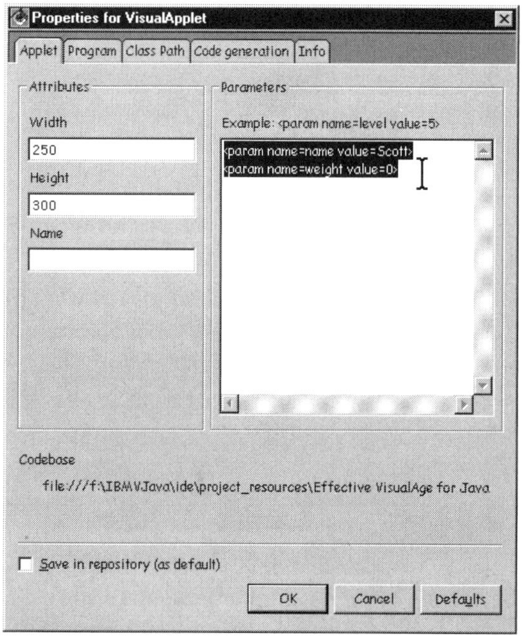

Figure 10.44 Applet Info page.

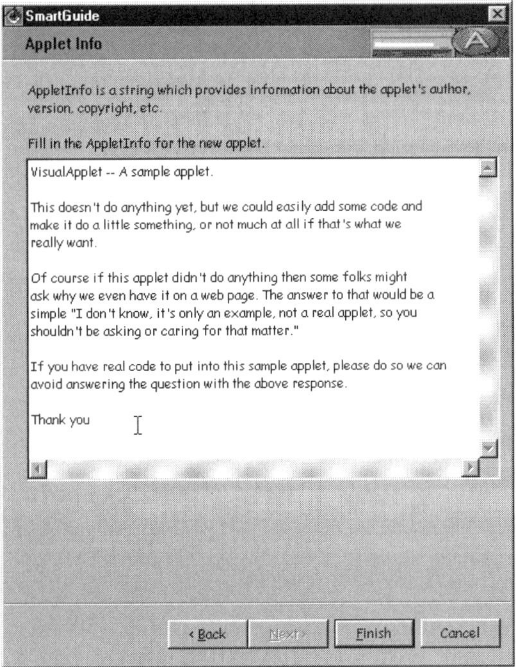

You start the application SmartGuide by choosing **Create Application** from the Quick Start window (**File->Quick Start**), or the Create Application tool bar button. The SmartGuide consists of two pages: Create Application and Application Details. On the Create Applications page, specify the project, package, and class names as well as the type of GUI (AWT or Swing). On the Application Details page, you decide which graphical controls should be added to the application, and whether a splash screen and an About dialog should be created or not. The application that you are going to create must belong to package and a project. If the package already exists, you can select it before starting the SmartGuide.

The Create Application Page

The Create Application page, shown in Figure 10.45, is the first that appears when you launch the application SmartGuide. You must supply the following information:

Project Name. The project to contain the generated application. If you want to create a new project for this class, type a project name in the field. If you want to select an existing project, click the **Browse** button or select the project before you invoke the SmartGuide.

Figure 10.45 The Create Application page.

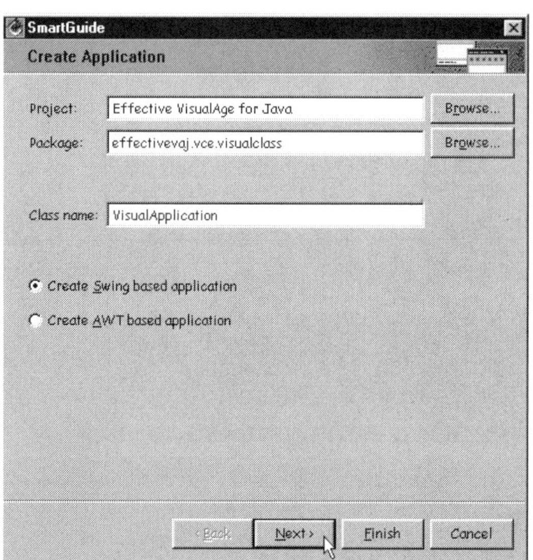

Package Name. The containing package for the application. If you do not specify a package name, the SmartGuide creates the application in a default package in the specified project. If you specify a non-existing package, the SmartGuide creates the package when creating the application.

Class Name. The name of the application class to generate. If you choose to generate a splash screen and/or About dialog, this name acts as a prefix in the class names for those classes. You cannot specify an existing class name in this field. However, there are cases in which you want to reuse an existing class name. For example, suppose that you just created a TypicalApplication class and want to regenerate the class again but with different options. To do this, you can proceed as follows: Version the existing TypicalApplication class and then delete it. Remember that the delete action just unloads the class from the workspace; it still exists in the repository. Then, invoke the SmartGuide with the same class name to recreate the application. You can then reload any methods or code that you had added to the first version of the TypicalApplication class from the repository. For details on version control and team programming features, please see Chapter 4.

Application Type. Choose whether you would like an AWT- or Swing-based application.

For this example, we create a Swing-based application named VisualApplication.

You can click the **Next** button to move to the application details page. If you click **Finish** here, the SmartGuide creates the application with the following default options and dialogs:

- A tool bar with a Cut, Copy, and Paste buttons.
- A menu bar with File, Edit, View, and Help entries. Each has several typical submenus.
- A status bar with two message areas.
- A splash screen.
- An About dialog.
- The class name as the title of the application.

We strongly recommend that you click Next to enable customization of menus and tool bars in the Application Details page.

> **TIP**
>
> Unless you want to create a project and package to store the class, select the package in the browser tree or list first. If it already belongs to a project, then the corresponding project name is loaded automatically.

The Applications Details Page

You use the Application Details page, shown in Figure 10.46, to specify which graphical controls to add to your application, the title of the application, and which additional dialogs should be created. You can customize the following information:

Application's title. By default, the class name is the application title. This title appears in the title bar for the Frame or JFrame of the application.

Menu bar. Adds a customizable menu bar to the application. We describe customization in detail in the *Customizing the Menu Bar* section later in this chapter.

Tool bar. Adds a customizable tool bar to the application. We describe customization in detail in the *Customizing the Tool Bar* section later in this chapter.

Status bar. Adds a status bar to the application. You can customize the status bar in the VCE after application generation.

Figure 10.46 The Application Details page.

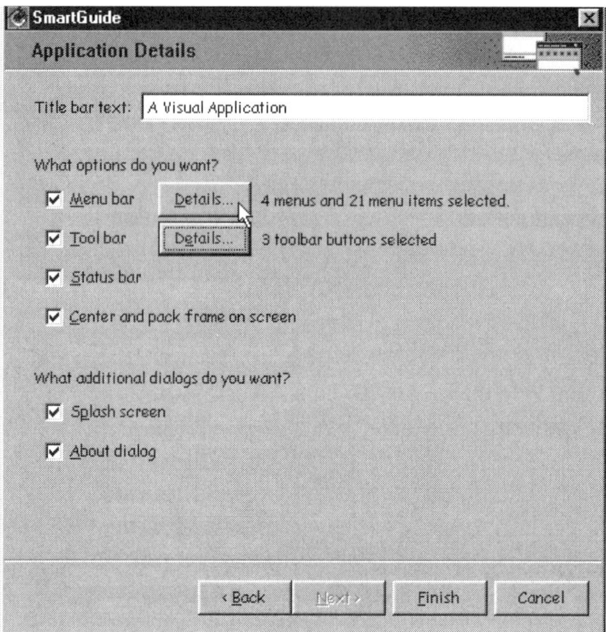

Frame position and size. Selecting the center and pack frame option sizes and positions the frame on the screen when it starts. The application calls the frame's pack() method to resize the frame to its preferred size. The application will also appear centered on the screen. If you do not choose this option, the frame appears at the top left corner of the screen at the same size as it appears in the VCE.

Create additional dialogs. Select the corresponding check boxes if you want a splash screen to start when launching the application, or if you want to create a dialog that displays information about your application. The splash screen and the About dialog are created as separate classes that can be edited with the VCE.

Customizing the Menu Bar

The default menu bar contains File, Edit, View, and Help menus. Each of these menus contains a number of menu items. Use the menu details window, shown in Figure 10.47, to add, delete, and reorder menus and menu items. To add a new menu:

Figure 10.47 The Menu Details window.

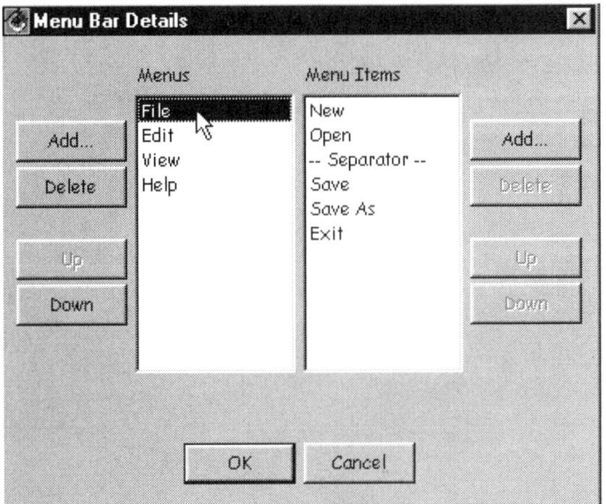

1. Click the **Details** button to show the menu details window.
2. Click the **Add** button on the left of the window.
3. A dialog appears, asking for a menu name. Enter the new menu name (for example, *Window*) and click **Ok**. The SmartGuide adds the menu at the bottom of the menu list. Select the new item and click the **Up** and **Down** buttons to reorder it.
4. When you select a menu, the dialog displays the list of menu items for it on the right. File, Edit, View, and Help have predefined menu items. If you delete them, you can retrieve them from a predefined list.

   To add a menu item:

1. Select the menu you wish to modify (*Window*, for example).
2. Click the **Add** button on the right side of the menu details window.
3. You have three options: Create a menu item by entering a menu item text, create a predefined menu item, or create a separator. Select the radio button that corresponds to your choice. The Create predefined menu item option is available only if you have selected a predefined menu.
4. Click **Ok** to confirm your choice, and repeat those steps to create all menu items. Then, use the **Up** and **Down** buttons to reorder menu items and separators in the list.

Customizing the Tool Bar

The tool bar contains a number of tool bar buttons. Use the tool bar details window shown in Figure 10.48 to add or remove predefined buttons and separators to the tool bar. You cannot create new tool bar buttons from this dialog. If you want to do so, you have to edit the application with the VCE once after application creation. To customize the tool bar:

1. Click the **Details** button on the right of the tool bar to start the Toolbar Details window.
2. Select one or several available buttons, and click the >> button.
3. If necessary, reorder the tool bar buttons using the **Up** and **Down** buttons. You can also drag and drop icons in the list.

Generating Code

Clicking the **Finish** button generates the code for the described application. Do not worry if you see messages such as "4 problems found" during code generation. The first generated class is the application itself; it contains references to the nonexistent splash screen window and About dialog classes. When the SmartGuide generates the splash screen and About dialog classes, you should see a message such as "4 problems fixed" at the bottom of the dialog.

After code generation, the SmartGuide opens the class to the Visual Composition Editor. The look and feel is different depending on your choice of an AWT-based or Swing-based application, but the logic is the same.

Figure 10.48 The Toolbar Details window.

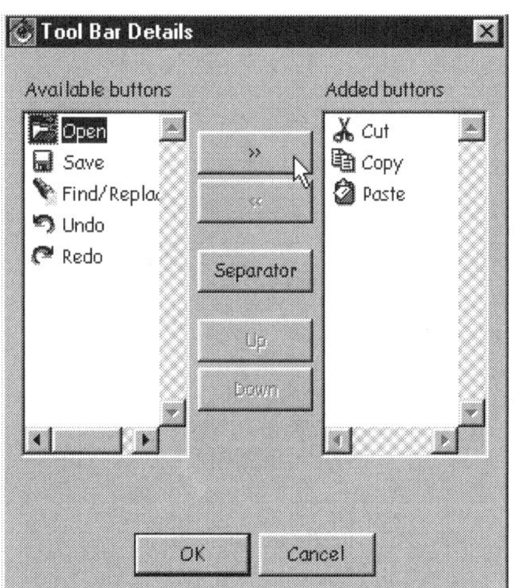

Summary

So far, we have explored the basics of the Visual Composition Editor. We have shown how to add, modify, and remove beans from a visual design. However, we have said nothing of how the GUI is structured. The next chapter discusses how you can compose components to create flexible user interfaces.

11 LAYOUT MANAGEMENT

There are two ways to design a GUI in the Visual Composition Editor (VCE): with or without layout managers. You can design GUIs without a layout manager (also referred to as "using a null layout," because the container's *layout* property is null), explicitly positioning and sizing each component. Such an implementation creates a fixed GUI; components will not move or resize when the user changes the size of the window. Alternatively, you can implement your GUI using layout managers, algorithms that control size and position of components.

The VCE provides tools to assist your design regardless of which implementation method you choose. There are tools to equalize component sizes and align them when using a null layout, and there are tools to adjust component constraints (hints about how to place components) within layout managers. Both sets of tools provide significant help when implementing a GUI. However, you should *always* use layout managers in your released applications; because Java applications can run on many different platforms, font and screen sizes, as well as internationalized text, require your GUI to adapt.

This chapter describes how you can use the tools provided in the VCE to implement GUIs for your application. Note the word *implement*: The VCE is an implementation tool, not a design tool. We'll examine this point in the next section, *GUI Design versus GUI Implementation*. Next, we'll discuss how to use the absolute positioning tools, helping you implement GUIs using a null layout. We then discuss using each of the basic layout managers defined in the Java Runtime Environment in the VCE.

> **NOTE**
>
> This book assumes you know the Java language and Java Runtime Environment well. Currently, *no* book does a proper job explaining how to use layout managers. Most books simply introduce layout managers and show a simple example of that manager *by itself*. The real power of layout managers is their interaction when nested. Because of this, we strongly recommend that you read Scott Stanchfield's article, *Effective Layout Management*, at http://java.sun.com/developer/onlineTraining/GUI/AWTLayoutMgr.

GUI Design versus GUI Implementation

There is an important difference between GUI design and GUI implementation. Many people mistakenly believe that GUI building tools are *design* tools. This is incorrect. GUI builders are *implementation* tools. In the last chapter, we explored the VCE, including its "design area." This is a misnomer. It is really a place to draw your GUI *implementation.*

Just as you write code to implement a program design, you draw GUIs to implement a GUI design. The biggest problem with GUI builder tools is that it is far too easy to forget that you need to *design* the GUI. Programmers sit down in front of a tool like the VCE and just start dropping components and drawing connections (discussed in Chapter 12, "Connections"). This is *not* GUI design. This is hacking together a GUI.

GUI design starts with a picture. Do *not* attempt to create a GUI from a mental picture. Get a piece of paper or use a simple drawing tool and draw your GUI. This applies whether you decide to use layout managers to control the GUI or not. Drawing the picture on graph paper can help with alignment, especially if you choose to use a null layout.

Next, you need to annotate the picture to describe component-sizing behavior. Which components expand or shrink when the user resizes the window? Which components remain fixed in width and/or height? Which components should appear the same size? We can annotate the diagram using arrows and I-bars to represent expansion or fixed sizing.

Finally, you need to determine the layout design. Draw boxes on your diagram (preferably in different colors) to group components into containers, and then group these containers into larger containers. This usually works best if you examine the GUI from the outside edge. Write a tree-form description of the layout design (and/or a constraint table, if using a GridBagLayout).

The format of this design is crucial to easy GUI implementation. A tree maps exactly to the Beans List representation of the GUI, so it is very easy to add components to implement the design. It's also very easy to read and makes clear where components belong. It's a good idea to keep a copy of this written form in the comments for your GUI class to help maintainers see the design. This applies even if you decide to create the GUI by writing code by hand, because it helps anyone who reads your code to visualize the GUI structure.

Once you have your GUI layout designed, you can implement it in the VCE. We'll discuss both of the following methods of GUI implementation:

Absolute Positioning. Place and size components in a null layout by using absolute coordinates and dimensions. If you use this strategy, the components will not resize or move when the user resizes the window or changes font size.

Layout Managers. The right way to do things, specifying hints to a layout manager on where you would like components to appear; the layout manager positions and sizes the component. Components will resize and move to react to changes in window size, fonts, displayed text, and other appearance-changing factors.

> **TIP**
>
> To design your GUI layout:
>
> 1. Draw a picture!
> 2. Annotate the picture to describe resize behavior.
> 3. Determine the layout design.

We start by exploring the absolute positioning controls in the VCE. We'll then move on to using the layout managers provided in the Java Runtime Environment effectively to create your GUIs in the VCE.

Absolute Positioning of Components

The Visual Composition Editor (VCE) provides several tools to position components within the GUI that you are composing. These alignment tools allow absolute positioning and sizing of components. The user will see the components in the exact size and position that you set in the visual design. If the user resizes the window, nothing will change. If the user changes fonts, nothing will change. The components will look the same.

> **WARNING**
>
> Only use these tools for simple prototypes! You should *never* use them for production work. Layout managers are necessary for production quality work.

Alignment Tools

The alignment tools in the VCE enable you to position components relative to each other when you're using a null layout. There are two sets of alignment tools: horizontal alignment tools and vertical alignment tools.

The VCE has three horizontal alignment tools:

- left alignment

- center alignment

- right alignment

The *left-alignment control* aligns all selected components to the left, based on the position of the anchor component. The *anchor component* is the *last* component selected. For example, if you select three buttons by shift-clicking each in turn, the *last* one selected is the anchor. The anchor component is indicated with black selection dots at each corner and on the middle of each edge. All other components are marked with white selection dots. Figure 11.1 shows examples of anchor and non-anchor components.

The *center horizontal alignment control* centers components relative to the position of the anchor component. If some selected components are wider than other selected components, the components will be aligned at their midpoints.

The *right alignment control* is similar to the left alignment tool, but the selected components align to the *right* edge of the anchor component. Examples of components positioned using the left, center, and right alignment tools appear in Figure 11.1.

VCE also has three vertical alignment tools:

- top alignment

- middle alignment

- bottom alignment

Figure 11.1 Left-, center-, and right-aligned components.

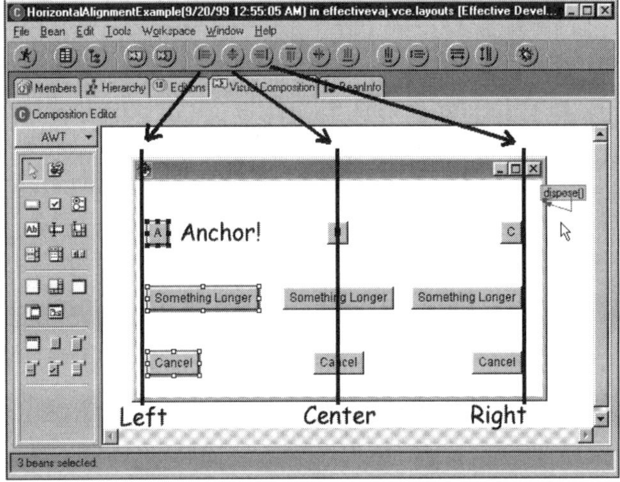

These tools function in the same manner as the horizontal alignment tools. Figure 11.2 shows examples of components that have been positioned using the three vertical alignment tools.

Distribution Tools

The *distribution tools* position components within a parent container based on their sizes. Each selected component is spaced such that there is equal space between each component. Distribution tools do not use the anchor component when placing the selected components. Components can be distributed horizontally or vertically, as shown in Figure 11.3.

Sizing Tools

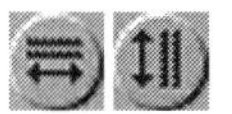

Sizing tools enable you to set the size of all non-anchor components to the size of the anchor component. To use these controls, select all of the components that you want to have the same size and press the match width or match height button in the tool bar. You can use these buttons to make selected components the same height or the same width. The width or height of all selected components will now be the same as the anchor component. Note that if you want them aligned as well, you still need to press one of the alignment tools. Examples of components sized using the sizing tools appear in Figure 11.4.

> **TIP**
>
> Unless you are building a quick prototype, you should *always* use layout managers to construct your GUI. Absolute positioning not only frustrates users but can also result in improper display based on font sizes or locale.

Figure 11.2 Top-, middle-, and bottom-aligned components.

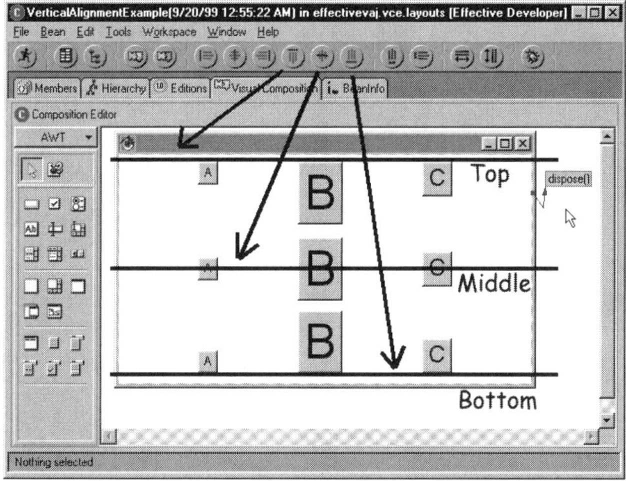

Figure 11.3 Component horizontal and vertical distribution.

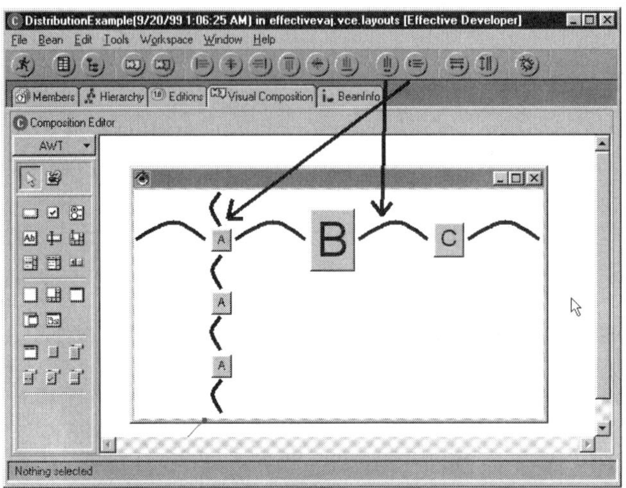

Layout Management in the VCE

The proper way to implement GUIs is to use the Java Runtime Environment's layout managers. The Visual Composition Editor provides support for the standard layout managers as well as custom layout managers that you may develop. In this section, we'll explore how you use the standard layout managers in the VCE. Later in this chapter, we'll discuss how you can use your own layout managers.

Figure 11.4 Sizing tools for width- and height-matching.

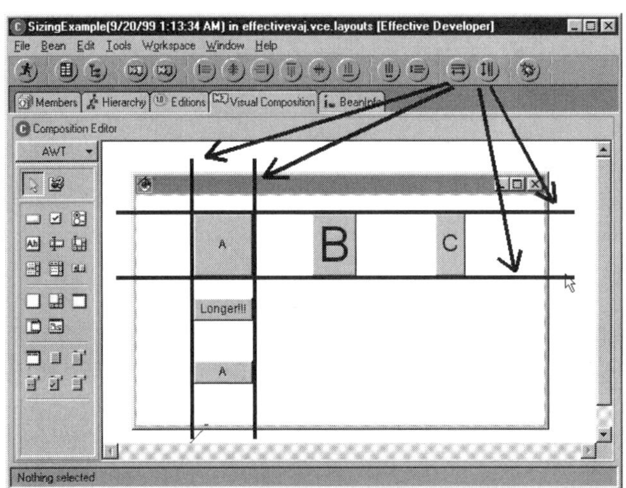

> **NOTE**
>
> We don't cover the concepts of layout management in this book. However, Scott Stanchfield has written an excellent article on layout management, and it is available online at http://java.sun.com/developer/onlineTraining/GUI/AWTLayoutMgr.

FlowLayout

This is the simplest of the AWT layout managers. Its layout strategy is:

- Respect the preferred size of all contained components.
- Lay out as many components as will fit horizontally within a container as a single row.
- Start a new row of components if more components exist.
- If all components can't fit in the displayed container, too bad!

To use FlowLayout in the VCE, set the *layout* property of a container to FlowLayout in its property sheet. To do this:

1. Bring up the Property sheet for the container by double-clicking it.
2. Change its layout property to FlowLayout, as seen in Figure 11.5. Notice that the layout property lists all LayoutManager classes in the workspace.

The VCE provides special support for the standard layout managers, BorderLayout, FlowLayout, CardLayout, GridLayout, GridBagLayout, and BoxLayout. You can use other, custom layout managers (third-party or your own), but the VCE provides little visual support for their manipulation.

When you select one of the standard layout managers, a small plus sign appears to the left of the layout property in the property sheet. If you click this plus sign, the layout parameters appear. This enables you to customize the use of the layout in your GUI design. FlowLayout lists two parameters: hgap and vgap. These parameters specify how much space should appear between adjacent components. For this example, we set hgap and vgap to 5, as shown in Figure 11.6. Most layout managers have hgap and vgap parameters.

FlowLayout provides three parameters to customize its appearance: alignment, hgap, and vgap. The alignment affects the arrangement of components in each row. If alignment is CENTER, FlowLayout centers the components in each row as a group. The layout separates adjacent components by the hgap and vgap. If alignment is RIGHT or LEFT, FlowLayout groups the components near the right or left edge of the container. Figure 11.7 shows some example flow layouts.

Figure 11.5 Setting the layout property.

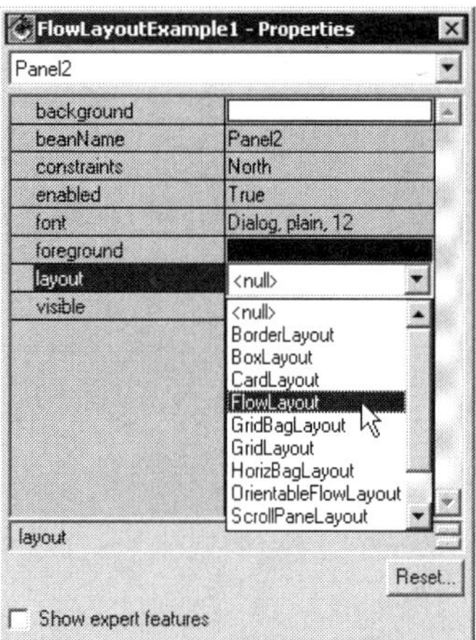

When the layout has been set to FlowLayout, add components to its container by clicking *and holding* the mouse button in the container. While holding the mouse button, you'll see a hint line appear, as shown in Figure 11.8. You can add components before or after any other component, based on the left-to-right, top-to-bottom layout strategy. By dragging the mouse, the hint line will move to tell you if the component will be placed before or after existing components.

As you add more and more components to FlowLayout, the layout reorganizes them based on how many will fit per line.

Figure 11.6 Setting the layout parameters.

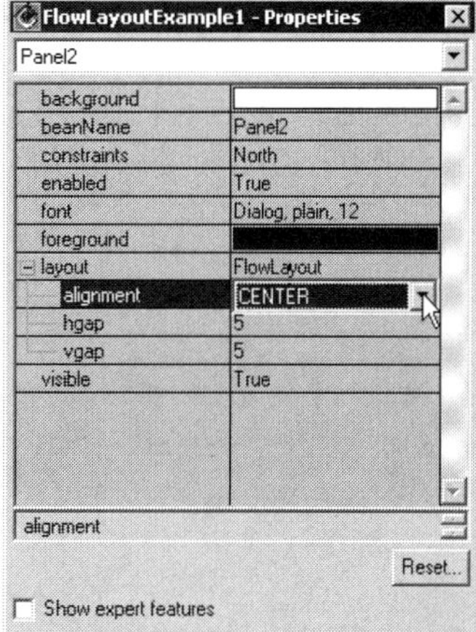

Figure 11.7 Example flow layouts.

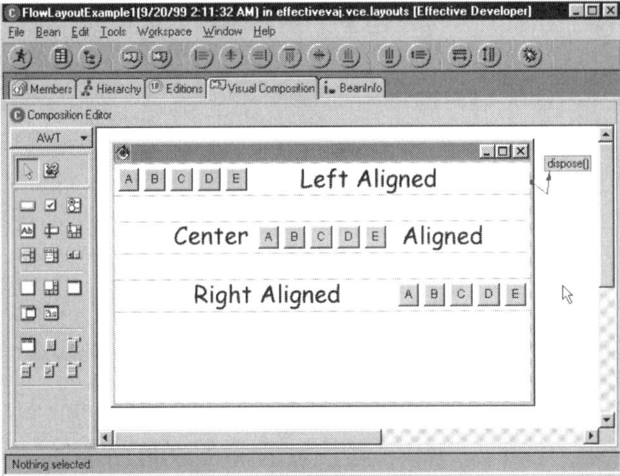

BorderLayout

BorderLayout is probably the most useful of the standard layout managers. It defines a layout scheme that maps its container into five logical sections: NORTH, SOUTH, EAST, WEST, and CENTER.

Figure 11.8 Adding a button to FlowLayout.

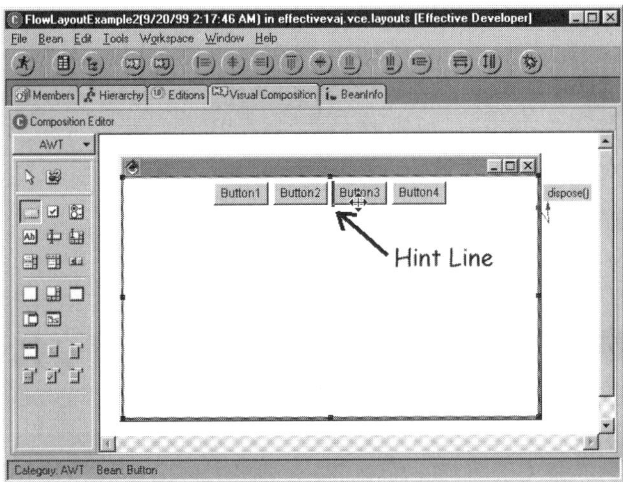

You can use BorderLayout in the VCE in much the same way as you did FlowLayout. First, you need to set the layout property of the container to BorderLayout. You can choose it from the list of available layout managers seen in Figure 11.5. BorderLayout only has hgap and vgap parameters, which determine how much space is left between adjacent components in the container. After setting the layout manager to BorderLayout, you can drop components inside the container, holding and dragging the mouse to set their position.

In Figure 11.9, you'll see a five-component border layout in the VCE. Note that this is *definitely* not a typical GUI. In fact, *no* GUI *ever* looks like this. This is the first lesson of layout management: most layout managers are useless on their own; however, they are incredibly powerful when well nested. Together, each layout manager can constrain *part* of a GUI. Each part of a GUI contributes to the overall GUI, and by nesting layout managers we can build larger and larger GUIs

The Visual Composition Editor provides direct support for positioning BorderLayout components. Whenever you are adding components to a layout-managed container, the VCE gives you visual hints about the location of the component. As you did for FlowLayout, do not simply click to drop components inside a parent container! When you place a component, click and hold the mouse button, then *drag* it to see its target location. It is very easy to drop a component into the wrong position. Visual hints appear when a component is dragged, which ensures that the component drops in the proper position when the mouse button is released.

As an example, let's build a simple labeled text field:

1. Create a new class with superclass java.awt.Frame.
2. Select a Label component from the beans palette.
3. Press and hold the mouse button near the center of the BorderLayout panel. A small dotted rectangle appears near the center of the panel, as shown in Figure 11.10. *Keep holding the mouse button.*
4. Drag the label around, watching for the other hint lines to appear. The other hint lines representing the NORTH, SOUTH, EAST, and WEST positions of BorderLayout appear in Figure 11.11.
5. Place this label in the WEST position of the border layout.

Figure 11.9 A five-component border layout.

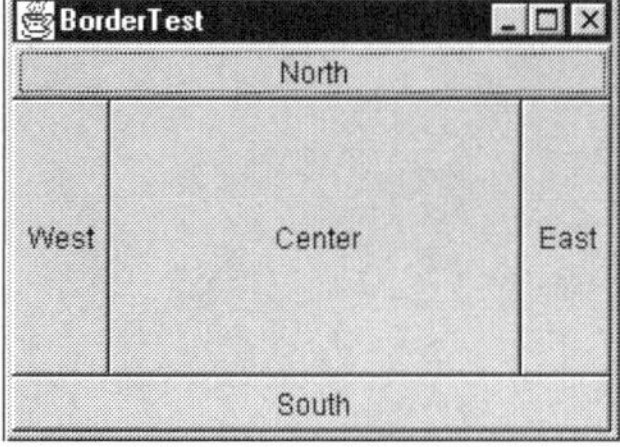

Figure 11.10 The CENTER position visual hint.

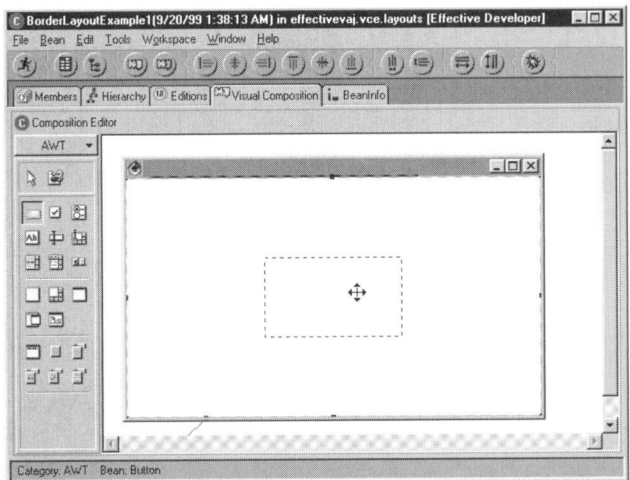

6. Change the *text* property of this Label to "Name." The label automatically resizes itself inside the displayed GUI, as in Figure 11.12.
7. Next, place a TextField component in the CENTER position of the GUI. To do this, press and hold the mouse button near the center of the GUI, and drag the component until the CENTER area hint appears. Then drop the TextField component. After dropping it, the text field expands to fill the entire center section of the GUI. This is not exactly what we wanted. The TextField and Label components are too big. What we really want is to restrict the heights of the text field labels to their preferred height. Once again, this is the job of BorderLayout.

To restrict the height of the Label and TextField components, let's create another panel to contain these two components in the WEST and CENTER positions, and place *that new panel* in the NORTH part of the overall GUI. By placing it in the NORTH, it is bound to its preferred height. The name label will not get any taller, nor will the text field.

To create the nested border layouts:

1. Start by dropping a new Panel component *outside* the first panel, as shown in Figure 11.13. This gives you more room to work. The VCE is very flexible, allowing you to place extra components *anywhere* you want to in the design area. By placing this new panel in an unoccupied part of the design area, you can create a sub-GUI and then drag it into the overall GUI.

Figure 11.11 BorderLayout hint lines.

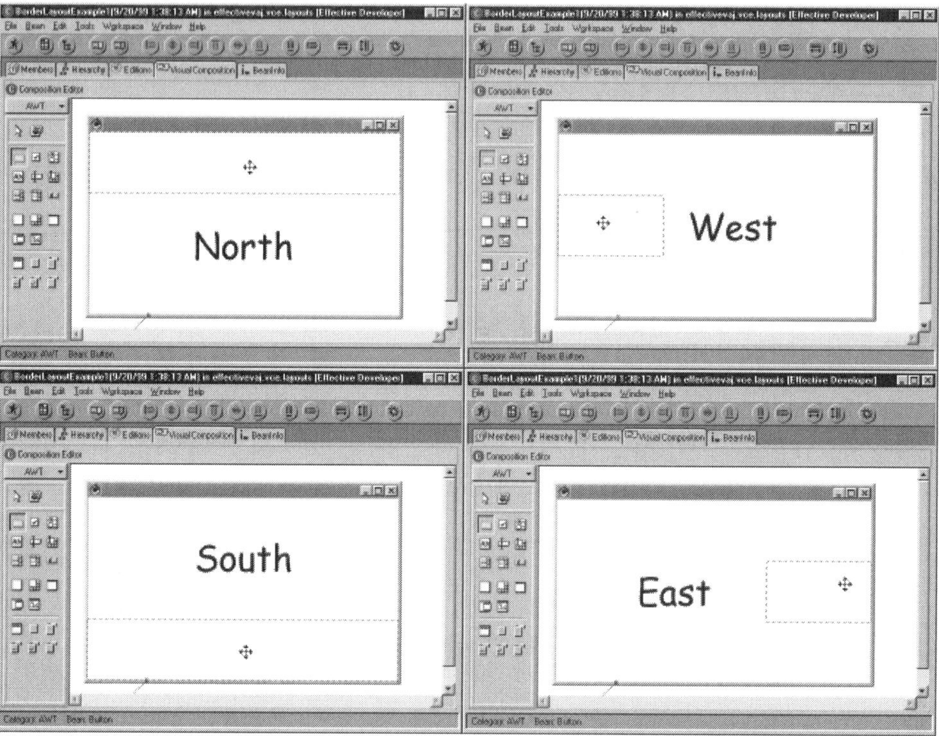

Figure 11.12 The label in the WEST position.

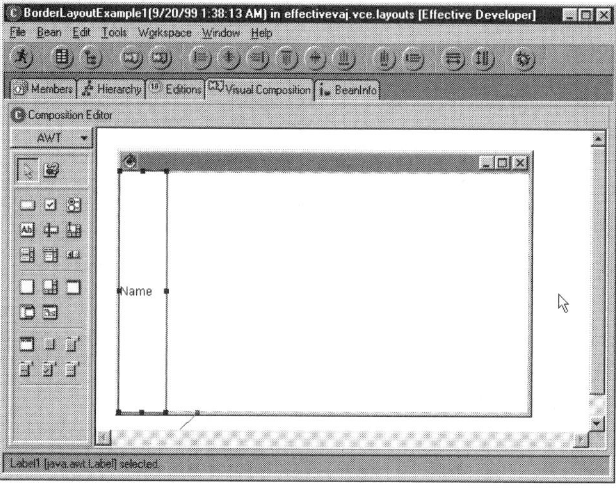

Figure 11.13 The new sub-GUI panel.

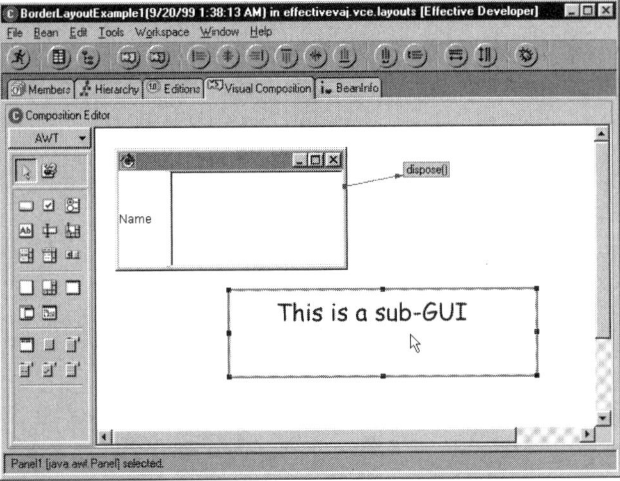

2. Set the layout of this new panel to BorderLayout, as described previously.
3. Drag the Label and the TextField components *from* the old panel into the WEST and CENTER positions of the new panel. The new panel should look very much like the original GUI. Our current work appears in Figure 11.14.

Figure 11.14 The filled-in Sub-GUI.

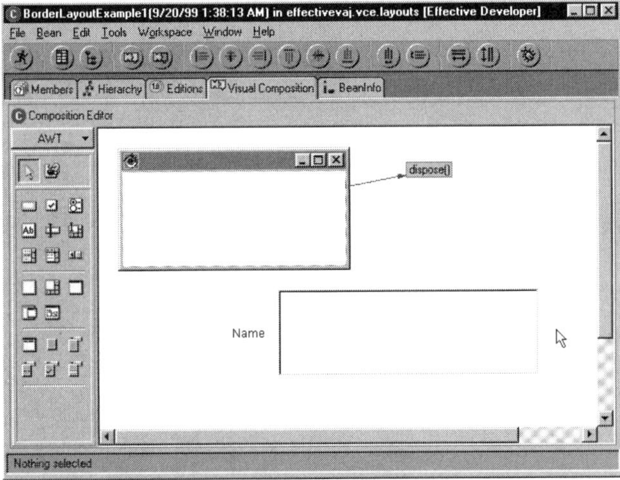

Once we have created this sub-GUI, look at the Beans List, shown in Figure 11.15 (recall that you can bring up the Beans List by pressing the third-from-left toolbar button. BorderLayoutExample is the topmost component. This represents the class you are creating. Inside it is a frame that is also named BorderLayoutExample. This is the main frame of the GUI, which represents the superclass of the composite bean. Inside this frame is a contentsPane panel.

Next, look at the panel that has been dropped. VisualAge for Java labeled this panel *Panel1*. Underneath Panel1 are *Label1* and *TextField1*. These are the Label and TextField components that we just dragged into the new panel.

4. Select Panel1 in the Beans List. This also selects it in the GUI. This allows us to interact with Panel1 in the GUI. This is the *only* way to select Panel1 in the GUI. If you had attempted to click on it in the visual representation, only the Label or the TextField would be selected since the Label and the TextField completely fill Panel1.

NOTE

contentsPane is an extra component that VisualAge for Java generates for all AWT GUIs. Although you do not really need this, it helps if you decide to convert your GUI to Swing. Swing JFrame beans *always* contain a contentsPane panel, which allows it to provide extra support for things such as tool tips, drag-and-drop support, and menus. If you are interested in why this is necessary, please see the MageLang Institute's Swing tutorial, Part II, located at the Java developer connection, http://java.sun.com/jdc, under its online training section.

5. Carefully drag the *border* of Panel1.
6. Move Panel1 to the NORTH part of *BorderLayoutExample*, as seen in Figure 11.16.

Figure 11.15 The Beans List for the sub-GUI.

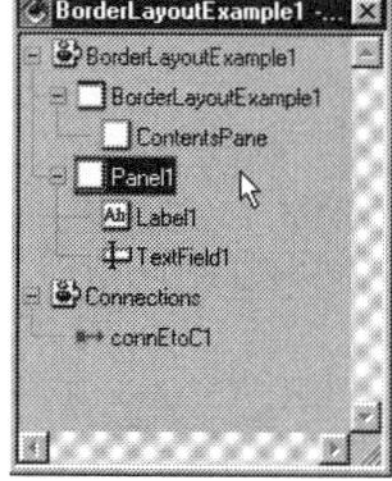

Figure 11.16 Moving the sub-GUI into the overall GUI.

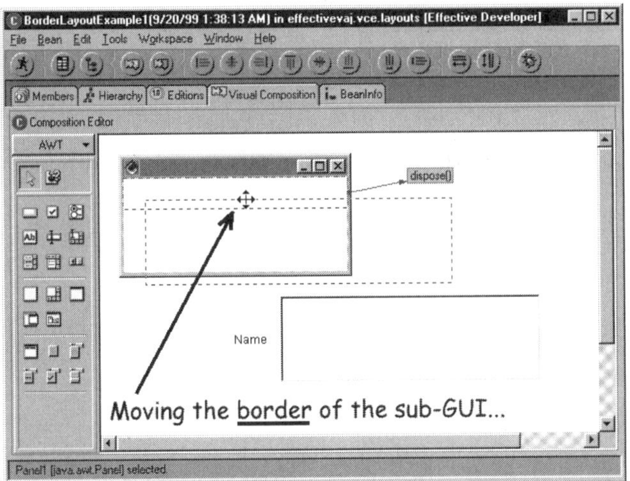

When you move this component, watch the location of the cursor, *not* the outline of the component. The cursor determines the target location of the component. The outline of the component being dragged is simply a distraction. Drag the sub-GUI into the BorderLayoutExample Frame until the NORTH hint lines appear. Then release the mouse button. The result appears in Figure 11.17; you have now bound the Label and TextField components by their preferred height. In the Beans List, contentsPane now contains Panel1.

Figure 11.17 The height-bound sub-GUI.

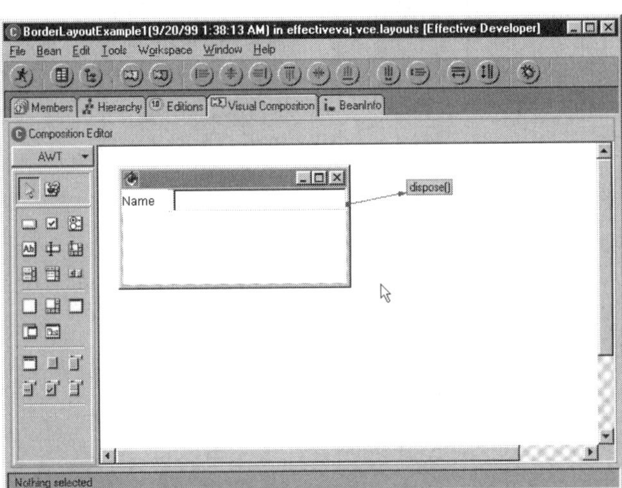

By border layouts are nested like this, the label is bound by *both* its preferred height and its preferred width. However, the text field is bound *only* by its preferred height. If the sub-GUI contained multiple rows of components, this would bind all of them to their preferred heights.

GridLayout

GridLayout lays out its components in a grid. Each component is given the same size and is positioned left-to-right, top-to-bottom.

Using GridLayout in the VCE is very similar to how you use FlowLayout. As a simple example:

1. Set the layout property of a container to GridLayout.
2. Click the "+" next to the layout property to see its parameters. GridLayout provides fourparameters: rows, columns, hgap, and vgap.
3. For this example, set hgap and vgap to 5.
4. Set rows to 3 and leave columns set to 0.

> **NOTE**
>
> If you want to set rows to 0 for a grid layout in the VCE, *you must set columns to a non-zero number* ***first***. Otherwise, if you set rows to 0 and then click on columns in the property sheet, the VCE will automatically set rows back to 1. (It detects that you have both rows and columns set to 0 at that point and wants to avoid the IllegalArgumentException.)

To add components to a grid layout, move the mouse over the container it manages and press and hold the mouse button. As you move the mouse, hint lines appear that indicate placement of the component when the mouse button is released. This does not make any difference for the first-dropped component. You can position other components relative to previously dropped components.

CardLayout

CardLayout uses a different strategy than the other layout managers. Instead of assigning locations in the container for *all* nested components, it displays only *one* component at a time. The displayed component fills the entire container, with an empty space of size hgap and vgap as a border that surrounds it.

The VCE gives some support for CardLayout as well, though you need to be a careful how you use it. To demonstrate CardLayout:

1. Create a new class that extends Frame and open it to the VCE.

2. Set contentsPane's layout to CardLayout.
3. Drop several Button components in contentsPane. Each of these buttons now has an extra pop-up menu item: **Switch to**. The VCE gives any components that reside inside a card layout the **Switch to** option. You can use this option to move to other components inside the card layout. You can also select the other components directly in the Beans List.
4. Change the order of components in the card layout by dragging the components *in the Beans List*. The order in which components are listed under their container in the Beans List is the order in which they appear when you call the next() method of CardLayout. An example of calling the next() method is covered in Chapter 13, "Variables and Instances."

When designing a card layout for a SmartGuide or tabbed panel application, do not attempt to add *all* of your GUI components in one visual composition. A better strategy is to create a separate class for each page in a separate visual composition, such as a user-information entry page, a billing information page, and a shipping information page. You then drop instances of each of these pages in the main GUI class (another separate visual composition), in a card layout. This makes developing and maintaining the GUI much easier, because you have fewer components to work with in a single visual composition. If you need to change the contents of one of the pages, you just edit the class for that page; you do not need to involve the other pages.

BoxLayout

BoxLayout exists as part of the Swing library. Swing is an enhanced GUI kit available from Sun for JDK 1.1.6 and beyond, and is part of the standard Java2 Platform. Although they have bundled BoxLayout with Swing, there is no reason you cannot use it for non-Swing layouts. However, you still need to include the Swing libraries in your application class path to find the layout.

BoxLayout enables you to arrange components along either an x-axis (horizontally) or y-axis (vertically). In a y-axis box layout, components are arranged from top to bottom in the order they are added. In an x-axis box layout, they are arranged left to right.

BoxLayout allows components to occupy different amounts of space along the primary axis. A TextField component in a top-to-bottom BoxLayout can take much less space than a TextArea component. The space allocations of a layout are determined by examining the minimumSize, maximumSize, and preferredSize properties of all contained components.

Box Beans

Swing provides a Box class that is a JPanel with a box layout and several convenience methods. These convenience methods allow you to add *struts* and *glue* to your layout. A strut is an invisible, fixed-size component that provides space between two components in a box layout. Glue is an invisible component that can expand to fill all remaining space in a box layout.

The Box class, as defined in Swing, presents some problems for visual design tools such as the VCE. The main problem is that it defines struts and glue as inner classes to assist development, but struts and glue are not beans. Because they are not beans, you cannot use them in builder tools. Additionally, because BoxLayout respects the preferred, maximum, and minimum sizes of its components, you would need to subclass components to define their resizing behavior.

To address these problems, Scott created some beans called BoxBeans. The companion CD-ROM contains BoxBeans, and you can obtain updates at http://javadude.com/tools/boxbeans. The BoxBeans provide strut and glue components *that are beans*. The strut and glue beans have a design-time appearance that makes them easier to work with as well. The BoxBeans also include a decorator that controls the resize behavior of a contained component.

Once you have installed the BoxBeans according to their included instructions, you must add its feature to VisualAge for Java. Do this by invoking the **File->Quick Start** menu option (or press F2), select **Features** in the left pane and **Add Feature** in the right pane. Choose the feature named *JavaDude Box Beans*. This adds the BoxBeans project to your workspace and adds the BoxBeans to the Swing and AWT beans-palette pages in the VCE.

The beans palette now contains the following BoxBeans:

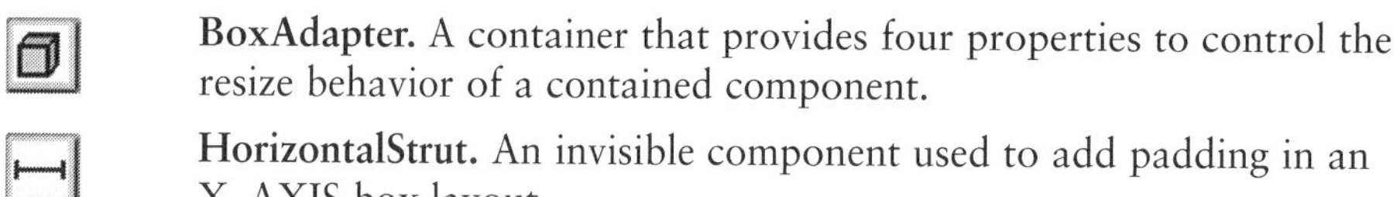

BoxAdapter. A container that provides four properties to control the resize behavior of a contained component.

HorizontalStrut. An invisible component used to add padding in an X_AXIS box layout.

VerticalStrut. An invisible component used to add padding in a Y_AXIS box layout.

HorizontalGlue. An invisible component used to fill available space. It expands horizontally as much as needed.

VerticalGlue. An invisible component used to fill available space. It expands vertically as much as needed.

BoxAdapters control the size of their contained component via their *stretchHorizontal*, *stretchVertical*, *shrinkHorizontal*, and *shrinkVertical* properties. These properties determine the return values when a layout asks the BoxAdapter for its maximum and minimum sizes. All of the BoxBeans provide design-time representations, making them easier to work with in the VCE.

For example:

1. Create a BoxLayoutTest class that extends Frame.
2. Open it to the VCE.
3. Set its contentsPane's layout to BoxLayout.

BoxLayout takes a parameter that describes whether it controls a horizontal or vertical arrangement of components. An X_AXIS orientation lays out components in a single horizontal row. AY_AXIS orientation lays out components in a single vertical column. We'll create an example as seen in Figure 11.18.

Examining the GUI closely, we can see that it is really a horizontal box layout containing five components.

1. The leftmost List component, set to expand horizontally and vertically.
2. A horizontal strut for spacing.
3. A container for the two Button components, set to stay a fixed size.
4. Another horizontal strut for spacing.
5. The rightmost List component, set to expand horizontally and vertically.
6. Set the contentsPane's BoxLayout orientation to X_AXIS.
7. Drop a BoxAdapter into contentsPane.
8. Drop a HorizontalStrut to the *right* of the BoxAdapter.
9. Drop a BoxAdapter, HorizontalStrut, and a final BoxAdapter to the right of the Horizontal Strut in the layout.
10. Set the *stretchHorizontal* and *stretchVertical* properties of the leftmost and rightmost BoxAdapters to true. The result is shown in Figure 11.19. Next, we'll use the middle BoxAdapter as the container for the buttons.
11. Set the layout property of the middle BoxAdapter to BoxLayout with a Y_AXIS orientation.
12. Add a BoxAdapter, VerticalStrut, and another BoxAdapter to the middle BoxAdapter using the Beans List. The BoxAdapters, by default, set their stretch and shrink properties to false, meaning whatever component you place inside them will remain its preferred size. The visual design now looks as shown in Figure 11.20.

We have created a GUI structure composed completely of BoxBeans that control padding and resize behavior. All that remains is to drop the List and Button components into place. The resulting design appears in Figure 11.21.

Figure 11.18 A simple BoxLayout example.

Figure 11.19 The horizontal box layout.

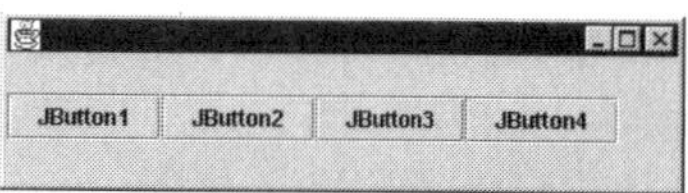

Fixed-size components in a BoxLayout

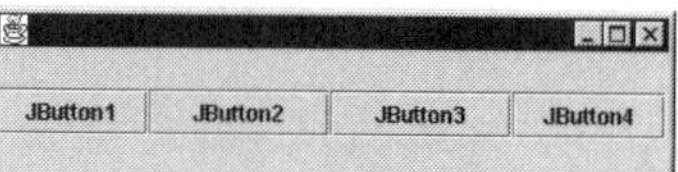

Horizontally expanding components in a BoxLayout

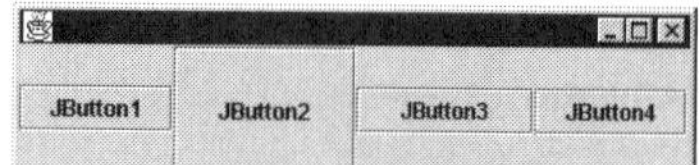

Vertically expanding components in a BoxLayout

We have used only struts so far, providing fixed spacing between components. Glue components provide variable spacing, growing or shrinking as needed. For example, if you wanted to position a button in the center of the screen, you could drop a HorizontalGlue, a BoxAdapter, and another HorizontalGlue in an X_AXIS box layout. The Glue components expand equally, and the BoxAdapter, by default, keeps the button fixed at its preferred size. This causes the button to float in the center of the GUI, as shown in Figure 11.22.

Figure 11.20 The layout structure.

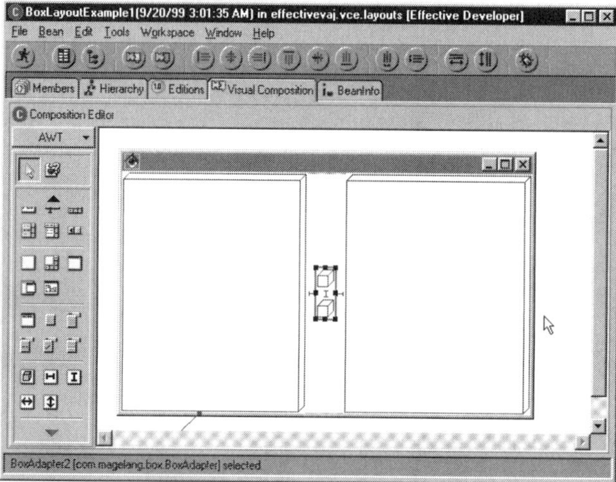

Figure 11.21 The final BoxLayout design.

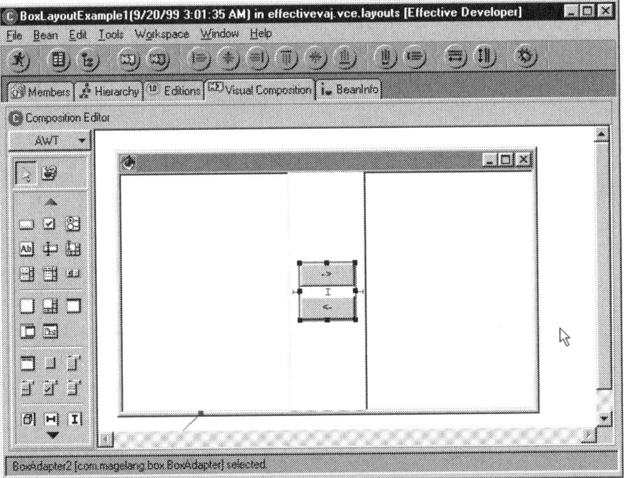

If you did not include the second HorizontalGlue component, the first one would be the only one that expands, pushing the button against the right edge of the GUI, as shown in Figure 11.23. This has the same effect as if you had placed the component in a right-aligned flow layout.

Figure 11.22 Glue used to center a component.

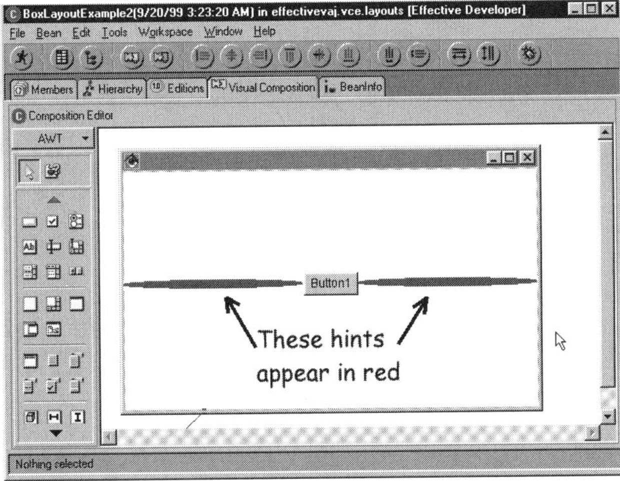

NOTE

The BoxBeans are free for any use (other than selling them just as a library) and are distributed with source code.

GridBagLayout

GridBagLayout tends to be one of the most difficult layout managers to understand.

We'll show how to use GridBagLayout in VisualAge for Java; however, we *strongly* recommend that you avoid its use. Instead, we recommend nesting the other, simpler layout managers, using the strategies discussed in *Effective Layout Management* at http://java.sun.com/developer/onlineTraining/GUI/AWTLayoutMgr.

When you develop a grid-bag layout, as with any other layout, it is *critical* that you first write your design on paper. GridBagLayout has a huge number of constraint parameters for each component, and if you attempt to simply drag and drop a GUI, your chances of creating inconsistent constraints is significantly greater.

A simple GridBagLayout example looks like the GUI in Figure 11.18. This design represents two components on either side of some middle components. The two outermost components expand horizontally and vertically, while the center components float in the center, keeping their preferred sizes. This GUI can be implemented using a six-cell grid-bag layout. The easiest way to determine this is to draw horizontal and vertical lines completely through the GUI between adjacent components, until no two components share the same cell. The set of cells appears in Figure 11.24.

It is important that you draw this picture and the GridBagLayout cells when you design your grid-bag layout. This picture gives you all the information you

Figure 11.23 Glue used to right-align.

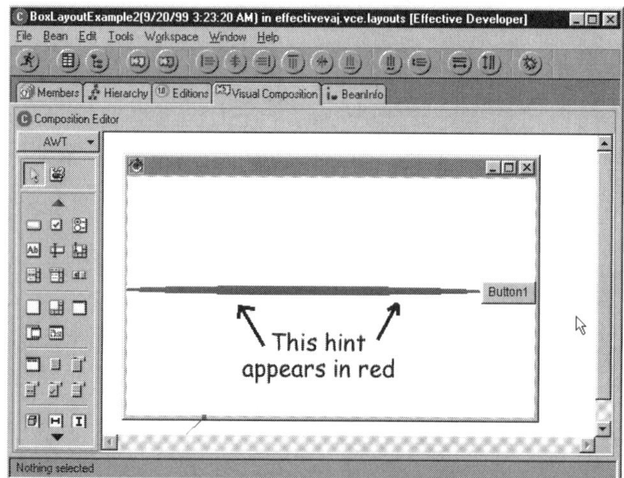

Figure 11.24 Breaking the GUI into GridBagLayout cells.

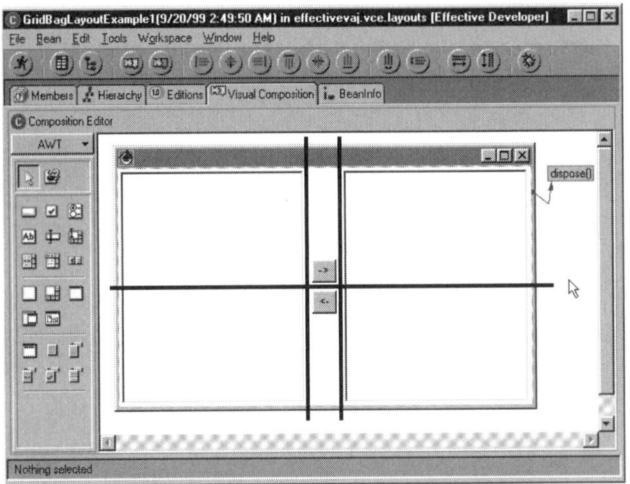

need to properly decide the grid-bag constraints for each component. After examining this picture, we determine the grid-bag constraints seen in Table 11.1.

When you place components in the VCE, you should follow a simple placement strategy. Always start with the upper-left-most component, and add components to the left and below it. Never add components to the left of or above others, as this can sometimes confuse GridBagLayout.

To create this GUI:

1. Create a new class named GridBagLayoutExample, extending Frame.
2. Open this class to the VCE and set its contentsPane's layout to GridBagLayout. When you set a layout to GridBagLayout, there are no parameters to the layout; it does not have a plus sign next to it in the property sheet. GridBagLayout does not have parameters because you set a complex constraint object each for each of its components.
3. Place a List component in the grid-bag layout. Notice that it expands to fill the entire container.
4. Open the property sheet for the list, and click the plus sign next to its *constraints* property. (Note that constraints is not really a property, but it acts like one in the property sheet.) The VCE tries to assume how you want to use certain types of components in a typical grid-bag layout. In the case of a list, it assumes you want it to expand, so it sets some initial values for the grid-bag constraints for the component.
5. Add a Button component to the layout. Be very careful when you add these components. Because the list expanded to fill the container, there is

Table 11.1 Grid-bag Constraints for the Example

	Component 1 List (left)	**Component 2 Button (top)**	**Component 3 Button (bottom)**	**Component 4 List (right)**
GridX	0	1	1	2
GridY	0	0	1	0
GridWidth	1	1	1	1
GridHeight	2	1	1	2
Fill	BOTH	NONE	NONE	BOTH
Anchor	CENTER	SOUTH	NORTH	CENTER
Insets	(4,4,4,4)	(0,4,2,4)	(2,4,0,4)	(4,4,4,4)
IpadX	0	0	0	0
IpadY	0	0	0	0
WeightX	0.5	0.0	0.0	0.5
WeightY	1.0	0.5	0.5	1.0

not much room to work. Select a button, and *click and hold* the mouse button on top of the list. As you drag near the borders of the list, watch for the hint lines at the border. You should see straight hint lines, *not* BorderLayout hint lines. If you see BorderLayout hints (surrounding large areas of the layout), you have moved too far. Figure 11.25 shows the hint line when dropping this button. Drop it to the *right* of the list.

6. The button appears at its preferred size; the VCE assumes you want the button to stay a fixed size.
7. Drop another Button component *below* the first button, and another List component to the *right* of the first button. The resulting visual design should look like Figure 11.26.

Notice how the second button floats below the lists. This is because the VCE set the initial value of *gridHeight* for the lists to 1. You can stretch the lists by either setting *gridHeight* to 2 in their property sheet constraints, or visually by dragging the bottom edge of each list. To expand it visually:

1. Click in a list to select it.
2. Drag the bottom edge of the list at its bottom-center selection dot down until you see the hints seen in Figure 11.27. The dark hint line should snap into the new, 2, grid position as you drag down.

Figure 11.25 Dropping the button.

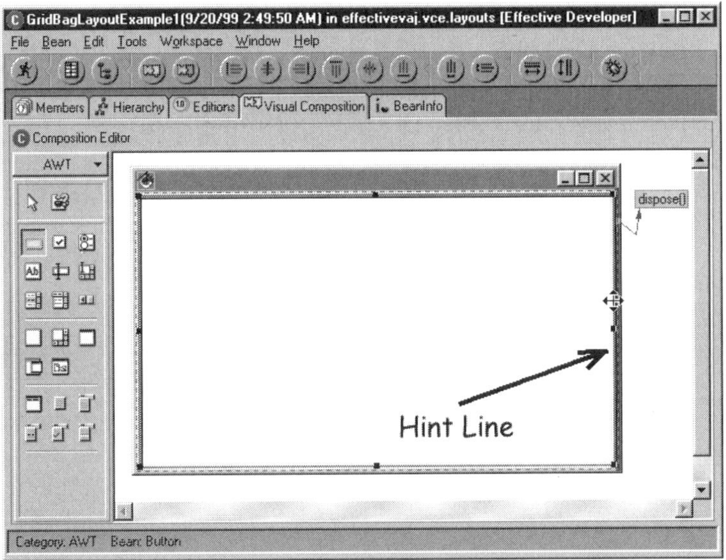

Figure 11.26 The initial visual design.

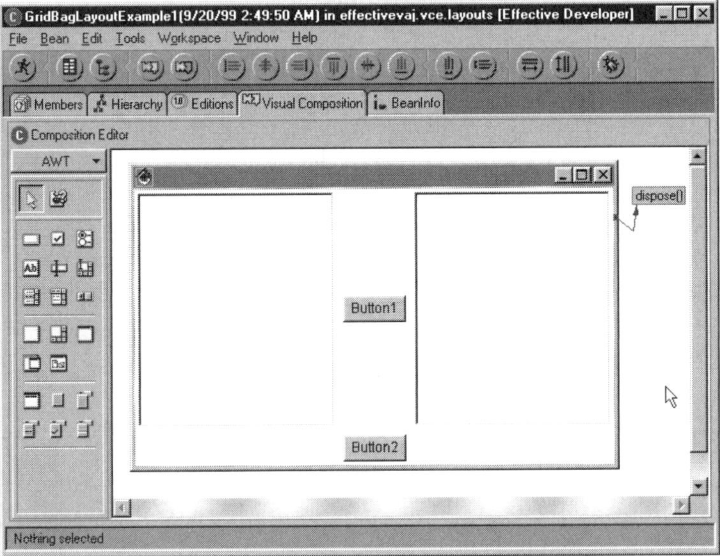

Figure 11.27 Changing gridHeight.

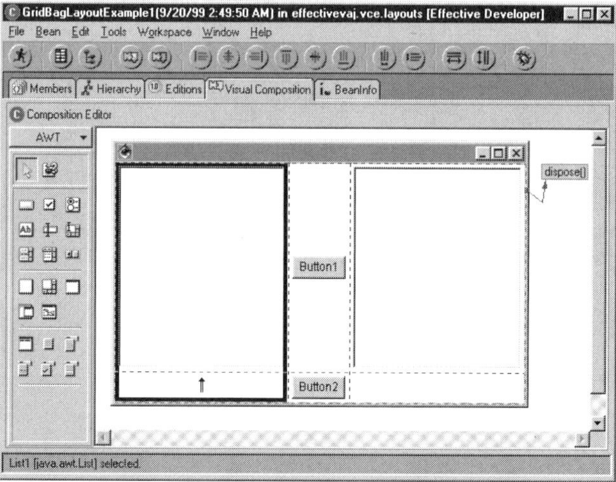

3. Expand the height of the other list in the same manner. The resulting visual design appears in Figure 11.28.

Next, finish setting the grid-bag constraints for the components. The visual manipulation has set the gridX, gridY, gridHeight, and gridWidth constraints, but you need to set more to match the design. Notice in Table 11.1 that the constraints for the two lists are the same, with the exception of gridX. You can multiply select the two lists and set their constraints at the same time by clicking on one, then, shift-clicking on the other. You can then select Properties from either one's pop-up menu if the property sheet is not visible.

The only constraint that does not match the design in Table 11.1 is weightX. While the current weights perform as you like, you should match the design, so change weightX to 0.5. This results in no change to the GUI appearance.

You need to edit the constraints of the buttons separately to set their anchors, although you could use multiple selection to set the insets and weighty values. Change the constraints for the buttons to match the design in Table 11.1. The resulting GUI looks as we expected, shown in Figure 11.18. This layout required quite a bit of design thought, not to mention that if we are not careful, the grid-bag layout in the VCE can become confused.

A Useful GUI Pattern

Many GUIs require the input of several String values. For example, let's create a simple address form GUI that accepts a person's name, address, city, state, and phone number. This GUI is shown in Figure 11.29.

Figure 11.28 The lists with proper gridHeight values.

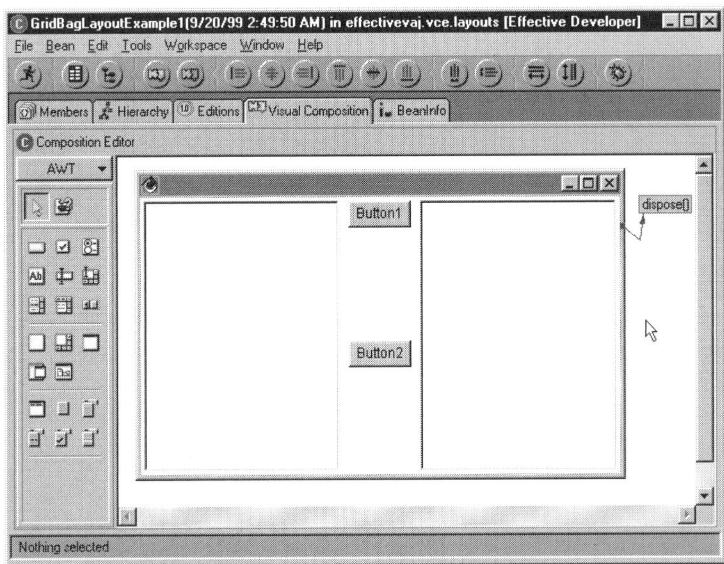

The strategy for designing this GUI is to separate it into two sections at the top of the panel. The leftmost section contains one set of Label and TextField components; the rightmost section contains the other set of Label and TextField components.

Each of the sections has the same type of structure: a column of labels, and a column of text fields. The labels should not expand horizontally, but the text fields should. To accomplish this, put all labels in the WEST part of a border layout, and the text fields in the CENTER part of a border layout. This binds the width of the labels, but not the text fields. A grid layout controls each of these columns. Bind the height of the labels *and* the text fields by placing their layouts inside a border layout.

Figure 11.29 An address GUI.

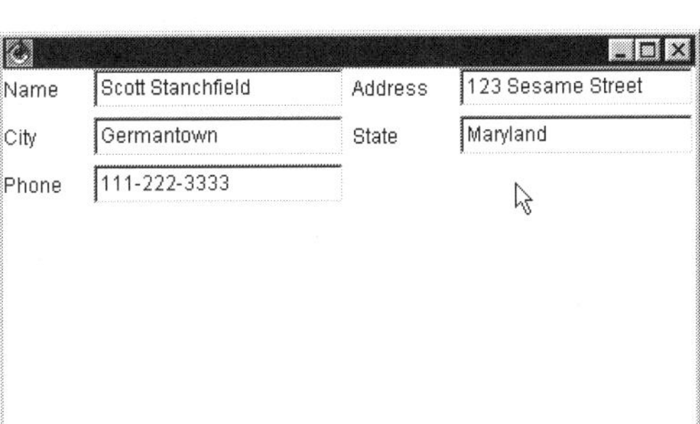

To create our GUI class:

1. Begin with a class named SimpleAddressGUI, extending Frame. This GUI is going to get very complicated very quickly. Because of the number of components involved, especially the panels we need to arrange the layout, we will use the Beans List to do most of our work. Assuming we had designed our GUI before we started dropping components (which is a very good idea if you do not want to incur the wrath of this author), we should have a direct mapping between our GUI design and what we will be dropping in the Beans List. The design we are using for our GUI is:

```
Frame[BorderLayout]                        SimpleAddressGUI
  NORTH=Panel[GridLayout(1 row)]            topPart
    Panel[BorderLayout]                        topLeftPart
      WEST=Panel[GridLayout(3 rows)]             topLeftLabelPart
        Label["Name"]                                nameLabel
        Label["City"]                                cityLabel
        Label["Phone"]                               phoneLabel
      CENTER=Panel[GridLayout(3 rows)]           topLeftEntryPart
        3 TextFields                                 nameField...
    Panel[BorderLayout]                        topRightPart
      WEST=Panel[GridLayout(3 rows)]             topRightLabelPart
        Label["Address"]                             addressLabel
        Label["State"]                               stateLabel
      CENTER=Panel[GridLayout(3 rows)]           topRightEntryPart
        2 TextFields                                 addressField...
```

By writing the design in a tree form, creation of the GUI inside the VCE is very simple, using the Beans List. Simply read down the previous tree and add components to the Beans List. It is up to you whether you prefer to use the Beans List or drag –and drop components in the design area. Sometimes you have no choice but to use the Beans List, because you may not be able to select some containers because their components completely fill them. Sometimes you may find it effective to use a combination of adding some components through the Beans List and some components through the design area. The best advice is to use what feels most comfortable to you. When you are initially learning VisualAge for Java, try to use both methods equally.

2. Open class SimpleAddressGUI to the VCE; open the Beans List. All of the work will be performed there.
3. Set SimpleAddressGUI's contentsPane's layout to BorderLayout.

Follow through the design tree to create the GUI, dropping the panels and components in the Beans List. The following steps create the GUI. All actions take place in the Beans List. For all layouts, set their hgap and vgap parameters to 5.

Watch how the GUI looks in the design area as you build it. In many cases, panels appear too small to add any components, forcing use of the Beans List. If we were not using the Beans List, we would be creating these sub-GUIs in other parts of the design area and then moving them into place.

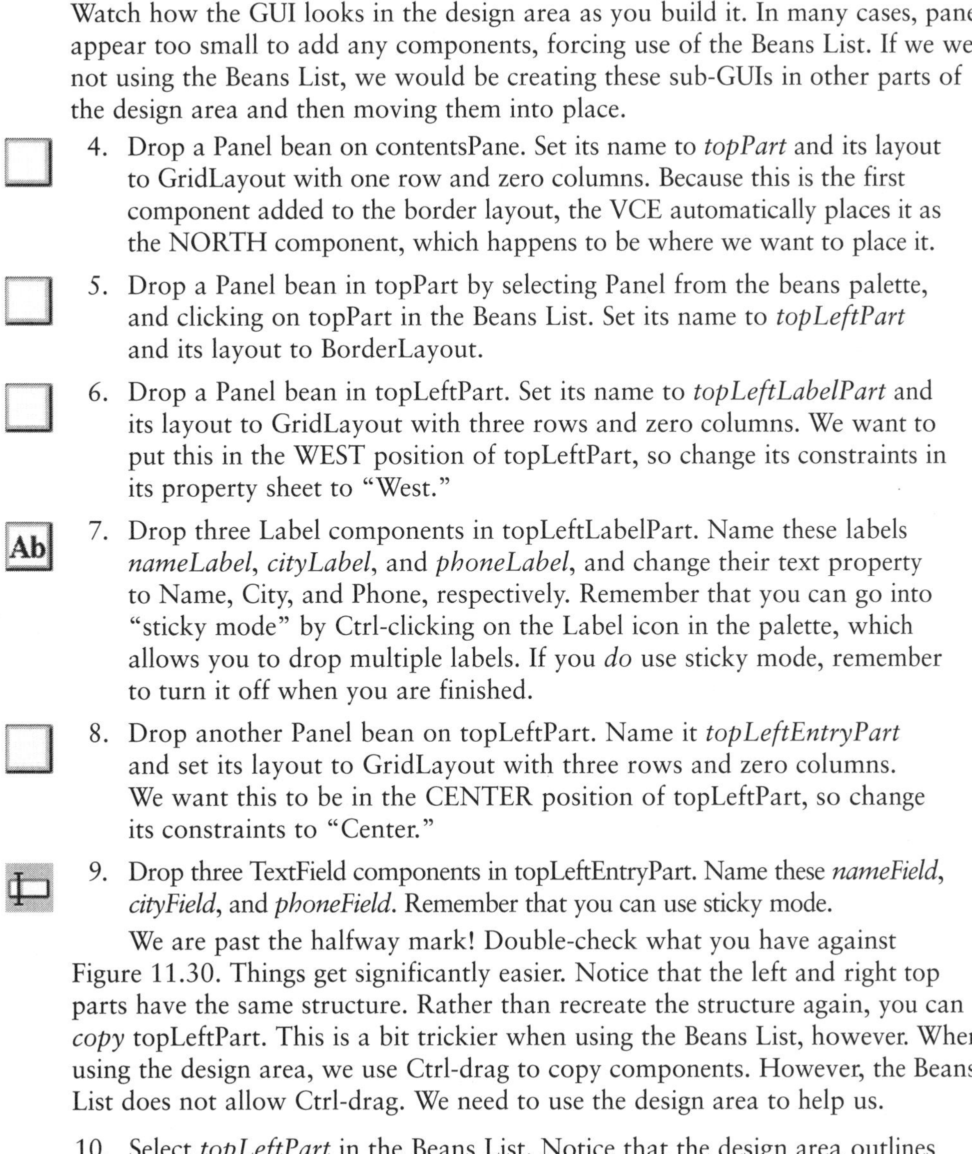

4. Drop a Panel bean on contentsPane. Set its name to *topPart* and its layout to GridLayout with one row and zero columns. Because this is the first component added to the border layout, the VCE automatically places it as the NORTH component, which happens to be where we want to place it.
5. Drop a Panel bean in topPart by selecting Panel from the beans palette, and clicking on topPart in the Beans List. Set its name to *topLeftPart* and its layout to BorderLayout.
6. Drop a Panel bean in topLeftPart. Set its name to *topLeftLabelPart* and its layout to GridLayout with three rows and zero columns. We want to put this in the WEST position of topLeftPart, so change its constraints in its property sheet to "West."
7. Drop three Label components in topLeftLabelPart. Name these labels *nameLabel*, *cityLabel*, and *phoneLabel*, and change their text property to Name, City, and Phone, respectively. Remember that you can go into "sticky mode" by Ctrl-clicking on the Label icon in the palette, which allows you to drop multiple labels. If you *do* use sticky mode, remember to turn it off when you are finished.
8. Drop another Panel bean on topLeftPart. Name it *topLeftEntryPart* and set its layout to GridLayout with three rows and zero columns. We want this to be in the CENTER position of topLeftPart, so change its constraints to "Center."
9. Drop three TextField components in topLeftEntryPart. Name these *nameField*, *cityField*, and *phoneField*. Remember that you can use sticky mode.

We are past the halfway mark! Double-check what you have against Figure 11.30. Things get significantly easier. Notice that the left and right top parts have the same structure. Rather than recreate the structure again, you can *copy* topLeftPart. This is a bit trickier when using the Beans List, however. When using the design area, we use Ctrl-drag to copy components. However, the Beans List does not allow Ctrl-drag. We need to use the design area to help us.

10. Select *topLeftPart* in the Beans List. Notice that the design area outlines it as well.
11. Ctrl-drag the outline of topLeftPart (make sure you are *between* the selection dots, not on them) into a free spot of the design area, and release. This creates a copy of topLeftPart and its contents. The VCE names the copy *topLeftPart1*. Likewise, all contained components mirror their original's names.

Figure 11.30 Halfway done.

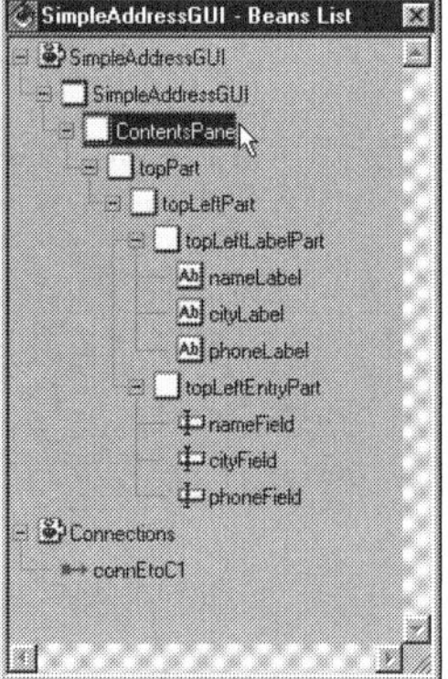

12. Using the Beans List, rename:
    a. topLeftPart1, to topRightPart
    b. topLeftLabelPart1, to topRightLabelPart
    c. topLeftEntryPart1, to topRightLabelPart
13. Delete phoneLabel1 and phoneField1 from the new copy; the top right part of the GUI has only two labels and entry fields.
14. Rename nameLabel1 to *addressLabel*, and set its text to Address.
15. Rename cityLabel1 to *stateLabel* and set its text to State.
16. Rename nameField1 to *addressField.*
17. Rename cityField1 to *stateField.*
18. Finally, drag topRightPart into topPart in the Beans List, and you should see the proper results, shown in Figure 11.31.

You can extend this GUI by adding buttons in the bottom right corner (using the previously discussed GridLayout-nested-in-a-FlowLayout-in-a-BorderLayout technique). Chapter 14, "Design Patterns for the VCE," discusses ways to make sub-GUI components interact using only events. This will allow us to easily reuse our dialog button sub-GUI.

Quick Form

Version 3.0 of VisualAge for Java provides a new tool in the VCE to help you quickly define layouts that map to properties in a bean. The Quick Form tool examines the properties in a bean and creates labeled text fields for each property. It also connects the fields in the form to the properties such that when a field changes, the property is updated (and vice versa). In this chapter, we'll discuss

Figure 11.31 The completed visual design.

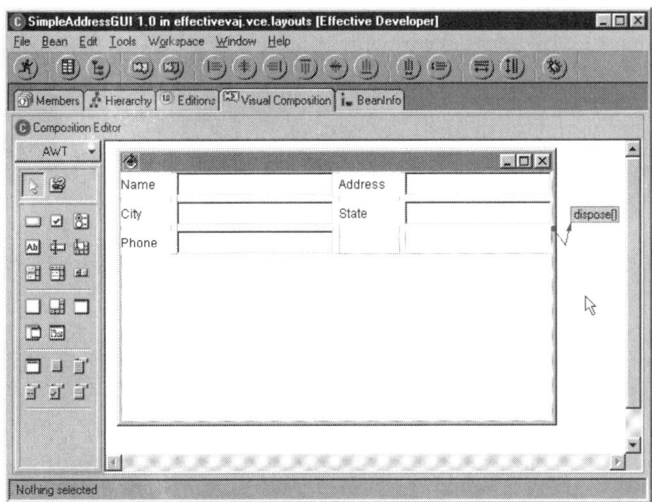

how Quick Form generates a grid-bag layout. Quick Form generates property-to-property connections, which you can read about in Chapter 12.

We've got mixed feelings about the Quick Form tool. Although it can generate some very useful connections automatically, it creates a GridBagLayout GUI. As we discussed earlier, GridBagLayout is pure evil, and can be very difficult to understand. However, the grid-bag layouts produced by the Quick Form tool are consistent from one Quick Form to another, and are fairly simple. This makes it more maintainable than a hand-implemented grid-bag layout, but you should still be careful how you manipulate it once the Quick Form tool is done.

Generating a Quick Form

The Quick Form tool is a *one-shot* code-generation tool. You use it to generate an initial GUI and then add, remove, or move components within that GUI to finish your implementation.

> **NOTE**
>
> We *strongly* recommend that you isolate Quick Form generated GUIs from the rest of your GUI. This is easy to do if you apply the Model-View-Controller paradigm to your application. See Chapter 15, "Model-View-Controller in the VCE," for details on separation of parts of your GUI from each other and from the business logic behind your application.

We'll walk through the same example shown in Figure 11.31, using a Quick Form. We'll do this as follows:

1. Define a bean that has the properties we want to display.
2. Drop an instance of that bean in a VCE session.
3. Start the Quick Form SmartGuide for that bean.
4. Define the field-to-property mapping we want for the form.
5. Arrange the layout for the form.

We'll discuss each of these steps in the following sections.

Defining a Bean for Our Quick Form

The first thing we need to do is to define a bean to represent our data. As you'll see in Chapter 15, separation of business logic and data from the GUI results in much more maintainable and extensible applications. Quick Form helps us achieve this goal by automating the creation of a form from a bean. To create the bean:

1. Create a new class called AddressData.
2. Open AddressData to the BeanInfo editor. See Chapter 8, "The BeanInfo Editor," for details on its operation and how to create properties.
3. Create the following properties. All of these properties will be read/write/bound Strings:
   - Name
   - Address
   - City
   - State
   - Phone
4. Create a new class named AddressForm. Use java.awt.Frame as the superclass and select the **Compose the class visually** check box.
5. Drop an instance of AddressData in the design area *outside* the rectangular dotted line that represents the Panel superclass.
6. Bring up the pop-up menu for that instance of AddressData.
7. Choose **Quick Form** from the pop-up menu. You'll see the QuickForm SmartGuide, seen in Figure 11.32.

   This page of the SmartGuide contains the following options:

   Select a parent for the quick form. This box lists all containers in your GUI. You can choose which container you want to contain the generated form. Later you'll be given the choice if the generated grid-bag layout is added to this container, or if you want to directly add the components in the container (setting its layout to GridBagLayout).

Figure 11.32 The Quick Form SmartGuide.

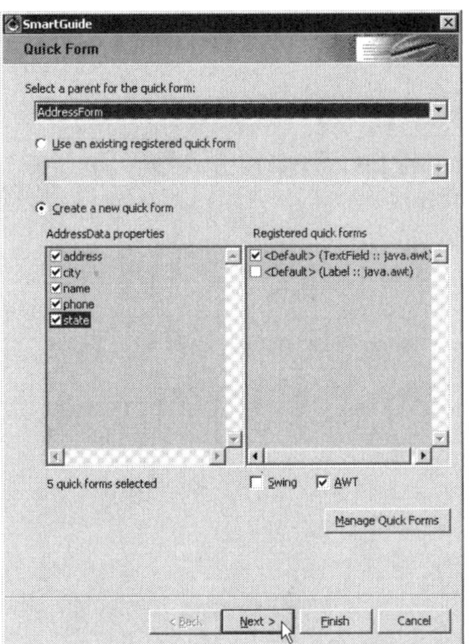

Use an existing registered quick form. If you select this radio button, you can choose an existing quick-form mapping. The quick-form mapping defines how properties in your bean will be represented in the GUI.

Create a new quick form. If you select this radio button, you will define a new quick-form mapping using the following fields.

AddressData properties. This section lists all of the properties in the bean you selected. In this case, the bean was an AddressData bean, but the name over this list and its contents will change for other beans. In this list, you'll select which properties should be included in the generated form. As you select each property, you can define which type of property mapping to use for that field under **Registered quick forms.**

Registered quick forms. You can select which type of component will be used to represent each property in the generated GUI. Select the property you want to customize; then choose the Registered quick form property mapping to use (usually a TextField or Label mapping).

Swing. If selected, registered quick forms that use Swing components will be displayed.

AWT. If selected, registered quick forms that use AWT components will be displayed.

NOTE

Unfortunately, IBM chose to use the term *Quick Form* at several levels. The term is used at two levels:

Mapping a bean to a GUI. At the topmost level, the term *Quick Form* means a mapping from a bean to a GUI, defining which properties are connected to which GUI components. You manipulate these Quick Forms by choosing the **Quick Form** option from a bean's pop-up menu. After you've finished the Quick Form SmartGuide, you can choose to save the form, which you can use later for beans with the same properties by choosing **Use an existing registered quick form.**

Mapping a property to a GUI component. At the lower level, the term *Quick Form* means a mapping from a specific property to a GUI component. These are the Registered Quick Forms that you can edit by pressing the Manage Quick Forms button or choosing **Window->Options->Visual Composition->Quick Form Manager**.

Manage Quick Forms. If pressed, you will be taken to the Quick Form manager, which enables you to define mappings from a specific property type to a GUI control to represent it.

8. Choose which properties should be included in the generated GUI. In this example, leave all properties selected.
9. Select each property in turn (by clicking on its name, not its check box) and choose the property mapping for it. For this example, we'll use the default mapping for each. This default mapping will map String properties to TextField components in the GUI.
10. Press **Next** to move to the layout page of the SmartGuide, seen in Figure 11.33.

    On this page of the SmartGuide, you'll see the following options:

    Number of columns per row. This number represents the maximum number of *properties* that may appear in each row. Each property could be represented by two components (usually a label and a text field), and the label could appear above or to the left of the text field. A property could span multiple columns.

NOTE

It is important to think of this setting as the number of *properties* rather than the number of components that appear.

Figure 11.33 Defining the quick form layout.

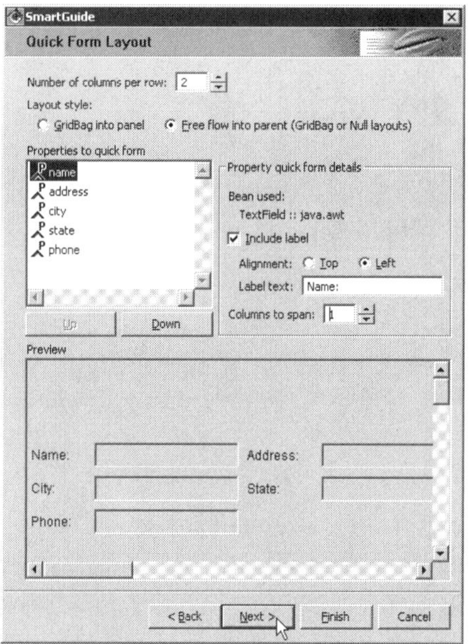

GridBag into panel. If selected, the Quick Form tool will create a new Panel that uses GridBagLayout and drop that panel into the selected container (from the previous page).

Free flow into parent. If selected, the components will be placed directly in the parent container. This is valid only if the layout of the parent container is GridBagLayout or null. Remember, **never** use a null layout unless you want Scott to hunt you down like a rampaging moose!

Properties to quick form. This is a list of the properties you selected on the previous page. You can select each property in turn and modify **Property quick form details** to the right of this list.

Up and **Down** buttons. Select a property and press Up or Down to set the order of properties. Properties will be arranged from left to right and then top-to-bottom.

Bean used. This is a reminder of the GUI component you selected on the previous panel for the property mapping. If you notice this is incorrect, you'll need to go back to the previous page and choose the correct **Registered quick form.**

Include label. If selected, the generated GUI will include a label above or to the left of the GUI component for the field.

Top or **Left.** Defines where the label appears relative to the GUI component for the property. These options are only available if you selected **Include label**.

Label text. The text to appear on the generated label. The SmartGuide guesses what this should be based on the property name, but you will probably have to change this for many properties.

Columns to span. Specifies how many columns a property (including the label and GUI component) should cover in their row.

Preview. Gives you an idea what the GUI will look like when it's generated.

11. Select how many columns you want (in this case two).
12. Decide if you want to place the components in the selected container or in their own panel. You can usually get better results by placing them in their own container (the **GridBag into Panel** option). In this example, we choose GridBag into Panel.
13. Change each property's details to use a label on the left.
14. Press **Next.** If you want to save the quick form for use with the same bean later, check the box and give it a name.

The resulting quick form looks as shown in Figure 11.34.

By setting the layout of the main panel (the outer dotted rectangle in Figure 11.34) to BorderLayout and moving the generated panel to the main panel's NORTH position, we'll get the same GUI we had in Figure 11.31.

Figure 11.34 A Quick Form generated GUI.

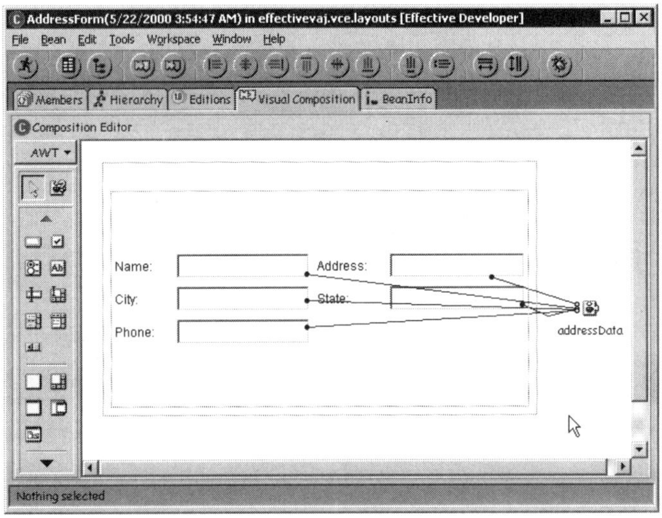

Custom Layout Managers

Version 3.0 of VisualAge for Java now enables you to use *any* layout manager in your GUI designs. The layout property of containers will list all defined layout managers in your workspace. However, if the layout manager you want to use requires custom constraint objects, you need to provide special support for VisualAge in that layout manager to be able to use those constraints in the VCE.

To use a custom layout manager, simply select it as the layout property value for a container. All layout managers that exist in your workspace appear in the list of layout values. Once selected, you can add components to it by dropping them in the container in the VCE design area or Beans List. We recommend that you use the Beans List, because it shows the ordering of the components in the container.

For layout managers that are positional, like FlowLayout or GridLayout, you only need to change component order by dragging contained components in the Beans List. For layout managers that require constraints, like BorderLayout or GridBagLayout, you need custom support.

Suppose we had downloaded a simple custom layout manager called MaxMinLayout. (The code for this layout manager is available as effectivevaj.vce.layouts.MaxMinLayout in the sample code on the CD.) This layout manager manages two components, one labeled "max," the other labeled "min." The max component will never be sized larger than its preferred width, and the min component will never be sized smaller than its preferred width (unless the container is too small). This means that if there is more room than their combined preferred widths, the min component will expand horizontally. If there isn't enough room for their preferred sizes, the max component will shrink horizontally. This behavior is demonstrated in Figure 11.35.

To use this layout, you would write code as follows:

```
Panel p = new Panel(new MaxMinLayout());
p.add(new Label("Enter your name in this field"),
       "max");
p.add(new TextField(20), "min");
```

The max constraint means, "Respect the requested maximum size of this component." The min constraint means, "Respect the minimum size of this component."

Figure 11.35 MaxMinLayout in action.

For the simple implementation of the MaxMinLayout provided in the sample code on the CD, the max component is always the leftmost, and the min component is always on the right.

We can *almost* use this layout in the VCE, but there is a slight problem. The VCE has no way of knowing what type of constraint objects it needs to ask the user about. We can select this layout for the layout property of any container in the VCE, but the VCE will not allow you to enter constraints. This makes the VCE initially useless for this layout. If you add any components to the layout, they can only be arranged based on the order in which they were added to the container (the order in which they appear in the Beans List).

The following sections describe what you must do to ensure that your custom layout manager works in the VCE.

> **NOTE**
>
> The following required customizations are specific to the VCE and will *not* work in other bean builder tools. However, that they are simply additions to the layout manager class (or subclass) and will not hurt use of the layout manager in any other environment.

The Public Default Constructor

The first thing you must do with your custom layout manager is to provide a public default constructor. The VCE will create instances of custom layout managers only by calling the public default constructor for the class. This is the constructor that takes no arguments.

> **NOTE**
>
> If your layout manager class does not have a public default constructor, it will not appear in the list of available layout managers when you select the layout property in a Container's property sheet.

For MaxMinLayout, you would need to have the following defined:

```
public MaxMinLayout() {}
```

It could contain some code if you want or need it to.

Layout Constraints

If your layout manager requires that constraints be passed to the add() method of the container (like the min and max constraints mentioned previously), you must explicitly tell the VCE what type of object to ask for.

For the MaxMinLayout example, all you need to do is add the following method to your layout manager or to a subclass of the layout manager:

```
public static final Class getConstraintsClass() {
  return String.class;
}
```

The VCE calls this method whenever a property sheet is shown for a component contained in your layout manager. It then looks to see which property editor is registered for the constraint type and uses that property editor to edit the constraints for the class. See Chapter 20, "Bean Customization," for details on defining and registering property editors.

Layout Parameters

You'll probably want to provide parameters to your custom layout managers, like hgap and vgap. The VCE provides a way to find out what parameters are needed. The VCE will *not* look at the parameters passed to the constructor of the layout manager. Instead, the VCE examines the custom layout manager class for get and set methods. Anytime it sees a pair of get/set methods, such as getHgap() and setHgap(), defined like JavaBeans properties (see Chapter 7, "Introduction to JavaBeans Components"), it adds these values under the layout property in the property sheet for the container. To access these properties, you must click on the "+" button to the left of the layout property in the property sheet. For example, if you wanted your layout manager to have an hgap parameter, you would add something like the following to your layout manager:

```
public void setHgap(int hgap) {
  this.hgap = hgap;
}
public int getHgap() {
  return hgap;
}
```

> **NOTE**
>
> If your layout manager does not provide get/set methods for the parameter, you must either change the code of the layout manager or create a subclass that provides the get/set methods for that parameter.

Using the Custom Layout Manager

After you've made sure you have a public default constructor, layout constraint specification, and layout parameters, you can use your custom layout manager in the VCE. Any layout manager that defines a public default constructor will appear in the list of possible layout managers when you're setting the layout property of a container. After selecting the custom layout manager, you may or may not see a "+" to the left of the layout property in the property sheet. If you have any get/set methods defined in the layout manager, you'll see the "+" and can click it to set those parameters for the layout manager.

Once you've told the VCE which layout manager to use, you can add components to the container the same way you would add them to a grid layout or flow layout. The VCE will provide hint lines to help you determine the order of components within the container. This is the only visual support you'll receive from the VCE for components within custom layouts.

If you have defined the getConstaintsClass() method in your layout manager, you can click on components added to the container and edit their *constraints* properties. This will be your primary interaction with the layout manager for telling it how to position and size components.

Focus Ordering in the VCE

An application's focus order is the order in which components gain focus when the Tab key is pressed. Focus order determination depends on whether you are using an AWT or Swing GUI.

If you are using an AWT GUI, the order in which you add components to containers determines the focus order. If you are using a Swing GUI, a separate FocusManager class determines which component gains focus next. For Swing, the DefaultFocusManager class determines the order based on the position of components on the screen. It orders components from top to bottom, with components at nearly the same vertical position ordered from left to right.

AWT Tab Ordering

The VCE provides support for the AWT model of focus ordering. We will see in a moment how to adapt a Swing application to take advantage of this VCE support. To activate VCE focus-order support, select **Set-Tabbing** from the pop-up menu of any container. Note that you may have to select the container from the Beans List to see its pop-up menu. Tab order icons appear as shown in Figure 11.36.

You can change the focus order by dragging the yellow and blue tab icons. Yellow tab icons represent the focus order of non-container components. Blue tab icons represent the position of containers within another containers.

The VCE will let you change the tab ordering only for containers that either have no layout manager (their layout property is null) or use BorderLayout or

Figure 11.36 Tab icons.

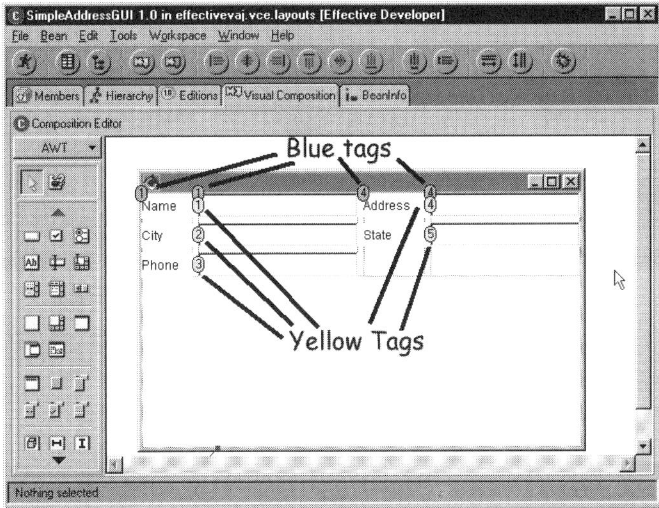

GridBagLayout. If you use any layout manager that depends on component order when laying them out, you will not be able to change the tab ordering with these icons. This is because changing the tab order with the icons actually changes the order in which the generated code adds components to the container.

Changing the focus order with tab icons is actually just a shortcut for rearranging components in the Beans List. In other words, you can accomplish the same effect by dragging components to another location in the same container in the Beans List.

Swing Tab Ordering

If you try to change the focus order of a Swing container using the tab icons, you will not get the desired results. The problem is that swing uses a separate FocusManager class to determine the order of components. To enable the VCE support when designing a Swing container, you must design your own FocusManager subclass that determines component order based on their position within a container. A simple implementation of such a class follows. We will not provide details in this book on how FocusManager classes work, but we feel it's important to give you this code so you can effectively use tabbing support in the VCE with Swing.

```
import javax.swing.DefaultFocusManager;
// OR import com.sun.java.swing.DefaultFocusManager;
//     for VisualAge for Java version 3.0
```

```
import java.awt.Point;
import java.awt.Component;
import java.awt.Container;

/** A Simple Swing FocusManager that walks through components in the
 *    order they were added to containers, the same way AWT works
 */
public class ContainerOrderFocusManager extends DefaultFocusManager {
  /** Return order based on order in which
   *    components were added to containers
   */
  public boolean compareTabOrder(Component a,Component b) {
    // find a common container for the two components
    Container commonContainer;
    for(Component lookA = a; a != null; a = commonContainer) {
      commonContainer = lookA.getParent();
      for(Component lookB = b; b != null; b = b.getParent())
        if (commonContainer.isAncestorOf(b))
          // determine which is found first
          return (depthFindFirst(commonContainer, a, b) == 1);
    }
    // if neither share a parent container,
    //   do the normal focus search
    return super.compareTabOrder(a,b);
  }

  /** Helper method that walks through containers, depth-first,
   *  returning
   *    0: container doesn't contain either a or b
   *    1: found a first
   *    2: found b first
   */
  protected int depthFindFirst(Container c,
                               Component a,
                               Component b) {
    Component[] comps = c.getComponents();
    for(int i = 0; i< comps.length; i++)
      if (comps[i] == a)
        return 1;
      else if (comps[i] == b)
        return 2;
      else if (comps[i] instanceof Container) {
        int result =
```

```
          depthFindFirst((Container)comps[i], a, b);
        if (result > 0)
          return result;
      }
    return 0;
  }
}
```

By using such a class, you can change the focus order of your components by using the tab icons, and see the expected movement when you press the Tab key in your application. Use this class by adding the following code to the main () method:

```
FocusManager.setCurrentManager(new ContainerOrderFocusManager());
```

NOTE

If you have an import for java.awt.* in your code, you will need to fully qualify the FocusManager class in the previous statement, as it exists in both the Swing package (com.sun.java.swing or javax.swing) and AWT. In these cases, the previous code would look as follows:

```
// for VisualAge for Java, version 3.0
com.sun.java.swing.FocusManager.setCurrentManager(
    new ContainerOrderFocusManager());

// for VisualAge for Java, version 3.5
javax.swing.FocusManager.setCurrentManager(
    new ContainerOrderFocusManager());
```

Summary

Layout managers are incredibly powerful, once you become familiar with them and how to nest them. VisualAge makes it easy to create and maintain GUIs in the VCE, but remember that it is an *implementation tool*, not a *design tool*. Draw your GUI and write your design before even starting VisualAge for Java. In addition, never use a null layout. Always use a layout if you want to survive the experience.

Now that we can design the *appearance* of our GUIs, we move on to designing the *behavior* of the GUI by drawing connections between components.

Connections

12

Drawing a user interface is only half the battle. An attractive interface is worthless if the buttons and other controls don't work. Fortunately, the VCE provides a way to define what happens when a user interacts with your interface.

The JavaBeans specification provides a very flexible event model. Some objects fire events; others act as listeners that respond to events. VisualAge for Java's BeanInfo editor makes it easy to create event sources. The VCE makes it easy to listen and react to events. Even more importantly, it makes the interaction *visual*. You no longer need to write code to program bean interaction; you can *draw* that interaction in your visual design in the VCE.

A visual representation of an application design greatly helps you to understand the design. It is much easier to see that a button click updates a text field when a line exists between them instead of reading the code to find all event handlers. More importantly, if you want to delete the action, you delete the line. If you want to modify the action, you modify the line. This is less error-prone than searching code for the proper event handlers and deleting/modifying them.

A *connection* is a line drawn between beans in the VCE's design area that represents a *listener* for events from a particular event source. The connection listens for an event and, when the source fires that event, performs some action.

The VCE uses introspection to determine which events a bean can fire (see Chapter 7, "Introduction to JavaBeans Components," for a discussion of the introspection process). This makes it possible for the VCE to present simple menus and dialogs that list these events. You select which source event you would like to listen for, starting a connection from that source bean, and draw a line between that bean and a target bean, to specify the bean with which you want to interact when the source fires the event. You pick an action to perform on the target, setting a property or calling a method.

This chapter presents the types of connections available. Each has significant power, especially the often-misunderstood property-to-property connection. We will walk through several examples of connections, explaining when and why you would want to use each type.

> **NOTE**
>
> The examples in the chapter, while useful for explaining connections, are not necessarily good examples of design in the Visual Composition Editor. When designing a GUI application in VisualAge, you should strive for as much separation of user interface and the actual logic and data as possible. The problem with tools such as the VCE is that they make it easy to forget about this separation; most users simply drop beans and create connections. We discuss GUI/logic separation and how to achieve it in VisualAge for Java in Chapter 15, "Model-View-Controller in the VCE." For now, follow these examples to get used to the power of VCE connections.

Types of Connections

Several types of connections are available in the VCE. Some are slight variations of others, while others are much more complex than they seem. All connections start with an event, which could be a PropertyChangeEvent fired when a bound property changes, or any other type of event. Connections end by calling a method to modify a property value or perform another action.

Each connection type is discussed in detail in the following sections.

To start a connection, choose the **Connect** option of a bean's pop-up menu, as shown in Figure 12.1. You can select this option either in the design area of the VCE or through the beans list.

The **Connect** option brings up a submenu that contains preferred events and properties. If the event or property in which you are interested is present, you can select it. If it is not present in the submenu, you can select it by choosing the **Connectable Features** option shown in Figure 12.2.

Once a connection has been started, you can cancel it by pressing the Esc key, or, if a connection pop-up menu is visible, click outside that menu.

Connection Sources and Targets

Every connection has a *source* and a *target*. The connection source is a bean that fires the event that triggers the connection, or another connection that requires a parameter value. The connection target is a bean that contains the intended method to invoke or the property to change.

> **NOTE**
>
> The source and target *can* be the same bean. For example, to change the label on a button when it is pressed, treat the button as the source (the button press is the triggering event), and treat the same button as the target (you want to change one of its properties, such as its *enabled* state).

Figure 12.1 Start a connection.

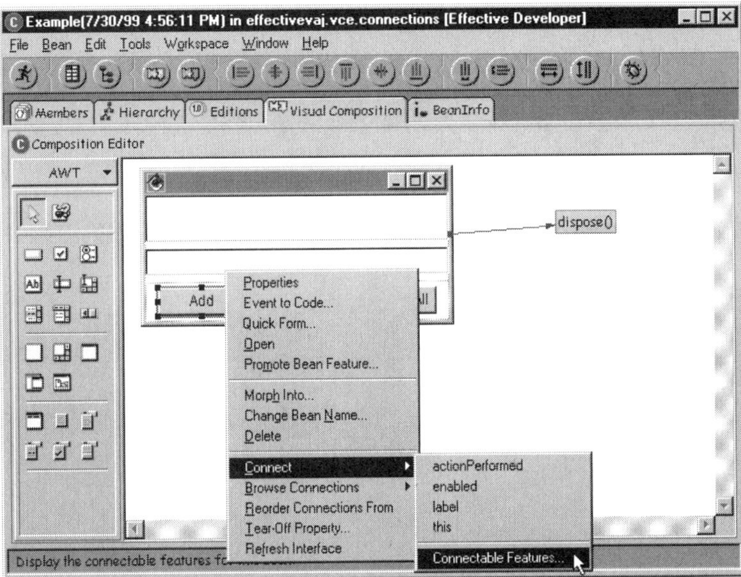

Figure 12.2 Connectable features.

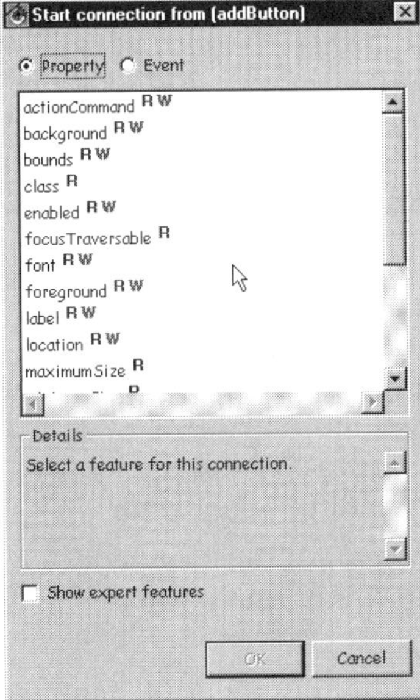

Source and target beans can be a bean dropped in the design area or the bean that you are visually composing. If you want to use a dropped bean, click on it when you start or end a connection. If you want to use the bean you are composing, click in an empty section of the design area. If the bean you are composing is a visual component, you can also click on the superclass image in the design area. For example, if the superclass were Frame, click on the Frame bean in the design area to choose methods and properties of the bean you are composing.

> **TIP**
>
> If you want to interact with the "this" instance (the instance of the composite bean), click in an empty spot in the design area. If you want to interact with a particular dropped bean, click on it.

Event Connections

Event connections start by selecting an event in a source bean. The event can be any type of event: a button click, a key press, a change of focus, adjustment of a component value, or even a custom event. Start the connection by choosing **Connect** from a bean's pop-up menu and selecting an event feature. Some event features are present in the **Connect** submenu; these are the preferred events (see Chapter 8, "The BeanInfo Editor," for details on preferred features). You can select other events from the Events page of the Connectable Features dialog, shown in Figure 12.3.

Notice that the Events page contains some property names. These property names represent the PropertyChangeEvent fired when these property values change. This type of event is discussed in more detail in the *Property Connections* section later in this chapter. We'll start by concentrating on simple event-set features.

The listed events contain two types of event names:

Event-handler method names. The names of the methods defined in event-set listener interfaces. For example, a Button instance would list *actionPerformed*, the name of the method defined in the ActionListener interface. A Frame instance would list methods *windowClosing*, *windowClosed*, *windowOpened*, and the other methods defined in interface WindowListener. Selecting a particular method name creates an event handling connection that responds only when the event source calls that particular handler method.

Event-set names. The names of the event sets fired by a source bean. Continuing the previous example, a Button instance would list

Figure 12.3 Choosing a connectable event.

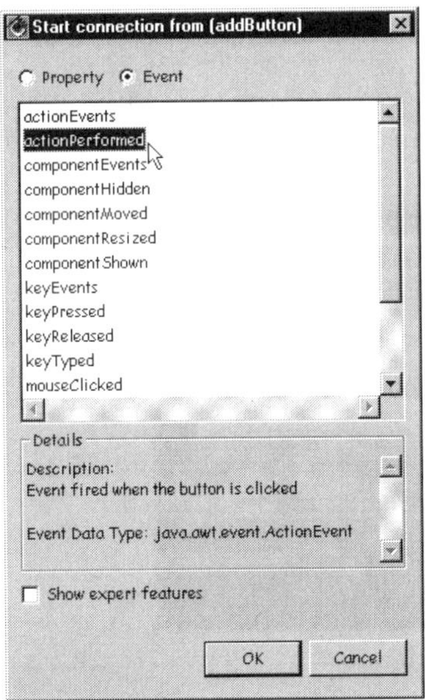

actionEvents as an event set; Frame would list *windowEvents*. If you select an event-set name as the source event, *any* event handler defined in that event set activates the connection. If you choose actionEvents, the actionPerformed method triggers the event handling. If you choose windowEvents, the windowClosing, windowOpened, windowClosed, and the other WindowListener event methods invoke the event handling. Choosing the event set name acts as though you had created connections for *all* of the event-handler methods available for that event set. Note that actionEvents versus actionPerformed makes no difference, as there is only one method in the actionEvents event set. However, windowEvents versus windowClosing is a major difference in behavior, as the windowEvents event set contains seven event-handler methods.

When you select an event handler or event-set name from the list, you are saying, "When this event happens, do *someAction*." The *someAction* is the topic of the next three sections. All three of the following connection types start with this choice of event-handler or event-set name.

Event-to-Method Connections

The first and simplest type of connection is the *event-to-method connection*. Event-to-method connections tell the VCE to call a method when a specific event

> **NOTE**
>
> The display name of the event set may not have "events" as part of its name. In VisualAge for Java version 3, IBM gave AWT event sets nice names like actionEvents so the meaning of the name would be more obvious. If you define your own events or add third-party libraries to your workspace, you will see simpler names. For example, if you create a SunListener interface, the default name for the event set is simply *sun*. If you prefer it to be sunEvents, you can alter the display name by using the BeanInfo editor for the source bean.

occurs. To keep things simple for our initial discussion, we only discuss methods that have no parameters or return value and that do not throw exceptions. Later, we discuss how to pass parameters, use the return value, and handle thrown exceptions.

Start an event-to method connection as you would any other event connection: Choose the source bean and source event. Then select a target bean and a target method to invoke on that bean.

For example, suppose that you have the GUI depicted in Figure 12.4. Without event handling, this GUI is rather useless. For this example, we want the Remove All button to remove all items from the list. Event-to-method connections make this is an easy task.

Perform the following steps to create the remove-all action:

1. First, choose **Connect->actionPerformed** from the button's pop-up menu, shown in Figure 12.5. The event *actionPerformed* represents the button click. (Notice that it appears directly on the pop-up menu, as it is a preferred feature.) The cursor turns into a spider-like cursor. As you move it, the VCE draws a line between the button and the current cursor position. The spider cursor is used to select a target bean.

Figure 12.4 A simple GUI.

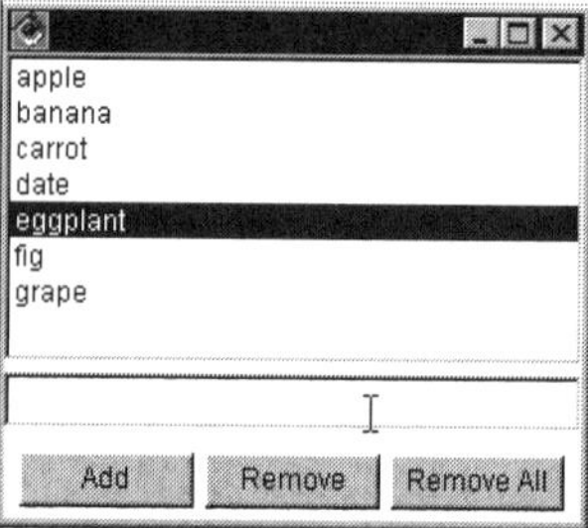

Figure 12.5 Starting the button click connection.

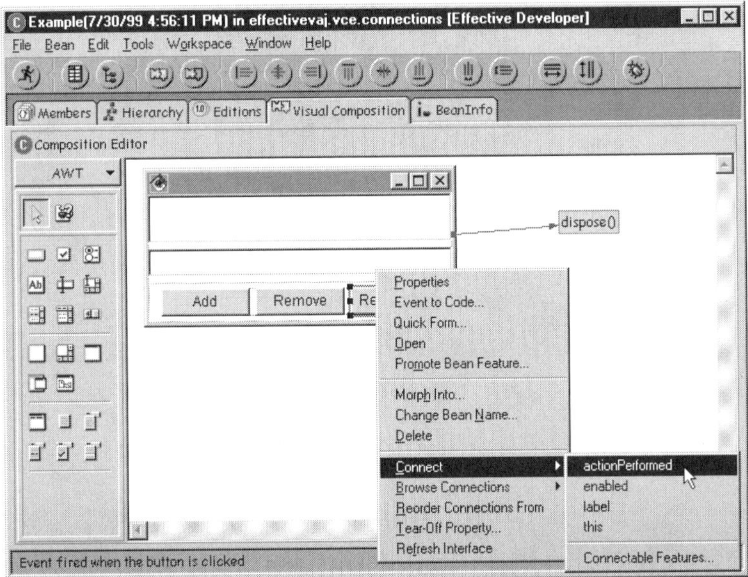

2. The target bean for this example is the List component, which appears as the large white space inside the Frame in Figure 12.6. To select the target bean, click on it with the spider cursor.
3. A pop-up menu appears with a list of the target's preferred methods and properties, as in Figure 12.7. The method that you want to invoke in this example does not appear in the preferred feature list. To find it, select **Connectable Features**.
4. To find the method removeAll(), select the **Method** radio button in the Connectable Features dialog, and then select the removeAll() method. When you select a method, the dialog displays that method's description information in the details box. Remember that you can specify the information to display when editing the BeanInfo for your beans. Because this makes it easier for someone to select the appropriate methods, properties, and events, we always recommend taking the time to carefully specify the description.

There is a **Show expert features** checkbox at the bottom of the Connectable Features dialog. By default, this option is unchecked, assuming you do not need the expert features. If a method you require does not appear in the list, check this box and it will most likely appear. If it still does not appear, there are a few possibilities:

- The feature is marked hidden in its BeanInfo description.

Figure 12.6 Choosing a target bean.

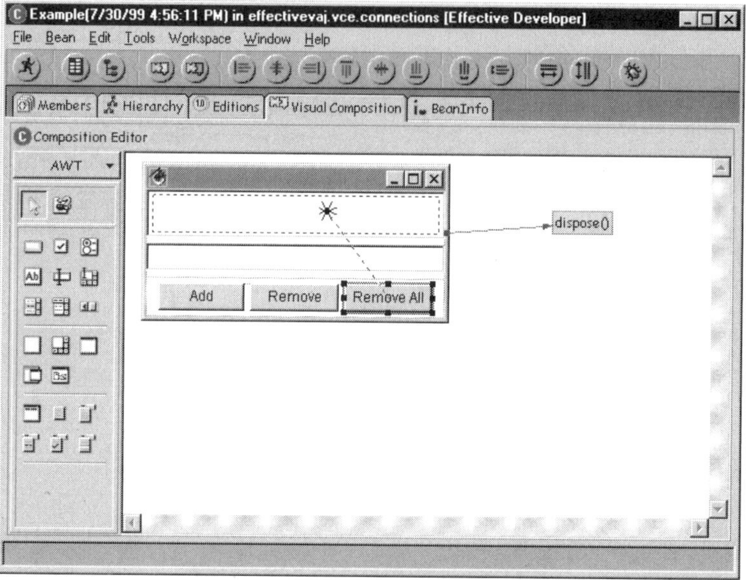

Figure 12.7 Target bean preferred features.

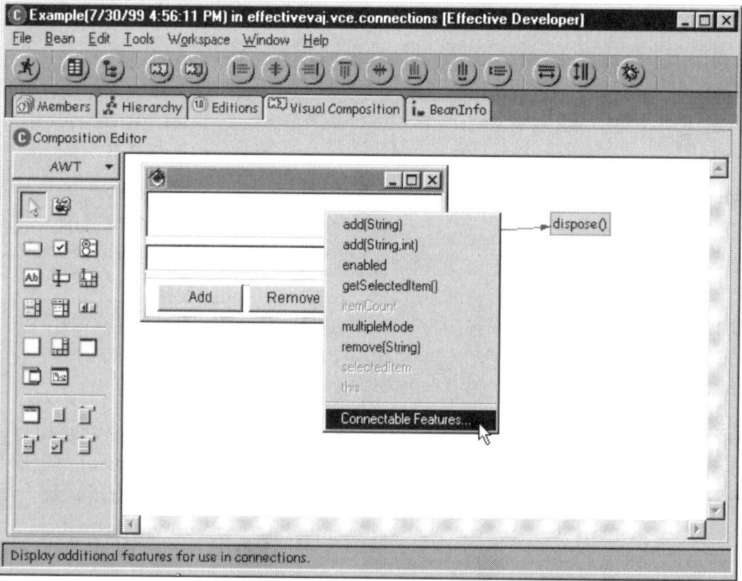

- The feature was added outside the BeanInfo editor. Select **Add Available Features** from the BeanInfo editor's Features menu to inform the BeanInfo class of the new addition.
- It is not a feature—perhaps it is not public.
- The VCE may not have refreshed the feature list for the bean. Try choosing **Refresh** interface from the bean's pop-up menu.

5. After you select the method and click **Ok**, a connection arrow will appear in the design area. Event-to-method connections appear as green arrows. These arrows will appear as solid or dashed, shown in Figure 12.8, depending on whether they require parameter values. In this example, the result is a solid green arrow because the method did not require any parameters. If parameters were required, the result would have been a dashed green arrow. How to pass values using parameter connections and setting constant parameter values is discussed later in this chapter.

The finished connection represents a *listener* to the Button, acting when the Button is clicked. The listener's actionPerformed() method calls the List's removeAll() method. Do not worry about the generated code at this point; it is discussed in detail in Chapter 19, "Handwritten Code versus Generated Code."

Event-to-Code Connections

Event-to-method connections are only valid for method *features*, which must be public. If you want to call non-public methods, you must use an *event-to-code connection.* Event-to-code connections enable you to execute any code as the result of a connection. You can select *any* method in the composite bean (the class you are composing). This means that you can define a method containing some code in the composite bean, or use any method inherited from the superclass of the composite bean.

There are two ways to create event-to-code connections. You can start the connection as a normal event connection and then select Event-to-Code in an empty spot in the design area. You can also choose Event-to-Code directly from

Figure 12.8 Finished event-to-method connections.

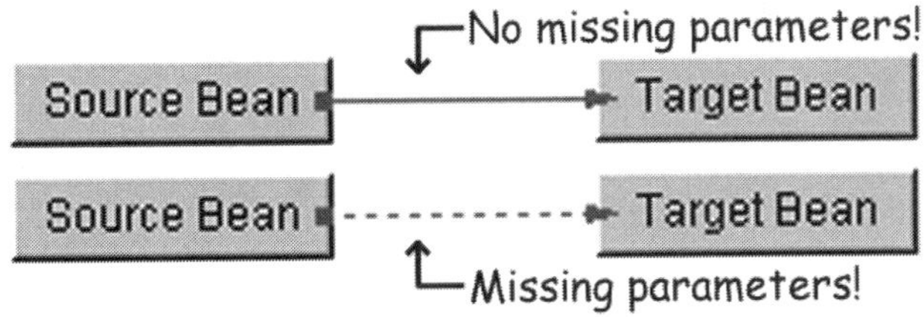

the source bean. Suppose that you have the GUI in Figure 12.9 and you want to print "Hello" when the button is clicked. The following examples walk through both ways of creating this event-to-code connection.

Method 1

Perform the following steps to create the event-to-code connection:

1. Choose **Connect->actionPerformed** from the Press Me button (same process as in Figure 12.5. Once again, the logic is "when the button is pressed, do something." The difference here is that you want to execute a scrap of code rather than a target method.
2. Click in an empty spot of the design area and choose **Event-to-Code**, as in Figure 12.10.
3. Continue with *Filling in the Details* later in this section.

Method 2

Instead of starting with the trigger event, you can simply choose **Event-to-Code** from the source bean's pop-up menu. For this method:

1. Bring up the pop-up menu for the Press Me button, selecting **Event-to-Code**, as shown in Figure 12.11. This brings up the Event to Code dialog, where you can select the source bean event as shown in Figure 12.12.
2. Select *actionPerformed* as the source event.
3. Continue with *Filling in the Details*.

Filling in the Details

At this point, an event-to-code connection has been started. Clicking the button executes the code in the selected method. The event-to-code dialog, shown in Figure 12.13, contains:

Event. The event in the source bean that triggers the connection.

Figure 12.9 A hello world GUI.

Figure 12.10 Picking Event-to-Code as a connection target.

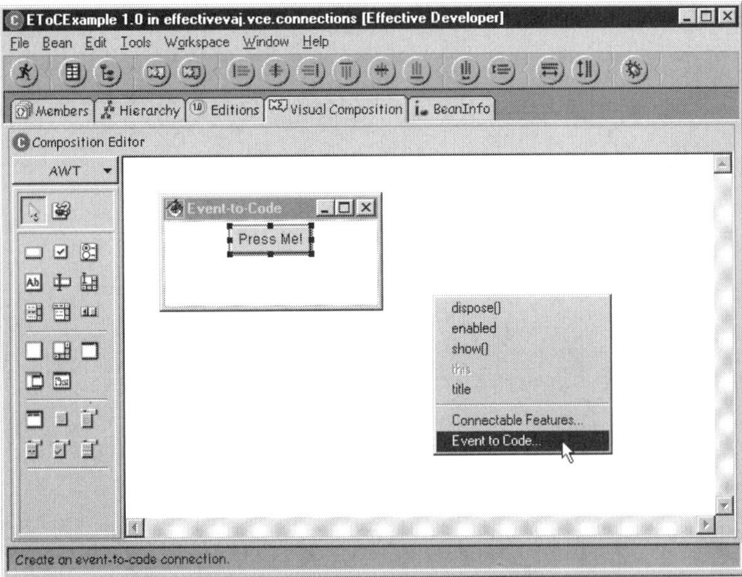

Figure 12.11 Choosing Event-to-Code to start a connection.

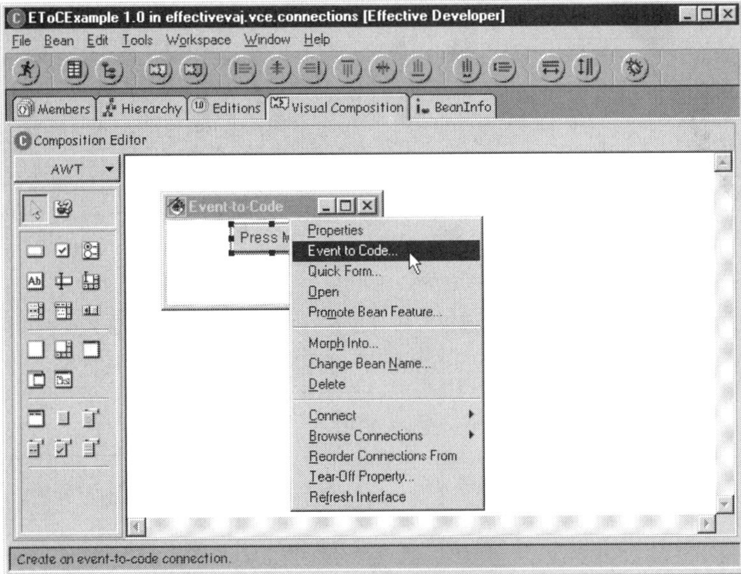

Figure 12.12 Selecting the event-to-code source event.

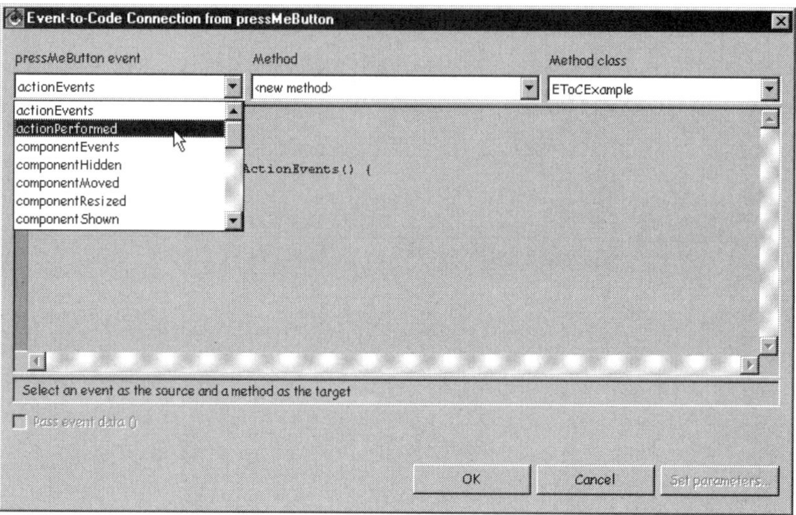

Method. The target method to execute. The selected method's code will appear in the method source pane. When you initially enter this dialog, this field displays "<new method>" and fills the method source pane with a skeleton method. You can select another method if an appropriate one already exists. The method may or may not have parameters.

Method Class. The class in which the target method resides. This defaults to the class you are composing, but you can choose any superclass as well. The Method field lists only the methods in the selected Method Class. For example, if you were composing a bean named MyApp that extends class java.awt.Frame, you would see MyApp, Frame, Window, Container, Component, and Object in this list.

Method Source. The Java source for the selected method (if available in the repository). You can edit this source as long as you have access to it and it is not a method in the Java core libraries.

Generally, use event-to-code connections to enter code you want to execute. If the code simply is calling a method feature in another bean, using an event-to-method connection is preferable. When you choose the event-to-code option, the dialog initially contains a skeleton method named after the source event.

For this example, start an event-to-code connection from the Press Me button using one of the above methods. You need to modify the skeleton method to perform the desired operation:

Figure 12.13 The event-to-code connection dialog.

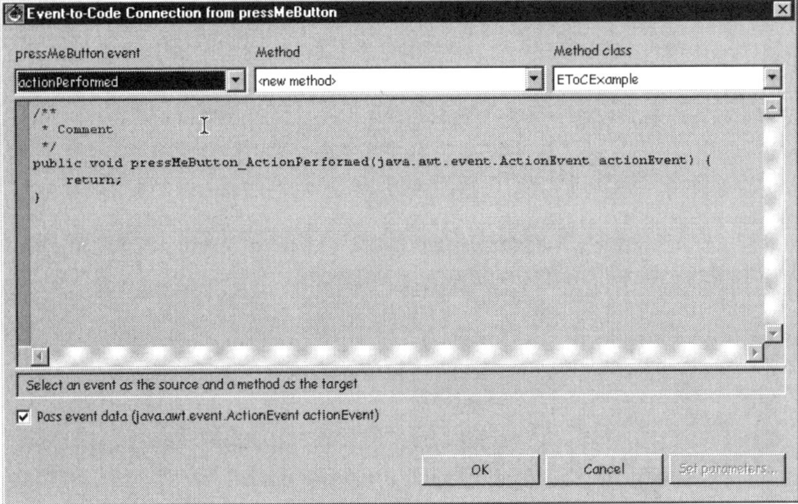

> **TIP**
>
> We strongly recommend you change the method name to reasonably describe what you want to do.

4. You do not need to pass the ActionEvent associated with the button click, so deselect the **Pass Event Data** check box. This option is discussed in more detail later, when passing parameter values to connections. Notice that this automatically deletes the parameter from the skeleton method. If you want to deselect this option, make sure you do so *before* editing the skeleton method, or you will need to delete the parameter manually.
5. Change the name of the method. The default name, pressMeButton_ActionPerformed, is rather ugly and does not indicate the meaning of the method. Edit the source code to change the name to *sayHello*.
6. Add the actual code to perform the task. Add the following code before the return statement (you can actually remove the return statement if you would like).

```
System.out.println("Hello");
```

When you are finished, the dialog should look as it does in Figure 12.14. After you click **Ok**, the VCE draws a connection from the button to a box in the design area with the method name in it, as shown in Figure 12.15.

Property-to-Method and Property-to-Code Connections

Property-to-method and *property-to-code* connections are variations of event-to-method and event-to-code connections. If you select a property as the source of a connection, what you are really doing is selecting the PropertyChangeEvent for that property as the connection source.

These types of connections perform the connection action when a certain property value changes. Note that you can only create property-to-method and property-to-code connections starting on a *bound* property. Refer to Chapter 7 for details about bound properties.

Event-to-Property Connections

Event-to-property connections are a special case of an event-to-method connection. Rather than selecting a method to invoke in the target bean, you select a property in the target. The result of the connection is to call the set method for that property. You can only use *writeable* properties as the target of an event-to-property connection, because read-only properties do not have a set method. This type of connection will appear as the same green dashed line of an event-to-method connection.

Figure 12.14 The finished event-to-code dialog.

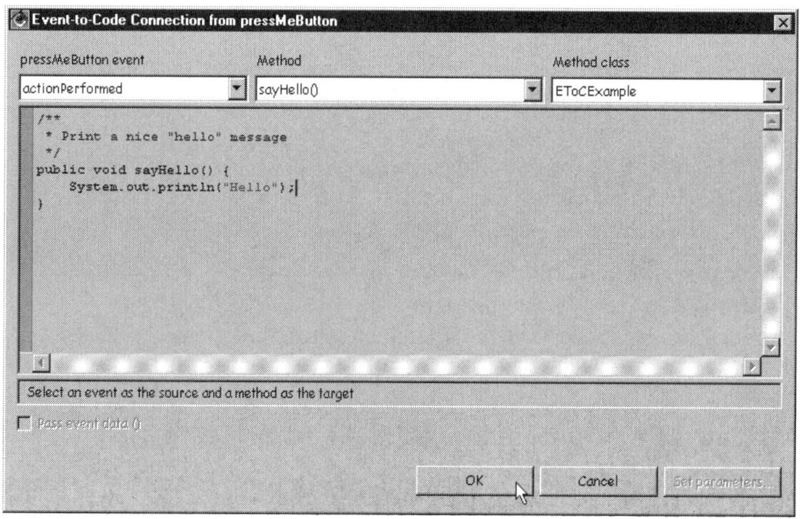

Figure 12.15 An event-to-code connection.

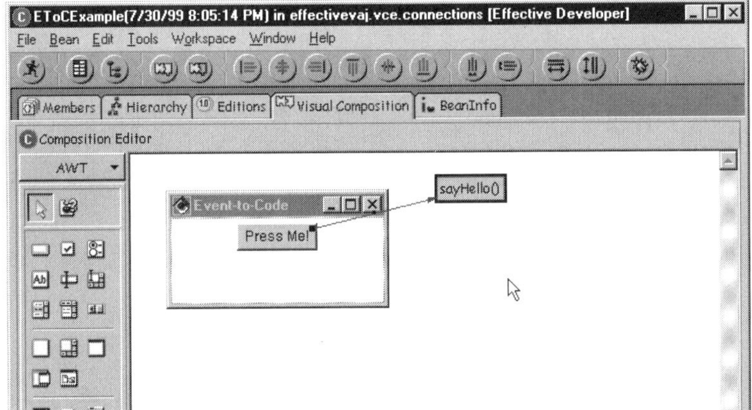

The effect of this connection is that the target property value is changed when the source event occurs. Of course, this begs the question "change it to what value?" Next we discuss how you can provide a value for such a connection.

Connection Parameters

Many connections need parameters. If you create an event-to-method connection and the target method requires parameters, a dashed green line appears. If you create an event-to-property connection, the same dashed green line appears, because you need a value for the property. Dashed connection lines represent missing parameters.

You can provide the parameter values in several ways:

- Set a constant value for the parameter.
- Pass *event data* to the target method.
- Create a connection that retrieves the value from another method or property.

Setting Constant Parameter Values

The first way to indicate a parameter value is to provide constant values for each parameter. To do this, you need to bring up a property dialog for the connection in question, click its **Set parameters** button, and specify the constant values you want. For example, suppose you have a GUI that looks like the one in Figure 12.16. This GUI is a simple application that displays the text "Hello" in the Label at the top of the frame when you click the Press Me button. So far, a connection has been created between the button and label that sets the text property of the label when the button fires actionPerformed. (To do this, use **Connect->actionPerformed** from the button's pop-up menu to the text property on the label's pop-up menu.) The connection appears dashed because you need to specify the target value for the text property.

In this example, the target property value is a constant String value. This is set through the property dialog for the connection. To display the connection's property dialog, you can either double-click on the connection line or choose **Properties** from the connection's pop-up menu. The event-to-method connection property dialog appears in Figure 12.17.

This dialog contains the names of the source event and target method for the connection. To change these, select the desired values from the lists. Click the **Set parameters** button; the VCE displays the property sheet in Figure 12.18. Note that other connection types, such as event-to-code, also have a **Set parameters** button.

Set the *value* parameter to "Hello" (without quotation marks).

You can reset parameter values in the same manner as in the normal VCE property sheets (by clicking the **Reset** button). If you are providing parameters for

Figure 12.16 A dashed connection indicates a missing parameter value.

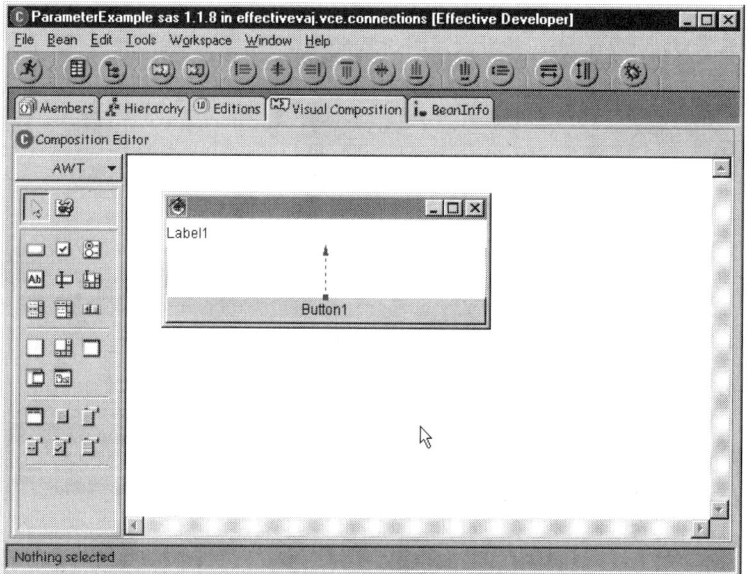

Figure 12.17 The event-to-method connection property dialog.

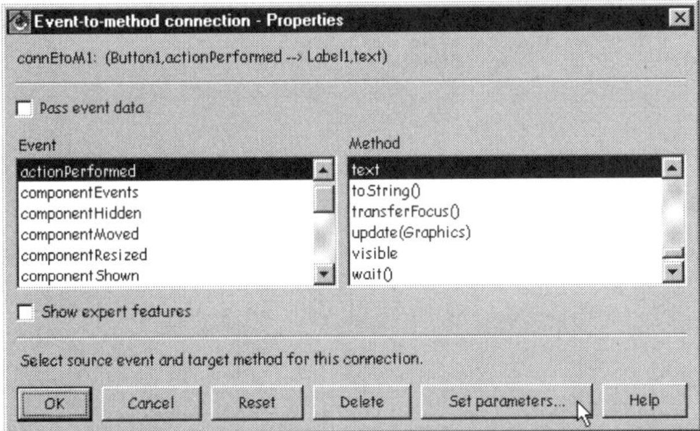

> **NOTE**
>
> The value for Strings should *not* be enclosed in quotation marks unless you want the quotes to actually appear!

a method, the actual formal parameter names appear in this property sheet. If you are providing a property value, the name "value" appears in this property sheet.

Be careful if you are providing a value for an object type. Object values will be enclosed in curly braces, as shown in Figure 12.19. For example, if the parameter type was of type Person and you wanted to pass a Person object as the parameter value, you could type:

```
new Person("John", "Doe")
```

as the parameter value. *Note that you must type a complete and valid Java expression.* The VCE performs very limited checking on the value you type.

Figure 12.18 A constant-parameter property sheet.

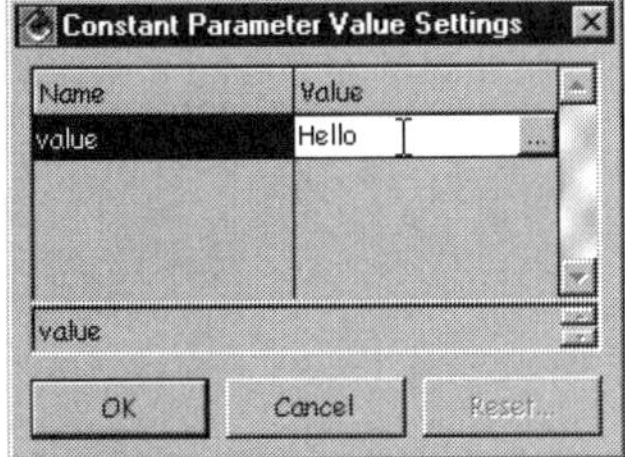

Most often, the VCE inserts it as is into the generated code, not reporting any problems until you save the visual design (which compiles the generated code). For example, if you were passing the above Person instance to an addPerson() method, the generated code would look as follows:

```
addPerson(new Person("John", "Doe"))
```

The bold text in the previous code is the parameter value. If you had mistyped the *new* expression, the generated code would have an error. Suppose you had added a semicolon after the *new* expression. The resulting code is incorrect; when you save the bean, the VCE reports the error. It is easiest to see the error by switching to the Hierarchy tab of the class browser and looking for the red X.

> **WARNING**
>
> Do *not* fix the error in the code itself! It is *very* easy to make this mistake. The VCE *regenerates* the code each time you save the bean in the VCE. You *must* fix the error in the parameter property sheet for the connection.

Once you have finished setting the parameter values, click **Ok** to exit the property sheet and click **Ok** to exit the connection property dialog. The VCE generates code including the constant value.

Passing Event Data

The second way to pass parameter values is by passing the actual event object to the target method. For example, suppose that you wanted to examine the ActionEvent that the button passes to the actionPerformed method. Each event-connection property sheet has a **Pass event data** check box. If you check this box, the VCE generates code to pass the event object *as the first parameter to the target method.*

Figure 12.19 Entering an object value.

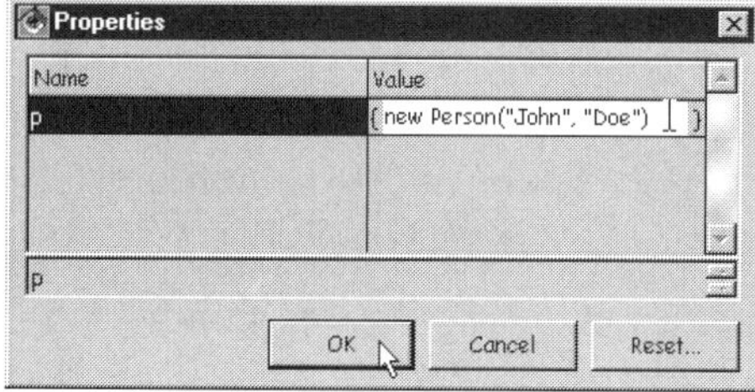

> **NOTE**
> If you press the **Set parameters** button and one or more parameter values are already correct, *you need to change them so VisualAge knows that you want those values.* Simply change the value to some other value and then change it back. This causes VisualAge to detect that you have really set the value; it changes the connection to a solid line. If you do not change the values, the connection will remain dashed. The generated code will *use* the correct values, *but, the design appears unfinished; another programmer may attempt to "complete" it, possibly incorrectly.*

This option acts slightly different for property connections (discussed later). Property connections are triggered when a property value changes (firing a propertyChanged event). For property connections, the VCE uses the *value* of the property as the event data, and passes it as the first parameter to the called method.

> **NOTE**
> If you set a constant parameter value *and* pass event data for the first parameter, the *constant* value takes precedence; the VCE does *not* pass the event data!

Parameter Connections

You can pass the result of a method call as a parameter, enabling you to compute or create the required value. This is one of the strongest features of the VCE's visual design paradigm. You can use *connections* to fill in the parameters to *another* connection! Parameter connections can get the parameter value from method or property features in another bean, or from any method in the composite bean.

Start all parameter connections by bringing up a pop-up menu for a dashed-line connection and choosing **Connect->*parameterName***, where parameterName is the name of the missing formal parameter. Note that if the connection is setting a property value, parameterName is "value". An example of this appears in Figure 12.20.

The next three sections demonstrate the types of parameter connections possible in the VCE:

Parameter-from-Method. Obtain the parameter value from a method in a bean.

Figure 12.20 Starting a parameter connection.

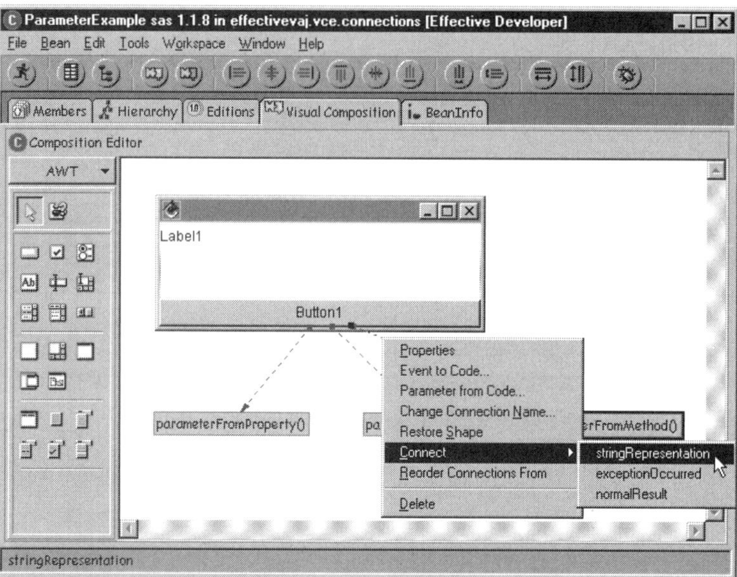

Parameter-from-Property. Obtain the parameter value from a property in a bean.

Parameter-from-Code. Obtain the parameter value from a scrap of code.

The examples use the VCE design in Figure 12.21. Pressing the button triggers the three event-to-code connections, parameterFromMethod, parameterFromProperty, and parameterFromCode. Each requires a parameter that we supply via the three parameter-connection types.

> **NOTE**
>
> Parameter connections are the strongest way to pass necessary data to an existing connection. They take precedence over the other two ways of passing parameters (constant values and passing event data). You can, of course, use them in combination with the other forms of parameters, by setting some parameters as constants, others as parameter connections, and possibly passing event data as the first parameter.

Figure 12.21 VCE session for parameter examples.

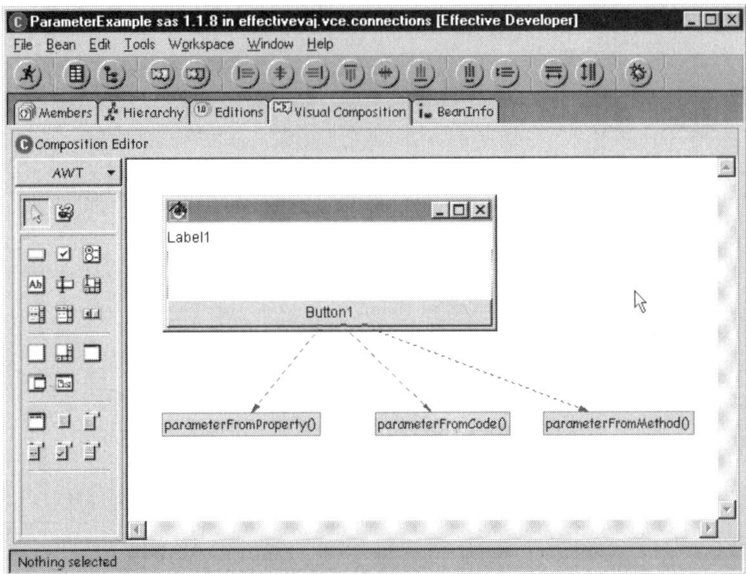

Parameter-from-Method Connections

Parameter-from-method connections fill in the missing parameter values by calling methods in other beans. The example *parameterFromMethod* event-to-method connection calls a method that takes a single String parameter named *stringRepresentation*. We select **Connect->stringRepresentation** from the connection's pop-up menu, as already seen in Figure 12.20. For this example, we call the toString() method of Button1. We do this by dragging the connection to Button1, clicking, selecting **Connectable Features** and then method toString(). (This is exactly like selecting the target end of an event-to-method connection.)

The called method may or may not require its own parameters. If it does require parameters, pass them by setting constant values or using parameter connections. You can create a chain of as many parameter connections as necessary to provide the values you need. You also can have multiple parameter connections if your method requires multiple parameters. For example, examine Figure 12.22.

This may seem difficult to figure out at first, but be sure to look carefully at the connection lines. First, parameter connections are violet, while event connections are green. Next, parameter connections start with an open circle *in the middle of another connection* and have an arrowhead at their target end. Some connections might not be obvious; in this example picture, the first parameter connection is selected, to help

Figure 12.22 A complex parameter scenario.

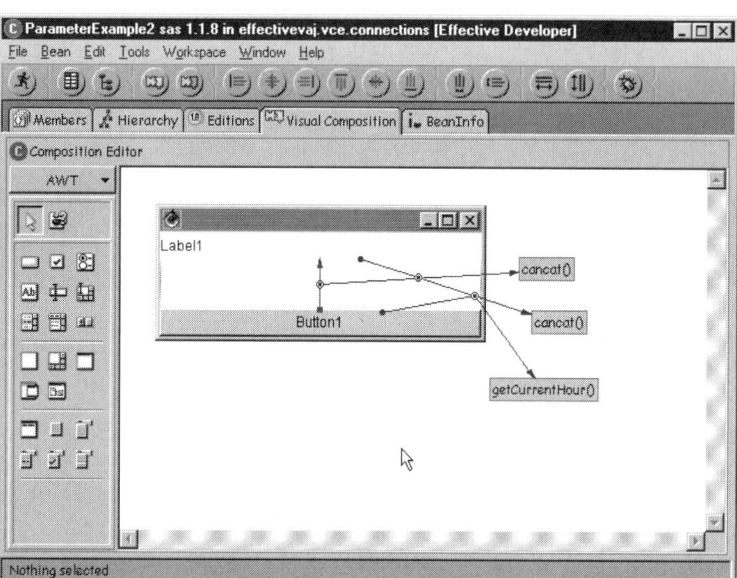

you locate its source and target. Looking carefully at Figure 12.22, you can see the connection structure is:

```
Button1->Label1 (event-to-method)
   PARAMETER: from call to method concat()
      PARAMETER: from Label1
      PARAMETER: from another call to concat()
         PARAMETER: from Button1
         PARAMETER: from call to method getHour()
```

The method *must* return a value; you cannot use a void method to provide a parameter value.

Parameter-from-Property Connections

If you need to get a parameter value from a bean property, you create a *parameter-from-property connection.* Connect the name of a parameter in the connection's pop-up menu to a property in some other bean. The connection uses the current value of that property as the parameter value.

The example connects the text parameter of the parameterFromProperty connection, shown in Figure 12.23, to Button1's label property. Note that the target end of the connection appears as a solid dot, rather than an arrow. Remember, an arrow means "call a method," and a dot means "access a property." The connection ends the same way you end an event-to-property connection.

Figure 12.23 Starting the parameter-from-property connection.

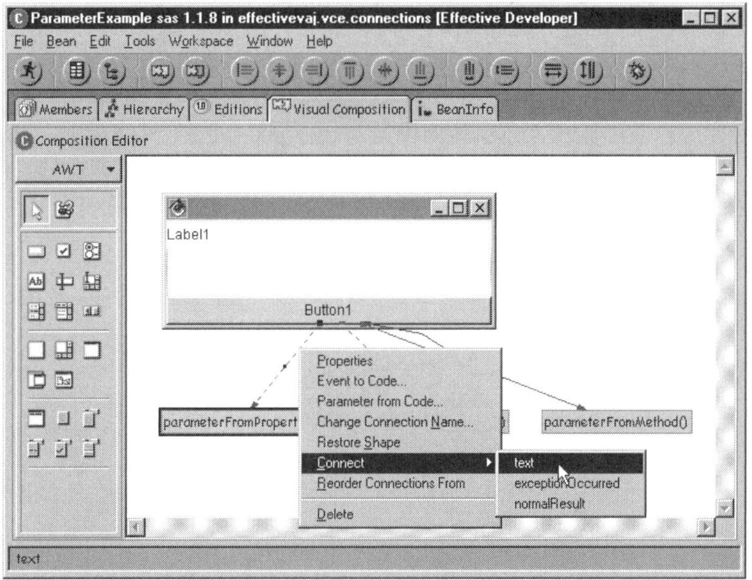

Parameter-from-Code Connections

Finally, if you want to write your own code to create the parameter value, you can create a *parameter-from-code connection*. You create this as you would a parameter-from-method connection, but you end it in an empty spot of the design area and select **Parameter from Code** from the pop-up menu, as shown in Figure 12.24.

Create or select a method to invoke the same way you would for an event-to-code connection. This is particularly useful when you need to compute a parameter value from other methods or properties. Figure 12.22 uses parameter-from-code connections to concatenate two strings as a parameter value. Common uses include string concatenation, Boolean operations such as *not/and/or*, and arithmetic operations.

Property-to-Property Connections

Property-to-property connections are the most powerful and useful connections available in the VCE. This is one of the main features that really separate the VCE from any other GUI builder on the market. The connection itself is very

Figure 12.24 Ending a parameter-from-code connection.

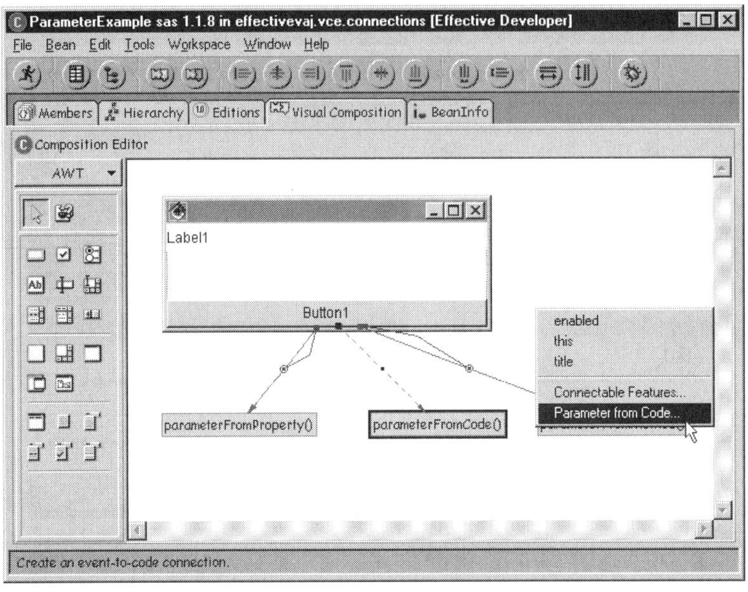

simple, but there is much more to it than a simple line on the screen. There are two reasons for this:

- They perform a great deal of work in one simple line drawn in the design.
- They provide excellent support for several visual design paradigms discussed in later chapters.

  Property-to-property connections perform two basic tasks:

  Target initialization. You can use property-to-property connections to initialize a bean's property to the value of another property in the same or another bean.

  Synchronization of bound properties. You can keep the values of two bound properties synchronized with property-to-property connections. When one property value changes, the other property is set to the new value.

Create a property-to-property connection by selecting **Connect->*propertyName*** (where propertyName is the name of a preferred property) from a bean's pop-up menu (or **Connect->Connectable Features**, selecting a property in the dialog.) Then select a property in the target bean to complete the connection. For example, select the label property on Button1 in Figure 12.25 to start the property-to-property connection, and select the text property of the TextField bean in Figure 12.26 to end it.

Figure 12.25 Starting a property-to-property connection.

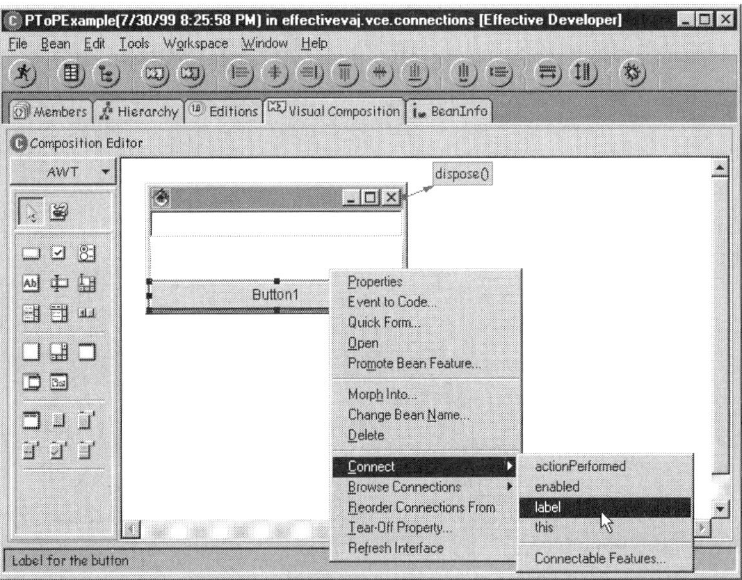

Figure 12.26 Ending a property-to-property connection.

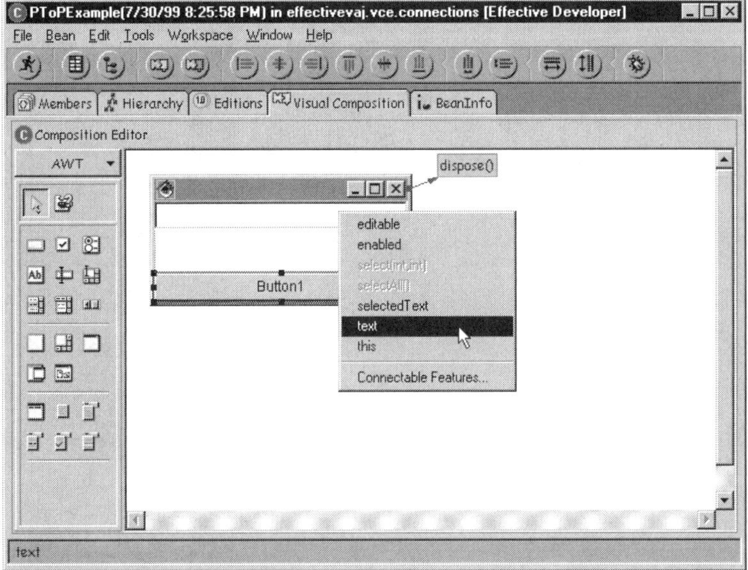

Note that there is an important distinction between the source and target of a property-to-property connection. To help visualize this distinction, the source end of the connection has an empty circle, while the target end has a filled circle. See Figure 12.27 for a close-up view of the connection line. The connection line appears blue in the VCE design area, to help distinguish it from other connection types.

You must create property-to-property connections between two properties of compatible types. *The target property must always be able to accept the source property's value.* VisualAge will create some type conversion code for you, but you cannot create a property-to-property connection between two unrelated object types like Vector and Button.

The effects of a property-to-property connection depend on certain details of the source and target property. The connection may behave differently or even become reversed.

Target Property Initialization

The VCE-generated code assigns the source values to the target values for *all* property-to-property connections when your bean initializes. Think of this as copying values across every property-to-property wire from source to target. This makes the source/target selection for property-to-property connections critical. Did you want to initialize the TextField bean with the value from an address book, or did you want to blank out that value in the address book with the initial value from the TextField bean? Be *very* careful when creating property-to-property connections. The selection of source and target *does* matter!

Figure 12.27 A property-to-property connection line.

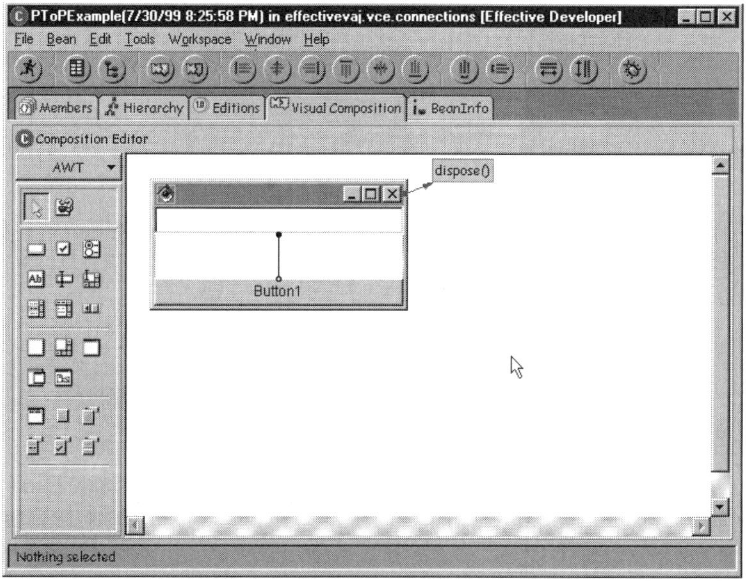

However, the properties could dictate the order, rather than the way you draw the connections. For a property-to-property connection to work, the target property must be writeable. When you think about it, this makes sense, as you cannot copy a value into a read-only property. If you create a connection from a writeable property to a read-only property, *the connection automatically reverses*. Be careful of this. Normally, it produces the correct results, but occasionally it can be quite confusing.

Target initialization becomes even more useful when the source bean is actually a *variable*. Variables can point to any instance of their type, enabling our visual design to be more dynamic. We discuss variables in detail in Chapter 13, "Variables and Instances," but for now it is enough to know that their value can change. Anytime a variable's value changes, the target initialization executes again. This makes property-to-property connections incredibly useful from a data-display standpoint. If you had a variable of type Person and had several Person instances in a data store, you could change that variable to point to those different Person instances. By creating property-to-property connections from that Person variable to text fields on the screen (for the person's name, address, phone, and so on), you have instant screen updates anytime the variable points to a new instance. This technique is used often in the next several chapters.

Synchronization of Bound Properties

No other tool has harnessed the power of the JavaBeans component model as much as VisualAge for Java. This feature of property-to-property connections stands out from all other bean-builder tools. The VCE keeps property values synchronized, utilizing bound properties. While this may seem like a trivial task, several visual design patterns discussed in the next several chapters make this an indispensable tool.

If the source and target properties are *both* bound, the VCE keeps them synchronized. Whenever one property changes, it fires a PropertyChangeEvent (recall that that is the definition of a bound property). The VCE generates code to catch the event and update the *other* property. This communication works both ways.

Recall that initialization runs from source to target. When the application starts, the source and target both contain the source's initial value. Whenever either of the values changes, the generated code updates the other, keeping the values completely synchronized.

If *neither* the source nor the target properties are bound, no synchronization occurs. The effect of such property-to-property connections is only to execute the initialization. These types of property-to-property connections can still be useful, though, especially when the source bean is a variable.

If only one of the two properties is bound, the synchronization only flows in one direction, from the bound property to the unbound property. Note that if the unbound property is read-only, no synchronization takes place.

NOTE

Many people worry about infinite update loops between two bound properties. Most bound properties contain code to check that the value *really* changed before firing the PropertyChangeEvent. Of course, some beans might not be as diligent. The VCE is overprotective, and ensures that rogue beans cannot create infinite loops. The generated code guarantees that the update only proceeds once. We discuss this in detail in Chapter 19.

An Example

An example of the power of property-to-property connections is a simple relay system. While the example itself is not useful in real life, it demonstrates how easy it can be to synchronize properties and not worry about where data comes from. This type of indirection is key to several very useful visual design patterns.

This example is a simple name-display GUI, shown in Figure 12.28. The two TextField beans map to the firstName and lastName properties of the Person bean. Clicking a button sets firstName and lastName in the Person bean. This triggers the property-to-property connections, setting the text fields. Note that the button processing directly touches only the Person; the GUI updates independently.

Figure 12.28 A simple phone book GUI.

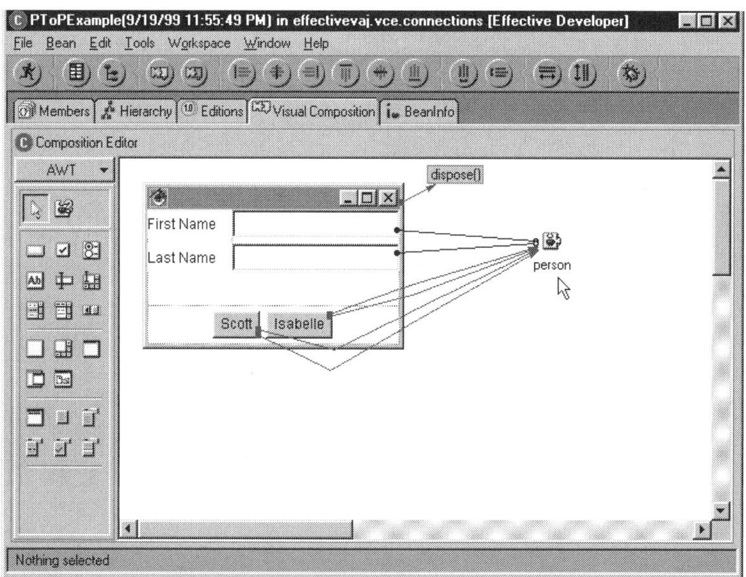

To create this set of connections:

1. Create the simple name GUI (Label, TextField, and Button beans).
2. Drop an instance of Person, named *person*.
3. Connect the firstName property of person to the text property of the top TextField bean.
4. Connect the lastName property of person to the text property of the bottom TextField bean.

> **NOTE**
> Because firstName and lastName are bound properties, they send their values across the connection anytime they change. The text properties are not bound properties, so they do not attempt to update the Person instance.

5. From each button, create two event-to-property connections. These connections span from the actionPerformed event of the Button to the firstName and lastName properties of person.
6. The value parameter of these connections is set to "Isabelle," "Mauny," "Scott," and "Stanchfield," depending on the button and target property. Use constant parameter values on these connections.

When someone presses the Isabelle button, the first event-to-property connection sets firstName in person to "Isabelle." The person bean detects the change and fires a PropertyChangeEvent. This triggers the firstName property-to-property connection to send the value to the text field. Then the second event-to-property connection sets lastName, which propagates to its text field through the other property-to-property connection.

The buttons have no idea that the values are going anywhere *but* the person properties. The text fields have no idea that a user clicked a button. A chain reaction has been created based solely on the bound property notification. Property-to-property connections are used very heavily in Chapter 14, "Design Patterns for the VCE," when we discuss visual design patterns in the VCE.

Property-to-Property versus PropertyChangeEvent-to-Property

There is a difference between synchronizing two properties and updating an unrelated property when another changes. Using property-to-property connections, the values of two properties are synchronized. Each property mirrors the other. There are times, however, when you could want to update an unrelated property.

For example, suppose that you have a Person bean that has two bound properties: firstName and lastName. Perhaps your program has another bean, named

Reservation, which has a *fullName* field. You would like your program to update the fullName property whenever firstName or lastName changes.

Be *very* careful when drawing these connections. If you simply choose **Connect->firstName** from the Person bean and connect it with fullName in the Reservation bean, fullName and firstName are synchronized. Further, if you create a similar connection between lastName and fullName, things get trickier. Whenever *any* of the three involved properties change, *all* will take that new value.

This is obviously not the intent. To create these connections, choose **Connect->Connectable Features** from the Person bean and select firstName from the event pane, as in Figure 12.29. This tells the VCE that you mean to create an event-to-property connection *instead of* a property-to-property connection. To finish this connection, select the fullName property in the Reservation bean. You can then create an event-to-code connection to pass the value for fullName (concatenating firstName and lastName).

Changing Property-to-Property Direction

Suppose that you create a property-to-property connection from a TextField bean's text property to a Person bean's firstName property. After testing, you realize that the connection is going the wrong way. Instead of sending the current firstName value to the TextField bean, the connection clears the firstName. You have two choices in this situation.

Figure 12.29 Explicitly choosing a PropertyChanged event.

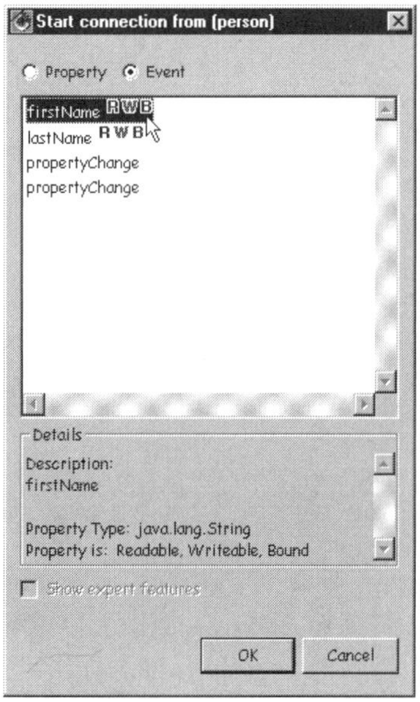

You *can* delete and recreate the connection. However, there is a better way. Bring up the property sheet for the connection and click its Reverse button, as shown in Figure 12.30. This swaps the source and target properties of the connection, reversing the effect of its initialization action.

Changing Source and Target Events

We have seen that property-to-property connections synchronize bound properties. However, their usefulness does not stop there. Many properties in existing beans are *not* bound. This includes AWT and Swing components. For example, AWT's TextField and Swing's JTextField components both have text properties; neither is bound.

This prevents automatic synchronization of text displayed in a TextField bean and a String property of a nonvisual bean (Person, for example). What we would like is to create a property-to-property connection from our firstName property to the text property of the TextField bean, and, when either changes, update the other. Because text is not bound, the VCE-generated code does not update firstName when text changes.

There is hope, however: Look at Figure 12.31. The two highlighted drop-down lists specify the source and target events of the property-to-property connection. For bound properties, the property name appears in these fields. The firstName property is bound in this example, so it appears as the source event. However, the target event is “<none>” because the target property, text, is not bound. For this example, you can use another event to detect when text changes. Whenever an AWT TextField bean's text changes, it fires a textValueChanged event. In Figure 12.32, the target event is set to textValueChanged, and the connection performs the desired two-way synchronization.

Figure 12.30 Reversing a property-to-property connection.

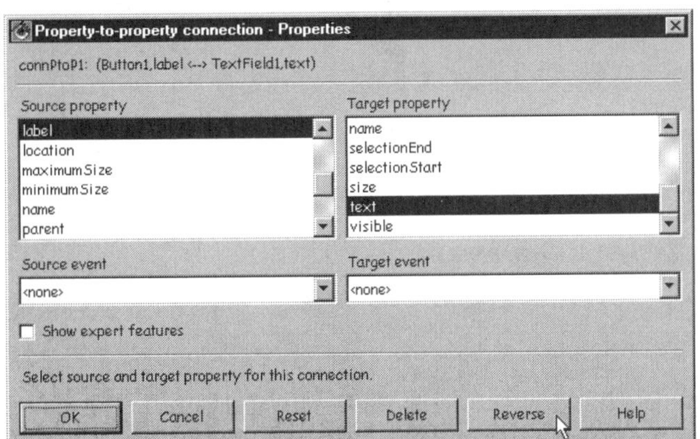

Figure 12.31 Source and target events.

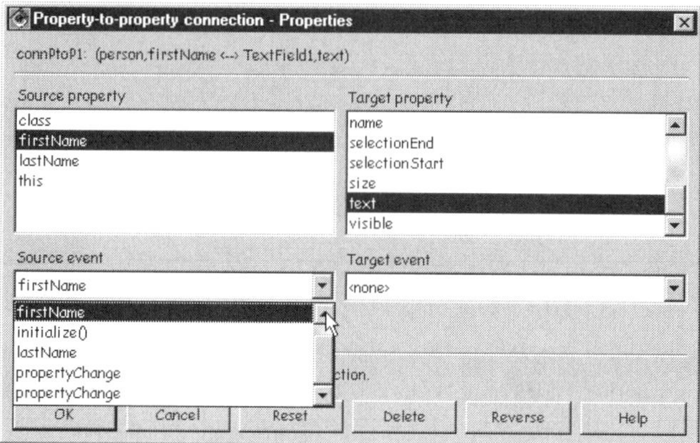

While this works, *we do not recommend this approach*. The problem is the appearance of the connection in the VCE. If someone else looks at your visual design, a property-to-property connection is the only visual cue. There is a hidden changed-target event, and it appears as though you only get default property-to-property behavior: The update would proceed only in one direction.

Rather than using this approach, we recommend that you create or otherwise obtain bound versions of the components you want to use. In Chapter 10, "Bean Composition in the VCE," we created a class called BoundTextField, which watches for its own changes and fires a PropertyChangeEvent. If you use BoundTextField rather than TextField, you can create property-to-property connections between your bound data and the text properties. This makes the visual design more apparent and easier to create.

Figure 12.32 Using a different target event.

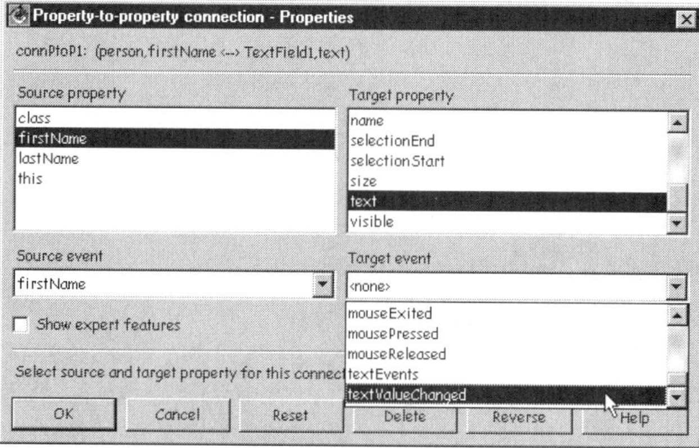

Result Connections

So far, we discussed using parameter connections to *pull* data from methods. For example, suppose that you want to display the number of elements within a Vector instance in a label when the user clicks a button. You can create a connection from the button's actionPerformed event to the label's text property (an event-to-property connection) and then create a parameter-from-method connection, calling size() in the Vector instance.

However, there is another way to create this connection. All event-to-method connections provide a *normalResult* event. The generated code triggers a normal Result event when the method call ends without throwing an exception. This provides a more direct approach to connection design. Call the method *first* and pass its value to the target property. For example, the GUI could look like Figure 12.33, where the button's actionPerformed event is connected to the Vector instance's size() method.

Next, choose **Connect->normalResult** from the connection's pop-up menu, as seen in Figure 12.34. Finish this connection on the label's text property, effectively *pushing* the return value to the label. This connection ordering seems more straightforward and can sometimes save a connection. However, many people avoid using it because they do not know it as well. Our advice: Try both directions and use what feels comfortable and makes the most sense to you.

Figure 12.33 Starting a normal result connection routing.

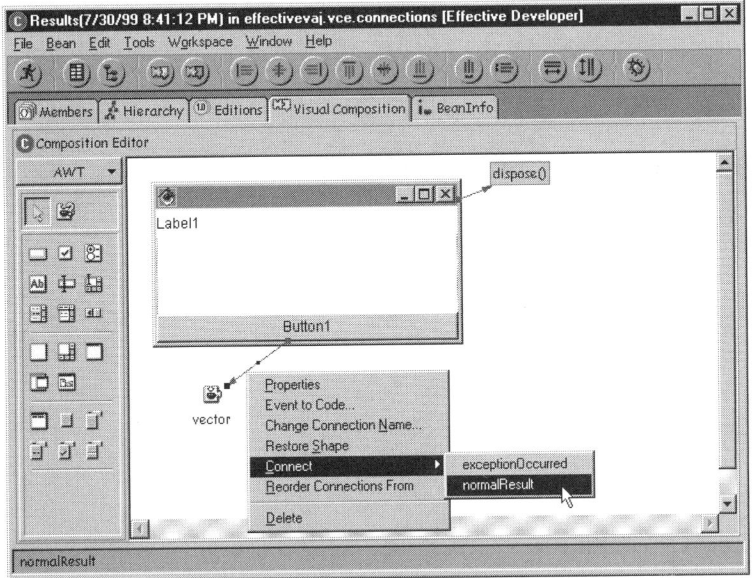

> **NOTE**
>
> The normalResult connection is *not* a true Java event. It is a special connection for use in the VCE, generating code to pass a return value to another connection.

Exceptions During Connection Processing

If a called method throws an exception, normalResult does not fire. Instead, a generated try-catch block catches the exception and passes the exception to a generated handleException() method. The generated handleException() code looks as follows:

```
/**
 * Called whenever the part throws an exception.
 * @param exception java.lang.Throwable
 */
private void handleException(Throwable exception) {

     /* Uncomment the following lines to print uncaught
        exceptions to stdout */
```

Figure 12.34 The normalResult connection.

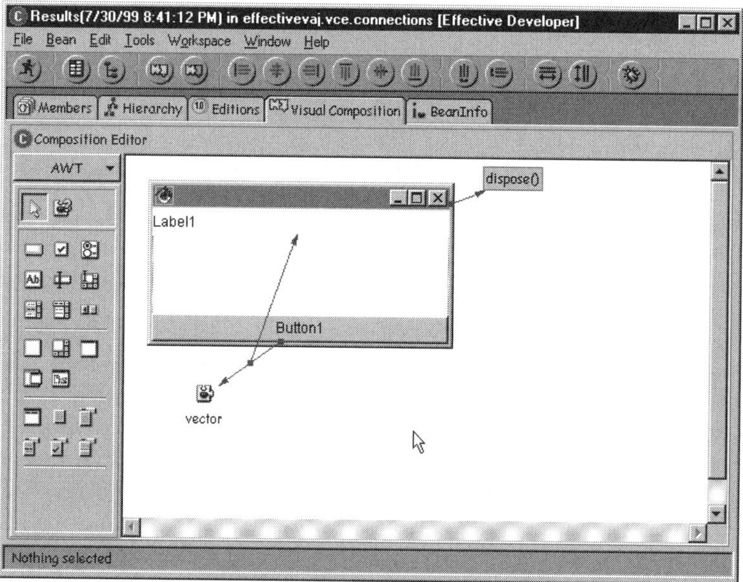

```
    // System.out.println("------ UNCAUGHT EXCEPTION ------");
    // exception.printStackTrace(System.out);
}
```

Notice that this method does nothing. It essentially hushes any uncaught exceptions, which is actually *very* bad for you as a developer. You should *always* uncomment the last two comments in this code, or you may never realize that your code throws exceptions.

> **TIP**
>
> *Always* uncomment the code in handleException() or add your own code that tells the application what to do if it catches an exception.

The handleException() method acts as a catch-all for uncaught exceptions. This enables you to inform the user that something unexpected has occurred and exit as gracefully as possible. You could also use it to examine the application status, and repair bad situations. When handleException() exits, processing continues after the connection that failed.

Handling Specific Connection Exceptions

There are often specific exceptions that you would like to handle without falling out to the handleException() method. For example, a connection could call a lookup() method in a PhoneBook class that throws a PhoneListingNotFoundException. You should catch this type of exception and respond to it; it is not a programmer error like most NullPointerExceptions.

Similar to normalResult, each connection can fire an *exceptionOccurred* event. While the VCE does not implement this as a true Java event, you can use it as the source of another connection. For example, suppose that you have the design shown in Figure 12.35. The user inputs a name in the name field and clicks Find. The find button triggers a lookup() call in a PhoneBook object. Connect normalResult of the connection to the phone number field's text property; if the find succeeds, it displays the phone number. Connect exceptionOccurred of the connection to the label at the bottom of the window to report "Not Found." Figure 12.36 shows the selection of the exceptionOccurred event. "Not Found" is set as a constant value to pass to the label's text property (using the Set Parameters button on the connection's property dialog).

Figure 12.35 A simple PhoneBook GUI.

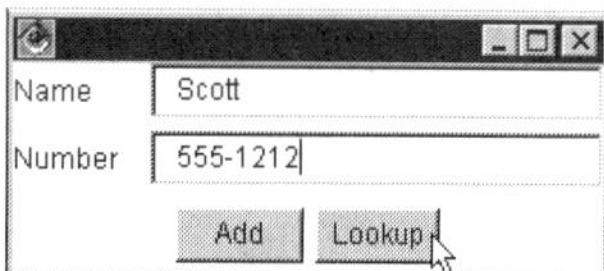

Renaming Connections

The VCE generates connections with certain naming conventions. The default names begin with "conn" and the connection type, such as "EtoC" for event-to-code, and finally a unique connection number. For example, connections could be named "connEtoC4" (event-to-code), "connPtoP2" (property-to-property), or "connEtoM6" (event-to-method).

The name of a connection appears in the status line of the VCE when you select that connection, as seen in Figure 12.37. This enables you to know which methods are involved for that connection, possibly setting breakpoints or adding code to those methods. (The generated methods are discussed in Chapter 19.)

While these names are somewhat descriptive, many developers want to customize them. You can change a connection's name by selecting **Change Connection Name** from the connection's pop-up menu, shown in Figure 12.38.

Figure 12.36 Starting an exception connection.

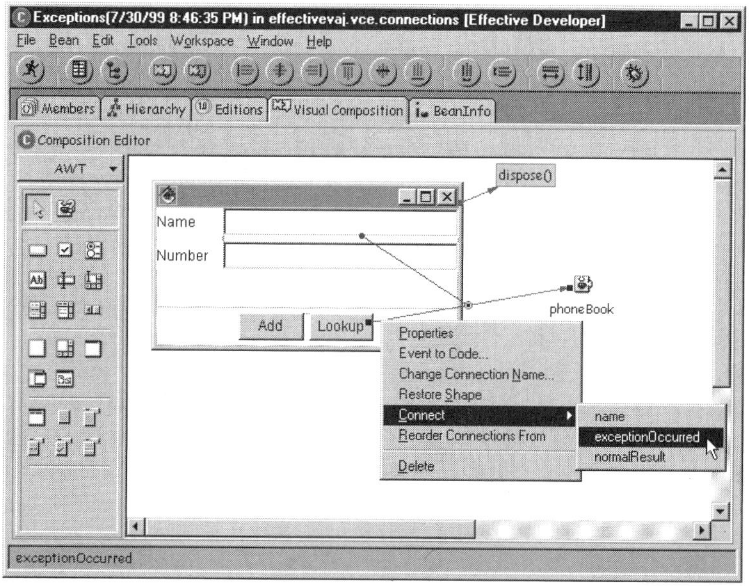

Figure 12.37 The connection name.

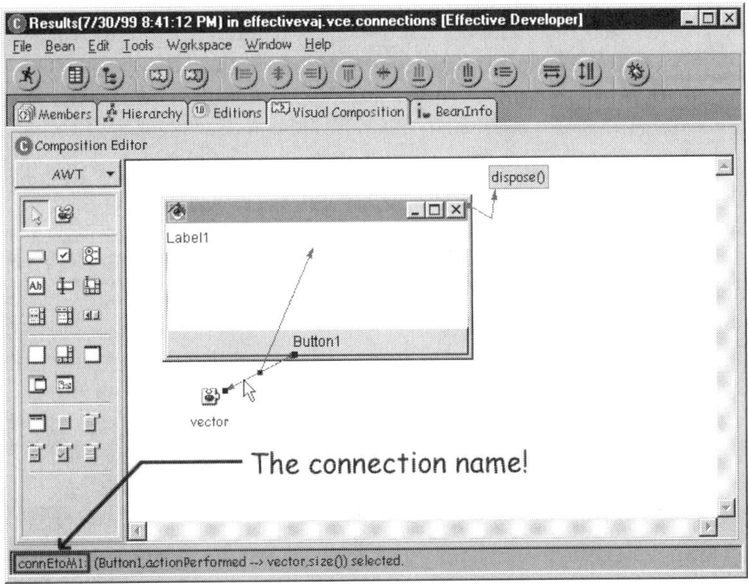

Figure 12.38 Changing a connection's name.

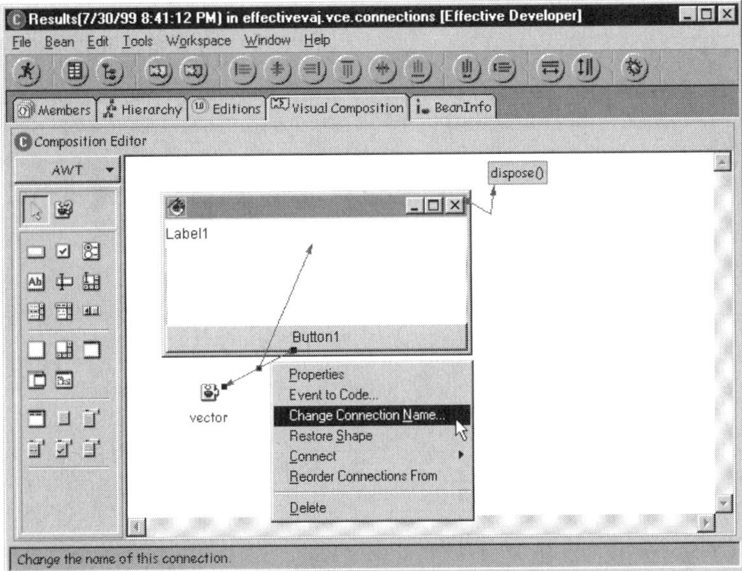

> **WARNING**
>
> You can pick any name you like, but be careful not to pick an existing method name. If you select an existing method name, the VCE replaces the method with the generated connection code!

Descriptive names can make your design more readable but can be fraught with danger. It is incredibly easy for the newly generated connection name to conflict with existing method names. However, there is an easy way to avoid these problems. If you start all of your connection names with "zz," the chance of conflict becomes nearly non-existent. It also has the advantage that when you view the list of methods for a class, all of the generated connection methods sort to the bottom of the list.

> **TIP**
>
> If you rename connections, choose names that start with "zz". These have less chance of conflict *and* sort to the end of displayed method lists. For example, you might call a connection that displays the time when you click a button "zzDisplayTime".

Changing the Source or Target Bean

If you decide that you would rather use a different bean as the source or target of a connection, you can easily change this. To change the source or target of a connection:

1. Select the connection by clicking on it in the design area or in the beans list.
2. Move the cursor over the source or target end (the one you want to change) of the connection until it turns into the spider cursor.
3. Drag that end of the connection to the bean you want to assign it to.
4. If asked, choose the appropriate feature in the new bean.

If the new source or target bean is not compatible with the old source or target bean, the VCE will warn you and ask if you want to continue. This is most often not a real problem, but it is better that the VCE warn you to double-check the change.

If the connected feature exists in the old source or target *but not* in the new source or target, the VCE will prompt you for the new feature. For example, if you dragged the source of an event-to-method connection from a Button bean's actionPerformed event to a ScrollBar bean, the VCE would ask what source event you want to use in the ScrollBar bean.

Changing Connection Shape

The VCE attempts to draw connection lines to avoid overlapping and make them accessible. Sometimes it is successful. Other times, the connection lines cross other connections or are difficult to see. The VCE enables you to change the shape of connections to suit your taste and make the visual design easier to read.

When you select a connection, selection anchors appear at the ends and midpoint of the connection, shown in Figure 12.39. As explained previously, if you drag the endpoint anchors of a connection, you change the source or target of that connection. If you drag the *midpoint* anchor of the connection, you *bend* that connection.

Whenever you drag a connection midpoint, you change the shape of the connection. This is like grabbing the center of an elastic cord and pulling it. The endpoints remain fixed but the center moves. Once you release the midpoint, *two new anchors appear on the connection*, as shown in Figure 12.40. These new anchors help further shape the connection. You can drag the new anchors to bend a segment of the connection, which in turn creates two new anchors. You can repeat this as needed to shape the connection.

Figure 12.39 A selected connection.

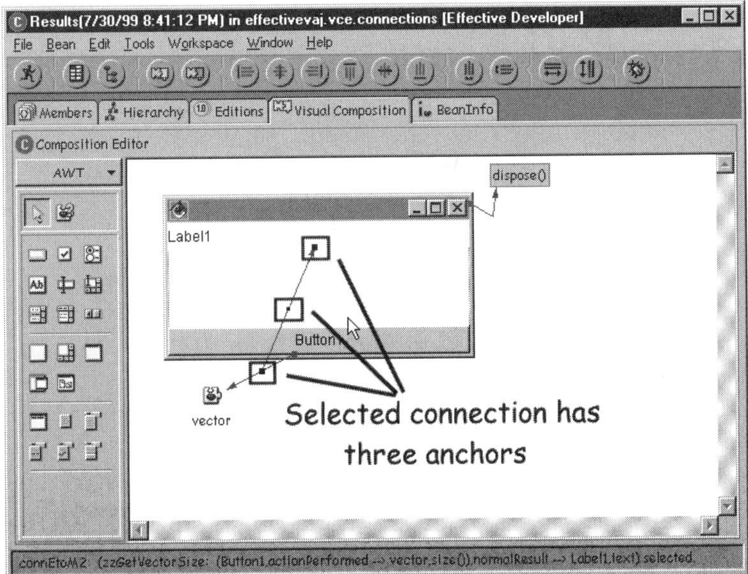

Figure 12.40 New anchors appear after reshaping.

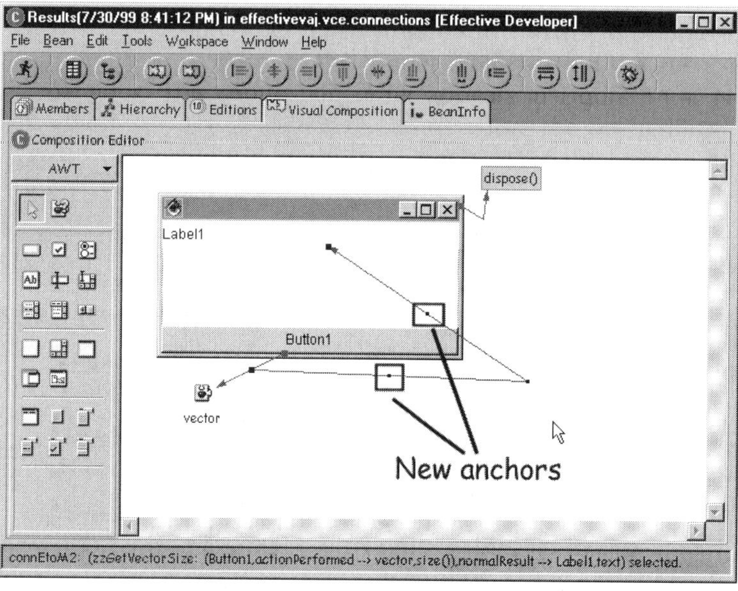

If you decide you do not like the shape change, you can enable the VCE to manage the connection shape by selecting **Restore Shape** from the connection's pop-up menu, shown in Figure 12.41.

Order of Connection Execution

When you start multiple connections from the same bean, using the same event, order of execution becomes an issue. For example, suppose that you have a button that performs a long task. You want the button press to:

- Display a "working" message in the status line.
- Perform the task.
- Display a "done" message in the status line.

You can create these connections *in the previous order* in the VCE. The order in which you create connections is the order in which they execute. When the user clicks this button, the generated event handler responds. That event handler calls the connection code for the above three actions in the order in which they were created. This example could look as shown in Figure 12.42.

Suppose you had created the connections in a different order. Perhaps you had first created the connection to perform the task, then the connection for the

Figure 12.41 Restoring a connection shape.

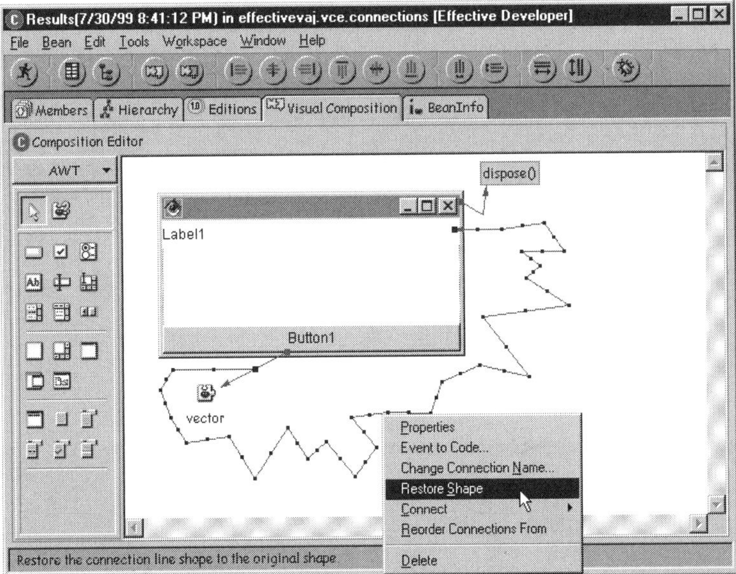

Figure 12.42 Three connections from the same event.

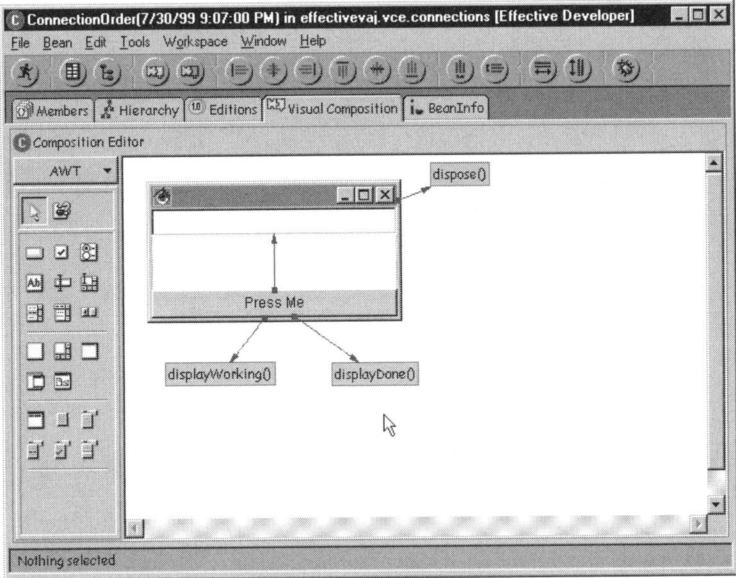

completion message, and then the connection to display a "working" message. When the button is clicked, the task executes, followed by a "done" message and, finally, a "working" message. Obviously, this is not the intent.

The order in which the connections execute needs to be changed. To do this, select **Reorder Connections From** from the button's pop-up menu, shown in Figure 12.43. This displays the Reorder Connections dialog shown in Figure 12.44. Note the order of the connections. You want to perform the "working" message connection first, not last. Do this by *dragging* the last connection *above* the first connection in this connection list. As you drag the connection, note the dark hint l ine appearing before or after connections. This hint line helps you see where the connection will appear when dropped.

Figure 12.43 Preparing to reorder connections.

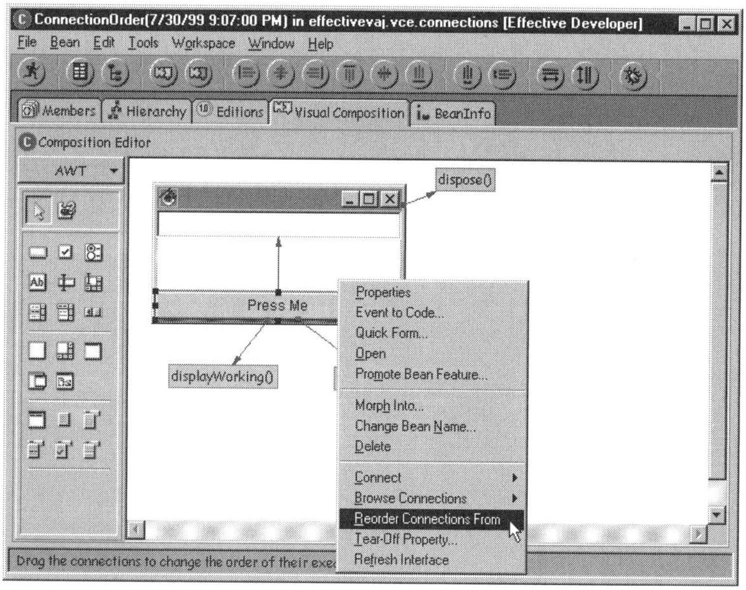

Figure 12.44 Reordering connections.

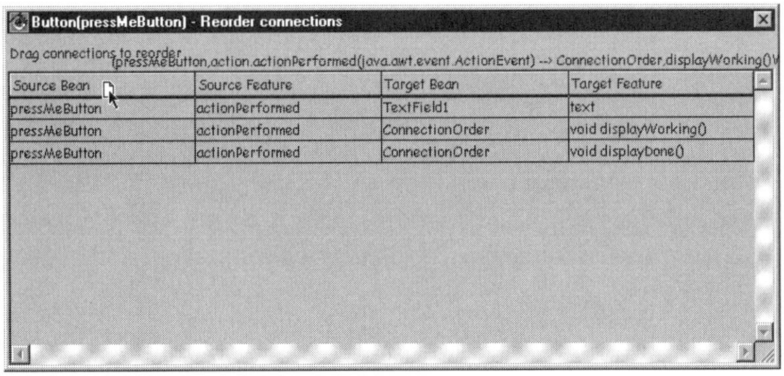

Button(pressMeButton) - Reorder connections

Drag connections to reorder
(pressMeButton,action.actionPerformed(java.awt.event.ActionEvent) --> ConnectionOrder.displayWorking()

Source Bean	Source Feature	Target Bean	Target Feature
pressMeButton	actionPerformed	TextField1	text
pressMeButton	actionPerformed	ConnectionOrder	void displayWorking()
pressMeButton	actionPerformed	ConnectionOrder	void displayDone()

Summary

VisualAge for Java's connections are the most powerful visual design tools available for Java today. They provide significant flexibility, enabling you to chain connections as parameters, customize connection order and appearance, and react to thrown exceptions. As you read the following chapters, you'll see how effective connections can be when applying visual design paradigms in the VCE.

Connections can connect visual *and* nonvisual beans, but the flexibility does not stop there. Connections can even connect bean instances that do not yet exist, passed in at run time. In the next chapter, we discuss variables, acting as placeholders for bean instances, providing the next important key to creating a maintainable visual design.

Variables and Instances

13

So far, we have covered completely static GUIs; that is, nothing inside them changes. Once you decide where you want to put your components in your GUI, they stay there; the running application adds no new components, nor does it remove existing components. For many applications, this is perfectly fine. However, some applications require dynamic data. That is, you will get the data from some other data source and present it to the user. Alternatively, you can get the data from the user and store it in some external data source. In cases like this, an instance of a class cannot be dropped in the VCE. The problem is, the data will change.

To help us with the situation, VisualAge for Java provides us with something called a *variable*. A variable is used in place of an instance of a class or interface. You can use a variable in much the same way as you would use instances in the VCE, drawing connections to it to interact with other components. This gives you a great deal of flexibility in your application. Rather than relying on a single instance of data and setting its properties, you can change *which* instance you are working with, and it interacts instantly with the rest of the GUI. This is ideal for many design patterns that we look at in later chapters. In particular, you can use variables as sockets in which to plug data values after you have created a visual design. This makes the component *completely* generic with regard to what type of data is expecting. We discuss how this is possible in Chapter 15, "Model-View-Controller in the VCE."

This chapter covers the use of variables in the VCE. We discuss how you can use variables to explore properties of beans and create plugs through which the outside world can communicate with our composite bean. In later chapters, we will use variables as an integral part of some design patterns, such as the Model-View-Controller paradigm.

Tearing Off Properties

A common use of variables in visual composition is to access properties of other properties. By pointing a variable to some instance's property, you can access that property's properties directly. There is no other way to get to "properties of properties" directly in the VCE. VisualAge for Java sets up such a pattern for you automatically by tearing off a property.

Let's begin the tear-off discussion by examining exactly how this works without using the tear-off feature, and then examine how tear-offs implement this.

Manually Reaching Our Goal

Suppose that you want to create a bean that describes relationships between people. The Person bean contains two read/write/bound String properties: an address and a name. Two read/write/bound mother and father properties, of type Person, are also added to describe relationships between a person and his parents. If this bean is used in the VCE, you can access the name and address of the person, as well as the mother and father person objects. However, you *cannot* directly access the father or mother's name.

Suppose that you design a GUI as seen in Figure 13.1. This GUI displays the name and address of a person, and the name of that person's mother and father. What you would like to do is to set the data for the instance of the person and have it displayed in the GUI.

Figure 13.1 A GUI for the Person bean.

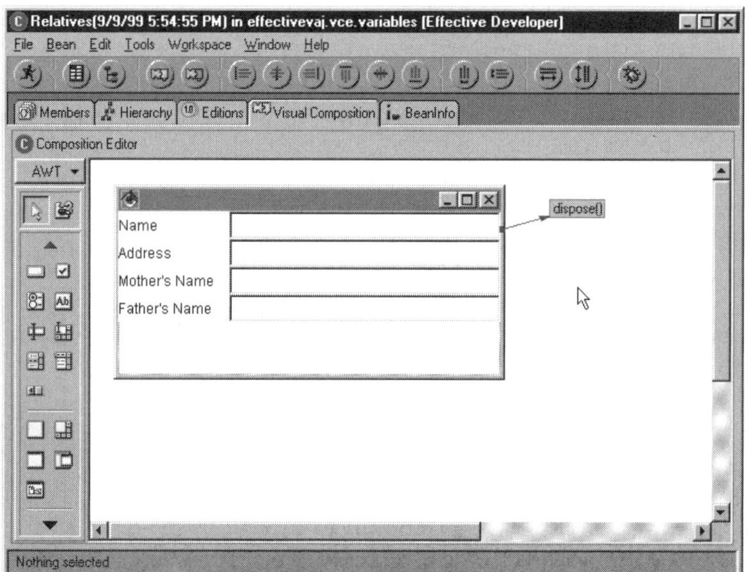

To create the example, perform the following steps:

1. Begin by developing the GUI. We assume you can now develop this GUI on your own.
2. Drop an instance of Person in a free part of the VCE design area, as seen in Figure 13.2.
3. Connect the name and address of the person to the name and address field, using property-to-property connections.

> **NOTE**
>
> You *cannot* draw a connection between the Person bean and the mother or father text fields. There is no mother's name property or father's name property in the Person bean.

Rather than worry about this right now, imagine that you actually have mother and father person objects sitting in the design area of the VCE. You can reference these imaginary people using two *variables*, rather than real instances.

Figure 13.2 The GUI in the VCE.

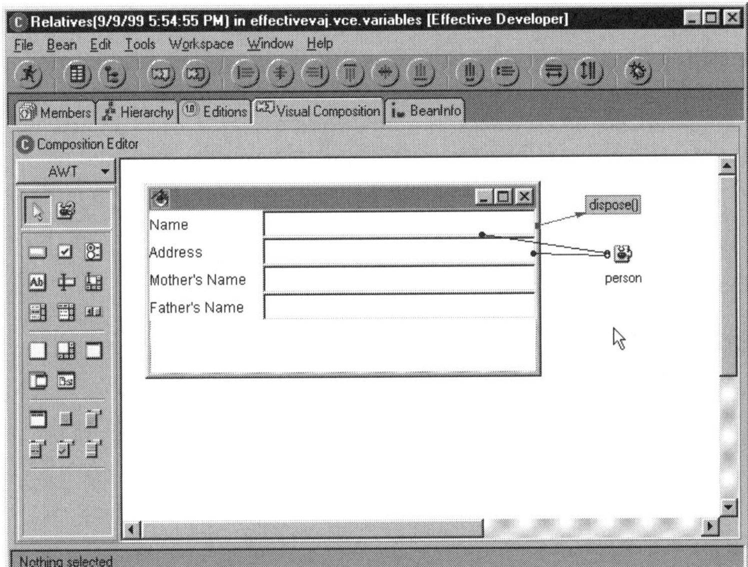

4. Create these variables using the VCE's Choose Bean command. Select **Variable** as the bean type, as shown in Figure 13.3. Note that when you open up the Choose Bean dialog, you have three types of beans:
   - Class
   - Variable
   - Serialized

   You have already added beans of type Class in Chapters 10 through 12. This creates an *instance* of the bean in the VCE. For this example, select **Variable** as the bean type, and Person as the class name.

5. Add two variables: one named *mother*, and one named *father*. Note the difference in appearance of these variables when you drop them in the VCE, as shown in Figure 13.4. Brackets surround the variable icons, distinguishing them from instances. Think of these brackets as showing you where you can plug in an instance of the bean.
6. Now, treat these two variables as though they were instances in the VCE. Connect the name property of the mother variable to the text property of the mother's text field. This is a simple property-to-property connection. Whenever the name property changes, the generated code updates the TextField bean's text property.
7. Connect the name property of the father variable to its TextField bean's text property in the same manner. The resulting connections appear in Figure 13.5.

Assuming these variables actually point to real Person data, this should work properly. This is no different than if you had started the connections from two Person *instances*. Assuming the data exists, the GUI displays the name and address of the Person, and the name of some mother and father. Now you just need to provide some link between the mother and father variables and the Person instance.

Figure 13.3 Creating a variable.

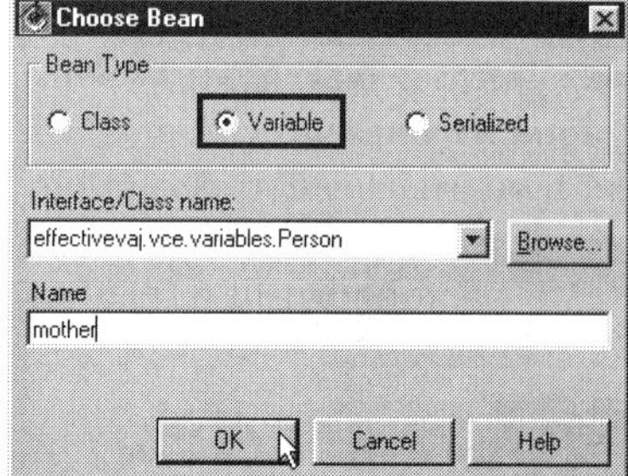

Figure 13.4 Variables in the VCE.

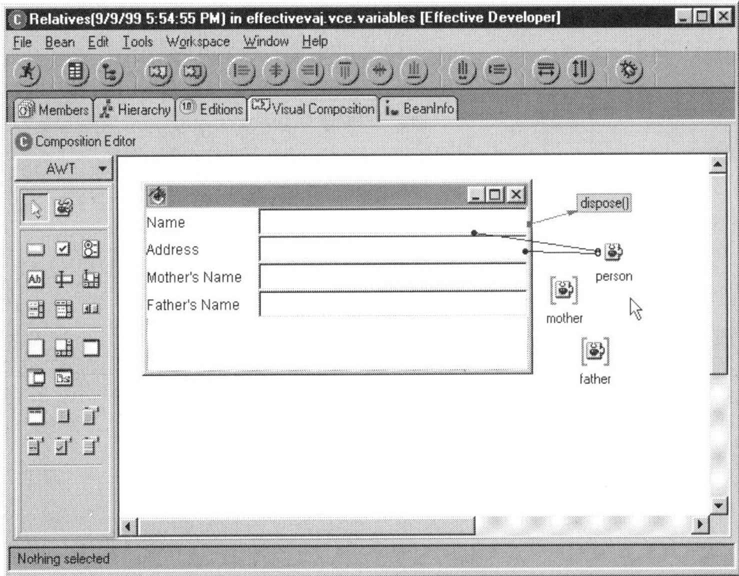

Figure 13.5 The mother and father connections.

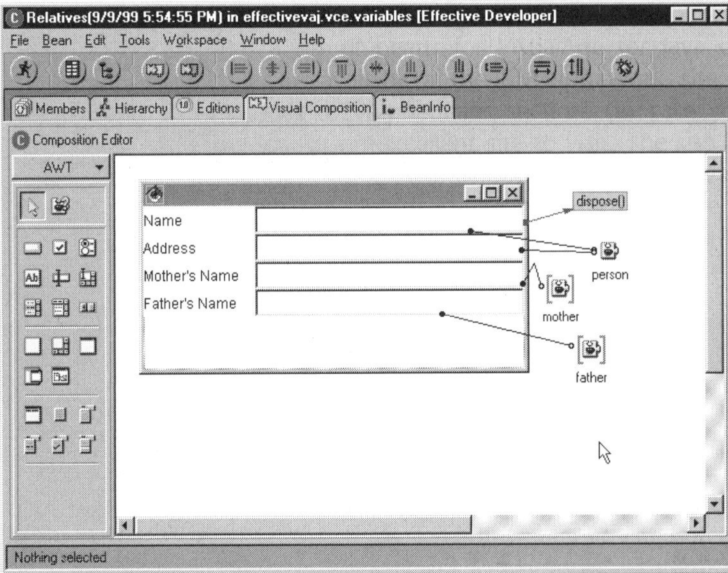

Before you can do that, you need to find out how to set the value of a variable. Each variable has a special property called *this*. The *this* property is not a true bean property; that is, there is no setThis() or getThis() method. The *this* property represents the value of the variable itself. You can set it use it as the source of a connection. When used as a connection source, it means "when the variable has been assigned," and it acts like a bound property.

8. To connect the variables to the Person instance, set the variable values to the mother and father properties of the Person bean by connecting the *this* property of the mother and father variables to the mother and father properties of the Person bean. These connections start from the Person instance and end on the variables, causing the property-to-property initialization to flow *from* the Person instance's mother and father properties to the variables. Anytime these values change in the person, the generated code sets the variables to the new values. Anytime the variables change, the properties in the Person bean change. This synchronizes the variables with the mother and father properties. If someone outside the GUI sets the person's mother to something, the mother variable updates automatically.
9. Connect the mother variable to the Person instance by starting a connection from the Person bean's mother property (**Connect->mother**, or **Connect->Connectable** Features if mother is not preferred) to the this property of the mother variable.
10. Similarly, connect the Person's father property to the *this* property of the father variable. After adding these connections, the VCE appears as shown in Figure 13.6.

There is one little gotcha in the generated code. You have connections from the mother and father variables to the TextField beans, and connections from the Person bean going to those mother and father variables. The order of the connection execution is extremely important. If the generated code has the mother and father variables send their data to the TextField beans first, you have some problems: There is no data to send. You have not executed the connections from the Person instance to the variables yet.

What you really want is to make sure that the Person bean sends the mother and father property values to the variables *before* updating the TextField beans; do this by reordering the connections.

11. Choose **Reorder Connections From** on the mother variable. This opens the dialog shown in Figure 13.7.
12. Drag the Person connection to the top as seen in Figure 13.8; then click OK.
13. Repeat the connection reordering for the father variable. Changing the order in this way ensures variable initialization before you attempt to access their features.
14. Save the visual design.

Figure 13.6 The finished relatives GUI.

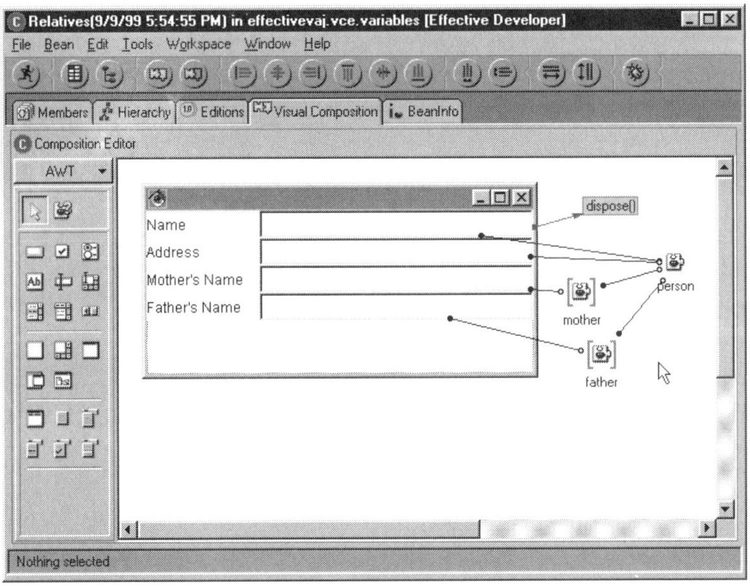

> **TIP**
>
> Remember to uncomment the handleException() method in your composite bean. This will disclose some of the problems caused by bad connection ordering.

In version 2 of VisualAge for Java, incorrect ordering caused problems. The VCE-generated code did not check if the variables were null before it attempted to set the TextField beans. This led to NullPointerExceptions. In VisualAge for Java version 3, the generated code checks for null variables before trying to access them. Therefore, in version 3, the order is not as important; the null checks

Figure 13.7 The connection reordering dialog.

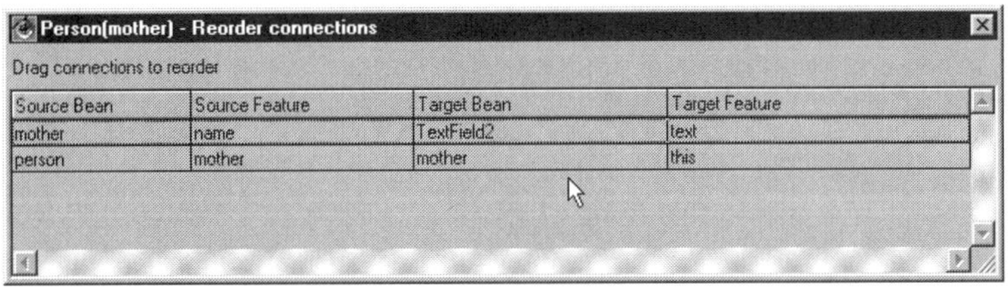

Figure 13.8 Reordering connections.

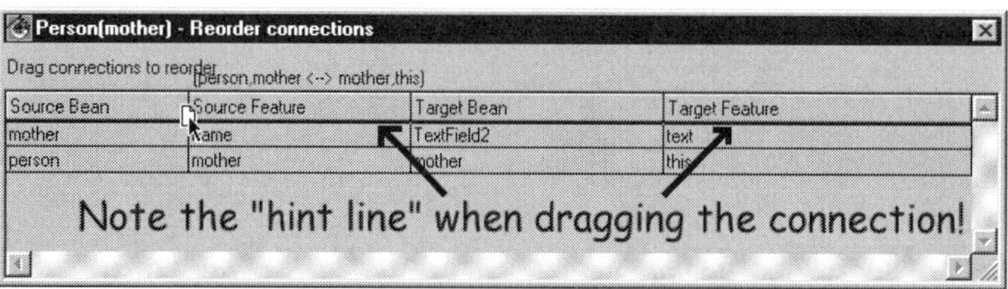

ignore the initial TextField connections; then it sets the variables, which in turn update the TextField beans.

15. After you save the visual design, write code to access the Person instance, and set its name, address, mother, and father properties. Performing these actions automatically updates the GUI. The code for the main method looks as follows:

```
public static void main(java.lang.String[] args) {
   // Create a new instance of our class
   Relatives aRelatives;
   aRelatives = new Relatives();

   // Grab a reference to the person instance
   Person me = aRelatives.getperson();
   me.setName("Scott");
   me.setAddress("Somewhere, USA");

   // Create his father and mother
   Person father = new Person();
   father.setName("Oliver");
   father.setAddress("Somewhere, USA");

   Person mother = new Person();
   mother.setName("Margaret");
   mother.setAddress("Somewhere, USA");

   // associate the person with the parents
```

```
    me.setMother(mother);
    me.setFather(father);

    // add a window-closing event-handler
    aRelatives.addWindowListener(new java.awt.event.WindowAdapter()
  {
      public void windowClosing(java.awt.event.WindowEvent e) {
        System.exit(0);
      }});
    aRelatives.setVisible(true);
  }
```

When this executable is run, you will see the expected results, shown in Figure 13.9.

Using Tear-Off Properties to Automate the Process

The previous scenario uses variables to provide access to a property of a property. Think about it this way: If you wrote some code to access the name and address of a person, the code could look as follows:

```
person.getName()      // access the name of a person
person.getAddress()   // access the address of a person
```

If you wanted to access the father or mother, you could use:

```
person.getFather()    // access the father of a person
person.getMother()    // access the mother of a person
```

All of these provide *direct* access to the properties of the person. You can represent these accesses using single connections in the VCE. However, to access the name of the father or mother, you would have to write code that looks as follows:

```
person.getFather().getName() // get mother's name
person.getMother().getName() // get father's name
```

Figure 13.9 The resulting Relatives GUI run.

Notice the number of dots in the code. If you use two dots, you are accessing a *feature of a feature*. You have added an extra level of indirection. You cannot directly represent this extra level of indirection in the VCE. To provide it, you must add variables to represent the first feature you access, and then access features that the *variable* contains. If you were to write code for this, it would look as follows:

```
Person father = person.getFather();
Person mother = person.getMother();
father.getName(); // get father's name
mother.getName(); // get the mother's name
```

Note the number of dots in each of the above accesses: one. These accesses can be represented using connections in the VCE.

This type of processing is often required in VisualAge for Java. Because of this, IBM has provided an easy way to create this pattern. They call it "tearing off properties." To demonstrate this, let's re-create the relatives GUI. You still want the same processing, but you can create it automatically.

1. Start by dropping the Person instance in the VCE and connecting it to the name and address ext fields as before. Then choose **Tear-Off Property** from the Person instance's pop-up menu, displaying the Tear-Off Property dialog shown in Figure 13.10. This dialog presents a list of all properties in the Person instance.
2. Select the mother property. The VCE creates a new variable of type Person, connecting to the Person instance through a property-to-property connection. This is *exactly* what you created before, but this time, it was much easier to create. The biggest advantages of this approach, however, are that it ensures the variable is of the proper type *and* the property-to-property connections occur in the right direction.
3. Repeat the process, tearing off the father property.

Figure 13.10 Tearing off a property.

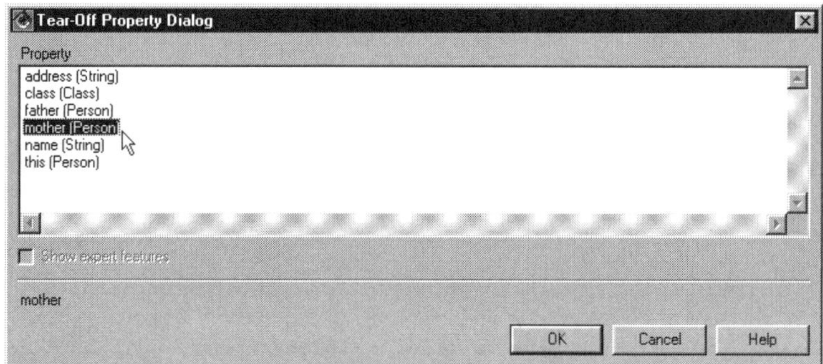

4. Once you have the torn-off mother and father variables, connect their name properties to the TextField beans' text properties. This is slightly easier than before, because you do not have to worry about what the mother and father variables actually are. If you compare Figure 13.11 (this new visual design) with Figure 13.6 (the previous visual design), you will notice that they have exactly the same effect. In fact, the two designs are nearly identical. The only difference is the name of the variables. By default, the VCE names torn-off properties with the name of the property followed by a unique number. In this case, the VCE generates variables named *mother1* and *father1* (you can rename these, of course, by choosing **Change Bean Name** from the variable's pop-up menu). You just used the VCE's Tear-Off Property command to automate some of the creation for us. Running the application produces the same result as before, shown in Figure 13.9.

Casting Using Variables

Sometimes you need to access a value as a different type. The Java language calls this *casting* the value to a different type. The Java language enables casting from one type to a compatible type, whether the type is a primitive or class. To do this in the VCE, create a variable of the desired type and draw a property-to-property

Figure 13.11 The new relatives GUI.

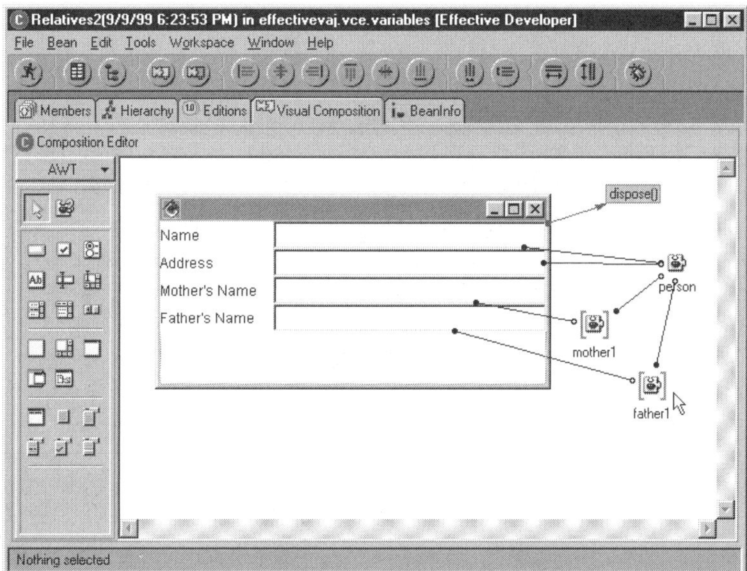

connection from the old property to the new variable's *this* property. The VCE generates the appropriate conversion code for you.

This also applies when you need to pass a compatible property value to a method. For example, if you want to pass a double to a method that requires an int, the VCE generates a cast for you.

The VCE generates code for many object conversions. Basic value conversion code is simply a cast. For example, if you need to use an int where a method takes a double as its parameter, the VCE generates code to cast the int into a double:

```
someMethod((double)x);
```

The VCE also performs some special conversions. There are many cases where you would want to convert a String to a primitive value, or the reverse. The VCE generates code for these conversions where possible:

- To convert an Object type to String, the VCE generates code to call String.valueOf() on the object. This normally invokes the toString() method of the object in question. There is no reverse (String to Object) available for this conversion.
- To convert a primitive type to String, the VCE generates code to call String.valueOf() on the primitive. This normally invokes the toString() method of a wrapper class like java.lang.Integer to create the String value.
- To convert a string to a primitive type, the VCE generates code to parse the string using one of the wrapper-class static methods, like Integer.parseInt(), or by creating a new instance of a Wrapper class, passing it a string.

The VCE always attempts to create a conversion between different types, such as casting up or down an inheritance hierarchy. However, if it detects that you are performing a potentially illegal cast, it will warn you, giving you the chance to cancel the connection.

Casting Example: Manipulating a Card Layout

If you use a card layout in your GUI design, you may want to call its next(), previous(), or show() methods to change the currently-displayed component. These are methods that exist in the CardLayout class, but not in the LayoutManager interface. To use them, you need to look at a container's layout manager as though it were actually a CardLayout. Therefore, you need to visually cast the *layout* property, of type LayoutManager, to type CardLayout using a variable.

As an example, suppose that you had a Frame bean that used CardLayout to display Button, CheckBox, Label, and TextArea beans. Further, suppose you want to switch between these components using Previous and Next buttons. You can do this as follows:

1. Create the GUI, as shown in Figure 13.12. This GUI consists of a panel, managed by CardLayout, that contains the Button, CheckBox, Label, and TextArea beans. At the bottom of the GUI, we have the Previous and Next buttons.
2. To interact with the layout, add a *variable* of type CardLayout to an empty part of the VCE design area.
3. Create a property-to-property connection from the layout property of contentsPane to the *this* property of the variable. The resulting visual design appears in Figure 13.12. You can then interact with that variable to move between cards in the layout.
4. Create an event-to-method connection between the actionPerformed event of the Previous button and the previous() method of variable theCardLayout. Name this connection "zzPrevInCardLayout" (choose Change Connection Name from the connection's pop-up menu).
5. Connect the parent parameter of zzPrevInCardLayout to the this property of the panel with CardLayout. Note that you will need to create this connection using the beans list, as the contents of the card layout completely fill the panel and you cannot directly click on the panel.
6. Repeat steps 4 and 5 to connect the Next button to the next() method of variable theCardLayout.

Figure 13.12 Accessing a card layout via a variable.

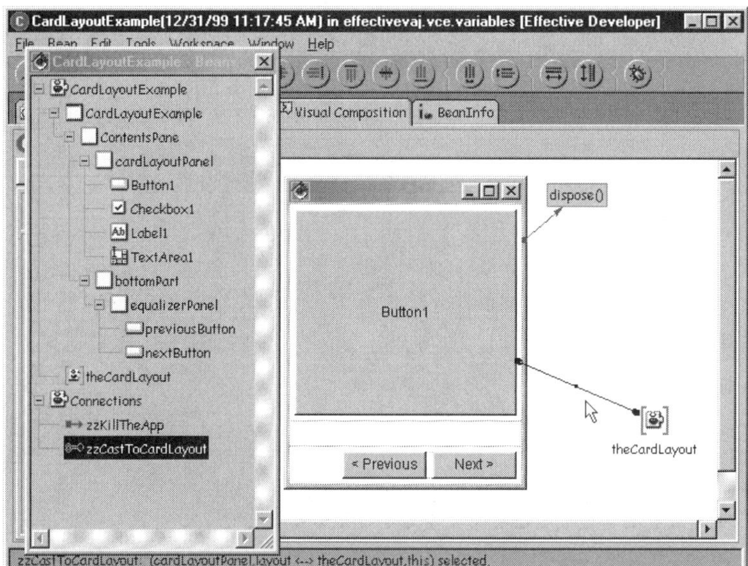

The final visual design appears in Figure 13.13. When you run this example, you initially see Button1 in the CardLayout area. If you click Next or Previous, the card layout switches which component is displayed.

Variables as Plugs for External Classes

You may have noticed that the first example in this chapter used an *instance* of Person and actually set some of its properties. It would be a lot more flexible to actually use a *variable* of type Person, which would enable someone *outside* of the class to pass in the person instance. This would make the relatives example *entirely generic*; simply pass a Person, *any* Person, and the GUI examines that Person to see its details. You can do this by changing the *instance* of Person to a *variable*. You would then promote the variable so it is visible *outside* the Relatives class. Modify the Relatives GUI with a few minor changes. We will use a variable for the Person, enabling us to plug in *any* person we want while the application is running. Later chapters will use variables to provide external plugs into our GUI.

The easiest way to accomplish this is to:

1. Open the existing Relatives class to the VCE.
2. *Morph* the instance of Person to a variable by selecting **Morph into** from the Person instance's pop-up menu. (Morphing is discussed in Chapter 10,

Figure 13.13 Connecting to cycle a card layout.

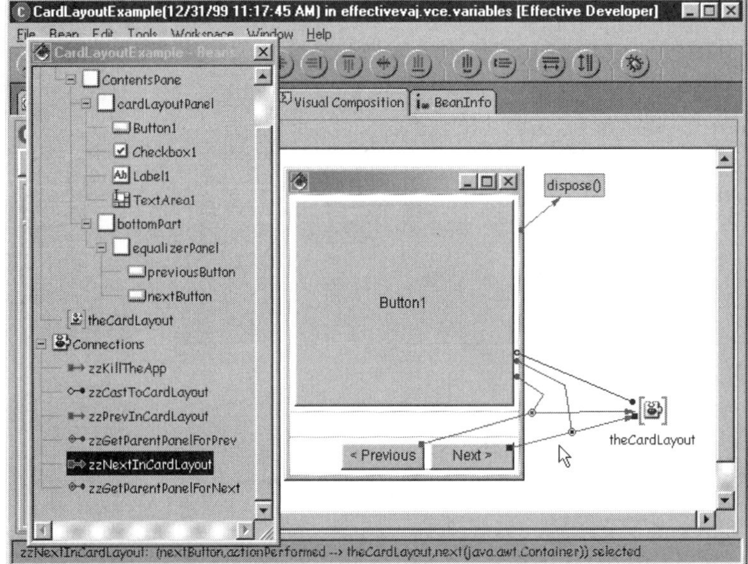

"Bean Composition in the VCE.") This enables you to change the type of the instance, or change it from an instance to a variable.

3. Change the bean type at the top of the Morph Into dialog to **Variable**.
4. Click **Ok.** Poof! The instance becomes a variable. You will notice that the person puzzle piece now has brackets around it: It is a variable, as seen in Figure 13.14.

For this example, we want to enable external classes to set the person variable. To do this, *promote* the *this* property of the variable.

1. Choose **Promote Bean Feature** from the person variable's pop-up menu.
2. Move the *this* property to the right pane by selecting *this* under properties and clicking the >> button.
3. Change the property's promote name to *thePerson*. (Feature promotion is discussed in Chapter 10.) Note that you cannot pick person as the name as it is already the name of a bean in the visual design. This creates a new property called thePerson that, when set, changes the value of the variable. Remember that the *this* property of the variable represents the variable itself.

Figure 13.14 The GUI, with person as a variable.

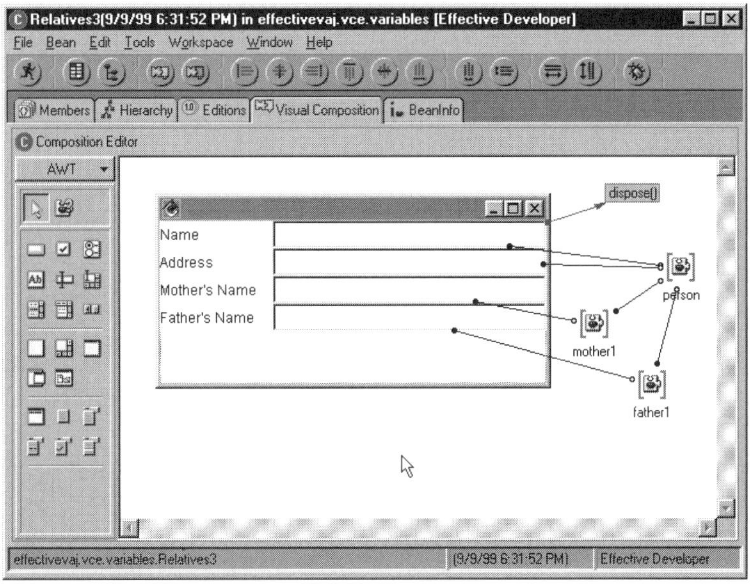

4. Change the main code to the following. The changes are in bold type: This code creates a new instance of Person and sets the variable in the VCE to that new instance.

```
public static void main(java.lang.String[] args) {
  // Create a new instance of our class
  Relatives3 aRelatives;
  aRelatives = new Relatives3();

  // Create a new Person and set it in the
  //   relatives class
  Person me = new Person();
  aRelatives.setThePerson(me);
  me.setName("Scott");
  me.setAddress("Somewhere, USA");

  // Create his father and mother
  Person dad = new Person();
  dad.setName("Oliver");
  dad.setAddress("Somewhere, USA");

  Person mom = new Person();
  mom.setName("Maragaret");
  mom.setAddress("Somewhere, USA");

  // associate the person with the parents
  me.setMother(mom);
  me.setFather(dad);

  // add a window-closing event-handler
  aRelatives.addWindowListener(new java.awt.event.WindowAdapter()
{
    public void windowClosing(java.awt.event.WindowEvent e) {
      System.exit(0);
    }});
  aRelatives.setVisible(true);
}
```

Now the *only* communication you have to the Relatives GUI is via the person variable. Everything else happens automatically, as determined in the visual design. When you execute this application, you see the same results as before, seen in Figure 13.9.

This is the key to effective separation of GUI and program logic in your application. The real data is defined outside the GUI, and passed to it. The GUI interacts with a variable, enabling it to use *any* piece of data of its type that we may pass in. We discuss this in more detail in Chapter 15.

Providing a promoted variable gives us a "socket." The GUI becomes generic, and you can plug in any instance of that type that you want. In Chapter 15 we will see that making this variable an interface type can greatly increase the flexibility of the GUI application. You can plug in any type of data that implements that interface. This can make your GUI much more reusable.

When a Variable Changes

What happens when the value of the variable changes? As you can see in the main code, you set the value of the person variable. When you set a variable, several things happen:

- If we had set up event handlers to process connections to that variable, the generated code disconnects them. VCE connections only apply to a single instance at a time. The latest value is the *only* value that connects to anything in the visual design.
- After dropping all connections, the generated code sets the variable to the new value.
- Once the new value is in place, the generated code reinstates the connections to that new value. The generated code connects any event necessary listeners to process the connections to the new variable value.
- After all connections are set up, the generated code re-executes any property-to-property initializations. This makes variables very powerful for setting values in the GUI. Anytime you set a variable, its property values magically appear in the GUI.

Variables in the VCE also act like bound properties; you can start the connection from the *this* property of the variable, and whenever the variable changes, the connection will take effect. You can use this to your advantage, as we will see in Chapter 14, "Design Patterns for the VCE."

Switching between Variables and Instances

As we demonstrated in the previous example, you can change an instance into a variable by selecting the **Morph into** command in the VCE. You can create the reverse effect by choosing **Morph into** for a variable and change the bean type back to Class. Note that this will not work if the variable is of an interface type. This makes the **Morph into** command very convenient if you accidentally create a variable or instance when you intended to create the other type. This also enables you to make your application more generic later, by changing instances into variables.

Variable Initialization

Sometimes you want to provide initial values for variables in a visual design. Initially, the value of a variable is null, but null may not be a useful default value. Perhaps the Person variable in your GUI is not set until the user performs an action, and you would like the fields to initially contain the text "not available".

There are two main ways to initialize variables. You can push a variable's value in from the outside (as we did previously with the promoted thePerson variable) or connect it with an instance of the same type. By dropping in an instance of the same type in the design area of the VCE, you can initialize the variable via a property-to-property connection. The property-to-property connection starts on the *this* property of the *instance* and ends on the *this* property of the *variable*. This sets the variable to point to that instance on initialization. You can bring up the property sheet for the instance and set some initial values if you so desire. This is demonstrated in Figure 13.15.

Figure 13.1 Initializing a variable with an instance in the VCE.

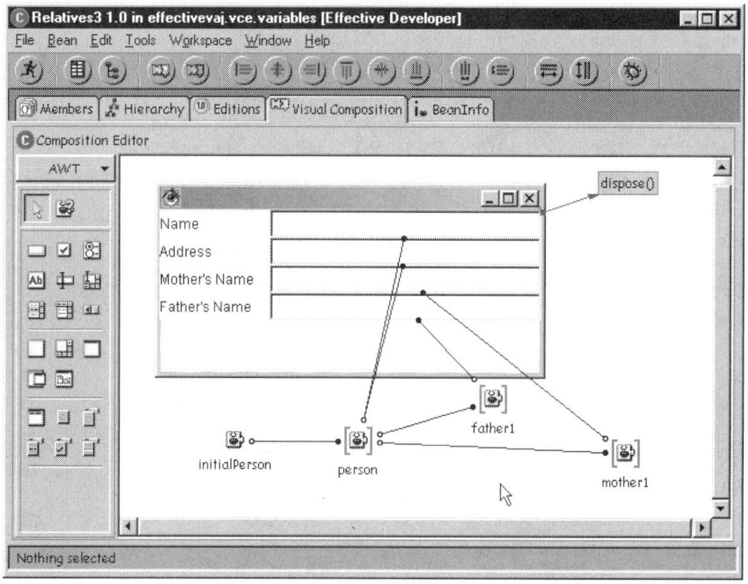

The Person instance named *initialPerson* provides a default Person instance to use in the GUI. When the GUI initializes, it triggers the property-to-property connection from initialPerson to person. This sets the person variable to point to initialPerson. Note that the value of initialPerson cannot change; it is an instance of Person. This means that it will never change the value of person when the GUI is running, and it cannot change when person changes. This property-to-property connection *only* performs initialization.

If the code that uses this GUI does not set the thePerson property (the promoted *this* property of the person variable), you will see the initialPerson values displayed in the text fields. If the code that uses the GUI sets the thePerson property, you will see that new Person's values displayed in the text fields.

Summary

Variables are one of the powerful tools provided in the VCE to enable you more flexibility in your application design. You can use variables to access nested features in your visual design and provide access to your GUI from the outside world. They are key to effective separation of your GUI and program logic.

Now that we have discussed the tools available to create your application, we move to a discussion of effectively applying these tools in your application. Each tool, from the BeanInfo editor to GUI building to VCE connections and variables, provides an important part of your application. In the next three chapters, we examine some design patterns to help you apply these tools. These design patterns can greatly simplify your life and, more importantly, help generate more maintainable code.

14 DESIGN PATTERNS FOR THE VCE

Now that we have covered the tools available in the VCE, we examine some strategies for using those tools. In this chapter, we discuss some design patterns that you can use to simplify both development and maintenance of your application. Consider these techniques as extra tools in your arsenal. Think simplicity!

Design patterns are proven methods for solving common problems. They can range from low-level code templates (such as the get and set methods for bean properties) to complete system architectures. Patterns have been around for quite some time but have recently come to the forefront of program design, thanks to the book *Design Patterns: Elements of Reusable Object-Oriented Software* [(Gamma, Helm, Vlissides, Johnson), Addison-Wesley 1995]. This is commonly known as the "Gang-of-Four" book, or GOF for short.

Design patterns fill two roles:

Vocabulary. Many design patterns have been in use for quite some time. However, communicating patterns can take a lot of explaining. Usually near the end of the explanation, the other person says, "Oh, I know what you're talking about. We used that approach on project X." Rather than explain the pattern each time you want to communicate it, books and articles containing design patterns assign them names. You can now say "use the Visitor pattern" and people who have read GOF know what you mean.

Education. Many programmers have heard of several patterns, but would benefit from seeing many more. GOF presents several patterns, and programmers are bound to learn new techniques by reading it.

This chapter presents some patterns that you may or may not have used. Hopefully you'll learn some new techniques and adopt the names we've chosen to help you communicate the patterns.

NOTE

You can blame the pattern names chosen in this chapter on the authors of this book. Any similarity to existing pattern names is coincidental and unintentional. As far as we know, these patterns have not been documented elsewhere.

General Strategies

The VCE is meant to be a productivity tool. It allows you to *draw* your user interface and interaction between the interface components. While this *can* help speed up development and maintenance, it can *also* hinder those same processes. You still need to consider the design of your application. Remember, the VCE is *not* a design tool; it is an implementation tool.

There are several strategies you should keep in mind when using the VCE:

Less is more. Just because you *can* do something in the VCE, doesn't mean you *should* do it in the VCE. VisualAge for Java provides many ways of modifying your code; consider them all.

Code is okay if it is visible. Don't be afraid to write code that helps your GUI. Just make sure that a maintenance programmer can easily see that the code exists.

Break down for maintenance. If a visual design starts looking crowded, consider breaking it into sub-GUIs. If you can't see the design easily, neither can a maintenance programmer.

Separation is key. Keep clean separation between your user interface and program logic. This can help if you need to change the GUI or logic later, without affecting the entire application.

We'll start by explaining each of these strategies. You should make sure you're thinking about all of these concepts while creating your visual design. Then, we'll present some methods you can use to help your implementation of these strategies.

Less Is More

The most important thing to realize when you use the VCE is that *less is more.* Just because you *can* create connections very easily does not mean that you *should.* Visual connections are the most abused and overused features of VisualAge for Java. Because they are so easy to create, many people feel they should create their *entire* application using connections. This can lead to a visual design like the one shown in Figure 14.1.

Figure 14.1 A fine mess.

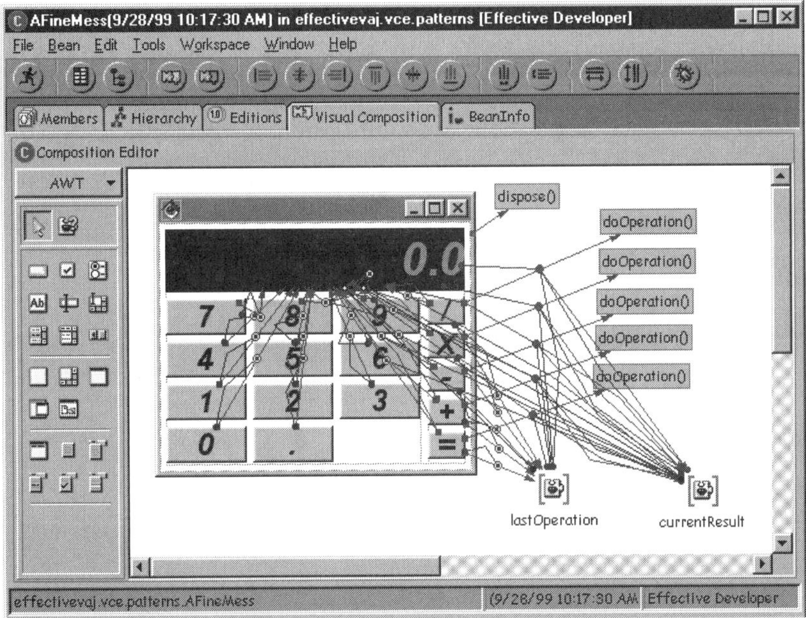

Such a design is completely unreadable. It may have been fun to create, but it is certainly no fun to read. Chances are, even the original designer would have trouble reading this design. While it may seem difficult to believe, designs like this are abundant in the wild. The goal is to simplify the design, making it readable to both designer *and* maintainer.

There are several ways to simplify designs. While using connections can save you from writing lots of code, too many of them can obscure the design. By using some of the strategies and patterns we discuss in this chapter, you can create visual designs that are not only more readable, but also easier to create in the first place. For example, a much simpler calculator design is shown in Figure 14.2. By utilizing several patterns, we created a readable visual design, and vastly eased maintenance. Note the significant reduction in the number of connections that was achieved by using a small amount of code instead of the extra connections. Overall, the amount of handwritten code *is nearly the same.*

Code Is Okay *If* It Is Visible

Many people forget that *writing code is okay*. While connections save you from writing code, there are actually times when it is easier to perform the same task

Figure 14.2 A simpler calculator visual design.

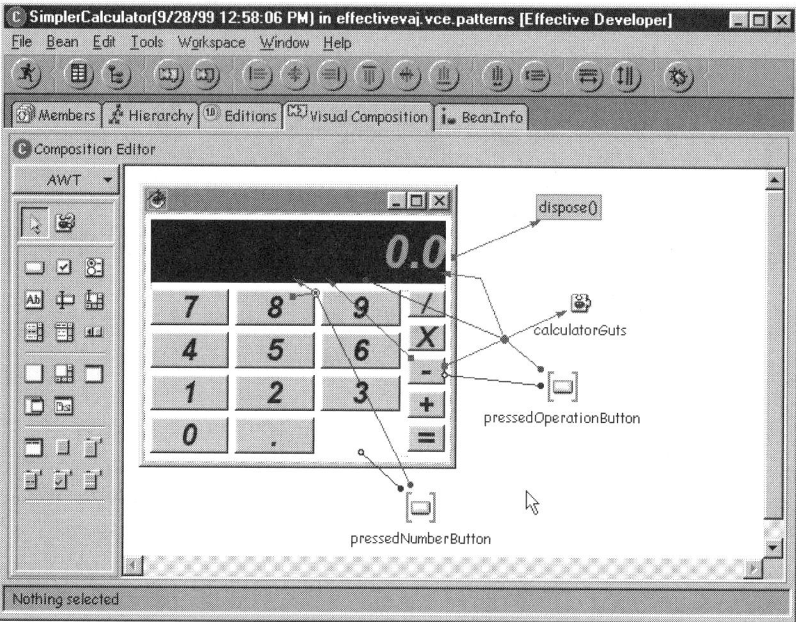

by writing code instead of creating connections. Some of the more interesting patterns presented in this chapter involve writing a small piece of code to act as an intermediary.

However, it is very important not to add handwritten code to generated methods. The VCE provides *user code* blocks in each generated method. (We discuss the VCE-generated code in Chapter 19, "Handwritten Code versus Generated Code.") If you add code in these blocks, the VCE preserves it when regenerating the method. This may seem like a nice feature when you develop an application, but it can quickly become a maintenance nightmare. When the maintainer examines the application to determine the cause of a bug, or how to add new functionality, the *last* place he will think to look for your code is in the VCE-generated methods. Think of the amount of code that the VCE generates. If you had added a single line of handwritten code to any of these generated methods, the maintenance programmer's task becomes significantly more difficult. He must examine *all* generated methods, in case you added your own code to *any* of them!

If you need to add your own code, do so via an event-to-code connection. This adds visual documentation to the design, informing a maintenance programmer where your handwritten code exists. Your method does not look like a generated method, and the VCE shows the call.

Break Down for Maintenance

As seen in Figure 14.1, a single visual design with many connections can be quite difficult to read. If you decide that connections are the best way to create an application, think about breaking the GUI down into smaller sub-GUIs. Each sub-GUI can handle its own connections locally, possibly firing some events to notify the GUI that contains it. This also helps to create reusable partial GUIs. For example, the Ok and Cancel buttons found at the bottom of nearly every dialog could be a reusable sub-GUI.

Separation Is Key

Chapter 15, "Model-View-Controller in the VCE," adds one of the best maintenance patterns to your arsenal. Clean separation of GUI and business logic is imperative to effective and maintainable application design. This enables you to change the business logic without affecting the GUI or to change the GUI without affecting the business logic. It enables you to add multiple GUIs that view the same data or to give each GUI separate data. Most importantly, however, the application readability increases, because there are fewer connections between GUI components and the data on which they act.

Connection Patterns

In this section, we present five patterns that are designed to reduce connections as well as add some visual logic to the application. You can factor connections, moving common functionality from several places to a centralized location. You can conditionally execute connections, changing the way the application behaves.

Factorization Patterns

When developing an application, you may notice that several connections are virtually identical among many controls. Look again at Figure 14.1. Notice the connections that start from each of the operator buttons (you may need to squint). These connections perform the following tasks:

- Execute the *previous* operation (+, -, x, /), storing the result in the variable *currentResult*
- Save the name of the clicked operator button as *lastOperation*
- Set the text of AppendableLabel to *currentResult*
- Tell AppendableLabel to overwrite its text on the next number-key click

All five operation buttons perform these same tasks. This redundancy is a waste of development time as well as a source of confusion when maintaining the code.

Trigger Pattern

The Trigger pattern resolves this by factoring the redundant operations. A *trigger* is a bean that has a single bound property. The PropertyChangeEvent of the trigger is used as the starting point of the common connections. Then, wherever the common connections used to exist, a single connection is used to set the bound property. In the calculator example, rather than have four connections from each of the five operation buttons (a total of 20 connections, plus parameter connections), there are four connections from the trigger, and one from each button (a total of nine connections, plus parameter connections). If you have a GUI with several common connections, this can significantly increase the readability and maintainability of your design.

The following is an example trigger class. Note the bound property can be of any type; often, you should make it of type Button if the trigger will handle multiple button clicks. Likewise, if you are using different types of components, have the bound property be of those types.

```
import java.awt.*;
import java.beans.*;
/**
 * A Simple Trigger Class
 * This Trigger tracks a pressed button, firing PropertyChangeEvents
 *   whenever the button is set. This is useful for factoring
 *   connections when several buttons require the same connections
 */
public class ButtonTrigger {
  private Button fieldButton;

  public Button getButton() {return fieldButton;}

  public void setButton(Button button) {
    fieldButton = button;
    // Note: We changed this to _always_ fire the change by
    //         passing null as the old value. Otherwise our
    //         trigger would not work if the same value is set
    //         twice in a row
    firePropertyChange("button", null, button);
  }

  // Typical Bound property support methods
  public synchronized void addPropertyChangeListener(
                              PropertyChangeListener listener) {...}
  public synchronized void removePropertyChangeListener(
                              PropertyChangeListener listener) {...}
```

```
  public void firePropertyChange(String propertyName,
                                 Object oldValue,
                                 Object newValue) {...}
}
```

The trigger is easy to create. Create a new class and add a bound property to it using VisualAge for Java's BeanInfo editor. Then make a slight modification to the property's set method to pass *null* as the old value, which forces the event to *always* fire when the set method is called.

To demonstrate the trigger pattern, take a look at the partial GUI representation of the problem, shown in Figure 14.3. Note that the four operations do not map to the above operations; they are presented as a simple example. Event-to-property connections set the *button* property of the trigger to the clicked button.

These connections cause each button to set the button property of the trigger when pressed. This, in turn, triggers the event-to-code connections starting at the button PropertyChangeEvent of the trigger. The changed object (the clicked button) is passed to each event-to-code connection, because we selected the **Pass Event Data** check box for each connection. The event-to-code connection that calls doFourthThing() requires a String parameter, and the label property of the clicked button is passed as that parameter. Note that to access that label property, we had to tear off the button property of the trigger.

Figure 14.3 A trigger in action.

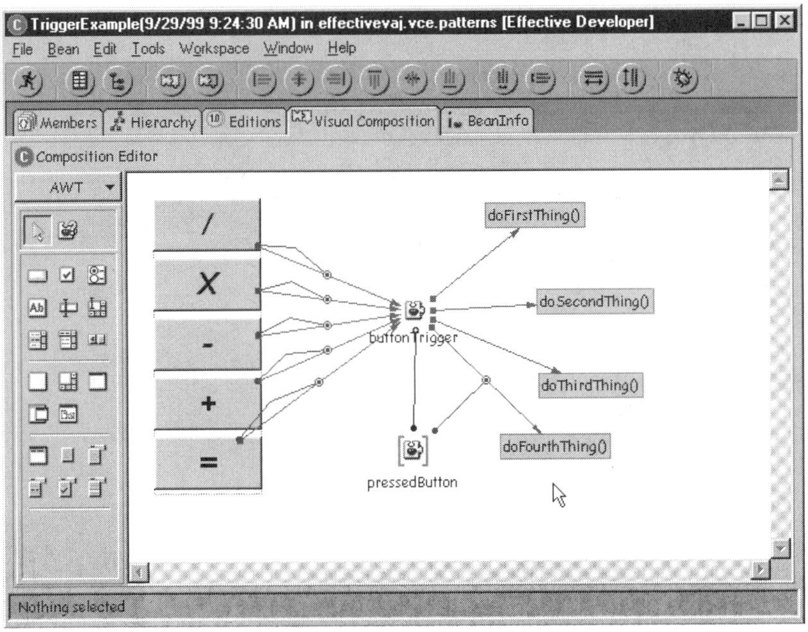

> **NOTE**
>
> The connection order is *very* important. You are in trouble if you tear off the button property of the trigger *after* creating the event-to-code connections. This connection order appears in Figure 14.4. Note that the event-to-code connections execute before the pressedButton variable is set! This means that doFourthThing() will see the *previous* button clicked. Be careful with connection order!

Some people complain that this is a performance hit. Yes, this requires an extra level of event-firing method calls. However, method call overhead is trivial compared to nearly any operation performed in your GUI application, especially in light of the high processor speeds today. *It all boils down to a minute performance impact versus maintainability*. If your visual design contains several common connections, we urge you to apply a trigger, funnel, or other pattern to factor your connections.

Figure 14.4 Incorrect connection order!

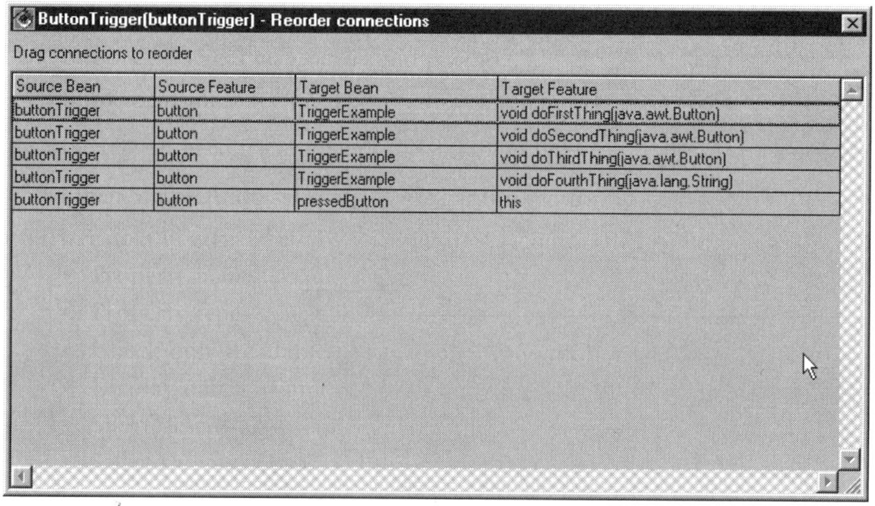

ButtonTrigger(buttonTrigger) - Reorder connections

Drag connections to reorder

Source Bean	Source Feature	Target Bean	Target Feature
buttonTrigger	button	TriggerExample	void doFirstThing(java.awt.Button)
buttonTrigger	button	TriggerExample	void doSecondThing(java.awt.Button)
buttonTrigger	button	TriggerExample	void doThirdThing(java.awt.Button)
buttonTrigger	button	TriggerExample	void doFourthThing(java.lang.String)
buttonTrigger	button	pressedButton	this

Funnel Pattern

A *funnel* is a container that watches for events on some or all of its contained components, and fires its own event in response. This is somewhat like a trigger, except the events that cause the trigger to fire are hidden. Funnels are very easy to create. The following is a simple funnel that watches for button clicks and sets its own *pressedButton* property. This is only useful for managing adjacent components in the GUI, as the components need to reside in the same container.

```
import java.awt.*;
import java.awt.event.*;
import java.beans.*;

/**
 * A simple Funnel that watches its Buttons
 * When any button inside it is pressed, the funnel sets its
 *   pressedButton property to that button. Because pressedButton
 *   is a bound property, it fires a property change event that
 *   can be used as the source of connections in the GUI
 */
public class ButtonActionFunnel extends Container
                                 implements ActionListener {
  // Bound property support ommitted for brevity

  // -- bound property pressedButton ----------
  private Button fieldPressedButton;

  public Button getPressedButton() {
    return fieldPressedButton;
  }

  public void setPressedButton(Button pressedButton) {
    fieldPressedButton = pressedButton;
    // force to fire by passing null as old value
    firePropertyChange("pressedButton", null, pressedButton);
  }

  // ---------- the trigger ---------------
  /** When notified that a button is pressed, set our
   *    pressedButton property to that button
   */
  public void actionPerformed(ActionEvent e) {
    setPressedButton((Button)e.getSource());
  }
```

```
// —— handle added/removed components——————————
/** Intercept Container's addImpl call:
 *    When adding a Button, add the funnel as a listener.
 */
protected void addImpl(Component comp,
                       Object constraints,
                       int index) {
  super.addImpl(comp,constraints, index);
  if (Beans.isInstanceOf(comp,Button.class))
    ((Button)comp).addActionListener(this);
}

/** When a Button is removed, remove us as a listener */
public void remove(int index) {
  Component comp = getComponent(index);
  if (Beans.isInstanceOf(comp,Button.class))
    ((Button)comp).removeActionListener(this);
  super.remove(index);
}

public void remove(Component comp) {
  if (Beans.isInstanceOf(comp,Button.class))
    ((Button)comp).removeActionListener(this);
  super.remove(comp);
}

public void removeAll() {
  Component[] comps = getComponents();
  for(int i = 0; i < comps.length; i++)
    if (Beans.isInstanceOf(comps[i],Button.class))
      ((Button)comps[i]).removeActionListener(this);
  super.removeAll();
}
}
```

The above funnel code detects components as they are added. Anytime it detects a Button instance as the added component, it adds itself as an ActionListener. Whenever a user clicks one of the buttons, the funnel sets its *pressedButton* property. Because this is a bound property, the funnel fires a PropertyChangeEvent. This PropertyChangeEvent is used in the VCE to perform the desired actions. If you use a funnel in place of the trigger in the previous example, the VCE design looks as displayed in Figure 14.5.

Figure 14.5 A funnel in action.

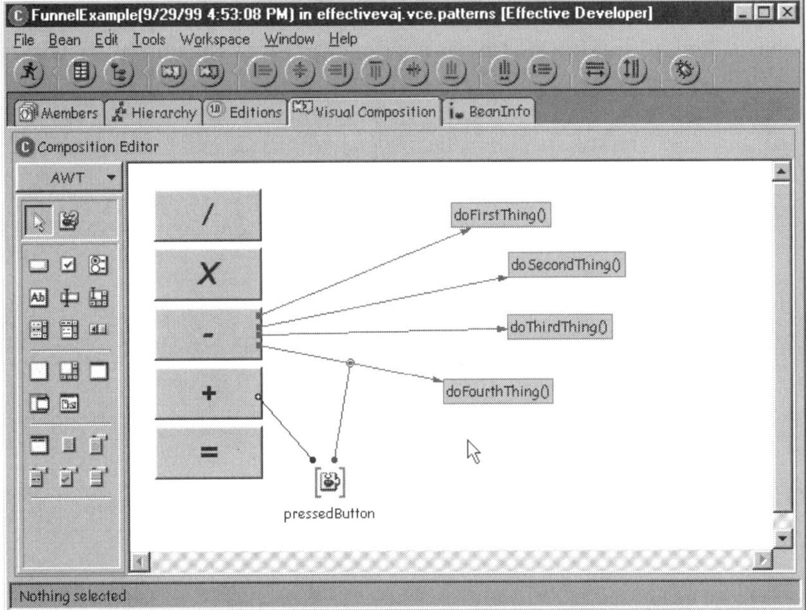

As you can see, this visual design is significantly simpler. The only disadvantage to this approach is that the connections *appear* to originate from some of the buttons. Whenever you have connections that originate from a container instead of from one of its contained components, you should document that fact. The best way to do this is to document that you are using the Funnel pattern and reference this book for its explanation. (Alternatively, you can create a single document that describes your interpretation of the pattern, using the name "Funnel," and include that document in your design notes for the application. The point is to use a consistent name anytime you use the same pattern, so that it becomes part of your group's vocabulary.)

Funnels provide an excellent blend of a small amount of handwritten code and VCE connections. Keep this trade-off in mind, especially when you could reuse such a component in several applications.

Enabler Pattern

An *enabler* is a trigger that watches over a bound Boolean property. The purpose of this type of trigger is to associate the enabled status of several components with a single trigger. By creating several property-to-property connections from the enabler to some components, we create an easy means to turn them all off or on. This is especially useful if you have a group of components in a GUI to enable or disable based on a check box in the same GUI. Figure 14.6 shows a GUI with an enabler in action. The code for an enabler is the same as that for a trigger with a Boolean property. The Enabler pattern is really a specialization of the Trigger pattern.

A better way to provide this support is to combine the Funnel and Enabler patterns. This is called an EnablingContainer. The idea is that the container passes its enabled status to each of its components. This makes the entire enable/disable processing invisible in the VCE. The code for an EnablingContainer follows. Note that if you use this type of container in your design, you must make sure that all *nested* containers are also EnablerContainers, or it cannot enable/disable deeply nested components.

```
import java.awt.*;
/**
 * A Container that sets the enabling status of its components
 */
public class EnablingContainer extends Container {
  /**
   * Intercept enable/disable requests, and propagate them to
   *   our contained components
   */
  public void setEnabled(boolean enabled) {
    boolean oldValue = isEnabled();
```

Figure 14.6 An enabler in action.

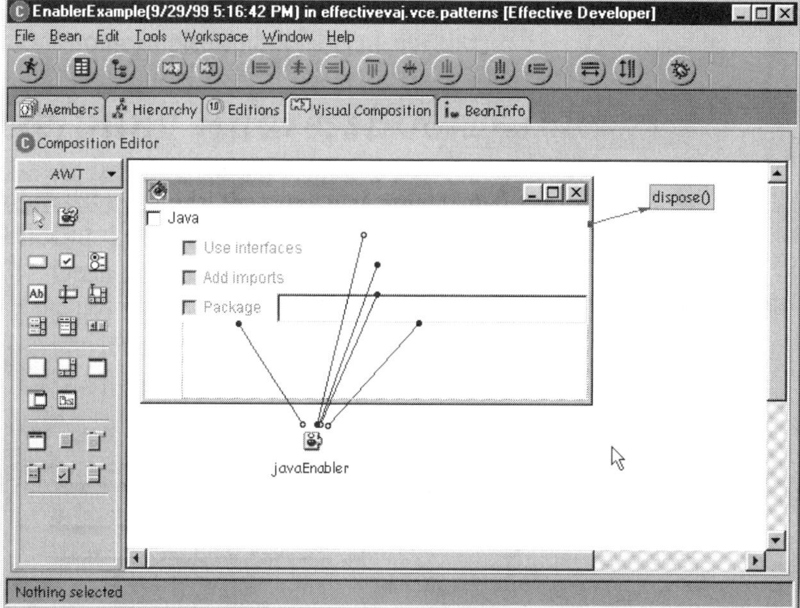

```
      super.setEnabled(enabled);
      if (enabled != oldValue) {
        // walk through all components and enable/disable them
        Component[] comps = getComponents();
        for(int i = 0; i<comps.length; i++)
          comps[i].setEnabled(enabled);
      }
    }
  }
```

Once again, writing a small amount of code saved several connections. The VCE design for this example is trivial; it is the same as Figure 14.6, without the connections (except the property-to-property connection that sets the EnablerContainer's enable property). However, instead of using panels to contain components, we use EnablerContainers. The result appears in Figure 14.7.

Conditional Patterns

Sometimes it is desirable to execute different connections based on a condition. For example, if the user types some text in a field and clicks an Add button, the text could be added to a database. However, if the field were empty, clicking the

Figure 14.7 An EnablerContainer in action.

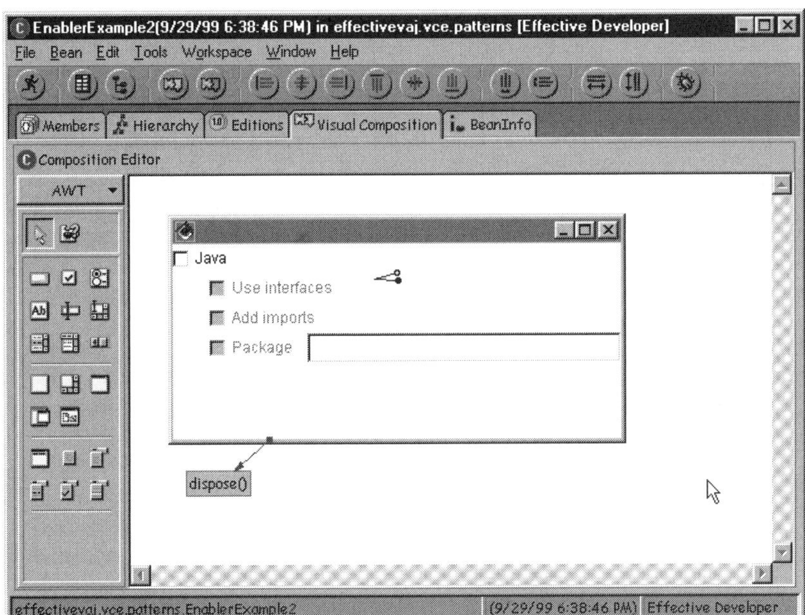

Add button should display an error message. This section examines two patterns that can provide conditional functionality in the VCE.

> **NOTE**
>
> While these patterns are conceptually interesting, in practice it is much easier to write code and use event-to-code connections. Before using these patterns, think carefully about whether you would rather write some code. However, these patterns are still useful to explore, to help you become more aware of different ways of using the VCE for application design. Part of the key to success with the VCE is simply to be willing to think about problems in alternative ways.

Visual Assertion Pattern

An *assertion* is a test performed to check that a certain condition is true at a certain point in a program. You can visualize this in the VCE with a VisualAssertion class. A VisualAssertion class has methods to provide comparison; each method either throws an exception or does nothing. By connecting to these methods, you can fork your logic via the *exceptionOccurred* and *normalResult* connections. The following is a simple VisualAssertion class.

```
package effectivevaj.vce.patterns;

/**
 * A Simple class for assertion testing in the VCE
 */
public class VisualAssertion {
  /** Test that two ints are equal */
  public void assert(int i, int j) throws Exception {
    if (i != j)
      throw new Exception("assertion failed!");
  }

  /** Test that two Strings are equal */
  public void assert(String i, String j) throws Exception {
    if (!i.equals(j))
      throw new Exception("assertion failed!");
  }

  /** Test that a condition is true */
  public void assert(boolean condition) throws Exception {
```

```
        if (!condition)
          throw new Exception("assertion failed!");
    }
}
```

Use a VisualAssertion class by dropping an instance of it in the VCE, and calling its assert() methods. To decide what to do when an assertion fails, create an exceptionOccurred connection from the original connection. As a simple example, consider the visual design shown in Figure 14.8. When a user clicked the button, it tests the value of the check box using a VisualAssertion instance. If all goes well, it sets the TextField to "done"; if the assertion fails, it sets the TextField to "there was a problem."

The Visual Assertion pattern can prove useful in some circumstances; however, we recommend that you think very carefully about your design and alternative means of providing conditional logic. For example, you could use constrained properties to perform your validation.

Because exceptions are expensive, only use a VisualAssertion class in cases that you normally would expect processing to end *without* throwing the exception. If you need conditional connections based on a value that normally varies, such as the sex of a person (male or female), you should use a different type of conditional pattern: a conditional fork.

Figure 14.8 A VisualAssertion class in action.

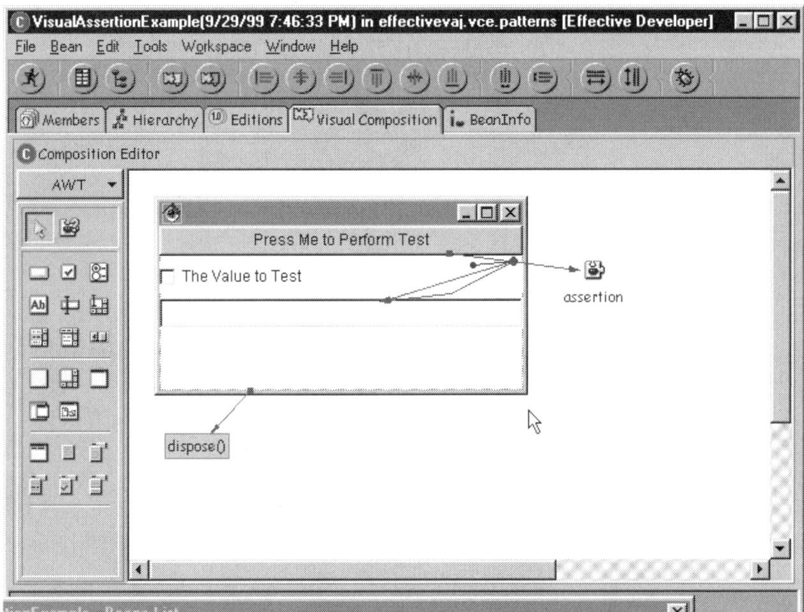

Conditional Fork Pattern

A *conditional fork* is similar to VisualAssertion but uses events rather than exceptions to distinguish the alternatives. The method in a conditional fork is called as the target of a connection. The method then fires one of several events, each of which can be the source of other connections. You can use variations on this type of pattern for several types of conditional logic. For example, take a look at the If bean that follows:

```
/**
 * A Sample Conditional Logic Bean
 * When tested, it fires truePart or falsePart events
 */
public class If {
  /** Test a boolean value, and fire the corresponding
   *    truePart or falsePart events
   */
  public void test(boolean condition) {
    if (condition)
      fireTruePart(new IfConditionEvent(this, true));
    else
      fireFalsePart(new IfConditionEvent(this, false));
  }

  // Methods to fire events in IfConditionListener
  // These were added via "New Listener Interface" in the
  //   BeanInfo editor and are standard bean event set methods
  public void addIfConditionListener(
                 IfConditionListener newListener) {...}
  public void removeIfConditionListener(
                 IfConditionListener newListener) {...}
  protected void fireFalsePart(IfConditionEvent event) {...}
  protected void fireTruePart(IfConditionEvent event) {...}
}
```

The If bean has a method named test(), which takes a boolean expression as its argument. This method fires either a truePart or falsePart event based in the value of the parameter. An example of its use appears in Figure 14.9. Note that this is nearly the same example as Figure 14.8. The difference is that truePart and falsePart events are used instead of normalResult and exceptionOccurred. This is a more appropriate pattern to use when the condition values occur in a more even distribution.

Figure 14.9 The If bean in action.

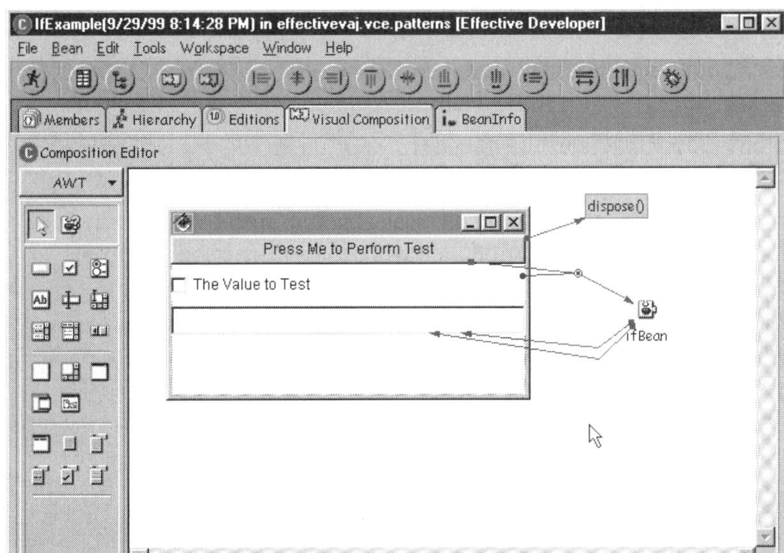

> **TIP**
>
> If you like this style of connection programming, there are many variations available. IBM has a set of beans for VisualAge for Java called *Wiring Helpers*. These beans are available at the IBM alphaWorks site, www.alphaworks.ibm.com, under the AlphaBeans section. (In case you have not been there before, this is an excellent site to visit. The site hosts several very useful beans). The Wiring Helpers package contains beans similar to the If bean that we just discussed, although a bit more complex. It includes beans to perform conditional processing, such as if and switch statements, and loop processing, such as for and while statements.

GUI Composition Patterns

You can use several patterns when composing a visual design. Composition involves dropping beans into the VCE to create a more complex, compound bean. One of your primary design strategies should be to break down the design into several smaller sub-GUIs. This has several advantages for maintenance of the program, as well as keeping the design simple as you develop it.

Encapsulated Promotion

The *Encapsulated Promotion* pattern allows a sub-GUI to expose selected features. The exposed features can be any bean feature: property, event set, or method. The sub-GUI can implement its functionality and layout in any way. By promoting certain features, you define the public programming interface of the sub-GUI. Compound GUIs can only communicate with the sub-GUI via this programming interface. You can change the sub-GUI without worrying about impacts, as long as you still provide the same public programming interface.

For example, suppose that you define the sub-GUI shown in Figure 14.10. This sub-GUI accepts input from the user in several text fields. In the application, the important thing is the text in those text fields. That is, it is only important that the user has input a first name, last name, and prefix. It is *not* important that they actually entered the data in a text field; that is simply an implementation detail. Using these text fields in a sub-GUI hides them from the compound GUI. The only thing the compound GUI knows about the sub-GUI is that it is a subclass of Panel, and the compound GUI has access to the features of the sub-GUI as a Panel.

Because the compound GUI will most likely need to access the information that the user has entered, that information needs to be exposed. However, rather than exposing the text fields, you only expose the text properties of the TextField beans by promoting the text property of each TextField bean.

Figure 14.10 A simple sub-GUI.

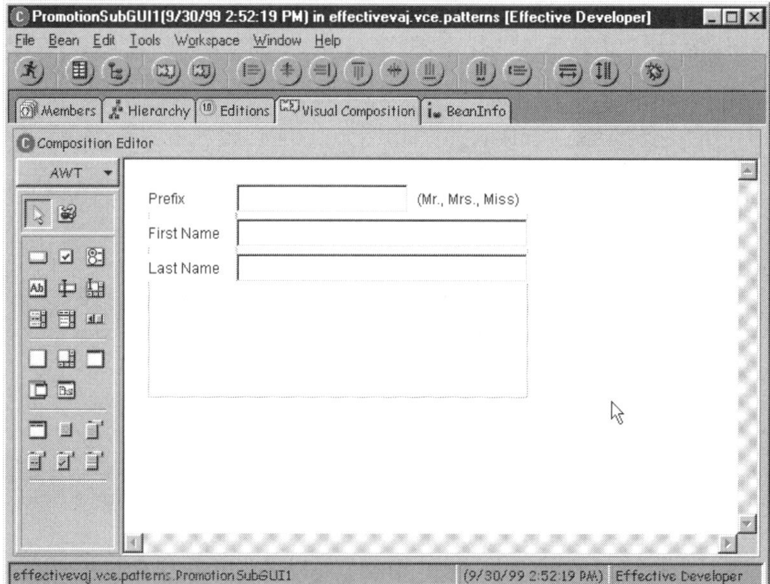

The example in Figure 14.11 uses this simple sub-GUI. This compound GUI asks the sub-GUI for the prefix, first name, and last name whenever the user clicks the Ok button. The Cancel button simply prints, "Canceled." The compound GUI does *not* actually look at the text fields in the sub-GUI; it uses the promoted text properties of the sub-GUI exclusively. It does not have access to the text fields at all.

The advantage to the Encapsulated Promotion pattern is that the sub-GUI can change without affecting any bean that uses it. For example, if the sub-GUI is changed to look as shown in Figure 14.12, its set and get methods are modified slightly for the promoted text properties, you can now use radio buttons to set the prefix string.

> **NOTE**
>
> Notice that the GUI pictured in Figure 14.12 could benefit from use of a factorization pattern, possibly a funnel. The processing on each of the radio buttons is similar.

Figure 14.11 Using the promoted strings.

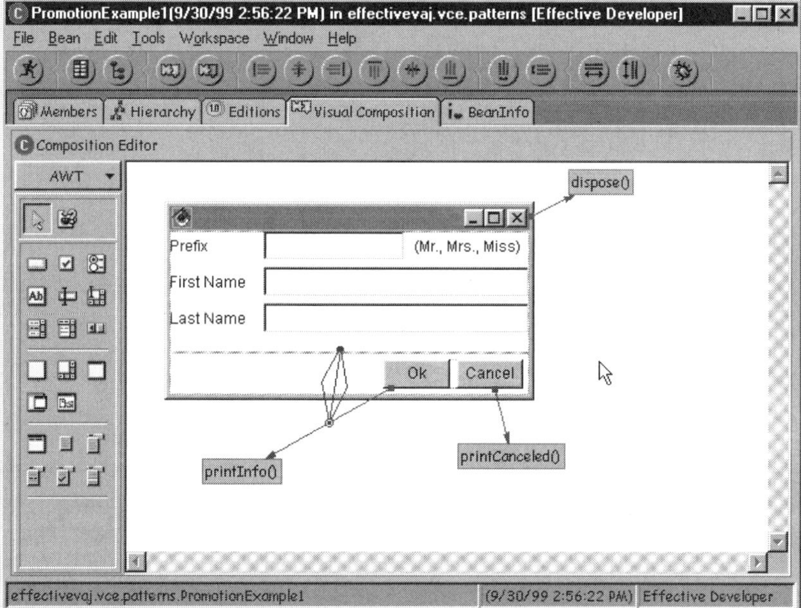

Figure 14.12 Changing the sub-GUI.

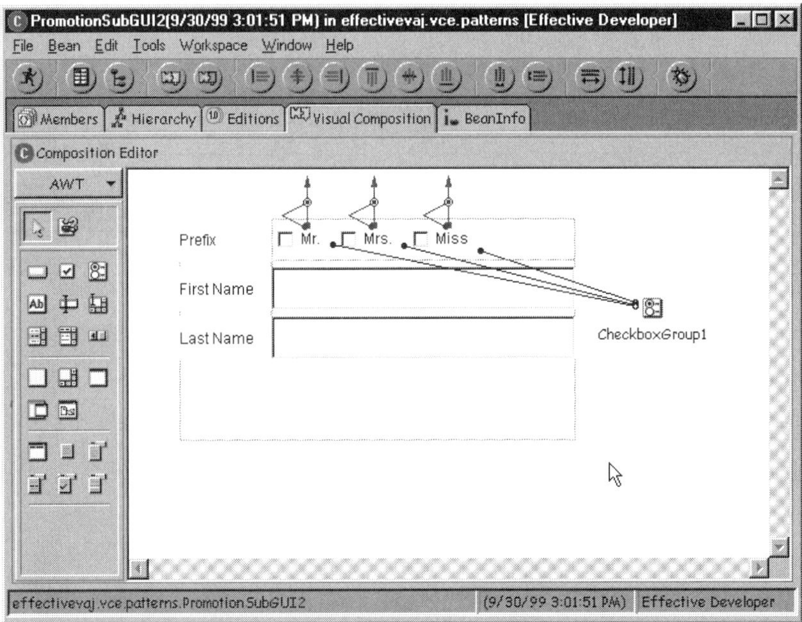

The compound GUI does not change. Even though the sub-GUI looks different, *its programming interface is the same.* (See Figure 14.13.) The compound GUI still asks the sub-GUI for the promoted text properties.

This approach can help increase maintainability of sub-GUIs. However, it lacks some flexibility. The next pattern, the Hook pattern, allows the compound GUI to have more input in the sub-GUI.

Hook Pattern

The *Hook* pattern is a more sophisticated means of communication between a GUI and a sub-GUI. The basic idea is that the sub-GUI interacts with *variables* rather than actual instances, and promotes the *this* property of the variable. This pattern allows compound GUIs to "plug in" an actual instance in place of the variable in the sub-GUI. The sub-GUI can be generic; it does not know which actual instance is used, and the instance could be of a *subclass* of the class that the variable represents. It can be even *more* generic, if the variable is of an interface type: The actual instance used merely has to implement the interface. This type of generic hook communication is the key to making the Model-View-Controller pattern work in VisualAge for Java.

Figure 14.13 Usage does not change!

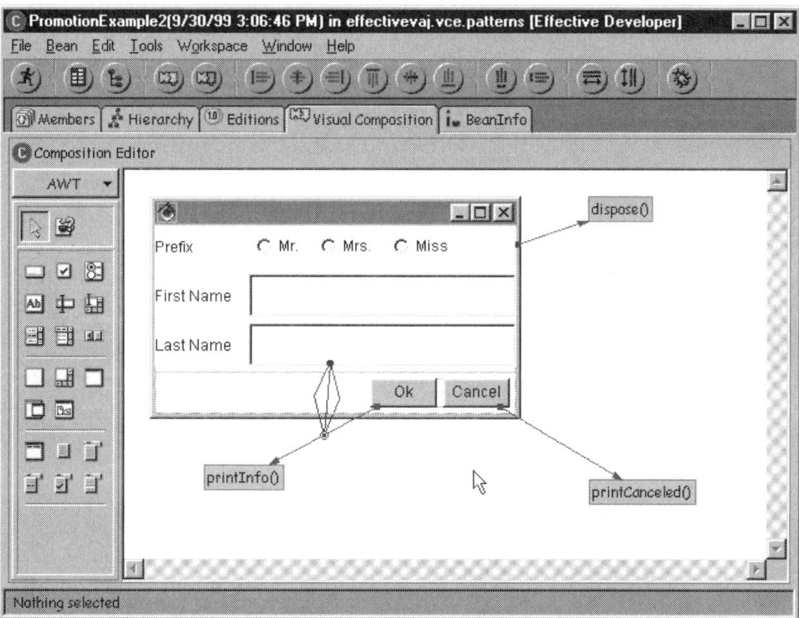

Let's reexamine the previous name-entry sub-GUI. Instead of allowing access to the text properties of the TextField beans, drop an instance of a Person bean in the VCE design area. Connect this Person bean to each of the TextField beans via property-to-property connections. This appears in Figure 14.14. You could now promote the Person bean, enabling an external compound bean to access it. However, it would be much more flexible to allow the external compound bean to set which Person bean should be used. Do this by using a *variable* in place of the Person instance.

The advantage to using a variable is twofold:

- The external compound GUI can pass in *any* instance of Person.
- The external compound GUI can pass in an instance of a *subclass* of Person.

This provides significant flexibility in your application. The sub-GUI simply concerns itself with interacting with the variable. The external compound GUI passes in the actual data. This separates the sub-GUI from the actual data. This is a significant step towards a Model-View-Controller architecture. Keep this in mind as you read Chapter 15. Morphing the Person instance in Figure 14.14 to a variable yields the design in Figure 14.15. Then promote the *this* property of the

Figure 14.14 Storing the data.

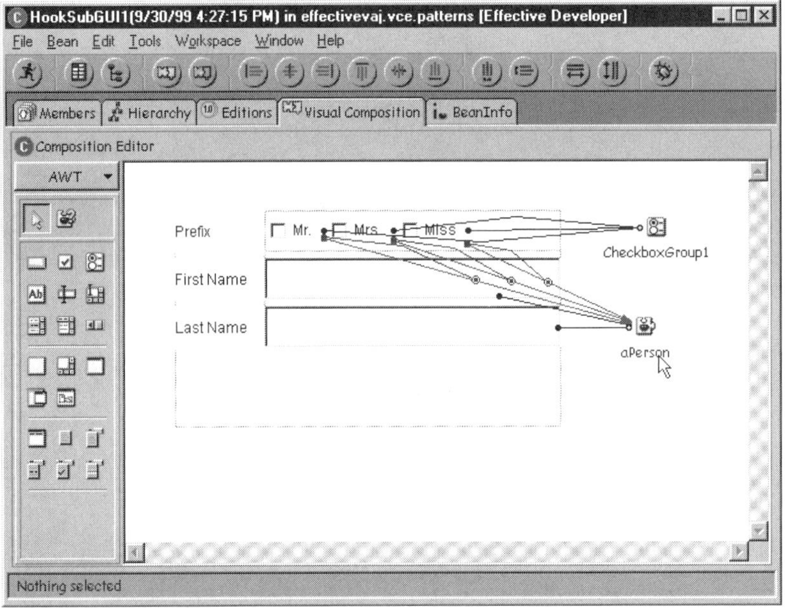

Figure 14.15 Storing the data in a variable.

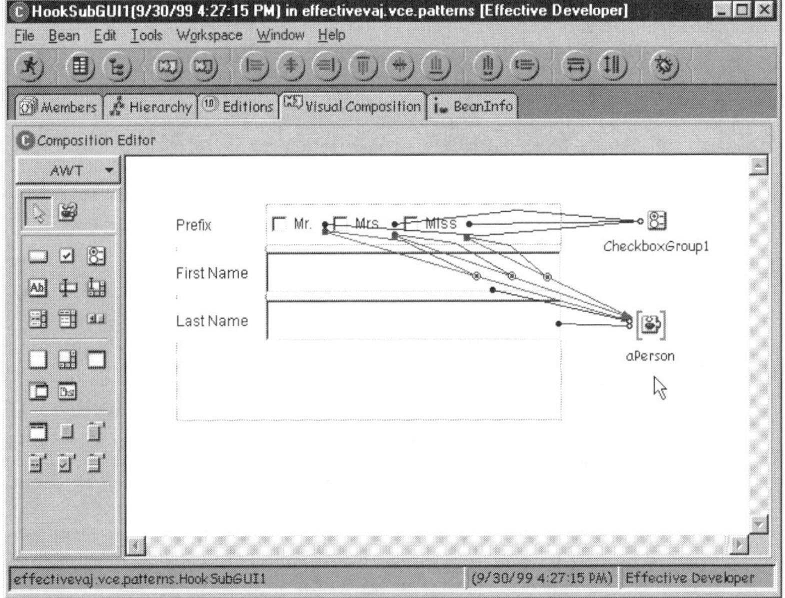

variable to make it accessible to compound GUIs. The possibilities of this pattern are explored in more detail in the next chapter.

Event Catcher

An *event catcher* is a variable that is set in response to a bean firing an event. This variable has the same type as the event data passed as part of the event notification. This allows easy access to the details of the event notification. For example, suppose that you want to append the actionCommand property of an ActionEvent instance to a TextArea bean when a button is clicked. You could define a GUI is seen in Figure 14.16.

The connections from the buttons simply set the value of the variable, connecting actionPerformed from the buttons to the *this* property of the variable. Then tell the connections to pass their event data by double-clicking a connection and selecting the **Pass Event Data** check box, shown in Figure 14.17. The result of these connections is to set the variable to the actual event objects that the buttons send to their listeners.

Once the variable has been set, it triggers the other two connections. The first connection starts at the *this* event of the variable and ends on the append() method of the TextArea bean. Use a parameter connection to pass the actionCommand of

Figure 14.16 Catching an event object.

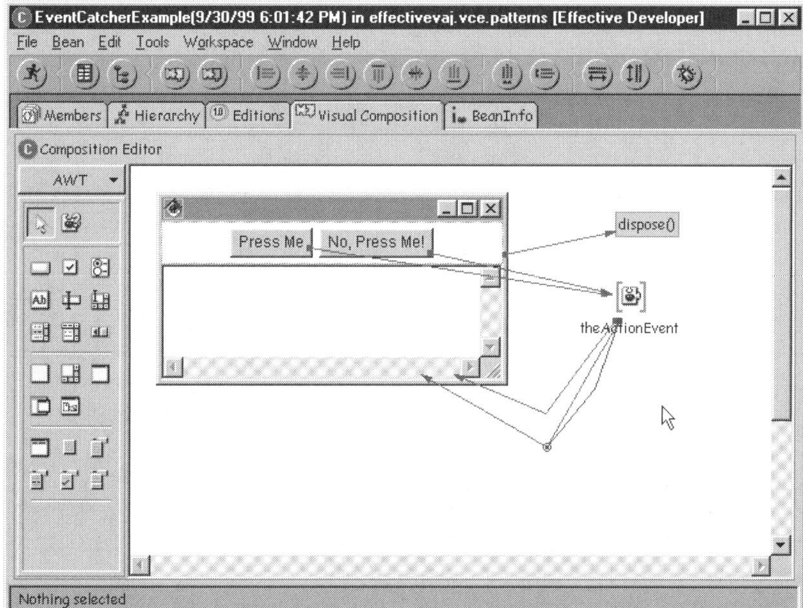

Figure 14.17 Passing event data.

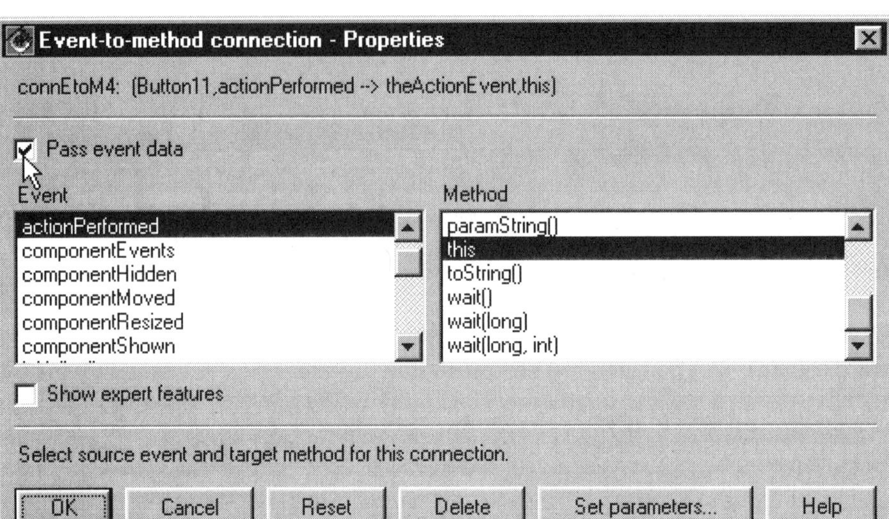

event object. The second connection also starts at the *this* event of the variable but appends a constant new-line character to the TextArea bean.

This pattern is extremely useful, especially when used with the Event Percolation pattern discussed next.

Event Percolation Pattern

Event percolation is the process by which a sub-GUI notifies a containing compound GUI of an action. The sub-GUI manages the events of its contained components and fires its own events to notify the outside world. This provides a great deal of separation between the functionality that a sub-GUI provides and its user interface. This is similar to the Hook and Encapsulated Promotion patterns. As long as the programming interface (the fired events) remains the same, the sub-GUI's user interface can change at any time.

For an example, create a useful Ok/Cancel sub-GUI. This sub-GUI contains the familiar layout, the GridLayout nested in the FlowLayout, to arrange and size the buttons nicely. The sub-GUI catches the Ok and Cancel buttons to see when the user clicks them. In response, it fires a new event to represent the clicked button. This sub-GUI appears in Figure 14.18.

To use this sub-GUI in a sample application, drop the sub-GUI in the South part of a border layout. The connections watch for the *okPressed* and *cancelPressed* events from the sub-GUI. It responds by either setting some text in the label at the North of the border layout, or quitting the application. This sample application appears in Figure 14.19. By using such a subclass, all of your applications could

Figure 14.18 An Ok/Cancel sub-GUI.

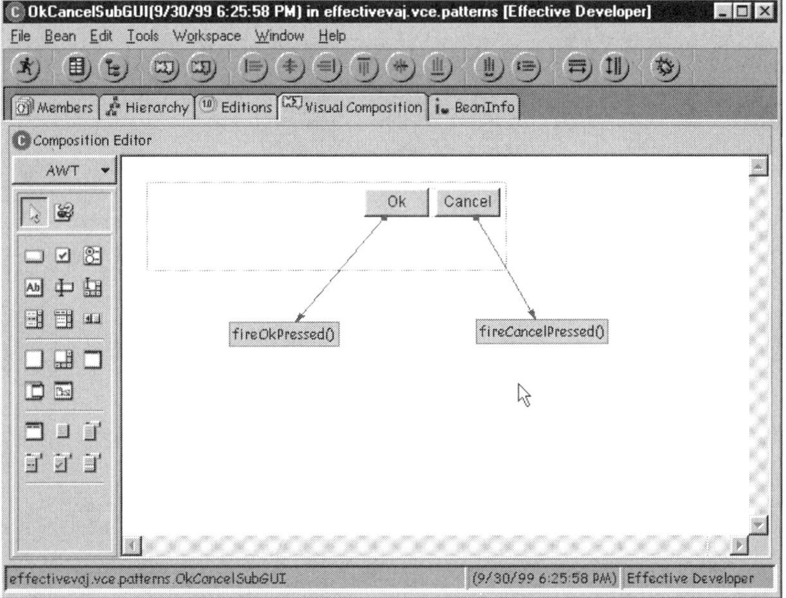

Figure 14.19 Percolating events.

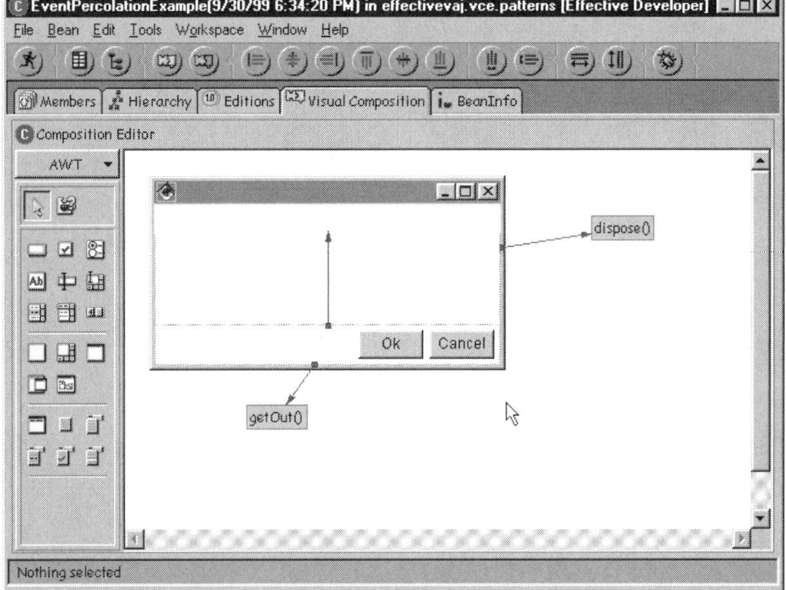

have Ok and Cancel buttons that look and behave in exactly the same way. If you want to change their appearance, you change it in one class, and all applications that use that class pick up the change.

The Event Percolation pattern is one of the most useful patterns presented in this chapter. Think about sub-GUI separation as the design your application. Think about percolating events to communicate between sub-GUIs. This provides maximum reusability and maintainability of your sub-GUIs.

> **NOTE**
>
> We will use the Event Percolation pattern again when we discuss the Factory Bean component in Chapter 17, "Factory Beans."

Boolean and Arithmetic Operations

Sometimes, when creating a visual design, you need to modify the value of a parameter that you pass to a connection. Typically, this modification involves a Boolean *not* operation or simple arithmetic. By creating some helper classes, this type of operation can be quite simple in the VCE.

First, think about Boolean operations, such as *and*, *or*, and *not*. If you create a helper class called BooleanLogic that contains methods for each of these operations, you can simply drop an instance of this class in the VCE and call its methods. A simple BooleanLogic class follows.

```
/**
 * A helper class that provides boolean logic functionality
 */
public class BooleanLogic {
  public boolean and(boolean v1, boolean v2) {
    return v1 && v2;
  }

  public static boolean not(boolean value) {
    return !value;
  }

  public boolean or(boolean v1, boolean v2) {
    return v1 || v2;
  }
}
```

> **NOTE**
> You might think the above methods should be static, because they do not require any instance data. However, making them instance variables allows you to use them as bean features. In particular, you can mark them as preferred for easy access in the VCE.

You can drop an instance of this BooleanLogic class in the VCE, and call its methods to modify parameters to other connections. For example, Figure 14.20 shows a sample GUI. When the value of the Male check box changes, its connection calls the not() method of the BooleanLogic instance, passing its state. The normalResult connection passes the result to the state of the Female check box. Note that it would be a better idea to use a CheckboxGroup in a case like this; however, this serves well to demonstrate how to use a BooleanLogic helper.

Similar to the BooleanLogic helper, you can create an Arithmetic class for simple arithmetic operations. The simple Arithmetic class looks as follows.

Figure 14.20 BooleanLogic in action.

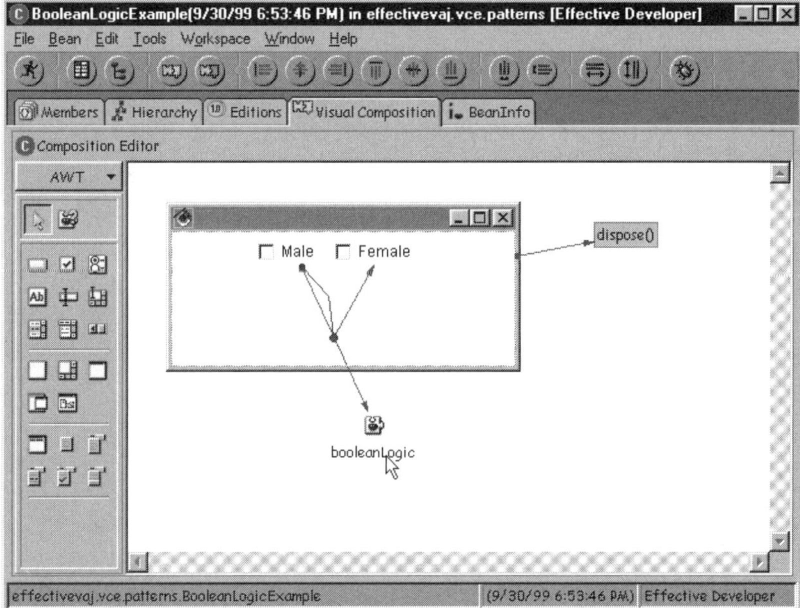

Figure 14.21 Arithmetic in action.

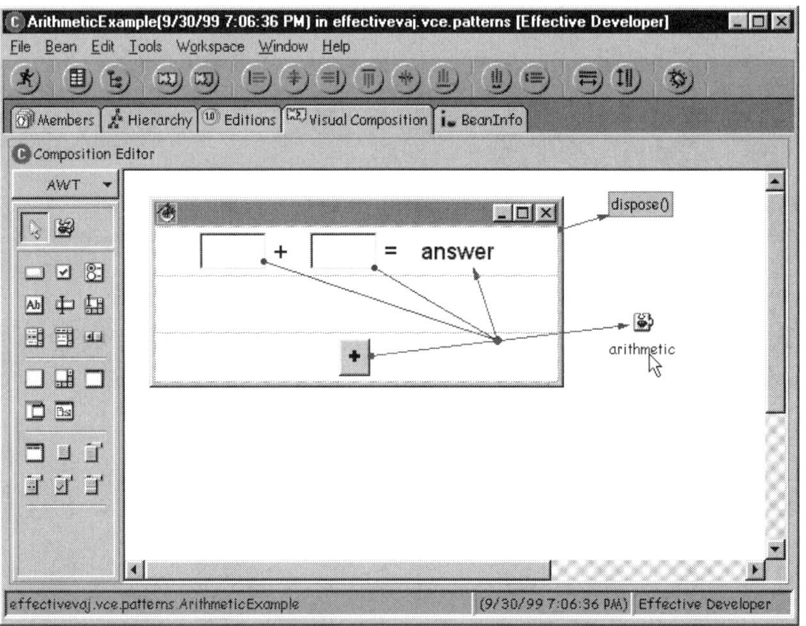


```
/**
 * A Simple Helper to provide artithmetic operations in the VCE
 */
public class Arithmetic {
  public int add(int a, int b) {
    return a + b;
  }

  public int divide(int a, int b) {
    return a / b;
  }

  public int multiply(int a, int b) {
    return a * b;
  }

  public int subtract(int a, int b) {
    return a - b;
  }
}
```

The example shown in Figure 14.21 uses an Arithmetic instance to add two numbers, placing the result in a Label bean. You can create helper classes for these and other operations such as string concatenation.

Summary

The patterns discussed so far apply to small sections of your visual design. You can use them to help simplify creation and maintenance of your visual designs. The next chapter discusses a more broadly applicable pattern: Model-View-Controller. The Model-View-Controller pattern is widely accepted as a useful paradigm for separation between a GUI and the business logic. You can use it to develop your application at a high level or possibly at a low level, such as a component. Keep in mind, though, that you can use the patterns discussed in this chapter to help implement parts of your views.

Model-View-Controller in the VCE

15

The Model-View-Controller (MVC) design paradigm is an incredibly useful tool for writing maintainable programs. MVC lets you separate business logic from Graphical User Interfaces (GUIs), making it easier to modify either one without affecting the other. Initially, MVC requires a little extra planning and coding, but the long-term benefits are well worth it.

When MVC was first publicized, visual composition tools were limited in capability and not nearly as popular as they are today. The visual composition tools of today, such as the VisualAge for Java Visual Composition Editor (VCE), support true visual programming, enabling you to visually create much of an application's GUI and business logic.

Unfortunately, this kind of simple visual programming has eroded solid design techniques. Many developers simply sit down at their desk, open the VCE, and start clicking the mouse. Rather than thinking through GUI and application designs, they experiment. Eventually they get things to "look right" and then draw lines to "make the application work."

This chapter discusses the MVC design paradigm and demonstrates its application in visual programming. Keep in mind that MVC is but a single technique in a developer's design arsenal, and should be used in combination with other techniques, including object-oriented analysis and design.

What Is MVC?

The MVC paradigm was introduced by Smalltalk developers at Xerox PARC (Palo Alto Research Center) in the late 1970s. The basic idea is to split your application into three distinct parts, each of which can be replaced without affecting the others:

> **Model.** The data of your application, along with the business logic that defines how to change and access that data. The model can be shared among any number of view and controller objects.

View. The means of presenting the model's data to the outside world. This could take the form of a GUI, generated speech, audible tones, printouts, or even non-user oriented output, such as turning on an air conditioner.

Controller. The means of gathering user or other environmental input and providing feedback to the model, normally changing some of the data in that model.

Let's examine the interaction between these pieces.

Interaction between Components

Initially, the view, and possibly the controller, asks the model for its current state. The view may present data to the user, and the controller may check the data to help decide how to handle user interaction.

As seen in Figure 15.1, the view and controller will typically "listen" for changes to the model. The Java language implements this notification using events. Whenever the model says, "I have changed," the view and controller can ask for the new state of the model's data and then update their presentation to the user.

Figure 15.2 shows user interaction in the application. If the user decides to interact, the controller takes charge. It watches for user input, such as clicking or moving the mouse or pressing keyboard keys. It decides what the interaction means, and asks the model to update its data and/or the view to change the way it displays the data.

For example, you could have a view that displays a set of data in a Swing JList component. You add a scroll bar as a controller, which directs the view to change which items are displayed. Further, you could add *another* controller, perhaps a Swing JTextField component, to take user input and ask the model to add the new

Figure 15.1 Model and user interface communication.

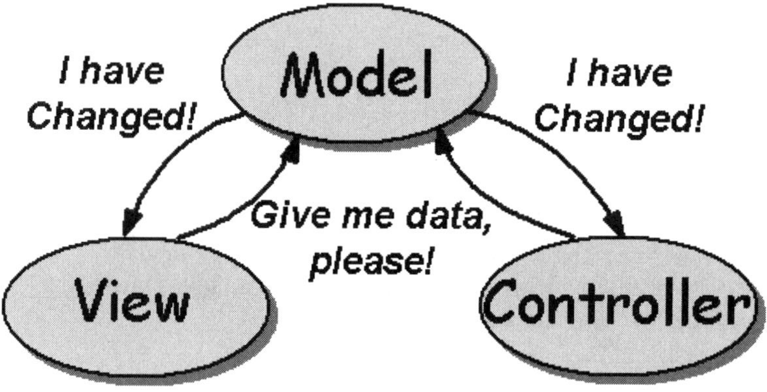

Figure 15.2 Controller-to-model communication.

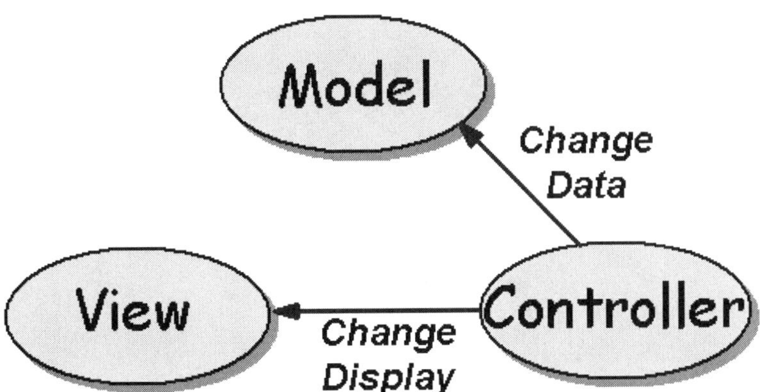

value to the set. Of course, this would cause the model to shout "I have changed!" to which the view responds by asking for the set of data.

The above scenario has two controllers. One watches for mouse interaction with a scroll bar, while the other accepts user input to add to the model. You can have any number of controllers and any number of views in your application.

Suppose that you have an application that presents information from a database in a table and pie chart. The table can be scrolled using horizontal and vertical scroll bars, and new data can be entered via a pair of text fields. The MVC pattern could be applied as shown in Figure 15.3.

This example includes a model, two views, and three controllers. The scroll bar controllers update only the table view, while the text field controller updates the model.

Delegates—Combining View and Controller

You may be concerned at this point about separation between the scroll bars and the table they scroll. In theory this separation is good, but in practice it can make life much more difficult:

- You would need to separate the GUI among multiple VCE sessions, and provide promoted variables and events to communicate between the controller GUI and the view GUI. Separation of view and controller requires separate classes, which means multiple VCE sessions.

Figure 15.3 Multiple views and controllers.

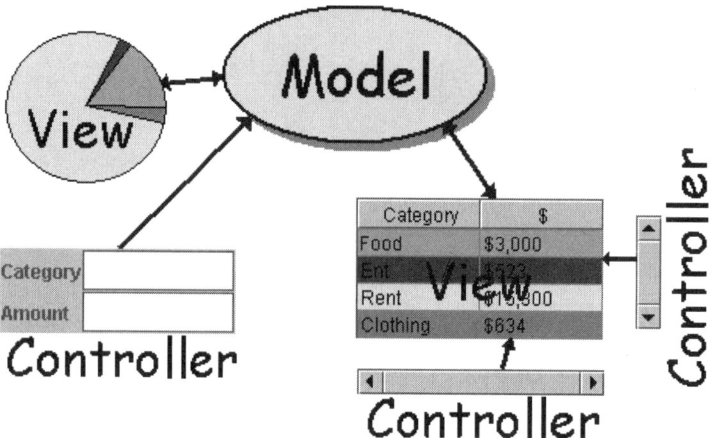

- Where does an AWT TextField bean go? It acts like a view to display existing data, and like a controller to change the data.
- Many components have built-in support for user interaction such as scrolling.
- Interaction between multiple controllers and views can be quite heavy and complex.

Because of such issues, the MVC paradigm is often simplified by *combining* views and controllers. There are several names for this approach—this chapter uses the name *delegate* to refer to a combined view/controller. (This is the term used by Sun in describing the Swing GUI components.) This combination into a delegate is shown in Figure 15.4.

In a delegate, the view and controller communicate as necessary to perform their duty. It is a good idea to keep this communication separate when possible, but often it's impossible to break a component into a view or a controller. And, in practice, the separation doesn't provide nearly as significant a benefit as separation of the model and delegate.

The delegate *as a whole* communicates with the model in the same way described earlier for the view and controller. The separation between the model and the user interaction of the delegate is the key to the success of this model. Although this version of MVC is somewhat simplified by the combination of the view and controller into the delegate, the design is still MVC-based. You can use it to create some interesting and very flexible applications in VisualAge for Java.

Figure 15.4 Combining view and controller into a delegate.

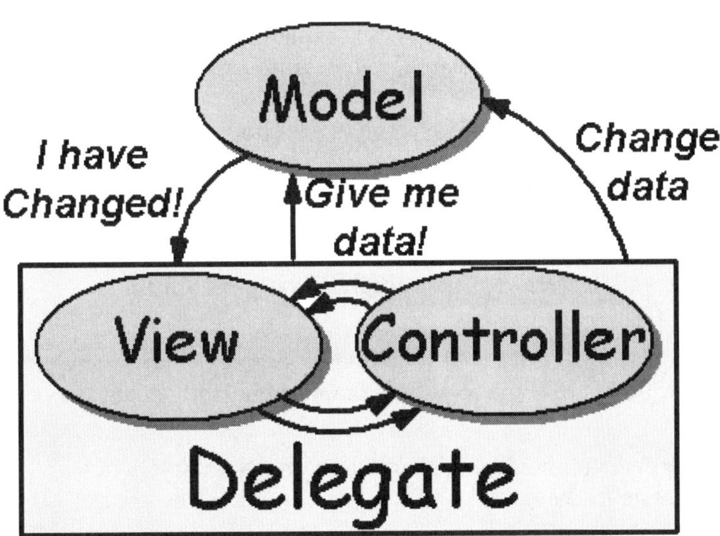

Why Is MVC So Important?

By this point you may be thinking, "Sounds like neat theory, but it also sounds like a lot of work!" You're right on the first point, but as you'll see later, implementation in VisualAge for Java is actually very easy. Development typically occupies 10 percent or less of a program's life cycle. Therefore, program maintenance should be a developer's *number one* concern. A clean, understandable design is a good start, but to be effective, the design should separate business logic from user interface.

Think about some of the ways a program changes over time:

- The current state of GUI design evolves, and a company decides to update their GUIs. (Often this is referred to as "making the GUI look more professional.")
- A company changes network architectures and wants to port their applications.
- A company decides to create a limited-feature demo of their application.
- A company wants to add a new way of examining existing data.

Changes like these often involve *either* the GUI *or* the business logic of an application. If the GUI code and business logic are tightly coupled, making these changes can be quite difficult. Using an MVC-based design makes the changes less extensive, and more importantly, more isolated, reducing the chance of introducing bugs in unrelated code.

Using an MVC-based design, the above changes are simple:

- Updating the GUI requires *only* changing GUI code. The stable business logic is not touched.
- Updating network architectures, perhaps changing from a two-tier to three-tier database architecture requires modifying only part of the model. The stable GUI is not touched.
- Creating a limited feature demo might merely be a matter of subclassing the model to block access to some features. Again, there is no change to the GUI.
- Adding a new way to examine data is simply a matter of adding a new view. Often *no* change to the model is necessary, nor is it necessary to change other views!

A final thought on the importance of MVC: By separating the business logic from the GUI, you can also separate the coding tasks. Separate developers can work on each part, for instance—a GUI specialist coding the GUI and a domain expert coding the business logic.

Implementing MVC in VisualAge for Java

Now that we've laid out the concepts and rationale, let's look at implementation details by walking through a simple address book application. Being a good MVC designer, you split the application into models and delegates. For this sample application, use a two-level model:

Address Book. A model that stores a collection of addresses. The interface that defines this model requires methods to add and look up individual address records.

Address Data. A model that represents a single address record. Many of these will be stored in an AddressBook implementation class.

This two-level model helps show that MVC can be applied at many levels in an application. You can use MVC when creating GUI components (such as Sun's Swing components) as a good division of labor for your entire application, or at any level in between. Models can contain references to other models and delegates can contain references to other delegates.

To understand the creation of this application, you can break the design into four phases:

1. **Define a model interface.** Define how the model and delegate communicate. Defining a protocol (or contract) between them is best represented in Java by writing an interface class.
2. **Define concrete model(s).** Implement the interface to create actual model classes for use in an application.
3. **Create delegate(s).** Create a delegate (GUI) class that has a variable of the model interface type. The GUI can communicate with the model, and any model class that implements that interface can be plugged in at run time.
4. **Connect as an application.** Finally, create an application by simply connecting one or more delegate classes with a concrete model class.

In this chapter, you will create a concrete model that stores the data in a hash table, but the actual data location does not matter. In Chapter 16, "Advanced Model-View-Controller Techniques," you will implement filtering and sorting models and discuss how you can use data from other sources, stored in databases or on other machines.

Defining a Model Interface

The first step in defining an MVC application is to define how your model and delegate will communicate:

- How will the model inform the delegates that it has changed?
- What data can the delegates obtain from the model, and how do they access it?
- What data can the delegates request be changed, and how do they request it?

Several issues are involved with change notification. The first and most important is the granularity of the notification. You can notify at several levels. For example:

You can fire an event that says, "something's changed," without giving details. The delegate then needs to examine *all* the data to determine what has changed. This is effective if the delegates will normally need to reread all the data after any change. For example, Swing provides a generic ChangeEvent for just this purpose.

You can simply use JavaBeans bound properties as the available data in your bean. PropertyChangeEvents are fired any time one of the properties changes, which effectively limits the scope of the change notification. This approach works well when you have a one-to-one correspondence between properties and the GUI components that represent them to the user.

You can create a custom event class and listener interface that captures specific information about the nature of a change. For example, Swing's TreeModel fires a TreeModelEvent to its TreeModelListeners. The TreeModel can be more specific about the type of change, telling its listeners that nodes were added or removed from other nodes, structure has changed for some subtree, and so forth. This allows the delegate to update its presentation more efficiently; if the updated area doesn't affect the current display, nothing changes.

Bound Properties and GUI Components

You could take advantage of the JavaBeans specification's definition of bound properties to assist in creation of your models. Bound properties are properties that fire a PropertyChangeEvent any time their value changes. You could use this as the "I've changed" notification from your model.

You could also take advantage of bound properties in your GUI components. VisualAge for Java provides excellent support for bound properties in the form of property-to-property connections. Two bound properties connected via a property-to-property connection will update each other's values when they change.

Assuming you have bound properties in the model and in the delegate, much of the communication between a model and a delegate can be accomplished through a property-to-property connection.

The problem is that Swing and AWT do *not* bind properties that should be bound. For example, TextField does not bind its text property. Fortunately, you'll be using the Quick Form dialog in the VCE, and that makes dealing with changes in TextField easy. For Swing components, however, you would need to create a BoundJTextField bean. For a discussion on how to do this, see *Extending to Bind an Unbound Property* in Chapter 9, "Extension and Composition."

> **NOTE**
>
> Note that in this chapter you will be using TextField.

Making Things Easier in VisualAge for Java

VisualAge for Java provides excellent tools for developing *classes*, but not much support for developing *interfaces*. The above four-step process assumes you define the interface first, then implement that interface with concrete classes. Because you're using bound properties in your model, it would be much easier to *start* with a concrete model. The BeanInfo editor in VisualAge for Java provides a very easy way to define a bean with bound properties. You will use the BeanInfo editor to flesh out a concrete model, then create a model interface based on that concrete class.

Once you have the interface, you can implement any other models you like and plug them into your application.

To create this interface, you can use the AutoGut tool, a plug-in for VisualAge for Java. AutoGut examines a class and creates an interface by "gutting" the methods from that class. (The name "AutoGut" comes from the act of copying the methods defined in a class and removing the "guts" of the methods, so all that is left is the method declaration.) We'll walk through the use of AutoGut in a moment, but first you need to install the tool. AutoGut is located on the CD-ROM that accompanies this book, and its installation is described in Appendix D, "The CD-ROM."

> **TIP**
>
> Start with a concrete model in VisualAge for Java, and use AutoGut to create your model interface.

Example Models

Using the JavaBeans bound property approach mentioned above, you will create an example that tracks telephone and address information for various users. Two levels of models are involved—a small model to track a particular address record, and an overall model to track *all* addresses.

AddressDataModel. A model that represents a single address record. This will contain the following properties (all are of type String and are readable, writeable, and bound):

- name
- address
- city
- state
- country
- postalCode
- businessPhone
- homePhone

AddressBookModel. A model that represents a collection of addresses. This will contain the following methods:

- `public AddressDataModel find(String name) throws Exception` - Locate a name in the address book. If not found, throw a simple exception.
- `public void add(AddressDataModel data)` - Add a new record in the address book.

AddressBookModel also contains the following property:

- addresses - Bound, indexed, read-only String

Implement these models by first creating the following two concrete implementations of the models:

SimpleAddressData. An implementation of AddressDataModel that uses String variables to store the address information.

HashAddressBook. An implementation of AddressBookModel that stores addresses in a Hashtable instance.

By defining these two classes and gutting them, you can automatically create the required interfaces.

Defining SimpleAddressData

Start by creating the SimpleAddressData class:

1. Use java.lang.Object as its superclass.
2. Don't select the **Compose this class visually** check box; this is a nonvisual model bean.
3. Import packages java.beans and java.io.
4. Implement interface java.io.Serializable, making this class a bean.

   Next, you need to add properties to the model to track its data.

5. Open SimpleAddressData to the BeanInfo editor.
6. Create a new property by clicking the P icon on the tool bar.
   - **Property name** = name
   - **Property type** = java.lang.String
   - Check only **Readable, Writeable,** and **bound.**
   - **Display name** = name
   - **Short description** = a person's name
   - Select the **preferred** check box.
7. Create the properties listed in Table 15.1, using the same settings as above.

Table 15.1 SimpleAddressDataModel Properties

Property	Display Name	Short Description
address	address	the street where the person lives
city	city	the city where the person lives
state	state / province	the state or province where the person lives
country	country	the country where the person lives
postalCode	zip / postal code	the zip or postal code where the person lives
businessPhone	business phone	the person's business telephone number
homePhone	home phone	the person's home telephone number

Congratulations! You now have your first concrete model.

Defining AddressDataModel

Now you can easily create your model interface for your address data records.

8. Make sure you installed AutoGut as mentioned earlier in this chapter.
9. Open the pop-up menu for SimpleAddressData and select **Tools->Create Interface from Class.**

   This invokes the AutoGut tool, seen in Figure 15.5.
10. Fill in the information shown in Figure 15.5 and click the **Ok** button. Note that if you choose a package that is in the workspace, the project field will automatically fill in for you.

Figure 15.5 Specifying the interface to create.

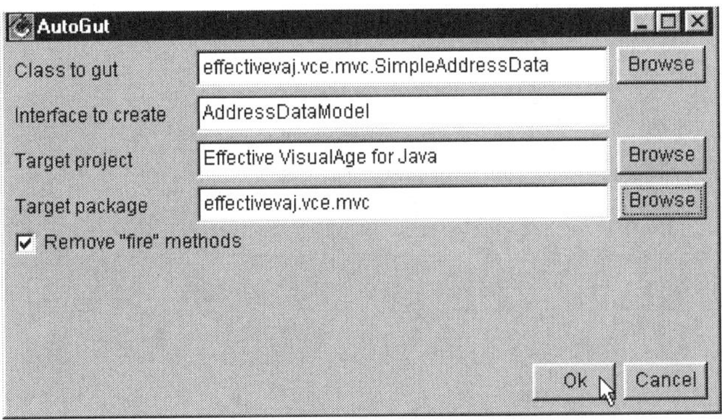

> **NOTE**
>
> AutoGut can only work on a single class at a time; if there are multiple classes selected, it will fill in the name of the first-selected class.

11. Click the **Ok** button; AutoGut creates the specified interface in the specified package and project (creating the package and project if they do not exist). AutoGut copies the method declarations of all *public* methods (excluding constructors) from the class to the new interface. If you check the **Remove fire methods** box, it skips any methods that begin with the word *fire*.

In this example, you do not need to modify the resulting interface. However, keep in mind that AutoGut does not currently copy import statements to the new interface, and you may need to add import statements by hand.

You now have an interface that represents any piece of address data. You need to change the definition of AddressDataModel slightly to ensure other beans that use it can serialize their referenced components.

12. Modify the AddressDataModel interface definition to look like the following. The bold text shows the changes.

```
import java.io.*;

public interface AddressDataModel extends Serializable {
}
```

Your SimpleAddressData is currently unrelated to the AddressDataModel interface. To finish the address data models, you need to add AddressDataModel to the implements clause of SimpleAddressData.

13. Edit SimpleAddressData and change its declaration to look as follows. The bold text indicates the change. You do not need to change anything else in this declaration.

```
public class SimpleAddressData implements Serializable,
AddressDataModel {
   ...
}
```

Now you can use a SimpleAddressData instance anywhere you need to talk to an AddressDataModel.

Defining HashAddressBook

HashAddressBook is a concrete model that tracks a collection of AddressDataModels in a Hashtable instance. Define this class as follows:

1. Start the Create Class SmartGuide.
   - **Class name** = HashAddressBook
   - **Superclass** = java.lang.Object
   - Do not select the **Compose this class visually** check box.
   - Import packages java.beans, java.io, and java.util. You need java.util because you're using Hashtable for the implementation.
   - Implement interface java.io.Serializable (this is a bean!).
2. Open HashAddressBook to the BeanInfo editor.
3. Add property *addresses*:
   - **Property name** = addresses
   - **Property type** = AddressDataModel
   - Select only the **Readable, Indexed,** and **bound** check boxes.
   - **Display name** = addresses
   - **Short description** = list of all addresses
   - Select the **preferred** check box.

The **Indexed** box is checked, and the **Writeable** box is *not* checked. When you choose the property type, do *not* type the open and close square brackets (" [ ] "). These are added by VisualAge for Java when you select the **Indexed** check box. By using interface AddressDataModel as the type, you can store any kind of address data in this address book as long as that address data implements AddressDataModel. This includes, but is not limited to, SimpleAddressData, as it implements AddressDataModel.

> **TIP**
>
> Keep your models as generic as possible. If they need to use instance of other models, *refer to the other models' interfaces,* not to other concrete models.

4. Add the find() method by clicking the M icon on the tool bar:
   - **Method name** = find
   - **Return type** = AddressDataModel
   - **Parameter count** = 1
5. Click **Next** to enter the parameter description:
   - **Parameter name** = name
   - **Parameter type** = java.lang.String

- **Display name** = name
- **Short description** = the name of the person to look up

6. Click **Next** to finish the method details.
   - **Display name** = find
   - **Short description** = search for an address method
   - Select the **preferred** check box.
7. Click **Finish** to create the find() method.
8. Create the add() method by clicking the M icon on the tool bar.
   - **Method name** = add
   - **Return type** = void
   - **Parameter count** = 1
9. Click **Next** to enter the parameter information:
   - **Parameter name** = address
   - **Parameter type** = AddressDataModel
   - **Display name** = address
   - **Short description** = the address entry to add to the book
10. Click **Next** to enter the method details:
    - **Display name** = add
    - **Short description** = add an address entry to the phone book
    - Select the **preferred** check box.

You now have the basic HashAddressBook. We'll come back to it later to add in some implementation details for the find() and add() methods.

Defining AddressBookModel

Like AddressDataModel, AddressBookModel is an interface. Create AddressBookModel the same way you created AddressDataModel: using AutoGut. To do this:

1. Open the pop-up menu for HashAddressBook.
2. Select **Tools->Create Interface from Class**. This invokes AutoGut (seen previously in Figure 15.5).
3. Specify AddressBookModel for the interface name.
4. Choose the same package that contains your other classes and interfaces.
5. Click **Ok** to run AutoGut.
6. Add *extends Serializable* to the created interface. Edit AddressBookModel's interface definition to look as follows. The changes are in boldface.

```
import java.io.*;

public interface AddressBookModel extends Serializable {
}
```

7. Add AddressBookModel to the implements clause of HashAddressBook. Edit HashAddressBook and change its declaration to look as follows. The bold text indicates the change. You do not need to change anything else in this declaration.

```
public class HashAddressBook implements Serializable,
AddressBookModel {
  ...
}
```

Now you can use a HashAddressBook instance anywhere you need to talk to an AddressBookModel.

Filling in the Implementation Details for HashAddressBook

So far, you have defined your concrete models and model interfaces. The interfaces are finished, but your HashAddressBook is missing the details it needs to perform its task.

1. Edit the class definition for HashAddressBook adding the text in bold:

```
public class HashAddressBook implements Serializable, AddressBookModel
{
  private Hashtable records = new Hashtable();
  private int count = 0;
...
}
```

This creates a Hashtable instance named *records* in which you store your addresses, and a count of how many addresses you have. You need *count* to help you process the *addresses* property, as we'll see in a moment.

2. Edit the add() method and change its code to the following:

```
public void add(AddressDataModel address) {
  if (records.get(address.getName()) == null)
    count++;
  records.put(address.getName(),address);
  firePropertyChange("addresses",null, getAddresses());
}
```

This code stores the record in the hash table and increments the count if there wasn't already a record with the same key.

3. Edit the find() method and change its code to the following:

```
public AddressDataModel find(String name) {
  AddressDataModel data = (AddressDataModel)records.get(name);
  if (data == null)
    throw new RuntimeException(name + " not found");
  return data;
}
```

The find() method searches for an entry and returns it, or throws an exception if not found. Note that we're using RuntimeException for convenience here. You can replace it with a custom exception, perhaps a PhoneListingNotFoundException. Keep in mind that this would affect your model interface, as you would need to add a throws clause to the method declaration. For this example, stay with RuntimeException, which does not require a throws clause.

4. Modify the getAddresses() method. This method returns the list of addresses in the model. For this particular model, your data is stored in a Hashtable. The getAddresses() method simply creates an array with the hash table's contents and returns it. Note that a more efficient implementation could provide a cache array—once you generate the array, keep it until a new address is added.

```
public AddressDataModel[] getAddresses() {
  // convert the contents of the Hashtable into an array
  Enumeration e = records.elements();
  AddressDataModel[] result = new AddressDataModel[count];
  int i = 0;
  while (e.hasMoreElements())
    result[i++] = (AddressDataModel) e.nextElement();
  return result;
}
```

The getAddress(int index) method will work okay as it is, as it calls the above getAddress() method. Note that there is no setAddresses(); the add() method acts like a way to change the address list.

You now have all the models you need for your application!

Creating Delegates

Now the fun part: developing a delegate! You'll create a simple GUI to present the models, and connect the GUI components to those models.

> **NOTE**
>
> This chapter explains how the GUI and the model are connected but does not discuss the layout design. For details on layout management, see Chapter 11, "Layout Management."

The first delegate you create represents a single AddressDataModel instance, allowing the user to easily edit the data. This delegate contains fields for each property in the AddressDataModel, with property-to-property connections between those fields and the model. VisualAge for Java, version 3.0, provides a tool that can automatically create this delegate for you. This option is called Quick Form, and we discussed it in detail in Chapter 11.

> **NOTE**
>
> Unfortunately, Quick Form generates a GridBagLayout for the form. While this is highly unsettling for this author, it is automated; it can make creating this delegate easier.

To create this delegate:

1. Create a class named AddressDataEntryFormUI. We're borrowing the naming convention of using *UI* from Swing's Model-Delegate implementation.
   - **Class name** = AddressDataEntryFormUI
   - **Superclass** = java.awt.Panel
   - Select the **Compose this class visually** check box.
   - Import packages java.awt, java.awt.event, java.beans, and java.io.
   - Implement interface java.io.Serializable.

2. After the class opens to the VCE, select the Choose Bean tool from the beans palette.
   - **Bean Type** = Variable
   - **Class name** = AddressDataModel
   - **Name** = anAddressDataModel
3. Drop the variable in an empty spot of the VCE design area.

Now the fun part: We'll use the Quick Form command to create a form that represents all of the properties in the variable. You want the GUI to look something like the GUI pictured in Figure 15.6.

Figure 15.6 An entry-form GUI.

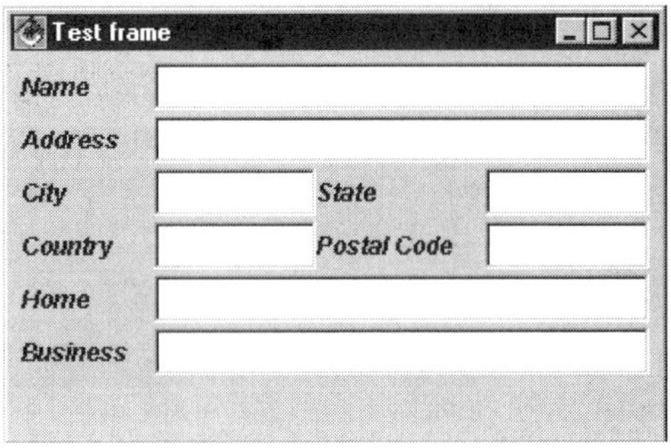

Figure 15.7 Choosing a quick form.

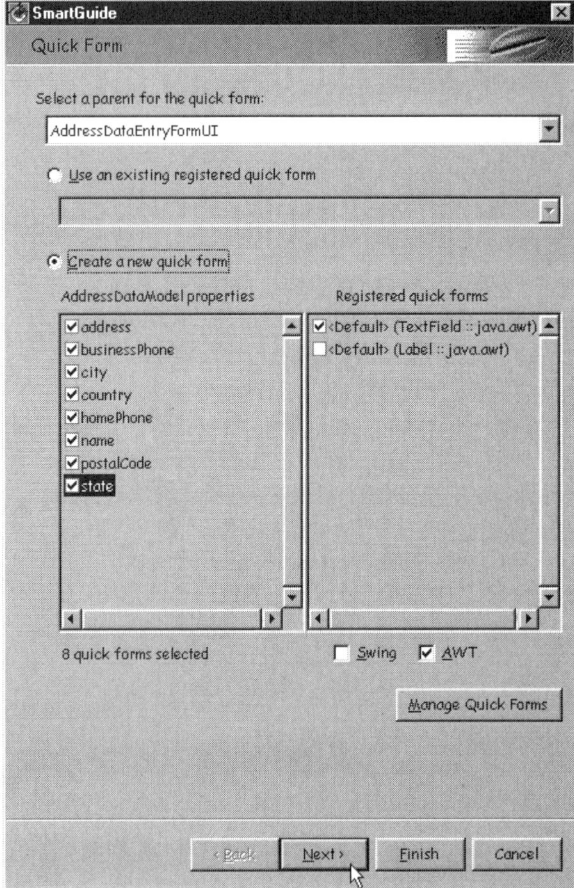

Quick Form uses GridBagLayout to display its contents, but we'd like that layout to reside in the top section of your panel. You need to set the layout of your panel to BorderLayout and place the resulting Quick Form in the NORTH position.

4. Double-click inside the dotted rectangle representing your panel and change its layout property to BorderLayout.
5. Open the pop-up menu for variable anAddressDataModel and choose Quick Form. This brings up the Quick Form dialog, seen in Figure 15.7.
6. In the Quick Form dialog, select the parent container in which you want to create the form (you are given a choice of all empty containers in your visual design) and the type of form to create. AddressDataEntryFormUI should already be selected, as it's the only container in your visual design.
7. Select *each* property in turn, and ensure that the quick form listed in the right-side list is "<Default> (TextField::java.awt)". Make sure you do this for *each* property. It should already have this value selected for each property, but you should double-check.
8. Click the **Next** button to continue to the Quick Form Layout page, seen in Figure 15.8.
9. Set Number of columns per row to 2. You want at most two properties displayed in a row (for City/State and Country/PostalCode).
10. Use the **Up/Down** buttons to change the order of the properties to *name, address, city, state, country, postalCode, homePhone*, and *businessPhone*. This defines the left-to-right, top-to-bottom order of the displayed component pairs for each property.

Table 15.2 Quick Form Layout Settings

Property	Label text	Columns to span
name	Name	2
address	Address	2
city	City	1
state	State/Province	1
country	Country	1
postalCode	Zip/Postal Code	1
homePhone	Home	2
businessPhone	Business	2

Figure 15.8 Defining the quick form layout.

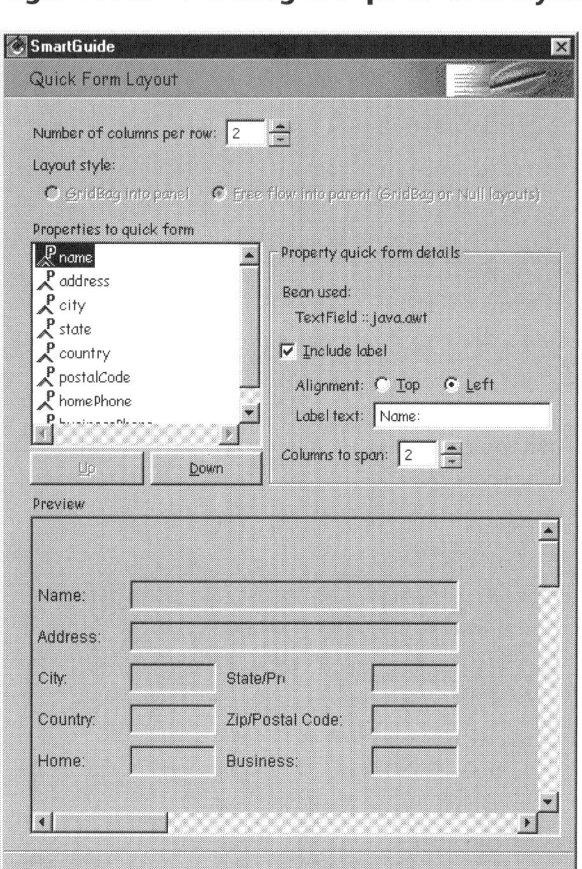

11. Select each property in turn, and set its quick form details. For all properties, leave the Include label check box selected (which adds a label for the specified property) and set Alignment to Left. Set Label text and Columns to span as defined in Table 15.2.
12. Click the **Next** button to continue.
13. The final page of the Quick Form dialog gives you a chance to save this form definition. This is useful if you want to create this same form again in other GUIs. Leave the options as it (no save) and click **Finish.**
14. Click the **Finish** button to complete the quick form. You don't want to save these options, so you can skip the last page of the Quick Form SmartGuide.

In general, it is a much better idea to create reusable delegate classes than constantly recreate the form using Quick Form. Delegates contain a GUI to display a model, and can be dropped into a new GUI that requires them. This ensures a consistent and correct delegate, rather than recreating the delegate GUI each time using the Quick Form SmartGuide. Using this Model-View-Controller-based strategy, you should rarely need to save these Quick Form-generated designs.

TIP

Don't overuse Quick Form. Rather than recreating the same form repeatedly, create reusable delegates that can display the contents of a model bean. You can plug these delegates into any other GUI you need that needs to manipulate the model's contents.

The resulting GUI appears in Figure 15.9. Note that it resides in the NORTH part of the border layout. The VCE treats NORTH as the first component of the layout, so when you generate the Quick Form, its panel is dropped in the NORTH section.

See the generated property-to-property connections? Each of these connections flows *from* the variable to the GUI. This means that any time the *variable* changes, all property values are passed to the GUI. Because the quick form specifies

Figure 15.9 The resulting form.

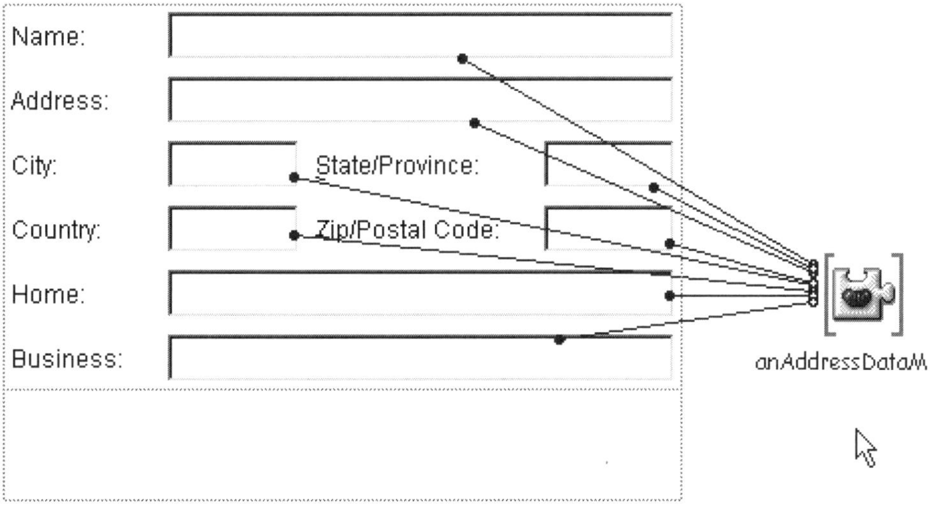

textValueChanged as the target event, any time the text in the field changes, the data in the object that the variable points to is updated.

The final step in your AddressDataEntryFormUI delegate is to make the model variable accessible *outside* this bean. You can do this by *promoting* it, as follows.

1. Open the pop-up menu for the variable and choose **Promote Bean Feature**. This option enables you to make a feature of a *contained bean* visible as a feature of the bean we're creating.
2. In this case, you want to make the variable visible, so you will promote its this property and call the resulting property model. In the Promote features dialog, select *this* under the Property list.
3. Click the >> button.
4. Double-click on **Promote Name** for the *this* property and change it to *model*.

Promoting the *this* feature creates getModel() and setModel() methods that directly access the anAddressDataModel variable. You can now access all of the form data from *outside* the AddressDataEntryFormUI bean!

After creating the form, you can modify the GUI components as you like. For example, you could change the fonts of the labels, text color, or anything else. The quick form is a one-time generation.

5. *Save the bean!* You should really save the bean as often as you think about it in the VCE.

This is a very simple design with only property-to-property connections, and *any* AddressDataModel implementer can be plugged in from the outside.

> **TIP**
>
> Always use variables of the model interface type, and promote them. This enables anyone to plug in a concrete model in place of that interface variable.

A Delegate for AddressBook

Your AddressBookUI delegate will contain an instance of your AddressDataEntryFormUI delegate, as well as buttons to add and look up names.

1. Create class AddressBookUI.
   - **Class name** = AddressBookUI
   - **Superclass** = java.awt.Panel
   - Select the **Compose the class visually** check box.
   - Import packages java.awt, java.awt.event, java.beans, and java.io.
   - Implement interface java.io.Serializable.

   Note that you should always use Panel (or JPanel for Swing GUIs) as the superclass of a delegate. This enables you to drop an instance of this delegate *inside* another delegate or application if you want to later. You are not limiting the GUI by using Frame, Dialog, or Window as the superclass.

2. Create the GUI seen in Figure 15.10. This GUI layout is

```
Panel BorderLayout (created by the VCE as the superclass)
   Panel BorderLayout (contentsPane, created by the VCE)
      CENTER=AddressBookEntryFormUI
      SOUTH=Panel FlowLayout(CENTER)
         Buttons for Find and Add
```

   Make sure you choose **Class** as the bean type when adding your AddressDataEntryFormUI!

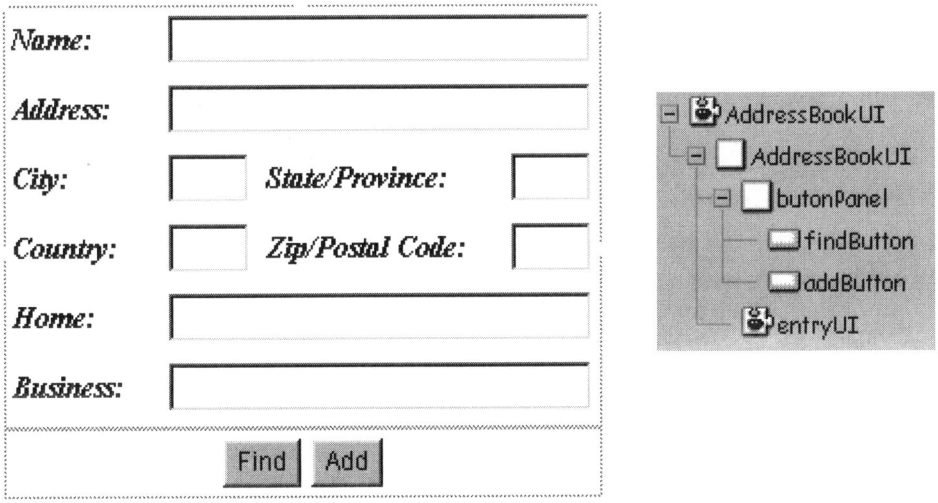

Figure 15.10 The Address Book user interface.

3. Save the bean.

You need to be able to work with models for the overall address book (so you can add/remove addresses) and for a specific address that you can display in the entry form. To do this:

Drop two variables in an empty part of the VCE design area using the Choose Bean tool. These variables are:

- anAddressDataModel, of type AddressDataModel
- anAddressBookModel, of type AddressBookModel

Make sure you choose **Variable** as the bean type for these.

You need to associate the anAddressDataModel variable with the AddressDataEntryFormUI instance. You want to set it up so that anytime the variable changes, the model in the UI changes. You can do this using a property-to-property connection.

4. Start this connection by opening the pop-up menu for anAddressDataModel and choosing **Connect**. This brings up the Start connection dialog.
5. Select **Properties** at the top of the dialog and *this* as the property name.
6. Click **Ok**; the pointer cursor will turn into a spider cursor.
7. Click on the AddressDataEntryFormUI delegate and choose **Connectable Features**. Note that if you had made the promoted model property of the entry-form delegate a preferred feature, you would see it directly in this pop-up menu.
8. Select **Connectable Features** to display the End connection dialog.
9. Choose model as the end property.
10. Click **Ok** to complete the connection. This is the solid connection that appears in Figure 15.11.

You need to create the actions that the Find command should perform. These actions are simple. The Find command should:

- Call find() in the AddressBookModel
- Pass in the value of the name property in anAddressDataModel
- Set anAddressDataModel to the result of the find method

To accomplish this:

11. Choose **Connect->actionPerformed** from the Find button's pop-up menu.
12. Click on anAddressBookModel; you'll see the End connection dialog.
13. Choose the find() method and click **Ok**. The resulting connection appears in Figure 15.11.

Figure 15.11 The first connection—the dashed line means it's incomplete.

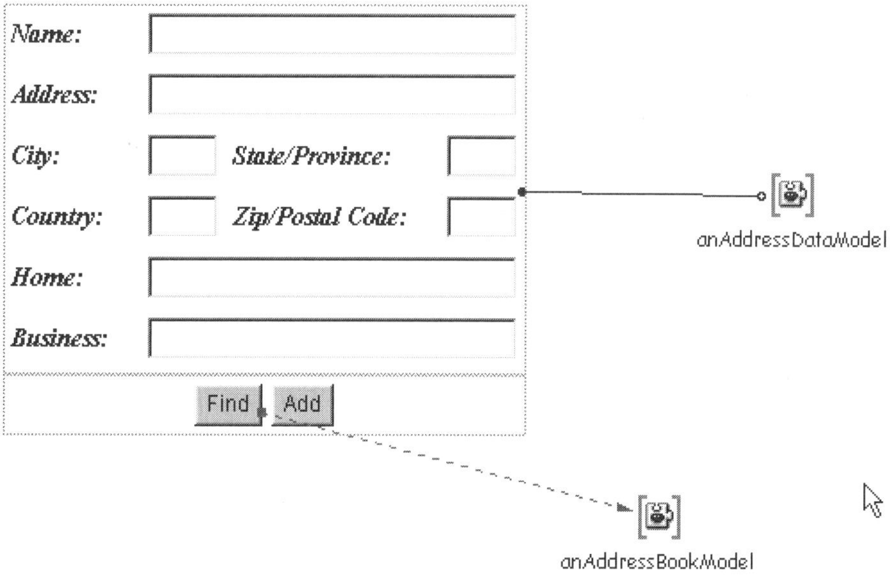

Figure 15.12 The parameter connection.

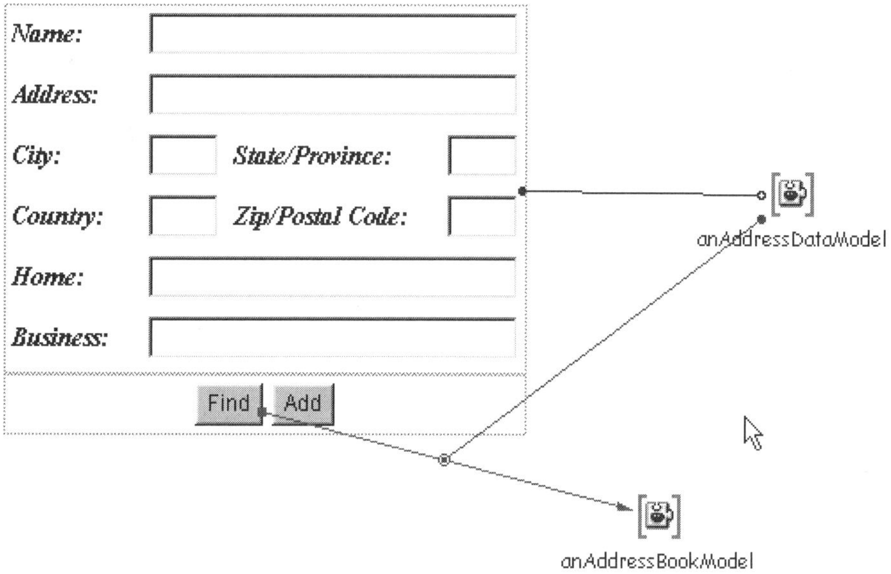

Note that the connection is dashed. This means it's incomplete. You need to provide a parameter to it, the name of the person to find in your phone book.

14. Open the pop-up menu for the dashed connection and choose **Connect->name**. Make sure the cursor is on the connection when you click, or you won't see the right pop-up menu.
15. Click on variable anAddressDataModel.
16. Choose *name* from the list of properties in the End connection dialog.
17. Click **Ok**; the resulting connection appears in Figure 15.12.

This connection grabs the name from whatever anAddressDataModel points to and passes it as the parameter to the find() method. This assumes that the variable has a value (we'll be setting that outside delegate). Note that the connection between anAddressDataModel and the entry form UI means that if the user types data in the Name field, that data is passed to the object that anAddressDataModel points to. This gives you access to the contents of the GUI, and you don't need to directly interact with the GUI to get the data!

Finally, you need to take the result of the find() method and stick it in anAddressDataModel.

18. Open the pop-up menu for the green connection and choose **Connect->normalResult.**
19. Click on variable anAddressDataModel.
20. Choose property *this* from the end connection dialog.
21. Click **Ok** to create the connection shown in Figure 15.13.

Figure 15.13 The complete find() processing.

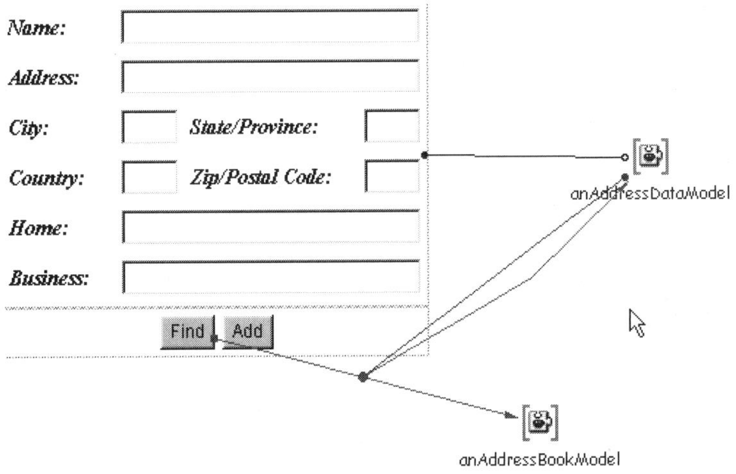

The resulting connections mean "when the Find button is pressed, set the anAddressDataModel variable to the result of finding the current name in the address book model."

Remember that you defined your find() method as throwing an exception if the name was not found. You could attach the exceptionOccurred event of the connection to display a dialog stating "not found." Right now, the exception will be ignored by handleException().

Next you examine what you need for the Add button. When Add is clicked, pass the current value of addAddressDataModel to add() in anAddressBookModel.

To create the Add button connections:

22. Choose **Connect->actionPerformed** from the Add button's pop-up menu.
23. Move the mouse to anAddressBookModel and click.
24. Choose method add() from the end connection dialog.
25. Choose **Connect->address** from the dashed connection's pop-up menu.
26. Move the mouse to anAddressDataModel and click.
27. Choose this from the list of properties. Make sure you have **Properties** checked at the top of the end connections dialog.

The resulting connections look as shown in Figure 15.14.

The last thing you need to do with this delegate is expose the variables so you can set them from the outside. You do this by promoting them, just as you did to create the model property in the AddressDataEntryFormUI. Here you want to promote the *this*

Figure 15.14 All connections for the AddressBookUI.

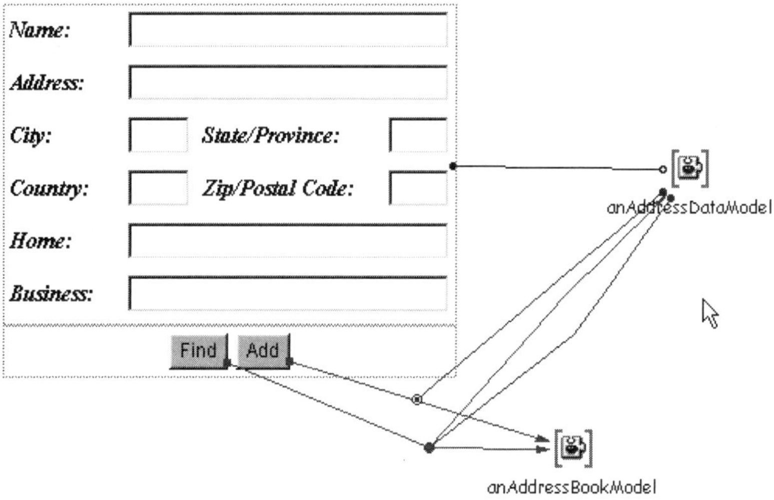

property of each variable. Promote the *this* property of anAddressBookModel as addressBookModel, and the *this* property of anAddressDataModel as addressDataModel.

When finished, *save the bean*!

Connecting as an Application

Creating an application now becomes an exercise in connecting models and delegates. Visual applications usually subclass Frame or Window (or their Swing equivalents). Usually the Application's visual design is simply dropping one or more UIs and one or more models, then connecting them together. This application is no exception.

1. Creating class PhoneApplication1:
   - **Class name** = PhoneApplication1
   - **Superclass** = java.awt.Frame
   - Select the **Compose the class visually** check box.
   - Import packages java.awt, java.awt.event, java.beans, and java.io.
   - Implement interface java.io.Serializable.
2. Change the ContentsPane's layout to GridLayout (the ContentsPane is the panel in the center of the main frame).
3. Drop an *instance* of AddressBookUI in the ContentsPane. Make sure you select **Class** as the bean type when choosing the AddressBookUI bean, as you want an instance, not a variable.
4. Drop two *instances*, one of type SimpleAddressData and one of type HashAddressBook, in an empty part of the design area.
5. Connect the *this* property of the SimpleAddressData instance to the addressDataModel property of the AddressBookUI.
6. Connect the *this* property of the HashAddressBook instance to the addressBookModel property of the AddressBookUI.

> **NOTE**
>
> To make the GUI look nicer, you can set the background color of the overall panel to SystemColor.control via its property sheet.
>
> When you set the background color, the TextField beans inherit that color (they looked gray). To fix this, you can open AddressDataEntryFormUI to the VCE and set all of its TextField beans' background colors to SystemColor.window.

The finished application appears in Figure 15.15.

Running the Application

Finally, we're ready to run. Watch out, though! It doesn't *quite* work right...

Try adding a couple sets of address data, clicking Add after each. Then type in an existing name and click Find.

Doesn't seem to work, does it?

The problem lies in your implementation of the model. We're using a Hashtable instance to hold the data. Let's think about what the hash table is doing.

> **TIP**
>
> If a data structure seems to act incorrectly, *draw a picture.* As you'll see in the following figures, the problem can become much easier to see.

You start off by creating an instance of SimpleAddressData. That's the simpleAddressData object in your PhoneApplication. You pass that to AddressBookUI, which passes it to the AddressDataEntryFormUI. When the user types data into the form, that data is sent to the SimpleAddressData instance. So far, your data looks as shown in Figure 15.16.

Figure 15.15 The application after changing some background colors.

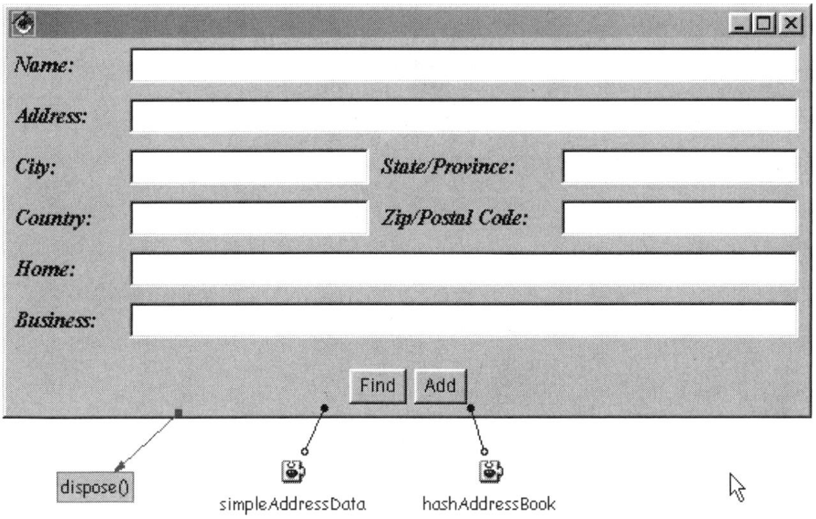

Figure 15.16 After typing in the data.

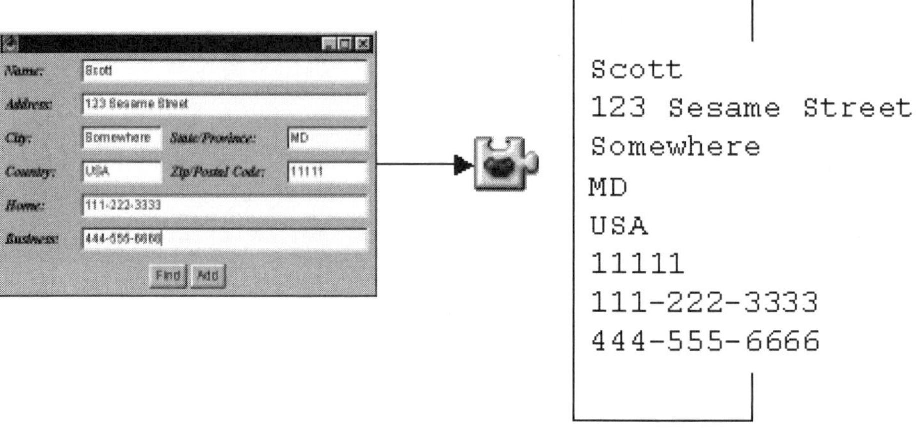

When the user clicks the Add button, the data is added to the Hashtable instance, keyed by the name. Your data now looks as shown in Figure 15.17.

Figure 15.17 After pressing the Add button.

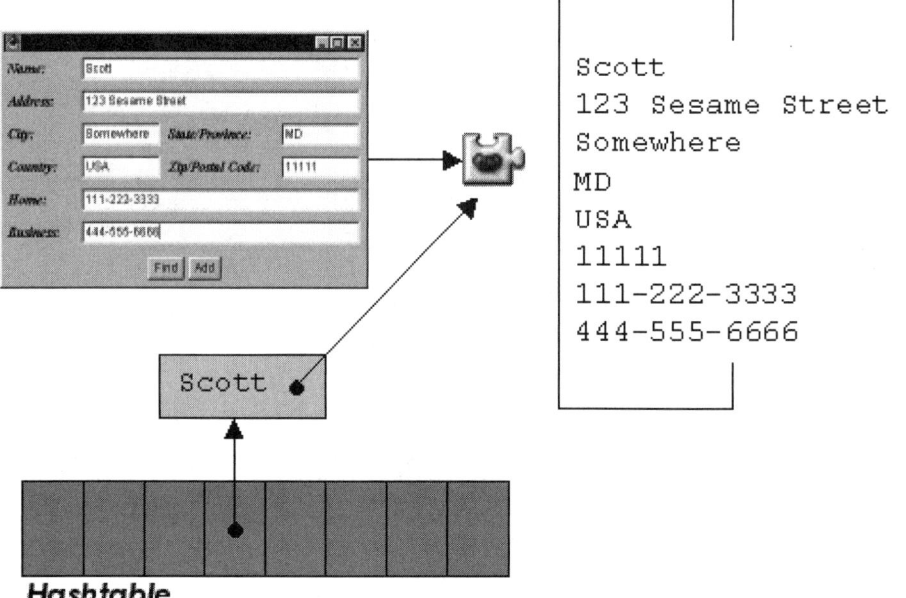

Note that the hash table keeps track of the key ("Scott") and a pointer to the value. (Technically, the key is just a pointer to some Object, in this case a String, but that's not important here.)

Now the user types the next set of address data, but does not click Add yet. Notice what the diagram looks like, seen in Figure 15.18.

Notice the problem so far. We've actually changed the object that "Scott" was keying in the hash table. After the user clicks Add again, you see the resulting data state in Figure 15.19.

The problem is that you have only a single piece of data, no matter how many keys you assign to it in the hash table. If you look up *Scott*, you find the last-entered data, whatever that was.

This is not a problem in the MVC paradigm; it is a problem in the implementation of your model.

This example makes you think about different kinds of model implementations. Some models directly *use* the data passed into them, as this one clearly does. Other models extract the data and store it somewhere else, perhaps in a database or across a network. You need to consider these types of problems when designing your model. Because of the differences between models, you do not want to build this knowledge into the model interface. You want to treat this situation as an implementation detail of a specific concrete model. Other models may not have this type of situation.

Figure 15.18 After typing new data.

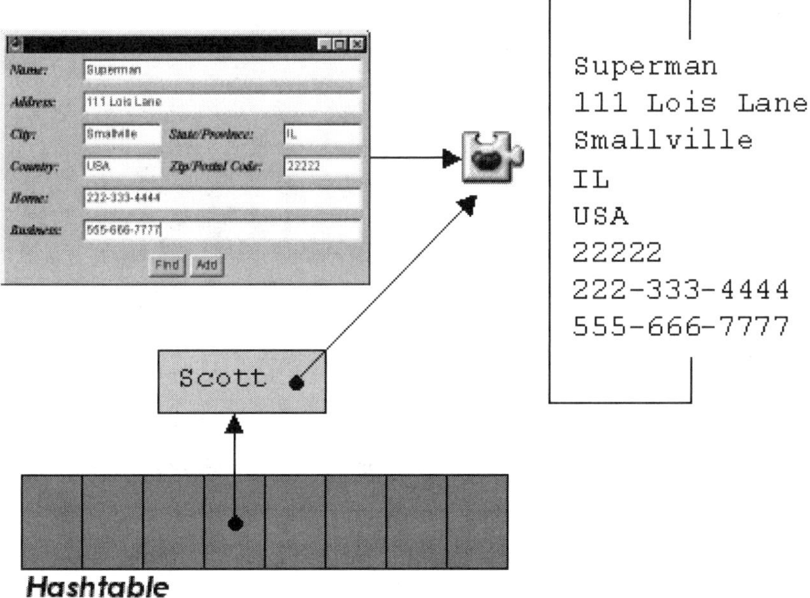

Figure 15.19 Two pieces of data in the hash table.

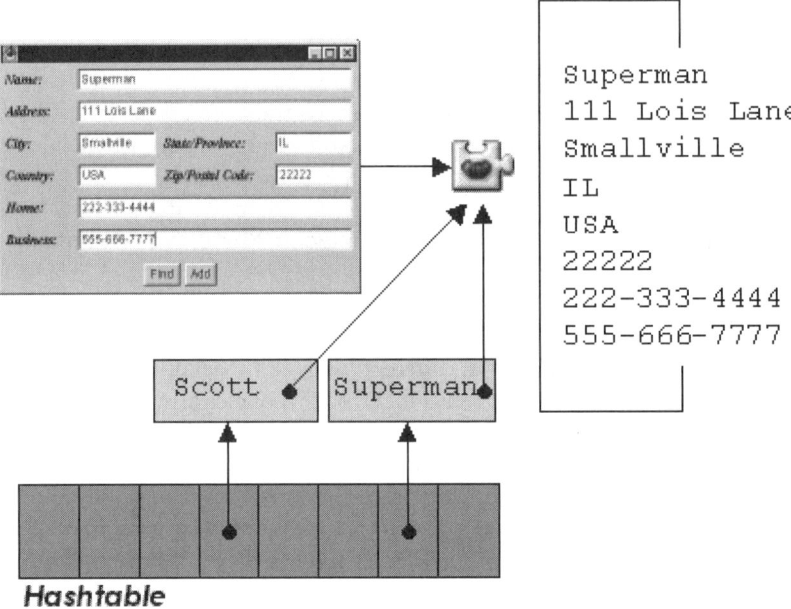

Fixing the Problem

There are several approaches to solving this problem. We'll examine three approaches, starting with "the wrong way."

At the heart of all solutions to this problem is that you need to make a copy of the data. If you think about it carefully, you'll see that you actually need to copy the data when adding *and* when finding. If you return the found record and the user types in the next name to find, it would overwrite the name in the old record!

Adding a Simple Copy to the add() Method

The first simple approach would be to just make a copy of the data. You *could* modify your add() method in HashAddressBook as follows:

```
public void add(AddressDataModel address) {
  if (records.get(address.getName()) == null)
    count++;
  SimpleAddressData copy = new SimpleAddressData();
  copy.setName(address.getName());
  copy.setAddress(address.getAddress());
  copy.setCity(address.getCity());
  copy.setState(address.getState());
```

```
    copy.setCountry(address.getCountry());
    copy.setPostalCode(address.getPostalCode());
    copy.setHomePhone(address.getHomePhone());
    copy.setBusinessPhone(address.getBusinessPhone());
    records.put(copy.getName(), copy);
    firePropertyChange("addresses",null, getAddresses());
}
```

The find() method would perform a similar copy, returning a fresh copy of the retrieved data.

This seems like an easy fix, but it's dead wrong. Think about the data types. Any AddressBookModel is supposed to store *any* type of AddressDataModel. In this naive patch, you *assume* that you should be storing SimpleAddressData objects. This is *not* an acceptable solution.

> **TIP**
>
> The only place you should ever directly use a concrete model is in the application. The application only chooses which concrete models work with which delegates. In your code, you should only reference the model interfaces. That keeps you application generic.

Using the Prototype Pattern

A really nifty alternative is to employ the Prototype pattern to make the copy. A prototype is an object that can make a copy of itself. The copy is a new object *of the same type* as the prototype, and contains a copy of the data in the prototype. In Java, you would use the Cloneable interface to represent a prototype and call the clone() method in that interface to make the copy. You could use this in the add() method as follows:

```
public void add(AddressDataModel address) {
  if (records.get(address.getName()) == null)
    count++;
  AddressData copy = (AddressData)address.clone();
  records.put(copy.getName(), copy);
  firePropertyChange("addresses",null, getAddresses());
}
```

There is obviously much less code here, and making the address data Cloneable is an easy task (the Java Virtual Machine provides support for the actual bitwise shallow-copy). However, look at *what* needs to be Cloneable: AddressDataModel.

This is not a good solution, because we're *requiring* all AddressDataModels to be Cloneable just so this *one* concrete address book model can do its job.

Once again, this is not an acceptable solution.

> **TIP**
>
> The prototype pattern *can* be quite useful, but be careful when applying it to a model interface. Anything you add to the interface is *required* by *all* classes that implement that interface, so think carefully when modifying the model interface.

Using a Factory Model

Fortunately, an acceptable alternative is easy. Define an additional object called a Factory. (Note that this is unrelated to the VCE's Factory bean, discussed in Chapter 17, "Factory Beans.") This Factory creates instances of a specific class but follows a nice generic interface for flexibility. Start by defining an interface for this Factory. Give this interface two methods: one that creates an empty instance of a class, and one that creates a copy of an existing instance.

> **TIP**
>
> Factory *models* are not the same as the VCE's Factory *bean*. Factory *models* are classes that you write to create instances of other classes. The VCE's Factory *bean* is a pseudo-bean that you can drop in the VCE to create an instance of a class. The main difference is that you cannot pass the Factory bean between classes, whereas you *can* pass a Factory model.

1. Define the factory model interface:
   - **Interface name** = AddressDataFactoryModel
   - Extend interface java.io.Serializable.
   - Import package java.io.
2. Add the following method declarations to the interface (you can type them directly in the interface definition):

```
public AddressDataModel create();
public AddressDataModel create(AddressDataModel address);
```

Note that you use the model type. The generic concept of the AddressDataFactoryModel is to create *any* type of AddressDataModel. Specific implementations of AddressDataFactoryModel will create specific types of AddressDataModels.

3. Now, create a concrete implementation of the factory model. Create class SimpleAddressDataFactory"
   - **Class name** = SimpleAddressDataFactory
   - **Superclass** = java.lang.Object
   - Do not select the **Compose the class visually** check box.
   - Implement interface AddressDataFactoryModel.

   Note that you don't need to specify implements Serializable, as the implemented interface does that for you. (It doesn't hurt to add it if you would like.)

4. Edit the two create() methods in SimpleAddressDataFactory to look as follows:

```
public AddressDataModel create() {
  return new SimpleAddressData();
}

public AddressDataModel create(AddressDataModel address) {
  SimpleAddressData copy = new SimpleAddressData();
  copy.setName(address.getName());
  copy.setAddress(address.getAddress());
  copy.setCity(address.getCity());
  copy.setState(address.getState());
  copy.setCountry(address.getCountry());
  copy.setPostalCode(address.getPostalCode());
  copy.setHomePhone(address.getHomePhone());
  copy.setBusinessPhone(address.getBusinessPhone());
  return copy;
}
```

Although this is a very simple class, it provides total flexibility in HashAddressBook. And speaking of HashAddressBook:

5. Add a property to HashAddressBook using the BeanInfo editor:
   - **Property name** = addressDataFactory
   - **Property type** = AddressDataFactoryModel
   - Select the **readable, writeable, bound,** and **preferred** check boxes.

6. Update the add() and find() methods as follows in HashAddressBook to use the factory model. Updated code is in bold text.

```
public void add(AddressDataModel address) {
  if (records.get(address.getName()) == null)
    count++;
```

```
    AddressDataModel copy =
      getAddressDataFactory().create(address);
    records.put(copy.getName(), copy);
    firePropertyChange("addresses",null, getAddresses());
}

public AddressDataModel find(String name) {
    AddressDataModel data = (AddressDataModel)records.get(name);
    if (data == null)
      throw new RuntimeException(name + " not found");
    return getAddressDataFactory().create(data);
}
```

7. Open PhoneApplication1 to the VCE.
8. Drop an *instance* of SimpleAddressDataFactory in an empty spot in the design area.
9. Connect the *this* property of the SimpleAddressDataFactory to the addressDataFactory property in the HashAddressBook.

   The resulting visual design appears in Figure 15.20.

   Overall, this was a very small change to provide the fix in a very flexible manner.

10. Run PhoneApplication1 again. You should see appropriate results. Add several items, and when you look up any of them, the fields are properly found.

Adding Another Delegate

Suppose that you want to add a window that displays a list of everyone in the phone book. You can simply plug in *another* delegate! This is where some of the power of MVC really starts to show.

1. Create the AddressBookListUI class:
   - **Class name** = AddressBookListUI
   - **Superclass** = java.awt.List
   - Select the **Compose the class visually** check box.
   - Import packages java.awt, java.awt.event, java.beans, java.io, and java.util.
   - Implement interface java.io.Serializable.
2. Drop a *variable* of type AddressBookModel in the VCE and call it anAddressBookModel.
3. Choose **Connect** from the variable's pop-up menu.

Figure 15.20 Adding SimpleAddressDataFactory to the application.

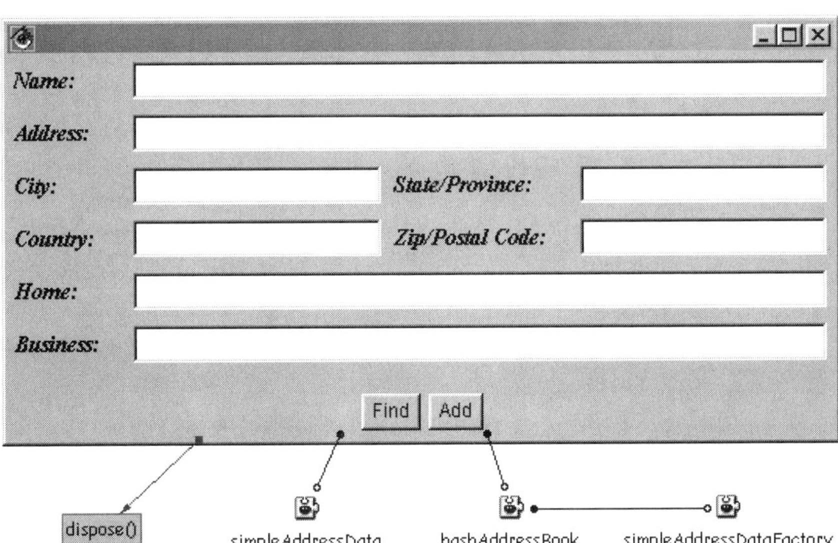

4. Select **Event** at the top of the Start connection dialog.
5. Choose *addresses*. This means "perform this connection when the addresses property changes."
6. Click on any empty spot in the VCE design area and choose **Event to Code.**
7. Make sure **Pass event data** is selected in the Event to code dialog.
8. Modify the code in the Event to Code dialog to look as follows. This clears the current list and adds all items to it. This is not terribly efficient, but easy to do for an example.

```
public void loadList(AddressDataModel[] addresses, List list) {
  list.removeAll();

  for(int i = 0; i<addresses.length; i++)
    list.addItem(addresses[i].getName());
}
```

9. Click **Ok** to exit the dialog. If asked to save the method, pick "Yes."
10. Choose **Connect->list** from the dashed connection.
11. Click on the List component (the List component is the rectangle in the VCE).

12. Select property *this*.
13. Promote the *this* property of the *variable* as addressBookModel.

That's it! This is a very simple view-only delegate. There is no way for the user to change the model using this delegate.

Using the New Delegate

To use this delegate, you simply need to drop it in an application and connect it to a model. Rather than modify your original application, let's make a copy of it.

1. Select **Reorganize->Copy** from class PhoneApplication1's pop-up menu in the Workbench (or some other browser).
2. Choose the same package but rename the class PhoneApplication2.
3. Note that you will get an error in the copy. Edit the class definition for PhoneApplication2 and change the PhoneApplication1 reference to PhoneApplication2. (If you are not using one inner class for all events, the error may appear in a different location, like in the initConnections() method.)
4. *Delete the main() method in PhoneApplication2.* The VCE will regenerate a correct one when you save the class. If you don't do this, you will end up running the PhoneApplication1 GUI when you run PhoneApplication2.
5. Open PhoneApplication2 to the VCE.
6. Drop an instance of AddressBookListUI in the GUI (place it in the grid layout to the left of the entry form UI).
7. Connect the *this* property of the HashAddressBook to the addressBookModel property of the AddressBookListUI.

The resulting design appears in Figure 15.21.

> **TIP**
>
> Note that you can add or remove *either* delegate without hurting the other. They are completely unrelated. You can add other delegates; the existing delegates do not need to change.

When you run PhoneApplication2, any phone entries that you add will also appear in the list on the left. Note that selecting items in the list will *not* cause them to be displayed in the entry form. Also, note that the list is not sorted. We discuss how to handle selections and sort results in Chapter 16.

Figure 15.21 The second phone application, with two delegates.

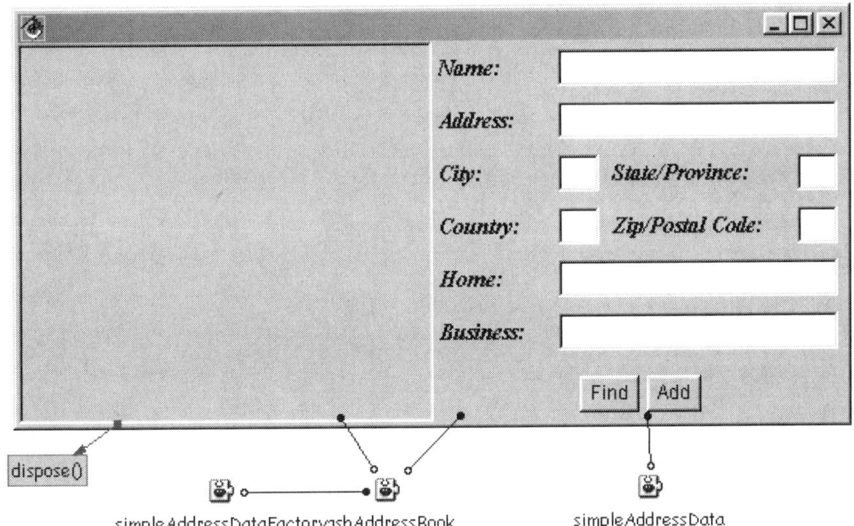

Summary

GUI builder tools have helped steer developers away from good separation of GUI and business logic, but fortunately it is possible to still use the MVC paradigm, which provides an excellent way to improve the maintainability and flexibility of your applications. It just takes a little extra planning and conscious separation of tasks.

VisualAge for Java's Visual Composition Editor provides all of the tools necessary to make this separation easy, using variables, bound properties, and property promotion to keep model details out of the GUI design process. While it's a little less direct than traditional "GUI building," it's the key to a cleaner design.

Separating GUI from business logic helps reduce errors when adding features; it lets you easily change either the GUI or the business logic without affecting the other. Using MVC may seem like extra work during development but can really save time and prevent trouble during program maintenance and debugging.

In the next chapter, we'll expand your knowledge of MVC by using new models that filter data and allow you to handle selections between delegates.

Advanced Model-View-Controller Techniques

16

In Chapter 15, "Model-View-Controller in the VCE," we introduced the Model-View-Controller paradigm and walked through an example implementation. This chapter covers advanced techniques and strategies for applying the Model-View-Controller paradigm. Much of this chapter is conceptual, with examples given in VisualAge for Java so you can see how to implement the strategies. Keep in mind that the key to MVC is abstraction and separation of classes. The techniques described in this chapter add more power and flexibility to your use of MVC to achieve these goals.

Advanced MVC Strategies

The previous chapter presents the basic concepts of the Model-View-Controller paradigm. In that chapter, you applied the MVC paradigm by creating a simple phone book application. Your final phone application contained a model that tracked address entries in a hash table, and two delegates. One delegate displayed a single address entry, enabling the user to add and find entries. The other delegate presented a list of all names registered in the address book.

However, your implementation of the phone application was incomplete:

- The data in the list was unsorted.
- There was no way to associate the selected data in two different delegates. Presented with a list of names in a phone book application, users would assume that selecting a name would display its details in the entry form. In this chapter, we will describe how to associate the notion of selection with multiple delegates.

In this chapter, we will address these issues as well as several others that can help improve any Model-View-Controller design. We'll start with some concepts and then come back to the phone application as well as some other example applications.

NOTE

Sun's Java Foundation Classes (JFC) library provides an extremely useful tool kit called Swing. The Sun developers based Swing firmly on the Model-View-Controller paradigm, which makes it a very effective tool set for developing a delegate. For some examples in this chapter, you will use Swing as the basis for new models and delegates. You will use Swing's TableModel, showing ways to enhance its behavior and use it in VisualAge for Java. TableModel is an interface that defines the following methods:

```
public interface TableModel {
  public int getRowCount();
  public int getColumnCount();
  public String getColumnName(int columnIndex);
  public Class getColumnClass(int columnIndex);
  public boolean isCellEditable(int rowIndex,
                                int columnIndex);
  public Object getValueAt(int rowIndex,
                           int columnIndex);
  public void setValueAt(Object aValue,
                         int rowIndex,
                         int columnIndex);
  public void addTableModelListener(
                TableModelListener l);
  public void removeTableModelListener(
                TableModelListener l);
}
```

Advanced Models and Delegate

Models and delegates do not actually need to store their data. They can provide means to interpret existing data, even if that data is stored on another machine or if they want to change the appearance of the data. In this section, we examine models used as proxies for other data, delegates that proxy the view to another machine, and helper models that assist MVC development and usability.

Models as Proxies

One of the biggest mistakes that people make when designing and using models is copying data. When they adapt existing data structures into new models, they *copy* data to the new model. When they want to reinterpret the data, for example sorting it, they *copy* the data. When they want to join two separate sources of data, they *copy* the data.

This copying is often unnecessary and extremely expensive. This is one of the key reasons why many Swing applications display poor performance. What most programmers do not think about is that models are merely interfaces; they do *not* need to actually store any data!

A proxy is something that acts on behalf of another object. Whether that object exists on the current machine or across a network, the idea is that any other object can interact with the proxy in the same manner as it would interact with the real object. The proxy implements the same interface as the real object, obtains data from the real object, and possibly translates that data.

> **TIP**
>
> Apply proxy models to adapt existing data rather than copy the data into a new structure.

This is the key to developing effective models. If you already have data in an existing data structure or database, you can write a proxy to *adapt* communication with that data to fit a model.

Models as Simple Filters

Filters are simply proxies. A filter obtains data from some source (possibly another model that implements the same interface) and translates or hides some of that data. For a simple example, look at Swing's JTable class and define a model that can limit the displayed columns.

Suppose that you have a table model that contains 20 rows of data in six columns. An example of such a model follows. Note that this table model hard-codes its data, but it could easily have obtained the data from a database. The data in this model helps to demonstrate the effect of applied filters.

> **NOTE**
>
> 3.5 In version 3.5 of VisualAge for Java, use the following Swing imports (the ones that start with javax.swing. In version 3.02 of VisualAge for Java, you would need to use Swing packages starting with com.sun.java.swing.

```
import javax.swing.*;
import javax.swing.event.*;
import javax.swing.table.*;
```

```
/**
 * A simple table model with hardcoded data
 * Each cell displays (r,c) where r and c
 *   are integer row and column numbers
 * This model helps to show the effect of
 *   an applied filter model
 */
public class FixedTableModel extends AbstractTableModel {
  /**
   * Return the number of columns
   *   in the model - we explicitly use 6
   */
  public int getColumnCount() {
    return 6;
  }

  /**
   * Return the number of rows
   *   in the model - we explicitly use 20
   */
  public int getRowCount() {
    return 20;
  }

  /**
   * Return a string that describes the
   *   location in the data
   */
  public Object getValueAt(int rowIndex,
                           int columnIndex) {
    return columnIndex + "," + rowIndex;
  }
}
```

To simplify this and other examples, create an abstract class named FilteredTableModel. FilteredTableModel keeps track of another table model. This FilteredTableModel delegates all of its methods to the *real* table model. Each of the delegations alter the requested row and column using the mapRow() and mapColumn() method. This enables subclasses to create simple filters just by changing the mappings.

```
import javax.swing.*;
import javax.swing.event.*;
import javax.swing.table.*;
```

```
/**
 * A sample abstract filtering model
 * This model delegates nearly all its
 *   methods to another TableModel, but
 *   subclasses can change the way columns
 *   are mapped
 * Note that we have omitted error checking
 *   such as "is the real model null" for
 *   brevity/clarity in this example
 */
public abstract class FilteredTableModel
                implements TableModel {
    // The realTableModel property. This property
    //   tracks the real model we use
    private TableModel fieldRealTableModel;

    /**
     * Gets the realTableModel property (TableModel) value.
     * @return The realTableModel property value.
     * @see #setRealTableModel
     */
    public TableModel getRealTableModel() {
        return fieldRealTableModel;
    }

    /**
     * Sets the realTableModel property (TableModel) value.
     * @param realTableModel The new value for the property.
     * @see #getRealTableModel
     */
    public void setRealTableModel(TableModel realTableModel) {
        fieldRealTableModel = realTableModel;
    }

    /** Provides a mapping from a requested
     *     column to the column in the real model
     *  Subclasses can override this to
     *     define special mappings
     */
    protected int mapColumn(int columnIndex) {
        return columnIndex;
    }
```

```
/** Provides a mapping from a requested
 *    row to the row in the real model
 *  Subclasses can override this to
 *    define special mappings
 */
protected int mapRow(int rowIndex) {
    return rowIndex;
}

public void addTableModelListener(TableModelListener l) {
    getRealTableModel().addTableModelListener(l);
}

public Class getColumnClass(int columnIndex) {
    return getRealTableModel().
            getColumnClass(mapColumn(columnIndex));
}

public int getColumnCount() {
    return getRealTableModel().getColumnCount();
}

public String getColumnName(int columnIndex) {
    return getRealTableModel().
            getColumnName(mapColumn(columnIndex));
}

public int getRowCount() {
    return getRealTableModel().getRowCount();
}

public Object getValueAt(int rowIndex,
                         int columnIndex) {
    return getRealTableModel().
            getValueAt(mapRow(rowIndex),
                       mapColumn(columnIndex));
}

public boolean isCellEditable(int rowIndex, int columnIndex) {
    return getRealTableModel().
            isCellEditable(mapRow(rowIndex),
                           mapColumn(columnIndex));
}
```

```
    public void removeTableModelListener(TableModelListener l) {
        getRealTableModel().removeTableModelListener(l);
    }

    public void setValueAt(Object aValue, int rowIndex,
                           int columnIndex) {
        getRealTableModel().
            setValueAt(aValue, mapRow(rowIndex),
                       mapColumn(columnIndex));
    }
}
```

Define two subclasses that provide interesting filtering. First, OmitColumnTableModel hides a single column. OmitColumnTableModel extends FilteredTableModel, changes the column mapping to omit a column, and reduces the column number report.

```
import javax.swing.*;
import javax.swing.event.*;
import javax.swing.table.*;

/**
 * A sample filtering model that omits
 *   a single column in a table
 */
public class OmitColumnTableModel extends FilteredTableModel {
    // The hiddenColumn property tells us which column to omit
    private int fieldHiddenColumn = 0;

    /**
     * Gets the hiddenColumn property (int) value.
     * @return The hiddenColumn property value.
     * @see #setHiddenColumn
     */
    public int getHiddenColumn() {
        return fieldHiddenColumn;
    }

    /**
     * Sets the hiddenColumn property (int) value.
     * @param hiddenColumn The new value for the property.
     * @see #getHiddenColumn
     */
    public void setHiddenColumn(int hiddenColumn) {
        fieldHiddenColumn = hiddenColumn;
    }
```

```
    // Change the column mapping to skip the hidden column

    /** Returns a fewer columns than the real
     *    TableModel actually has, as we hide one
     */
    public int getColumnCount() {
        return getRealTableModel().getColumnCount() - 1;
    }

    /** Provides a mapping from a requested
     *    column to the column in the real model
     */
    protected int mapColumn(int col) {
        if (col >= getHiddenColumn())
            col++;
        return col;
    }
}
```

This simple extension effectively hides a column in the model. Define another filter that reverses the order of the columns. This is even simpler than the column-omitting filter.

```
/**
 * This TableModel reverses the column display
 */
public class ReverseColumnTableModel
        extends FilteredTableModel {
    /** Change the column mapping
     *    to return the columns in
     *    reverse order
     */
    protected int mapColumn(int col) {
        return getColumnCount() - col - 1;
    }
}
```

Apply these filters when assembling your application. The JTable instance acts as your delegate, while the previous two filters act as the models. You will assemble a simple GUI containing two JTable instances, each using one of the previous models and attaching a single FixedTableModel instance as the real table model for the filters.

To create this test application, perform the following steps in the VCE:

1. Create a new class that extends JFrame.
2. Set contentsPane's layout property to GridLayout.
3. Add two JTable beans to contentsPane.
4. Drop instances of FixedTableModel, ReverseColumnTableModel, and OmitColumnTableModel in an empty spot in the design area.
5. Connect FixedTableModel's *this* property to the realTableModel properties ofReverseColumnTableModel and OmitColumnTableModel, so they can filter its data.
6. Connect the *this* properties of the filters to the model properties of the two JTable beans.

The resulting test application appears in Figure 16.1.

When you run this example, *both* tables share the same actual model data from FixedTableModel. However, their actual models filter that data to present an altered view of it. Figure 16.2 shows the running application. The left table displays all columns except the fourth column (numbered column 3). The right table displays all data, reversing the column numbers.

Filtering Existing Data

Filters provide some of the real power of a Model-View-Controller application. One of the most common mistakes that people make when using Swing components is to *copy* the data into the default Swing models. The proper way to use existing data is to *adapt* it via a filter.

Figure 16.1 A filtering model sample.

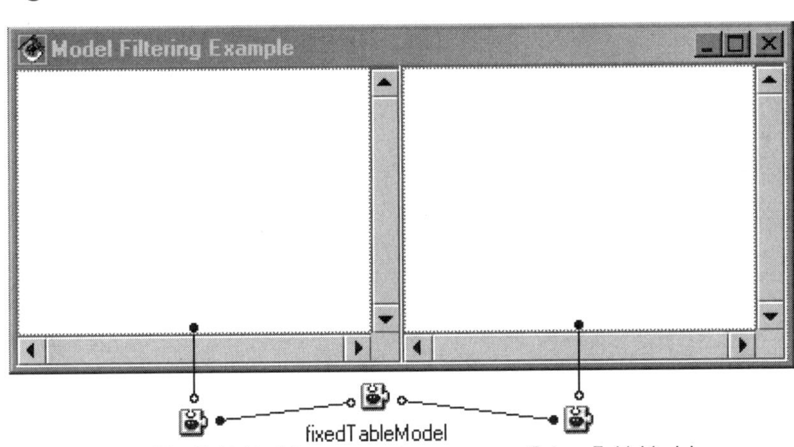

Figure 16.2 Filtering in action.

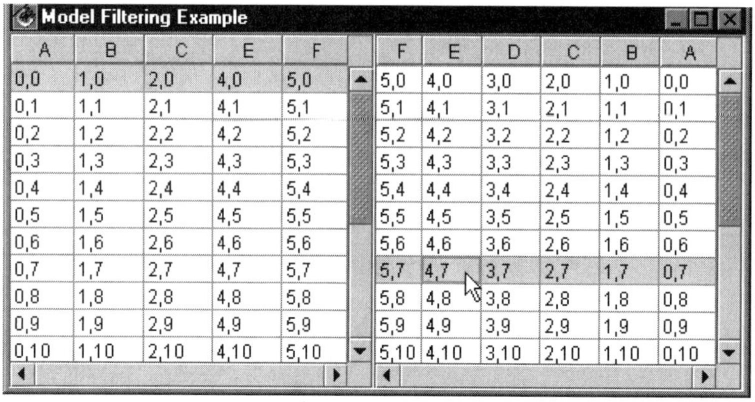

Model Filtering Example

A	B	C	E	F
0,0	1,0	2,0	4,0	5,0
0,1	1,1	2,1	4,1	5,1
0,2	1,2	2,2	4,2	5,2
0,3	1,3	2,3	4,3	5,3
0,4	1,4	2,4	4,4	5,4
0,5	1,5	2,5	4,5	5,5
0,6	1,6	2,6	4,6	5,6
0,7	1,7	2,7	4,7	5,7
0,8	1,8	2,8	4,8	5,8
0,9	1,9	2,9	4,9	5,9
0,10	1,10	2,10	4,10	5,10

F	E	D	C	B	A
5,0	4,0	3,0	2,0	1,0	0,0
5,1	4,1	3,1	2,1	1,1	0,1
5,2	4,2	3,2	2,2	1,2	0,2
5,3	4,3	3,3	2,3	1,3	0,3
5,4	4,4	3,4	2,4	1,4	0,4
5,5	4,5	3,5	2,5	1,5	0,5
5,6	4,6	3,6	2,6	1,6	0,6
5,7	4,7	3,7	2,7	1,7	0,7
5,8	4,8	3,8	2,8	1,8	0,8
5,9	4,9	3,9	2,9	1,9	0,9
5,10	4,10	3,10	2,10	1,10	0,10

For example, suppose that you had an existing array of Person objects. The Person bean provides String properties *name*, *address*, and *phone*. A naive TableModel implementation might copy the properties from each Person instance into a two-dimensional array, and use that array in Swing's default TableModel support as follows:

```
// define the target data for the table
String[][] data = new String[10][3];

// copy the property values to the array
for(int i = 0; i < people.length; i++) {
  data[i][0] = people[i].getName();
  data[i][1] = people[i].getAddress();
  data[i][2] = people[i].getPhone();
}

// define the names of the columns
String[] columnNames =
    {"Name","Address","Phone"};

// create a default table model with the data
DefaultTableModel tableModel =
  new DefaultTableModel(data, columnNames);

// use the default model with a table
table.setModel(tableModel);
```

This is a horribly slow implementation. Data copying must be avoided whenever possible.

> **NOTE**
>
> There are times when copying data to a cache can help performance. For example, suppose that your model retrieves some data from a database, and the user will repeatedly use that same data. Copying the data into another data structure can improve performance under these circumstances. However, if you already have your data directly accessible in a data structure, do *not* copy it to another data structure. In a case like this, create a new filtering model that re-interprets the existing data.

For this example, a better approach would be to define a table model that simply interprets the existing data and returns it. For example, the getValueAt() method of such a table model might look as follows:

```
public Object getValueAt(int row, int col) {
  switch(col) {
    case 0: return people[row].getName();
    case 1: return people[row].getAddress();
    case 2: return people[row].getPhone();
    default: throw IllegalArgumentException("Bad Column");
  }
```

Using a filter model such as this provides access to the existing data *in its existing format*. You simply interpret the existing data, adapting it to the model's interface. Remember: Never copy data that you can simply interpret!

Narrowing Your Phone List

For another example of filtering, write an address book model that limits the list of displayed names based on a simple pattern. This filter wraps around any existing AddressBookModel implementation (defined in Chapter 15). To provide the pattern, you need an extra property named *pattern*.

> **NOTE**
>
> To provide this extra property, define another interface called Patterned with a getPattern() and setPattern() method. This enables you to use any model that implements both AddressBookModel and Patterned in your application. You do not want to simply add the pattern property to the AddressBookModel, because you do not want to require that all address books support the pattern filtering. Nor should you allow the delegate to assume which class it uses; always abstract the communication via an interface!

Start by defining the Patterned interface. This interface defines the required methods to support a bound read/write String property named *pattern*. This interface looks as follows.

```
import java.beans.*;

/**
 * An interface that describes and object
 *   that keeps track of a pattern
 */
public interface Patterned {
  // the pattern property
  public String getPattern();
  public void setPattern(String pattern);

  // Bound property support
  public void addPropertyChangeListener(
                  PropertyChangeListener listener);
  public void removePropertyChangeListener(
                  PropertyChangeListener listener);
}
```

Your strategy for the pattern filter must ensure that:

- You track an address book model that really contains the data. Note that this real model can be *any* model that implements the AddressBookModel interface introduced in Chapter 15.
- You modify the *addresses* property of that real model to limit the returned results to those that match the pattern. For this example, you provide support only for a prefix pattern; that is, you only check to see if the pattern matches the beginning of a name.
- You properly deal with PropertyChangeEvents. This can be tricky. There are two main concerns here:
  - When a delegate receives a propertyChange notification, the *source* must be the model passed to it. This will be the filter, not the real model.
  - The delegate can receive notification for bound properties in *both* the real model and the filter model. However, it thinks all events originate from the *filter*.
- When the pattern changes, you must make the *addresses* property appear to change as well.

The PropertyChangeEvent issue can be somewhat complex. The solution presented in the following code has the filter listen for property changes in the real model and then fire duplicate property change events itself. This ensures that all events appear to originate from the filter, rather than some coming from the real model and others from the filter.

The code for the filter follows. Note that this filter is slightly complex and represents some of the issues you need to consider when writing a filter. At first, it may seem that a filter is simply a set of delegated methods with a few small changes. However, you need to carefully consider event handling, especially bound properties and ensuring that the event source is correct. The VCE's generated code depends upon a proper event source specification in order to perform connection processing.

```
import effectivevaj.vce.mvc.*;
import java.beans.*;

/**
 * An AddressBookModel filter.
 * This filter allows specification of a pattern that
 *   restricts which address are returned by the addresses
 *   indexed property
 */
public class PatternedAddressBook
     implements AddressBookModel, Patterned {
  private AddressBookModel fieldRealAddressBook;
  protected transient PropertyChangeSupport propertyChange;
  private String fieldPattern;

  // pcl is a holder for the PropertyChangeListener that
  //   we add to the real model. We need to hold a reference
  //   to it in case we change the real model later
  private PropertyChangeListener pcl;

  // Define addresses property to filter based on the
  //   pattern property
  public AddressDataModel[] getAddresses() {
    AddressDataModel[] data = getRealAddressBook().getAddresses();
    String pattern = getPattern();

    // if no pattern or it's empty, return data
    if (pattern == null || pattern.equals(""))
      return data;

    // find out how many match the pattern
    int count = 0;
    for (int i = 0; i < data.length; i++)
      if (data[i].getName().startsWith(getPattern()))
        count++;
```

```
    // if pattern matches all, return all
    if (count == data.length)
      return data;

    // Otherwise Make the new data array
    // Unfortunately, there is no other way to
    //   do this for an indexed property other
    //   than copy the String refs to a new
    //   array
    AddressDataModel[] patterned = new AddressDataModel[count];
    for (int i = 0, j = 0; i < data.length; i++)
      if (data[i].getName().startsWith(getPattern()))
        patterned[j++] = data[i];
    return patterned;
  }

  public AddressDataModel getAddresses(int index) {
    return getAddresses()[index];
  }

  // the pattern string property
  public String getPattern() {
    return fieldPattern;
  }

  public void setPattern(String pattern) {
    String oldValue = fieldPattern;
    fieldPattern = pattern;
    firePropertyChange("pattern", oldValue, pattern);
    firePropertyChange("addresses", null, getAddresses());
  }

  // the realAddressBook property, tracking the real model
  //   that we filter
  public AddressBookModel getRealAddressBook() {
    return fieldRealAddressBook;
  }

  public void setRealAddressBook(AddressBookModel realAddressBook) {
    AddressBookModel oldValue = fieldRealAddressBook;
    // if we used to have a value, remove the
    //   old property change listener
    if (oldValue != null)
      oldValue.removePropertyChangeListener(pcl);
```

```
    // set the property value
    fieldRealAddressBook = realAddressBook;

    // set up listener to delegate events
    if (pcl == null)
      pcl = new PropertyChangeListener() {
      public void propertyChange(PropertyChangeEvent e) {
        firePropertyChange(e.getPropertyName(),
                     e.getOldValue(),
                     e.getNewValue());
      }
    };

    realAddressBook.addPropertyChangeListener(pcl);

    // report that the property has changed
    firePropertyChange("realAddressBook", oldValue,
               realAddressBook);
  }

  // Simply delegate the add & find methods
  public void add(AddressDataModel data) {
    getRealAddressBook().add(data);
  }

  public AddressDataModel find(String name) {
    return getRealAddressBook().find(name);
  }

  // support methods for the bound properties
  public void addPropertyChangeListener(
          PropertyChangeListener listener) {
    getPropertyChange().addPropertyChangeListener(listener);
  }

  public void removePropertyChangeListener(
          PropertyChangeListener listener) {
    getPropertyChange().removePropertyChangeListener(listener);
  }

  public void firePropertyChange(String propertyName,
                     Object oldValue,
                     Object newValue) {
```

```
    getPropertyChange().firePropertyChange(propertyName,
                          oldValue,
                          newValue);
  }

  protected PropertyChangeSupport getPropertyChange() {
    if (propertyChange == null) {
      propertyChange = new PropertyChangeSupport(this);
    };
    return propertyChange;
  }
}
```

Once you define the model, you need to use it in a delegate. Create a new delegate that wraps the previous AddressBookListUI, adding a pattern. You can use this new delegate only when a Patterned object is present. The delegate appears in Figure 16.3. Note that there are two variables for delegate model communication. First, provide an AddressBookModel variable that the old AddressBookListUI (the top part of the delegate) sets as its model. Second, provide a Patterned variable that connects to the pattern text field. You use a TextField bean for entry and connect it with the pattern property of the patterned variable. (When doing this, you need to modify the property-to-property connection to specify textValueChanged as the target event.) Note that this delegate makes *no* assumption about a relationship between the AddressBookModel and the Patterned object. In this example, you will use the same object for both. However, you could pass in two separate objects that implement these interfaces and communicate in another manner.

Figure 16.3 AddressBookPatternListUI.

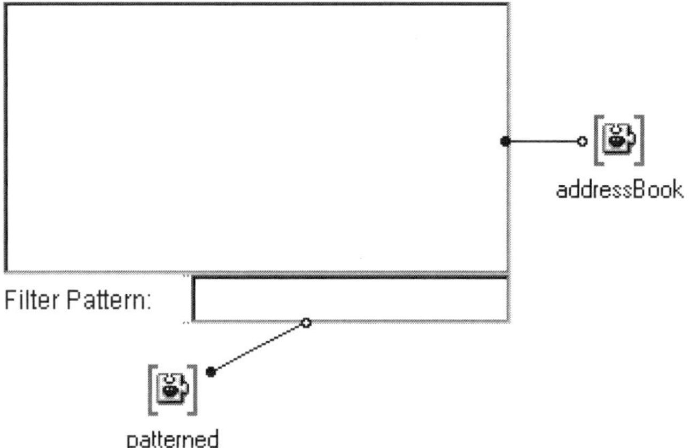

As you have done for all other delegate model variables, promote the *this* property of the variables so you can set the variables outside the delegates. You can now add this delegate to another application in the VCE.

To assemble your new application:

1. Create a new class that extends java.awt.Frame.
2. Drop instances of your new AddressBookPatternListUI and the old AddressBookUI into contentsPane.
3. Drop instances of PatternedAddressBook and HashAddressBook in an empty spot of the design area.
4. Connect the PatternedAddressBook instance as the AddressBookModel model for both delegates *and* the Patterned modelfor the AddressBookPatternListUI.
5. Use the HashAddressBook instance as the real model for the PatternedAddressBook instance.

This design appears in Figure 16.4. The rest of the design is the same as in Chapter 15 (use an instance of SimpleAddressData as the addressDataModel of the AddressBookUI, and an instance of SimpleAddressDataFactory as the addressDataFactory for HashAddressBook).

A sample execution appears in Figures 16.5 and 16.6. In Figure 16.5, all names in the list appear. Figure 16.6 shows the same list after typing the letter S in the filter field. Note that you do not change the real model; you simply provide a filter that restricts which data you see in it.

Figure 16.4 Designing the pattern filter test.

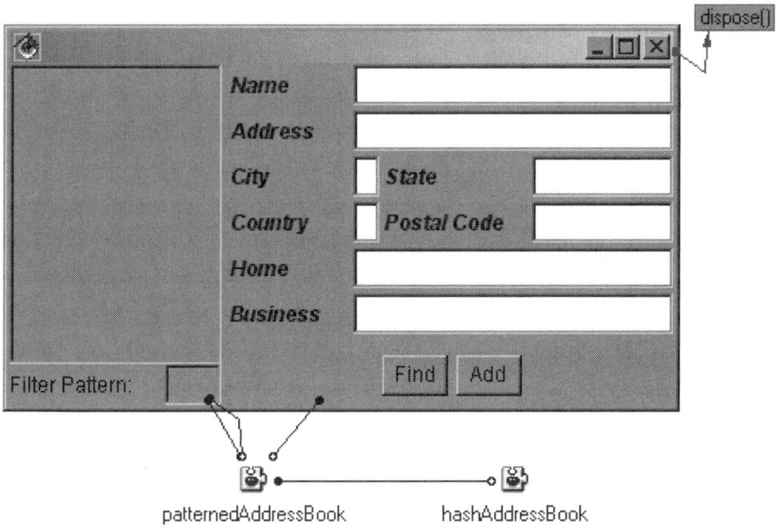

Figure 16.5 Without a pattern.

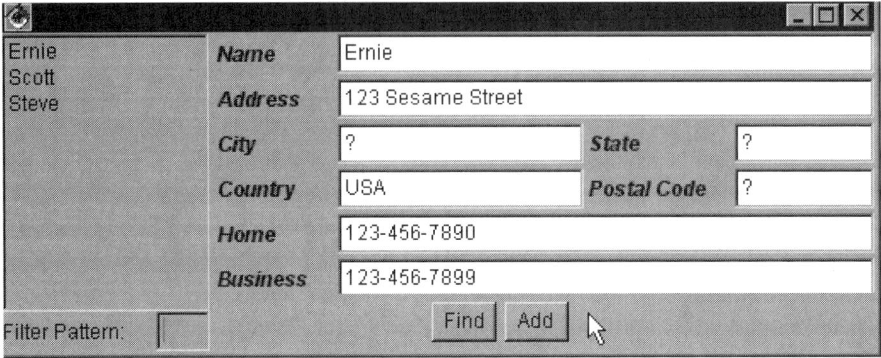

Filtering Is Only the Beginning

The above examples demonstrate some simple filters and some of the techniques involved in their creation. You can apply similar filtering to sort the names in the list. Note that you do not want to change the real data order with a sort, only the order in which the data appears. The following code provides a sort for the displayed names. The entire model is similar to the PatternedAddressBook example, without the pattern property.

```
public AddressDataModel[] getAddresses() {
  AddressDataModel[] data = getRealAddressBook().getAddresses();
  AddressDataModel[] sorted = new AddressDataModel[data.length];
  System.arraycopy(data, 0, sorted, 0, data.length);
```

Figure 16.6 With a pattern.

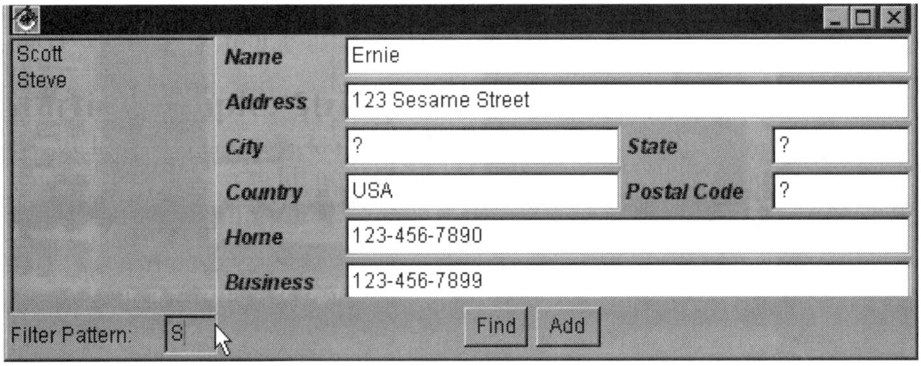

```
  // do a simple inefficient bubble sort
  for (int i = 0; i < sorted.length - 1; i++)
    for (int j = i + 1; j < sorted.length; j++)
      if (sorted[i].getName().compareTo(sorted[j].getName()) > 0) {
        AddressDataModel temp = sorted[i];
        sorted[i] = sorted[j];
        sorted[j] = temp;
      }
  return sorted;
}
```

Apply this filter *around* the pattern filter, so that you sort only the reduced data. A sample application design appears in Figure 16.7. For this example, you have the unfortunate necessity to actually create extra arrays to represent the reduced and filtered data. For other cases, such as with JTable, a sorting model can simply track a mapping of rows and modify the requested row number, similar to the column mapping you used to omit and reverse the table columns.

Note that this example shows how useful the separate Patterned interface has become. In this example, the list delegate uses the sorting model as its model, but it uses the pattern model to set the filter pattern. The separation of the two interfaces enables you this flexibility. Otherwise, you would have needed to provide the pattern in the sorting model.

Figure 16.7 A sorted list application.

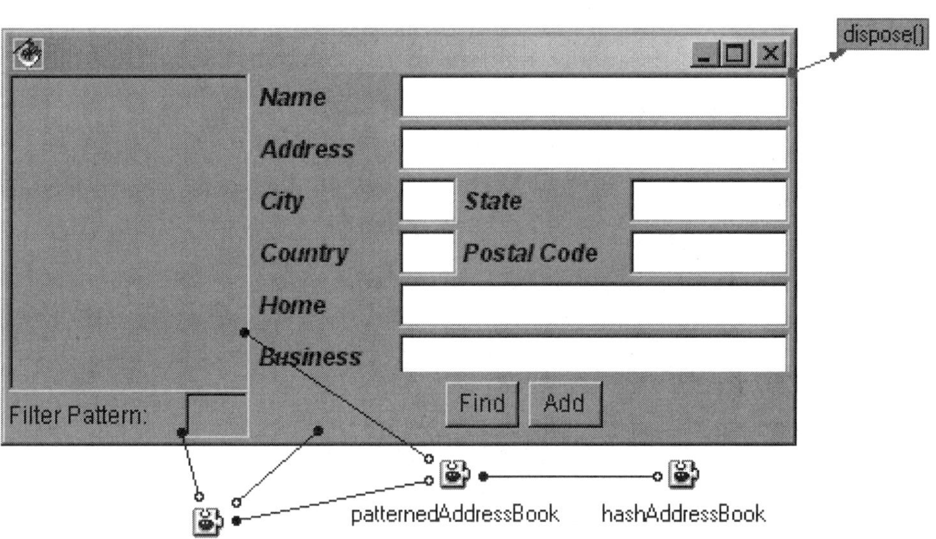

Models as Joins

Sometimes the data you need is not available in a single location. Suppose, for example, that your address data resides in two different models (but both models still implement the same model interface). Some of the data might be in your personal address book, while other data might be in your work address book.

Filter models can have more than one source of their real data. A filter could combine data from two or more real models. A join filter enables a delegate to display data from multiple sources as though there were a single source. As an example, you will use an implementation of Swing's TableModel as a joined model.

```
import javax.swing.*;
import javax.swing.event.*;
import javax.swing.table.*;
import java.beans.*;

/**
 * A Join Model, combining the columns in two models
 */
public class TwoTableJoinTableModel
       extends AbstractTableModel
       implements TableModelListener {
  protected transient PropertyChangeSupport propertyChange;
  private TableModel fieldModel1 = null;
  private TableModel fieldModel2 = null;

  /** Return the type of the column, mapping the column into
   *  the appropriate table
   */
  public Class getColumnClass(int columnIndex) {
    int col1Count = getModel1().getColumnCount();
    if (columnIndex < col1Count)
      return getModel1().getColumnClass(columnIndex);
    else
      return getModel2().getColumnClass(columnIndex - col1Count);
  }

  /** Return the number of columns, which is the sum of the
   *  the number of columns in each joined table
   */
  public int getColumnCount() {
    return getModel1().getColumnCount() +
           getModel2().getColumnCount();
  }
```

```
/** Return the name of the column, mapping the column into
 *  the appropriate table
 */
public String getColumnName(int columnIndex) {
  int col1Count = getModel1().getColumnCount();
  if (columnIndex < col1Count)
    return getModel1().getColumnName(columnIndex);
  else
    return getModel2().getColumnName(columnIndex - col1Count);
}

/** return the number of rows in this table — we'll use
 *  the maximum number of rows in either joined table
 */
public int getRowCount() {
  return Math.max(getModel1().getRowCount(),
                  getModel2().getRowCount());
}

/** get the row/column value, mapping it to the appropriate
 *  real table position. If an empty position is requested,
 *  we return null
 */
public Object getValueAt(int rowIndex, int columnIndex) {
  int col1Count = getModel1().getColumnCount();
  if (columnIndex < col1Count) {
    if (rowIndex < getModel1().getRowCount())
      return getModel1().getValueAt(rowIndex, columnIndex);
  }
  else
    if (rowIndex < getModel2().getRowCount())
      return getModel2().getValueAt(rowIndex,
                                    columnIndex - col1Count);
  return null;
}

/** set the row/column value, mapping it to the appropriate
 *  real table position. If an empty position is requested,
 *  we return null
 */
public void setValueAt(Object aValue, int rowIndex,
                       int columnIndex) {
  int col1Count = getModel1().getColumnCount();
  if (columnIndex < col1Count)
```

```
      getModel1().setValueAt(aValue, rowIndex, columnIndex);
    else
      getModel2().setValueAt(aValue, rowIndex,
                             columnIndex - col1Count);
  }

  /** delegate the check to see if a cell is editable to the
   *  appropriate real model
   */
  public boolean isCellEditable(int rowIndex, int columnIndex) {
    int col1Count = getModel1().getColumnCount();
    if (columnIndex < col1Count) {
      if (rowIndex < getModel1().getRowCount())
        return getModel1().isCellEditable(rowIndex, columnIndex);
    }
    else
      if (rowIndex < getModel2().getRowCount())
        return getModel2().isCellEditable(rowIndex,
                                     columnIndex-col1Count);
    return false;
  }

  // properties to track the two real models
  public TableModel getModel1() {
    return fieldModel1;
  }

  public TableModel getModel2() {
    return fieldModel2;
  }

  // The set methods need to add us as a listener
  //   so that we can forward the events to _our_ listeners
  public void setModel1(TableModel model1) {
    if (fieldModel1 != null)
      fieldModel1.removeTableModelListener(this);
    TableModel oldValue = fieldModel1;
    fieldModel1 = model1;
    fieldModel1.addTableModelListener(this);
    firePropertyChange("model1", oldValue, model1);
  }

  public void setModel2(TableModel model2) {
    if (fieldModel1 != null)
```

```
      fieldModel1.removeTableModelListener(this);
    TableModel oldValue = fieldModel2;
    fieldModel2 = model2;
    fieldModel1.addTableModelListener(this);
    firePropertyChange("model2", oldValue, model2);
  }

  /** Catch the table model events of the real
   *  models and refire it to _our_ listeners
   */
  public void tableChanged(TableModelEvent e) {
    fireTableChanged(new TableModelEvent(this,
                                         e.getFirstRow(),
                                         e.getLastRow(),
                                         e.getColumn(),
                                         e.getType()));
  }

  // standard bound property support
  public synchronized void addPropertyChangeListener(
                               PropertyChangeListener listener) {
    getPropertyChange().addPropertyChangeListener(listener);
  }

  public void firePropertyChange(String propertyName,
                                 Object oldValue,
                                 Object newValue) {
    getPropertyChange().firePropertyChange(propertyName,
                                           oldValue, newValue);
  }

  public synchronized void removePropertyChangeListener(
                               PropertyChangeListener listener) {
    getPropertyChange().removePropertyChangeListener(listener);
  }

  protected PropertyChangeSupport getPropertyChange() {
    if (propertyChange == null) {
      propertyChange = new java.beans.PropertyChangeSupport(this);
    };
    return propertyChange;
  }
}
```

Figure 16.8 A join model.

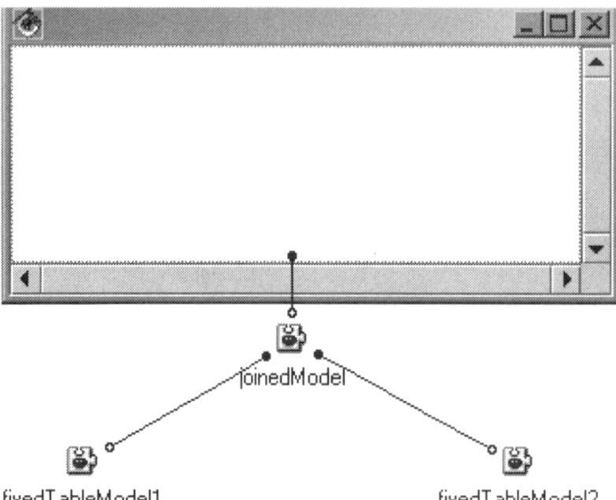

To use this new model, you simply need to connect two real models to a join model and then connect the join model to one or more delegates. An example of this appears in Figure 16.8.

Figure 16.9 shows the results of running the previous application.

Figure 16.9 Running the join model application.

A	B	C	D	E	F	A	B	C	D	E	F
0,0	1,0	2,0	3,0	4,0	5,0	0,0	1,0	2,0	3,0	4,0	5,0
0,1	1,1	2,1	3,1	4,1	5,1	0,1	1,1	2,1	3,1	4,1	5,1
0,2	1,2	2,2	3,2	4,2	5,2	0,2	1,2	2,2	3,2	4,2	5,2
0,3	1,3	2,3	3,3	4,3	5,3	0,3	1,3	2,3	3,3	4,3	5,3
0,4	1,4	2,4	3,4	4,4	5,4	0,4	1,4	2,4	3,4	4,4	5,4
0,5	1,5	2,5	3,5	4,5	5,5	0,5	1,5	2,5	3,5	4,5	5,5
0,6	1,6	2,6	3,6	4,6	5,6	0,6	1,6	2,6	3,6	4,6	5,6
0,7	1,7	2,7	3,7	4,7	5,7	0,7	1,7	2,7	3,7	4,7	5,7
0,8	1,8	2,8	3,8	4,8	5,8	0,8	1,8	2,8	3,8	4,8	5,8
0,9	1,9	2,9	3,9	4,9	5,9	0,9	1,9	2,9	3,9	4,9	5,9
0,10	1,10	2,10	3,10	4,10	5,10	0,10	1,10	2,10	3,10	4,10	5,...
0,11	1,11	2,11	3,11	4,11	5,11	0,11	1,11	2,11	3,11	4,11	5,...
0,12	1,12	2,12	3,12	4,12	5,12	0,12	1,12	2,12	3,12	4,12	5,...
0,13	1,13	2,13	3,13	4,13	5,13	0,13	1,13	2,13	3,13	4,13	5

Figure 16.10 Filters are models too.

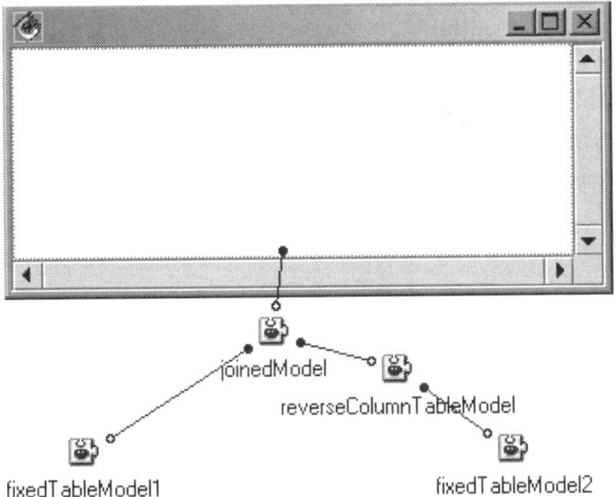

Note that the join model communicates with its real models only through the model interface. This means that you could plug in any other model into that interface. For example, you could use ReverseColumnTableModel from earlier in this chapter to change the behavior of one of the real models before joining them, as shown in Figure 16.10. You can see the difference this makes in Figure 16.11.

Figure 16.11 The data appears different, but the GUI looks the same.

A	B	C	D	E	F	F	E	D	C	B	A
0,0	1,0	2,0	3,0	4,0	5,0	5,0	4,0	3,0	2,0	1,0	0,0
0,1	1,1	2,1	3,1	4,1	5,1	5,1	4,1	3,1	2,1	1,1	0,1
0,2	1,2	2,2	3,2	4,2	5,2	5,2	4,2	3,2	2,2	1,2	0,2
0,3	1,3	2,3	3,3	4,3	5,3	5,3	4,3	3,3	2,3	1,3	0,3
0,4	1,4	2,4	3,4	4,4	5,4	5,4	4,4	3,4	2,4	1,4	0,4
0,5	1,5	2,5	3,5	4,5	5,5	5,5	4,5	3,5	2,5	1,5	0,5
0,6	1,6	2,6	3,6	4,6	5,6	5,6	4,6	3,6	2,6	1,6	0,6
0,7	1,7	2,7	3,7	4,7	5,7	5,7	4,7	3,7	2,7	1,7	0,7
0,8	1,8	2,8	3,8	4,8	5,8	5,8	4,8	3,8	2,8	1,8	0,8
0,9	1,9	2,9	3,9	4,9	5,9	5,9	4,9	3,9	2,9	1,9	0,9
0,10	1,10	2,10	3,10	4,10	5,10	5,10	4,10	3,10	2,10	1,10	0,10
0,11	1,11	2,11	3,11	4,11	5,11	5,11	4,11	3,11	2,11	1,11	0,11
0,12	1,12	2,12	3,12	4,12	5,12	5,12	4,12	3,12	2,12	1,12	0,12

> **NOTE**
>
> Be careful with connection order—make sure the connections fire from the bottom up. The lowest level models should send their values to the filters before the filters send their values to the delegate. Use the **Reorder Connections From** command from the pop-up menu for each model object to see which connections are fired first.

Keep in mind that filters are models too. Because of this, you can nest filters as deeply as you would like with very little overhead (unless they perform a very complex filtering operation).

Thinking More about Proxies

The idea of using models as proxies is incredibly powerful. Not only can you filter local data, but you could also use proxy models to access data in a database or across a network. This behavior is similar to the filters presented so far, but rather than use a realModel property, you can obtain the actual data using JDBC calls, Java Remote Method Invocation (RMI), or through your own custom network protocol.

Proxy models extend your reach and enable you to use *existing* data, *wherever* that data may be. Remember that models simply provide interpretation of your data so that a delegate can obtain that data.

Selection Models

So far, your phone application contains a list of names and an entry/display area for a specific record. The next logical step is to enable the user to select a name from the list delegate and have it displayed in the other delegate. Where do you store the current selection?

A common reaction is to put the selection information into the model. Because both delegates share the same model, they can access the same selection status. When one changes the selection, the other can see it.

Unfortunately, this does not enable you to display data from the same model in two different delegates *with different selections*. For example, it may be useful to display a list of addresses in three different lists in the user interface, perhaps in an application that maps a route between several locations. The immediate reaction might be to move the selection status to the delegate.

Again, you lose, because you cannot share the selection. If you cannot put the selection in either the delegate or the model, you must put it somewhere else. That other place is called a selection model.

Figure 16.12 Selection models: to share...

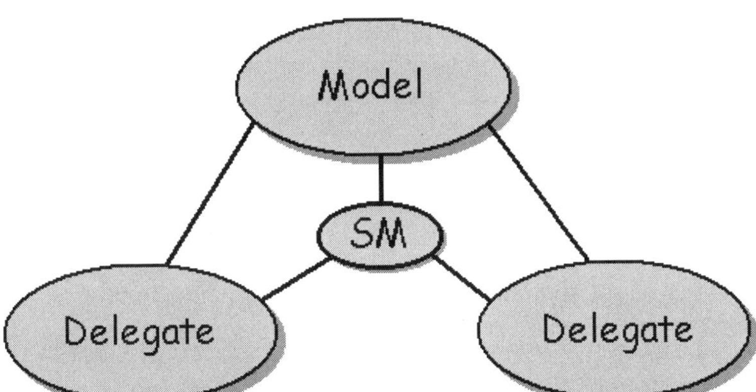

Enter the Selection Model

A selection model fits between a delegate and its model. The delegate may use a selection model, or it may not. The delegate could share the same selection model used by other delegates, or it may use a separate selection model. This provides a great deal of flexibility in your application. The delegates and models do not care about each other or how anyone is using a selection. Figure 16.12 displays the general pattern of a selection model, with two delegates sharing the same selection model (labeled "SM" on the diagram). Figure 16.13 displays a similar arrangement, but each delegate uses a separate selection model.

Figure 16.13 ...or not to share.

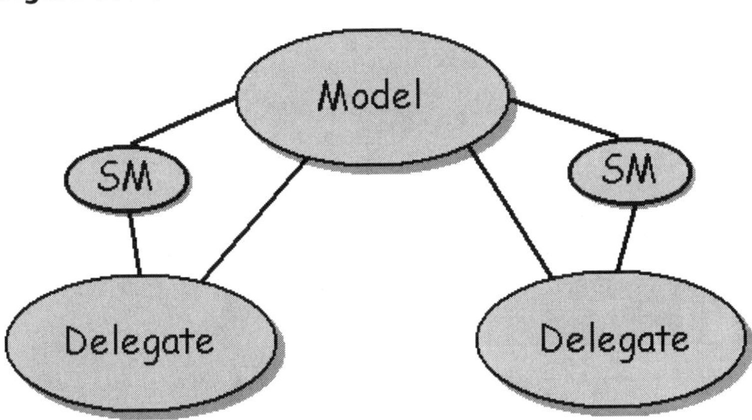

Note the paths of communication in both scenarios. The delegates communicate with the model normally, but they also communicate with a selection model. The selection model tracks the details of which item they should display as selected. Note the extra communication between the selection model and the model. The selection model is a delegate of the model. This is necessary in case someone removes the selected item from the model or its structure changes. This presents an interesting situation: You can use an object as *both* a model *and* a delegate!

Implementing a Selection Model

Your example application would benefit greatly from the addition of a selection model. You will share a selection model between the list delegate and the entry/display delegate.

A selection model needs to track a current selection status. This status can be either a single selection or multiple selections. This is useful for components such as a list, table, or tree, where you can enable a user to select several items. A very generic selection model would provide a set of selection information and enable an application to determine how much data a user can select. For your sample application, implement a simpler selection model that tracks a single selection using a bound property.

The selection model follows. Note that once again you choose an interface to represent the selection model. This enables you to replace the model (if needed) without requiring changes to a delegate. This model interface defines a single bound property of type AddressDataModel and the bound-property support methods.

```
import effectivevaj.vce.mvc.*;

import java.beans.*;
public interface AddressDataSelectionModel{
  public void addPropertyChangeListener(
                PropertyChangeListener listener) ;
  public AddressBookModel getModel() ;
  public AddressDataModel getSelection() ;
  public void removePropertyChangeListener(
                PropertyChangeListener listener) ;
  public void setModel(AddressBookModel model) ;
  public void setSelection(AddressDataModel selection) ;
}
```

Implement this using a very straightforward bean implementation. The only trick is handling changes in the model from which it gets data. Whenever the model changes, you need to check if the selection still exists in the model.

```
import effectivevaj.vce.mvc.*;
import java.beans.*;
```

```
/**
 * A simple selection model that tracks
 * and address in a phone book
 */
public class AddressDataSelectionModel
       implements PropertyChangeListener {
  protected transient PropertyChangeSupport propertyChange;
  private AddressDataModel fieldSelection;
  private AddressBookModel fieldModel;

  // standard bound property support omitted for brevity

  // model property keeps track of the model that contains the
  //   selection
  public AddressBookModel getModel() {
    return fieldModel;
  }

  public void setModel(AddressBookModel model) {
    // if we had a model before, remove us as a listener
    if (fieldModel != null)
      fieldModel.removePropertyChangeListener(this);
    AddressBookModel oldValue = fieldModel;
    fieldModel = model;

    // add us as a listener so we can make sure the selection
    //   still exists in the model
    fieldModel.addPropertyChangeListener(this);
    firePropertyChange("model", oldValue, model);
  }

  // selection property tracks which address is currently
  //   selected
  public AddressDataModel getSelection() {
    return fieldSelection;
  }

  public void setSelection(AddressDataModel selection) {
    AddressDataModel oldValue = fieldSelection;
    fieldSelection = selection;
    firePropertyChange("selection", oldValue, selection);
  }
```

```
  /** listen for changes in the model where the selection
   *    comes from. If we find out that the selection is
   *    no longer in the model, we kill it...
   */
  public void propertyChange(PropertyChangeEvent evt) {
    // if the model's list of addresses changes,
    //   check to be sure that the selection is still
    //   there
    if (evt.getPropertyName().equals("addresses")) {
      AddressDataModel[] data = getModel().getAddresses();
      for (int i = 0; i < data.length; i++)
        if (getSelection().getName().equals(data[i].getName()))
          return;
      // if not found, clear the selection
      AddressDataModel sel = getSelection();
      sel.setAddress("");
      sel.setBusinessPhone("");
      sel.setCity("");
      sel.setCountry("");
      sel.setHomePhone("");
      sel.setName("");
      sel.setPostalCode("");
      sel.setState("");
    }
  }
}
```

Once you have defined the interface for the selection model, you can update your delegates to interact with the selection. Figure 16.14 shows the patterned list delegate, updated with a selection model.

Figure 16.14 Using selection in the list delegate.

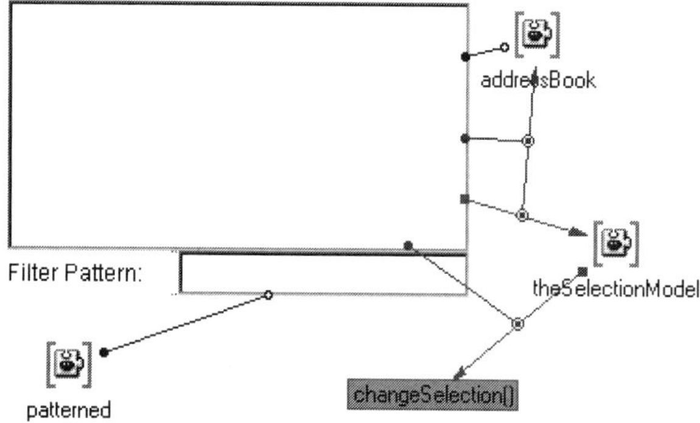

This new delegate provides two-way communication with the selection. When the user selects an item in the list, it fires an itemStateChanged event. You use this event to set the selection in the selection model variable. The value for the selection comes from the model's find() method, which is passed the selectedItem property of the List bean.

The other direction is a bit simpler. When the selection property in the selection model changes, call the changeSelection() method via an event-to-code connection. Pass the AddressDataModel from the selection property as the first parameter by selecting the **Pass event data** option for the connection. Then, pass a reference to the List bean so you can update it. The code for changeSelection, shown below, walks the items in the list to see which item number matches the selection's name; then it selects the item.

```
public void changeSelection(AddressDataModel data, List list) {
  // find which item matches the selection
  for(int i=0; i<list.getItemCount(); i++)
    if (list.getItem(i).equals(data.getName())) {
      list.select(i);
      return; // we are done!
    }
}
```

Finally, promote the *this* property of the selection model variable so you can set it from the outside. You now have a list delegate that can set its selection data. If other delegates use the same selection model instance, the selection model notifies them of the change and can update their appearance.

Figure 16.15 shows the changes you make to the entry/display delegate. Build on the AddressBookUI from Chapter 15. Make a copy of it and change the way it accesses the selection information.

Figure 16.15 Using selection in the entry/display delegate.

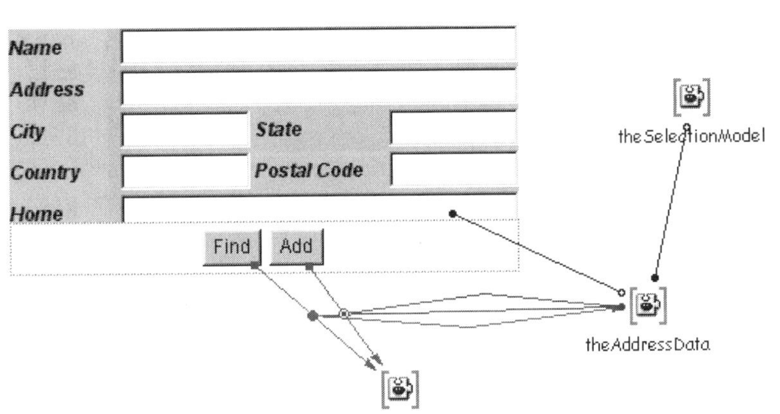

Figure 16.16 The new application assembly.

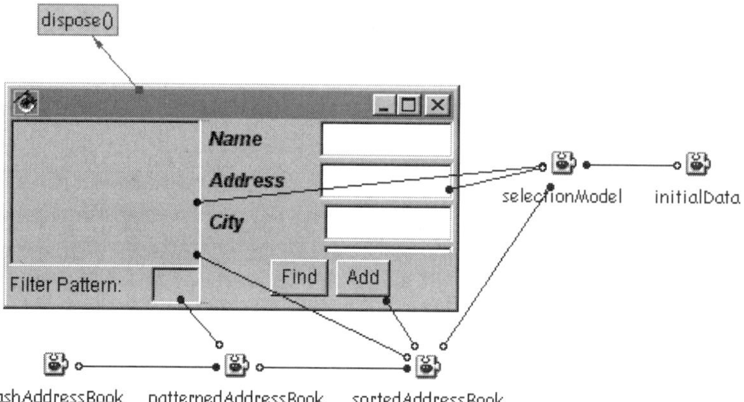

Add a selection model, and link its selection property to the address data variable. This updates the selection whenever you find an entry, and updates the address data whenever the selection changes from outside. By promoting the selection model variable, you enable the data to be set from the outside.

One key issue here is that you must have an initial piece of data. You set this initial data in the selection model outside the delegate, passing it to the selection model as the initial selection.

Assemble the application as shown in Figure 16.16. This new application passes an instance of the selection model to each delegate. Whenever you select an item from the list, the result appears in the entry/display delegate. Whenever you find an entry in the entry/display delegate, the name appears selected in the list delegate.

The final application has combined several of the elements you have used in this chapter. At the heart of the application is a HashAddressBook instance containing the real data. Filter the data through a PatternedAddressBook instance so you can limit the accessed entries via a pattern. Pass the results through a SortedAddressBook instance for a more natural display.

Add an AddressDataSelectionModel implementation into the picture, linking it to both delegates so they share the selection. Because the selection model should watch the real data, connect it to the SortedAddressBook model. Finally, to give you an initial AddressDataModel object, use a SimpleAddressData instance called initialData set to the selectionModel's selection property. The results of a sample execution appear in Figure 16.17.

Figure 16.17 Running your final application.

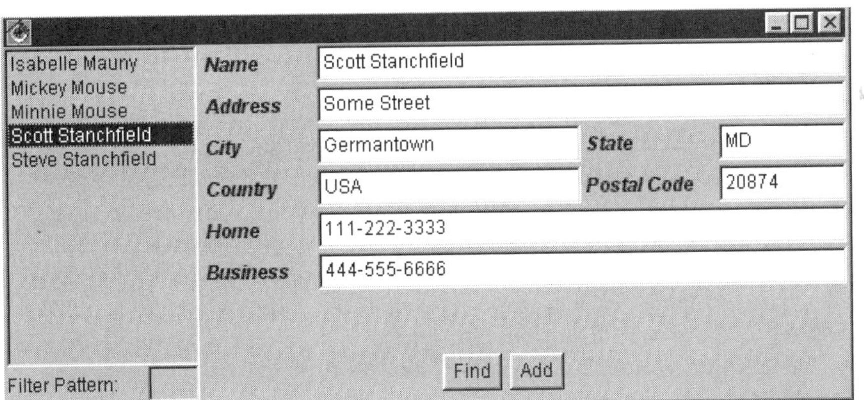

Food for Thought

We could keep expounding the benefits of the Model-View-Controller paradigm, but space and time simply do not permit. We leave you with the following ideas to pursue, keeping in mind the key ingredients in any good Model-View-Controller design: abstraction and indirection.

Documentation

While thoughts of documenting your use of Model-View-Controller may send shudders down your spine, it is *very* necessary. First, do not be afraid to state in your comments that you are applying MVC (though you should spell it out "Model-View-Controller" when possible). Placing statements at the top of each class can help your maintenance programmer know what to look for.

Second, provide design documents that list the model and listener interfaces you use and which delegates listen to which models. This can actually be a very simple and short document, but it will be one of the most useful ones available to maintenance programmers.

Third, point to resources, such as this chapter and Chapter 15, which explain the MVC usage in your code. Some maintenance programmers may not agree with a design pattern, and providing sources of explanation may help them see the benefits.

Finally, document the intended use of your interfaces and stress that later delegates should talk *only* to the model interfaces. Sometimes a class diagram, using a tool such as Rational Rose, can help the explanation, but at least provide a description of the interactions and why you chose the design.

Advanced Delegates

You can expand delegates in the same manner as you did for models, though it is not as common. One possible scenario that is quite easy to implement is a remote view of a model. The delegate that speaks to the model acts as a proxy for a *real* delegate on another machine. The proxy obtains data from the model and forwards it across a network to another delegate that reads that data and displays it for the remote user.

Such a proxy can make remote technical support significantly easier. The application normally attaches a local delegate to the model for the user interaction. The user can turn on a special technical support option, which simply adds another delegate to the model. This new delegate proxies the display to a technical support representative at your site. This type of delegate proxy can provide a significant benefit during a technical support call, as the support personnel can see and possibly modify the behavior of the application as it runs.

Debugging is another use of extra delegates. You can attach a debugging delegate to your model to dump the model contents and report the event notification. If your model provides additional methods to expose its details, such a debugger could present an ideal view of those inner workings. One of the key advantages of the Model-View-Controller paradigm is that the debugger does not affect the other delegates, and the isolation from the model helps ensure that the behavior while debugging does not differ from the behavior during normal execution.

Of course, if you combine these ideas, your technical support personnel can remotely debug the user's application.

Summary

We have spent a great deal of time discussing the Model-View-Controller paradigm. The nature of VisualAge for Java and its support for beans and visual composition, make it an ideal tool to implement this paradigm. Likewise, the Model-View-Controller paradigm is ideal for VisualAge for Java, as it greatly simplifies visual design and maintenance of your programs.

If Model-View-Controller is new to you, take some time to carefully read the examples we have presented as well as try some simple examples of your own. The pattern may seem complex at first, but once you become accustomed to it, you can easily apply it and recognize it in other applications. Your maintenance programmers will thank you for a more flexible design.

In the next chapter, we discuss an often-misunderstood part of the VCE, factory beans. When reading the next chapter, keep in mind that this is very different from the factory we discussed in Chapter 15. Nevertheless, it can be a very useful tool when constructing your application.

FACTORY BEANS

17

Sometimes your visual design requires some dynamic components. Maybe you want to add an extra button to your GUI, create an instance of a class to hold some data, or fire a new event. The VCE provides a pseudo-component called a *Factory* bean to help you create new instances of classes. Factory beans act as variables that you can easily set to a new instance. However, there is a difference: You have access to additional constructors.

In this chapter, we'll examine the Factory bean and some common uses for it. We'll see some examples of how the Factory bean can make your application more dynamic and enable you to work with non-beans in the VCE.

When to Use Factory Beans

The Factory bean is one of the least understood tools in VisualAge for Java. However, it is actually quite easy to work with. Look at the example shown in Figure 17.1. When a user clicks the Add button, buttonFactory creates a new instance of Button and sets itself to point to that instance. The two connections leading from buttonFactory start on its *this* property (that is, when the variable changes). These connections end by adding the button to contentsPane and validating the Frame bean. Thus, whenever the user clicks the Add button, a new button appears.

While the above example is interesting, it is not a realistic use of a Factory bean. In a real application, you could use Factory beans to:

- Create storage for user input values.
- Create event objects to fire (see Chapter 7, "Introduction to JavaBeans Components," for details on the bean event model).
- Create instances of a dialog.
- Create instances of another frame.
- Create an instance of a class that is not a bean. (That is, a class that is not Serializable. Note that the VCE can directly use non-beans that have a public default constructor, but they are still not considered beans.)

Figure 17.1 A simple Factory bean example.

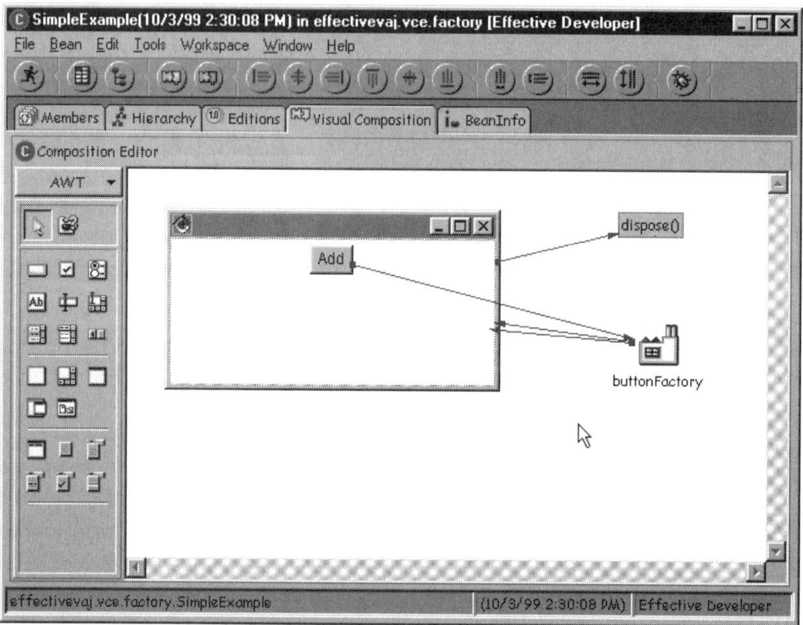

These uses fall into two categories: temporary storage creation and lazy instantiation.

Temporary Storage Creation

A Factory bean provides a visual way to create new instances of data objects. For example, let's create a CD catalog program. This CD catalog program stores its data in a hash table.

> **NOTE**
>
> The purpose of this example is to help you understand how a Factory bean works; we would not expect you to create an actual program in this manner. Instead, if you were to create such a program, we recommend applying the Model-View-Controller paradigm discussed in Chapters 15 and 16.

Suppose that you create the GUI shown in Figure 17.2. This GUI provides entry fields for the artist and title of a CD. These entry fields are associated with two bound string properties of a CDData bean. Anytime the user changes the

Figure 17.2 A problematic application.

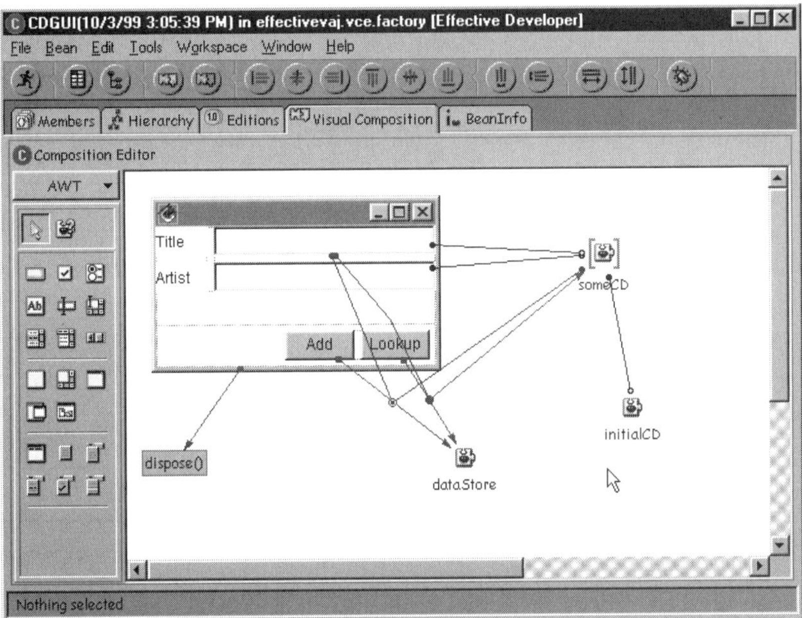

strings in the entry fields, the generated code updates the CDData bean. Because the CDData bean is represented as a variable in the visual design, it can be changed to point to another instance of CDData. Because the variable is initially null, you drop an instance of CDData to initialize it via a property-to-property connection.

This application has a critical flaw in its connection logic. The Add button adds the current CDData instance to the Hashtable instance (via its get() method), and the Lookup button finds a matching instance. At first glance, this application may appear to do the right thing. Watch what happens in a typical scenario. Note that if you do not share our taste in music feel free to replace the titles and artists used in this example with anything of your choice (except "Mambo No. 5," please).

1. The user types "Goodbye Yellow Brick Road" for the title and "Elton John" for the artist.
2. initialCD's title and artist properties synchronize with the TextField beans as the user types them.
3. The user clicks the **Add** button. The generated code calls the put() method of the dataStore hash table, passing in the Title text and whenever instance someCD happens to be pointing to. This means that

"Goodbye Yellow Brick Road" is associated with the initialCD instance of CDData in Hashtable. Note that someCD still points to initialCD.

4. The user types "52nd Street" for the title and "Billy Joel" for the artist.
5. The property-to-property connections update the title and artist properties of whenever someCD happens to point to. Herein lies the problem: The someCD variable still points to the CD you just added to the hash table.
6. The user clicks the Add button. The generated code calls the put() method of the dataStore hash table, associating "52nd Street" with whatever someCD points to. Unfortunately, you now have two music titles pointing to the same piece of data.

The result: Whenever the user looks up a CD, they will always see the artist of the *last* CD information entered. This is obviously not the desired behavior.

To correct this problem, you need to create separate CDData instances for each entry in the hash table. You can do this in two places: before you add the data to the hash table, or after you add the data to the hash table. If you create the new instance before you add the data to the hash table, the problem is that when the user starts entering data for the *next* entry, they change the data stored for the *previous* entry. Therefore, you want to add the current data to the hash table and then create a new instance to work with.

To do this, drop a Factory bean in the design area of the VCE. The Factory bean is available on the Other page of the beans palette, as seen in Figure 17.3. Drop an instance of the Factory bean in the design area. Before you can do anything useful with it, you need to change its type by selecting **Change Type** from its pop-up menu. Change the Factory bean to represent type CDData; and change the bean's name to cdDataFactory. The result appears in Figure 17.4.

> **NOTE**
>
> In case you're wondering, the icon to the left of the Factory icon in Figure 17.3 is the variable tool. You can choose a variable by clicking on this and dropping it in the free-form area of the VCE, then changing its type via the **Change Type** option from its popup menu. However, it is much easier to drop a variable using the Choose Bean tool.

Factories are easy to use. In this example, all you want to do is point *someCD* to a new instance of CDData. Do this by adding another connection from the Add button's actionPerformed event to the desired constructor in the Factory bean. Figure 17.5 shows constructor selection as the target of an actionPerformed connection. This connection creates a new instance of CDData and points cdDataFactory to it. From this point on, cdDataFactory acts like a variable.

Figure 17.3 The Factory bean.

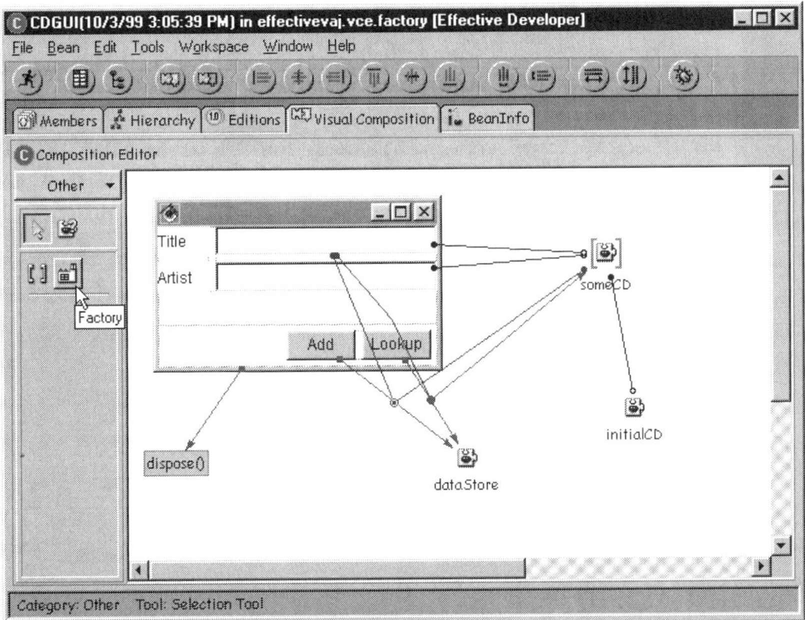

Figure 17.4 A CDData factory.

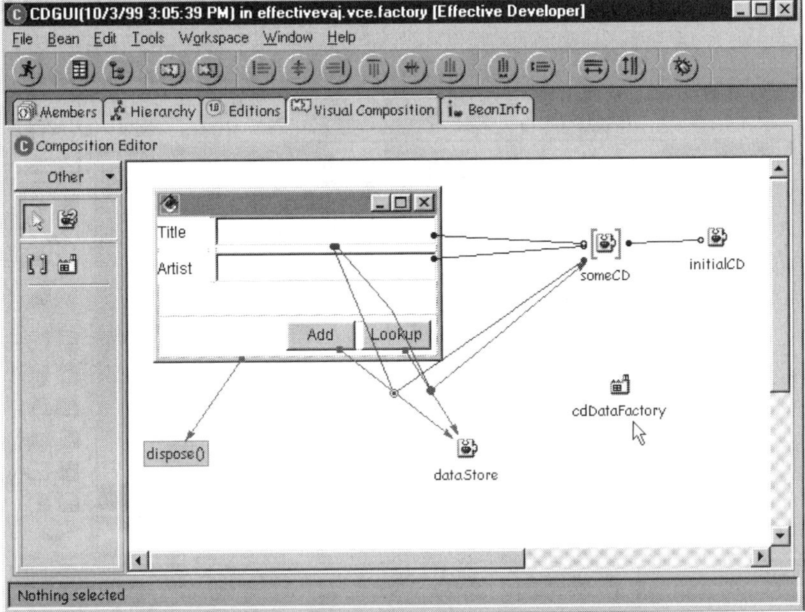

Figure 17.5 Selecting a constructor.

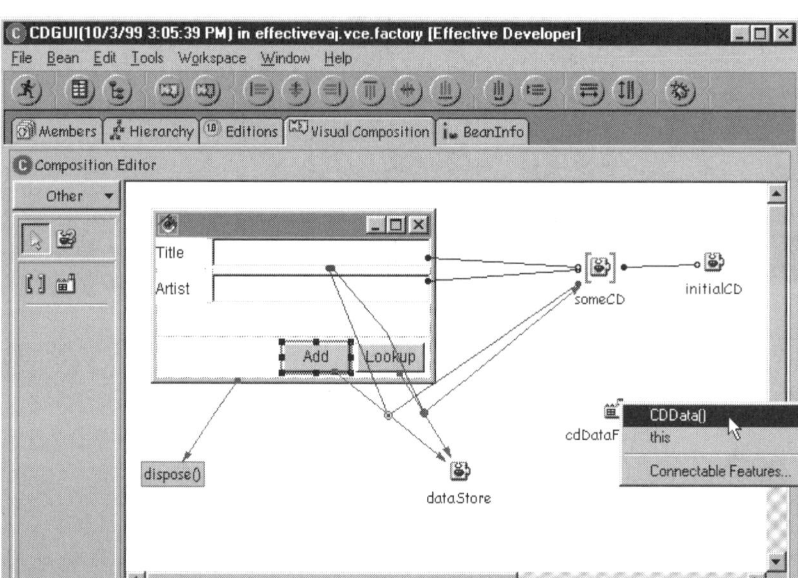

You can then create a property-to-property connection between the *this* property of cdDataFactory and the *this* property of someCD. This connection sets someCD to the new instance as soon as the factory creates it. The result appears in Figure 17.6.

The resulting visual design works exactly as expected. Each time the user clicks the Add button, the current instance is added to the Hashtable instance, and

> **NOTE**
>
> Think about the Factory bean *as a variable.* Looking at Figure 17.6, you should see that you could combine cdDataFactory and someCD. Remember, you can treat a Factory bean the same as a variable. To do this, you could drag the ends of all connections that touch someCD to cdDataFactory.
>
> Unfortunately, there is currently a bug that prevents this from working properly. Until the bug is fixed, you cannot set the Factory bean via the normalResult connection. IBM has acknowledged this bug and it will fix it in a later release.

Figure 17.6 Using the Factory bean.

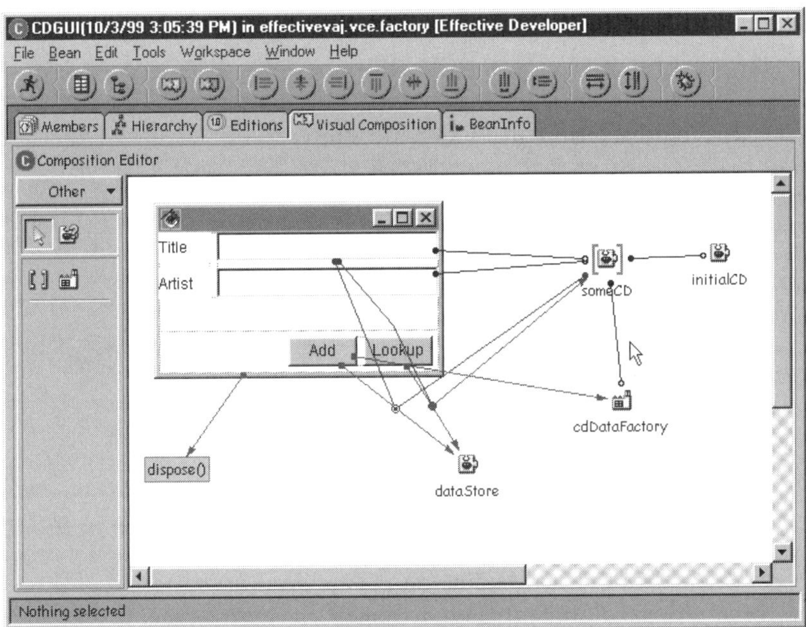

a new instance is created for them to play with. However, note the lack of flexibility in this application. The application is locked into using instances of a particular class. Use of factory models, as discussed in Chapter 16, "Advanced Model-View-Controller Techniques," or the Prototype pattern, is often a much better choice for these types of applications. In other words, this example should help explain *how* Factory beans work, but you should not pattern your applications after it.

Lazy Instantiation

A typical user may use only 10 to 20 percent of a large application. Think of a large word processing application. Many users only use simple editing and movement commands, occasionally spell-checking their document. Some users use a few extra features. Very few people use all (or even a large percentage) of a complex application's functionality.

Lazy instantiation means "delay creating an object until necessary." Applications accomplish this by providing a method to create an object if it does not exist. For example, a lazy instantiation method might look something like the following:

```
public Button getAddButton() {
  if (addButton == null) {
    addButton = new Button("Add");
```

```
        addButton.addActionListener(...);
        addButton.setForeground(Color.blue);
    }
    return addButton;
}
```

Note the basic logic of such a method: If the object is null, create it. In either case, return it. Exclusive use of such a method to access the button guarantees two things:

- The button will definitely exist when used.
- The button will *only* exist when used.

In your code, you would write:

```
getAddButton().setEnabled(false);
```

rather than directly use:

```
addButton.setEnabled(false);
```

The advantages to this type of programming is that you never need to worry *if* a variable was assigned before using it, and, if you never use it, you never perform the processing to create it. Depending on the application, performing lazy instantiation could provide a noticeable improvement in startup time. For example, if your application could present 45 different dialogs, waiting to create them until needed could boost startup performance, especially if any of them need to read or calculate data during initialization. However, if your application used only one or two simple dialogs, the difference probably would not be noticeable.

In the VCE, lazy instantiation is performed at two levels. First, *all instances in the visual design are lazily instantiated.* Each Button, Panel, sub-GUI and other form of bean are instantiated through a method like the one above. This allows you to reference any bean in the visual design without worrying whether it already exists. However, because all visual components and instances that have connections must be instantiated during startup, this level of lazy instantiation is only useful for the guarantee of existence. We discuss this in detail in Chapter 19, "Handwritten Code versus Generated Code."

The second level of lazy instantiation is user-controlled. You can create objects using Factory beans when you want to use them. The basic pattern is to drop a Factory bean that represents a subclass of Dialog, for example, then create and show() that dialog when needed. For example, suppose that you develop a HelloWorldDialog as shown in Figure 17.7. This dialog gets a user's name so we can say "hello."

You can use this visually in two ways. First, you could directly drop an instance of it in a design and call its show() method, as in Figure 17.8. Because the generated code must set up event handling, it instantiates the dialog as it initializes the application.

Figure 17.7 The HelloWord dialog.

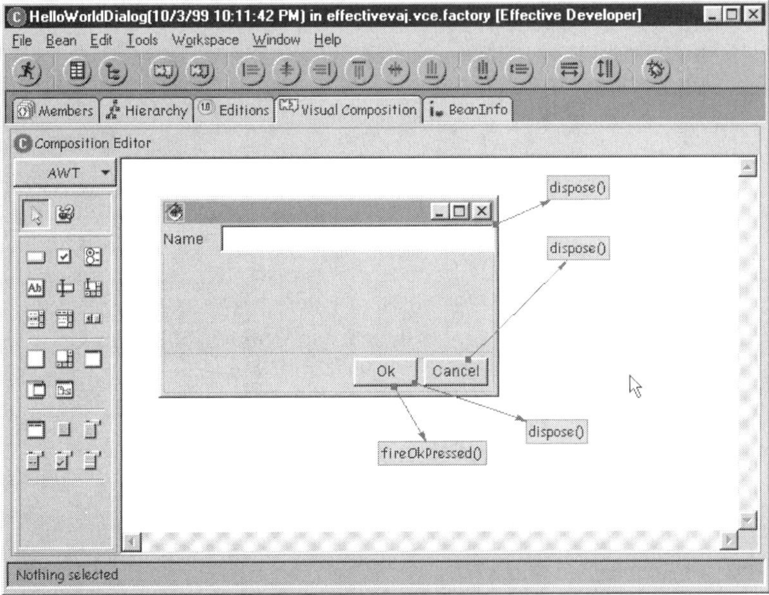

Figure 17.8 Explicit visual instantiation.

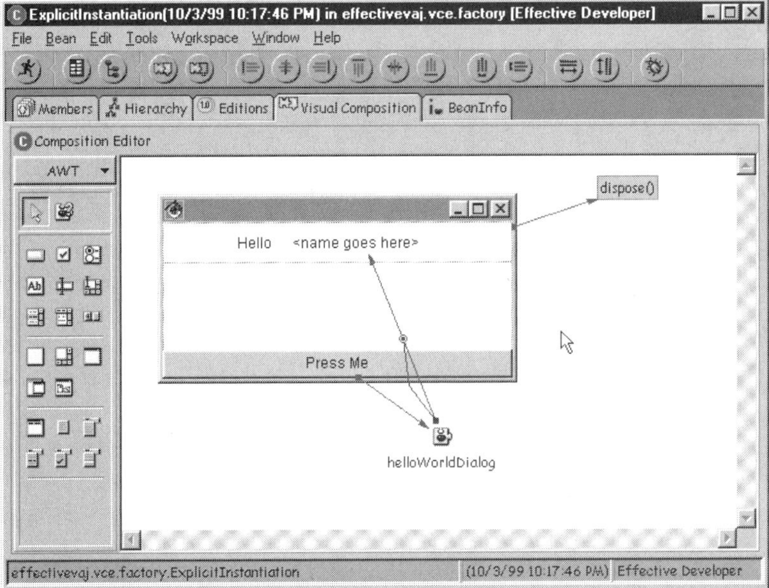

If the dialog had been large or needed to obtain some data during initialization, this could really slow down application startup. This is especially wasteful if the user never uses the dialog. To lazily instantiate the dialog, drop a Factory bean of type HelloWorldDialog and instantiate it when used. Figure 17.9 shows this scenario. Note that the Add button now creates an instance of the dialog before calling show().

Be aware that this creates a *new instance* each time the user clicks the button. If you no longer hold a reference to the old dialog, the old dialog becomes a candidate for garbage collection. This can cause unexpected behavior in your application, if, for example, you set state in the old dialog and expect that state to be present after clicking the button. If this is not the desired behavior, we suggest you write code to present the dialog rather than use a Factory bean. Alternatively, you could use a conditional pattern, such as the If bean discussed in Chapter 14, "Design Patterns for the VCE," but this is a case where a bit of code could be easier.

Implementing Event Percolation

In Chapter 14 we discussed a pattern called Event Percolation. The basic strategy of this pattern is to have a sub-GUI fire events that notify a compound GUI that it has performed a task. In some cases, you can easily implement this by promoting events in the sub-GUI. For example, you could implement the Ok/Cancel dialog like the one

Figure 17.9 Lazy visual instantiation.

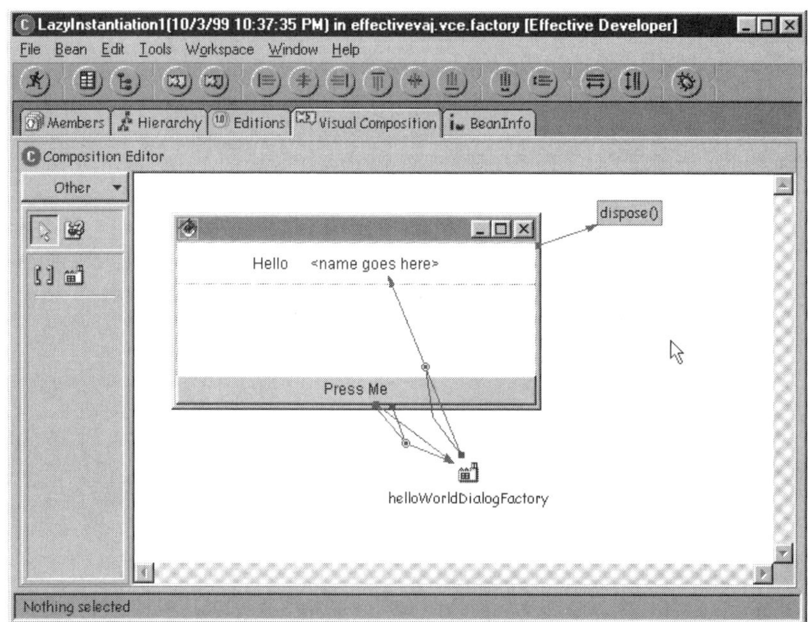

discussed in Chapter 14. This dialog provides two buttons, Ok and Cancel, and communicates with the composite bean via two events: okPressed (when the Ok button is clicked) and cancelPressed (when the Cancel button is clicked). We can do this by promoting the actionPerformed events of the Ok and Cancel buttons; the composite bean simply watches for these promoted events.

Sometimes, however, you need to pass data collected in the sub-GUI. Suppose, for example, that you designed the Find dialog shown in Figure 17.10. You can use event percolation to pass data from the dialog to whatever invokes it. This is an extremely useful application of the pattern. The invoker creates an instance of the dialog, registers a listener for the percolated event, and displays the dialog. If the user clicks the Find button, the dialog collects the user-entered information into an event and fires the event. If the user clicks the Cancel Button, it disposes the dialog.

For this example, we created the GUI shown in Figure 17.10 and then added a new listener interface called FindListener to it via the BeanInfo editor. The FindListener interface contains a single method: findRequested().The generated FindEvent was modified to hold the search string and match case value. The FindEvent receives these values via its constructor.

This is where the Factory bean comes in. Drop an instance of Factory bean in design area of the VCE; change its type to FindEvent and its name to findEventFactory. Then hook up the Find button to create a new FindEvent via

Figure 17.10 A simple Find dialog.

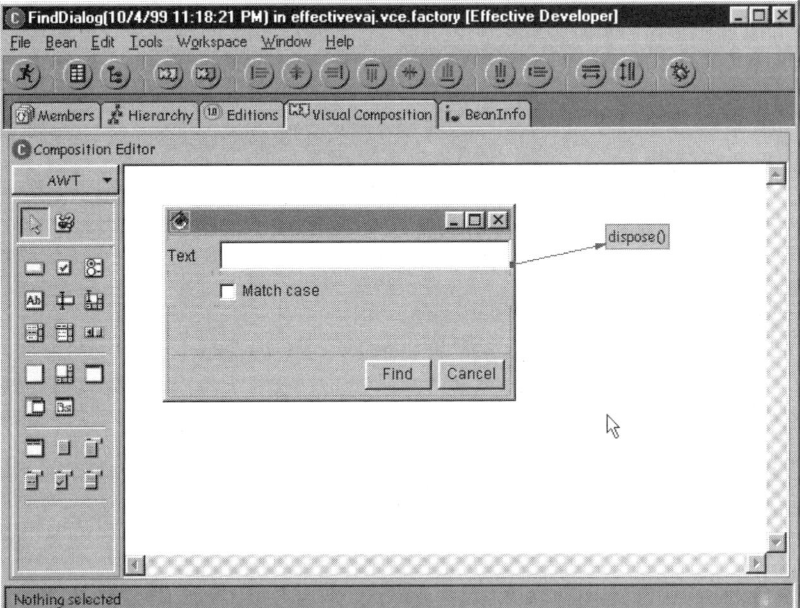

the Factory bean, shown in Figure 17.11. Then fill in the data for the event object's constructor. Once the Factory bean has created the event object, it is passed as event data to the fireFindRequested method via an event-to-code connection. Finally, have the Cancel button simply dispose the dialog. In the screenshots, we used a subclass for the Find/Cancel buttons that percolate their events.

The result of this dialog appears in Figure 17.12; it has some significant benefits:

The dialog is separate from whatever invokes it. The invoker knows only that the dialog fires an event and can interrogate the event for the required data. This enables you to change the dialog at will, as long as you pass the appropriate data via the event. The invoker never knows about the text field or check box, so you could change these implementation details anytime.

The invoker does not need to *wait* for the result of the dialog. This gives you an easy way to handle non-modal dialogs, simply by registering an event handler to do the processing. You can also create several instances of the same dialog, using the same or different event handlers.

Neither the dialog nor the invoker need know each other's details. You can reuse the dialog in other applications because it does not rely on this application's details to process the find request.

Figure 17.11 Creating a new FindEvent.

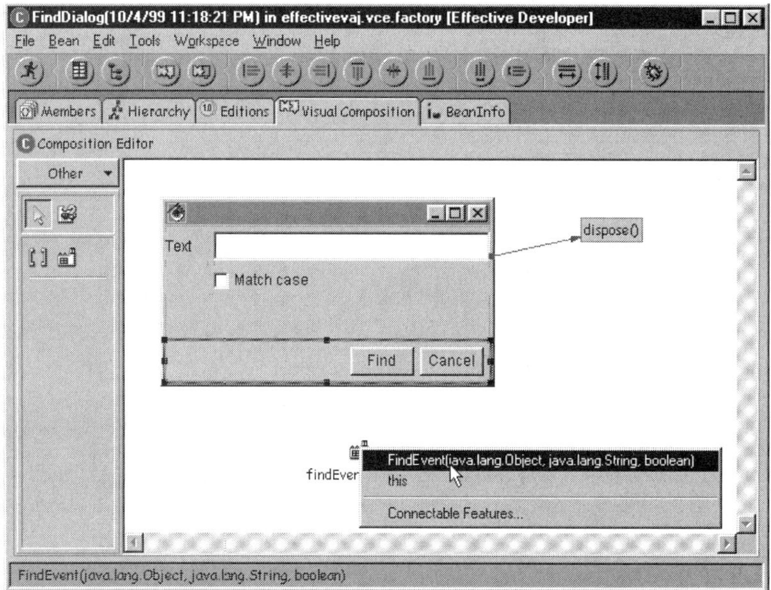

Figure 17.12 The final Find dialog.

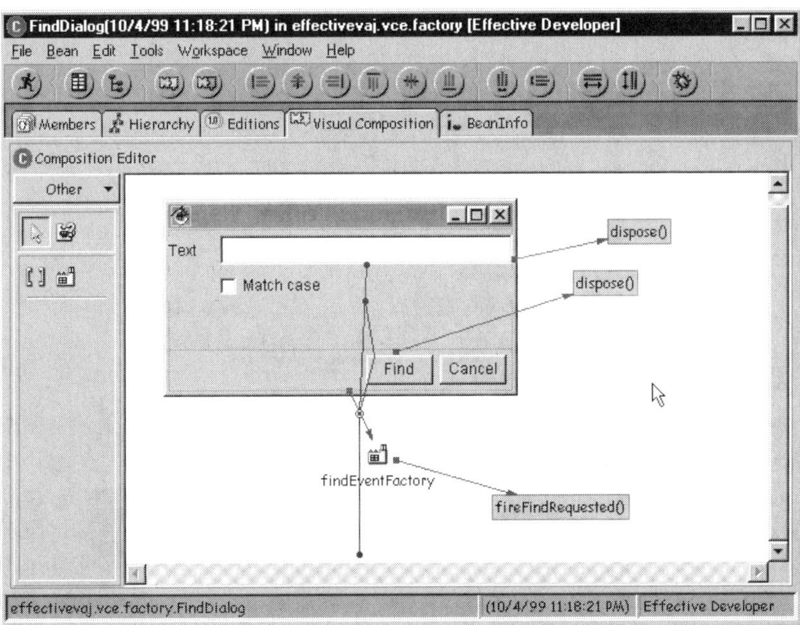

We use this as shown in Figure 17.13. In this example, the Find menu item calls show() on the FindDialog. If the FindDialog fires findRequested, set findEvent to the event data (using the event catcher pattern, described in Chapter 14). The variable detects that it has been set and fires connections to set the blank label to the search text.

Note how the invoking GUI obtains data only through findEvent. This provides excellent separation between the GUI parts of your application. You should always strive for this type of separation, as it provides excellent reusability and maintainability of your applications.

The application in Figure 17.13 can display a single FindDialog. A more flexible application would enable a user to bring up multiple dialogs, so they could have multiple searches ready, executing them by clicking their buttons. If you make a simple change to the application, you can display a new FindDialog each time the user chooses Find by using a Factory bean.

Modify the application shown in Figure 17.13, changing the instance of FindDialog to a Factory bean that creates FindDialogs, and adding a connection to create it before showing it. This results in the design shown in Figure 17.14. When the user chooses Find, the generated code creates a FindDialog and then displays it. When the factory creates the FindDialog, it then sets up the event handler to set findEvent.

Figure 17.13 Using the Find dialog.

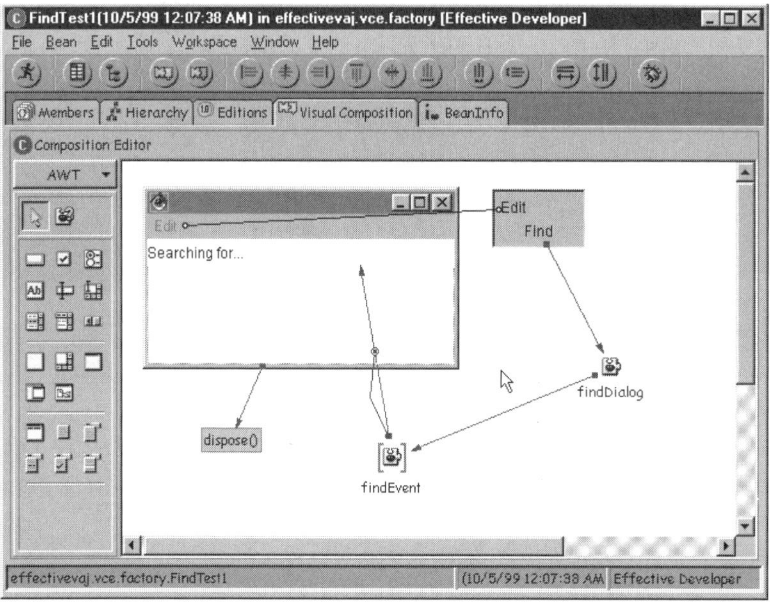

Figure 17.14 Creating multiple Find dialogs.

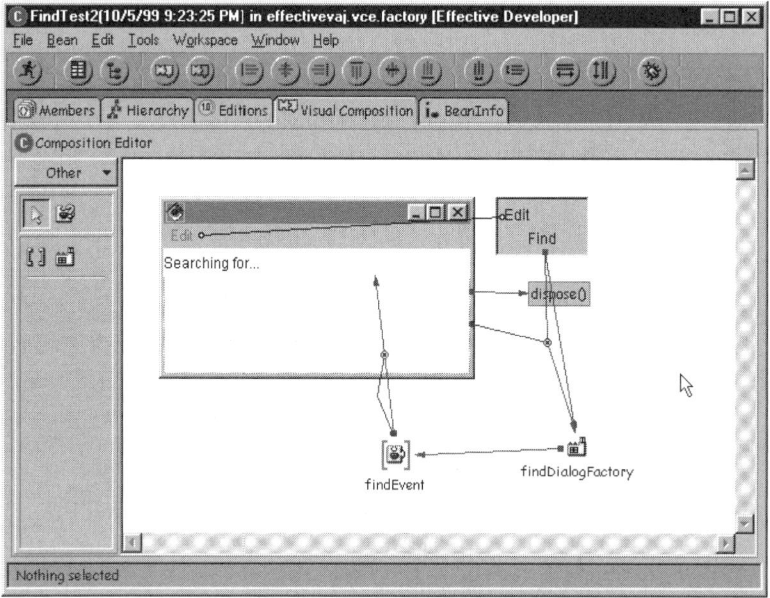

There is a small problem with this approach. When the user selects Find, a dialog appears. The user can enter some text and click the Find button; it fires the event. When the user selects Find again, a new dialog appears and its Find button fires an event. All seems well until the user clicks Find on the *first* dialog again.

The first dialog no longer fires events!

The problem is that when the factory creates a new FindDialog instance, *it disconnects the connections for the previous instance*. Again, the factory acts exactly like a variable, and a variable only holds connections to its current instance. We need to determine a method to work around this problem.

Looking at Figure 17.15, the problem is the connection between the findDialogFactory and findEvent. You need to replace this connection with your own code to perform the same function. Do this by deleting the problematic connection, and replacing it with an event-to-code connection to set up an event handler. This event-to-code connection starts on the *this* property of findDialogFactory and calls the following method:

```
public void registerFindEventCatcher(FindDialog dialog) {
  dialog.addFindListener(new FindListener() {
    public void findRequested(FindEvent e) {
      setfindEvent(e);
    }});
}
```

Figure 17.15 The final multiple dialog design.

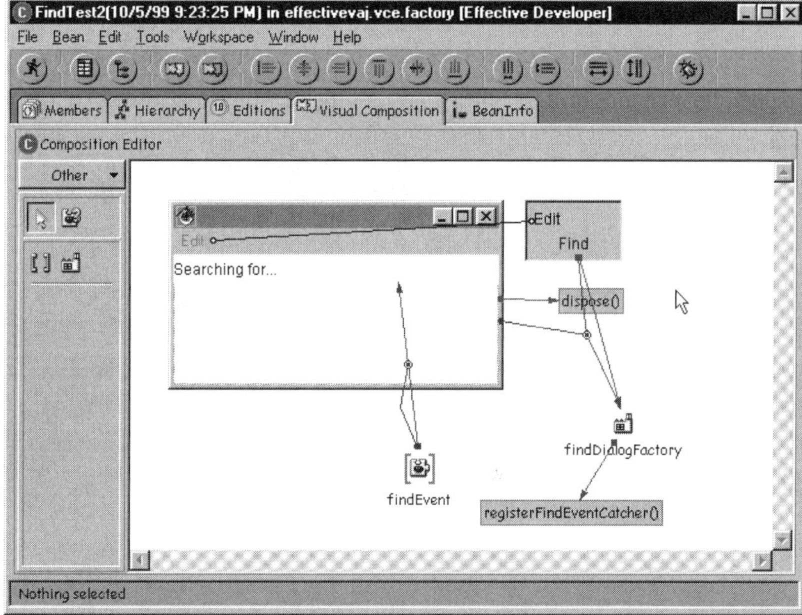

This simple piece of code performs the same function as the connection, but changing the factory's value does not remove it. Whenever the user clicks the Find button in one of the dialogs, this listener sets findEvent. Because there is an event starting on the *this* property of findEvent, this triggers the real action to perform. The final visual design appears in Figure 17.15.

Summary

Use of Factory beans provides dynamic capabilities to your visual design. While there are often better ways to implement your applications, Factory beans can sometimes provide an easy means for simple object creation. We recommend you use them for dialog event generation and possibly for dialog creation, but pay close attention to the amount of work involved versus writing the code yourself.

We now move on to some tips on how you can use the VCE with specific class libraries, such as AWT and Swing. The next chapter outlines some of the strong and weak spots in AWT and Swing support, and some general advice for using these GUI toolkits in the VCE.

Using AWT and Swing in the VCE

18

The Visual Composition Editor (VCE) provides some excellent tools to create composite beans. The composite beans can be either visual or nonvisual beans. In earlier chapters, we discussed how to use the VCE for general composite bean creation. We intentionally omitted any detailed discussion of the AWT and Swing components, showing you VCE operations that work with any JavaBeans component.

This chapter describes some of the AWT and Swing components and how you can use them in the VCE. We assume you are familiar with the components. If you would like additional information on the components, see the books listed in Appendix E, "Additional Resources."

Swing and AWT are both user interface libraries. Swing builds on top of some of the classes in AWT, providing more varied and customized user interface elements. However, there are some significant differences between AWT and Swing, many of which affect how you can use these beans in the VCE.

In this chapter, we cover several issues that you may encounter while using AWT and Swing in the VCE:

Heavyweight and Lightweight Components. What makes a component heavyweight or lightweight and what problems this can cause.

AWT versus Swing and MVC. Swing uses MVC as the basis for component operation. While most Swing components can mimic the behavior of their AWT counterparts, sometimes you must interact with their model instead of the component.

Swing Borders and Icons. Many Swing components provide decorative borders and icons. This section describes how you can easily set borders and icons in your visual design.

Look and Feel. Swing can paint its components differently based on the current look and feel settings. You can change the way the components look at run time or in the VCE.

Top-Level Components. The VCE treats top-level components such as Frame and JWindow a bit differently than other components. Be aware of the differences and how to manage these components.

Menus. The VCE provides an easy-to-use menu setup scheme, but it might not be obvious at first.

Dialogs. Find out how dialogs and their parent frames interact, and why modal is evil.

Grouping Radio Buttons. Find out how you can associate radio buttons so they are mutually exclusive.

Scrolling Swing Components. Swing components do not provide built-in scrolling behavior. VisualAge can make this easier for you, but you need to know what to do.

JTabbedPane. The VCE provides pseudo-properties for components added to JTabbedPane. Find out what these pseudo-properties are and how you can use them to set up JTabbedPane.

Swing Model Usage. If you need to look at the data in a Swing component, you'll probably need to get to its model. Find out how to visually access the model in this section.

Table Columns. You can set up JTable to automatically generate columns, or you can explicitly define columns in the VCE. This section explains how to deal with table columns.

Desktop Pane and Internal Frames. Interested in an MDI (Multiple Document Interface—all windows are contained by a parent window) application? JDesktopPane and JInternalFrame are here for just that purpose, but there are a few gotchas.

Using Swing 1.1.1 in the VCE. So you want to upgrade the Swing support in VisualAge for Java? Here's how!

Heavyweight and Lightweight Components

The standard AWT visual beans provide a native GUI component that interacts with the user. When running in a Java application on Windows, an AWT Button is *really* a Windows button. When running the same application on Motif, that same AWT is Button is *really* a Motif button. Each of these components is a *real* GUI component on the execution platform. This means they consume extra windowing system resources, but more importantly, they are all opaque rectangular windows. Because of this resource utilization, these are called *heavyweight* components.

If you directly extend the AWT Component or Container classes, your component *will not* have a real GUI component behind it. Your component simply defines a rectangular *area* in their parent container into which they can draw. Because these components do not have a real GUI component behind them, they do not consume the extra resources and may choose *not* to draw in part of their rectangular area. These *lightweight* components can be partially transparent; you can see through parts of the component to whatever lies underneath it, leading to some very interesting GUI designs.

Most Swing components extend AWT's Container class; they are lightweight components. A few, like JFrame and JApplet, extend their AWT heavyweight counterparts (Frame and Applet). JFrame, JApplet, JWindow, and JDialog are heavyweight components because any lightweight components inside them must have *something* on which to draw. The top-level windows in your application must be heavyweight.

You need to be careful not to combine heavyweight and lightweight components. Because lightweight components paint only on a parent component, the basic paint algorithm must paint any child components within their parent component *before* any heavyweight children appear. This means that if a container contains overlapping heavyweight and lightweight components, the heavyweight components always win, appearing on top of any of their lightweight siblings.

You might not think this is a major problem, that layout managers should always be used to arrange components so they do not overlap. The problem is that Swing menus (normal and pop-up) are lightweight. The menus paint within the container that holds them, usually the top-level JFrame or JApplet. This means that menus are painted long before any contained heavyweight components. The disastrous result is that heavyweight components appear *on top of* selected menus!

The general rule of thumb is *never to mix heavyweight and lightweight components*. More specifically, if at any level in your GUI design you include a lightweight component, make sure it has no heavyweight siblings or children. This is especially important for JFrame, JApplet, and JWindow. These high-level components display many lightweight elements, such as tool tips, and menus, as well as the drop-down list for a contained JComboBox bean and others. If you use JFrame, JApplet, or JWindow as your top-level component, we strongly recommend that you do not put any heavyweight components inside it.

AWT versus Swing and MVC

AWT components contain their own data. Swing components use the Model-View-Controller paradigm. (See Chapter 15, "Model-View-Controller in the VCE," for a description of the paradigm.) Some Swing components provide delegation methods to access their models. While this can make it easier to interact with these Swing components, you may need to interact differently with others.

A good example is AWT's TextField and Swing's JTextField components. These components perform the same UI function, enabling a user to see and edit a String. Their implementations are vastly different.

AWT's TextField has a text property that the user can change by calling setText() or changing the value in the displayed field. When the value changes through either of these means, TextField fires a textValueChanged event. TextField manages the user interaction and the data.

Swing's JTextField does things a bit differently. It has a model called Document that holds the text of the field. While JTextField provides a text property, it merely delegates this property to the Document model. The problem is that you cannot listen to JTextField for a textValueChanged event, as it does not manage the data. If you want to know when JTextField's value changes, you must listen to its model for a DocumentEvent (you will be notified whenever text in the model is inserted, deleted, or changed).

For this reason, we strongly recommend using the BoundJTextField component discussed in Chapter 9, "Extension and Composition." This extension binds the text property by watching its model for changes. This can greatly assist your use of JTextField in the VCE, as you do not need to tear off JTextField's model to watch for changes.

Other components may be more difficult to use in the VCE. Some components, like JTable and JTree, have complex models. While both provide default models and some simple delegation methods to add items to the models, it is not effective or efficient to attempt to add items through the components themselves. The easiest way to interact with them is to tear off their model properties. You can then interact directly with the models.

To truly use Swing components like JTable and JTree in an efficient manner, you often have to write your own models. You can then drop an instance of your model in the VCE, interact with it to change the data contained within the model, and use a property-to-property connection to associate it with the JTable or JTree component. This provides you full control over how the model stores its data and what you can do with that model, and you can choose the most efficient means of interacting with it.

Swing Borders and Icons

Swing components have some special properties that can make your user interface much more attractive and effective. One of the most useful properties is the *border* property. This provides a decorative border around your component or container. You can use these borders to add space around components, add a three-dimensional appearance to your GUI, or group parts of your GUI that provide associated functions. The VCE provides a very simple property editor for the border property. It enables you to write a line of code to define the border to use or to choose a border class from a list. The main problem is that this editor enables you to modify the borders only if they have properties; Swing border properties are all set through their constructors.

A more powerful solution is to use the Swing Border editor provided on the CD-ROM. This editor enables you to easily select from several common Swing borders or provide your own code for a border. To use the Border Editor:

1. Install the Border Editor as directed in Appendix D, "The CD-ROM."
2. While working on a Swing GUI in the VCE, double-click on a Swing component to display its property sheet.
3. Select the **Expert** check box in the property sheet to see the border property.
4. Click on the border property in the property sheet. This will display a "..." button.
5. Click the "..." button. The GUI seen in Figure 18.1 appears.
6. Choose the border options you would like. The border of the border editor changes as you select options so you can see what the resulting border will look like.

Many Swing components can also have one or more associated icons. The VCE provides a property editor for these icons that enables you to specify a file name or URL that references an image file. Normally, you should place the image you want

Figure 18.1 The Swing border editor.

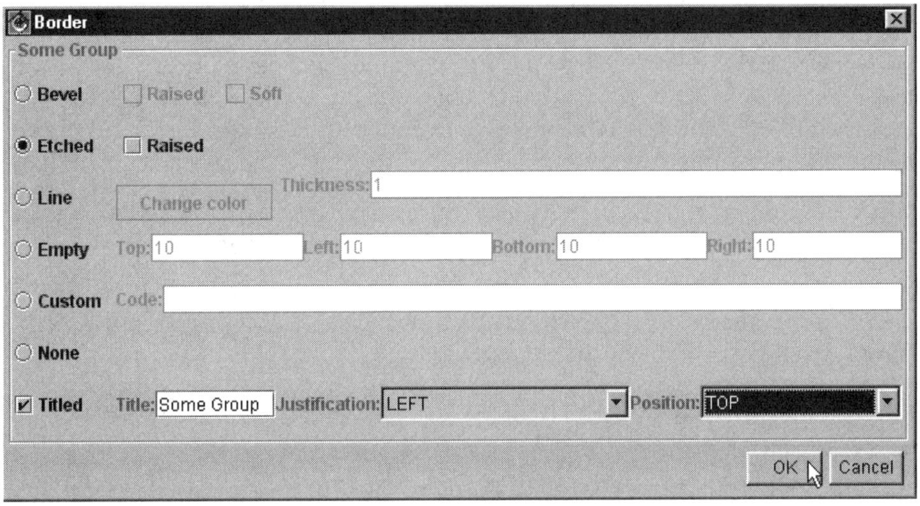

to use in a subdirectory of the project_resources directory for the current project. For example, if you name your project SampleProject, you could use an image named *installDirectory*\ide\project_resources\SampleProject\images\somePic.gif. By using images in this directory, you can easily export the images as resources.

> **NOTE**
>
> You specify the *installDirectory* when you install VisualAge for Java. The default installation directory varies upon which version of VisualAge for Java you're using. If you're using VisualAge for Java, version 3.02, the default installation directory is *c:\IBMVJava*. If you're using version 3.5, the default installation directory is c:\Program Files\IBM\VisualAge for Java.

Look and Feel

Swing components display differently based on the specified look-and-feel library. By default, the Java Look and Feel (the MetalLookandFeel class) paints all components. This platform-neutral appearance is what you see typically when you edit Swing components in the VCE. Your application can change which look-and-feel it uses by using the UIManager class to set the look-and-feel to another class. However, this does not affect how the components appear in the VCE.

To change the default look and feel in the VCE, create the file *installDirectory*\ide\program\lib\swing.properties (see the note above regarding the installation directory). This file should contain a single property definition: swing.defaultlaf. You can choose any of the following look-and-feel libraries for this property definition. You should include only one of the following lines in your swing.properties file. Note that Sun dropped MacLookAndFeel, and the version that is present in VisualAge for Java, Version 3.0, does not currently work.

```
swing.defaultlaf=com.sun.java.swing.plaf.motif.MotifLookAndFeel
swing.defaultlaf=com.sun.java.swing.plaf.windows.WindowsLookAndFeel
swing.defaultlaf=javax.swing.plaf.metal.MetalLookAndFeel
```

You can change this file without restarting VisualAge for Java. However, you must restart the VCE to see the change.

Top-Level Components

All visual applications must have a top-level component. The top-level component presents your GUI to the user. The top-level components are Frame, JFrame,

> **NOTE**
>
> 3.5 If you are using VisualAge for Java, version 3.5, use the above names. If you are using version 3.0, use "com.sun.java.swing.plaf.metal.MetalLookAndFeel" for the last one. This change will affect the way your application appears in the VCE *and* the way the application appears when you run it inside VisualAge for Java. However, if you explicitly set the look-and-feel in your application code, the application uses that setting when running the application.
>
> This change will *not* affect the application appearance when run outside VisualAge for Java. If you desire a specific look-and-feel when running the application, you should explicitly set that look-and-feel in your application code.

Applet, JApplet, Window, JWindow, Dialog, and JDialog. The most effective way to use these components is to subclass these classes and then edit the subclass in the VCE. For use as an applet in a Web page, your class *must* extend Applet or JApplet. You can either extend the other top-level classes or drop them in another visual design. We recommend extension because this enables you to easily reuse the developed GUI in other applications, and the VCE generates a main() method to automatically start your application.

Many of the top-level components have a *content pane*. This concept comes from the Swing components. JFrame, JApplet, JWindow, and JDialog all contain a nested container named the content pane. When you add components to a Swing top-level component, you must add them to the content pane rather than directly to the JFrame, JApplet, JWindow, or JDialog instance. Because of this, the VCE generates a special container to act as the content pane when dealing with these components.

To provide some consistency with this in AWT, the VCE also applies a content pane to AWT's Frame and Dialog. Applet and Window do not have a content pane. The names of the content pane vary between the components, but always contain the words *content* and *pane*, so you should be able to recognize these components.

You can delete the content pane from the AWT versions of these components if you want to. Your application will function correctly without them. If you remove them from the Swing components that require them, however, you *must* replace them. When you remove them, you will see the warning displayed in Figure 18.2. The Swing content pane can be *any* component, and you can drop the replacement content pane on top of this warning message to correct the design.

Figure 18.2 A missing content pane in a Swing component.

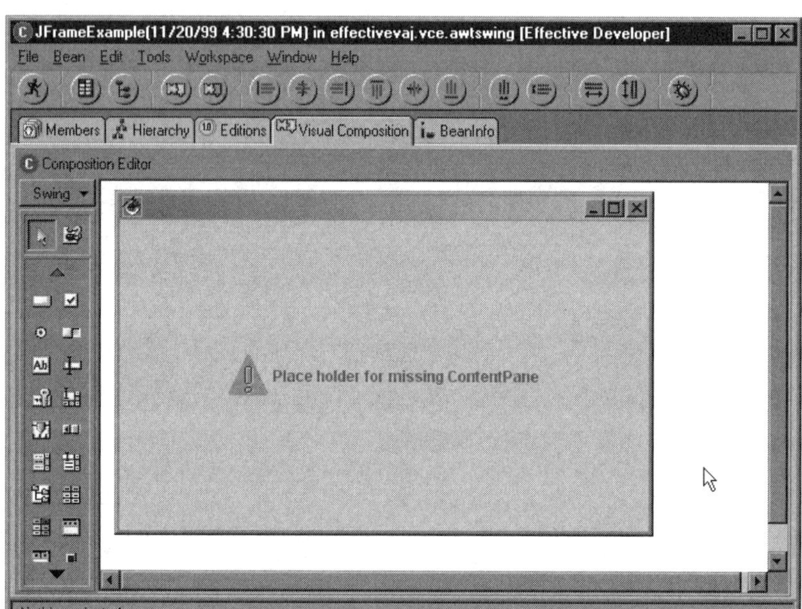

> **TIP**
>
> Only use top-level components for assembling an application. The *real* GUI for your application should subclass Panel, JPanel, or Container. By composing your entire GUI in Panel, JPanel, or Container, you can either drop it in a top-level component to create an application, *or* add it inside *another* Panel, JPanel, or Container as part of another GUI. This gives you quite a bit of flexibility. If you decide later to reuse your GUI inside another GUI, you can do so without changing the superclass of your GUI.

Menus

The VCE enables you to create AWT and Swing menus and pop-up menus. There is a slight difference between menus in AWT and Swing. When you design an AWT component, you can add a menu bar only to a frame. AWT menus are special components that map directly to native GUI menus. No other AWT component can have a menu bar. Swing menu bars act differently. Swing implements menu bars as normal lightweight components. Because of this, you can add a Swing menu to *any* Swing container, as a member of any layout manager.

You create both types of menus the same way in the VCE. You drop an AWT MenuBar instance in the target Frame instance or a Swing JMenuBar instance in any Swing container; then you add Menu or JMenu instances to them. You can add MenuItem and JMenuItem instances to Menu or JMenu. In addition, because Menu extends MenuItem, you can drop a Menu instance inside another Menu instance to create a cascaded menu. The same applies to Swing JMenu.

You can also create pop-up menus, dropping PopupMenu or JPopupMenu in an empty spot in the VCE design area, adding Menu or JMenu instances inside them.

To construct AWT menus:

1. Select MenuBar.
2. You can only drop this component into an AWT Frame. The easiest way to do this is to drop it on the title bar of the frame.
3. Once dropped, you will see the design shown in Figure 18.3. VisualAge for Java represents the menus as separate strips in the design area. You can drop menu items into these menus but not in the menu bar. To change the menu names, double-click them on the menu bar to access their property sheets.

Figure 18.3 Picking AWT MenuItem.

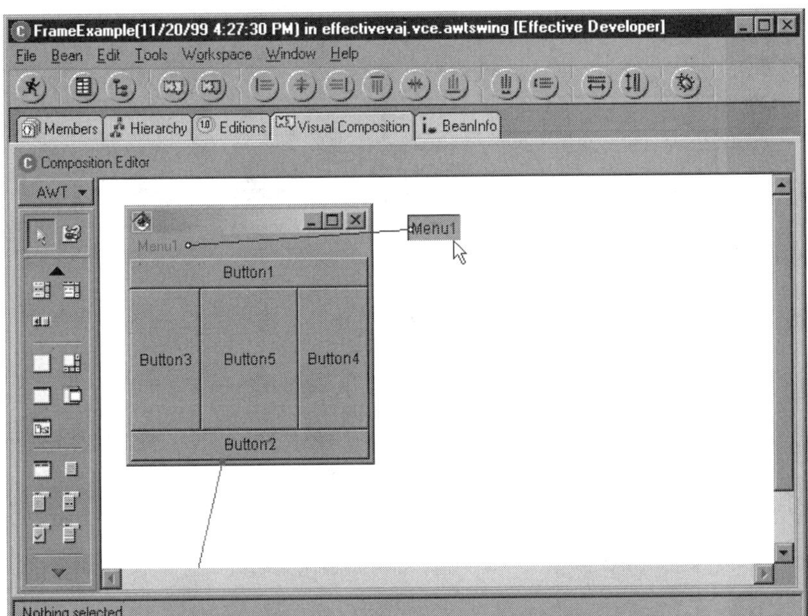

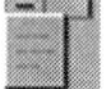

4. To add more menus to the menu bar, select Menu from the palette and drop it on the *MenuBar instance*. The VCE will automatically create a torn-off view of the menu.
5. You can then add other menus to a menu to create a cascading menu. You can also add any of the following components to a menu.

   MenuItem. An item that a user can select from a menu. When the user selects a menu item, the component fires an actionPerformed event.

   CheckboxMenuItem. An item in a menu that has a true/false state. The user can toggle the state by selecting the item. Whenever the user toggles the state, CheckboxMenuItem fires an itemStateChanged event. Note that you cannot attach a CheckboxGroup to CheckboxMenuItem instances.

   MenuSeparator. A horizontal line between two items in a menu. This helps break menus into groups. The user cannot interact with a menu separator.
6. After adding menus and menu items, your visual design will appear as shown in Figure 18.4. You can connect actionPerformed events from any of the MenuItem components, or itemStateChanged events from a CheckboxMenuItem component. MenuItem components act just like Button components when used in a visual design.

Figure 18.4 Visual design of menus.

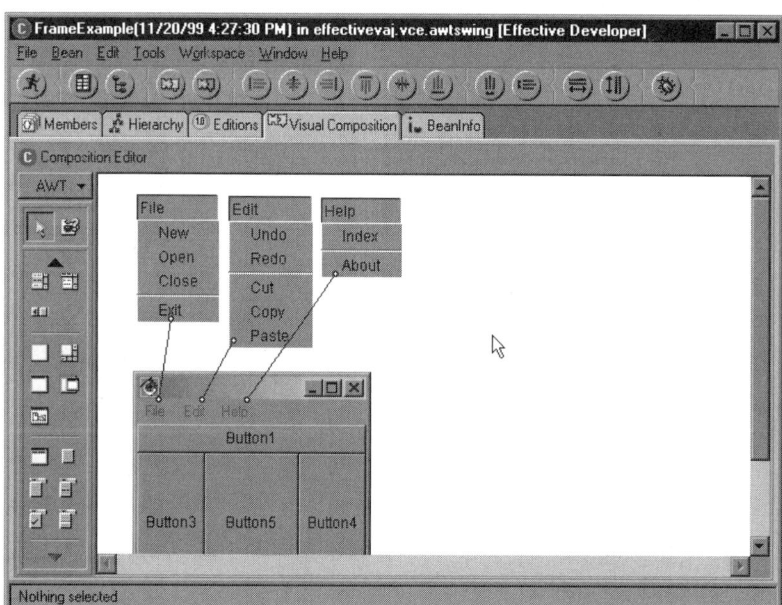

To build a pop-up menu instead of a normal menu, drop a PopupMenu in an empty space in the VCE design area. You can display the pop-up menu by calling its show() method.

> **NOTE**
>
> The mouse button used to display a pop-up menu varies between platforms. If you want to display a pop-up menu based on a mouse click, you should call a method like the following from both the mousePressed and mouseReleased events of the component controlling the pop-up menu.
>
> ```
> protected void displayPopup(MouseEvent e, PopupMenu m) {
>   if (e.isPopupTrigger())
>     m.show((Component)e.getSource(), e.getX(), e.getY());
> }
> ```

Swing Menu Construction

Swing menus, while similar, have a few differences to keep in mind. You select JMenuBar instead of MenuBar, but you now have the choice to place it anywhere you would like. You can add it to JFrame (by clicking on the JFrame's title bar) or to any container, *including* JApplet.

Swing provides the following menu components:

JMenu. Can be added to JMenuBar, JPopupMenu, or another JMenu.

JMenuItem. An item in a menu. Like MenuItem, it fires actionPerformed when selected by the user.

JSeparator. A component that draws a horizontal or vertical line. This can provide visual separation between groups of items in a menu. Note that because this is a normal component you can use it outside of menus if you want, helping to separate parts of your GUI.

JCheckBoxMenuItem. A menu item that tracks a state. The user can toggle the state, and JCheckBoxMenuItem fires an itemStateChanged event.

JRadioButtonMenuItem. A menu item that tracks a state *but* can be added to a Swing ButtonGroup. Note that you *cannot* add JRadioButtonMenuItem to ButtonGroup visually; you must write some code to do that. If you had JRadioButtonMenuItem instances named asciiModeItem and hexModeItem and a ButtonGroup named editModeGroup, you could write the following code to set up the group.

The code could appear in an event-to-code connection from the initialize() event of your composite bean.

```
geteditModeGroup().add(getasciiModeItem());
geteditModeGroup().add(getbinaryModeItem());
```

Dialogs

As mentioned earlier (see *Top-Level Components*, previously), Dialog and JDialog have the same content pane considerations as other top-level components. However, there are a few more considerations to keep in mind.

Dialog instances have a parent Window associated with them. When the parent closes or hides, it automatically hides the child dialogs. Using Dialog in the VCE can be a bit tricky because of this. There are a few rules:

- If the composite bean extends Frame, Dialog, or Window (or the corresponding Swing versions of these), the VCE passes *this* as the parent to any dialogs dropped in the design area. This means that if the composite bean closes or hides, so do any of its dialogs.
- If the composite bean extends any other class, the VCE generates code to pass a new Frame as the parent of any dropped Dialog instances. If your composite bean is nonvisual and displays Frame and Dialog instances, *there will be no association between the frames and dialogs!*
- If your composite bean is *not* a Frame, Dialog, or Window (or the Swing equivalent), you *must* use a Factory bean (see Chapter 17, "Factory Beans") to create Dialog instances if you want to associate them with a specific Frame, Window, or Dialog.

Finally, dialogs can be modal, meaning they will block control of the application until the user answers them. *Use modal dialogs sparingly, only where necessary (usually to prevent the user from destroying data).* Modal dialogs block input to all other top-level frames or dialogs (unless they are children of the dialog in question). To be blunt, modal dialogs are generally *evil* and quite often overused. If you're going to use a modal dialog, think carefully before doing so. Remember that the user cannot do anything else until they answer the dialog.

Grouping Radio Buttons

Radio buttons can be tricky to use in the VCE, depending on whether you use AWT or Swing.

AWT does not have radio button components; you apply CheckboxGroup to AWT Checkbox components and their appearance changes to look like radio buttons. To create and group radio buttons in AWT:

1. Drop Checkbox components into your visual design where you want your radio buttons.
2. Drop a CheckboxGroup instance in an empty part of the visual design area.
3. Create property-to-property connections from the *this* property of the CheckboxGroup instance to the checkboxGroup properties of the Checkbox components.

When done, your design should look like Figure 18.5. Note that you will *not* see a visual change to the Checkbox components at design time. However, when you run the application, the checkboxes will appear as radio buttons.

Swing provides class JRadioButton for mutually exclusive radio buttons. You can place JRadioButton components in your layout just like any other component. To act mutually exclusive, you must add JRadioButton instances to ButtonGroup, a nonvisual bean. Unfortunately, *there is no convenient way to do this visually*!

Figure 18.5 AWT radio button design.

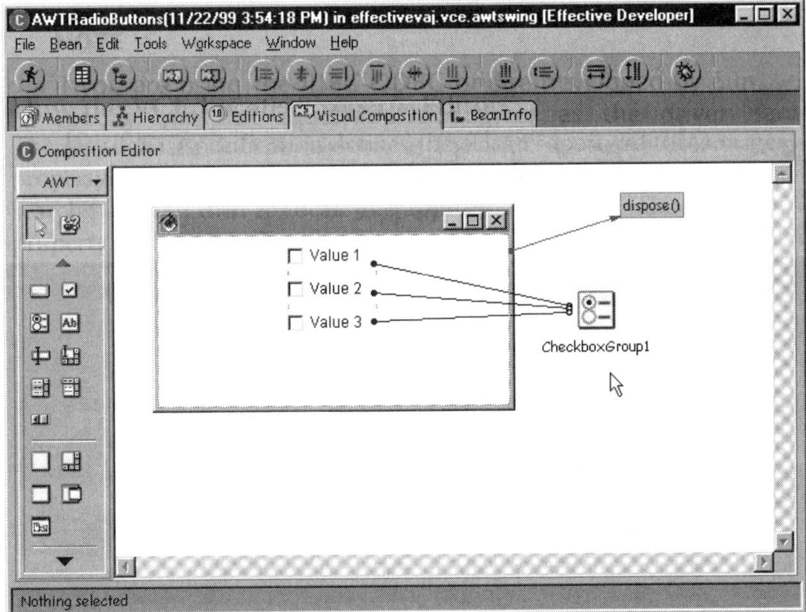

The best way to handle these is to create an extension of JPanel that handles the ButtonGroup registration. A simple version of such a class follows. Note that this ButtonGroupJPanel tracks any JToggleButton, JCheckBox, or JRadioButton component (JCheckBox and JRadioButton extend JToggleButton).

```
package effectivevaj.vce.awtswing;

import com.sun.java.swing.*;
import java.awt.*;
import java.io.*;
/**
 * A simple extension of JPanel that assigns any
 *   added JToggleButtons to a ButtonGroup
 */
public class ButtonGroupJPanel extends JPanel
     implements Serializable {
  // the ButtonGroup that tracks the selected
  //   JToggleButton (if any)
  private ButtonGroup bg = new ButtonGroup();

  /** Add a component to this container
   *  If the component is a JToggleButton,
   *     add it to our ButtonGroup
   */
  protected void addImpl(Component comp,
                         Object constraints,
                         int index) {
    super.addImpl(comp, constraints, index);
    if (comp instanceof JToggleButton)
      bg.add((JToggleButton)comp);
  }

  /** Remove a component from this container
   *  If the component is a JToggleButton, remove
   *     it from the ButtonGroup
   */
  public void remove(int index) {
      Component comp = getComponent(index);
      if (comp instanceof JToggleButton)
      bg.remove((JToggleButton)comp);
    super.remove(comp);
  }
```

```
  /** Remove a component from this container
   *  If the component is a JToggleButton, remove
   *     it from the ButtonGroup
   */
  public void remove(Component comp) {
      if (comp instanceof JToggleButton)
      bg.remove((JToggleButton)comp);
    super.remove(comp);
  }

  /** Remove all components from this container
   *  Start a new ButtonGroup to clear it
   */
  public void removeAll() {
    super.removeAll();
    // easiest to just start a new ButtonGroup
    bg = new ButtonGroup();
  }
}
```

Using this class, you can drop a ButtonGroupJPanel instance in your design and then drop JRadioButton components inside it; they are instantly mutually exclusive. You can use a similar technique for AWT, watching for added Checkbox components and assigning their *checkboxGroup* property.

Scrolling Swing Components

Swing provides select components that may require scrolling when they contain many data. When Sun designed Swing, they decided *not* to include scrolling support in these components. Instead, they required users to place these components inside JScrollPane to provide the scrolling support. The reason for this is simple flexibility. By keeping the scrolling outside the component, a programmer could combine multiple tables, trees, or lists into a single large scrolling area.

The three components that this affects are JTree, JTable, and JList. You can drop these components into your visual design by selecting them in the palette. When you drop JTable, the VCE automatically adds a JScrollPane instance around it. When you drop JTree or JList, the VCE drops *only* the JTree or JList component.

If you do not want JScrollPane for JTable, you can drag the JTable instance out of the JScrollPane instance into the desired parent component and then delete the JScrollPane instance. Most of the time, you will probably want the JScrollPane instance, however, or the user would not be able to scroll the table.

When dealing with JTree and JList, you must drop the JScrollPane instance yourself. If you do not, any off-screen items they contain will not be accessible.

JTabbedPane

JTabbedPane is a nifty component that enables you to have several pages in your GUI, each accessible by clicking on a tab on one of its edges. You can drop JTabbedPane anywhere you can drop other components. To add pages inside it, drop components on top of the tabs of the JTabbedPane instance. This creates a new page, named after the component dropped inside it. A sample appears in Figure 18.6.

Pages in JTabbedPane can be any type of component, including another JTabbedPane instance. If you want a page to contain more than one component, drop JPanel in the JTabbedPane instance. You can then drop components directly inside JPanel, which will cover the body of the JTabbedPane instance.

To switch between components in JTabbedPane, simply click on the tab for that component. This makes the page visible, *but you still have JTabbedPane selected*! Keep this in mind when trying to delete components from JTabbedPane. If you *just* click the tab for the component and press delete, you delete the JTabbedPane. If this happens, just press Ctrl-Z (undo).

To work with the component, click *inside* the component or select it from the beans list. Note that if the page is a JPanel instance and its contained components completely fill it, you will need to select it from the beans list. When you select the actual contained component, the VCE adds a few extra properties to the property sheet, seen in Figure 18.7.

Figure 18.6 JTabbedPane in a visual design.

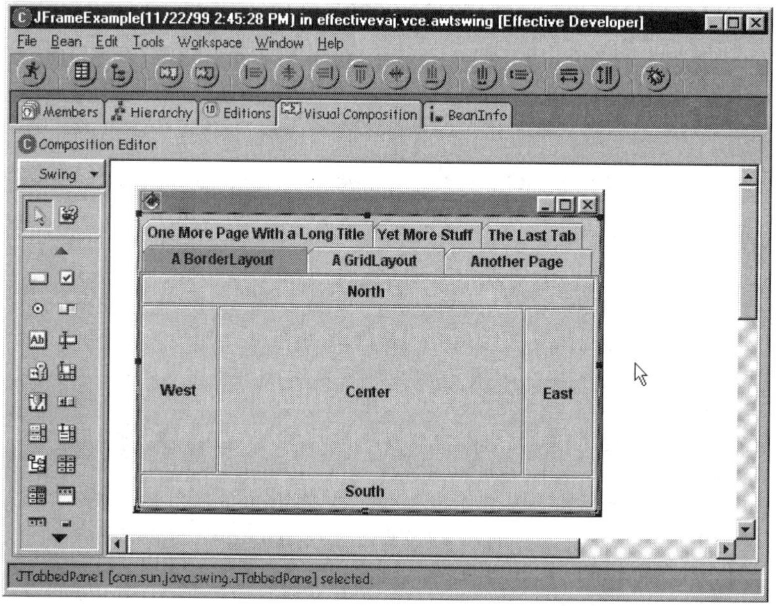

Figure 18.7 Extra properties for JTabbedPane.

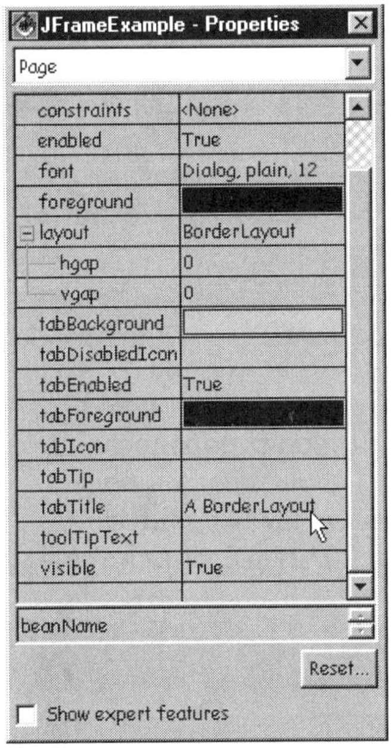

While these are not true properties of the contained bean, they act as settings for that item in JTabbedPane. These special properties are:

tabBackground / tabForeground. The color of the tab and foreground text for this component. Note that the background color changes when the user selects the tab.

tabIcon / tabDisabledIcon. Optional icons that appear in the tab.

tabTitle. The text that appears in the tab. By default, this is the bean name of the component.

tabTip. The tool tip text that appears when the user floats the mouse over the tab for this component.

tabEnabled. Can the user select this tab?

> **WARNING**
>
> If the component happens to have any properties with these names, *the real component properties will not appear in the property sheet.* We have reported this bug to IBM. See Appendix E, "Additional Resources," for information on obtaining patches for VisualAge for Java.

Swing Model Usage

One of the most confusing issues when using Swing components is how to use the model of the components. Swing components follow the same Model-Delegate pattern discussed in Chapter 15. We present a few tips on using components like JTable in the VCE, helping you interact with their models.

For example, sometimes DefaultTableModel is adequate for your data storage. It stores an Object[][] (two-dimensional object array) of data values and an Object[] used as column names. The trick to using the default model is to drop a *Factory bean* (see Chapter 17) to create the model, passing in the data you want it to contain.

Figure 18.8 shows a simple GUI where we fill a model with some data and column names, then set *it* as the model for the table. The connections create a DefaultTableModel instance when the bean initializes and then set the JTable's model to that DefaultTableModel.

Once you have a DefaultTableModel instance, you can interact with it by calling its methods. You can add and remove rows or columns, as well as move rows, change data, or set a new Object[][] for the data. However, DefaultTableModel is rather limited. You must tailor your data to fit its view of the world. Instead, you may want to create your own model. This enables you complete control over data

Figure 18.8 Starting DefaultTableModel.

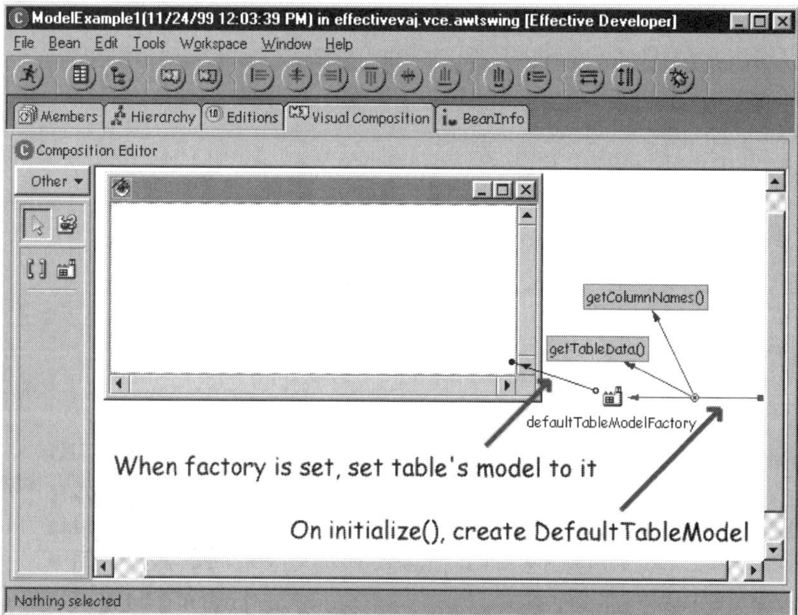

storage and retrieval. You can also apply filters as covered in Chapter 16, "Advanced Model-View-Controller Techniques."

Keep in mind that *all* Swing components have a model. Many, like JButton, provide methods that access the parts of the model that you need to access. Others, like JTable, JTree, and JList, usually require that you work with the model separately from the component.

TableColumn

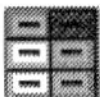

The VCE provides a special visual component called TableColumn. Swing's JTable has an associated object called TableColumnModel that tracks which columns to display. TableColumnModel tracks a set of TableColumn objects, which specify a mapping to a column in TableModel, a header, a renderer, and other information such as column sizing. Figure 18.9 shows a JTable instance that contains two added TableColumn objects.

If you want to display only certain columns, you can add TableColumn objects to JTable in the VCE and edit the properties. Make sure you select the **Show Expert Features** check box, as you need to set the modelIndex property for the column! Figure 18.10 shows the property settings for TableColumn. For the example shown in Figure 18.9, we added two TableColumn objects, representing

Figure 18.9 Added TableColumn objects.

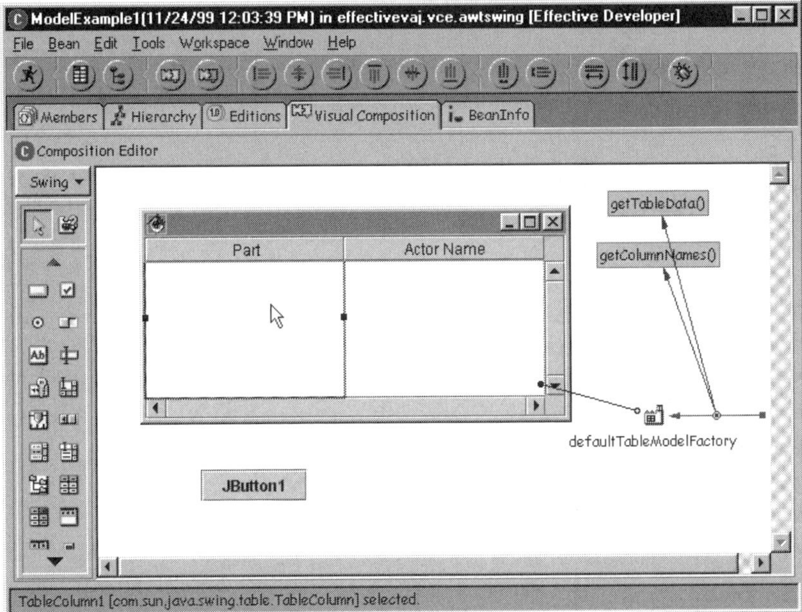

columns 1 and 0 in the model. Using these TableColumn objects, you can easily limit which columns JTable displays and can specify an ordering and size for those columns.

Desktop Panes and Internal Frames

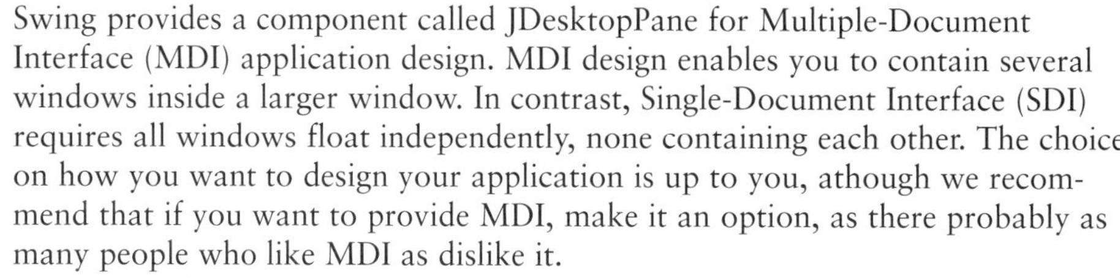

Swing provides a component called JDesktopPane for Multiple-Document Interface (MDI) application design. MDI design enables you to contain several windows inside a larger window. In contrast, Single-Document Interface (SDI) requires all windows float independently, none containing each other. The choice on how you want to design your application is up to you, athough we recommend that if you want to provide MDI, make it an option, as there probably as many people who like MDI as dislike it.

To implement an MDI design, drop JDesktopPane somewhere in your GUI, usually at the top level of the GUI. You then drop JInternalFrame instances inside it as the internal windows. These internal windows can contain whatever components you want. However, there are a few things to watch out for.

Internal frames can float inside JDesktopPane. That is their purpose. You *should not* set a layout manager for JDesktopPane, as it will preclude the internal frames from floating. You should explicitly position and size internal frames within JDesktopPane.

By default, internal frames reside in the same *layer* in the JDesktopPane instance. The layer in which an internal frame resides determines its position

Figure 18.10 Changing TableColumn properties.

ModelExample1 - Properties

TableColumn1

beanName	TableColumn1
cellRenderer	
headerRenderer	(TableColumn$1)
headerValue	Part
identifier	Part
maxWidth	2147483647
minWidth	15
modelIndex	1
resizable	True
width	157

beanName

Reset...

☑ Show expert features

above or below other internal frames in the JDesktopPane instance. Any internal frames with a higher layer number *always* appear on top of those with a lower layer number. If multiple internal frames reside in the same layer, the active (or focused) internal frame appears on top of all others at that layer.

When you place internal frames inside JDesktopPane, the VCE assigns them the default layer, 0. There is currently no property you can set to change the layer in which an internal frame resides. However, you *can* specify the layer by calling a method in JDesktopPane.

Suppose you wanted to put one of the internal frames at layer 10, so it always appears above the others. Figure 18.11 shows a simple JDesktopPane instance containing two JInternalFrame components. To set the layer for an internal frame:

1. Start a connection from the initialize() event of the composite bean (found by choosing **Connect** from the pop-up menu of an empty part of the design area).
2. Click on the JDesktopPane instance as the target of the connection.
3. Choose the setLayer() method of the JDesktopPane instance.
4. The setLayer() method takes two parameters. Attach the component parameter to the *this* property of the JInternalFrame instance.

Figure 18.11 DesktopPane with JInternalFrame instances.

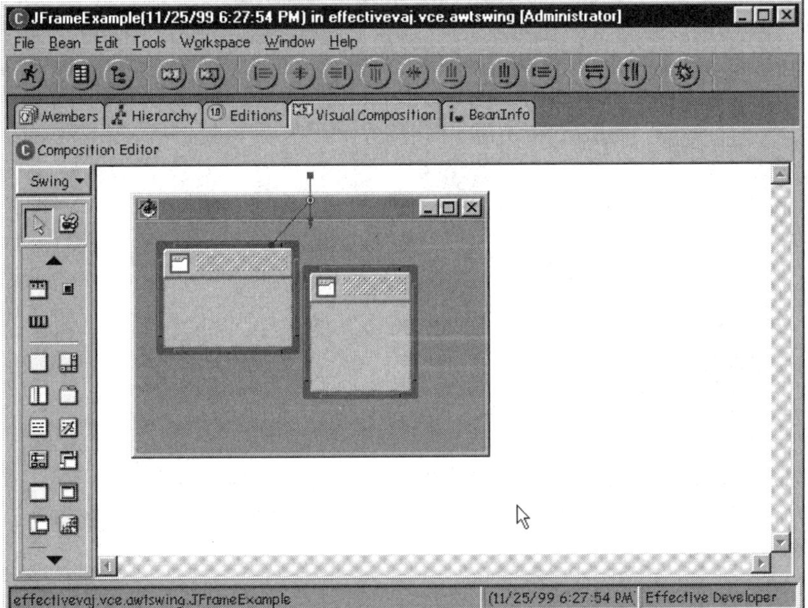

5. Set the layer number to a constant 10 in the connection's Set Parameters dialog.

If you want to set several component layers, we suggest you create an event-to-code connection to a method that calls the setLayer() method.

Using Swing 1.1.1 in VisualAge for Java, version 3.0

> **NOTE**
>
> 3.5 VisualAge for Java, version 3.5, includes the most recent version of Swing. If you are using version 3.5, you should ignore the following information on using and importing Swing 1.1.1.

VisualAge for Java, version 3.0, comes with Swing 1.0.3. This is a source of great grief for many, but you *can* import Swing 1.1.1 and use it fairly effectively. If you want to use a newer Swing with JDK 1.1, you must install the newer version of Swing in VisualAge for Java 3.0.

> **WARNING**
>
> Neither IBM, the authors of this book, nor John Wiley & Sons (publisher) provides support for this method. If you perform the following procedures, you do so *at your own risk*. We provide this information because many people have successfully done this and more would like to know how.

Current Swing Support

VisualAge for Java, version 3.0, distribution ships with JDK 1.1.7 and Swing 1.0.3. You will probably want to upgrade your Swing support to Swing 1.1.1. This section describes how you can import and use Swing 1.1.1.

VisualAge for Java, version 3.0, currently needs to do some special processing to support Swing:

The VCE contains knowledge that JFrame, JDialog, JApplet and JWindow use a content pane to hold their children. It uses this information anytime it sees the following class names:

- com.sun.java.swing.JFrame

- com.sun.java.swing.JApplet
- com.sun.java.swing.JDialog
- com.sun.java.swing.JWindow

Note that these names all begin with the old Swing package name prefix com.sun.java.swing. Because of this, if you import Swing 1.1.1, which uses prefix *javax.swing*, some of the components will not function properly in the VCE.

There are a few more classes, like JScrollPane and JTabbedPane, with similar concerns: knowing where to add the component and adding extra properties to those components.

If you pick BoxLayout when choosing a layout manager, the VCE explicitly chooses com.sun.java.swing.BoxLayout.

Setting up Swing 1.1.1 in VisualAge for Java, version 3.0

> **NOTE**
>
> Do *not* attempt to perform these steps in VisualAge for Java, version 3.5!

First, you need to import the Swing 1.1.1 classes into VisualAge for Java, version 3.0. To do this, you must grab the Swing distribution from Sun at http://java.sun.com/products/jfc and then install the *full* developer's release.

Start up VisualAge for Java and create a new project named Swing. Import the file swingall.jar from the directory into which you installed Swing. Be sure to import any resources contained within this file as well.

> **NOTE**
>
> When performing this import, you will need to deselect any classes whose package name starts with com.sun.java.swing. These classes already exist in VisualAge for Java and you cannot import them. You can deselect these by clicking the **Details** button next to the check box for importing class files.

When asked, create a new VCE palette category called Swing 1.1.1 and add all imported beans to that category.

After completing the import, version the Swing project using your initials and 1.1.1 as the version tag. For example, version it as "sas 1.1.1." This is important so you will not have any problems if IBM wants to add "Swing 1.1.1" to your workspace at a later date.

Now you are ready to use Swing 1.1.1 in VisualAge for Java.

Writing Swing 1.1.1 Applications in VisualAge for Java, version 3.0

> **NOTE**
>
> 3.5 This section only applies to VisualAge for Java, version 3.0. You can use Swing normally in version 3.5.

There are three ways to write Swing 1.1.1 applications in VisualAge for Java:

- Write code by hand. This approach will work, but can be a lot of work.
- Use the VCE with the original Swing classes to initially develop your GUI and then replace all references to com.sun.java.swing with those to javax.swing. You will lose the visual design unless you make the change in another package or outside of VisualAge for Java.
- Use the newly imported Swing beans, except JFrame, JApplet, JDialog, JWindow, JScrollPane and, JTable.

When developing your GUI, *if* you choose BoxLayout as a layout property, you will need to rename the generated names. A better choice for using BoxLayout is to create a subclass of JPanel that sets its own layout to BoxLayout. That way you can have it import javax.swing.BoxLayout instead of allowing the VCE to generate com.sun.java.swing.BoxLayout.

Create your classes by avoiding the unusable beans mentioned above. Then, write a small class by hand to wrap your VCE-created GUI in JFrame, JDialog, JApplet or JWindow. This code might look as follows:

```
public class FunkyApp extends JFrame {
  public FunkyApp() {
    setContentPane(new ThingCreatedInVCE());
    addWindowListener(new WindowAdapter() {
      public void windowClosing(WindowEvent e) {
        System.exit(0);
      }
    });
```

```
  }

  public static void main(String[] args) {
    new FunkyApp().setVisible(true);
  }
}
```

Remember, it is always a good idea to create your GUIs as JPanel extensions rather than JFrame extensions anyway. (This enables you to combine your GUI into another more complex GUI.)

Make sure you add the Swing project to the CLASSPATH for your application (the one that has the JFrame)!

You can deal with JScrollPane by adding one to the GUI in the VCE and then setting up an initialize() connection to call its setViewportView() method, passing the thing to stick in it.

Migrating Swing Code to VisualAge for Java, version 3.5

3.5 VisualAge for Java version 3.5 includes Java version 1.2.2, which includes support for the latest version of Swing. If you were using an earlier version of VisualAge for Java and want to transfer your code to version 3.5, you'll have to migrate any code that uses Swing. Older versions of Swing used package names starting with *com.sun.java.swing*. The current version of Swing starts most of its package names with *javax.swing*. You need to migrate your applications to change the Swing class names.

> **NOTE**
> If you were using VisualAge for Java, version 3.0, Early Adopters Environment, you will not need to perform this migration. The Early Adopters Environment already includes the correct Swing package names.

If you used the Visual Composition Editor to create your Swing user interfaces, it is *very* important that you use the Migration tool to perform these changes. If you just change the references to the Swing classes, the visual design data stored in the repository will not be changed. See *Fixing or Migrating References* in Chapter 2, "Creating Code."

To perform this migration, choose the **Reorganize->Fix/Migrate** option for a class, package, or project. Select the **Include JDK 1.2 renamed packages** option to automatically select the packages that need to be renamed for the Swing migration.

Summary

This chapter showed you some of the key points to keep in mind when using AWT and Swing in the VCE. We recommend that you examine some of the books listed in Appendix E, "Additional Resources," if you need more explanation on the components themselves.

Next, we delve into the gory details that make our applications run: generated and handwritten code. The next chapter is rather long, so we recommend that you get some rest or coffee if needed before proceeding.

HANDWRITTEN CODE VERSUS GENERATED CODE

19

As we have seen, VisualAge for Java can generate a great deal of code for you. However, it cannot generate every piece of code you need for your application. *Programs always need handwritten code*. This chapter explains how you should integrate your handwritten code with VisualAge for Java's generated code.

If you're interested in understanding the code that VisualAge for Java generates, please visit the VisualAge for Java Tips and Tricks site at http://javadude.com/vaj.

All applications require *some* handwritten code. The Visual Composition Editor is a great tool, but it cannot generate your entire application for you. You need to write the logic yourself. The trick is where to put that logic so it can peacefully coexist with the generated code.

Adding User Code to Generated Methods

Most of the generated code above contains comments that show where you can put user code. It *is* possible to add your own code to the generated methods, though we have some advice regarding this approach.

General Advice: *Do Not Do It!*

The best advice we can offer regarding adding your own code to generated methods is *do not do it*! It is incredibly tempting to add a bit of code here and there in the generated methods. After all, they provide some nicely marked places for your code, right?

Think about the poor maintenance programmer who has to figure out what you have done. (If you realize it or not, you will not be maintaining that code forever... or at least you should not want to.) If you insert a few lines of code here and there in the generated methods, the maintenance must really dig to find those lines of code.

Look at the following generated method.

```
private String zzOnAddPressed$GetText(ActionEvent arg1) {
  String zzOnAddPressed$GetTextResult = null;
```

```
  try {
    // user code begin {1}
    // user code end
    zzOnAddPressed$GetTextResult =
      getitemTextField().getText();
    zzPassTextToAdd(zzOnAddPressed$GetTextResult);
    // user code begin {2}
    // user code end
  } catch (java.lang.Throwable ivjExc) {
    // user code begin {3}
    // user code end
    handleException(ivjExc);
  }
  return zzOnAddPressed$GetTextResult;
}
```

Note the location of the three user-code blocks. One occurs *before* the action, one occurs *after* the action, and one occurs if the processing throws an exception. Rather than add code in these blocks, add an event-to-code connection before, after, or triggered by exceptionOccured.

For example, the previous connection describes what to do when the user clicks the Add button. That connection starts on the actionPerformed event of the button. Suppose that you want to execute some handwritten code before or after the previous connection adds the text to the list. Simple: Add an event-to-code connection *from the actionPerformed event of the Button bean*. You can always reorder these connections such that the newly added action executes before or after the existing connection. Alternatively, if you require custom exception handling, add a connection to the *exceptionOccured* event of the initial connection.

The result is the same. You custom code executes before or after the connection code. However, there is a huge maintenance benefit by doing this. A maintenance programmer can *see* that you have added code. If you had written the code in a user-code block, the maintenance programmer would need to examine *every* generated method *just* to see *if* one of them has user code.

> **TIP**
> Avoid writing code in the user-code blocks of generated methods. Doing so is a potential maintenance nightmare!

Try to think of the generated code as a black box. If you can avoid adding your code in there, a programmer can edit the generated code using *only* visual composition. This simplifies the GUI parts of your application significantly, while still giving you the power to write your own code separately.

Where It Is Safe to Add User Code

As we have seen, the generated code provides user-code blocks delimited by comments. If you choose to add code in these blocks (again, we recommend against this), the VCE will preserve your code any time it regenerates the methods. However, just because it preserves your code, this does not mean that your code will still recompile. Depending on how you have changed your visual design, other code you depend on in that handwritten code may no longer exist or may have changed in a non-compatible manner.

The VCE also preserves comments inside the generated methods as well as changes to make the generated methods more publicly visible. Feel free to modify comments to help describe what the methods are doing. However, be careful about changing the visibility of the generated methods. If you change one of the private generated methods to be public or protected, a subclass could accidentally override that method. This can cause some very-difficult-to-diagnose problems in your code.

Keep Clean Separation

Ideally, keep your code as far from the generated code as possible. You can accomplish this most easily by providing clean separation between your GUI and your business logic. We discussed how to do this in Chapter 15, "Model-View-Controller in the VCE."

Keep Interfaces Simple

Whenever you do need your generated code and handwritten code to communicate, do so through a well-documented interface. Using the Model-View-Controller paradigm is one approach. Other approaches involve use of event-to-code connections to make it obvious where your code executes, as we discussed previously. In addition, other approaches involve minimizing the methods that provide interaction with the user interface and documenting exactly where the communication takes place.

Use Beans Consistently

If most of your classes are beans, you can easily assemble applications in the VCE. IBM designed the VCE to work with beans, so it knows the bean patterns and can provide a great deal of assistance in your application. If the VCE can provide a simple event connection to make your beans communicate, you have that much less code to write, test, and document.

Summary

Take advantage of the code that VisualAge for Java generates. The tools provided in VisualAge for Java can do a great deal of very tedious work for you. Not only does this increase your productivity, but it also helps ensure consistency and correctness of your code.

Apply design patterns to link your code to the generated code, especially the Model-View-Controller paradigm. This minimizes the places where your code and the generated code interact, making it easier for maintenance programmers to understand your application, correct problems, and add new functionality.

Next, we move on to some nice details that can help your beans stand out from the crowd. Providing easy ways to customize a bean increases usability of that bean, and helps insure correct bean initialization. Whether that customization is at the property level or for the entire bean, this extra attention to detail separates the useful beans from those that you grind each morning.

BEAN CUSTOMIZATION

20

As we saw in earlier chapters, beans are easy to define and use in bean-builder tools like the Visual Composition Editor (VCE). Many beans are simple to edit by using the property sheet in the VCE. However, some beans can become quite complex and could benefit from easier methods of changing their properties.

You can provide easier customization of your beans by using:

Property Editors. These provide a friendlier interface for setting a specific property's value.

Customizers. These provide a wizard-like interface to set all of the properties in a bean.

In this chapter, you'll learn how to write property editors and customizers. You can use these property editors and customizers in VisualAge for Java or any other JavaBeans-compliant environment.

Property Editors

Property editors provide a simple or controlled editing interface for bean properties. Bean-builder tools can determine quite a lot about your bean just by examining it and its corresponding BeanInfo, but they provide only very simple and generic interfaces to edit the properties in the bean. Many properties are primitive types, Strings, or Colors, and most bean design tools have built-in editors for these types. If a property is another type of object, however, you must tell the design tool how to edit it.

The JavaBeans specification defines the java.beans.PropertyEditor interface to define custom property editors. This interface has several ways of reading and writing information about a property:

String Editors. The user types a String that you can modify.

Enumerated List Editors. The user selects a String value from a list of possible values.

Simple GUI with String values. The user interacts with a GUI to set a String value.

Non-String property editors. The user interacts with a GUI to set a *non-String* value.

Painted value property editors. The user interacts with a non-String property editor, and you paint the current value in the property sheet.

All bean development tools are required to support property editors. This means that any property editors you create in VisualAge for Java will also be usable in other bean-builder tools. In this chapter, we discuss property editors from the point of view of VisualAge for Java, but keep in mind that these property editors will also work in any compliant bean-builder tool.

Saving the Last Property Value in Bean Builders

Once users have set properties for bean, they would like to see those properties again the next time they bring up the property sheet. Property editors define setValue() and getValue() methods to support saving the value. The VCE saves the value between invocations of the property editor.

The setValue() Method

The setValue() method gives the VCE a way to tell the property editor the current property value. This value will initially be null, zero, or false (represented as objects). As the user edits the property, the VCE stores the value and passes it to the property editor for display in the property sheet. The property editor can *look* at this value, but it should *not* directly modify it! The property editor should create a new object to hold the new value for the property and then return that new object when the VCE asks for it.

The getValue() Method

The getValue() method provides a way for a VCE to ask for the edited property value. The VCE stores this value and passes it to setValue() any time the user opens a property sheet for the bean instance. The property editor is responsible for creating an object that contains the value for the property, and returning that object when a bean tool asks.

Starting Simple: String Editors

The VCE displays a text field to edit String property values. There is no validation done on this text field. In the first property editor example, you will define a Color editor in which the user types in a color name and the editor verifies that it is one of the basic colors.

The interaction for each property is as follows, as shown in Figure 20.1.

Figure 20.1 Initial communication: String-only editor.

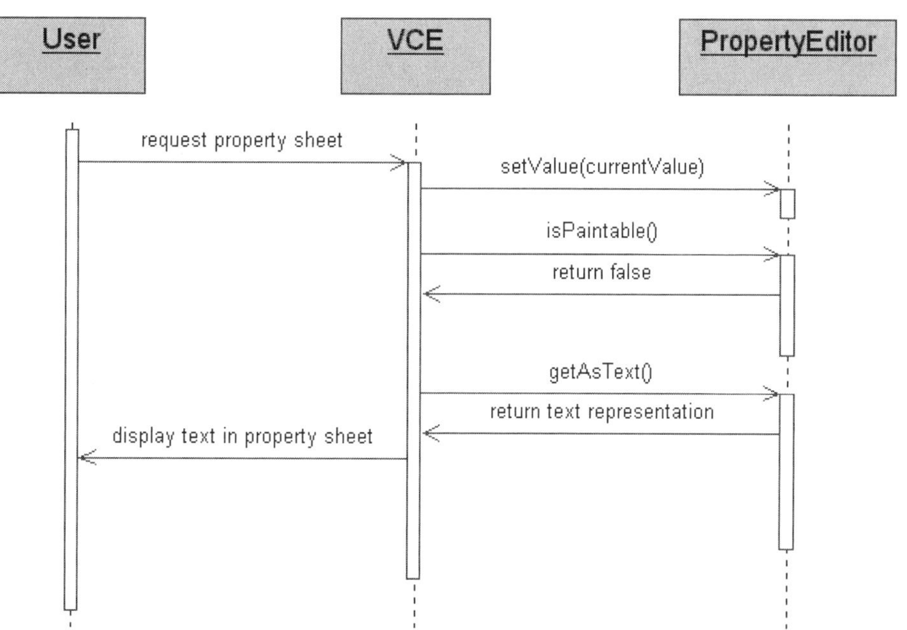

> **NOTE**
>
> Some of the communication between the VCE and the property editor can seem quite redundant. There are often what seem to be extra calls to many of the methods. These extra calls are often necessary to ensure the property editor processes the correct value, in case some of its methods modify the value. These are most often extra calls to the property editor's setValue() method. We omit some of these calls from the following sequence diagrams to save space. The sequence diagrams represent the basic communication between the VCE and the property editor.

1. The user asks for a property sheet by double-clicking a component, choosing *Properties* from its pop-up menu, or by pressing the Properties button on the toolbar.
2. The VCE tells the property editor the current value by calling the setValue() method.

3. The VCE asks if the property editor wants to handle the representation presented in the property sheet by calling isPaintable(). So far, we return false, so the VCE will handle display of the value.
4. The VCE asks, "What String should be displayed" by calling the getAsText() method.
5. The VCE displays the value in a text field on the property sheet for the bean.

After the VCE displays the property sheet, the user can interact with it. There are two main forms of user interaction: The user selects or edits the value, and the user finishes the edit to that value. The user selects a value by clicking on it in the property sheet, and the user finishes an edit by pressing Enter or clicking somewhere other than the edited value. Note that pressing Enter usually causes a few extra calls to get, set, or display the value, and these calls will not appear in the sequence diagrams.

Figure 20.2 describes the interaction when a user selects the String value using the previous simple property editor. This interaction is as follows:

1. The user selects the value in the property sheet by clicking on it.
2. The VCE tells the property editor the current property value.

Figure 20.2 User selects a value: String-only editor.

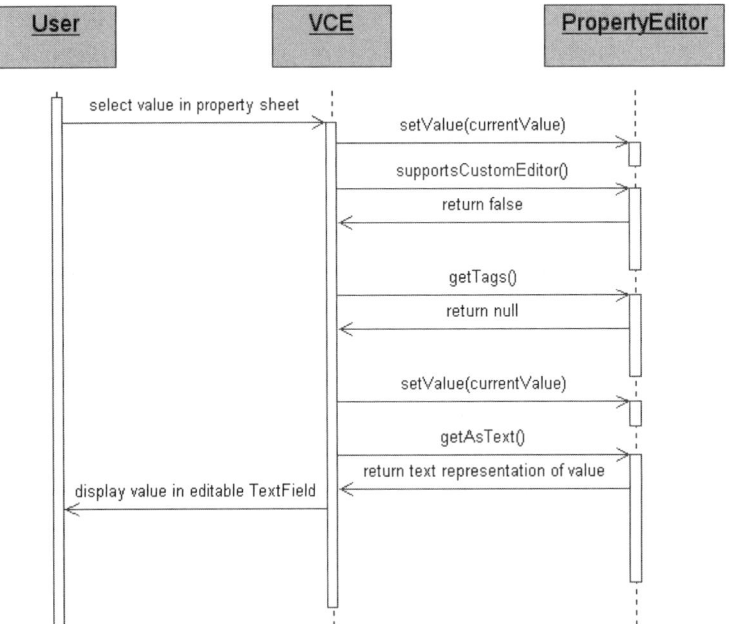

3. The VCE asks the property editor whether it provides special editing capabilities as a custom editor or tag list. This type of property editor answers no in both cases.
4. The VCE tells the property editor the current value again, in case the edit checks modify the value.
5. The VCE asks for the value as a String, and displays it in an editable text field.

Now the user performs the edit, typing changes in the text field. He or she ends the edit by pressing Enter or clicking somewhere other than the field being edited. The resulting communication between the VCE and the property editor follows; it is shown in Figure 20.3.

1. The user finishes the edit.
2. The VCE asks for the final object value by calling the getValue() method.

Figure 20.3 Finishing the edit: String-only editor.

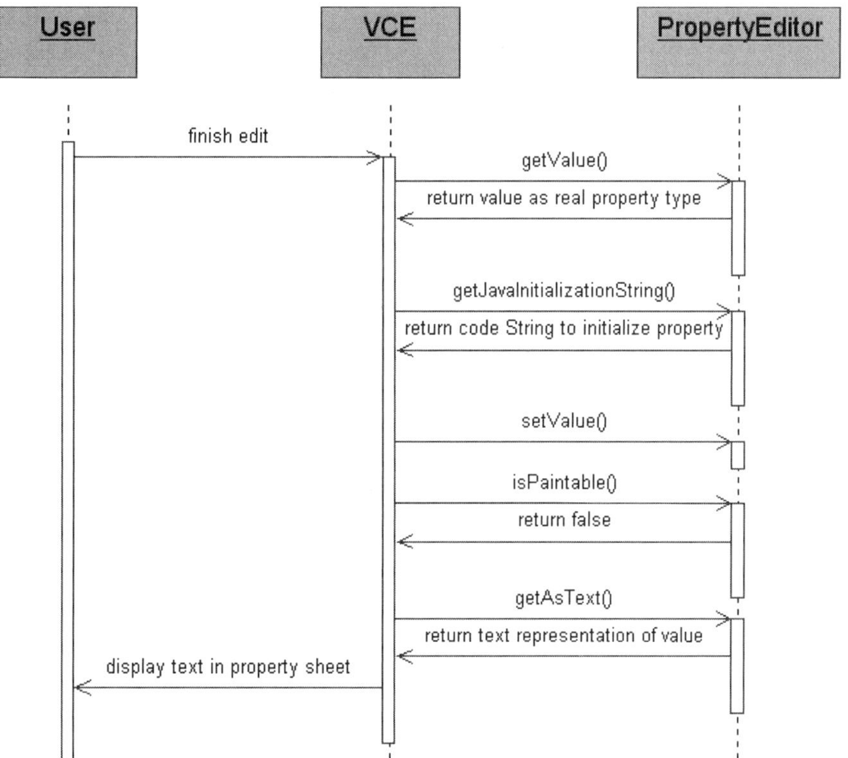

3. The property editor returns the real object value. In this example, the property editor converts the user-typed String to a real Color object.
4. The VCE requests source code to initialize the property by calling the getJavaInitializationString() method.
5. The property editor returns that String.
6. The VCE re-presents the value to the user as it did initially.

> **NOTE**
>
> The VCE handles all user interaction, and informs the property editor when the displayed text changes. The property editor does not need to inform anyone of the property value change. (This will become an issue when the property editor handles the user interaction, because it's the only thing that knows the user has changed a value.)

The following is an implementation of this property editor. While property editors are easy to write, some aspects of them can be tedious. The Java Development Kit provides a class, java.beans.PropertyEditorSupport, to make defining a property editor easier. PropertyEditorSupport provides default implementations of all PropertyEditor methods, including some event-firing routines that you will need when defining more complex property editors.

```
package effectivevaj.vce.customizing;
import java.awt.*;
import java.beans.*;
/**
 * A Simple Property Editor that edits Colors
 * This editor only allows the user to type
 *   String values, converting them to Colors
*/
public class ColorEditor1 extends PropertyEditorSupport {
  private static final String colorNames[] =
    { "white", "lightGray", "gray", "darkGray",
      "black", "red", "pink", "orange", "yellow",
      "green", "magenta", "cyan", "blue"};
  private static final Color colors[] =
    { Color.white, Color.lightGray, Color.gray,
      Color.darkGray, Color.black, Color.red,
      Color.pink, Color.orange, Color.yellow,
      Color.green, Color.magenta, Color.cyan,
```

```
    Color.blue};
private int selected = 0;

/** tell the VCE the current value when asked */
public Object getValue() {
  return colors[selected];
}

/** allow the VCE to tell us the current value */
public void setValue(Object value) {
  selected = 0;
  if (value != null)
    for (int i = 0; i < colors.length; i++)
      if (value.equals(colors[i])) {
        selected = i;
        break;
      }
}

/** return a String representation of the value */
public String getAsText() {
  return colorNames[selected];
}

/** set the value based on a user-entered String */
public void setAsText(String text)
            throws IllegalArgumentException {
  for (selected = 0;
       selected < colorNames.length &&
       !colorNames[selected].equals(text); selected++);
  if (selected == colorNames.length)
    selected = 0;
}

/** return a piece of code as a String that can be used
 *  in the VCE-generated code to set the property value
 */
public String getJavaInitializationString() {
  return "java.awt.Color." + colorNames[selected];
}

// the colorNames property — mainly used by subclasses
public String[] getColorNames() {
```

```
    return colorNames;
  }

  public String getColorNames(int index) {
    return getColorNames()[index];
  }

  // the colors property — mainly used by subclasses
  // gets the actual color objects
  public java.awt.Color[] getColors() {
    return colors;
  }

  public Color getColors(int index) {
    return getColors()[index];
  }

  // the selected property -- mainly used by subclasses
  public int getSelected() {
    return selected;
  }

  protected void setSelected(int selected) {
    this.selected = selected;
  }
}
```

This property editor converts the set Color value to a String representing that color's name. It validates that name whenever it changes and converts it to a Color object.

The getJavaInitializationString() Method

You probably noticed the getJavaInitializationString() method in the previous code. This method is called by the VCE *after* the property value has changed to get the code to include when generating the class. The String returned from this method *must* be a valid expression that can be used in a call to set the property value.

In the above example, our getJavaInitializationString() looked as follows:

```
  /** return a piece of code as a String that can be used
   *  in the VCE-generated code to set the property value
   */
  public String getJavaInitializationString() {
    return "java.awt.Color." + colorNames[selected];
  }
```

Note that we return the entire constant name, like java.awt.Color.orange, for example. If we were editing the *color* property of ColorBean, the VCE would generate code that looks like:

```
ColorBean aColorBean = new ColorBean();
aColorBean.setColor(java.awt.Color.orange);
```

Note the code in boldtext. That's the exact String returned by getJavaInitializationString(). In this example, we referenced a class constant (java.awt.Color.orange.) If you needed to create a new instance of some class, your getJavaInitializationString() method might look like this:

```
/** return a piece of code as a String that can be used
 *  in the VCE-generated code to set the property value
 */
public String getJavaInitializationString() {
  return "new java.awt.Color(" +
            red + "," + green + "," + blue + ")";
}
```

It might generate the following code:

```
ColorBean aColorBean = new ColorBean();
aColorBean.setColor(new java.awt.Color(45, 100, 214));
```

Again, note the code in bold text. In this example, we create an instance of the Color class, passing values to its constructor. These values would have to be entered by the user as a String, or through a dialog that the property editor displays. (See *Taking Control of the Property Edit* later in this chapter for details on how your property editor can display its own dialog.)

NOTE

There are two important things to think about when returning values from getJavaInitializationString():

- Never put a semicolon at the end of the returned String. Remember that the String will appear inside the parenthesis when calling a set method. The String must be a valid expression that returns a value of the property's type.
- Always fully qualify any class names that are not in package java.lang. You have no way of determining whether or not the user has an import statement for the class in question, so you must fully qualify the class name.

Using the Property Editor

The VCE needs to know which property editors you want to use for which properties. You can associate property editors with properties in three ways:

- Explicitly associate a property editor with specific properties in a BeanInfo class.
- Explicitly register the property editor with the PropertyEditorManager to provide all editing for a specific type.
- Associate a property with a specific type using a naming convention.

We discuss each of these methods in the following sections. Note that the order of these items is the order in which property editors are located. More on this in *How the VCE Locates Property Editors*, later in this chapter.

Explicit Property Editor Association Using BeanInfo

If you specify a property editor for a property in a BeanInfo class, the VCE will always use that property editor for that property. Any other means of registering property editors are ignored. This enables you to define general editors (through other registration means) for all properties of type Color, for example, and use a different property editor for specific properties in specific bean classes.

To demonstrate explicit association via BeanInfo, the following example defines a simple Panel subclass that has a color property (representing its background color). The real *background* property is left intact to allow you to compare this property editor and the default Color editor in VisualAge for Java.

A simple way to create this bean is to:

1. Create a class named ColorBean that extends java.awt.Panel.
2. Open ColorBean to the BeanInfo editor.
3. Add the *color* property using the New Property Feature SmartGuide in the BeanInfo editor. Define it as type java.awt.Color and make it a read/write property. For this example, do not make it a bound property (it depends on your application, but for this example, keep the code shorter).
4. Change the code in the getColor() and setColor() methods to call getBackground() and setBackground(), respectively. See the following code for details on how this is done.
5. Delete the generated fieldColor instance variable from the class definition.

The resulting class should look as follows:

```
package effectivevaj.vce.customizing;

import java.awt.Panel;
import java.awt.Color;
```

```
import java.io.Serializable;
/**
 * A Sample ColorBean, providing a color property for
 *    us to edit.
 */
public class ColorBean extends Panel
                          implements Serializable {
  // the color property -- delegate to background property
  public Color getColor() {
       return getBackground();
  }
  public void setColor(Color color) {
       setBackground(color);
  }
}
```

To set the property editor for the color property, open ColorBean to the BeanInfo editor. Select feature *color* and change its property editor to effectivevaj.vce.customizing.ColorEditor1, as seen in Figure 20.4.

Figure 20.4 Specifying a property editor.

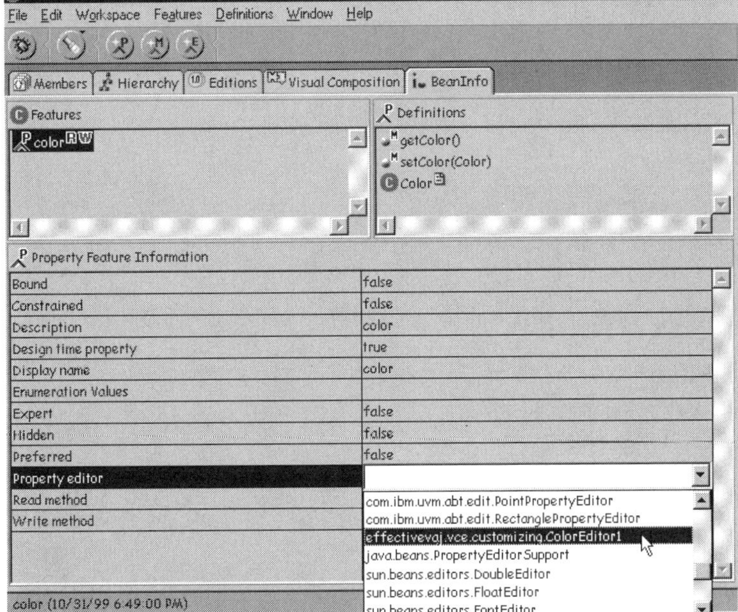

To see the property editor in action, follow these steps:

1. Create a subclass of java.awt.Frame and open it to the Visual Composition Editor.
2. Set the layout property of its ContentsPane to GridLayout.
3. Drop an instance of effectivevaj.vce.customizing.ColorBean in the ContentsPane.
4. Bring up the property sheet for the ColorBean instance. The property sheet appears in Figure 20.5.
5. Type various color names ("green," "blue," "red," without quotation marks) in the color field. Press the Enter key after each name and watch what happens. (You should see the background color in the bean change, but the background property does not change.)
6. Change the value of the background property. Notice what happens. (You should see the background color in the bean change, but the color property does not change.)

Figure 20.5 The color bean's property sheet.

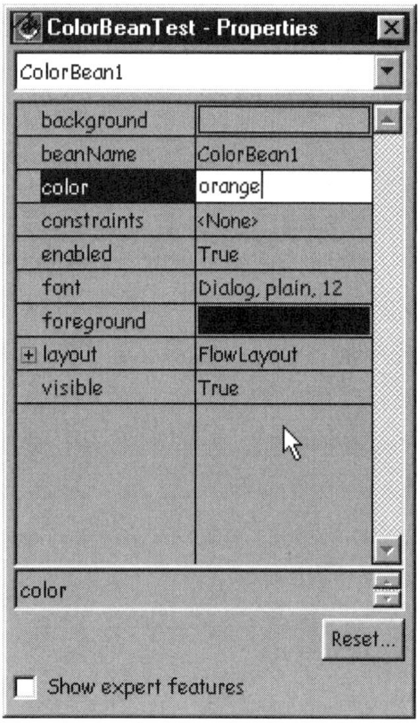

> **NOTE**
>
> When you change the background color via the background property in the property sheet, it *will not* change the value of the color property. This is because the VCE sees them as two independent properties, with two separate values. Because the color property delegates to getBackground() and setBackground(), changing it initially causes the background property to change, but once we explicitly set the background property, it is now separately managed.

In real beans, it is rare to define a property that shadows another property like this, so this will not be an issue. We present it here to demonstrate the different appearances of property editors.

Explicit Property Editor Registration

You can tell VisualAge for Java to use a specific property editor for *all* properties of a given type (except those whose BeanInfo explicitly lists another editor). This allows you to specify your own property editor for *all* properties of a given type.

To register property editors:

1. Create file ivj-property-editor-registry.properties in the installDirectory\ide\program\lib directory.

> **NOTE**
>
> You specify the *installDirectory* when you install VisualAge for Java. The default installation directory varies upon which version of VisualAge for Java you're using. If you're using VisualAge for Java, version 3.02, the default installation directory is *c:\IBMVJava*. If you're using version 3.5, the default installation directory is c:\Program Files\IBM\VisualAge for Java.

2. Add lines of the form property-type=property-editor-class to that ivj-property-editor-registry.properties file. For example, this file might look like this:

```
java.awt.Color=com.javadude.MyColorEditor
java.lang.String=com.funstuff.MyStringEditor
javax.swing.border.Border=com.javadude.border.BorderEditor
```

3. Save the ivj-property-editor-registry.properties file.

4. Exit any open VCE sessions. *You do not need to exit VisualAge for Java.*

The next time you open a class to the VCE, your new property editors will be used to edit properties of the specified types in the property sheet.

Note that this type of property editor registration is new in version 3.0 of VisualAge for Java.

Using Naming Conventions to Edit Properties

In general, it is good idea to name your property editors after the type of data they edit. For example, if you write a property editor to edit Swing Border objects, you should name it BorderEditor. This naming convention can also be useful to help the VCE (and other bean development tools) locate the appropriate property editor.

When the VCE searches for property editors, it first looks for explicit registrations in BeanInfo classes and then for editors registered in the ivj-property-editor-registry.properties file, as discussed in the previous section. If an appropriate editor is not found, it searches based on the name of the property type.

In general, if you're defining a property editor that you always want to use for a given type called *SomeType*, you name the property editor *SomeType*Editor *and place it in the same package as SomeType*. If the VCE finds an appropriately named property editor in the same package, it will use it (after the previously-mentioned explicit registrations).

If you prefer, you could place the *SomeType*Editor in a different package. This package needs to be added to the BeanInfo search path, by selecting **Window->Options->Visual Composition.** This enables your user to select between various editing packages, arranging them in whatever order they would like. As a last resort, the VCE looks in the BeanInfo search path for property editors. If none are found, it uses its default property editors (which are usually a simple text field where the user can enter a code String).

Recommended Registration Strategies

Based on whether you defined the property type and whether you want a consistent way to edit all properties of that type (versus defining property editors for a specific property), use Table 20.1 to determine how to register properties.

The basic strategies we're suggesting are:

- If the property editor is for someone else's property type, define it in any package that you own.
- If you want the property editor to apply to any property of a given type, either deliver it in the same package as the original type (if you own that package) or explicitly register it in the ivj-property-editor-registry.properties file.
- If you want the property editor to apply to specific properties, define a BeanInfo class that explicitly registers the editor for those properties.

Table 20.1 Registration Strategies

Did you define the property type?	Do you want to edit all properties in the same way?	Then define the property editor in this package	Then register the property editor in...
Yes	Yes	Same package as the property type	No explicit registration
Yes	No	Any package	BeanInfo
No	Yes	Any package	ivj-property-editor-registry.properties
No	No	Any package	BeanInfo

> **WARNING**
>
> Wherever "Any package" appears in the previous table, it means any package *that you own*. This usually means any package starting with your reversed domain name. Do not place it in the original type's package if you don't own that package!

How the VCE Locates Property Editors

The JavaBeans specification defines the class PropertyEditorManager to locate property editors. Users and bean-builder tools use it to register editors and a search path and then to locate the appropriate editors. The VCE searches for property editors any time the user requests a property sheet. This search proceeds as follows:

1. If the BeanInfo explicitly specifies an editor for a property it lists, that property editor is used.
2. The VCE asks PropertyEditorManager to locate the editor by calling its findEditor() method. This method performs the remainder of the search.
3. If PropertyEditorManager has an explicitly registered editor for the property type, that editor is used.
4. If PropertyEditorManager finds a class named *SomeType*Editor in the same package as a property type *SomeType*, that editor is used.
5. If PropertyEditorManager finds a class named *SomeType*Editor (where the property type is *SomeType*) in any of the packages in its search path, that editor is used.

Making the Property Editor a Bit Nicer

Suppose that you want a finite set of values to be the only values available for the property. For example, you can improve the user interface for ColorEditor by presenting a list of specific color choices. The getTags() method of PropertyEditor provides this functionality. If getTags() returns null (which is the default in PropertyEditorSupport) the VCE presents a text field to edit the value. If getTags() returns an array of Strings, the VCE presents a drop-down list with those String values. You can extend the ColorEditor as follows:

1. Create a ColorEditor2 class that extends ColorEditor1.
2. Add a getTags() method, changing its code to simply return the color names indexed property.

   The code for this new subclass follows.

```
package effectivevaj.vce.customizing;

/**
 * Another ColorEditor, this time presenting a list
 *   of valid color names for the user to choose
 */
public class ColorEditor2 extends ColorEditor1 {
  /** return a list of valid color names */
  public String[] getTags() {
    return getColorNames();
  }
}
```

3. Change the BeanInfo of ColorBean to use ColorEditor2 as the property editor for its *color* property.

Try editing the color property of the ColorBean in your test frame. You should see a list when you select the *color* property in the property sheet, as shown in Figure 20.6.

The communication between the VCE and the property editor is similar to the first property editor. However, the interaction is slightly different when the user selects the value in the property sheet. This interaction is as follows, and appears in Figure 20.7.

1. The user selects a property in the property sheet.
2. The VCE passes the current value to the property editor by calling setValue().
3. The VCE asks if the property editor wants to handle the edit. It does this by calling supportsCustomEditor(). This particular property editor returns false to let the VCE handle the edit.

Figure 20.6 Selecting tag values.

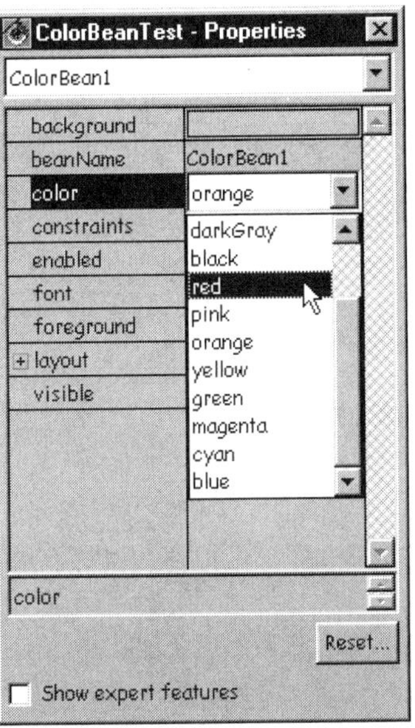

Figure 20.7 Tag selection interaction.

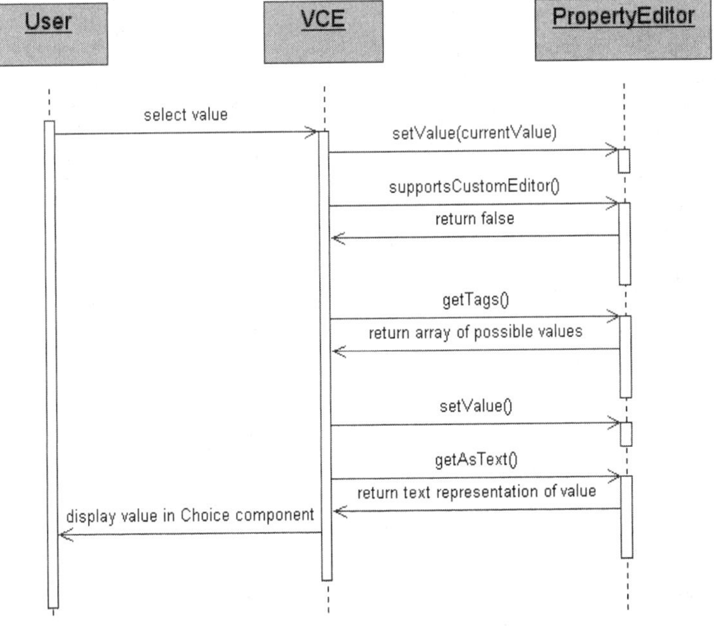

4. The VCE asks the property editor if it has a list of possible values by calling getTags(). This property editor returns an array of Strings that represent the color names.
5. The VCE (once again) tells the property editor the current value.
6. The VCE then asks for the current String representation of the value. Note that this *should* be one of the values returned from getTags().
7. The VCE displays a drop-down list in the property sheet.
8. When the user selects a new value, the VCE repeats the process, informing the editor of the selected value.

Taking Control of the Property Edit

Until this point, the VCE has handled all user interaction. This works well for simple properties that have a String representation. (For example, perhaps you want to have the user type a name and you want to make sure it is a valid word in a dictionary. Your property editor could be similar to ColorEditor1 but perform a spelling check on the value instead of checking the color.) You can represent complex properties, such as Colors, as something more "colorful."

Let's take a small step toward a better property editor by presenting *our* own GUI, a Choice component. This requires the following steps:

1. Create a simple GUI, the Choice component.
2. Tell the VCE that we provide the GUI.
3. Pass the GUI to the VCE when asked.
4. Tell the VCE when the property has changed.

Look at the last item first: You need to tell the VCE when the property has changed. The PropertyEditor interface requires methods addPropertyChangeListener() and removePropertyChangeListener(), which allow other classes to listen for property changes. In this case, the other class is the VCE itself.

Class java.beans.PropertyChangeSupport already provides this functionality. All you need to do is call its firePropertyChange() method whenever the property value changes.

To do this, modify your color editor to provide the GUI. Define supportsCustomEditor() to return true. When the VCE asks if our editor supportsCustomEditor(), and the editor returns true to tell it that *we* want to control the user interaction. The VCE responds by adding a "..." button to the property sheet whenever the user selects the color property. This interaction is as follows, and appears in Figure 20.8.

1. The user selects a value in the property sheet by clicking on it.
2. The VCE informs the property editor of the current value.
3. The VCE asks if the editor wants to handle the user interaction (through supportsCustomEditor()) and the editor responds "yes."

Figure 20.8 Preparing for a custom edit.

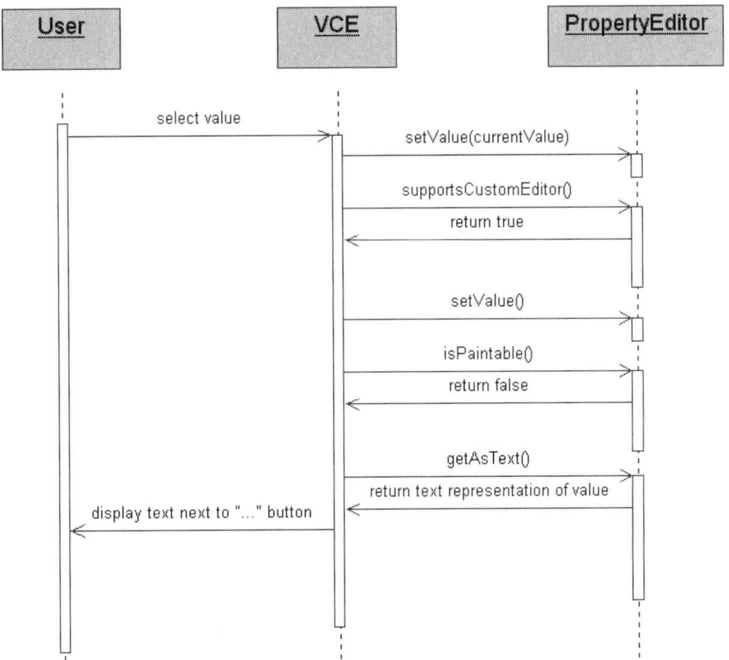

4. The VCE once again tells the editor the current value.
5. The VCE asks if the editor has a specific way it would like to paint the current value in the property sheet. This editor returns false, so the VCE will display the property as a String.
6. The VCE then calls getAsText() to get the value to display in the property sheet.

The big difference here is the "..." button that appears next to the text. The user is still shown the value as a String, *but they cannot directly edit that String.* The VCE provides a "..." button, shown in Figure 20.9, which means "press me to edit this property."

When the user presses the "..." button, it triggers the following interaction, shown in Figure 20.10.

1. The user presses the "..." button.
2. The VCE tells the property editor what the current value is (through setValue()).
3. The VCE asks for the custom editor component (through getCustomEditor()). The property editor returns an AWT Component. Note that this component *cannot* be a Dialog, Frame, or Window. It *must* be a Component that

Figure 20.9 The "..." button.

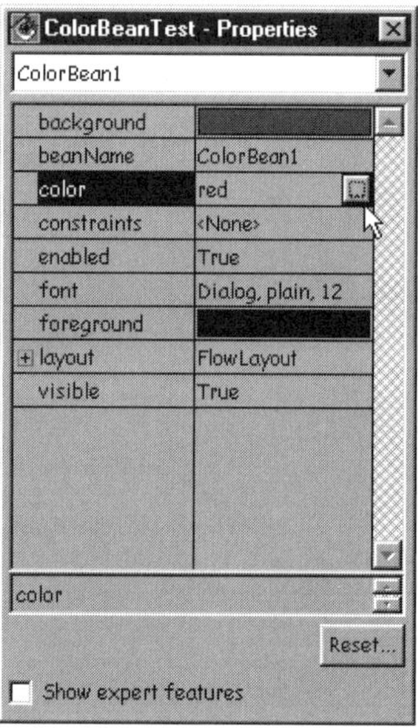

can be inserted into another Container, as the VCE manages the actual dialog. The Component *could* be a Panel, of course.

4. The VCE once again passes the value to the property editor.
5. The VCE asks if the property editor has a custom way to paint the value. This editor answers "no."
6. The VCE asks for the current representation of the value as a String (through getAsText()). It then updates the text next to the "..." button.
7. The VCE then displays the custom editor.
8. The user interacts with the custom editor. Anytime the user changes the value in the custom editor, it should call setValue() in the property editor.
9. If the user clicks **Cancel**, the VCE simply discards the custom edit dialog and makes no changes. Note that the custom editor *has no idea* that this has happened, as the VCE manages the dialog itself, including the Ok and Cancel buttons.
10. If the user clicks **Ok**, the VCE asks for the value.
11. The VCE then asks for a piece of code it can put in the generated code, by calling getJavaInitializationString() in the property editor.
12. The VCE then repeats its process to obtain a textual value for the field from the property editor.

Figure 20.10 The custom editor process.

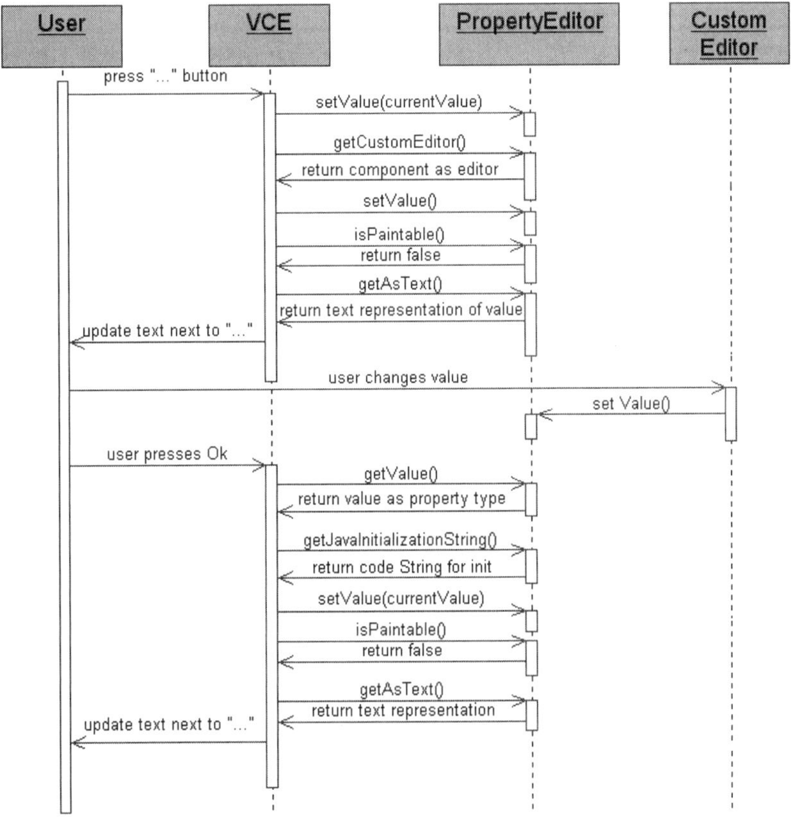

The property editor in this example:

Creates a Choice component filled with color names. This component *is* the GUI that interacts with the user to change the color property value. Register an ItemListener with the Choice component to track when its value is changed. This ItemListener sets the value of the editor, and PropertyChangeSupport fires a PropertyChangeEvent to tell the VCE that the property has changed. The VCE can then ask for the value.

Returns that Choice component through the getCustomEditor() method. When the user presses the "..." button, VisualAge asks for the custom editor and adds it to a dialog. It displays the dialog to allow the user to change the property value.

The resulting custom dialog appears in Figure 20.11.

Figure 20.11 A custom property editor.

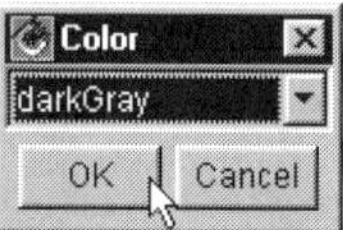

The code for this extension looks like the following. Remember to use the hierarchy view of the class browser to override methods easily.

```
package effectivevaj.vce.customizing;

import java.awt.*;
import java.awt.event.*;
import java.beans.*;
import java.io.*;
/**
 * A ColorEditor with a custom GUI. Nothing fancy,
 *   just a simple Choice component
*/
public class ColorEditor3 extends ColorEditor1
       implements Serializable, ItemListener {
  private Choice myGUI;

  /** tell the VCE that we want to do the edits
   *    with our own GUI
   */
  public boolean supportsCustomEditor() {
    return true;
  }

  /** return a populated Choice component to do the
   *  editing */
  public Component getCustomEditor() {
    if (myGUI == null) {
      myGUI = new Choice();
      String[] colorNames = getColorNames();
      for (int i = 0; i < colorNames.length; i++)
        myGUI.addItem(colorNames[i]);
        myGUI.addItemListener(this);
    }
    return myGUI;
  }
```

```
  /** an event hander to watch for changes in
   *    the Choice component */
  public void itemStateChanged(ItemEvent e) {
    setAsText((String) e.getItem());
  }
}
```

A More Natural Interface

The interface in the custom property editor is still not as simple as it could be. What does cyan look like? Why not provide buttons with the colors as their background? If a natural representation of the data is available, you should try to use that representation. Showing what a color looks like is much more natural than printing its name. Many people don't know what cyan looks like, but they recognize the color when they see it on the screen.

> **NOTE**
>
> Some versions of the JDK have a bug in AWT's Button class that does not paint the background color of the button. The current version of VisualAge for Java contains this AWT bug, so we use Swing's JButton class instead of AWT's Button class in this example.

The interface between the property editor and the bean builder remains the same; you just change the GUI a bit. Extend ColorEditor3 to create ColorEditor4, as seen in the following code.

```
package effectivevaj.vce.customizing;

import java.awt.*;
import java.awt.event.*;
import java.beans.*;
import java.io.*;
import javax.swing.JButton;

/**
 * A more natural color editor, allowing the
 *   user to press a colored button
*/
public class ColorEditor4 extends ColorEditor3
```

```
        implements Serializable, ActionListener {
    private Panel myGUI;

    /** An event handler to watch for pressed buttons */
    public void actionPerformed(ActionEvent e) {
      setAsText(((JButton) e.getSource()).getText());
    }

    /** The new GUI that interacts with the user
     *     to select the color */
    public Component getCustomEditor() {
      if (myGUI == null) {
        myGUI = new Panel(new GridLayout(0, 2));
        String[] colorNames = getColorNames();
        Color[] colors = getColors();
        for (int i = 0; i < colorNames.length; i++) {
          JButton b = new JButton(colorNames[i]);
          b.setBackground(colors[i]);
          b.addActionListener(this);
          myGUI.add(b);
        }
      }
      return myGUI;
    }
}
```

All that has changed is the GUI. If you are careful, you can change the appearance of the GUI with very little effort. This GUI is now Panel-based with a two-column grid of JButton beans. Each JButton bean has the color name and the color it selects. When pressed, the color value is set. This new editor appears in Figure 20.12.

Interaction between the VCE and this property editor is the same as with ColorEditor3.

The Final Touch

What about that textual color name in the property sheet? Why not present it as a color as well? You can!

The PropertyEditor interface provides a means to graphically display a property value in the property sheet. You only need to implement the isPaintable() and paintValue() methods. Instead of passing a text value for the property to VCE, tell it that you can paint a value for the property, and provide a method to do that painting. The changes to the class are very simple:

- Add an isPaintable() method that returns true (the default defined in PropertyEditorSupport returns false), telling the VCE that you want to draw the property value.

Figure 20.12 A more natural color chooser.

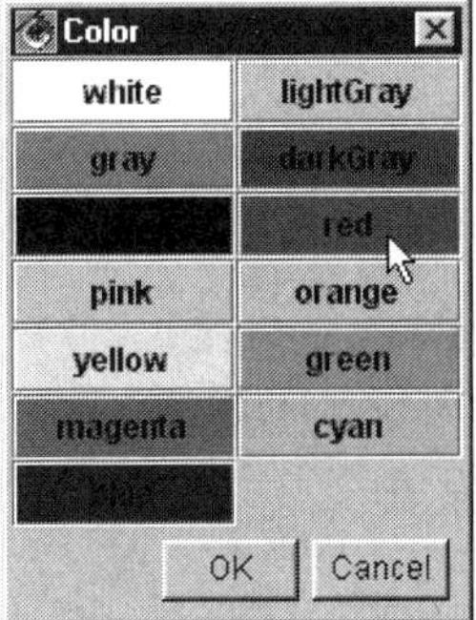

- Add a paintValue() method to represent the property value.

The VCE passes a graphics context and a bounding rectangle to paintValue(). These parameters tell you where you should draw. *Make sure you respect that bounding box*, or the property sheet graphics could end up looking rather ugly! Our implementation for ColorEditor5 draws a raised box in the selected color. Code for the new property editor follows:

```
package effectivevaj.vce.customizing;

import java.awt.*;
import java.awt.event.*;
import java.beans.*;
import java.io.*;
/**
 * Enhance our property editor by drawing the
 *   current value in the property sheet
*/
public class ColorEditor5 extends ColorEditor4
       implements Serializable {

  /** tell the VCE that we want to paint the current value
  public boolean isPaintable() {
    return true;
  }

  /** perform the painting */
  public void paintValue(Graphics gfx, Rectangle box) {
    gfx.setColor(getColors(getSelected()));
      // we use three 3-d rects to over-emphasize the
```

```
        //    3-d effect -- you many want to be more subtle
        // (this way you can be sure this editor is working...)
        gfx.fill3DRect(box.x + 2, box.y + 2,
                       box.width - 5, box.height - 5, true);
        gfx.fill3DRect(box.x + 3, box.y + 3,
                       box.width - 7, box.height - 7, true);
        gfx.fill3DRect(box.x + 4, box.y + 4,
                       box.width - 9, box.height - 9, true);
    }
}
```

The interaction for this property editor is slightly different, because you control how it appears in the property sheet. When the user requests a property sheet, it triggers the following interaction, shown in Figure 20.13.

1. The user requests a property sheet.
2. The VCE tells the property editor what the current value is.
3. The VCE asks if the property editor wants to paint the value in a special way. This property editor responds true.
4. The VCE then asks the property editor to paint the value in a specified area.

Note that the VCE does not ask for a String representation of the property. That's because it does not need to display a String representation in the property editor.

Figure 20.13 Property sheet display, custom painting.

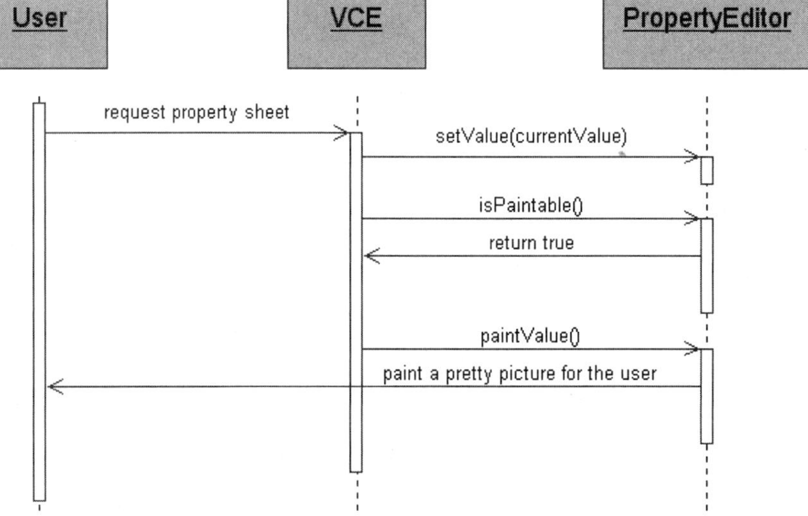

When the user selects the value to edit it, the following interaction, shown in Figure 20.14, begins.

1. The user selects the value.
2. The VCE asks if the property editor wants to paint (true) and asks it to update the current painting.
3. The VCE then passes the property editor the current value and goes through the paint update again.

When the user presses the "..." button, it triggers the interaction in Figure 20.15. Note that this interaction is similar to that for property editors that want to handle the edit without a custom painting. The difference is that this particular property editor must refresh the painted value rather than return a String.

Locating Property Editors, Revisited

Earlier in this chapter we mentioned an option for associating property editors with property types. The JavaBeans specification provides a naming pattern for associating property editor classes with the types they edit. Let's explore this option by providing a new property type and an editor for it. The "new type" and editor will actually be simple subclasses of java.awt.Color and the ColorEditor5.

Figure 20.14 User selection, custom painting.

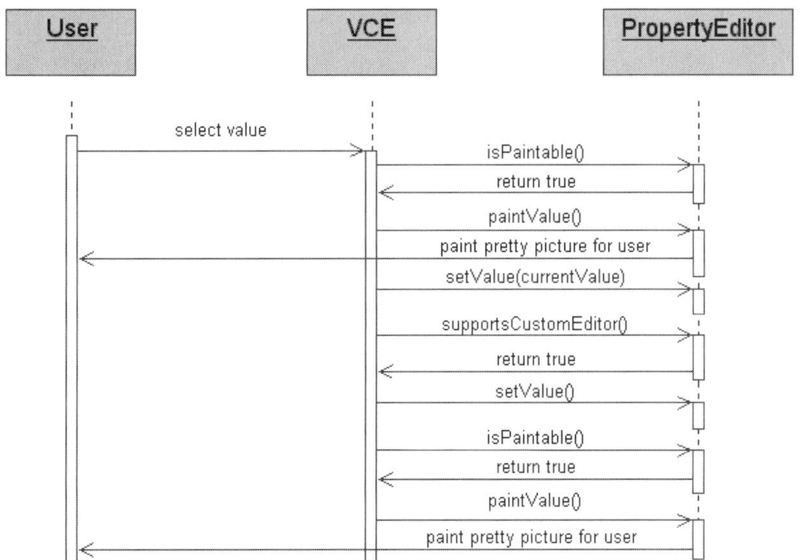

Figure 20.15 Editing the property, custom painting.

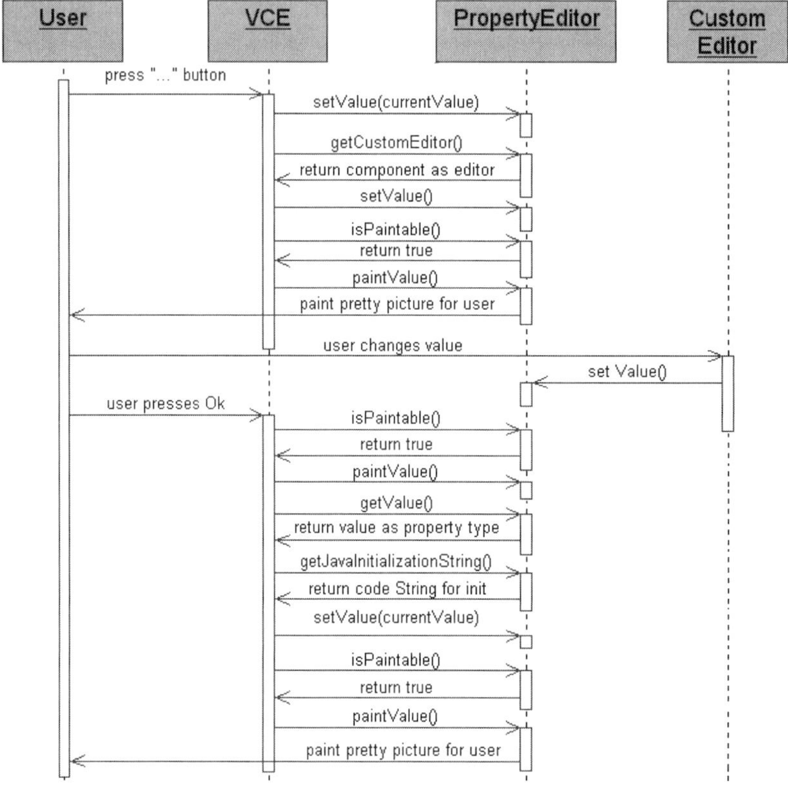

Create a new class MyColor as an extension of java.awt.Color in order to create a new type name. Create a new class MyColorEditor as an extension of ColorEditor5. These two classes must reside in the same package (this example places them in effectivevaj.vce.customizing, but they could be in any package you desire). Note the similarities in the name: MyColor and MyColorEditor. The editor class is named the same as the property type class, with *-Editor* added on the end.

```
package effectivevaj.vce.customizing;

import java.awt.*;
/**
 * A silly extension of Color to provide
 *   and example of property editing by type.
 */
public class MyColor extends Color {
  public MyColor(float r, float g, float b) {
```

```
    super(r, g, b);
  }
  public MyColor(int rgb) {
    super(rgb);
  }
  public MyColor(int r, int g, int b) {
    super(r, g, b);
  }
}

package effectivevaj.vce.customizing;

/**
 * An editor specifically to edit properties of
 *    type MyColor
 */
public class MyColorEditor extends ColorEditor5 {
}
```

Because these classes are in the same package, and because nothing registers MyColor with PropertyEditorManager, MyColorEditor is the property editor for *any* properties of type MyColor.

To test this, add a new property *anotherColor* of type MyColor to the ColorBean. Open ColorBeanTest in the VCE, and bring up the property sheet for the ColorBean instance. When you edit the *anotherColor* property, the VCE uses MyColorEditor to edit it. Any beans that define a property of type MyColor and do not explicitly associate a property editor with that property will use MyColorEditor to edit it.

Customizers

Customizers give you total control over the user interaction with your beans. Because property editors only edit one property at a time, you cannot manage dependencies between them. For example, if a Person bean has a *zipCode* property, you could not automatically set the *city* and *state* properties of that bean based on the value of zipCode.

By using a customizer, you have complete control of the edit. You return a GUI that the user can use to edit the entire bean at once. This allows you to have interproperty relationships such as the zipCode property outlined above. Customizers act like SmartGuides for a bean.

The JavaBeans specification defines an interface called Customizer. The Customizer interface defines three methods:

- `void addPropertyChangeListener(PropertyChangeListener l);`

- `void removePropertyChangeListener(PropertyChangeListener l);`
- `void setObject(Object bean);`

These three methods allow simple communication between your bean builder (in this case, the VCE) and the customizer. The bean builder registers itself with the customizer to allow immediate visual updates whenever properties in the customizer change. When the user initially requests a customizer, the bean builder calls its setObject() method to pass the bean to customize. The customizer directly modifies that bean, whereas property editors should never directly modify their property.

> **NOTE**
>
> The VCE *does not* register for change notification. This means that you may not see updates to the bean until the user closes the customizer dialog. If the target bean is an AWT component, you may see some changes immediately due to the processing provided by the peer classes.

Note that there are currently some problems in the way VisualAge for Java handles customizers. IBM is working to fix them, but we provide some workarounds here to assist development.

Simple and Direct Property Edits

Let's start with an example that demonstrates one possible use of a customizer. This customizer edits a simple Person bean. The Person bean provides *name*, *phone*, *street*, *city*, *state*, and *zipCode* String properties. To make the data entry easier for the user, you automatically set the *city* and *state* properties for known *zipCodes*. In example code below, we hardcode for zip codes; for a real application, we would read this data from a database.

The PersonCustomizer class must provide the three methods that the Customizer interface requires. These methods and a few support methods follow the next paragraph. The rest of the PersonCustomizer class is composed visually, and appears in Figure 20.16.

Note that this customizer extends Container. The bean builder tool creates its own dialog to contain your customizer. *Do not extend Dialog yourself*, or the bean builder tool will not be able to use your customizer. The methods that appear in bold are those required by the Customizer interface.

```
package effectivevaj.vce.customizing;

import java.awt.*;
import java.beans.*;
```

Figure 20.16 The customizer's visual design.

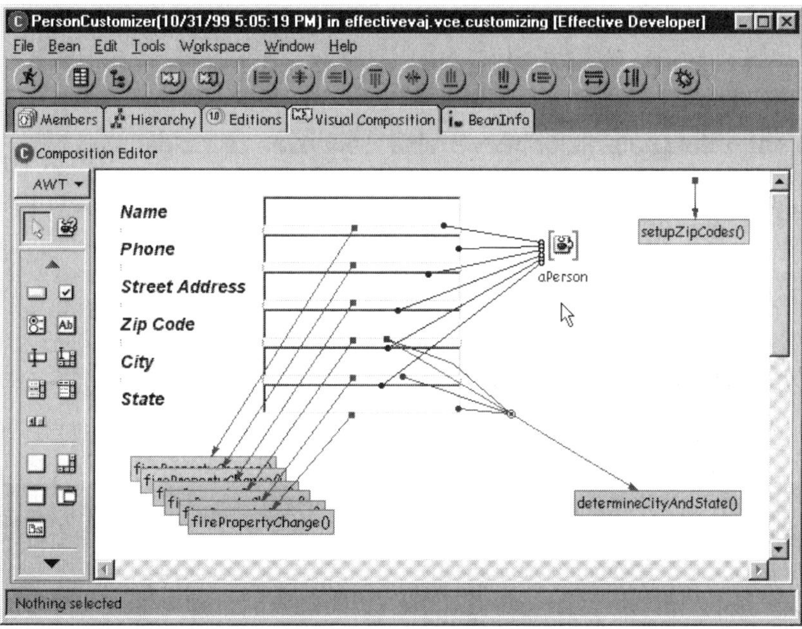


```
import java.io.*;
import java.util.Hashtable;

/**
 * A simple customizer that sets the city and state
 *   of a person based on the zipcode
*/
public class PersonCustomizer extends Container
       implements Customizer, Serializable {
  private Hashtable cities = new Hashtable();
  private Hashtable states = new Hashtable();
  private static final Object[][] zipInfo =
    { {"20874", "Germantown", "Maryland"},
      {"20877", "Gaithersburg", "Maryland"},
      {"48103", "Ann Arbor", "Michigan"},
      {"95065", "Santa Cruz", "California"}};

  public synchronized void addPropertyChangeListener(
                                PropertyChangeListener l) {
    getPropertyChange().addPropertyChangeListener(l);
```

```
  }

  public void determineCityAndState(String zip,
                                    TextField stateField,
                                    TextField cityField) {
    String city = (String) cities.get(zip);
    String state = (String) states.get(zip);
    if (city != null)
      cityField.setText(city);
    if (state != null)
      stateField.setText(state);
  }

  public synchronized void removePropertyChangeListener(
                              PropertyChangeListener l) {
    getPropertyChange().removePropertyChangeListener(l);
  }

  public void setObject(Object bean) {
    Person person = (Person) bean;
    setaPerson(person);
  }

  public void setupZipCodes() {
    for (int i = 0; i < zipInfo.length; i++) {
      cities.put(zipInfo[i][0], zipInfo[i][1]);
      states.put(zipInfo[i][0], zipInfo[i][2]);
    }
  }
}
```

The visual design requires some explanation. It performs the following tasks:

- When the customizer is initialized, it calls setupZipCodes(). This initializes the zip code data for later processing.
- The property-to-property connections between the aPerson variable and the TextField beans provide initialization from the variable, and set the properties in the variable whenever the TextField beans change. *The connections do not provide update capability when the properties in the variable change.* The source event of each connection is set to **<none>**. This is extremely important, because if you provide this communication, it requires that you add PropertyChangeListeners to the bean that you are customizing. The problem with this is that there is no way to know when the customization is finished; those listeners cannot be removed.

You should make sure that your customizer never adds listeners to the bean it is customizing!

- The textValueChanged event of the zip code field triggers a call to determineCityAndState(). This method checks the zip code data in the customizer and sets the text of the city and state TextField beans. Because of the processing in the property-to-property connections, this results in changes to the bean properties.
- Finally, when any of the TextField beans change, firePropertyChange() is called. This method simply notifies any listeners that something has changed. In this case, null is passed as the property name. The firePropertyChange method looks as follows:

```
public void firePropertyChange() {
  getPropertyChange().firePropertyChange(null, null,
                                         getaPerson());
}
```

To use the customizer, you must associate it with the Person bean. To do this, open the Person bean to the BeanInfo editor and change its customizer attribute to the PersonCustomizer, as demonstrated in Figure 20.17.

Figure 20.17 Setting a customizer.

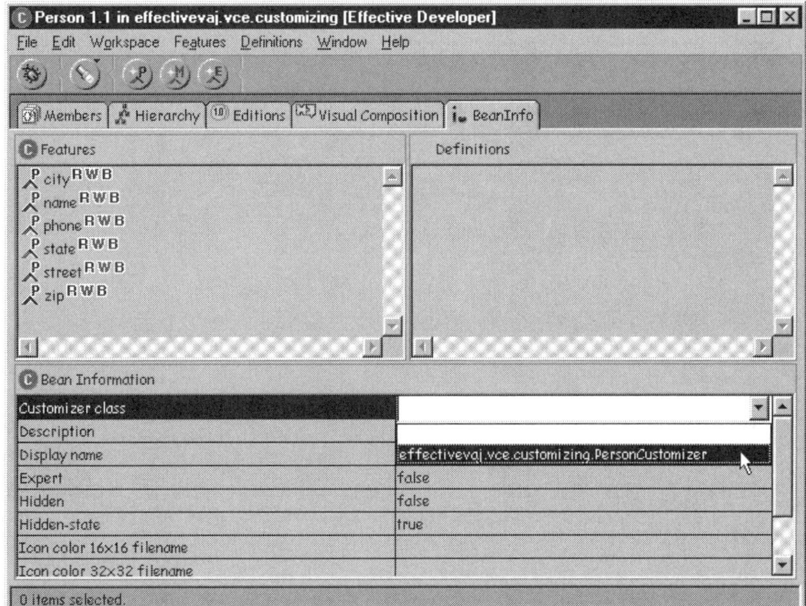

To test the customization, create a simple nonvisual class and drop a Person bean in it. When you bring up the property sheet for that Person bean, the **Custom Properties** button appears, shown in Figure 20.18.

If you click the **Custom Properties** button, the VCE displays the customizer GUI, as seen in Figure 20.19. When the user types in a recognized zip code, it automatically sets the city and state fields. The resulting property sheet appears in Figure 20.20.

Customizers Assist Interproperty Relationships

There is a relationship between the zip code and the city and state properties of Person. The customizer helps the user fill in some potentially redundant information. This is a very effective use of a customizer. This example worked perfectly well, because all of the properties were of types that VisualAge knows how to deal with. Unfortunately, if one of the properties is itself another bean that is not built into VisualAge, you can experience some problems.

Problems with Complex Property Edits

Suppose that you move the address data into a separate Address bean. The Address bean would contain the *street*, *city*, *state*, and *zipCode* properties. The Person bean would contain *name*, *phone*, and *address* properties, where the address property is of type Address.

Figure 20.18 A property sheet for a customizable bean.

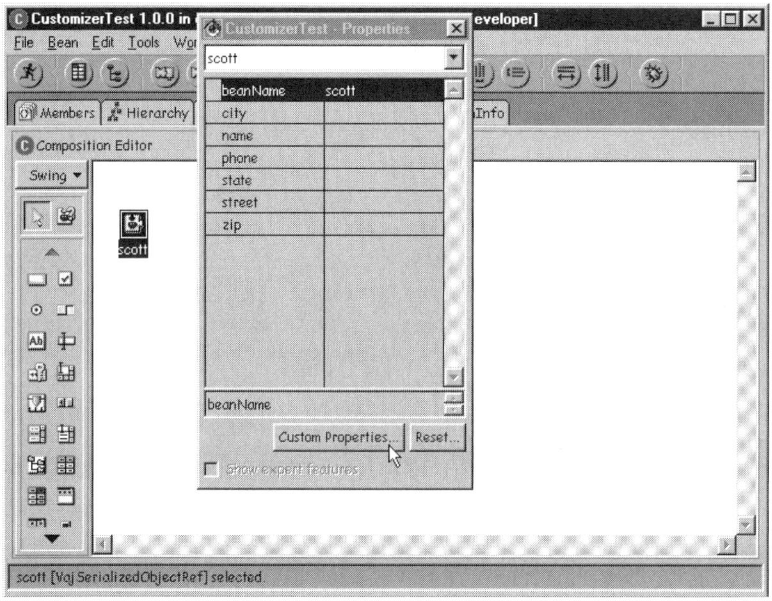

Figure 20.19 The customizer in action.

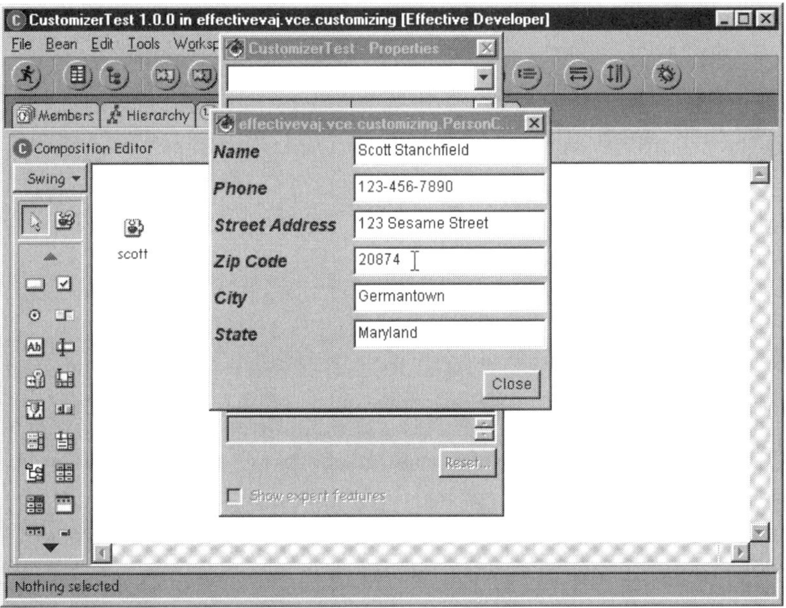

Figure 20.20 The property sheet after customization.

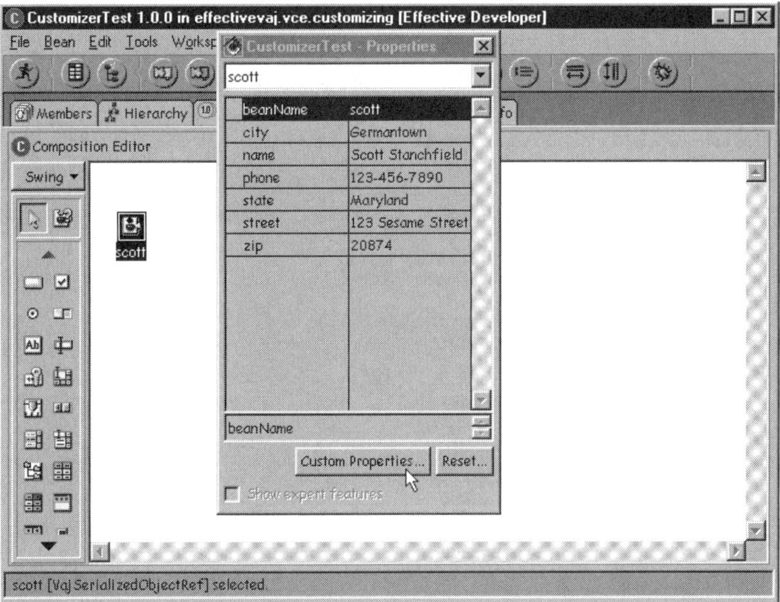

You want to keep the interface of the customizer the same. The visual design changes slightly, as seen in Figure 20.21.

The difference in this design is that the address property of the person variable is torn off. Now, instead of person properties actually changing, address properties change. The problem is that VisualAge does not realize the person has changed, *because it has not changed.* All of its properties remain the same.

You must do two things to make this example work properly:

Mark the Person Bean as using Hidden State. The hidden-state attribute of a bean tells the bean-builder tool that it must use serialization to save and recreate the bean. Because you are setting information *inside* a property of customized bean, rather than changing the property itself, VisualAge does not realize that needs to save any data. Furthermore, VisualAge would not have any idea how to generate code to create that property.

By marking the bean as a hidden-state bean, the VCE serializes the customized bean when the user saves the visual design. It also generates code in the composite bean to read that serialized bean at run time.

Explicitly regenerate code. Because VisualAge does not realize that the bean changed, it may not realize that it needs to save the visual composition. If you customize a bean with complex properties, and the VCE does not allow you to save the visual design, make sure you select

Figure 20.21 The new customizer design.

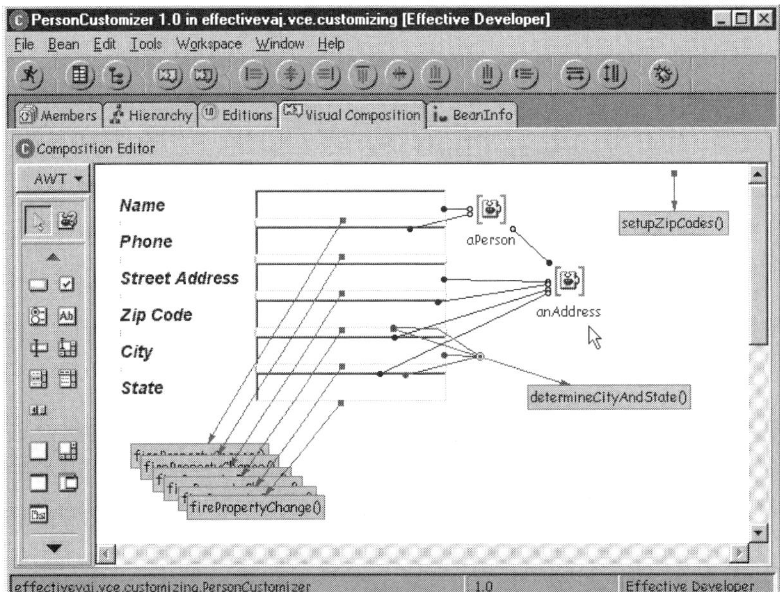

Regenerate Code from the Bean menu in the VCE. If you make other changes during a VCE session, you will not need to worry about this. However, if the only change you make is to a complex property in a customizer, you may need to regenerate the code.

When to Provide Property Editors and Customizers

When should you use customizers or property editors? The answer is threefold.

- If you require relationships between properties, you should provide a customizer and hide those properties. This forces the user to use your customizer to set those property values. This gives you complete control over how the user can use your bean in a bean-builder tool.
- If you do not require relationships, and the properties are simple (primitive types or Strings), you probably do not need a property editor *or* a customizer.
- For complex property types, or ones that require the user to type code, property editors are a very good idea. The only alternative for the user would be to type complex code Strings to define the property. Your bean is much easier to edit if you ask a few questions in a property editor and generate that code String for the user.

Note that because property editors can provide a GUI component, you can build a customizer by composing several property editor GUIs into a larger GUI. This is often quite helpful, since you do not need to reinvent any of the processing that the property editor already provides.

Neither property editors or customizers are *necessary*; however, they can make the difference between a *good* bean and a *usable* bean when your user is using a bean–builder tool. Your bean can be the most amazing bean in the world, but if it's difficult for people to use in a tool, developers will not use it. By providing property editors and customizers, you make it much easier for developers to use your bean

Summary

This concludes our coverage of visual composition. The next chapters move into some more advanced Java API programming concepts, starting with database programming. VisualAge provides many tools to simplify database programming, as well as assist in development with other enterprise APIs. We will guide you through these APIs, helping you to learn when and how to use them.

DATABASE PROGRAMMING

21

VisualAge for Java comes with several tools and class libraries that you can use to access and manipulate the data stored in relational databases:

- The *Data Access Beans*, part of all VisualAge for Java editions (Entry, Professional, and Enterprise), enable you to build SQL queries using wizards. You can then invoke those queries using predefined beans in the Visual Composition Editor.
- The *Data Access Builder*, part of VisualAge for Java since version 1.0, enables you to generate beans to manipulate rows in a table (select, insert, delete, and update) from an existing database schema or invoke SQL queries through customized SELECT statements. It helps you manage database connections and transactions (commit, rollback). You can customize the generated beans to extend their functionality. This tool is available only in version 3.0.x, and has been *removed* in version 3.5. Therefore, we highly advise not to use it, and to make sure you don't, we will not explain how it works!
- The *Persistence Access Builder* enables you to define an object model, define which object attributes are persistent, and map the object model to a database schema. You can also start from a database schema and create the object model, or map an existing model to an existing schema.
- The Stored Procedure Builder enables you to build, install, register, and run DB2 stored procedures on the server on which they will execute. You can also debug them remotely using the Distributed Debugger. You must have DB2 version 6.1 to use the Stored Procedure Builder.
- *SQLJ Supporting Tools*. SQLJ is static SQL in Java programs. VisualAge for Java comes with a set of tools to edit, run, and debug SQLJ programs.

NOTE

The Persistence Builder deserves a book all by itself. Rather than just scratching the surface, we recommend that you read the Redbook SG24-5426 available from www.redbooks.ibm.com. We cover some of the Persistence Builder functionality in Chapter 23, "Developing Enterprise JavaBeans." Most Persistence Builder mapping tools are used to create persistent enterprise beans.

In this chapter, we walk you through a complete database application-development project. First, we use the Data Access Beans to insert rows in a table and display the contents of a table. Then, we create a stored procedure using the Stored Procedure Builder and invoke it from a client application by using the Data Access Beans. Finally, we write an application based on SQLJ to display the contents of a table.

NOTE

We assume in this chapter that you have basic knowledge about SQL and relational databases. In addition, most samples are developed with the Visual Composition Editor. If you have never worked with this tool, please refer to Chapters 10 through 13 before reading the following sections.

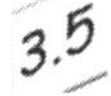

Throughout this chapter, we have identified version 3.5 changes by using this icon.

Populating Data in a Table

One of the Data Access Beans, the Modify bean, can be used to insert data into a database table. In this section, we will use the Data Access Beans tools to create a customized Modify bean, and use this Modify bean in the Visual Composition Editor. Throughout this chapter, we assume you have created a database called MUSIC. This database contains two tables:

CLASSICS. It describes classical-music CDs. This table can be created by using the following SQL statement:

```
CREATE TABLE CLASSICS (
 ID CHAR(6) NOT NULL,
 TITLE VARCHAR(30) NOT NULL,
```

```
  COMPOSER VARCHAR(40) NOT NULL,
  TRACKS INTEGER,
  TYPE VARCHAR(20),
  LENGTH CHAR(5),
  CONDUCTOR VARCHAR(30));

ALTER TABLE CLASSICS ADD PRIMARY KEY(ID);
```

TRACK. This table describes tracks on a classical CD. This table can be created by using the following SQL statement:

```
CREATE TABLE TRACK (
  ID INTEGER NOT NULL,
  CDID CHAR(6) NOT NULL,
  TITLE VARCHAR(30),
  LENGTH VARCHAR(6));
ALTER TABLE TRACK ADD PRIMARY KEY (ID, CDID);
```

The two tables are linked by a foreign-key relationship on the CLASSICS ID column. This foreign-key relationship can be created using the following SQL statement:

```
ALTER TABLE TRACK
ADD CONSTRAINT TRACKCD FOREIGN KEY(CDID)REFERENCES CLASSICS;
```

The first application you will create, InsertClassicsApp, lets you insert rows into the CLASSICS table. After checking all prerequisites, you will use the Visual Composition Editor to create a GUI to gather the data that will be inserted in the table. Next, you will use the Data Access Beans tools to generate a customized Modify bean, used to insert the data itself. Finally, you will complete the application by linking the GUI and the Modify bean.

Checking Prerequisites

Before developing the InsertClassics application described in this section, you must make sure that the Data Access Beans feature is installed and that the JDBC drivers you intend to use are correctly working.

Adding the Access Beans Feature

To load the Data Access Beans feature in your workspace, you must:

1. Go to the Quick Start dialog by selecting **File->Quick Start** or pressing F2.
2. Select the Features category and then **Add Feature**; press **Ok**.
3. Select **Data Access Beans**, and press **Ok**.

You should now see the **IBM Data Access Beans** project in your workspace. In addition, a **Database** category has also been added to the Visual Composition Editor beans palette. This category contains all of the base beans delivered with the Data Access Beans library. You will use most of the beans available in the Data Access library in the various applications described in this chapter.

Adding JDBC Drivers to the Class Path

The Data Access Beans use the Java Database Connectivity (JDBC) API to connect to a database and retrieve schema information. They can be used to connect to virtually any database that has a JDBC driver. You must ensure that this JDBC driver is listed on the workspace class path. You do not need to import the drivers in VisualAge to use them, because you will only use them at run time and not at compile time. You must import only the workspace classes that VisualAge for Java needs to analyze at compile time. For example, if you write

```
mydriver = new JDBCDriver();
```

the JDBCDriver class must be imported in the workspace. If you load a class dynamically at run time (for example, using

```
Class.forName("JDBCDriver"))
```

you need only to reference the archive file or directory containing that class on the workspace class path. It will not hurt if you import a JDBC driver that you reference dynamically: It is just not mandatory.

To add a JDBC driver to the workspace class path, you must:

1. Open the IDE customization window from **Window->Options** and select the **Resources** category.
2. Press the **Browse** button near the workspace class-path entry field.
3. Add either a directory or JAR/ZIP file name for the JDBC driver you want to load. For DB2, the driver is stored in the db2java.zip file located under c:\sqllib\java, as shown in Figure 21.1.

> **NOTE**
>
> If your database vendor does not provide a JDBC driver but does provide an ODBC driver, you can use the JDBC-ODBC driver developed by SUN instead. The JDBC-ODBC driver is part of the base JDK: therefore, you have nothing to add to the workspace class path.

Once the workspace class path has been modified, you can test the connection to a database by writing a few lines of code in the Scrapbook, such as:

Figure 21.1 Setting the workspace class path.

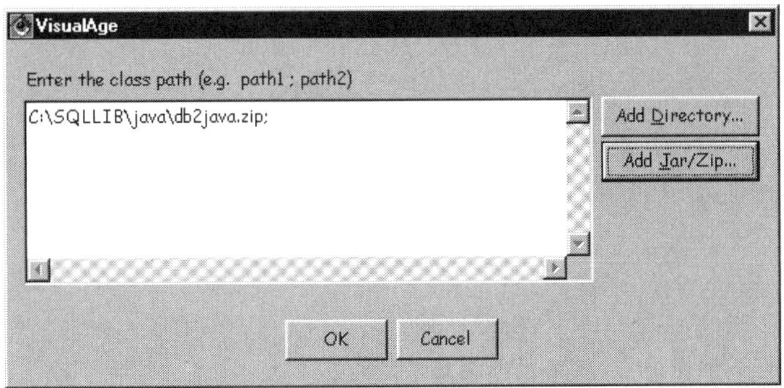


```
Class.forName ("COM.ibm.db2.jdbc.app.DB2Driver");
java.sql.Connection conn =
  java.sql.DriverManager.getConnection ("jdbc:db2:MUSIC",
                                        "userid",
                                        "password");
com.ibm.uvm.tools.DebugSupport.inspect(conn);
conn.close(); // Do not forget to do this!
```

These lines of code dynamically load the DB2 native driver (application driver) and try to open a connection to the MUSIC database using a URL (jdbc:db2:MUSIC), a logon ID, and a password. If you select the code in the Scrapbook (Ctrl-A) and choose **Edit->Run**, an inspector window opens on the Connection object, shown in Figure 21.2. Do not forget to close the connection, or it will stay open until the IDE is closed! For more details on the Scrapbook and inspector windows, please refer to Chapter 5, "Testing and Debugging."

NOTE

Occasionally, you will get an UnsatisfiedLinkError in the debugger. There is a variety of reasons why this may happen, but the most probable is that the DLL that contains the code called by the driver via JNI can't be located. Make sure that the path to the DLL (such as c:\SQLLIB\bin) is on your system PATH (on the LIBPATH or LD_LIBRARY_PATH if you are using a UNIX platform).

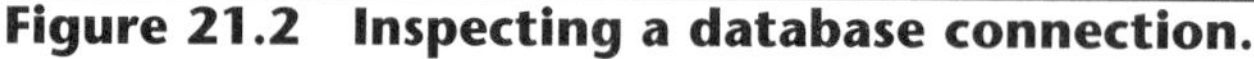

Figure 21.2 Inspecting a database connection.

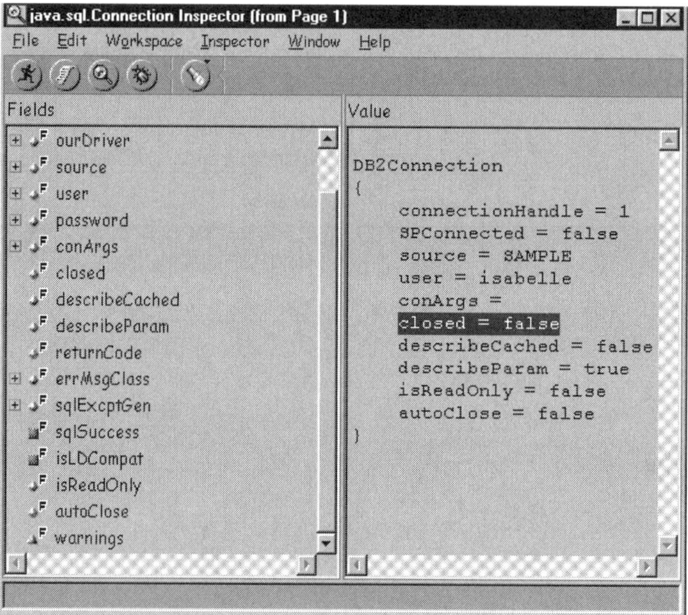

Creating the InsertClassics Application GUI

The InsertClassics application will be created in three steps. In this first step, you will create the application base GUI. InsertClassics is a Swing-based application that you will create with the Visual Composition Editor. This application inherits from com.sun.java.swing.JFrame. Follow those steps to create the InsertClassics base GUI:

1. Select **Add->Class** from the Selected menu.
2. Specify *Effective VisualAge for Java* as the project name.
3. Specify *effectivevaj.data.applications* as the package name.
4. Specify InsertClassicsApp as the class name and JFrame as the superclass. You can use code completion to automatically insert the package name in front of JFrame by placing the cursor right after JFrame and pressing **Ctrl-Space**.
5. Select the **Browse the class when finished** and **Compose the Class visually** options: We want to use the Visual Composition Editor to create this sample.
6. Press **Finish**.

The class browser will open to the VCE. You will now customize the base GUI by following those steps:

1. Change the JFrameContentPane layout property to BorderLayout.
2. Drop a JPanel component (ButtonsPanel) on the free-form surface, change its layout to FlowLayout, and set its layout alignment property to LEFT.
3. Drop a JButton bean on ButtonsPanel.
4. Rename this button ExecutePB and change its text property to Execute.
5. Move ButtonsPanel to the SOUTH position of JFrameContentPane.

Customizing the Modify Bean

In the next step, we will create a database connection and SQL statement using the SQL Assist SmartGuide provided with the Data Access Beans. First, we will create a package to contain all of the code generated by those tools. Then, we will use the SQL Assist SmartGuide to create a database connection and SQL statement.

Creating a Package for the Database Access Class

When you define a database connection or an SQL statement, a method is generated for it. You must specify the class (called a Database Access class) that will contain this method. You can use an existing Database Access class, or create a new one using a wizard. This class must be placed in an existing package. If you supply a non-existing package name, the tool will not create this package for you, and the code generation will fail.

You can group all connections that you define in one package, and name the class after the database name. This makes the generated code easier to understand. In addition, it makes deployment easier: You do not need the database access classes at run time. To create the package that will contain all Data Access classes:

1. Select the *Effective VisualAge for Java* project
2. Invoke **Add->Package** from the pop-up menu.
3. Enter *effectivevaj.data.test.dab.connections* as the package name.
4. Press **Finish**.

> **NOTE**
>
> If you are using the Enterprise Edition, make sure you are a package group member of this package! You will not receive any warning when you start the SmartGuide; the code generation will simply fail.

Creating a Modify Bean

The com.ibm.ivj.db.uibeans.Modify bean can be used to insert, update, and delete data from a table. To use it, you must drop it on the VCE free-form surface and customize its *action* property. The action property is of type **com.ibm.ivj.db .uibeans.Query**. This property defines how to connect to the database and what SQL statement to execute. A property editor is provided to edit this property. Follow those steps to create a Modify bean and start the action property editor:

1. Select the Database category in the palette, select the Modify bean and drop it on the free-form surface. This creates an instance of the Modify bean called Modify1.
2. Double-click on the Modify1 bean to open its properties.
3. Change the **beanName** property to insertClassicRow.
4. Invoke the action property editor by clicking on the button on the right-hand side of the action property field.

The property editor is started after a short while. The next sections describe how to use this property editor. First, you will create a database access class and define a database connection. Then, you will use the SQL Assist SmartGuide to create the SQL statement to execute.

Defining the Database Connection

First, you need to define the class that will contain the database connection and SQL statement definitions (the database access class). To do this:

1. Press the **New** button on the right-hand side of the **Database Access Class** field. A dialog similar to Figure 21.3 appears.
2. Specify *effectivevaj.data.test.dab.connections* as the package name and ClassicsDAC as the class name.
3. Press **OK**.

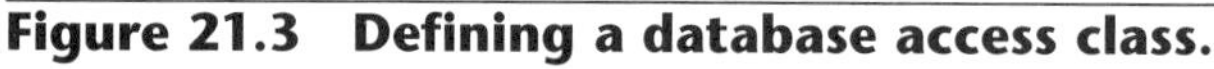

Figure 21.3 Defining a database access class.

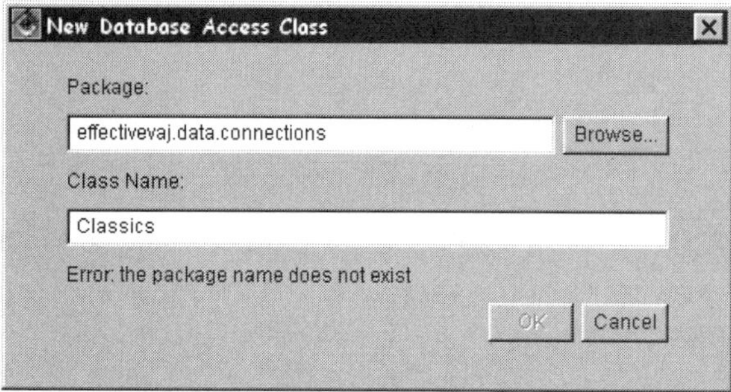

Next, you must define a database connection. You can define a database connection by pressing the **Add** button to the right of the Connections list; specify the following properties in the Connection Alias Definition dialog, shown in Figure 21.4.

Connection name. The name of the connection you are defining (for example, ClassicsConnection).

Database URL. You must use the proper URL in the form of jdbc:*subprotocol*:*subname* to address the database, such as jdbc:db2:alias-name for DB2, or jdbc:oracle:thin:@servername:port:instance-name for Oracle databases.

JDBC driver. There are several types of JDBC drivers: Some are pure Java (Type 4); others use the native database interface for faster performance (Type 2). Type 2 drivers use the Java Native Interface (JNI) to talk to the native database interface, such as CLI for DB2 or OCI for Oracle. VisualAge for Java has some problems with JNI support. Some native drivers, such as the Oracle OCI driver, can't be loaded by VisualAge for Java. This results in an UnsatisfiedLinkError when you try to use the database driver. If you encounter this type of error, use the pure Java driver while developing in VisualAge for Java, and then switch to the native driver in production.

NOTE

If you are using the JDBC-ODBC bridge developed by Sun, you must specify sun.jdbc.odbc.JdbcOdbcDriver as the driver name, and jdbc:odbc:ODBCSourcename as the URL. Be aware that this configuration will give poor performance results, and that the jdbc:odbc bridge provided by Sun is a non-supported production environment.

If you use a database driver that is not listed in the JDBC drivers list, you can select **Other: enter a driver name below** from the list of possible drivers and specify an alternate driver name in the **JDBC Driver Input** field.

Connection parameters. If you need to pass parameters other than the userID and password to the connection, you can define them in the Connection properties field like this:

```
property=value;property=value.
```

For example, you can specify TXNISOLATION=1 to set the DB2 transaction isolation level to 1 (Read Uncommitted) for this connection.

> **WARNING**
> Do not put a semicolon (;) at the end of the properties' list, or it won't be tokenized properly.

Auto Commit option. If you select the **Auto Commit** check box, all changes you make to database rows are systematically committed. This can be dangerous, because it is too late to roll back after that! We recommend that you control commit and rollback of changes using the commit() and rollback() methods available on the Modify bean at production time. However, for this sample, you can leave the **Auto Commit** on.

User ID and password for the connection. If you select the **Prompt for logon ID and password** check box, you will be asked for the logon ID and password each time you access the database. This can be a burden at development time, because you test quite often. We recommend that you leave this option off and supply a user ID and /password pair in this dialog during development, until final testing. If you plan to use those classes from a servlet, you must leave the option unchecked, even in production. If you specify a password, it is encoded in the generated code. If you gather the user ID and password from an HTML form or from a dialog, you must use the following lines of code to set the user ID and password values on the database connection:

```
getInsertClassicRow().getDatabaseConnection().setUserID("USERID");
getInsertClassicRow().getDatabaseConnection().setPassword("PASSWORD");
```

> **NOTE**
> You should probably read the user ID and name values from a file or other source, rather than hardcode them in your code.

Once you have supplied all parameters, you can click the **Test Connection** button to establish a connection. A message box with a "The connection is successful" message should be displayed.

Using DataSources

In VisualAge for Java, version 3.5, you can use datasources to connect to a database. Datasources are part of the JDBC 2.0 specification. A datasource is defined from a JDBC driver name and a database name. The main advantage in using datasource is connection pooling. For each datasource, you can specify the minimal/maximal number of connections to the database. The application server or database server that manages the datasource takes care of the life cycle of the connections, creating connections as necessary, serving connections to clients, and automatically returning connections that are considered idle to the pool. A client application will obtain a connection from the pool, and return it to the pool when it is no longer needed.

> **NOTE**
>
> If you are developing servlets that you intend to deploy in the IBM WebSphere Application Server, you can switch to the Advanced tab and check the **Use WebSphere database connection pools** option. By using this option, you take advantage of the WebSphere database connection pooling mechanism.

Defining a Datasource

Datasource definitions are stored in a naming service. In VisualAge for Java, version 3.5, you define datasources using the WebSphere Test Environment window, which

Figure 21.4 Defining a database connection alias.

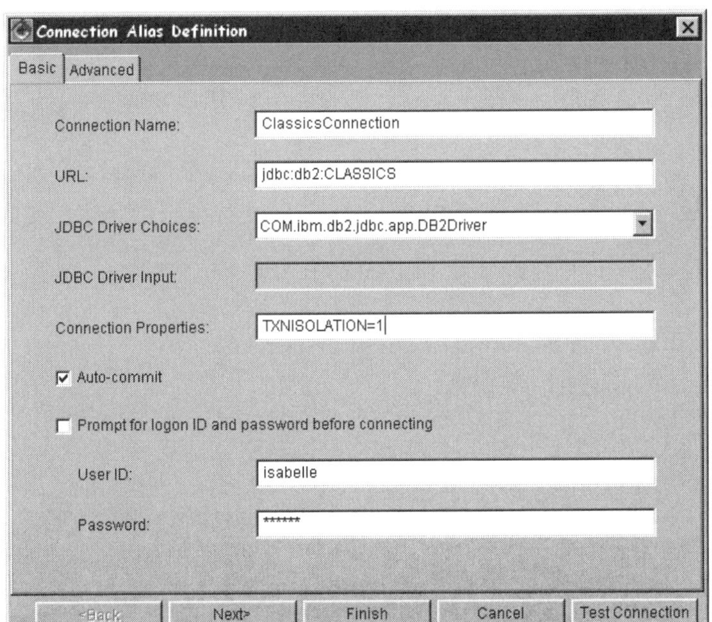

can be started from **Workspace->Tools->WebSphere Test Environment...** To define a datasource for the MUSIC database:

1. Start the Persistent Name Server. Select the **Servers->Persistent Name Server** entry, and press the **Start Name Server** button. Wait until you see a "Server open for business" message in the Console window to proceed further.

> **WARNING**
>
> There seems to be some stability problems with the Persistent Name server when used with the InstantDB (IDB) database. In addition, we saw the IDE crash when the PNS was failing. We fixed those problems by using DB2 or Oracle as a persistent database rather than IDB.

2. Select the Datasource Configuration entry, and press the **Add...** button. A dialog similar to Figure 21.5 is started. The following information must be supplied to create a datasource definition:

   Datasource name. This name is used to reference the datasource in the naming service, for example MUSIC.

   Database driver. The name of the JDBC driver used to connect to the database, such as COM.ibm.db2.jdbc.app.DB2Driver.

   Database URL. The URL by which you would normally address the database, such as jdbc:db2:MUSIC or jdbc:oracle:thin:@eagle:1521:ORA_INST

   Database type. This property lets you specify whether you want to use the two-phase commit support of the JDBC driver. Unless you need two-phase commit (for example, if you want to commit changes in two different databases within a same transaction), you should use JDBC, not JTA. When the JTA mode is activated, the access to the database is usually slower.

   Description (Optional). A description of the datasource.

   Minimum/maximum connections. The minimal and maximal number of connections for this datasource. The application or database server dealing with datasources would create a minimal set of connections, then increase the number of connections until maximal connections is reached. If the maximal number of connections has been reached, the next request will have to wait for a connection to be returned to the pool or freed by the application server. For testing purposes, a minimum value of 1 and a maximum value of 5 are probably sufficient.

Connection timeout (in seconds). If a connection is not made available to your application after this timeout, an exception will be raised. The default of 300 seconds is fine for testing purposes.

Idle timeout (in seconds). If a connection has been taken by an application, but not used for idle timeout, the application server considers that the application has forgotten to close the connection and returns it to the pool of free connections. The default value of 1800 seconds is fine for testing purposes.

> **NOTE**
>
> In production mode, the connection pool size and the various timeout values are critical for performance. If you are using the WebSphere Application Server, we recommend that you read the WebSphere V3 Performance Guide Redbook, available from www.redbooks.ibm.com.

3. Press **Ok** to insert the database definition in the persistent name server.

Figure 21.5 Defining the MUSIC datasource.

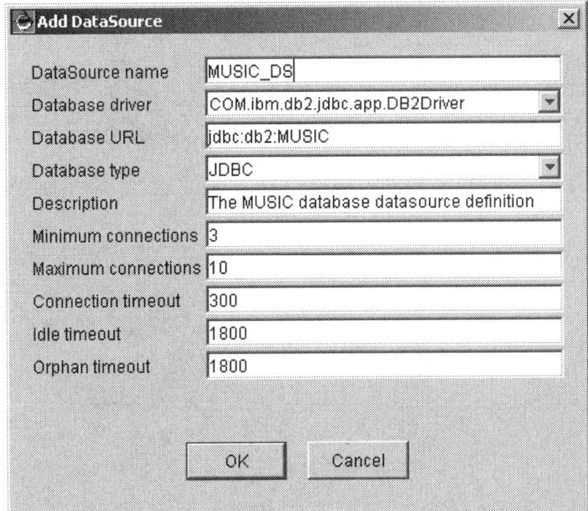

Testing a Datasource Programmatically

Once you have defined a datasource, you can test that it works by executing a few lines of code in the scrapbook. First, you must connect to the Persistent Name Server, which is running by default on port 900. This is done using the Java Naming Directory Interface (JNDI). The INITIAL_CONTEXT_FACTORY and PROVIDER_URL values used in this sample are specific to the WebSphere Application Server. You must use those values when connecting to a datasource running in VisualAge for Java, but you would use different values to connect to a datasource running in DB2, Oracle, or another application server. Therefore, you should isolate those strings in a property file.

The following code lets you connect to a naming service running on port 900 on machine eagle. The IIOP protocol is used to connect to the naming server.

```
java.util.Hashtable parms = new java.util.Hashtable();
parms.put(
    javax.naming.Context.INITIAL_CONTEXT_FACTORY,
    "com.ibm.ejs.ns.jndi.CNInitialContextFactory");
parms.put(javax.naming.Context.PROVIDER_URL, "iiop://eagle:900");
javax.naming.InitialContext ctx =
                              new javax.naming.InitialContext(parms);
```

Once you have obtained a naming context, you can look for the datasource definition. By naming convention, the datasource name you have given at creation time must be prefixed with "jdbc/", as shown in the following code:

```
javax.sql.DataSource DS =
             (javax.sql.DataSource) ctx.lookup("jdbc/MUSIC");
ctx.close();
```

Finally, you can obtain an SQL connection from the datasource. Once you have obtained a connection, you can use it the same way you used a connection obtained using a DriverManager (in JDBC 1.0). As usual, be a good citizen, and free resources as soon as you do not need them anymore! The following lines of code obtain a connection from the pool and open an inspector for this connection.

```
java.sql.Connection conn = DS.getConnection("isabelle", "******");
com.ibm.uvm.tools.DebugSupport.inspect(conn);
conn.close(); // Don't forget to do this!!
```

> **NOTE**
>
> The retrieval of an initial context and the datasource lookup are rather slow, and can greatly impact performance if they are done repeatedly. You should make sure they happen only once. You can do this either by putting the code in the init() method when using servlets, or by creating a datasource factory class, based on the singleton pattern. See an example of factory class in Chapter 23.

Using a Datasource In a Database Connection

Once you have defined a datasource, you can use it in a database connection by following these steps:

1. If you are using VisualAge for Java, version 3.5, you should see an option named **Obtain Connection From** on the database connection dialog. Make sure to select DataSource rather than DriverManager as the connection source.
2. In the provider URL field, specify the URL of the naming server. If this field is left blank, the tool assumes you want to connect to a local naming service, that is iiop:///.
3. In the InitialContextFactory field, select com.ibm.ejs.ns.jndi. CNInitialContextFactory. This assumes you want to connect to a datasource defined in the VisualAge for Java naming service. When you select this entry in the drop-down, VisualAge for Java automatically connects to the naming service running in VisualAge for Java. Therefore, you must make sure the persistent name server is up and running before selecting this option.
4. If the connection to the naming server is successful, the datasource name drop down will be populated with datasource definitions found in the naming tree. Select the jdbc/MUSIC datasource.
5. Press the **Test Connection** button to make sure everything works.

Defining the SQL Specification

Once you have defined a connection to the database, you are ready to define a SQL specification to insert a row in the CLASSICS table. A SQL specification consists of a SQL statement and metadata about the statement. To do this, follow these steps:

1. Select the SQL tab on the action property editor.
2. Give the SQL specification a name such as InsertRowInClassics.
3. You can then choose whether you want to write the SQL yourself or use the SQL Assist SmartGuide. Even if you know SQL, we recommend that you use the SQL Assist SmartGuide. It will generate meta-information about the SQL statement. This meta-information is then used by the Visual Composition Editor.

The SQL Assist SmartGuide uses the connection previously defined to connect to the database and retrieve a list of tables or views whose schema matches the current user ID (here, ISABELLE). If no schema matches the current userid, all tables or views are retrieved. You can use the View Schemas and Filter tables options to narrow the amount of information you wish to see in the SmartGuide. The **View schemas** button lets you select the list of schemas for which you want to see tables, while the **Filter tables** button lets you choose whether you want to see tables, system tables, views, or aliases.

Using the SQL Assist SmartGuide, you can create insert, update, and delete SQL statements. For this application, we want to insert data in the CLASSICS table. Select the **Insert** radio button, and choose schema_name.CLASSICS as the table name, as shown in Figure 21.6. In this example, the schema name is ISABELLE, because we were logged with this Windows NT ID when the database and tables were created.

The next page, the Insert page, lets you specify values for each column of the row that is inserted in the CLASSICS table. For each column, you can specify a null value, a default value, or a host variable. You define host variables by specifying **:hostvarname** in the value column. For each host variable, a corresponding property is added to the Modify bean interface. For example, a Parm_title property allows you to easily initialize the value of the :title host variable from a GUI, as shown in the section *Completing the Application.* Required columns (defined as not null in the database) are marked with a + (plus) and highlighted in dark blue. Because you want to enter values for each of the columns in the InsertClassicsApp GUI, you must define a host variable for each of them, as shown in Figure 21.7.

Once you have declared all host variables, you can view and test the corresponding SQL statement from the SQL page. If you press the **Run SQL** button, you can test the SQL statement by entering data for each column, as shown in Figure 21.8.

Figure 21.6 Selecting tables.

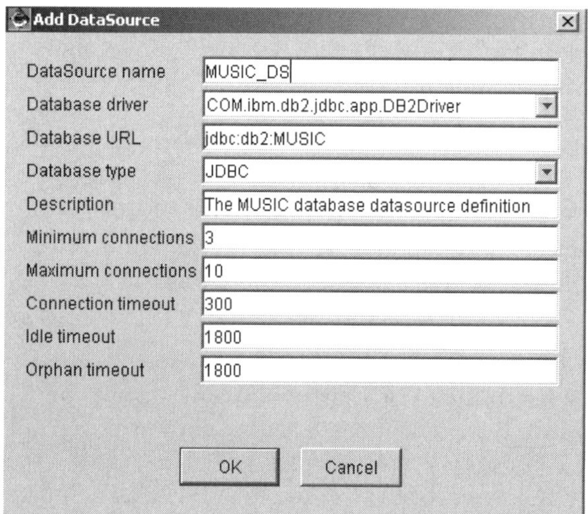

Figure 21.7 Setting host variables on the Insert page.

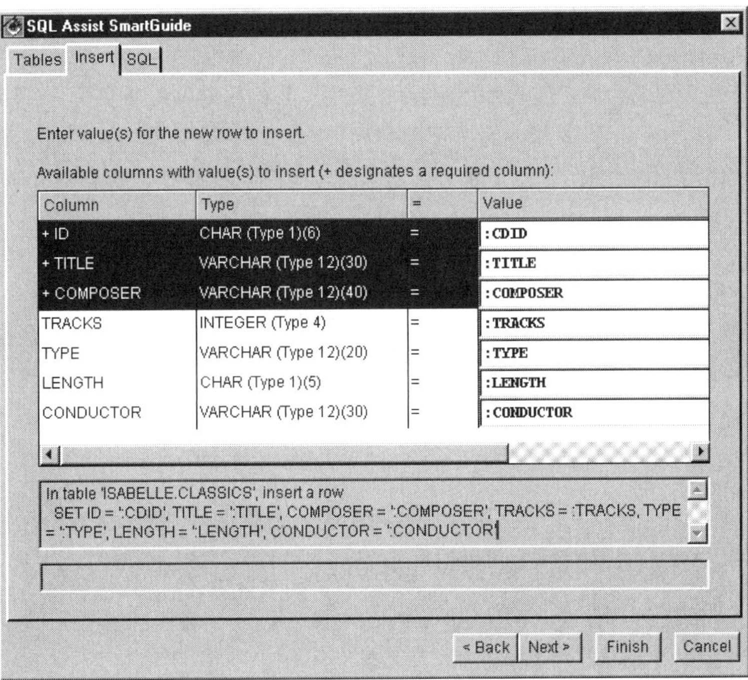

Figure 21.8 The SQL test page.

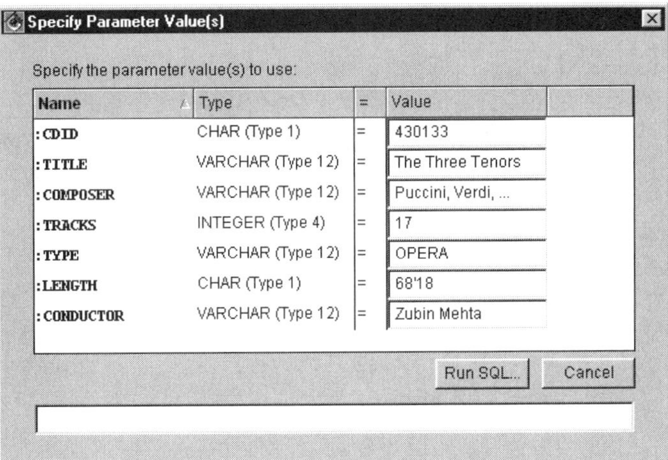

WARNING

Changes you make (inserting a row, in this example) are committed to the database, *even if* you have unchecked the Auto Commit flag on the connection definition. If you test a DELETE statement, the corresponding record(s) will really be deleted!

By selecting the **Schema qualified names** option, you decide whether the schema name (ISABELLE in this example) should or should not be part of the SQL statement. If the schema is part of the query (for example, SELECT * FROM ISABELLE.CLASSICS), you must have an ISABELLE schema defined in the database, and the CLASSICS table must belong to that schema. If the schema is not specified, the current user name is used as the schema name: If the user SCOTT is logged on DB2, running SELECT * FROM CLASSICS looks for CLASSICS in the SCOTT schema.

A Look at the Generated Code

If you look at the effectivevaj.data.test.dab.connections package, you find one class called Classicals and two methods:

- ClassicsConnection, which corresponds to the connection alias
- InsertRowInClassics, which corresponds to the SQL statement

The connection method looks like this:

```
public static com.ibm.db.DatabaseConnection ClassicsConnection()
              throws java.lang.Throwable,
              com.ibm.db.DataException {
              com.ibm.db.DatabaseConnection connection = null;
  try{
    connection = new com.ibm.db.DatabaseConnection();
    connection.setConnectionAlias(

"effectivevaj.data.dab.connections.Classics.ClassicsConnection");
    connection.setDriverName("COM.ibm.db2.jdbc.app.DB2Driver");
    connection.setDataSourceName("jdbc:db2:CLASSICS");
    connection.setUserID("isabelle");
    connection.setPromptUID(false);
    java.util.Properties props = new java.util.Properties();
    props.put("TXNISOLATION", "1");
    connection.setProperties(props);
    connection.setAutoCommit(true);
```

```
    connection.setPassword("acedg0574g06737473353167", true);
  } // try
  catch(com.ibm.db.DataException e){throw e;}
  catch(java.lang.Throwable e){throw e;}
 return connection;
}
```

This is the default connection code. You can change a connection specification by creating and customizing a DatabaseConnection instance and then calling the setConnection() method on the Modify bean to replace the default connection definition with the new one. You need to call this code before calling the execute() method on the Modify bean. The following lines of code create a database connection and assign it to an existing Modify bean instance:

```
DatabaseConnection conn = new DatabaseConnection();
conn.setDriverName("COM.ibm.db2.jdbc.app.DB2Driver");
conn.setURL("jdbc:db2:SAMPLE");
conn.setUserID ("userid");
conn.setPassword ("password");
aModifyBean.setDatabaseConnection(conn);
```

The InsertRowsInClassics method returns a StatementMetaData object that describes the INSERT statement defined in the SmartGuide. Each host variable is defined as a parameter to the statement. Note in this method the set of lines after the ***start of SQL Assist data*** comment. This metadata is used by the SQL Assist SmartGuide to rebuild the information you entered in the SmartGuide. If you alter this data, the only way to reopen the SQL Assist SmartGuide is to revert to the previous method edition (VisualAge for Java creates a new edition each time you save a method). The code of the InsertRowInClassics method looks like this:

```
public static com.ibm.db.SQLStatementMetaData InsertRowInClassics()
       throws java.lang.Throwable {
String name =  "effectivevaj.data.dab.connections."+"
                  Classicals.InsertRowInClassics";
 String statement = "INSERT INTO CLASSICS (ID,TITLE,COMPOSER,TRACKS,
 TYPE,LENGTH,CONDUCTOR) VALUES (:CDID,:TITLE,:COMPOSER,:TRACKS,
 TYPE,:LENGTH,:CONDUCTOR )";
  SQLStatementMetaData aSpec = null;
  try{
    aSpec = new com.ibm.db.SQLStatementMetaData();
    aSpec.setName(name);
    aSpec.setSQL(statement);
    aSpec.addParameter("CDID", 1, 1);
    aSpec.addParameter("TITLE", 12, 12);
    aSpec.addParameter("COMPOSER", 12, 12);
    aSpec.addParameter("TRACKS", 4, 4);
```

```
    aSpec.addParameter("TYPE", 12, 12);
    aSpec.addParameter("LENGTH", 1, 1);
    aSpec.addParameter("CONDUCTOR", 12, 12);
    // user code begin {1}
    // user code end {1}
  }
  catch(java.lang.Throwable e){
    // user code begin {2}
    // user code end {2}
    throw e;
  }
  return aSpec;

/*V2.0
**start of SQL Assist data**
504b030414g08g08g6abe5d27gggggggggggg0cg81b5b48841
243ada272bb12c512f27312f5d2fb8a428332fddc4a38481d0690563232b
620329f274296160b57276f1744196e204191de21f9b159881a6
d908593397159c83e67a6324d7a35ac16a089434f64064g86fb
19cd80581545c41488add102c6181c30a85a994d606461826191a
1802c58c300c82c526bb158485a6c0186e13aa79104b0708b601
3a5c2e01gg8a02gg504b010214g14g08g08g6abe501g3aggg6801gggg
**end of SQL Assist data**/
}
```

Completing the Application

The customization of the Modify bean is now complete. You can complete the application by connecting the Modify bean to the base GUI you created earlier. You will first use the quick-form facility provided by the Visual Composition Editor to easily complete the GUI; then you will complete the application by connecting the Execute and Exit GUI buttons to appropriate actions.

Registering a Quick Form

Quick form is a VCE tool that enables you to create a default form for data manipulation from the properties of a bean. You can define which properties you want to display, which GUI control should be associated to a particular property, and a label to describe the property on the GUI. Property-to-property connections will be created between the GUI control and their corresponding properties. In this sample, we reuse a bean called BoundJTextField created in Chapter 9, "Extension and Composition." This bean is an extension of the JTextField Swing bean, where the bean's text property is a bound property (an event is sent each time that this property changes).

To use BoundJTextField in a quick form, you must first register it and then associate it to properties of type java.lang.String. To do this, you must:

1. Open the IDE customization window from **Window->Options.**
2. Select the **Visual Composition->Quick Form Manager** category.
3. Press the **Register New** button. A dialog similar to Figure 21.9 appears.
4. Enter BoundJTextField as the quick form name.
5. Specify java.lang.String as the type this quick form should registered against.
6. Specify effectivevaj.bean.extension.binding.BoundJTextField as the visual bean.
7. Choose the text property as the target property for the bean. The text event should be automatically selected as the target event.
8. Enter a description such as "Bound Swing Text Field."

Figure 21.9 Registering the BoundJTextField quick form.

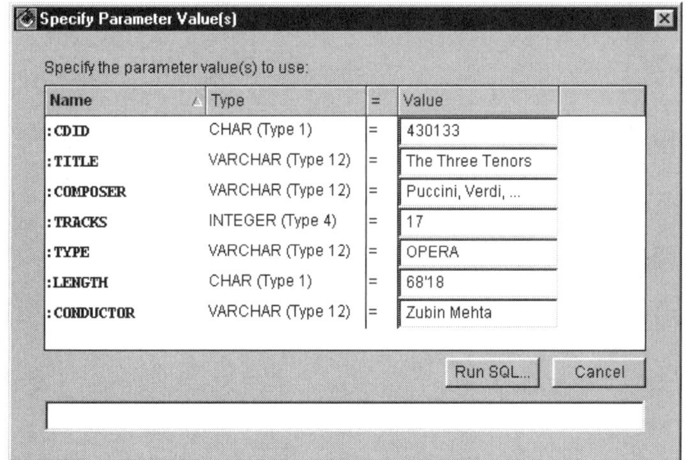

9. To include a label to the left of the BoundJTextField in a GUI, select the **Include Label** option.
10. Press **OK** to register the quick form.

Using Quick Form on the Modify Bean

To use the quick form facility on the Modify1 bean, select it, right-click, and select **Quick Form**. The Quick Form dialog, shown in Figure 21.10, enables you to choose which properties you want to display in the form, and the GUI control (Swing or AWT) you will use to display the property's value. Displayable properties are preselected in the **Modify properties** column. Registered quick forms are displayed in the right column.

Figure 21.10 The Quick Form dialog.

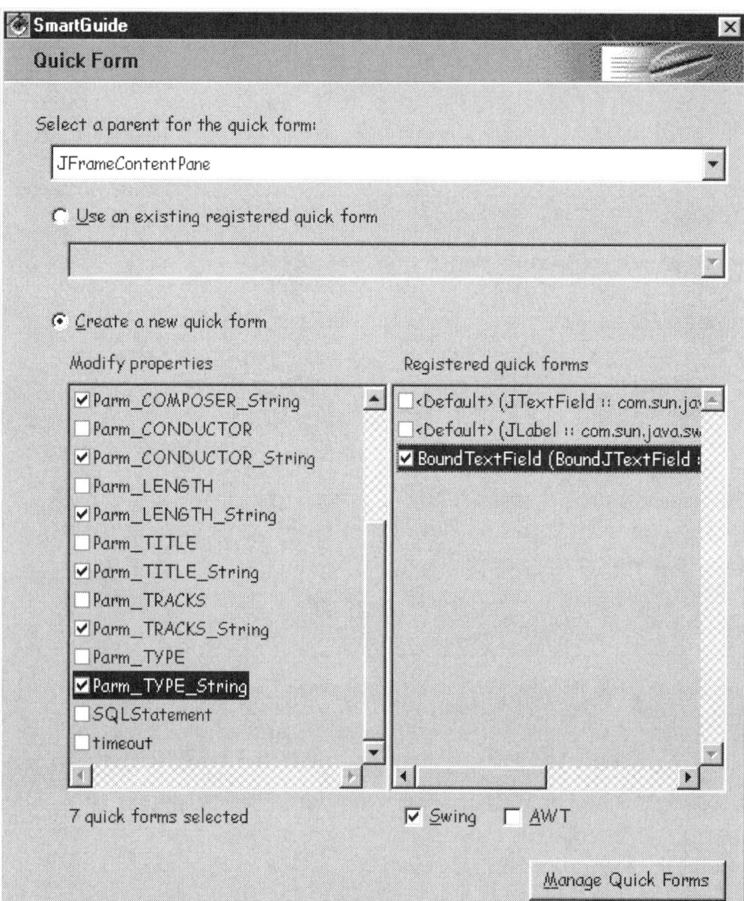

For each host variable that you have defined for the InsertRowInClassics SQL statement, two bound properties are generated: one in the native data type, and another one as a String type. For example, the :CDID host variable maps to Parm_CDID and Parm_CDID_String. The Parm_xxx_String properties are useful in the VCE, where you can easily connect them to GUI controls, such as a text field or a label. Follow these steps to create a form corresponding to the InsertRowInClassics SQL statement:

1. Select the Panel component in which you want to put the form; in this example, it is JFrameContentPane.
2. Select the properties you want to display on the form. The parameters that correspond to host variables defined in the INSERT statement are preselected. Some other properties, such as the connected status, the executed status, or the number of affected rows, are also preselected. For our sample, you only want to leave the Parm_xxx_String properties.
3. For each selected property, select BoundJTextField in the registered quick forms list.
4. Customize the label for each property as well as the order in which you want to display the properties in the form. You can reorder properties in the form by using the **Up** and **Down** buttons. For each property, you can define a custom label that can be placed on the left or on top of the property entry field. Fields and labels are arranged in a grid-bag layout. By setting the Numbers of Columns per row option, and changing the Columns to Span value for each property, you can easily organize elements inside the layout. In Figure 21.11, the number of columns is set to 2, which spanned the CD ID field over two columns.
5. Optionally, register the quick form. By registering a quick form, you associate a quick form to a certain type, the Modify type in this example. Each time you call Quick Form on an instance of a Modify bean, the registered quick form is used to display the data. Registering a quick form for the Modify bean is not appropriate, because its set of properties changes each time you customize the action property. However, it is very useful to create quick forms for beans you use often, such as a database connection. You then have a predefined dialog that you can use in any application to request a URL, a user ID, and a password from a user. Even better, the generated dialog can be edited with the VCE and customized. In the case of a database connection form, you could add *Connect* and *Exit* buttons, for example.

Once you press **Finish**, the quick form (a JPanel) is added to JFrameContentPane. Property-to-property connections are created between the entry fields in the form and the Modify bean. You can change the quick-form constraints so the quick form is located in the CENTER position of JFrameContentPane.

Figure 21.11 Customizing quick form properties.

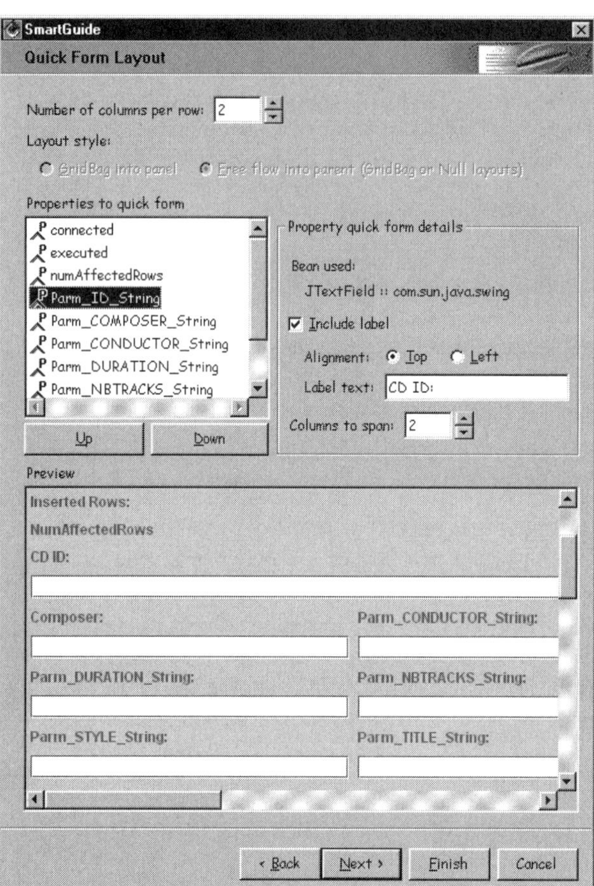

Finalizing the Application

You are now ready to complete the application. This is the easy part! You have a few connections to create:

1. To execute the SQL statement, connect the **actionPerformed** event of the Execute button to the **execute**() method of the Modify1 bean.
2. Connect the **windowClosing** event of the main window to the **disconnect** method of the Modify bean. If you had not set the **AutoCommit** flag to true on the connection, it would be good practice to commit or roll back changes before disconnecting from the database. There should be no active transactions when you disconnect from a database.

The application is complete! You can now save the bean, run the application, and try to insert rows in the database.

TIP

If you neglect to disconnect before your application closes, the connection will remain open until garbage collection occurs. This may not happen immediately. If this happens repeatedly, you may end up with many unwanted connections. In addition, you may quickly reach the limit of possible connections to the database. You can close connections by stopping VisualAge for Java or by manually forcing the applications to close. On DB2, you can use the **LIST APPLICATIONS** statement to list all opened connections and clean up the connection using the **FORCE APPLICATION (connection number)** command. The FORCE APPLICATIONS ALL command closes all open connections.

Displaying a List of Rows

Another Data Access bean, the **Select** bean, enables you to retrieve data from one or multiple tables and easily display them in a Swing table. Although JDBC 1.0 supports only forward navigation in a result set, rows retrieved using a Select bean are stored in a cache, allowing forward *and backward* navigation. The following example demonstrates the different caching and navigation options.

Using the Select bean is very similar to using the Modify bean. You must create a database access class, set up a connection, and use the SQL Assist SmartGuide to build the SELECT statement. In this example, we reuse the same connection to the database and describe in more detail the new pages in the SQL Assist SmartGuide. Options that are common to the Modify and Select beans are silently ignored, since we explained them previously.

WARNING

You must be careful when you reuse database connections. Sharing database connections provides some sort of connection pooling, which is good. However, because multiple applications share a same *physical* connection to the database, it also means that if you commit changes in one application, you implicitly commit any uncommitted changes made by other applications.

The ListClassics application will be built in three steps: First, you will create a base GUI for the application. Then, you will use a Select bean to create an SQL SELECT statement. Finally, you will complete the GUI by connecting the Select bean to the base GUI.

Creating the GUI

The ListClassics application is a Swing-based application that you will create with the Visual Composition Editor. This application inherits from com.sun.java.swing.JFrame. Follow those steps to create the ListClassics base GUI:

1. Select **Add->Class** from the Selected menu.
2. Specify *Effective VisualAge for Java* as the project name.
3. Specify *effectivevaj.data.applications* as the package name.
4. Specify ListClassicsApp as the class name and JFrame as the superclass. You can use code completion to automatically insert the package name in front of JFrame by placing the cursor right after JFrame and pressing Ctrl-Space.
5. Select the **Browse the class when finished** and **Compose the Class visually** options: We want to use the Visual Composition Editor to create this sample.
6. Press **Finish.**

The class browser will open to the VCE window. You will now customize the base GUI, shown in Figure 21.12. The Data Access Beans library comes with a customizable navigation panel called DBNavigator. This panel has a set of predefined buttons (such as commit, rollback, execute, nextRow, previousRow). You will use this panel to navigate within the set of rows retrieved by the Select bean. You can open the DBNavigator properties and select a subset of buttons to show. For example, you could keep only the execute, nextRow, and previousRow buttons.

You will use a Swing JTable component to display the rows retrieved from the database. Follow those steps to customize the GUI:

1. Change the JFrameContentPane layout to BorderLayout.
2. Change the application **title** property to List All Classicals.
3. Drop a JPanel component on the free-form surface and change its layout to FlowLayout. Change the bean name to navigationPanel, and the layout alignment to LEFT.

4. Switch to the Database category in the palette, select the DBNavigator bean, and drop it on navigationPanel.
5. Drop a JLabel and a JTextField bean to the right of the DBNavigator bean. Change the label's **text** property to Current Row: and the text field's **columns** property to 5.
6. Move navigationPanel to the NORTH position of JFrameContentPane.
7. Drop a JTable component to the CENTER position of JFrameContentPane.
8. Save the bean. Your current GUI should be similar to the one in Figure 21.12.

Customizing the Select Bean

Similarly to the Modify bean, the Select bean has a property called query that you will customize to provide a connection alias and define an SQL specification. To create and customize the Select bean:

1. Drop a Select bean from the Database category on the free-form surface, open its properties list, and launch the query property customizer.
2. Select the effectivevaj.data.test.dab.connections.ClassicsDAC database access class and the ClassicsConnection connection.
3. Switch to the SQL page, make sure the effectivevaj.data.test.dab.connections.Classics is selected, and press the **Add** button to create a new SQL specification. This SQL specification should be called RetrieveAllClassics.

Figure 21.12 The basic ListClassicsApp GUI.

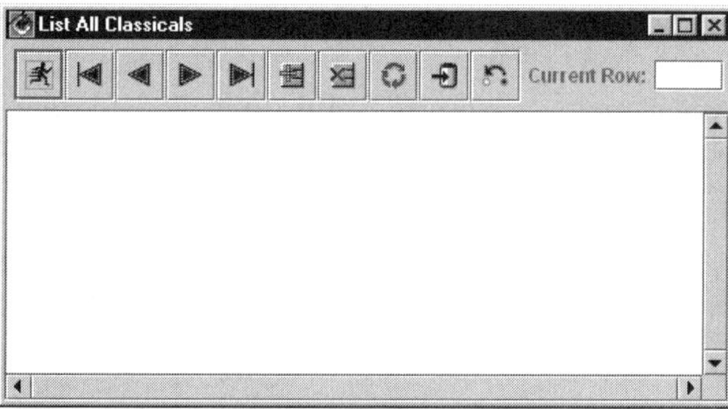

Choosing Database Tables

The first page you see in the SQL Assist SmartGuide is the Tables page. It should list all tables whose schema matches the current user ID (here, ISABELLE). Two types of SELECT statements can be created: **Select** or **Select Unique.** If you choose "Select Unique," you generate a SELECT DISTINCT statement: All duplicate rows are eliminated from the result set. For this example, we use a SELECT statement by checking the Select radio button. In the ListClassics application, we want to list all classic CDs and their associated tracks. Therefore, you must select both the CLASSICS and TRACK tables in this page.

Defining Joins

Since we chose to display data coming from both the CLASSICS and TRACK tables, we must define a join. The Join page lets you define one or multiple table-joins. Joins can be of three types: inner—which is the default—left outer, or right outer. You choose the join type by pressing the **Options** button on the Join page. To define a join on the ID column:

1. Select the ID column in ISABELLE.CLASSICS.
2. Select the CD ID column in ISABELLE.TRACKS.
3. Press the **Join** button on the right side. You should now see a red line joining the CDID and ID columns.

Defining Conditions

The next step would be to define one or more conditions. In this example, you want to retrieve all rows that result from the join. Therefore, we do not need to create any conditions, but let's explain how it works anyway. Each condition consists of a column, a comparison operator, and a value. All tables involved in the query are listed in the **Selected tables** drop-down list. To specify a condition, select a column from one of the tables in the drop-down list, select a comparison operator, and enter a value. The list of operators (in the middle column) changes depending on the column type. For example, you have different operators for DATE and VARCHAR SQL types.

A condition value can be either a host variable (:TITLE) or a hardcoded value. The SQL Assist SmartGuide comes with a very handy option to retrieve a condition value directly from the database. For example, suppose that you want to define a condition on the ID column in the CLASSICS table. If you want to list tracks for a specific CD identified by its ID, but you can't remember what the ID is, you can:

1. Select the ISABELLE.CLASSICS table in the selected tables drop-down list.
2. Select the **ID** column.
3. Select the "**is exactly equal to**" operator.

4. Press the **Find** button. A dialog similar to Figure 21.13 appears. If you know the ID starts with the digit **4**, you can specify **4%** in the *Search For* field. Then, specify the maximum hits value and press the **Find now** button.
5. Select one or multiple values in the results list and press the **Use Values** button to add those values to the condition.

You can define only one condition on a page. By default, there is one condition page (Condition 1), but you can use the **Find on another column** button to define additional conditions. For each additional condition, you can use radio buttons to choose whether it should be AND'd or OR'd with the other conditions.

You should check the Distinct Type option on the condition page if you know the column on which you are defining a condition has a user-defined (distinct) type. The SQL generated for the column will cast the column to the native SQL type on which the user-defined type is based before evaluating the condition. If you do not check the option, you will get a database error when executing the query.

Selecting Columns to Show

After defining conditions, you can press the **Next>** button to switch to the Columns page. The Columns page lets you choose which columns should be retrieved in the result set. Just select a table, select one or multiple columns to include in the result set, and use the **Add>>** button to add them to the Columns to include list. For this example, you want ID, TITLE, and COMPOSER columns from the CLASSICS table, as well as the TRACK NUMBER and TITLE column from the TRACK table. You can then use the **Move Up** and **Move Down** buttons to reorder columns in the list.

Ordering the Rows

The Sort page enables you to define on which column's value the order of the rows should be based. To define a column to sort results on, you must *first* select a sort

Figure 21.13 Retrieving condition values.

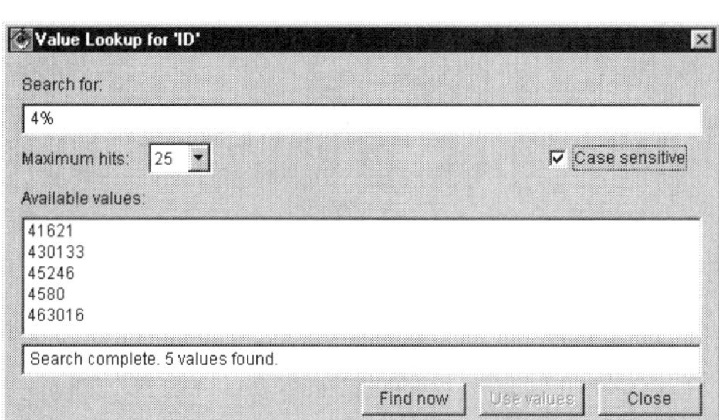

order (ascending or descending) and *then* select a column and add it to the **columns to sort on** list. You won't be able to change the sort order once the column has been added to the sort list without removing the column from the list and adding it again with the right sort order. For this example, you should sort results first on the ID column and then on the track number column, both in ascending order.

Reviewing the Mapping

The SELECT statement is now complete. You can review the default mapping options in the Mapping page. SQL Types are mapped to Java types according to the table below. If you want to map a column to a different SQL type and, thus, to a different Java class, you can select a different SQL type in **the Map to New data type** column. You can restore default mapping by pressing the **Use Defaults** button.

Testing the SQL Statement

Finally, you can test the SQL statement from the SQL page the same way you tested the INSERT statement for the Modify bean. You should see a list of rows displayed in the Results page.

Changing Caching Options

When you execute a query, you obtain a result set, that is, a set of rows that satisfy your SELECT statement. By setting caching options on the Select bean, you decide how many of those rows will be cached in memory. Remember that you can navigate forward and backward in the cache, not in the result set. The Select bean contains a few expert properties that let you specify caching characteristics. Those properties are listed below:

fillCacheOnExecute. If this property is set to true (the default), the cache is filled up to its capacity from the result set right after executing the query. The cache size is defined according to the properties described below. If you set this property to false, the cache is filled on demand each time you call nextRow() on the Select bean.

maximumRows. This property sets the maximum of rows to fetch. If your query returns 45 rows, and you set the maximum rows property to 30, only the 30 first rows are added to the cache. There is no way to retrieve the additional 15 rows. A value of 0 (the default) indicates no limit on the number of rows.

packetSize. A packet is a set of rows in the cache. If the packet size is set to 5, you add rows to the cache five at a time. A value of 0 has the same effect as a value of 1 (the default).

maximumPacketsInCache. If this property is set to 3 and the packet size is set to 5, the maximum number of rows in the cache is 15. The size of the cache is set to **packet size*maximum packets in cache** or **maximum rows**, whichever is smaller. A value of 0 (the default) indicates no limit on the number of packets in the cache.

Table 21.1 Default SQL Type Mapping

SQL Type	Java class
CHAR	java.lang.String
VARCHAR	java.lang.String
LONG VARCHAR	java.lang.String
INTEGER	java.lang.Integer
TINYINT	java.lang.Integer
SMALLINT	java.lang.Short
DECIMAL	java.math.BigDecimal
NUMERIC	java.math.BigDecimal
BIT	java.math.Boolean
BIGINT	java.lang.Long
REAL	java.lang.Float
FLOAT	java.lang.Double
DOUBLE	java.lang.Double
BINARY	java.lang.byte[]
VARBINARY	java.lang.byte[]
LONGVARBINARY	java.lang.byte[]
DATE	java.sql.Date
TIME	java.sql.Time
TIMESTAMP	java.sql.Timestamp

You must choose among several caching strategies. You can take the default values for these properties and place no limits on the cache size. In this case, you can move forward and backward through all the rows in the result set. Alternatively, you can limit the cache size by setting the maximumRows property. However, this may prevent you from fetching all the way to the end of the result set. The last strategy (which we recommend) is to set maximumRows to 0 and tune the packetSize and maximumPacketsInCache values. In this case, all possible results are added to the result set and the packet size and number options are used to determine how many rows are put in the cache. With the last strategy, you can still fetch all the way to the end of the result set. You can then view the cache as a "window" over a certain number of rows in the result set.

You can move backward and forward within the window and move the whole window forward when you request more rows. You can't move the whole window backward, though: After you fetch the last row, the first row(s) in the result set may not be visible anymore.

Navigating in the Result Set

You navigate in the result set using the nextRow() and previousRow() methods. If you have chosen the strategy we recommended (setting the packet size and packets in cache properties) and if you are positioned on the last row in the cache, calling nextRow() causes **packetSize** rows to be fetched into the end of the cache. You are then positioned at the first new row added to the cache. The firstRow and lastRow methods move the cursor to the first and last row in the *result_set*. The **currentRow** and **currentRowInCache** properties represent the current row index in the result set and in the cache, starting at 0.

Let's look at a quick example. Suppose that you run a query that returns 30 rows. The packetSize is 5, the maximumPacketInCache is 2, and maximumRows is set to 0 (all rows are added to the result set). When you execute the query, rows 0 to 9 are added to the cache, and the currentRow and currentRowInCache are equal to 0. If you call nextRow(), both currentRow and currentRowInCache are equal to 1. Suppose you now move to row 9, and call nextRow() again. Rows 10 to 14 are added to the cache, currentRow is 10, and currentRowInCache is 5. When you call lastRow(), rows are added 5 at a time to the cache until row 29 is in the cache. Since the packet size is 5, rows 20 to 29 are available in the final cache (remember, indexes start at 0: Row 29 is actually the 30th row). The current row in the cache is now 9, and the current row is 29.

You can navigate backward only within the cache. For example, calling firstRow() now would raise a com.ibm.db.DataException exception, since row 0 is not available in the cache anymore. Note that this exception is caught in the Data Access Beans code.

Handling Exceptions

If you use the DBNavigator bean, the methods of the Select bean will be executed on a separate thread. Whenever an exception occurs, the DBNavigator bean catches it and fires the exceptionOccurred event, passing the exception as a parameter. If you want to handle this exception in your application, you should create an event-to-code connection from the DBNavigator bean's exceptionOccurred event to a method you write.

If you do not use DBNavigator, exceptions are by default in the handleException() method. Remember that the method body is commented out by default. You must uncomment it to see evidence of an exception, such as the exception stack in the Console window.

Completing the GUI

We now complete the GUI by connecting the Select bean to the base GUI created earlier. The DBNavigator and Select beans are very easy to connect to a GUI. The Select bean implements the Swing com.sun.java.swing.table.TableModel interface. You can simply connect the object itself (through the **this** property) to a Swing JTable to display the contents of a result set. JTable columns are automatically built from the table model. The DBNavigator has a **model** property that you can connect to the Select bean. Then you can navigate through the result set retrieved by the Select bean using the DBNavigator buttons. To complete this application, you need to:

1. Connect the **this** property of the Select bean to the **model** property of the JScrollPaneTable component.
2. Connect the **this** property of the Select bean to the **model** property of the DBNavigator bean.
3. Connect the **currentRow** property to the **text** property of the currentRow entry field.
4. To highlight the current row in the table, connect the currentRowInCache event to the method showCurrentRowInTable (event-to-code connection), which looks like this:

   ```
   protected void selectRowInTable(int currentRowInCache) {
   getScrollPaneTable().setRowSelectionInterval(currentRowInCache,
   currentRowInCache);
   }
   ```

   Alternatively, you could create a connection between the currentRowInCache *event* and the setRowSelectionInterval method of the JScrollPaneTable component, passing currentRowInCache as a parameter to this method.
5. Connect the **windowClosing** event of the application to the **disconnect()** method of the Select bean.

6. Save the bean to execute the application. When you click on the **Execute** button, the table should be populated as shown in Figure 21.14.

> **NOTE**
>
> Step 4 only allows you to move in the result set by using the DBNavigator bean, and to get the corresponding row highlighted in the JTable component. If you want to select a row in the table and get the corresponding row selected in the result set, you need to synchronize the selectedRow property of the JScrollPaneTable component with the currentRowInCache property of the Select bean.

Creating Table Columns Manually

As you can see in Figure 21.14, the table-column header name has been set to the actual column name in the database. You can fix this by adding table columns directly to the table and then mapping each table column to the appropriate column in the result set. The modelIndex property can be set for each table column to match the SQL column indexes in the result set. Result-set column indexes start at 0. For example, suppose that you are executing the following query:

```
SELECT CLASSICS.ID,                 (modelIndex => 0)
       CLASSICS.COMPOSER,           (modelIndex => 1)
       CLASSICS.TITLE,              (modelIndex => 2)
       CLASSICS.TRACKS,             (modelIndex => 3)
       CLASSICS.CONDUCTOR           (modelIndex => 4)
FROM CLASSICS
ORDER BY CLASSICS.COMPOSER
```

To display the results in a table that has columns in the order of ID, Title, Track, Composer, and Conductor, you must set the **modelIndex** property of each table column to the value indicated in the previous code example.

Figure 21.14 Running the final application.

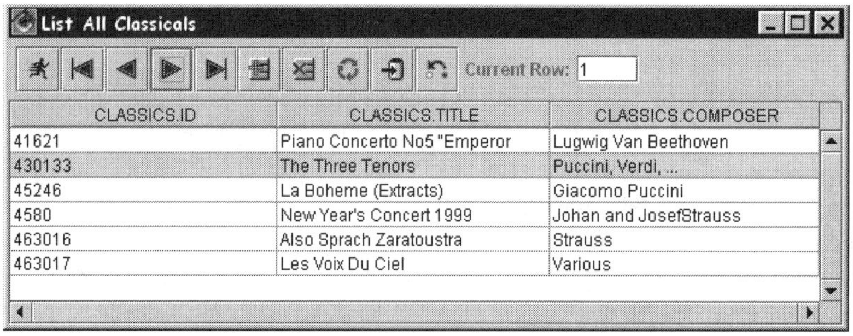

List All Classicals

Current Row: 1

CLASSICS.ID	CLASSICS.TITLE	CLASSICS.COMPOSER
41621	Piano Concerto No5 "Emperor	Lugwig Van Beethoven
430133	The Three Tenors	Puccini, Verdi, ...
45246	La Boheme (Extracts)	Giacomo Puccini
4580	New Year's Concert 1999	Johan and JosefStrauss
463016	Also Sprach Zaratoustra	Strauss
463017	Les Voix Du Ciel	Various

Using the Select Bean to Update Data

The Select bean supports updating and deleting rows in the result set, as well as inserting new rows. The SQL statements used to do this are automatically generated: You don't have to create them. In fact, the application you have built already supports updating data. For example, you can directly update one or multiple cells in the current row, and move to another row. If you have set AutoCommit to true, changes are committed to the database as soon as you move to another row (using nextRow(), for example). Otherwise, you need to call commit() to commit all changes in the database.

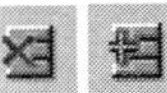

To delete the current row, use the **Delete** button on the DBNavigator bean. To insert a new row, press the **Insert** button on the DBNavigator bean, edit the cells of the current row, and move to the next row to commit the changes.

To prevent direct editing, you can set the Select bean's **readOnly** property to true. If this flag is set to true, the JTable component used to display the data is also in read-only mode (you can't do direct cell editing).

Understanding Other Expert Properties

You can change four other expert properties on the Select bean. Those properties are:

distinctTypesEnabled. The Select bean generates code that enables you to find, update, insert, and delete rows without writing your own SQL. If this property is set to true, all columns in the query are treated as potentially having user-defined (distinct) data types. This implies that the generated code casts the column to a native SQL type before evaluating conditions on it. If any column in your query has a user-defined type and you do not set this property to true, you will get a database error when trying to select, update, insert, or delete data. If your database supports the CAST syntax, it is okay to set this flag to true even if you do not use any user-defined types. However, the generated SQL code will be somewhat more complex than necessary.

forceSearchedUpdate. By default, the Select bean performs positioned updates if the JDBC driver supports them. If your JDBC driver does not support positioned updates, you can force searched updates by setting this property to true. Searched updates are supported by all JDBC drivers.

lockRows. If this property is set to true, a lock is acquired on a row as soon as you are positioned on it. If this property is set to false, the lock is acquired only before an update or delete. You can control locks on rows by using the lockRow() and unlockRow() methods.

timeout. This property represents the number of seconds you will wait before the query times out. A value of 0 means the query never times out. This property is also available on the Modify bean.

Using the Database Application SmartGuide

All right, you are probably going to hate us for this, but you could have created the exact same GUI without writing a line of code! How? By using the Create Database Application SmartGuide. This SmartGuide provides an easy way to create an application using the Select bean: It lets you pick a tabular view, a details view (current row only), or both. This SmartGuide is available from a project or package pop-up menu. It lets you create or reuse a connection alias and an SQL specification, and it generates a base GUI to execute the SQL statement and display the data. The GUI can then be customized in the VCE.

The SmartGuide is composed of four pages:

Create Database Application Page. This page lets you specify the project, package, and class name for your application.

Database Connection and SQL Specification Page. This page lets you specify the connection alias and a SQL specification. You can select existing specifications or create new ones.

Database Views Specification Page. From this page, you choose which components should be added to the GUI, as shown in Figure 21.15. Three components can be added: a navigation bar, a master view, and a details view. By selecting the navigation-bar option, you add a DBNavigator

Figure 21.15 Specifying GUI components.

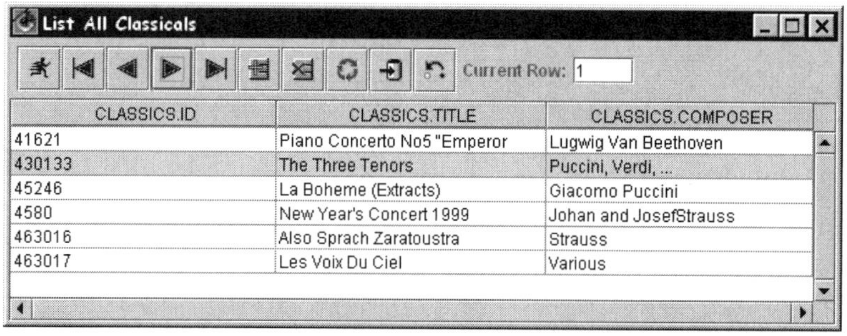

List All Classicals

Current Row: 1

CLASSICS.ID	CLASSICS.TITLE	CLASSICS.COMPOSER
41621	Piano Concerto No5 "Emperor	Lugwig Van Beethoven
430133	The Three Tenors	Puccini, Verdi, ...
45246	La Boheme (Extracts)	Giacomo Puccini
4580	New Year's Concert 1999	Johan and JosefStrauss
463016	Also Sprach Zaratoustra	Strauss
463017	Les Voix Du Ciel	Various

bean to the GUI. The master view is generally a JTable bean, while the details view is a JPanel bean with a grid-bag layout that shows all or a subset of the columns returned in the result set. You can use the positioning options to design the layout of components in the GUI.

Details View Specification Page. If you have decided to create a details view, you can use this page to select which columns should be displayed. Column names will be displayed only if you used the SQL Assist SmartGuide to create your SQL statement and there is metadata available for the SQL statement. By default, all result-set columns are shown in the details view.

When you are done, press **Finish** to start code generation. Before running the application, you should modify it to properly disconnect from the database on exit. This can be done by adding a connection from the **windowClosing** event of the application to the **disconnect** method of the Select bean. In addition, the application is built in such as way that the execute() method is invoked as soon as the application starts. If your query contains parameters that require user input, you need to modify the application further.

Using the Selector Beans

The Selector beans can be used to retrieve a subset of a result set. You can use them to display rows in a list or to pass the contents of a selected row (or just a cell) to another application. By providing a row number, a column number, or both, you can select a row, a column, a cell, or even a range of cells. Note that the Selector beans lets you work on cached data: The rowNumber property you specify indicates which row in the cache you want to work with. If you are using the expert properties that let you set caching characteristics, setting rowNumber to 5 in a Selector bean does not imply you are working with row 5 in the result set.

The RowSelector and ColumnSelector beans implement the Swing ComboBoxModel. Therefore, they can be easily connected to JList or JComboBox components. To illustrate the use of these beans, we will slightly modify the application we just created. We will create an additional dialog: This dialog will display the contents of the cell selected in the main JTable component, and the contents of the row and columns corresponding to that cell. To complete the application:

1. Add a JDialog bean to the free-form surface. This is not good VCE practice, but it is good enough to illustrate usage of the selector beans.
2. Add two JList components (ColumnDataList, RowDataList), a JLabel bean (CellDataLabel), and a JTextField bean (CellDataField) to this dialog. Feel free to arrange those controls as you like. You should also change the label text to *Current Cell.*

3. Connect the **initialize**() event of the main window to the **show**() method of the dialog.
4. Drop a RowSelector, a ColumnSelector, and a CellSelector bean on the free-form surface. Those beans can be found in the Database category.
5. Connect the **model** property of each of the selector beans to the **this** property of the Select bean. The data you want to display is taken from the model of that bean.
6. Connect the **this** property of the Row Selector to the RowDataList model property.
7. Connect the **this** property of the Column Selector to the ColumnDataList model property.
8. The next step is to initialize the rowNumber and columnNumber properties of each Selector bean from the corresponding properties in the table. The easiest way is to create a method that updates those properties each time the mousePressed event occurs in the table, like this:

```
public void displayCurrentData() {
 int selectedRow = getScrollPaneTable().getSelectedRow();
 int selectedColumn = getScrollPaneTable().getSelectedColumn();
 getColumnSelector1().setColumnNumber(selectedColumn);
 getRowSelector1().setRowNumber(selectedRow);
 getCellSelector1().setColumnNumber(selectedColumn);
 getCellSelector1().setRowNumber(selectedRow);
 // Initialize JTextField from Cell Selector data.
 getCellDataField().setText(getCellSelector1().getString());
 return;
}
```

The application is now complete. You can run it and check that the data in the dialog is updated each time you select a cell in the table.

Querying Data with Stored Procedures

A stored procedure is stored on a database server. It executes and accesses the database locally to return information to client applications. Stored procedures save the overhead of having a remote application pass multiple SQL commands to a database on a server. With a single statement, a client application can call the stored procedure, which then executes on the server and returns the results to the client application. Stored procedures are specific to a database; you can't port them from UDB 6.1 to Oracle, for example.

The DB2 Stored Procedure Builder lets you create the procedure stored on the server in Java. The ProcedureCall bean from the Data Access Beans lets you call this stored procedure from a client application.

In this section, you will create a stored procedure to list all tracks for a particular classical CD. We do not review in detail the stored procedure builder functionality, since this is beyond the scope of this book. Please refer to the online documentation for more details on the Stored Procedure Builder.

Configuring DB2

The KEEPDARI configuration parameter must be set to NO before you start working with the Stored Procedure Builder. Otherwise, you will not be able to execute a new version of an installed procedure without stopping and starting DB2 (the JAR files containing the procedure will be locked by DB2). To change the KEEPDARI parameter, you can issue the following command in a DB2 command window:

```
DB2 UPDATE DATABASE MANAGER CONFIGURATION USING KEEPDARI NO.
```

Alternatively, you can use the DB2 command center by choosing **Configure** on the DB2 instance, switching to the Applications page, and setting the Keep DARI process indicator to No. Note that you must set this parameter back to YES in production.

> **NOTE**
>
> The Stored Procedure Builder requires the UDB Version 6.1 software development kit (SDK). You must install this SDK before using the Stored Procedure Builder from VisualAge for Java.

Invoking the Stored Procedure Builder

The DB2 Stored Procedure Builder can be started on a project's tools contextual menu. Saving a stored-procedure project creates a **.spp** file that is saved as a resource for the VisualAge for Java project from which you started it. If the .spp file already exists, it is automatically loaded when you start the Stored Procedure Builder.

To create a stored procedure to access the MUSIC database, select the **Effective VisualAge for Java** project and invoke **Tools->IBM DB2 Stored Procedure builder** from the project's pop-up menu. If you can't find this entry in the menu, you probably forgot to select the **Enhanced Database Support** component at VisualAge for Java installation time. Restart the installation, select **Custom Installation**, and select this component.

Creating a Database Connection

When you start the Stored Procedure Builder for the first time, you must set up a database connection, as shown in Figure 21.16. From this dialog, you can choose the alias of the database you want to work with, and provide a user ID and password to access the database.

You can also create a database connection by selecting the project name in the left pane (here, *Effective VisualAge for Java*), and select **Insert Connection** from the pop-up menu.

Creating a Stored Procedure

Once you have defined a database connection, you can start the stored procedure SmartGuide by selecting the stored procedure folder under the MUSIC database connection, and choosing **Insert Java Stored Procedure** from the pop-up menu. In the following steps, you will create a stored procedure to retrieve all TRACK records corresponding to a certain ID:

1. **Specify the stored-procedure name.** You must provide a name for the stored procedure, preceded by the schema name (for example, ISABELLE.SHOWALLTRACKS). This name will be used to register the stored procedure in DB2. If you supply SHOWALLTRACKS as the stored-procedure name, the Stored Procedure Builder generates a class

Figure 21.16 The MUSIC database connection.

Inserting Database Connection - MUSIC
Database Connection | Filter
Specify identifying information for this connection.
Driver: IBM DB2 alias
Database
Alias: MUSIC — Create...
Comments:
Location (URL): jdbc:db2:MUSIC
Driver class: COM.ibm.db2.jdbc.app.DB2Driver
User ID: isabelle
Password: ******
Use your current user ID and password
OK | Cancel | Apply | Reset | Help

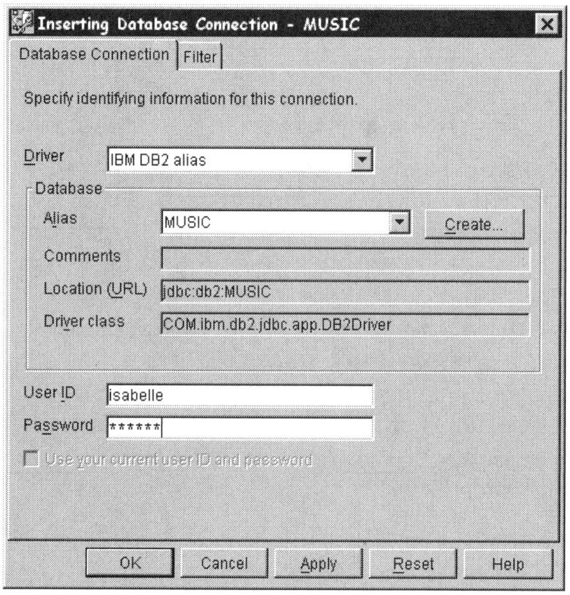

with that name that contains one static method sHOWALLTRACKS (the first letter is put in lowercase).

2. **Specify the number of queries to run.** A stored procedure can contain one or multiple queries that you can invoke separately. From the pattern page, you can decide whether you want to create one or multiple queries, return a result set or not, and how to want to handle exceptions. For this example, you want a single query, return a result set, and throw an SQLException when something is wrong.

3. **Create an SQL specification.** Using the SQL query page is very similar to using the Select or Modify beans' query customizers. You can either enter the SQL code manually, or use an SQL Assist SmartGuide by pressing the **Define SQL** button. What you want to define is a query that retrieves all TRACK records: This query takes a parameter with a compact disc ID. The results should be ordered by track number. To achieve this, you should create a condition on the Condition 1 page that requires the CD-ID column of the TRACK table to be equal to an host variable called :CDID. Do not forget to test the SQL to make sure you query works. The generated SQL code should look like this:

```
SELECT
 ISABELLE.TRACK.ID,
 ISABELLE.TRACK.TITLE,
 ISABELLE.TRACK.LENGTH
FROM
 ISABELLE.TRACK
WHERE
(
   (
      ISABELLE.TRACK.CDID = :CDID
   )
)
ORDER BY ISABELLE.TRACK.ID
```

TIP

When you define the CDID host variable, make sure you use the **Variable** button to create it, rather than type :CDID directly in the field (the host variable must be in bold letters). Otherwise, you will not see the :CDID variable on the parameters page.

4. **Rename the stored-procedure parameters.** The :CDID host variable is supplied to the stored procedure as a parameter to the procedure call. From the parameters page, you can rename the parameter or add extra parameters, if necessary. For this example, you should rename CDID to compactDiscNumber. You can directly type a new name, or use the **Change** button to edit the parameter properties.
5. **Specify code-generation options.** The options page lets you specify:
   - The specific name of the stored procedure: A specific name serves as a unique name among all stored procedures. You can keep the default generated one, or specify your own (for example, ListAllTracks).
   - A package name, for example, effectivevaj.data.spb.
   - Whether you want to generate SQLJ or pure JDBC code: For this example, select the **Dynamic SQL using JDBC** option.
   - Whether the stored procedure should be generated and built when you exit the SmartGuide. If you select the **Generate Only** option, you will have the choice to modify the generated code before the tool starts to compile and register it. There are many cases in which you may want to modify the generated code for a stored procedure before building it. For example, if you wanted your stored procedure to return output parameters instead of a result set, you would need to modify the stored-procedure code to initialize those output parameters from the query results. In this example, we do need to modify the generated code: You can leave the **Generate and Build** option selected.
   - Whether you want to generate the stored procedure in debug mode: If you select this option, you will be able to debug your stored procedure remotely. We do not want to debug this stored procedure, so you do need to generate it in debug mode.

TIP

If the package that you specify on this page exists, make sure it is an open edition and that it is loaded in the project from which you started the Stored Procedure Builder. If you work with the Enterprise Edition, make sure you are a group member for this package. If the Java code was not imported to your workspace after you build the stored procedure, have look at the Log window for possible error messages.

Because we have chosen the Generate and Build option, the stored procedure will be built as soon as we close the stored procedure SmartGuide. The Stored Procedure Builder compiles the stored-procedure code, creates a JAR file, installs this JAR file in the \SQLLIB\FUNCTION\JAR\<SCHEMA_NAME> directory on the DB2 server, and registers the stored procedure in the server. Because you have started the builder from VisualAge for Java, the stored-procedure code will be imported in the repository and loaded in your workspace after a successful build.

> **TIP**
>
> If you have not set the KEEPDARI configuration parameter to NO as explained in the *Prerequisites* section, you may receive an error message during a build that states that the JAR files can't be removed. To fix the problem, you must stop and restart DB2, and start another build.

You should now test the stored procedure by selecting it in the stored procedures folder and choosing Selected->Run from the menu bar. A dialog should pop up, asking for the value of the CDID parameter: Enter some data, and press OK. The query results should be printed at the bottom of the window.

Special Considerations for VisualAge

Once a stored procedure is generated, you can modify its source code from the Stored Procedure Builder editor. If you have chosen to generate pure JDBC code, you can also use the VisualAge for Java IDE to edit the generated code. However, you should always modify the generated code from the Stored Procedure Builder editor. Although the VisualAge for Java editor is a much better Java editor, it is easier to modify the code in the Stored Procedure Builder, since you have to start the stored procedure builds from there.

After each successful build, if you are using pure JDBC code, the Java source code is imported in the workspace. If you version your class after each successful build, you will be able to revert to any working version by loading versions from the VisualAge for Java repository into the Stored Procedure Builder editor, using **File->Get Another Edition.**

Stored procedures written in SQLJ are stored as resources in the project from which you started the Stored Procedure Builder. Upon a successful build, the SQLJ file is copied there. This implies that you can always revert to the last working version of your stored procedure by using **File->Get Another Edition**, even if you are dealing with SQLJ files.

When you save a Stored Procedure Builder project file, a corresponding .spp file is created under the project's resources directory (in this example, Effective

VisualAge for Java). If you export a VisualAge for Java project to another repository, do not forget to also export its associated resources. See Chapter 6, "Integrating with the File System," for details on this topic.

Calling the Stored Procedure from an Application

Once you have created a stored procedure on the server, you can call it from a client program using the ProcedureCall bean. This bean can be found in the Database category in the VCE palette. Because a ProcedureCall bean implements the Swing TableModel interface, using this bean from the VCE is very similar to using the Select or Modify bean.

If you want to call a stored procedure, you can create a GUI similar to the Select bean example. The GUI should inherit from JFrame, contain a JTable component, and contain a BoundJTextField bean to supply the compactDiscNumber parameter and an Execute button to start the procedure-call execution.

Then, drop a ProcedureCall bean on the free-form surface. You must then customize it to call the stored procedure with the following steps:

1. Open the ProcedureCall bean's properties list, and edit the procedure property.
2. Select the effectivevaj.data.test.dab.connections.ClassicsDAC database access class and the ClassicsConnection database connection.
3. Switch to the SQL page, make sure the effectivevaj.data.test.dab.connections.Classics is selected, and press the Add button to create a new SQL specification. You should name it GetAllTracksSP (to differentiate from a straight SQL statement) and start the SQL Assist SmartGuide.
4. The first page of the SQL Assist SmartGuide displays the list of stored procedures. If the stored procedure you have created is not in the list, it has not been built properly. You should go back to the Stored Procedure Builder and test the stored procedure there first. Select the SHOWALLTRACKS procedure and switch to the Parameters page.
5. The COMPACTDISCNUMBER parameter should be listed on the Parameters page. You can't modify the parameter name or type, but you can supply a value in the input value column. Because we supply the parameter from the GUI, you do not need to enter any values in that page. Switch to the Result Set page.
6. If your stored procedure returns a result set, you can describe it on the Result Set page. This description will be used by the SQL Assist SmartGuide to generate update, delete, and insert SQL statements for this result set. If you do not describe the result set, you can still retrieve data using the result set, but those customized statements will not be generated. If your stored procedure returns multiple result sets, you can add more Result Set pages to describe them. In this sample, you do not

care about updating or deleting data in the applications (just consulting). Therefore, you do not need to describe a result set.

7. Finally, the SQL page lets you review and run the SQL statement. Note that the generated SQL is very simple; just a call to the procedure, passing the right parameters, like this:
   CALL SHOWALLTRACKS(:COMPACTDISCNUMBER)

Once you have customized the ProcedureCall bean, you can complete the application by following those steps:

1. Connect the **model** property of the ProcedureCall bean to the **this** property of the JScrollPaneTable bean.
2. Create a property-to-property connection between the BoundJTextField text property and the stored-procedure parameter (Parm_COMPACTDISCNUMBER_String).
3. Create a connection to call the stored procedure when the Execute button is pressed.
4. Create a connection to disconnect from the database when the windowClosing event occurs.

You can test the final application by supplying a parameter in the text field, and pressing the Execute button.

Developing SQLJ Programs

The most frequent concern with database access is probably performance. Data retrieval must be efficient and fast. Using statically bound SQL (or static SQL) is a well-known solution to performance problems. By binding SQL statements to a database, you take advantage of data indexes, for example. The SQL statement is optimized when you bind it to the database.

SQLJ is an ANSI standard that enables the use of static SQL in Java programs. Basically, you inline SQL statements in Java code, and process this .sqlj file to replace all static SQL calls by the corresponding supporting SQLJ code. The translation process also creates a profile (.ser) that can be customized for a particular database. Customizing this profile is the only way to get a significant performance improvement; the customizing process generates bind files and binds them to the database. If you do not customize the profile, SQLJ calls are simply translated to equivalent JDBC calls. When you use static SQL, most semantic and logic checking is done at compile time (bind time) and not at run time. By doing those checks only once, you improve execution time considerably.

Prerequisites

Working with SQLJ requires that you install the SQLJ Runtime Library. To do this, use the Quick Start window (F2) and add the **SQLJ Runtime Library 3.0** feature. If you can't find this tool, it probably means you haven't installed it. You should restart the VisualAge for Java installation process, select a Custom Installation, and install the Enhanced Database Support component.

If you want to execute and debug SQLJ programs inside the IDE, you must also add the SQLJ run-time classes to the workspace class path. For DB2, SQLJ run-time classes can be found in the **runtime.zip** file, located under x:\sqllib\java.

Editing SQLJ Files

Editing SQLJ files is not the most evolved feature in VisualAge. First, SQLJ files can't be stored by the repository, so they are treated as project resources. You can either create the .sqlj file there and edit it, or create the SQLJ file using your favorite editor and then import it using the SQLJ tool. Then, you will be able to edit and translate this file from the project's resources page. If you open a pop-up menu on an SQLJ file, you see a default **SQLJ Tools->SQLJ** menu item with three entries: edit, translate, and create SQL Debug Class File, as seen in Figure 21.17.

The Edit action brings up an editor pane that is SQLJ-sensitive. This editor has no tool bar though, no menus, and no help in the documentation! Of course, it is very different from the integrated editor. The commands reference listed in Table 21.2 belongs to the Stored Procedure Builder help, since this builder comes with the same editor (known as LPEX).

Figure 21.17 Handling SQLJ files from the Resources page.

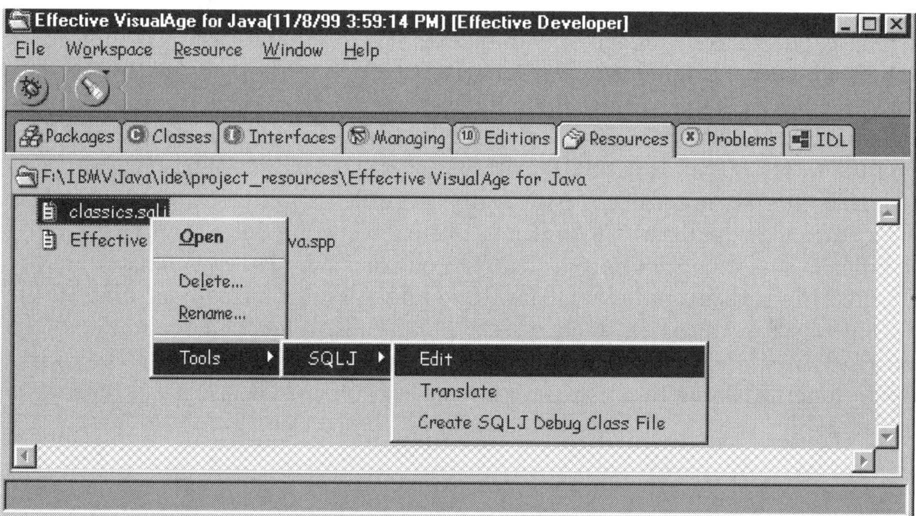

Table 21.2 SQLJ Editor Command Reference

Keyboard Command	Command Description
Ctrl-C	Copies selected text to the clipboard
Ctrl-V	Pastes text from the clipboard
Ctrl-X	Cuts selected text from the editor and places it in the clipboard
Ctrl-Backspace	Deletes the line containing the cursor
Ctrl-Enter	Inserts a new line beneath the cursor
Ctrl-Shift-End	Selects all text from the cursor downward
Ctrl-Shift-Home	Selects all text from the cursor upward
Ctrl-Shift-Left Arrow	Selects the previous word (or selects a portion of the current word)
Ctrl-Shift-Right Arrow	Selects the next word (or selects a portion of the current word)
Alt-L	Selects line of text containing the cursor; move cursor and press Alt-L again to select a group of lines
Alt-B	Selects a block of text starting with cursor; move cursor and press Alt-B again to mark the end of the block
Alt-R	Selects a rectangular block of text starting with the cursor; move cursor and press Alt-R again to mark the end of the block
Alt-U	Deselects selected text
Ctrl-Z	Undoes changes; press Ctrl-Z repeatedly to undo multiple changes
Ctrl-Shift-Z	Redoes changes; press Ctrl-Shift-Z repeatedly to redo multiple changes
Ctrl-F	Finds specified text
Ctrl-J	Finds the last change made
Ctrl-M	Finds the matching bracket
Ctrl-N	Finds the next occurrence of specified text (searching downwards)
Ctrl-U	Finds the previous occurrence of specified text (searching upwards)

(Continues)

Table 21.2 SQLJ Editor *(Continued)*

Ctrl-A	Displays all lines in file
Ctrl-Home	Moves the cursor to the top of the file
Ctrl-End	Moves the cursor to the end of the file
Ctrl-Left Arrow	Moves the cursor to the beginning of the previous word
Ctrl-Right Arrow	Moves the cursor to the beginning of the next word
Ctrl-L	Moves the cursor to the specified line number

Using a Different Editor

If you want to use a different editor for SQLJ files, you can associate this editor to the .sqlj extension in the IDE customization window. To create the association, start the IDE customization window from **Window->Options** and go to the *Resources-Resources Association* page. Then:

1. Enter .sqlj in Resource Extension entry field, and press **Add.**
2. Select either **External Program** or **Java Class.** The external program option lets you choose any executable on the file system. The Java class option lets you choose a Java class in your workspace.
3. Press **Apply** or **OK** to commit changes.

Once the association is created, double-click on an .sqlj file in the resources page to open your favorite editor.

Creating SQLJ Files

To illustrate SQLJ usage, we have created this simple SQLJ program to list all classical CDs from the CLASSICS table. There is no builder available here, so you need to create this yourself. Here is the source code:

```
// File: ListClassicApp.sqlj
// Author: Effective Developer.

package effectivevaj.data.sqlj;

import java.sql.Connection;
import java.sql.DriverManager;
import java.sql.SQLException;
import sqlj.runtime.*;
import sqlj.runtime.ref.*;
```

```
// Declare a named cursor, to hold the results of the
// query. This generates an extra Java class called App_Cursor1.
#sql iterator App_Cursor1(String ID, String title, String composer);

class ListClassicsApp {
  static {
   try {
    //  register the driver with DriverManager
    Class.forName("COM.ibm.db2.jdbc.app.DB2Driver");
   }
   catch (Exception e) {
     e.printStackTrace();
   }
  }
  public static void main(String argv[]) {
   try {
     App_Cursor1 cursor1;
     String str1, str2, str3 = null;
     Connection con = null;
   //URL is jdbc:db2:dbname
   String url = "jdbc:db2:MUSIC";
   DefaultContext ctx = DefaultContext.getDefaultContext();
   if (ctx == null) { // if1
    try { // try1
     if (argv.length == 0) {
       // Connect with default id/password
     con = DriverManager.getConnection(url);
      }
      else
       if (argv.length == 2) {
         String userid = argv[0];
         String passwd = argv[1];
           //connect with user-provided username and password
         con = DriverManager.getConnection(url, userid, passwd);
       } else {
         System.out.println("\nUsage:"+
                              ListClassicsApp[userid password]\n");
         System.exit(0);
       }
       con.setAutoCommit(false);
       ctx = new DefaultContext(con);
      } // end try1
      catch (SQLException e) {
```

```
        System.out.println("Error: could not get a default context");
        System.err.println(e);
        System.exit(1);
      }
      DefaultContext.setDefaultContext(ctx);
    } // end if1

   //  retrieve data from the database
   System.out.println("Retrieving CLASSICS from the database...");
   #sql cursor1 = {SELECT ID, TITLE, COMPOSER from CLASSICS};
   //  display the result set using the cursor.
   //  cursor1.next() returns false when there are no more rows

   System.out.println("Results:");
   while (cursor1.next()) {
     str1 = cursor1.ID();
     str2 = cursor1.title();
     str3 = cursor1.composer();
     System.out.print(" CD ID: " + str1 + "\t");
     System.out.print(" Title: " + str2 + "\t");
     System.out.println("Composer: " + str3 + "\n");
   }
   cursor1.close();
  } // end try2
   catch (Exception e) {
    e.printStackTrace();
   } // end catch
  } // end main
} // end class
```

You should always give the same name to the SQLJ source file and the Java class name declared in the SQLJ source file, as you would do in pure Java programming. This is particularly important for generating debugging files (see section on debugging later in this chapter). In this example, the SQLJ file name is **ListClassicsApp.sqlj.**

The Translation Process

The translation process takes an .sqlj file as input (again, the extension is case sensitive), and generates the corresponding Java source files as well as a profile file (with extension .ser). The Java source code is imported into the repository and loaded in your workspace, while the .ser file is added as a resource to the current project.

TIP

Once you have translated the SQLJ file, use F5 to refresh the resources page contents. They do not refresh automatically.

Setting the Right Translator

VisualAge for Java is customized by default to use the DB2 translator classes. However, you may want to change this to point to your favorite database-translator class. Those properties can be changed in the **SQLJSupportToolTranslator.properties** file located under x:\ibmvjava\ide\tools\com-ibm-ivj-sqlj. You must provide in this file the names of a translator class and the main method in the class, as follows. Please refer to your database documentation to find the right class and method names.

```
Additionalclasspath =
          lib\\sqlj-translator.zip;C:\\sqllib\\java\\db2java.zip
translatorclassname         = sqlj.tools.Sqlj
translatormethodname        = statusMain
```

Changing Translation Options

Each time you translate an SQLJ file, the current values of a set of translation options are used. The translation properties can be edited from **Workspace->Tools ->SQL->Properties**. One option governs the NLS encoding that will be used. The other one indicates whether online semantics checking will be performed as part of the translation process. By default, this option is off. By turning it on, you will check the semantics of the SQLJ statement against the database at translation time. The translator process will takes a bit more time, but this is a great saver at debug time. We recommend that you always select this option. If you turn this option on, you must also the following properties, as shown in Figure 21.18:

Driver Name. The full JDBC driver name. There is no list available here; you must enter the full name manually. If you plan to paste data in this field, use Ctrl-V, not Shift-Insert.

Default URL. The URL of the database where semantic checking should performed.

UserID/Password. The proper authorization information.

Calling Translate

You translate a SQLJ file by calling the **Translate** function from the resources page. The translation process is a happy process. If the translation fails, it says it's completed. If the translation works, it says it's completed. The truth is out there in the Console window!

Figure 21.18 Specifying translation properties.

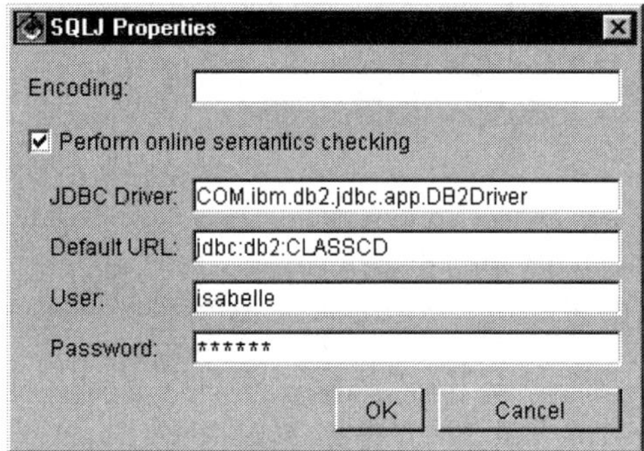

There are two possible sources for translation errors. Some of the SQLJ code could have syntactic or semantic errors, or the Java code around it could have errors. If there are no SQLJ errors, the Java code is imported in the repository and loaded in the workspace. However, the Java code may still have errors. Although it is (very) tempting, you must not fix the errors directly in VisualAge. You must *always* fix errors in the master SQLJ file located in the resources directory and translate the file again.

Profile Customization

When translation finishes, a profile file, ListClassicsApp.ser, is created in the resource directory, in the leaf directory based on the package name (effectivevaj\data\sqlj). A ListClassicsApp_SJProfileKeys class is also imported in the VisualAge for Java IDE. This class describes the profile keys information. If you want to take advantage of database performance improvements, you must use the tool provided by your database vendor to customize the profile, generate bind files, and bind them against the database. Note that this must be done outside of VisualAge.

DB2 provides a tool to list the contents of the profile file in text form. If you run profp ListClassicsApp_SJProfile0.ser, you get the following output:

```
====================================================
printing contents of profile
effectivevaj.data.sqlj.ListClassicsApp_SJProfile0
created 942166716993 (11/9/99 5:58 PM)
```

```
associated context is sqlj.runtime.ref.DefaultContext
profile loader is sqlj.runtime.profile.DefaultLoader@18a626
contains no customizations
original source file: ListClassicsApp.sqlj
contains one entry
==================================================
profile effectivevaj.data.sqlj.ListClassicsApp_SJProfile0 entry 0
#sql { SELECT ID, TITLE, COMPOSER from CLASSICS };
line number: 65
PREPARED_STATEMENT executed via EXECUTE_QUERY
role is QUERY
descriptor is null
contains no parameters
result set type is NAMED_RESULT
result set name is effectivevaj.data.sqlj.App_Cursor1
contains 3 result columns
1. mode: OUT, java type: java.lang.String (java.lang.String),
   sql type: VARCHAR, name: ID, marker index: -1
2. mode: OUT, java type: java.lang.String (java.lang.String),
   sql type: VARCHAR, name: title, marker index: -1
3. mode: OUT, java type: java.lang.String (java.lang.String),
   sql type: VARCHAR, name: composer, marker index: -1
```

You can optimize the query and bind it with the database. Make sure to optimize the profile file located in the Effective VisualAge for Java resources directory. Otherwise, the updated profile (changed after optimization) will not be used when you run your program from VisualAge.

For DB2, you must use the **db2profc** command to optimize a profile and bind it to a database, like this: db2profc –url=jdbc:db2:MUSIC ListClassics-App_SJProfile0.ser. This command gives the following results:

```
[IBM][SQLJ Driver] SQJ0001W Customizing profile
"ListClassicsApp_SJProfile0".
PROFILE NAME:   ListClassicsApp_SJProfile0
SOURCE PROGRAM: ListClassicsApp.sqlj

ENTRY   LINE    MESSAGES
------  ------  ------------------------------------------------
                 SQL0060W  The "SQLJ" precompiler is in progress.
                 SQL0091W  Precompilation or binding was ended with
"0"
                           errors and "0" warnings.
```

You are now ready the run an optimized SQLJ program!

Debugging SQLJ Programs

The VisualAge integrated debugger can be used to debug the Java generated code; however, it will display the generated Java code source, which is not very convenient. We'd rather step in the original SQLJ file when debugging. To do this, you can generate from the SQLJ file a special .class file that is instrumented from the original SQLJ source code rather than from the Java code created during the translation process. However, the integrated debugger can't debug those files; you must use the VisualAge Distributed Debugger instead. The distributed debugger is installed separately from VisualAge for Java. If you haven't installed it, you should do so now, from the original VisualAge for Java installation CD-ROM.

The first step is to generate the special class file. You must select the SQLJ file in the resources page and select **Tools->SQLJ->Create SQLJ Debug File.** The .class file is created in the same directory as the SQLJ source file, regardless of what the package name is. Suppose that the SQLJ file is at the root of the project's resources folder. The .class file will be created in this directory, although the name of the class is effectivevaj.data.sqlj.ListClassicsApp. Therefore, the .class file should have been created under the effectivevaj\data\sqlj directory.

Deploying the Code

The distributed debugger can load classes located on the file system only. Therefore, you must export the SQLJ and .class files before debugging the application. To deploy the application:

1. Select the effectivevaj.data.sqlj package, and choose **File->Export**.
2. Select **Directory** as the export destination.
3. Specify a directory for export, for example **C:\SQLApps**.
4. Select the .class and resources options: For the .class files, make sure that the ListClassicsApp file is not selected (we want to use the special version created in the resources directory instead).
5. Press the **Details** button near the resources option. Select the ListClassicsApp.sqlj file and the ListClassicsApp.class files at the root. Normally, you don't need the SQLJ source file at execution time, but you need it for stepping into source code. Then, use the + on the left of **Effective VisualAge for Java** to expand the directory tree down to effectivevaj\data\sqlj. Select the sqlj directory by clicking in the square on the left. This will select the profile file contained in this directory.
6. Close that window, and press **Finish**.
7. After the code is generated, you must move the .sqlj and .class files from the C:\SQLApps directory to the C:\SQLApps\effectivevaj\data\sqlj directory. This will avoid errors when loading the .class file in the debugger.

Creating an Environment File

We have found a few problems when starting the distributed debugger if the PATH and CLASSPATH variables were not kept minimal. Therefore, we highly recommend that you create a setenv.bat file such as the one that follows, and run this file before starting the debugger. Make sure to list on the class path all directories and JAR/ZIP files that your application may require to run. In addition, if your source code is located in a different directory than the compiled code, you can set the debugger environment variable DER_DBG_PATH to point to the source code locations.

```
@set PATH=c:\sqllib\bin;f:\ibmdebug\bin;%JAVA_HOME%\Bin;c:\winnt;
@set CLASSPATH=c:\sqllib\java\db2java.zip;c:\sqllib\java\runtime.zip;c:\sql-
lib\java\sqlj.zip;C:\SQLApps;%JAVA_HOME%\classes;%JAVA_HOME%\lib\classes.zip;
```

A few words about this file: **db2java.zip, sqlj.zip,** and **runtime.zip** are required to run an SQLJ-based application. **C:\SQLApps** is the root for the code you exported in the previous step and, as such, must be added to the class path. Finally, the JDK run-time classes must be added to the class path as well.

c:\sqllib\bin must added to the PATH variable, because it contains the JDBC driver native DLLs. **F:\ibmdebug\bin** is the binaries directory for the distributed debugger, and **%JAVA_HOME%\bin** is the path for the java and java_g executables.

Debugging the Application

Ready to debug? Run the setenv.bat file from a command window and invoke **idebug** to start the distributed debugger. The load program dialog, shown in Figure 21.19, lets you select which program you want to debug, which language you are debugging, and whether you debugging in local or remote mode. To start debugging the ListClassicsApp class:

1. Switch to the **Interpreted (Intel/AIX)** tab.
2. Press on the Browse button to locate the class you want to debug.
3. Select the C:\SQLApps directory in the class-path components list.
4. In the bottom pane, expand the successive directories (effectivevaj\data\sqlj) until you reach the ListClassicsApp.class, select it, and press OK.
5. The dominant language should be **Interpreted Java**.
6. Make sure the **Local** mode is selected, and press **Load**.

If everything is in place, the debugger now invokes the application in debug mode using java_g and stops at the first line in the main() method. As you can see in Figure 21.20, the SQLJ source code has been loaded in the Source pane. Please refer to Chapter 5 for more information about the distributed debugger. We also recommend that you read the documentation that comes with the debugger. The debugger.pdf file is located in the x:\ibmdebug\help\<locale_name>\pdf directory, where locale_name is locale name you used to install this debugger. The default locale is en_US.

Figure 21.19 The Load program window.

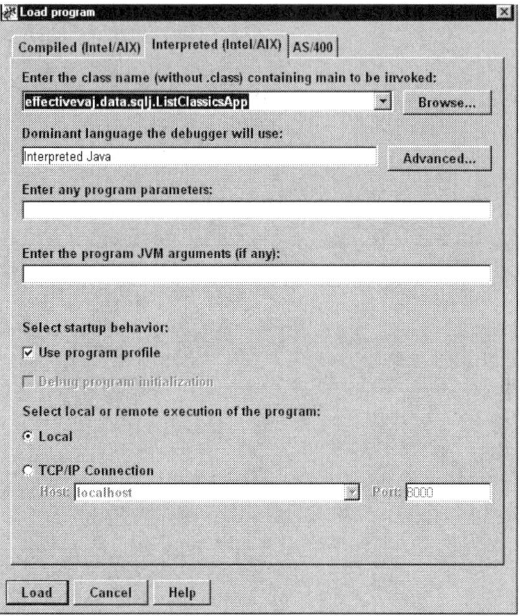

Figure 21.20 Finally, debugging!

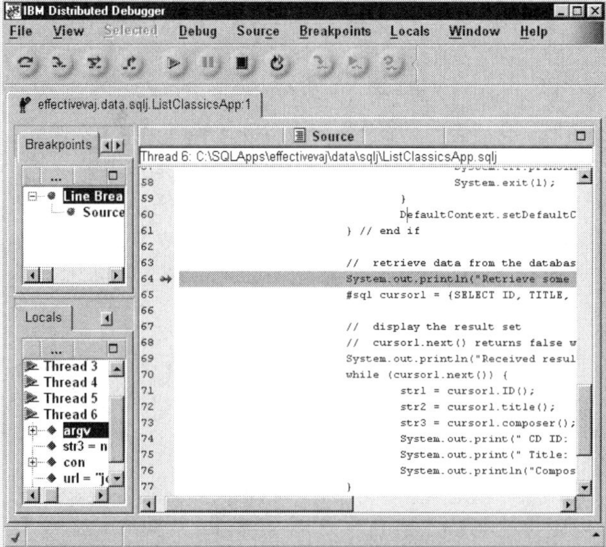

Summary

VisualAge for Java comes with many features to help you create database applications. The Data Access Beans let you create and invoke SQL statements without being an SQL expert. The DB2 Stored Procedure Builder eases the task of creating stored procedures in Java. The SQLJ support lets you create, run, and debug SQLJ programs.

In the next chapter, we jump into a complete different world: distributed objects. Should you want to use RMI or create CORBA-based applications, VisualAge for Java comes with tools to help you achieve your goal.

DEVELOPING DISTRIBUTED APPLICATIONS

22

In this chapter, we concentrate on building distributed applications using VisualAge for Java. In a distributed application, the different application components, such as the GUI, the business logic, and the data, are spread across multiple machines. Such architecture lets you split the workload across multiple machines and share some parts on the application (mainly the business logic) across applications. Distributed applications can be difficult to implement. On top of dealing with business-logic problems, developers need to define and implement how the application components will communicate over a network. In other words, they spend their time dealing with "plumbing" rather than concentrating on the application business logic.

Distributed-object technologies provide a framework of services on which developers can rely to get components to communicate over a network. The JDK provides a Java-to-Java solution with the Remote Method Invocation (RMI) API. However, RMI supports only the distribution of components written in Java. If you need to integrate with applications written in C, C++, COBOL, or other languages, you can rely on the Common Object Request Broker Architecture (CORBA). CORBA, which is an Object Management Group (OMG) specification, defines a common format, the Interface Definition Language (IDL), to represent an object that can be distributed across applications. Enterprise JavaBeans combine the best of the RMI and CORBA technologies: We cover EJB components in Chapter 23, "Developing Enterprise JavaBeans."

In this chapter, we cover how to develop an RMI-based application and test it in the IDE. Then, we cover the IDL Development Environment, which allows you to create and manage object definitions in IDL. Those definitions then can be mapped to an equivalent Java definition by using an IDL-to-Java compiler. Finally, we explain how to integrate a third-party tool for CORBA development in VisualAge for Java.

NOTE

The RMI Access Builder, which was available in VisualAge for Java, version 3.0.x, has been removed in version 3.5. Therefore, we do not expose it in this chapter. If you are using version 3.0.x, and are interested in using this builder, please refer to the book's companion web site for more information.

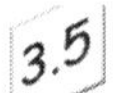

Throughout this chapter, we have identified version 3.5 changes by using this icon.

Overview of Distributed Objects

Before diving into RMI and CORBA, let's do a quick review of distributed-object basics. If you are already familiar with distributed objects, you may skip to *Developing RMI Applications.*

Suppose that you have defined the basic behavior of a counter object. This counter presents the following *remote interface* to client objects: You can increment the counter, decrement it, and get the current counter value. The remote interface is the contract between a client and the counter-server object. A client object can call the methods of the server counter object by using a proxy called a *stub.* A stub is a representation of a server object on the client machine. It implements all methods of the counter remote interface.

The client object uses the stub to pass messages to the server object: The stub's implementation packages the client call and sends it to the server. This packaging phase is called *marshalling.* On the server side, a *skeleton* receives the remote call, unmarshals the data, and calls the server object code (for example, the real decrement() method code). If data needs to be passed back to the client, the skeleton marshals data that the stub will unmarshal.

The stub and the skeleton are generated classes. They contain all of the code that the client and server objects need to communicate, that is, the "plumbing" code we mentioned in the chapter introduction. For RMI, stubs and skeletons are generated by a compiler called **rmic**. For CORBA, the stubs and skeletons are generated using an IDL compiler.

Developing RMI Applications

In this section, you will develop a sample RMI application: write the remote interface, implement the server object, and generate stubs and skeletons. You will generate the stub and skeleton—invoke the rmic compiler—from the IDE. By developing this sample, you will have a complete overview of RMI-based development with VisualAge for Java.

To create an RMI application, you define a remote interface, create a server application, and, finally, create a client application. For this example, we have chosen a very simple fictitious counter, which lets you manipulate its value using increment and decrement methods. You can get the current counter value via getValue(). You should create all types in an effectivevaj.adv.dist.traditionalrmi package.

Writing the Remote Interface

The remote interface is the contract between the client and the server objects, that is, the list of methods the client object can call on the server object. All remote interfaces must inherit from the java.rmi.Remote class. You can create the remote interface by following those steps:

1. Start the Interface SmartGuide by selecting **Selected->Add->Interface.**
2. Specify Effective VisualAge for Java as the project name.
3. Specify effectivevaj.adv.dist.traditionalrmi as the package name
4. Specify Counter as the interface name.
5. Press **Add** and choose java.rmi.Remote as an interface to extend.
6. Press **Finish.**

Next, you must complete the interface definition to add the decrement, increment, and getValue methods as shown in the following code. Each method must throw a java.rmi.RemoteException: This exception is thrown if the client call to the server fails (for example, if the network is down). We have also added in our definition a SERVER_NAME final string: This string contains the name of the server where the counter object will run, as well as the name of the server object. Since the interface is implemented by both the client and the server, it is a convenient way to know where the object is running. This is not mandatory; it's just a programming tip. The final Counter interface code looks like this:

```
import java.rmi.RemoteException;
public interface Counter extends java.rmi.Remote {
   // CounterServer is the name of the server object, eagle
   // the name of the machine where the RMI registry runs.
   // Change this variable according to your machine name,
   // or to CounterServer if you are running the
   // application locally.
   static final String SERVER_NAME = "rmi://eagle/CounterServer";
   // Decrements the counter value by step.
   void decrement (int step) throws RemoteException;
   // Increments the counter value by step.
   void increment (int step) throws RemoteException;
```

```
    // Returns the current counter value.
    int getValue () throws RemoteException;
}
```

Creating the Server Application

The remote interface is the contract between the server and the client objects. Once this contract is defined, you must create the server implementation of the methods, in other words, the business logic of the counter object. The server object must implement the remote interface we just defined and inherit from UnicastRemoteObject. To create the CounterImpl class, use the Class SmartGuide as follows:

1. Select the Counter interface in the IDE. The interface is then added automatically to the list of interfaces that the CounterImpl class must implement.
2. Start the Class SmartGuide from **Selected->Add->Class**.
3. Specify CounterImpl as the class name.
4. Specify java.rmi.server.UnicastRemoteObject as the superclass name. You can type the first letters of the class name (Uni) and then press Ctrl-Space to fill in the package name or use **Browse** to pick the class from a list.
5. Press **Next** and select the **main(String)** option, because we need a main entry point in this class.
6. Press **Finish**.

Next, add a *private int counterValue;* field definition to the class, and complete each method of the remote interface that has been added to your class as follows:

```
public void decrement(int step) throws RemoteException {
 counterValue = counterValue - step;
}
public void increment(int step) throws RemoteException {
 counterValue = counterValue + step;
}
public int getValue() throws RemoteException {
 return counterValue;
}
```

Finally, you complete the main() method for this implementation class. First, you must register your server object to the RMI naming service. A client object will connect to the RMI naming service to look up an object by name and obtain the stub that lets it call methods on the server object. Naming services are handled by the RMI registry, a process that runs on port 1099 by default. We have defined a string called SERVER_NAME in the remote interface, which is used by the server object to register with naming services. If the application is run locally, you can omit the machine name in SERVER_NAME. With all this in mind, the main() method looks like this:

```
public static void main(String[] args) {
try {
   CounterImpl aCounterServer = new CounterImpl();
   // Bind to local registry.
   Naming.rebind(Counter.SERVER_NAME, aCounterServer);
   System.out.println ("Server Running and waiting for incoming
calls");
 }
 catch (Exception e) {
   System.out.println("Server could not start" + e.getMessage());
   e.printStackTrace();
   System.exit(0);
 }
}
```

> **TIP**
>
> SERVER_NAME is built from the machine name (here, eagle) and the server-object name (CounterServer). If you want to test an RMI application locally (client and server object on the same machine), we strongly advise that you always have a TCP/IP stack. For Windows NT, this implies that you install the MS Loopback Adapter. You must be able to ping your machine *by name* (not through localhost), should you be connected to a network or not.

Generating RMI Stubs and Skeletons

The server code is complete, but an essential piece of the RMI framework is missing: the stub and the skeleton. You do not have to exit from VisualAge for Java to generate stubs and skeletons; just select the CounterImpl class and choose **Tools->Generate RMI**. Calling this option is equivalent to running the JDK's **rmic** compiler.

The rmic compiler is slightly different in the JDK 1.1 and Java 2. If you are using VisualAge for Java, version 3.5, you will see three options:

JDK 1.1 stubs/skeletons. This option allows you create stubs/skeletons that will only work with JDK 1.1. It is equivalent to the –v1.1 option of the rmic compiler.

JDK 1.2 stubs/skeletons. This option lets you create Java2 stubs. Note that with Java2, skeletons are not needed anymore. Therefore, this option generates only one class, not two! This option is equivalent to the –v1.2 option of the rmic compiler.

JDK 1.1&1.2 stubs/skeletons. Finally, this option lets you generate stubs/skeletons that will work with both JDKs: this is probably the best choice for portability. This option is equivalent to the –vcompat option of the rmic compiler.

After generation is complete, you will have at least one class: CounterImpl_Stub and eventually CounterImpl_Skel (if you are using JDK 1.1). You will never use these classes directly, but they must be there, because they do all the plumbing work! Because those classes implement the Counter remote interface, you must regenerate them anytime the Counter interface changes.

> **NOTE**
>
> RMI passes local objects as parameters by value. In other words, a copy of the object has to travel between the client and the server. RMI uses the serialization mechanism to do this: Therefore, if a method returns an object or takes an object as a parameter, this object must implement the Serializable interface.

Creating a Client Application

We are now ready to create a client application to interact with the counter. Eventually, you must set a proper security manager. This security manager is used to control the operations the stubs can perform. RMI uses dynamic stub loading: When the stub bytecodes can't be found locally, the RMI class loader tries to dynamically download them from the server machine. If no security manager has been provided, dynamic stub-loading fails: Stubs can be loaded only from the local file system as defined by the class path. In our sample, the stubs can be found locally, and the security manager is optional. If the client does not have access to stubs locally, you must set a security manager to ensure that the downloaded code does not contain any malicious bytecodes. The only security manager available for RMI is RMISecurityManager.

Then, the client application locates the server object by name through the naming services. The latter call returns a stub interface that you use as a handle to the remote object. You can then interact with the remote object exactly as if it was local. To create the client application:

1. Start the Class SmartGuide from **Selected->Add->Class.**

2. Specify CounterClient as the class name.
3. Leave java.lang.Object as the superclass name.
4. Press **Next** and select the **main(String)** option, because we need a main entry point in this class.
5. Press **Finish**.

Once the class has been generated, you can complete the main() method using the following example. We first look up the RMI naming services using the SERVER_NAME attribute stored in the remote interface. We perform a cast on the lookup result to obtain a local stub. This stub is then used to call the different methods of the counter remote object:

```
public static void main(java.lang.String[] args) {
  // Local Variables
  Counter aCounter;
  try {
    aCounter = (Counter) Naming.lookup(Counter.SERVER_NAME);
    System.out.println (">> Incrementing Counter");
    aCounter.increment(4);
    System.out.println ("The new value is: " +
                        aCounter.getCounterValue());
    System.out.println (">> Decrementing Counter");
    aCounter.decrement(2);
    System.out.println ("The new value is: " +
                        aCounter.getCounterValue());


  }
  catch (Exception e) {
    System.out.println ("Connection to server failed" +
e.getMessage());
    e.printStackTrace();
    System.exit (0);
  } // catch
 } // main
```

Running the Application

The RMI application can be tested in three steps:

1. Start the RMI registry.
2. Start the server application.
3. Start the client.

When you start the RMI registry, it uses the workspace class-path to find classes. Because the RMI runtime must access the Counter_Stub class, you must add the Effective VisualAge for Java project to the workspace class-path. Only directories and Jar/Zip filenames can be added to the workspace class-path, not project names. However, if you add the project-resources path to the workspace class-path, VisualAge for Java magically "knows" it has to look for classes in the project with the same name! If you add x:\ibmvjava\ide\project_resources\Effective VisualAge for Java to the workspace class-path, the RMI registry and the server application will start successfully.

The RMI registry can be started in VisualAge from the IDE customization window. Choose **Window->Options**, go to the RMI registry page, and press the **Restart RMI registry** button to start the registry on the default port. Once the registry is started, you can start the server application (CounterImpl). If all goes well, a *Server Running and waiting for incoming calls* message is displayed in the Console window. Now start the client and watch the counter moving in the Console window.

The Transition to CORBA

RMI can be used to distribute pure Java applications. If you want objects written in different languages to be part of a same application, you must use the CORBA programming model. In the CORBA model, remote interfaces are defined in a neutral language called the Interface Definition Language (IDL). RMI uses a proprietary transport protocol called JRMP, which supports the transport of only Java objects across the wire. The Internet Inter-ORB protocol (IIOP) is the CORBA transport protocol. RMI has evolved in Java 2 to support IIOP as a transport protocol: This is known as RMI/IIOP.

RMI/IIOP lets you use the RMI programming model, which is simpler than the CORBA programming model, on top of the IIOP protocol. This transition requires minimal changes to your code. Mainly, you must use the CORBA naming services (CosNaming) in place of the RMI registry to bind your objects. After your object is registered to the CosNaming services, it can be located by any client and used from a different language, such as C++. However, it also means that a C++ interface equivalent to your Java interface has to be generated. In the CORBA environment, interfaces are described in a neutral language: the Interface Definition Language (IDL).

You can generate an IDL version of a RMI remote interface by selecting **Tools->Generate RMI->IDL**. The RMI compiler is invoked with the **–idl** option: The corresponding IDL files are generated in the project_resources directory. You would then use an IDL-to-C++ compiler to generate the appropriate C++ stubs that can be used from a C++ client program.

> **NOTE**
>
> For more information about RMI/IIOP and examples of migration from the JRMP protocol to the IIOP protocol, you can refer to the JavaSoft site: www.javasoft.com/products.

Developing CORBA Applications

The Common Object Request Broker Architecture (CORBA) is a specification adopted by the Object Management Group (OMG). It addresses the development of distributed applications written in heterogeneous programming languages. Objects distributed across a network use the services of an Object Request Broker (ORB) to communicate with other objects. A Java ORB is an ORB written in Java. An application written in Java can use the services of a Java ORB to communicate with objects running on another ORB. The application uses CORBA naming services to look up an object, get a handle on that object (the stub), and call methods on this object as if it were local.

CORBA makes a clear separation between the definition and the implementation of an object. An object interface is always described in IDL, which is language-neutral. Once an object has been defined in IDL, you can generate the implementation class in a given language using an IDL compiler, also known as an *emitter*. Those classes are also called *bindings*. Nothing prevents you from writing the object implementation in Java and a client application in C++. In this case, you will need a C++ emitter (for the client side) and a Java emitter (for the implementation).

The IDL Development Environment supports the creation of IDL interfaces. By invoking an IDL Java emitter, you generate the client and implementation classes. Those classes are then imported in the repository. Only Java ORBs are supported. You can't generate C++ bindings inside the environment.

Prerequisites

In order to manage IDL code in the IDE, you must first add the **IDL Development Environment 3.0** feature to the workspace. A project named IBM Enterprise IDL Development Environment appears in the workspace. This project may seem empty because it has no packages attached, but in fact, it is not! Some mysterious metadata is hidden in this project. Do not alter this project in any way; if you do, the IDL Development Environment may be corrupted. Once the feature is added, a new IDL page is available for all project browsers.

The IDL Page

The IDL page, shown in Figure 22.1, can be used to edit IDL code. The source code editor is IDL-sensitive and comes with a few shortcuts to add modules, interfaces, and methods to an IDL source. From the IDL page, you can version IDL files the same way you would version a class or package. There are few restrictions to this: See *Versioning the IDL and Generated Classes* later in this chapter for more details.

When you invoke an IDL2Java compiler, classes generated during compilation are automatically imported in the repository. You can view in the same page the source IDL code and the generated classes; therefore, you do not need to switch back to the Workbench to view the generated code. In addition, you will be able to debug the client and server side of the CORBA application inside the integrated debugger.

Figure 22.1 The IDL page.

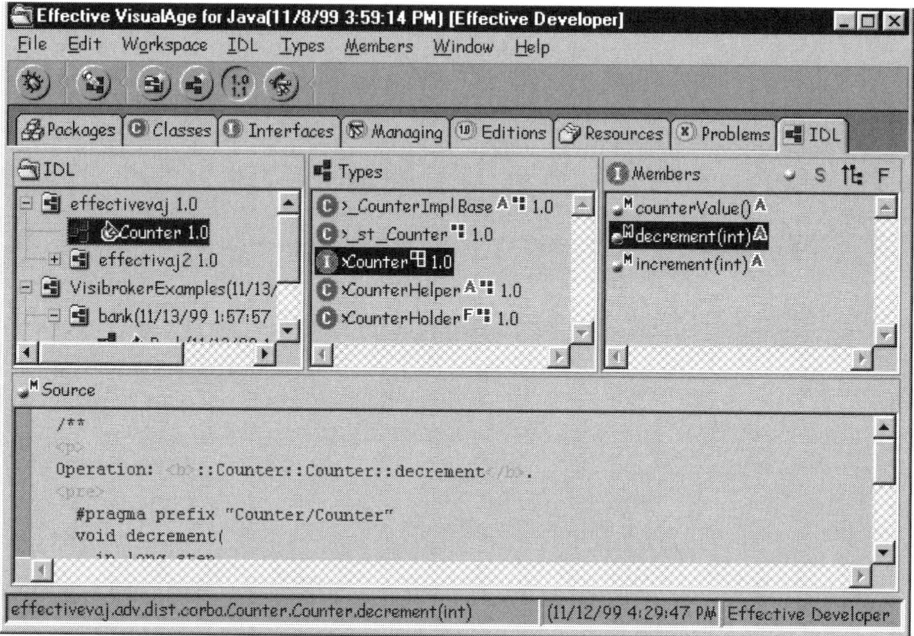

You can create IDL code in this page or import it from the file system. In the IDL page, IDL source is stored in an IDL object. IDL objects are grouped under IDL groups. To illustrate the usage of the IDL Development Environment, we explain how to create an application similar to the RMI one, but this time in CORBA. First, create the Counter interface in IDL; then generate the proper bindings and write the object implementation and a client application.

> **NOTE**
>
> Although code generated by the Java2IDL compiler can be viewed and edited from the Workbench, resist the temptation: *Don't do it!* All editing and versioning must be done from the IDL page. If you lose information on the IDL page, it means you are doing something wrong. However, you might lose information, but not code! Our brave repository is keeping it. The IDL group and object definitions as well as the generated code are still available from the repository; they can be added to the IDL page if they get lost.

Creating the Counter Interface

IDL is easy to understand if you already know Java, so the following code should be easy to interpret:

```
module Counter {
 interface BaseCounter {
  readonly attribute long counterValue;
  void decrement (in long step);
  void increment (in long step);
 };
};
```

A *module* defines an IDL namespace. A module is equivalent to a Java package. When you generate code, module names are converted to Java package-names. Therefore, the "Java name" of the BaseCounter interface is Counter.BaseCounter. If you declared a module CorbaObjects inside the Counter module, the Java name of the BaseCounter interface would be Counter.CorbaObjects.BaseCounter, and so on.

The *interface* keyword is used to declare an interface in a module, here, Counter. The notion of an interface in IDL is very similar to the notion of an interface in Java, with the exception of attributes. An attribute in IDL is very similar to a bean property. By defining an attribute, you define a field of a certain type (here, long) and its accessors. Because we have declared that counterValue is a read-only attribute, only a counterValue()get-accessor—method will be generated by the IDL2Java compiler. If you remove the read-only qualifier, a counterValue(int) set-accessor method is generated as well. Finally, we declare the decrement and increment methods: Both take an *in* parameter called step. In IDL, you must specify whether parameters are supplied only to a method (*in*), if they will be returned by a method (*out*), or if a supplied parameter can be modified in the method body (*inout*).

Creating an IDL Group

To add this IDL code to the Effective VisualAge for Java project, you must open a project browser to the IDL page. Then, you must create an *IDL group* that will contain the Counter IDL object.

Create an IDL group by right-clicking in the IDL pane and choosing **Add IDL Group** in the pop-up menu. You can add an IDL group into another IDL group by first selecting the containing IDL group. The following options are available in the IDL group SmartGuide, shown in Figure 22.2:

Place Group In. An IDL group can be attached either to the root of the IDL groups tree or to another IDL group. You can either choose the **Root** option, or press **Browse** to select an existing IDL group to attach to.

Create a Group Named. IDL groups are used to organize IDL objects, not for code generation. An IDL group name cannot contain a dollar-sign ($). This character is reserved for use by the IDL Development Environment.

Figure 22.2 Creating the effectivevaj IDL group.

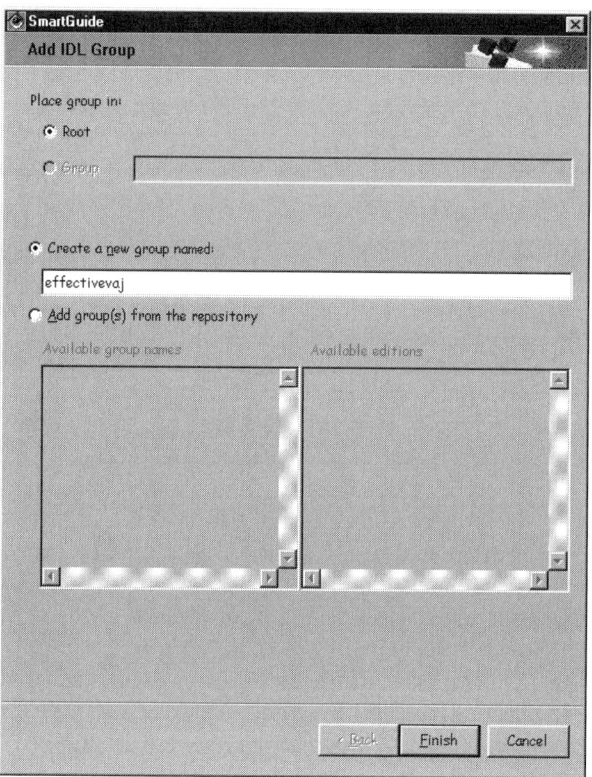

Add IDL Groups from repository. If you have imported IDL groups and objects into the repository, you can add them to the IDL page by selecting this option and choosing an IDL group name. Non-root IDL groups (attached to another IDL group rather than to Root) do not show up in that list. The only way to add an IDL group attached to another IDL group is by adding the outermost IDL group first.

Adding an IDL Object

The next step is to create an IDL object inside the IDL group by selecting the effectivevaj IDL group, right-clicking, and choosing **Add IDL Object** from the pop-up menu. The name of the IDL object should be Counter. VisualAge for Java creates the IDL object and inserts a base module-definition in the IDL Source pane, shown in Figure 22.3. Just complete the code according to the source listing provided previously; you can use the code generation helpers as shown in Figure 22.3 to go a bit faster!

Figure 22.3 Completing the Counter IDL object.

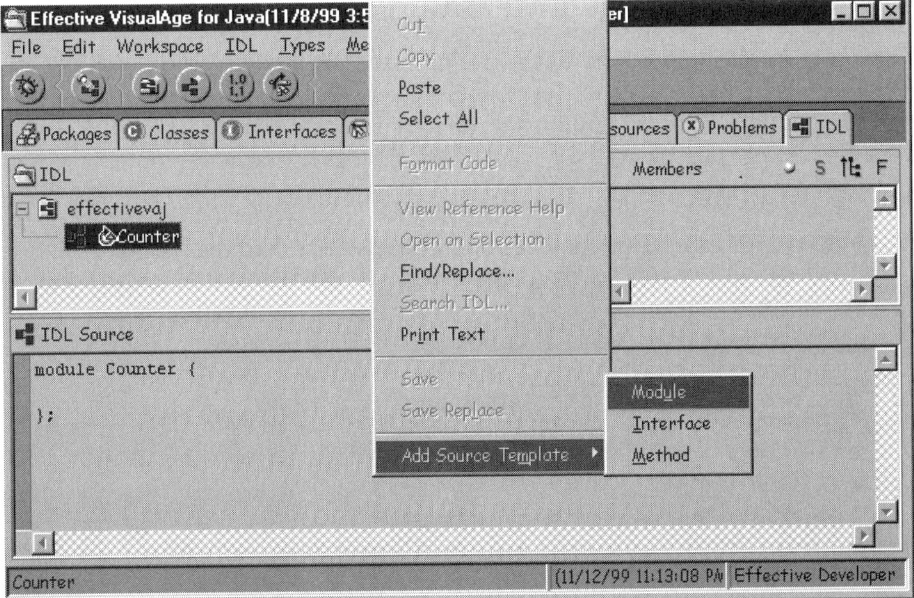

The Evil Reserved Package

What we gently call the evil package is actually a central piece of the IDL Development Environment. If you switch back to the Workbench, you can see that an *Effective$VisualAge$for$JavaEABPMReserved* package has been added to the Effective VisualAge for Java project. This package contains metadata used by VisualAge for Java to display information in the IDL page. In addition, it contains IDL versioning information. In other words, this package is more than precious: Do not touch it or alter it in any way.

Another important point: The reserved package is added to a project the first time that you create an IDL group. It contains the definition of all IDL groups created in that project. If you have read carefully Chapter 4, "Using Version Control," you should know that only project owners can create packages inside a project. In other words, only the project owner can create the reserved package. Similarly, only the package owner or a package-group member can add a class to a package. Each time you create an IDL object or version an IDL object, you add a class inside the reserved package.

Therefore, you should ask the project owner to create the IDL group for you and then add package-group members to the reserved package. Those package-group members can now work safely in the IDL page.

Installing a Third-Party ORB

You can customize VisualAge for Java to use different IDL compilers. The default compiler is the Component Broker Series compiler, now part of the IBM WebSphere Application Server, Enterprise Edition. The second option is the CICS IIOP compiler. CICS TS Version 1.3 comes with CORBA support and, therefore, an IDL compiler. The third option is to use a third-party vendor Java ORB. The IDL compiler provided with the Java ORB must respect two rules, though:

1. The IDL-to-Java compiler must work from the command line.
2. If the compilation fails, compiler output must be sent to the standard-error stream: Otherwise, VisualAge will not detect that the compilation has failed. VisualAge considers the compilation to be successful when files have been generated and no messages have been sent to the standard-error stream. All messages are redirected to the Console window.

For our tests, we used an evaluation copy of Visibroker for Java, from Inprise Corp. Evaluation copies are available from the www.inprise.com Web site.

If you want to create and run the application in the IDE, you must first import a Java ORB. Actually, code generation would work, but all classes would be marked with problems because ORB classes would be missing. Vendors who implement CORBA-compliant ORBs must implement a certain number of classes, contained in packages starting with org.omg.corba. The implementation is obviously different from Vendor A to Vendor B. The Inprise implementation comes with Visibroker for Java; the IBM implementation, with the WebSphere Test Environment, a feature that you need to develop servlets, JavaServer Page components, and Enterprise JavaBeans components. There is no problem with having several editions of a same package in the repository, but that's not true for the workspace. In other words, you *cannot* have the IBM implementation and the Inprise implementation of CORBA classes loaded *at the same time* in the workspace. It is one *or* the other. Note that this also occurs with the CICS IIOP environment and the Notes Library Version 5.0.

One solution to this problem is to isolate the common packages into a separate project, and switch between the version that WebSphere (or CICS, or Notes) uses and the version that the third-party ORB uses every time you need to. Although this is painful because dependencies are analyzed every time (dependent classes are recompiled), you can live with it. But if you want to develop a servlet that talks to a third-party ORB, you are stuck. To the best of our knowledge, there is no solution to this problem, but we were told that IBM was working on it.

The Visibroker for Java ORB is contained in the **x:\vbroker\lib\vbjorb.jar** file. Therefore, you must create a project and import this JAR file in that project before generating any classes with the IDL-to-Java compiler.

> **WARNING**
> Because the org.omg.corba packages are already versioned in the repository, an open edition of the packages must be created at import time. Those system packages are owned by Administrator. Therefore, you must be Administrator to import a third-party ORB!

With all this in mind, you can now switch to the Administrator user (or ask your administrator to do this for you), create a Visibroker project, and import the vbjorb.jar code inside that project. We recommend that you version this project after the import ends. Use a version name such that you can easily recognize the Inprise version of the CORBA packages, for example, **VBJ 3.0**.

Setting Compilation Options

The IDL-to-Java compiler name and its options can be set at the workspace or at the IDL-group level. You can set an IDL-to-Java compiler name at the workspace level from the IDE customization window in the IDL-to-Java Compile category. The same options can be set for an IDL group by selecting the group and choosing **Change Compile Options** from the pop-up menu.

The compiler name can be either an executable name or a Java class name, preceded with **java**. IDL compilers are executed outside VisualAge for Java; the JDK must be installed to execute a Java program, because the VisualAge virtual machine will not be used. You can specify the compiler options in the **Compile Options** entry field. Options set at the workspace level apply only to new IDL groups. Existing IDL-group compilation options are not modified.

The IDL2Java compiler is invoked outside VisualAge for Java. Generated classes are then imported in the repository. If you specify a file mask, only those classes are imported. The Visibroker compiler is **x:\vbroker\bin\idl2java.exe**. We used the **–no_tie** and **–no_examples** options to generate the code.

Generating the Java Classes

That's the easy part! Just select an IDL group or an IDL object and select **Generate Java**. Java code can be generated for **All Objects** or for **Modified objects** only. Modified objects are indicated in the IDL page by a specific icon.

Under the covers, VisualAge for Java exports the IDL file to the x:\ibmvjava\ide\project_resources\.idls\<project.name>\<IDL.Group.Name> directory. Blanks in project and IDL-group names are replaced with periods (.). Then, the IDL compiler is invoked outside VisualAge and the generated code is loaded in the workspace.

NOTE

In real-life applications, an IDL file includes other IDL files. If an IDL file requires another IDL file located in a *different project or IDL group*, you must set the INCLUDE variable to the path indicated in the previous paragraph. You can use the **%PATH%** string as a substitute for x:\ibmv-java\ide\project_resources\.idls. Setting the INCLUDE path is often done through a compiler option (**-I** in Visibroker for Java).

Several classes have been created. If you switch to the Workbench, you see that they belong to a <module_name> package (Counter). If you specify a package name for code generation (using the –p option), classes are generated in <specified_package_name>.<module_name>.

Versioning the IDL and Generated Classes

You can version and manage editions of IDL objects and groups in the same fashion as any program element (although the compare facility is not available). The main difference is that IDL source is not stored directly in the repository. It is stored as metadata in classes stored in the repository. Those classes are part of the now-famous reserved package. IDL object and IDL group versioning *must* be done from the IDL page, *not* from the Workbench.

When you version an IDL object or group, the corresponding Java class in the reserved package is versioned as well. In addition, the generated classes are versioned, and the same version name is used for all. If you replace an IDL object- or group-edition by another edition, the corresponding generated classes are loaded as well. In other words, you should manage only the IDL group and IDL objects, and let VisualAge for Java do the rest for you. That's the best way to stay out of trouble.

After all IDL groups are versioned in a project, the corresponding reserved package can be versioned from the Workbench. However, you may forget to version all IDL groups: Nobody's perfect! To avoid major problems, the AVersionMonitor class will be executed and version all opened editions on your behalf before versioning the reserved package. But the recommended way is still to do this yourself.

Importing and Exporting IDL Files

IDL code can be created in the IDL page but also imported from the file system. IDL code can be imported to an existing group, but you may also specify a group name in the import SmartGuide. When you select a directory, all IDL files located in that directory and its subdirectories are selected for import. You can use the Select button to select the IDL you want to import from that list.

Directories will be imported as group names if you select the corresponding option. Although IDL groups do not influence package naming, this option is interesting if you want to modify the IDL in VisualAge for Java and export it under the same directory structure. Note that those IDL groups are added to the root IDL group specified in the next paragraph.

Finally, you must provide the name of an existing or new root IDL group for the imported IDL objects. In Figure 22.4, we are importing two of the Visibroker for Java samples in a VisibrokerExamples group. Because we have checked the Import Directories as groups option, a *bank* and *bank-with-tie* IDL group will be created under the VisibrokerExamples group.

Exporting IDL files is straightforward: If you export the effectivevaj IDL group under f:\Export, a Counter.idl file is created under f:\Export\effectivevaj\Counter.

Searching IDL

A special search facility can be used to find IDL objects in the current project or the workspace. You can search for modules, interfaces, or a string by using the **All text** option, as shown in Figure 22.5. Search results are displayed in the Search Results window.

Figure 22.4 Importing IDL files.

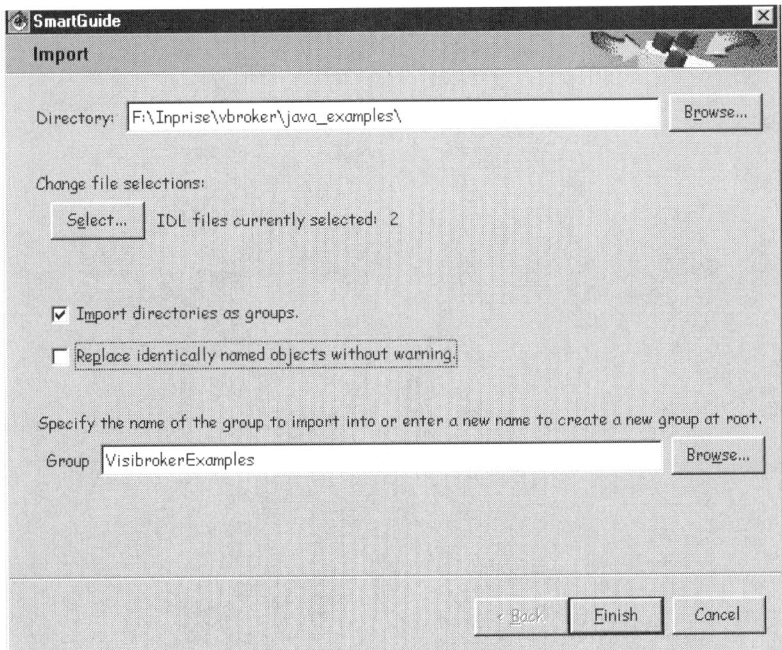

Figure 22.5 The Search IDL dialog.

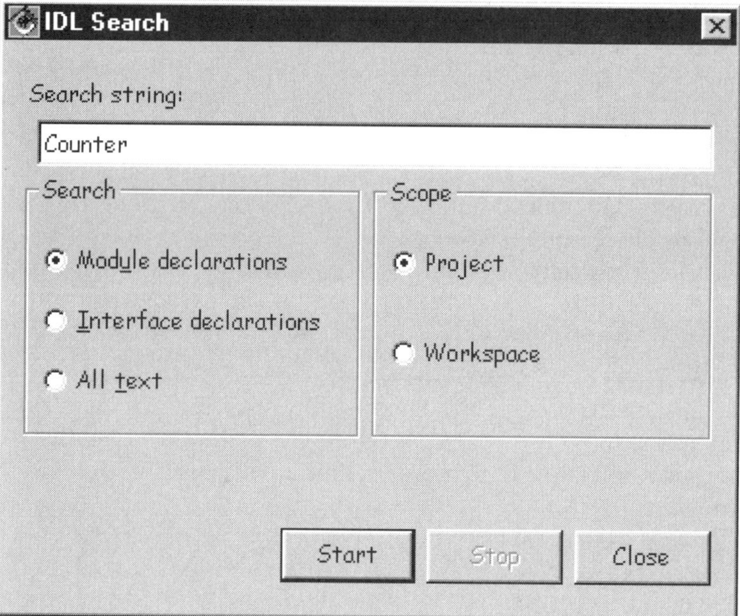

Summary

VisualAge for Java can be of great help in developing distributed applications, whether you are following the RMI or the CORBA path. Code can be created and tested within the IDE, without the need to invoke or use external tools. Distributed computing has recently made a big leap with the arrival of Enterprise JavaBeans components. Learn it all in the next chapter: VisualAge for Java is very good at EJB components.

DEVELOPING ENTERPRISE JAVABEANS

23

The Enterprise JavaBeans specification defines a services framework for component-based distributed computing. Enterprise beans are Java server-side components that can use those services. In this chapter, we give you an overview of the Enterprise JavaBeans (EJB) architecture and then present how you can use the VisualAge for Java tools to create, test, and debug enterprise beans. It is not our intent to cover extensively when, how, and why you should use enterprise beans or to provide you with a detailed tutorial; this could be several hundred pages long! Rather, this chapter shows how to take advantage of VisualAge for Java once you have decided to use enterprise beans in your applications.

For VisualAge for Java, version 3.02, Enterprise-bean development support is available in the Windows NT and AIX versions of VisualAge for Java, Enterprise Edition only. VisualAge for Java, version 3.5 is not available on AIX.

Throughout this chapter, we have identified version 3.5 changes by using this icon.

Introduction to Enterprise Beans

The Enterprise JavaBeans specification is a foundation for the Java 2 Platform for the Enterprise (J2EE) defined by Sun. Vendors use this specification to implement an infrastructure in which components can be deployed, and use a set of services such as distributed transactions, security, or life-cycle management. As a developer, you just reuse the services detailed in the specification: For example, you do not need to include any code in your components to make them transactional. This lets you concentrate on the business logic of the application. Enterprise beans are designed to be *portable* from one vendor's execution environment to another, independently of the choices made by the vendor to implement the services described in the specification.

The quality of service required by an enterprise bean is described *outside* of the component in a deployment descriptor. The deployment descriptor is analyzed at deployment time by a tool provided by the vendor. This feature provides a great level of flexibility for reusing your component. For example, if you wish to change the transactional behavior of an enterprise bean, you need to change only the transaction attribute stored in the deployment descriptor, not the EJB business logic. Changes are taken in account when you re-deploy the enterprise bean in the container.

Enterprise JavaBeans Architecture

The architecture defined by the Enterprise JavaBeans specification is depicted in Figure 23.1. In this architecture, an Enterprise Java Server (EJS) manages one or more containers.

EJB containers provide services to a set of enterprise bean instances. First, a container controls the enterprise bean's life cycle: It creates beans instances, manages pools of instances, and destroys them. Containers are also responsible for providing services such as persistency and security to the beans they manage. Containers are transparent to client programs. However, you always use the services of a container when you invoke an enterprise bean. The container takes care of providing the level of service you requested at deployment time. For example, it will start a transaction before calling a method if you specified in the deployment descriptor that this method had to execute within a transaction context.

The container does not actually provide this service itself. It must communicate with the enterprise server, which implements the services, and obtain access to the service on behalf of the enterprise-bean instance. At a minimum, an Enterprise Java Server must provide naming services accessible through a Java Naming Directory Interface (JNDI) and transaction services. The EJS can be an application server (such as WebSphere Application Server) or a database server (such as Oracle 8i).

Enterprise beans are distributed objects: You must use the services of a factory to manipulate enterprise-bean instances. The *EJBHome* class provides this service. There is one EJBHome per enterprise-bean type. A client must first locate the EJBHome class and then use it to create and find instances. The EJBHome class

Figure 23.1 Enterprise JavaBeans architecture.

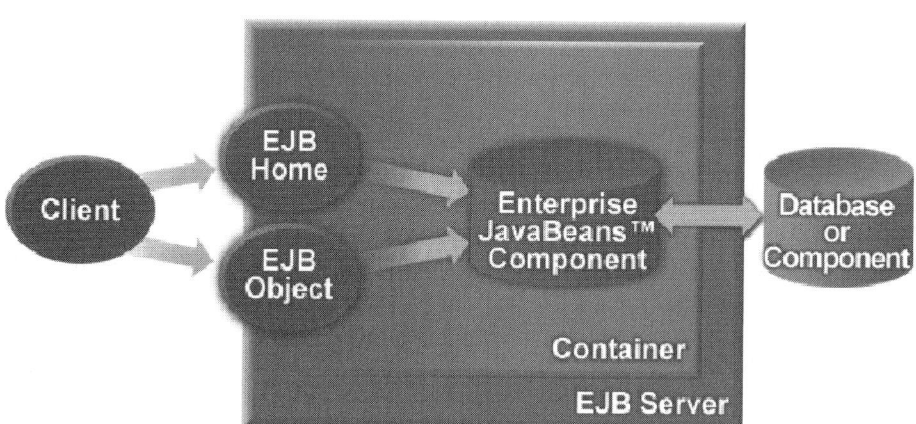

implements the *home interface*, which lists the methods that client programs use to create and find bean instances. As a developer, you only define the home interface. The container is responsible for creating the EJBHome class from this interface definition and for instantiating the EJBHome class when the server is started.

The EJBObject class implements the *remote interface*, which defines the business methods of the enterprise bean. As a developer, you provide only the remote interface. At deployment time, the container creates the EJBObject class from this interface definition. After a client program has access to the home object, it asks the container to create an enterprise-bean instance. In return, it obtains a reference to an EJBObject. In fact, a client program never accesses a bean instance directly; it always goes through the EJBObject. The EJBObject intercepts all requests and forwards them to the bean instance. In the process, it works closely with the container to provide the necessary services. This architecture also lets the container efficiently manage bean instances: For example, a bean that has been idle for some time can be transparently swapped to disk and re-activated when the client program requests it. This would not be possible if the client held a reference to the bean instance.

The *enterprise bean class* contains the implementation of the methods defined on the remote interface, as well as other mandatory methods defined in the specification, such as ejbCreate(), ejbActivate(), or ejbRemove(). Those methods will be called by the container whenever needed. For example, when you call a create() method on the EJBHome, the container will create an EJBObject, create an execution context, create an instance, and then invoke ejbCreate() on the instance.

Enterprise Bean Types

There are two types of enterprise beans: session beans and entity beans. Sessions beans are attached to a specific client: At any one point in time, a session-bean instance is used by only one client. Although session beans may maintain a state on behalf of a client, this information is transient: The state will not be saved when the bean instance is destroyed and will be lost if the server crashes. A typical example of session bean usage is a shopping cart. For each client connecting to the online shop, a session bean instance is created. When the client conversation ends, the session bean is destroyed. Although it is important to maintain the shopping cart contents during the client conversation, this data is not vital and does not need to be persistently saved.

However, if we edit an invoice for our online shopper, this invoice must be persistently saved. For that, we would use an Invoice entity bean. Entity beans represent data, typically a row in a database table. In this case, creating an entity bean is equivalent to adding a record to the table. Even if the bean instance is removed or if the server crashes, the bean instance can be recreated from its persistent state. Entity beans may be shared by multiple clients: The invoice could be simultaneously edited by the finance department and consulted by the shipping department.

Session Beans

There are two types of session beans: stateless and stateful. A container typically creates a pool of session-bean instances to serve multiple clients. With stateless session beans, the container may elect a different bean instance from the pool at each method call. In other words, if a client calls *method1()* on a session bean, and then calls *method2()*, those requests may be served by a different bean instance! This means that a stateless session bean does not maintain any state on behalf of a client. Stateless session beans are very efficient: The container can use a small number of instances to serve a large number of clients, and therefore use a minimal amount of memory.

When a session bean is declared as stateful, a client program is sure to talk to the same bean instance between method calls. It maintains a conversational state with the client. Stateful session beans are not pooled. A new instance is created each time a client invokes create() on the home interface. With stateful beans, you can save data in the bean instance; the container guarantees this data is still available on the next method call.

Entity Beans

Entity beans persistency can be handled either by the developer or by the container. With container-managed persistence (CMP), you totally delegate the persistency to the container: Only the business logic of the enterprise bean is left to the programmer to write. In bean-managed persistence (BMP), the developer must provide the code that runs each time the container decides to save or restore the enterprise bean's state.

Enterprise Beans and "Normal" Beans

Enterprise JavaBeans and JavaBeans components (as described in Chapter 7, "Introduction to JavaBeans Components") do not have much in common beside their name. Whereas the JavaBeans specification focuses on defining how components behave in a visual builder tool, the Enterprise Java Beans specification focuses on defining a framework of standard services that server-side Java components can rely on. Enterprise beans do not have properties or events, nor do they have a BeanInfo class.

However, do not make the mistake of thinking that JavaBeans components are for the client and EJB components, for the server. You could as well use JavaBeans as a component model on the server. The difference is that for a bean, you would have to write the middleware code yourself, whereas for the enterprise bean you use the services offered by an Enterprise Java Server. If you want to make an analogy between those two technologies, you should think of the term "JavaBeans" as the equivalent to "software component."

This concludes our introduction to EJB components. For further information about Enterprise Java Beans, we suggest you refer to the EJB 1.1 specification.

Developing a Simple Session Bean

VisualAge for Java, Enterprise Edition, comes with an integrated support for Enterprise JavaBeans. It provides SmartGuides to create both session and entity beans and their supporting classes, as well as support for deploying, testing, and debugging enterprise beans inside VisualAge for Java. VisualAge for Java is tightly integrated with IBM's WebSphere Application Server, Advanced Edition (WAS AE), which is written mostly in Java. WAS AE is "EJB1.0+" (or "EJB1.1-") compliant. It misses a few things to be EJB-1.1 compliant, the main one being XML deployment descriptors, but it supports entity beans, which are mandatory only in EJB 1.1.

Although the two environments are highly integrated, enterprise beans developed and tested in VisualAge for Java can be deployed to other application servers (see the *Deploying to Other Application Servers* section).

Introduction to the EJB Page

All EJB work is done from the Workbench EJB page. All enterprise beans loaded in the workspace can be managed from the EJB page. The EJB page is added to the Workbench when you add the IBM EJB Development Environment to the workspace. You must do all EJB work (editing, versioning, and so on) from the EJB page; do not attempt to modify the generated classes from the Workbench, or you may "confuse" the EJB Development Environment! To install the EJB development environment:

1. Go to the Quick Start dialog: select **File->Quick Start** or press F2.
2. Select **Add Feature**, and click on **Ok**.
3. Select **IBM EJB Development Environment**, and click on **Ok**.

Adding this feature takes some time depending on your machine. It actually loads over 5000 classes to the workspace, most of it being the WAS AE runtime. Once you start using the EJB Development Environment, 128 megabytes of memory is a bare minimum.

The HelloWorld Enterprise Bean

Let's start simple with the infamous HelloWorld session bean. In this section, we concentrate on learning the environment; advanced EJB development techniques come a bit later! Creating enterprise beans with VisualAge for Java is very easy. It hides all the intricacy of enterprise beans development. The EJB SmartGuide creates the home interface, remote interface, and enterprise bean class, as well as all of their required methods. You can then enrich the enterprise bean with business logic, add methods to the remote interface, generate the deployment code and a test client, run and test the enterprise bean, all within the EJB page.

> **WARNING**
>
> If you are using VisualAge for Java, version 3.0.x, *do not remove* the EJB Development Environment feature once it is loaded! If you do, you will receive a "Can't unload IC" error message. The EJB Development Environment is now corrupted, and adding the feature does not fix the problem. The only way to fix the problem is to start from a fresh workspace. You do not lose any code, but you need to rebuild the workspace from the repository. This takes a bit of time. See the "Maintenance and Troubleshooting" appendix for detailed instructions on this procedure. This problem has been fixed in VisualAge for Java, version 3.5: just be patient as the IDE user interface gets refreshed.

Adding an EJB Group

Before creating an enterprise bean, you must create an EJB group. EJB groups are used to logically group enterprise beans. Session and entity beans can be added to a same EJB group. You can start the EJB group SmartGuide, shown in Figure 23.2, by choosing **EJB->Add->Add EJB Group** in the menu bar, from the corresponding icon in the tool bar, or from the Enterprise Beans pane pop-up menu.

> **WARNING**
>
> When you create an EJB group, you must specify a project name. A package is added to this project for each EJB group you create. Therefore, you must be the project owner to create an EJB group in a given project. In addition, this project must be an open edition. Similarly, multiple classes are created for each enterprise bean. You must make sure you are a group member of the package where the classes are generated, and that this package is an open edition.

An EJB group must be created in a project. You can specify an existing or a new project name, but you need to make sure this is a project you own. Then, specify an EJB group name, for example *EffectiveVAJPart1*, and press the **Finish** button. The EffectiveVAJPart1 group is now listed in the Enterprise Beans pane.

The Evil Reserved Package

If you have just read Chapter 22, your reaction is probably "Again?" and, yes, the EJB information page is also kept in a reserved package. There is actually one reserved package for each EJB group. The *EffectiveVAJPart1EJBReserved* package

Figure 23.2 Creating an EJB group.

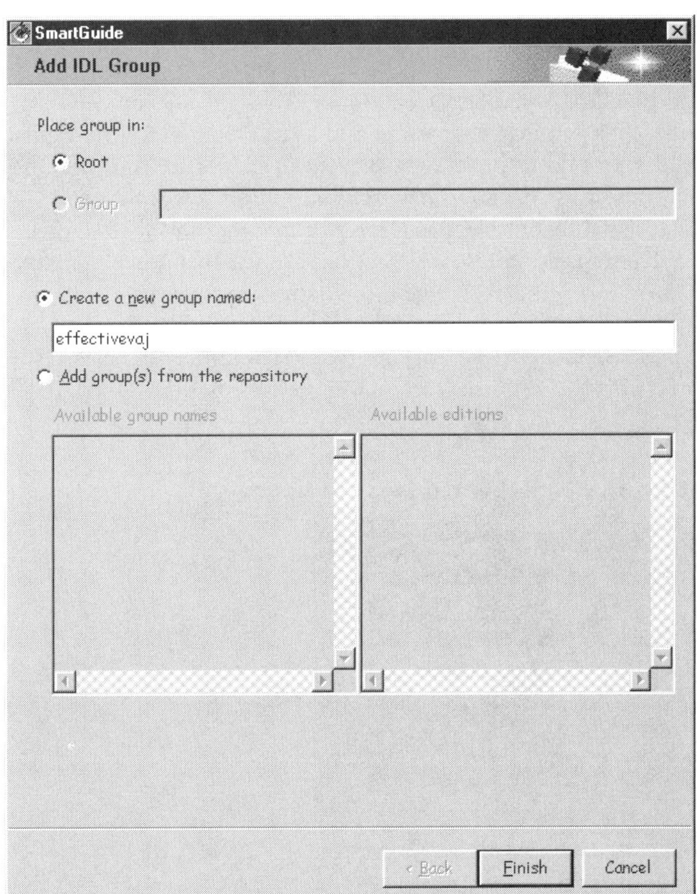

contains essential information about the enterprise beans created in the *EffectiveVAJPart1* EJB group. Of course, you must not change, delete, or alter this package and the classes it contains in any way.

Only repository files can be used to preserve the information kept in a reserved package. If you want to give enterprise beans to another developer, you must version the EJB group *from the EJB page*, and export all versioned packages to a repository file.

Once the repository file contents are imported in another repository, enterprise beans can be added to a project from the EJB page. Start the EJB Group SmartGuide and select the option to add from the repository. The EJB groups that have been imported should be listed there. If you add reserved packages to a project directly from the workbench using **Add Package**, the EJB page may not be properly updated.

Creating the Session Bean

The enterprise bean SmartGuide lets you create enterprise beans. This SmartGuide generates an enterprise bean class, a home interface, and a remote interface. Enterprise beans are listed in the Enterprise Beans pane. Enterprise bean classes are shown in the Types pane. If you call an enterprise bean *HelloWorld*, the enterprise bean's class name is *HelloWorldBean*, the home interface is *HelloWorldHome*, and the remote interface is *HelloWorld*. Those basic naming conventions are widely adopted, and we recommend following them, but you can change those names if you wish.

To create the HelloWorld enterprise bean, select the EffectiveVAJPart1 group and select **Add->Enterprise Bean** from the pop-up menu. The Enterprise Bean SmartGuide shown in Figure 23.3 requires the following information:

Figure 23.3 Creating the HelloWorld session bean.

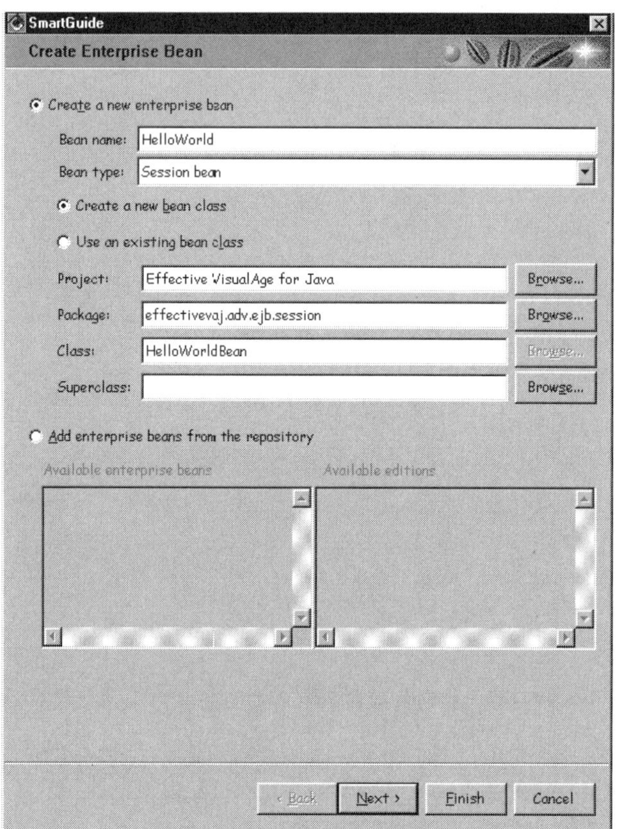

Bean Name. The name of the enterprise bean, here, HelloWorld.

Bean Type. Use this drop-down list to select whether you want to create a session bean, an entity BMP bean, or an entity CMP bean. The HelloWorld bean is a session bean.

Project Name. A valid VisualAge for Java project name, existing or new! By default, the project in which you created the EJB group is selected. The HelloWorld bean is created in the Effective VisualAge for Java project.

Package Name. A valid package name. Be careful when choosing the package name: Although it is very easy to create code with this SmartGuide, it is much more difficult to move generated code from one package to another. This mistake is actually easy to make, because VisualAge for Java displays in this field the name of the first package (in alphabetical order) loaded in the project. The package name should be effectivevaj.adv.ejb.session. In addition, make sure you are a group member of this package, or the code generation will fail.

Class. The enterprise bean's class name. It is recommended that you leave the suggested name.

Super Class. The enterprise bean class can inherit from any class listed in the workspace. This field should be left empty for this example.

You can create an enterprise bean class or use an existing one. If you choose to use an existing enterprise bean class, you actually do not create any code; rather, you create a reference between your enterprise bean and existing implementation code. You must use this option if you want to create an enterprise bean from an existing enterprise bean class. Please refer to the *Importing Enterprise Beans Definitions to the EJB Page* later in this chapter for more details on this topic. For now, you want to select the **Create a new bean class** option.

If you press **Next**, you can change the name of the home and remote interfaces. Although it is possible, we do not recommend changing the default names, because they follow commonly used naming conventions.

After you press **Finish**, VisualAge for Java generates all necessary classes and their default methods. The HelloWorld interface is empty, the HelloWorldHome interface contains a *create()* method, and the HelloWorldBean class contains the methods as defined in the javax.ejb.SessionBean interface, as well as an *ejbCreate()* method.

If you select the HelloWorldBean class, you will see a small icon to the right of the ejbCreate() method. This icon indicates that the method is present on the home interface. Each create() method on the home interface must correspond to an ejbCreate() method in the enterprise bean class. An ejbCreate() method is very similar to a constructor: You call it to create an instance of a enterprise bean. However, the difference is that you can't directly call ejbCreate() on the enterprise bean class; you have to go through the home interface. The EJB container will take care of creating an instance for you, or serve you an instance from a pool.

Each time you define a new "constructor" on the enterprise bean class, you must add it to the home interface. To do this, you must select the ejbCreate(...) method, and invoke **Add To->Home Interface** from the pop-up menu.

> **NOTE**
> Stateless session beans can have only one zero-argument ejbCreate() method. If you add an *ejbCreate(int i)* method to a stateless session bean, the bean is marked with errors (a red X).

Adding Business Logic

The HelloWorld enterprise bean is not very useful as is. We must add a method *sayHello()* to the enterprise bean class and promote it to the remote interface. Remember: Only methods listed in the remote interface can be invoked by a client application. The enterprise bean class is similar to any other Java class, so proceed as usual to add a method. For example:

1. Select the HelloWorldBean class, and choose **Add->Method** from the pop-up menu.
2. Enter

   ```
   public String sayHello(String someone)
   ```

   as the method name.
3. Press **Finish.**
4. Complete the sayHello() method body to look somewhat similar to this:

   ```
   public String sayHello(String someone) {
    return "Hello From the EJB world: " + someone;
   }
   ```

   The method is complete, but you must add it to the remote interface.

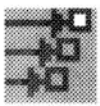

5. Select the sayHello() method and choose **Add To->Remote Interface** from the pop-up menu. You should see an icon to the right of the sayHello() method. This icon indicates that the method is part of the remote interface. A method must be promoted to the remote interface each time you change its signature.

By writing exactly two lines of code, you have created a simple, but complete, enterprise bean. VisualAge for Java allows you to really concentrate on the business logic, and completely takes care of the infrastructure.

Modifying the Deployment Descriptor

By selecting an enterprise bean, and choosing **Properties** from the pop-up menu, you can modify the contents of the bean deployment descriptor. The deployment descriptor contains information such as the bean home JNDI name, the transaction attribute, or the database isolation level. The Properties page shown in Figure 23.4 is divided in four tabs: Info, Bean, Environment, and Method. The Info page gives versioning and ownership information of the enterprise bean. The Bean page lets you edit enterprise bean deployment attributes: session bean type (stateless, stateful), transaction level, database isolation level, as well as the JNDI name.

In VisualAge for Java, version 3.5, the method tab has been removed. You can set method-level attributes from a method contextual menu.

The default JNDI name is the enterprise bean name. You can change it to create your own branch in the JNDI naming tree, for example, with **/VAJBook/Part1/HelloWorld**. You will use this name in client applications to find the enterprise-bean home object by its name. By default, the HelloWorld bean is defined as a stateless bean. This is a good choice, because there is no state to preserve from one method call to another. The HelloWorld bean does not need to maintain a conversation with a client, which would make it stateful.

The transaction level, isolation level, and security information can also be set at the method level on the Methods page. The Environment page is used to create environment variables that will be added to the bean execution context. Please refer to *Advanced Topics* later in this chapter for details on those pages.

Figure 23.4 Setting deployment attributes.

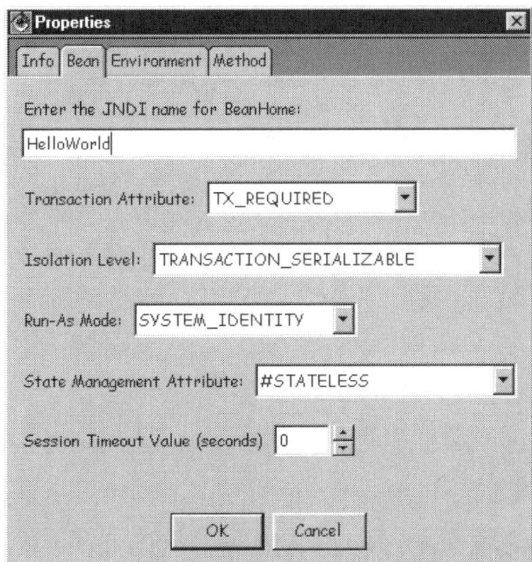

> **NOTE**
>
> The transaction-level and isolation-level attributes must be chosen with great care at deployment time. It is beyond the scope of this chapter to go into the business rules that drive those choices. Some excellent books have been written on the subject.

Testing the HelloWorld Bean

To test the HelloWorld bean, you must first generate the deployment code. The deployment process uses information stored in the deployment descriptor to generate appropriate stubs and skeletons used by the WAS runtime. Next, you install this code in the EJS and start the EJS processes. Finally, the test client is used to interact with the HelloWorld bean class.

Generating Deployment Code and Test Client

The deployment code is generated by selecting the enterprise bean and choosing **Generate->Deployed Code** from the pop-up menu. Once generation is finished, you see a few more classes in the Types pane. You can hide or show the deployment classes by using the *Show Generated Types* icon as shown in Figure 23.5.

Figure 23.5 Deployment code in the Types pane.

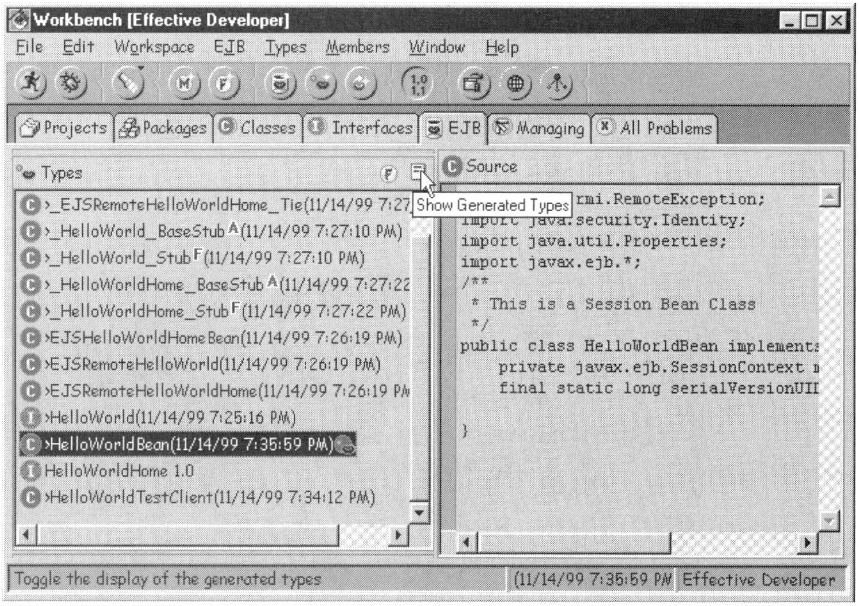

> **NOTE**
>
> You must regenerate the deployment code anytime you change the enterprise bean class, the home interface, or the remote interface. In general, the enterprise bean is marked with errors (a red X) if the deployment code is de-synchronized with the actual bean code. This happens if you add or remove a method from the home or remote interface for example. Deployment code cannot be generated if the enterprise bean is already deployed and running.

Setting Up the Execution Environment

The next step is to add the EJB group to the server configuration. To do this, select the *EffectiveVajPart1* EJB group and then **Add To->Server Configuration.** The server-configuration dialog shown in Figure 23.6 is started. In VisualAge for Java, version 3.0.2, three servers are listed in the Servers pane: a *Location Service Daemon*, a *Persistent Name Server*, and an EJB server named *server1* (the one you just created). Enterprise beans that are part of the *EffectiveVAJPart1* EJB group will run in the *server1* EJB Server. The Location Service Daemon serves no purpose and does not need to be started.

3.5 In VisualAge for Java, version 3.5, the Server Configuration window lets you manage EJB Server. The location service daemon has been removed (it was useless anyway), and the Persistent Name Server can be started from the WebSphere Test Environment control center, which you start from **Workspace->Tools->WebSphere Test Environment.**

The Persistent Naming Server (PNS) is an EJB-based application. It stores naming information in a database by using entity enterprise beans. Therefore, the PNS requires a valid database configuration to run. For version 3.0.2, the supported databases are IBM DB2 Version 5.2 with Fixpack 11, DB2 Version 6.1 with Fixpack 2 or 3, Oracle 8.0.5 with the latest *Thin* driver, and InstantDB. For VisualAge for Java, version 3.5, the supported databases are IBM DB2 6.1 with Fixpack 4, Oracle 8.16 with the latest *Thin* driver, as well as Sybase 12.0 and InstantDB. For each of these databases, you must make sure that the ZIP/Jar file containing the JDBC driver is listed on the workspace class path.

InstantDB is a lightweight database from Instant Computer Solutions Ltd. By default, the PNS is configured to use InstantDB. If you want to use DB2 or Oracle, you must edit the Persistent Naming Services properties and set up an appropriate URL, user ID, and password. We recommend using InstantDB for the PNS with version 3.02 to avoid all database-related issues. However, there seems to be some stability problems with the Persistent Name server when used with InstantDB in VisualAge for Java, version 3.5. In addition, we saw the IDE crash when the PNS was failing. We avoided those problems by using DB2 or Oracle as a persistent database rather than InstantDB.

WARNING

Starting the PNS and server processes when you are disconnected from the network can be a problem because those processes require an IP stack. On Windows NT 4, this means you must install the MS Loopback Adapter. This adapter is part of your Windows NT CD. You should make sure you can ping your machine by the same host name, should you be connected to the network or not (and not through the 127.0.0.1 address, or localhost). If you configure the MS Loopback adapter with address 10.0.0.1, then you must add to your hosts file a line similar to *10.0.0.1 eagle eagle.lagaude.ibm.com*, so that *ping eagle* works fine.

Once the various servers have been configured, you can start them individually. Start the PNS first and then server1. Servers must be started in that order, because they depend on each other. For the PNS server, wait until you see the "Server open for business" printed in the Console window to start the server1 server. When you start an EJB server, it adds an entry in the JNDI naming tree for each deployed enterprise bean: Therefore, the naming service (the PNS) must be up and running. The server1 server is ready to serve client requests when the *Server open for business* message is displayed in the Console.

If one of the servers fails to start, you can print a more detailed trace in the Console window by modifying the **Trace Level** property to *Medium* or *High* in the properties page. You should use the Medium/High settings for debugging purposes only, because using them has a considerable impact on the servers' performance.

Figure 23.6 The server configuration window.

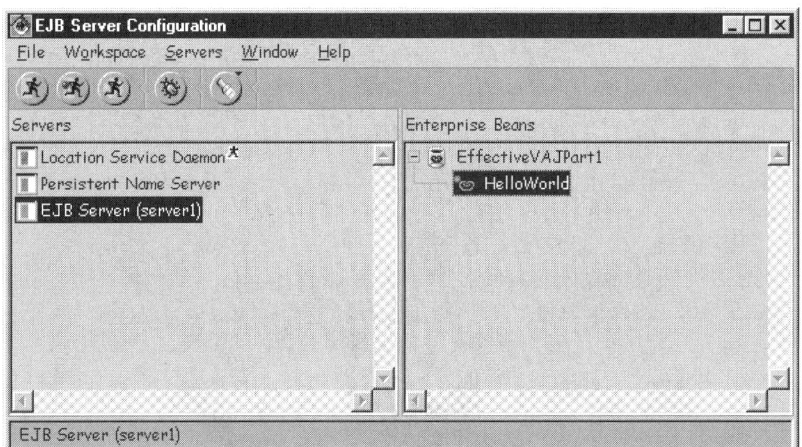

Running the Test Client

To test the HelloWorld bean behavior, you normally would write a client application. The test client lets you interact with an enterprise bean to test its behavior before creating a client application.

Using the Test Client in Version 3.0.2

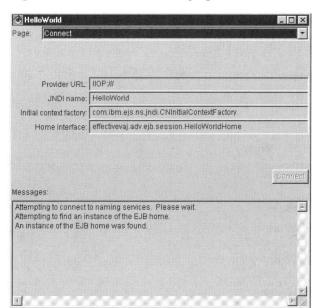

To generate a test client, select the enterprise bean, right-click, and choose **Generate->Test Client**. Then, select **Run->Test Client** from the same menu to execute the test client. The test client can also be started from the Run icon on the tool bar. The test client, shown in Figure 23.7, can be used as follows:

1. When you press the Connect button, the test client tries to connect to the naming services, looks up the enterprise bean name, and retrieves a home interface. If the home interface is found, the test client GUI changes to the Home Interface page, shown in Figure 23.8.
2. The Home Interface page presents the list of available methods on the home interface. Select a method in the Methods pane, and press **Send** to execute the method. Typically, you call the create method on the home interface to create an enterprise-bean instance, and obtain a proxy object. If the *create()* call is successful, the Remote Interface page is displayed, as shown in Figure 23.9.

Figure 23.7 The Connect page.

Figure 23.8 The Home Interface page.

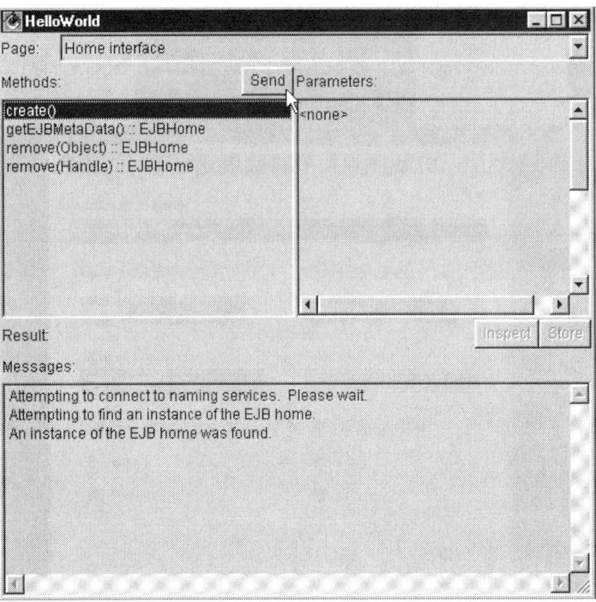

Figure 23.9 The Remote Interface page.

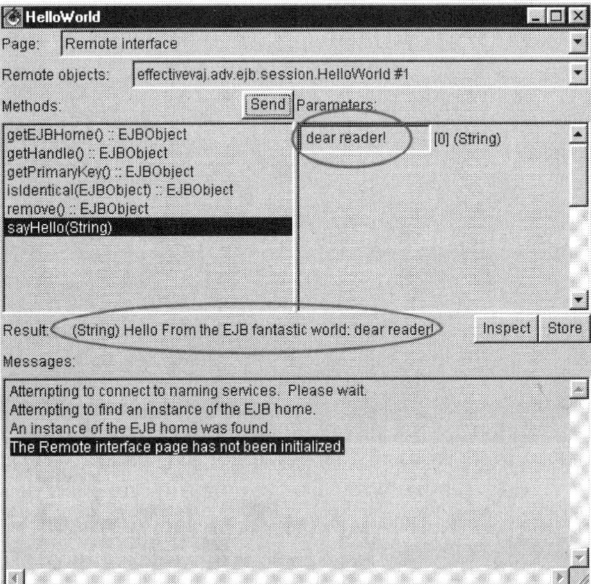

3. Call *sayHello()* on the remote interface. Finally, you can select the *sayHello()* method, provide a parameter in the right pane, and press *Send* to call the method. Results returned by the call are displayed in the middle of the window. You can open an inspector window on the results by pressing the Inspect button, or store the results for later usage by pressing the Store button.

If an exception occurs, the exception stack trace is displayed in the Messages pane.

Using the TestClient in Version 3.5

With VisualAge for Java, version 3.5, the EJB Test Client no longer needs to be generated. A same EJBTestClient application can be used to connect to any EJB running in VisualAge for Java. To test the HelloEJB in the new test client, you must:

1. Start the EJB Test Client by clicking on the yellow Running Man in the EJB Page.
2. Select HelloWorld in the JNDI name drop down, and press **Lookup**. The default Provider URL and Context Factory values are fine if you test inside VisualAge for Java.
3. A new dialog should then appear, with two pages: Home and Remote. First, you need to select the *create()* method on the home page, and call **Invoke** from the contextual menu. If the create call is successful, the tool automatically switches to the Remote page.
4. On the Remote page, select the *sayHello()* method, provide a parameter in the details pane, and call **Invoke** from the method contextual menu. The results will be displayed under the method (as String Result) and in the details pane.

Methods and properties that have been declared on the parent classes are not visible by default. If you want to invoke them, select the home or remote class name (such as HelloWorldHome), and invoke **Show Object Features**. You can customize in this dialog the amount of information you want displayed, such as fields, properties, or static members. If you select the **extends** option in Superclasses pane, inherited properties and methods will be displayed, allowing you to invoke them.

Modifying Code on the Fly

Enterprise bean code may be modified even if the bean is deployed and running in the enterprise server. You can't change the signature of a method or a class definition on the fly, but you should be able to modify the body of a method without any problems. For example, you can put a breakpoint in the sayHello() method in the enterprise bean class. When the method is called from the test client, the integrated debugger comes up, and you can step inside the code, modify, and save it. For more information on the integrated debugger, please refer to Chapter 5, "Testing and Debugging."

Creating a Client Application

The Enterprise JavaBeans programming model is a distributed object model. As in CORBA or RMI development, a client application that wants to use an enterprise bean must perform the following steps:

1. **Locate the EJB Home object.** This is done by connecting to the naming services provided by the EJS and querying a handle to an EJBHome object based on its JNDI name, for example, "HelloHome."
2. **Create or find an EJB Object.** You then use the handle to the home object to create or find a bean. If you are using session beans, you need to create a bean instance; otherwise, you may create or find an entity bean using a unique key. Once you have a handle to an EJBObject, you can invoke the services defined in the bean's remote interface.

Here are the detailed steps you must follow to create a client application for our HelloWorld enterprise bean:

1. **Obtain a naming service context.** A naming context is of type javax.naming.InitialContext. To create an initial context, you must construct a java.util.Properties object, assign values to this Properties object, and finally use this object as an argument to the initial context constructor. Properties you provide vary from one EJS vendor to another. The following instructions are valid only for the WebSphere Application Server; you must use those values when accessing an enterprise bean running in the WebSphere Test Environment.

   A WebSphere naming context is created from two parameters. The first parameter is the location of the name service or **PROVIDER_URL**, that is, iiop://*<hostname>*:*<port>* URL, where the naming services can be contacted. The *iiop:///* URL can be used to connect to a naming service running locally, regardless of the port number. The second parameter is the INITIAL_CONTEXT_FACTORY, that is, the class used by the EJS to create the initial context. For WAS Advanced Edition, this value must be set to "com.ibm.ejs.ns.jdni.CNInitialContextFactory".

   The code to obtain a naming service context should be isolated in a different method; it will be different for each application server. In addition, you should not hardcode the different properties but, rather, store them in an external properties file or resource bundle. The getInitialContext method() for the client application should be similar to this:

```
private static InitialContext getInitialContext()
                                throws NamingException
{
  InitialContext namingContext;
  Properties namingProps = new Properties();
  namingProps.put (javax.naming.Context.PROVIDER_URL,
                   iiop://eagle:902");
  namingProps.put
            (javax.naming.Context.INITIAL_CONTEXT_FACTORY,
             "com.ibm.ejs.ns.jndi.CNInitialContextFactory");
  namingContext = new InitialContext (namingProps);
  return namingContext;
}
```

Next, we will complete the main() method to locate the EJBHome object, and obtain a proxy to the enterprise bean EJBObject.

2. **Look up the home interface** of the enterprise bean using its home JNDI name (here, HelloWorld).

```
namingContext = getInitialContext();
java.lang.Object o = namingContext.lookup("HelloWorld");
```

3. **Obtain an EJB home object for the enterprise bean.** The static method javax.rmi.PortableRemoteObject.narrow() takes two parameters: the object to be narrowed and the class of the home object returned by the method call. The narrow call checks that the object returned by the lookup call is actually of the HelloWorldHome type. This makes sure you haven't looked up the wrong JNDI name. The result of the method call must be cast to the home interface class (here, HelloWorldHome).

```
ejbHome = (HelloWorldHome)
     javax.rmi.PortableRemoteObject.narrow(o,
                                  HelloWorldHome.class);
```

NOTE

You should avoid retrieving the home object each time you need it. The lookup process is rather slow, and this can be a performance hit. You can achieve this by implementing a singleton pattern for the ejbHome object. See the *Creating a EJB Home Factory* section later in this chapter for a full example.

4. **Create an enterprise bean instance** using the create() method on the enterprise bean home. This call returns a proxy to an EJBObject that implements the Hello interface (you do not have the cast the result):

   ```
   HelloWorld aHelloBean = ejbHome.create();
   ```

5. **Call the remote methods** of the enterprise-bean instance through the proxy object.

   ```
   System.out.println (aHelloBean.sayHello(userName));
   ```

> **NOTE**
>
> Before running the client application, make sure to check the class path! Select the HelloClient, choose **Run->Check Class Path** from the pop-up menu, and press **Compute Now** to update the project class-path.

As you have seen from the previous steps, accessing an enterprise bean from a client application is rather heavy: You have quite a few lines of code to write to obtain an enterprise bean proxy. This code is basically the same each time you want to access an enterprise bean, whatever the client type (servlet, application, or another enterprise bean). In addition, each method call on the enterprise bean proxy is a remote call. For example, you may encounter significant performance problems when retrieving the value of 15 attributes to display in a JavaServer Page component. VisualAge for Java solves those problems by introducing Access Beans.

Using Access Beans

An **Access Bean** adapts an enterprise bean to the JavaBeans programming model by hiding the home and remote interfaces from the users. You do not have to manipulate those interfaces directly. In addition, an access bean provides fast access to enterprise bean data, because it maintains a local cache of attributes. Access beans have been designed specifically to support servlet and JavaServer Page programming, but they can also be used to access an enterprise bean from another enterprise bean or any application. Note that access beans do not contain any proprietary code, so they can be used with any application server. There are three types of access beans:

Java bean wrapper. Using this access bean, an enterprise bean can be easily consumed by a visual builder tool. This is the only access bean available for session beans.

Copy helpers. A copy helper access bean contains a local copy of entity bean attributes. A servlet or JavaServer Page component does not need to make remote calls to obtain the attribute values. A copy helper access bean also has all of the characteristics of a Java bean wrapper.

Row Set. Row-set access beans contain multiple copy helpers. They are used to manipulate a collection of access beans.

Access beans are created using the Access Beans SmartGuide. In the next section, we create a Java bean wrapper access bean for the HelloWorld session bean. In Chapter 24, "Developing Servlets and JavaServer Pages," we use a Row Set access bean to display database information in a JavaServer Page component.

Creating a Java Bean Wrapper Access Bean

Start the Access Bean SmartGuide, shown in Figure 23.10, by selecting the HelloWorld enterprise bean, right-clicking, and choosing **Add->Access Bean.** Only Java bean wrapper access beans can be created for session beans.

To instantiate an enterprise bean, the access bean invokes one of the create() or finder methods defined in the home interface. If the no-argument access bean constructor is used, the access bean performs lazy instantiation of the enterprise bean. The enterprise bean is instantiated only when the first business method is called. You must define which create or finder method will be called during the enterprise bean initialization on the *Define Zero Argument Constructor* page, shown in Figure 23.11. If the constructor takes an argument, a corresponding *init_XX* property is defined on the access-bean interface, where XX is the name of the original argument in the home interface. This property can be easily initialized from any visual builder tool or JavaServer Page component.

Figure 23.10 The Access Bean SmartGuide.

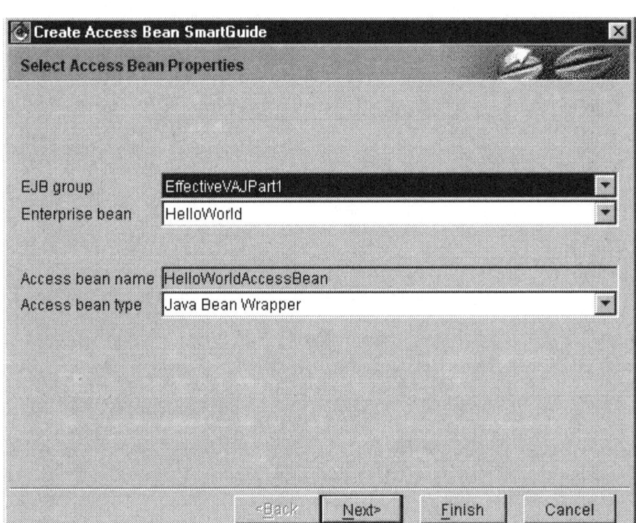

Figure 23.11 Specifying the zero-argument constructor.

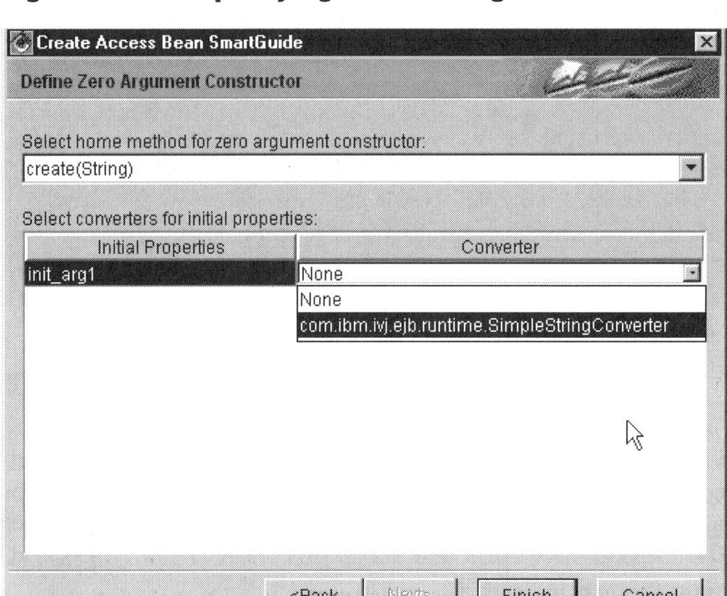

All init_XX properties are of type String. For each argument that is not of type String, you must provide a converter from String to the argument type, and vice versa. A default converter, *com.ibm.ivj.ejb.runtime.SimpleStringConverter*, can be used to convert primitive types such as *float* or *int* to String. For all other types, you must provide your own converters. All converters must implement the com.ibm.ivj.ejb.runtime.StringConverter interface. For each type you want to support, you must provide a StringToType (String arg1) method and a TypeToString (Type aType) method. As an example, the following converter can be used for java.math.BigDecimal types:

```
package effectivevaj.ejb.utils;

import java.math.BigDecimal;
import com.ibm.ivj.ejb.runtime.StringConverter;

public class BigDecimalStringConverter implements StringConverter
{
   public final static String BigDecimalToString(BigDecimal value) {
    return (new Double(value.doubleValue()).toString());
    // Used instead of value.toString() which creates huge strings...
```

```
    }
    public final static BigDecimal StringToBigDecimal(String value) {
     return ( new BigDecimal(value));
    }
}
```

The HelloWorld enterprise bean, which is a stateless bean, has only a default no-argument constructor. This constructor is therefore used as the default zero-argument constructor for the HelloWorld access bean.

A Look at the Access Bean Code

The Access Bean SmartGuide generates a HelloWorldAccessBean class that inherits from com.ibm.ivj.ejb.runtime.AbstractSessionAccessBean. This class has two constructors: the zero-argument constructor defined previously, and a constructor that lets you create an access bean from an existing EJB object. Here is the definition of the HelloWorldAccessBean class:

```
import javax.ejb.*;
import javax.rmi.*;
import com.ibm.ivj.ejb.runtime.*;

public class HelloWorldAccessBean extends AbstractSessionAccessBean {
 transient private HelloWorld __ejbRef= null;
 static final long serialVersionUID = 3206093459760846163L;
   public HelloWorldAccessBean () {
     super();
   }
   public HelloWorldAccessBean(javax.ejb.EJBObject o)
          throws java.rmi.RemoteException
   {
     super(o);
   }
 }
```

A default home JNDI name is generated in the access bean from the information found in the enterprise-bean properties. This JNDI name can be changed by using the *setInit_JNDIName()* method. The initial context construction is done using the PROVIDER_URL and INITIAL_CONTEXT_FACTORY properties. You can change those properties using the *setInit_NameServiceURLName()* and *setInit_NameServiceTypeName()* methods. The service type name must not be changed unless you are deploying the enterprise bean to an application server other than WAS 3.0.2, Advanced Edition.

For each business method on the remote interface, a corresponding method exists on the access bean. The sayHello() method looks like this:

```
public java.lang.String sayHello(java.lang.String arg0)
        throws java.rmi.RemoteException,
                javax.ejb.CreateException,
                javax.naming.NamingException
{
  instantiateEJB();
  return ejbRef().sayHello(arg0);
}
```

If the *ejbRef* instance variable, declared in the AbstractAccessBean class, is null, the *instantiateEJB()* method creates an initial context and does a lookup on the home interface; a proxy EJBObject is obtained on the enterprise bean in the *ejbRef()* method. Finally, the business method *sayHello()* is called on the proxy object.

> **NOTE**
>
> If several access beans share the same home (same JNDI name and initial context parameters), the access bean class will look up the home only once. This is a good point for performance improvement, since the lookup process is relatively slow.

Modifying the Client Program

The HelloClient is much simpler now. You just need to instantiate an access bean and call the sayHello() method. The enterprise bean is instantiated only when sayHello() is called. You can basically replace all the code we have detailed previously by those two lines of code in the main():

```
HelloWorldAccessBean aHelloWorld = new HelloWorldAccessBean();
System.out.println (aHelloWorld.sayHello (userName));
```

> **TIP**
>
> Before running the client application, make sure to check the class path, because your Hello Client is now using the access beans library. Select the HelloClient, choose **Run->Check ClassPath** from the pop-up menu, and use **Compute Now** to update the project class-path.

Working with Entity Beans

So far, you have seen how to create and test session beans. Entity beans introduce a new level of complexity by dealing with data persistence. In Chapter 21, "Database Programming," we told you that the Persistence Builder tools can be used to map business objects attributes to database schema columns. The Persistence Builder mapping tools are heavily used in the EJB Development Environment to define entity-bean persistence.

Entity-bean persistence can be managed by the developer (bean-managed, or BMP) or managed by the container (container-managed, or CMP). In this chapter, we concentrate on container-managed persistence. From now on, we will use the term *entity CMP* to refer to a container-managed persistent enterprise bean. In the next section, we will create a Song entity bean, and show you how to map its attributes to a database table.

Creating the Song Entity Bean

The Song entity bean has three attributes: the song *title*, its *composer,* and *interpret*. An additional ID attribute is used as the enterprise bean's primary key. You could perfectly create the Song entity bean in the EffectiveVAJPart1 EJB group, but EJB groups should be used to group enterprise beans by affinity, and the HelloWorld session bean has no affinity with the Song entity bean.

Therefore, you'd better create a new EJB group in the *Effective VisualAge for Java* project: Name it *EffectiveVAJMusic*.

Creating the Entity Bean

Session and entity beans are created using the same SmartGuide. Start the enterprise bean SmartGuide by selecting **Add->Enterprise Bean** on the EffectiveVAJMusic group; provide the following information:

1. The enterprise bean name is Song.
2. The enterprise bean type is "Entity bean with container-managed (CMP) field".
3. The project name is Effective VisualAge for Java.
4. The package name is effectivevaj.adv.ejb.entity.
5. The enterprise bean class name is SongBean.

The next SmartGuide page defines the entity-bean fields and interfaces. In addition to the home and remote interfaces, an entity bean requires a key class that is used to ensure the bean uniqueness. You can think of a key class as the primary key of a record in a database. The default key class name is SongKey.

The default finder method, *findByPrimaryKey,* retrieves an enterprise bean using its unique key. You can define finder methods on an entity bean to retrieve a collection of enterprise beans, for example, *findAllSongsForComposer(String aComposer)*. A custom finder method requires that you define a custom SQL query. This SQL query definition must be added to a finder helper interface. If you intend to create finder methods, which are very common in real-life applications in which you need to manipulate sets of enterprise beans, select the *Create finder helper interface* option. An example of finder method is given in the *Advanced Topics* section of this chapter.

Defining Container-Managed Fields

The next step is to define the container-managed fields. First, define the key field as shown in Figure 23.12:

1. Press the **Add** button to the right of the *Add CMP fields to the bean* label. This starts the CMP field SmartGuide.
2. Enter *ID* as the field name.
3. Enter *int* as the field type.
4. Select the *Key Field* option. In this example, the key is formed with one field, but you could add several fields to the key definition. Those fields

Figure 23.12 Creating the ID key field.

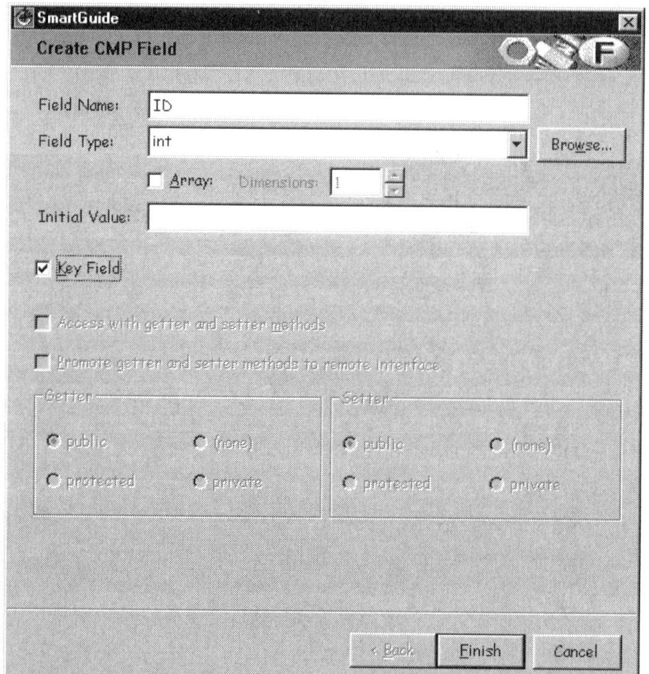

are used to create a SongKey instance; they are passed as arguments to the SongKey class constructor.

5. Press Finish to create the field definition. The ID field appears in the fields list. You can only add or remove a field's definition, not change them! If you make a mistake in the field definition, you must remove the current definition and re-create it. You could also fix the problem by modifying the bean class code afterwards, but it is much faster and easier to remove a field and use the *CMP field SmartGuide* to create a new definition.

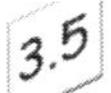

6. In VisualAge for Java, version 3.5, you can press the **Create CMP field and continue...** button to automatically restart the CMP SmartGuide.

Next, create the other container-managed fields. Start the CMP SmartGuide again, and provide the following values:

1. Enter *title* as the field name.
2. Enter *String* as the field type.
3. Fields are declared as private to the enterprise bean class definition. If you want to access a field value, you must at least generate a getter method and eventually a setter method. Accessors are public, because you are likely to add them to the enterprise bean's remotel interface. Use the (none) option to prevent the method generation. For the Song entity bean, use both accessors.
4. Once you have defined accessors, you can automatically add them to the remote interface by selecting the corresponding option.

5. If you promote the getter method to the remote interface, you can declare it as read-only in the deployment descriptor by selecting the **Make getter read-only** option. Please refer to the *Declaring Const Methods* section later in this chapter for details on read-only methods.
6. Press **Finish** to create the field definition.
7. Repeat steps 1 through 5 for the additional *interpret* field, of type String.

Once you have defined all fields, you can press **Finish** to start the code generation. You can toggle to the fields view in the Types pane by clicking on the Field icon. As depicted in Figure 23.13, the ID key field is represented by a little key icon.

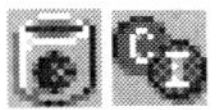

Container-managed fields are indicated with a small container icon. If you decide to delete a field or transform a container-managed field into a transient field, you should switch to the Field view and use the various options available on the pop-up menu displayed in Figure 23.13. You can revert to the Types view by selecting the Types icon.

If you want to add a container-managed field to an existing entity bean, you can select the enterprise bean and start the CMP Field SmartGuide from

Add->CMP Field in the field pop-up menu. This is different from selecting the enterprise bean class and choosing **Add->Field**. Using this option would only add a field to the bean implementation class.

> **NOTE**
>
> Container-managed fields are automatically added to the bean deployment descriptor.

Modifying ejbCreate Methods

Container-managed fields must be initialized in each *ejbCreate(..)* method. When you create the enterprise bean instance by calling *create()* on the home interface, it calls the ejbCreate () method on the enterprise bean, and a row is inserted in the corresponding SONG table. If container-managed fields are not properly initialized, the enterprise bean instantiation may fail, for example, if one of the corresponding columns in the SONG table has been declared as non-nullable. Moreover, the container is using a pool of instances. The create() call may return from the pool an instance that has already been used. Consequently, the bean fields may already contain some data. By

Figure 23.13 Modifying CMP fields from the EJB page.

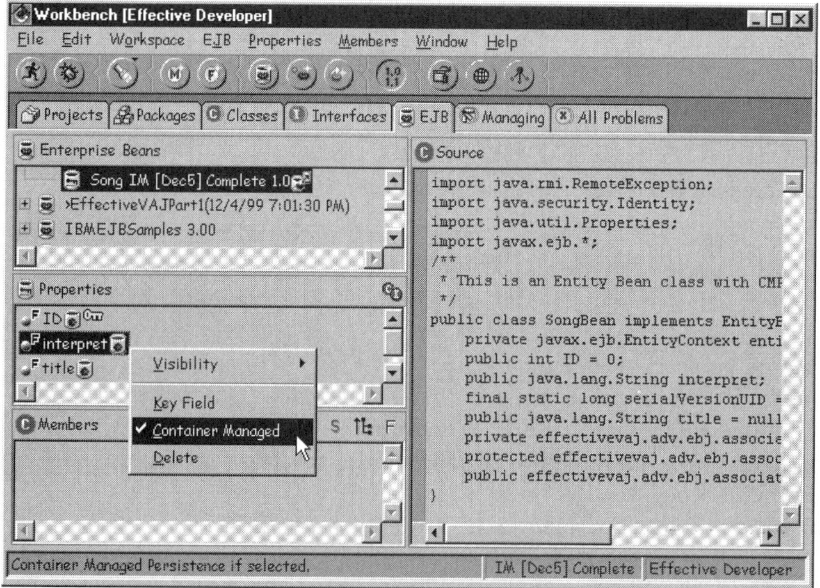

default, the key field is initialized in the ejbCreate() method. You should complete the *ejbCreate()* method to look like this:

```
public void ejbCreate(int argID)
            throws javax.ejb.CreateException,
                   java.rmi.RemoteException
{
  // All CMP fields should be initialized here.
  ID = argID;
  interpret = "";
  title = "";
}
```

> **NOTE**
>
> In EJB-1.1 compliant servers, the container is responsible for proper initialization of CMP fields. In EJB 1.0, it is the developer's responsibility.

Database Mapping

The next step is to map the fields in the entity bean to columns in a relational database table. In the Enterprise JavaBeans specification, this step is part of the deployment phase, and therefore, it should be done at deployment time using the application server deployment tool. If you plan to deploy your code to a server other than the WebSphere Application Server, you should skip the following sections and go directly to the *Deployment Considerations* section.

> **TIP**
>
> The mapping information generated by VisualAge for Java can be deployed only to the WebSphere Application Server, Advanced Edition, version 3.0.2.

There are three approaches you can take when mapping entity beans to relational data:

Bottom-up approach. In this approach, you want to create entity beans from an existing database schema. You use the Schema Browser (one of the Persistence Builder tools) to import a database schema from a database, and select *Add-EJB Group From Schema or Model* in the enterprise beans pane. This option can also be used to migrate business object models created with the Persistence Builder to an EJB-based implementation. This option is very powerful. Each table is mapped to an entity bean, whereas table relationships, such as foreign keys, are mapped to entity-bean associations. Associations are described in the *EJB Associations* section in this chapter. It is definitely too late for us to use that approach, because we just created the Song bean. Although we will not go directly over this approach, you will have enough knowledge to try it for yourself on an existing schema after reading the following sections.

If you modify an enterprise bean that has been created using this approach, those changes are not preserved if you generate the bean again from an existing database schema.

> **NOTE**
>
> This approach makes it very easy to create enterprise beans, maybe too easy! Remember that your data model is not your business model. Converting all your tables to enterprise beans is not a good design approach. First, create an object model; then, map it to a data model.

Top-down approach. The reverse approach is to go from the entity bean definition and create the appropriate database schema. This is definitely the easiest way to make an entity bean persistent. To create the database schema, you must select an EJB group and invoke *Create Schema from EJB Group*. We will first use that approach to create a table for the Song entity bean.

Meet-in-the-middle approach. The most flexible approach is to map an entity bean to an existing database schema.

In the next examples, you will use the top-down approach to create a relational database table from the Song entity bean, and test the bean persistence. Then, you will use the meet-in-the-middle approach to import an existing schema and map the enterprise bean fields to an existing database schema. In the following sections, we assume that you have created a database called MUSIC. This database contains a table called SONG1 that you use in the meet-in-the-middle approach. In the top-down approach, we create a SONG table in the same database.

> **NOTE**
>
> All entity beans in an EJB group must be mapped in the same way. An EJB group cannot contain entity beans that have been mapped using a combination of the top-down and bottom-up approaches.

Introducing VisualAge Mapping Tools

VisualAge for Java comes with a complete persistence framework called VisualAge Persistence. The development of an application is usually done in three steps:

1. Describe the object model.
2. Define a relational database schema.
3. Map the object model to the relational database schema.

The framework comes with three different tools:

- **Model Browser.** Lets you create the object model and specify relationships between the classes that compose your object model.
- **Schema Browser.** Lets you create a relational database schema or import one from an existing database.
- **Map Browser.** Lets you map an object model to a database schema. You can then generate domain and services classes on top of the framework.

You already have an object model: the enterprise beans. Nevertheless, you can reuse the Schema and Map browsers to define how the enterprise beans persist in a database. The Schema Browser is used to create a relational database schema or import a database schema from a database. The Map Browser is then used to define the mapping between entity beans fields and columns of a relational database table. The enterprise bean deployment tool uses this information to generate the bean deployment code. This deployment code must be deployed as-is in the WebSphere Application Server, Advanced Edition and in this application server only.

Typically, a table is created for each entity bean. Then, columns are created for each enterprise bean field, and the field (or fields) you declared as the EJB key field is used to define the table's primary key.

Using the Top-Down Approach

In the top-down approach, the schema and mapping information are automatically generated from the entity-bean definition. To generate the schema and map information, select the Song enterprise bean, and choose **Add->Schema and Map from EJB Group** from the pop-up menu. If you select the same action on the EJB group, this action is applied to all CMP beans in the group.

> **NOTE**
>
> All entity beans within an EJB group use the same database schema. In other words, you can't have in a same EJB group an entity bean that persists in database MUSIC and another entity bean that persists in database SONG.

Handling the Database Schema

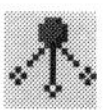

When the generation is finished, you can open the Schema Browser by selecting the EJB group and then **Open to->Database Schema**, or by using the corresponding tool-bar icon. By default, the database schema has the same name as the EJB group. If you select the SONG table and choose **Edit Table** from the pop-up menu, you are able to modify the default table and columns definition in the Table Editor, shown in Figure 23.14.

Typically, you would change the physical table and column names. Table and columns names are usually limited in length, and you may have to change the physical database name to comply with your database rules. For DB2 5.2, the limit for table and columns names is 18 bytes. In DB2 6.1, the table name limit has been increased to 128 bytes, and the column name limit has been increased to 30 bytes. You can validate all physical names by selecting **Validate Physical Names** on a database schema and specifying your database physical-name limits. Note that this action trims names that exceed the specified limit.

> **NOTE**
> Changes you make to a database schema are preserved if you regenerate the schema from the enterprise-bean definition.

Figure 23.14 Editing the Song table schema.

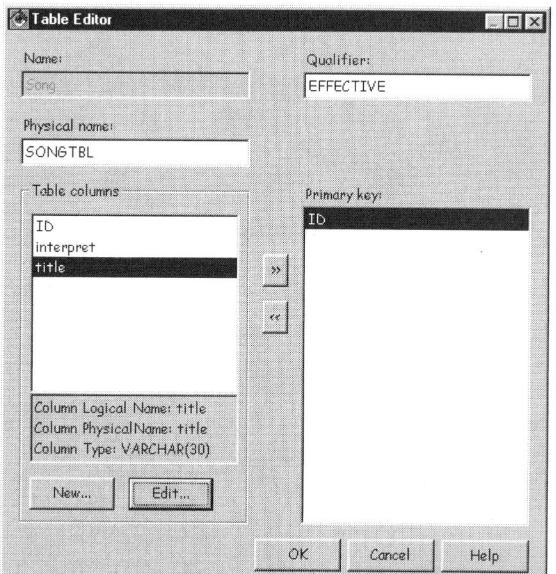

Creating the Schema in the Database

The top-down approach implies that the database schema does not exist. Before testing the Song entity bean, you must export the database schema to a database. You can either export an entire schema or export individual table definitions. To export a entire database schema:

1. Select the database schema name, and choose **Schemas->Import/Export Schema->Export Entire Schema to database** from the menu bar.
2. Enter the JDBC driver to use, the database URL (this database must exist; it will not be created), and a valid logon and password. We have created a MUSIC database to contain the SONG table.
3. Press **Ok** to start exporting the schema. You can trace the export process in the Console window.

> **WARNING**
>
> The export process first attempts to *drop* any existing tables. You will lose all data contained in existing tables.

Converting Java Types to SQL Types

A converter is used to translate an enterprise bean field type to the appropriate SQL type. You specify a converter when editing a table-column definition. The default converter, *VapConverter*, specifies that no conversion should be done. Data is stored as-is in the database, according to the default Java-to-SQL mappings defined in Table 23.1. The persistence framework comes with numerous converters, but you can also write your own. All converters must inherit from the *VapAbstractConverter* class. Source code for the default converters is available to use as a base for your own converters. The online documentation provides a full converter sample.

Handling the Schema Map

A schema map defines the mapping between fields in the entity bean and columns of the database schema. The Map Browser, shown in Figure 23.15, can be launched from the tool bar or by selecting **Open To->Schema Maps** on the enterprise bean pop-up menu. In the top-down approach, you typically have nothing to customize, but it is interesting to check what the tool did: a *song (primary)* table map has been created. You can edit this table by selecting it and then **Edit Property Maps**. A dialog similar to Figure 23.16 specifies how the enterprise-bean fields map to the table columns.

Table 23.1 Default Java/SQL Type Mappings

Java Type	SQL Type
String	VARCHAR
Short / short	SMALLINT
Integer / int	INTEGER
Float / float	FLOAT
Double / double	DOUBLE
Byte / byte	SMALLINT
Long / long	VARCHAR(22)
Character / char	CHAR(1)
Boolean / boolean	SMALLINT
java.math.BigDecimal	NUMERIC
java.sql.Date	DATE
java.sql.Time	TIME
java.sql.Timestamp	TIMESTAMP
Other (serialize)	BLOB

For each entity-bean field, you can define the corresponding column in the database schema and a mapping type. A *simple mapping* is a one-to-one mapping between an entity-bean field and a table column. A *complex mapping* lets you map a single field to multiple table columns. For example, you could define an *authors* field in the entity bean as a combination of the COMPOSER and INTERPRET columns in the database schema. Complex mapping is defined using a composer class: Please refer to the online documentation for instructions on creating composer classes.

Using the Meet-in-the-Middle Approach

In the meet-in-the-middle approach, you import a database schema from an existing database and create the schema map between the enterprise-bean fields and table columns available in the schema. Suppose that you have created a table SONG1 in database called MUSIC. This table can be easily created from that SQL definition:

```
CREATE TABLE SONG1 (
   TITLE VARCHAR(40),
   ID INTEGER NOT NULL,
```

Figure 23.15 Song schema-map definition.

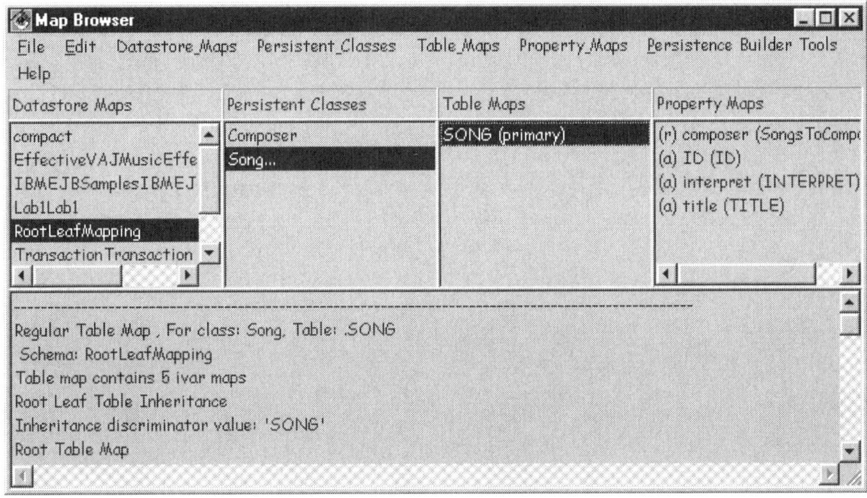

> **NOTE**
> Make sure you have only one schema map for each EJB group.

Figure 23.16 The property-map editor.

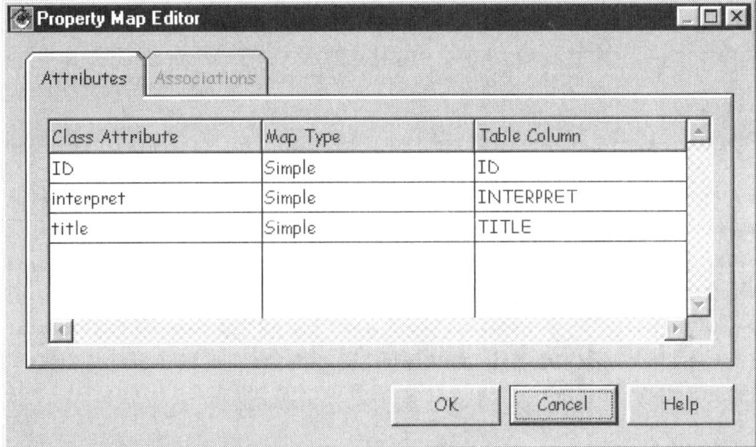

```
INTERPRET VARCHAR(40),
primakey key (ID))
```

You want to map the Song entity bean to the SONG1 table in the music database. This can be done in two steps: importing the database schema and then creating the schema map.

Importing the Database Schema

You can import a database schema by selecting **Schemas->Import/Export Schemas->Import Schema from database** from the Schema Browser's menu bar. Enter a name for the schema (such as *MUSIC*), and supply the following information on the database connection dialog:

JDBC Driver Name. Select the JDBC driver you want to use, in this example, the DB2 application driver.

Database URL. For example, *jdbc:db2:MUSIC.*

Userid/Password. The logon and password used to connect to the database.

You can use the **Test** button to check that the connection definition is valid. Once you press Ok, the tool retrieves the list of available qualifiers. To retrieve a list of tables:

1. Select one or more schema qualifiers.
2. Press the **Build Table List** button.
3. Select one or multiple tables from the table list, and press **Ok**. You do not want to select views, because views are read-only and can't be used in an EJB schema map.

Creating the Schema Map

The next step is to create a schema map. Open the Map Browser and select **Database Schemas->New EJB Group map** from the menu bar. You must supply the following data to create an EJB schema map:

Schema map name. For example, SongInMusicDB.

EJB Group name. Select the *EffectiveVAJMusic* EJB group name from the list.

Database Schema name. Select the MUSIC database schema you just created.

A schema map can contain multiple table maps. A table map usually associates an entity bean to a table in a database schema. To create and customize a table map for the Song enterprise bean:

1. Select the persistent class (the entity bean) that you want to map to a table.
2. Select **Table_Maps->New Table Map->Add Table Map with no inheritance** from the menu bar.
3. Select the SONG1 table from the proposed list, and press **Ok**.
4. Select the new table map, and choose **Table_Maps->Edit property maps** from the menu bar.
5. You can now use the property map editor described in the top-down approach section, shown in Figure 23.16, to create a simple mapping between the entity bean attributes and the SONG1 table columns.
6. Press **Ok** to validate the mapping.

> **NOTE**
>
> Errors messages are displayed in the browser information pane as you build the table map. Do not worry about them; they will disappear when the mapping is complete unless you do something wrong, such as not mapping a container-managed field to a table column. If you forget to map the title entity bean field, you should see a message similar to *Validation error in a VapPersistentClassMap('Song', 'Music'), the error is: 'Could not find map with name: 'title' '*. This message disappears as soon as you correctly map the title field to the appropriate table column.

Saving the Mapping Information

Database schemas and schema maps are kept by default *only* in the workspace. You must explicitly save them in a package to store them in the repository. A storage class is created for each database schema and schema map. Those classes contain metadata used by the persistence browsers to rebuild the mapping and schema information. Exporting this package to a *repository* format file (.dat file) is the only way to save the mapping information properly. If you export only your enterprise beans to a repository file, you will lose all mapping information! There are two other advantages in saving the schema map and database schema:

- You can revert to the state you were the last time you saved the schema or map by selecting **Revert to Selected Map** or **Revert to Selected Schema**.
- You can retrieve saved schema maps or database schemas after deliting them. If you delete a database schema or schema map *without* saving them in a storage class first, they are lost forever, because they were saved only in

the workplace. A saved storage class can be reloaded in the workspace by invoking **Load Available Schemas** or **Load Available Maps**.

If the database schema or schema maps have been changed since the last time you saved them, an "Entity is Dirty and should be saved" message is displayed in the browser information pane. This does not mean the entity bean has errors, just that you need to save the schema or map information. We recommend that you save the database schema and the schema map in a separate package, such as effectivevaj.adv.ebj.mappingInfo.

Testing an Entity Bean

Once the mapping is complete, you can generate the deployment code. The deployment code *must be* generated inside VisualAge for Java. The database schema and schema map information is used by the VisualAge for Java persistence tools to create special classes in the deployed code (EJSJDBCPersister*BeanName* classes).

> **TIP**
>
> If you have followed the steps described previously, you have two schema maps for the same EJB group. This was only done for illustration purposes. First, make sure to save all mapping information (schemas and maps); then delete one of the schema maps (the SongInMusicDB, for example). This must be done *before* generating the deployed code.

After the deployed code is generated, you can add the EffectiveVAJMusic group to the server configuration. A little bit more setup is required for entity beans than for session beans. Open the server2 properties (it should be called server2 if you haven't deleted the HelloGroup server1) and specify the database JDBC driver, database URL, logon, and password to connect to the database used by the entity bean. You must use the database to which you either exported a schema (in the top-down approach) or from which you imported a schema (in the meet-in-the-middle and the bottom-up approach). In this chapter, we used the MUSIC database.

> **NOTE**
>
> If you used the top-down approach and you haven't exported the database schema yet, you can create the schema by selecting the server2 server, right-clicking, and selecting **Create Database Tables**. The table(s) must exist *before* you start the server process, or it will fail to start.

Once the server2 is configured, you can start the PNS and the server2 server, and test the behavior of the bean as you did for the HelloWorld session bean.

Using Inheritance and Associations

Defining an enterprise bean as a subclass of another enterprise bean or defining associations between enterprise beans is not part of the Enterprise JavaBeans specification. However, it is quite hard to create real-life applications without those essential features of object-oriented programming. Direct inheritance and association support is specific to WAS 3.0.2, Advanced Edition. Code generated by the VisualAge for Java mapping tools can be deployed only in this application server.

> **NOTE**
>
> You should be aware that relationship support is a technical preview, which means this may very well change in future versions.

In this section, we implement the UML object model depicted in Figure 23.17. A Song entity bean is used to describe a generic piece of music. The classic and pop enterprise beans inherit from this generic entity bean. Finally, a song is associated to a composer. For this example, we assume there is only one composer for a specific song, but that a composer can compose multiple songs. This association is navigable both ways; you can retrieve all songs written by a composer, and the composer of a specific song.

Enterprise Beans Inheritance

You will now build on the example we started earlier by subclassing the Song enterprise bean and creating Classical and Pop enterprise beans. Bean inheritance is possible only within the same EJB group, so the Classical and Pop enterprise beans must be created in the EffectiveVAJMusic group. Select the EffectiveVAJMusic EJB group, and select **Add->Add Enterprise Bean With Inheritance** to start the bean creation SmartGuide. The SmartGuide requires the following information:

Bean Name. The enterprise bean name, here, Classical.

The enterprise bean from which you want to inherit. Select Song from the list.

Additional CMP fields. By inheriting from the Song entity bean, you inherit its CMP fields. You should only define additional CMP fields (*key* and *movement*, of type java.lang.String) here.

Figure 23.17 Songs object model.

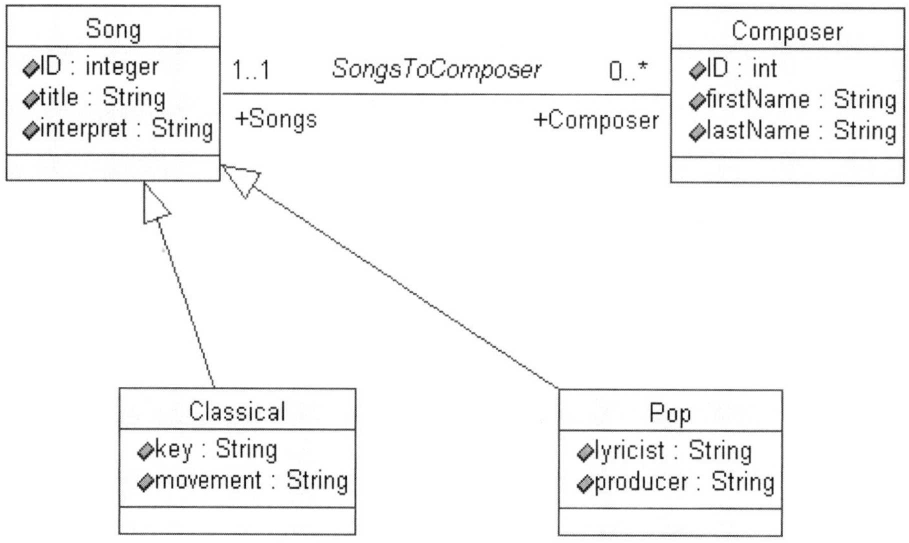

Import statements. Specify any package or class you need to import. For this sample, this list can be left blank.

You can repeat the same steps to create the Pop enterprise bean, which also inherits from Song. The additional CMP fields are *lyricist* and *producer* of type java.lang.String.

Looking at the Generated Code

When you create an enterprise bean by subclassing another enterprise bean, the new enterprise bean has the following characteristics:

- The remote interface of the child enterprise bean extends the remote interface of the parent enterprise bean:

```
public interface Classical extends Song {
   java.lang.String getKey()throws java.rmi.RemoteException;
  void setKey(java.lang.String)throws java.rmi.RemoteException;
   java.lang.String getMovement()throws java.rmi.RemoteException;
   void setMovement(java.lang.String)
                          throws java.rmi.RemoteException;
}
```

- Key classes are common to the parent and child classes: This means that the key class in the child enterprise bean is identical to the key class in the parent enterprise bean.
- The bean class of the child enterprise bean extends the bean class of the parent enterprise bean. You do not define parent methods in the child bean class.

```
public class ClassicalBean extends SongBean {
  private javax.ejb.EntityContext entityContext = null;
  public java.lang.String key;
  public java.lang.String movement;
  final static long serialVersionUID = 3206093459760846163L;
    <<key/movement getter/setter methods omitted>>
}
```

- Home-interface classes are specific to child and parent enterprise bean. When the child bean is created, the parent home-interface methods are copied to the child-bean home interface. If you add methods later to the parent home interface, you must manually correct the child home interfaces. The child bean home interface still extends javax.ejb.EJBHome.

```
public interface ClassicalHome extends javax.ejb.EJBHome {
    Classical create(int argID) throws javax.ejb.CreateException,

java.rmi.RemoteException;
    Classical findByPrimaryKey(SongKey key) throws
              java.rmi.RemoteException,
              javax.ejb.FinderException;
}
```

The schema for inheritance supports two different mappings: single table mapping and root-leaf table mapping.

Using Single Table Mapping

In the single table mapping approach, all enterprise beans within a single hierarchy are stored in one table. A special column, the discriminator column, is used to differentiate bean instances. The discriminator column is not an attribute of any enterprise bean: It is used only for mapping. Figure 23.18 depicts the table structure. Each CMP field corresponds to a table column. The additional *songType* column is used as a discriminator column. A discriminator column value must be set for each class in the inheritance hierarchy.

Single table mapping should be used only when there are more CMP fields in the base enterprise bean than in the child beans. Otherwise, the table will contain lots of unused space, represented in Figure 23.18 by grayed cells.

You can create a default single table mapping for the Song bean and its child enterprise beans by selecting the EffectiveVAJMusic group and selecting **Add->Schema and Map for EJB Group**. The tool will define a discriminator column with the same name as the EJB group name and use the enterprise-bean name as the discriminator-column value.

You can change the discriminator-column value by editing the persistent class' table map from the Map Browser. To edit a table map, you must first select a enterprise-bean name in the persistent classes pane; then select **Edit Table Map** on the *Song(primary)* table map shown in Figure 23.19.

> **TIP**
>
> You must double-click on the Song entry in the persistent classes pane to view its child enterprise beans.

Using Root-Leaf Mapping

In root-leaf mapping, you create one table for each enterprise bean in the inheritance hierarchy. The root table for the parent bean contains the shared columns and the discriminator column. A leaf table is created for each child enterprise bean. Each child bean's table has a foreign key pointing to the primary key of the root table, and columns for each field specific to the child bean, as depicted in Figure 23.20.

In this example, the ID field is used as the primary key for the Song enterprise bean. Therefore, you must create an ID column for each enterprise bean in the hierarchy, and define a foreign key relationship between this ID column in each child enterprise bean and the ID column defined in the parent enterprise bean (Song). When you call create() on the Classical enterprise-bean home interface, it inserts a row in the SONG and in the CLASSICAL tables, linked by the ID column.

Using root-leaf mapping is more efficient, because it does not leave unused space in tables, but it requires much more work on your part! You must first create one table for each enterprise bean and define the appropriate foreign keys in the each table. Then, you must map those tables to each enterprise bean's fields.

Creating the Tables

Tables can be created from the Schema Browser. First, create a new database schema called RootLeafMapping. Then, for each enterprise bean, follow these steps:

1. Select **Tables->New Table** from the menu bar.
2. In the Table Editor, provide a table name, such as SONG, and optionally a qualifier and physical name.

Figure 23.18 Single table mapping example.

ID	title	interpret	songType	key	movement	lyricist	producer
1	La Boheme	La Callas	CLASSICAL	e-minor	none		
2	My Way	F. Sinatra	POP			C.Francois	Whoever
3	Symphony 41	London Philharmonic Orchestra	CLASSICAL	c-major	Allegro		
4	Piano Concerto 5	Dresden State Orchestra	CLASSICAL	e-flat	Allegro		

3. For the SONG table, create a SONG_TYPE column of type VARCHAR(15): This column is used as the discriminator column and must only be created in the root table.
4. For each field in the enterprise bean, create the appropriate table column by pressing the **New** button. Use the tables provided in Figure 23.20 to properly define the table columns. Do not forget to create an ID column for each enterprise bean, and define it as the table primary key. You should use the default VapConverter for each column (the default Java/SQL types mapping described in Table 23.1 are used).
5. Press **Ok** to save the table definition.

Figure 23.19 Editing the discriminator-column value.

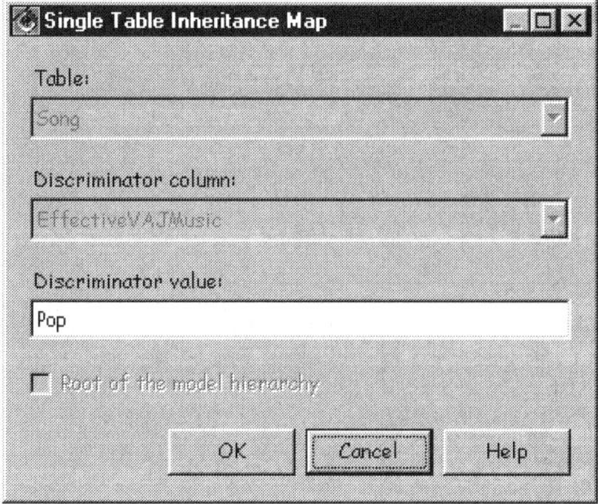

Figure 23.20 Root-leaf mapping example.

ID	title	interpret	songType
1	La Boheme	La Callas	CLASSICAL
2	My Way	F. Sinatra	POP
3	Symphony 41	London Philharmonic Orchestra	CLASSICAL
4	Piano Concerto 5	Dresden State Orchestra	CLASSICAL

Table: SONG

ID	lyricist	producer
2	C.Francois	Whoever

Table: POP

ID	key	movement
1	e-minor	none
3	c-major	Allegro
4	e-flat	Allegro

Table: CLASSICAL

Defining Foreign-Key Relationships

Once you have defined all tables, you must create two foreign-key relationships using the Foreign Key Relationship Editor, shown in Figure 23.21: one between Classical and Song and one between Pop and Song. With this relationship, you link the ID primary key of the root table (that is, Song) to the ID primary key of the leaf table (that is, Classical/Pop). To define a relationship between the SONG and CLASSICAL:

1. Call **Foreign_Keys->Create Foreign Key Relationship** from the menu bar.
2. Supply a relationship name, usually the composition of the two table names, such as SONG_CLASSICAL.
3. Select the **Constraint Exists in Database** option. This ensures that a referential constraint is added to the database. A referential constraint rules that the values of the foreign key are valid only if they appear as values of a parent key.
4. Choose SONG as the primary-key table.

Figure 23.21 Defining a foreign-key relationship.

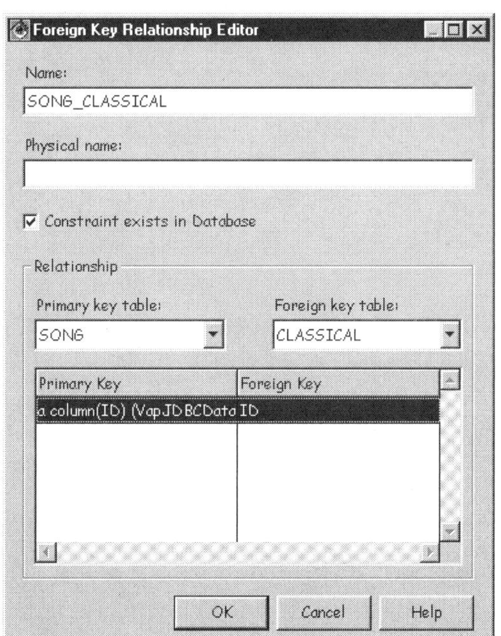

5. Choose CLASSICAL as the foreign-key table.
6. Select ID as the foreign key (the primary key is already selected and can't be changed).
7. Press **Ok** to create the foreign-key relationship.
8. Repeat those steps to create the SONG_POP relationship.

Mapping Tables to Enterprise Beans

The database schema definition is complete. You can now create a new schema map, and associate the tables you just created to the enterprise beans:

1. Create a new EJB group map in the schema map Browser.
2. Create the root class mapping. Select the Song persistent class, and choose **Table Map->New Table Map->Add Root-Leaf Inheritance Table Map.**
3. Specify *SONG_TYPE* as the discriminator column and *SONG* as the discriminator value.
4. Press **Ok** to create the Table Map.
5. Select the SONG table map, and choose **Table Map->Edit Property Map.**

6. In the property map editor, define a simple mapping between the enterprise bean fields and the corresponding SONG table columns.
7. Repeat the same process for the Classical and Pop persistent classes.

You're done! The mapping is complete. If you want to test the Song, Classical, and Pop enterprise beans, you must export the *RootLeafMapping* database schema to the music database. Then, you must stop the server2 server if it was running, generate the deployed code, restart the server2 server, and generate a test client for each enterprise bean.

EJB Associations

You have seen how to implement enterprise beans inheritance: The object model in Figure 23.17 specifies an association, *SongsToComposer*, between the song and composer. There is almost a one-to-one mapping between the information available in this UML schema, and the information you must supply to create an association between two enterprise beans. Let's take a bit of time to explain this UML schema: Once you understand its structure, creating an association is very easy.

> **NOTE**
>
> Associations can be created only between enterprise beans contained in the same EJB group.

An association is represented by a solid line between two classes. This solid line simply means some kind of "link" exists between them. Each association is named (SongsToComposer) and must be customized to provide the following information:

Navigability. Navigability indicates whether you can traverse the link. In other words, it indicates whether you can retrieve a composer from a song, or songs from a composer. An arrow on the association link shows the direction in which the link can be traversed. A plain link indicates an association that can be traversed both ways.

Role names. A role name is the name by which a class is known to the other object in the association. A composer sees *songs*, and a song sees a *composer*.

Multiplicity. For each role, multiplicity specifies how many values of an association an object may have. In this model, we have defined a 1..1 multiplicity for the composer role, assuming that a song can't exist without a composer but can have only one composer. The 0..* multiplicity of the *songs* role indicates that a composer may be a newbie and hasn't composed any songs yet, or it may have written multiple songs!

With all this in mind, you can create an association between the Song enterprise bean and a new Composer CMP entity bean. We assume at this point that you have enough knowledge about the EJB development environment to create a Composer entity bean that complies with the object model. The ID field should be used as the entity bean's primary key.

Once you have created the Composer enterprise bean, an association can be added to the Song enterprise bean. Select the Song enterprise bean and choose **EJB->Add->Association** from the menu bar. Using the Association Editor is very easy if you compare the UML model settings to the editor settings, as we did in Figure 23.22. Information in this editor reads as follows: The *Song* enterprise bean has a *composers* view on the *Composer* enterprise bean. The *Composer* enterprise bean has a *songs* view on the *Song* bean. The association is navigable both ways. A song must have an associated composer (required), and a composer may have composed 0 or more songs (many, not required). You can use Table 23.2 as a mapping between UML multiplicity and settings in the Association Editor.

A Look at the Generated Code

Many things happen behind the scenes when you create an association: First, the *composer* role is added to the Song enterprise bean and the *songs* role is added to the Composer enterprise bean. Roles are listed with CMP fields, as shown in Figure 23.23.

> **NOTE**
>
> A role is usually represented in a database as a foreign key and, therefore, is considered as an entity bean property. As such, it can be added to the bean primary key. You can select a role as key field by choosing **Add Role to Key** (as shown in Figure 23.23).

Table 23.2 Multiplicity Settings

Many?	Required?	Multiplicity
Yes	Yes	1..*
Yes	No	0..*
No	Yes	1..1
No	No	0..1

Figure 23.22 Mapping the UML model to an association.

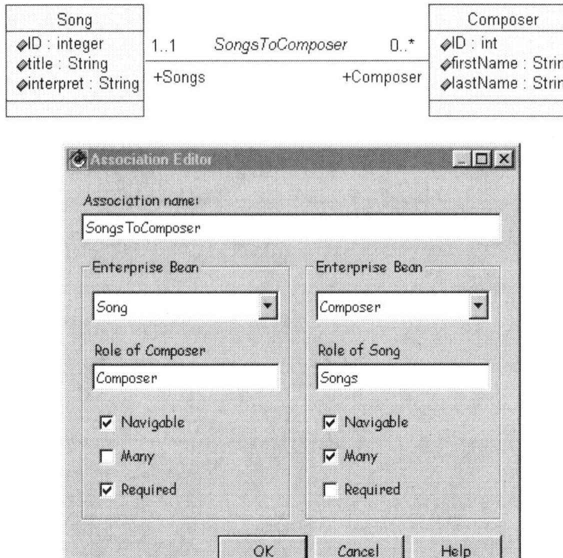

When you create an entity bean, the following methods are generated to support associations. They are updated each time you edit or delete an association, and must not be changed manually:

_initLinks(). This method initializes association links for the enterprise bean. Each enterprise bean involved in an association holds a reference to the other end of the association. For example, Song holds a *private transient SingleLink composerLink* object, which is initialized by the _initLinks method. The _initLinks method is called in ejbCreate(), ejbActivate(), and ejbLoad().

_removeLinks(). This method is used in the ejbRemove() method to maintain the list of associations.

_getLinks(). This method is used to retrieve the list of associations for the bean.

The composer role is inherited by the Classical and Pop child beans. You see inherited properties if you have set the visibility attribute to **All Inherited Properties** in the Types pane. The following user methods have been added to the Song enterprise bean class, and promoted to the remote interface:

- The *ComposerKey getComposerKey()* method returns the key for the composer associated to a song.

- The *Composer getComposer()* method returns a reference to the remote interface of the associated composer.
- Finally, the *setComposer(Composer)* method can be used to update the association from a song to a Composer.

  Similarly, the Composer enterprise bean class has been modified as follows:
- The *getSongs()* method returns an enumeration of songs written by the composer.
- The *addSongs(Song)* and *removeSongs(Song)* methods can be used to manage the list of songs associated to a composer.

> **NOTE**
>
> Many other methods such as secondaryAdd<RoleName> or get<RoleName>Link have been generated for each end of the association. However, you should not use those methods directly. They are used by VisualAge for Java for association support.

Figure 23.23 Displaying roles in the Types pane.

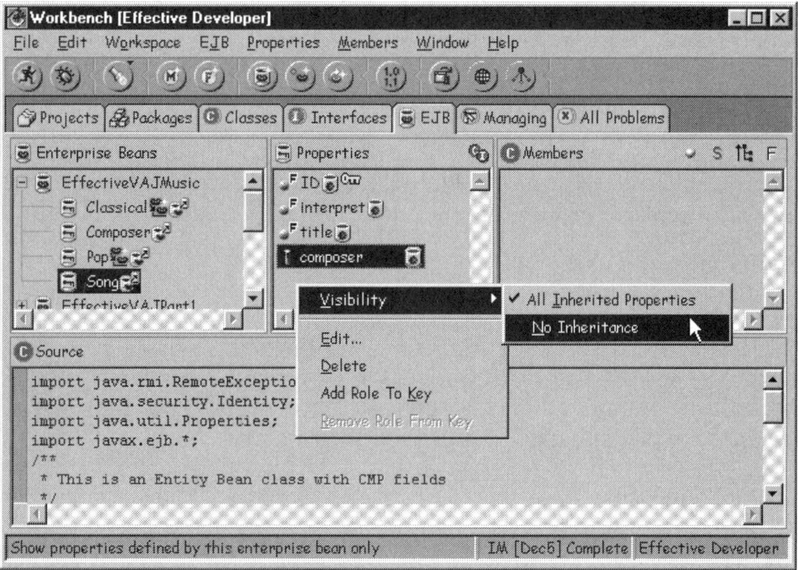

Modifying the ejbCreate and ejbPostCreate Methods

The object model shown in Figure 23.17 states that a song can't exist without a composer. This implies that a song cannot be created before its composer exists. To enforce this rule, you must initialize the reference to the composer using the privateSetComposerKey() method. Once the composer key is initialized, it can be used in the getComposer() method to retrieve the song's composer. If you don't make this change, you will get a NULL COLUMN database error when trying to create a Song enterprise bean instance.

You can achieve this by adding an *int composerID* parameter to the ejbCreate() method of the Song enterprise bean. Replace the current ejbCreate() method definition with this one:

```
public void ejbCreate(int argID, int composerID)
             throws javax.ejb.CreateException,
                    java.rmi.RemoteException
{
   // All CMP fields should be initialized here.
   ID = argID;
   privateSetComposerKey(new ComposerKey(ComposerID));
}
```

> **NOTE**
>
> You could also use a *Composer aComposer* as a parameter, and modify the last line of the ejbCreate() method like this: privateSetComposerKey ((ComposerKey) aComposer.getPrimaryKey());

Remember that the ejbPostCreate method must be modified accordingly. Therefore, you must replace the current ejbPostCreate() definition with this one:

```
public void ejbPostCreate (int argID, int composerID)
           throws java.rmi.RemoteException {}
```

Use the **Save replace** option when saving those methods. Because the ejbCreate() method signature has changed, you must add it to the home interface again. Although this is required, do not worry about generating the deployment code for now; we have more changes to make on the enterprise bean!

Completing the Table Mapping

An association is implemented in a database using a foreign-key relationship. In our sample, the Song table holds a foreign key to the associated composer. We

NOTE

You must also correct the create() method definition for all child enterprise beans. Remember that home interfaces do not inherit from each other, and that create() methods must match the ejbCreate() methods defined on the enterprise bean class. Therefore, create() methods on each child bean must match ejbCreate() methods of their parent bean.

must first add a COMPOSER_ID column to the SONG table, and associate this column to the ID column of the COMPOSER table in a foreign-key relationship. Next, we must create a COMPOSER table and map its columns to the corresponding CMP fields. Finally, we must map the *songs* and *composer* roles to the foreign-key relationship created earlier. This indicates how the association is represented in the database schema. To complete the database schema, you must:

1. Open the Schema Browser.
2. Add a COMPOSER_ID column of type INTEGER to the SONG table: Select the SONG table, and choose **Columns->New**.
3. Create a COMPOSER table composed of ID (INTEGER), FIRSTNAME(VARCHAR(30)), and LASTNAME (VARCHAR(30)) columns. You can add a table by selecting **Tables->New Table** in the menu bar. Then, use the New button to add the columns listed previously and define the ID column as the table primary key.
4. Create a SongsToComposer foreign-key relationship between the SONG and COMPOSER persistent classes. You can add a foreign-key relationship by invoking **Foreign Key->New Foreign Key Relationship**. Then, define COMPOSER as the primary-key table and SONG as the foreign-key table. Finally, map the COMPOSER table's ID column to the SONG table's COMPOSER_ID column.
5. Export the entire schema to the database. This will erase any records you may have inserted in the inheritance section.
6. Open the schema map Browser.
7. Select the Composer persistent class, and create a table map using **Table Map->New Table Map->Add Table Map with no Inheritance**.
8. Edit the COMPOSER table map by selecting **Edit Property Maps** from the pop-up menu.
9. Map the Composer entity bean fields to the appropriate table columns.
10. Switch to the Associations page, and map the *songs* association to the SongsToComposer foreign-key relationship.

11. Select the SONG table map, and edit its property maps.
12. Switch to the Associations page, and map the *composer* association to the SongsToComposer foreign-key relationship.
13. Save the database schema and schema map.

Congratulations, you now have implemented the complete object model! Select **Generate->Deployed Code** on the EJB group to regenerate the deployment code for all entity beans in the group. Then, regenerate all test clients, because you have changed the ejbCreate() methods. After you start the server2 process, you can create a composer, create several songs for this composer, and use the getSongs() method to retrieve them from the Composer instance.

Deployment Considerations

Several deployment options are available from VisualAge for Java version 3.0. You can export a base EJB JAR file that can be read by any enterprise-bean deployment tool, a WAS 3.0.2-ready JAR file, or a specific JAR file for the Component Broker tool that is part of WebSphere Application Server, Enterprise Edition.

Deploying to WebSphere Advanced Edition

If you intend to run your enterprise beans in the WebSphere Application Server, Advanced Edition, you must use the **Export->Deployed Jar File** option. This is the only way to preserve the code generated by the VisualAge for Java persistence tools. You can use only VisualAge for Java to generate the persistence code used in EJB inheritance and associations. The resulting JAR file will contain all base classes (remote interface, home interface, key class, and enterprise bean class) as well as all classes generated by the deployment tool and Persistence Builder tools. The deployment descriptor is also stored in the JAR as a serialized class (.ser).

Deploying to Other Application Servers

If you want to deploy your enterprise bean to a non-IBM application server, you must use the **Export->EJB JAR** option. The resulting JAR contains only the base classes and the deployment descriptor. Note that if you have any WebSphere-specific extensions (inheritance, associations), it is very unlikely that your application server will be able to use those classes properly. If you intend to port your enterprise beans to multiple application servers, you should not use any of the extensions provided by the VisualAge tools (inheritance, association, complex mapping).

> **NOTE**
> A deployed EJB JAR file must be deployed as-is in the WebSphere Application Server. You must not use the WebSphere Application Server's deployment tool (jetace) to deploy the code, or you will lose all database mapping information.

Deploying to Component Broker

Component Broker is part of WebSphere Enterprise Edition. It is a CORBA-compliant ORB, with support for enterprise beans. One of the main advantages of Component Broker over WebSphere Advanced Edition is its support for enterprise beans persistence in CICS and IMS. When you select **Export->EJB Jar for CB**, the Component Broker deployment tool is started (cbejb). This requires Component Broker to be installed on the machine. If you want to create the deployed code later, or if Component Broker is not installed on your development machine, use the **Export->EJB Jar** instead. Please refer to the Component Broker documentation for deployment instructions.

Troubleshooting

Manipulating enterprise beans in the EJB Development Environment is quite easy when you add bean definitions, methods, or fields. However, deleting or renaming beans requires some manual processing on your side. The following sections cover the most common problems you may encounter.

Deleting an Entity CMP Field

If you delete a CMP field *after* creating the database schema and schema map, you must manually remove the corresponding column from the table definition. You must also fix the schema map by deleting the property map that corresponds to the field you removed. To remove a column from a table definition and fix the schema map, follow those steps:

1. Open the database schema browser.
2. Select the name of the column you want to delete in the Columns pane.
3. Choose **Delete Column** from the pop-up menu.
4. Open the schema map.
5. Select the table map you want to fix.
6. In the property maps pane, select the property that corresponds to the field you deleted—it should be marked with errors—and choose **Delete Property Map** from the pop-up menu.

7. Regenerate the deployment code for the entity bean by selecting **Generate->Deployed Code** from the bean's pop-up menu.

> **NOTE**
>
> If you have used the top-down approach, just regenerate the schema map and database schema after deleting the entity CMP field by selecting the enterprise bean and choosing **Add->Schema and Map from EJB Group** from the pop-up menu.

Deleting Enterprise Beans

You should always manipulate beans from the EJB page. If you want to delete a bean definition from the EJB page, or remove generated code, do not delete the classes directly from the Workbench: Select Delete on the EJB group or enterprise bean instead. When you select **Delete** on an enterprise bean, you have the choice between:

Deleting the bean itself. This option removes only the enterprise bean definition from the EJB page. It actually deletes the bean definition from the reserved package. Use this option when you want to rename an enterprise bean or move it to another package. Since this information—the bean name or package name—is stored in the reserved package, the only way to move the bean is to delete the bean information and recreate. Check the next section for details.

Deleting the generated access beans. This option deletes access beans generated using the access bean SmartGuide.

Deleting the deployed code. This option deletes only the deployed code. You may have to delete the deployment code to fix some errors on the bean before being able to generate the deployment code again.

Deleting all. This option deletes all classes related to the enterprise bean.

> **NOTE**
>
> Remember that deleting just unloads information from your workspace, but that all of this information is kept in the repository. Even if you delete an enterprise bean, you can still retrieve it from the repository by selecting **Add enterprise beans from the repository** in the enterprise beans SmartGuide.

Renaming Enterprise Beans

You can't directly rename an enterprise bean. To rename an enterprise bean, you must rename its generated classes and create the bean again in the EJB page as follows:

1. Make sure the project in which you created the bean is an open edition. If you do not remember the project name, look at the Info page of enterprise bean properties (right-click; select Properties).
2. Make sure the EJB group is not versioned: You can check this by looking at the Info page of the enterprise bean properties (right-click; select Properties). If it is versioned, create an open edition by selecting **Manage->Create Open Edition** from the pop-up menu.
3. Delete the enterprise bean by selecting **Delete** and pressing the **Bean Only** button. This will erase only the bean definition from the EJB page, not the generated classes/interfaces.
4. Switch to the Packages page and locate the package in which you generated the enterprise bean class and interfaces.
5. Rename each of those types (for example, replace HelloWorld by HelloEJB in every type name). We recommend that you adhere to the commonly used naming conventions: *<beanName>Home* for the home interface, *<BeanName>* for the remote interface, and *<BeanName>Bean* for the enterprise bean class.
6. Switch back to the EJB page and select **Add->Enterprise Bean** on the EJB group into which you want to place the enterprise bean.
7. Select the **Use Existing bean class** option.
8. Specify the new enterprise bean name.
9. Select the project, package, and class names using the Browse button.
10. If you have respected the VisualAge for Java naming conventions, the next page should be filled with the correct home interface and remote interface names. Otherwise, use the Browse button to select the correct interface name.

After you press **Finish**, you should see the enterprise bean definition added to the EJB group.

Changing an EJB Package Name

If you have chosen the wrong package name at enterprise-bean creation time, or if you want to move the enterprise bean class and interfaces to another package, you have a bit of work to do! To change an EJB package name, you must follow roughly the same steps we used for renaming the enterprise bean. However, in step 5, you must rename the package or copy the enterprise bean classes to another package rather than rename the enterprise bean interfaces and classes themselves.

Importing Enterprise Bean Definitions to the EJB Page

You can add existing enterprise beans to the EJB page in two ways. If the enterprise beans have been packaged in an EJB JAR file that contains a *serialized* deployment descriptor, you can directly import this JAR in an EJB group. If you just have the enterprise bean class and the home and remote interfaces, you must import them in the workspace and create the bean definition in the EJB page. Once an enterprise bean has been added to the EJB page, and assuming you have the source code, you can work with it as if you had created it using the VisualAge for Java SmartGuides. To import an EJB-JAR file, you must:

1. Create an EJB group from **EJB->Add->EJB Group** in the menu bar, or use an existing EJB group.
2. Select the EJB Group and choose **Import Enterprise Beans** from the pop-up menu.
3. Press the Browse button, and pick the JAR file you want to import.
4. Select whether you want to import source or bytecodes (please refer to Chapter 6, "Integrating with the File System," for more details on import and export).
5. Press **Finish**.

You should now see the definition of the enterprise beans added in the EJB group. If you do not have the source code of an enterprise bean, you can't use it in an association, because this requires changes to the enterprise bean class.

If you have only the enterprise bean class and home and remote interfaces, you must first import them into a project in your workspace; then switch to the EJB page and:

1. Create an EJB group from **EJB->Add->EJB Group** in the menu bar, or use an existing EJB group.
2. Select **Add->Enterprise Bean** on the EJB group.
3. Select the **Use Existing bean class** option.
4. Specify the enterprise bean name.
5. Select the project, package and class names using the Browse button.

6. If you have respected the VisualAge for Java naming conventions, the next page should be filled with the correct home interface and remote interface names. Otherwise, use the Browse button to select the correct interface names.

After you press **Finish**, you should see the enterprise bean definition added to the EJB group.

Transporting EJB Definitions

If you want to move complete enterprise bean definitions from one VisualAge for Java repository to another, follow these steps:

1. Save database schemas and schemas as described in *Saving the Mapping Information*, and version the package that contains this information.
2. Version the EJB groups. By versioning an EJB group, you version all enterprise beans contained in that group, their associated classes, and the EJB group reserved package.
3. Version the project that contains the enterprise bean code and mapping information.
4. Export the packages you just versioned to a repository file (or the full project if you have grouped all EJB-related packages in a project). Make sure you export the EJB group reserved package, the package that contains the database mapping info, as well as the packages that contain the enterprise bean's associated classes and interfaces. If you need help about import or export, you can refer to Chapter 6.
5. Import the resulting repository (.dat) file into the other VisualAge for Java repository.
6. Switch to the EJB page.
7. Select **EJB->Add EJB Group** from the menu bar.
8. Select the **Add EJB groups from repository** option.
9. Select the EJB group in the list. The reserved package and the packages containing the enterprise bean classes are automatically loaded in the workspace.
10. Add the *MappingInfo* package to the workspace, and load the database schema and schema map from their respective browser (using the **Load Database Schema** and **Load Schema Map options**). They will be automatically associated to the EJB group.

Migrating from Version 3.02 to Version 3.5

We have encountered no difficulty when we migrated the code created for this chapter from VisualAge for Java, version 3.0.2 to version 3.5. Just follow these steps to migrate your code:

1. Make sure to save all metadata information (schemas, maps), version the EJB groups, version the packages containing the EJB classes and interfaces, and export everything in a repository file.
2. After importing this repository file in VisualAge for Java, version 3.5, you should see the EJBs on the EJB page, and the schemas/maps should have been automatically loaded and migrated to version 3.5.
3. If you have used associations, select them, invoke edit, and press OK to regenerate the code.
4. Delete all generated test clients, which are useless.
5. Finally, regenerate the deployment code, to migrate it to Java 2.

You should now be ready to test your enterprise beans in VisualAge for Java, version 3.5!

Advanced Topics

In this section, we cover some advanced topics: advanced settings of the bean deployment descriptor, and the creation of finder methods.

Declaring Const Methods

When dealing with entity beans, a container systematically synchronizes the attributes of the entity bean with the underlying database when the transaction is committed. Suppose you have specified the TX_REQUIRED transaction attribute on an entity bean. When you call a method on this entity bean from a servlet, the container starts a transaction at the beginning of the method, synchronizes the underlying database data with the bean attributes (SELECT call), executes the business method, synchronizes the attributes with the underlying database (UPDATE call), and commits the transaction. The UPDATE call will always occur, even if you have just called a getxxx() method.

In version 3.0.2, to prevent the UPDATE call, you can mark methods as read-only by following those steps:

1. Select the entity bean you want to customize (it must be a CMP entity).

2. Open the Properties page from the popup menu.
3. Switch to the Method page.
4. Press the **Add** button and select the method you want to mark as read-only, then press Ok.
5. In the Control Descriptor window that opens, select the **Const Method** option, and press Ok.
6. Repeat steps 4 and 5 for all read-only methods.

In VisualAge for Java, version 3.5, method-level deployment information is set from the EJB Deployment Attributes contextual menu. To declare a method as read-only, select the method and invoke **EJB Deployment Attributes->Read-only Method.**

When you export a deployed JAR, this setting will be added to the deployment descriptor. This setting is valid only for the IBM WebSphere Application Server, Advanced Edition.

Defining Environment Variables

You can use the Environment page of the properties window to add variables to the enterprise-bean execution environment. For example, follow those steps to add a USERNAME variable to the Song execution context:

1. Select the Song enterprise bean.
2. Open the Properties page from the pop-up menu.
3. Switch to the Environment page.
4. Enter a variable name—USERNAME—and a value—TheBoss—and press **Set.**

According to the EJB 1.0 specification, an environment variable can be retrieved from the bean EJBContext, using the following line of code:

```
public String getDefaultUser() {
 return mySessionCtx.getEnvironment().getProperty("USERNAME");
}
```

Creating Finder Methods

Finder methods are used on CMP entity beans to retrieve a set of enterprise beans, for example, to find all songs written by such composer, or find all composers whose first name starts with C. You can think of finder methods as an equivalent for a SELECT SQL query on a database. In this section, you will create a finder method for the Song entity bean that retrieves all existing songs.

The Enterprise JavaBeans specification does not detail how a finder method must be implemented. However, it specifies that finder methods must be listed on the home interface, like this:

```
public Enumeration findAllSongs()throws java.rmi.RemoteException,
                                        javax.ejb.FinderException;
```

The EJB container is smart, but not smart enough to create the implementation code based just on the method declaration. You must give it a little hint. For WebSphere, the choice has been to declare a string with the SQL query that must be executed when the finder method is called. This string must be added to an interface called *<BeanName>BeanFinderHelper*, for example, SongBeanFinderHelper. This interface is automatically created if you select the **Create Finder helper Interface** option when creating a CMP entity bean. Two types of string can be used:

<finderName>QueryString. This string would contain the complete SELECT statement, that is, SELECT * FROM SONGBEANTBL. The main problem is that this form forces you to know the database structure (the table name), but the main point about CMP entity beans is that you should not care about this. This form has been deprecated, and was left in version 3.0 only for compatibility with version 2.0. Do not use it in any new development.

<finderName>WhereClause. In this form, you specify only the "where" part of the query, for example, "ITEM_PRICE > 100". If you specify an empty WHERE clause (to retrieve all songs), you must use a statement that is always true, such as "1=1".

To complete the findAllSongs finder, you must add the following string to the SongBeanFinderHelper interface. Make sure to match exactly the name you have specified on the home interface (findAllSongs) to the name of the string.

```
static final string findAllSongsWhereClause="1=1";
```

If you need to pass parameters to the finder method, you must represent them by question marks (?) in the query string. For example, you can define a findAllSongsForComposer(int compID) finder method, with the following associated string:

```
static final string findSongsForComposeWhereClause="COMPOSER_ID=?";
```

Creating a EJB Home Factory

EJB homes are obtained through a JNDI lookup, an operation will is expensive and can drastically impact a performance application when used repeatedly. One of the development best practices for WebSphere Application server is to create an

EJB Home factory class. This class is based the singleton pattern. Here is an example of such a class, for you own reuse:

```
import java.rmi.RemoteException;
import javax.naming.InitialContext;
import javax.ejb.EJBHome;
import java.util.PropertyResourceBundle;
import java.util.Properties;
import java.util.Hashtable;

/**
 * <h3> Class: EJBHomeFactory</h3>
 * <h3> Description : </h3>
 * <p> This class is based on the singleton pattern. It creates
 * a static Hastable that contains the homes already referenced.
 * Home lookups are rather slow, and MUST be done only once.
 * </p>
 * @version  1.2
 * @author Isabelle Mauny (IBM)
**/

public class EJBHomeFactory {
  private static EJBHomeFactory singleton = null;
  private static Hashtable homeCache = null;
  private static PropertyResourceBundle regProperties = null;
  private static InitialContext _initContext = null;

  static {
   homeCache = new Hashtable(25);
   regProperties = UtilityClass.loadPropertyFile("ejbprop");
  }

/**
 * This private constructor ensures than clients
 * of this class use the getSingleton() method rather than
 * the constructor to access an instance.
 */
private EJBHomeFactory() {
  _initContext = getInitContext();
}
/**
 * Returns an Initial Context.
```

```
 * @return javax.naming.InitialContext
 */
public static InitialContext getInitContext() {
// Create an Initial Context.
InitialContext namingContext;
Properties namingProps = new Properties();
namingProps.put(javax.naming.Context.PROVIDER_URL,
                 regProperties.getString("ejb.provider.url"));
namingProps.put(javax.naming.Context.INITIAL_CONTEXT_FACTORY,
                 regProperties.getString("ejb.initial.factory"));
 try {
   return new InitialContext(namingProps);
 }
 catch (javax.naming.NamingException ne) {
   System.err.println ("[EJBHomeFactory:getInitContext]
                          Could not  retrieve context");
   return null;
 }
}
/**
 * Returns the unique instance of the class.
 */
public static EJBHomeFactory getSingleton() {
if (singleton == null) {
singleton = new EJBHomeFactory();
}
return singleton;
}
/**
 * Returns an EJB Home based on Its JNDI name and class name.
 * The EJB Home may have already been cached or not.
 * @return javax.ejb.EJBHome
 * @param jndiName java.lang.String
 */
public static EJBHome lookupHome(String jndiName,
                                   Class homeClassName)
{
  // Local Variables
  EJBHome home;
  // Check whether the home is already in the cache.
  home = (EJBHome) homeCache.get(jndiName);
  if (home != null)
  {
    // Home is already in Hashtable.
```

```
      return home;
    }
    // Time to Lookup the new home. The Initial Context has already
    // been retrieved at class initialization.
    if (_initContext == null)
    {
      return null;
    }
    try
    {
      // Lookup the home.
      Object homeObject = _initContext.lookup(jndiName);
      home = (EJBHome)
              javax.rmi.PortableRemoteObject.narrow(homeObject,
                                                    homeClassName);

      synchronized (homeCache)
      {
        homeCache.put(jndiName, home);
      }
    }
    catch (javax.naming.NamingException ne)
    {
      System.err.println("[EJBHomeFactory] - Lookup Failed" +
                         ne.getMessage());
      return null;
    }
    return home;
  } // end lookupHome
  /**
   * Returns a String that represents the value of this object.
   * @return a string representation of the receiver
   */
   public String toString() {
    return homeCache.toString();
   }
  } // end class
```

A client application would first access the singleton using the getSingleton() method, then lookup an EJB home, as shown in this sample code:

```
EJBHomeFactory homeFactory = EJBHomeFactory.getSingleton();
cashRegisterHome =(CashRegisterHome)homeFactory.lookupHome
                                    ("ejb/CashRegister",
                                     CashRegisterHome.class);
```

Summary

In this chapter, we covered the development of enterprise beans in VisualAge for Java. You can easily generate all of the required classes and interfaces for any bean type, customize the deployment descriptor, and generate the deployment code. Thanks to the integration with the WebSphere Application Server, you can test and debug your enterprise beans without leaving the IDE. In addition, we covered WebSphere-specific extensions, such as inheritance and associations. In the following chapter, we cover another great feature of VisualAge for Java: the servlet and JavaServer Pages development environment.

Developing Servlets and JavaServer Pages

24

Servlets and JavaServer Pages (JSP) components are essential technologies for developing e-business applications. Servlets extend the functionality of a Web server and replace server-side scripting solutions with a pure Java-based solution. Servlets can be combined with JSP components to provide a programming model in which the view and the model of the application are clearly separated. Servlets and JSP components are two foundation technologies for the J2EE architecture.

VisualAge for Java uses the WebSphere Application Server servlet engine to serve servlets and JSP components. Servlets and JSP components can be created in the Professional and Enterprise editions of VisualAge for Java, on the Windows NT and AIX platforms. However, enterprise beans can be developed only in the Enterprise Edition.

In this chapter, we explain how to install the WebSphere Test Environment, briefly review servlet and JSP concepts, and walk through the implementation and test of a sample application using servlets, JSP components, and enterprise beans.

> **NOTE**
>
> In this chapter, we assume you know a bit about the HTTP protocol, HTML forms, and XML syntax.

3.5 Throughout this chapter, we have identified VisualAge for Java, version 3.5 changes by using this icon.

Installing and Testing the Environment

Servlets and JSP components can be executed directly in the VisualAge for Java IDE: The WebSphere Application Server has been totally integrated with VisualAge for Java. Because its servlet engine is written in Java, it can be run inside the IDE. Servlets and JSP components are then loaded and executed as if you were using the actual application server. After the WebSphere Test Environment starts, the VisualAge for Java IDE becomes an HTTP server and servlet engine. It can serve HTTP requests, servlets, and JSP components.

In the following sections, we explain which features to load, how to start the WebSphere Test Environment, and verify that your installation works correctly.

Prerequisites

Before you develop servlets or JSP components, you must load the IBM WebSphere Test Environment feature. Note that this feature is a prerequisite for the EJB Development Environment. If you have already developed and tested enterprise beans, you can skip to *Using the WebSphere Test Environment.*

To install the IBM WebSphere Test Environment:

1. Go to the Quick Start dialog by selecting **File->Quick Start** or pressing F2.
2. Select the Features category, select Add Feature, and press **Ok.**
3. Select **IBM WebSphere Test Environment**, and press **Ok.**

Adding this feature will take some time, depending on your machine. Be patient! Once the feature is installed, five projects should added to your workspace:

- IBM IDE Utility class libraries
- IBM Servlet IDE Utility class libraries
- IBM WebSphere Test Environment
- IBM XML Parser for Java
- Servlet API Classes

Using the WebSphere Test Environment

To test servlets and JSP components, you must start a base HTTP server and the servlet engine. VisualAge integrates a base HTTP server, which provides an HTTP entry point, and the WebSphere servlet engine. The servlet engine can serve servlets loaded in the workspace or located outside the IDE. We cover this in more detail in *Advanced Configuration*, later in this chapter. The base HTTP server and the servlet engine are launched simultaneously when you start the WebSphere Test Environment.

The WebSphere Test Environment (WTE) can be started from **Workspace->Tools->Launch WebSphere Environment**. In VisualAge for Java, version 3.0.2, calling the WTE automatically starts the servlet engine. In VisualAge for Java, version 3.5, it starts the WTE control center, from which you can start the servlet engine.

Starting the WebSphere Test Environment (version 3.0.2)

When you start the WebSphere Test Environment, a dialog similar to that shown in Figure 24.1 should appear. If the dialog does not start and you don't see any execution

Figure 24.1 The WebSphere Test Environment dialog.

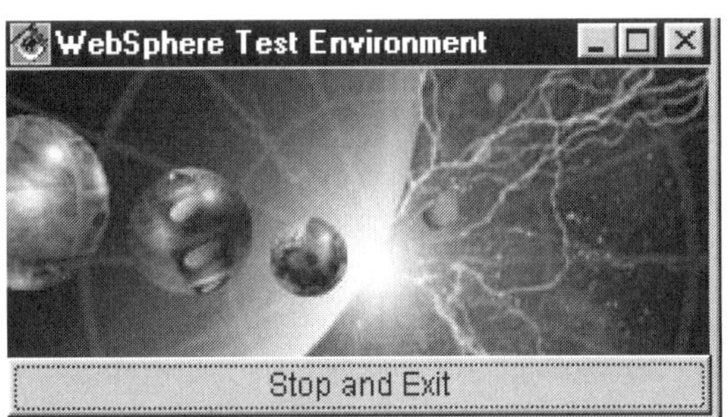

trace in the Console window, it usually means that the port that is required by the HTTP server is busy. You can verify this by running the netstat—a command on any operating system. By default, the HTTP server runs on port 8080.

SERunner is the actual class that gets executed when you start the WTE. The SERunner class will read some property files, then start the servlet engine class.

After the WebSphere Test Environment starts, the servlet engine configuration is displayed in the Console. This information is useful when you modify the initialization parameters and you need to check whether those changes are effective. We describe the servlet engine configuration in *Advanced Configuration*, later in this chapter.

When you start the WebSphere Test Environment, all projects loaded in the workspace are automatically added to the servlet engine class path, which means that any servlet loaded in your workspace can be served by the servlet engine.

Stopping the WebSphere Test Environment (version 3.0.2)

The WebSphere Test Environment can be stopped by using the **Stop and Exit** button. This normal shut-down process ensures that servlets are properly unloaded and resources freed. On some occasions, the WebSphere Test Environment won't stop. In these cases, manually terminate the SERunner main thread from the debugger or the Console window.

Starting/Stopping the WebSphere Test Environment (version 3.5)

In VisualAge for Java, version 3.5, all WebSphere related servers and configuration tasks have been grouped in the WebSphere Test Environment control center. You must start the servlet engine from that dialog. Note that SERunner is not used anymore; the ServletEngine class is started directly. The other change is that you must explicitly list the projects or JAR/ZIP files that contain the code of the servlets you want to execute. For example, you must edit the class path and select the *Effective VisualAge for Java* project before starting the servlet engine if you want the servlets loaded in this project to be found at execution time.

WebSphere users will be familiar with the icons used in the WTE. When you start the servlet engine, wait until the white and red icon on the servlet engine entry changes to white and blue. You can also look at the trace in the Console, and wait for the "***Servlet Engine is started***" message.

Stopping the servlet engine is as easy as starting it: simply press the **Stop Servlet Engine** button.

> **WARNING**
>
> Closing the WTE control center stops (or better, kills) all running servers, such as the servlet engine or the Persistent Name Server. We highly recommend you stop all servers *before* closing the WTE control center, or you may experience IDE crashes.

Testing the Installation

After the WebSphere Test Environment is started, you can test it by opening a static HTML page, a JSP file, and a servlet. By default, the WebSphere Test Environment waits for HTTP requests on port 8080. Therefore, you can use the localhost:8080/index.html URL to open the WebSphere Test Environment index page. The input shown in Figure 24.2 should be displayed in your browser.

Figure 24.2 WebSphere Test Environment test pages.

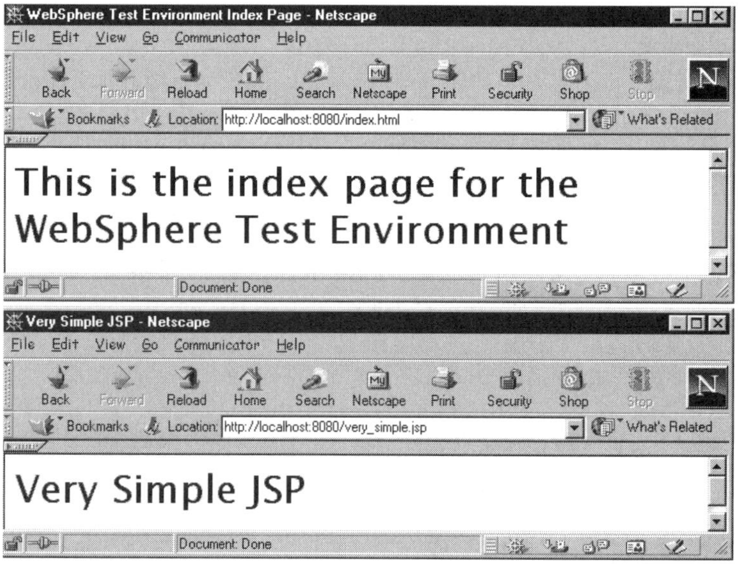

WebSphere Test Environment Index Page - Netscape

File Edit View Go Communicator Help

Back Forward Reload Home Search Netscape Print Security Shop Stop

Bookmarks Location: http://localhost:8080/index.html What's Related

This is the index page for the WebSphere Test Environment

Document: Done

Very Simple JSP - Netscape

File Edit View Go Communicator Help

Back Forward Reload Home Search Netscape Print Security Shop Stop

Bookmarks Location: http://localhost:8080/very_simple.jsp What's Related

Very Simple JSP

Document: Done

Similarly, you can open the localhost:8080/very_simple.jsp page. The result should be similar to the page shown in Figure 24.2. Finally, you can invoke a sample servlet, TestServlet, which can be found in the IBM WebSphere Test Environment project's default package. This servlet prints out the WebSphere Test Environment's system properties as well as the HTTP request headers. It is also useful to check the contents of the class path. You can start this testing servlet using the localhost:8080/servlet/TestServlet URL. If you have seen the correct output for each of these resources, congratulations, you are ready to work!

Configuring the WebSphere Test Environment

So you have tested some HTML files and servlets, and they worked. But how did they work? Where are the files located, and how did the servlet engine find them? Remember, each time you create a project, a corresponding folder is created under X:\ibmvjava\ide\project_resources. This rule also applies to the IBM WebSphere Test Environment project; a folder with the same name can be found under X:\ibmvjava\ide\project_resources. This folder contains critical configuration files (mostly in XML), as well as run-time classes and samples. The main configuration files are:

SERunner.properties. This file lets you specify the HTTP port number and the WebSphere Test Environment's document root. You must use to configure the document root and HTTP ports **only for VisualAge for Java, version 3.02.** For version 3.5, you must modify the two files listed below.

default_servlet.engine. Describes the servlet engine configuration. This file contains the definition of all Web applications and hostname bindings. We describe this file in more detail in *Advanced Configuration.*

hosts\default_host\default_app\servlets\default_app.webapp. Describes the contents of the *default_app* Web application. We describe this file in more detail in *Advanced Configuration.*

Modifying the HTTP Port and Document Root Properties (version 3.02)

The SERunner.properties file is read each time that you start the WebSphere Test Environment. This implies that you must restart the WebSphere Test Environment each time you modify this file. The default SERunner.properties file looks like this:

```
# SERunner.properties                                          #
# VisualAge for Java WebSphere Test Environment Properties     #
# docRoot -  location the server expects to find html, jsp and #
#             various other resources.                         #
# httpPort - The port the server listens on for HTTP requests. #
```

```
#                                                               #
# Note: form the path using either single forward slash "/" or  #
# double \\                                                     #
httpPort=8080
docRoot=F:\\IBMVJava\\ide\\project_resources\\IBM WebSphere Test
Environment\\hosts\\default_host\\default_app\\web
serverRoot=F:\\IBMVJava\\ide\\project_resources\\IBM WebSphere Test
Environment
```

By changing the httpPort and docRoot properties, you influence two things: the port the WebSphere Test Environment listens on for HTTP requests, and the location where the server looks for HTML files, JSP files, or other resources such as images. Suppose that you set docRoot to F:/EffectiveVAJ/web and change httpPort to 80. By opening localhost/index.html, you load the F:/EffectiveVAJ/web/index.html file. If you want to test a complete application, you must copy all files (HTML, images and other resources, JSP files) to the document root folder.

The default docRoot points to F:/IBMVJava/ide/project_resources/IBM WebSphere Test Environment/hosts/default_host/default_app/web. The index.html and very_simple.jsp files you have previously opened are located there, as well as all JSP examples.

You should not change the serverRoot property. It is used by VisualAge to locate some configuration files. Please check *Advanced Configuration* for more information on this.

> **TIP**
>
> If you set the httpPort value to whatever port your *real* Web server runs on, you can use the same URLs to make requests to the real Web server or the WebSphere Test Environment. Moving from the development environment to the deployment environment is then very easy to do.

Developing Servlets

Now that the environment is set up, let's create a simple servlet. This servlet takes your date of birth and returns the day you were born (Monday, Tuesday, and so on). It's nothing fancy, but enough to illustrate the principles. Moreover, if you don't know the day you were born, you have extra motivation for getting this to work! You will first develop a pure servlet and then modify it to use JSP components.

Quick Introduction to Servlets

A servlet is a Java program that works as an extension to a Web server. Similar to a Common Gateway Interface (CGI) program, it can receive client requests, handle them, and send a response. If a servlet is called through HTTP, the response is typically an HTML flow. Unlike CGI programs that are loaded in memory each time a client makes a request, a servlet is loaded in memory once by the application server and can serve multiple requests in parallel using threads. By using servlets as a server-side programming model, you have access to the full range of Java APIs. In addition, servlets usually perform better than CGI programs (because they are preloaded and initialized), are more scalable (unlike CGI, servlets are multithreaded), and portable. You can use the same servlet code on a Linux or OS/390 system.

You develop servlets using the Java Servlet Development Kit (JSDK). The WebSphere Test Environment supports JSDK 2.1. The JSDK provides a specialized type of servlets: HTTP servlets. HTTP servlets provide a framework to handle the HTTP protocol, such as GET and POST methods. We uniquely use HTTP servlets in the following example. All HTTP servlets must inherit from the javax.servlet.http.HttpServlet class. A servlet's life cycle is composed of three phases:

init() method. This method is called by the application server when the servlet is loaded in memory. This method is called only once. You rarely need to override this method, but if you do, make sure you do not open connections to critical resources in here. For example, do not open a database connection, or it will stay open for the lifetime of the servlet (until destroy() is called). Instead, you should manage a pool of database connections, and grab or release them in the service() method. You can provide initialization parameters for a servlet in the Web application's configuration files. Please refer to *Adding User Servlets to a Web Application*, later in this chapter.

service() method. This method is called for each client request. For HTTP requests, the service method has been specialized to dispatch the request to the appropriate doGet, doPost, doPut, or doDelete methods, depending on the HTTP request method (DO, POST, PUT, DELETE). If you write HTTP servlets, you should not override the service() method, but rather override the appropriate doXXX method.

destroy() method. This method is called when the application server unloads the servlet from memory. You should free any resources used by the servlet in this method.

Servlets are managed by the application server's run-time library. They are loaded in memory upon the first client request, or at server startup. Each client request is then served on a different thread. Your servlets must be coded to be thread-safe, because multiple clients access the same code in parallel. It is the developer's responsibility to synchronize the access to shared resources. However, for performance reasons, you must avoid synchronizing the service or doXXX methods yourself. Instead, synchronize the access to shared resources in a synchronize{} block of code.

Servlets are multi-threaded by default. You can create a single threaded servlet by implementing the javax.servlet.SingleThreadModel interface. An application server usually creates a pool of single-threaded servlets to handle multiple requests.

That's it for the introduction. Let's put all this in practice by implementing CalcdayServlet.

Creating the Calcday Servlet

We will now take you step by step through the creation of the CalcdayServlet, a servlet that takes date-of-birth information from an HTML form, calculates the day of the week, and returns the data it has calculated.

> **NOTE**
>
> The Servlet Builder, which comes with VisualAge for Java, version 3.0.2, has been removed in version 3.5. Therefore, we highly recommend that you do not use it, other than for prototyping purposes.

The *calcday.html* file, which calls the servlet, looks like this:

```
<!DOCTYPE HTML PUBLIC "-//W3C//DTD HTML 4.0//EN">
<HTML><HEAD>
  <META name="GENERATOR" content="IBM WebSphere Page Designer">
  <TITLE> Welcome to the servlets' world!</TITLE>
</HEAD>
<BODY bgcolor="#ffffca">
  <H1 align="left">Hello There!<BR>
  Tell me when you were born<BR>
  I'll tell you which day it was!</H1>

  <FORM NAME="GREETING"
    ACTION="/servlet/effectivevaj.adv.servlets.CalcdayServlet"
    METHOD="POST">
    <TABLE>
      <TR>
        <TD>Enter your name here:</TD>
        <TD><INPUT TYPE="text" SIZE=20 MAXLENGTH=50 NAME="NAME"></TD>
      </TR>
      <TR>
        <TD>When were you born?</TD>
```

```
          <TD><TABLE>
            <TR>
              <TD>Day</TD>
              <TD><INPUT size="2" type="text"
                           maxlength="2" name="DAY" value="1"></TD>
            </TR>
            <TR>
              <TD>Month</TD>
              <TD>
                <SELECT NAME="MONTH" SIZE=1>
                  <OPTION SELECTED>January
                  <OPTION>February
                  <OPTION>March
                  <OPTION>April
                  <OPTION>May
                  <OPTION>June
                  <OPTION>July
                  <OPTION>August
                  <OPTION>September
                  <OPTION>October
                  <OPTION>November
                  <OPTION>December
                </SELECT>
              </TD>
            </TR>
            <TR>
              <TD>Year</TD>
              <TD><INPUT TYPE="text" SIZE=4 MAXLENGTH=4
NAME="YEAR"></TD>
            </TR>
          </TABLE></TD>
        </TR>
        <TR>
        <TD></TD> <!—Blank cell —>
        <TD><INPUT type="submit" name="Submit"
                    value="Click to Submit"></TD>
      </TR>
    </TABLE>
</FORM>
</BODY>
</HTML>
```

The HTML form contained in this page is used to gather four pieces of information: a NAME, the DAY, MONTH, and YEAR (highlighted in bold in the previous HTML source). When the Submit button is pressed, the /servlet/effective-vaj.adv.servlets.CalcdayServlet servlet is called using the POST method. Therefore, CalcdayServlet must overwrite the doPost method and gather the NAME, DAY, MONTH, and YEAR parameters from the HTTP request.

> **NOTE**
>
> You must precede the full servlet name—package name plus class name—with /servlet to start it, as specified in the default servlet-engine configuration. In the *Advanced Configuration* section later in this chapter, we explain how this default path can be customized, and how you can name servlets to start them using a specific web path (for example, /vajbook/CalcdayServlet).

A Reusable Basic Servlet

All HTTP servlets perform similar tasks: gather information from an HTML form, execute some business logic, and return an HTML flow. Therefore, you could create a basic servlet that factorizes some of this behavior and specialize it to create other servlets. The BasicHttpServlet class is available in the effective-vaj.adv.servlets package. Its class definition looks like this:

```
import java.io.IOException;
import javax.servlet.ServletException;
import java.io.PrintWriter;
import java.util.Enumeration;
import javax.servlet.http.*;
import java.util.Properties;

public abstract class BasicHTTPServlet extends HttpServlet {
}
```

This servlet does several things: First, it gathers information coming from an HTML form and stores the gathered name/value pairs in a Properties object. This method is called getFormParameters and looks like this:

```
protected Properties getFormParameters (HttpServletRequest req)
{
  Properties formData = new Properties();
  Enumeration fieldNames = req.getParameterNames();
  while (fieldNames.hasMoreElements())
  {
    String paramName = (String) fieldNames.nextElement();
```

```
    String paramValue = (String) req.getParameterValues(paramName)[0];
    formData.put(paramName, paramValue);
  }
  return formData;
}
```

The getParametersNames() method is used on an HTTPServletRequest object to retrieve the list of parameters present in the form. In this example, they are NAME, DAY, MONTH, and YEAR. Then, for each parameter, we get its value using the getParametersValue() method. This method returns an array of strings. In fact, nothing in HTML prevents you from giving a same name to multiple fields or lists. In such a case, getParametersValue returns the list of values for that specific name. In this example, all names are different, and we therefore take only the first element of the array ([0]). If you are sure that a name is unique, you can use getParameter(String parameterName) instead.

Next, the basic servlet contains doGet and doPost methods that simply call an execute method. This assumes that HTTP requests of type GET and POST are handled equally, which might not be the case. A GET method means that the servlet has been directly invoked through an URL, and you may want to prevent this. If necessary, you can tailor this basic servlet to suit your needs.

The execute method is an abstract method that needs to be implemented by all subclasses. Finally, the sendResponse and sendErrorResponse abstract methods are used to send an HTML flow to the response output stream. The rest of the class definition follows:

```
public void doGet(HttpServletRequest req, HttpServletResponse res)
             throws ServletException, IOException {
     execute(req, res);
}

public void doPost(HttpServletRequest req, HttpServletResponse res)
             throws ServletException, IOException {
     execute(req, res);
}

protected abstract void execute( HttpServletRequest req,
                                    HttpServletResponse res)
                          throws ServletException, IOException;
protected abstract void sendErrorResponse(HttpServletRequest req,
                                            HttpServletResponse res)
                          throws ServletException, IOException;
protected abstract void sendResponse(HttpServletRequest req,
                                       HttpServletResponse res)
                          throws ServletException, IOException;
```

Finally, the getOutputStream() method returns an HTML stream from the HTTP response. This output stream can then be used to send the HTML response:

```
protected PrintWriter getOutputStream(HttpServletResponse res)
                          throws IOException {
// Assumption: this servlet only returns HTML
PrintWriter out = null;
res.setContentType("text/html");
out = res.getWriter();
return out;
}
```

Creating the Day Bean

The Day bean we use is very simple. It has two properties (username and dayOfWeek) of type java.lang.String and one method, calculateDay(). It will be used by the servlet to calculate the day a person was born. If you have carefully read Chapter 7, "Introduction to JavaBeans Components," creating this bean should be an easy task. Here is the complete code for the Day bean:

```
import java.util.GregorianCalendar;
import java.text.SimpleDateFormat;

public class Day implements java.io.Serializable {
private String fieldDayOfWeek = new String();
private String fieldUsername = new String();
static private Properties MonthIndexes = null;
public Day() {
  super();
}

public String getDayOfWeek() {
  return fieldDayOfWeek;
}

public String getUsername() {
  return fieldUsername;
}

public void setDayOfWeek(String day) {
  fieldDayOfWeek = day;
}

public void setUsername(String username) {
  fieldUsername = username;
```

```
}

public void calculateDay(String day, String month, String year)
            throws NumberFormatException
 {
   GregorianCalendar cal = null;
   SimpleDateFormat sdf = new SimpleDateFormat("MMMM");
   int monthNumber = sdf.parse(month).getMonth();
   cal = new GregorianCalendar(Integer.parseInt(year),
                              monthNumber,
                              Integer.parseInt(day));
   // EEEE means we want the day in week, in full form.
   setDayOfWeek(new SimpleDateFormat("EEEE").format(cal.getTime()));
 }

 public String toString() {
   // For debugging purposes
   return "{User="+getUsername()+"DayOfWeek="+getDayOfWeek()+ "}";
 }
} // End Day class definition.
```

Creating CalcdayServlet

To create CalcdayServlet, you simply need to create a subclass of the BasicHttpServlet class. Follow these steps to create the servlet:

1. Select **Selected->Add->Class** from the menu bar.
2. Enter *Effective VisualAge for Java* as the project name.
3. Enter *effectivevaj.adv.servlets* as the package name.
4. Enter *CalcdayServlet* as the class name.
5. Enter *effectivevaj.adv.servlets.BasicHTTPServlet* as the superclass name (you can use code completion in this field to automatically insert the package name).
6. Make sure the **Compose the class visually** option is *not* selected.
7. Press **Finish.**

> **NOTE**
>
> For the sake of simplicity, we have not included the otherwise mandatory code to check the validity of the user input (such as a wrong day or year). Of course, this must be done in a real-life application!

The execute() method is called for each client request. It calls he getFormParameters() method and uses a reusable component, the Day bean, to calculate the day of the week. If the calculateDay() method does not throw an exception, sendResponse is called; otherwise, sendErrorResponse is called. The execute() method's source code follows:

```
protected void execute(HttpServletRequest req,
                        HttpServletResponse res)
                throws ServletException, IOException
{
// Local Variables
Properties DOBInfo = null;
Day aDay = new Day();
String day, month, year = null;

// Get the input form contents
DOBInfo = getFormParameters(req);

// Initialize day, month, year from the FORM data.
day = DOBInfo.getProperty("DAY");
month = DOBInfo.getProperty("MONTH");
year = DOBInfo.getProperty("YEAR");
// Initialize the username parameter
// This will be used when we do JSP.
aDay.setUsername(DOBInfo.getProperty("NAME"));
// Now, calculate the dayOfWeek
try {
   aDay.calculateDay(day, month, year);
   sendResponse(req, res);
  }
  catch (NumberFormatException nfe) {
    // A requested parameter is wrong (badly formatted)
    sendErrorResponse (req, res);
  }

}
```

sendErrorResponse and sendResponse first request an output stream from the response and then send an HTML flow in the stream, like this:

```
protected void sendResponse(HttpServletRequest req,
                             HttpServletResponse res)
```

```
                throws ServletException, IOException
{
  PrintWriter out = getOutputStream(res);
  out.println("<html>");
  out.println("<head><title>The day you were born</title></head>");
  out.println("<body bgcolor=\"#ffffca\">");
  out.println("<P> Thanks " + aDay.getUsername() + "! </P>");
  out.println("<P> I think you were born on a <FONT
color=\"#ff3399\">"
                + aDay.getDayOfWeek() + "</FONT></P>");
  out.println("<P> Would you like to
       <A HREF=\"javascript:history.back(1)\"> try again</A> ? </P>");
  out.println("</body></html>");
  out.flush();
  out.close();//Make sure to close the flow before returning.
}

protected void sendErrorResponse(HttpServletRequest req,
                                    HttpServletResponse res)
                throws ServletException, IOException
{
  PrintWriter out = getOutputStream(res);
  out.println("<html>");
  out.println("<head><title>Servlet Execution Failed</title></head>");
  out.println("<body bgcolor=\"#ffffca\">");
  out.print("<h2>Sorry, we could not calculate the day
                  you were born</h2>");
  out.print("<h2>Make sure you have provided valid data!</h2>");
  out.println("<p>Please press the <strong>Back</strong> button,
                and resubmit.</p>");
  out.println("</body></html>");
  out.flush();
  out.close(); //Make sure to close the flow before returning.
}
```

Testing Servlets

Congratulations, your servlet is complete; you can now test it. The problem is that you can't just select a servlet and select Run, because this class does not have a main() entry point. You must make a request to the WebSphere Test Environment for that servlet. This can be done in two ways: using the servlet launcher or by opening the *calcday.html* page.

Using the Servlet Wizard (version 3.5 only)

3.5 VisualAge for Java, version 3.5 introduces a new tool called the servlet wizard. This wizard generates a servlet class skeleton for you. To create the CalcdayServlet skeleton from this wizard:

1. Select the effectivaj.adv.servlets package, and invoke **Add->Servlet** from the pop-up menu.
2. Enter a servlet name, such as CalcdayServlet35.
3. Press the **Next>** button.
4. Select the methods you want your servlet to implement, such as doGet(), doPost(), or init().
5. Press **Finish.**

In the generated code, you will find a performTask() method, called by both doGet and doPost. This method is equivalent to the execute method we created in the BasicHTTPServlet.

Unit Testing with Servlet Launcher

The Servlet Launcher lets you specify in a property sheet the list of parameters that would be typically entered in an HTML form. The WebSphere Test Environment is then started and your servlet started with the right parameters. You have nothing to do! One point though: The servlet is started from a URL, which means your servlet must support GET HTTP requests. This is not a problem for CalcdayServlet, because we override the doGet() method in BasicHTTPServlet.

First, you must set the properties for the servlet launcher by selecting CalcdayServlet, right-clicking, and selecting **Tools->Servlet Launcher->Properties.** A dialog similar to Figure 24.3 is displayed (be patient; it takes some time to start this dialog). For each parameter you expect to receive from the HTML form, you can create a name/value pair and press the **Add** button to add this data to the query string. The complete URL string is visible at the bottom of the window. For the CalcdayServlet, you must supply the NAME, DAY, MONTH, and YEAR. The final URL should look like this (all on one line):

```
http://127.0.0.1:8080/servlet/effectivevaj.adv.servlets.CalcdayServlet?
NAME=Isabelle&DAY=25&MONTH=12&YEAR=1999
```

> **NOTE**
>
> Parameter names are case-sensitive; make sure to spell them correctly.

Figure 24.3 The Servlet Launcher properties window.

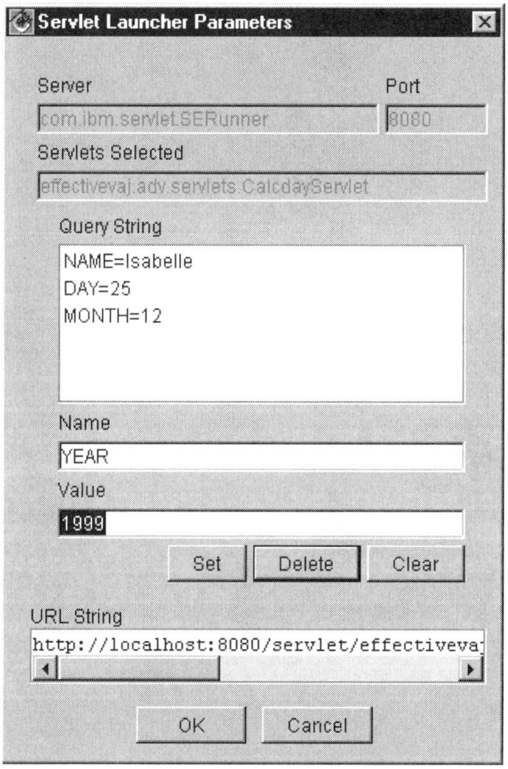

Once you have set the correct launch properties, you can launch the servlet by selecting it and then **Tools->Servlet Launcher->Launch**. The WebSphere Test Environment is started if it was not running, the default Web browser is launched, and the URL is automatically invoked. If all goes well, you should see a result similar to that shown in Figure 24.4. You can check that the servlet has been correctly instantiated by the server by looking at the Console window. A trace similar to Instantiate: effectivevaj.adv.servlets.CalcdayServlet is created each time a servlet is loaded in memory by the application server.

TIP

If you select **Tools->Servlet Launcher->Launch** on a project or package, a list of available servlets in this project or package is displayed.

Figure 24.4 Results from CalcdayServlet execution.

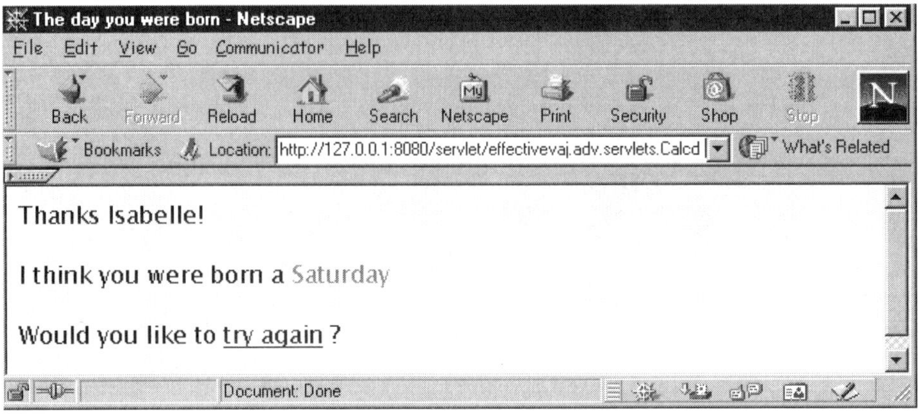

Calling a Servlet from an HTML Page

Once you have determined that CalcdayServlet works, you can test the complete calling chain by opening the *calcday.html* file and submitting a request. The *calcday.html* file must be placed in the docRoot directory defined in SERunner. properties to be found by the server. If you haven't reset the docRoot property, you must place the *calcday.html* file in the default directory, that is:

```
X:/ibmvjava/ide/project_resources/
    IBM WebSphere Test Environment/hosts/default_host/default_app/web.
```

Then, simply start the WebSphere Test Environment from **Workspace->Tools ->Launch WebSphere Test Environment**, and open localhost:8080/calcday.html, assuming you have not changed the default httpPort in SERunner.properties. Otherwise, just specify the port number you have chosen, that is, localhost:1234. After the HTML is displayed, put some input values into the form and press the Submit button to start CalcdayServlet. If it works, that's great! Otherwise, read the next section.

Debugging Servlets

The most tedious task in developing servlets is probably debugging. After a servlet is deployed to an application server, your usual choice is to attach a remote debugger to the servlet-engine virtual machine and spend your time switching between the development and test environments.

With VisualAge for Java, you debug servlets like any other program: If you put a breakpoint in any servlet method, the debugger starts automatically when this method is called. All normal debugging features are then available to you. You can step into the code, change the code on the fly, and continue the execution from the point you stopped. If you want to step into the execution of the *execute* method, simply put a breakpoint at the beginning of this method, and start the servlet again. The debugger starts automatically when the execute method is called. If you want to check the DOBInfo variable contents, you can proceed as follows:

1. Step over the code (F6) until the getFormParameters method has run and the DOBInfo variable has been initialized.
2. Leave the mouse pointer over the DOBInfo variable for a few seconds. A string should display the contents of the object. You can also select the DOBInfo variable and open an object inspector.

If you modify code on the fly, remember that the execution thread is restarted from the beginning of the method you have changed. Changes to variable values are not undone. Moreover, any HTML you have already sent to the output stream will appear twice in the resulting HTML page. You can easily test this by stepping in the sendReponse method and modifying the method after the fourth or fifth line of code has been executed. Each line of HTML sent to the output stream before you modified the code should be duplicated in the resulting HTML page. These results must not be interpreted as bugs in your code.

TIP

After a servlet is deployed in your favorite application server, you can use the distributed debugger to remotely debug the servlet code (provided that your application server can run in debug mode). The distributed debugger back-end is integrated in the WebSphere Application Server. This lets you automatically start the distributed debugger as soon as a servlet is started. You can learn more about the distributed debugger in Chapter 5, "Testing and Debugging."

Developing JSP Components

So far, you have developed a pure servlet, which can respond to a request and send a response. In this servlet, the response is an HTML flow: You ended up writing HTML in your Java code. VisualAge for Java is definitely a great Java editor, but not an HTML editor.

The example we have developed so far is very simple, but in a real-life example, creating the entire HTML page manually in the servlet code is a real burden. In addition, your application view (the HTML page) and the business logic (the servlet and reusable components) are developed by very different people. By mixing HTML and

Java in a servlet, you must ask a graphic designer to update a servlet (Java code) to change the company logo. This is the main motivation behind JavaServer Pages components.

A Quick Introduction to JSP Components

In a Model-View-Controller model (MVC model), the data, the logic manipulating the data, and the presentation (view) of the data are designed to be independent. If the data changes, the controller takes care of updating the view. If the view evolves, the business logic and the data must not be affected. The servlet/JavaServer Pages programming model is based on the MVC model. In this model, shown in Figure 24.5, the servlet receives a request from a client, accesses the data through a set of reusable components (beans or enterprise beans), and invokes a JavaServer Pages (JSP) component to display the results of the request.

A JSP component is very similar to an HTML page. You can view a JSP component as a template for the HTML result page, with "holes" for the dynamic data that vary on each the request. These holes are filled at run time with dynamic data coming from the servlet. If you consider the example servlet you just created, the result page is mostly static but has two dynamic elements, the user name and the day of the week. The servlet must query the dynamic data, package it, and pass it to the JSP component. A bean is used as the contract between the servlet and a JSP component; the servlet stores dynamic data in a bean instance and places the bean instance somewhere the JSP component can access it. The JSP component retrieves the bean instance and inserts the dynamic data (typically bean properties) into the HTML page using special JSP tags.

Figure 24.5 Servlets and the MVC programming model.

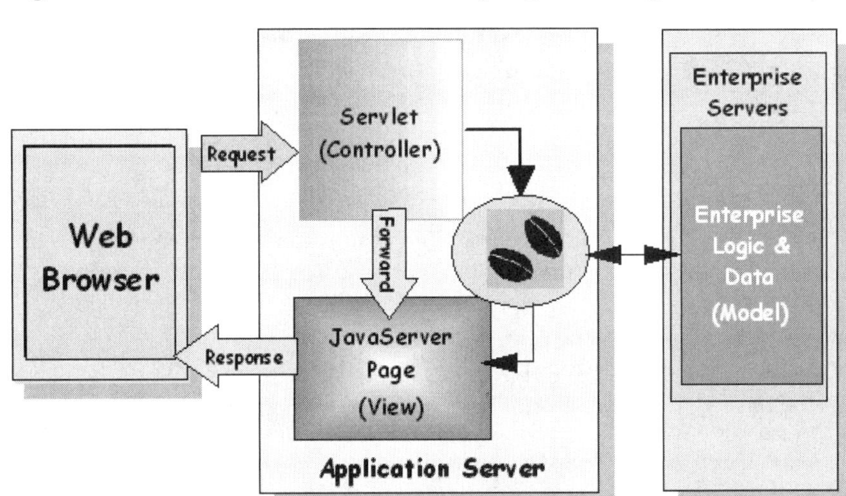

What happens when you open a JSP component? This file is compiled by a JSP compiler. The compilation process transforms the original mix of HTML and JSP tags into a... servlet. The servlet is then loaded in memory and run. This compilation process occurs each time that you change the JSP source code, not each time you invoke the JSP component. Once a JSP page has been compiled and loaded in memory, it performs as fast as a handwritten servlet.

The full JSP syntax lets you insert complex Java code fragments in HTML, declare variables, create methods, or influence the code generated by the JSP compiler; you could actually write more Java than HTML in a JSP component. By doing this, you reverse the problem: You now have to look in the view to find some business logic. This is no better than editing a servlet to change the view of your application. Maintenance of your JSP files is much easier if you keep the Java code to a minimum.

In the following example, we have chosen to demonstrate how to transfer data from to servlet to a JSP component through a Java bean. We use only a fragment of the JSP syntax in this example, and we encourage you to refer to the JSP specification, available on the JavaSoft Web site (www.javasoft.com), for a more complete syntax description.

Choosing the Right JSP Compiler (version 3.02 only)

Both JSP 0.91 and JSP 1.0 are supported by the WebSphere Application Server. Version 0.91 is supported essentially for migration purposes and backward compatibility with the WebSphere Application Server, version 2.0. This level of the specification should not be used for new development. By default, the WebSphere Test Environment is configured to support JSP 0.91 (the VisualAge for Java samples are at the 0.91 level). The example is written to the JSP 1.0 specification, so you should switch JSP compilers now.

You can change the settings to support JSP 1.0 by editing *the default_app.webapp* properties file located under x:\IBMVJava\ide\project_resources\IBM WebSphere Test Environment\hosts\default_host\default_app\servlets:

1. Find the following line in the XML file: <description>JSP support servlet</description>.
2. Change <code>*com.ibm.ivj.jsp.debugger.pagecompile.IBMPageCompileServlet* </code> to: <code>*com.ibm.ivj.jsp.runtime.JspDebugServlet*</code>.
3. Save the file and restart the WebSphere Test Environment if it was running.

NOTE

3.5 In VisualAge for Java, version 3.5, the JSP compiler is already configured at JSP 1.0 level. All samples have been ported from V0.91 to V1.0.

Modifying CalcdayServlet

The HTML output is isolated in two methods of CalcdayServlet: sendResponse and sendErrorResponse. The rest of the servlet logic is mostly unchanged. In each of these methods, you must replace the existing code by a call to the corresponding JSP file. A servlet forwards a request to a JSP component by using a request dispatcher. A request dispatcher is available through the servlet context object. You could actually dispatch the request to another servlet or HTML page; dispatching to a JSP file is just a special case. The new versions of the sendResponse and sendErrorResponse methods look like this:

```
protected void sendResponse(HttpServletRequest req,
                              HttpServletResponse res)
                throws ServletException, IOException
{
 RequestDispatcher reqDispatch = null;
 reqDispatch = getServletContext().
                  getRequestDispatcher("displayDay.jsp");
 reqDispatch.forward(req, res);
}
protected void sendErrorResponse(HttpServletRequest req,
                                   HttpServletResponse res)
                throws ServletException, IOException
{
 RequestDispatcher reqDispatch = null;
 reqDispatch = getServletContext().getRequestDispatcher("error.jsp");
 reqDispatch.forward(req, res);
}
```

Recall from the introduction to JSP programming that a Java bean is used as the contract between the servlet and the JSP component. In this example, the bean we want to use is *aDay*, which contains the user name and day of the week. A JSP component can access this bean instance in a certain scope. The most used scopes are *request* and *session*. Objects stored in an HTTP request do not exist beyond the life of the HTTP request, while objects stored in HTTP sessions can be reused across requests. If we had to pass the bean data across multiple requests, using an HTTP session would be mandatory. In the example, we want to pass the data from the servlet to the JSP component; therefore, storing the bean instance in the HTTP request is sufficient.

NOTE

The JSP specification defines two other scopes: page and application. If you create a bean instance in a JSP component, this instance is available in the page scope. Objects stored in the servlet context are accessible using the application scope. Please refer to the JSP specification for more details about this topic.

To store the *aDay* bean instance in the request, you add an attribute to the request. This attribute has a unique name (here *DAY*), and points to the bean instance, like this:

```
<beginning of execute method goes here>
// Initialize the username parameter
aDay.setUsername(DOBInfo.getProperty("NAME"));
// Now, calculate the dayOfWeek
try {
 aDay.calculateDay(day, month, year);
 // Add bean to request object
 // This must be done before forwarding the request to the JSP.
 req.setAttribute("DAY", aDay);
 sendResponse(req, res);
}
catch (NumberFormatException nfe) {
 // A requested parameter is wrong
 sendErrorResponse(req, res);
}
```

The new version of the servlet is complete. You must now create the *displayday.jsp* and *error.jsp* files.

Completing the JSP Files

You can use any HTML editor to create JSP files, although some of them do have specific JSP tag support, which makes the page development easier. We use two JSP tags in this example:

<jsp:useBean> This tag is used to retrieve the bean instance stored by the servlet in the request object. The basic syntax is that a bean of type *type* is searched within the *scope* using the specified *ID*. If the object can't be found in the scope, an exception is raised. If you specify *class* instead of *type*, and the specified object can't be found in the scope, an object with name *ID* is created.

<jsp:getProperty> This tag is used to insert the value of the bean properties inside the HTML code. It takes two parameters: the bean ID (here, DAY) and the property name. You must have defined a read accessor for those properties (that is, getUsername()). The property is implicitly converted to a String. You must make sure that a String object can be built from this property (primitive types are fine), or provide a toString() method on your own types.

The displayDay.jsp and error.jsp are similar to this:

```
<!—DISPLAYDAY.JSP-->
<HTML><HEAD>
```

```
<TITLE>The day you were born</TITLE>
</HEAD><BODY bgcolor="#ffffcc">
<jsp:useBean id="DAY"
    type="effectivevaj.adv.servlets.util.Day" scope="request" />
<H2>Welcome to this wonderful WebSphere application!</H2>
<P>Thanks,<jsp:getProperty name="DAY" property="username" />
<P>We think the day you were born was a
<FONT color="#ff3399">
<jsp:getProperty name="DAY" property="dayOfWeek" />
</FONT>.<P>
Would you like to <A HREF="javascript:history.back(1)">try again</A>?
</BODY></HTML>

<!--ERROR.JSP-->
<html>
<head><title>Servlet Execution Failed</title></head>
<body bgcolor="#ffffca">
<p><h2>Sorry, we could not calculate the day you were born</h2>
<p><h2>Please, make sure you have provided valid data!</h2>
<p>Press the <strong>Back</strong> button, and resubmit.</p>
</body></html>
```

It is useful to look at the code generated by the JSP compiler to understand the exact meaning of the different tag options. For the <jsp:useBean> tag specified in displayday.jsp, the following Java code is generated:

```
synchronized (request) {
  DAY= (effectivevaj.adv.servlets.util.Day)
        pageContext.getAttribute("DAY",PageContext.REQUEST_SCOPE);
  if (DAY  == null)
    throw new java.lang.InstantiationException ("bean DAY not found
within scope ");
}
```

Running and Debugging JSP Components

If you invoke the calcdayServlet again, the displayday.jsp file is compiled as a servlet and executed. The first request usually takes a bit of time, since the JSP

> **NOTE**
>
> Both JSP files (displayDay.jsp and error.jsp) must be put in the folder specified by the docRoot property in the SERunner.properties file to be found at run time. By default, this directory is X:/IBMVJava/ide/project_resources/IBM WebSphere Test Environment/hosts/default_host/default_app/web.

file must be compiled. Further requests just start the resulting servlet, with little overhead compared to a static HTML page call.

If the displayDay.jsp file does not contain any errors, you will see the resulting HTML page in the browser. If your JSP component has syntax errors, or if you have inserted bad Java statements in it, the debugger automatically starts up. Usually, the information given in the debugger is of little help when you try to understand why the compilation or execution of the JSP file failed.

Several options are available in VisualAge for Java to help you debug JSP components. First, you can use the JSP execution monitor to view in a single window the JSP source file, the Java source created by the JSP compiler, and the HTML output. Second, you can choose to retrieve syntax error information to visually indicate errors in the JSP source code.

Setting JSP Debugging Options

You enable the JSP debugging options from the JSP Execution Monitor options dialog shown in Figure 24.6. In VisualAge for Java, version 3.02, this dialog is launched from **Workspace->Tools->JSP Execution Monitor**. In version 3.5, those options are available from the WTE control center. The following options can be set from this dialog:

> **Internal Port Number.** This port number should not be changed unless the default port (8082) is already in use. You must not give the same port number for the HTTP port and the JSP execution monitor port; they have nothing in common! Use any number between 1024 and 65536.
>
> **Enable monitoring JSP execution.** If this option is selected and the JSP file compilation is successful, the JSP Execution monitor is started as soon as the JSP file is loaded.

Figure 24.6 The JSP Execution Monitor options dialog.

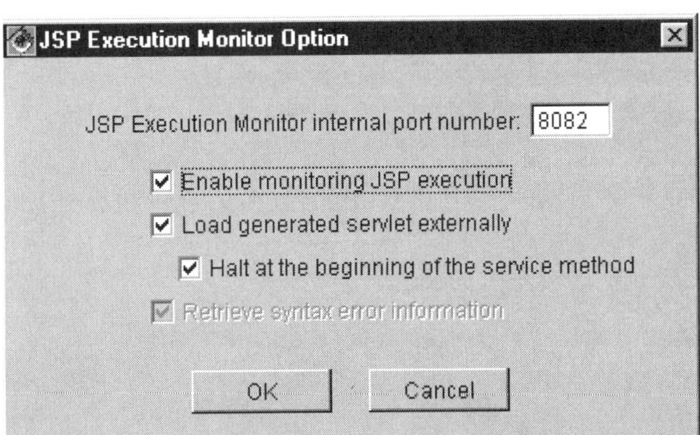

Retrieve Syntax Information. When this option is set, the JSP compiler adds debug information to the Java code it generates; this debugging information is then used to visually indicate errors in the JSP source code. The Retrieve Syntax Information option is automatically set when *Load Generated Servlet externally* is set.

Load Generated Servlet Externally. You have the option to either import the Java source code created by the JSP compiler in the workspace or leave it on the file system. If you choose the Load Generated Servlet Externally option, the JSP file is compiled and the generated servlet is left on the file system. Otherwise, the generated code is automatically imported to the workspace in a project called *JSP Page Compile Generated Code*. If you leave the generated code on the file system, you will be able to step into the generated code line by line. However, you will not be able to modify the generated code on the fly, or modify variables. You must select *Halt at the beginning of the service method* for the debugger to start automatically when the generated servlet is executed. If you import the code in the workspace, you can put breakpoints anywhere in the generated code, change variable values on the fly, and even modify the generated servlet. Limitations when debugging classes loaded externally are covered in Chapter 5.

> **NOTE**
>
> 3.5 For VisualAge for Java, version 3.5, the last setting is available from the servlet engine properties page, not from the JSP properties page.

Working with the JSP Execution Monitor

If you enable the JSP Execution Monitor, a dialog similar to Figure 24.7 is automatically started when the JSP component is loaded. The JSP execution monitor comports four panes:

***JSP File List* pane.** All loaded JSP files are added to this list.

***JSP Source* pane.** Contains the JSP source code. You can double-click in the left margin of this pane to set a breakpoint in the JSP source code, as shown in Figure 24.7.

***Java Source* pane.** Displays the source code of the servlet created by the JSP compilation process.

***Generated HTML Source* pane.** Displays the HTML flow created during the execution of the JSP component.

You can minimize, maximize, or detach a selected pane from the **View** menu.

Figure 24.7 The JSP Execution Monitor.

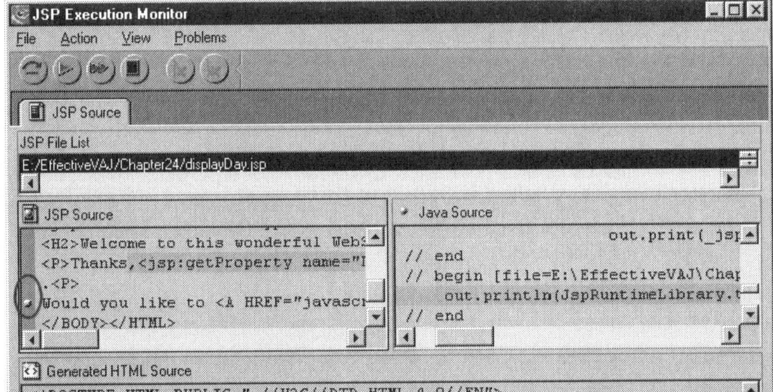

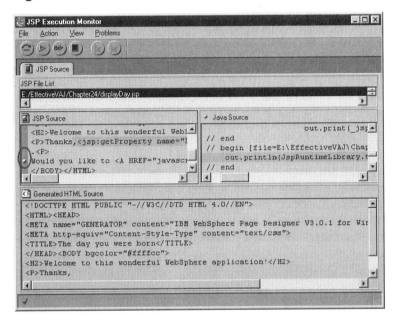

> **TIP**
>
> If the WebSphere Test Environment refuses to start, make sure the JSP Execution Monitor is stopped.

Debugging JSP Components

A JSP execution can fail for one of two reasons:

- The JSP syntax is wrong.
- There is a mistake in the Java code inserted in the JSP component.

Dealing with JSP Syntax Errors

If the JSP component is syntactically wrong, the JSP compiler will fail to generate a proper servlet. The JSP Execution Monitor will not be started, and the error message returned by the JSP compiler will be displayed in the browser. If you want to test this behavior, you can change the displayDay.jsp file and modify the <jsp:getProperty> tag to point to a nonexistent property, for example, *user* instead of *username*. If you start the servlet, a message similar to this should appear in the browser:

```
com.sun.jsp.JspException:
```

```
    "getProperty(DAY): can't find method to read {1}"
java.lang.Throwable(java.lang.String)
java.lang.Exception(java.lang.String)
javax.servlet.ServletException(java.lang.String)
com.sun.jsp.JspException(java.lang.String)
void com.sun.jsp.compiler.GetPropertyGenerator.generate(…)
```

Because the servlet generation failed, the JSP Execution Monitor does not start, even if you have selected the appropriate option in the JSP Execution Monitor dialog. This error message is your only indication of what went wrong.

Dealing with JSP Java Errors

Even if a JSP file has been successfully compiled, it may still contain Java errors. If you insert chunks of Java code in a JSP component, they are not interpreted by the JSP compiler. They are just inserted as-is in the generated servlet. For example, you can replace:

```
<jsp:getProperty name="DAY" property="username" />
```

with:

```
<%= DAY.getUserName() %>
```

The code enclosed in <%= %> is inserted as-is in the servlet generated by the JSP compiler. If this code is wrong, the execution of the servlet will fail. In such cases, we recommend that you select the Load Generated Servlets Externally option. The generated servlet will be instrumented with debugging information that allows you to point the line of code that triggered the error in the JSP file. If you set the Enable Monitoring JSP Execution option, the wrong JSP statement is highlighted in the JSP Execution Monitor's Source pane, and the corresponding error message is displayed at the bottom of the window, as shown in Figure 24.8. If you introduce an error by calling DAY.getUser(), an message similar to this is displayed in the browser:

```
com.sun.jsp.JspException:
…\_displayDay_xjsp_debug_1778187557.java:192: Method getUser() not
found
in class effectivevaj.adv.servlets.util.Day.
line(192);    out.print( DAY.getUser() );
```

However, this message only indicates which line (192) is in error in the generated servlet. It says nothing about the statement in the original JSP file that triggered the error. If you select the Enable JSP Execution Monitor option, the JSP Execution Monitor will be started when the error occurs. The JSP Execution Monitor will show you exactly which statement in the JSP source code is wrong, as shown in Figure 24.8.

Figure 24.8 Displaying Java errors in the JSP Execution Monitor.

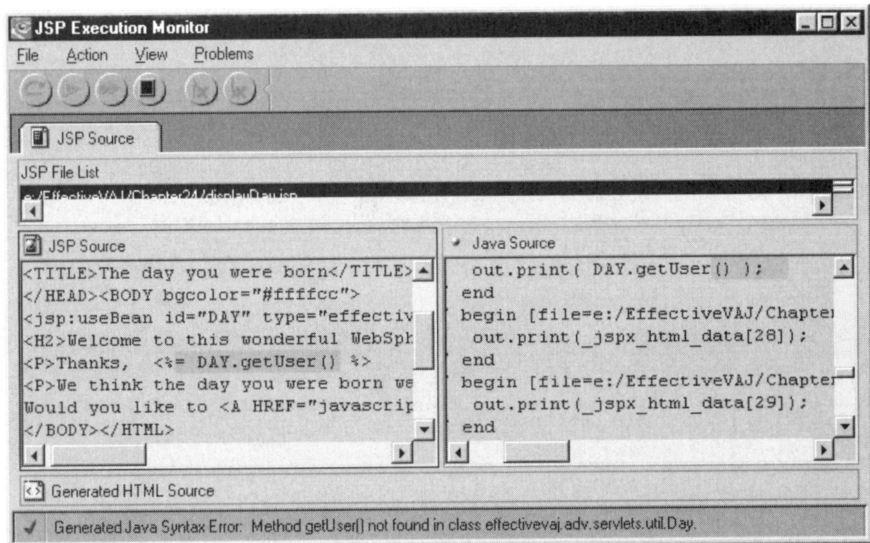

Stepping in JSP Source Code

Once all JSP and Java errors have been eliminated, you can step into the JSP source code in the JSP Execution Monitor. We recommend the following approach:

1. Set the Enable Monitoring JSP Execution option.
2. Do not set the Load Generated Servlet Externally or Retrieve Syntax Error options. The JSP compile process will be much faster.
3. Start the CalcdayServlet that will call the JSP component. After the JSP Execution Monitor starts, you can:

- **Step into the JSP code.** If you select Action->Step (F6), you step into the JSP code. For each JSP statement, the corresponding Java source code is highlighted in the Java Source pane, and the resulting HTML is displayed in the generated HTML Source pane.

- **Execute the JSP code in stepping mode.** If you select Action->Run (F5), you will step in the JSP source code until a breakpoint is found. If you haven't set any breakpoint in the JSP source code, you step in the execution until the end of the JSP file is reached.

- **Execute the JSP in fast forward mode.** To run the JSP file without stepping, use the fast forward option from Action->Fast Forward (Ctrl-F5). If you use fast forward, the generated HTML source is not displayed.

Import Troubleshooting

If you select the Retrieve Syntax Information option, you may get an error message stating that the servlet file can't be imported. You should check at least one thing: the project owner (assuming you are working with the Enterprise Edition). The first time you call a JSP component, the *JSP Page Compile Generated Code* project is created, and the current workspace owner becomes the project's owner, for example, Effective Developer. The resulting servlet is then placed in the default package for this project or in a specific package. The current workspace owner becomes the package owner and the *unique* package group member. If you change the workspace owner to WebSphere Student and call the JSP again, the import step will fail. The WebSphere Student user does not have the right to create a class in the package, because he/she is not a package group member.

This error is quite difficult to find, because you do not get any feedback that would indicate the origin of the problem. One way to find why the import fails is to do it manually. You can open the generated code in the Scrapbook and manually import the code in the workspace from **File->Import Page** into the *JSP Page Compile Generated Code* project. The generated code (for JSP 1.0) is kept under <VAJ_InstallRoot>\ide\project_resources\IBM WebSphere Test Environment\temp\JSP_10\default_app. You should open the Java source file (displayday_jsp_xxxx.java), and try to import it. If you have ownership problems, you should receive a message similar to Figure 24.9.

There are several ways to correct this problem. The easiest way is to delete the JSP Page Compile project. It will be recreated with the right ownership. If you can't do this, and if you are trying to import a class into an existing package, you must add the current user—WebSphere Student—as a package group member of this package. If you are trying

Figure 24.9 Servlet import process fails.

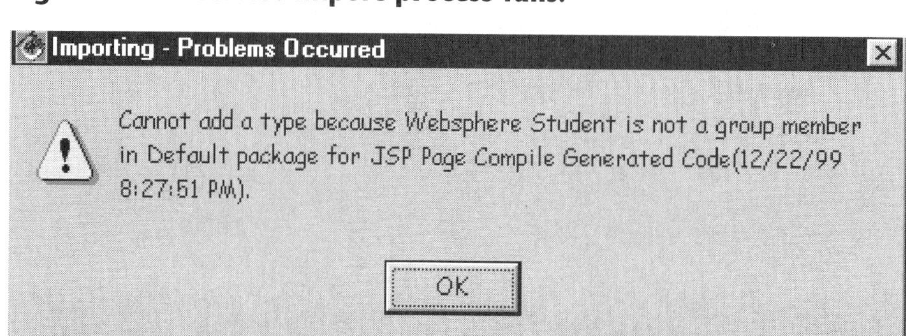

to create a new package, you must change the JSP Page Compile project's owner to be WebSphere Student. Please refer to Chapter 4, "Using Version Control," for details on users and how to change project and packages ownership.

Calling Enterprise Beans from Servlets

According to the MVC model, servlets use components to access back-end data. Those components can either be beans or enterprise beans. In this section, we use *access beans* to call enterprise beans from a JSP component. Access beans, which were introduced in the previous chapter, enable you to perform local caching of EJBs attributes. In other words, the JSP component performs a local call instead of a remote call to retrieve attributes from the Song entity beans, and displays them.

In this architecture, the servlet creates an instance of the rowset SongAccessBean, calls the finder method on the access-bean instance, and populates a SongAccessBeanTable instance from the result. An access bean table is an enumeration of copy helper access beans. This table is then stored in a request or HTTP session object, and retrieved by the JSP component. Because this table already contains all results, the JSP component just has to exploit them by walking the SongAccessBeanTable instance and displaying the cached data it contains.

Only the entity bean attributes are stored on the client side. A JSP component can directly get the data without generating a remote call (the remote call is made in the servlet, when the table is populated). An implicit refreshCopyHelper() is done the first time a get method is called on an access bean. You can also call refreshCopyHelper() explicitly to refresh the cached data from the actual enterprise-bean data. Similarly, you can use the commitCopyHelper() method to update the enterprise beans data from the cached values.

In the following example, we call a finder method on the Song entity bean to retrieve existing songs and display the results of the finder using a JSP component. This example in built in four steps:

1. Create an access bean copy helper for the Composer entity bean and a rowset access bean for the Song entity bean. You must create the Composer access bean due to the association between those two EJB components. If you want to update an enterprise bean from a copy helper, you must use the commitCopyHelper() method.
2. Test the access-bean code from the Scrapbook (just to make sure it works).
3. Create a ListSongsServlet component that creates a Song access bean, call the findAllSongs finder, and populate the table.
4. Create a JSP component that prints out the results of the finder method in an HTML table.

Creating the Song Access Bean

The first step is to create a row-set access bean for the Song enterprise bean. Because there is an association between the Composer and Song enterprise beans, you must create an access bean for both, although we will use only the Song access bean in this example. In addition, you must regenerate the deployment code for the whole EJB group. To create the Song access bean:

1. Select the Song enterprise bean and choose **Add->Access Bean** from the pop-up menu.
2. Select *Rowset for multiple entity bean instances* as the access-bean type. You need a rowset because we want to call a finder that returns an enumeration of entity-bean instances.
3. Click on **Next**.

The next page lets you choose a default zero-argument constructor. This constructor is used if you create a copy helper access bean instance and call a method of the bean's remote interface. The copy helper attributes are initialized only when the first method is called, not when you call the constructor. Suppose that you have set the zero-argument constructor to be findByPrimaryKey (SongKey) and you execute the following piece of code:

```
SongAccessBean SAB = new SongAccessBean();
SAB.setInitKey_ID (100);
SAB.getTitle();
```

When the getTitle() method is called, a SongKey instance is created using the argument passed to the setInitKey_ID() method—100— and the findByPrimaryKey(aSongKey) finder is called. To set the zero-argument constructor, you must:

1. Select findByPrimaryKey(SongKey) as the home method.
2. You need to supply a converter if you choose to create a song access bean by passing a string as a parameter. For example, if you gather data from an HTML form and want to create a song access bean from this data, you could write the following code:

   ```
   SongAccessBean SAB = new SongAccessBean();
   SAB.setInitKey_ID (request.getParameter("SONG_KEY"));
   SAB.setTitle (request.getParameter("SONG_TITLE"));
   ```

The SimpleStringConverter can be used to convert basic types to strings, and vice versa. You can create your own converters by implementing the com.ibm.ivj.ejb.runtime.StringConverter interface. Please refer to the source of this interface for instructions. If you create a converter, it is added automatically to the converter list. In our sample, we do not deal with strings, so you can keep the converter value to *None*.

> **NOTE**
>
> Converters that are used with access beans are different from the converters we described in Chapter 23, "Developing Enterprise JavaBeans," used to map entity bean attributes to SQL types.

3. The last dialog page lets you choose which enterprise bean attributes should be cached in the copy helper. In this example, we need to access only the title and the composer: Therefore, we select only those two attributes. Both attributes are strings, so we do not need to specify any converter. You must supply a converter if the attribute is not a string and you want to display it in a JSP component. When you supply a converter, it will be used in the attribute accessors of the access bean, like this:

```
public String getAmount() throws java.rmi.RemoteException,
                                    javax.ejb.CreateException,
                                    javax.ejb.FinderException,
                                    javax.naming.NamingException
{
  return SimpleStringConverter.doubleToString(((Double)
          _getCache("amount")).doubleValue());
}
```

You can now click on **Finish** to start the access-bean code generation. When the code generation is finished, you should see some errors in the song access bean. To fix those errors, you must create a copy helper access bean for the Composer enterprise bean the same way in which you just created the access bean for the Song enterprise bean. Then, you must regenerate the deployed code for the whole EJB group.

Testing the Access Bean

To make sure the access-bean code works, we will first test it in the Scrapbook. For details on the Scrapbook, please refer to Chapter 5. In the example code provided below, we first create a SongAccessBean instance and then call the findAllSongs() finder. The finder returns an enumeration that is used to initialize a SongAccessBeanTable instance. This table contains the cached attributes of the multiple enterprise-bean instances returned by the finder, that is, multiple copy helpers. Finally, we loop on the table to display the data it contains. To test this code in the Scrapbook, you need to:

1. Start the enterprise-bean testing environment, as explained in Chapter 23. Make sure in the Console window that the Enterprise Java Server for the EffectiveVAJMusic EJB group is "open for business."

2. Start the Scrapbook from **Window->Scrapbook**.
3. Change the page execution context to the SongAccessBean class by selecting **Page->Run In**.
4. Type the code below, select it, and select Run.

```
SongAccessBean songAB = new SongAccessBean();
java.util.Enumeration enum = songAB.findAllSongs();
SongAccessBeanTable songABT = new SongAccessBeanTable();
// Populate Table from Enumeration
songABT.setSongAccessBean (enum);
for (int i = 0; i < songABT.numberOfRows(); i++){
  SongAccessBean tmpAB = songABT.getSongAccessBean(i);
  tmpAB.refreshCopyHelper(); // Initialize Attributes.
  // The get accessors do not trigger any remote call.
  System.out.println("Title: " + tmpAB.getTitle() +
                    "\t Interpret: " + tmpAB.getInterpret());
} // end for
```

You should see a list of songs printed on the Console window. We will now use a servlet and a JSP component to display these results in an HTML table.

Creating the ListSongs Servlet

The code we tested in the Scrapbook calls the findAllSongs() finder and displays the results on the standard output stream. In a servlet/JSP model, the servlet will call the finder and pass the results to the JSP component for display.

> **NOTE**
>
> You could also take the code tested in the Scrapbook and insert it in the JSP component. Although this is technically possible, it is not a recommended approach. The main problem with running large chunks of Java code in a JSP component is exception handling. It is much easier and cleaner to catch any exception thrown during the creation of the access bean or the invocation of the finder in the servlet than in the JSP component. If an exception is thrown, the servlet takes the appropriate course of action and calls an error in the JSP component. As the controller, the servlet handles the execution flow. The JSP is in charge of displaying whatever data the servlet may return.

You should create ListSongsServlet the same way you created CalcdayServlet, by inheriting from BaseHTTPServlet. Then, you should override the execute method so that the servlet creates an access bean, calls the findAllSongs() finder, and populates the access-bean table from the returned enumeration. The table now contains all cached attributes for all enterprise beans returned by the finder. Then, the access-bean table is added to the HTTP request under the SONGS_TABLE id, where the JSP component is able to find it. The final execute() method looks like this:

```
protected void execute(HttpServletRequest req, HttpServletResponse res)
                throws ServletException, IOException
{
  // Local Variables
  SongAccessBean songAB;
  SongAccessBeanTable songABT;

  // Create a Song Access Bean
  try {
    songAB = new SongAccessBean();
    Enumeration enum = songAB.findAllSongs();
    songABT = new SongAccessBeanTable();
    // Populate Table from Enumeration
    songABT.setSongAccessBean (enum);
    // Initialize Cached Attributes
    for (int i = 0; i < songABT.numberOfRows(); i++){
     songABT.getSongAccessBean(i).refreshCopyHelper();
    }
    // Put the Access Bean Table in the request for display
    req.setAttribute("SONGS_TABLE", songABT);
    sendResponse(req, res);
}
  catch (Exception e) {
    sendErrorResponse(req, res);
  }
}
```

WARNING

In this example, the numbers of enterprise beans returned by the findAllSongs() finder is limited. For performance reasons, you should not populate the access-bean table with a large enumeration (for example, 1000 elements) in one shot but, rather, use the addRow() method to populate the table block by block.

Finally, you should complete the sendResponse and sendErrorResponse methods to respectively call the listSongs.jsp and error.jsp files:

```
protected void sendResponse(HttpServletRequest req,
                              HttpServletResponse res)
                throws ServletException, IOException
{
  RequestDispatcher reqDispatch = null;
  reqDispatch = getServletContext().
                  getRequestDispatcher("listsongs.jsp");
  reqDispatch.forward(req, res);
}

protected void sendErrorResponse(HttpServletRequest req,
                                   HttpServletResponse res)
                throws ServletException, IOException
{
  RequestDispatcher reqDispatch = null;
  reqDispatch = getServletContext().getRequestDispatcher("error.jsp");
  reqDispatch.forward(req, res);
}
```

Completing the ListSongs JSP Component

In the ListSongs JSP component, you must retrieve the song access-bean table from the HTTP request and loop on this table to display the data. There is no standard JSP tag for loops, so we must use some Java code to perform the loop. You can enclose a chunk of Java code in a scriptlet by using <% and %> to delimit the Java code. The JSP compiler will insert the code, unchanged, in the generated servlet. We can also use expressions to insert the string returned by the getTitle() and getComposer() methods in the generated servlet. Results of an expression are inserted in place of the expression itself: An expression must evaluate to a string.

> **NOTE**
>
> WebSphere provides a <tsx:repeat> tag as an extension to the base JSP syntax. If you intend to use your code in WebSphere only, use this tag rather than the Java loop described in the following paragraph.

In the ListSongs JSP component, we first retrieve the song access-bean table from the request and then loop over the table to display its contents. Make sure to close the *for* loop in a separate scriptlet, as indicated in the following code:

```
<HTML>
<HEAD>
<TITLE>List of Songs</TITLE>
</HEAD>
<BODY bgcolor="#FFFFCC">
<H1 align="center">List of Songs in the Music Database</H1>
<P>The following songs have been entered in
the MUSIC database:<BR>
<jsp:directive.page import="effectivevaj.adv.ejb.entity.*" />
<jsp:useBean id="SONGS_TABLE"
             type="SongAccessBeanTable"
             scope="request" />
<TABLE border="1">
<TBODY>
<TR bgcolor="#cccccc" >
<TH>Interpret</TH>
<TH>Title</TH>
   </TR>
   <%
     for (int i = 0; i < SONGS_TABLE.numberOfRows(); i++){
       SongAccessBean tempAB = SONGS_TABLE.getSongAccessBean(i);
   %>
    <TR>
<TD><%= tempAB.getInterpret() %></TD>
<TD><%= tempAB.getTitle() %></TD>
</TR>
<%}%> <!-Make sure to close the loop!! -->
</TBODY>
</TABLE>
</BODY></HTML>
```

Now that the JSP files are complete, we can test the full solution in the VisualAge for Java IDE.

Testing the Whole Solution

One of the main advantages of VisualAge for Java over other Java IDEs is its flexibility and power for testing a typical Java-based application from end-to-end. If you want to test the full servlet/JSP/EJB solution, you can start the WebSphere Test Environment and the enterprise bean test environment simultaneously. After all servers are running, simply open localhost/servlet/effectivevaj.adv.ejb.servlets.ListSongsServlet; you should see the list of songs in the MUSIC database listed in an HTML table in your browser.

Advanced Configuration

In this section, we explain how to configure the WebSphere Test Environment. These settings are especially useful if you are planning to deploy to a WebSphere Application Server. The goal is to configure the WebSphere Test Environment in such a way that the code you are writing runs unchanged in the test environment and the real application server. First, we describe Web applications and their various properties. Then, we explain how to name servlets, and install the ServletEngineConfigDumper servlet in the test environment. Finally, we explain how to create multiple independent Web applications.

> **WARNING**
>
> Back up the original properties files before playing with them. These files are essential to the WebSphere Test Environment, and you want to make sure you can revert to a working version.

Setting Servlet Engine Properties

The servlet engine properties are described in a file called default.servlet_engine. In VisualAge for Java, version 3.0.2, all properties files are located under x:\ibmvjava\ide\project_resources\IBM WebSphere Test Environment. In version 3.5, they are located under x:\ibmvjava\ide\project_resources\IBM WebSphere Test Environment\properties.

You are likely to edit this file for two reasons: changing hostname bindings and working with Web applications. As a rule of thumb, do not try to change properties we do not expose in the following sections.

Changing Transport Definitions (version 3.5 only)

If you are using VisualAge for Java, version 3.0.2, please skip this section, you should not edit transport definition, but rather use the SERunner.properties file to change the HTTP Server port! If you are using VisualAge for Java, version 3.5, you must change the transport definition to define which port the HTTP Server is running on. This can be done by editing the transport definition below:

```
<active-transport>http</active-transport>
 <transport>
  <name>http</name>
  <code>com.ibm.servlet.engine.http_transport.HttpTransport</code>
  <arg name="port" value="8080"/>
  <arg name="maxConcurrency" value="5"/>
  <arg name="server_root" value="$server_root$"/>
</transport>
```

> **NOTE**
>
> You should not change any other value, especially the active transport, which should always be *http*.

Changing Hostname Bindings

A virtual host is defined like this in the default.servlet_engine file:

```
<websphere-servlet-host name="Host for VisualAge for Java WebSphere
Unit Test Environment">
```

When defining a virtual host, you define which host aliases are valid for this virtual host. When an HTTP request is sent, the application server looks at the URL to check whether it can handle the request. For example, if you want to handle www.myco.com/servlet/MyServlet in the WebSphere Test Environment, you must add www.myco.com as a valid hostname alias to the default virtual host. Some host aliases have been defined for you and are shown in the Console when you start the WebSphere Test Environment.

Although you can define multiple virtual hosts, we highly recommend that you keep the default one. You should be able to test all your code with a single virtual host, even if you later need to define multiple virtual hosts in the real application server. For VisualAge for Java, version 3.02, the name of the default virtual host must be left unchanged. SERunner will fail to start if the virtual host name is not *Host for VisualAge for Java WebSphere Unit Test Environment.*

If you want to add the www.myco.com to the default virtual host, you must add the following line at the end of the default.servlet_engine file. Do not add a port number after the hostname (i.e, www.myco.com:82), it will be done automatically for you.

```
<hostname-binding hostname="www.myco.com" servlethost=
     "Host for VisualAge for Java WebSphere Unit Test Environment"/>
```

> **NOTE**
>
> You can't just use any arbitrary name as a host alias; it has to be a valid hostname, defined in a name server or a hosts file. In other words, you should be able to ping www.myco.com and get an answer. If you want to practice with this, just add www.myco.com to your hosts file like this: *127.0.0.1 localhost www.myco.com.*

3.5 For VisualAge for Java, version 3.5, the default host name is *default_host*, and can be changed provided you change it accordingly in the <hostname-binding>

definitions. Note that for VisualAge for Java, version 3.5, you *must* specify the port number in the hostname-binding definition, like this:

```
<hostname-binding hostname="www.myco.com:8080"
                                    servlethost="default_host"/>
```

If an alias is found for a specific virtual host, a Web application attached to the virtual host is used to answer to the request.

Working with Web Applications

The Web application concept is described in the Java Servlet Development Kit (JSDK) specifications. You use a Web application to logically group HTML files, JSP files, and servlets that relate to each other. A Web application has the following characteristics:

A document root. When you request a resource that belongs to a certain Web application, the application server looks for static HTML pages, JSP files, and other static resources (images, and so on) in the document root of the Web application.

A classpath. When you call a servlet that belongs to a Web application, the application server looks for servlet classes, dependent classes, and servlet resources (such as properties files) on the Web application class path.

A unique identifier (or URI). This identifier is used in a URL to specify which Web application you are addressing. If your Web application has a URI of /vajbook and you call http://<host-alias>/vajbook/index.html, the application server tries to find the index.html file in the document root of the vajbook Web application. The default Web application has a URI set to /, which means that http://<host-alias>/index.html loads the index.html file located in the document root of the default Web application.

The WebSphere Test Environment defines a Web application called default_app. This Web application is defined in the default.servlet_engine file as follows:

```
<websphere-webgroup name="default_app">
  <description>Default WebGroup</description>
  <document-root>$approot$/web</document-root>
  <classpath>$approot$/servlets$psep$$server_root$/servlets</classpath>
  <root-uri>/</root-uri>
  <auto-reload enabled="true" polling-interval="3000"/>
  <shared-context>false</shared-context> // Do not change this value.
</websphere-webgroup>
```

The default_app Web application has a URI set to /, which means that all requests are handled by this Web application. The document root is set to $approot$/web, where $approot$ is $server_root$/hosts/default_host/<web application name>. The $server_root$ variable is set to x:\ibmvjava\ide\project_resources\IBM WebSphere Test

Environment. The class path is set to $approot$/servlets$psep$$server_root$/servlets, where $psep$ represents a platform-dependent path separator (";" on NT, ":" on UNIX). If the auto-reload feature is enabled, the application server will check every "polling-interval" whether the code has changed and will automatically reload the new servlet bytecode. This feature is useful only if you run servlets stored on the file system. The <shared-context> attribute must always be set to false.

> **NOTE**
>
> When you call a servlet, the application server *first* looks for the code in the workspace and then in the Web application class path.

Creating Your Own Web Application

You can create your own Web application by adding a new entry to the default.servlet_engine file. To define a Web application that will contain all the servlets created in this chapter, you could add the following entry to this file:

```
<websphere-webgroup name="vajbook">
  <description>Effective VisualAge for Java book samples</description>
  <document-root>$approot$/web</document-root>
  <classpath>$approot$/servlets</classpath>
  <root-uri>/vajbook</root-uri>
  <auto-reload enabled="true" polling-interval="3000"/>
  <shared-context>false</shared-context>
</websphere-webgroup>
```

You must use the <websphere-webgroup> XML tag to define a Web application. The Web application name is vajbook, which means we must create a **vajbook.webapp** file to contain the Web application servlet definitions. The URI for our Web application is /vajbook, which means that all requests addressing servlets in this Web application must start with <host-alias>/vajbook. The vajbook.webapp file must be placed in the Web application class path. You can easily create this file by copying the default_app.webapp file and modifying it.

If you have correctly defined your Web application, you should see a similar trace in the Console when starting the WebSphere Test Environment:

```
[WebGroup:name]:vajbook
[WebGroup:document-root]:e:\EffectiveVAJ\Chapter24
[WebGroup:root-uri]:/vajbook
[WebGroup:classpath]:f:\ibmvjava\ide\project_resources\
   IBM WebSphere Test Environment\hosts\default_host
```

```
    \default_app\servlets
[WebGroup:shared-context]:false
[WebGroup:shared-context-JNDI-name]:SrdSrvltCtxHome
[WebGroup:auto-reload-enabled]:true
[WebGroup:auto-interval]:3000
```

Customizing Default Servlets in a Web Application

Once you have defined a Web application, you must configure it by installing special servlets in that Web application. Specifically, you must define which level of JSP compliance the Web application supports, and whether the servlet can serve static HTML pages or let you call servlets by their fully qualified class name. You will find the following definitions in the default_app.webapp file, which can be found under $approot$/servlets. Just copy and paste this information in your own .webapp files.

Invoker servlet. Used whenever you want to call a servlet by its fully qualified class name, as we did for CalcdayServlet and ListSongsServlet. The <servlet-path> attribute indicates a Web path you can use to call this servlet. In other words, when you call localhost/servlet/effectivevaj.adv.servlet.MyServlet, the invoker servlet is called and tries to serve the effectivevaj.adv.servlet.MyServlet servlet. If the invoker servlet is not present in a Web application, you can only call a servlet by naming it. See the section *Adding Your Servlets to a Web Application* for details. The definition of the invoker servlet looks like this:

```
<servlet>
  <name>invoker</name>
  <description>Auto-registration servlet</description>
  <code>com.ibm.servlet.engine.webapp.InvokerServlet</code>
  <servlet-path>/servlet</servlet-path>
  <autostart>true</autostart>
</servlet>
```

JSP servlet. Handles JSP files. It is actually the JSP compiler. If you want to serve JSP files in your Web application, you must define a JSP compiler. A Web application supports JSP technology at level 0.91 *or* 1.0 (not both). The workingDir parameter points to the path where servlets generated by the JSP 0.91 compiler will go, while the scratchDir parameter points to the path where servlets generated by the JSP 1.0 compiler go. The keepGenerated flag indicates whether the Java source of the generated servlet should be kept on the file system, or deleted as soon as the corresponding bytecode has been generated. We recommend that you leave this option set to true, because it is always useful to have a look at the generated code. The definition of the jsp servlet looks like this:

```
<servlet>
    <name>jsp</name>
    <description>JSP 1.0 support servlet</description>
    <code>com.ibm.ivj.jsp.runtime.JspDebugServlet</code>
    <init-parameter>
        <name>workingDir</name>
        <value>$server_root$/temp/default_app</value>
    </init-parameter>
    <init-parameter>
        <name>jspemEnabled</name>
        <value>true</value>
    </init-parameter>
    <init-parameter>
        <name>scratchdir</name>
        <value>$server_root$/temp/JSP1_0/default_app</value>
    </init-parameter>
    <init-parameter>
        <name>keepgenerated</name>
        <value>true</value>
    </init-parameter>
    <autostart>true</autostart>
    <servlet-path>*.jsp</servlet-path>
</servlet>
```

File serving servlet. Used to serve static HTML pages. In a real test environment, an HTTP server such as Apache or IIS would serve static HTML pages. However, the HTTP server provided in the WebSphere Test Environment serves only as a base entry point and does not serve HTML static pages. Therefore, you **must** have a file-serving servlet enabled in a Web application to serve static HTML pages or static resources such as images. The file-serving servlet has a default servlet-path of /, which means that this servlet will try to serve any request the invoker servlet or JSP servlet can't serve. The definition of the file servlet looks like this:

```
<servlet>
    <name>file</name>
    <description>File serving servlet</description>
    <code>com.ibm.servlet.engine.webapp.SimpleFileServlet</code>
    <servlet-path>/</servlet-path>
    <init-parameter>
        <name></name>
        <value></value>
    </init-parameter>
```

```
    <autostart>true</autostart>
  </servlet>
```

> **NOTE**
>
> All basic servlets have their autostart attribute set to true. They are loaded in memory as soon as the application server starts.

Error reporter servlet. Necessary for each Web application. This servlet will be called whenever something goes wrong in the Web application, for example, if you call a nonexistent servlet. The default error-reporter servlet is ErrorReporter. The <error-page>/ErrorReporter</error-page> attribute is a mandatory tag of the XML file; the webapp file will not be loaded properly if this entry is not specified. In other words, you should always have those entries in a Web Application:

```
<error-page>/ErrorReporter</error-page>

<servlet>
 <name>ErrorReporter</name>
 <description>Default error reporter servlet</description>
 <code>com.ibm.servlet.engine.webapp.DefaultErrorReporter</code>
 <servlet-path>/ErrorReporter</servlet-path>
 <autostart>true</autostart>
</servlet>
```

Adding User Servlets to a Web Application

If you choose to call your servlets by name rather than by their fully qualified class name, you must create a new entry in the Web application definition file.

> **NOTE**
>
> We highly recommend to name your servlets way in production mode, where leaving the invoker servlet running is a security flaw (if it is running, then anybody can call a servlet available on the web app class path). Moreover, only named servlets can be secured or loaded at server startup. By naming them in test mode, you can test them in the exact same conditions as in production mode.

To add the CalcdayServlet servlet to the vajbook Web application, you must add a definition similar to the following one to the vajbook.webapp file:

```
<servlet>
 <name>calcday</name>
 <description>
    A servlet to calculate the day you were born>/description>
 <code>effectivevaj.adv.servlets.CalcdayServlet</code>
 <servlet-path>/CalcdayServlet</servlet-path>
 <servlet-path>/CalculateDayOfBirth</servlet-path>
 <autostart>false</autostart>
 <init-parameter>
   <name></name>
   <value></value>
 </init-parameter>
</servlet>
```

The servlet name (calcday) is an arbitrary name used to identify the servlet in the Web application; it is not used to call the servlet. The <code> attribute points to the fully qualified class name of the servlet. Whenever you call the servlet by its name, the server will try to find and load this code. The <servlet-path> attribute contains the name by which the servlet is called. You can have one or multiple <servlet-path> entries for a same servlet, as shown previously. We could call the calcdayServlet using either *<host-alias>/vajbook/CalcdayServlet* or *<host-alias>/vajbook/CalculateDayOfBirth*. When you call a servlet by its name, the invoker servlet definition is *not* used. The <init-parameter> block is used to pass parameters to a servlet. Those parameters are added to the servlet context when the servlet is loaded by the application server. Use the <name> and <value> attributes to declare one or many initialization parameters.

If you have correctly defined CalcdayServlet in the vajbook.webapp file, you should see the following trace in the Console window:

```
[Servlet:name]: calcday
[Servlet:description]:  A servlet to calculate the day you were born
[Servlet:code]: effectivevaj.adv.servlets.CalcdayServlet
[Servlet:autostart]: false
[Servlet:servlet-path]: /CalcdayServlet
[Servlet:servlet-path]: /CalculateDayOfBirth
```

Starting the Servlet Engine Manually (version 3.02 only)

If you start the WebSphere Test Environment using SERunner, the value of the document root and class-path attributes *are the same for all Web applications* you define in the default.servlet_engine file. In other words, the values you set in the Web application definition are ignored. The document-root value set in the

SERunner.properties file is used, while the class-path value is set to <ServerRoot> /hosts/default/hosts/servlets. ServletRoot is also defined in the SERunner.properties file. To specify a different document root and class path for each Web application, you must start the servlet engine manually by running the com.ibm.servlet engine.ServletEngine class. Before running this class, you must configure its class path and define command line arguments and an environment variable.

The ServletEngine class path must be set properly. First, you must add to the project class-path all projects that contain servlets the servlet engine will have to load, as well as all projects that contain classes those servlets are using. In our case, you should find the Effective VisualAge for Java, IBM EJB tools (for the access beans) on the project class-path. Moreover, you need to add some extra directories to the class path: The best way to do this is to copy this information from the SERunner class-path definition. Then, you must open the ServletEngine properties sheet and add:

- serverRoot "X:/IBMVJava/ide/project_resources/IBM WebSphere Test Environment" as a command-line argument
- ivj.version=3.0.2 as an environment property

For each Web application, you need to set a proper document root and class path, and ensure that the .webapp file is correctly located on this class path. For example, if you configure the vajbook Web application like this:

```
<websphere-webgroup name="vajbook">
  <description>Effective VisualAge for Java book samples</description>
  <document-root>F:/EffectiveVAJ/Chapter24/web</document-root>
  <classpath>F:/EffectiveVAJ/Chapter24/servlets</classpath>
  <root-uri>/vajbook</root-uri>
  <auto-reload enabled="true" polling-interval="3000"/>
  <shared-context>false</shared-context>
</websphere-webgroup>
```

You need to place the vajbook.webapp file in F:/EffectiveVAJ/Chapter24/servlets. Be careful when using the $approot$ variable: If you start the servlet engine class by using ServletEngine, the $approot$ variable is equivalent to $server-root$/hosts/ <virtual-host name>/<webapp-name>. In other words, if you leave the class path as $approot$/web, the class-path value is X:/IBMVJava/ide/project_resources/ IBMWebSphere test environment/Host for VisualAge for Java WebSphere Unit Test Environment/vajbook.

You can fix this by renaming the virtual host to default_host, which is the default name of the WebSphere virtual host. You can also hardcode a path as we did in the previous example. The advantage of the second alternative is that you can keep the same default.servlet_engine file, should you start the WebSphere Test Environment by using SERunner or ServletEngine. Otherwise, you would have to rename the virtual host to *Host for VisualAge for Java WebSphere Unit Test Environment* each time you want to use SERunner (SERunner will not start if the virtual host is named differently).

> **NOTE**
>
> This behavior is the default behavior implemented in VisualAge for Java, version 3.5.

Summary

In this chapter, we covered how to create an application based on servlets, JSP components, and enterprise beans, and to test inside the VisualAge for Java IDE. We also covered how you can configure the WebSphere Test Environment to match the code organization and naming used in the WebSphere Application Server. In the next chapter, we cover how to integrate your own tools in the VisualAge for Java IDE.

25 TOOL INTEGRATION

In version 2.0 of VisualAge for Java, IBM added a tool integration API. This API enables you to write Java code that controls VisualAge for Java, export and import code, generate new methods, delete others, version and display code. While the Tool API is not yet complete, the current implementation can provide hours of good clean fun and save you quite a bit of work while you develop other applications.

This chapter covers two types of extension in VisualAge for Java. The more complex of these is the Tool API, a set of classes and interfaces that enable you to control VisualAge for Java programmatically, so we will discuss that last. The simpler, feature integration, enables you to distribute applications and libraries with an easy setup inside VisualAge for Java. Using features and tool integration, you can provide greater functionality inside VisualAge for Java and distribute that functionality to coworkers and friends.

> **WARNING**
>
> You should be familiar with team programming and repository concepts before attempting to write any tool. Even if you use the Professional Edition of VisualAge for Java, other people could use your tool in the Enterprise Edition, and the tool needs to handle it properly. For example, your tool may need to create open editions of projects or packages, but the user may not have authority to do so.

Features

Simply put, *features* are repository export files with a nice installation description. You can export any projects to a repository file, describe where any contained beans should be placed in the beans palette, and zip it up. You deliver it to a friend who unzips it, starts VisualAge for Java, and asks to install the feature. Poof! The project appears in his workspace, and the beans appear in the palette.

Feature bundling is an easy and convenient way to distribute your applications to other users. It is a nice touch, making it easier for other users to install your library of beans.

Creating Features

Creating features is very simple. In Chapter 6, "Integrating with the File System," you learned how to export code as a repository. You will use this skill to create much of the feature package. As an example, we will look at the Box Beans feature. We developed the classes for the Box Beans in project "JavaDude Box Beans" (under domain name javadude.com) and placed the resource files in the appropriate project resources directory.

When developing beans to be used in a feature, it is very important to provide useful information, such as descriptions of properties and icons in the BeanInfo for the beans, as well as icons for the beans. (The icons are 16x16 or 32x32 GIFs.) You should also provide adequate documentation on the feature, usually in the form of javadoc comments. We will walk through the steps necessary to create the feature bundle, assuming the code, BeanInfo, and documentation comments are in place.

Step 1: Export the Projects

The first thing you need to do is export the projects that you require for this feature to a repository file. These projects should be ones that are unique to *this feature*; if you have a common project that several features require, you should treat that common project as a separate feature, listing it as a prerequisite for this feature. We will discuss how to do that later.

> **NOTE**
> In order to export to a repository file, the project *must* be versioned.

The feature will exist in a special directory in the VisualAge for Java installation. IBM calls this directory the feature's *base* directory, naming it *installDirectory*\ide\features\<*feature-name*>

The <*feature-name*> part of the directory must be unique, so a good choice is to use the name of one of the packages in the feature and replace dots with dashes. For this example, we called the main package com.javadude.boxbeans, so the feature base directory is *installDirectory*\ide\features\com-javadude-boxbeans.

> **NOTE**
>
> If you are using VisualAge for Java, version 3.0, the default installation directory is *c:\IBMVJava*. If you are using VisualAge for Java, version 3.5, the default installation directory is *c:\Program Files\IBM\VisualAge for Java*. Whenever we mention *installDirectory* in this chapter, it refers to this installation directory. If you have chosen a different directory for installation, use that directory instead.

You must export the required projects to a file named projects.dat in the feature's base directory. You cannot use any other name, or VisualAge will ignore your feature. For this example, we export project JavaDude Box Beans to repository file *installDirectory*\ide\features\com-javadude-boxbeans\projects.dat. You can have only a single version of any project in this repository file. Be careful; you should delete the file before performing another export to it.

> **WARNING**
>
> If you uninstall VisualAge for Java and delete the product directory, your feature bundle will be gone. We *strongly* recommend that you keep a zip of each feature outside of the VisualAge for Java installation directory so you can easily add the feature to a new installation of the product. Otherwise, you will need to recreate the feature bundle.

Step 2: Copy the Project Resources

Next, ensure that all the resources required by the feature are present by copying the appropriate project_resources directories to the right directory. For this example, create a new directory called project_resources under the base directory and then copy the resource directories for each project to it. We created directory *installDirectory*\ide\features\com-javadude-boxbeans\project_resources and copied *installDirectory*\ide\project_resources\JavaDude Box Beans into that directory. Note that you should copy the entire directory, not its contents. The result is directory *installDirectory*\ide\features\com-javadude-boxbeans\project_resources\JavaDude Box Beans and its contents.

You must copy each of the project resource directories to the feature's project resources directory. When you add the feature to your workspace, VisualAge copies the contents of these directories into the corresponding project resource directories. Make sure these directories contain the proper resources (and that those resources are current) under the feature, or you may lose changes to your resource files.

Step 3: Create Help HTML

Next, you need to create HTML help files for your feature. These help files can provide important information to users of your feature. The user can access these from the Help menu in the IDE.

The easiest way to create help files is to run javadoc on the projects, specifying <*feature base*>/doc as the target directory. After generating the HTML, you should copy the *installDirectory*\ide\javadoc\images directory into your <*feature base*>/doc directory.

If you do not have appropriate javadoc comments, or you have better documentation available separately, you can simply add your HTML documentation to the <*feature base*>/doc directory.

> **NOTE**
>
> Features do not *require* help pages, but we strongly recommend them to help the folks who use your bundled beans. You were nice enough to bundle them; you might as well go the extra step to document them. In addition, you can put the HTML into any directory under the feature base directory. Just use that directory when specifying the help page location.

As of the general release of Version 3.0, VisualAge for Java does not list the help page for features. We have reported this bug to IBM and they are working on it. We recommend that you do provide the help pages, as a patch may correct the problem. Just make sure you tell your users where they can find the documentation (in the feature base directory). See Appendix E, "Additional Resources," for information on where you can obtain patches for VisualAge for Java.

Step 4: Create the Control File

Each feature must have a control file. The control file describes the feature and how to install it in VisualAge for Java. You should name this file default.ini and place it *directly* in the feature base directory.

> **NOTE**
>
> See *Internationalization and Features/Tools* at the end of this chapter for information on when you would name this file differently.

The file has the following format. The order in which these entries appear is not important.

```
Name=feature name
Version=version id string
Help-Item=menu text,HTML file name
Palette-Items=category1,class1,class2,...,classN ;
category2,class1,...
Prereq-Features=base dir1,base dir2,...
```

Name. A unique name for the feature. Note that it is very important that you make this name as unique as possible. As more and more people provide features, distinguishing them will become more difficult. Do *not* use feature names like "Buttons"; rather, use names like "JavaDude's Fancy Image Buttons." This name does not need to be related to any of the project or package names contained within it.

Version. A version string that helps you identify the *release* number of the feature. This version is independent of the versions of any of the contained projects or packages.

Help-Item. An optional entry that provides help for how to use your feature. The specified help text appears in the Help menu. This feature does not currently work in versions 2.0 or 3.0.

Palette-Items. An optional list of the beans inside the feature that VisualAge should add to the beans palette. You can specify to which category to add the beans, followed by the fully qualified class names of the beans to add. Make sure that the beans you add specify icons, and that those icons reside in the appropriate project resources directory in step 2. These icons appear at the bottom of the palette, preceded by a separator. If you specify a dash ("-") as a palette item, it creates a separator in the palette.

Prereq-Features. An optional entry that automatically adds other required features. VisualAge makes sure it adds this feature last if possible. Note that prerequisites do not affect unloading features from the workspace. If you delete a feature, you will need to delete prerequisites by hand if you want them removed as well.

VisualAge for Java requires only the name and version lines. For this example, the control file looks as follows:

```
Name=Box Beans
Version=1.2.2
Help-Item=Box Beans,doc/packages.html
Palette-Items=AWT,com.javadude.boxbeans.BoxAdapter,          \
                 com.javadude.boxbeans.HorizontalStrut,   \
                 com.javadude.boxbeans.VerticalStrut,     \
                 -,                                       \
                 com.javadude.boxbeans.HorizontalGlue,    \
```

```
            com.javadude.boxbeans.VerticalGlue;        \
        Swing,com.javadude.boxbeans.BoxAdapter,         \
              com.javadude.boxbeans.HorizontalStrut,   \
              com.javadude.boxbeans.VerticalStrut,     \
              -,                                        \
              com.javadude.boxbeans.HorizontalGlue,    \
              com.javadude.boxbeans.VerticalGlue
```

The Palette-Items entries must either all appear on a single line or be followed by backslash characters as in this control file. Note the grouping of the palette items. In this example, we add the same four beans to the AWT and Swing palettes in order to allow the user to easily use them from either palette page.

Step 5: Delete the Projects from Your Workspace

Delete the feature projects from your workspace, as described in Chapter 2 "Creating Code". This enables you to truly test the feature and see if it properly modifies the palette. If you do not delete the projects from your workspace, VisualAge for Java does not allow you to add the features (as it already exists in the workspace).

Step 6: Shut Down and Restart VisualAge for Java

At this point, you must shut down and restart VisualAge for Java. This is necessary because VisualAge checks for new features only when it starts. Note that you should see a small dialog stating that VisualAge is installing your new feature as it starts up again. This does not mean that it added the feature to your workspace. It simply means the feature is available for inclusion.

VisualAge for Java now knows about the new feature, so we're ready to add it to the workspace.

Step 7: Add the Feature

There are two ways to add the feature to the VisualAge for Java workspace. You can use the Quick Start menu, available from the File menu or by pressing F2; or you can choose the Available page of the beans palette. If you opt to use the Quick Start menu, select Add Feature from the Features category. Selecting Add Feature from Quick Start or Available from the beans palette presents a list of features that exist in the *installDirectory*\ide\features directory that you can add. Any features that you have already added do not appear in the list.

For this example, select "Box Beans 1.2.2" from the list. VisualAge adds the appropriate projects to your workspace, adds the beans to the palette, and adds any prerequisite features.

Step 8: I Say "Zip it! Zip it Good!"

Finally, you should zip the feature base directory so you can keep a safe copy of it and distribute it to other users. Some people like to zip just the base directory, and instruct users to unzip it into *installDirectory*\ide\features. Others like to make a copy of the entire directory structure in the zip file (just the paths leading to the features directory, not their contents) and instruct the users to unzip it to their C:\ drive.

Both methods are acceptable, just be sure to tell the user exactly what to do. Make sure that the entire directory is in the zip, including the projects.dat, default.ini, help files, and any resources the feature requires.

> **NOTE**
>
> If you plan for others to use your beans in other environments, you must provide alternate packaging. We recommend that you package the beans in a JAR file for usage in other IDEs.

Updating Existing Features

Whenever you want to update an existing feature, copy the code for the feature into the feature's base directory, *and modify the feature's control file.* VisualAge for Java will only re-load existing features if the control file's modification time actually changes. Once you have perfomed the updates, shutdown and restart VisualAge for Java to pick up the changes.

Tool Integration

Features are the simplest form of VisualAge for Java code integration. While they provide additional beans that you can use when designing new applications, they cannot *control* the IDE or modify your code. To provide this control, VisualAge for Java includes a Tool API that gives your Java code a good deal of control.

Using the Tool API, you can version, export, import, execute, delete, and generate code. You can also add objects to the workspace and ask the user to select which objects to work with. The interface is flexible but not complete. While it exposes a great deal of control, there are still several missing functions, like being able to modify the visual design of an application. Nonetheless, the Tool API is quite powerful, and you can create some very interesting plug-ins for VisualAge for Java without much effort.

Let's start by explaining how you create, use, and install tools. Pretend for a moment that you have already written a tool, and just need to set it up. After that, we explain how to perform several tasks in your code.

Developing Tools

Tool distribution is very similar to feature distribution. Each tool has a *base directory*, which contains the code for the tool, resources, and a control file. The biggest difference is that instead of providing a repository file, you export the code to a directory. You cannot use a JAR file or repository here.

This example uses the AutoGut tool. AutoGut is a simple tool that creates an interface by gutting an existing class. It essentially copies the method declarations, and guts the method bodies (hence the name of the tool). Suppose that AutoGut exists in the workspace as project JavaDude AutoGut. The steps for setting up a tool are similar to those used to create a feature.

Step 1: Add the Tool API Feature

To run tools inside VisualAge for Java, you must add the Tool API feature to the workspace by selecting **File->Quick Start** (or pressing F2) to see the Quick-Start dialog. Then select **Features**, in the left pane, and **Add Feature**, in the right pane. After you press Enter, you will see a list of available features, including the Tool API (unless you have already installed it). The Tool API feature appears as **IBM IDE Utility class libraries** in this list.

This will add the tool libraries to your workspace. You need these to develop tools in the IDE. Note that you do *not* need to have these libraries in your workspace to execute tools from the menus or Quick Start dialog.

> **NOTE**
>
> The end user does *not* need the Tool API in your workspace to *run* your tool. You only need the Tool API in your workspace when you are *developing* the tool.

Step 2: Write the Tool Code

Once you have the tool API in your workspace, you can develop code for your tool. See *Writing a Tool* later in this chapter for details.

Step 3: Export the Code

Next, you need to export your code to a directory for use as a VisualAge for Java tool. Perform a *directory* export of the class files for your tool code, as well as any necessary resource files. (Exporting is covered in Chapter 6.) You can export the source code if you like, but it is not required. The code must reside in a tool-specific base directory in *installDirectory*\ide\tools*<tool base>*. We use the same convention for tool base-directory names as we did for features: Pick a package in the feature and replace its dots with dashes. For this example, the directory looks like *installDirectory*\ide\tools\com-javadude-vaj-autogut. Use this base directory as the target of the export. VisualAge for Java will create the appropriate subdirectories under it.

Step 4: Copy Resources and Help

Copy the resource and help files into the tool's base directory as you would for a feature. The only difference here is that the tool help link actually works. When the user loads a tool into VisualAge for Java, a Tools menu is placed in the Help menu. Each tool has an entry in this menu, which displays the tool's help page.

Step 5: Create the Control File

The tool's control file is similar to that of a feature, but it contains a bit more information. Like a feature's control file, you must name the file default.ini and place it in the tool's base directory.

> **NOTE**
>
> See *Internationalization and Features/Tools* at the end of this chapter for information on when you would name this file differently.

The file has the following format. The order in which these entries appear is not important.

```
Name=feature name
Version=version id string
Help-Item=menu text,HTML file name
Menu-Group=menu group name
Menu-Items=menu item text,class,context; menu item text, ...
Action-Items=menu op name,class,context; menu op name, ...
Quick-Start-Group=quick start category
Quick-Start-Items=quick start text,app class; quick start text, ...
```

Name. A unique name for the tool. Note that it is very important that you make this name as unique as possible. As more and more people provide tools, distinguishing them will become more difficult. This name does not need to be related to any of the project or package names contained within it.

Version. A version string that helps you identify the release number of the tool. This version is independent of the versions of any of the contained projects or packages.

Help-Item. An optional entry that provides help on how to use your tool. The specified help text appears in the Help->Tools menu. If the user selects the tool option, the tool help page appears in the registered web browser.

Menu-Group. An optional name of a submenu to add to the Tools menu of projects, packages, classes, or the **Workspace->Tools** menu. If you have more than one menu item, you should define a menu group for your tool. The menu group appears only in the contexts specified by the menu items (see the next section for details on the contexts). If specified, all menu items appear in this menu group. If not specified, menu items appear directly in the Tools menus.

Menu-Items. Optional items that are added to the **Tools** menus of projects, packages, classes, or the main Workspace menu. Each item has three parts: a name that VisualAge displays in the menu, the name of the main tool class to execute when the user selects that name, and the context in which the command appears. If you specify a Menu-Group entry for the tool, the menu items appear underneath that Menu-Group in the appropriate **Tools** menu.

NOTE

If you want separators between menu items, use a hyphen (-) as the menu name and class to execute.

Action-Items. An optional list of tool classes to run when the user selects Open for various types of resource files. Resource files appear only in the Resources page of project browsers, and you can provide your own editors and viewers for resource files using these options. The context entries for these items specify which types of resource files the tool classes affect. The context can be -R. ("dash –R –dot"), running the tool application for resource files without a suffix (ones that do not contain a dot in their name), or -R.*suffix*, which affects only the resources ending with the specified suffix.

Quick-Start-Group. By specifying an optional Quick-Start-Group and Quick-Start-Items, the user can run your tool from the Quick Start dialog. The Quick-Start-Group specifies the group name that appears in the left side of the Quick Start dialog. You must provide *both* Quick-Start-Group and Quick-Start-Items if you want your tool to appear in the Quick Start dialog.

Quick-Start-Items. An optional list of the items that should appear in the specified Quick-Start-Group in the Quick Start dialog. Note that you do not specify a context for these items.

VisualAge for Java requires only the name and version of the tool, but you must specify locations in which to run the tool to make it useful.

> **NOTE**
> Your tool can run from any or all of these locations, and you can use different classes for different contexts if you like.

Tool Contexts

Users can run your tool under many contexts. A context is the set of projects, packages, or classes that users have selected when they execute the tool. Tools can only be run on a single type of program element at any given time. For example, you could run a tool against several classes at once, or several projects at once, but not on both projects and classes at the same time. Depending on the context options you specify in your control file, the tool may or may not be available from the Tools menus of projects, packages, classes, the Workspace menu, or the Quick Start dialog.

When you specify a Menu-Items entry, you list the name of the menu entry, the application class, and the context in which it runs. The context can be one of the following:

-c The menu item appears on the **Tools** menu for selected classes.

-p The menu item appears on the **Tools** menu for selected packages. This is a *lower-case* p.

-P The menu item appears on the **Tools** menu for selected projects. This is an *upper-case* P.

-R.*ext* The menu item appears on the **Tools** menu for selected resource files that have the specified extension.

-R.* The menu item appears on the **Tools** menu for resource files that have *any* extension, or no extension at all.

-R. The menu item appears on the **Tools** menu for selected resources that have no file extension.

-R/ The menu item appears only on the **Tools** menu for resource directories.

-R The menu item appears on the **Tools** menu for any resource file or directory.

(nothing) If you leave the context blank, the tool appears on the **Workspace->Tools** submenu in all browsers.

If you want the tool to appear in more than one context, you must repeat the Menu-Items specification for each context. Note that there is still only a single Menu-Items line in the control file, just multiple tool specifications.

When your tool runs, VisualAge for Java passes context information as parameters to the main() method of the specified class. The first parameter is the context indicator, -c, -p, or -P. The rest of the parameters are the names of the selected classes, packages, or projects. The tool can run only in one of these contexts. If the user runs the tool from the **Workspace->Tools** menu or from the Quick Start dialog, VisualAge passes it no parameters. Make sure your tool checks in which context it runs by looking for its first argument.

If your tool runs against a resource file, you can add Action-Items entries for it as well as Menu-Items. If you specify Action-Items entries, these actions replace the behavior of the Open command for the resource file. When a tool is run for a resource, VisualAge passes **-R** as the first argument, followed by *pairs* of strings (project name followed by resource file name).

> **NOTE**
>
> Your tool must handle *all* of the listed objects passed to it. VisualAge for Java does not invoke your tool separately for each selected object.

Some examples of Menu-Items lines follow.

```
Menu-Items=Explode,com.foo.Exploder,;Explode,com.foo.Exploder,-c
```

This specification provides a **Workspace->Tools->Explode** item in the menu bar and a **Tools->Explode** item in a class' pop-up menu. Both items run the same class, though the parameters passed to the main() method will differ.

```
Menu-Group=External Fun
Menu-Items=Configure,com.foo.SetUp,;      \
            Configure,com.foo.Setup,-c;    \
            Run in JDK,com.foo.Runner,-c; \
            Configure,com.foo.Setup,-P;    \
            Add to ClassPath JDK,com.foo.ClassPathSetter,-P
```

This specification creates the following options:

- **Tools->External Fun->Run in JDK** for classes, running com.foo.Runner.
- **Tools-> External Fun->Configure** for classes, running com.foo.Setup.
- **Tools-> External Fun->Add to ClassPath** for projects, running com.foo.ClassPathSetter.
- **Tools-> External Fun->Configure** for projects, running com.foo.Setup.

- **Workspace->Tools-> External Fun->Configure,** running com.foo.Setup.

It will often be necessary to repeat information to make the tool available in multiple contexts.

Sample Control Files

The control file from the AutoGut tool is a good example of a general control file:

```
Name=AutoGut
Version=1.0
Quick-Start-Group=Scott Stanchfield's Tools
Quick-Start-Items=Create an interface based on a class
Help-Item=Create an interface based on a class,doc/index.html
Menu-Items=\
  Create interface from a class,          \
      com.javadude.vaj.autogut.AutoGut,;     \
  Create interface from these classes,      \
      com.javadude.vaj.autogut.AutoGut,-c
```

In this control file, the text for the menu and quick-start items does not simply list the name of the tool (AutoGut). Instead, the item names describe the *action* that the user is taking. This makes it easier for the user to determine the available options without needing to know the tool names. Note the subtle difference between the text for the workspace-level tool execution and that for running with a class. For a class, we say "Create interface from these classes"; from the workspace, we say "Create interface from a class." Try to be descriptive, using words like "these" or "a" to help the user determine if the selected object is involved.

Suppose that you wrote a tool that opens a graphics editor on various graphical resource files. Its control file might look as follows. This control file contains actions that act on resource files such as images. Resource files use the Action-Items specification to describe how to run a tool, rather than a Menu-Items specification as previously seen in the AutoGut tool control file.

```
Name=Graphic Editor
Version=1.0
Quick-Start-Group=Resource File Tools
Quick-Start-Items=Edit Graphical Resources
Menu-Items=\
  Edit this JPG,com.foo.GraphicsEditor,-R.JPG;\
  Edit this GIF,com.foo.GraphicsEditor,-R.GIF;\
  Edit all JPG & GIFs in this dir,com.foo.GraphicsEditor,-R/;\
  Give this file a suffix,com.foo.SuffixGiver,-R.
Action-Items=\
  OPEN, com.foo.GraphicsEditor,-R.JPG;\
  OPEN, com.foo.GraphicsEditor,-R.GIF;\
  OPEN, com.foo.GraphicsEditor,-R./
```

The menu and actions are available only from the resources panel of the project browser.

Step 6: Shut Down and Restart VisualAge for Java

To finish the tool installation, you must shut down and restart VisualAge for Java. Note that we do *not* need to delete the tool project from the workspace. Tools are executed from their base directory and are never brought into the workspace unless you explicitly import them.

Step 7: Run It!

Next, run the tool by selecting it from the appropriate contexts. Normally, this will be from the **Tools** menu of a selected class, package, or project, but you could also have placed it in the **Workspace->Tools** menu or in the Quick Start dialog. Your tool may perform different functions based on its execution context.

Step 8: When a New Tool Comes Along, You Must Zip It!

Once again, we *strongly* recommend that you zip the tool directory and store it safely. This allows you an easy way to reinstall the tool on other machines or if you uninstall and reinstall VisualAge for Java.

Updating Existing Tools

Whenever you want to update an existing tool, copy the code for the tool into the tool's base directory, *and modify the tool's control file.* VisualAge for Java will only re-load existing tools if the control file's modification time actually changes. Once you have perfomed the updates, shutdown and restart VisualAge for Java to pick up the changes.

VCE Tool Setup

Sometimes it is useful to run a tool inside a property editor or customizer. For example, you may want to obtain a list of all classes that implement a specific interface, or allow the user to select a class using VisualAge's class selection dialog. Using VisualAge's Tool API inside a property editor or customizer provides a huge advantage to your beans' users, because they won't need to type class or package names, and your customizer could even add new methods to the class!

To use the Tool API in a property editor or customizer, you need to know two things.

- The tool code can reside directly in the property editor or as a separate class in the workspace. You do not place these types of tools in the external tools directory. This also means you do not need a control file for this type of use.

> **WARNING**
>
> If you access the Tool API inside your property editor or customizer, your property editor or customizer will run properly only inside VisualAge for Java. Other IDEs do not support this API. To take advantage of these extensions, we recommend that you have your property editor or customizer check to see if running under VisualAge for Java before using these extensions. If not, you should provide an alternate way to process input if you want a portable bean. We discuss how to perform this check later.

- You must add the Tool API libraries to your design-time class path. VisualAge for Java needs to know where to find the Tool API libraries, or you'll get ClassNotFoundExceptions when you try to run the tool.

To make your Tool API calls work in the VCE, you must add the following directories to your design-time class path:

```
installDirectory\ide\project_resources\IBM IDE Utility class
libraries\
installDirectory\ide\project_resources\IBM IDE Utility local
implementation\
```

You can modify the design-time CLASSPATH setting by choosing Window ->Options to access the options dialog and then choosing the Visual Composition page. You can click the Edit button to add these directories. We recommend you click Add Directory to choose these. They will appear as relative names in the displayed design-time CLASSPATH specification.

Testing and Execution

If you want to test your tool inside VisualAge without exporting and creating the control file, you can do so, but you must make sure the Tool API libraries are available. You can either add the two project directories mentioned above to the workspace class path (available via **Window->Options->Resources**), or add the IBM IDE Utility class libraries project to the tool application's class path. We recommend you set up the workspace class path, because it makes testing several tools much easier.

You can then test your tool by running its application class. You can pass different parameters to it by setting the arguments in the Program page of the class' Properties dialog. Make sure the first argument is the context (-c, -p, -P, or -R) followed by the names of the objects.

We recommend that you *first* try your tool in the proper place and try to run it inside VisualAge only if you need to debug it. Getting the command-line arguments correct can be tricky.

Writing a Tool

Now we come to the fun part, at least the fun part for *this* author to type: the Tool API. In this section, we describe the process and considerations for writing tool code.

The current Tool API documentation provided with the product is rather light. The product provides good concept descriptions of tool integration, but it can be difficult to really determine how to use all of those methods. We describe most of the API in this section, providing you the knowledge to write some nifty tools of your own.

> **NOTE**
>
> The CD-ROM that accompanies this book contains several VisualAge for Java tools. Some of the tools describe their tool design in their documentation, and most provide source code for you to examine. See Appendix D, "The CD-ROM," for details on these tools.

First, a little note on mucking with other people's code...

Version Considerations

The VisualAge for Java Tool API enables you to create, delete, and modify a user's code. You should not take this power lightly. Yes, VisualAge *does* automatically version methods for you, but in general, you should try to make "undoing" code changes easy for your user.

We recommend that you work only on versioned code. You can do this in three ways. For all three methods, begin by checking to see if the type has been versioned (using the isVersion() method). If not, the user has versioned it, and you can simply continue. Otherwise, choose one of the following ways to deal with the open edition.

Refuse to process the code and exit. This is the easiest way to handle the situation, but the least user-friendly. In general, people don't like to run tools that say, "You need to version first! Try again later!" Users prefer to have the tool ask, "Would you like me to version this for you?" Many existing tools, including functions like the Fix/Migrate command (found on the Reorganize menu) perform their processing this way.

Version it before proceeding. The problem with this approach is that the user has no input for the version name. We do *not* recommend this approach.

Ask the user what they want to do. Always the best option, though it involves more work. The main problem is that the user may not have the authority to version an object if they are using the Enterprise Edition of VisualAge for Java. This is the ideal handling of the problem, but you need to be very careful in your implementation.

No matter how you handle open editions, you must deal with cases where the containing object is *not* an open edition. If you want to edit a class, the containing package must be either a scratch edition or an open edition. If it is versioned, you should ask the user what they want to do. In general, you should *not* simply try to create an open edition of the package or project in question. Many times the user will not be the owner of the containing object and cannot create that open edition.

Finally, be aware that enterprise users have additional constraints. This is the toughest thing to do when creating a tool. The biggest problems this can cause are creating open editions of containing objects, and versioning a package or project that contains unreleased objects. Keep in mind that a user may *not* have authority to create an open edition or release an object. Write your tool's error handling accordingly.

The Tool API Packages

IBM provides the Tool API in two packages.

com.ibm.ivj.util.base The main Tool API; provides all non-code manipulation.

com.ibm.ivj.util.builders The builder API; provides code generation, deletion, and modification.

You should normally include these two packages in your tool class, as follows:

```
import com.ibm.ivj.util.base.*;
import com.ibm.ivj.util.builders.*;
```

> **NOTE**
>
> Package com.ibm.ivj.util.builders contains interfaces BuilderFactory, TypeBuilder, and MethodBuilder. All other classes mentioned in this chapter are in package com.ibm.ivj.util.base. You need to import com.ibm.ivj.util.builders only if you are writing a tool that modifies or generates code.

Are We Running in VisualAge for Java?

The first thing you need to check is if you are running inside VisualAge for Java. Because the Tool API runs your class' main() method, the class *could* be run on its own outside of VisualAge for Java. It would be nice to exit gracefully in cases like this.

The Tool API provides a method that tells you whether you are running inside VisualAge for Java. Static method ToolEnv.hostedByVAJava() returns true when running in VisualAge for Java, false otherwise. The problem with using this method is that it assumes the presence of the Tool API libraries. A better method of determining where you are running is to use the following code.

```
boolean inVisualAge = false;
try {
  Class.forName("com.ibm.ivj.util.base.ToolEnv");
  inVisualAge = ToolEnv.hostedByVAJava();
}
catch (ClassNotFoundException ignoreMe) {}
```

This method ensures that you do not try to use classes that do not exist. However, if your class includes references to the Tool API (instance variables, for example), the JVM cannot load it. If you intend to write a tool that works with or without VisualAge for Java, you must separate the VisualAge parts. We recommend you write an interface that describes actions to take, and if using VisualAge, plug in a class that uses the Tool API and implement that interface. If not using VisualAge for Java, plug in a class that does not use VisualAge for Java.

A Simple Example

For example, suppose that you were writing a property editor that needed to ask the user for a class name. Using the Tool API, you could prompt the user to choose the class name from a list. This is great, because VisualAge for Java provides you extra information that can help the user select an appropriate response. If you are running in some other environment, you would need to ask the user to type the name, because we don't know what classes are available. You can implement this as follows:

```
public interface Helper {
  public String askUserForClassName();
}


public class VisualAgeHelper implements Helper {
  public String askUserForClassName() {
    //  use Tool API to prompt the user for a class
    //     and return its name
  }
}
```

```
public class NonVisualAgeHelper implements Helper {
  public String askUserForClassName() {
    //  display a simple dialog asking user to type
    //    class name and return that class name
  }
}

public class MyPropertyEditor ... {
  private Helper helper;
  public MyPropertyEditor() {
    try {
      Class.forName("com.ibm.ivj.util.base.ToolEnv");
      helper = new VisualAgeHelper();
    }
    catch (ClassNotFoundException ignoreMe) {
      helper = new NonVisualAgeHelper();
    }
  }

  // in some method where needed...
    String name = helper.askUserForClassName();
}
```

Using a scheme like this enables you to provide the added benefit of the Tool API function when using VisualAge for Java, but the scheme still enables the property editor in other IDEs

Interfaces Everywhere!

Throughout the rest of this section, you will see that nearly all of the Tool API types are interfaces. Why? Because that is all you should care about! All you need to know is *what* features the Tool API provides. VisualAge for Java hides the implementation details, returning an instance of some class that implements a requested interface by using a *factory method*. This allows IBM to change the implementation of the Tool API at any time, as long as the interface remains compatible. They can add new methods to the interfaces but not remove them if they want to preserve existing tools. However, they can change how the tool performs its job quite easily, even using native methods where necessary.

Connecting to the Workspace

After you confirm that you are running inside VisualAge for Java, you need to connect to the workspace in order to use the Tool API. The Tool API provides a bootstrapping class called ToolEnv, which acts as a starting point by providing a factory method to obtain access to the workspace. You write code such as the following to grab a handle to the workspace:

```
Workspace workspace = ToolEnv.connectToWorkspace();
```

You place this code inside your tool class and then access the rest of the tool API through that workspace reference.

> **NOTE**
>
> We omitted most exception handling from the examples for clarity. You will normally have to catch IvjException or one of its subclasses.

Workspace is an interface that describes how you can interact with VisualAge for Java. You access all other Tool API features from the returned Workspace-implementing instance.

Once you have a connection to the workspace, we recommend you access the workspace log. If you want to write messages about the status of your tool, you should write them to the log, *not* to System.out or System.err. The simplest way to write messages to the log is to use the logMessage() method of Workspace:

```
workspace.logMessage("This is a message\n", true);
```

The logMessage() method writes a String to the log; you must provide newline escape sequences where you want them. The second parameter specifies whether you want to raise the log window in front of all other windows.

If you want more control over the output, or you need to pass an OutputStream to one of your methods for output, you can grab the log by executing the following code:

```
WorkspaceLog log = new WorkspaceLog(workspace);
```

WorkspaceLog is a subclass of java.io.OutputStream, which means you can use it wherever you would need an OutputStream. Note that output written to the log may not appear unless your call its flush() method.

> **NOTE**
>
> It is a good idea to write a new-line ("\n") sequence to the log before writing any other messages, because the previous tool may not have written one.

Are We Running Team Version Control?

One of the most difficult tasks when writing a tool is handling version control issues. The difficulty compounds when running in team mode. If you ever need to determine if VisualAge is running in team mode, use the following code:

```
if (workspace.isTeamMode()) {
  // we are running in team version mode!
}
```

Team mode can greatly affect versioning issues like whether or not you can version a project, package, or class, and if you can create open editions. Be aware that users of your tool may be running the Enterprise Edition of VisualAge for Java.

Workspace and Repository Contents

Now we get to the meat of the Tool API. We can use the API to inspect the repository and workspace, in order to find available types, packages, and projects. This section should familiarize you with the available API, but it does not provide the full details of which parameters each method takes. Please see the online help under "Reference" for the IBM Tool API class javadoc documentation. We discuss the Workspace interface methods in each section that they manage.

Workspace and Repository Models

VisualAge for Java represents types, packages, and projects as *model objects* in the Tool API. The Model interface defines the identification of a type, package, or project. This identifying information includes the name of the program element, its version, and owner. You can examine this identification information by using the following methods in any Model implementation. (We will see the specific models in a moment.)

Each program element in the repository or workspace is represented by a model. The specific types of models (Project, Package, Type, and so on) all extend the Model interface and thus inherit the common functionality provided by it.

getName() Perhaps the most important method in all models. This method allows you to see the name of the type, package, or project. Default packages use the name you see for them in the workspace, similar to "Default package for My Funky Project."

getOwnerName() Returns the name of the owner of the model. This is useful if you are running the Tool API with Enterprise Edition Team Support.

getVersionName() Returns the name of this version of the model. If the model is an open edition, this returns null.

getVersionStamp() Returns a timestamp that represents when this model was versioned or when the open edition was created.

isEdition() Returns true if this model is an open edition. If the model is versioned or a scratch edition, this method returns false.

isPackage(), isProject(), isType() These methods return true or false to tell you the model type.

isVersion() Returns true if this model has been versioned. Be careful with this method! If you have deleted a package and a project references it, and you try to call isVersion() on that package version, you will get an IvjUnresolvedException. Watch for this when using this method.

The Model interface is extended by two more interfaces:

WorkspaceModel. Represents a project, package or type that is loaded into the user's workspace.

RepositoryModel. Represents an edition of a project, package, or type in the repository.

You can use all of the Model methods from any *WorkspaceModel* or *RepositoryModel.*

WorkspaceModel

WorkspaceModel represents your view of a type, package, or project that is in your workspace. It provides extra methods to create open editions of a model, version an open edition, and allow you to save some extra data, such as the last settings the user used when running a tool against a type, that the tool can access later. We will discuss this extra data later in this chapter in *Storing Tool Options.*

WorkspaceModels provide the following additional methods. There are additional tool data methods, but we will omit them for now, because we will discuss them later in *Storing Tool Options.*

createNewEdition() Creates a new open edition of this model.

createVersion(String versionString) Versions this model, using the passed-in String as the new version name.

delete() Removes the model from the workspace. Remember, removing something from the workspace does *not* delete it from the repository.

Each of the subinterfaces of WorkspaceModel (Project, Package, Type) provides the methods you need to interact with those types. WorkspaceModel and Model merely provide the identification and versioning methods.

RepositoryModel

As a subinterface of Model, RepositoryModel has the same identifying information available. RepositoryModel represents a specific model *version* in the repository.

Thus, a class represented by a single WorkspaceModel in your workspace might have several RepositoryModels representing it in the repository. Your workspace can contain only a single version of any object, while the repository stores them all.

RepositoryModel adds a single method, **isLoaded()**, which allows you to check if a specific version of a model exists in the user's workspace.

Each of the subinterfaces of RepositoryModel (ProjectEdition, PackageEdition, TypeEdition) provides the methods you will need to use to interact with the models.

The Workspace Interface

So far, we have connected to the workspace but done little else. The returned Workspace object is your main handle into the Tool API. Its primary use is a handle to the loaded types, packages, and projects, as well as keeping track of which repository you use. Workspace tracks the loaded types as WorkspaceModel objects. Throughout this section we will frequently come back to Workspace, so do not forget about it.

The Repository Interface

The Repository interface describes the repository manager. You can access the repository from the Workspace object with the following code. You would type this code in your tool anytime you need to examine the repository's contents.

```
Repository repository = workspace.getRepository();
```

Other versions of getRepository() take a String or two to access alternative repositories, either on the local machine or through a team server. Most often, however, you will use the current repository to which the workspace is connected.

The Repository interface contains methods getName() to identify the name of the repository, and isCurrentRepository(), which returns true if the returned Repository object represents the current repository.

The returned Repository object also contains methods to access the contained ProjectEdition and PackageEdition objects. We will see more on this in a moment.

> **WARNING**
>
> The Repository interface also contains a compact() method. This method attempts to compact the repository. Use extreme care with this method, if you use it at all! You can use compact(String reposName) to specify a target directory for the compaction. See Chapter 4, "Using Version Control," for details on what a repository compact does.

Working with Projects

A VisualAge for Java project is essentially a collection of packages. As such, the interfaces you use allow you to access those packages. There are two flavors of projects in the Tool API: Project and ProjectEdition.

Project

Project is an interface that describes a version of a project that has been loaded into the workspace. You can edit the project through this interface in the Tool API. You *cannot* edit a project through its repository view, ProjectEdition. Project extends WorkspaceModel (which extends Model) to provide identification information and adds a few extra methods. You can obtain Project objects by asking Workspace for them. Workspace provides the following methods to access Projects:

> **getProjects()** Returns an array of Project objects, listing all projects in the workspace.
>
> **loadedProjectNamed(String name)** Returns a Project object that matches the specified name.
>
> **loadedProjectsNamed(String[] names)** Returns an array of Project objects that match the specified names.

You can also access projects by grabbing a ProjectEdition from the repository, and asking it for the getLoaded() Project (see the next section).

Project defines the following methods:

> **createDefaultPackage(boolean ignoreRepository)** Creates a default package for this project if one does not already exist. This method takes a single Boolean parameter, *ignoreRepository*. If false and some version of the default package exists in the repository, the method throws an IvjException. If true, the processing ignores the fact that another default package already exists for the project in the repository.
>
> **createPackage(String name, boolean ignoreRepository)** Creates a package with the specified name in the project in the workspace.
>
> **getAllEditions()** Returns an array of ProjectEdition objects to tell you which editions are available in the repository.
>
> **getComment()** Returns the comment string that was saved with this edition of the project.
>
> **getDefaultPackage()** Returns the default package for the project, or null if one does not exist in the workspace.
>
> **getEdition()** Returns a ProjectEdition representing the edition of the project that is in the workspace. If this is a scratch edition of the project, you will see the edition on which the scratch edition is based. Remember, scratch editions do not appear in the repository.
>
> **getPackages()** Returns an array of Package objects that tell you which packages are in this project in the workspace.
>
> **getTypes()** Returns an array of Type objects that tell you which classes and interfaces are in this version of the project.

isScratchEdition() Returns true if the version of the project in the workspace is a scratch edition.

openBrowser() Opens a project browser for the project.

setComment(String comment) Allows you to change the comment associated with the project.

For example, you print the name of all projects in the workspace using the following code:

```
// connect to the workspace
Workspace workspace = ToolEnv.connectToWorkspace();

// get the projects in the workspace
Project[] projects = workspace.getProjects();

// log their names
workspace.logMessage("\n",false); // ensure we start on new line
for(int i=0; i< projects.length; i++)
  workspace.logMessage(projects[i].getName() + "\n", true);
```

If you use this code in your tool, a list of all projects in the workspace will appear in the VisualAge for Java log window.

ProjectEdition

ProjectEdition is an interface that describes a specific version of a project in the repository. You can access ProjectEditions from Repository or from a Project object in the workspace. Repository defines the following methods to work with ProjectEditions:

getProjectCount() Returns the number of projects (not project editions) in the repository.

getProjectNames() Returns an array of Strings containing the names of all projects in the repository.

getProjectEditions(String name) Returns an array of ProjectEdition objects that describe versions of the specified project in the repository.

The ProjectEdition interface extends RepositoryModel (which extends Model) to provide identification information, and adds a few extra methods.

getAllEditions() Returns an array of ProjectEdition objects, allowing you to access any version of a project, no matter which version you start with.

getComment() Returns the String comment that the user saved with the project.

getLoaded() Returns the Project object that represents the view of this project edition in the workspace. This method returns null if this edition is *not* the one that is loaded into the workspace. Use the isLoaded() method (inherited from RepositoryModel) to determine if you have the loaded edition.

getPackageEditions() Returns an array of the repository models (PackageEdition) that represent the specific versions of packages contained in this specific version of the project.

getTypeEditions() Returns an array of TypeEdition objects (the repository models for the specific versions of classes and interfaces) that appear in this project. Note that Repository does not directly track this information. Instead, it obtains it by asking its PackageEditions for *their* lists of classes and merges them together. If you need only class or interface information but not a list of packages, this method can make your life much easier.

loadIntoWorkspace() Places this edition of the project into the workspace, replacing any previous edition that happened to be there. Be very careful if you use this method, as it can cause a great deal of confusion to the user.

purge() Attempts to mark this version of the project for deletion. This will not work if the user does not own the project. Use this method with care.

The following example lists the names and versions of all projects in the repository:

```
String versionName = "";

// connect to the workspace
Workspace workspace = ToolEnv.connectToWorkspace();

// grab the current repository
Repository repository = workspace.getRepository();

// get a list of the names of all projects in the
//   repository
String[] projectNames = repository.getProjectNames();

// for each name...
workspace.logMessage("\n",false); // ensure we start on new line
for(int i = 0; i<projectNames.length; i++) {
  // report the name
  workspace.logMessage(projectNames[i] + "\n", true);

  // get a list of all editions of the project
  ProjectEdition[] editions =
    repository.getProjectEditions(projectNames[i]);

  // for each edition
  for(int j=0; j< editions.length; j++) {
    // determine the version name - if not versioned, use
```

```
    //   open edition format for the name
    if (editions[j].isVersion())
      versionName = editions[j].getVersionName();
    else
      versionName = "(" + editions[j].getVersionStamp() + ")";

    // print the edition name
    workspace.logMessage("   " + versionName + "\n", true);
  }
}
```

Working with Packages

A VisualAge for Java package is a representation of a Java-language package. VisualAge represents packages using the Package and PackageEdition interfaces. VisualAge treats packages as groups of classes and interfaces.

Package

Package is the WorkspaceModel view of a Java package. You can use it to edit the contents of a package, specifying which classes and interfaces it contains, as well as performing version-control operations. A package is a specific version of a Java package that is currently loaded into the workspace. The Package object contains references to the specific versions of classes and interfaces that its Java package contains.

You can obtain Package instances by asking for them in Workspace, or by asking their containing Project instance. The Workspace interface provides the following methods to access packages:

getPackages() Returns an array of Package objects for all packages that are currently loaded in the user's workspace.

loadedDefaultPackageFor(String name) Returns a Package object for the default package in the named project.

loadedDefaultPackagesFor(String[] names) Returns an array of Package objects that represent the default package in the named projects.

loadedPackageNamed(String name) Returns the Package object for the named package.

loadedPackagesNamed(String[] names) Returns an array of Package objects for the named packages.

You can also access packages using methods in the Project class or by calling getLoaded() from the PackageEdition object that is currently loaded in the workspace.

Package defines the following methods:

createVersion(String versionString, boolean releaseMe) Versions the package using the new *versionString*. If you specify true for the *releaseMe* parameter, VisualAge will attempt to release the package into an open project edition. Releasing can fail for several reasons, such as the project is not an open edition or the user does not own the package.

getAllEditions() Returns an array of PackageEdition objects that represent all versions of the package in the repository.

getComment() Returns the String comment that the user entered with this version of the package.

getEdition() Returns a PackageEdition for this specific version of the package.

getProject() Returns the Project that contains this package in the workspace. Note that a package *could* appear in several different project versions in the repository but only in a single project in the workspace. Even the same version of a package could appear in different projects in the repository.

getTypes() Returns an array of Type objects that represent the classes and interfaces defined in this package in the workspace.

isDefaultPackage() Returns true if this is the default package for its project in the workspace, false if it's a named package.

isReleased() Returns true if this package has been released, associating it with its parent project version in the repository.

isScratchEdition() Returns true if this is a scratch edition of the package in the workspace.

openBrowser() Opens a package browser for the package in the workspace.

release() Attempts to release the package into its containing project version. This will fail if the project is not an open edition or if the user does not own the package.

setComment(String comment) Sets the comment String for the package.

Adding to the earlier project example, the following example displays the packages contained within each project. The bold code is what we have added for this example.

```
// connect to the workspace
Workspace workspace = ToolEnv.connectToWorkspace();

// get the projects in the workspace
Project[] projects = workspace.getProjects();

// log their names
```

```
workspace.logMessage("\n",false); // ensure we start on new line
for(int i=0; i< projects.length; i++) {
  workspace.logMessage(projects[i].getName() + "\n", true);

  // write names of all packages in this project
  Package[] packages = projects[i].getPackages();
  for(int j=0; j< packages.length; j++)
    workspace.logMessage("   " + packages[j].getName() + "\n",
true);
}
```

PackageEdition

PackageEdition describes a specific version of a package in the repository. You can access package editions from a Package object's getEdition() method, or from a ProjectEdition's getPackageEditions() method. The Repository interface provides the following methods to work with PackageEditions:

getPackageCount() Returns the number of packages (not the number of package editions) in the repository.

getPackageNames() Returns an array of Strings containing the names of the packages contained in the repository.

getPackageEditions(String name) Returns an array of PackageEdition objects that represent the versions of the specified package in the repository.

The PackageEdition interface contains the following methods:

getAllEditions() Returns an array of all package editions in the repository for this package.

getComment() Returns the comment String stored by the user for this package version.

getLoaded() Returns the corresponding Package object if this project is currently loaded in the workspace,and false otherwise.

getTypeEditions() Returns an array of TypeEdition objects representing the classes and interfaces contained in this edition of the package in the repository.

isDefaultPackage() Returns true if this package is the default package for its containing project version in the repository.

loadIntoWorkspace(Project project) Adds the version of the package to the workspace, replacing any existing version in the specified project. If a different version of the same package exists in a different project in the workspace, the Tool API throws an IvjException.

purge() Attempts to mark this version of the project for deletion. This will not work if the user does not own the project. Use this method with care.

The following code extends the previous example to print the names and editions of all packages inside the project versions. The additional code appears in bold text.

```
String versionName = "";

// connect to the workspace
Workspace workspace = ToolEnv.connectToWorkspace();

// grab the current repository
Repository repository = workspace.getRepository();

// get a list of the names of all projects in the
//   repository
String[] projectNames = repository.getProjectNames();

// for each name...
workspace.logMessage("\n",false); // ensure we start on new line
for(int i = 0; i<projectNames.length; i++) {
  // report the name
  workspace.logMessage(projectNames[i] + "\n", true);

  // get a list of all editions of the project
  ProjectEdition[] editions =
    repository.getProjectEditions(projectNames[i]);

  // for each edition
  for(int j=0; j< editions.length; j++) {
    // determine the version name - if not versioned, use
    //   open edition format for the name
    if (editions[j].isVersion())
      versionName = editions[j].getVersionName();
    else
      versionName = "(" + editions[j].getVersionStamp() + ")";

    // print the edition name
    workspace.logMessage("   " + versionName + "\n", true);

    // for each package edition in the project edition
    PackageEdition[] packageEditions =
                        editions[j].getPackageEditions();
    if (packageEditions != null)
      for(int k=0; k < packageEditions.length; k++) {
        // determine the version name
```

```
            // note the necessary try-catch!
            try {
              if (packageEditions[k].isVersion())
                versionName = packageEditions[k].getVersionName();
              else
                versionName =
                  "(" + packageEditions[k].getVersionStamp() + ")";
            }
            catch(IvjUnresolvedException e) {
              versionName = "UNRESOLVED: " +
                            packageEditions[k].getVersionName();
            }
            // print the package info
            workspace.logMessage(
              "     " + packageEditions[k].getName() +
              "   " + versionName + "\n", true);
          }
    }
}
```

Working with Types

Types are VisualAge's way to refer generically to classes and interfaces. The type of data stored by VisualAge for Java for classes and interfaces is nearly identical. As with projects and packages, types come in two flavors: Type and TypeEdition.

Type

Type is a representation of a class or interface in the workspace. You can use it for versioning and editing types (described later under *Generating Code*). You can obtain a Type from its containing Package or Project via their getTypes() method. However, the Workspace object provides the most effective means to access Types.

The Workspace interface defines the following methods to access loaded types:

getTypes() Returns an array of all Type objects loaded into the workspace.

loadedTypeNamed(String name) Returns the Type object matching the package-qualified name in the workspace.

loadedTypesNamed(String[] names) Returns an array of Type objects matching the package-qualified names in the workspace.

Once you have a Type object, you can call the following methods:

createVersion(String versionString, boolean releaseMe) Versions the type using the new *versionString*. If you specify true for the *releaseMe* parameter, VisualAge will attempt to release the type into an open package edition. Releasing can fail for several reasons, such as the package is not an open edition or the user does not own the type.

getAllEditions() Returns an array of TypeEdition objects that represent all of the versions of this type in the repository.

getAllSubtypes() Returns an array of Type objects that extend this class or interface, *and* if this is an interface, all of the classes that implement this interface. This is a complete list of all extensions or implementations, direct or indirect (meaning that subclasses of subclasses are included). This can be an incredibly useful method, especially in property editors and customizers. Note that if this type is an interface and you are only interested in subinterfaces *or* implementing classes, you must check each returned item by calling isClass() or isInterface().

getDeveloperName() Returns the name of the user who developed this version of the type. Remember, any user can develop and version a type, but only the owner can release it.

getEdition() Returns the TypeEdition object that represents the specific version of the type in the workspace.

getPackage() Returns the Package object that represents the package containing this type in the workspace.

getProject() Returns the Project object that represents the project containing this type in the workspace.

getQualifiedName() Returns the package-qualified name of the type. Note that getName() only returns the type name itself without package qualification.

hasError() Returns true if there are any errors in the source code. This is helpful because you cannot export .class files for source code that contains errors.

hasSourceCode() Returns true if source code is available for a class.

isApplet() Returns true if this type is an applet (a class that extends java.applet.Applet).

isApplication() Returns true if this type is an application (a class that has a main() method).

isClass() Returns true if this type is a class.

isInDefaultPackage() Returns true if this type is in the default package for the containing project.

isInterface() Returns true if this type is an interface.

isReleased() Returns true if this version of the type has been released.

openBrowser() Opens a class or interface browser for the type.

release() Attempts to release the type into its containing package version. This will fail if the package is not an open edition or if the user does not own the type.

For example, suppose that you want a tool that lists all classes that implement selected interfaces. You can do this with the following code:

```
import com.ibm.ivj.util.base.*;

/** A Simple VisualAge for Java tool that displays
 *    all classes that implement the selected interfaces
 */
public class ListImplementers {

  /** The main tool processing */
  public static void main(String[] args) throws IvjException {

    // connect to the workspace
    Workspace workspace = ToolEnv.connectToWorkspace();
    workspace.logMessage("\n", true);

    // we only run in context -c so
    //   there will alwayss be at least two args
    // first is "-c", second and after are the list
    //   of selected type names
    for(int i=1; i<args.length; i++) {
      String interfaceToFind = args[i];

      // find the selected type in the workspace
      Type interfaceType =
              workspace.loadedTypeNamed(interfaceToFind);

      // if it's not an interface, report, but continue
      if (!interfaceType.isInterface())
        workspace.logMessage(interfaceToFind +
                            " is not an interface!\n", true);

      // otherwise, it's an interface
      else {
        // write a small header
        workspace.logMessage("Classes that implement interface " +
                            interfaceToFind + "\n", true);

        // get a list of all implementers and sub-interfaces
```

getSimpleName() Returns in the unqualified name of the type (no package name in front of it).

loadIntoWorkspace() Attempts to load this type into the workspace.

We can extend the edition example again to dump all versions of all classes in all versions of all packages in all projects in the repository. Note that this is just a silly example and can take quite a while to run. This example is provided here to help show the relationship between the various edition objects. Once again, the additional code appears in bold text.

```
String versionName = "";

// connect to the workspace
Workspace workspace = ToolEnv.connectToWorkspace();

// grab the current repository
Repository repository = workspace.getRepository();

// get a list of the names of all projects in the
//   repository
String[] projectNames = repository.getProjectNames();

// for each name...
workspace.logMessage("\n",false); // ensure we start on new line
for(int i = 0; i<projectNames.length; i++) {
  // report the name
  workspace.logMessage(projectNames[i] + "\n", true);

  // get a list of all editions of the project
  ProjectEdition[] editions =
    repository.getProjectEditions(projectNames[i]);

  // for each edition
  for(int j=0; j< editions.length; j++) {
    // determine the version name - if not versioned, use
    //   open edition format for the name
    if (editions[j].isVersion())
      versionName = editions[j].getVersionName();
    else
      versionName = "(" + editions[j].getVersionStamp() + ")";

    // print the edition name
    workspace.logMessage("  " + versionName + "\n", true);
```

```
          Type[] implementers = interfaceType.getAllSubtypes();

          // walk the list
          for(int j=0; j<implementers.length; j++)
            // check if it's an implementing class
            if (implementers[j].isClass())
              // if so, report it!
              workspace.logMessage(
                  "     " +
                  implementers[j].getQualifiedName() +
                  "\n", true);
        }
      }
    }
  }
```

The control file for the above tool looks as follows:

```
Name=List Interface Implementers
Version=0.2
Menu-Items=\
  List implementers,\
      effectivevaj.under.toolapi.ListImplementers,-c
```

Set this tool up outside VisualAge for Java (in the tools directory, as explained previously) and then shut down and restart VisualAge. You now have a simple tool that displays the names of all classes that implement the selected interfaces. You could later add a GUI to allow users to select interfaces from a list and display the results in a window instead of the log.

TypeEdition

VisualAge tracks classes and interfaces in the repository using TypeEdition. TypeEdition represents a specific version of a class or interface. You can access type editions from a Type's getEdition() method or a PackageEdition's getTypeEditions() method. There is no direct way to access a type edition from the Repository object.

TypeEdition provides the following methods:

getAllEditions() Returns an array of TypeEdition objects that represent all versions of this type that exist in the repository.

getDeveloperName() Returns the name of the user who developed this version of this type.

getLoaded() Returns the Type object that represents this version of the type as loaded into the workspace. This method returns null if this version of the type is not currently in the workspace.

```
    // for each package edition in the project edition
    PackageEdition[] packageEditions =
                      editions[j].getPackageEditions();
    if (packageEditions != null)
      for(int k=0; k < packageEditions.length; k++) {
        boolean validEdition = true;
        // determine the version name
        // note the necessary try-catch!
        try {
          if (packageEditions[k].isVersion())
            versionName = packageEditions[k].getVersionName();
          else
            versionName =
              "(" + packageEditions[k].getVersionStamp() + ")";
        }
        catch(IvjUnresolvedException e) {
          versionName = "UNRESOLVED: " +
                      packageEditions[k].getVersionName();
          validEdition = false;
        }
        // print the package info
        workspace.logMessage(
          "     " + packageEditions[k].getName() +
          "   " + versionName + "\n", true);

        if (validEdition) {
          TypeEdition[] typeEditions =
            packageEditions[k].getTypeEditions();
          if (typeEditions != null)
            for(int l=0; l < typeEditions.length; l++) {
              if (typeEditions[l].isVersion())
                versionName = typeEditions[l].getVersionName();
              else
                versionName =
                  "(" + typeEditions[l].getVersionStamp() + ")";
              workspace.logMessage(
                  "       " + typeEditions[l].getName() +
                  "   " + versionName + "\n", true);
            }
        }
      }
  }
}
```

Running a Class

Inside your tool, you may need to run other classes or applications. The Tool API provides a method to invoke another class' main() method.

The Workspace interface's runMain() method provides the functionality to invoke another class' main() method from within the tool. This enables you to ask the user for a class to run and run it, possibly with a set of arguments. The runMain() method takes two arguments: a Class object that represents the class you want to execute, and an array of Strings to pass as arguments. A sample invocation could look as follows:

```
// the following string for the class name could come from a
//   parameter, or could be selected by the user while the
//   tool is running
String className = "effectivevaj.SomeClass";

// get a class object for the named class
try {
  Class theClass = Class.forName(className);

  // run the application
  workspace.runMain(theClass,
                    new String[] {"Larry", "Curly", "Moe"});
}
catch(ClassNotFoundException e) {
  // deal with the bad class name
}
```

Sometimes these other applications require different CLASSPATH settings to find resources, and you may not know which resource directories you need until run time. You can view and modify the current CLASSPATH setting using the following methods, defined in the Workspace interface:

getClassPathEntries() Returns an array of entries that represent the current CLASSPATH setting. These entries are either Strings or Project objects. If Strings, they contain the full file-system path of the CLASSPATH entry. This could be a directory name or the name of a JAR or ZIP file. If this is a Project, it represents the project_resources directory of the indicated project.

getDefaultClassPathEntries() Returns an array of entries that represent the required VisualAge for Java CLASSPATH entries. Note that these *must* appear on the CLASSPATH setting. If you use setClassPath() to change the CLASSPATH setting, you must ensure that these entries appear in your new class path, or VisualAge may not be able to find its own required classes. This method exists to allow you to determine where you want to place the required VisualAge for Java libraries, before or after your own libraries.

Entries are either Strings or Projects as previously described in getClassPathEntries().

setClassPath(Object[] entries) Enables you to set CLASSPATH for the current execution. The entries are Projects and Strings, as previously described in getClassPathEntries(). You *must* include the entries required by VisualAge for Java, obtained by calling getDefaultClassPathEntries().

removeClassPathEntries(Object[] enties) Removes the specified entries from the current CLASSPATH setting. Entries can either be Strings or Projects, as previously described in getClassPathEntries.

For example, suppose that you want to add a jar named c:\jars\cookie.jar to the class path, as well as the Swing class libraries. The following code prepends the required jar file and project to the current CLASSPATH setting:

```
// connect to the workspace
Workspace workspace = ToolEnv.connectToWorkspace();

// get the entries that VisualAge requires
Object[] requiredStuff =
            workspace.getDefaultClassPathEntries();

// create the new (bigger) class path array
Object[] newClassPath =
            new Object[requiredStuff.length + 2];

// set the new entries
newClassPath[0] = "c:\\jars\\cookie.jar";
newClassPath[1] =
workspace.loadedProjectNamed("JFC class libraries");

// copy the required entries
System.arraycopy(requiredStuff, 0,
                  newClassPath, 2, requiredStuff.length);


// set the CLASSPATH in the workspace
workspace.setClassPath(newClassPath);
```

Helping the User Pick an Object

Often during the execution of the tool, you need to ask your user which project, package, class, file, or directory they want to work with. Rather than just presenting them with a text field where they need to type the entire name, you can ask VisualAge to present them with the same dialogs it uses when asking users for these types of data. In this section we'll examine some convenience methods that display these dialogs.

Common Parameters

Most of the methods we discuss in this section accept the same parameters. We explain these parameters once before even talking about what the methods do. Each prompting method uses some or all of these parameters.

Title and Prompt

The *title* parameter is the String that appears in the title bar of the dialog that VisualAge displays. This String should be a very short description of the activity. "Choose Class" or "Select Directory" are good choices when choosing a title.

The *prompt* parameter is the actual request displayed for the user. This String should be a full sentence and can be as descriptive as you like. "Please select the target directory" or "Please select the class you want to delete" might be appropriate prompts.

Scope and Mask

Scope and mask parameters help decide what items actually appear in the list. The *scope* parameter limits items to those contained with a given WorkspaceModel. If you pass null as the value, the entire workspace is the scope. If you pass a Project or Package as the scope, the user will see only those entries that reside under that Project or Package. Generally, using a Type as the scope is not very useful, because only a single entry is visible at a time in the list. The *mask* parameter is the initial String that helps whittle the list to just those starting with a certain sequence of letters. Normally, you would leave this parameter null or set it to the previously selected name (not fully-qualified, of course).

The user can change the mask while interacting with the dialog, but they cannot change the scope.

Workspace Prompting Methods

The Workspace interface provides the following methods for prompting the user for an object. Workspace provides some variations on these methods that provide more control. Some methods enable you to specify an array of WorkspaceModels, and these are the only choices presented to the user. This is extremely useful for cases where you might want to allow only classes that implement a certain interface, for example.

promptForApplet(String title, String prompt, WorkspaceModel scope, String Mask) Displays only classes that extend java.applet.Applet.

promptForApplication(String title, String prompt, WorkspaceModel scope, String Mask) Displays only classes that have a main() method.

promptForClass(String title, String prompt, WorkspaceModel scope, String Mask) Displays only classes.

promptForInterface(String title, String prompt, WorkspaceModel scope, String Mask) Displays only interfaces.

promptForPackage(String title, String prompt, WorkspaceModel scope, String Mask) Displays only packages

promptForProject(String title, String prompt, String Mask) Displays only projects. This method does not have (or need) a scope parameter.

promptForType(String title, String prompt, WorkspaceModel scope, String Mask) Displays only classes or interfaces.

promptForModel(WorkspaceModel[] models, String title, String prompt, String mask) Displays only the models you pass in. The list can contain a mix of Projects, Packages, and Types.

promptForPackage(Package[] models, String title, String prompt, String mask) Displays only the specified packages.

promptForProject(Project[] models, String title, String prompt, String mask) Displays only the specified projects.

promptForType(Type[] models, String title, String prompt, String mask) Displays only the specified Types.

promptForDirectoryName(String title, String initialDir) Allows the user to browse for a directory.

promptForFileName(String title, String initialFile, String extension) Allows the user to choose a file, possibly limited to a specific extension (null for any extension).

You can use these methods just as though you were asking a question. If the user clicks Cancel, the methods return null. For example, if you wanted to ask the user to select a class that they have loaded into the workspace, use the following code:

```
// connect to the workspace
Workspace workspace = ToolEnv.connectToWorkspace();

// Find the example project for this book
Project book = workspace.loadedProjectNamed(
                "Effective VisualAge for Java");

// Ask the user to choose a class. Only classes
//   in this book's package appear in the selection list
String className =
    workspace.promptForClass("Select Class",
                             "Please select the class to use!",
                             book, null);
```

Exporting and Importing

Often, your tools work with code inside VisualAge for Java. Sometimes, however, you may want to send the code outside (perhaps to check it into an external version-control tool) or bring external code into VisualAge for Java. The Tool API provides export and import capabilities that allow you to move code in and out of the IDE.

The Workspace interface provides methods importData() and exportData() to perform the import and export, respectively. These methods each take import and export specification objects that describe what is imported or exported and how.

Import and Export Specifications

The import and export specifications are objects that describe what to export and provide parameters to how that export occurs. There are two types of specifications: code and interchange. Code specifications describe directory exports and imports. Interchange specifications describe repository file exports and imports. You create instances of the specification classes and call some methods to set the parameters of the export or import. We describe each of the classes in the following sections.

ExportCodeSpec

The ExportCodeSpec class defines the details needed to export code to a directory. If you want to create a JAR file, you must run the jar tool yourself after performing the export. You create an ExportCodeSpec instance using its default constructor.

```
ExportCodeSpec exportData = new ExportCodeSpec();
```

ExportCodeSpec provides the following methods:

getExportDirectory() Returns a String value that contains the current target directory for the export.

getPackages() Returns an array of Package objects that are to be exported to the target directory.

getProjects() Returns an array of Project objects that are to be exported to the target directory.

getTypes() Returns an array of Type objects that are to be exported to the target directory.

includeClass() Returns true if you are set to export .class files.

includeClass(boolean value) Allows you to specify that you want to export .class files.

includeClassDebugInfo() Returns true if you are set to include debug attributes in the exported .class files.

includeClassDebugInfo(boolean value) Allows you to specify that you want to include debugging attributes in the exported .class files.

includeJava() Returns true if you are set to export .java source files.

includeJava(boolean value) Allows you to specify that you want to export .java source files.

includeResources() Returns true if you are set to export resource files from the projects' project_resources directory.

includeResources(boolean value) Allows you to specify that you want to export resource files from the projects' project_resources directory.

overwriteFiles() Returns true if you are set to overwrite existing files without warning. If false, VisualAge asks the user if they want to overwrite any existing files.

overwriteFiles(boolean value) Allows you to specify that you want to overwrite existing files without warning. If you pass in false, the user must verify each file to overwrite.

setExportDirectory(String directory) Allows you to specify the target directory for the export. VisualAge for Java will create this directory if it does not already exist.

setPackages(Package[] packages) Allows you to specify which packages to export.

setProjects(Project[] projects) Allows you to specify which projects to export.

setTypes(Type[] types) Allows you to specify which types to export.

useSubdirectories() Returns true if you are set to create the proper subdirectory structure in the target directory.

useSubdirectories(booelan value) Allows you to specify that you want VisualAge for Java to automatically create the proper directory structure for exported classes. Each class resides in a directory structure built from its package's name.

As an example, the following code exports the contents of two packages, effectivevaj.gencode and effectivevaj.vce.factory to directory c:\\targetdir:

```
Workspace workspace = null;

try {
  // connect to the workspace
  workspace = ToolEnv.connectToWorkspace();

  // create a list of packages to export
  Package[] packages = new Package[2];
  packages[0] =
```

```
    workspace.loadedPackageNamed("effectivevaj.gencode");
  packages[1] =
    workspace.loadedPackageNamed("effectivevaj.vce.factory");

  // set up the export specification
  ExportCodeSpec exportData = new ExportCodeSpec();
  exportData.includeClass(false);
  exportData.includeJava(true);
  exportData.includeResources(true);
  exportData.overwriteFiles(true);
  exportData.setPackages(packages);
  exportData.setExportDirectory("c:\\targetdir");

  // perform the export
  workspace.exportData(exportData);
}

// if we had an export problem, list the errors
catch(IvjExportException e) {
  String[] errors = e.getErrors();
  workspace.logMessage("\nErrors during export!\n", true);
  for(int i=0; i<errors.length; i++)
    workspace.logMessage(errors[i]+"\n", true);
}
```

ExportInterchangeSpec

The ExportInterchangeSpec class describes an export into another repository. Recall that repository format exports *only* export projects or packages from the repository, not from the workspace. If you use these methods, make sure that the user has versioned the objects being exported, or perform the versioning in your tool. You create an instance of ExportInterchangeSpec using its default constructor and then set the parameters on that instance.

```
ExportInterchangeSpec exportData = new ExportInterchangeSpec();
```

ExportInterchangeSpec provides the following methods:

allowRepositoryCreation() Returns true if this export specification will allow VisualAge for Java to create a new repository (if the specified repository does not exist).

allowRepositoryCreation(boolean value) Allows you to specify that you want to allow VisualAge for Java to create a new repository as the target of the export if the specified repository does not already exist.

getPackageEditions() Returns an array of PackageEdition objects that represent the versions of packages to be exported.

getProjectEditions() Returns an array of ProjectEdition objects that represent the versions of projects to be exported.

getRepository() Returns the target repository.

setPackageEditions(PackageEdition[] packages) Allows you to specify which package versions to export. You can export several versions of the same package.

setProjectEditions(ProjectEdition[] projects) Allows you to specify which project versions to export. You can export several versions of the same project.

setRepository(Repository repository) Sets the target repository. You will need to use the getRepository() methods in Workspace that take Strings to specify the target repository. Although VisualAge for Java can create the target repository, the directory containing that target repository must already exist.

For example, suppose that you want to export all versions of project "Big Bad VooDoo Scotty" to repository file c:\sample\transfer.dat. We could do so with the following code:

```
Workspace workspace = null;
try {
  // connect to the workspace
  workspace = ToolEnv.connectToWorkspace();

  // get the current repository
  Repository myRepository = workspace.getRepository();

  // specify the target repository
  Repository targetRepository =
    workspace.getRepository("c:\\sample\\transfer.dat");

  // Find all versions of the project to export.
  ProjectEdition[] projects =
    myRepository.getProjectEditions("Big Bad VooDoo Scotty");

  // fill in the export details
  ExportInterchangeSpec exportData = new ExportInterchangeSpec();
  exportData.allowRepositoryCreation(true);
  exportData.setProjectEditions(projects);
  exportData.setRepository(targetRepository);

  // perform the export
```

```
  workspace.exportData(exportData);
}

// report any errors
catch(IvjExportException e) {
  String[] errors = e.getErrors();
  workspace.logMessage("\nErrors during export!\n", true);
  for(int i=0; i<errors.length; i++)
    workspace.logMessage(errors[i]+"\n", true);
}
```

ImportCodeSpec

The ImportCodeSpec class describes the parameters needed when importing source, .class, or resource files from a directory. ImportCodeSpec defines the following methods:

getClassFiles() Returns an array of Strings, the fully-qualified names of the .class files to be imported.

getDefaultProject() Returns the Project object that represents the project into which any new packages and types within those packages are imported.

getJavaFiles() Returns an array of Strings, the fully-qualified names of the .java files to be imported.

getResourceFiles() Returns an array of Strings, the names of the resource files to be imported. These names are relative to the resource path.

getResourcePath() Returns the base path of resources to be imported.

setClassFiles(String[] fileNames) Sets the names of the .class files to import. These names are all fully qualified.

setDefaultProject(Project project) Sets the project into which all new packages and their types are imported. Types within existing packages are imported into their project in the workspace.

setJavaFiles(String[] fileNames) Sets the names of the .java files to import. These names are all fully qualified.

setResourceFiles(String[] fileNames) Sets the names of the resource files to import. These names are all relative to the resource path. This is necessary so that VisualAge for Java knows how to copy the resources into the project_resources directory. You need to choose a resource path that maps to the project_resources directory, and VisualAge will set up the appropriate directory structure under the project_resources directory that matches the names of these files.

setResourcePath(String path) Sets the name of the base directory for resources. All resource files are relative to this directory.

useSharedResDir() Returns true if set to import resources into the shared project_resource directory.

useSharedResDir(boolean value) Specifies whether to import resources into the shared project_resource directory.

For example, to import several .java files into a new project in the workspace, use this code:

```
Workspace workspace = null;
try {
  // connect to the workspace
  workspace = ToolEnv.connectToWorkspace();

  // create an import specification
  ImportCodeSpec importData = new ImportCodeSpec();

  // create a new project to import into
  Project targetProject =
    workspace.createProject("Sample Project", true);

  // list the files to import
  String[] javaFiles = {
    "C:\\sample\\test\\FirstClass.java",
    "C:\\sample\\test\\SecondClass.java",
    "C:\\sample\\test\\AnotherClass.java",
    "C:\\sample\\test\\StillAnotherClass.java"
  };

  // set up the parameters for the import
  importData.setDefaultProject(targetProject);
  importData.setJavaFiles(javaFiles);

  // perform the import
  workspace.importData(importData);
}

// report any errors
catch(IvjImportException e) {
  String[] errors = e.getErrors();
  workspace.logMessage("\nErrors during import!\n", true);
  for(int i=0; i<errors.length; i++)
    workspace.logMessage(errors[i]+"\n", true);

}
```

ImportInterchangeSpec

The ImportInterchangeSpec class provides the information necessary to import project or package versions from another repository into the current one. ImportInterchangeSpec provides the following methods:

getPackageEditions() Returns an array of PackageEdition objects that represent the versions of packages that are to be imported.

getProjectEditions() Returns an array of ProjectEdition objects that represent the versions of projects that are to be imported.

getRepository() Returns the source repository for the import.

setPackageEditions(PackageEdition[] packages) Sets the package versions to import.

setProjectEditions(ProjectEdition[] projects) Sets the project versions to import.

setRepository(Repository repository) Sets the source repository.

Note that if you want to bring the loaded project or package into the current workspace, you must use a separate call to the relevant loadIntoWorkspace() method.

For example, the following code imports all versions of the JavaDude Box Beans project in an external repository file:

```
Workspace workspace = null;
try {
  // connect to the workspace
  workspace = ToolEnv.connectToWorkspace();

  // get the source repository
  Repository sourceRepository =
    workspace.getRepository("c:\\sample\\boxbeans.dat");

  // get all versions to import
  ProjectEdition[] projects =
    sourceRepository.getProjectEditions("JavaDude Box Beans");

  // setup the import parameters
  ImportInterchangeSpec importData = new ImportInterchangeSpec();
  importData.setProjectEditions(projects);
  importData.setRepository(sourceRepository);

  // perform the import
  workspace.importData(importData);
}
```

```
// report any errors
catch(IvjImportException e) {
  String[] errors = e.getErrors();
  workspace.logMessage("\nErrors during import!\n", true);
  for(int i=0; i<errors.length; i++)
    workspace.logMessage(errors[i]+"\n", true);
}
```

Generating Code

One of the most useful things a tool can do is code generation. You can add, delete, and modify methods and classes, even provide your own user-code blocks. The following sections describe the VisualAge tool API's builder classes. We separate this section into two parts:

> **The Code Generation Interfaces** describes each of the interfaces you interact with to generate code.
>
> **Code Generation Tasks** describes how you would accomplish several common tasks in a tool that generates code.

The Code Generation Interfaces

The Tool API provides code generation classes in the com.ibm.ivj.util.builders package. This package contains three interfaces that provide code generation capabilities.

BuilderFactory

BuilderFactory is your handle into the code generation capabilities, providing the functionality to create MethodBuilders, TypeBuilders and user-code blocks. All code generation starts here. BuilderFactory provides the following methods:

> **createMethodBuilder(String builderName)** Creates a new MethodBuilder that you can use to add a new method. If you want to modify or delete an existing method, ask the TypeBuilder to find the appropriate MethodBuilder for you. The name passed in to this method is simply a unique name for *you* to work with; it has no effect on the name of the method you are creating. Each MethodBuilder must have a unique name, so it is probably a good idea to use a name that encodes the signature of the method you want to create. For example, if you are creating method callDoctor(Child, Symptoms) you may want the string to be "callDoctor(Child,Symptoms)" to make it easy to distinguish from other MethodBuilders. See *Add a Method to a Class or Interface* later in this chapter for an example of creating a new MethodBuilder.
>
> **createTypeBuilder(String name, Package pkg)** Creates a new TypeBuilder for adding a new class or interface. You cannot use this method to work

with an existing type. See *Create a New Class or Interface* later in this chapter for an example of creating a TypeBuilder for a new class.

createTypeBuilder(Type type) Creates a TypeBuilder to modify an existing type in the workspace. You cannot use this method to work with types that do not exist yet. See *Add a Method to a Class or Interface* later in this chapter for an example.

createUserCodeBlock(String identifier, String indent) Creates a special block comment that delimits a safe place for the user to add their own code. The identifier can be any String you would like, but it must be unique within the block of code you are generating. You can use the saveMerge() method in the TypeBuilder interface to merge code containing user-code block comments with existing user code, keeping the user code. The *indent* parameter is a spacing String that enables you to line up the comment blocks with the rest of the generated code. See *Modify Method with Embedded User Code* later in this chapter for an example.

TypeBuilder

TypeBuilder represents an interface or class that you want to add or modify. If you want to delete a type, you can just go ahead and delete it from the workspace. You access TypeBuilders by calling the BuilderFactory createTypeBuilder() methods.

The concept of contained MethodBuilders bears some explanation. TypeBuilder uses MethodBuilders to describe the *actions* you want to take on methods. MethodBuilders are *not* the methods themselves. For example, if you call removeAllMethodBuilders(), it does *not* remove all methods in the class; the method removes the *actions* you wanted to take on those methods. Each MethodBuilder enables you to change source code or specify deletion of that method. When you save() or saveMerge() a TypeBuilder, the tool API executes the *actions* you specified through MethodBuilders.

When you first access a TypeBuilder, it contains no MethodBuilders. You can ask it to create MethodBuilders for its existing methods, but unless you explicitly add those MethodBuilders to the TypeBuilder through its addMethodBuilder() method, the TypeBuilder will not contain the MethodBuilders. This enables you to choose which methods to modify or delete, and add *only* those MethodBuilders to the TypeBuilder.

> **NOTE**
>
> Accessing an existing method builder for a particular method is very difficult. Usually, the only reason you would want to do so is to see its source or mark it for deletion. If you want to modify or delete a method, just create a *new* MethodBuilder and set the source or mark it for deletion. If you need to access the old source code, we describe how to do that in *Obtaining the Source of an Existing Method.* We describe the methods of MethodBuilder in the next section.

TypeBuilder provides the following methods:

addMethodBuilder(MethodBuilder methodBuilders) Adds a MethodBuilder to the TypeBuilder to represent the change you want to make to a method in this type. When you save() or saveMerge() this TypeBuilder, the Tool API executes the actions specified by your added MethodBuilders.

checkMethodExists(MethodBuilder methodBuilder) Checks if this TypeBuilder contains a method with the same signature as the specified method builder. This method compares only the name and parameter types of the specified MethodBuilder to the methods in this type, not the method body, return type, or access modifier. Note that if this method returns true, it does *not* mean that the specified MethodBuilder is in the return list from getExistingMethods(). It just means that a method with that signature exists. When specifying the signature of the MethodBuilder, fully qualify the type names you use to describe the parameters. See *Delete a Method* later in this chapter for an example.

getBuilderName() Returns the name of this builder, which is not necessarily the same as the name of the type. This should be used only for internal distinction between TypeBuilders.

getExistingMethods() Returns an array of MethodBuilder objects, describing the methods contained in this type.

getExistingMethodSource(MethodBuilder methodBuilder) Returns a String that contains the source code of a method that matches the signature of the passed-in MethodBuilder. See *Obtaining the Source of an Existing Method* later in this chapter for an example.

getExistingSource() Returns a String that contains the entire source of this type, which does *not* contain the method source (as in the Workspace view of a class or interface definition). In other words, this returns just the class header.

getMethodBuilders() Returns an array of MethodBuilder objects that represent the actions to take against methods. Note this is very different from getExistingMethods(), which creates MethodBuilders for each method in this type.

getSource() Returns a String representing the current set source. This will be the source that replaces the existing source if this type is saved.

removeAllMethodBuilders() Removes the MethodBuilders that you added to make changes. This does *not* delete any methods from the type.

removeMethodBuilder(MethodBuilder methodBuilder) Removes a specific MethodBuilder from the list of those you had added to make changes to the type. This does *not* delete the actual method from the type.

save() Saves the type, setting its source in the workspace to the source you set by setSource() and executing the actions of all MethodBuilders added to this type. This save ignores any user code in changed methods.

saveMerge() Same as save(), except user code is merged with the new versions of methods that define user code blocks.

setSource(String source) Overwrites the source of this type. If this source contains any methods they are extracted from the source as their own new MethodBuilders.

MethodBuilder

MethodBuilder represents a method that you want to add, modify, or delete. If you add a MethodBuilder to a TypeBuilder, you indicate that you want to perform an action on that method, adding it, replacing its contents, or deleting it.

MethodBuilder defines the following methods:

getBuilderName() Returns the builder name for this MethodBuilder. As mentioned several times previously, remember that the builder name might not be related to the method signature.

getSource() Returns the source that you have set for the method. If you obtain an array of MethodBuilders from a TypeBuilder's getExistingMethods() method, calling getSource() on those MethodBuilders will return null. If you want the source, you must pass the MethodBuilders to the getExistingMethodSource() method of the TypeBuilder.

isMarkedForDeletion() Returns true if you have marked the method for deletion.

markForDeletion(boolean deleteMe) Allows you to specify that this method should be deleted.

setSource(String source) Enables you to set the new source for this method. When you add the MethodBuilder to a TypeBuilder and call save() or saveMerge() on the TypeBuilder, the new source is updated in the workspace.

Code Generation Tasks

Throughout the rest of this section, we describe several tasks that you may want to perform in a tool that generates code. With each task is an example of the code you would write to perform that task.

Create a New Class or Interface

The first basic task you may want to do is define a new class. There are two main ways to do this. The easiest is to define the entire source for the class in a TypeBuilder and save that TypeBuilder.

```
String projectName = "Generated Code Samples";
String packageName = "sample.generated.code";

// connect to the workspace
Workspace workspace = ToolEnv.connectToWorkspace();

// get a builderfactory to start the generation
BuilderFactory factory = workspace.createBuilderFactory();

// find or create the specified project
Project targetProject = workspace.loadedProjectNamed(projectName);
if (targetProject == null)
  targetProject = workspace.createProject(projectName, true);

// find or create the specified package in that project
Package targetPackage = workspace.loadedPackageNamed(packageName);
if (targetPackage == null)
  targetPackage = targetProject.createPackage(packageName, true);

// if the package is in the wrong project, complain!
else if (targetPackage.getProject() != targetProject)
  workspace.logMessage("The target package " + packageName +
                       " is already in another project!!!", true);

// create a TypeBuilder for the new Class
TypeBuilder typeBuilder =
  factory.createTypeBuilder("HelloWorld", targetPackage);

// Use a StringBuffer for building the code -- it's much
//   faster than concatenating Strings
StringBuffer b = new StringBuffer();

// Write the code for the class
// the leading space in the following code
//   is actually one or two tab characters
b.append("public class HelloWorld {\n"                        );
b.append("  public static void main(String[] args) {\n"      );
b.append("    System.out.println(\"Hello, World!\");\n"      );
b.append("  }\n"                                              );
b.append("}\n"                                                );

// set that code as the source for the new class
typeBuilder.setSource(b.toString());
```

```
// save the class
typeBuilder.save();
```

The other method is similar to the next section. Create the TypeBuilder and add MethodBuilders to it for each of the methods you need in that class.

Add a Method to a Class or Interface

To add a method to a type, you create a new MethodBuilder for that method, set its source, add the MethodBuilder to the TypeBuilder for your type, and save it. The following code demonstrates how to do this.

> **NOTE**
>
> There is currently a minor bug in the tool API that removes any leading space in front of the first line of your method. There is no workaround for this; the Tool API removes all leading white-space characters. See Appendix E, "Additional Resources," for details on where you can obtain patches when they become available.

```
// connnect to the workspace
Workspace workspace = ToolEnv.connectToWorkspace();

// find the specified class
Type helloWorld =  workspace.loadedTypeNamed("SomeClass");

// create a builder factory to start code generation
BuilderFactory factory = workspace.createBuilderFactory();

// find the type builder for the existing type
TypeBuilder typeBuilder = factory.createTypeBuilder(helloWorld);

// create a new method builder for the new method
MethodBuilder mainMethod = factory.createMethodBuilder("main");

// Use a string buffer for efficiency
StringBuffer b = new StringBuffer();

// write the code for the new method
// the leading space in the following code is
//    actually tab characters
b.append("  public void foo() {\n"   );
b.append("    System.out.println(\"We're doing something\");\n" );
```

```
b.append("    }\n");

// set the source for the new method
mainMethod.setSource(b.toString());

// tell the type builder to add this method when save()d
typeBuilder.addMethodBuilder(mainMethod);

// save the type
typeBuilder.save();
```

Modify the Code in a Method

To modify code in a method, you generally ignore the old code and just replace it with new code. The code to do this is exactly the same as the code for adding a method. If you want to allow the user a safe place to put their own code, you can define user blocks for them and merge your changes with theirs. We show how to do this in the next sections.

If you want to obtain the previous source and modify it, see *Obtaining the Source of an Existing Method* later in this chapter to access the source as a String, make some changes, and then save it using this technique.

Defining User Code Blocks

Sometimes users may want to add their own code inside one of your generated methods. You can provide blocks inside the generated code that are "safe" for users to add code to. When you later regenerate the code, the code in their safe blocks remains in a block in the new code, while the rest of the generated method could change.

In general, you should provide a user-code block before or after actions in any methods that you want to have this feature, and between actions where you think the user might want more control. BuilderFactory provides a convenience method, createUserCodeBlock() that creates the block comments for you. These comments are merged with existing code when you call saveMerge() in a TypeBuilder.

You can use any String as the identifier for user code blocks. We recommend that you pick textual names rather than numbers like the VCE uses. This gives you more flexibility if you want to add more user blocks later.

```
// connnect to the workspace
Workspace workspace = ToolEnv.connectToWorkspace();

// find the specified class
Type helloWorld =  workspace.loadedTypeNamed(args[1]);
```

```
// create a builder factory to start code generation
BuilderFactory factory = workspace.createBuilderFactory();

// find the type builder for the existing type
TypeBuilder typeBuilder = factory.createTypeBuilder(helloWorld);

// create a new method builder for the new method
MethodBuilder mainMethod = factory.createMethodBuilder("main");

// Use a string buffer for efficiency
StringBuffer b = new StringBuffer();

// Define the source for the method, including some
//   user code blocks before and after the action
// the leading space in the following code is actually
//   one or two tab characters
b.append("  public static void main(String[] args) {\n"    );
b.append(factory.createUserCodeBlock("before action","\t\t"));
b.append("\n");
b.append("    System.out.println(\"Hello, World!\");\n" );
b.append(factory.createUserCodeBlock("after action","\t\t"));
b.append("\n");
b.append("  }\n"                                          );

mainMethod.setSource(b.toString());
typeBuilder.addMethodBuilder(mainMethod);
typeBuilder.saveMerge();
```

Modify Method with Embedded User Code

As long as you keep specifying where the user blocks are, you can keep the user's code by calling the saveMerge() method of your TypeBuilder. You only need to use saveMerge() when at least one of your added MethodBuilders contains a user code block. If none of the changes you are making modify methods with user code blocks, you can still use save().

> **NOTE**
>
> Be careful to keep the same name for the user code block. If you change the name, the code entered by the user (in the block with the old name) will be discarded.

The following code modifies an existing method with user code blocks. Note that we used the same user code block names as we did in the previous example.

```
// connnect to the workspace
Workspace workspace = ToolEnv.connectToWorkspace();

// find the specified class
Type helloWorld =  workspace.loadedTypeNamed(args[1]);

// create a builder factory to start code generation
BuilderFactory factory = workspace.createBuilderFactory();

// find the type builder for the existing type
TypeBuilder typeBuilder = factory.createTypeBuilder(helloWorld);

// create a new method builder for the new method
MethodBuilder mainMethod = factory.createMethodBuilder("main");

// Use a string buffer for efficiency
StringBuffer b = new StringBuffer();

// Create the new code with user blocks. In this
//   example we add a new user block
// the leading space in the following code is actually
//   one or two tab characters
b.append("  public static void main(String[] args) {\n"   );
b.append(factory.createUserCodeBlock("before action","\t\t"));
b.append("\n");
b.append("     System.out.println(\"This is different!\");\n" );
b.append(factory.createUserCodeBlock("after action","\t\t"));
b.append("\n");
b.append("     System.out.println(\"So is this!\");\n" );
b.append(factory.createUserCodeBlock("final action","\t\t"));
b.append("\n");
b.append("  }\n"                                              );

// set the source for the method builder
mainMethod.setSource(b.toString());

// tell the type builder that we want to change
typeBuilder.addMethodBuilder(mainMethod);

// merge the changes, keeping the user-entered code
typeBuilder.saveMerge();
```

Checking if a Method Exists

Sometimes you may want to check if a method exists. What you really want to check is if a method exists *with a specific signature*. To do this, create a new MethodBuilder and set the source to an empty method. You do this just so you have a new method with the signature you want to find. You pass this method to checkMethodExists, which compares its method signature with those in the type.

> **NOTE**
>
> When specifying parameters to the test method, you should fully qualify all types other than those in package java.lang. This ensures that the Tool API will be able to match the parameter types even if the necessary imports are not present in the type.

You do not need to specify the access modifier for the method, or any code within the method.

```
// connect to the workspace
Workspace workspace = ToolEnv.connectToWorkspace();
Type type = workspace.loadedTypeNamed(args[1]);

// get the type builder for the class
BuilderFactory factory = workspace.createBuilderFactory();
TypeBuilder typeBuilder = factory.createTypeBuilder(type);

// create a new method builder for the search
// note that it just needs to define the signature
//    -- no method body needed
//    -- no access modifier needed
//    -- parameter types should be fully-qualified
//       in case imports are not present
MethodBuilder test = factory.createMethodBuilder("test");
test.setSource("void paint(java.awt.Graphics i) {}");

// check to see if we have a method with the signature
if (typeBuilder.checkMethodExists(test))
  System.out.println("FOUND!!!");
```

Delete a Method

Method deletion is actually very simple. First, create a *new* MethodBuilder with the same signature as the method you want to delete. Then, mark that MethodBuilder for deletion. Finally, add it to the TypeBuilder. When the TypeBuilder executes save() or saveMerge() calls, the method is deleted.

```
// connect to the workspace
Workspace workspace = ToolEnv.connectToWorkspace();

// find the specified type
Type helloWorld =  workspace.loadedTypeNamed(args[1]);

// get a builder factory to start code generation
BuilderFactory factory = workspace.createBuilderFactory();

// get the type builder to change the specified class
TypeBuilder typeBuilder = factory.createTypeBuilder(helloWorld);
MethodBuilder mainMethod = factory.createMethodBuilder("main");

// specify enough source for the method signature
mainMethod.setSource("void main(java.lang.String[] args) {}");

// check if it exists...
if (typeBuilder.checkMethodExists(mainMethod)) {
  // ... if so, mark it for deletion
  mainMethod.markForDeletion(true);

  // tell the type builder that we'd like to make changes
  typeBuilder.addMethodBuilder(mainMethod);

  // save the type, deleting the method.
  typeBuilder.save();
}
```

Obtaining the Source of an Existing Method

If you need to work with the existing method source, you *cannot* simply grab a MethodBuilder from the TypeBuilder and call getSource(). Instead, you should create a new MethodBuilder that has the proper signature of the method you want. Then check that it exists in the type. Finally, call getExistingMethodSource() for that MethodBuilder in the TypeBuilder. This finds the method with the same signature and returns its code as a String.

```
// connect to the workspace
Workspace workspace = ToolEnv.connectToWorkspace();
```

```
// find the specified type
Type helloWorld =  workspace.loadedTypeNamed(args[1]);

// get a builder factory to start code generation
BuilderFactory factory = workspace.createBuilderFactory();

// get the type builder to change the specified class
TypeBuilder typeBuilder = factory.createTypeBuilder(helloWorld);

// create a method builder to help us find main
MethodBuilder mainMethod = factory.createMethodBuilder("test");

// set enough source so we have the signature
mainMethod.setSource("void main(java.lang.String[] args) {}");

// check to see if a method with that signature exists
if (typeBuilder.checkMethodExists(mainMethod)) {
  String source = typeBuilder.getExistingMethodSource(mainMethod);
  workspace.logMessage("Source code for main:\n" + source, true);
}
```

Storing Tool Options

A nice touch to add to your tool is persistence of tool options. Most tools require the user to provide some input, such as classes to export, and some output, such as where to export the classes. Users can quickly grow to hate a tool if they must input the same data every time they use the tool.

To resolve this situation, tools can save ToolData objects. ToolData acts as a keyed piece of information that VisualAge for Java tracks for you. Your tool accesses it through a key, which usually maps uniquely to the tool name. The data stored within it can be *any* Serializable object, allowing you to store any amount of necessary data. ToolData can be stored at the workspace level or with any WorkspaceModel subclass.

Setting Tool Data

Set tool data by creating an instance of some Serializable class, storing your data within that class, and then calling setToolOptions() with that data. For example, suppose that you want to store the last-used class, package, and project names. Start with the following code, defining a bean that holds the data:

```
import java.io.*;

public class LastUsedOptions implements Serializable {
```

```
  private String lastClass;
  private String lastPackage;
  private String lastProject;
  public String getLastClass()   {return lastClass;}
  public String getLastPackage() {return lastPackage;}
  public String getLastProject() {return lastProject;}
  public void setLastClass(String lastClass) {
    this.lastClass = lastClass;
  }
  public void setLastPackage(String lastPackage) {
    this.lastPackage = lastPackage;
  }
  public void setLastProject(String lastProject) {
    this.lastProject = lastProject;
  }
}
```

Then write the code to store the current values from the tool in this object and save it as tool data.

```
// connect to the workspace
Workspace workspace = ToolEnv.connectToWorkspace();

// set up the options for later retrieval
LastUsedOptions options = new LastUsedOptions();
options.setLastClass("SomeClassName");
options.setLastPackage("some.package");
options.setLastProject("A Sample Project");

// store the options, keyed by this tool name
ToolData toolData = new ToolData("my.class.ThisToolName", options);
workspace.setToolOptions(toolData);
```

Checking if Tool Data Exists

If you need to check if a ToolData exists for a project, simply call testToolOptions() in the Workspace interface. For example:

```
// connect to workspace
Workspace workspace = null;
workspace = ToolEnv.connectToWorkspace();

// check to see if the tool options exist
if (workspace.testToolOptions("my.class.ThisToolName")) {
  // get the options...
}
```

Reading the Tool Data

As soon as you know the tool data exists, you can read it via the getToolOptions() method in the Workspace interface. For example:

```
// connect to the workspace
Workspace workspace = ToolEnv.connectToWorkspace();

// grab the tool data
ToolData toolData = workspace.getToolOptions("my.class.ThisToolName");

// get the data we want from it
LastUsedOptions options = (LastUsedOptions)toolData.getData();

// use the data
workspace.logMessage(options.getLastClass() + "\n", true);
workspace.logMessage(options.getLastPackage() + "\n", true);
workspace.logMessage(options.getLastProject() + "\n", true);
```

Deleting the Tool Data

If you no longer need the data, or perhaps your user requests so, you can delete the tool data by calling clearToolOptions(). For example:

```
// connect to the workspace
Workspace workspace = ToolEnv.connectToWorkspace();

// delete the tool data
workspace.clearToolOptions("my.class.ThisToolName");
```

Storing Other Files

You can also get a tool-specific directory in which you can place whatever you want. Note that there is a *single* instance of this directory, as opposed to one tool directory per project. This is a good place to store other files and data that you want to apply to the tool no matter on which project you invoke it. You can get this name by calling the getToolDataDirectory() method of the Workspace class.

Workspace and Repository Data

You can store ToolData for *any* Workspace model. You can do this by calling the following methods, available from Project, Package, or Type. The Tool API defines these methods in interface WorkspaceModel.

> **setToolWorkspaceData(ToolData data)** associates the data with the Project, Package, or Type, and the ToolData key.

getToolWorkspaceData(String key) obtains the data for this Project, Package, or Type with the specified key.

testToolWorkspaceData(String key) checks to see if this Project, Package, or Type has data for the specified key.

clearToolWorkspaceData(String key) removes the data from the Project, Package, or Type has data for the specified key.

Using these methods, you can store information *for the user* in their workspace. Think of these as personalized tool options.

You can also store data in the repository instead of in the workspace. This makes the settings available to *all* users who connect to that repository. The repository versions of these methods are:

setToolRepositoryData(ToolData data) associates the data with the Project, Package, or Type, and the ToolData key.

getToolRepositoryData(String key) obtains the data for this Project, Package, or Type with the specified key.

testToolRepositoryData(String key) checks to see if this Project, Package, or Type has data for the specified key.

clearToolWorkspaceData(String key) removes the data from the Project, Package, or Type has data for the specified key.

Usage for all of these methods is similar to the getToolOptions() and setToolOptions() methods.

Miscellaneous Features

There are still a few features left in the API. They do not seem to fit in with any of the above topics, so we lump them together here.

Temporary directories. Sometimes you need a temporary directory while processing a tool. You might use it to export code that you need to process outside VisualAge for Java, for example. The Tool API can create a temporary directory for you through Workspace's getTempDirectory() method. This method returns a String, the name of the temporary directory. After your tool exits, VisualAge deletes the temporary directory and its contents.

Users. You may need to know which users can access this workspace, as well as name of the current workspace owner. You can access this information through the following methods in Workspace:

getValidUsers() returns an array of Strings that are the names of the users who can access this workspace.

getCurrentOwnerName() returns the name of the current workspace owner.

Shutting down VisualAge for Java. You can shut down VisualAge for Java by invoking the shutdown() method of the Workspace interface. This is normally only used in tool servlets (see *Remote Tool Access* later in this chapter), but if you have a need you can use it in a normal tool as well. If you do use it, make sure the user is well aware that you plan to shut down, or they may think the IDE has crashed.

Removing Features and Tools

To remove features, open the Quick-Start dialog (press F2 or select **File->Quick Start**) and choose **Features->Remove Feature.** Select the feature in question; VisualAge will remove that feature from your workspace as well as any additions for it in your palette.

> **NOTE**
>
> This does *not* remove it from the features directory. If you want to completely delete it, remove the feature as previously mentioned, exit VisualAge for Java, and delete the feature's base directory. If you do not delete the directory, you can add the feature back any time you want.

To remove tools, exit VisualAge and delete the tool base directory. The next time you start VisualAge for Java, the tool menu options disappear.

Internationalization and Features/Tools

If you want your control file to act differently based on the user's locale, you can simply define an .ini file for the desired locale. The default.ini file is just that: a set of defaults. Specific locale files override the default's behavior.

Suppose that you wanted to create a British English control file. You would simply define en_GB.ini in the feature or tool's base directory. If you wanted to define a set of general French control file settings, you would define fr.ini. To specify French in Canada, define fr_CA.ini. You need only define the settings that differ from the default.ini file in each of these. The more specific the locale in the file name, the higher its precedence. For example, entries in en_GB.ini take precedence over any in en.ini, which takes precedence over default.ini (assuming the locale is British English, of course).

> **NOTE**
>
> All control files *must* be ASCII files. If you need to use non-ASCII characters, you must use UNICODE escapes (\uxxx) to specify those characters.

Summary

The VisualAge for Java Tool API provides a powerful means for you to extend your development environment. This chapter has provided all of the information you need to create some very useful tools, helping you to generate commonly used code and automate tasks such as exports, imports, and repository maintenance.

Next, we move on to a few maintenance and troubleshooting tips, keeping your environment in tip-top shape and performing as fast as possible.

INTERNATIONALIZATION

A

VisualAge for Java provides some very useful support for internationalization of your applications. Internationalization is the process of making your program generic enough to run in any country using any language in the world. Through a few simple tools, VisualAge for Java can pull *all* of your Strings out of your code into external resource bundles, making it easy to provide localized resource bundles for each end user's language. These resource bundles provide the key to adapting your application to a specific language or region in the world.

In this appendix, we describe the tools provided with VisualAge for Java to help you internationalize your applications. This appendix is not intended to fully educate you on the topic of internationalization, and VisualAge for Java will not automatically do everything you need.

What Is Internationalization?

Internationalization, often called I18N because there are 18 letters between its leading 'I' and trailing 'N', is the process of making your program language-independent. Each country, and regions within that country, has different languages and customs for presenting data to the user of your application. We call these languages and customs *locales*. Although many people in the world speak English, you can much more effectively communicate with your users in their native language and using their customary ways of representing numbers, dates, and messages. Respecting the native language and formatting customs of your users makes your application stand out as significantly more user-friendly.

While internationalization is the process of making your site language-independent, localization is the process of *rebinding* your application to a specific locale. Java provides some great support for I18N, but it can be a lot of work during application development. Note that this appendix assumes you have internationalization knowledge or can acquire it from another source. We overview the concepts but cannot go into detail on exactly how internationalization works. See Appendix E, "Additional Resources" for some places you can find more details on internationalization.

What Must Be Internationalized?

There are many things that cause problems when non-English speakers interact with your application. Displayed text is the most obvious problem to spot, but other concerns, such as how numbers and dates are formatted, can make it difficult for your users to properly interpret the data you display.

The basic concerns with I18N are:

- Do not hardcode any Strings that the user will see. All Strings should appear in the user's native language.
- Do not assume a particular sorting order. Different languages use different character sets and may order characters differently.
- Do not hardcode any date formatting. Dates should appear in the user's expected format. For example, 5/4/99 means May 4, 1999 in the United States, but April 5, 1999 in Germany.
- Do not hardcode decimal formatting. Some countries use periods for decimal placement, while others use commas.
- Do not hardcode word order in messages. Messages like "You selected the green cat" where "green" varies should internationalize the *format* of the message. In Spanish, you would want to place the adjective *after* the noun, yielding "gato verde" instead of "verde gato".
- Do not use absolute positioning of GUI components. Suppose that you change the text on a button from "Bye" to "Auf Wiedersehen" when you move the application from the United States to Germany. If you had sized the button for the word "Bye", you could end up with just "Wieder" (which unfortunately means "again").

VisualAge for Java provides some excellent assistance for hardcoded Strings. The rest of the I18N issues are up to you to resolve, using the types and methods of the java.text package. In brief, you can solve these other issues as follows:

- Sort with the help of a java.text.Collator.
- Format dates using the java.text.DateFormat class.
- Format numbers using the java.text.NumberFormat class.
- Assemble messages using the java.text.MessageFormat class.
- Use layout managers in your GUIs to ensure they can resize internal components if their text changes.

The remaining issue, hardcoded Strings, is quite easy to resolve in VisualAge for Java, as we will see in the next section, String internationalization.

String Internationalization

The easiest way to deal with String-independence is to *ignore* it until you are nearly done with your application. Yes, we said *ignore* it.

VisualAge for Java provides some great tools to pull Strings out of your application, as well as ways to prevent each String from being hard coded. It is *much* easier to fix all of your Strings at once than one at a time. Suppose that we create the GUI shown in Figure A.1. This GUI contains several Strings that are only meaningful to an English speaker.

When implementing this GUI, we hard coded the values of each of the label texts. Now comes the fun part: asking VisualAge to remove this language dependency!

The Externalize Strings Command

The class pop-up menus contain an **Externalize Strings** command, shown in Figure A.2. This command helps you by removing *all* Strings from your code, placing them in either a property file or a resource class. *This makes your application generic with regard to which Strings it presents to the user.* When running the application, you only need to use Java's support for finding the appropriate resource bundle for the current locale, and the users will see the right text in their language.

Figure A.1 A sample English GUI.

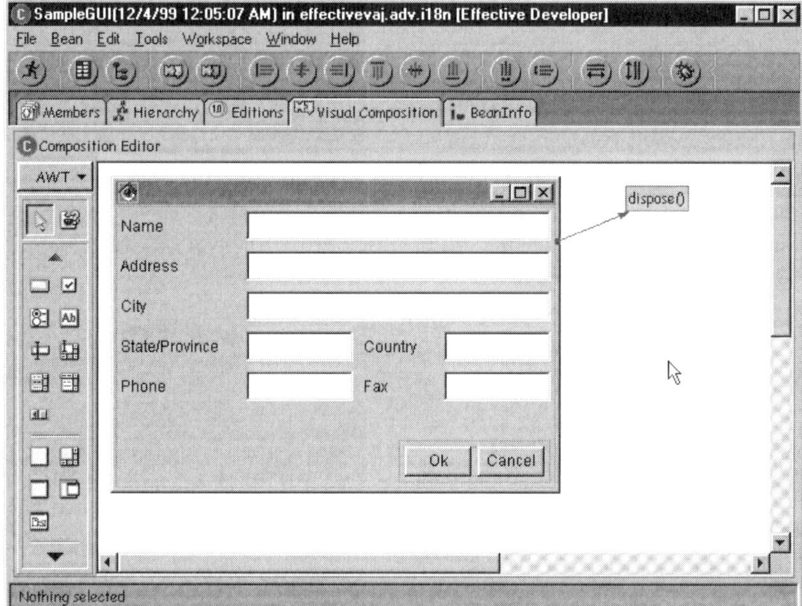

Figure A.2 The Externalize Strings command.

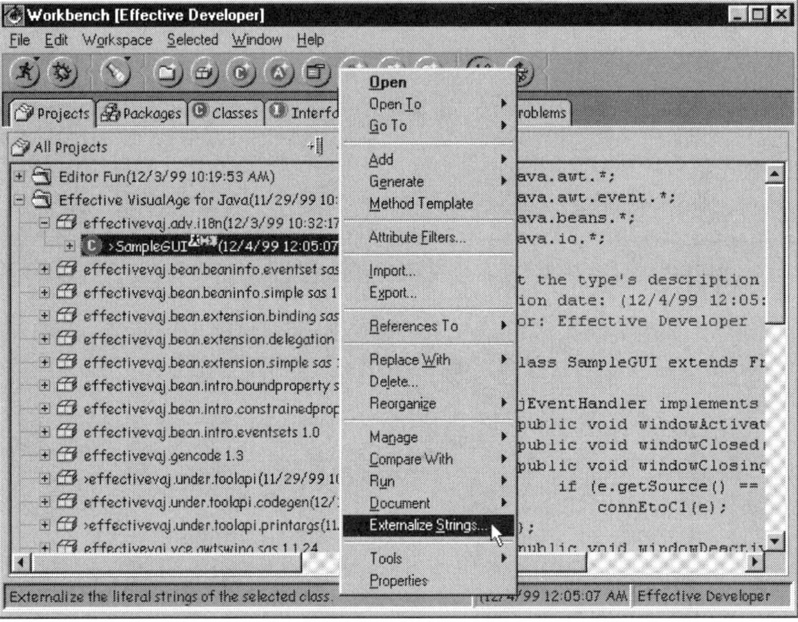

The dialog shown in Figure A.3 appears when you select **Externalize Strings**. The command extracts *all* Strings from your code, presenting them to write to resource bundles. You can specify the type of resource bundle to use:

List resource bundle. A class that contains a table of name/value pairs. These pairs describe the actual text to use for a key in your code.

Property resource file. A file that contains Java language property assignments. The assignments describe the text to use for keys in your code. We recommend that you place these files in the project_resources directory for the current project.

Both types of resource bundles accomplish the same task. List resource bundles are compiled code, and can perform a bit faster, but they cannot be as easily modified by the end user.

The dialog also allows you to specify the names of the keys to use for each String. Initially you will see *no* keys. You must first choose the list resource bundle class or property resource file to make the keys appear, as shown in Figure A.4. The context pane shows the code that contains the String.

Within the table in the center of the dialog, you can change the keys by clicking on them. You can also change the action to perform. By default, the dialog contains check marks, instructing the tool to perform the translation by moving the

Figure A.3 The externalize strings dialog.

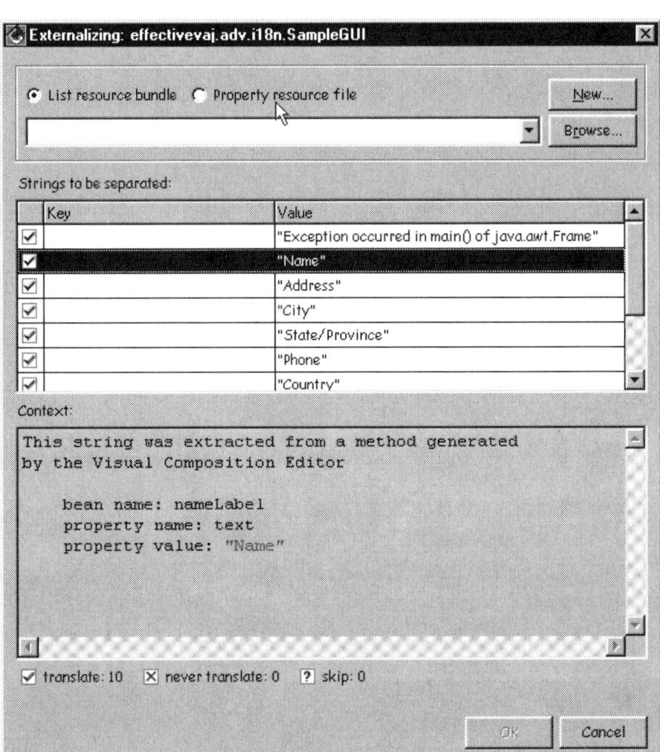

String out of your code. If you select **never translate**, the red X, you will never see theX'd items in an externalize request again. If you just want to skip certain Strings, choose **skip** ("?").

> **WARNING**
>
> Use **never translate** with extreme caution. Once you set strings to never translate, you cannot access them via **Externalize Strings.**

Where Did All My Strings Go?

After you click Ok, VisualAge for Java replaces the selected strings with resource bundle calls. These calls look up the needed text from the resource bundle created when externalizing Strings.

Figure A.4 After choosing property resource file.

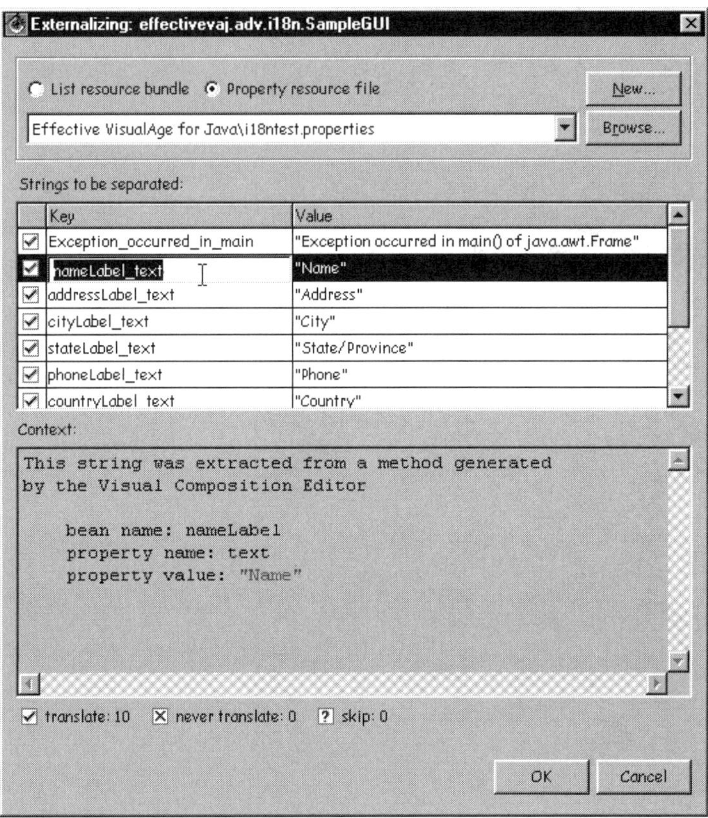

Looking at the following code, you can see that VisualAge has added a ResourceBundle and replaced the text that we had set for the label's text. Methods for the other Labels are similar.

```
private static ResourceBundle resi18ntest =
       ResourceBundle.getBundle("i18ntest");   //$NON-NLS-1$

private Label getaddressLabel() {
  if (ivjaddressLabel == null) {
    try {
      ivjaddressLabel = new Label();
      ivjaddressLabel.setName("addressLabel");
      ivjaddressLabel.setText(
                  resi18ntest.getString("addressLabel_text"));
```

```
      // user code begin {1}
      // user code end
    } catch (java.lang.Throwable ivjExc) {
      // user code begin {2}
      // user code end
      handleException(ivjExc);
    }
  }
  return ivjaddressLabel;
}
```

For this example, we generated a property resource file that looks as follows. Note that VisualAge generated the above code and this resource file.

```
Exception_occurred_in_main = \
      Exception occurred in main() of java.awt.Frame
nameLabel_text = Name
addressLabel_text = Address
cityLabel_text = City
stateLabel_text = State/Province
phoneLabel_text = Phone
countryLabel_text = Country
faxLabel_text = Fax
okButton_label = Ok
cancelButton_label = Cancel
```

If we had instead used a list resource bundle, VisualAge generates the following definition for the resource bundle.

```
private static ResourceBundle resi18test =
    ResourceBundle.getBundle(
      "effectivevaj.adv.i18n. I18NTestBundle");  //$NON-NLS-1$
```

This refers to a Java class that defines the key/value pairs rather than a property file. This list resource-bundle class looks as follows.

```
public class I18NTestBundle extends ListResourceBundle {
  static final Object[][] contents = {
    {"Exception_occurred_in_main",
          "Exception occurred in main() of java.awt.Frame"},
    {"nameLabel_text", "Name"},
    {"addressLabel_text", "Address"},
    {"cityLabel_text", "City"},
    {"stateLabel_text", "State/Province"},
    {"phoneLabel_text", "Phone"},
    {"countryLabel_text", "Country"},
```

```
        {"faxLabel_text", "Fax"},
        {"okButton_label", "Ok"},
        {"cancelButton_label","Cancel"}
    };

    protected Object[][] getContents() {
        return contents;
    }
}
```

Our program is now hardcoded-String-free!

Now What?

The above application still has the same effect. The English names appear in the GUI. We can change that, however. For example, to make the text appear in French, copy and edit the generated resource file, naming is i18ntest_fr.properties:

```
Exception_occurred_in_main = \
      Exception occurred in main() of java.awt.Frame
nameLabel_text = Nom
addressLabel_text = Adresse
cityLabel_text = Ville
stateLabel_text = Etat/Province
phoneLabel_text = Telephone
countryLabel_text = Pays
faxLabel_text = Fax
okButton_label = Valider
cancelButton_label = Annuler
```

If the user runs the program in locale "fr", they will see these Strings instead of the English defaults we provide.

> **NOTE**
>
> Depending on the locale, sometimes it's okay for certain messages to remain in English. In the above example, in some French-speaking countries it might be okay to use "Exception occurred in main() of java.awt.Frame." In other French-speaking countries it could cause a riot. Situations like these require research into specific regions' use of the language.

Changing VCE Properties after Externalizing Strings

Besides using the **Externalize Strings** command, you can also set the Strings on a property-by-property basis in the VCE. When you display a property sheet in the VCE, any String values look as displayed in Figure A.5. Note the ... button. Clicking it displays the Text property editor shown in Figure A.6.

Using this dialog, you can choose the resource bundle to use, the key name, and the default value. After you make changes and save the visual design, the VCE updates the resource bundle to contain the new values.

General Internationalization Strategy

The general strategy for internationalizing your code boils down to the following:

- Ignore Strings until the end.
- Make sure you properly handle numbers, dates, and sorting where you use them.
- Always use layout managers.

Then, when your application is complete:

- Externalize all user-visible Strings.
- Copy the resource bundle class or property file to ones for the proper locales.
- Change the contents of the property files to be language-specific Strings.

Figure A.5 A VCE string property.

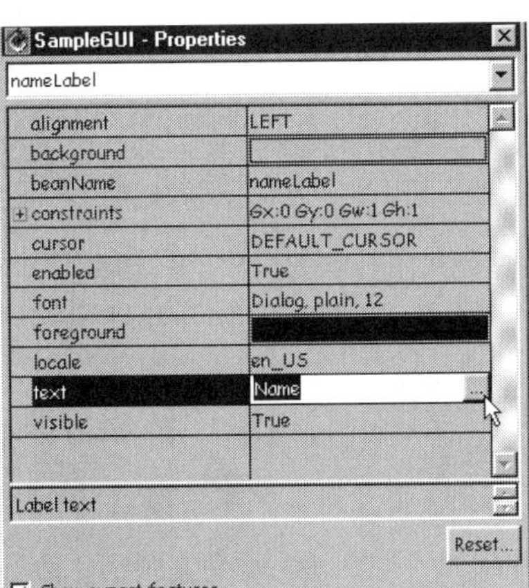

Figure A.6 String internationalization in the VCE.

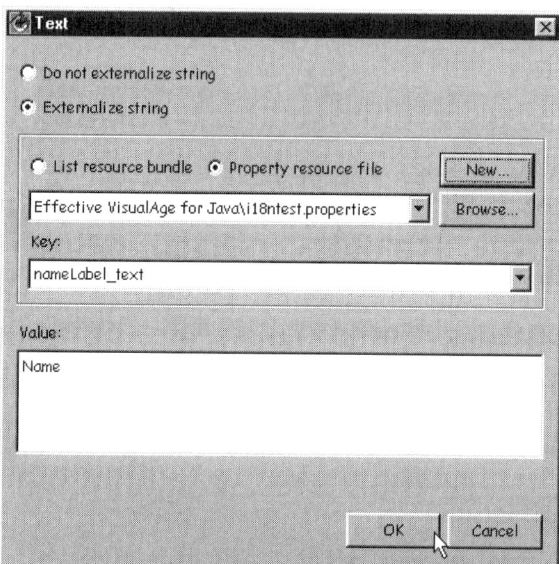

Keep an eye on the VisualAge for Java Tips and Tricks page (www.javadude.com/vaj) for some tips on other internationalization issues.

Summary

Internationalization makes your application stand out from the rest. Respecting the language of your user makes using the application more pleasant for them. VisualAge provides some great tools to help, but you still need to think globally while writing code, using the java.text package for date, number, and message formatting.

Maintenance and Troubleshooting

B

In this appendix, we present a few tips on improving performance and correcting problems when they occur. This appendix is not a complete troubleshooting guide, however, and we recommend that you take advantage of the VisualAge for Java newsgroups and FAQs to help diagnose and solve your problems. See Appendix E, "Additional Resources" for details on available newsgroups and FAQs.

Performance

For many users, VisualAge for Java performance is not even an issue. For some, performance can be dreadful. In this section, we examine some of the causes of performance problems and how you can correct them.

Fragmentation and Disk Speed

The VisualAge for Java repository is rather large, usually over 50MB, and grows much larger for the Enterprise Edition. Large files fragment *very* quickly. By defragmenting your drive often, perhaps daily, you can significantly speed up access to the repository.

This seems to be the number-one culprit of performance problems. Machines are getting *so* fast that disk access is a significant bottleneck. Any time you access the hard drive, whether it is to access data, like VisualAge retrieving or saving source, or page virtual memory, you take a performance hit. If your disk is badly fragmented, the disk access time increases significantly.

If you are using OS/2, fragmentation is not an issue because you use HPFS (High Performance File Systemdrives)! HPFS prevents or reduces fragmentation.

If you are using Windows 95/98/2000, use the defragmenter that comes with the operating system. Access it from the tools page of a disk's property sheet or from **Start->Programs->Accessories->System Tools**.

Windows NT does not come with a defragmentation tool. You must buy a defragmenter. There are a few sources for defragmentation tools:

Diskkeeper (www.diskeeper.com). This product has a boot-time directory consolidator that can help even more by arranging all directories in one chunk on the disk.

PerfectDisk (www.raxco.com). This product has an interesting placement algorithm. It places less-recently-used files at the start or end of the disk, and more-recently-used ones at the center. This reduces disk head movement and because fragmentation usually only occurs near the center (rather than spread over the disk) reduces later defragmentation run times.

From experience, it seems that VisualAge runs faster on a FAT or HPFS drive than on an NTFS drive. And if you have FAT32 it seems to be a slight improvement as well.

Other than fragmentation issues, you should place the VisualAge installation on the fastest hard drive you have available. VisualAge for Java is *very* I/O intensive, and even a slightly faster disk can make a world of difference. If you are looking for optimal performance, a high-speed SCSI drive is usually a good choice. If you are installing a team server, you should ensure you do so on a very fast file-server machine. Preferably the file server should be dedicated to serving the team repository.

Workspace and Repository Size

The size of your workspace and repository can have an impact on performance. The workspace image is loaded into RAM when VisualAge for Java starts. The larger the workspace is, the more RAM that VisualAge consumes, and the higher the probability that the operating system will need to swap RAM to disk. The larger the repository, the faster it fragments and the sooner search speed slows.

Three things you can do to help improve performance here are:

1. Remove unused code from the Workbench.
2. Store rarely used code in a separate repository (sometimes called a Warehouse).
3. Purge code or old editions of code that you know you'll never need.

Smaller repositories can mean better access times for the data you are looking for. Delete items from the repository that you no longer need. However, the repository size isn't nearly as big of a concern as the size of the workspace.

Keeping a Lean Workspace

Any time you save a method, VisualAge checks dependencies in your workspace and recompiles *anything* that needs recompilation. The larger the workspace, the slower this process can become. In addition, VisualAge for Java loads the workspace contents into memory. The bigger your workspace, the more RAM VisualAge will consume.

If you've got code in your workspace that you don't use (like that copy of IBM's huge San Francisco library that you evaluated last month and have not used, you should remove it from your workspace.

To clean your Workspace:

1. **Version the code you are no longer using.** By versioning the code, you lock the current incarnation of it in the repository. If you do end up needing the code later, you can just bring it back in from the repository.
2. **Delete the code from the workspace.** After you have versioned the code, you can delete it from the workspace; it will still exist in the repository. Any compiles that you now do in the workspace will no longer need to check this code for dependencies and possibly recompile it. If you need the code later, you can bring it in from the repository again. When you bring it back in, VisualAge will compile it against what is currently in the workspace.

Warehousing

If you have some code that you use very rarely, export it to a separate repository file and delete it from your workspace and repository. For example, suppose that you were developing exercise solutions for a class you are presenting. You probably do a lot of work to create the exercises, write them out to a CD-ROM or Web site, and then don't need to modify them for a while, at least until you find a problem or add a new exercise.

When you are not actively using the code, you can *warehouse* it by exporting it to a different repository file and then delete it from your primary repository. When you need it again, just import the warehouse repository file and then add the projects into your workspace.

Purging

Make sure you purge and compact your repository regularly. Whether that means once per month for a single-user repository or bi-weekly for a team repository is up to you. However, you should make it a habit to get rid of old editions that you are certain you no longer need. If you connect to a team repository, you are responsible for purging old editions of projects and packages that you own. If you do not own any projects or packages, you do not need to perform this task. By regularly purging your packages and projects, the repository administrator can compact the repository to reduce its size. See Chapter 4, "Using Version Control," for details on purging program elements from the repository. Keep an eye on the

VisualAge for Java Tips and Tricks site (http://javadude.com/vaj) for tools that will help make the purging process simpler.

System Resources

System resources, such as memory and CPU speed, can make a large difference in performance as well.

One of the best and least expensive ways to gain performance in VisualAge for Java is to add more RAM. As computers get faster, the speed of file I/O becomes more of a bottleneck. If you do not have enough RAM to run the program, the operating system must swap memory out to your disk, and that can be *very* slow compared to other operations on your computer.

Memory is incredibly inexpensive right now, and it seems that the prices keep dropping. By adding more memory, you will encounter less swapping and much improved performance.

IBM specifies 64MB RAM as a minimum, recommending 96MB. 96MB seems to perform well, assuming you are not running much else besides VisualAge for Java. (Note that there have been reports that some combinations of chips to create 96MB RAM perform very poorly.) We recommend 128MB RAM or more, depending on how many other applications you run at the same time. For example, while writing this paragraph, I am currently running VisualAge for Java, Word, UltraEdit, Outlook, Excel, Internet Explorer, and Paint Shop Pro. I notice no performance problems, running with 256MB RAM on a Pentium III 550MHz.

Not everyone has a 500MHz+ machine available, but that usually is not a problem. Many users report excellent performance on 200MHz machines. RAM, disk speed, and defragmentation contribute much more significantly than CPU speed once you are past 200MHz.

Some users have reported running the VisualAge for Java Version 3.0 beta for Linux on a 486 with 16MB RAM, and called the performance acceptable. While we cannot recommend that configuration, you may want to try the Linux edition if you have a Linux-loaded machine available.

Maintenance and Recovery

In this section, we look at some of the things you should do to ensure you don't lose data in VisualAge for Java. Of all the available Java IDEs, VisualAge for Java is by far the most stable. However, other programs that you run at the same time can cause your operating system to crash, or you could experience a power failure. We'll explore what data you should back up, how to recover it, and how to ensure your data is safe when upgrading VisualAge for Java.

Backups

There are two important files in VisualAge for Java that you should back up: the repository and the workspace. The repository stores all of your source code, visual designs, and version information, while the workspace views a slice of the repository contents. It is important to back these files up so that you do not lose your source code or a clean view of it from the workspace.

The Repository

It is extremely rare for the repository to become corrupt, but if it does, *you lose data*: plain and simple. Because of this, we *strongly* recommend that you back up the repository nightly. This ensures that you never lose more than a day's worth of work. You can copy and zip the repository file. Make sure you zip it, as it compresses *very* well, and you can save a great deal of disk space.

You can usually find the repository file at **installDirectory\ide\repository\ivj.dat** (the location can be slightly different based on platform and VisualAge installation directory). Depending on the edition of VisualAge for Java, you may have changed the location of this file, or it may be on a team server machine. The repository administrator must perform regular backups.

> **NOTE**
>
> You specify the *installDirectory* when you install VisualAge for Java. The default installation directory varies upon which version of VisualAge for Java you're using. If you're using VisualAge for Java, version 3.02, the default installation directory is *c:\IBMVJava*. If you're using version 3.5, the default installation directory is c:\Program Files\IBM\VisualAge for Java.

You can also export the items you are working on more often to a separate repository file. See Chapter 6, "Integrating with the File System," for details on exporting to another repository. This not only helps for transfer between computers, but also can serve as somewhat of an incremental backup.

> **NOTE**
>
> The only times the repository usually becomes corrupt are in extreme cases such as power failure or a disk crash. One way to help avoid this is to obtain an Uninterruptable Power Source (UPS) for your computer or team repository server. As for disk failure, the only way to protect against them is to back up your data often.

The Workspace

The workspace file exists at ***installDirectory*\ide\program\ide.icx** (the location can be slightly different based on platform and VisualAge installation directory). You need to back this up only when you apply patches to the environment. If anything goes wrong, you can replace the workspace with a clean workspace (described later in this appendix under *Corrupt Workspace Recovery*); then, you can simply add the items you were working on. We do *not* recommend that you back up the workspace daily because it changes too quickly. If you restore it, you will likely be looking at versions of methods and classes that are several hours back-level. It is much easier and safer to re-add the items you need, adding the latest versions.

> **TIP**
>
> Before doing *anything* else, *right now*, make a backup of a clean workspace. To do this, version *everything* in your workspace, delete all projects except the basics, and copy the ide.icx file somewhere safe. If you have not backed one up and need to recover, one is available on the VisualAge for Java installation CD (it's in a backup folder that varies by location based on the edition of VisualAge). It is generally better to keep your own backup any time you apply a patch to VisualAge for Java, as the base workspace image may change with the patch and the backup on the CD would be outdated

Other Files

In addition to the workspace and repository, there can be other files used by VisualAge for Java and your application. While these files may not be critical, they can save you a great deal of time in the event of a problem.

User Options. There is a file called ***installDirectory*\ide\program\ide.ini** that contains the user options. Unless you want to make all of your changes in the options dialog after a workspace problem, back up this file. To restore it, just copy it back. Always copy this file outside the c:\IBMVJava directory, preferably to a separate drive or tape.

Resource Files. You should also back up resource files regularly, though they do not usually change as often as source code. The resource files reside in ***installDirectory*\ide\project_resources**. You should back up this directory weekly or daily, depending on how much resource file activity occurs.

Tools and Features. Tools or features are installed in directories under ***installDirectory*\ide\tools** and ***installDirectory*\ide\features**. You should back up these directories before and after you install new tools.

Corrupt Workspace Recovery

Occasionally, VisualAge reports that the workspace has become corrupt. There are various reasons this happens, such as VisualAge bugs, machine crashes, bad Karma, but corruption is actually easy to correct.

There are several things to remember when VisualAge reports the Workspace is corrupt:

You will only lose data you did not save. Previous versions remain intact in the repository. If the workspace becomes corrupt while you are visually designing, you probably will not be able to save the visual design. Because of this, we recommend you save anytime you think of it in the VCE. If you visually design for three hours and the workspace crashes or you lose power, you have lost three hours of visual design work. If you save every 10 minutes, you have lost 10 minutes of visual design.

Save any pages you want to save in the Scrapbook. If the workspace becomes corrupt and you were working in the Scrapbook, make sure you save the pages to a file.

If you were editing a method and cannot save it, save its text to the clipboard. When VisualAge reports the problem, promptly select the code, copy it to the clipboard, and paste it into another editor like Notepad. This way you can copy and paste it back after you recover.

If you have done everything else, shut down and restart VisualAge for Java. This will usually rebuild the workspace properly.

Recovering Workspaces that VisualAge Could Not

If the workspace *cannot* be rebuilt, VisualAge will complain rather bitterly when you try to start it. You must then recover it yourself as follows:

1. Copy the saved ide.icx file (you backed it up when I said so, right?) to the ***installDirectory*\ide\program** directory. If you do not have a backup, *delete* the current ide.icx file and reinstall VisualAge for Java. This will replace *only* the workspace file, and all should be well. Then, promptly kick yourself for not following that tip about backing up the workspace before.
2. Restart VisualAge for Java.

3. If you had switched repositories during your last run, you need to switch to that repository now.
4. Add the items you were working on.

We recommend you read the online help under **Help->Reference->IDE Hints and Tips->IDE Failure** or corrupted workspace for more details on how you can recover. It is especially important that you read this section if you use the team server and the server goes down.

Version Upgrades

There are a few things you need to keep in mind when you migrate from one version of VisualAge to another.First, *read the release notes on the new version.* While release notes *can* be tedious, they can save your code in case of problems. The only safe path for migration is to read all of the migration information provided with the new release or patch. Then, perform the following actions to upgrade to the new version:

1. Version *everything* in *everyone's* workspaces before upgrading.
2. Make a copy of the repository and the tools, features, and project_resources directories.
3. If you want to ensure a clean start, uninstall the old version. This is not necessary, but if you find yourself having problems it might help.
4. Install the new version.
5. Import the old code *from the old repository.*
6. Copy in the appropriate tools, features, and project_resources.

Summary

We have provided a few key tips to help you improve VisualAge performance and correct some problems. We cannot stress enough how important it is to back up your code. It is far too easy for hard disks to crash, causing you to lose real data.

OVERVIEW OF CHANGES IN VISUALAGE FOR JAVA

C

This appendix presents a list of known changes made between versions of VisualAge for Java. We present two lists: Changes between versions 3.02 and 3.5, and changes between versions 2.0 and 3.02. This list may not be complete, but represents all changes that we are aware of in the product. This list can serve as a quick means to find some very nice improvements in the tool. We do not describe these changes in detail here, though most of the changes appear in the book.

Changes Between Versions 3.02 and 3.5

The following changes were made between version 3.02 of VisualAge for Java and version 3.5. Most of the changes made were bug fixes and usability enhancements, though some interesting new features were added.

The Workbench

- The JDK version has been updated to The Java2 Platform, Software Development Kit, version 1.2.2.
- You can now edit the entire source of a class or interface at once. A new Source View is available from class browsers and the popup menu of projects, packages and classes. Note that the order of the methods you edit in the source view is preserved when importing source code from outside VisualAge for Java.
- A Resources tab was added at the top of the Workbench, allowing you to manage resource files for all projects very easily.
- Top-level inner classes now appear in the tree views of your code, allowing you to see which inner classes are defined and work directly with their methods. Note that local and anonymous inner classes will *not* appear in the tree views, as their location within methods is important to their function.

- **Run->Run main with** and **Run->In applet viewer with** options were added to allow you to specify parameters to your application/applet for each run individually.
- A new Servlet SmartGuide helps create servlet classes.
- You can seal jars when exporting code to JAR files.

Editor

- Hovering the mouse over a variable or class name provides a tool-tip that describes the variable or class name. This can be very helpful when viewing code that you're not familiar with.
- Code formatting options have improved significantly. You can now specify more details, such as how to deal with extra blank lines in the code and how long lines should be.
- You can now specify breakpoint options (such as conditions) when creating a breakpoint, using the **Breakpoint** option of the source pane's popup menu.
- Supports bi-directional text, enabling languages that read right-to-left.
- Context-sensitive help for types and keywords is now available by selecting the word and pressing F1.

Version Control

- A new external Source Code Management bridge was added to provide stronger/simpler communication with external tools that you want to use for version control.
- Non-Java resource files are now versioned along with your projects.
- Solution maps were created to associate multiple project versions. These solution maps act like collections of projects that you can manage from the Repository explorer.
- Users can specify a default initial version name to use for any new program elements.

Removed Features

The following features have been removed from VisualAge for Java, version 3.5. If you need these features, you will need to continue using version 3.02.

- RMI Builder
- Servlet Builder. Note that if you require support for running existing Visual Servlets, you can download a Servlet Builder runtime environment

for version 3.5 from VisualAge Developer Domain (www.software.ibm.com/vadd).

WebSphere Test Environment

- Provides a central control center for the following functions. The separate control and configuration of these features no longer exist.
  - JSP Execution Monitor
  - Datasource management
  - Servlet Engine
  - Persistent Name Server
  - Enterprise JavaBean control

Database Programming

- Datasource object support has been added to help manipulate database connections.
- BLOB support has been added.

Other Features

- IBM's XML Parser is delivered and documented with VisualAge for Java.
- XML Generator function can generate random sample XML documents from a DTD. This is quite helpful for testing your parsers.
- XMI (XML Metadata Interchange) Toolkit provides support for importing Rational Rose diagrams into VisualAge for Java and generating code, as well as sending code to Rational Rose for viewing as diagrams.

Changes Between Versions 2.0 and 3.02

The following changes were made between version 2.0 of VisualAge for Java and version 3.02. The changes include new functionality, usability enhancements, and bug fixes.

The Workbench

- The Quick Start menu (available via **File->Quick Start**) has more options, helping you access tools to build applications and applets, manage the repository, and others.

- Three new menu items appear at the top of the **Workspace** menu. These items enable you to open a project, type, or package browser without changing the current selection in your browser. This is a great benefit, because you don't need to save one method or class to view another.
- Resource files now appear in a tab in the project browser. You can open, delete, and rename these files. You can assign which program or Java class opens each type of resource file.
- A new application wizard helps you build visual applications.
- The run command keeps track of the last several runs. You can right-click on the running-man button on the tool bar to choose a previously run class to run. This helps because you do not need to select the class again to run it.
- A version button now appears on the toolbar to version any selected objects.
- A **Generate->Required methods** command for classes adds stub methods required by interfaces or abstract superclasses.
- **Generate->Accessor Methods** (get/set) for fields: Using this option, you can choose a field and VisualAge will create get/set methods to access and modify that field.
- A **Reorganize->Fix/Migrate** command can rename package references in classes *and* in their visual design information. This is useful if you rename a package or want to move from Swing 1.0.3 to Swing 1.1.1.
- The **Window->Orientation** menu has changed to provide a simpler **Window->Flip orientation** option.
- The tree views store their last tree expansion states. This is optional and can be set in the **Window->Options** dialog.
- You can now open browsers in the same window, moving between windows using a forward and back button in the tool bar. This behavior is disabled by default and can be enabled in the **Window->Options** dialog.
- Bookmarks are a bit easier to manage via pop-up menus in the All Projects pane title.
- The status bar is now segmented, showing a more organized view of its data. You now have the choice of seeing the developer or owner of types in the status bar by right-clicking on the user name in the bottom-right corner of the window.
- The All Projects pane has filter buttons at top to limit public items, static methods, and field display.

- The panes of the Members page have filter buttons at the top that limit public items, static methods, visibility to root-minus-one, and field display.
- The online help format is significantly improved.
- Browsers open to the last-selected tab.
- A new Problems page appears in property dialogs for projects, packages, classes, and interfaces, showing a summary of problems. You can access this by choosing the **Properties** option from pop-up menus of projects, packages, classes, or interfaces.
- The **Reorganize->Rename** option for classes now has a check box to find references to the old name. When checked, the class is renamed and you will then see the search dialog. This can help you replace the name wherever it's referenced in your workspace.
- A new warning has been added for unconventional package names.
- Attribute filters have been added to enable you to limit displayed items in lists (protection, fields, abstract, final, constructors, and so on).
- SmartGuides can add imports for selected fully-qualified types. For example, if you enter java.awt.Frame in a superclass field, VisualAge can add *import java.awt.**; to the generated class.

Keyboard Features

- A new whatis command is available by pressing F6. You then can press another key, and VisualAge tells you what command it binds.
- You can run a class by using a keyboard assignment. By default, this is bound to Ctrl-E.
- You can maximize the pane that has focus by using (by default) Ctrl-M.
- You can change key bindings in the Options dialog.
- Multiple keys can be bound to the same action.
- Emacs-style key presses are available.

Code Assist

- Code assist is available in more places.
- You can choose completion using other keys.
- It can automatically insert code if there is only one possible completion.
- It does not require all text to be correct in the Scrapbook.
- Types are now shown for fields and macros in selection list.

- It now works case-insensitive, except for first character.
- Code assist is available in SmartGuide fields that ask for existing class or field names.
- Method parameter names now appear in tool tips.

Editor

- You can comment a block of code by selecting the code and pressing Ctrl-/. You can uncomment it by selecting the commented code and pressing Ctrl-\.
- A new incremental text search has been added. You can press Ctrl-I to start the search, and as you type letters, the first word after the cursor position that starts with all of those letters is selected.
- You can open an object browser based on selected text by pressing F3.
- Deeper undo (20 levels). Previous versions of VisualAge only allowed you to undo the last change.
- Cursor movement no longer loses undo data. In previous versions of VisualAge, if you changed the cursor position, you could no longer undo the last change.
- Backspace and delete now undo properly.
- You can view reference (API) help by pressing Ctrl-H.
- You can set a breakpoint by pressing Ctrl-B.
- HTML tags in documentation comments are now color-coded to aid readability.
- Keyword completions can create entire language constructs.
- User-defined macros, including some that have already been defined for you:
  - You can specify any text you want.
  - Predefined <user> inserts the current user name.
- Predefined <timestamp> inserts the current time.

Searching

- The search facility keeps track of previous searches. You can rerun previous searches by right-clicking the flashlight icon in the tool bar.
- Working sets allow performing a search across a specific set of projects, packages, or types.

- Textual find and replace is available across multiple objects, and it can now do whole-word matching.
- Navigation to next occurrence is easier (up and down buttons were moved to Matches pane).
- You can sort results by method or class.
- You can remove some results from view.
- You can replace matches with something else.
- Search scope is consistent across all search dialogs and Management Query window.
- Search scope is now clearly visible and modifiable.
- Common scope choices were added to method pop-up menu search-items.
- Field search menus were combined into single dialog.
- The search facility has options for called methods and used variables (method pop-up menu).
- Restructured "references to" and "declarations of" menu items.
- Management Query improvements, as follows:
  - Simpler interface.
  - Common queries were added in a drop-down menu.
  - Allows projects, packages, and types in the same search.

Import/Export

- You can automatically version after import.
- You can automatically add the most recent version of a project in a repository import file to the workspace.

Debugging

- You have more control of conditional breakpoints:
  - They can be set for a specific iteration.
  - They can be set for specific threads.
- Watch window was added to watch variable and expression values.
- The Evaluation window enables you to evaluate any code without modifying the source code.
- You can inspect selected thread in the debugger.
- Caught exceptions now appear as a debugger page instead of a dialog.

- You can set breakpoints inside a method of an external class.
- External .class file breakpoints now appear in the breakpoints list.
- Visible variables list can appear in its own window.

Scrapbook

- Goto line number (Ctrl-G) allows you to jump to a specific line number in your source code.
- Execution contexts are added only when needed.

VCE

- It now uses inner classes for event handling.
- If import-on-demand is used, the VCE generates unqualified class names in most cases.
- Custom layout manager support.
- Reset button is available to "unset" properties.
- Fix-unresolved-references command.
- Generated code no longer uses custom classes (for example, WindowCloser).
- You can register property editors for types.
- Null layout-to-GridBagLayout converter.
- Quick-form generation based on a bean definition.
- Property-to-property connection code now checks if source or target variable is null.
- The "add beans from project" option for palette management now sorts by bean class name rather than package name.
- GridLayout now allows rows=0 setting.

BeanInfo

- Ctrl-S key combination works (if it is set to save/new; otherwise, use Ctrl-Shift-S).
- **Preferred** check box in SmartGuides makes it easier to define preferred features.
- Delete dialog now includes fields for deleting properties.
- Delete dialog now selects methods by default when deleting properties.

WebSphere Test Environment

- Available in Professional and Enterprise editions on Windows/NT or Windows/2000. VisualAge for Java Version 2.0 provided this only in the Enterprise Edition.
- In the Professional Edition, it supports servlets and JavaServer Page (JSP) files.
- In the Professional Edition, the JSP Execution Monitor helps to debug JSP coding errors.
- In the Enterprise Edition, it supports Enterprise JavaBeans (EJB) components as well.

Other Features

- The Stored Procedure Builder was added.
- New Data Access Beans were added.
- SQLJ support is now provided. You can edit and compile SQLJ files.

Tool API

- New methods were added:
    - purge() in ProjectEdition and PackageEdition
    - compact() in Repository
    - hasError() in Type
    - hasSourceCode() in Type
- Remote access to tool API
- Tool data directory
    - An Early Adopters Edition supports the Java 2 platform.

THE CD-ROM

D

This book contains a CD-ROM that contains the full Professional Edition of VisualAge for Java, the sample code from this book, as well as several useful tools. This appendix describes how to install and use the tools and code.

The products (VisualAge for Java and VA Assist/J) contained on this CD-ROM will only work under Windows. However, the sample code and tools can be used in any environment that supports VisualAge for Java. The sample code and tools are included as directories rather than zip/gzip/compress files so they'll be easy to install on any platform.

System Requirements

To use this CD-ROM, your system must meet the following requirements:

- Pentium Class processor
- Windows 98/NT/2000
- 64 MB Minimum, 128MB or more *highly* recommended. (Note that IBM states that 48MB is the minimum for VisualAge for Java. While VisualAge will run in 48MB RAM, performance will be significantly degraded.)
- 800 × 600 Minimum screen resolution
- 1024 × 768 or larger recommended
- 500MB Free Hard Disk space.
- CD ROM drive

> **NOTE**
>
> For best performance, we strongly recommend that you defragement your hard drive after installing VisualAge for Java. If you are running Windows NT, you can purchase a defragmentation tool from http://www.diskeeper.com (Diskeeper) or http://www.raxco.com (Perfect Disk)

Prerequisites for VisualAge for Java, Version 3.5

This edition of VisualAge for Java, Version 3.5 has the following hardware and software prerequisites:

- Windows 98, Windows 2000, or Windows NT 4.0 with Service Pack 4 or higher.
- TCP/IP installed and configured
- Pentium® II processor or higher recommended. If you plan to work in the WebSphere™ Test Environment we recommend a minimum processor speed of 400 MHz.
- SVGA (800 × 600) display or higher (1024 × 768 recommended)
- 48 MB RAM minimum (96 MB recommended)
- To use the Distributed Debugger, you will need 128 MB RAM minimum (196 MB recommended)
- 128 MB RAM minimum is required if you wish to work in the VisualAge for Java WebSphere Test Environment. We strongly recommend 256 MB to avoid disk thrashing.
- Frames-capable Web browser such as Netscape Navigator 4.7 or higher, or Microsoft Internet Explorer 5.0 or higher. You should not use anything lower than Netscape Navigator 4.7 or Internet Explorer 5.0 to view any online documentation.
- Disk space requirements: (based on NTFS) 350 MB minimum (400 MB or more recommended). Disk space on FAT depends on hard disk size and partitioning: if you are installing to a very large FAT drive, then the space required for VisualAge for Java is almost doubled (due to 32KB cluster overhead).
- If you want to run the WebSphere Application Server with DB2(R) and VisualAge for Java concurrently, then a minimum of 512 MB is recommended.

IMPORTANT

The installation code for VisualAge for Java makes use of VB script. If you encounter an installation error message that refers to "DoCosting" or VB script runtime errors, then you do not have VB script support installed on your system. VB script support is included in Windows® 98 and Windows 2000, but not in Windows NT® 4.0. You can download Windows Script 5.5 from http://msdn.microsoft.com/scripting.

Installation of VisualAge for Java, Version 3.5

To install VisualAge for Java, version 3.5:

1. Insert the CD-ROM into your CD drive.
2. If autorun is disabled on your system, run setup.exe from the root of the CD drive.
3. Select **Install Products.**
4. Select **Install VisualAge for Java** to begin the installation of VisualAge for Java.
5. If you intend to debug any classes are developed outside the VisualAge for Java IDE or debug programs running on a separate machine, select **Install Distributed Debugger.**
6. Follow the on-screen instructions.
7. Start the VisualAge for Java IDE.

   Installation instructions giving more detail are available from the initial screen by following: **Start Here** > **Installation and Migration Guide.**

The CD-ROM Organization

The following products, samples, and tools are available on the CD-ROM:

- **IBM VisualAge for Java, Professional Edition, version 3.5**
  A full, unrestricted version of IBM's Java development environment. (Of course, if you didn't know that, you probably wouldn't have bought this book...)
- **Instantiations VA Assist/J**
  An excellent add-on to VisualAge for Java, modifying some features of the IDE to make it even easier to use.
- **Effective VisualAge for Java Sample Code**
  The sample code that appears in this book. Two versions of the sample code are included, one for use with the Enterprise Edition of VisualAge for Java, one for use with the Professional Edition.
- **JavaDude Swing Border Editor**
  A plug-in feature for the Visual Composition Editor that makes it easier to choose borders for Swing components.
- **JavaDude BoxBeans**
  A plug-in feature for the Visual Composition Editor that makes BoxLayout easy to use when building a GUI.
- **JavaDude AutoGut**
  A plug-in tool for the IDE that creates a Java interface based on a class definition. This allows you to use tools like VisualAge's BeanInfo Editor

to create a JavaBean component, then strip it down to create an interface to communicate with that component.

- **JavaDude Importify**
  A plug-in tool for the IDE that expands Java import-on-demand (".*" imports) statements into the much preferred fully-qualified import statements.

We've set up the CD-ROM with the following structure:

```
/
  products/
    IBM VisualAge for Java/
    Instantitiations VAAssist/
  samples/
    ide/
      features/
        com-javadude-bordereditor/
        com-javadude-boxbeans/
        com-javadude-effectivevaj-enterprise/
        com-javadude-effectivevaj-professional/
      program/
        lib/
          javadude-ivj-property-editor-registry.properties
      tools/
        com-javadude-autogut/
        com-javadude-importify/
```

We'll discuss how you install each part shortly.

IBM's VisualAge for Java

This CD-ROM contains a complete, commercial copy of IBM's VisualAge for Java, Professional Edition, version 3.5. When installing VisualAge for Java, please read the license agreement for terms of use.

Why We Included the Professional Edition

IBM granted us the rights to include either the full Professional Edition of VisualAge for Java, or a limited Enterprise Edition. We felt that a full professional copy would be more useful to most of the readers of this book.

The drawback to including the Professional Edition is that you cannot use it to try the Enterprise JavaBeans features described in this book. We felt that the Enterprise features wouldn't be useful to readers *unless* they were also using the Enterprise Edition at their workplace, in which case they would have access to an Enterprise Edition. In addition, the Enterprise Edition would have been limited in the number of classes you can develop and the right to create commercial applications.

Finally, the number of Enterprise-only features (such as Enterprise JavaBeans development) discussed in this book is minimal. The vast majority of this book's content applies equally to both the Professional and Enterprise Editions.

Therefore, we decided to include the full Professional Edition. We hope that you'll find it useful for Java language development for many years to come.

Installing VisualAge for Java

To install VisualAge for Java, insert the CD-ROM into your CD-ROM drive. Run **\products\IBM VisualAge for Java\setup.exe** on the CD to start the VisualAge for Java installer.

You can access the setup program using a Windows Explorer, or by double-clicking on **My Computer** and choosing the CD-ROM drive, then **products**, then **IBM VisualAge for Java**, then double-clicking on **setup.exe**.

Follow the prompts to install the product. If the installer asks you to restart your computer, please do so. We *strongly* recommend you use the default path settings, as this will help you match the product location with directories named in this book. If you need to change the installation path or drive, please note the location you select, as you'll need to know where VisualAge for Java is installed to install tools and work with resource files.

> **NOTE**
>
> To use the sample code you *must* install the **Enhanced Database Support** and **JSP Development Environment**. If you do not install this, you cannot use the WebSphere Test Environment for testing Java Servlets and JavaServer Pages, and the sample code features will not install. You can either choose **Complete** as the setup type or choose these options during a **Custom** setup.

Instantiation's VA Assist/J

Over the life of VisualAge for Java, several usability requests have been made though IBM's VisualAge for Java newsgroups. While IBM has had to spend its development efforts on new features and fixing bugs, another company, Instantiations (www.instantiations.com), has created a patch to VisualAge for Java to address many usability requests.

The CD-ROM for this book includes the preview version of VA Assist/J. This is a completely free, unlimited version of the product that runs only with the Professional Edition of VisualAge for Java. (There is no "pay version" for the Professional Edition. Instantiations also sells a version that runs with the Enterprise Edition of VisualAge for Java.)

NOTE

Instantiations has worked with IBM on these patches, starting from the actual source of VisualAge for Java. These patches are not "hacks" into the code, but are actual subclasses of the source code, extending and modifying functionality.

Features of VA Assist/J

VA Assist/J provides enhancements in four key areas:

- Version Control
- Browser/Ergonomic
- Visual Composition
- Import and Export

A brief overview of these enhancements follows. You can see all of the details and online documentation at www.instantiations.com/assist/Products/Preview. Product features are described in detail at www.instantiations.com/assist/productfeatures.htm.

We *strongly* recommend you install and use VA Assist/J, as the enhancements can make VisualAge for Java even more useful. There are far too many enhancements to list them all here, but a few of the most important ones are mentioned below.

Version Control Enhancements

VA Assist/J opens up many new ways to manage your source code. These enhancements start with version templates, making it easy to provide, and possibly require, consistent version naming conventions across your code. You can also rename versions.

Other enhancements to version control include enhancements to comparison options, easy changes to owners of projects, packages, and their contents, and combinations of operations like creating and releasing an open edition.

Browser/Ergonomic Enhancements

This is the area where VA Assist/J really shows its true colors. Quite literally, in fact.

VA Assist starts by coloring the items in the trees and lists that appear in browsers. These colors indicate the version status of the program elements, whether they are versioned, released, open editions or scratch editions. In addition, you can directly edit the names of program elements by a simple click combination.

On the various problem pages, you can filter certain types of problems, such as the dreaded Deprecation warnings. Searches provide more options, and the Running man toolbar button works the same across all pages on which it appears.

Among the many other ergonomic enhancements, many fields in the SmartGuides provide "memory", so you can easily select a previously-entered choice, and you can exit without saving the workspace.

Visual Composition Enhancements

In the Visual Composition Editor, you can directly edit the labels on many AWT and Swing components by Alt-clicking on them. You can also filter which connections should appear, helping to untangle your visual design. (However, if you've applied the Model-View-Controller paradigm as discussed in Chapters 15 and 16, your designs should not appear very tangled to begin with.) Connections can be filtered statically or based on which component is currently selected.

Other enhancements are available, but the most popular VCE enhancement is the ability to change the size of the Event-to-Code dialog.

Import and Export Enhancements

Some of the most useful enhancements fall under the realm of exporting and importing code. One of the most important such enhancements is that Export and Import sessions are remembered, so you can repeat them.

You can now choose how you want the exported code to appear, including keeping the methods in the same order in which you imported them, and formatting the exported code by indenting methods and adding a blank line between each. Finally, you can define a "batch export" that performs several export sessions at once. You can even schedule the batch export to run at a later time, providing a means to perform a nightly build outside VisualAge for Java.

Installing VA Assist/J

To install VisualAge for Java, insert the CD-ROM into your CD-ROM drive. Run **\products\Instantiations VAAssist\ VAAssistPreviewJ_v1.5.5.exe** on the CD to start the VA Assist installer.

You can access the setup program using a Windows Explorer, or by double-clicking on **My Computer** and choosing the CD-ROM drive, then **products**, then **Instantiations VAAssist**, then double-clicking on **VAAssistPreviewJ_v1.5.5.exe.**

Follow the prompts to install the product. When asked, choose the edition of VisualAge for Java that you have installed. (If you installed VisualAge from this CD-ROM, you should choose version 3.5). If the installer asks you to restart your computer, please do so.

The Book's Sample Code

In the sample directory of the CD is a collection of sample code and tools that you can use in VisualAge for Java. The sample code and tools will work in *both* the Enterprise and Professional Editions of VisualAge for Java.

License and Disclaimer for the Sample Code

The following license applies to the sample code distributed with the book. This includes the Features named

> **Effective VisualAge for Java Sample—ENTERPRISE EDITION ONLY**
>
> **Effective VisualAge for Java Sample Code—PROFESSIONAL EDITION ONLY**

Installing the Sample Code

> **WARNING**
>
> Check to see if you already have an *installdir*/program/lib/javadude-ivj-property-editor-registry.properties file. If so, you should save a copy of it somewhere before proceeding. The sample code includes a copy of this file to set up the property editor for Swing borders.
>
> If you have a copy of this file, you will need to merge the contents of the sample code's version of it with your version.

To install the sample code:

1. If VisualAge for Java is currently running, exit it.
2. Copy the directory \samples\ide from the CD-ROM to the directory you installed VisualAge for Java. For example, if you installed VisualAge for Java in its default directory, you would copy the \samples\ide directory to the c:\Program Files\IBM\VisualAge for Java directory. Note that you should copy the entire **ide** directory (not the samples directory.)

Start VisualAge for Java. You should see a dialog stating that the features and tools copied are being installed.

Choose **File->Quick Start** (or press F2).

Select **Features** in the left pane of the **Quick Start** dialog.

Select **Add Feature** in the right pane of the **Quick Start** dialog.

Press **Ok**.

Choose either
Effective VisualAge for Java Sample Code—ENTERPRISE EDITION ONLY or
Effective VisualAge for Java Sample Code—PROFESSIONAL EDITION ONLY
depending on which version of VisualAge for Java you have installed.
Do not select both.

> **NOTE**
>
> If you receive a message that some required features were not already installed, you must rerun the VisualAge for Java installer and choose to install the **Enhanced Database Support** and **JSP Development Environment**. You can either choose **Complete** as the setup type or choose these options during a **Custom** setup.

Adding the feature will take some time, as it needs to install pre-requisite features as well.

Sample Code Contents

The following is a list of all chapters in the book and which packages contain the sample code for those chapters. Any chapters that are not listed do not have any sample code. To see the sample code for a chapter, find the chapter in the following list. Then look at the listed packages in the Effective VisualAge for Java project in the Workspace.

Chapter 5 Testing and Debugging

- effectivevaj.env.debug

Chapter 7 Introduction to JavaBeans Components

- effectivevaj.bean.intro.boundproperty
- effectivevaj.bean.intro.constrainedproperty
- effectivevaj.bean.intro.eventsets

Chapter 8 The BeanInfo Editor

- effectivevaj.bean.beaninfo.eventset
- effectivevaj.bean.beaninfo.simple

Chapter 9 Extension and Composition

- effectivevaj.bean.extension.binding
- effectivevaj.bean.extension.delegation
- effectivevaj.bean.extension.simple

Chapter 10 Bean Composition in the VCE

- effectivevaj.vce.beancomp
- effectivevaj.vce.beancomp.promotion

Chapter 11 Layout Management

- effectivevaj.vce.layouts

Chapter 12 Connections

- effectivevaj.vce.connections
- effectivevaj.vce.visualclass

Chapter 13 Variables and Instances

- effectivevaj.vce.variables

Chapter 14 Design Patterns for the VCE

- effectivevaj.vce.patterns

Chapter 15 Model-View-Controller in the VCE

- effectivevaj.vce.mvc

Chapter 16 Advanced Model-View-Controller Techniques

- effectivevaj.vce.mvc.adv

Chapter 17 Factory Beans

- effectivevaj.vce.factory

Chapter 18 Using AWT and Swing in the VCE

- effectivevaj.vce.awtswing

Chapter 19 Handwritten Code versus Generated Code

- effectivevaj.gencode

Chapter 20 Bean Customization

- effectivevaj.vce.customizing

Chapter 21 Database Programming

- effectivevaj.data.applications
- effectivevaj.data.dab.connections

Chapter 22 Developing Distributed Applications

- effectivevaj.adv.dist.traditionalrmi

Chapter 23 Developing Enterprise JavaBeans

- effectivevaj.adv.ejb.association
- effectivevaj.adv.ejb.entity

- effectivevaj.adv.ejb.mappingInfo
- effectivevaj.adv.ejb.session
- EffectiveVAJMusicEJBReserved
- EffectiveVAJPart1EJBReserved

Chapter 24 Developing Servlets and JavaServer Pages

- effectivevaj.adv.servlets
- effectivevaj.adv.servlets.util

Chapter 25 Tool Integration

- effectivevaj.under.toolapi
- effectivevaj.under.toolapi.codegen
- effectivevaj.under.toolapi.printargs

Appendix A Internationalization

- effectivevaj.adv.i18n

Tools and Features

Four additional tools and features are provided on the CD-ROM:

JavaDude AutoGut. Creates a Java interface based on a class definition.

JavaDude BoxBeans. Provides easy visual manipulation of BoxLayout in the Visual Composition Editor.

JavaDude Importifier. Expands import-on-demand statements in your source code.

JavaDude Swing BorderEditor. Provides an easy way to change the borders used on Swing components.

> **NOTE**
>
> "JavaDude" refers to the name of Scott Stanchfield's Web site, http://javadude.com. You can obtain updates for these tools and features, as well as additional tools and Java information, from http://javadude.com.

License and Disclaimer for Tools and Features

The following license applies to the sample tools and features included with the book. This includes the Features and Tools named

JavaDude Swing Border Editor

JavaDude Box Beans

AutoGut (Create interface from class)

JavaDude Importifier (Expand import statements)

```
Use this code at your own risk!  Scott Stanchfield is not
responsible for any damage caused directly or indirectly
through use of this code.

I reserve no legal rights to this code—it is fully in the
public domain. An individual or company may do whatever they
wish with source code distributed with it, including the
incorporation of it into commerical software.

However, this code cannot be sold as a standalone product.

I encourage users to develop software with this code. However, I do
ask that credit is given to me for developing it. By "credit", I mean
that if you use these components or incorporate any source code into
one of your programs (commercial product, research project, or other-
wise) that you acknowledge this fact somewhere in the documentation,
research report, etc... If you like these
components and have developed a nice tool with the output, please men-
tion that you developed it using these components. In addition, I ask
that the headers remain intact in this source code. As long as these
guidelines are kept, I expect to continue enhancing this system and
expect to make other tools available as they are completed.
```

Tool Installation

These tools are installed when you install the sample code for the book. Copying the \sample\ide directory into your VisualAge for Java installation directory places these tools and features in the proper place, and restarting VisualAge for Java completes the installation.

Tool Descriptions

The tools are maintained on Scott Stanchfield's http://javaDude.com site. You can see the description of each tool in the following locations:

JavaDude AutoGut. http://javadude.com/tools/autogut

JavaDude BoxBeans. http://javadude.com/tools/boxbeans

JavaDude Importifier. http://javadude.com/tools/importifier

JavaDude Swing BorderEditor. http://javadude.com/tools/borderedit

ADDITIONAL RESOURCES

E

What follows are some useful sources of information on VisualAge for Java, the Java language, and updates/errata for this book. You'll find a list of web sites, Frequently-Asked Question lists, newsgroups, and books that we recommend for additional information.

Web Sites

There are several useful Web sites promoting the use of VisualAge for Java, and general Java programming. The following are some of the our favorites.

- **Effective VisualAge for Java Book Site—**
  www.wiley.com/compbooks/stanchfield
  Home page on the Web for this book. We'll post updates and errata here.
- **VisualAge for Java Tips and Tricks—**http://javadude.com/vaj
  A collection of useful techniques to improve your VisualAge for Java productivity. Many of these tips appear in this book, but keep an eye on the site for new tips!
- **IBM VisualAge Developer Domain—**http://www.software.ibm.com/vadd
  Home to and excellent collection of articles and downloads related to VisualAge for Java. This site requires free registration to access most content, and they reserve some content for paid subscribers. Paid subscribers can download the Professional Edition of VisualAge from this site. Think of this as IBM's development view of the tool.
- **IBM VisualAge for Java Product Home—**
  http://www.software.ibm.com/vajava
  The product homepage for VisualAge for Java. Think of this as IBM's marketing view of the tool.
- **Developerworks Java—**http://www.ibm.com/developer/java
  IBM's excellent Java language programming site.

- **AlphaBeans**—http://www.alphaworks.ibm.com/alphabeans
Excellent JavaBeans that play in VisualAge for Java. This site gives free previews of future IBM commercial beans (which usually have a very reasonable price once they "graduate" to commercial beans.)
- **Sun's Java Language Home Page**—http://java.sun.com
Home of the Java Language. Lots of great information on the language, including future plans, articles, and product downloads.
- **The Swing Connection**—http://www.theswingconnection.com
A great online magazine from Sun on using the Swing toolset. Make sure you read the archived articles as well!
- **The Java Tutorial**—http://java.sun.com/docs/books/tutorial
An excellent online tutorial for most Java concepts. Also available in book form (see the site).
- **Java Developer Connection Training and Tutorials**—
http://developer.java.sun.com/developer/onlineTraining/Several tutorials on the Java language, including many by MageLang Institute (now known as jGuru.com).

> **NOTE**
>
> This site includes the article "Effective Layout Management," a must-read article that helps you understand how layout managers can be nested to achieve your desired results. The perfect way to avoid the big bad evil GridBagLayout! (A totally unbiased opinion, by the way...)

- **IBM Websphere Product Home Page**—
http://www.software.ibm.com/websphere
The product homepage for IBM's Webpshere Application Server. Provides links to invaluable information about WebSphere, including the WebSphere Java Zone at the VisualAge Developer Domain.

Frequently Asked Questions

There are two sources for VisualAge for Java FAQs.

jGuru.com VisualAge for Java FAQ

First, the "FunkMaster Portal of the Java Universe", http://www.jGuru.com, has a searchable VisualAge for Java FAQ under its resources page. The name of the VisualAge FAQ module is FAQ: VAJ.

The jGuru.com VisualAge FAQ is open for new submissions. We encourage everyone to add new FAQ entries to help grow the FAQ. Note that question submissions and answers are moderated to limit duplicates and ensure relevancy.

IBM VisualAge Developer Domain FAQ

The VisualAge Developer Domain site also includes a VisualAge for Java FAQ. The main VisualAge Developer Domain page, http://www.software.ibm.com/vadd, contains a link to IBM's VisualAge FAQs.

Newsgroups

There are several great resources for finding the answers to your questions. Newsgroups often provide the greatest source of both answers and frustration. Be sure when using the newsgroups that you ask nicely and use a meaningful subject. Above all, *please* search the newsgroup archives before asking questions like, "Can I upgrade to JDK 1.3?" If you have not used newsgroups before, please subscribe to news:news.announce.newusers and read all entries before posting. These entries cover basic "netiquette", standards of behavior for newsgroup participation.

> **NOTE**
>
> You can access newsgroups using a tool like Microsoft's Outlook Express, Eudora, or Free Agent. If you do not have NNTP access due to firewall restrictions, you can also access newsgroups by visiting http://www.deja.com/usenet.

VisualAge for Java Newsgroups

IBM provides seven newsgroups dedicated to VisualAge for Java. The discussions on these groups are the most civil newsgroups of any on the Internet, so they can be quite a pleasant place to visit. (Please keep this in mind when asking or answering questions.) IBM provides support on these groups on a "best effort" basis. The technical support personnel make no guarantees that they will answer your questions. Fortunately, many other users know the product well and answer questions on the groups too!

IBM hosts its product newsgroups on NNTP server news.software.ibm.com. The VisualAge newsgroups are:

- **ibm.software.vajava.beans**—For discussion of JavaBean components in VisualAge for Java. Discussion can range from building beans to finding and using beans in the environment. VCE issues usually end up either here or in the ide group.
- **ibm.software.vajava.beta**—For discussion of beta versions of the product.

- **ibm.software.vajava.enterprise**—For discussion of enterprise edition questions. This usually means team version control, EJB, and other features that are only in the enterprise edition.
- **ibm.software.vajava.ide**—For discussion of general IDE operation. Some VCE issues wind up here though most should probably go in the beans group.
- **ibm.software.vajava.install**—For discussion of installation issues.
- **ibm.software.vajava.language**—For discussion of Java language issues, and how they relate to VisualAge for Java. Note that you should post general Java questions to the Java newsgroups listed below.
- **ibm.software.vajava.non-technical**—For discussion of non-technical issues like "is version 3 out yet?" or pricing issues.

Java Newsgroups

Usenet provides many Java language newsgroups as well. If your question is relating to the Java language and not use of VisualAge for Java, we recommend that you use the following usenet newsgroups.

- **comp.lang.java.advocacy**—Where you can go to praise or curse Java. Note that this often turns into fairly religious battles over the language, usually when comparing it to other languages like C++.
- **comp.lang.java.3d**—For discussion of the Java3D API.
- **comp.lang.java.announce**—General announcements. This is a very low traffic group, and was mainly intended for announcements like "JDK 1.1 has been released". Now it sees almost no activity.
- **comp.lang.java.beans** —For discussion of JavaBeans components.
- **comp.lang.java.corba**—For discussion of use of Java and CORBA integration.
- **comp.lang.java.databases**—For discussion of JDBC and other database fun in Java.
- **comp.lang.java.gui**—For discussion of GUI development.
- **comp.lang.java.help**—Generally considered the newbie group, helping get people up and running with Java.
- **comp.lang.java.machine**—For discussion of the Java Virtual Machine and writing emulators/interpreters for it.
- **comp.lang.java.programmer**—For general Java language programming. This group gets the most traffic of all of these groups. Note that some people in this group tend to flame more often than in the help group, so be careful of asking, "What is java?" here...

- **comp.lang.java.softwaretools**—For discussion of Java language development environments, like VisualAge for Java. This group tends to be almost completely composed of the question "what is the best IDE" followed by religious incantations of each person's favorite IDE. Note that there are some "how do I do *x* in VisualAge" questions here, though we suggest you post those types of questions in IBM's VisualAge for Java groups.

Newsgroup Archives

Whenever you have a question, you should always check to see if it was already asked and answered. The easiest way to do this is to surf to http://www.deja .com/usenet and search the discussion archive. We recommend you choose the "Power Search" and enter *vajava* for the forum if you are looking for VisualAge for Java questions.

Books

There are several good books on the Java language and its various APIs. We list a few of our favorites here.

- **Thinking in Java,** (Bruce Eckel), Prentice Hall Computer Books, 1998
  This book should be your first stop on the road to reading about Java! Covers all of the basics and a great deal of enterprise concepts with excellent examples all around.
  ISBN 0-13659728-8
  Note: The latest edition of this book is available **free** *online at http://www.bruceeckel.com. We strongly recommend you check out the downloadable book!*
- **Core Java 2, Volumes 1 & 2,** (Cay Horstmann, Gary Cornell) Prentice Hall, 1998
  An excellent introduction to the Java language.
  ISBN 0-13081933-6
- **Graphic Java 2, Volume 1 (AWT),** (David M. Geary), Prentice Hall, 1998
  The best book available on AWT GUI development, even if he *does* like GridBagLayout.
  ISBN 0-13079666-2
- **Graphic Java 2, Volume 2 (Swing),** (David M. Geary), Prentice Hall, 1999
  An excellent book on Swing, covering nearly every aspect of the Swing API.
  ISBN 0-13-079667-0

- **Java Swing,** (Robert Eckstein, Marc Loy, Dave Wood), O'Reilly & Associates, 1998
  Another excellent Swing book. Complements Geary's book quite well, as they both seem to cover each other's weaknesses.
  ISBN 1-56592-455-X
- **Developing Java Beans,** (Rob Englander), O'Reilly & Associates, 1997
  A good introduction to the JavaBean component model, delving a bit deeper than we could in this book.
  ISBN 1-56592-289-1
- **Design Patterns,** (Erich Gamma, Richard Helm, Ralph Johnson, John Vlissides), Addison-Wesley, 1995
  A must-have for every design group, though it *can* be incredibly difficult to read at times. This book describes several common patterns for application design, giving each a name. The main benefit of the book is providing a common vocabulary for patterns like "Visitor", "Factory Method", and so forth. They were a bit overly formal in specification of the patterns, but once you get used to it the information is excellent.
  ISBN 0-20163361-2
  Note that this book is now available in CDROM HTML format, ISBN 0-20163498-8, published 1998.
- **Enterprise JavaBeans, Second Edition,** (Richard Monson-Haefel), O'Reilly & Associates, 1999
  If you want to know Enterprise JavaBeans, you want *this* book.
  ISBN 1-56592-869-5
- **Java Enterprise Applications,** (Steven Asbury, Scott Weiner), John Wiley & Sons, 1999
  Provides great overview and details on many of the Enterprise Java APIs, such as JDBC, RMI, JNDI, JSP, JMS and EJB.
  ISBN 0-47132756-5
- **Mastering Enterprise JavaBeans** (Ed Roman), John Wiley & Sons, 1999.
  Provides the clearest explanations of Enterprise JavaBeans including excellent examples and details of related technologies. A must-have for learning Enterprise JavaBeans.
  ISBN 0-471-33229-1
- **Client/Server Programming with Java and CORBA,** (Robert Orfali, Dan Harkey), John Wiley & Sons, 1998
  The book to get if you need to know CORBA integration with JavaBeans components and Enterprise JavaBeans.
  ISBN 0-47124578-X

INDEX

T

For System Requirements, please see Appendix D.